D0686983

INTERNATIONAL HANDBOOK OF TEACHERS AND TEACHING

Kluwer International Handbooks of Education

VOLUME 3

Volume 1
International Handbook of Educational Leadership and
Administration
Edited by Kenneth Leithwood, Judith Chapman, David Corson,
Philip Hallinger, Ann Hart
ISBN 0-7923-3530-9

Volume 2
International Handbook of Science Education
Edited by Barry J. Fraser and Kenneth G. Tobin
ISBN 0-7923-3531-7

Volume 3
International Handbook of Teachers and Teaching (I and II)
Edited by Bruce J. Biddle, Thomas L. Good, Ivor F. Goodson
ISBN 0-7923-3532-5

Volume 4
International Handbook of Mathematics Education
Edited by Alan J. Bishop, Ken Clements, Christine Keitel,
Jeremy Kilpatrick, Colette Laborde
ISBN 0-7923-3533-3

Volume 5
International Handbook of Educational Change
Edited by Andy Hargreaves, Ann Lieberman, Michael Fullan,
David Hopkins
ISBN 0-7923-3534-1

International Handbook
of Teachers and Teaching

Volume II

Edited by

Bruce J. Biddle
University of Missouri-Columbia, USA

Thomas L. Good
University of Arizona, USA

Ivor F. Goodson
*University of East Anglia, England,
and University of Rochester, USA*

KLUWER ACADEMIC PUBLISHERS
DORDRECHT / BOSTON / LONDON

ISBN 0-7923-3532-5

Published by Kluwer Academic Publishers,
P.O. Box 17, 3300 AA Dordrecht, The Netherlands

Sold and distributed in North, Central and South America
by Kluwer Academic Publishers,
101 Philip Drive, Norwell, MA 02061, U.S.A.

In all other countries, sold and distributed
by Kluwer Academic Publishers Group,
P.O. Box 322, 3300 AH Dordrecht, The Netherlands

Printed on acid-free paper

Printed in the Netherlands

Table of Contents

Chapter 1: The Study of Teaching: Modern and Emerging Conceptions

THOMAS L. GOOD, BRUCE J. BIDDLE, IVOR F. GOODSON
University of Arizona, University of Missouri-Columbia, and University of East Anglia and University of Rochester

In the past 30 years, research on teaching has displayed an amazing burst of energy and has generated many important concepts and research findings. One prominent feature of this effort has been researchers' willingness to observe instructional process and to conceptualize the complex interactions of classrooms as fast moving social settings. Prior to 1960 most educational research (whether conducted by educators, sociologists, or psychologists) used research methods that excluded direct examination of instructional process. Modern research, in contrast, has included observation of classroom processes and detailed interviews with students and teachers. These data sources have generated greater awareness of the complexities of classroom life and have begun to steer theory away from simple notions to more complex, contingent, contextualized knowledge about what makes for good teaching.

Although identifying the start of modern research in any area is difficult, clearly the first *Handbook of Research on Teaching* (Gage, 1963) had an important impact upon the field. This publication provided authoritative account summaries of research to that date and called for better observational studies of teaching. The dominant paradigm for the study of teaching immediately prior to the onset of observational research had been research on teacher personalities. Teachers who had certain personalities (warmth, openness) had been thought to be better facilitators of student achievement in the classroom than teachers who did not have these characteristics. By the mid 1960s, however, many researchers were beginning to debunk the myth that there was a 'personality for teaching' (Getzels & Jackson, 1963), and this led to calls for better research on the *processes* of teaching.

It is beyond the scope of this introductory essay to provide a historical analysis of the various ways researchers responded to this call (for extensive coverage see Anderson, 1995; Good, 1996). However, it is instructive to understand that several different research paradigms for exploring instruction and learning in classrooms became influential within a short time period.

B.J. Biddle et al. (eds.), International Handbook of Teachers and Teaching, 671-679

Research Perspectives and Progress

One major goal of researchers, especially in the 1960s and 1970s, was to demonstrate that variation in the behaviors of teachers could be related to student learning. The title 'teacher behavior' subsumes hundreds of studies with different intentions, research methods, and findings. For example, included within this research tradition were studies of specific teaching behaviors such as 'indirectness,' clarity, or enthusiasm (see, for example, Flanders, 1970); investigations of teachers' management behavior toward the whole class (e.g., Kounin, 1970); wait time research (e.g., Rowe, 1969); naturalistic process-product studies (e.g., Brophy, 1973); research on instructional pace and content coverage (Barr & Dreeben, 1983); and experimental studies of process-product relations (Clark, Gage, Marx, Peterson, Stayrook, & Winne, 1979; Evertson, Anderson, Anderson, & Brophy, 1980).

Another emphasis that flourished in the past 30 years has been research on the effects of teacher cognition. Many types of teacher thought have been explored within this broad tradition including teacher expectations for students (Good & Brophy, 1973); teacher conceptions of the teacher's role (Biddle, Rosencranz, & Rankin, 1961); teacher decision making (Borko, Cone, Russo, & Shavelson, 1979); teachers' conceptions of lessons (Leinhardt & Putnam, 1987); teachers' ideas about subject matter (Shulman, 1987); teachers' expert knowledge (Berliner, 1992); and teacher responsibility, morality, and ethics (e.g., Jackson, Boostrom, & Hansen, 1993; Tom, 1984).

More recently, a flurry of research interest has appeared concerned with student mediation of instructional behaviors. Although research had long demonstrated the effects of instructional behavior in the classroom (see Dunkin & Biddle, 1974), some scholars have also argued that true understanding of classroom events and their implications for student learning cannot be achieved without an understanding of student thinking and student mediation of classroom events. Research responding to this insight has included studies of student social cognition (Rosenholtz & Simpson, 1984; Rohrkemper & Corno, 1988); student learning in small groups (e.g., Webb, 1983); student task literature (Alton-Lee, Nuthall, & Patrick, 1993; Anderson, 1981; Mergendoller, Marchman, Mitman, & Packer, 1988); student passivity (Good, Slavings, Harel, & Emerson, 1987; Sizer, 1984); students' self-regulated learning (Corno & Mandinach, 1983; Pressley & Levine, 1983); student volition (Corno, 1992; Snow, Corno, & Jackson, 1996); and student goal-regulation (McCaslin & Good, 1996).

And if these various traditions of research were not sufficient, other insights about classroom teaching have been generated by the recent flowering of works on the lives of teachers (see Goodson, 1981; Goodson & Hargreaves, 1996). (Chapter 1 of the first volume of this *Handbook* provides a more detailed introduction to this latter tradition, and several chapters representing it appear in that volume.)

Given both the amount of effort and the breadth of perspectives that have characterized recent research on teaching, it is little wonder that scholars have begun to comment on the gains in knowledge that have resulted. Weinert and Helmke (1995) have recently noted, for example, 'It was only 20 years ago that Good, Biddle, and Brophy (1975) wrote, "Do teachers make a difference? No definite answer exists because little search has been directed to the question in a comprehensive way." (p. 3). Since then, we have gained a good deal of convincing empirical evidence' confirming large differences in the quality of instruction among teachers and classrooms and that these differences have significant impact on students' academic performance (see also Gage, 1991).

New Directions and Contributions

As important as research within these traditions has been, most chapters in this volume assert the need for radical changes in the conceptualization of teaching and learning in American classrooms. These calls for new conceptualization of classroom teaching and learning are based upon various considerations. For example, obvious changes have appeared as many countries in the world have moved from economies based on agriculture and mining, to those based on industry, and are now entering a post-industrial world focused on the provision of services, the exchange of information, and global interdependence. The demographic characteristics of students and teachers are also changing in many countries, and much more information is now available from governments and other sources concerning the status and 'progress' of education in many societies. In addition, competition for tax-supported services has become more acute, and this has led to the flowering of conservative ideologies and attacks on public education (see, for example, Berliner & Biddle, 1995, who deal with the American case). Given such societal changes, it is apparent that goals for schools in the year 2000 will differ sharply from goals that were expressed for schools in 1900, 1950, 1970, or even 1990. And, if there are new goals, it follows that there must be new instructional processes and new forms of learning opportunities for students. The chapters of this volume provide an exciting set of arguments, images, and recommendations about the transformations needed in the teaching-learning process to accommodate these changes.

The volume begins with four chapters focused on student thought and its importance in understanding the processes and effects of teaching. In chapter 2, Graham Nuthall argues that a radical change has recently appeared in educators' conception of students' thinking and learning in classroom settings. He argues that it is no longer possible to retain the concepts and theories that provided the foundation for virtually all classroom research until a decade ago and that the field is in the midst of a profound paradigm shift. To help with this reconceptualization, he reviews three different traditions of research that beg for synthesis: studies of student thinking in which students are seen as creating or constructing their own knowledge and skills; studies that are sociocultural in orientation in which learning and thinking are conceived as social processes that are laid within specific contexts; and studies that have a sociolinguistic orientation in which the language of the classroom conceived as both the content and the medium of learning and thinking. Chapter 3 by Deborah Ball maintains that no task is more fundamental or difficult for teachers than understanding what students are learning. She argues that there are major challenges in trying to listen to students. For example, teachers must learn from individuals who are quite different from themselves. She suggests that what a student is thinking 'here and now' may not be what they are thinking later in the week and that teachers need to listen to students through multiple contexts. She also asserts that because teachers want children to understand and to learn, they are prone to over-interpret what children might say and do. Her chapter includes suggestions about how teachers may improve their ability to listen and understand students' perspectives – a fundamental necessity if teachers are to implement the perspectives of constructivists.

The fourth chapter – by Phyllis Blumenfeld, Ronald Marx, Helen Patrick Joseph Krajcik, and Elliot Soloway – focuses upon the instructional importance of teaching for understanding. The authors provide a rich historical analysis of how the field of research on teaching has evolved from models stressing the transmission of information to current conceptions of practice which emphasize students' transformation of knowledge. They compare a variety of extant programs that incorporate elements of constructivist thought and identify issues that merit further research. Importantly, these authors also explore issues of emerging technologies in their pursuit of integrating new technology with modern constructions of students' learning.

In the fifth chapter, Barbara Bank reviews research on the peer cultures of children and adolescents and their effects on teaching. She argues that such peer cultures often conflict with teacher's goals and the official school culture, that many discussions of teaching ignore the tensions and contradictions created by peer cultures, and that the latter have important theoretical and instructional implications. She suggests that it is useful to separate three aspects of school culture – academic goals, extra curricular activities, and school discipline policies – and she discusses how each interacts with the peer cultures that students create. She also examines the implications of peer cultures for teaching and offers suggestions about what schools and teachers can do to deal more effectively with peer concerns.

The next few chapters focus on changing conditions in the society that affect teaching. Chapter 6, by Joseph Blase, explores recent research on the social and cultural aspects of the teacher's work with particular emphasis on the micropolitics of teaching. His analysis begins by discussing how individuals and groups use power to advance their interests in various kinds of relationships, such as those that are nominally democratic, collegial, or conflictful. He notes that most micro-political studies of teachers have so far been conducted in traditional school settings. Not surprisingly, these studies suggest that teachers are vulnerable to pressure from other adults in their work, especially to thoughtless, self-serving, or manipulative school principals. He argues that current research illustrates a substantial discrepancy between the expected and actual political roles of teachers in the school restructuring process. Thus, current reforms that stress greater teacher empowerment and more democracy in school decision making may be more illusionary than real.

In chapter 7, Peter Cookson and Charlotte Lucks argue that schools are becoming increasingly politicized and suggest that if the United States continues to adhere to market solutions for public policy, it is likely that public education as a unifying social force will be seriously weakened or destroyed. Although this unfortunate outcome is possible, they argue that the picture need not necessarily be gloomy and that greater teacher autonomy might leave teachers with a strong voice if they can increase their professional autonomy. The authors contend that this can best be achieved by setting higher standards for those who enter and who stay in the profession.

Chapter 8 by Hans Vonk notes that many policies regarding social welfare and the labor market are no longer the primary domain of an individual nation but are also influenced by regional or global events and policies. His analysis leads to the conclusion that the work of teaching in Europe is now becoming more narrowly defined and more thoroughly supervised. He maintains that if teachers want to see themselves as professionals that are fully recognized by governing bodies, they will have to gain some degree of control over the decisions that affect their work and the curricula of teaching.

In chapter 9, Linda Darling-Hammond and Marcella Bullmaster contend that challenges faced in America are also being more affected by the global economy than has been the case historically. They assert that changing social contexts and expectations for learners in the twenty-first century require teachers who can teach for understanding – who can scaffold key ideas in part by anticipating misconceptions that students have. Such skills should allow teachers to create learning experiences that build upon students' own thinking, while at the same time reflecting the standards of inquiry in a particular discipline. This suggests that teachers must diversify classroom practice and must allow for greater variability rather than assuming uniformity in learners.

John Smyth, in a provocative essay, chapter 10, contends that schools may be one of the few remaining social institutions that can help youth to be socialized in a way that places a value on social relationships – by generating trust, establishing shared expectations, and creating and enforcing social norms. An alternative vision suggests that for too long teachers have been treated in ways that diminish the value of teaching as a social practice. He contends that teachers are influenced by social policy simultaneously as they help to shape it. This implies that teachers can and need to be more than passive purveyors of educational edicts that have been developed by those external to classroom situations.

In chapter 11, Philip Wexler argues that teaching in the post-modern world must not be limited to skill transmission but should be aimed at growth, transformation, and creativity. This suggests the need for teachers who are not only strong pedagogic models but who also concentrate on the social world and its possibilities. The new forms of teaching he thus envisions are 'remptive' and call for more attention to students and teachers as social beings and not just subject matter purveyors and learners.

The next two chapters place special emphasis on the need for teachers to learn new ways of reasoning and thinking. Chapter 12 by Judi Randi and Lyn Corno notes that teachers often act as innovators, adapting and revising curriculum on the basis of individual needs and conditions within the communities in which students live. The authors argue that researchers have much to learn from teachers' creative adaptation of curriculum to particular learners in specific social settings. They assert that, unless researchers develop a clear understanding of how teachers generate new practices in response to changing demographics and other contextual features of their work environments, it is unlikely that researchers will be able to support innovation at the classroom level. This suggests the need for more careful understanding of how teachers learn, grow, and adapt.

In chapter 13, Ralph Putnam and Hilda Borko provide a comprehensive and integrative review of research on cognition and explore its implications for teacher learning. They argue that recent scholarship on teacher learning and education can be captured in four images:

a) teachers should be treated as active learners who construct their own understanding;
b) teachers should be empowered and treated as professionals;
c) teacher education must be situated in classroom practice; and
d) teacher educators should treat teachers as they expect teachers to treat students.

They argue that teachers, like students, need to learn new ways of reasoning, communicating, and thinking through their participation in classroom discourse communities.

The final three chapters point out the need for clearer conceptualizing and the important role of evidence as educators (and others) help to transform schools. Chapter 14 by Andy Hargreaves debunks simple assumptions about the desirability of teacher cultures. He notes that teacher cultures can be positive or negative and that we need to learn not only from their ethical and romantic features but also from their ironic and sometimes even tragic consequences. He argues that, as we continue to explore the evolution of leadership in school settings, we need to avoid simple-minded notions such as that collegiality and collaboration are always virtues, whereas individualism and isolation should be eradicated for cause.

Doug Noble provides, in chapter 15, a comprehensive and insightful analysis of the history of computer-based education over the past two decades. He renders a startling account of how various individuals and companies have attempted to commercialize technology in educational settings. He contends that schools are typically sold an unexamined bill of goods – through effective advertisements and advocacy rather than through evidence concerning the effectiveness of the technologies. His analysis leads to the conclusion that computer-based education is more about using schools to sell technological products for profit than it is about using technology to improve education for students.

Finally, chapter 16 by Thomas Good, Sally Clark, and Donald Clark analyzes the tendency of educators to move from fad to fad, often with little if any evidence to support a new organizational structure or instructional strategies. Along these lines, the authors raise the question as to whether certain aspects of the new paradigm 'teaching for understanding' is anything more than faddism. The authors conclude their chapter by presenting several hypotheses as to why faddism is so prevalent in educational settings and provide recommendations that may help instructional practice to evolve from an advocacy base to an evidential base.

Taken together, these chapters provide exciting new images of teaching that should stimulate considerable debate about curriculum and instruction as well as help to generate new research. It is our hope that future teachers, current teachers, and policy makers will benefit from the thoughtful analyses of modern conceptions of teaching and learning that these chapters provide. But since the tasks and challenges of teaching will continue to evolve, we again stress that this *Handbook* represents a good cross-section and broad overview of up-to-date, innovative thinking and scholarship concerning teachers and teaching. It is not, nor can it be, the final word on these important topics.

REFERENCES

Alton-Lee, A., Nuthall, G., & Patrick, J. (1993). Reframing classroom research: A lesson from the private world of children. *Harvard Educational Review, 63*, 50-84.

Anderson, L. (1981). Short-term student responses to classroom instruction. *Elementary School Journal, 82*, 97-108.

Anderson, L. (Ed.) (1995). *International encyclopedia of teaching and teacher education* (2nd ed.). Oxford: Pergamon.

Barr, R. & Dreeben, R. (1983). *How schools work*. Chicago: University of Chicago Press.

Berliner, D. C. (1992, February). *Educational reform in an era of disinformation*. Paper presented at the annual meeting of the American Association of Colleges for Teacher Education, San Antonio, TX.

Berliner, D. C. & Biddle, B. J. (1995). *The manufactured crisis: Myths, fraud, and the attack on America's public schools*. New York: Addison-Wesley.

Biddle, B. J., Rosencranz, H. A., & Rankin, E. F., Jr. (1961). *Studies in the role of the public school teacher* (5 volumes). Columbia, MO: University of Missouri Press.

Borko, H., Cone, R., Russo, N., & Shavelson, R. (1979). Teachers' decision making. In P. Peterson & H. Walberg (Eds.), *Research on teaching: Concepts, findings and implications* (pp. 136-160). Berkeley, CA: McCutchan.

Brophy, J. (1973). Stability of teacher effectiveness. *American Educational Research Journal, 10*, 245-252.

Clark, C., Gage, N., Marx, R., Peterson, P., Stayrook, N., & Winne, P. (1979). A factorial experiment on teacher structuring, soliciting, and reacting. *Journal of Educational Psychology, 71*, 534-552.

Corno, L. (1992). Encouraging students to take responsibility for learning and performance. *Elementary School Journal, 93*, 69-84.

Corno, L. & Mandinach, E. (1983). The role of cognitive engagement in classroom learning and motivation. *Educational Psychologist, 18*, 88-108.

Dunkin, M. J. & Biddle, B. J. (1974). *The study of teaching*. New York: Holt, Rinehart and Winston.

Evertson, C., Anderson, C., Anderson, L., & Brophy, J. (1980). Relationships between classroom behaviors and student outcomes in junior high mathematics and English classes. *American Educational Research Journal, 17*, 43-60.

Flanders, N. A. (1970). *Analyzing teacher behavior*. Reading, MA: Addison-Wesley.

Gage, N. L. (Ed.) (1963). *Handbook of research on teaching*. Chicago: Rand McNally.

Gage, N. L. (1991). The obviousness of social and educational research results. *Educational Researcher, 20*, 10-16.

Getzels, J. & Jackson, P. (1963). The teacher's personality and characteristics. In N. Gage (Ed.), *Handbook of research on teaching* (pp. 506-582). Chicago: Rand McNally.

Good, T. L. (1996). Teaching effects and teacher evaluation. In J. Sikula, T. Buttery, & E. Guyton (Eds.), *Handbook of research on teacher education* (2nd ed., pp. 617-665). New York: Macmillan.

Good, T. L., Biddle, B. J., & Brophy, J. (1975). *Teachers make a difference*. New York: Holt, Rinehart and Winston.

Good, T. L. & Brophy, J. (1973). *Looking in classrooms*. New York: Harper and Row.

Good, T. L., Slavings, R., Harel, K., & Emerson, H. (1987). Student passivity: A study of student question-asking in K-12 classrooms. *Sociology of Education, 60*, 181-199.

Goodson, I. F. (1981). Life history and the study of schooling. *Interchange* (Ontario Institute for Studies in Education), *11*(4), 62-76.

Goodson, I. F. & Hargreaves, A. (Eds.) (1996). *Teachers' professional lives*. London, New York, and Philadelphia: Falmer Press.

Jackson, P., Boostrom, R., & Hansen, D. (1993). *The moral life of schools*. San Francisco: Jossey-Bass.

Kounin, J. (1970). *Discipline and group management in classrooms*. New York: Holt, Rinehart and Winston.

Leinhardt, G. & Putnam, R. (1987). The skill of learning from classroom lessons. *American Educational Research Journal, 24*, 557-587.

McCaslin, M. & Good, T. (1996). *Listening in classrooms*. New York: Harper Collins.

Mergendoller, J., Marchman, V., Mitman, A., & Packer, M. (1988). Task demands and accountability in middle-grade science classes. *Elementary School Journal, 88*, 251-265.

Pressley, M. & Levine, J. (Eds.) (1983). *Cognitive strategy research: Educational applications*. New York: Springer-Verlag.

Rohrkemper, M. & Corno, L. (1988). Success and failure on classroom tasks: Adaptive learning and classroom teaching. *Elementary School Journal, 88*, 297-312.

Rosenholtz, S. & Simpson, C. (1984). The formation of ability conceptions: Developmental trend or social construction? *Review of Educational Research, 54*, 31-63.

Rowe, M. (1969). Science, silence, and sanctions. *Science and Children, 6*, 11-13.

Shulman, L. (1987). Knowledge and teaching: Foundations of the new reform. *Harvard Educational Review, 57*, 1-22.

Sizer, T. (1984). *Horace's compromise: The dilemma of the American high school*. Boston: Houghton Mifflin.

Snow, R., Corno, L., & Jackson, D., III (1996). Individual differences in affective and conative functions. In D. Berliner & R. Calfee (Eds.), *Handbook of educational psychology* (pp. 243-310). New York: Simon & Schuster Macmillan.

Tom, A. (1984). *Teaching as a moral craft*. White Plains, NY: Longman.

Webb, N. (1983). Predicting learning from student interaction: Defining the interaction variable. *Educational Psychologist, 18*, 33-41.

Weinert, L. & Helmke, A. (1995). Interclassroom differences in instructional quality and interindividual differences in cognitive development. *Educational Psychologist, 30*, 15-20.

Chapter 2: Understanding Student Thinking and Learning in the Classroom

GRAHAM NUTHALL
University of Canterbury

INTRODUCTION

The original purpose of this chapter was to provide an account of student thinking in the classroom. There was a time, some years ago, when the content of such a chapter would have been self-evident. It would have included research on the development of problem solving skills and on the ways in which teachers could encourage students to use higher-order cognitive skills by asking appropriate questions and setting appropriate problems. My own early studies of 'classroom interaction' were concerned with the logical demands made by teachers' questions and the effects these had on students. The results were published under the title of *Thinking in the Classroom* (Nuthall & Lawrence, 1965). The categories and concepts that were used to set clear boundaries around different types of classroom behaviour were largely borrowed from research in the psychological laboratory (e.g., Bruner, Goodnow, & Austin, *A Study of Thinking*, 1956; Skinner, *Verbal Behaviour*, 1957) or from logic and analytic philosophy (e.g., Hirst & Peters, *The Logic of Education*, 1970; Smith & Ennis, *Language and Concepts in Education*, 1961).

As recently as 1986, a review of student thought processes in the classroom (Wittrock, 1986) could make a clear distinction between thinking and learning and achievement. Thinking was seen as a distinct set of processes that took place in the student's head and mediated between teaching or instruction and classroom behaviour and learning. The range of processes included in thinking had widened since the previous decade, but there was no question that thinking processes were distinct and easily distinguishable from learning and achievement. Thinking was considered 'higher order,' while learning (especially of knowledge and practical skills) was seen as important but of a lower order.

There has, however, been a radical change in conceptions of thinking and learning in the classroom in recent years. New perspectives, introduced from a range of different disciplines (e.g., linguistics, sociolinguistics, aesthetics, semiotics, social anthropology, literary criticism), a range of different methodologies (e.g., ethnomethodology, phenomenography, discourse analysis, textual criticism) and cultural perspectives (e.g., Soviet psychology) have produced

B.J. Biddle et al. (eds.), International Handbook of Teachers and Teaching, 681-768
© *1997 Kluwer Academic Publishers, Printed in the Netherlands*

what appears at first glance to be a confusion of new ways of conceptualising and understanding student experience in the classroom.

Whether we like it or not, it is no longer possible to retain the concepts and theories that lay behind most classroom research until a decade ago. Distinctions that used to be made between thinking and learning, between language and thought, between the individual and the social, have all become problematic. New processes and concepts are being suggested that do not fit within the traditional disciplines that used to inform classroom research. For those who believe in the value of constant challenge and change, or who accept the postmodernist perception of everything as endlessly evolving particularities and subjectivities and delight in disrupting established discourses (Lather, 1991), these are exciting times. For the writer of a review of recent research on student thinking in the classroom, it presents considerable problems.

What I have attempted to do in this chapter has been to bring together as many recent studies of student experience in classrooms as I could and try to identify the common themes and issues that seem to hold them together. This led me to group the studies into three broad categories based on the conceptual background or interests of the researchers. These categories are not sharply defined. They represent approaches or perspectives rather than theories, and many of the studies included in one category have elements in common with studies included in one of the other categories. This is partly because many of the researchers (such as Wells, 1994) have tried to take a multi-disciplinary approach, incorporating insights from several disciplines into their studies.

The first category includes those studies that appear to be primarily psychological in their orientation. Learning and thinking are incorporated into a broad concept of cognition, and students are seen as creating or constructing their own knowledge and skills. The second category contains those studies that are primarily sociocultural in their orientation. Learning and thinking are seen as social processes occurring in social contexts, between rather than within individuals. Students progress through a process of apprenticeship within significant social groups. In the third category there are those studies that have a primarily language or sociolinguistic orientation. In these studies, the language of the classroom is both the content and the medium of learning and thinking. What students acquire are the linguistic 'genres' of the disciplines. These genres contain the concepts and ways of perceiving and thinking that characterise the disciplines.

While each of these three broad types of studies contributes something different to our understanding of students' classroom experience, they are more than just complementary perspectives on the same processes. They challenge and compete with each other over a number of central issues. As I worked to bring the studies together and find common themes I became increasingly aware that the differences between the studies occurred around these central issues. They concern the nature of mind and of the processes of the mind. They bring into question the way we have traditionally described and understood the changes that education is supposed to produce in students.

Beneath a diversity of different perspectives and methods of analysis, I have become aware that a paradigm shift is occurring that is as significant as any that has occurred in classroom research. The nature of the new paradigm is not yet clear. The debate is still in progress and radical ideas that challenge the basis of our thinking are being proposed alongside minor modifications to familiar and accepted ideas.

The purpose of this chapter is to inform the reader about the nature of the current debate. This is done in the first three sections of the chapter by describing the three different approaches to understanding student cognition in the classroom. In so doing I become involved in the debate myself. In the fourth section of the chapter I examine the major points of conflict between the three approaches. These concern the existence of mind and the processes by which students learn from classroom experience. I then describe, using data from our own studies, a new perspective on classroom learning and thinking that incorporates the currently conflicting perspectives.

Throughout this chapter I have tried to keep the discussion in touch with the realities of student classroom experience. To do this I have made use, wherever possible, of examples of classroom observations, transcripts and interviews. Most of these come from studies that I have undertaken with Adrienne Alton-Lee (Alton-Lee & Nuthall, 1992; Alton-Lee, Nuthall, & Patrick, 1993; Nuthall & Alton-Lee, 1993). I am aware that extensive use of classroom observational data is unusual in a handbook chapter of this kind, but I hope it will constantly remind the reader of two things. First, the concepts and ideas that are debated in this chapter are supposed to provide insights and understanding of students' classroom experience. Second, it is a major strength of most of the research referred to in this article that it has been based in classrooms and can, without difficulty, be referenced back to its original classroom context.

THE COGNITIVE CONSTRUCTIVIST PERSPECTIVE

The studies that share the greatest continuity with earlier research on student thinking and learning in the classroom are those studies that have a broadly defined 'cognitive' perspective on student experience. With the development of cognitive science and of the concept of 'cognition' as a way of understanding all mental processes, the careful distinctions that used to be made between concepts such learning, thinking, problem solving, and remembering, are no longer tenable. As a consequence, it no longer makes sense to talk of knowledge simply as a behavioural response or as a kind of substance that is transferred from the mind of the teacher, or the page of the textbook, to the mind of the student. Instead, it is now commonly accepted that knowledge is a product of the ways in which the student's mind is engaged by the activities and resources of the classroom. Recent research studies on teaching and learning in science education (Carey, 1986; Driver, Asoko, Leach, Mortimar, & Scott, 1994; Magnusson, Boyle, & Templin, 1994), in mathematics education (Brown, 1993; Carpenter, Fennema, & Romberg, 1993; Cobb, 1994; Ernest, 1989), and in social studies education (Brophy & Alleman, 1992; Gregg & Leinhardt, 1994) have increasingly been based on the view that students construct their own knowledge as they engage in the processes of interpreting and making sense of their classroom experience. Learning is seen as the conceptual restructuring that results from this cognitive processing.

As a consequence of this view, it is no longer possible to make the assumption that there can be a direct link between teaching and learning. The way that tasks are structured, the questions that teachers ask, the examples that students practice, can only have indirect effects on student learning (Hiebert & Wearne, 1993). As students encounter new experiences, their minds construct representations of those experiences that are structured by their own previous knowledge and beliefs. These individually constructed representations interact with each other in the production of new knowledge and beliefs.

How this process works can be illustrated with an example from one of our studies. Kim was a third-grade student we observed in a class that was studying a social studies unit on England in the Middle Ages. The concept of a 'charter' as a social contract was a concept that came up several times during the unit. The teacher expected the students to learn about a charter although she did not discuss it directly.

Our observations showed that Kim came across references to a charter on three occasions during the unit. First, he read a work sheet (supplied by the teacher) that described the occasion when the English barons forced King John to sign the Magna Carta. This work sheet described the Magna Carta as a 'great charter' that 'sets out all the rights of free men.'

Three days later the teacher conducted a class discussion about life in medieval towns. The teacher summarised the discussion by writing a set of sentences on the blackboard. These included 'The marketplace was in the centre of town. People bought and sold goods there, the town crier made announcements, and it was a place where criminals were punished. A charter was a written promise giving the town its freedom.' Along with the other students, Kim copied the sentences into his project book. The teacher also gave each student an outline picture of the central square of a medieval town with instructions to colour it and paste it into their project book alongside the sentences. This picture showed a marketplace at a cross roads, with shops, various people and animals, and a person throwing objects at a man locked into the stocks. Kim coloured his picture and pasted it into his project book.

Each morning during the unit, the teacher gave the students a list of spelling sentences containing key words related to the content of the unit. The students were required to copy these sentences into their project books and learn to spell the relevant key words. Two days after the previous experience, the teacher included a sentence about a charter in the morning spelling activity. On this morning, the teacher put a set of sentences on the blackboard that related to the previous class discussion of medieval towns. In each sentence the key word had been omitted and the students were expected to identify this key word and learn to spell it as part of their homework. Before beginning the task the teacher discussed the sentences with the class.

Student:	(reading sentence from blackboard) 'A written promise called a something showed that the town had been given its freedom.' [Student knocks on door of classroom, enters to find out the number of students who needed to order food for lunch.]
Teacher:	What was it called? Celia?
Celia:	Charter?
Teacher:	Right. [To lunch-order student] Are you coming with the charter?
Lunch-order Student:	Any lunch orders? [Students indicate orders.]
Teacher:	Right. Good girl. I wonder if anyone can tell me what the root word is for charter? Bev?
Bev:	Chart.
Teacher:	Right. Er. Chart - er …

This discussion continued for the other sentences about the mayors and market places of medieval towns. Later Kim wrote these sentences in his spelling book.

This was the last of the three occasions when Kim experienced anything related to the concept of a charter during the unit. When we interviewed Kim about two weeks after the unit, he described a charter in the following way.

Kim:	Charters. I think it was, showed people directions for moving about the towns, 'cause there was charters in the middle where the market was, I think.
Interviewer:	Describe one to me … anything you can tell me will help.
Kim	Um, I can remember a person in the middle of the road with a scroll.
Interviewer:	Right.

Kim:	Um, and reading things. Yes, Ms A. was telling us about it. I hope I haven't muddled.
Interviewer:	You think you might have muddled?
Kim:	Yeah.

Kim's description of a charter is a coherent and sensible interpretation of some of the information that he had picked up from the work sheet, and the picture colouring and spelling activities. From the picture and the sentences he copied beside it, and the spelling sentences, he had remembered the marketplace and the reference to the town crier. From the class discussion of the spelling sentences, he recalled the teacher's reference to a 'chart.' His prior knowledge of the role of the town crier and of charts must have suggested the connection between the scroll used by the town crier in the town centre and a map.

When we interviewed Kim again 12 months later and asked him about a charter, he gave the following description.

> Kim: ... I think, ah, no, um, there's this thing I can remember. Well, there, something, in the picture was a cross road, well, lots of roads joining into it and there was the stocks and people were throwing eggs at this person in the stocks, and then I think I heard something about a man stands in the middle there, and if someone wants to go somewhere, they go and ask him where to go.

These interview responses make it clear that Kim constructed in his mind a descriptive account of a charter that brought together the elements of his original classroom experiences (a picture of a crossroads marketplace with a man in stocks, the root word of charter being a chart, associated sentences about a town crier, etc.) and presumably reflected his attempts to give these experiences a kind of logical coherence. What he remembered was not just what he had been told (or read) about a charter ('sets out all the rights of free men,' 'a written promise that showed that the town had been given its freedom') but an interpretation of those statements embedded in the contexts in which he had experienced them.

Understanding how knowledge construction occurs has become the focus of a considerable number of research studies in the last few years (cf. Carey, 1991; Driver et al., 1994). Three kinds of variables have become the central concerns of this research. First, there has been concern for how classroom tasks and practical activities engage and structure cognitive processing. Second, there has been interest in how the social processes of the classroom influence learning and knowledge construction, especially the interaction of peers in small cooperative groups. Third, the role of the teacher in motivating, structuring and guiding student cognition has been investigated. In the following sections, I will try to tease out from this research those critical variables that seem to have the most effect on the way students construct their own knowledge and beliefs.

The Structure and Demands of Classroom Tasks

Researchers concerned with identifying how students' minds engage with subject matter in the classroom have been confronted with a reality in which many different and conflicting demands are constantly being made on students' attention and involvement. Some years ago, Doyle suggested that student experience in classrooms could be understood best as work and that students involvement in this work was a function of the task demands imposed on them (Doyle, 1983). Student engagement, he argued, is a product of the clarity of task instructions, the ambiguity of task outcomes, and the level of risk and effort involved in task completion. An early report by Doyle and Carter (1984) suggested that students will work to reduce the ambiguity of task outcomes in order to reduce the cognitive effort involved in carrying out the task. More recent studies suggest that students may, on occasions, prefer more ambiguous task outcomes when this reduces the risk of failure (Good, McCaslin, & Reys, 1992). Although teachers design tasks to engage students' minds with critical aspects of the curriculum, as Brophy and Alleman (1992) have pointed out, when the efforts of students to reduce the risk and effort are combined with poor task design, tasks may make only minimal relevant cognitive demands on students. A mismatch between task design and student knowledge and motivation is common (Bennett & Desforges, 1988).

Understanding the effects of tasks on students' cognitive processing is further confused by the disparity that often exists between the teacher's and the students' understanding of the resources and requirements of a task. For example, Cobb, Yackel, and Wood (1992) have pointed out that the materials often used in mathematics classrooms (e.g., cuisenaire rods, blocks, coloured cards, symbol systems) may have a transparent mathematical meaning to teachers but remain confusingly opaque to students. Students may have to spend considerable time searching for the teacher's perspective in order to make any kind of sense of the activity. Failing this, the students will develop strategies for getting by and avoiding the appearance of failure (Perret-Clermont, Perret, & Bell, 1991).

In an interesting study of how students coped with the typical tasks of mathematics classrooms, Frid and Malone (1994) asked fifth-grade students how they knew when they understood the mathematics they were learning in their class. The students reported two simple criteria. First, they knew they understood a mathematical procedure when they got it right. Second, they knew they had got it right when the teacher said it was right. Mathematical understanding in these classrooms had become equated with getting the same answer as the teacher (or sometimes, the calculator). For the students, classroom tasks had become matters of doing what the teacher wanted, and 'understanding mathematics' meant nothing more than getting the answers right. Managing task requirements had replaced genuine engagement with mathematics.

Accounts of the private talk that takes place between students during classroom activities reveals that it is frequently related to task requirements and ways of obtaining the teacher's approval (Alton-Lee et al., 1993). The following example is typical of a group of students trying to translate a teacher's instructions into reality. In this third-grade class the teacher was setting up a demonstration to show that air has weight. Each group of students had been asked to inflate two balloons and tie them onto each end of a metre-long stick. The stick was then to be suspended on a piece of string at the point of balance so that the stick was horizontal and the balloons were hanging from the ends of the stick at the same height (see diagram below). Finally one of the balloons was to be gently pricked so that the air came out slowly.

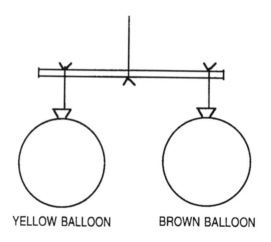

YELLOW BALLOON   BROWN BALLOON

At the time of the following excerpt, the students had reached the stage of pricking one of the balloons to let the air out.

Teacher: [talking to class as a whole as the students work in groups] It's going to go down slowly. While it does that, hold the string bit very tightly and very still and watch what happens. Alright.

Student [in Tui's group]: I'm going to do it, OK?

Tui [holding stick]:   What do you have to do?

Student: You have to make a hole at the top.

Student 2:   I want to hold it.

Student 3:   Don't cut it.

Student 2:	You've got to.
Student 3:	No.
Tui:	Here. I'll do it. I'll do it. You just get this end
Student 2:	You're meant to hold it up like this.
Student:	Yeah, you're meant to. Get ready! [pricks balloon with point of scissors, but doesn't make hole]
Student 2:	We done one!
Student 3:	Have you?
Student:	Do you mean you have to make a hole?
Student 3:	What with?
Tui:	With scissors. Who's got a pair of snips [scissors]? Do that one after [pointing to balloon at other end of stick].
	Student pokes point of scissors into balloon, balloon swings away and nothing happens.
Tui:	Don't! Don't! You're not meant to do that. Leave it!
Student:	Hold it properly.
Tui:	You hold it. I'll put it under. You made me bump the snips.
Student:	Tui! [Tui walks away from the group]

During this discussion the students were trying to relate what they thought they were 'meant to do' to what actually happened with unstable balloons. The task was a difficult one and the discussion between the students was almost all concerned with the mechanics of the activity itself. How much student talk is taken up with concerns about understanding instructions, and with the details of tasks, can be seen in Table 1. This data is taken from the same study in which the balloon episode occurred. The context was a science unit about the weather that lasted over a period of 8 days. The student talk was recorded from individual transmitter microphones worn by each of the students. This meant that the proportion of private talk (to self and peers) to public talk was higher than the proportion found in studies that depend on observers or public microphone systems. The private talk went on more or less continuously through whole-class discussions and through group and individual activities. Only the private talk that was relevant in some way to the curriculum or to curriculum-relevant classroom activities has been included in this table.

Type of Talk	Percent of all relevant utterances				
	Jan	Pam	Rata	Tui	Total
Public Talk					
Contributing to class discussion	28.8	17.5	7.6	8.7	13.1
Reading aloud & chorus	3.8	2.1	2.3	1.0	2.1
Private talk (to self & peers)					
Content related talk					
Asking & answering	10.7	13.4	17.1	11.2	14.1
Elaborating	7.7	19.0	19.8	17.8	18.0
Evaluating & arguing	4.0	11.1	5.2	9.2	7.9
Total content related	22.4	43.4	42.1	38.2	40.0
Task related talk					
Instructions & requirements	14.7	7.5	15.8	18.0	13.3
Organization & resources	6.0	7.8	4.8	6.3	6.2
Presentation & completion	2.0	2.7	1.5	3.0	2.2
Evaluating content & process	7.1	3.8	5.1	0.8	4.0
Total task related	30.0	21.6	27.2	28.0	25.7
Social & personal talk					
Asking for & giving help	6.2	6.2	12.5	16.3	10.4
Polite & expressive	4.4	1.3	2.5	1.5	2.0
Negative & competitive	2.0	2.7	1.2	3.5	2.2
Total social and personal	12.5	10.1	16.1	21.2	14.7
Metacognitive talk	2.8	5.2	4.4	1.7	4.0
Singing & sounds	0.0	0.1	0.4	1.1	0.4
Total number of utterances	**504**	**1918**	**2077**	**1064**	**5563**

Table 1: Recorded Curriculum and Task-Relevant Utterances of Four Students During an Eight-Day Science Unit in a Fourth-Grade Classroom

About a quarter of all private student talk appears to be concerned with carrying out and completing tasks. As in the above excerpt, students spend a significant amount of time clarifying instructions, organising and preparing equipment and resources, worrying about how to complete or present the results of the task, and commenting on how difficult or boring the task is. This is in addition to the time spent listening to the teacher's instructions and asking questions about those instructions in the whole-class context. Given the problems that students typically have understanding instructions and determining what to do, designing tasks in ways that engage the students' minds directly, continuously, and effectively with the relevant subject matter is the essential first step to ensuring that relevant cognitive processing actually takes place (Brophy & Alleman, 1992). Good, McCaslin, and Reys have developed a set of categories to describe the level and type of involvement that tasks might engender (1992, pp. 145-147).

The Content of Effective Classroom Tasks

There are two major problems relating to the content of tasks that have been identified in studies of students' thinking about subject matter. The first concerns the issue of transfer. Researchers in science and mathematics education have long been aware that effective cognitive engagement within the context of a specific classroom activity may not produce the understanding or knowledge needed in later learning or different contexts. Hiebert and associates (Hiebert et al., 1994) have argued that it is critically important to ensure that students are engaged in 'authentic problem solving' in the classroom. It is the nature of the problem that determines the type of learning that occurs. For example, if mathematical learning is to occur, then the problem as it is understood by the student must involve mathematical thinking. It should be 'owned' by the student in the sense that the solution relates to goals that the student feels are personally worth achieving. It must engage the student in significant intellectual reflection on, and communication about, the mathematical content of the task. And it must involve the use of specifically mathematical 'tools' such as the use of mathematical procedures, and mathematical representation and notation.

The second problem concerns the significance of the content being learned in the classroom. Brophy and Alleman (1992) note that designing effective tasks is likely to be a very time-consuming activity for the teacher. For this reason, well-designed tasks should focus on the most central and powerful concepts and principles in a discipline. Carey (1986), in her descriptive analysis of the constructivist approach in science education, notes that research on commonly held misconceptions has provided science educators with a challenge and a direction for designing effective classroom activities. But she suggests that specific misconceptions reflect larger underlying cognitive structures and belief systems that need to become the focus of science education. The resistance of some important misconceptions to change, or the failure of students to transfer classroom learning to their understanding of everyday events, may reflect the fact that classroom activities do not engage with these important underlying conceptual structures.

What these problems bring to the fore is the uncertain connection that exists between the acquisition of specific knowledge and skills and the development of those underlying conceptual structures and control processes that have been the focus of Piagetian and neo-Piagetian research on children's cognitive development (cf. Case, 1991). Tasks that connect to the daily lives of students may not, by their very nature, engage those underlying structures and processes that shape the evolution of students cognitive development. Tasks that challenge established ways of thinking are likely to fall outside the areas that are familiar and attractive to students.

Peer Interactions and the Social Processes of the Classroom

Another set of variables affecting students thinking about subject matter in the classroom relate to the ways in which students interact with each other. Piaget (1928) and more recently a group of European researchers (cf. Doise & Mugny, 1984; Gilly, 1991; Perret-Clermont, 1980; Perret-Clermont et al., 1991) have identified the apparently privileged role that peer interactions play in changing students' cognitive structures. Their research has found that differences in point-of-view or beliefs between students can lead to advances in their understanding even when the beliefs are initially incorrect or inadequate (Glachan & Light, 1982).

Two related reasons have been suggested to explain why peer interaction appears to have a privileged role in changing students cognitive structures. The first is the difference in perceived status between adult views and student views. Students expect that teachers will have different knowledge and different beliefs. Being made aware of these differences is not necessarily a challenge, especially if the student is culturally and socially distant from the teacher and has developed ways of appearing to be involved or get the right answers without actually engaging with the curriculum. Students, however, generally expect other students to see the world in the same way as they do. Confronting other students' different beliefs presents a more immediate and personally significant challenge (Flavell, 1963; Piaget, 1928). However, as Driver and her associates have pointed out, children can, and often do, hold alternative or conflicting beliefs that they learn to select and apply only in socially appropriate contexts (Driver et al., 1994). Without the active involvement of the teacher, students may come to accept holding incompatible beliefs as socially acceptable.

The second related reason arises from the interrelated nature of the cognitive and the social in peer relationships in the classroom. Perret-Clermont has suggested that when students try to resolve the differences between their knowledge and beliefs, they are driven more by social imperatives than by the need for logical coherence.

> Cognitive processes and social relations are so intricately interwoven in learning at school that it is difficult to separate them. (1991, p. 58)

This is the view that underlies the 'socio-constructionist' theories of Doise and Mugny (Doise, 1991; Doise & Mugny, 1984). The driving force behind the developmental effects of peer interaction is the social disequilibrium that differences in perceptions and beliefs creates: 'without this social conflict, the child would be unlikely to feel cognitive conflict' (Doise & Mugny, 1984, p. 160).

Although conflict or disagreement is the occasion for change, it is the search for agreement, resolution of differences, and establishment of mutual understanding that creates cognitive change (Amigues, 1988, 1990). For example, in a study of young children's attempts to solve binary matrix problems, Blaye (1990) found that the children made most progress when the experimenter required the children to reach agreement. The resolution of their differences required the children to take several points of view into account and to develop persuasive explanations for their own perspectives.

In the classroom, conflict about subject matter frequently arises as a result of specific task requirements that require agreement or the coordination of individual viewpoints. The following excerpt from a sixth-grade classroom illustrates the interaction of social processes with knowledge construction. The student group was working on the task of identifying and making a list of the similarities and differences between two photographs of people working on the snow in Antarctica. The students had not been told what the photographs were about.

Paul:	(looking at one picture) They're studying something. Oh, a little penguin!
Pupil:	Oh cool!
Paul:	In one of them there's a penguin and in the other there isn't ...
Joy (to self):	Mm ... They're just telling the weather or something aren't they?
Paul:	That [picture] there's definitely meteorology. I'm not sure about that [other picture].
Joy:	Yeah. What's that?
Maude:	They might be actually two women here.
Paul:	(responding to Joy, talking at the same time as Maude) Yeah. That's what I want to know. Unless that's about the weather too.
Koa:	They might be looking for, no, they might be looking for ah, say ...

Joy:	Yeah. They might be testing how cold or …
Koa:	Yeah. They might be testing how cold it is. They might be testing how, if there's any life in it [inaudible].
Paul:	(talking at the same time as Koa) They might be pretending not to look and catch the penguin when it comes walking by. What penguin is that? That's an Adelie isn't it?
Joy:	Don't know …
Maude:	Its so sweet.
Paul:	I'll give you one difference. You see people in this one and there's one person in this one. Maude, there's two people in the top one and there's one in the bottom one. That's different (talking over the top of a discussion between Joy and Maude about how to spell 'similarity'). The bottom one's doing meteorology. I don't know about the top one.
Koa:	… What exactly is that [object in picture]?
Joy:	They were telling the weather. [It's a] weather something.
Paul:	(talking at the same time as Joy) Ah, there's a meteorology thing. Yeah, meteorology.
Maude:	They look it up or something or do something to it at the end of the day.
Koa:	They see how cold it is.
Paul:	(talking at the same time as Koa) Yeah that's how they tell the weather.

The students in this group were engaged in coordinating their different perceptions of the content of the two pictures. What each contributed was determined by their relative social status and the accommodations they made to the others. Paul was sure of himself and his knowledge. He interrupted the other students (who were girls) and either ignored what they said (e.g., Maude's comment that 'they might be actually two women here') or redefined what they said in his own words (e.g., 'there's definitely meteorology'). The conflict of ideas paralleled and was part of the gender conflict occurring within the group. What this group recorded about the similarities and differences between the two photographs was largely defined by Paul rather than the girls in the group.

Several researchers have attempted to identify the ways in which conflict between students can lead to cognitive development. Miller, for example, argues that students' beliefs are like scientific theories. It is the accumulation of negative evidence that ultimately results in the theory being overturned and replaced. Students, like scientists, are unlikely to perceive or pay attention to negative evidence while they are perceiving and processing experience from within their own existing cognitive structures. Miller suggests that the social interaction of the classroom can create the circumstances in which students are forced to pay attention to negative evidence. However, if social interaction is to lead to a change in belief and to more advanced cognitive structures, the participants must abide by a set of cooperative principles that allow for the productive resolution of arguments. For example, students must agree to accept a statement as valid if no one can find contrary evidence or a good reason for denying it. This leads to what Miller calls the 'co-construction of negations' (1987, p. 237). One student makes a claim on the basis of experience, and another student makes a contrary claim on the basis of different personal experience. If both claims cannot be denied by either, then they have co-constructed a negation that must be resolved. It is the reflective resolution of such negations that leads to the creation of more advanced cognitive structures.

Mason and Santi (1994) studied a fifth-grade class in which the teacher taught the students to engage in productive argumentation. The class was studying a science unit on pollution. Mason and Santi used transcripts of class discussion to identify the way differences of opinion and belief were resolved by the students. They classified the argument steps the students used (e.g., making a claim, rebutting a claim, using a generalisation as a backing for a claim), their epistemic moves (e.g., referring to personal experience, describing an analogy, referring to evidence), and the references the students made to their own meta-cognitive processes (e.g., 'I think that …,' 'I like to see evidence first …,' 'You think that because …').

Their analysis provides examples of how students, trained by a teacher to argue productively, can arrive at collective solutions. Mason and Santi describe the way ideas can be collectively developed as they pass from student to student during the discussion. They detail the ways differences can be resolved as the students examine each others' ideas and submit them to rational examination. As the argumentation becomes more complex and more articulate, the students express higher levels of meta-cognitive awareness. This in turn stimulates more complex and articulated argumentation.

Wood has argued that students need to engage in 'reflective relational activity' (1994a, p. 5). He describes an incident from a mathematics classroom in which the class was discussing ways of subtracting multi-digit numbers (e.g., $53 - 17$). One student (Jeff) was puzzled about a mistake that several other students (including Mark) were making and finally identified why.

Jeff: Oh, I know how they did it! The switched it [the digits] around.
             What Mark was doing was switching it around … all he was doing was switching it around!

Mark had been puzzled about his mistake and now was further puzzled by Jeff's description of how he must have made the mistake ('switching it around'). As the class discussion proceeded Mark was observed trying to solve the problem again, this time counting with his fingers. This procedure produced the same answer as the other students and he immediately called out, 'Yeah. Now I understand! ... Now I understand!' (Wood, 1994a, p. 11). For Mark, Jeff's comment had been the trigger that, combined with his own concern about why he had got the answer wrong, had provoked him into trying a different method. The different method worked.

Wood is careful to point out that, in the classroom he observed, the students were encouraged to seek their own solutions to mathematics problems and were expected to be able to describe and justify their procedures to other students. In this context discussions between students played an important role in the creative acquisition of new mathematical procedures and insights. Hiebert and Wearne (1993) have also reported an analysis of the talk occurring in classes in which problem solving, reflection, and the communication of reasons and explanations were encouraged. They concluded that the critical aspect of successful classroom discussion was the way in which it focused student thinking for continuous periods of time on the relevant subject matter.

What remains unexamined in these studies is the relationship between the cognitive quality of the interactions occurring between teachers and students and changes that might be occurring in the cognitive structures in individual student minds. The research of Mason and Santi has shown that, in the right classroom context, with the appropriate curriculum content, relatively young students (10-11 years) can, through their own interactions, escalate the complexity and sophistication of their social argumentation. Although they suggest that experience with such argumentation changes the complexity and sophistication in the students' own thinking processes, it is not clear how this might occur.

Peer Tutoring and the Structuring of Student Thinking

An account of the cognitive constructivist perspective would not be complete without including some reference to those studies of cooperative learning that focus on the intellectual quality of student interactions in cooperative and peer tutoring groups. Early studies of why peer tutoring worked in some contexts and with some students better than with others suggested that it was the frequency and quality of explanations that was the critical factor. While giving and receiving directions and demonstrations was not related to measures of learning, the giving and receiving of explanations was related to learning (Fuchs, Fuchs, Bentz, Phillips, & Hamlett, 1994; Swing & Peterson, 1982). It has been suggested that giving and receiving explanations is effective because it involves more complex and elaborated cognitive processing (Cohen, 1994).

On the basis of these findings, several researchers have developed ways of training students to participate more effectively in peer tutoring and cooperative learning groups. Implicit in these studies is the belief that students, left to their own devices, will not normally engage in intellectually engaging discussion. Students need to be shown how to ask the right questions of each other and how to provide the right kinds of explanations. King, in a series of studies, has looked at the effects of training students to use 'guided cooperative questioning' (King, 1994; King & Rosenshine, 1993). According to King, students will normally identify associations, elaborate and draw inferences when they first encounter, and try to make sense of new knowledge. However, with specific training, these processes can be made 'intentional' and consequently more likely to produce 'highly elaborated and richly integrated mental representations' (1994, p. 340).

In King's studies, fourth- and fifth-grade students working on health science topics were trained and given prompt cards to guide their questioning of each other. The purpose of the questions was to focus their thinking on the connections between different aspects of the topics and between the topics and out-of-school experiences. The students were also trained in how to answer the questions with explanations and reasons. The training produced improvements in the students' comprehension of the topics and their ability to draw inferences and to make connections to other knowledge.

An alternative approach to getting students to engage in more effective thinking about subject matter has been to focus on the classroom climate and the kinds of student behaviours that the teacher encourages and models. Wood, for example, has argued that if students are to be encouraged to talk about and share ideas, they need to feel confident that their ideas, their explanations, and the conclusions they reach, will be treated with respect (Wood, 1994b). This requires the teacher to both encourage and model the sharing and justification of one's own ideas and the constructive criticism of other people's ideas. The difficulty for the teacher is to avoid a climate in which the teacher's own ideas are accepted as authoritative or privileged, while at the same time assisting the students to construct for themselves the most adequate and coherent ideas.

> Teachers struggle to find a balance between probing, pushing, and offering suggestions to encourage student reflection and hindering or interrupting the flow of the child's thought. (1994b, p. 15)

Several research groups are currently working on experimental programs designed to create mathematics classrooms in which students are encouraged to construct their own mathematical knowledge through both individual and social cognitive processes (see, for example, Carpenter et al., 1993; Cobb et al., 1992; Hiebert & Wearne, 1993). The purpose, as Hiebert and Wearne describe it, is to create classrooms in which students 'express their beliefs and opinions with their classmates, defend them in the face of questions and question others' ideas' (Hiebert & Wearne, 1993, p. 396). By working together, they are made aware of different perspectives and potential solutions. This leads them to 'recognise incongruities and elaborate, clarify and reorganise their own thinking' (Hiebert & Wearne, 1993, p. 396).

Constructing the 'Right' Knowledge

Although the constructivist view of student cognition emphasises the personal and/or social nature of the knowledge that students acquire from classroom experiences, most of those concerned with designing classroom tasks and activities to enhance student knowledge construction are aware that students cannot be expected to discover or create for themselves the important concepts and ways of thinking that characterise the major curriculum areas.

> Learners need to be given access not only to physical experiences but also to the concepts and models of conventional science. The challenge lies in helping learners to appropriate these models for themselves, to appreciate their domains of applicability and, within such domains, to be able to use them. (Driver et al., 1994, p. 7)

This issue is a critical one because it brings to the fore the potential conflict that exists between the role of the teacher (or the task) as the motivator or facilitator of student thinking, and the role of the teacher as the source of established and effective knowledge. Consider the example, described above, of the fourth-grade teacher who was trying to get the students to understand that air has weight. He gave his students instructions about how to carry out an experiment in which they could see for themselves that a balloon inflated with air was heavier than an uninflated balloon. However, students at this age do not normally conceive of air as a material substance (Carey, 1991). They were unable to understand the experiment in terms of the weight of the air in the balloons. The teacher found that he needed to explain the meaning of the experiment before the students could understand what happened. As several researchers have noted (e.g., Brickhouse, 1994; Driver et al., 1994), many of the important concepts in science and mathematics conflict with the common sense knowledge that is widely accepted in our culture. Such concepts (e.g., that air has weight) are either counter intuitive or based on evidence that is not available within ordinary experience. They are never likely to be discovered by the students without the active involvement of the teacher.

However, if the teacher intervenes and tries to introduce alternative scientific concepts and ways of interpreting data, the student can easily reach the conclusion that, in the end, it is the teacher who holds the key to all important knowledge. This invites students to try to subvert or short circuit even the best designed activities in order to discover the 'real' answers in the head of the teacher or the back of the textbook. It may also prevent any significant connection being made between the new knowledge and the underlying conceptual structures that students use to understand and assimilate their experiences.

This concern has led several researchers to suggest that the important focus of classroom tasks should be those underlying conceptual structures that play a significant general role in determining how students acquire specific knowledge and skills. A series of studies initiated by Case and his associates have been concerned with identifying the 'central conceptual structures' that determine how children understand and learn from experience in broadly defined domains of experience (Case, 1991). Their studies indicate that these central conceptual structures can be affected by forms of instruction that encourage students to assemble and coordinate simpler conceptual structures into increasingly complex structures and cognitive control processes (see, for example, Case & Sandieson, 1991; McKeough, 1992). The effects of this instruction generalises to a range of different tasks and experiences within the same general domain (e.g., logico-mathematical relationships, spatial representations, understanding of personal intentionality).

Research of the kind being carried out by Case and his associates comes from within a neo-Piagetian tradition and like the research of Perret-Clermont and others in the socio-constructionist tradition, is concerned with the enhancement of developmental processes that have previously been seen as biologically or genetically determined. Quite how this cognitive developmental research relates to studies of knowledge and skill acquisition within such curriculum areas as mathematics, science, or social studies, remains at this stage an open question.

Summary of the Cognitive Constructivist Perspective

As the discussion above indicates, research within the cognitive constructivist perspective is in a state of evolution, pushing at the boundaries with developmental research and research on social and cultural processes in the classroom. If there is a centre to the cognitive constructivist view of students' classroom experience it is the claim that students construct their own knowledge. This occurs as their minds are engaged by classroom activities and as they try to make their own sense of the experiences that arise from those activities. Learning has been described as the 'residue' of the mental processing that occurs in the classroom.

On this view, learning and thinking are not distinct from each other. Mental processes are motivated by the need to make sense of experience. Making sense of experience involves integrating that experience with established knowledge within the constraints of existing cognitive structures. It involves resolving apparent contradictions not only between parts of what is known but also between what is known and what is implied by what is known. And it involves creating new knowledge and ultimately new conceptual structures wherever the available knowledge or conceptual structures appear incomplete, inadequate, or contradictory.

Because new experience is filtered through existing knowledge and beliefs, creating significant cognitive change appears to present a 'paradox.' How can new knowledge and understanding be created when existing knowledge determines how experience is perceived and understood (Bereiter, 1985; Fodor, 1980). Interaction with the knowledge and beliefs of peers within significant social groups appears to play a privileged role in generating new beliefs and knowledge structures.

The major problem that confronts the teacher is how to structure and guide the students' mental processes so that the 'residue' of these mental processes is consistent with desirable curriculum outcomes. This is especially critical when common sense and commonly held beliefs are inconsistent with significant concepts in the disciplines and when students underlying conceptual structures are inadequate for comprehending and acquiring complex skills and abilities. Somehow the student must also be helped to appropriate and make use of the cultural concepts and tools that are the essential to the disciplines (Driver et al., 1994).

THE SOCIOCULTURAL AND COMMUNITY FOCUSED PERSPECTIVE

The cognitive constructivist theories of student thinking and learning have been criticised for being too closely tied to a technocratic, positivist, and individualist perception of education and the social order (cf. O'Loughlin, 1992). We must, it has been claimed, take much greater account of the important roles that social relations, community and culture play in cognition and learning (cf. Lave, 1988; Rogoff, 1990).

Mind and rationality are concepts that are central to the cognitive constructivist view of student experience and learning, but Lave argues that these concepts cannot be considered in isolation from the activities and settings in which they might be identified (Lave, 1991). It is a mistake to focus on students as individuals who construct their own knowledge and store it as disembodied mental representations in memory. Knowledge is not distinguishable from the process of knowing. Persons are not distinguishable from the activities and social settings in which they act. The processes of the mind are not universal and do not function in a uniform way across different social and cultural contexts.

According to this view, what we must understand is that the concepts of mind, rationality, and knowledge are themselves cultural concepts deeply embedded in an ideology that privileges the individualistic and technocratic power relations of Western culture. In order to free schools and students from the patterns of failure and alienation that continue to resist attempts to reform schools, we need a radical revision of the ways in which we conceptualise the socialisation of students (O'Loughlin, 1992; Rogoff, 1990, 1994).

Lave provides one of the more explicitly sociocultural critiques of the cognitive constructivist view. On the basis of her studies in a variety of non-Western and non-school settings, she proposes that the process of acquiring culturally significant knowledge should be seen as the process of becoming a member of a community. It is 'an emerging property of a whole person's legitimate peripheral participation in communities of practice' (1991, p. 63). A 'community of practice' is a group of people who are recognised as having a special expertise in some area of significant cultural practice (e.g., midwives, teachers, baseball players). The learner seeks to develop an identity as a member of a community of practice, and the process is driven and shaped by the self identity formation involved in becoming an 'old timer' in the community.

Behind this description of learning as a process of identity formation within a culturally structured community lies a conception of mind and knowledge as processes that occur as people interact with each other in communal activity. The person and the social activity are not distinct from each other. The boundaries between mind and community, between thinking and social interaction, between knowing and doing, are of little significance. Mind and the social and cultural world are said to 'constitute each other' (Lave, 1991, p. 63). Cognition is located 'in the experiencing of the world and the world experienced, through activity, in context' (Lave, 1988, p. 178).

Contained in Lave's view is a critique of present school practice as essentially artificial and alienating. Curriculum knowledge and thinking have become divorced from their real origins and turned into commodities that have little meaning or significance in the lives of the students outside the school. Such knowledge as students do acquire in school lacks authenticity because of its artificial separation from the communities and sociocultural practices of which it was originally an integral part. Failure is the inevitable product of isolating students from legitimate participation in authentic communities of practice.

Because thinking and learning are not seen as an activity of the mind in isolation, but rather as part of, or constituted by, the visible social interaction that takes place between members of a community, teaching is redefined as the activities of 'old timers' who are exercising their skill and knowledge in the legitimate practices of the community and assisting 'novices' to participate alongside them. The need for the community to replace its members and recreate itself is identified as the central goal of the process.

Situating cognition in the process of community activity leads to a view of cognition as 'distributed' across the context in which it occurs.

> Cognition observed in everyday practice is distributed – stretched over, not divided among – mind, body, activity, and culturally organised settings (which include other actors). (Lave, 1988, p. 1)

In order to identify and understand cognitive processes in everyday community settings, it is necessary to identify and describe:

a) the involvement of other persons,
b) the way the culture structures and gives meaning to the setting within which the cognition occurs, and
c) the tools and practices that are involved in the activity.

The work of Saxe (1988), on the mathematical knowledge and skills of the young children selling candy on the streets of a Brazilian city, provides an example of how this kind of analysis works. He found that the currency the children used had become for them an alternative representational system for making mathematical calculations. Instead of using the conventional rational number system, they used the currency denominations as the units of counting. The pricing ratios the candy-selling children used to make profits on their candy had evolved as a set of conventions among successive generations of the young sellers. These pricing conventions structured the mathematical procedures the children invented and became skilled at using. What Saxe's research shows is that understanding the invented mathematical knowledge and skills of these children required an understanding of the material, social, and cultural conditions of their work on the streets. We lack this kind of understanding of the development of mathematical knowledge and skills in schools because we are, ourselves, part of the cultural conventions that structure and give meaning to mathematics in schools. To understand fully what children must learn, we need to step back from the culture of the school and see how mathematics forms a part of the larger cultural context. This was the purpose of one of Lave's studies of the shopper's use of mathematics in the supermarket (Lave, 1988).

Rogoff's work has also played a significant role in developing the sociocultural view of learning and cognition (cf. Rogoff, 1994; Rogoff, Matusov, & White, in press). Like Lave, Rogoff defines learning as a function of the transformation of roles that occurs as a person participates in, and becomes an experienced member of, a community of learners. She emphasises the 'situated' nature of learning. Instead of making distinctions between the development in a child of behaviour, cognition, language, and affective responses, all aspects of development should be seen as constituting each other within the cultural activity in which they occur. The child's development is the process that occurs as the child comes to identify, understand, and handle particular problems or types of activities. For this reason, it is the problems or types of activities that must become the unit of analysis and understanding, not the child as an individual or the child's individual characteristics or skills (1990, p. 190).

Again, like Lave, Rogoff makes significant use of the concept of 'apprenticeship' (Lave, 1991; Rogoff, 1990, 1994). This concept draws attention to the active role that children take in initiating and organising their own learning, the socially interactive nature of the learning process in which the expertise and support of experienced others (adults, teachers) is essential, and the way the process is structured by technologies and cultural institutions. According to Rogoff, children learn early to use adults as sources of information and guidance for interpreting, understanding, and learning to participate in new situations (Rogoff, 1990).

How Are Learning and Cognition Socially and Culturally Constituted?

If, as Rogoff and Lave assert, the mind and social interaction 'constitute each other,' how are we to understand the changes that take place as a child acquires expertise within a community of practice?

Central to their analysis is the change that takes place in an activity as the expert and novice participate in the activity together. 'Learning is a process of the transformation of participation itself' (Rogoff, 1994, p. 209). Rogoff cites as examples the parent-child interaction that occurs as a child learns to become competent at some mutual activity. As the child tries to participate in the activity and is guided by the parent, the behaviours of both the parent and the child change. Initially the child is expected to do very little, and the parent adapts to the child's level. Progressively the child contributes more to the joint activity with the parent. As this happens, the parent's involvement moves up again towards the expert level. The motivation and focus is on sustaining the joint activity. Participating is the immediate and all-absorbing problem, and it is through the increasing participation of the child that changes in the nature of the activity occur.

The process of progressive change from novice to expert can be illustrated with examples of parent-child interaction from Dimitracopoulou's study of the development of conversational competence in children (Dimitracopoulou, 1990). As part of her study she asked mother-child pairs to find a way to play a simple board game. The following excerpts from conversations between parent-child pairs engaged in this task illustrate the progressive changes that occurred in the children's conversational competence. The first excerpt comes from the interaction between a mother and her 3.8 year old child (Dimitracopoulou, 1990, p. 104).

Mother:	(pointing to object) What is that?
Child:	Pig.
Mother:	What shall we do with the little pig?
Child:	(shrugs)
Mother:	Shall we use it in our game?
Child:	Yes.
Mother:	OK. Do you want to be the pig?
Child:	(nods head)
Mother:	OK, and I'll be the cow.
Child:	(points at alligator on board) Alligator.
Mother:	Yes an alligator! Scary!

The child's involvement in this interaction is minimal. The mother structures the progress of the game, and the child, who is very interested in playing, does little more than respond to the mother's questions. An excerpt from the interaction between a 4.6 year old and her mother shows some progression towards the increasing involvement and control by the child (Dimitracopoulou, 1990, p. 146).

Mother:	You know what we could do?
Child:	(shakes head) What?
Mother:	(rolling dice) We could roll the dice and whatever colour comes on top (points at colours on dice) we go there!
Child:	(nods head, takes dice) OK!
Mother:	(Looking at board) And where are we going to?
Child:	(Leaning forward, pointing) The finish line is here.

By the age of 6.9 years, the child is capable of more active participation and has the social and linguistic skills to organise the game for both of the participants (Dimitracopoulou, 1990, p. 144).

Child:	OK! Let's play it.
Mother:	(pointing to board) What is this?
Child:	Go. This is the starting point. And you move into here (pointing to pathways on board) into two turns.
Mother:	And how do you get turns?
Child:	Eh, we, … We, eh, pick a number on this! (points at the dice)

Rogoff describes this progression in the nature of adult-child interaction as 'participatory appropriation' and identifies it as the substance of cognitive development.

> People make a process their own through their (necessarily creative) efforts to understand and contribute to social activity, which, by its very nature, involves bridging between several ways of understanding a situation. (Rogoff, 1993, p. 141)

What becomes progressively the same between expert and novice is not only the skill, but the understanding and knowledge. The novice comes to think and perceive as well as behave like the expert.

This progressive appropriation of the expert's knowledge and skill is distinguished from the concept of 'internalisation' that cognitive constructivist theorists use to describe the acquisition of mental skills (cf. Carey, 1986; Piaget, 1978). Whereas internalisation refers to the incorporation of behaviour and knowledge into the cognitive processes of an individual mind, appropriation is the process by which two people come to understand each other and work effectively together. They each appropriate the product of their mutually evolving partnership in the activity. The process is inherently mutual, creative, and situation specific (Rogoff, 1993).

As with some behaviourist views, concepts like 'memory,' 'mental representation,' and 'internalisation' are seen as unnecessary and misleading. The focus of analysis must be on the process of participation. Changes in participation are the substance of development. According to Rogoff, cognitive theorists make the mistake of seeing behaviour as merely surface features that need to be penetrated in order to identify the real development taking place underneath (Rogoff, 1993, p. 145). For Rogoff, however, while interactive behaviour is the focus of analysis, it needs to be understood in terms of the goals and understandings that it involves. Becoming a member of a community is more than just learning the requisite behaviours. It also involves taking on the goals and perspectives of members of that community. As Schoenfeld describes it, membership 'subtly shapes one's interpretive frameworks' (1989, p. 79). According to Lave

> It is not that behaviour is all there is to it, but that behaviour is the same thing as culture, that cognition is the same thing as social interaction, that 'mind, culture, history, and the social world ... constitute each other.' (1991, p. 63)

The Theories of Vygotsky and the Soviet Psychologists

The sociocultural theories of Lave, Rogoff, Lemke, Wertsch, and others cannot be fully understood without taking into account the work of Vygotsky on the social origins of intellect. The focus of Vygotsky's psychological research and writing was to explain the nature of mind by tracing its development and maturation in the child. In a much quoted excerpt, Vygotsky described his general genetic law of psychological development:

> Any function in the child's cultural development appears twice, or on two planes. First it appears on the social plane, and then on the psychological plane. First it appears between people as an inter-psychological category, and then within the child as an intra-psychological category. This is equally true with regard to voluntary attention, logical memory, the formation of concepts, and the development of volition. (1981, p. 163)

For Vygotsky, the origins of all mental processes were to be found in the social interactions that children had with other people. The forms and structures of the higher mental processes are the same as the forms and structures of social interaction. These forms and structures are largely determined by the technical and psychological tools available in a culture. These tools include, as well as technical machinery, such cultural artifacts as works of art, maps, mathematical symbols, and most importantly, language itself. The tools that make up our culture structure, and are the context for, social interaction. Consequently they have a profound effect on socialisation and development.

Although the concept of mental function implicit in Vygotsky's writing is one in which the social, the psychological, and the technical (cultural tools) are all embedded, he described development as the process by which the social becomes psychological through the medium of cultural tools. Vygotsky was impressed by the critical role that language plays in children's development.

> ... we have found that speech not only accompanies practical activity but also plays a specific role in carrying it out ... speech and action are part of one and the same complex psychological function directed toward the solution of the problem at hand. (1978, p. 25)

Initially speech is social and accompanies the child's activities. Progressively this activity-related speech becomes internal and occurs before rather than during activity. In this way speech becomes the basis for planning, self-awareness, and personal control.

Critical to the process of development is Vygotsky's concept of a 'zone of proximal development.' This 'zone' is defined as the distance or space between what a child can do alone and what a child can do with adult or expert assistance (1978, p. 86). It identifies those aspects of a child's development that are in the transitional state between the social (aided) and the psychological (independent), 'functions that will mature tomorrow but are currently in an embryonic state' (1978, p. 86).

There are three important characteristics of the transitional processes that go on in the child's zone of proximal development. First, it involves interaction between participants of unequal expertise or knowledge. The language and activities through which they interact have different meanings for the participants, but in order for the social interaction to work, they behave as though they had the same meanings. According to Newman, Griffin, and Cole (1989) it is this difference between the expert's and the novice's meanings and skills that is essential to the development that occurs in the zone of proximal development. During the process of transition from the social to the psychological, the understandings, perceptions, and the skills of the participants move together, each modifying the other. It is the motivation for social interaction that drives this progressive coordination of perceptions, understandings and skills.

Second, during the process of interaction, the child internalises a transformed version of the interaction. These internalised interactions become mental processes, not in their original form but in what Vygotsky calls a 'quasi-social' form (1981, p. 164). They retain the sense and basic structures of the original but not the specific surface features. For example, as the language used in the social interaction becomes internalised, it loses the surface features of syntax and morphology and becomes more fluid and richer in personal associations (Wertsch, 1991).

Third, the outcome of the transitions that take place within the child's zone of proximal development is the ability of the child to act and think independently. The child does not individually construct new knowledge, understandings or skills. Critical aspects of the child's development take place within the mutual interaction between adult and child. A cognitive constructivist view sees the mind of the child struggling to accommodate new experience to existing knowledge and sees the construction of new knowledge as continuous with old knowledge. In Vygotsky's view, the accommodation takes place in the social interaction, not within the mind of the child. The child develops first as a 'collective subject' in collective activities before developing as an independent individual (Davydov, 1995, p. 15).

Vygotsky himself was aware that the process of internalising or acquiring the structures of social interaction was not well understood. He saw it as a series of transformations in which external activities were 'reconstructed' internally (1978, p. 56). This occurred during collective (social) activities as the acquisition of the signs and symbols that constitute the child's culture. The essential point is that development takes place during social activities. What matters is not the child's maturation or prior experience or ability but the specific cultural and social context in which the child's life is embedded.

Transferring the Sociocultural Perspective to the Classroom

If social process becomes the substance of cognitive process, then the problem for educators becomes one of creating a social process in the classroom that models effective cognitive processing. Brown and Campione and their associates have undertaken a series of experiments in which they have attempted to translate the sociocultural perspective into specific classroom practice (Brown, 1992, 1994; Brown, Ash, Rutherford, Nakagawa, Gordon, & Campione, 1993; Brown & Campione, 1994). They have called these experiments the 'community of learners' project (COL).

The first problem that needs to be faced in making this translation is to decide what kind of community the classroom should become. If learning is an apprenticeship involving the gradual transformation of the identity of a student from that of novice into that of expert in the classroom community, what kind of transformation should be involved?

Brown and her associates argue that although it is tempting to see the science classroom as the place where students become apprentice scientists or the mathematics classroom as the place where students become apprentice mathematicians, such an interpretation is unrealistic. Within the limitations of the time and resources available, students are not going to become experts in the disciplines. However, it is critical that students become expert learners within the contexts of the different curriculum areas. Thus it makes sense to try to create, within the classroom, a community of learners in which the teacher models the role of an expert, self-motivated and intelligent learner. Students can then be encouraged to take on the role of 'learning apprentices' (Brown et al., 1993, p. 190).

Two things need to be done to establish a community of learners. First the activities of learning have to be defined, modelled, and practised. Second, norms of practice have to be established that will structure effective participation in learning communities. In the classroom community described by Brown and Campione and the participating teachers (Brown et al., 1993; Brown & Campione, 1994), two reciprocal activity structures were set up. In one activity structure the students worked together in teaching-learning groups to share their newly acquired knowledge and develop new research questions. The method used was reciprocal teaching with the jigsaw technique for structuring group cooperation (Palincsar & Brown, 1989). Students learned to participate in these teaching-learning groups taking the roles of both teacher and learner.

In the second activity structure, the students worked together in research groups asking and finding out the answers to questions on a designated segment of the curriculum topic. Each research group contained one member of each teaching-learning group, so that each member of the teaching-learning groups had a different area of expertise to bring to the group (hence the 'jigsaw' technique). Technology and resources were made available to the students as they helped each other to search for information and to prepare what they discovered for later teaching to the others in their teaching-learning groups.

Structuring the whole process were the norms of cooperative collaboration among students. Students were encouraged to take responsibility for their own learning and to share their expertise with others. Underlying this was an emphasis on mutual respect between students, and between the teacher and students and others who provided resources for the students. The use of the jigsaw method and the deliberate seeding of the classroom with ideas and resources meant that each student had, on appropriate occasions, expertise that she or he could share with others. Students were also assisted to become experts in social facilitation and dispute reconciliation. The goal of these norms was to establish a classroom in which 'constructive discussion, questioning and criticism were the mode rather than the exception' (Brown et al., 1993, p. 200).

The outcome of this kind of classroom, according to Brown and her associates, is the development of students as members of a community of research practice in which they adopt the ways of knowing, the cultural practices, the discourse patterns and belief systems of scholars (Brown et al., 1993, p. 223). Scholarly ways of learning and thinking are appropriated by students as they discuss and negotiate with each other the meanings of their jointly constructed activities.

Rogoff has described a public school which exemplifies her concept of a community of learners (Rogoff, 1994; Rogoff et al., in press). This school, which has been in operation for more than a decade, involves students, teachers, and parents in cooperative learning activities. Relationships of power and control are replaced by relationships in which adults and students see themselves as primarily learners willing to assist each other in achieving their learning goals. Adults serve as facilitators not as authorities.

The emphasis is on the learning process and not on outcomes. Projects are initiated out of the interests of the students and students learn to take responsibility for their own learning and the choices that they make. Assessment of progress occurs through participation with the students rather than by external means. Students 'learn how to coordinate with, support, and lead others, to become responsible and organised in their management of their own learning, and to be able to build on their inherent interests to learn in new areas and to sustain motivation to learn' (Rogoff, 1994, p. 225).

A more formal approach to creation of an effective community of learners has been described by a Russian school psychologist working in Moscow (Zuckerman, 1994). The program she described was set up to prepare young students for the transition from kindergarten to the more formal Russian first grade. Students were involved in a training program designed to enhance their skills as effective students in grade school. This involved teaching them to know how and when to ask for information from the teacher or other students, how to evaluate their own knowledge, and how to develop mutual trust and discuss their ideas with peers. The effects of the program were evaluated, not only through gains in the targeted skills, but also through changes in the students' intellectual development. Specifically measures were taken of changes in the students' ability to decenter their own thinking by coordinating the beliefs, perceptions, and emotions of other students with their own. At this stage in a child's intellectual development, the decentration of thinking is a critical transition.

What is significant about Zuckerman's study is that the development of effective social and classroom skills is seen as integral to the development of intellectual skills. Training in one area produces gains in the other. Where Rogoff, and Brown and Campione, approached the development of an effective classroom as a matter of developing a learning-focused community, Zuckerman approached it as a matter of developing specific socio-intellectual skills. She did, however, emphasise the critical role of mutual trust and the use of 'unauthoritarian teachers with a gentle, democratic style of interacting with children.' (1994, p. 412)

The Culture of Studenting

The sociocultural perspectives described so far in this section have been focused primarily on the integration or 'mutual constitution' of the social and the cognitive. Closely related to these perspectives is the sociological analysis of how students learn to be students within the traditional school system (see, for example, Woods, 1980). Schools, and the classrooms within them, are communities that inherit and develop their own institutional culture. As students enter school and as they are assigned to each new class and teacher, they also inherit and must negotiate anew their own individual positions, roles, and status (Ball, 1980). In the process of this negotiation, students develop and use strategies that allow them to assert their own needs and pursue their own goals.

> To a greater or lesser extent, the social order of the classroom is a negotiated phenomenon with teachers and pupils adopting strategies which promote their particular interests. (Denscombe, 1980, p. 55)

Within the framework of the positions and roles that students negotiate with their teachers and other students in their classrooms, there are the changing patterns of friendships and personal relationships that make up the total life of the students within the school (see, for example, Deegan, 1993). Creating a full account of the ways in which sociocultural processes and cognition are interrelated requires all aspects of the school life of students to be taken into account. As yet such an integrated account has not been produced.

Summary of the Sociocultural Perspective

The sociocultural perspectives described in this section were developed from the desire to see school learning within a larger cultural context. This led to a focus on the culturally embedded nature of classroom processes and the central role that cultural norms and artefacts play in structuring the nature of the learning and the way we view learning. So long as we take the cultural and social context of school classrooms for granted and keep them in the background of our thinking, we will focus on individual students and on cognition as a process of individual minds. If we step back and see the whole integrated system of schools, classrooms, students (and the norms, beliefs and concepts, that bind them together) as an example of a specific cultural practice, we will begin to see the concept of individual cognition as nothing more significant than an embedded fragment of larger and more inclusive cultural processes. Seen from outside, or from the perspective of other cultures and other cultural practices, learning and cognition take on a different appearance. They are distributed across or spread between all aspects of the activities and contexts in which they occur.

From this perspective, social groups or communities, and the collective activities they engage in, should be the focus of analysis. Shaping the nature of the educational process involves shaping the nature of the community in which it occurs. This means that educational change should be seen as cultural change. Rogoff, and Brown and Campione and their teachers, have understood this very well when they describe their experiments as creating 'communities of learners,' and see their task as creating a new culture in the classroom.

It is fortunate, though probably not an accident, that the writings of the Soviet psychologists Vygotsky and Leont'ev have recently become more widely available (cf. Wertsch, 1991). The Marxist view of human nature as the product of the social relations created by the conditions of human labour has much in common with a sociocultural analysis of human learning and thinking. Vygotsky has been credited with being the first psychologist to develop the view, from research evidence, that in the child's development, the mind is socially constructed (Leont'ev, 1981). It is for this reason that Vygotsky's work has played a central role in the development and support of the sociocultural perspective (cf. Newman et al., 1989).

THE LANGUAGE FOCUSED PERSPECTIVE

Implicit in the sociocultural theories of Lave and Rogoff is the importance of language as the primary sociocultural tool through which membership of communities of practice is socially negotiated. The significance of language in education has long been recognised, but in recent years a number of researchers have developed theories of student cognition and learning that focus primarily on the ways in which language is used in the classroom.

It is possible to distinguish three somewhat distinct kinds of language-focused theories of classroom process. The first type of language-focused theory is based on concepts and methods of analysis used in linguistics and in sociolinguistics (cf. Halliday, 1978). It is exemplified by the work of Green and her associates in the Santa Barbara Classroom Discourse Group (cf. Dixon, de la Cruz, Green, Lin, & Brandts, 1992). Their concern has been with the ways in which knowledge and opportunities to learn are negotiated and 'talked into being' in the classroom. The second is more closely related to the sociocultural perspective and is based on a view of language as a cultural artefact. Language is seen as consisting of a set of genres or discourses that embody the concepts, ways of thinking, acting, and valuing that define the different curriculum areas (e.g., Hicks, 1993; Holland, Anderson, & Palincsar, 1994; O'Loughlin, 1992; Wells, 1994, in press-a). Like the sociocultural perspective, this language-based analysis of student cognition and learning has been developed from the ideas of Vygotsky, Leont'ev, and Bakhtin. It also incorporates important concepts from the growing field of sociolinguistics (cf. Romaine, 1994). The third language-focused perspective includes those who see a specific linguistic genre as having central significance in cognition (cf. Egan, 1989, 1993; Hicks, 1993; Schank, 1990). These writers argue that the narrative genre is the primary organising structure that lies behind the way we process, come to understand, and remember experience.

Talking Knowledge Into Being

Green and Dixon have described the Santa Barbara Classroom Discourse Group as being concerned with 'understanding how everyday life in classrooms is constructed by members through their interactions, verbal and other, and how these constructions influence what students have opportunities to access, accomplish, and thus 'learn' in schools' (Green & Dixon, 1993, p. 231). They have attempted to identify the ways in which language both reflects and is a part of the negotiation of roles, responsibilities, norms, and mutual expectations between teacher and students. Language is used to construct a commonly held understanding of the purposes, events, tasks, and curriculum content of each of the activities occurring in the classroom.

Central to the view of the Santa Barbara Group is the claim that the events that occur in a classroom are the product of two intersecting dimensions. In one dimension, the social life of the students and teachers is developed and played out through the negotiation of roles and status. In time, a unique classroom culture is developed that embodies the results of many specific ongoing negotiations and events (Baker, 1992; Heras, 1993). Each classroom has its own evolving culture that is understood and known implicitly by its participants. The second dimension involves the evolution of curriculum knowledge and the opportunities and processes of learning. As students and teacher interact with each other, new and unique knowledge, or what is accepted and understood as knowledge, emerges: 'kinds of knowledge (academic and social) are talked into being by a range of discursive practices that coexist in teachers' and students' talk' (Heras, 1993, p. 295).

Because the knowledge emerging in a particular classroom is a social construction, it is a fluid, constantly evolving by-product of the students' and teacher's social interactions (Dixon et al., 1992). This is illustrated in the analysis that Brilliant-Mills carried out of the discourse and social interactions occurring in a mathematics classroom (1993). Brilliant-Mills describes mathematics as a 'language variety' or 'register' that, in a particular classroom, is 'socially and discursively constructed' (1993, p. 307). As the teacher introduces the activities to be carried out in the classroom, social and mathematical terms are introduced and social and discursive practices are established that, taken together, constitute 'talking mathematics into being.' Mathematics and the culture of the classroom evolve as the discourse continues. The classroom becomes a unique language community.

The following (abbreviated) transcript of a class discussion from one of our own studies illustrates how a teacher negotiates the norms and procedures which structure behaviour, understandings, and beliefs in the classroom. The class (sixth grade) was starting an integrated science and social studies unit on Antarctica. Teacher and students were discussing, on the first day of the unit, the homework they were to do on Antarctic animals.

Teacher: Okay. Shhhh. Right listening very carefully. Once you get this sheet, I'd like you just to read through it quietly ... and then we'll discuss it and I'll tell you what I expect. Your expectations. Okay? ... It says choose one Antarctic animal that you are interested in studying. Okay, the Adelie penguin, the skua, the blue whale, snow petrel, Weddel seal and the wandering albatross ... Okay, you might think of others that you wish to study ... Alright?

Student: Is this a type of project?

Teacher: It is sort of like a project. Thank you Kurt. Okay. Right. [Teacher then lists five things they could find out about the animal]

Teacher: Yes Kurt?

Kurt: Can we do all of them? Are you allowed to do all of them — all five things?

Teacher: Yeah, the reason that I asked for only two, rather than the whole lot is that I want you to do two at least really, really well. Okay. If I gave you the whole lot then you might find that you ran out of time and were just doing them, just really quickly ...

Maude: Um, what book, are we going to do it in?

Teacher: Okay. Um, I expect it, ... expect it to be done on refill paper ... Okay? I expect it to be your own work. Now that's very important. I don't want to read bits of the *Encyclopaedia Britannica* or the Greenpeace book on animals. Alright? I want to hear what you know and what you can tell me. Right?

Leigh: Can we do it in our social studies books?

Teacher: No. Right. The reason it's to be done on refill paper is that, every day next week you must be prepared to show me what you have done. Because if you carry on and I don't check up what you've done it will come to Thursday night and you'll spend probably five or eight hours, cram packing what you haven't done. I know that's how some people work. Okay. So every day you need to bring it to school, to work on. Kurt?

Kurt: Are we allowed to read the Greenpeace, Greenpeace books and stuff and then put our own words there?

Teacher: That's what's called paraphrasing. That's fine. Okay?

Leigh: How long does each section have to be?

Teacher: You have to um, make that decision. I want quality not quantity okay and I want quality in your own words. Alright. Okay.

What the teacher was negotiating was the nature of the process and product that will make up the students' study of Antarctica. This included the content (penguin, skua, blue whale, etc.), the procedures to be used ('I expect it to be done on refill paper') and the reasons for these procedures (so the work is not left until the last day), the emphasis on quality not quantity, the names for procedures

('That's what's called paraphrasing'), and the importance of different expectations ('I expect it to be your own work. Now that's very important.'). As the students were learning what to do, they were learning the words, the norms, and the ways of talking that constituted the 'genre' of the science and social studies in that classroom.

In parallel with the public negotiation of norms and expectations (illustrated above) the students also negotiate amongst themselves, establishing their own culture of norms and expectations. Just after the time of the preceding excerpt, the students in the same class were preparing for the next activity. The following private conversation was recorded between two boys as they prepared for that activity. The teacher had just asked them to write their notes with a pen not a pencil.

Jim:	[to himself as teacher mentions pen] Sorry I don't use pen. [to Ben] I don't use pen. (laughs)
Ben:	I do.
Jim:	I prefer not to. It's too messy for me.
Ben:	I can hardly even see ... I can hardly ... even see pencil.
Jim:	I hate using pens cause with me it's too messy 'cause my hand shivers when I try to do fine detail.
Ben:	Well um, well you know how I write messy right?
Jim:	Mmm.
Ben:	Well if I did it in ... pencil because the, I, my pencil's always blunt, 'cause I never bother to sharpen them very often, um I can hardly see the words so I have to use pen as well.
Ben:	Excuses, excuses!
Jim:	Yeah but it's a good one.

Although the teacher told all the students to use a pen, Jim decided not to. Between them Jim and Ben established their own set of norms based on their own reasons ('it's too messy 'cause my hand shivers,' 'Excuses, excuses!'). Such private conversations established further layers of mutual understandings and expectations between specific groups of students that shaped the social processes and the ways language was used and understood in that classroom.

What the Santa Barbara Group have drawn attention to is the critical role that mutual understanding plays in communication. Linguists have long understood that meaning is referred to by words, not contained in words (cf. Clark & Clark, 1977; Clark & Schaefer, 1989). The way words refer to meaning is a function of the cooperation and mutual understanding that is established or expected between speakers. Language works because of the specific experiences and understandings that speaker and listener share and attribute to each other (Grice, 1989). For example, in the course of normal conversation, speakers are expect-

ed to use the smallest number of words that will effectively convey their meaning (Grice's maxim of avoiding unnecessary prolixity). When speakers share
common experience and a common history, the words they use are few in
number and rich in reference to that common history. They are very different
from the words that would be used between speakers who did not share a common history.

In the classroom discussion quoted above, the teacher said that putting something in your own words was called paraphrasing. If, two or three days later, the
teacher looked at the homework done by one of the students and asked: 'Is this
a paraphrase?', the student would be expected to understand not only what the
word 'paraphrase' meant, but also that the teacher expected the homework to be
a paraphrase. Mutual understanding of this meaning and the implicit expectation was established during the class discussion (quoted above) and gave a
class-specific meaning to any subsequent use of the word by the teacher and students.

Lemke takes a more radical view of the way language shapes classroom experience (Lemke, 1990). His analysis of the language of science classrooms explores, not only the social interaction structures that provide the framework for
talking and understanding talk about science, but also the ways in which the
meanings of science concepts and ideas are constructed and elaborated in the
classroom. Lemke proposes a semantic as well as a sociocultural analysis of
classroom language. He is interested in the ways in which underlying meanings
come together and interact with each other. Ideas and concepts make sense by
virtue of their relationships with other ideas and concepts: 'Everything makes
sense only against the background of other things like it' (1990, p. 204). For example, dictionary definitions of words normally describe meanings by reference to the meanings of other words that are also defined in the dictionary. The
web of semantic relationships that define ideas and concepts are usually embedded in the way these ideas and concepts are talked about. As a consequence,
whenever a teacher is discussing a topic there is an enormous potential array of
meanings that are implicated and from which the student must select and adapt
appropriate meanings.

The following transcript illustrates the nature of the semantic web that Lemke is referring to. It is an extract from a discussion in another sixth-grade class
that was studying Antarctica. As part of this unit, the teacher invited a geologist
(who had carried out a mapping survey of mountains in Antarctica) to talk to
the class. She started her talk with a description of how cold it was in Antarctica.

… when I got out of the plane, the cold hit me so dramatically it's like
being hit in the head with a hammer. There's a cold comes into your
forehead just here. It's a really painful cold. If you've ever taken a glass
of water out of a fridge and gulped it down in a big hurry, especially if

you're very hot. Have you ever done that? And felt a sort of pain here? [students nod, murmur agreement] Yes. Or even an ice block in a hurry. Well that's what it's like, this really strong pain. And the other thing that happens, is that all the moisture inside your nose freezes into icicles. So your nose goes crickle, crickle, crack, crack, crack. Because it's full of icicles. Your nose drips all the time in the Antarctic because it's cold. It's not that your nose needs blowing, it's just the cold makes the moisture run in your nose and you sniff. So one way to deal with this, for the people who work in the Antarctic, we're given big gloves on top of our clothes with a big piece of artificial fur, fluffy fur on the back. And these are so you can wipe your nose and wipe the drips off. Because if you didn't wipe the drips off they would freeze and you would have big icicles on your nose. And that becomes very difficult and then your nose would get frostbite.

In this example, the geologist was faced with the task of explaining something outside the experience of the students. She tried to make the experience meaningful to the students by referring to an array of concepts and ideas (pain, forehead, hammer, hit, glass of water, hot day, fridge, ice block, icicles in your nose, crickle, etc.). According to Lemke, 'every action is made meaningful by placing it in some larger context. In fact we place every action or event in many different contexts in order to make it meaningful' (1990, p. 187).

What Lemke is claiming is that meaning is not some mysterious substance that is to be found in the minds of individuals. Meaning is created in and through the social interactions that occur between people. When we talk to each other and make connections between each other's experiences, we are, in that process, 'making meaning.' The network of semantic connections that the geologist created as she talked with the class about the cold in Antarctica was the substance of the 'thinking' that occurred in that class at that time. She made sense of cold in Antarctica by weaving together a context of familiar images and ideas through the words that she used. Later when the students recalled what she said, they expressed that understanding by recalling that context.

For Lemke, and for the Santa Barbara Discourse group, discourse is both the medium and the expression of the norms, expectations, understandings, and cognitions that occur in the classroom. Like other researchers who have taken similar approaches, understanding what students experience, think about, and learn from classroom activities requires a detailed analysis of the multilayered nature of classroom discourse (see also Alvermann, O'Brien, & Dillon, 1990; Floriani, 1993; Gutierrez, 1993).

Student Cognition and Learning as Semiotic Apprenticeship

A group of other researchers have focused on classroom language, not only as the medium of student cognition, but also as the primary source of the content and structure of student cognition. Classroom discourse is said to consist of a variety of genres (Wells, 1994). There are the genres specific to each discipline and the genres of everyday life that the teacher and students bring to the class-room. Although linguists have a specific technical definition for a genre (cf. Andersen, 1990), in this context it is broadly defined as the ways of talking and interacting through symbols that are characteristic of a social role or active membership in an expert community. Thus the way parents talk to their children, the way physicists talk to each other at work, the way wives talk to husbands, are all different genres. Muscovici (1961, quoted in Doise, 1991) has described such genres as cognitive meta-systems that control, verify, and select the products of other cognitive systems in accordance with socially constructed and regulated linguistic structures and norms.

This approach to classroom language is based on ideas derived from the work of Vygotsky and especially of Leont'ev (cf. Leont'ev, 1981). Vygotsky's work has been briefly described in a previous section. Leont'ev's work is more recent than Vygotsky's and places greater emphasis on the mastery of cultural tools. According to Leont'ev the development of mental processes such as thinking and memory occurs through the mastery of cultural tools within a social context.

> Every object made by man – from hand tool to modern electronic computer – embodies mankind's historical experience and at the same time embodies the mental aptitudes moulded in this experience. (1981, p. 421)

The mastery or appropriation of these cultural tools (which include language, science, and works of art) is the way in which children acquire the mental faculties and skills that are embodied ('objectified') in these tools. Mastery, however, always occurs in a social context, so that social interaction is always part of the process of appropriation.

> This activity cannot, however, be formed by itself in the child; it is formed in practical, speech contact with the people around it and in joint activity with them ... (1981, p. 425)

Through mastery of cultural tools, the knowledge and concepts embodied in the tools are inherited by the child. The activities involved in using the tools are initially external and proceed through 'actions on the verbal plane' to acquire the character of 'reduced mental operations, mental acts' (1981, p. 314)

Within education, the most important set of cultural tools are the language genres. Each curriculum area is made up of a set of genres or discourses that embodies the concepts and ways of thinking of that area. What students learn in a particular curriculum area is not just a collection of concepts and principles, but ways of perceiving, thinking about, and classifying experience that are embedded in the language, the symbol systems, and technology, used by experts in the area. From this view, students can be described as 'semiotic apprentices' as they participate in the discourse and the technical and cultural practices of a curriculum area such as mathematics, science, or history. As Wells describes it, semiotic apprenticeship involves the appropriation and mastering of the ways of making meaning through activities and representations that define each discipline (Wells, 1996; Wells, personal communication, 1995).

An example may help to explain the nature of this process. An important part of appropriating the genre of scientific discourse is learning to use scientific terms to describe and explain observations. The following example is from the fourth-grade science classroom in which the teacher was trying to demonstrate that air has weight. The teacher was trying to structure the students' observations. At the time of the discussion in this excerpt, the teacher himself was demonstrating the experiment to the class and was about to put a pin hole in one of the two coloured balloons to let the air out (see diagram above).

Teacher:	Now, if it was, one was heavier than the other, if the brown one was heavier by a lot, what would it do? If the brown one was heavier, how would the thing look at present? Tui?
Tui:	Oh, the brown one would be down and the yellow one would be up.
Teacher:	Sort of like that? [Teacher tilts rod with the end with the brown balloon down]
Tui:	Yep.
Teacher:	Right. It would be balanced.
Student:	No.
Teacher:	Is that what you're saying? If they were even, they'd sort of look like they are now?
Student:	Yeah.
Teacher:	OK. Now if I let the air out of one, say, let the air out of this yellow one and it does that [demonstrates the end of the rod with the yellow balloon going up], what does it show?
Pam:	One's lost more air than the other.
Teacher:	Yes. And?
Pam:	One's heavier than the other.

Teacher:	And?
Mary:	It's not balanced.
Teacher:	Right. Because? Mary?
Mary:	Because one's heavier than the other. One's, the brown one's heavier.
Teacher:	Heavier, isn't it. It's not the size, it's the weight isn't it? Heaviness. OK. Let's see what happens. [The teacher pricks a hole in the top of the yellow balloon.]

In this discussion, the teacher provided the students with a description of how they were to describe and understand what they would see when the demonstration was carried out. The status of the two suspended balloons was described as 'balanced.' If one balloon went up and the other went down, it would be because of its 'weight' and not because of its 'size.' If the air was let out of one balloon that would make one balloon 'heavier' than the other. Implicit in this discourse is a particular relationship of language to observation and experience – the precise, descriptive, technical genre of physical science.

The next day, because the demonstration did not go as planned, the teacher told the students that 'the balloon experiment was meant to show us that air has weight.'

Anderson, Palincsar, and their associates in the Collaborative Problem Solving Project (e.g., Anderson, 1994; Vellom, Anderson, & Palincsar, 1994) have also described curriculum learning in terms of genres. They have been exploring those factors that affect the acquisition of the language and concepts of science when students are working in collaborative groups. Their observations suggest that students can be affected and confused by the competing genres they are already familiar with. Out-of-school experience gives some students access to models of scientific explanatory discourse that other students have not experienced. Cultural and status differences within groups caused discussions to be undermined and individual students to be excluded from opportunities to practice and develop their scientific discourse skills (Holland et al., 1994; Kollar, Anderson, & Palincsar, 1994). They suggest that productive engagement in group processes involving scientific discourse is the way in which students acquire such discourse. When social and cultural factors interfere with the effective involvement of students in group discussions, they fail to master the discourse.

Wells has investigated another way in which language processes affect the acquisition of curriculum knowledge (Wells, 1994). He suggests that classroom discourse forms a bridge between:

    a) the informal language genres of everyday life and classroom management, and

b)   the formal genres of the curriculum.

The informal genres are those that are used to mediate activities, to negotiate the goals and means of activities, and to manage interpersonal interaction and relationships. In the formal genres of the curriculum, language is used to represent the world, to classify, interpret, and explain events, objects, and experiences. In these formal genres, language creates a semiotic world of its own – a parallel, representational world that can be entered and navigated through the representational meaning of language. It is the world of formal semantic networks described by the semantic analysis of Lemke (1990).

According to Wells, classroom discussion involves interpreting, in the informal language, the meaning and significance of texts in the formal representational language. For example, a teacher may get students to talk about what they understand from a text or to describe what they have observed in an experiment. This involves translation from the technical or visual observational 'text' into the informal genre of the 'student's own words.' On other occasions, teachers may formalise the students' informal descriptions by rewording them in more formal terms or by writing them up as lists or charts on the blackboard. Through this kind of class discussion, the teacher is assisting the students to work backwards and forwards between the different language texts or genres. Understanding, Wells suggests, consists of being able to interpret one genre into another.

An example of this kind of intertextual translation is contained in the following transcript. The teacher was discussing a thermometer with a fourth-grade science class. He had shown the class an actual thermometer and during the discussion drew on the blackboard an outline diagram of the thermometer with its central glass tube.

Teacher:	And if you're very clever, inside it you can see ... [draws outline of the thermometer on the blackboard] ... put a line around it. There is a hollow part here that the silver stuff goes up in [pointing to blackboard drawing]. What is the silver stuff called? Does anyone know?
Student:	Mercury.
Teacher:	Is that right?
Student:	Oh, glass tube.
Teacher:	It's called mercury. No question about that. Used to be called in ancient times, quick silver. Why might it be called quick silver? Noel?
Noel:	Because, when it, the heat, it would go up quickly.
Teacher:	Right. Carry on ... There's another reason. More on the silver bit. Why do you think it's called silver.
Student:	Because it's got silver on it.

Student:	It looks like silver.
Teacher:	Silver coloured. Yeah ... It's actually a sort of liquidy stuff, isn't it. Sort of flows a bit.

The teacher in this class is bringing together three different representations of the thermometer. There is the actual thermometer as the students see it, the diagram of the thermometer on the blackboard, and the verbal descriptions that emerge from the discussion. During the discussion the teacher also translates the technical genre (e.g., 'mercury,' 'silver coloured') into the more informal genre of everyday description ('sort of liquidy stuff,' 'sort of flows a bit'). This sequence of translations between the visual and the verbal – between the object, the diagram, the technical description, and the everyday descriptions – provides the students with a set of parallel 'texts.' According to Wells, the students understand these texts to the extent that they can translate effectively between one text and another.

The idea that the ability to translate between texts in different genres constitutes understanding comes from the work of Bakhtin. According to Bakhtin all language and thought is dialogic (see O'Loughlin, 1992; Wertsch, 1991). When we speak or write, we always have an audience in mind. When we try to understand a text, we speak back in our minds to the author, articulating our reactions to the author's words. If we experience discourse in our minds as dialogic or multi-vocal, we are creating a semiotic space within our minds that is shaped by alternative interpretations or depictions. Within this semiotic space we can be free to select or create our own interpretations and understandings. However, when a student in a classroom treats the teacher's or the text's words as univocal and authoritative, understanding and thinking about the words are precluded.

> The authoritative word demands that we acknowledge it, that we make it our own; it binds us ... we encounter it with its authority fused to it. (Bakhtin, quoted in Wertsch, 1991, p. 78)

By learning that discourse can be multi-vocal, and by learning how to translate from one genre to another, the student develops the ability to think about discourse and creates a rich understanding that is the product of such meta-linguistic thinking. In the discussion of a thermometer cited above, if the teacher had provided the students with nothing but a formal verbal definition of a thermometer, the semiotic space available to the students would have been narrowly limited to that definition and the possibility of their understanding and thinking about the thermometer consequently constricted.

Implicit in this analysis is the assumption that what students internalise from their social experience is not just the product or summary of a discussion, but the entire discussion with all its social and cultural processes. The student's mind is, as it were, furnished not just with knowledge but with all that was involved in experiencing that knowledge. The student can replay and rescript the roles, the discussions, the texts.

Cognition as Narrative

Egan (1989, 1993) and Hicks (1993) also take the view that the discourse structures of classroom language become the structures of student thought.

> As the child moves within the social world she appropriates the discourse forms that are available to her, which then, in turn, become the primary means for making sense of her world. (Hicks, 1993, p. 131)

However, while other researchers have claimed that the learning of curriculum is the learning of several different technical and specialised genres, Hicks claims that one genre (narrative discourse) plays a central or privileged role in shaping student thinking. She claims that narrative discourse structures are, arguably, the fundamental intellectual tools that enable children to make sense of their world. Narrative provides children with the symbolic means for structuring events into a meaningful and comprehensible whole. By creating a story context, it gives individual events form and significance.

According to Hicks, children are exposed to oral narrative in many forms before they enter school. They inhabit an oral culture and begin to make use of the narrative structures they experience in their community to structure and understand their world from an early age. What school does is to extend and formalise the range of discourse forms, and especially narrative discourse forms, that the child has available. Without saying so explicitly, Hicks' implies that the acquisition of narrative discourse structures provides the means by which children develop new cognitive structures and hence develop intellectually.

Schank has also argued for the central importance of narrative forms as the medium though which we organise our understanding and memory for experience (Schank, 1990). Schank claims that the stories we hear and tell ourselves and others, give meaning and significance to experience and provide formats for storing and using past experience. Telling a story about what happened is the mechanism by which the component parts of an experience get put together into a single entity. Narrative is the organising structure of memory. In a sense, experience does not exist until we tell others and ourselves a story about it. By giving it a plot, we give it meaning. Each of us has a set of primary narrative stories that represent our personal view of the world.

From this perspective, classroom discussion can be understood as the creation of a narrative. Teachers use classroom discussions to give coherence and structure to student experiences. In the following extract from a seventh-grade classroom the teacher was asking the students to recollect what a visiting speaker had said to them about her experiences in Antarctica. The teacher organised this recollection of the visiting speaker's narrative by asking each student to produce a short narrative of their own (What did you find interesting and why?). The teacher then used each student's contribution to weave together a coherent reconstruction of where the speaker had been in Antarctica (Dry Valley, Shackleton's hut, and Scott's hut).

Joy:	Um, I liked … seeing the old clothes and things. Yeah.
Teacher:	Right. The old clothes … What hut was that in? Can you remember?
Students:	Scott's.
Teacher:	Scott's. Right. Was in Scott's hut. Who else was the other explorer's hut that they had a look in?
Students:	Shackleton.
Teacher:	Right.
Leigh:	And another one.
Teacher:	And another one was there?
Students:	McMurdo.
Girl:	No. That's a base. Amundsen.
Teacher:	Amundsen they didn't have.
Maude:	They didn't have that. They only had two.
Leigh:	They went to three places.
Teacher:	They did go to three places too. You're right. They went to Scott, back to Scott Base I think it was.
Leigh:	Yeah.
Maude:	No. No. They went to the Dry Valley.
Leigh:	Yeah, they went to the Dry Valley …
Teacher:	That's it!
Leigh:	… and um …
Teacher:	Dry Valley, Shackleton's hut and Scott's hut. If I remember rightly. But I'll check that anyway and see.

By bringing the single pieces of information together into a single narrative statement, the teacher unified the students' recollections into a simplified and coherent entity. Together, the teacher and students had 'talked into being' a segment of the curriculum into a unified narrative (Brilliant-Mills, 1993).

Curriculum Learning as Language Learning

A number of writers have suggested that because language and curriculum are closely related to each other, curriculum learning should follow the same processes as language learning. According to Halliday (1993), the distinctive characteristic of human learning is that it is a process of making meaning – a semiotic process. The prototypical form of human semiotic is language, so the acquisition of language is in some way central to all human learning. When the child acquires the language of a particular community, such as the classroom, the child 'appropriates a powerful and versatile tool for participating in and reflecting on, activity in collaboration with others' (Halliday, 1993, p. 4).

The way young children acquire their first or home language is now understood to be a complex interactive process (Gee, 1991; Nelson, 1989; Rice & Schiefelbusch, 1989). The first and most important characteristic of language acquisition is that it is not an intentional activity but occurs in the process of accomplishing other (primarily social) goals. What children learn to understand, and participate in, are the activities of everyday life in which language is embedded. According to Halliday, language acquisition emerges from the predisposition of the very young child to try to organise and make sense of experience (Halliday, 1993). The need to give meaning to experience organises children's activities before the beginnings of language and dominates and subsumes the acquisition of language. Children are constantly exposed to contexts in which there are multiple sources of meaning, one of which is language. Acquiring vocabulary, sentence structure, and the pragmatics of language occurs through the interplay of these multiple parallel sources of meaning.

A second important feature of language acquisition is that it involves a process that Halliday calls 'filtering.' Children appear to select those aspects of their social experience that they are able to understand and appropriate. There is, as it were, a window within which the child is aware of the differences between their performance and that of adult or more expert models. Behaviour falling outside the view of this window is either not perceived or not perceived as usable. The child appears incapable of imitating or reproducing language models outside this window (Bloom, 1991). Unlike the zone of proximal development which is seen as socially constructed, this window or filter is determined by the developmental processes going on within the child. It places significant limits on what children can acquire at any one time regardless of the nature of adult intervention. According to Case (1991), such limits are predictable from the complexity of the learning required.

The primary mechanism of language acquisition is the interaction that occurs between the child and an expert language user (adult or older child) in the context of social interaction. In western European cultures, the norms of parent-child interaction structure common patterns of verbal interaction. Typically, as parents try to carry on conversations with their children, they repeat and recast segments of their children's speech in predictable ways. The following are typical patterns, taken from a study by Bohannon and Stanowicz (1988, p. 685).

Child:	The blue ball.
Mother:	Yeah, the ball is bouncing!
Child:	Monkey climbing.
Mother:	The monkey is climbing to the top of the tree.

Studies of these patterns of repeating and recasting children's language have shown that it plays a significant role in language acquisition. For example, children are more likely to imitate their mother's words following a recast than they other following any other kind of response, including positive and negative reinforcement (Farrar, 1992).

In a study of a science classroom, Wells and Chang-Wells (in press) have used the concepts developed to understand children's language acquisition in an analysis of verbal interaction patterns between teacher and students. They interpret the typical question-answer-comment cycle that characterises classroom discussions as an extension of typical pattern of interaction that characterises mother-child talk. By asking appropriate questions, the teacher invites the students to participate in the co-construction of a meaningful curriculum narrative. As the students' construct responses, they open up, and reveal to the teacher, their own understanding of the topic. Typically, the teacher then comments on the students' responses, rephrasing and/or adding to what they have said. In this way she can 'step up' their responses and model her understanding and way of thinking about the topic. Wells and Chang-Wells equate the semiotic space created by the question-response cycle with the zone of proximal development. Within this zone, the teacher's comments provide the students with 'an opportunity to take over and internalise her organising cognitive structures and associated language' (Wells & Chang-Wells, in press, p. 19).

How this can happen is illustrated in the following transcript of a discussion in a seventh-grade social studies class. The teacher was discussing the reasons why forests of kauri trees in New Zealand were cut down during the nineteenth century.

Teacher:	Why do you think perhaps they cut down all the kauri trees before? What was the reason for this? Trevor?
Trevor:	Building houses and homes and things like that.
Teacher:	Yes, they wanted to do that with it. Yes?
Brian:	Um, cut it down and put in place of it pine trees. It's a little bit faster.

Teacher:	They cut down the kauri trees so that they could replace them with pine trees because they grow faster? Mmmm. I don't think so. Warwick?
Warwick:	Kauris are timber that doesn't take so long to rot and it would be good for housing and that.
Teacher:	Yes. But there's another reason why the kauris were cut down. Can you tell me? Do you think they might have been wanting something else? Murray?
Murray:	Farmland?
Teacher:	Yes, perhaps they wanted to cultivate land. Yes. Might be something else.
Student:	The gum.
Teacher:	Yes. They wanted to get the gum underneath, so they went around and rather recklessly destroyed these great kauri forests. But, as I said before there's still a lot of kauri there.

The teacher's questioning gradually elicited from the students the conclusion that the trees were cut down to find the 'kauri gum' that the trees produced around their roots. The teacher appropriated and reworded most of the students' responses, usually adding information to them. For example, Brian's suggestion that they had 'cut it down and put in place of it pine trees. It's a little bit faster' is reworded by the teacher as 'They cut down the kauri trees so that they could replace them with pine trees because they grow faster.' The teacher's question (Why do you think perhaps they cut down all the kauri trees before?) asked for the students to provide a reason and she reworded Brian's statement using the linguistic markers of a reason, 'so that they' and 'because.' Later the teacher got the explanation she was looking for, but the student's response was only a single word ('gum'). She took this response and, to use Wells and Chang-Wells term, 'stepped up' the response into a complete explanation ('They wanted to get the gum underneath, so they went around and rather recklessly destroyed these great kauri forests'). The teacher's questions and suggestions ('Do you think they might have been wanting something else?') engaged the students in cognitive processing of relevant background knowledge. The discussion that ensued produced new meanings and knowledge at the intersection of the students' own knowledge and informal language with the teacher's 'expert' knowledge and language.

If this recasting of student knowledge and language is successful, then the discussion is readily absorbed or appropriated by the students. It works because it makes use of the students own ideas and their own words. The teacher's language adapts to the students' language as the students' responses are adapted to the teacher's knowledge. If the teacher is less sensitive to the students' understandings and language, is less able to articulate the new knowledge or linguistic forms clearly, or is working in a classroom where there is a wide variation in the students' knowledge and linguistic or cultural backgrounds, then the teacher's reconstruction of the students' responses will fall outside each student's zone of proximal development. When this occurs, as it may do frequently in traditional classrooms, then, as Baker has argued, many students have to learn to extract (or abstract) from quite complex sequences of talk 'what it is they might or should be noting or remembering, i.e. what counts as the knowledge in the lesson' (Baker, 1992, p. 11).

It is not clear from Wells and Chang-Wells research how many students in a class need to be involved in the process of co-constructing meaning. An interactive process that works well with mother-child dyads may only be superficially effective in classroom discussions where only a minority of students are actively involved at any one time. It is clear from previous research that students do not have to participate in class discussions in order to learn from them (Hughes, 1973) and that listening to class discussion is more effective than listening to a lecture or monologue (Nuthall & Church, 1973). The process of co-construction of meaning that Wells and Chang-Wells have identified may be the characteristic of class discussion that makes it vicariously effective in shaping student learning.

The Classroom as a Writing Environment

The development of 'process writing' as a method of ensuring that students acquire effective writing skills has lead to research on how the classroom can become a 'writing community' (Graves, 1983). While the focus is not on the acquisition of knowledge or thinking skills, it is difficult to make any clear distinctions between the 'writing skills' that students acquire in a process writing program and general cognitive development. If language and the narrative genre are central to cognitive development, then acquiring story writing skills must also be seen as part of this development.

There is not space in this chapter to explore all of the ways in which the classroom as a writing community is related to the classroom as a language or knowledge community, but there are some concepts that are almost identical. For example, Parecki and Palincsar (1994) have developed the concept of 'intersubjectivity' to explain the ways in which the teacher and students develop mutual understandings of the writing process. They draw on Grice's notion of 'conversational implicature' (Grice, 1989) and Clark's 'common ground theory' (Clark & Schaefer, 1989) to emphasise the mutuality of communication. The effective use of language depends on speaker (writer) and listener (reader) sharing a common understanding of what is mutually known and mutually assumed in any communication. Developing the classroom as a community of writers requires the teacher and students to 'decenter' their own individual perspectives and to construct shared understandings. By building a community of trust in which each student is seen as both a learner and an expert with specific skills and knowledge, students become able to accept and incorporate ideas and comments into their own work. Sharing and exchanging the roles of writer and reader leads to the incorporation of both perspectives in the writing process.

In the classroom as a community of writers it is the nature of language that determines classroom process. The mutuality essential to effective communication becomes the goal of classroom process. The decentering and building of inter-subjective understanding becomes the 'curriculum' of teaching writing.

Summary of the Language Focused Perspective

The language focused perspective on classroom cognition and learning that has been described in this section has drawn into sharp focus the ways in which language works to structure the social relationships between students and teachers and to create the knowledge and meanings that constitute the experienced curriculum. The research undertaken from this perspective has made it clear that language is not the transparent or neutral medium through which preordained knowledge is transferred from the mind of the teacher to the minds of the students. Curriculum knowledge, and the conditions for thinking about experience and acquiring knowledge, are created in the process of using language. Classrooms are language communities that develop their own forms of language. Using, and learning to use language, are creative processes that depend on, and are part of, the mutual understandings that constitute and hold together a community such as a classroom.

What I have not been able to include in this section is research on the culture of classroom language. For all its diversity and involvement in the creation of each classroom as a unique community, there are culture-specific forms that characterise classroom language. Studies involving micro-analyses of classroom language have identified standardised language forms that are common across teachers and classroom contexts (e.g., Chinn, Waggoner, Anderson, Schommer, & Wilkinson, 1993). There is, in fact, a considerable and growing diversity in the ways in which classroom language is being analysed by researchers. The underlying disciplines on which these analyses are based (such as sociolinguistics, pragmatics, discourse analysis, and text analysis) are themselves rapidly evolving areas of research. No summary is likely to do justice to the variety of understandings of classroom discourse that have emerged in recent years and are likely to emerge as new linguistic understandings are applied to the classroom.

THE ROLE OF MIND AND COGNITION IN THE CLASSROOM

So far in this chapter, I have tried to provide a descriptive summary of the three major approaches to understanding student cognition and learning in the classroom: the cognitive or constructivist perspective, the community-focused or sociocultural perspective, and the language-focused perspective. I have used the term perspective because the studies included within in each approach do not have the coherence or comprehensiveness of theories. What unites the studies within each perspective are similar theoretical backgrounds, similar approaches to the analysis of classroom data, and similar explanatory concepts. However, it is also true that each of the three perspectives shares a number of characteristics with the other two perspectives. It is tempting to conclude this chapter by drawing together these common elements, thereby implying that the points of agreement must be of more importance, if not validity, than the points of disagreement.

I would like, however, to focus this final section on the areas of disagreement between the three perspectives. It is these areas that highlight the distinctive characteristics of the different approaches, and it is in these areas that the most important issues arise. In particular, there are three related issues that are of critical importance to our understanding of the way students' classroom experience affects their learning and thinking skills.

The first, and seemingly most dramatic point of contention concerns the existence of the mind and cognition as it is normally understood. Specifically, do mental processes exist as a property of individual minds, or are they located, if they exist at all, in social interaction between people and in the processes of communities?

The second major point of contention is a consequence of the first. If the mind and cognition are located in the processes of social interaction, how are we to understand learning and the changes in students that result from students' classroom experience? The cognitive constructivist struggles with the problems of how students incorporate or translate the structure and content of experience into the structure and content of their minds. The sociocultural theorist claims that there is no such problem. They use terms like 'semiotic apprenticeship' and 'mutual appropriation' to indicate that the only processes of significance occur in students' interactions with their teachers or peers.

The third point of contention arises over the nature and site of cognitive change. Again, the sociocultural theorists locate change in the processes of social interaction. Learning occurs during the interaction of expert and novice, as the behaviour of one accommodates to the behaviour of the other. The restructuring and self-organisation of knowledge that concerns the cognitive theorists, occurs during and through social interaction.

I would like, in this fourth section of the chapter to look more closely at these areas of contention and explore how they relate to our understanding of students' thinking and learning in the classroom.

Do Mind and Cognition Exist?

The cognitive constructivist view of student cognition implies a largely 'scientific realist' approach to the nature of mental processes (cf. Haig, 1987; House, 1991) although von Glasersfeld and Cobb take a more pragmatic view (Cobb, 1994; von Glasersfeld, 1989). The assumption is made that the mind exists as a property of the individual student and is the site of those representations of the social and physical world that guide students' understanding and behaviour. These representations (or mental models) are seen as the product and content of cognitive processing. When a student encounters new information or experience she relates it to the representations that already exist in her mind. The form of this cognitive encounter is structured by classroom activities that require the student to engage in relevant logical and semantic operations (cf. Fuchs et al., 1994; King, 1994). The effects of these operations include the construction of new knowledge and the reconstruction of existing knowledge. As Ohlsson describes it, a 'shallow, poorly articulated, fragmented, inconsistent and inaccurate world view' gets changed into a 'deep, richly elaborated, integrated, coherent, and accurate world view' (Ohlsson, 1990, p. 563). The mind is seen as inherently dynamic (Bereiter, 1985; Magnusson et al., 1994), self-organising (von Glasersfeld, 1989), and affected by social processes such as argumentation (cf. Alton-Lee & Nuthall, 1992; Cobb et al., 1992), but ultimately the unique property of the individual student. The mind works on its own representations.

The most radical attack on this constructivist view has come from those who claim that the concepts of mind and cognition are both unnecessary and misleading if we are to understand how students are affected by classroom experience. Lemke in a detailed analysis of the structure and meaning of the language of the mathematics classroom argues that the only thing we need to take into account is the interaction that occurs between teacher and students.

> What we call thinking is simply the material processes which enact the meaning-making practices of a community; the use of language and other semiotic resources. (Lemke, 1990, p. 194)

Lemke goes on to explain that giving meaning to an action or an event involves placing it in a relevant context. For example, we understand a word by knowing how it is used, who uses it, and in what physical, social, and historical contexts it gets used. These are what we know when we 'understand' a word rather than some mental entity called 'meaning.' Making meaning is contextualizing. It fol-lows from this view that thinking is a socially visible process, occurring 'out there' in the social world. The words used to talk about mental processes refer to nothing more than the things we do in interaction with others when we are engaged in 'thought-related' activities.

Lave's critique is also based on the primacy of the social and cultural context of human activity. 'Learning, thinking and knowing are relations among people engaged in activity in, with, and arising from, the socially and culturally struc-tured world' (Lave, 1991, p. 67). She claims that no real boundary exists be-tween the inside and the outside of the head. The inside and the outside have a recursive, reciprocal relationship and are 'partially incorporated into each oth-er' (1991, p. 68). Cognition is said to be distributed or stretched over mind, body, activity, and setting. Similarly, for Rogoff, learning is not the property of the individual but of the interaction process itself (Rogoff, 1994). The specific processes by which students and teachers interact and share in the decision mak-ing and the progress of an activity are the substance of cognitive development (Rogoff, 1993, p. 393).

In order to try to make sense of these claims about the nonexistence of indi-vidual mind and cognition, we need to distinguish between claims that are pri-marily methodological and claims that are primarily substantive. The former are claims about the perspective that we should take when we analyse and interpret classroom process data. They are concerned with the kinds of data that should be included in the analysis and how that data should be understood. The latter are claims about the reality or theoretical value of the concepts we use when we construct explanations for student experience and development.

Both Lave and Rogoff appear to be aware of the methodological nature of their critique of the cognitive perspective. Lave, for example, argues that we need to 'cross-cut' the traditional distinctions between mind and body, between cognition and practice, between person and culture, and make use of units of analysis that bind them together. A 'person-acting-in-a-setting' is an appropri-ate basic unit that can include indivisibly all relevant aspects of mind, body, cognition, activity, social relationships, and culture (Lave, 1988). She does not deny the existence of individual mind or cognition, any more than she denies the existence of individual persons or activities. Her primary claim is that indi-vidual mental entities should be replaced by sociocultural entities as the basic units of analysis. To focus on the individual mind is to forget the ever-present significance of the social and cultural context.

From a similar perspective, Rogoff argues that all thinking is 'functional, ac-tive and grounded in goal-directed actions' (1990, p. 8). The context of such goal-directed thinking is an essential part of the action and it cannot be studied separately from the context. For Rogoff, the primary unit of analysis is the event or activity and its entire social, cultural and historical context. Furthermore, it is the material surface of this event or activity that is the object of analysis, not any underlying or hypothetical mental processes. The product is there in the process itself.

On the other hand, the positions taken by Lemke (1990) and O'Loughlin (1992) are more radical. They deny the functional significance of individual mental processes. The cognitive constructivist view, they claim, fails to acknowledge the fundamentally social and contextual nature of the activities we describe as thinking and understanding. Because their position is a relativist rather than a realist one, their claims cannot be construed as a denial of the 'reality' of mind and cognition so much as a denial of the value of talk about mind and cognition. From a relativist or post-modernist philosophical point of view, nothing is independently 'real.' What matters is what is accepted by a significant community as important or valuable. From this perspective, all claims are primarily methodological because any substantive claim is seen as inherently methodological.

Calling the claims of the sociocultural theorists about the nature of mental processes primarily methodological is not intended to deny their importance. Behind the claims made by writers like Lave and Rogoff lies one of the most important shifts in perspective to have occurred in classroom research since it came of age in the 1960s. Put simply, classroom data cannot and should not be reduced to the purely psychological. The classroom is more than just the scene of many different individual psychological causes and effects. Its complexity gives it an order of being that is beyond the psychological, or the sociological, or the linguistic. This position parallels the position that is now widely accepted in the biological sciences. Biologists understand that complex living systems cannot be reduced to the sum of their component parts. Their complexity gives them a new order of being with emergent properties beyond physical and chemical explanations. According to Gould:

> The insufficiency of physics and chemistry to encompass life records no mystical addition, no contradiction to the basic sciences, but only reflects the hierarchy of natural objects and the principle of emergent properties at higher levels of organisation. (Gould, 1991, p. 388)

In the same way, writers like Lave and Rogoff are claiming that neither the experience of the student, nor the processes of the classroom, can be fully understood from either the perspective of the individual student's mind or the perspective of the group. The classroom is a complex social and cultural system and the thinking and learning that occur there are a function of the system as a whole, not of a collection of individual minds. The social processes are the cognitive processes.

Given the force of their arguments, the important question then becomes one of deciding, not whether the mind or cognition exist, but what roles these concepts should play in understanding students' classroom experience. If we expand our understanding of mind and cognition and start to see them as sociocultural processes, how can these concepts usefully contribute to a more complete and comprehensive understanding of classroom processes?

Salomon in the book he edited on 'distributed cognition' (Salomon, 1993) agrees that cognition is usefully seen as a property of persons acting together in culturally structured settings, such as classrooms, but points out that individuals also act in socially isolated settings. In other words, we sometimes think together with others, we sometimes think in and through cultural tools (such as language, television, computers), and we sometimes think alone.

As communities and cultural tools have an identity of their own across individuals, across occasions, across settings, and across times, so individuals have an identity of their own across settings, across communities, across cultural tools, and across times. In persons, it is the mental representations of their experiences that provide the continuity that constitutes this identity. Salomon does not to deny that the relationship between individual representations and social activities is a constantly fluid and 'transactional' relationship. He describes it as a spiral of mutually influencing effects (Salomon, 1993, p. 122). Unless we are to introduce the concept of a collective or communal consciousness or memory, the individual mind provides the essential continuity between the occasions and settings of sociocultural activity whether that activity is social or individual. Put another way, an individual may participate in many different communities and play several different roles within those communities. The individual may be partly a different person in each different setting, but will also be partly the same person. Personal representations of experience are carried by individuals from one setting or community to another and influence the enactment of social roles in individual ways.

Another way of understanding this issue is to consider discarding the notion of the individual mind as a single internally coherent entity or self-contained ego. Recent analyses of the nature of human consciousness suggest that individual minds are better understood as sites of multiple parallel processes. Dennett (1993) has described this as the 'multiple drafts' model of mind. He argues that there can be no 'I' sitting in the head and controlling perception and thinking from some central site. The sense we have of single personal identity or self-looking-out-on-the-world is no more than a functionally useful, but culturally created, myth. As the language we use consists of many genres or ways of saying things, so the mind is a system of parallel processes. The mind is itself a community (Lee, 1987). It is a complex system of multiple representations of experience, a community within that reflects, and is in some way a creation of, the community without.

How Is Experience Internalised to Create Representations?

The second major issue of contention concerns the way in which the mind represents experience. Cognitive theorists refer to a process of 'internalisation' to describe the way the student's interactions with the world become represented in the student's mind. On the other hand, sociocultural theorists dismiss the concept of internalisation because it implies the individual mind is the repository of experience. They either claim that there is no satisfactory account of the way external behaviours become mental processes (cf. Brown et al., 1993, Cobb, 1994) or they suggest an alternative account based on the work of Vygotsky in which the internal is seen as the same as, or continuous with, the external (cf. Newman et al., 1989; Rogoff, 1993). Development is described as 'appropriation' (Rogoff, 1993) or 'acquisition' (Halliday, 1993) and is seen as an essentially social process.

Much of the debate on this issue reflects, I believe, an unnecessarily narrow interpretation of the concept of internalisation. While Piaget's account of the process was largely confined to understanding the development of children's representations of the physical world, there is no reason to believe that it does not apply equally well to children's representations of the sociocultural world.

In Piaget's account of the way representations of experience form in the mind and start to organise themselves into mental structures, imitation plays a critical role (Piaget, 1962). In the life of young children, imitation is common especially in play. During play, children imitate the language and behaviours of people around them and the activities of animals and objects such as automobiles and planes. Imitation involves the reproduction of those elements of their experiences that they perceive as significant and that they need to use in understanding and controlling their environment. Imitations are usually created from memories and are both a copy and an abstraction of the initial experience. As a behaviour or perception is imitated in increasingly different contexts, the imitations become separated from their original sources and become increasingly representative and abstract.

Once experiences have been abstracted from their original context through imitation, they can also be imitated in a 'mental' form in the mind. This internal imitation is a repetition of the original experience without its external or behavioural components. It is thus a decontextualized or abstracted representation of the original experience that we normally call an image. As Piaget has described it, an image is an internal imitation of a perception or behaviour, dislocated not only from its original context (as an imitation is) but from the material world altogether (Piaget, 1962). Images are, in this sense, mental representations or proto-models. They can serve the same function as the original perception or behaviour without being attached to the original material context or constraints.

Young children's drawings of human figures and houses are interesting examples of the way imitation produces representations. They are reproductions of the images that children hold in their minds. Such images arise as the child attempts to imitate the original perceptions in the mind. Like the imitations of actions that are enacted in children's in play, they are structured abstractions of the original experience.

In Piaget's account, this process of internalisation is driven by the child's need to anticipate and plan effective participation in the physical and social world. It arises in and through play as children reproduce behaviours and experiences in contexts in which they can reconstruct, control and vary the behaviours and their consequences and contexts at will. The imitations that occur in play become the mental representations that children can use to understand and anticipate the consequences of their actions. Thinking is a way of acting on the world by imitating appropriate actions and consequences within the mind.

There is evidence to show that this account of internalisation applies equally well to children's experiences of the social and cultural worlds. Research on children's play, especially their pretend play, shows that it commonly takes place in social contexts and involves the imitation of social roles including the language genres that are part of those roles (Andersen, 1990). Research on the development of language in children shows that acquisition processes are primarily social and that selective and managed imitation plays a critical role in the acquisition of vocabulary and those syntactic structures that Vygotsky saw as the progenitors of mental structures (Bloom, 1991; Farrar, 1992; Levy & Nelson, 1994).

Internalisation in the Classroom

It is clear that, as children grow older, language plays a critical role in the process of internalisation. Classrooms are not places in which students are generally free to engage in the varieties of play and imitative experimentation that characterise their early development. However, as students acquire the concepts and structures of language, language itself becomes an important medium or channel for the process of internalisation in the classroom. As Vygotsky has shown, the transition between the external and the internal occurs through the transitional language of self-talk (Lucy & Wertsch, 1987; Vygotsky, 1981). Self-talk is a kind of personal imitation of social talk freed from the constraints and structures of social talk.

Recent classroom research suggests that self-talk among elementary and middle school students is relatively common (cf. Berk, 1986; McCaslin Rohrkemper, 1989). In our own studies, recordings from individual broadcast microphones showed that a considerable proportion of the talking that students did was self-talk (Alton-Lee et al., 1993; Nuthall & Alton-Lee, 1993). An analysis of the student talk recorded in a fourth-grade science classroom illustrates this point (see Table 2). Recordings were made over an eight-day period when the class was studying a unit on the weather. During the unit the class was engaged in a variety of whole class, small group, and individual activities.

Analysis of the recordings made from individual broadcast microphones indicated that about 15 per cent of student utterances consisted of self-talk that did not elicit a response from anyone else. It was often difficult to distinguish between self-talk and private talk to a nearby peer. A significant proportion of each student's private utterances occurred within hearing of other students and may or may not have been intended to be heard.

	Percent of all utterances			All utterances	
	Related to content or task	Unrelated to content or task	Ambiguous or inaudible	Total number	Percent
Public discussion & talking to teacher	11.10	0.0	0.26	747	11.36
Reading aloud & chorus responses	1.78	0.40	0.27	161	2.45
Talking to peers	57.32	3.92	7.56	4523	68.80
Talking to self	14.09	0.24	0.82	996	15.15
Singing & sounds	0.33	1.78	0.12	147	2.24
	84.62	6.34	9.04	6574	100.00

Table 2: The Contexts and Relevance of the Utterances of Four Students During an Eight-Day Science Unit in a Fourth-Grade Classroom.

Research by Berk (1986) identified a similar frequency of self-talk among younger students. She reported a study of the self-talk among first- and third-grade students during mathematics classes. She identified three different types of self-talk:

a) self-stimulating and task irrelevant self-talk such as word plays, expressing feelings, talking to absent others or things,
b) task relevant self-talk such as describing one's own activity, answering one's own questions, reading aloud to oneself, and
c) inaudible but clearly evident (from lip and tongue movements) sub vocal speech

Berk found that self-talk was relatively common (about 60 per cent of the time) when the students were working on mathematics problems. Consistent with Vygotsky's claim that social speech is transformed through self-talk to inner (cognitive) speech, Berk found a progressive reduction in the first two types of self-talk (audible speech) and a corresponding increase in the third type (inaudible speech) as the students moved from first grade to third grade.

The following examples of self-talk from our recordings illustrate some of the different ways students use self-talk. In the first excerpt, recorded in a sixth-grade classroom, the student (Jim) was sitting at a table writing a report about the talk a visiting speaker had given to the class. He began by ruling a line across the page and writing the name of the speaker (Amanda Hamlin).

Jim (talking to self as he looks at blackboard where the visitor's name is written) Amanda Hamlin. (writes two letters of her name) Wait, wait. Jim do this. (gets ruler out of desk, rules line on top of page) Now, that's better! (fiddles with hair, with pen) Yeah ... no, it was from this ... (waves ruler round) I say, oh damn, I've ruled it wrongly ... (glances round, no one is listening) Yeah. (looks at blackboard again) Amanda ... (starts writing visitor's name) H-A-M, Amanda Ham ... (looks up at blackboard): L-I-N. (gestures as teacher approaches his desk): Now, Amanda Hamlin. Yeah ...

Jim's self-talk is a parallel behaviour accompanying his task behaviour. It is both a description and verbal commentary on his task behaviour. It is as though he is watching himself, taking the roles of observer and instructor as well as of student.

Students also talked to themselves in ways that suggested they were using language to clarify and organise ambiguous information or confused situations.

In the following excerpt, Teine, in the same sixth-grade class, tried to clarify (and remember?) the name of an Antarctic explorer.

Public discussion	Parallel private talk
Teacher: … Who else was the other explorer's hut that they had a look in?	
Pupil: Shackleton.	Teine (to Cory): Shacknill?
Teacher: Right … And another one was there?	Cory: Shackleton. Teine: Shambleton? What? Shackleton?
Pupil: McMurdo.	Teine (to self): Shackleton. Shackleton.
Girl: No. That's a base … etc.	

The organising and clarifying functions of self-talk are more apparent during whole class discussions. Self-talk occurs quite frequently during public discussion and reflects students' parallel personal involvement in the discussion. Ideas and information that are new or controversial appear to generate a higher frequency of self-talk. It is as though public debate generates internal debate and the students imitate the process in their self-talk in order to reach resolution inside their heads. In the following excerpt, also from the same class, the teacher and students were discussing the pronunciation of the name of the Adelie penguin.

Public discussion	Private talk
Teacher: OK. Which, what penguins were they? Can you remember?	
Maude: It's Adèlie.	
Teacher: What are they called?	Jim (whisper to self): Adelly.
Several pupils: Adèlie penguins.	Paul (to self): Adderley.
Maude: Are they pronounced Adelly or Adaily?	Joy (to self): She said 'Adaily.'
Girl: Adaily.	
Teacher: I'm not sure.	Paul (whisper to Cory) Say Adelie.
Teine: Adelly.	Cory (whisper to Paul): Adaily.

Public discussion	Private talk
Maude: She said 'Adaily.'	
Joy: No, she said it.	Jim (whisper to self): Adelly.
Nevin: (spelling word) A-D-E-L-I-E.	Jane (to self): Adaily.
Maude: (inaudible)	Paul (to Cory): Adaily. Adaily.
Teacher: Just have to be aware that there might be different pronunciations of things as well. Good. OK. Thanks Carl. Nathan?	Cory (to Paul): I call them Adelly. Teine (to peer): He, she said Adelly. Peer (to Teine): No she didn't. Adaily. Adaily.
Teacher: Pardon? ... etc.	Teine (sings softly): There's no way, man, I can win.

This incident was unusual in the amount of recorded self-talk and private debate between peers (more was recorded than could be included above), but it reflects the way students become involved in the public discussion. In the classrooms in which we have used individual broadcast microphones to record student talk, the borders between public discussion, private peer discussion, and personal self-talk are fluid. If self-talk is interpreted as a transitional behaviour between the external world of sociocultural processes and the internal world of cognitive processes, then an incident such as the one above suggests that the social space defined by the interaction of alternative and competing points of view is being internalised by the students as a correspondingly complex cognitive 'space.' There is what Salomon (1993) has described as a 'transactional relationship' between social interaction and cognitive process.

The Evolution of Concepts and Mental Structures

The third major area of contention between the sociocultural and linguistic perspectives and the cognitive constructivist perspective lies in the way existing knowledge or beliefs are changed or restructured to produce new knowledge or beliefs. At issue is the site and cause of change in knowledge and skill. In the sociocultural view, change occurs during the process of acquisition. Change is a function of the social interaction between parent and child or between expert and novice as each accommodates to the behaviour of the other (Rogoff, 1990). In the cognitive constructivist view, change is seen as largely internal, driven by the need for consistency and coherence between new experience and existing knowledge structures. The mind is said to be self-organising (Ohlsson, 1990). Representations of experience must identify relevant existing knowledge structures and adapt to them. Once stored in memory, they become active in the continuing reorganisation of past experience and interpretation of new experience.

The problem with the sociocultural and linguistic perspectives, with their emphasis on the here and now qualities of experience, is that they fail to describe how knowledge, once it has been acquired through social and linguistic interaction, is maintained through the passage of time. They fail to explain how individual experience provides the link between different occasions and different contexts. On the other hand, the problem with the cognitive constructivist perspective is that it overlooks the critical roles played by social experience, language, and culture in structuring the way individual minds carry out their self-organisation.

What is needed to resolve the conflict between these alternative perspectives is an analysis of knowledge acquisition that incorporates Salomon's 'transactional' relationship between sociocultural experience and the self-organisational activities of the mind. Recent neo-Piagetian research on the way interactive social processes and structures determine the course of children's cognitive development suggests the way such an analysis might be developed (cf. Doise & Mugny, 1984; Perret-Clermont, 1980).

Piaget described the development of children's knowledge structures (schemas) as the constant reorganisation of evolving representations of experience (Piaget, 1978). The process of developing complex and effective mental representations goes through three stages. Early representations of experience are little more than memories (i.e., internal imitations of the original experience). When the child first learns to carry out an appropriate action or procedure, the child's memory for the action includes the entire context and circumstances in which the action took place. The child is not aware of the boundaries between the context, the action, and its consequences. Consequently, the child cannot distinguish functional from peripheral elements or the relationship between them (Piaget & Inhelder, 1973).

The undifferentiated nature of the child's memory for a behaviour-in-context means that when the behaviour is reproduced it is likely to result in unforeseen consequences. The difference between the actual consequences of the behaviour and the consequences recalled (and expected) on the basis of memory produces a conflict that leads to changes in the representation of the behaviour-in-context. The child learns from this conflict to identify the functional elements in the behaviour and restructures the representation of the behaviour-in-context to distinguish these elements. As representations become more functionally accurate or viable (von Glasersfeld, 1989), they become less closely tied to specific experiences. They become progressively more generalised with use and consequently better guides for planning and carrying out further action. They replace the role of specific memories in the reproduction and control of behaviour.

With further experience, representations of different behaviours-in-context are coordinated into complex schemas that include an increasing variety of behaviours and their consequences. These schemas are mental structures that contain representations of how behaviours lead to consequences in a variety of contexts. They are, as it were, a mental map of alternative actions and their consequences and connections. As they get used for planning and interpreting behaviour, they become thinking processes. '… the material and causal coordinations of movements and logical and implicative connections are but two faces of the one and the same organisation' (Piaget, 1978, p. 215). Physical effects become logical implications. For example, representations of events in which hitting resulted in hurting become, in the child's mind, a knowledge schema in which hitting *implies* hurting.

In a series of studies, Doise (1991), Gilly (1991), Portecorvo (1990), Perret-Clermont and her associates (1991), and others working within the European sociocultural perspective, have shown how Piaget's analysis of the development of the mind of can be extended to incorporate the sociocultural world of the child. While Piaget saw the conflict between the child's evolving mental representations of the physical world and the child's experience of that world as the primary source of cognitive development, these researchers include social conflict as a primary mechanism for change. When a child's perceptions and beliefs conflict with another person's while interacting with that person in a socially binding context, the child tries to find ways to resolve the disagreement. The social processes involved in creating agreement and mutual understanding are the means by which children disrupt their existing beliefs and perceptions and create new understandings and cognitive structures. According to Portecorvo (1990) 'the social need for keeping the relationship, even in the conflict, supports the cognitive and emotional effort of finding and developing new ways of reasoning' (p. 15). Studies exploring the effects of debate and disagreement between peers from a cognitive constructivist perspective have been reviewed above (e.g., Mason & Santi, 1994; Miller, 1987).

These researchers claim that, in addition to social processes, social structures are also implicated in the development of cognitive structures (Doise, 1991). For example, social demands can provide both the model and the motive for cognition. When children are required to divide up a quantity of objects (such as candies) into containers of unequal proportions, they are much better at getting the quantities equal when the outcome has significant social consequences (such as ensuring they get as much as their friend). 'Social marking' is the term used to describe the correspondence that may exist between the structure and regulation of the social relationships and social context of a problem and the structure and regulation of the physical variables involved in the problem. The sociocultural schema that children develop to understand and represent social relationships are available for, and implicated in, understanding and representing the relationships of the physical world.

If, for example, a student acquires knowledge of a concept by being told the relevant information by a teacher, the students' understanding will incorporate the single dependent perspective of the student-teacher relationship. If, on the other hand, the student acquires the knowledge in the context of a classroom discussion in which different perspectives are described, explained and debated, the student's representation of the schema will incorporate a larger network of intertwined social and logical relationships. Such a network defines the dimensions of a mental space within which the student can explore, interact with, and try out alternative beliefs, arguments, and conclusions.

One of the important implications of this research is that the representations that children internalise and the cognitive structures that evolve from these representations are more complex than those that Piaget envisaged. Not only are social relationships and structures embedded in the cognitive structures that represent the physical world, but the child needs to develop multiple structures to represent the same aspects of the physical world from the perspectives of different social roles and contexts. For example, there are understandings and structures appropriate to the sociocultural context of the child's home that are different from the understandings and structures appropriate to the sociocultural context of the child's school experiences with teachers and peers. These are, as it were, the mental 'genres' of the cultural communities that the child participates in.

This neo-Piagetian sociocultural analysis of the evolution of cognition is not only consonant with the sociocultural perspectives of Lave and Rogoff but also provides an important developmental explanation for the concept of the mind as a community of multiple parallel processes (Crick, 1994; Johnson-Laird, 1988). Once we understand that the mind acquires the multiple perspectives and roles involved in the sociocultural contexts of our experience, then it is not difficult to understand the claim made by philosophers such as Dennett (1993) that the single perspective that is familiar to us through our own conscious experience is an incomplete representation of the way our mind works. Although we have the experience of taking a single point of view, the underlying processes of which we are not necessarily aware incorporate the complexities of our sociocultural experience. As Vygotsky suggested, 'consciousness must be regarded as a particular case of social experience' (Vygotsky, 1979, p. 31).

The Evolution of Knowledge and Mental Structures in the Classroom

If sociocultural processes and structures are a major determinant of cognitive development, then how do the sociocultural processes and structures of the classroom affect the cognitive development of students? Specifically, what kind of transactional relationship exists between the sociocultural processes of the classroom and the cognitive processes that students use to acquire knowledge?

Knowledge acquisition involves a set of cognitive processes that allow new experience or information to be assimilated into existing knowledge structures. These processes are required in order to adjust what is known to what is being experienced and to resolve any conflict between the two. Two distinct sets of processes are involved. First, connections must be identified between the incoming experience and existing knowledge. How this is done depends on available knowledge structures that predict where and how useful connections may occur. Second, the mind must evaluate the consistency or coherence of the incoming experience (and its implicit implications) with existing knowledge. Points of agreement and disagreement must be identified and changes made that will keep the existing knowledge structures pragmatically viable (Alton-Lee & Nuthall, 1992; Nuthall & Alton-Lee, 1992, 1993; Ohlsson, 1990; von Glasersfeld, 1989).

Our studies of students' classroom experience suggest how students' use of these two sets of knowledge acquisition processes is structured by the social interaction that occurs in the classroom. Again it is the data on self-talk that provides the critical link between the individual use of these processes and their evolution through social interaction.

Creating associations, elaborations and implications.

Knowledge acquisition involves identifying the ways in which new experience or information is connected with existing knowledge. Associations need to be identified and potential implications inferred. The following examples illustrate the ways in which students identify associations to the ideas they were working with. The first example was recorded in the fourth-grade class that was working on the unit on weather. The teacher had asked each group in the class to think of as many 'weather' words as possible. Tui was talking partly to himself and partly to anyone who would listen as other members of his group were suggesting and recording words.

Tui: … Sunny. We've got sun. Yeah, but sunny?
Peer: That's to do with sun.

Tui: Muvver, muvver, wevver, wevver, weather ... So we got all of them. Stick one here at the top [of the page], at the top, at the top ... damp, damp, dump ... doo, doo, black, black ... (inaudible) Ice, ice, icy, ice block. Tornado. We've got tornado, potato, squashed potato ...

Tui's word associations were spontaneous, imitative, and playful, similar to the imitative variations on prototype phrases that are a significant part of children's acquisition of language structures (Levy & Nelson, 1994). His self-talk reflected the associative processes required by the task. Characteristically there was little to distinguish his self-talk from his social talk. The two flowed into each other without pause. In the next example, the same playful exploration of associations occurred as a group activity. This excerpt was recorded in another group in the same fourth-grade classroom carrying out the same task.

Student 1:   ... No, it's not snow.
Student 2:   Doesn't snow in New Zealand.
Jan: It does not.
Student 2:   Not in Christchurch.
Jan: It only snows in the mountains.
Student 2:   And Mount Cook.
Jan: Yeah.
Student 2:   And Mount Egmont and Mount everything.
Jan: Mount Egmont I love. I've been over there. I've got a T shirt of Mount Egmont.
Student 2:   Mount Tekapo?
Jan: Yeah.
Student 2:   I suppose that is.
Jan: No. And there's, um ...
Student 1:   It just about snowed the other Friday. Last Friday. That was thick cloud.
Jan: The clouds are, um, ...
Student 2:   Sheep clouds.
Jan: Yeah. Sheep clouds, all puffy sheep clouds. Baa lamb clouds.

Jan and her two peers created a chain of associations to the word 'snow' by cuing each other's responses. The associative process of a single mind (illustrated by Tui in the example above) is replicated in this example as the socially coordinated activities of several minds engaging in the same process. Again, it is playful and imitative.

In the next excerpt from a sixth-grade class, two boys (Jim and Paul) co-constructed a set of associations by using a cultural artifact (an adventure story structure) to cue and coordinate their connections. The students had been asked by the teacher to work together in groups, making notes about the talk given by a visiting speaker. Jim wanted to know whether the speaker had been to the magnetic south pole. He had not asked her but inferred that she had not been.

Jim:	Because she would have said [if she had been there], told us in the slides. She would have said 'Now this is the magnetic pole.' I don't think she's been there.
Koa:	She sort of stayed in one place really.
Jim:	Yeah. Exactly. The magnetic pole is basically right in the middle.
Koa:	(inaudible)
Jim:	Yeah. And you can get lost. You have to go by chopper. You have to go by chopper and then you get, and then the magnetic um, energy would kind of give you a down pull [gestures with hands], a down draught and you'd get in more trouble than its worth.
Paul:	I don't think its that strong, Jim.
Jim:	No, but the, well look, if they can pick it up in America, then it will be quite strong. Quite strong. I mean it would interfere with the radio contact. If they took them in too close, by the chopper …
Paul:	Hey, Jim, Jim. What you do is you get down onto a sledge. You hold a magnet and you throw yourself off your sledge [makes screeching noise, mimes a sledge out of control]. Oh, slow down! Cause there's this massive pull.
Jim:	So I went [makes crashing noise, also mimes out-of-control sledge].
Paul:	No Jim. You go straight through the centre of the earth and pop back out at the magnetic pole at the North pole. Oh! This is the Arctic! Errgh! A bit hot, though …

The knowledge of the two boys about the magnetic south pole was shared and elaborated into an imaginary story about using a magnet to find the magnetic south pole and being dragged through the centre of the earth to the north pole. The result was a jointly created spontaneous elaboration of the original content using the cultural structure of an adventure story.

Each of the examples above illustrates the process of knowledge acquisition through the playful creation of associations. They form a progression, from the spontaneous but culturally structured elaboration co-constructed by peers (Jim and Paul), through the spontaneous unstructured flow of associations also co-constructed by peers (Jan and her peers), through the spontaneous flow of asso-

ciations by an individual talking to himself (Tui). There is a transactional relationship between the individual and social versions of the processes illustrated
in the examples. The socially structured versions of the process are internalised
and imitated by individual students. The individual versions of the process form
the basis on which the each student participates in the social co-construction of
the process.

However, the socially co-constructed versions of the process are not just coordinations of individual versions. They are also shaped by the social relationships that exist between the students and the cultural norms that structure those
relationships. The contributions of different students to the co-construction
process are weighted according to their status and role in the group. Not only
does the cognitive content reflect the sociocultural structure of the group but the
co-construction of cognitive associations is itself a playing out of social processes.

Monitoring validity, coherence and consistency.

Another process involved in knowledge acquisition is the evaluation of the consistency or fit between new knowledge, with its associations and implications,
and existing knowledge. This process takes many forms in which the teacher often plays a critical role as the judge of the truth and value of new knowledge. In
the following example, taken from the fourth-grade class that was studying the
unit on the weather, Rata was evaluating her knowledge against the teacher's
knowledge. Rata was both participating in the class discussion and talking to
herself.

Public discussion	**Private talk**
Teacher: What's another word for [air] pressure? Another way to explain pressure if we don't understand pressure? Rata?	
Rata: How heavy the air is.	
Teacher: Simple as that. Did you hear what she said, Sue?	Rata (to self): I got it right.
Sue: No.	
Teacher: Say it again, Rata	
Rata: How heavy the air is.	

Public discussion	Private talk
Teacher: It's the weight of air. What information can we use that tells us the weight of air? …	Rata (whisper to peer): I didn't even know that was right.

It was not enough for Rata to hear the teacher accept her public response. she also told herself and whispered to her neighbour that she had the right answer, implying that she was not as capable as it might have seemed ('I didn't even know that was right'). The next example comes from later in the same unit. The teacher was discussing a thermometer.

Public discussion	Private talk
Teacher: What is the silver stuff called? Does anyone know?	
Student: Mercury.	
Teacher: Is that right? It is called mercury. No question about that. Used to be called in ancient times quick silver. Why do you think its called quick silver?	Rata (to self): Good. I got it right then.
Student: 'Cause its got silver in it.	Rata (to self): Cor, I got it right.

Rata's self-talk suggests a constant personal process of self-evaluation. On this occasion, Rata did not contribute to the public discussion, but her self-talk suggests that she was both answering the teacher's questions to herself and evaluating her own answers in imitation of the teacher's evaluations of public student answers. In the next example, the evaluation of knowledge was translated into a process of social evaluation. It occurred in the sixth-grade class studying Antarctica. Teine's self-talk expressed her evaluation not of herself but of Lapana as a 'stupid idiot' and 'dick' because he gave a wrong answer to the teacher.

Public discussion	Private talk
Teacher: Did you think they would have to wear so much clothing?	
Lapana: Yeah.	

Public discussion	Private talk
Teacher: You did? You thought that they would have to wear all that gear? Would you wear that if you were in Christchurch?	Teine: [to self, watching Lapana] Oh, dick! Stupid idiot! [laughs to self]
Lapana: I don't know.	
Teacher: No. Probably not. Not unless you had a really cold icebox of a house like mine.	Teine: [to self, looking at Lapana] Doesn't even know!

While Teine's evaluation of Lapana was expressed privately, the next example reflects the way the same connections between knowledge claims and personal status can be played out as social processes. Pam and her group were outside their fourth-grade classroom recording the day's weather. They were debating the name of the clouds they could see in the sky.

Pam:	What's the clouds like?
Student:	Nimbus. Nimbus.
Pam:	It is not. Look! Clouds aren't nimbus.
Student:	They are so. Look!
Pam:	What is nimbus, anyway?
Student:	Big black. They're big and black.
Pam:	Oh, you are [black]!
Student:	Big black rain clouds.
Student 2:	Don't look like rain clouds to me.

The argument between Pam and the others in her group developed over alternative claims about the name of the clouds. Relevant evidence ('They're big and black') became mixed with personal comment ('Oh, you are [black]!') and assertions of truth ('Don't look like rain clouds to me'). The evaluation of knowledge had become, in this incident, mixed up with the constant social negotiation of personal status and credibility.

The next example comes from a sixth-grade class that had been discussing the multi-ethnic nature of New York as part of a unit on understanding ethnic differences. The teacher asked each group to make a list of the advantages and disadvantages of a multi-ethnic population. Joe was working in a group with Ricky and Derek. Unlike Joe and Derek, Ricky was a member of a minority ethnic group.

Joe:	Ricky, I'm with Derek.

Ricky:	Ooh!
Joe:	Because you don't come with good ideas.
Ricky:	Ooh!
Joe:	Ha ha! I'll go with you next time … Hey! I've lost my bloomin' chair [grabbing Ricky's chair]
Ricky:	Give me that one.
Joe:	Na! Give me that, nig nog. Give me that, nig nog. Give me that! … [returns with chair to desk] Shut up nig nog … Oh! Get your stupid bag out of there Ricky.
Ricky:	I don't want to.
Joe:	You're dumb.
Ricky;	[inaudible]
Joe:	Get stuffed!
Ricky:	Do you know what we have to do?
Joe:	Yeah.
Ricky:	What?
Joe:	Read it.

In this class, Ricky was constantly surrounded by the kind of talk illustrated in the example above. Joe mixed remarks about ability ('You're dumb!', 'You don't come with good ideas') with racial name-calling ('nig nog') and with personal attacks ('Get stuffed!').

These examples illustrate the ways in which knowledge acquisition processes occur as social processes as well as cognitive processes. Examples of the same processes occurring in student self-talk suggest the transactional relationship that exists between the social and the cognitive. Because the social versions of knowledge acquisition processes are structured as much by the social and cultural processes of the classroom as they are by the cognitive demands of the task, the versions of knowledge acquisition processes that are internalised incorporate the ongoing social and cultural dimensions of the classroom. For example, each student's ideas and contributions to class activities are evaluated according to the student's position and status within the class or group. The processes by which students like Pam, Teine, Lapana, Joe, and Ricky develop a sense of self-worth and self-efficacy are the same processes by which they argue about and evaluate their ideas and beliefs. Together, their individual knowledge acquisition processes evolve as they use and reuse them within the changing social contexts of their classroom experience.

How Do Cognitive Representations Develop and Change?

In addition to the processes involved in knowledge acquisition, there are those processes that serve to sustain and protect knowledge once it has been acquired. These are, as it were, the housekeeping processes of the mind that ensure that knowledge is organised and accessible for future use. If the mind provides the continuity of experience between social settings, between communities and between occasions (Salomon, 1993), how does it sustain that continuity? It is in this area that the sociocultural and linguistic perspectives have little to say. However, classroom evidence suggests that the same kind of transactional relationship exists between the processes of knowledge maintenance (or memory) and social processes as exists between knowledge acquisition and social processes.

Recent research on the nature of memory suggests that there are at least three processes involved in the storage and retrieval of experience. The first is the retrieval process itself. In the classroom it occurs not only when the teacher or the task require students to recollect or review past experience but also whenever new experiences are related to previous experience. Retrieval may involve several processes. Simple recollection of readily available knowledge is supplemented by 'reconstruction' (Brewer, 1987) and 'deduction' (Nuthall & Alton-Lee, 1995) from a variety of alternative and associated forms of knowledge. The second process involves the integration of related representations of experience into a single complex representation. This process has been described as 'integration' (Alber & Hasher, 1983; Bransford, Barclay, & Franks, 1972) and 'unitization' (Mandler, 1989). The third process involves the coordination of specific representations into a hierarchical structure through summarisation or abstraction of common elements (Neisser, 1989). In this process a more abstract or summary representation is created that provides a structure for the hierarchical organisation of the original representations (Conway, 1990). This process of the progressive integration and hierarchical organisation of mental representations is the basis for the Piagetian account of the development of intelligence (cf. Piaget, 1978).

The retrieval of representations in memory.

The following example illustrates some of the important characteristics of how students retrieve memories of classroom experience. Amy, a student in the fourth-grade class that studied life in the Middle Ages, was asked to recall (during two interviews) what she remembered about what castles were made of. Amy had some prior knowledge about castles because she had lived in England with her family and could recall visiting a castle some years before. During the class activities on the Middle Ages (discussions, workbook activities, reading of books, etc.), there had been several references to castles – how they were constructed, what they are made of, what they looked like, and what they contained. The following excerpts are an abbreviated description of the class activities relevant to what castles were made of. Amy's first encounter with relevant content occurred during a class discussion about William the Conqueror taking over England after the Battle of Hastings.

Teacher:	… William had to settle his army safely in England. He did this by building wooden castles, which could be made very quickly. First he forced the English to build a huge mound of earth … on top was a wooden tower or keep … the keep was protected by a fence of sharp stakes called a palisade …
Teacher:	[later, reviewing the previous discussion] Right. True or false? He built them in a hurry?
Student:	True.
Teacher:	Good girl. The walls were made of stone? True or false?
Student:	False.
Teacher:	Good … Give me one disadvantage of a wooden castle? Just one? Jim?
Jim:	It could burn.
Teacher:	Good …

Several days later, the teacher discussed the history of the Tower of London.

Teacher:	What was the keep made from? Stan?
Stan:	Wood.
Teacher:	Why was it made from wood? Mary?
Mary:	So, um, it, it's difficult.
Teacher:	The keep is the tower, Mary, OK?
Mary:	Oh, 'cause it was easy to build.
Teacher:	[later in discussion] … But don't forget. It was wood to start off in a hurry, and then it would have been rebuilt … It was started by William the First in 1078. At first there was a wooden castle on a mound of earth.

Subsequent to this discussion, the students studied work sheets that described the construction of early castles out of wood, and the construction of later castles out of stone. There were several coloured pictures of medieval scenes, including castles, posted around the walls of the classroom that were visible to the students during the unit. In addition, Amy looked at coloured pictures of castles when she was reading a reference book about knights and castles.

When we interviewed Amy about two weeks after the completion of the unit on the Middle Ages, she recalled that castles were made of wood and stone.

Amy:	Wood and stone.
Interviewer:	How do you know?
Amy:	Well Ms A told us that the early castles were built of wood because they needed them to get up quickly.
Interviewer:	They needed to get the castles up quickly. Right. And what about stone?
Amy:	I don't think I heard about it.
Interviewer:	Right.
Amy:	Seen pictures though.
Interviewer:	Right, where would you have seen pictures?
Amy:	This book called *Knights and Castles* ...
Interviewer:	Yeah.
Amy:	The pictures of the knights coming into the castles and they were brick, grey bricks, stone stuff.
Interviewer:	Right. That's a good, good answer.

A year later, when we interviewed Amy again, she thought she recalled that castles were made of clay bricks.

Interviewer:	How do you know?
Amy:	I've seen pictures of them [castles] before, and they certainly weren't wood and stone ... they were large clay bricks.
Interviewer:	Right. Where did you see these pictures?
Amy:	On castles, pictures, in the rooms of castles.
Interviewer:	Right. That's good. Did Ms A ever talk about what they were actually built of?
Amy:	I think she talked about what the mud and thatch type serfs' type house was made of. I think she talked about that as well.
Interviewer:	Right. What did she talk about the mud and thatch in relation to?
Amy:	Um the serfs houses not, not the castles.
Interviewer:	Right.

Several important characteristics of the memory retrieval process are evident in this example. First, the memory representation that Amy described in the first interview contained not only the relevant semantic content ('wood and stone') but also the contexts in which this was learned ('Ms. A told us,' 'this book called *Knights and Castles*'). She had a clear recollection of the use of wood to build castles ('because they needed them to get up quickly'), but relied on her visual memory of pictures of castles to recall the use of stone ('brick, grey bricks, stone stuff'). Her representation of castles in her memory was a complex structure of semantic and contextual detail from which she both retrieved and deduced the appropriate answers.

A year later, however, critical elements of her representation of her relevant classroom experiences had disappeared. What the teacher said about castles had disappeared. An image of castle walls had been retained that may have been based on her prior experience of visiting a castle and, as she believed, the pictures she had seen of castles. She deduced from this image that castle walls must have been made of 'large clay bricks.' This deduction about clay bricks brought to mind (through an association of clay with mud) an associated memory of the teacher talking about the cottages of serfs being made of mud and thatch.

The evidence from our interviews suggests that the initial representations that students construct of classroom experiences contain much of the social and cognitive complexities of the original experiences. This may include representations of the associative and evaluative processes that occurred during the internalisation of the experiences. Retrieval of knowledge involves the use of any or all of the details contained in this complex representation (Nuthall & Alton-Lee, 1995).

Over time elements of this original representation disappear making it increasingly necessary to infer or deduce the nature of the original experiences. Well-established prior knowledge (such as Amy's early experience of visiting a castle) absorbs the details and more abstract memory structures are used to deduce, rather than retrieve, the content of the original experiences.

The integration of related experiences.

All the classroom experiences relevant to a specific idea or piece of information are unlikely to occur in close proximity to each other. During the course of classroom activities they may be dispersed over time and often inter-leaved with experiences relevant to other unrelated ideas or information. In addition, within a specific curriculum unit or topic, experiences relevant to one concept may also be relevant in different ways to several different concepts. Consequently, in order to develop coherent knowledge structures, a student's mind must be constantly sorting and organising experiences. Much of this sorting and organising appears to occur automatically and unconsciously during the process of internalisation (Bransford et al., 1972).

Because the process of integration is largely automatic and unconscious it is easier to identify when it goes wrong. The next example illustrates the effect of a failure in the integration process. Near the beginning of this chapter, I described Kim's recollections of the concept of a charter in medieval society. The first time Kim had come across a reference to a charter during the unit on the Middle Ages was in a work sheet about the signing of the Magna Carta. This work sheet described the Magna Carta as a 'great charter' that 'sets out all the rights of free men.' When we asked Kim to remember what he learned about a charter, he appeared to have forgotten the content of this work sheet. In fact, he appeared to have forgotten about the Magna Carta entirely. However, in a later interview, when Kim was asked about the Magna Carta itself, he seemed to remember it.

Kim:	I thought it was a treaty signed by King Harold, I mean King John.
Interviewer:	What's a treaty?
Kim:	Oh, um, a treaty. When we studied Antarctica we had an Antarctica treaty, Antarctic Treaty …
Interviewer:	What are you thinking of when you're remembering Magna Carta?
Kim:	Um, the King signing a treaty.
Interviewer:	Right, how did you learn that?
Kim:	We did um, there's a picture on a number line about that and we learned it [sitting] on the mat.
Interviewer:	Who taught you?
Kim:	Ms. A.

In this context, Kim recalled the work sheet about the signing of the Magna Carta. He remembered the teacher discussing it and placing it on the time line on the classroom wall. This memory for the Magna Carta had, however, been integrated with his prior knowledge about a treaty. Consequently, although there is reference in the work sheet to the Magna Carta being a 'charter,' it was not integrated with Kim's memory for his other experiences related to a charter. As reference to the earlier example will show (pp. 4-7), his representation of a charter was created by integrating other experiences relating to town criers, scrolls, and a picture of the cross roads and square in a medieval town.

In the next example, the integration process led directly to a misunderstanding. Integration is a selective organising process guided by the semantic structures that make up the student's prior knowledge. One of the semantic structures that get used for integrating experience is the story or narrative structure (Schank, 1990). Jim and Paul used it in their discussion of the magnetic pole (described above). During part of the unit on the Middle Ages, the teacher gave the class an account of the changes in medieval society that led to the peasants' revolt. With the help of a pictorial history book, she gave a narrative account of the events leading up to the peasants' revolt.

Teacher:	... It [the feudal system] was becoming more like, um, a sort of market society where you worked and were given ... money for the work you did ... and also about this time there were lots of new inventions, ... um, for example?
Student:	The printing. Printing.
Teacher:	The printing press. William Caxton, he invented the printing press. Right. And firearms were invented too ... Anyway. To get back to the peasants' revolt ... Wat Tyler isn't actually mentioned in this story ... and if anyone is interested in this book, there is some more information about the peasants' revolt ...

When we asked Amy, during an interview after the unit, about why William Caxton was famous, she referred to the peasants' revolt.

Amy:	I thought it might have been the peasants' revolt ... we had the peasants revolt.
Interviewer:	Yes, you remember doing something about the peasants' revolt.
Amy:	Read a story.
Interviewer:	Did you. Did Ms A read it or did you read it or?
Amy:	I think Ms A read it I can't remember.
Interviewer:	Do you remember what it was about?
Amy:	About the peasants revolting. Just how lots of people got together ...

Amy's representation of the story of the peasants' revolt retained its narrative structure. Because the reference to William Caxton occurred in the middle of this narrative, it was integrated into it. There are several examples in our data of misunderstandings caused by integration based on temporal or contextual contiguity. The nature of the underlying cognitive structures that guide integration determines how experience gets stored and used in memory.

Summarisation and abstraction.

During the passage of time there is a tendency for representations in memory to produce more abstract or generalised representations. As Neisser describes it, the original representations come to contain 'multiple levels of description' from the more abstract to the more specific (Neisser, 1989, p. 75). The multiple levels of representation (or 'descriptions' as Neisser refers to them) are the product of the way experience is interpreted during internalisation and during subsequent integration in memory. The multiple levels provide a set of alternative points of access to the representation at the time of retrieval. It is interesting to note that recent research on the neurophysiology of the human brain has also identified the multiple layers involved in the processing of experience. According to Crick (1994):

> The secret of the neocortex, if it has one, is probably its ability to evolve additional layers to its hierarchies of processing, especially at the upper levels of those hierarchies. (p. 159)

The easiest to access, and usually the longest retained, are the more abstract or generalised representations. This is illustrated in the following example from the sixth- grade classroom that was studying life in New York. One of the work sheets contained an outline diagram of the official seal of the city of New York, and an account of the meaning of symbols on the seal. When Ann was asked, 12 months after the unit, to remember what was on the seal of New York, she had forgotten all of the details.

Ann:	... I can't really remember this. (laughs)
Interviewer:	Can't you? Have you got any vague mem, memories of things happening during the unit about that?
Ann:	I can remember we did something about it but I can't really remember ... Something to do with trading or something, I can't really remember.
Interviewer:	Yeah. Was it talked about or was there?
Ann:	I think ... yes we did talk about it for a while but I can't really remember.
Interviewer:	Did you do anything about it?
Ann:	... I don't know ... really.
Interviewer:	That's OK. Something to do with trading?
Ann:	Mm.

The class discussion of the symbols (which represent trade and industry) and the visual appearance of the seal had disappeared from Ann's memory. What remained was the abstraction that the seal was 'to do with trading or something.' It is abstract representations such as this one that provide the mind with the knowledge structures that are used for organising and integrating new experiences.

The processes of self-organisation and memory that I have described in this section appear to be largely individual in nature. Since they represent, as it were, the housekeeping activities of the mind, they have traditionally been thought of as individual cognitive processes. However, like the knowledge acquisition processes described in the previous section, they too occur in a transactional relationship with the sociocultural processes of the classroom. Recalling past experiences, integrating and abstracting information, occur during interactions between teachers and students and between students and students. Edwards and Middleton (1988) have shown how social interaction can model and structure the ways in which children recall their representations of past events. Wells and Chang-Wells (in press) have described how, during the process of classroom discussions, teachers can model and invite students to participate in their ways of understanding, integrating, and generalising about, a topic.

CONCLUSIONS

My purpose in this chapter has been to describe the current state of research and debate on student thinking and learning in the classroom. Because I believe we are in a process of radically reconceptualizing the way we understand student classroom experience, there are no comfortable conclusions to be drawn from the content of this chapter. What is clear is that the traditional definitions of thinking and learning, and the traditional distinctions between the social, the linguistic, and the cognitive, no longer apply.

In the final section of this chapter I have focused on the major areas of contention between the three different perspectives on student thinking and learning in the classroom. What I have attempted to show is that if we incorporate the sociocultural and linguistic perspectives into a cognitive constructivist model of the development of mental processes, then it is possible to see how the language and social processes of the classroom construct the ways in which students acquire and retain knowledge.

The implications of the recent research on student thinking and learning in the classroom are, in one sense, clear, but in another sense, quite unclear. It is clear from the general implications of this research that teachers need to see teaching as the management of the classroom as a community rather than simply as instruction in specific curriculum areas. All the evidence we have now about how language shapes classroom experience, about how social processes structure the content of what is talked about and how, about how students remember both the context and content of their classroom experiences, all these make it clear that it is the whole of what goes on in classrooms that determines how students think and learn. What is not so clear from the recent research is how teachers should manage the classroom as a learning community. There are a number of experiments being carried out that are attempting to identify the management skills that teachers need (e.g., Brown et al., 1993; Hiebert et al., 1994), but readers who had hoped to find in this chapter a set of recommendations about how to get students to think and learn more effectively in their classrooms, will be disappointed. There are two reasons for this. One is historical and the other is practical, but they are closely linked to each other.

If the research described in this chapter is put into the context of the history of research on learning and teaching in the classroom, it can be seen as an important stage in the development of this research, but not a stage that has immediate practical implications for teachers. Some years ago, in a report on a series of experimental studies of the effects of teaching, John Church and I suggested that classroom research should evolve through a series of four stages (Nuthall & Church, 1973). First, observational and descriptive studies should be carried out to explore and understand how teachers and students experience life in classrooms. Second, attempts should be made to identify the relationships between classroom experiences and student learning. These studies should be informed by, and closely linked to, the observational and descriptive studies in the first phase. Third, attempts should be made to verify, through carefully designed classroom trials and experiments, the significance and generality of the relationships identified in the second phase. Fourth, explanations should be developed to describe, in general terms, how classroom experiences and learning are related to each other. Such explanations should provide teachers with the theoretical insights and understandings that they need to guide and develop their own teaching.

It was envisaged that the four phases should constitute a loop or cycle with information feeding backwards and forwards between studies being carried out in each of the four phases. In this way the research could be kept constantly in touch with the evolving realities of life in classrooms as it produced increasingly reliable and general knowledge about teaching.

What has happened in the last 30 years of research on classroom learning and teaching is that some studies have progressed from the observational and descriptive phase through the correlational and experimental phases, but in so doing, they have became increasingly narrow and limited in their conceptions of the nature of teaching and learning (Brophy & Good, 1986; Gage & Needels, 1989). The early observational and descriptive studies that had been reported through the 1970s included a wide range of concepts and methodologies from sociology, anthropology, linguistics, and philosophy. But the correlational and experimental studies that followed that first phase were dominated by conceptions of learning and teaching that were primarily psychological and behavioural. In the reductionist climate of the time, rigor meant narrowness.

In this historical perspective, the radical reconceptualization of our understanding of classroom learning and teaching that underlies the studies reported in this chapter represents nothing less than an explosive reaction against the paradigm that dominated the correlational and experimental research of the last two decades. This chapter is an account of how new disciplines and new methodologies have been introduced into the study of classroom experience. But the price of this radical reconceptualization of our understanding of the classroom is that most of the recent research has been descriptive and observational. In terms of our research cycle, it has gone back to the first phase.

Returning to the first phase of the research cycle should not, however, be interpreted as a regressive development. This return does mark a paradigm-breaking increase in the conceptual and methodological sophistication of the research. The cycle has become an upward spiral. Of greatest significance is the clear acknowledgement of the multi-layered and multi-dimensional nature of classroom processes. The reductionist conception of research that favoured simplicity and objectivity has been abandoned for a conception of research that embraces the considerable complexity and subjectivity of much of what we need to observe, describe, and understand in classrooms.

However, having acknowledged the considerable step forward that has occurred in returning to the observational and descriptive phase of classroom research, we also need to acknowledge that the ultimate value of this research depends on incorporating the other phases of the cycle. We need to focus once again on the relationships that actually occur between classroom experience and changes in students' cognitive and social skills. We cannot continue to depend on assumptions and theoretical predictions about how students are affected by their classroom experiences. Teachers need to know how the classroom processes that they manage, and have responsibility for, affect the lives and development of their students. As Hiebert has put it, 'Unless the results allow us to begin building explanations of superior performance, in terms of relationships between teaching and learning, the studies are of limited use' (Hiebert, 1993, p. 237).

As several writers have indicated, moving on to the other phases of the research cycle will require us to develop new and much more sophisticated research procedures. We need to match the complexity of our evolving conceptual understanding of the classroom with an equally complex set of procedures for investigating and verifying that understanding (Nuthall & Alton-Lee, 1993). Data of an individual and specific nature will need to be handled within studies that incorporate a wide range of different types and sources of information about student experience. Enclosed individual research studies will need to be replaced by open-ended programmes of research. In short we will need to find ways of identifying and exploring multiple inter-relationships between complex social processes and complex mental processes in a variety of settings and over longer periods of time (Marshall, 1995).

The practical consequence of the increasing complexity of our research and understanding of classroom processes is that there is no longer the possibility of simple answers to questions about how to improve the quality of students' thinking and learning in classrooms. The research reported in this chapter indicates quite clearly that there has been a major shift in the sophistication of research in classrooms. The informed and reflective teacher must come to understand that classroom research on student thinking and learning is nothing less than research on the development of the human mind. It would be foolish to underestimate the complexity, and ultimate value, of the journey that this research is undertaking.

ENDNOTE

1. Most of the transcripts used in this chapter come from the studies in the Understanding Learning and Teaching Project whose co-director is Adrienne Alton-Lee. We would like to thank all the teachers and students who have been involved in this project and especially the research assistants (Greta Bowron, Anthea Clibborn-Brown, Kerry Hancock) and the technician (Roger Corbett) who have worked with us as observers, recorders, transcribers, and data processors.

    I would like to acknowledge the considerable assistance I have had in preparing this chapter from the editors and from authors of the work I have described. In particular Gordon Wells, Terry Wood, James Hiebert, and Hermine Marshall who went out of their way to share their experience and wisdom.

REFERENCES

Alber, J. W. & Hasher, L. (1983). Is memory semantic? *Psychological Bulletin, 93*, 203-231.

Alvermann, D. E., O'Brien, D. G., & Dillon, D. R. (1990). What teachers do when they say they're having discussions of content area reading assignments: A qualitative analysis. *Reading Research Quarterly, 25*, 296-322.

Alton-Lee, A. G. & Nuthall, G. A. (1992). A generative methodology for classroom research. *Educational Philosophy and Theory, 24*, 29-55.

Alton-Lee, A. G., Nuthall, G. A., & Patrick, J. (1993). Reframing classroom research: A lesson from the private world of children. *Harvard Educational Review, 63*(1), 50-84.

Amigues, R. (1988). Peer interaction in solving physics problems: Sociocognitive confrontation and metacognitive aspects. *Journal of Experimental Child Psychology, 45*, 141-158.

Amigues, R. (1990). Peer interaction and conceptual change. In H. Mandl, E. de Corte, N. Bennett, & H. F. Friedrich (Eds.), *Learning and instruction: European research in an international context* (Vol.2, pp. 27-43). Oxford: Pergamon Press.

Andersen, E. S. (1990). *Speaking with style: The sociolinguistic skills of children.* London: Routledge.

Anderson, C. W. (April, 1994). *Engagement in explanation and design in middle school science.* Paper presented at the annual meeting of the American Educational Research Association, New Orleans.

Baker, C. D. (1992). Description and analysis in classroom talk and interaction. *Journal of Classroom Interaction, 27*, 9-14.

Ball, S. J. (1980). Initial encounters in the classroom and the process of establishment. In P. Woods (Ed.), *Pupil strategies: Explorations in the sociology of the school* (pp. 143-161). London: Croom Helm.

Bennett, N. & Desforges, C. (1988). Matching classroom tasks to students' attainments. *Elementary School Journal, 88*, 221-234.

Bereiter, C. (1985). Toward a solution of the learning paradox. *Review of Educational Research, 55*, 201-226.

Berk, L. E. (1986). Relationship of elementary school children's private speech to behavioral accompaniment to task, attention, and task performance. *Developmental Psychology, 22*, 671-680.

Blaye, A. (1990). Peer interaction in solving a binary matrix problem: Possible mechanisms causing individual progress. In H. Mandl, E. de Corte, N. Bennett, & H. F. Friedrich (Eds.), *Learning and instruction: European research in an international context* (Vol. 2, pp. 45-46). Oxford: Pergamon Press.

Bloom, L. (1991). *Language development from two to three.* New York: Cambridge University Press.

Bohannon, J. N. & Stanowicz, L. (1988). The issue of negative evidence: Adult responses to children's language errors. *Developmental Psychology, 24*, 684-689.

Bransford, J. D., Barclay, J. R., & Franks, J. J. (1972). Sentence memory: A constructive vs interpretive approach. *Cognitive Psychology, 3*, 193-209.

Brewer, W. F. (1987). Schemas versus mental models in human memory. In P. Morris (Ed.), *Modelling cognition* (pp. 187-197). New York: John Wiley & Sons.

Brickhouse, N. W. (1994). Children's observations, ideas, and the development of classroom theories about light. *Journal of Research in Science Teaching, 31*, 639-656.

Brilliant-Mills, H. (1993). Becoming a mathematician: Building a situated definition of mathematics. *Linguistics and Education. 5*, 301-334.

Brophy, J. E. & Alleman, J. (1992). Planning and managing learning activities: Basic principles. In J. E. Brophy (Ed.), *Advances in research on teaching: Planning and managing learning tasks and activities. Vol. 3* (pp. 1-45). Greenwich, CT: JAI Press.

Brophy, J. E. & Good, T. L. (1986). Teacher behavior and student achievement. In M. Wittrock (Ed.), *Handbook of research on teaching* (3rd ed., pp. 328-375). London: Collier Macmillan.

Brown, A. L. (1992). Design experiments: Theoretical and methodological challenges in creating complex interventions in classroom settings. *The Journal of the Learning Sciences, 2*, 141-178.

Brown, A. L. (1994). The advancement of learning. *Educational Researcher, 23*(8), 4-12.

Brown, A. L., Ash, D., Rutherford, M., Nakagawa, K., Gordon, A., & Campione, J. C. (1993). Distributed expertise in the classroom. In G. Salomon (Ed.), *Distributed cognitions: Psychological and educational considerations* (pp. 188-228). Cambridge: Cambridge University Press.

Brown, A. L. & Campione, J. C. (1994). Guided discovery in a community of learners. In K. McGilly (Ed.), *Classroom lessons: Integrating cognitive theory and classroom practice* (pp. 229-270). Cambridge, MA: MIT Press/Bradford Books.

Brown, C. (1993). A critical analysis of teaching rational number. In T. P. Carpenter, E. Fennema, & T. A. Romberg (Eds.), *Rational numbers: An integration of research* (pp. 197-218). Hillsdale, NJ: Erlbaum.

Bruner, J. S., Goodnow, J. J. & Austin, G. A. (1956). *A study of thinking.* New York: John Wiley & Sons.

Carey, S. (1986). Cognitive science and science education. *American Psychologist, 41*, 1123-1130.

Carey, S. (1991). Knowledge acquisition: Enrichment or conceptual change? In S. Carey & R. Gelman (Eds.), *The epigenesis of mind: Essays on biology and cognition* (pp. 257-291). Hillsdale, NJ: Lawrence Erlbaum Associates.

Carpenter, T. P., Fennema, E., & Romberg, T. A. (1993). Toward a unified discipline of scientific inquiry. In T. P. Carpenter, E. Fennema, & T. A. Romberg (Eds.), *Rational numbers: An integration of research* (pp. 1-11). Hillsdale, NJ: Erlbaum.

Case, R. (with Bruchkowsky, M., Capodilupo, A., et al.) (1991). *The mind's staircase: Exploring the conceptual underpinnings of children's thought and knowledge.* Hillsdale, NJ: Lawrence Erlbaum.

Case, R. & Sandieson, R. (1991). Testing for the presence of a central quantitative structure: Use of the transfer paradigm. In R. Case (with others) *The mind's staircase: Exploring the conceptual underpinnings of children's thought and knowledge* (pp. 117-134). Hillsdale, NJ: Lawrence Erlbaum.

Chinn, C. A., Waggoner, M. A., Anderson, R. C., Schommer, M., & Wilkinson, I. A. G. (1993). Situated actions during reading lessons: A microanalysis of oral reading episodes. *American Educational Research Journal, 30,* 361-392.

Clark, H. H. & Clark, E. V. (1977). *Psychology and language.* New York: Harcourt, Brace Jovanovich.

Clark, H. H. & Schaefer, E. F. (1989). Collaborating on contributions to conversations. In R. Dietrich & C. F. Graumann (Eds.), *Language processing in social context* (pp. 123-152). Amsterdam: Elsevier Science.

Cobb, P. (1994). Where is the mind? Constructivist and sociocultural perspectives on mathematical development. *Educational Researcher, 23*(7), 13-20.

Cobb, P., Yackel, E., & Wood, T. (1992). A constructivist alternative to the representational view of mind in mathematics education. *Journal for Research in Mathematics Education, 23,* 2-33.

Cohen, E. G. (1994). Restructuring the classroom: Conditions for productive small groups. *Review of Educational Research, 64,* 1-35.

Conway, M. A. (1990). *Autobiographical memory: An introduction.* Milton Keynes: Open University Press.

Crick, F. (1994). *The astonishing hypothesis: The scientific search for the soul.* London: Touchstone Books.

Davydov, V. V. (1995). The influence of L. S. Vygotsky on education theory, research and practice. *Educational Researcher, 24* (3), 12-21.

Deegan, J. G. (1993). Children's friendships in culturally diverse classrooms. *Journal of Research in Childhood Education, 7,* 91-101.

Dennett, D. C. (1993). *Consciousness explained.* Hammondsworth, Middlesex: Penguin Books.

Denscombe, M. (1980). Pupil strategies and the open classroom. In P. Woods (Ed.), *Pupil strategies: Explorations in the sociology of the school* (pp. 50-73). London: Croom Helm.

Dimitracopoulou, I. (1990). *Conversational competence and social development.* New York: Cambridge University Press.

Dixon, C. L., de la Cruz, E., Green, J., Lin, L., & Brandts, L. (1992). Do you see what we see? The referential and intertextual nature of classroom life. *Journal of Classroom Interaction, 27,* 29-36.

Doise, W. (1991). System and metasystem in cognitive operations. In M. Carretero, M. Pope, R-J. Simons, & J. Pozo (Eds.), *Learning and instruction: European research in an international perspective* (Vol. 3., pp. 125-139). Oxford: Pergamon Press.

Doise, W. & Mugny, G. (1984). *The social development of the intellect.* New York: Pergamon Press.

Doyle, W. (1983). Academic work. *Review of Educational Research, 53,* 159-199.

Doyle, W. & Carter, K. (1984). Academic tasks in classrooms. *Curriculum Inquiry, 14*(2), 129-149.

Driver, R., Asoko, H., Leach, J., Mortimar, E., & Scott, P. (1994). Constructing scientific knowledge in the classroom. *Educational Researcher, 23*(7), 5-12.

Edwards, D. & Middleton, D. (1988). Conversational remembering and family relationships: How children learn to remember. *Journal of Social and Personal Relationships, 5,* 3-25.

Egan, K. (1989). *Teaching as story telling: An alternative approach to teaching and the curriculum in the elementary school.* Chicago: University of Chicago Press.

Egan, K. (1993). Narrative and learning: A voyage of implications. *Linguistics and Education, 5,* 119-126.

Ernest, P. (Ed.). (1989). *Mathematics teaching: The state of the art.* London: Falmer Press.

Farrar, M. J. (1992). Negative evidence and grammatical morpheme acquisition. *Developmental Psychology, 28,* 90-98.

Flavell, J. H. (1963). *The developmental psychology of Jean Piaget.* Princeton, NJ: Van Nostrand.

Floriani, A. (1993). Negotiating what counts: Roles and relationships, texts and contexts, content and meaning. *Linguistics and Education, 5,* 241-275.

Fodor, J. (1980). Fixation of belief and concept acquisition. In M. Piattelli-Palmerini (Ed.), *Language and learning: The debate between Jean Piaget and Naom Chomsky* (pp. 142-149). Cambridge, MA: Harvard University Press.

Frid, S. & Malone, J. (1994, April). *Negotiation of meaning in mathematics classrooms: A study of two Year 5 classes.* Paper presented at the annual meeting of the American Educational Research Association, New Orleans.

Fuchs, L. S., Fuchs, D., Bentz, J., Phillips, N. B., & Hamlett, C. L. (1994). The nature of student interactions during peer tutoring with and without prior training and experience. *American Educational Research Journal, 31,* 75-103.

Gage, N. L. & Needels, M. C. (1989). Process-product research on teaching: A review of criticisms. *Elementary School Journal, 89,* 253-300.

Gee, P. G. (1991). What is literacy? In C. Mitchell & K. Weiler (Eds.), *Rewriting literacy: Culture and the discourse of the other.* New York: Bergin & Garvey.

Gilly, M. (1991). The social psychology of cognitive constructions: European perspectives. In M. Carretero, M. Pope, R-J. Simons, & J. Pozo (Eds.), *Learning and instruction: European research in an international perspective* (Vol. 3., pp. 99-123). Oxford: Pergamon Press.

Glachan, M. & Light, P. (1982). Peer interaction and learning: Can two wrongs make a right? In G. Butterworth & P. Light (Eds.), *Social cognition: Studies of the development of understanding* (pp. 238-262). Chicago: University of Chicago Press.

Good, T. L., McCaslin, M. M., & Reys, B. J. (1992). Investigating work groups to promote problem solving in mathematics. In J. Brophy (Ed.), *Advances in research on teaching: Planning and managing learning tasks and activities, Vol. 3* (pp. 115-160). Greenwich, CT: JAI Press.

Gould, S. J. (1991). *The flamingo's smile: Reflections in natural history.* Harmondsworth, Middlesex: Penguin.

Graves, D. H. (1983). *Writing: Teachers and children at work.* New Hampshire: Heineman.

Green, J. L. & Dixon, C. N. (1993). Talking knowledge into being: Discursive and social practices in classrooms. *Linguistics and Education, 5,* 231-239.

Gregg, M. & Leinhardt, G. (1994, April). *Constructing geography.* Paper presented at the annual meeting of the American Educational Research Association, New Orleans.

Grice, H. P. (1989). *Studies in the way of words.* Cambridge, MA: Harvard University Press.

Gutierrez, K. D. (1993). How talk, context, and script shape contexts for learning: A cross-case comparison of journal sharing. *Linguistics and Education, 5,* 335-365.

Haig, B. D. (1987). Scientific problems and the conduct of research. *Educational Philosophy and Theory, 19,* 22-32.

Halliday, M. A. K. (1978). *Language as social semiotic: The social interpretation of language and meaning.* London: Edward Arnold.

Halliday, M. A. K. (1993). Towards a language-based theory of learning. *Linguistics and Education, 5,* 93-116.

Heras, A. I. (1993). The construction of understanding in a sixth-grade bilingual classroom. *Linguistics and Education, 5*, 275-299.

Hicks, D. (1993). Narrative discourse and classroom learning: An essay response to Egan's 'Narrative and learning: A voyage of implications.' *Linguistics and Education, 5*, 127-148.

Hiebert, J. A. (1993). Benefits and costs of research that links teaching and learning mathematics. In T. P. Carpenter, E. Fennema, & T. A. Romberg (Eds.), *Rational numbers: An integration of research* (pp. 219-238). Hillsdale, NJ: Erlbaum.

Hiebert, J. A. & Wearne, D. (1993). Instructional tasks, classroom discourse, and students' learning in second-grade arithmetic. *American Educational Research Journal, 30*, 393-425.

Hiebert, J. A., Wearne, D., Carpenter, T. P., Fennema, E., Fuson, K., Human, P., Olivier, A., & Murray, H. (1994, April). *Authentic problem solving in mathematics.* Paper presented at the annual meeting of the American Educational Research Association, New Orleans.

Hirst, P. H. & Peters, R. S. (1970). *The logic of education.* London: Routledge & Kegan Paul.

Holland, J. D., Anderson, C. W. & Palincsar, A. S. (1994, March). *Appropriating scientific discourse in a sixth-grade classroom: The case of Juan.* Paper presented at the annual meeting of the National Association for Research in Science Teaching, Anaheim, CA.

House, E. R. (1991). Realism in research. *Educational Researcher, 20*(6), 2-9.

Hughes, D. C. (1973). An experimental investigation of the effects of pupil responding and teacher reacting on pupil achievement. *American Educational Research Journal, 10*, 21-37.

Johnson-Laird, P. N. (1988). *The computer and the mind: An introduction to cognitive science.* Cambridge, MA: Harvard University Press.

King, A. (1994). Guiding knowledge construction in the classroom: Effects of teaching children how to question and how to explain. *American Educational Research Journal, 31*, 338-368.

King, A. & Rosenshine, B. (1993). Effects of guided cooperative questioning on children's knowledge construction. *Journal of Experimental Education, 61*, 127-148.

Kollar, G. M., Anderson, C. W., & Palincsar, A. S. (March 1994). *Power, status and personal identity in small group problem solving: The effects of social power and task specific agendas.* Paper presented at the annual meeting of the National Association for Research in Science Teaching, Anaheim, CA.

Lather, P. (1991). *Getting smart: Feminist research and pedagogy with/in the postmodern.* New York: Routledge.

Lave, J. (1988). *Cognition in practice: Mind, mathematics, and culture in everyday life.* Cambridge: Cambridge University Press.

Lave, J. (1991). Situated learning in communities of practice. In L. B. Resnick, J. M. Levine, & S. D. Teasley (Eds.), *Perspectives on socially shared cognition* (pp. 63-82). Washington, DC: American Psychological Association.

Lee, B. (1987). Recontextualizing Vygotsky. In M. Hickman (Ed.), *Social and functional approaches to language and thought* (pp. 87-104). Orlando, FL: Academic Press.

Lemke, J. L. (1990). *Talking science: Language, learning, and values.* Norwood, NJ: Ablex.

Leont'ev, A. N. (1981). *Problems of the development of the mind.* Moscow: Progress Publishers.

Levy, E. & Nelson, K. (1994). Words in discourse: A dialectical approach to the acquisition of meaning and use. *Journal of Child Language, 21*, 367-389.

Lucy, J. A. & Wertsch, J. V. (1987). Vygotsky and Whorf: A comparative analysis. In M. Hickman (Ed.), *Social and functional approaches to language and thought* (pp. 67-86). Orlando, Fl: Academic Press.

Magnusson, S. J., Boyle, R. A., & Templin, M. (1994, April). *Conceptual development: Reexamining knowledge construction in science.* Paper presented at the annual meeting of the American Educational Research Association, New Orleans.

Mandler, G. (1989). Memory: Conscious and unconscious. In P. R. Soloman, G. R. Goethals, C. M. Kelley, & B. R. Stephens (Eds.), *Memory: Interdisciplinary approaches* (pp. 84-106). New York: Springer Verlag.

Marshall, H. H. (1995). New perspectives on learning and research on learning. In G. Imsen, E. Skaalvik, & A. Telhaug (Eds.), *Fronlijer I Pedagogisk Forskning* (pp. 57-83). Trondheim, Norway: Norsk senter for barneforskning, Universitetet i Trondheim.

Mason, L. & Santi, M. (1994, April). *Argumentation structure and metacognition in constructing shared knowledge at school.* Paper presented at the annual meeting of the American Educational Research Association, New Orleans.

McCaslin Rohrkemper, M. (1989). Self-regulated learning and academic achievement: A Vygotskian view. In B. J. Zimmerman & D. H. Schunk (Eds.), *Self-regulated learning and academic achievement: Theory research and practice* (pp. 143-176). New York: Springer-Verlag.

McKeough, A. (1992, April). *Program development criteria for curricula designed to teach central conceptual structures.* Paper presented at the annual meeting of the American Educational Research Association, San Francisco.

Miller, M. (1987). Argumentation and cognition. In M. Hickman (Ed.), *Social and functional approaches to language and thought* (pp. 225-249). Orlando, FL: Academic Press.

Muscovici, S. (1961). *La Psychoanalyse, son image et son public.* Paris: Presses Universitaires de France (quoted in W. Doise, System and metasystem in cognitive operations. In M. Carretero, M. Pope, R-J. Simons, & J. Pozo (Eds.), *Learning and instruction: European research in an international perspective* (Vol. 3., 1991, pp. 125-139). Oxford: Pergamon Press.

Neisser, U. (1989). Domains of memory. In P. R. Soloman, G. R. Goethals, C. M. Kelley, & B. R. Stephens (Eds.), *Memory: Interdisciplinary approaches* (pp. 67-83). New York: Springer Verlag.

Nelson, K. E. (1989). Strategies for first language teaching. In M. L. Rice & R. L. Schiefelbusch (Eds.), *The teachability of language* (pp. 263-310). Baltimore: Brookes Publishing.

Newman, D., Griffin, P., & Cole, M. (1989). *The construction zone: Working for cognitive change in school.* New York: Cambridge University Press.

Nuthall, G. A. & Alton-Lee, A. G. (1992). Understanding how students learn in classrooms. In M. Pressley, K. Harris, & J. Guthrie (Eds.), *Promoting academic competence and literacy in school* (pp. 57-87). San Diego: Academic Press.

Nuthall, G. A. & Alton-Lee, A. G. (1993). Predicting learning from student experience of teaching: A theory of student knowledge construction in classrooms. *American Educational Research Journal, 30*, 799-840.

Nuthall, G. A. & Alton-Lee, A. G. (1995). Assessing classroom learning: How students use their knowledge and experience to answer achievement test questions in science and social studies. *American Educational Research Journal, 32*, 185-223.

Nuthall, G. A. & Church, R. J. (1973). Experimental studies of teaching behaviour. In G. Chanan (Ed.), *Towards a science of teaching* (pp. 9-25). Slough, Berks: National Foundation for Educational Research.

Nuthall, G. A. & Lawrence, P. J. (1965). *Thinking in the classroom.* Wellington, NZ: Council for Educational Research.

Ohlsson, S. (1990). Cognitive science and instruction: Why the revolution is not here (yet). In H. Mandl, E. de Corte, N. Bennett, & H. F. Friedrich (Eds.), *Learning and instruction: European research in an international context* (Vol. 2, pp. 561-600). Oxford: Pergamon Press.

O'Loughlin, M. O. (1992). Rethinking science education: Beyond Piagetian constructivism toward a sociocultural model of teaching and learning. *Journal of Research in Science Teaching, 29*, 791-820.

Palincsar, A. S. & Brown, A. L. (1989). Classroom dialogues to promote self-regulated comprehension. In J. Brophy (Ed.), *Advances in research on teaching, Vol. 1* (pp. 35-71). Greenwich, CT: JAI Press.

Parecki, A. D. & Palincsar, A. S. (1994). *Expanding roles to advance understandings within a community of writers.* Paper presented at the annual meeting of the American Educational Research Association, New Orleans.

Perret-Clermont, A. N. (1980). *Social interaction and cognitive development in children.* New York: Academic Press.

Perret-Clermont, A. N., Perret, J., & Bell, N. (1991). The social construction of meaning and cognitive activity in elementary school children. In L. B. Resnick, J. M. Levine, & S. D. Teasley (Eds.), *Perspectives on socially shared cognition* (pp. 41-62). Washington, DC: American Psychological Association.

Piaget, J. (1928). *Judgement and reasoning in the child.* London: Routledge & Kegan Paul.

Piaget, J. (1962). *Play, dreams, and imitation in childhood.* New York: Norton.

Piaget, J. (1978). *Success and understanding.* London: Routledge & Kegan Paul.

Piaget, J. & Inhelder, B. (1973). *Memory and intelligence.* London: Routledge & Kegan Paul.

Portecorvo, C. (1990). Social context, semiotic mediation and forms of discourse in constructing knowledge at school. In H. Mandl, E. de Corte, N. Bennett, & H. F. Friedrich (Eds.), *Learning and instruction: European research in an international context* (Vol. 2, pp. 1-26). Oxford: Pergamon Press.

Rice, M. L. & Schiefelbusch, R. L. (Eds.). (1989). *The teachability of language.* Baltimore: Brookes Publishing.

Rogoff, B. (1990). *Apprenticeship in thinking: Cognitive development in a social context.* New York: Oxford University Press.

Rogoff, B. (1993). Children's guided participation and participatory appropriation of sociocultural activity. In R. H. Wozniak & K. W. Fischer (Eds.), *Development in context: Acting and thinking in specific environments* (pp. 121-153). Hillsdale, NJ: Lawrence Erlbaum Associates.

Rogoff, B. (1994). Developing understanding of the idea of communities of learners. *Mind, Culture, and Activity, 1,* 209-229.

Rogoff, B., Matusov, E., & White, C. (in press). Models of teaching and learning: Participation in a community of learners. In D. Olson & N. Torrance (Eds.), *Handbook of education and human development: New models of learning, teaching and schooling.* Cambridge: Basil Blackwell.

Romaine, S. (1994). *Language in society: An introduction to sociolinguistics.* New York: Oxford University Press.

Salomon, G. (1993). No distribution without individual's cognition: A dynamic interactional view. In G. Salomon (Ed.), *Distributed cognitions: Psychological and educational considerations* (pp. 111-138). Cambridge: Cambridge University Press.

Saxe, G. B. (1988). Candy selling and math learning. *Educational Researcher, 17*(6), 14-21.

Schank, R. C. (1990). *Tell me a story: A new look at real and artificial memory.* New York: Charles Scribner's Sons.

Schoenfeld, A. H. (1989). Ideas in the air: Speculations on small group learning, environmental and cultural influences on cognition, and epistemology. *International Journal of Educational Research, 13,* 71-88.

Skinner, B. F. (1957). *Verbal behavior.* New York: Appleton-Century-Crofts.

Smith, B. O. & Ennis, R. H. (Eds). (1961). *Language and concepts in education.* Chicago: Rand McNally.

Swing, S. R. & Peterson, P. L. (1982). The relationship of student ability and small group interaction to students achievement. *American Educational Research Journal, 19,* 259-274.

Vellom, P., Anderson, C. W., & Palincsar, A. S. (1994, April). *Constructing facts and mediational means in a middle school science classroom*. Paper presented at the annual meeting of the American Educational Research Association, New Orleans.

von Glasersfeld, E. (1989). Cognition, construction of knowledge and teaching. *Synthese, 80*, 121-140.

Vygotsky, L. S. (1978). *Mind in society: The development of higher psychological processes*. Cambridge, MA: Harvard University Press.

Vygotsky, L. S. (1979). Consciousness as a problem in the psychology of behavior. *Soviet Psychology, 17*(4), 3-35.

Vygotsky, L. S. (1981). The genesis of higher mental functions. In J. V. Wertsch (Ed.), *The concept of activity in Soviet psychology* (pp. 148-188). Armonk, NY: Sharpe.

Wells, G. (1994). Text, talk and inquiry: Schooling as semiotic apprenticeship. In N. Bird et al. (Eds.) *Language and learning*. Hong Kong: Institute for Language and Learning, Department of Education.

Wells, G. (1994). The complementary contributions of Halliday and Vygotsky to a 'Language-based theory of learning.' *Linguistics and Education, 6*, 41-90.

Wells, G. (1996). Using the tool-kit of discourse in the activity of learning and teaching. *Mind, culture and activity*, 3 (2),74-101.

Wells, G. & Chang-Wells, G. L. (in press). What have you learned: Co-constructing the meaning of time. In J. Flood, S. B. Heath, & D. Lapp (Eds.), *A handbook for literacy educators: Research on teaching in communicative and visual arts*. New York: Macmillan.

Wertsch, J. V. (1991). *Voices of the mind: A sociocultural approach to mediated action*. Cambridge, MA: Harvard University Press.

Wittrock, M. C. (1986). Heuristic models of teaching. In T. Husén & T. N. Postlethwaite (Eds.), *The international encyclopedia of education* (1st ed., pp. 2167-2177). Oxford: Pergamon Press.

Wood, T. (1996). Events in learning mathematics: Insights from research in classrooms. *Educational Studies in Mathematics, 30*, 85-105.

Wood, T. (1994b, April). *The importance of pedagogy in reforming mathematics education*. Paper presented at the annual meeting of the American Educational Research Association, New Orleans.

Woods, P. (Ed.). (1980). *Pupil strategies: Explorations in the sociology of the school*. London: Croom Helm.

Zuckerman, G. A. (1994). A pilot study of a ten-day course in cooperative learning for beginning Russian first graders. *Elementary School Journal, 94*, 405-420.

Chapter 3: What Do Students Know? Facing Challenges of Distance, Context, and Desire in Trying to Hear Children[1]

DEBORAH LOEWENBERG BALL[2]
University of Michigan

No task is more fundamental to teaching than figuring out what students are learning. Paradoxically, no endeavour is more difficult. In his well-known sociological analysis of teachers and teaching, Lortie (1975) found that questions about the assessment of student learning evoked significant emotional response from teachers. Although the teachers whom he interviewed believed that good teachers inform their practice by closely monitoring students, many despaired of really knowing about the effects of their teaching. Lortie nominates this as one of the endemic uncertainties of teaching, observing that

> ... [a]ll craftsmen must adjust and readjust their actions in line with hoped-for outcomes; must monitor their steps and make corrections as they proceed ... Yet the monitoring of teaching effectiveness, defined as achieving instructional goals, is fraught with complications. (p. 135)

Lortie analyses these complications from two perspectives. Viewed externally, he argues that assessing outcomes is complicated by the lack of shared standards, lack of clarity about cause or influence, multiple criteria and lack of consensus, ambiguity about timing of assessment, and student changeability. Comparing teaching with other occupations, Lortie claims that these complications do not exist in more 'tangible fields' (p. 136). Indeed, he argues, such complications are inherent to the practice of teaching. Lortie also views the complications of assessment from the inside. Interestingly, he reports a bimodal distribution in teachers' feelings about assessing their effectiveness. Over half reported that it was problematic. Yet another third claimed that knowing whether one was doing a good job is relatively easy (p. 142). This divergence suggests that teachers live with the uncertainties differently.

However uncertain it may be, figuring out what students know is central to the everyday work of teachers.[3] Teachers ask themselves many questions in the course of teaching: What should I do next? Is what I am doing working? Does this concept need to be reviewed? Are the girls feeling disconnected from this unit we are doing? What is that student saying? What is he thinking? Teachers are responsible for helping students learn. Minute to minute, day to day, and

B.J. Biddle et al. (eds.), International Handbook of Teachers and Teaching, 769-818
© *1997 Kluwer Academic Publishers, Printed in the Netherlands*

week to week, teachers must constantly 'read' their students, making judgments about how things are going – in general and for particular individuals. They give tests, quizzes, and assignments. They ask questions, observe, listen. Yet what teachers watch, ask, and listen for varies. This variation may underlie differences in how unsettling teachers find the task of assessing what students are learning.

One way of coping with teaching's 'intangibility,' including the uncertainty embedded in assessing outcomes, is to use approaches that evade or mask such complications. One oft-heard shorthand confounds classroom activities with learning. Teachers report what students have 'had,' or what has 'been covered.' Still, most people know that a description of what has been taught is not equivalent to an examination of what has been learned. A consequent desire for accurate 'measures' of learning can be seen in the widespread efforts to make systematic a technology of monitoring students.

Standardized multiple-choice tests, weekly quizzes checked and recorded, progress charts, carefully convergent questioning – all are measures that check students in a manner that controls both variation and sources of ambiguity. Pimm (1987) describes a discourse pattern typical of many mathematics classrooms in which the teacher talks but leaves small openings for students to fill in key blanks:

T: Supposing you started with that shape and you increased its length by two, what would have happened to the area. It would simply have …
P: Doubled.
T: Doubled – but that's only moving in, increasing in one dimension – if you've got to increase the width by two as well – then you've got to double it again. So you would be doing – first of all, times two to double the length – and then times two again – to double the width again, so altogether you must have multiplied …
P: By four.
T: By four, by two squared. (Pimm, 1987, p. 53)

In this exchange, the pupil does little more than play a part in the teacher's script. This typical pattern 'allows the teacher to maintain control of the discourse, while focusing attention on particular items along the way. It … acts as a check for the teacher that the particular pupil questioned has grasped what is being explained' (Pimm, 1987, pp. 53-54).

Enacting such approaches, teachers can feel they know something about what students know. Still, what is being examined about students' learning is constrained – evidence often restricted to short, unprobed, and standardized answers (Cohen, 1995). Much is left unknown that teachers, parents, and the public care about – for instance, the ability to reason, to be imaginative, to construct a convincing argument. And under the cover of simpler measures lie the tangled – sometimes wonderful, sometimes terrible – idiosyncrasies that are the products of children's sensemaking.

In a famous case study of a sixth grader named Benny, Erlwanger (1975) probed beneath the surface. Despite the fact that his teacher thought of him as advanced, the understandings lurking under Benny's consistently correct written work were wildly nonstandard. But in the individualized approach to teaching used in this classroom, it was possible for him to continue to progress officially, his personal constructions invisible to his unsuspecting teacher. Dramatic as this case is, it is likely not unusual. When all we ask students is to fill in answers in constrained spaces, we block our access to views of students' thinking.

A different way of coping with the ambiguities of assessment is to see it as ongoing, drawing on multiple and varied sources of evidence. To make the examination of learning more complex is to admit of its subtleties and requires broadening both the objects and methods of assessment. Students are presented with open-ended tasks that have no single constrained 'right answer' and which invite application, imagination, and extension. Such assessments seem more satisfyingly 'authentic,' to have more relevance to the enterprises for which teachers strive to prepare their students (Darling-Hammond, Ancess, & Falk, 1995). At the same time, the open-endedness increases the uncertainty of interpreting and appraising student progress and makes it more difficult to share common standards across students, groups, and settings (Cohen, 1995). Moreover, the context of the task, necessarily constructed by each individual student, make it that much more complex to ascertain what students know. How is the context affecting the student's response in ways that are idiosyncratic to the particulars of the situation? Issues like these challenge core epistemological and psychological assumptions about what it means to 'know' something. Although some researchers claim that students who engage in close reasoning about performance-oriented problems have deep 'insights into the structure of the subject matter' (Hiebert et al. 1996, p. 17), others express reservations about the assessment of abstract ideas which are usable across settings (Anderson, Reder, & Simon, 1996, p. 9). Cohen (1995, p. 9) synthesizes the issues:

> [W]e have little evidence about how well the newer assessments represent students' 'understanding' of mathematics or reading, in part because this assessment technology is very young. It seems reasonable to think that performance assessments could do a better job than norm-referenced standardized tests, but researchers are only now turning their attention to what understanding might be, how it might be assessed, and what satisfactory assessment of understanding might be.

Despite these uncertainties, enthusiasm is high for focusing on what students *understand* and *can do* through ongoing and performance assessment (Darling-Hammond et al., 1995). Widely eschewed among reform advocates are the traditional measures that constrain the problems of 'measuring' what students know. But this current press for 'authentic assessment' moves central ambiguities of practice to the public stage of school accountability. The new assessments reveal the uncertainties of interpreting what students know and have learned and yet situate such tenuous information in the political context of schooling.

In this chapter, I return to and extend Lortie's (1975) examination of the sources of endemic uncertainty resident in assessment. Writing from the perspective of practice,[4] I investigate challenges inherent in the central task of figuring out what students are thinking and learning. I explore the problem from three angles:

- Teacher knowledge: First, I review briefly recent work on teacher knowledge. What have researchers identified as key elements of teaching knowledge and how do these play a role in hearing and assessing students' thinking and learning? What kind of knowing *is* knowing students, and how well do we as teachers, researchers, teacher educators, and parents understand the nature of what we know (or think we know) about students?
- Challenges embedded in practice: Second, I analyse conceptually what makes the task of assessment so difficult in practice. From the perspective of the teacher, what persistent challenges influence efforts to figure out what students are learning?
- Learning to know about students: In the final section of the chapter, I turn to an examination of what is involved in preparing teachers to hear their students. What do teachers need in order to be prepared to figure out what students know, and what are some ways in which they can develop and enhance such capability?

TEACHER KNOWLEDGE: BEING BOTH RESPONSIBLE TO SUBJECT MATTER AND RESPONSIVE TO STUDENTS

I begin with a brief look at recent developments in research on teaching and teacher thinking where issues of what teachers need to know have occupied center stage. In particular, over the past decade the role of subject matter knowledge has claimed considerable attention among researchers and teacher educators. In a seminal presidential address to the American Educational Research Association, Lee Shulman (1986) referred to subject matter understanding as 'the missing paradigm' in research on teaching and teacher education. With a sweep of convincing argument, he attracted renewed interest in the nature and role of teachers' subject matter knowledge[5] – and in a new kind of knowledge, *pedagogical content knowledge*. Not only do teachers need personal understanding of the material they *were* teaching, Shulman and his colleagues argued, but they also need to know ways in which key ideas might be compellingly, engagingly, and helpfully represented. Teachers need a repertoire of metaphors and analogies, problems and tasks, pictures and diagrams. They need to be aware of topics with which students often had difficulty, and of common misunderstandings (Shulman, 1986; Wilson, Shulman, & Richert, 1987). In short, they need ways to see into the subject matter through the eyes, hearts, and minds of learners. And their task is to 'transform' the content in ways that make it accessible to students (Wilson et al., 1987) while maintaining its integrity (Ball, 1993b; Bruner, 1960; Lampert, 1992).

Responsibility to the subject matter is only one part of the equation. In making subject matter 'accessible,' teachers also need to know students. Teachers need understandings of students in general – patterns common to particular ages, culture, social class, geography, and gender; patterns in typical student conceptions of the subject matter. But, more to the point, teachers must know *their* students (Peterson, Carpenter, & Fennema, 1989). Face to face with actual children who are particular ages and gender, culture and class, teachers must see individuals against the backdrop of sociological and psychological generalizations about groups. Often to simplify the enormous complexity of teaching, teachers may presume a 'shared identity,' mistakenly assuming that students share their teachers' experiences of school and of the world (Jackson, 1986). Teachers are themselves particulars in the social tapestry and different from their students. They are separated at least by generation and in multiple other ways as well. For example, women teachers will teach boys and middle class teachers poor children, while non-religious teachers teach devout Christians (Delpit, 1988; Paley, 1995). Yet teachers must build bridges across the chasms of difference. In order to make the subject matter accessible to students, the more they know about student experiences, backgrounds, understandings, and interests, the better equipped they will be, so the argument goes.

Much of the recent work on pedagogical content knowledge has advanced our understandings of what teachers need to know about students to inform 'the ways of representing and formulating the subject that make it comprehensible to others' (Shulman, 1986, p. 9). In 'transforming' the content for instruction, teachers examine critically the topic or text at hand and select a way of representing it, adapting particular representation in light of what they know in general about students (Wilson et al., 1987). Wilson and her colleagues describe the interplay between the teacher's understanding of the specific content and of the particular students, one step in a cyclical process they call *pedagogical reasoning*:

> Student characteristics that might influence the ways in which material is represented include student misconceptions or misunderstandings of the material; student ability, gender, and motivation. When preparing a lesson on light, science teachers might think about the preconception that students may have about light that will interfere with their learning. Math teachers preparing to teach fractions might consider students' prior knowledge of coins and how best to use that prior knowledge in developing a more sophisticated understanding of the material. *Tailoring refers to adapting the material to the specific students in one class rather than to the student population in general.* (Wilson et al., 1987, p. 120; emphasis added)

But planning and selecting is but one element of teaching well. In order to know if they are effective, and to make adjustments as they go, teachers must assess how students are making sense and what they are learning. This must happen in the course of instruction as well as at landmark points (e.g., the end of a unit). To do this, teachers must do more than *use* knowledge of students. They must, on an ongoing basis, *construct* new knowledge of their students. They must observe, listen, and make conjectures. They must test and revise these conjectural understandings, from moment to moment and week to week.

Seeking to engage students productively, teachers adjust, make mid-course corrections, follow students' ideas (Duckworth, 1987). Dewey (1902/1990) saw the construction of curriculum as inherently constructive and interactive. He urged:

> [A]bandon the notion of subject-matter as something fixed and ready-made in itself, outside the child's experience; cease thinking of the child's experience as also something hard and fast; see it as something fluent, embryonic, vital; and we realize that the child and the curriculum are simply two limits that define a single process. Just as two points define a straight line, so the present standpoint of the child and the facts and truths of studies define instruction. It is continuous reconstruction, moving from the child's present experience out into that represented by the organized bodies of truth that we call studies. (Dewey, 1902/1990, p. 11)

Paley (1986) captures elegantly the shift that this requires of the teacher, from one who presents knowledge to one who supports its construction. Describing her own initial efforts to teach in ways that drew on and connected with students, she reflects,

> When my intention was limited to announcing my own point of view, communication came to a halt. My voice drowned out the children's. However, when they said things that surprised me, exposing ideas I did not imagine they held, my excitement mounted ... I kept the children talking, savoring the uniqueness of responses so singularly different from mine. The rules of teaching had changed; I now wanted to hear answers I could not myself invent ... Indeed, the inventions tumbled out as if they had been simply waiting for me to stop talking and begin listening. (Paley, 1986, p. 125)

In sum, teaching in ways that are responsible to content and responsive to students (Ball & Wilson, 1996) requires teachers to work continually to know students. What they need to know cannot be fully specified in advance. Instead, across multiple intellectual, personal, and cultural divides, teachers must work to see and hear students flexibly in the moment and over time. As they work to help their students develop understandings of content, teachers must listen to students – making use of their own knowledge of the content while not being limited by it. A teacher who knows little of the content, or knows it in only narrow and rigid ways, may miss children's often wondrous insights. But, paradoxically, a teacher with considerable depth of knowledge may fail to hear the nonstandard perspective, the novel insight, listening only for 'the answer.' Teachers, argues Hawkins (1974/1972), must be able to notice when children's observations and questions take them 'near to mathematically sacred ground' (p. 113) – that is, to the edges of wonder or to core foundations. In much the same way, teachers must use theories about adolescents and children, males and females, learning and development, social class and culture, as resources, not determinants (Duckworth, 1987). Teachers must know students both in general and in the moment – their knowledge always changing in light of the current and the particular (Ramsey, 1991). In order to be both responsive and responsible, teachers need to live in multiple worlds, moving back and forth between the wider disciplinary culture with its conventions, norms, and theories, and the idea-filled worlds of their students. The teacher cannot belong entirely to any single world, 'but [must be] an ambassador from one to the other' (Lampert, 1992, p. 310).

KNOWING STUDENTS

What does it take to know particular students, to construct, use, and revise knowledge of students? Much can of course be learned about students in general. But particular students – not the faceless students of general theory, or even the real and remembered students of previous classes – are the actual terrain of practice. It is *these* students, now, whom teachers must teach. Take the following example from my third grade mathematics class, early one October,[6] where I confronted a typically puzzling incident in which I did not know what a student was saying. It is important to understand that, as an experienced teacher of over 15 years, I did know a great deal about students of this age. I knew theories of child development. I knew what mathematical ideas third graders were likely to have encountered. I came into this episode with considerable knowledge of students. Still, what Mei said puzzled me, and knowing what she was thinking was critical in helping her – and probably, others – to make progress in the lesson. In the midst of a unit in which we had been exploring integers, we were struggling on this particular day to figure out a sensible answer to 6 + (-6). Two answers had been proposed: 6 and 0. Mei, a frequent contributor to class discussions, disagreed with both, because, as she explained, she had come up with the answer 9.

Betsy, a classmate, was incredulous. '*Nine?*' I, too, was puzzled. I asked her if she could show us. She went to the board and, using our paper model of a skyscraper with floors below and above the ground, placed a paper person on the building, on the sixth floor above the ground.

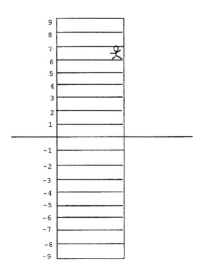

Mei explained, 'And then I, and then you plus six below zero, and six below zero is below zero, so I add three to that three, because when you go three and three is six, so I went up three more, and one, two, three — there. Oops, went too far. Yeah, and then I got nine, so I think it's nine.'

I still had no idea what she meant. Lucy's hand was up and I called on her.

Lucy *(to Mei)*:	Where did the other three go then?
Mei:	Well, see, 'cause it's *below zero*, so I …
Betsy interrupted:	*I* know what you're saying, *I* know what you're saying …
Mei continued:	So we put two in each group in order to make one because it's below zero.
Betsy:	Mei, is *this* what you're saying? (places a paper person on the building).
	There. And then you're saying six below, and since it's below, that we have to go up to the three?
Mei:	I'm saying that since it's below that we have to take the, you take three and go up three, 'cause it's like *three*, because three plus three is six, and then we

put two in each group in order to make one, so I added another three more to the six above zero.

Still quite unsure of what Mei was thinking, I pushed. 'I don't quite understand this 'put one, put three in each group in order to make one.' I don't understand that part.'

Mei: Well, see, I said that if we starting on six and we'd plus six below zero, and you start on six, plus – *(Mei starts to make a drawing, Betsy tries to help)* like, three, I start on six above zero and three and three is, three and three is six, and since this is below zero so I say three, and so I say that think that we, since this is six, then if we add six to it, we get twelve above zero, and it's below zero and three and three plus six, well three and three equals six, so we add three more to the six above zero and then I got nine.

Betsy: Is this what you're doing *(draws three circles with three hash marks inside each one)* – making three groups of three?

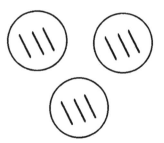

Mei: Let me see …
Betsy: Is that what you're doing, or are you making four groups? *(makes another group)*
Mei giggled: No! I'm making a group of … This is one of the numbers, these are two of the numbers below zero, and if two of these equals one, and if I have about, like

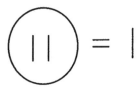

Betsy continued to press Mei. She erased the hash marks and asked Mei what the numbers were: 'Can you put the numbers in yet?' Mei paused, wrinkling her face. Trying to respond to Betsy's question, she put numbers in the circles:

> Okay, let's see, two below zero and three below zero, and this could be four below zero and five below zero, equals one.

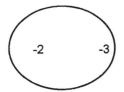 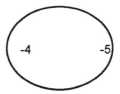

> And then I have two already, and that means you will go up to eight. *(She moved the paper person from the 6 to the 8 on the building.)* And then I make one more.

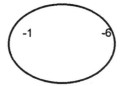

> One below zero and six below zero, so there's one more then to go up, and now I end up on nine.

And she moved the paper person up to the 9 on the building.

What was Mei thinking? What was she doing with her circles and numbers? Despite everything I knew, I could not quite hear in what she was saying a glimmer of anything familiar. I simply could not see in what way $(-2) + (-3)$, $(-1) + (-6)$, and $(-4) + (-5)$ could all equal 1. What was she thinking?

It was only later, in talking with others in my research group,[7] that it seemed most plausible that she had built an explanation on some vague idea that 'two negatives make a positive,' which her mother had told her. With 'six below zero,' Mei may have thought, each 'pair of the negatives' would combine to make a positive. Since we were starting with 6 (as in $6 + [-6]$), then each of the pairs of negatives in the 'six below zero' would be added to the 6 above zero. Since there were three pairs of negatives, then there were three 'ones' to add to the six above zero, for a result of nine. Looking at her diagrams, this conjecture was plausible, but not entirely satisfying.

When teachers seek to construct the curriculum in response to students' ideas and understandings, then moment-to-moment appraisals of student thinking are critical. This is hard work, bounded by the uncertainty of ever knowing what anyone means, and multiplied by the complexity of classroom teaching in which teachers are responsible for groups of students, not just individual learners (Jackson, 1968; Lortie, 1975). In this case, subsequent reflection on Mei's confusion, and the mess that was created in class that day, led me to rethink what I was doing. No simple adjustment would work. The problem here was not an inherently mathematical one in some respects but a problem emerging from the representation – the building with its floors above and below ground (see Ball, 1993b, for a thorough discussion of my deliberations about representational contexts for integers). Later I could see that ours was a problem of convention, not discoverable somehow, especially not in any meaningful way with the elevator rides as we were using them (Lampert, 1990a). Unlike problems of invention, conventions are not readily discoverable, for they are decisions interior to and agreed upon by a community. We would have to have defined and agreed what a 'negative number ride' meant and then use it that way. But once having taken this path, and not yet fully appreciating our situation, I was stuck in trying to make sense of Mei's thinking.

Duckworth (1987), writing about the 'virtues of not knowing,' proposes that knowing the right answers is not what really counts 'in the long run.' She argues, 'What you do about what you don't know is, in the final analysis, what determines what you ultimately know' (p. 68). Although Duckworth is writing about children's learning, her insight applies equally to teaching. Not knowing what Mei was thinking, what I did to understand her is what mattered. I let her continue to try to explain her interpretation. Betsy, a classmate, worked along with her, doing what children will often do, engaging in their peers' ideas even when they did not agree. As mathematical explorers, they would try to get inside another's thinking, to see what it might mean. 'Is this what you're saying?' asked Betsy. And, 'Where did the other three go?' asked Lucy. I, too, probed. Together, we assumed that Mei's thinking made sense to her, and that our challenge was to figure out what that sense was.

In the face of the uncertainty, what can a teacher do to see, hear, and interpret as flexibly as possible, assisted but not limited by her own background, habits of mind, and understandings about both children and mathematics? How can a teacher construct understandings of students in the moment, understandings that are robust enough to be able to take the next step in practice? What is good enough evidence for such an interpretation? What problems arise when trying to understand children's sensemaking? In this case, it was not until after class, that I thought I had a possible interpretation of what Mei was thinking. I still was not sure this was right, but it also made me question the task I had pursued. We ultimately agreed to consider 'negative number rides' as rides down the elevator. Hence, $6 + (-6)$ was defined as meaning a person starts on the sixth floor and take a ride *down* six floors. Even so, I was left humbled by the challenges of knowing what students think, and by the elaborate processes they use to construct solutions and understandings, often quite complex to follow.

While working in an environment that presses for demonstrable outcomes, confronting the ambiguities of assessing what students know creates endemic challenges for teachers. In what follows, I explore three such challenges. First, I situate my work and explain my methods of analysis.

USING MY OWN PRACTICE AS A SITE FOR RESEARCH ON TEACHING

The analyses in this chapter draw on my own daily teaching of mathematics in a local third grade classroom between 1988 and 1992. (This is also the school where, prior to the arrangement I describe, I was a regular, full-time classroom teacher from 1975 on.) Over half of the students in this school are from other countries and speak limited English; the American students are linguistically, culturally, and racially diverse and come from many parts of the United States. Sylvia Rundquist, the teacher in whose classroom I was working, taught all the other subjects besides mathematics. She and I would meet regularly to discuss individual students, the class, what each of us was trying to do, and the connections and contrasts between what we were trying to do with the children. We also investigated mathematical ideas, analysed representations generated by the students or introduced by me, assessed the roles played by me and by the students in the class discussions, and examined the children's learning.

In situating a strand of research inside my own practice, I seek to contribute to our collective understanding of what 'teaching mathematics for understanding' entails. My focus is on identifying and examining closely its endemic challenges – that is, issues with which teachers like myself must grapple, and which are *built in* to the intersection of vision and practice. For example, what it is like to try to teach for understanding while also maintaining a broad sense of responsibility to the school district and state goals and objectives? What does it mean to get students to be more centrally involved in deciding whether something is true or reasonable and yet, as the teacher, maintain an eye on accepted knowledge of the field? In this chapter, I take up the special problem of trying to know what students are thinking, a problem of critical importance in a pedagogy that seeks to be responsive to students. This first-person research on teaching seeks to investigate issues that arise in practice *from the inside*. It is a kind of research *into* teaching that is complementary to other approaches to research on teaching.[8]

The setting.

This chapter draws on data from my teaching during 1989-90. In this particular class, in which we had 22 students, 10 were from the United States and 12 were from other countries – Indonesia, Taiwan, Korea, Nepal, Nigeria, Kenya, Egypt, Ethiopia, Nicaragua, and Canada. Four of the ten U.S. students were African-American. Although no standardized or district testing is done in this school until the end of third grade, informal assessment showed that these students' entering levels of mathematics achievement varied widely in both mathematical skills and concepts.

The mathematics period was approximately one hour long. During this time, we often worked on just one or two problems. My intention was to select problems that would be generative, rich with mathematical possibility. Usually the problems were built from the previous day's work, with an eye to where we were heading. As such, the task of figuring out what students were learning was basic to the task of figuring out what to do next. The class often began with students exploring the problem of the day individually. As part of the class, students kept mathematics notebooks in which they recorded all their work and in which they also wrote about that work. Although I asked students to start by working on the problem alone, I also encouraged them to confer with others. After ten minutes or so (depending on the problem), students moved into small groups and worked together some more. We spent about half the class period in a large group discussion, during which individuals and groups presented their solutions and discussed their ideas.

Data collection and analysis.

Every class period was audiotaped, and most were video-taped as well. Many class periods have been transcribed, working from both video and audio records. I kept a daily journal about my thinking and work – a kind of all-purpose plan book and journal – which provides a record of my thinking on a day-to-day basis, including comments I made about students and their thinking and learning. In addition to the students' own math notebooks, there were also quizzes and homework and all student work was photocopied and saved. To complement what could be learned from their written work, students were interviewed regularly, sometimes informally – sometimes more formally – sometimes in small groups and sometimes alone.

The analysis for this chapter consisted of reading a sample of lesson transcripts, examining student talk and writing, and looking closely at evidence for my interpretations of students' thinking. I examined moves I made at that time to uncover or probe students' thinking and looked at the interpretations I seemed to be making. My journal and the students' written work gave me other angles on particular instances. Of particular interest to this analysis were instances where I, as teacher, was unsure about what students meant. Also of interest were instances where I appeared to have been sure of my interpretations at the time, but with the benefit of hindsight, my earlier interpretations now seem problematic. Uninterested in making general claims about my teaching or this class, my research focused on examining what seemed to influence my efforts to know what students were learning and to create better understanding of the general pedagogical task of trying to know students. I used my own teaching as a case that could contribute insights about specific challenges of that task.

CHALLENGES IN TRYING TO KNOW WHAT STUDENTS ARE LEARNING

Hearing students – understanding what they are saying, showing, feeling, doing – seems like the everyday work of communication. However, as I analysed instances where I had puzzled over what a child was thinking, I began to see particular features of the task that seemed to make it complex. These features did not seem specific to me as the teacher or to these children. As I understood them better, I began to see that these features were inherent in the task of listening to children. In this section, I identify three challenges that underlie this task and use instances from my teaching to ground and provide evidence for my claims. The instances reveal not only the temporality of practice and its fleetingness, but also the remarkable density of its intellectual and personal demands from moment to moment.

Content.

All the instances in this section come from a series of classes in January, during which the students and I were working on even and odd numbers – what makes a number even or odd, which numbers were even and which were odd, and patterns in adding even or odd numbers. In the course of this, we were also working on the epistemological issue of what it means to *prove* something in mathematics – pushing past the mere giving of examples to establish the plausibility of a claim to finding ways to show that a claim would hold true for *all* cases. For example, to show that 'an even number plus an even number equals an even number,' students were trying to do more than illustrate it with examples such as 6 + 8 = 14 or 2 + 10 = 12. To understand even numbers, they were trying to come up with a way to know if a number was even that did not involve alternately reciting numbers along the number line (e.g., '5 is odd, 6 is even, 7 is odd, so 8 is even') or drawing circles and trying to split them into two equal groups

Name*	Gender	Race	Country	English proficiency	How long at this school**
Lindiwe	M	African-American	U.S.A./South Africa	Fluent	2 weeks
Nathan	M	White	Ethiopia	Fluent	3 years
Betsy	F	White	Canada	Native speaker	4 months
Daniel	M	Asian	Indonesia	Developing	3 years
Jeannie	F	White	U.S.A.	Native speaker	3 years
Keith	M	African-American	U.S.A.	Native speaker	2 weeks
Tembe	M	African Black	Kenya	Fluent	3 years
Mei	F	Asian	Taiwan	Fluent	2 years
Lucy	F	White	U.S.A.	Native speaker	3 years
Maria	F	Latina	Nicaragua	Beginning	4 months
Mark	M	White	U.S.A.	Native speaker	2 years

* All names are same-gender culturally congruent pseudonyms.

** This column reflects the length of time the child has been in this school as of mid-January. No one had been in this class longer than four months (since September).

Table 1: Third-Grade Class Roster in Mid-January .

Name*	Gender	Race	Country	English proficiency	How long at this school**
Ofala	F	African Black	Nigeria	Fair	3 years
Devin	M	White	Nepal	Beginning	9 months
Riba	F	White	Egypt	Good	3 years
Harooun	M	Asian	Indonesia	Developing	16 months
Sean	M	White	U.S.A.	Native speaker	2 years
Sheena	F	African-American	U.S.A.	Native speaker	4 months
Tory	F	White	U.S.A.	Native speaker	2 weeks
Cassandra	F	African-American	U.S.A.	Native speaker	16 months

* All names are same-gender culturally congruent pseudonyms.
** This column reflects the length of time the child has been in this school as of mid-January. No one had been in this class longer than four months (since September).

Table 1: Third-Grade Class Roster in Mid-January (Continued).

(this becomes unwieldy with 1,421). Developing this more principled way of understanding what makes any number even or odd would extend the domain of their mathematical reach.

Students.

Although it was the middle of the school year, three students had joined the class less than a week before the instances I report here. Two students had already left the class since September. Table 1 offers a summary of the range of students who were in the class in January. The table illustrates some of this class's diversity. It is but a dim portrait, for there were many more differences among the children. The children's ages ranged over three years, and their home life varied, as did the kinds of experiences they had. Some had siblings, some did not. Some lived with one parent, some with two. Their religious backgrounds varied. I could not assume that my experiences of the world or of learning were similar to theirs. Hence, there was much for me to learn about each of them.

But there were some similarities as well. Most were from middle-class backgrounds, although what this meant varied given the diverse nationalities. They all lived in the identical brick barracks of student housing and had parents who were university or English Language Program students. And they were all in a common class, talking about even and odd numbers together.[9]

What did I know about this content and students in general?

I had taught even and odd numbers many times before. Personally, I am fascinated with number theory, and I enjoy the work of pattern-finding, explaining, and proving. I knew the formal definitions – $k2$ is an even number (k groups of 2) and $k2 + 1$ is odd – and I knew that the domain of these definitions was the integers. I also knew that a useful representation of even numbers for young children was to take a set of objects and define as even those quantities that could be divided into two equal groups without having to split any in half, even though this representation was effective mainly for natural numbers, elusive for 0, and inapplicable for negative numbers.

I was aware that third graders often could correctly label numbers as either even or odd but that their understandings were often more recognitional than principled. That is, they knew that 1 was odd and 2 was even, much as they knew that *A* was a capital letter and *a* lower case. Presented with a number such as 74, many would be unsure: 7 is odd and 4 is even – so what *is* 74? Those who said it was even would likely explain it on the basis of the maxim, 'You only have to look at the ones place.' These things I knew from other students, but I had never read any research probing children's understandings of even and odd numbers. I doubt it exists. As such, the knowledge I had about students in general and their understandings of this content was constructed from my own experience. I had also never talked with anyone else about students' understandings of even and odd numbers, so I knew little of what other teachers had encountered. My knowledge was personal – and idiosyncratic, for all I knew.

Challenge #1: Listening Across Divides

The first challenge is rooted in the fact that teachers are faced with learning what people quite different from themselves think, say, and mean. Children are different from adults. The divide of age is great; eight-year-olds see and think differently from adults. They talk, gesture, move, and think in ways that are special and not always familiar. And children may differ from their teachers in other ways as well – in gender, class, culture, religion, and native language, to name a few. How children think, talk, and represent their ideas is shaped by their varied identities and experiences. Trying to hear children challenges teachers with trying to listen across a gulf of human experience and meaning.

One day, near the end of class (1/17/90), I asked two girls – Betsy and Jeannie – to tell the rest of the class about a disagreement they had had. Jeannie explained that she thought that zero was 'even *and* odd' but that Betsy thought it was even. 'Why do you think 0 is both even and odd?' I inquired. Jeannie said she wasn't sure why but that that was what she thought. Betsy said she had not been convinced by Jeannie and that she had asked her parents and they had said that 'if you have zero things, zero things, and you cut it in two, you have zero stuff on both sides.' A student proposed that there was 'half on both sides,' and another offered, 'There's *air* on both sides,' but Betsy dismissed this firmly, 'We're talking about numbers, not the environment.' I asked if others wanted to comment. Sean raised his hand.

Sean: Uh huh, I just, I don't, I disagree. Well, I agree *and* disagree because um, because I think it's true that you can cut zero in half and there'd be zero on both sides, but that would, there, but I don't, I still don't, I don't think that um, that um, you can ever, you can ever have zero to begin with. Because, like, what um, like, like, how, how would you get zero then?

He continued:

> Lucy said that um, if you, if you, if you had um, if you had one below zero (-1) plus one (1), she said it would be zero, but I disagree and said it would be um, it would be 1 *above* zero, and it is.

He seemed to be claiming that $(-1) + 1 = 1$ instead of 0. What was he saying, and why? It seemed somehow related to the discussion of whether 0 was even or odd, because it had to do with exploring what you get if you 'split zero in half.'

I didn't know exactly what Sean was thinking or what he understood, but I could feel among the other children the rising tide of emphatic disagreement that occurs most often when one child says something that conflicts with something that other children think we have already agreed upon. And we had already agreed months ago that $(-1) + 1 = 0$. In fact, we had come close to proving the general claim that any number plus 'that same number below zero would always equal zero.' I asked Sean to show us on the number line how he thought about $(-1) + 1$.

He went up to the board, and used the pointer to work with the number line that stretched above the chalkboard. Starting at (-1) he moved one spot to the left, ending up on (-2). 'That's *backwards*!' called other children.

I didn't know what he was thinking. And I was therefore unsure of what to do or say next. It might be that he was merely making a clerical error, a misstep of direction, and that no fundamental or conceptual confusion existed. But it could also be that he was struggling to make sense of adding to a negative number. For eight-year-olds, I knew that there was something troubling about the fact that, to the left of 0 on the number line, smaller numbers have larger magnitudes. They are farther from zero, and, in this sense *more*. From this perspective, 5 and -5 are actually equal, for they are both at a distance of 5 units from 0. But -5 is also less, and in fact this is part of what had been puzzling for the children So why did Sean choose to work on $(-1) + (1)$?

Listening across a divide, teachers face a problem similar to most forms of cross-cultural communication. It centres on problems of understanding what students mean with their words, pictures, gestures, and tone. Students often do not represent their thinking in ways that match adult forms. They use nonstandard terms, draw pictures, and make analogies. They get apparently right answers for unsound reasons, and apparently incorrect answers for sound reasons. Their speech comes in parcels of expressive talk or few words. What is required to listen both generously and critically? Awash in eight-year-old speech, some of it in halting English, scrutinizing drawings unclear from lack of technical skill as well as from undeveloped thinking – teachers must seek to 'read' and 'hear' their students.

The students had moved into a space of the number system outside the domain to which their working definition had thus far applied. It seemed to make little sense to them to talk of 'splitting in half' the number zero. Moreover, they had developed no conventions for dealing with negative numbers; hence, their definition did not provide them with adequate guidance. I did not know what Sean was saying. I was not even sure if he was saying he thought zero was even, like Betsy, or both, as Jeannie was. It sounded as though he was disagreeing with Betsy's explanation that zero was even because if 'you cut it in two, you have zero stuff on both sides.' And his explanation? That one below zero plus one was not zero. Why?

I could guess. One conjecture might be that Sean was using this point to show that zero could not be even. If there are not two numbers that can be added to equal 0, then it is not even. Another hypothesis might be that Sean was feeling argumentative and was enjoying this exchange, that he was trying to say something that would provoke controversy. A third is that Sean was not really thinking about whether 0 is even or odd but was interested instead in whether it can be divided in half and was wrestling with whether that made sense or not. Yet another was that Sean was mixing up classes of numbers – positive/negative with even/odd. While thinking about even and odd numbers, perhaps he had fallen unwittingly into the category of positive and negative.

None of these hypotheses felt – or feels – satisfying. None seemed compelling. Not knowing what he meant, it was difficult to know what to do next. Was Sean misunderstanding something? If so, would it be a good move to engage everyone in what he was saying or preferable to talk with him later? Was he just playing around? Was he making a novel observation that would be intriguing to explore?

And this instance was no unusual event. From minute to minute, students say things, or say them in ways, that are unfamiliar to adults. A few days later, Ofala sought to explain what she thought an odd number was.

Ofala:	I just wanted to say if, um, you wanted an odd number, you just have to take one off of it.
Ball:	Why would that work?
Ofala:	Um, because usually odd numbers are ... like, *like* ... *(picks up chalk)*
Ball:	*(interrupting)* Cassandra, can you hear Ofala okay?
Ofala:	This, kind of like have ones in the middle? Like five *(she draws:*

and there's a one in the middle, or, um nine: *(she draws)*

Mei:	I think it's better with circles.
Ofala:	*(she circles groups of two in her drawing of nine hash marks)*
	This two together, this two together … this two together, and
	this two together.

There's one left. And even numbers — like six — *(she draws)*

— you can't get *anything* in the middle. There isn't one left.

Ofala, like many of her classmates, often used drawings and movements interspersed with words.[10] Her sentences would be better represented like this:

Um, because usually odd numbers are … like, *like* … this, kind of like have ones in the middle? Like five

here and there's a one in the middle, or, um nine.

Even with this representation, the reader cannot see Ofala, moving gracefully as she speaks, waving her slender arms, pointing and emphasizing. The drawings and the motions, it seemed, were not illustrations of the statement. They were an integral part *of* it. She, and many of the others, would make their drawing or movements *as* they spoke, rarely using a diagram or picture that was already on the board. Hearing the children meant watching. 'Reading' them meant integrating multiple media: facial expression and diagrams, words and body language.

Ofala's definition was not the textbook's. Structurally it was very close to the algebraic one — $k2 + 1$. (Note: k two's, not two k's.) Or so I thought at the time. I now see that Ofala was actually saying two things here and coupling her words with two sets of drawings.[11] One idea she had was that 'odd numbers are the ones with ones in the middle.' This she represented with a linear arrangement of units. Her idea was to consider the bilateral symmetry of the row: With a central reflection, odd numbers are those where a 'middle one' remains. But she never carried this idea out. Her drawing showed the linear arrangement only, but without representing a test for a 'middle one', e.g.:

Ofala's idea about 'odd numbers have ones in the middle' was never demarcated or used. Mei's simple comment, 'I think it's better with circles,' seems to have influenced Ofala to abandon the 'one in the middle' idea, and shift to

And I, trying to keep my eye both on what Ofala and each of her classmates were thinking *and* on making sure that we developed a more robust idea of even and odd numbers, did not at the time notice that she was actually proposing two solid — and distinct — ideas. I completely missed the power of her linear arrangement. When she drew the circles, she switched back to circling in groups of two, and proposed that what matters is whether there would be any left. But at the end, she also leaned back to her more linear image, and explained that 6 is even 'because you can't get any in the middle.' She used her long slender fingers to motion that there were none left, but she did not concretize her representation as she did for the circle diagrams.

Did Ofala simultaneously understand oddness in two different, both correct, ways? Circling by twos and asking if you have any left is an appropriate representation for even or odd numbers. Arranging in a line and establishing that 7 will have one in the middle is another. Ofala was often not easy to understand. Her speech was soft, halting, and falling. She was highly mobile and physically graceful, and movement was a pronounced channel of her communication. So, although she did not mark the linear arrangement of units with chalk, she did mark the lines with gestures. Still, I completely missed the two distinct ideas, and only picked up the standard, $k2 + 1$. Steered by Mei ('it's better with circles'), and unassisted by me, Ofala emphasized the more standard representation. I did not even notice her first and very interesting idea recede. And, my

own unfamiliarity with the mathematical distinction she was conjecturing also
made it harder to hear her complex contribution.

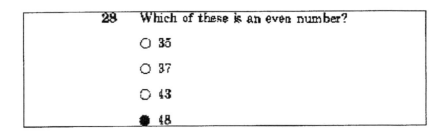

**Figure 1: Sean's response to the item on even/odd numbers on the
standardized test.**

With more conventional approaches to teaching and assessment, children may
represent their ideas in more standard, more adult – and, hence, more familiar –
terms. Indeed, teachers and curriculum developers often work to constrain children's expressions, channelling their thinking in ways that will help them remember things correctly (Edwards, 1993). In the third grade mathematics
workbook that I was *not* using there were six pages on even and odd numbers.
Students were asked to 'circle the even numbers' from a list of 15 numbers between 1 and 40. No zeroes, no negative numbers, no invitations to conjecture
and hence complexify. And on the standardized test which my students took in
late April, three months after these complicated class discussions, there was one
item on even and odd numbers. Figure 1 shows the item, reprinted from an actual test booklet.

   Not surprisingly, no one in the class missed this item. In its constrained opening, the children's varied and idiosyncratic expressions had no space. In such
openings, teachers are protected from the puzzling, the novel, the unfamiliar in
students' thinking and expression. In such openings, too, teachers are protected
from the problems with how children sometimes think, as well as from their insights and capacity for deep, complex thought. The constraints typical in much
teaching and assessment channel students' ideas in conventional directions,
perhaps supporting the development of standard knowledge but also masking
the existence of nonstandard understanding. What does it tell me that all the students got this item correct? Some may have gotten it right because they know
that 40 is even and 8 is even, others because they know the rule of thumb that
all you need to look at is the ones place and 8 is even, so 48 is even. Maybe some
got it right because 4 is even and 8 is even, and would not have chosen *38* of-

fered as the correct choice. Even these alternatives represent quite different understandings of even and odd numbers, covered over by the simplistic item response.

When schools constrain children's responses to familiar structures, the divide is masked. Students find ways to fit their ideas into the structured openings, their thinking shaped into recognizable forms, but that may not represent their meanings. I turn next to the role of context in shaping students' thinking.

Challenge #2: Listening through the Multiple Influences of Contexts

The second challenge to understanding what children understand is rooted in the contextual nature of human sense-making and presents a challenge to the kinds of claims we want to be able to make about what students are learning. Despite the fact that schools tend to treat knowledge as something that can be transmitted and then measured, understanding is variable, and not nearly as stable or externally consistent as we pretend. Children can think one thing under one set of conditions and quite another under other conditions. They can seem to 'get it' one day and have little clue the next. Contexts matter, and new insights can, at times, confound that which had previously seemed clear, or change that which had seemed solid. When Sean had thought zero was even and later been unsure, it is not necessarily that he forgot. Mei had been adding and subtracting negative and positive numbers accurately. When she encountered 6 + (-6), what was different to her? Why did she stop, think, and come up with an answer of 9 when she had added (or so I thought) many other similar problems? What was different in this particular case?

Edwards (1993) argues that talk (or other expressions) cannot be interpreted as 'windows on children's minds.' We are not answering the question, 'What does this child *really* think?' Instead, by listening and watching, we are asking, 'What is going on *here*?' We seek to make sense of what, given this social and psychological context, a child is thinking *here*, now. Yet schools and school talk support a shared illusion that claims we make about students are general and independent of time, person, task, and setting.

During the first part of class one day, the children were working on conjectures which they had formulated about adding even and odd numbers – for instance, (1) even + even = even; (2) odd + odd = even; (3) if you add an odd number of odd numbers, you will get an odd number; (4) any number of even numbers will always add up to another even number. Children looked for examples of the conjecture they were investigating and were trying to find a way to prove that the statement would 'always be true.'

During the first part of class, the children were working with partners. I leaned over Cassandra, who was exploring pairs of odd numbers. She had written:

$$35 + 35 = 70$$

When I asked her what this showed, she said it was an example for 'odd plus odd equals even.' I asked how she knew that, and she said that 35 was an odd number and that 70 was even. I knew that 70 was a challenging example for the children. Since their understanding of the structure of numbers was just developing, many would not be sure that the 7 represented 70, and hence, be even. Some would claim that the 7 was odd, and the uncertainties about what 0 was would lead them to be unsure about 70. I was curious what Cassandra understood, so I asked how she knew that 70 was even. She said that 70 came after 69 on the number line, and that 69 was odd, and numbers go 'even, odd, even, odd' – an explanation that had consistently been her favourite. Then, using the current class definition of even numbers, she said that 70 could also be split into two equal parts – 35 and 35 – without 'having to use halves.' When I asked if there was any other way to show that 70 was even, she added that since 0 was even, and you only have to look at the 'last number,' then 70 was even. I was impressed at her versatility and confidence. I resolved to call on her later during the whole group discussion so that her ideas could be available to others and also to give her an opportunity to shine with her thinking. I knew that Cassandra liked to be centre stage but did not always find a constructive way to take that part. This seemed to me an ideal opportunity since she had developed such elaborate explanations.[12]

In the large group discussion, I called on Cassandra to share her work on the conjecture, 'odd + odd = even.' She went to the board and carefully carried out 35 + 35 and explained her answer but then said nothing about its relationship to the conjecture. Then I probed gently, 'Okay, Cassandra, why did you do that? How does that fit with the conjecture?'

Cassandra:	That these two are odd numbers and it ends up with an even number.
Ball:	Cassandra, if somebody wanted you to prove that 70 was even, what would you say?
Cassandra:	Um, I would say that I would agree with them.
Ball:	No, if they wanted you to *prove* it. If they said, 'I don't believe you that it's even, what would you do?'
Cassandra:	Um, because um …
Ball:	What were you thinking about? Maybe you can tell us what you were thinking about.

Cassandra:	All right. Because 69 is odd and you would probably guess that 70 would be even.[13]
	I noticed that she did not use the number line or any more detailed explanation, so I asked her why that followed.
Cassandra:	Because you would say 69s odd, then 70s even.
	Recognizing this as her first, and preferred, theory, I pushed her.
Ball:	What if they didn't believe that explanation? Could you give them a different one?
Cassandra:	Um, let's see …
Ball:	Is there another way to prove that 70 is even?
Cassandra:	Um … I don't think so.
	I was disappointed at the receding of her ideas.
Ball:	You showed me three ways two minutes ago. Think about what you showed me.
Cassandra:	Um … what?

Cassandra either could not or would not continue. I was not sure what to make of this. Perhaps I had imagined her clarity in our private discussion earlier; perhaps I had assisted more than I realized in the production of her explanations. I could not remember vividly enough. Maybe her ideas about this were less stable than I had thought. Or possibly she was unnerved in front of the class. What did Cassandra understand about evenness and the different explanations we had been exploring as a class? Should I base this on what I remembered her saying to me when we talked alone? On what she did in the whole group discussion? Later, looking at her written work, I saw that she relied most on the alternation of even and odd numbers without establishing that a given number was even or odd. For example, when asked whether 72 was even or odd, and how you would prove it, she wrote, 'Even. Because 71 is odd, so 72 is even.'[14] In response to a question about definitions of even and odd numbers, she was able to use the pictures – although she did not explain them – and also the recognition of particular numbers:

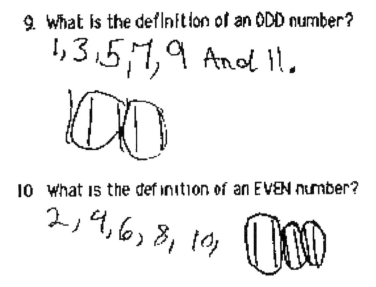

**Figure 2: Cassandra's written definitions of even and odd numbers
(2/1/90).**

Although it may appear from the pictures that she had a structural sense of even and odd numbers, what Cassandra meant by the pictures, or how she understood them, was not clear from her writing. What was more clear was that she could name certain even and odd numbers (i.e., odd numbers are 1, 3, 5, etc., and 2, 4, 6, and so on are even). What then should be made of her more elaborated explanations with me in an individual conversation in class? Did she understand in a more fleeting sense? Connected with me, without the social distraction of presenting before the group, was the depth of her understanding more visible? Or was it that I was doing part of the understanding for her? Did the nature of the specific mathematical question affect her understanding? In class, she sought to reproduce that, but the presentation was also to establish that 35 + 35 did equal 70. Did the social context and the task itself unsettle her understanding, or was it that my presence earlier had strengthened it? In her written work, was it the lack of social and personal connection, the isolation of writing, that did not draw her out to elaborate her thinking? Or was it that these represented her current understanding, unaffected by relationships with me or with her classmates? Which snapshot of Cassandra provided the best picture of her thinking? Or did they all?

Lots of questions; few clear or definite answers. Perhaps this is why teachers may avoid delving deeply into questions of what students know. The questions seem to multiply exponentially. And, given the fleeting and intangible nature of knowledge, no answer seems satisfying. To assume that there is a 'true' picture of a child's understanding is to blot from consideration the many elements that contribute to understanding being more fragile than is convenient to assume. We would like to think that understanding can be a state, or a destination, that we can observe and certify. That it is so sensitive to context – to social relations, to time and tiny filigrees of consideration – is to admit of an uncertainty in the very core of teaching and learning, one understandably unappealing for either teachers or researchers to acknowledge.

Cassandra's thinking illustrates the complexities within one individual child. As if this was not already sufficiently confusing and challenging, it is important to bear in mind that such attentiveness to what students think and understand takes place in a context where one must be concerned with not one but many individuals. But there is a multiplication involved, for sometimes the sensitivities of student thinking are matters of the collective, located in the shared assumptions of the group. A discussion later on this same day in class, January 26, was one such example. In the past, the children's way of approaching these conjectures had been to find many examples of the statement and to assume that if they supported it with many examples, that this was sufficient to claim that it was true for all cases. This notion was beginning to come apart. In the middle of class on this day, Jeannie raised her hand.

Jeannie: Me and Sheena were arguing together, but we didn't find one that didn't work. We were trying to prove that, um, Betsy's conjecture – um, that you *can't* prove that Betsy's conjecture always works.

Ball: Go on, Jeannie. Say more about why you think that.

Jeannie: Because, um, there's, um, like numbers go on and on forever and that means odd numbers and even numbers, um, go on forever and, um, so you couldn't prove that all of them aren't.

I was amazed that the two girls had extended the problem to a sophisticated epistemological issue ('we were trying to prove that you *can't* prove the conjecture'). I had wondered how young children could begin to make a shift toward establishing general mathematical validity of a claim, rather than merely illustrating a claim with finitely many verified cases. Thus far, all the children's work had been at this level of example-giving; their work more like inductive science than mathematics. Yet, Jeannie and Sheena seemed suddenly to have made two leaps: First, they were, for the first time, referring to the *set* of the integers as a mental construct, rather than to individual integers. Second, they seemed to be recognizing that giving examples could not establish general claims about this infinite set.

Touched by the magnitude of their new insight, I asked what others thought of this idea. Ofala immediately raised her hand and, looking at her intricate notebook page, filled with sums, said that she thought 'it can always work,' because she had tried eighteen of them and so she thought it could always work. I did not ask her what the 'it' was here – Betsy's conjecture, or the issue of method that was being challenged by Jeannie and Sheena. Ofala did not seem troubled by their objection. Many others nodded. Mei looked thoughtfully around the room at several posted ideas that had started in the class as conjectures at some point earlier in the year, and that the class had explored and decided to hold as true, based on their proofs. Suddenly Mei realized that Jeannie and Sheena's concern had the potential to unseat that earlier work.

> Mei: … with those conjectures, we haven't even tried *them* with all the numbers that there is, so why do you say *those* work? Well, we haven't even tried all *those* numbers that there ever could be … we haven't tried, we haven't … she said that it's not always true. Then why do you say that is, that those conjectures is not always true? *(She waved with her hand, indicating the lettered posters with the class's earlier agreements – such as, from October, 'Any number plus that same number below zero equals zero.')*

Jeannie paused, thoughtfully, and then replied, 'I wasn't thinking about it.' And Sheena added, 'We were just thinking about it today.' In a moment of inspiration, Mei's insight took Jeannie and Sheena's one step further. challenging the certainty and validity of all the children's previous work on conjectures.

I asked what other people thought about Jeannie and Sheena's claim. Sean, still very comfortable with the inductive example-based approach, said he thought you could prove that conjectures were always true, because he had been adding pairs of odd numbers and he kept getting even numbers for the answers and so he was convinced. Several others agreed and gave examples from their work. Riba nodded. She had tried sixteen examples and 'they all turned out to be even.' 'But that's not all the numbers in the world,' demurred Sheena, pressing her new realization.

The class's prior agreements about what would constitute a proof were beginning to disintegrate, but the children were in different places with respect to the girls' insight and subsequent challenge. What could I say about the children's understanding about the role of examples in establishing that a conjecture 'always works'? The collective understanding was coming apart, on the way to one of the central powers of mathematical reasoning – the capacity to reason abstractly and construct general claims about entire classes of objects. Some students had little glimpse yet of what Jeannie and Sheena were recognizing; others' ideas were being challenged or unsettled, and others also glimpsed the big shift in thinking that this insight would provoke.

On a subsequent day, some of the children began trying to prove that some of their conjectures would hold true for *all* even and odd numbers. They tried to show that an odd number plus an odd number would always have to add up to an even number. They used drawings like this:

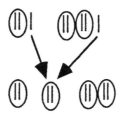

Figure 3: Drawing used to prove that any odd number plus any other odd number would always add up to an even number.

They seemed to intend these drawings to represent the general case of two odd numbers: Arguing that any odd number would always have one left over after grouping it by twos (using the currently accepted class definition), they showed, triumphantly, that two leftover ones would always be able to be combined; hence, yielding an even sum for the combination. Proud as these children were of their argument, many of their classmates were understandably unable to make the leap required to see the drawing in Figure 3 as something other than 3 + 5. They agreed with the claim that 3 + 5 = 8, and that 3 and 5 were both odd, and their sum, 8, even, but they could not see this argument as a support for a more general claim about *all* odd numbers. Moreover, many were not yet entirely – or even a little bit – convinced that there was any problem with using many examples to prove that the conjecture was true.

The limitations in their mathematical lexicon were creating a problem of understanding in context. The argument they wanted to make was an abstract one. Had they been able to represent an odd number comfortably as $2k + 1$, they might have been able to argue that $(2k + 1) + (2h + 1) = (2k + h) + 2 = 2 (k + h + 1)$, which would be, by definition, even. The symbolic form, after all, paralleled the intention of those who made the drawings in Figure 3, and which grounded the general conclusion for many of their classmates. Still, it was not clear that understanding that odd numbers are the ones with one left over after you group by twos was an abstraction yet for many of the children. Instead, some of the children understood the idea only as a linked set of examples, while others glimpsed something more patterned and general. Understanding what Jeannie, Sheena, and Mei were seeing requires first of all to see odd numbers as a set, with the common property of having one left over once divided by two. The particularity of numbers were needed for the children to grasp this idea, and yet the idea paradoxically also requires a conceptual lift-off from the particular. Unsure of the complex role of context in individual children's current thinking, I did not try at this juncture to offer symbolic notation that might have helped transport them into the world of mathematical proof.

Still, this major mathematical insight challenged what had been a common agreement in the sufficiency of an empirical approach to mathematical proof. Although arguments of this kind occurred in the group setting, individual children continued to believe in examples while others switched to efforts to establish the generality of claims. The rules of knowing and proving seemed ironically less stable than they had been before the girls' mathematical discovery.

The variability in students' thinking, shaped by context and moment, can be seen as the failure to attain the 'solid' understanding to which teachers aspire for their students. It can be frustrating, even discouraging, to try to figure out what students think. However, what appears as an instable fragility may be merely the reflection of the highly contextualized nature of knowing and learning. I move next to the emotional demands of trying to figure out what students think and the challenges that arise in caring that students learn.

Challenge #3: Listening With and Through Desire

A third challenge for teachers rests in the basic commitment of the role. Teachers want students to understand. One part intellect, three parts emotion, teaching involves hope and wish, prayer and care, worry and craving. I wanted to feel that my third graders understood even and odd numbers well and that they were developing some ideas about how a definition and a conjecture are different. Being a teacher is centrally about helping others learn, and feeling successful is wrapped up in accomplishing this. Teachers are disappointed when they confront their students' confusions, missing pieces, distorted understandings. They care about their students. After investing time and effort in a particular student, a teacher *wants* to hear right answers, sensible reasons, creative ideas. Teachers ask leading questions, fill in where students leave space, and hear more than what is being said because they so hope for student learning. The desire to have been effective, to have helped, is strong and affects pedagogical hearing in ways that shape the assessment of what students know. Teachers also want students to feel good about their own accomplishments and may shy away from pushing students for fear of being seen as critical and, subsequently, as silencing.

Desire is also related to a fear for the fragility of understanding. Desire not only makes interpretation more complicated, it also can instill the hesitation to probe. On hearing a student say something right, fear of destabilizing the child's thinking can hold a teacher back from probing. Maria, who was often shy in class and whose English was just emerging, raised her hand to offer an example for the conjecture 'an odd plus an odd equals an even':

Ball:	What about other people? Maria, did you try some? How many did you try?
Maria *(barely audible)*:	I just want to show one.
Ball:	You want to show just one? Okay. Okay, do you want to tell them why it, what that is?
Maria:	21 plus 21 equals 42.
Ball:	What does that show?
Maria:	That 42 is an even number.
Ball:	Cassandra, can you listen to Maria right now please? Go ahead, Maria.
Maria:	That 42 is an even number.
Ball:	And 21?
Maria:	21 is an odd number.
Ball:	Comments? Cassandra?
Cassandra:	I agree with her.
Ball:	Anyone disagree with Maria? Thank you, Maria.

Her short turn over, we moved on. I had protected Maria and myself from saying anything wrong or from getting confused. I *wanted* her to understand, to get it 'right.' In wanting it, I arranged the context so that she did. It is true that there were many good reasons not to press Maria here. She volunteered for few turns in class, and even in small group work she was quiet. She volunteered on this day, and I was pleased. I wanted it not to be an uncomfortable experience; I hoped it would encourage her to do it more often.

Because Maria talked less in class, though, I was far less sure about what she was understanding. Leaving her answer unprobed did not threaten the possibly fragile nature of her feelings or her understandings. I did not risk confusing or unsettling her. But I also had less information on what she was thinking. Although I heard that she could correctly identify 21 as an odd number and 42 as an even, I did not know how she understood the definition of even or odd numbers. Without questioning her, I could not help her take the next step.

Desire also shapes teachers' responses to students' ideas. After Ofala expanded the class's definition of odd numbers, I 'helped' by rephrasing more straightforwardly what (I thought) she had said:

Ball: So, you're saying the even numbers are the ones where you
                can group them all by two's and the odd ones are the ones
                where you end up with one left over?

Ofala had not said this precisely. What she had said was, 'I just wanted to say if, um, you wanted an odd number, you just have to take one off of it ... because usually odd numbers are ... like, like ... this, kind of like have ones in the middle? Like five

and there's a one in the middle, or, um nine.

This two together, this two together ... this two together, and this two together.'

There's one left. And even numbers – like six

you can't get *anything* in the middle. There isn't one left.' She had actually probably been saying two rather different, and both potentially valuable, things. However, as a consequence of my desire for Ofala to have a successful turn, and for the class to have a stable definition of odd numbers, I leaned into her contribution, heard it as correct, and restated it in my own terms to imbue it with still more stability.

Wanting students to 'get it right,' teachers rephrase, reshape, and reconstruct students' talk into more standard form (Edwards & Mercer, 1989). Was Ofala really saying what I said she was saying? I now am quite sure that she was saying both more and less. She was saying more in that she seemed to be making use of a linear arrangement, thereby having a 'middle' position, which conferred a geometric perspective on the number, and illustrated a particular aspect of oddness. She was saying less in that she did not articulate what I said when I transformed her words into a standard definition ('odd ones are the ones where you end up with one left over,' or $k2 + 1$). On one hand, a teacher can function as a learned listener of her students: Having come to know a particular child, the teacher can make sense of some of what that child is saying that a stranger would never hear. Sharing history with a class, both teacher and students can 'fill in' around idiosyncratic expressions. Ofala was a child for whom skilled listening was invaluable. An observer to our class would find Ofala particularly complicated to understand; the challenge of unfamiliarity heightened in listening to her. Up to this point, Ofala had mixed pictures and words to display odd and even numbers. I took her contribution and turned it all into words. I wanted the class, not just Ofala, to have access to this idea, to hold it in words, and so I sought to underscore her idea, reinforcing it with my succinctness. Whereas Ofala expressively showed one aspect of what she meant, using both narration ('this two together, this two together') and pictures,

I formulated the idea succinctly and less colourfully. Worrying about its fragile expression, and thinking it mathematically valuable, I did not want it to slip away. My words, I thought, would bolster it. My desire for particular ends overlaid what she said, adding and refining it, and leaving behind her second idea that odd numbers are 'the ones with something in the middle.'

On one hand, perhaps this is appropriate. That I wanted the students to develop their understandings is central to the role of teacher. On the other hand, my desire to move Ofala and her classmates in a particular direction affects what I hear them say, what I make of their expressions, and what I do next. I likely wanted Ofala to have said what I say she said. I wanted her to have made this distinction that if you divide a number into groups of two what matters mathematically is whether there is one left over or not. Inserting myself into her thought is entangled with my wanting to hear her as right. To have success with students is one of the few sources of reward in teaching (Lortie, 1975). Consequently, the incentives are high to hear students as right, to fill in the gaps in what they say, to read their words over-generously.

Listening is a balancing act: Hearing generously is critical to teaching well — listening sympathetically, leaning *into* rather than *away from* students, to believe rather than doubt (Elbow, 1986). It is not always unhelpful to put words in students' mouths. The language proffered can be a valuable scaffold for students' developing ideas. But it is also true at times that when teachers rephrase students' ideas, they take over, and obscure the students' own thinking. In many of the instances in this chapter, it would be possible to interpret and make sense of what students said, to come up with some explanation that would exclude a discrepant piece of evidence or interpret it more hopefully. How can teachers balance their desire for their students to have learned with the need to scrutinize the evidence carefully and skeptically? How can teachers be receptive and sympathetic listeners, working hard to see how students are making sense, and yet still be able to push and strengthen students' thinking and not settle for approximations?

PREPARING TO KNOW WHAT STUDENTS ARE THINKING

Trying to figure out what students are learning is central to teaching. However, although it is not popular to admit it, knowing with any certainty what students know is fundamentally impossible. Teachers listen across divides of human experience, through the vagaries of context, and with intense desire that their students succeed. Still, this of course cannot mean abandoning the quest to know students' thinking. In the fleeting moments of classroom talk, teachers must infer what students mean and interpret what they can do. Confronted with students' drawings and writings, teachers attempt to delve the layers of students' writing and drawing, and the relationships of writing and drawing to ideas and thinking. Teachers must convince administrators, parents, and the public of what students are learning, all the while reassuring themselves of what they are accomplishing.

What are the elements that interact in teachers' thinking as they listen and try to understand what students think? One element is knowledge of the particular ideas themselves, the content and the contexts of children's work. In the examples in this chapter, knowing flexibly what it means for a number to be even or odd makes a difference in listening to children's ideas. When Ofala talks of numbers that are odd having 'one left,' knowing that one mathematical representation of odd numbers is as groups of two with one left (one interpretation of $k2 + 1$) helps sharpen my hearing. When she simultaneously speaks of odd numbers having 'one in the middle,' it helps that I understand divisibility by two as meaning either dividing into *two groups (2k)*:

Ofala: This, kind of like have ones in the middle? Like five *(she draws:*

and there's a one in the middle, or, um nine: *(she draws)*

or into *groups of two (k2)*:

Ofala: *(she circles groups of two in her drawing of nine hash marks)* This two together, this two together ... this two together, and this two together.

Ofala was doing both, and I can track her thinking better for my own mathematical thinking. In the first instance, Ofala's idea seemed to be that suggested by the following drawing, which she did not, however, produce:

Some of the essential subject matter knowledge is epistemological rather than topical. For instance, appreciating the role of definitions in mathematics, and respecting the requirements of a functional definition would be important to listening to the children's attempts to capture what makes a number odd or even. At one point, when Sean tried to argue that 1 was even because it could be split into two parts $(1/2 + 1/2)$, understanding the incompleteness of the definition on which he was relying helped me to interpret what he was thinking.

And some aspects of subject matter understanding are about relations, connection, and development. Children's ideas are continually in motion, evolving, changing, and adapting. They bump into the boundaries of their current domains and assumptions, and press on these to accommodate their ideas. These discontinuities can closely resemble the paradigm shifts that occur with disciplinary communities, as entire perspectives, and hence, ideas and methods, change (e.g., Kitcher, 1984; Kuhn, 1962). When Jeannie and Sheena realized that they were unable to prove something about *all* numbers, they precipitated a major paradigm shift, first for themselves, and later for their classmates. Familiarity with how this has happened to these ideas within the discipline can help teachers to understand the mobility of children's thinking (Bruner, 1960; Kline, 1970). A broader perspective on the mathematical connections between topics divided by conventions of the school curriculum can also enhance listening, when children work across those traditional boundaries without realizing it. For example, I was unattuned to the geometric potential of Ofala's linear arrangement, and the illumination it made possible for our exploration of number theory.

In the episodes discussed in this chapter, what I understood sharpened my hearing; what I did not know constrained it. For instance, when Jeannie raised her concern that there was no way to prove whether Betsy's conjecture (that odd + odd = even) would be true for any numbers, I was able to hear that she was edging toward a fundamental element of proof – that is, the need to establish that something is analytically and not merely empirically true. I was also able to understand that she was not yet thinking of ways that that could be done, but that she did have a sense that numbers were infinite. In the case of Ofala, however, I missed one of two main parts of Ofala's contribution about what makes a number odd. While I noticed that she was saying that odd numbers were those numbers that, when grouped by twos, have one left over, I completely missed the potency of her other idea – that an odd number, arranged linearly, and reflected about a central line of symmetry, would have 'one in the middle.' My own understanding was such that I heard these two as the same: as an argument about 'one left over.' I did not recognize the elegance of the geometric perspective she was offering and, as such, missed one main component of her thinking.

At the same time, mathematical understandings are only part of the work. Knowing about eight-year-olds made a difference – what they are like, how they think, what they are likely to have had experience with, how they are likely to read, write, and draw. Knowing specific students mattered as well. For example, knowing Ofala also helped to hear her. I knew to watch, to pay attention to her drawings, and I understood her drawings as processes, not products. That is, Ofala made pictures as parts of her explanations, not as illustrations of them. Like those of some other children in the class, it was in their construction, not the pictures' final form, that the most vivid expression could be found. With other children, the pictures were only sensible once they were completed; these children had long periods of quiet as they prepared a drawing amid an explanation. I developed sense of how to interpret Sean's lanky body motions and Ofala's graceful hands. Knowing the rhythms of their communication and talk made a difference in hearing them. Across a year of video-taping class every day, and struggling with issues of camera location, and mikes and other supports for recording the sound, I discovered that technical acuity was but a minor part of hearing and seeing children. Instead, really hearing and seeing them was a an active accomplishment of comprehension.

As the instances in this chapter illustrate, the challenges to figuring out what children know are great. Facing two or three dozen students at a time, teachers must make ongoing, usable estimates about what individual students know. They must observe and listen, and they must interpret their observations, reach conclusions, and act. The interpretations on which they act are no more than conjectures – uncertain, provisional, evolving. Yet, in the moment, teachers' assertions have the epistemological status of knowledge and must function as such (Scheffler, 1965). That is, teachers make decisions and design moves based on what they know, and they must treat that knowledge as likely to be true. What they must know is much more than what they can know in advance; they must know *in* the context of their interactions with children.

Teachers' knowledge of students is most often private, and as such, lacks the support of community. When mathematicians, or scientists, or historians make claims, they first convince themselves of what they think, but soon they are in the position of trying to convince colleagues and others of the validity of what they are claiming (Lampert, 1992). Doing this locates their efforts to know in the context of shared opportunity to examine evidence and shared standards for appraising that evidence. When the children in my third grade class made assertions, they sought to explain and justify their ideas, and in so doing subjected their conjectures to the scrutiny of others, who raised questions, offered alternatives, and suggested additions. But teachers, on this most central aspect of their work, most often work alone.

Interactions of Method and Knowledge in Figuring Out What Students Think

Despite these challenges inherent in listening to and interpreting children's thinking, to conclude that knowing students is an impossible task, and hence is not worth attempting, misses the point. Hence, the question: How can teachers improve their capabilities to figure out reasonably what their students are learning? In the face of uncertainty, what underlies skilled interpretation and better conjectures, and what are promising avenues of developing these? In an essay on 'The Nature of Method,' Dewey (1916/1944) brings together knowledge and its construction. He argues that, in order to become a skilled artist of any practice, there is an interplay of ideas and 'classical methods,' threaded with flexibility and imagination:

> Part of ... learning, a very important part, consists of *becoming* master of the methods which the experience has shown to be more efficient in like cases of getting knowledge. (p. 171)

At the same time that Dewey highlights the discipline of methods already used, he also recognizes their limits without 'an animating idea.' Exploring what he calls 'intellectual methods,' he considers physicians' engagement in diagnosis and treatment:

> To be used intelligently, existing practices, however authorized they may be, have to be adapted to the exigencies of particular cases ... [methods] should indicate standpoints from which to carry on investigations; they economize a survey of the features of the particular case by suggesting the things to be particularly looked into. (p. 171)

Figuring out what students think seems like a similar investigative endeavour.[15] On one hand, knowing as much as possible about 'like cases' – other children of similar ages and circumstance engaged in other encounters with the mathematical ideas – can help fuel the interpretations a teacher can venture. When my students fell into a discussion of whether zero was even or odd, it certainly helped that I had heard many third graders before them wrestle with this question. It helped further that I myself had thought about zero, and about its relation to the definitions of even and odd. Still, as the instances in this paper demonstrate, many situations arise in the course of teaching which are not like anything the teacher has heard before. I had never heard a child claim that $6 + (-6)$ = 9 nor reason about negative numbers as Mei did. What gives teachers leverage on the complexities of interpreting students in such situations is similar to Dewey's idea of the blending of past knowledge with the skilled personal investigation of a novel situation at hand. Past experience – the teacher's own, or that of others – can guide, but not cover, the range of ideas and expressions that children will produce. Beyond the idiosyncrasies of individual manner is method, more than 'extemporized inspirations' (Dewey, 1916/1944, p. 17), comprising instead methods for constructing new knowledge. Such methods depend both on study of children and experiments with probing and interpreting them.

In this last section, I turn to three emergent approaches in professional development, all of which are centred on developing both knowledge and ways of knowing: discussing cases of student thinking, using redesigned curriculum materials, and investigating artifacts of teaching and learning. Each of these has promise for equipping teachers with the intellectual resources likely to be helpful in navigating the uncertainties of interpreting student thinking. Each of these represents an area in need of development and research. What the three share is a focus on learning to make sense of students' thinking in the fleeting moments of real-time practice. If figuring out what students think is a task localized in the particulars of moments, children, and content, and for which all knowledge cannot be had in advance, we need to design ways to support teachers' preparation for knowing students 'on-line.' Interesting, also, is the different potential each of these three approaches seems to hold for mediating the challenges of distance, context, and desire.

Discussing cases of student thinking.

The first approach focuses on developing a case knowledge of student thinking and the methods of its examination (e.g., Barnett, 1991; Schifter, Russell, & Bastable, in press). Working from written cases of episodes of children's mathematical work, teachers work together to examine, conjecture, and explore alternative interpretations of the children's thinking. At times, case discussions will focus on the mathematics at hand, at other times more on children's language and drawings, at other times on teacher questions (see Barnett & Sather, 1992). An important component of this approach is group discussion and analysis of written episodes, which has the possibility of moving teachers beyond the isolation of professional practice and the limits of idiosyncratic interpretation. Collectively, teachers can discuss mathematical and learning themes that arise across classrooms, comparing evidence and inference, and expanding their individual repertoire of interpretations and method.

Schifter et al. (in press) have engaged teachers with whom they work in authoring cases of student thinking. This design, which involves teachers in collecting and organizing information about particular children, has promise for helping teachers develop more finely tuned capacities for listening and watching children. Schifter and her colleagues (in press) quote several participating teachers who have remarked on the contribution that this simple opportunity provided. For example, one commented, 'When I knew I needed to write down what the children were saying, I started to pay attention in a different way.'

Looking and listening more closely is one component of this approach. The disciplined examination and interpretation of the collected information is another. But not to be overlooked in this approach is the expansion of case knowledge, of exposure to the range of possible ideas children might have. Such case knowledge enables teachers to expand beyond the happenstance of their own experience, to students they have not taught, and to analyses they have not made, and to animate the subsequent conjectures they can make. By broadening the cases of student thinking around particular mathematical topics, teachers may be able to hear students better through the multiple contexts of mathematical work. The analysis of several students' thinking on a specific mathematical topic may help teachers to parse better what students are working on and develop more detailed maps for listening and looking.

Using redesigned curriculum materials.

Curriculum could constitute a second resource for helping teachers prepare for hearing and making sense of students. Teachers' guides are well-positioned to guide teachers' listening and their interpretations of what they hear. Curriculum materials are centrally situated in teachers' practice, for most elementary teachers use teacher guides and texts extensively (Schwille et al., 1983). Moreover, unlike many resources for teaching, curriculum materials aim to guide practice at the close level of the daily lesson.

Despite this, curriculum materials do not usually provide much close, detailed information about students. Instead, teachers' guides traditionally emphasize content and ways to present the content, leaving teachers on their own to interpret what students produce in response to lessons and worksheets. Teachers' guides usually also lack practical discussions of students' likely thinking. And rarely do curriculum materials offer examples of student work accompanied by comments on assessment of such work. Similarly absent are the kinds of concrete guidance for teachers about ways to respond to particular student comments, questions, or interpretations.

In a poignant episode and analysis from her own teaching, Heaton (1994) describes her own lack of preparation for hearing students' answers to a problem she had so carefully prepared from the teacher's guide. The lesson focused on composition of functions and engaged students in the construction of a simple function table:

> As the teacher's guide suggested, I varied the process of filling in the table with numbers by asking some students to give ending numbers first, followed by an explanation of how they generated them. The teacher's guide also suggested that I call on someone different to offer these explanations ... I held high hopes for the next part of the lesson in which I planned to ask students to notice patterns. (pp. 127-128)

In the ensuing minutes, children produced examples of patterns that Heaton did not understand and did not seem the point of the lesson, and she began to falter. 'Hearing Pili's [one of the students] idea, I thought to myself, what sort of patterns were we looking for? Definitely not ones like this' (p. 129). She grew frustrated as the students gave examples of 'patterns' that did not seem mathematical, but for which she was unprepared. The teacher's guide had prepared her insufficiently to anticipate, hear, or manage what students might say in response to the problem and questions of the lesson.

> I wanted to be open to the idea that my students' ideas might vary from the teacher's guide. How was I to know which of my students' responses were reasonable variations ... and which were not? How would I figure out how to be responsive to these variations? ... *The script in the teacher's guide was designed with questions for me to initiate, but I felt frustrated with what little help it offered me in figuring out what to do next in the situation, especially when it seemed that what my students were saying did not match what the developers ... anticipated they might.* (p. 137, emphasis added)

Reflecting on her hopes for the teacher's guide to help her learn to teach mathematics in ways that were both deeper mathematically and more responsive to students, Heaton considers what might make curriculum more educative for teachers. Following Bruner (1960, p. xv), who argues that curriculum 'must be first and foremost a curriculum for teachers,' that curriculum materials can only affect pupils if they 'change, move, perturb, and inform teachers,' Heaton outlines elements central to practice that curriculum materials could be better designed to offer. She suggests that teachers' guides could, in addition to providing likely student responses, provide guidance for interpreting those responses:

> Verbatim quotes of likely student responses are not very useful without some understanding of *why* these might be typical responses. What mathematics might someone understand who would say these things? (p. 375)

What is needed, according to Heaton, is information for teachers to hear, assess, and make use of students' responses, all the while keeping their eye on the mathematical goals at hand.

Note that this sort of information and guidance are of a different kind than the usual content of teachers' guides, which typically concentrates on what teachers do and say. Including more information about students' thinking, alternative plausible responses to students' ideas, and examples and discussions of student work would be much less matters of what to do and say, and would instead be resources for the interactive work of constructing curriculum in classrooms.

Recently, mathematics curriculum materials have been developed that are designed to provide teachers with substantial resources for probing, hearing and reading, interpreting, and responding to likely student work (see, for example, Lappan, Fey, Fitzgerald, Friel, & Phillips, in press; Russell & Rubin, 1994). Such material has the potential to reduce the challenges of distance by better preparing teachers to hear what students might say. Plans for mathematical work, accompanied by well-developed material on students' thinking and ways to hear and respond, can provide teachers with better preparation for the territory in relation to both content and learners. If such development is grounded in pilot work in appropriately varied settings, curriculum materials have the potential of covering more of the variation in students ideas and expressions, hence for reducing some of the inherent distance between teachers and students. Such material is well-situated to provide such insights along with commentaries that relate student thinking to the mathematical goals of the curriculum.

Investigating artifacts of teaching and learning.

In preparing to know what students know, a third approach entails creating contexts for shared examination of unnarrated children's work, talk, and ideas. Different from the case work described above, this approach engages teachers in direct examination of information from a classroom – video-tapes of classroom lessons, and interactions and children's written work and drawing on the chalk-board and on paper (e.g., Lampert & Ball, 1995). Teachers can examine closely a video-tape of a class discussion and analyse what different students seemed to be thinking. To do this, they would have to listen closely, striving to hear and see what students are doing. Could they examine closely what Ofala was pre-senting, for instance? Watching her body's motions, her hands, her drawings, and listening to her nonlinear and expressive talk, they could try to make sense of what she was saying. Unassisted by the interpretation of a case writer or a curriculum developer, they would be in the position of practice, leaning toward children and trying to hear. Similarly, teachers could look at a set of student es-says and compare the kinds of comments they might write and why.

Such work is particularly well-designed for confronting the uncertainties of practice precisely because the information is unstructured and uninterpreted. In-vestigating puzzling comments or unclear writing, teachers would seek to make sense and to compare what they see and hear. Because the actual interactions and products are available, teachers have the opportunity to go back to the level of direct examination of the phenomenon.

That teachers cannot interact with the students provides an opportunity that they do not have in real time, in their own classrooms. That these are not their students creates a buffer of reflection that could support learning to make inter-pretations on-line. Unfettered by the desires to help their own students learn, or the sense of anxious responsibility for effecting learning, teachers are freed for the direct and focused examination of student thinking. They are left with the challenges of distance and context and may be able to consider and analyse more open-mindedly.

DIRECTIONS FOR FURTHER INQUIRY

Understanding better what makes knowing students – a central task of teaching – so complex creates an opportunity. It can seem daunting to think that the very thing for which teachers are most centrally responsible is so fundamentally im-possible. Yet, its difficulty is also at the heart of what can make teaching intel-lectually challenging and engaging work, and what makes teaching so professionally demanding.

The ideas of this chapter suggest several lines of continued inquiry that can contribute both to our collective understanding of teaching and its challenges and the consequent issues posed for teachers' professional development.

First are continued questions about the challenges of knowing students and what students are learning. One issue crucial to understand better is how different approaches to and contexts of teaching affect the task and expectations for assessing student thinking. For example, within direct instruction, what are the issues entailed in knowing what students are learning different? Are teachers interested in different outcomes, hence face different issues in ascertaining what their students know? Or are the problems of knowing what students have learned plagued by similar challenges? Another important variable is subject matter. I have contextualized these analyses in the topics of mathematics teaching and learning. How are the issues similar and different in other subject areas, or in more integrated, thematic teaching? Do teachers of English literature face comparable challenges? How do the pedagogical problems of knowing students vary when the goal is to read *Canterbury Tales* rather than to develop understandings of even and odd numbers? Finally is an issue of level. How are the issues faced by teachers affected by the age of their students? On one hand, it may seem that issues of distance and unfamiliarity are greatest in the case of very young children whose talk and manner is so different from adults.' On the other hand, older students, with greater self-consciousness and awareness of their vulnerability about performance, may mask their thinking and be less accessible.

Second is much-needed study of how different kinds of support affect teachers' learning to hear and interpret students. The approaches sketched in the last section of this chapter are plausible hypotheses, not substantiated methods. Examined logically, they hold promise because of their relationship to the work of knowing students in practice – particularly its interactive, situated, and uncertain features. But many questions remain: Do teachers learn subject matter from such resources and experiences? Does such situated learning of subject matter ideas, located pedagogically within student thinking, provide the kind of intellectual resources that can help teachers hear and read unexpected student responses? Does such learning affect teachers' capacities to hear students in mathematical areas different from those addressed in the cases, curriculum materials, or artifact investigations?

A related set of questions centre on design. That the approaches discussed here are hypotheses is also to say that they are under development. How can such materials and experiences be designed to support teachers' learning? How might they be designed so as to be accessible, engaging, and useful to a wide variety of teachers in facing the challenges of knowing students? How might they provide opportunities for teachers to develop the mathematical resources crucial to hearing students, as well as to have better anticipations of what students might say? What variations in design are worth trying? What related but distinct approaches are worth pursuing?

Another set of crucial questions has to do with what teachers can learn about students from such work. Do they develop expanded case knowledge? What is it like? And how does such knowledge affect the work of interpreting their own students amid the challenges of distance, context, and desire?

Finally, how does the experience of engaging in collective professional discourse about student thinking affect teachers' standards for student work and their skills at interpreting and assessing particular students' thinking? That teaching has been traditionally so isolated makes attractive the idea of building a professional discourse and sense of community around this core task of teaching. A reasonable hypothesis is that such collegial work can build and extend individual teachers' resources – what they know about and how they look at students, as well as their flexibility and imagination in reasoning. It can, in Lord's (1994) terms, yield resources developed in the context of professional communities in ways that individual teachers cannot do alone. However, we need to track the work of such teacher groups and examine closely how norms of discourse evolve and how standards for knowing develop. We need to document what is discussed and what participants take from their engagement in such collective work.

The task of hearing students is complex; interpreting what they may be learning still harder. This chapter analyses aspects of the challenge and explores possible approaches to helping teachers prepare for the work. I close by returning to the children, who seem often much more comfortable with the uncertainties of their own understandings and the ambiguities of something called knowledge.

After Jeannie announced her sudden realization, arrived at by arguing with Sheena, that they could not prove for all numbers that even + even = even because 'numbers go on forever,' several children took notice. Some argued that the conjecture was true, and they reported how many examples they had tried. Then Mei challenged her on the basis of what she thought Jeannie already believed about other, previously agreed-upon, 'theorems':

Mei: … we haven't tried every number that there was, so can't really say those (motions to conjectures posted on the wall) are true if you're saying that you want to try every number there ever was.

Jeannie: I never *said* they were true all the time.

Mei: Then why didn't you disagree when Lucy and everybody agreed with those conjectures?

Jeannie paused thoughtfully. With a matter-of-factness about changing her thinking, she answered simply, 'Because I wasn't thinking about it.' And Sheena piped in, 'She *just* thought about it. That's why we were trying to think about it.' Jeannie's thinking had changed, she had told Sheena about it, and they were both in the process of remodelling their assumptions and ideas.

Learning to figure out what students think is in many ways like learning to think mathematically. Conjectures improve from concentrated attention and exploration; interpretation and analysis become more complicated, and new problems emerge. Knowing students is a domain worthy of such development, and promising for increased understanding and consequent new challenges.

ENDNOTES

1. My work on this chapter has profited greatly from the critical comments and helpful suggestions of Suzanne Wilson, Hyman Bass, Hilda Borko, and Deborah Schifter, as well as the editors of this volume. I wish also to thank Kara Suzuka for her assistance.

2. This work was supported in part by a post-doctoral fellowship from the National Academy of Education and the Spencer Foundation, and a grant from the National Science Foundation (TPE 92-55242). The opinions herein are mine and do not reflect the position, policy, or endorsement of either of the grantors.

3. David Cohen (in preparation) has analysed and written about issues of endemic uncertainty and how teachers manage to constrain or open their access to students' thinking in what he calls 'teachers' acquaintance with students' knowledge.'

4. See Lampert (in press) for a helpful examination and analysis of what it might mean to conduct research on teaching *from the perspective of practice*.

5. Teachers' content knowledge was an early focus of researchers on teaching who sought to prove what seemed an obvious relationship between what teachers knew and what the students learned. When given the ways in which they conceived 'subject matter knowledge' and 'student learning,' the expected correlations did not appear, this line of investigation was shelved for over a decade (see Ball, 1991).

6. A more complete discussion of this episode and an analysis of it in light of issues of representation and discourse can be found in Ball (1993b).

7. Kara Suzuka, Margery Osborne, Sylvia Rundquist (my classroom teacher-collaborator), Jim Reineke, and Erin Eberz.

8. Other researcher-teachers who conduct research on teaching from the perspective of practice include Lampert (e.g., 1986, 1990a, 1992, in press); Chazan (1992); Hammer (1995); Heaton (1994); Lensmire (1993, 1994a, 1994b); Osborne (1993); Roth (1992); Wilson (1995, in press); and Wong (1995). See also Ball (in press) for a discussion of first-person research.

9. I argue elsewhere (see Ball, 1995) that collective engagement in such abstraction can serve as common ground for students in ways preferable to applications and connections to the everyday world.

10. See Osborne (1993) for more on children's multiple expressions, including art, movement, body in a first-grade science class.

11. My thinking about Ofala's mathematical understanding has been greatly enhanced by studying Hyman Bass's written commentary on an earlier version of this analysis.

12. See Ball (1993a) for other instances of my trying to help Cassandra find a spot for presenting her ideas to this class.

13. It was not clear why claiming that 69 was odd was so obvious to Cassandra.

14. Again, it is not clear why 71 was so clearly odd to Cassandra.

15. Magdalene Lampert and I have been engaged over the past several years in exploring 'investigation' as a central task in teaching and teacher education and drawing parallels between this way of thinking about practice and professional education on one hand and

children's learning of mathematics on the other (see, for example, Lampert & Ball, 1995). Dewey also makes this connection (1916/1944, p. 172).

REFERENCES

Anderson, J., Reder, L., & Simon, H. (1996). Situated learning and education. *Educational Researcher, 25*(4), 5-11.

Ball, D. L. (1991). Research on teaching mathematics: Making subject matter part of the equation. In J. Brophy (Ed.), *Advances in research on teaching* (Vol. 2, pp. 1-48). Greenwich, CT: JAI Press.

Ball, D. L. (1993a). Moral and intellectual, personal and professional: Restitching practice. In M. Buchmann & R. E. Floden (Eds.), *Detachment and concern: Topics in the philosophy of teaching and teacher education* (pp. 193-204). New York: Teachers College Press.

Ball, D. L. (1993b). With an eye on the mathematical horizon: Dilemmas of teaching elementary school mathematics. *Elementary School Journal, 93*, 373-397.

Ball, D. L. (1995). Transforming pedagogy – Classrooms as mathematical communities: A response to Lensmire and Pryor. *Harvard Educational Review, 65*(4), 670-677.

Ball, D. L. (in press). Working on the inside: Designing to use one's own practice as a site for studying mathematics teaching and learning. In R. Lesh (Ed.), *Designing research for reform: In mathematics and science education.*

Ball, D. & Wilson, S. (1996). Integrity in teaching: Recognizing the fusion of the moral and intellectual. *American Educational Research Journal, 33*(1), 155-192.

Barnett, C. (1991). Building a case-based curriculum to enhance the pedagogical content knowledge of mathematics teachers. *Journal of Teacher Education, 42*(4), 263-273.

Barnett, C. & Sather, S. (1992, April). *Using case discussions to promote changes in beliefs among mathematics teachers.* Paper presented at the annual meeting of the American Educational Research Association, San Francisco.

Bruner, J. (1960). *The process of education.* Cambridge, MA: Harvard University Press.

Chazan, D. (1992). Implementing the 'Professional Standards for Teaching Mathematics.' *Mathematics Teacher, 85*(5), 371-375.

Cohen, D. K. (in preparation). *Teaching practice and its predicaments.* Unpublished manuscript, University of Michigan, Ann Arbor.

Cohen, D. (1995). Rewarding teachers for students' performance. In S. Fuhrman & J. O'Day (Eds.), *Rewards and reform* (pp. 60-112). San Francisco: Jossey Bass.

Darling-Hammond, L., Ancess, J., & Falk, B. (1995). *Authentic assessment in action: Studies of schools and students at work.* New York: Teachers College Press.

Delpit, L. D. (1988). The silenced dialogue: Power and pedagogy in educating other people's children. *Harvard Educational Review, 58*, 280-298.

Dewey, J. (1902/1990). *The child and the curriculum.* Chicago: University of Chicago.

Dewey, J. (1916/1944). The nature of method. In *Democracy and education* (pp. 164-179). New York: Macmillan.

Duckworth, E. (1987). *The having of wonderful ideas and other essays.* New York: Teachers College Press.

Edwards, D. (1993). What do children really think? Discourse analysis and conceptual content in children's talk. *Cognition and Instruction, 11*, 207-225.

Edwards, D. & Mercer, N. (1989). Reconstructing context: The conventionalization of classroom knowledge. *Discourse Processes, 12*, 91-104.

Elbow, P. (1986). *Embracing contraries: Explorations in learning and teaching*. New York: Oxford University Press.

Erlwanger, S. (1975). Benny's conceptions of rules and answers in IPI mathematics. *Journal of Children's Mathematical Behavior, 1*, 157-283.

Hammer, D. (1995). *Epistemological considerations in teaching introductory physics*. Newton, MA: Center for the Development of Teaching, Education Development Center.

Hawkins, D. (1974). Nature, man, and mathematics. In *The informed vision: Essays on learning and human nature* (pp. 109-131). New York: Agathon. (Original work published in 1972.)

Heaton, R. (1994). *Creating and studying a practice of teaching elementary mathematics for understanding*. Unpublished doctoral dissertation, Michigan State University, East Lansing.

Hiebert, J., Carpenter, T., Fennema, E., Fuson, K., Human, P., Murray, H., Olivier, A., & Wearne, D. (1996). Problem solving as a basis for reform in curriculum and instruction: The case of mathematics. *Educational Researcher, 25*(4), 12-21.

Jackson, P. (1968). *Life in classrooms*. New York: Holt, Rinehart, and Winston.

Jackson, P. (1986). *The practice of teaching*. New York: Teachers College Press.

Kitcher, P. (1984). *The nature of mathematical knowledge*. New York: Oxford University Press.

Kline, M. (1970). Logic versus pedagogy. *American Mathematical Monthly, 77*, 264-282.

Kuhn, T. (1962). *The structure of scientific revolutions*. Chicago: University of Chicago Press.

Lampert, M. (1986). Knowing, doing, and teaching multiplication. *Cognition and Instruction, 3*(4), 305-342.

Lampert, M. (1990a). Connecting conventions with inventions. In L. Steffe & T. Wood (Eds.), *Transforming children's mathematics education* (pp. 253-265). Hillsdale, NJ: Erlbaum.

Lampert, M. (1990b). When the problem is not the question and the answer is not the solution: Mathematical knowing and teaching. *American Educational Research Journal, 27*, 29-64.

Lampert, M. (1992). Practices and problems in teaching authentic mathematics. In F. Oser, A. Dick, & J. L. Patry (Eds.), *Effective and responsible teaching: The new synthesis* (pp. 295-314). San Francisco: Jossey-Bass.

Lampert, M. (in press). Studying teaching as a thinking practice. In J. Greeno & S. G. Goldman (Eds.), *Thinking practices*. Hillsdale, NJ: Lawrence Erlbaum.

Lampert, M. & Ball, D. L. (1995). *Aligning teacher education with contemporary K-12 reform visions*. Paper prepared for the National Commission on Teaching and America's Future, Teachers College, New York.

Lappan, G., Fey, J. T., Fitzgerald, W. M., Friel, S. N., & Phillips, E. D. (in press). *Connected mathematics project*. Palo Alto, CA: Dale Seymour Publications.

Lensmire, T. (1993). Following the child, socioanalysis, and threats to community: Teacher response to student texts. *Curriculum Inquiry, 23*, 265-299.

Lensmire, T. (1994a). *When children write: Critical revisions of the writing workshop*. New York: Teachers College Press.

Lensmire, T. (1994b). Writing workshop as carnival: Reflections on an alternative learning environment. *Harvard Educational Review, 64*(4), 371-391.

Lord, B. (1994). Teachers' professional development: Critical colleagueship and the role of professional communities. In N. Cobb (Ed.), *The future of education: Perspectives on national standards in America* (pp. 175-204). New York: The College Board.

Lortie, D. C. (1975). *Schoolteacher: A sociological study*. Chicago: The University of Chicago Press.

Osborne, M. (1993). *Teaching with and without mirrors: Examining science teaching in elementary school from the perspective of a teacher and learner*. Unpublished doctoral dissertation, Michigan State University, East Lansing.

Paley, V. (1986). On listening to what the children say. *Harvard Educational Review, 56*(2), 122-131.

Paley, V. (1995). *Kwanzaa and me: A teacher's story.* Cambridge, MA: Harvard University Press.

Peterson. P. L., Carpenter, T., & Fennema, E. (1989). Teachers' knowledge of students' knowledge in mathematics problem solving: Correlational and case analyses. *Journal of Educational Psychology, 81*, 558-569.

Pimm, D. (1987). *Speaking mathematically: Communication in mathematics classrooms.* New York: Routledge & Kegan Paul.

Ramsey, P. (1991). Social dynamics of early childhood classrooms. In *Making friends in school: Promoting peer relationships in early childhood* (pp. 43-70). New York: Teachers College Press.

Roth, K. (1992). *The role of writing in creating a science learning community* (Elementary Subjects Center Series No. 62). East Lansing: Michigan State University, Elementary Subjects Center.

Russell, S. J. & Rubin, A. (1994). *Landmarks in the hundreds.* In *Investigations in number, data, and space.* Palo Alto, CA: Dale Seymour Publications.

Scheffler, I. (1965). *Conditions of knowledge: An introduction to epistemology and education.* Chicago: University of Chicago Press.

Schifter, D., Russell, S. J., & Bastable, V. (in press). Teaching to the big ideas. In M. Solomon (Ed.), *Reinventing the classroom.* New York: Teachers College Press.

Shulman, L. (1986). Those who understand: Knowledge growth in teaching. *Educational Researcher, 15*(2), 4-14.

Schwille, J., Porter, A., Floden, R., Freeman, D., Knapp, L., Kuhs, T., & Schmidt, W. (1983). Teachers as policy brokers in the content of elementary school mathematics. In L. Shulman & G. Sykes (Eds.), *Handbook of teaching and policy* (pp. 370-391). New York: Longman.

Wilson, S. M. (1995). Not tension, but intention. A response to Wong's analysis of the researcher-teacher. *Educational Researcher, 24*( ),

Wilson, S. M. (in press). Mastodons, maps, and Michigan: Exploring uncharted territory while teaching elementary school social studies. *Elementary School Journal.*

Wilson, S. M., Shulman, L. S., & Richert, A. (1987). '150 different ways of knowing': Representations of knowledge in teaching. In J. Calderhead (Ed.), *Exploring teacher thinking* (pp. 104-124). Sussex: Holt, Rinehart, & Winston.

Wong, D. (1995). Challenges confronting the researcher/teacher: Conflicts of purpose and conduct. *Educational Researcher, 24*(3), 22-28.

Chapter 4: Teaching for Understanding[1]

PHYLLIS C. BLUMENFELD, RONALD W. MARX, HELEN PATRICK,
JOSEPH KRAJCIK, ELLIOT SOLOWAY
The University of Michigan

This chapter examines current views of teaching for understanding. First we provide background information, describing the influence of both theory and research on changes in approaches that have led to the recent stress on students as active constructors of their understanding. Then we summarize and compare a variety of programs that incorporate elements of construction and review issues that merit further investigation. Finally, we consider problems entailed in dissemination, especially difficulties teachers might encounter and describe promising attempts to foster their ability to teach for understanding.

WHAT IS TEACHING FOR UNDERSTANDING?

Over the last twenty years, approaches to teaching for understanding have evolved from models which stress information transmission to ones which emphasize student transformation of knowledge. The progression has been from emphasis on teacher directed, well structured, organized delivery of information to emphasis on the role of the individual learner in constructing understanding and the influence of the social environment on that construction. Below we present theoretical and empirical bases for different approaches to teaching, describe educational applications of these approaches, and indicate limitations derived from research and practice that have contributed to the current approaches to teaching for understanding.

Transmission Models

Early approaches.

Several approaches to teaching through the 1960s and 1970s were based on a transmission model of teaching and learning. The view was of a teacher as authority who disseminates knowledge largely through lectures and verbal exchanges; knowledge is an entity that exists and can be transferred to students;

B.J. Biddle et al. (eds.), International Handbook of Teachers and Teaching, 819-878
© 1997 Kluwer Academic Publishers, Printed in the Netherlands

learning is based on the accretion and retention of presented information and skills.

Behaviorism was one of the major theories contributing to this approach. Behavioral learning theory, focusing on behavior rather than mental operations, identified concepts like discrimination learning, generalization gradients, stimulus control, and fading as the operating mechanisms that controlled learning. Early instructional approaches based on behaviorism emphasized the need to structure curricula carefully so that prerequisite behaviors were shaped prior to students attempting to learn newer behaviors. As a result, it was critical that teachers carefully build up behavior through shaping responses, assuring that students gain mastery over early material before attempting to learn more advanced material. The underlying assumptions were that learning is hierarchical; it involves the aggregation of simple behaviors into more advanced behavior complexes and that high rates of success, shaped by positive reinforcement, are necessary for learning.

One of the most widely disseminated programs with comprehensive research bases was DISTAR (Engelmann & Brunner, 1984). DISTAR is an instructional program based on Bereiter and Engelmann's (1966) attempt to develop a structured reading program to overcome the presumed educational disadvantage that some children have, particularly those coming from what was called 'culturally deprived' backgrounds. The program was designed to lead children through highly structured, compressed language experiences to overcome their linguistic disadvantage.

Early applications of computer technologies for schools also were based on behavioral notions. One of the most thorough of these programs was developed by Suppes and Atkinson (Suppes, 1966), later to become the Computer Curriculum Corporation's drill-and-practice materials. This early work, which is still in very wide use, is based on a model of technology application called computer assisted instruction (CAI). The major strength of CAI to support drill-and-practice is in the ability of software applications to present material, collect achievement data on-line, and then select an appropriate subsequent item based on the student's individual learning history. In this way, CAI can embody many of the central attributes of direct instruction (e.g., carefully sequenced material, guided practice, immediate and specific feedback).

Research on learning and instruction also was influential in contributing to transmission models of instruction. Gagné (1985) emphasized task analysis where components of final performance were identified and sequenced. Teaching involved hierarchical task analysis of the desired performance via specification of prerequisite knowledge and skills. Understanding involved mastery of lower levels of the task-like skills, before moving on to higher levels like learning principles. Transfer was presumed to be enhanced when tasks had common prerequisites and component elements.

From the realm of practice, a spate of studies conducted in classrooms focused on teacher behavior and its relationship to student achievement. From the work of Heokter and Ahlbrand (1969) and the pioneering linguistic analysis of classrooms by Bellack, Kliebard, Hyman, and Smith (1966), researchers showed that a small number of common elements could be identified with classroom teaching. This research was conceptualized around four behavior complexes – structuring, soliciting, responding, and reacting – that could be found in classrooms in many different countries. These four complexes could be used to subsume a large number of teacher behaviors thought to be associated with effective instruction, that is, instruction that fostered understanding.

Ausubel (1960) proposed a much more cognitive model of learning and memory with implications for structuring information via advance organizers. These ideas went beyond previous notions of learning as accrual of facts and skills. The importance of teachers' organizing information for learners is also reflected in Rosenshine and Furst's (1973) model of explicit instruction. The model identified six behaviors associated with student achievement. One was review during which teachers were to check homework, review material, and determine where students were having difficulty. Second was presentation. Here teachers were to orient students to the material to be covered, often using instructional manoeuvres such as advance organizers (Ausubel, 1960) and stating the objectives for the lesson (Mager, 1975). Lesson presentations were structured and teacher controlled with characteristics similar to recitation (i.e., structure, solicit, respond, and react). Third was guided practice, keeping students active and on task, which provided opportunities for students to demonstrate understanding. Here teachers were to ask many questions and evaluate student responses to check for understanding. Fourth was providing feedback during guided practice. The feedback was highly descriptive, precise, and task focused, referring to correct and incorrect features of the response. Fifth was engaging students in independent practice, so that students would overlearn the material, responses would be quick and automatic, and attain a high correct response percentage. Finally, teachers were to conduct a review at the end of the lesson in order to consolidate learning and help students with recall and retrieval from memory.

Process-product research.

A large and influential body of work, labelled process-product research, stemmed from a model developed by Dunkin and Biddle (1974). This model offered a classification for factors involved in research on teaching: presage variables (teacher characteristics), context variables (pupil, school, and community properties), process variables (actual activities of classroom teaching), and product variables (the outcomes of teaching, including what students learn). One type of knowledge this model suggests concerns process-product relations between observable classroom events and student learning. In practice, most process-product studies compared observations of teacher behaviors, usually expressed in terms of frequencies, with standardized measures of student achievement. This tradition was advanced through the work of Gage and his colleagues (Clark, Gage, Marx, Peterson, Stayrook, & Winne, 1979; Gage, 1978), Berliner and the well-known Beginning Teacher Evaluation Study that examined how teachers use time (Berliner, 1979; Denham & Lieberman, 1980), Rosenshine and his colleagues (Rosenshine, 1986; Rosenshine & Stevens, 1986) who advanced what they called the functions of teaching, Brophy and Good (1986), who examined teacher behavior and student achievement, and Hunter (1982) who promoted inservice training approaches. Although similar in focusing on process-product relations, these investigations differed in their educational theory and in their view of psychological principles of learning.

An influential series of process-product studies used achievement test scores to describe differences in behaviors of teachers who consistently produced better student learning. Moreover, experimental studies based on these results produced achievement gains in students. Brophy and Good (1986) summarized some of the main findings of this approach. Teacher behaviors correlated with student achievement included providing opportunities to learn in terms of quantity and pacing of instruction, managing to maximize students' engaged time and actively teaching rather than leaving students to learn on their own. Such active teaching involved examination of how teachers delivered information in terms of structuring, sequencing, clarity, and enthusiasm. It also entailed frequent questioning of students to check for understanding, providing feedback about correctness, and helping those who answered incorrectly to reach the right answer by rephrasing, prompting and giving clues.

Missouri Math was one example of the process-product approach. Good, Grouws, and Ebmeier (1983) identified patterns that characterized teachers whose students differed on achievement test scores. They developed an instructional program based on the principles of active teaching identified in the process-product research. Teachers are instructed to provide clear illustrations of mathematics concepts and to use demonstrations, concrete examples and illustrations, models and diagrams, and manipulatives. Lessons:

a) begin with an *opening* which briefly reviews material previously learned and reviews homework;

b) move to a *development* phase, in which teachers focus on prerequisites and then develop meaning through illustrations, examples and highlighting relationships among ideas, emphasize application, assess student comprehension frequently, and repeat and elaborate as needed;

c) proceed to seatwork to provide uninterrupted successful practice (trying to have students achieve 80 per cent correct responses);

d) usually conclude with assigning homework to take about 15 minutes.

Additionally, the teacher should present weekly and monthly reviews. It is interesting to note that while the approach focuses on the teacher as transmitter of information, aspects of the recommended development phase foreshadow more recent approaches to teaching for understanding that stress meaning-making as the basis for understanding.

Limitations.

The central goal of the rapidly growing research program in transmission models of instruction and related areas through the 1960s and 1970s was to improve teaching and schooling through the development of a scientific basis for teaching. This overarching goal implies that both theoretical and practical criteria need to be attained to judge the success of the research effort. Criticisms of the research at the time focused on both types of criteria, and researchers raised several concerns which eventually led to the emergence of an alternative framework.

One limitation of the research was that it relied on standardized tests as measures of learning; typically such tests tap what has been called inert rather than usable knowledge. That is, they assess isolated knowledge and skills rather than the ability to use knowledge both in and out of school situations. Critics also argued that direct instruction seemed most effective in teaching factual content to low ability students (Peterson & Walberg, 1979) but that it was less successful for promoting problem solving or 'higher level' thinking. A second limitation was that while it was successful in distinguishing effective from ineffective teachers, it was less successful in characterizing exemplary instructors. A third related limitation was that it did not sufficiently address subject matter differences. A fourth was that it was not sensitive to the effect of context.

Most importantly, several researchers (e.g., Doyle, 1977; Winne & Marx, 1978) argued that transmission models could not adequately identify mechanisms that accounted for student learning. By the end of the 1970s, theoretical and empirical work on learning had begun to move from primarily behavioral accounts to more cognitive frameworks. Theoretical objections to transmission models were derived from these newer, cognitive learning theories. For example, Winne and Marx (1978) argued that most, if not all, studies in the process-product tradition used mental constructs (e.g., 'remembering,' 'understanding,' 'analyzing') as the presumed mechanisms to account for how a teaching process (say for example, the teacher's use of higher order questions, or of wait time) lead to achievement. Yet the research methods and traditions did not provide convincing data that these mechanisms actually were in operation during the classroom learning activity.

Additional arguments attacked time-on-task research arguing that mere time cannot account for important learning; what is essential is how the learner uses the time to think (Peterson, 1979). For example, Salomon (1983) showed that children's learning from media could be at least partially accounted for by what he called the 'amount of invested mental effort.' It was not merely the time these children spent learning from media such as television that counted, but learners' perceptions of how they needed to think and their engagement of these mental operations that were key. Finally, others showed that students developed their own understandings and misconceptions of phenomena, which differed considerably from what they had been taught in school, were resistant to change, and influenced subsequent learning (e.g., Confrey, 1990).

These objections (among many others; see, for example, Weinstein & Mayer, 1986) gave rise to a new research on learning and new approaches to teaching for understanding. As described in the next section, these approaches emphasized the role of the student in transforming information presented by the teacher as the route to understanding.

Transformation Models

In contrast to transmission models which focus on the teacher, the focus of transformation models is on the *cognitive* processes that are engaged by students as they learn. These processes are important because they *mediate* between the instructional events organized by teachers and the ultimate learning that students achieve. In a sense, learning occurs not just because of what the teacher does in actively presenting information in terms of providing examples, drawing relationships, and illustrating applications, but because of the cognitive processes that the learner uses. From the point of view of scholars concerned with research on teaching and classrooms, the significant advance lay in the renewed centrality of the student in theories of classroom learning (see Prawat, 1989a). The term constructivism has been broadly applied to these approaches, in the sense that they all presume that students actively 'construct' their knowledge (Good & Brophy, 1994; Phillips, 1995).

Transformation models are still in the process of evolving. Early incarnations stemmed from information processing theory; more recently, ideas from linguistics, anthropology, and sociology have been influential. As a result, there are some important differences in how 'constructivists' view learning and the implications of those views for teaching. More specifically, some approaches accentuate individual construction, whereas others accentuate social construction. However, to facilitate presentation, descriptions of these transformation models are divided below into earlier and more recent formulations. It is important to note that instructional programs based on these ideas, reviewed in subsequent sections, often incorporate elements of both approaches.

Early Formulations: Information Processing and Individual Construction

Foundations.

A major impetus for the transformation model came from cognitive studies based on information processing. The emergence of information processing models of thinking, derived from earlier cognitive theories of learning and memory (e.g., Ausubel, 1960; Bartlett, 1932) and the growing use of computer architecture as the metaphor for human thinking (Newell & Simon, 1972). Collectively these provided a robust and generative theoretical account for how students learn in classrooms. Information processing provided a model that could generate hypotheses about how students learn meaningful and complex material. Consequently, information processing rapidly became the psychological foundation for a range of promising research.

Basically, information processing research examines how information is encoded or represented in memory, the processes that act on and transform information for purposes of encoding, and aspects of memory functioning that influence and constrain how information is encoded and retrieved. Knowledge is organized and stored in memory in different representational forms, called schemas. It can be stored as isolated disconnected pieces of information. Such knowledge, like that from memorization of discrete facts, is considered isolated or inert. Alternatively, knowledge can be organized into large, interconnected networks, with conceptual linkages among pieces. An interconnected knowledge network allows one to draw on and to use knowledge in more flexible ways (Hiebert & Carpenter, 1992).

In fact, research employing information processing psychology suggested that prior knowledge and its organization played a considerable role in learning new material. It also indicated that experts and novices differ both in the amount and organization of knowledge they have and in what they choose to represent. Examination of the performance of experts in a range of fields from physicists to chess players showed that expertise could be accounted for at least partially by the way these people thought about their work. For instance, in physics, novices represent and link pieces of domain knowledge based on surface level features whereas experts organize in terms of deeper level features. Novices often group problems in terms of objects involved, such as inclined planes or pulleys; experts group problems in terms of the physical principles embodied. These differences in representation are linked to differences in experts' and novices' ability to reason about and solve problems. Similarly, in contrast to novices, master chess players do not necessarily have phenomenal memories for every possible move; instead, they have a way of organizing what they know about chess and the possible configurations of pieces on a chess board that enables them to quickly, and seemingly effortlessly, perceive possibilities for the game (de Groot, 1965).

In addition, numerous studies (Weinstein & Mayer, 1986) demonstrated the effectiveness of memory, elaboration, and organizational strategy use for learning. A considerable number of investigations of specific strategies pointed to the benefits of, for example, rehearsal and underlining as a memory aid. Similarly, summarization and elaboration of ideas are effective ways to make new ideas easier to remember, to relate to prior knowledge and to generate interconnected networks. Organization of content via concept maps also facilitates making connections thereby enhancing understanding. Additional research on the role of metacognitive strategies, including planning, monitoring understanding or progress, and evaluating outcomes, showed that learners were more successful when they were able to use systematic approaches to help them think about their thinking. Studies contrasting successful and less successful readers pointed to the importance of strategy use in comprehension (Cross & Paris, 1988). This work highlighted the importance of types of strategic knowledge, including declarative knowledge about what strategies to use, procedural knowledge about how to use them, and conditional knowledge about when to use them.

Applications.

One application of information processing theory to analyses of classroom teaching and learning included an examination of the nature of classroom tasks as ways of influencing student learning. In contrast to task analysis schemes which broke down performance into hierarchies of knowledge types and skills, information processing researchers modelled the presumed cognitive operations that underlay complex thinking in order to create a theoretical map of the cognitive demands of performance. Among classroom researchers, Doyle's (1983) model was one of the most influential. Doyle argued that there were four types of classroom learning tasks based on the primary types of cognitive operations that they involved. These tasks are memory (recognize or reproduce information), routine procedure (apply a known solution strategy to generate an answer), comprehension (transform information to construct meaning), and opinion (state a preference); classroom activities based on the latter two task types are more likely to lead to the development of student understanding. Other researchers (Blumenfeld, Mergendoller, & Swarthout, 1987; Brophy & Alleman, 1991; Winne & Marx, 1989) also argued that an understanding of the cognitive demands of classroom tasks would help teachers create learning activities that could more effectively lead to students achieving higher levels of understanding.

Several developers created specific 'strategy instruction' approaches to enhance teaching for understanding in classrooms. As in transmission model applications, some of these were general approaches to classroom teaching, some focused on specific subject areas, and some were based on technological applications. In general, a majority of these programs attempted to teach students how to use specific cognitive strategies to learn or how to think about and process information in a manner similar to experts in a domain. In most cases, rather than be the primary dispensers of knowledge, teachers were to help students develop knowledge by enhancing their capacities to become deliberate and thoughtful learners (Winne & Marx, 1978).

One of the more influential approaches to general strategy instruction was Bransford's (Bransford & Stein, 1984) *Ideal Problem Solver*. In this program, based on a substantial body of theory and research on human problem solving that had been stimulated by information processing psychology, Bransford and Stein identified five central processes to teach students to use to help improve their problem solving skills. These process are: identify the problem, define and represent the problem, explore possible strategies, act on the strategies, and look back and evaluate the effects of the strategies. These strategies, based as they were on laboratory and applied research over a range of subjects, were presumed to provide students with a powerful and widely applicable set of tools to help them learn.

Another very influential approach to teaching general strategies was based on emerging process theories of intelligence, as opposed to earlier trait-factor theories. The newer process theories emphasized how intelligence operated, thus portraying intelligence more as a constellation of skills that could be learned, rather than a biologically determined entity. The most influential of these theories were advanced by Gardner (1983) in his theory of multiple intelligences and by Sternberg (1985) in his triarchic theory of intelligence. These two scholars propose somewhat different theories of ability and how those abilities lead to learning in school settings. However, they share the point of view that there is a substantial range of talents that enable people to learn in different contexts, and that these talents can be enhanced considerably by well developed interventions.

Gardner and Sternberg combined their research and development efforts in an attempt to demonstrate such an intervention through their program called Practical Intelligence for Schools, or PIFS (Gardner, Krechevsky, Sternberg, & Okagaki, 1994). They developed curriculum units that were both independent of particular subject matter and infused in subject areas such as reading and social studies. Research results show that children who worked in PIFS class-rooms gained on a number of measures designed to be sensitive to the PIFS intervention. However, Gardner et al. (1994) worry about the impact of PIFS on more conventional and universal measures of school learning (e.g., classroom tests, homework, and papers), the difficulty of reliably adopting PIFS in a range of classrooms (they have found some teachers and classrooms to be more suc-cessful than others), and pushing PIFS beyond conventional expectations of schools (i.e., enhancing teaching for understanding rather than transmission of knowledge).

A number of researchers developed programs specifically to help students who had difficulties learning to read (Duffy & Roehler, 1987a, 1987b; Paris, Cross, & Lipson, 1984; Pressley, Johnson, Symons, McGoldrick, & Kurita, 1989). Although all of these programs have enjoyed some success, perhaps the foremost among these strategy instruction approaches to reading was the pro-gram called reciprocal teaching developed by Palincsar and Brown (1984). Pal-incsar and Brown's analysis of failure to learn to read focused on six cognitive processes that are effectively used by competent readers who:

a)   understand the need to construct meaning from reading,
b)   activate background information while reading,
c)   allocate cognitive resources,
d)   evaluate their understanding,
e)   draw and test inferences, and
f)   monitor all of these processes to insure comprehension.

In order to help students engage in these processes, Palincsar and Brown devel-oped a set of strategies – summarizing, questioning, clarifying, and predicting – to be used in small group settings. With the teacher providing a model of ex-pert performance, all of the children in a group take turns as leader, while the entire group provides encouragement and supportive critique.

As with transmission models of classroom learning, the cognitive approach was applied to technology. The primary vehicle for this application was the growing field of artificial intelligence (AI). The promise of artificial intelli-gence lay in the claims made by computer scientists that human thinking could be modelled by sophisticated computer software applications. If computers could be made to think like humans, particularly expert humans, then they could be used to support novices as they learned how to think like experts. What was needed was to simulate an expert's thought in the software through a set of pro-duction rules ('if X is the case, then perform Y') that operated on a knowledge base, which was everything that the expert knew relevant to a domain of per-formance. Two well known intelligent computer assisted instruction programs were 'Act' and 'geometry tutor.'

In the subject areas this approach led to focusing on key ideas, representing those ideas in multiple ways and explicitly on having students relate new knowledge to prior knowledge. It replaced the prior hierarchical approach to teaching, such as those of Gagné, which separated cognitive levels of learning and addressed them in sequential order (Hiebert & Carpenter, 1992). In math, programs were designed to familiarize teachers with how young children naturally understand addition and subtraction and to help teachers develop cognitively guided instruction programs (Fennema, Carpenter, & Peterson, 1989).

Because student knowledge networks serve as a filter for how they process new information, several programs were designed to address student misconceptions and to promote conceptual change (Confrey, 1990). The rationale was that if misconceptions persist they distort subsequent learning. In science, work by Anderson and Roth (1989) and Driver and Oldham (1986) represent this approach. Drawing on Piagetian ideas of accommodation and information processing ideas of schema, conceptual change teaching seeks to alter students' frameworks for understanding phenomena. Four conditions of conceptual change teaching are that learners:

a) must be dissatisfied with current understandings or explanations of a phenomena,
b) must be made aware of and understand alternative explanations,
c) must see the new conception as plausible in terms of applicability and fit with other understandings, and
d) must view the new concept as fruitful in terms of explanatory power (Posner, Strike, Hewson, & Gertzog, 1982).

Students in these approaches were encouraged to verbalize their ideas and thought process as a way for teachers to diagnose learning.

Limitations.

The information processing model, with its emphasis on strategy instruction, engendered criticism from several fronts. One was that there was little evidence that explicitly teaching learners how to use learning strategies resulted in the kind of transfer that was anticipated. Brown (1992, 1995) voiced concern that despite the fact that children were taught and could use strategies, they often did not call upon them under appropriate circumstances. One explanation was that the strategies were taught in a decontexualized fashion. In a similar fashion, Salomon and Perkins (1989) argued that two models of transfer have been used by researchers in this field. In high road transfer, students are taught the learning strategy and then are expected to transfer its use to new settings or new content.

The assumption is that once learners know how to use a strategy, they will use it when it is applicable. In low road transfer, the strategy is embedded in a curriculum and taught as a way to learn that particular information. According to the authors, students taught through high road programs failed to transfer the use of the strategy to new situations, while students taught through low road programs failed to notice that the strategy could be used in other situations – they did not transfer either. Thus, the idea was to combine both; have students practice strategies in situations in which they are naturally encountered, but also be cognizant of principles behind strategy use to facilitate transfer.

Further problems raised by critics relate to the difficulties of actually carrying out strategy instruction in classrooms. Duffy (1993) showed how teachers concentrated on the specifics of the strategy rather than on its purposes. As a result, students learn the steps of the strategy but have little understanding of what the strategy is designed to achieve. Pressley et al. (1992) attempted to overcome this problem by studying the kinds of learning strategies that teachers found to be acceptable and useful for classroom work.

In addition, concerns were raised about the fact that often the strategies were generic; that is, they did not deal with subject matter disciplines. Some scholars argue that different disciplines require different teaching and learning strategies (e.g., Shulman, 1987). Philosophers claim that there are particular epistemologies that underlie the formal disciplines and that the school curriculum should include these different disciplines because students ought to be familiar with the epistemologies. One could infer from this argument that different epistemologies embody different learning strategies. From classroom research, Stodolsky (1988) has shown that in elementary school classrooms, teachers use quite different activity structures for different subject matters (e.g., much more whole group instruction and individual seatwork in math, far more small group work in social studies). Students working in these different settings, with access to quite different resources and tools, are likely to use different strategies for learning.

Finally, researchers became more sensitive to the social and situational influences on learning. While they continued to acknowledge that learners actively construct their understanding, they stressed the need to consider that such constructions were a function of social interaction and the settings in which such construction took place. Bruer (1995) writes:

> The significance of sociocultural context, communities and discourse for cognition and learning ... emerged in part because researchers have attempted to apply cognitive science to authentic classroom tasks rather than just artificial laboratory tasks ... focused on individual problem solvers ... When researchers brought ideas about domain specific

trajectories, active learning, and metacognition to the classroom they realized that other factors influence learning ... (p. 285)

Recent Formulations: Social Constructivism

Social influences on learning underlie newer transformation approaches to teaching. The impetus for change from an individual focus came from the shortcomings described above. A related impetus stemmed from an influential presidential address by Lauren Resnick to the American Educational Research Association. In considering the problem of helping learners develop robust knowledge, Resnick (1987) observed that, in contrast to in school learning, real world learning is characterized by shared cognition, social distribution of knowledge and skill, use of tools to enhance capacities and share effort, and contextualized use of objects and events to give meaning to situations. Thus she argued against the detached, generalized notion of learning practiced in school. Another paper by Brown, Collins, and Duguid (1989) reinforced these recommendations. Based on studies of everyday learning and cognition, they argued that 'knowledge is ... in part a product of the activity, context, and culture in which it is developed and used' (p. 32). Thus knowledge is contextualized and cannot be easily separated from the situation in which it develops. Consequently, knowing and doing are not separate; knowledge is not an abstract phenomena that readily can be transferred from how it is learned in the classroom for use in other situations.

Advances in learning theory came from the popularization in North America of theories of learning from the Soviet Union that reflected a disillusionment with the individualistic nature of psychology that had gained ascendance in the United States. In particular, Vygotsky's work on learning and development in social settings became influential through American translators like Wertsch (1985, 1991), with further elaboration by scholars such as Newman, Griffin, and Cole (1989) and Tharp and Gallimore (1988). This approach highlights the role of the individual in interpreting the world but also stresses the importance of the social milieu in influencing these interpretations. In addition, proponents claim that knowledge itself is a reflection of the social setting and social interactions; knowledge is interpretation, rather than something that is objective and fixed.

Foundations.

The fundamental idea in social constructivism lies in its emphasis on discourse, community, and context. Stress is given to the centrality of language and other symbol systems to learning. In fact, it is hard to overemphasize the importance of language and other symbol systems to constructivist thought.

Language, of course, does not exist without a community. While the intrapsychic functions of language enable the learner to construct understanding, the interpersonal functions allow the learner to engage in discourse. Hence, the learner becomes a member of a discourse community. The movement between the interpersonal and intrapsychic uses of language constitute one of the essential sites of learning. Learners are introduced into the language community by more competent others. Learners appropriate the symbolic forms of others and the functionality of those forms through language.

Communities exist in cultures, and cultures have developed both common and unique approaches to addressing problems of life. These approaches can be considered tools – cultural tools – that have an astounding range of functionalities. Learners appropriate many cultural tools, ranging from the meanings of words, to basic cultural myths (e.g., a country's founding myths, like the Revolutionary War in the United States or the Magna Carta in England), to ways identifying and solving problems, and even to the epistemologies of formal disciplines. Education involves helping learners appropriate the powerful cultural tools of discourse communities such as the key ideas and intellectual frameworks underlying the subject matter. That is, by entering into the discourse of a particular field like math, science, or history, students learn ways of knowing in the discipline, what counts as evidence, and how ideas are validated and communicated.

A basic idea that follows from the community of discourse concept is that the assistance of more competent others can be used to help learners accomplish more difficult tasks than they otherwise are capable of completing on their own. There is a hypothetical space between assisted and unassisted performance that Vygotsky (1978) identified as the zone of proximal development (known in constructivist circles as the ZPD). By identifying a learner's ZPD, a teacher can locate the psychological space in which assistance can help to propel the learner to higher levels of understanding. Because learners construct their understanding, the assistance provided in the ZPD has become known (to expand the construction metaphor) as scaffolding. In the educational applications of constructivism, the ideas of discourse community, the zone of proximal development, and scaffolding occupy preeminent roles.

It is important to note that what is now called constructivism spans a variety of different perspectives that give primacy to individual versus social influences on learning (Ernest, 1995; Phillips, 1995). One major source of difference is in the views of the nature of knowledge. Ernest indicates that earlier notions of active learning and construction, based on information processing, often use the computer as a metaphor for mind. Information processing approaches stress the individual nature of learning, highlighting the role of routines, procedures, and data retrieval from memory. At the basic level, for information processing theorists, knowledge preexists; it is received by the learner who must acquire, store, and retrieve it. What has been called trivial constructivism is close to information processing. It recognizes that the individual constructs knowledge rather than simply receiving it passively and acknowledges that these constructions may differ. Yet proponents remain concerned. That is, trivial constructivism assumes that such truths exist.

In contrast, more socially oriented constructivist approaches 'problematize' knowledge. One view, called radical constructivism, rejects the notion of objective knowledge. It does assume that knowledge develops as individuals engage in dialogue with others. Individuals check the fit between their understanding and their experiences with the world; those understandings that are incongruous are accommodated and give way to others that fit better with experience. However, a one-for-one match between what the individual understands and the world is not possible.

Another major source of difference is that sociocultural theorists typically stress the homogeneity of members of established communities and downplay qualitative differences in individual thinking; cognitive constructivists tend to stress heterogeneity of thought that result from active interpretation by individuals as they participate in prevailing social and cultural processes. Cobb (1994) characterizes the debate as being about the individual versus the social nature of knowledge construction. It is a 'dispute about whether the mind is located in the head or in the individual-in-social action, and whether ... learning is primarily a process of active cognitive reorganization or a process of enculturation into a community of practice ...' (p. 13)

Applications.

While there are strong philosophical differences among the branches of constructivism, there is some agreement that the field should strive for 'a pragmatic convergence' of the positions when discussing education (Cobb, 1994; Driver, Asoko, Leach, Mortimer, & Scott, 1994). What is noteworthy about recent constructivist approaches as compared with older transmission models and early transformation models is that there are no prescriptions for instruction. That is, newer constructivist-based approaches are strongly contextualized. Since local conditions are so important, all one can expect from the theory is a set of principles to help guide teachers as they create practices that are congruent with constructivist theory (Cobb, 1994; Driver et al., 1994; Ernest, 1995). Thus there are families of instructional enactments that are consistent with constructivism; in contrast, previous approaches produced programs for dissemination and implementation that specified teacher behaviors, classroom curriculum, and desired student outcomes. The differences are not subtle and give rise to quite different approaches to educational change (Marx, Freeman, Krajcik, & Blumenfeld, in press).

As with earlier transformation approaches, the newer socially oriented ones assign primary importance to the way in which learners attempt to make sense of what they are learning rather than to the way in which they receive information. Integrated and usable knowledge develops when learners create multiple representations of ideas and are engaged in activities that require them to use this knowledge. Moreover designers continue to assert that the content presented should reflect depth not breadth and emphasize ideas and themes central to the discipline (Tharp & Gallimore, 1988). However, their perspective on tasks, assessment, tools, social organization, and pedagogy differs from earlier transformation approaches.

Authentic tasks are a core component. Because learning is situated in tasks and contexts, the nature of the tasks students undertake to learn important subject matter concepts should have meaning beyond the context of school. The Cognition and Technology Group at Vanderbilt (1990) describes anchored instruction where information is contextualized within rich video-based presentations. Many instructional programs emphasize engaging students in projects, where they pursue investigations in the course of which they find answers to questions, or solve problems as a means to learning concepts and understanding the discipline (Krajcik, Blumenfeld, Marx, & Soloway, 1994). The investigations need to connect to students' prior understandings and to real world situations. They need to be worthwhile so that, in the process of pursuing questions or solving problems, students master important subject matter concepts. In addition, learners need to encounter problems where they must draw on knowledge in a variety of ways in order to best understand it. Constructivism, then, deals with the enduring problem of transfer by helping learners develop multiple representations of concepts while pursuing solutions to authentic problems, thereby increasing the chances that mental representations can apply to different problems.

Artifacts and assessment are also crucial. Students should produce artifacts that allow them to learn concepts, to apply information, and to represent conceptual knowledge and knowledge of the disciplines in a variety of ways. These artifacts can take different forms, such as multimedia reports, presentations, and demonstrations (Newmann, 1993). Assessment is closely tied to artifact development. Rather than rely on standardized tests, which promote fragmented and decontextualized knowledge, the use of alternative assessments is encouraged (Perkins, 1992; Wiggins, 1993). For instance, Perkins calls for the use of 'understanding performances' where students engage in a variety of relevant demonstrations of thoughtfulness surrounding the content with which they are dealing. The thoughtfulness may involve offering explanations, articulating rich relational knowledge, and revising and extending explanations. Similarly, Newmann and Archibald (1992) suggest that assessments should focus on students exhibiting mastery of the discipline, integrating prior knowledge with new knowledge, and should have some value beyond classroom evaluation.

Tool use is another core element of recent constructivist approaches to classroom learning. Recent interest has centred on the uses of computers and associated technologies, such as interactive videodiscs, telecommunications, and microcomputer based laboratories (Perkins, Schwartz, West, & Wiske, 1995). Technology can help learners solve complex and ambiguous problems by providing access to information and opportunities to collaborate, investigate, and create artifacts (Salomon, Perkins, & Globerson, 1991). Such tools can extend and amplify learners' thinking. Perkins and Unger (1994) argue that computers reduce cognitive load for students, moving some routine tasks like repeated calculations or storing large amounts of data from students to computer. Technology can also help clarify the problem space, eliminating some complexities of situations so students can concentrate on the most salient aspects of a problem. For example, by creating models on computers, learners can achieve sophisticated understanding about complex systems such as stream ecology or space travel. With their ability to compress time, computers reveal complex relationships among variables and the immediate implications of changes in the values of variables. Computers can also provide useful analogies that help students focus on the essential attribute of concepts, rather than on their superficial characteristics.

Collaboration and conversation are important elements of constructivist approaches. Collaboration involves building shared understandings. According to Webb and Palincsar (1996), 'collaboration is convergence – the construction of shared meaning for conversations, concepts, experiences.' In as much as learning is social in nature, learners' understanding of ideas and of the nature of the discipline develops as they engage in discourse with and collaborate with others. These others can be located in the classroom, in the school, in the community, or in distant locations. Through capitalizing on the expertise distributed across learners and other experts, learners can accomplish more sophisticated performance and appropriate for their own thinking the capabilities of others. As students engage in conversation they can draw on others' expertise, appropriate the knowledge of others, reflect on their own ideas, and internalize modes of knowledge and thinking represented and practiced in the community of the discipline (Bruer, 1995). For instance, each school subject has a special vocabulary, a body of knowledge, and rules for methods of gathering evidence and evaluating results that novices need to acquire. Collaboration on accomplishing authentic tasks with others who have mastered these conventions helps learners become part of these discourse communities.

Collaboration builds on, but should not be confused with, cooperative learning (Bossert, 1988-89; Slavin, 1990). It differs with respect to the degree of structure, the nature of the group, and the purpose of working with others. Cooperative learning is often highly structured; students are given specific roles, tasks, and procedures; collaboration is loosely structured with roles and direction and interactions largely negotiated among and with students. In addition, cooperative learning focuses on small groups within the classroom, whereas collaboration envisions a wider sphere of communities of learners that extends beyond the classroom walls. Collaboration can include students and teachers within a classroom as well as students, teachers, community members or experts in other locations. While cooperative learning typically highlights the reproduction of knowledge – students generally share answers and explanations in order to learn predetermined concepts and procedures – collaboration can encompass both the reproduction and production of knowledge.

Several roles for the instructor are posed in these formulations. The teacher serves as a guide, facilitator, and also as a learner along with students. Collins, Brown, and Newman (1989) use the analogy of a cognitive apprenticeship for the teaching learning situation. Like a master craftsman, the teacher should scaffold instruction by breaking down tasks, use modelling and coaching to teach strategies for thinking, provide feedback, and gradually release responsibility to the learner. Similarly, Driver et al. (1994) suggests that the role of the teacher is to acquaint learners with new ideas or cultural tools and to support and guide students as they make sense of these. The diaologic process is a critical feature. As class discourse unfolds, the teacher listens and interprets the ways in which learners understand instructional activities and ideas to guide further action. In this manner, the teacher helps students understand concepts and introduces them to the subject matter discipline. Driver et al. (1994), writing about science education, used the metaphor of a tour guide in which the teacher mediates between the child's every day world and the world of science. The idea is to foster critical perspectives on knowledge and scientific culture including the purposes of scientific knowledge, its limitations, and the basis on which evidence is gathered and claims are made.

Overall, as Table 1 illustrates, the newer transformation approaches involve considerable change from previous transmission approaches to instruction. As Schuell (1996) comments, conceptions of the teacher's role have changed from one in which

> an authority disseminates knowledge to one in which the teacher creates and orchestrates complex learning environments, engaging students in appropriate instructional activities so that the students can construct their own understanding of the material being studied, and working with students as partners in the learning process. (p. 35)

Conceptions of the learner have changed from individuals who receive and memorize information and practice skills to individuals who actively process information and construct understanding by relating it to what they already know. Conceptions of the role of verbalization have changed from teachers presenting information and individuals answering questions and thinking aloud so teachers can diagnose learning, to group collaboration and discourse as a means for enhancing learning and introducing students into disciplinary ways of knowing. Conceptions of the purpose of activities or tasks have changed from teachers presenting carefully sequenced discrete experiences that build to expected performances, to creating opportunities for experiencing authentic problems that students might encounter outside of school and mirror those encountered by experts in the field. Conceptions of tools, especially computers, have changed from serving as sources of drill and practice or of expert tutoring, to serving as sources for gaining access to and representing information, facilitating communication and collaboration, and enhancing thought. Finally, conceptions of evaluation have changed from teachers using tests and standardized assessments to tap inert knowledge of isolated facts and skills, to using alternative assessments that emphasize robust or usable knowledge based on understanding of core ideas and ways of knowing in a discipline.

	Now	**Then**
Learning	Active construction	Information accretion
	Connections	Hierarchies
	Situated	Decontextualized
Instruction	Content representation	Content delivery
	Transformation	Transmission
	Scaffolded	Direct
Curriculum	Interwoven matrix	Sequenced
	Malleable	Fixed
Tasks	Authentic	Isolated
	Sets of representations	Sequenced materials
	Artifacts	Worksheets
Social Mediation	Communities of learners	Individual
	Collaboration	Competition
	Discourse	Recitation

Table 1: A Table of Changes

	Now	Then
Tools	Interactive, integrated computer-based	Pencil, paper
	High-bandwidth telcom	Low-bandwidth telcom
Assessment	Performance-based	Achievement scores
	Individual portfolios	Standardized tests

Table 1: A Table of Changes

EXAMPLE PROGRAMS BASED ON CONSTRUCTIVIST THEORY

A number of programs currently are being implemented that attempt to put individual and social constructivist ideas into practice. The programs differ in their point of departure and in their degree of emphasis on and inclusion of the elements of constructivist approaches and in the extensiveness of the intervention. Most combine features of cognitive construction with features of social constructivism. Some are very specific in the concepts and topics they address; others are more general and provide an overall approach that can be applied to different topics. All seek to ultimately change student learning and understanding, but they choose different elements or combinations as the primary vehicle for affecting change.

Below we present summaries of six programs in science designed to teach for understanding. We limited the selection to one subject area to allow for easier comparison among the approaches and because there has been substantial program development in science. Brief descriptions are included of the content and nature of problems posed (how programs attempt to make learning authentic), the role of collaboration, the use of technological tools, the type of artifacts students create, and how learning is assessed. The subsequent section presents comparisons among the programs and raises issues for research, for dissemination, and for teacher professional development.

Computer as Learning Partner

The Computer as Learning Partner (CLP), developed by Linn and her colleagues (Foley, 1995; Linn, 1992, in press; Linn, Songer, Lewis, & Stern, 1993) provides a semester-long integrated curriculum for teaching middle school students about heat, light, and sound. The CLP curriculum, which emphasizes conceptual change, begins with students' naive explanatory heuristics and concepts, and guides the students through a series of predefined experiments and writing exercises that are designed to challenge students' previous beliefs.

The program is premised on the argument that instruction needs to begin with models of science which students can understand. The goal is to promote conceptual change. The work began when Linn found that after a 13 week unit students did not understand thermodynamics when it was presented in terms of kinetic theory. In contrast, CLP addresses principles of thermodynamics from a more pragmatic and accessible heat-flow model instead of the more abstract and microscopic molecular-kinetic theory. Accompanying specially developed software, The Electronic Laboratory Notebook (E-LabBook), is designed to help students collect, display, and explain findings. It contains a series of prompts that ask students to explain and relate their findings to their own experiences in order to help students construct new and more adequate scientific models. Students get considerable practice in applying the scientific principles they formulate to real-life situations. For instance, they are asked 'Why does a Styrofoam cooler keep drinks cold?'

CLP is based on laboratory activities which students engage in pairs at computers connected to a network. The curriculum is contained within a computerized laboratory book and includes a relatively structured and sequenced series of laboratory activities that students engage in to investigate principles of heat energy. An activity checklist is included so that students can take some responsibility for their progress. Many of the activities involve experiments that students either conduct in real-time with temperature probes that are attached directly to the computer or via computer simulations. For example, to investigate the insulation properties of different substances, students may measure the change in temperature of hot and cold substances like baked potatoes, hot chocolate, or cold soft drink cans when wrapped in different materials. They can manipulate variables, such as covering the drinks or the potatoes with aluminium foil or wool, and then compare different plots of temperature curves for each experiment.

The software tool students use, the E-LabBook, is specially designed to collect, graphically represent, and store data from students' experiments. It includes word processing software for students to write notes about their findings and illustrate how their results reflect scientific principles. Prompts are designed to help students recognize disparities between their prior predictions or explanations and the results of experiments, and to encourage them to reconcile those disparities with more correct scientific explanations. Notes are stored in a database so that students can refer to them throughout the unit to identify patterns in the data or share information with each other.

The procedure for conducting experiments begins with students responding to a prompt to fill in a 'prediction note' in the E-LabBook (e.g., 'Our predictions are that the aluminium will work best'). Students predict the shape of the graph of temperature change by selecting from differently shaped curves presented on the screen. The student pairs then conduct the experiment, either real or simulated, and the E-LabBook software automatically graphs the results, which are plotted on the same grid as their predicted curve to facilitate comparison. Students write 'reflection notes,' in which they compare their predictions with outcomes and reconcile any differences between them.

The students' notes are scaffolded by prompts in the software entered by the teacher to fit the situation. Prompts, which mainly take the form of questions or sentence openers, are designed to highlight salient points. They can draw attention to important features of the investigation such as directing students to consider particular shapes of data curves. Examples of prompts are 'My predictions were the same as the outcome in the following ways ... The reason for this is ...', and 'My predictions were different from the outcome in the following ways ...The reason for this is ...'

After students have conducted a number of related experiments they look for patterns between the experiments and create a synthesis of their findings by writing a 'pattern note' in the E-LabBook. Again the software directs students' attention through prompts and directions. An example is 'Describe the energy change, transmission, and detection patterns that show up in this lab.' Students can access previous graphs from the database and superimpose them to assist in visually identifying patterns. They also can refer to these pattern notes when making predictions in subsequent experiments.

Each activity is also linked to at least one 'principle' and one 'prototype,' both of which are presented in the E-LabBook. Prototypes present familiar situations that embody more abstract scientific principles and encourage students to make connections between their prior knowledge and new learning. An example of a prototype for thinking about whether metals are conductors or insulators is a picture of a girl trying to decide whether a metal stick or a wooden stick would be best for roasting marshmallows. Prompts associated with the prototype guide students in realizing that metals are conductors by requiring them to apply results of previous experiments in which metals such as soft drink cans and aluminium foil were used.

These prototypes are designed as scaffolds; they encourage students to formulate principles – statements that summarize the main idea of the laboratory activity. Principles are presented on screen as incomplete sentences with options of phrases that students can assemble into the correct sentence when they understand the underlying scientific principle. An example of a conductivity principle is 'A good conductor allows heat energy to flow faster than a poor conductor.' The computer monitors whether students assemble the principles correctly, provides feedback, and instructs them to seek help from the teacher if they have persistent difficulty in correctly constructing a principle.

In order to foster better interaction and collaboration between student pairs, the software features an 'agreement bar' where students indicate the extent to which they agree with what has been written in response to prompts like those calling for predictions or for synthesis. The teacher also frequently rotates the student pairings and roles, such as using the keyboard, so that all students have opportunities to participate in all aspects of the activities. Students also interact, via e-mail, with graduate student coaches who are responsible for approximately 15 students. In addition to responding to student questions, they read and comment on writing and also pose questions to stimulate further reflection. There also is a common database of notes students can consult. Pairs can sometimes select from different experiments or choose different variables to manipulate. Their description of results of the experiment can be used by others as an additional source of information in answering questions.

The artifacts that students produce are their experimental notes, completed worksheets, and reports with graphs. Students also compile portfolios of their work.

Learning Through Collaborative Visualization (CoVis)

Pea and his colleagues (e.g., Edelson, in press; Edelson & O'Neill, 1994; Gordin & Pea, 1995; Gordin, Polman, & Pea, 1994; Pea & Gomez, 1992) have developed Learning Through Collaborative Visualization (CoVis) for use with high school earth science and environmental science classes. CoVis emphasizes collaboration and investigation. Students pose questions about weather and climate such as 'What were the weather conditions like that led to the disastrous wild fires in the Los Angeles area in 1993?', 'Why is the altitude lower at the poles than near the equator?', and 'What is the impact of volcanoes on weather?' They then engage in research projects to answer the questions using National Meteorological Center (NMC) data. Students might work on these projects individually or in small groups, communicating with others in the classroom and in other schools and settings. Thus they use real data and tools that mirror ones used by scientists. The program does not have a fixed structure or curriculum; it leaves all decisions about the content and the project specifications (e.g., topic, outcome, duration) to the individual classroom teachers. Consequently the degree of structure and direction varies across classrooms.

The software includes a notebook, visualizers, and telecommunications. Customized computer interfaces enable students to access the NMC data and employ visualization features similar to those used by atmospheric scientists. Students enter their project questions, note their hypotheses, develop plans for answering their questions and keep track of the process of their investigations in the Collaboratory Notebook, which is a networked multimedia database organized like a collection of scientists' notebooks that can store text, tables, graphics, videos, and animation. There are several types of notebooks including private journals, accessible only by the author, public discussion books, or shared books relating to a specific project. Each notebook is structured with pages labelled for specific purposes to enable students to enter questions, plans, conjectures, evidence, and commentary on their investigations.

The software includes three types of visualizers, the Weather Visualizer, the Climate Visualizer, and the Greenhouse Effect Visualizer. Each visualizer displays real numeric meteorological data on the computer screen symbolically, so that students can quickly interpret the data visually and observe patterns in series of data. For example, the Climate Visualizer displays temperature as colour, wind as vectors, and atmospheric pressure as contours. These data, accessed from the NMC, may come from satellite photos, weather maps, or university weather station reports. The visualizers also overlay maps onto the visual images to make students' interpretations easier. For example, in answering the question – 'How do volcanoes influence weather?' – students could access weather data that covers many years for all of the northern hemisphere. Using the Climate Visualizor they might create graphs of climatic features such as temperature and humidity, in periods before and after an eruption. They might note their interpretations in the Collaboratory Notebook or work with others directly in interpreting the data. Moreover, they can save text, graphics, and media for use in their presentations or reports.

Students are encouraged to collaborate with each other and with outside experts throughout their investigations. In fact, engaging in conversations is deemed a vital component of learning. A unique feature of CoVis is that students can work synchronously at different computers. This functionality, accomplished via remote screensharing and desktop video teleconferencing, makes it seem as if students were sharing the same computer. That is, they can see and talk to each other, and each person can control the screen. They can communicate with students in their class or in other locations over the network. They can also send questions through e-mail to other students, to their teacher, or to scientist mentors at participating universities or at the Exploratorium in San Francisco, and post general queries over the Internet. Students are also encouraged to read and comment on what other people have written in the Notebooks. The conversations are about an authentic scientific investigation so the students learn the language of the discipline, learn how to do research supported by software that scaffolds the inquiry process, and work with others within a realistic context.

To summarize their findings, students may also compile multimedia reports, graphics, video, audio, and text, and present their findings to others. In addition, the notebook contents are included as part of the projects.

Computer Supported Intentional Learning Environment (CSILE)

The Computer Supported Intentional Learning Environment (CSILE), developed by Scardamalia and Bereiter (e.g., 1991, Scardamalia, Bereiter, & Lamon, 1994), promotes student understanding of subject matter through electronic conversations centred on building a common database. CSILE has been used predominantly with 5th and 6th graders to support student investigations of topics such as endangered species, fossil fuels, evolution, and human biology, although it has been used with other subject matter areas and other grade levels.

At the beginning of the year CSILE is empty; it is populated by students' contributions of text and graphical notes throughout the year. Eight computers are available for students in each classroom, and the computers are connected to a file server which provides simultaneous access to the database. More recently, a number of classes in different regions of the United States and Canada have shared access to their CSILE databases through electronic networking. This enables a larger pool of students to contribute to the students' knowledge building. Additionally, these classes have used desktop video conferencing to link with groups that are working on common problems and have used e-mail to question outside experts (Lamon, Secules, Petrosino, Hackett, Bransford, & Goldman, in press).

The electronic database includes four different categories of notes, or 'thinking types,' each represented by an icon. Each category corresponds to a stage in the investigation process described below. These categories include 'what I know,' 'high-level question,' 'plans,' and 'new learning' notes. Students' notes can be in text form or graphics (e.g., charts or pictures). They can be commented on or added to by other students but only deleted or changed by the author who determines the status of the notes. They may be private, public anonymous, public named, or be a candidate for publication. Published notes have higher status, based on a quality review by the teacher or peer committees.

Typically, teachers using CSILE begin units with an introduction to the general topic or theme. This introduction usually involves teacher-led whole-class discussion and may also include introductory lessons to the topic or showing video-tapes. During this introductory phase the students produce notes within CSILE detailing 'what I know' about the topic and compile a list of 'high level questions' that relate to and build on their previous knowledge. They will subsequently investigate some of these questions. Examples of such questions are 'Why are condors an endangered species?' and 'How do genes cause defects in birth?'

After the initial discussion phase, students prepare to research some of the questions they have developed by writing a 'plan' note in CSILE that details how they will investigate the question. As they enact the plan students compile text and graphic notes in the 'new learning' section of CSILE. They are encouraged to integrate information from different sources in their notes. Typically, as a result of their investigations or comments from others, students further refine their question or identify new questions for research.

Student collaboration in developing a database on the question under investigation is an integral feature of CSILE; the structure of the software encourages students to engage in continued conversations about their research and their notes. The aim is to scaffold discourse so that students will build on each others' comments to reach new understandings. Additionally, students have the option of conducting their investigation within small groups. Students are encouraged to read what other students have written on the common database by searching the database for contributions by topic, keyword, author, thinking type (I know, high level questions, plan, new learning) or note status. When a note is selected for reading it is viewed in the 'Read-a-note' window. A second window, 'Write-a-note,' simultaneously opens on the screen, which includes a set of commenting cues that are designed to foster thoughtfulness as the students comment on each others' notes. Types of comments students can make include asking further questions, raising counter-arguments, suggesting additional sources of information, or offering feedback in the form of praise or constructive criticism. The 'Write-a-note' window has sentence openers to structure comments. Examples include 'A reference I thought you might find useful is ...', 'One thing I didn't understand is ...,' and 'I'd find it helpful if I knew ...' The author of the note receives a message whenever a comment is made in response to their note. They then respond and continue the conversation. The teacher is a resource person and may also add comments to students' notes. The teacher also contributes to the decision about whether notes are of a sufficiently high standard to achieve published status. Ultimately students produce reports, composed of texts and graphics, that are a synthesis of the information they have gathered from multiple sources.

Fostering Communities of Learners

Brown and her colleagues (e.g., Brown & Campione, 1994, in press, Brown, Ash, Rutherford, Nakagawa, Gordon, & Campione, 1993) have developed the Fostering Communities of Learners (FCL) program for elementary and middle school classes. This approach begins with making changes to the general learning environment of classrooms. Although interdisciplinary approaches to scientific topics have been used frequently, the approach does not specify a curriculum nor is it linked to one particular school subject. In FCL classrooms the entire class studies a common theme that crosses traditional disciplinary boundaries. For example, a unit called 'Plagues and People' integrates perspectives from biology, anthropology, and history. FCL emphasizes broad and enduring themes that can be revisited at increasingly mature levels of understanding. The goal is to promote critical thinking and reflection skills that underlie higher literacy, including reading, writing, argumentation, and technological sophistication. Another aim is to create self-directed learners, with a sense of responsibility to the group and a sense of ownership of the investigation and the knowledge they have developed.

FCL pays particular attention to interactions among students and provides a structure for collaboration and co-operation through use of cooperative jigsaw groups, reciprocal teaching techniques, and a variety of commercially available software applications. Students conduct independent and group research, share information, and ultimately create class projects or reports documenting their findings. Students pursue different questions and learn different skills from others in the class, so that knowledge and skills are distributed throughout the classroom much in the way they are distributed across communities of experts.

At the beginning of examining a new theme, the teacher conducts a whole-class 'benchmark' lesson during which students learn foundational knowledge and important issues about the theme are raised. After this lesson the whole class generates a list of questions for research relating to the theme. The teacher and the class together then categorize these questions. Each category is assigned to a group for investigation. For example, for a theme on changing populations, research groups may be formed to explore extinct, endangered, artificial, assisted, and urbanized populations. As research groups examine their areas and subtopics, scientific issues emerge and are discussed. For example, the endangered species theme may lead to study of issues such as interdependence, adaptation, predator/prey relationships, ecological balance, and effects of toxic agents on animals' reproductive casualty.

The students gather information from text resources, videos, field trips, and hands-on experiments. They also use commercially available software applications such as word processing, desk-top publishing, and graphics – as well as Browser, a specially developed electronic filing system. Students also are encouraged to communicate electronically with appropriate 'communities of scholars' including scientists, computer experts, librarians, staff at zoos and museums, and graduate students. Students synthesize their findings within Browser.

An important component of the research process is student interaction using Reciprocal Teaching, in which students engage within their research groups. Reciprocal Teaching (Palincsar & Brown, 1984) is a structured method for improving students' reading comprehension that scaffolds students use of text-based reading strategies. This ensures that all students within each research group participate in learning about and understanding their group's sub-topic. Using the jigsaw approach to cooperative learning (Aronson, Blaney, Stephen, Sikes, & Snapp, 1978), once initial groups have examined a question, new learning groups are formed that contain a member representing each initial research group. In the new group each member is responsible for teaching their information to the remainder of the students. This cooperative jigsaw technique, where each member possesses important and different knowledge that must be shared, produces individual and group accountability for learning.

Students produce diverse artifacts such as printed class books that include a compilation of the research groups' reports, poster displays, and verbal presentations and demonstrations. Students' learning and understanding are typically assessed using class tests for each topic. These tests are constructed by both the teacher and research group and represent the information that students have compiled and presented during the course of the study. The tests stress students' understanding and application rather than the retention of facts. Additionally, whole-class discussion and analysis after taking tests occupy a central role in FCL classes.

Scientists in Action

Scientists in Action is a series of videodisc-based science units, targeted for 5th and 6th graders, that has been developed by the Cognition and Technology Group at Vanderbilt (Cognition and Technology Group at Vanderbilt, 1992a, 1993; Petrosino, Sherwood, Bransford, & CTGV, in press). This series is modelled on their previously developed mathematics program 'Adventures of Jasper Woodbury' (e.g., Cognition and Technology Group at Vanderbilt, 1992b). The emphasis of Scientists in Action is on developing students' scientific reasoning and problem-solving strategies and on integrating knowledge across subject areas.

The program is designed around the principle of anchored instruction (Cognition and Technology Group at Vanderbilt, 1990). Video helps to create complex contexts within which problems are situated. Each video presents a simulated realistic scientific dilemma comprised of several related problems. The video begins by introducing the scene. As the story develops, students are presented with a structured sequence of questions; there are pre-determined places to pause the video so that the students can answer the questions. For example, the pilot Scientists in Action video, 'The Overturned Tanker' is about an emergency faced by a hydrologist: a tanker truck has overturned, the driver is unconscious, and there is a hazardous but unidentified chemical leaking from the truck which may flow into an adjacent river and affect a water treatment facility. Students view a team of scientists discussing various elements of the problem in an attempt to decide what to do.

The video is stopped to allow time for students to answer the predetermined series of questions. Students are first asked how the unknown chemical may react with water and to decide which direction it will flow if it runs into the river. They go on to answer questions about what the chemical is, how best to treat the spill, how fast the chemical is flowing, and how long it will take to reach the water treatment plant. They break into small groups where they pool ideas and explanations, share materials, and arrive at a consensus. Once the groups have arrived at their answer, the class resumes watching the video. Experts' answers are given so that students can compare their responses with those of the experts. The videodisc scenario continues to unfold until the next problem arises. The cycle of questions, expert discussion, and student problem-solving is repeated. For example, after witnessing a chemist's laboratory tests that identify the chemical, the students are again requested to help solve the problem of how best to deal with the spill.

During the problem-solving process students may view excerpts from the video again, including information from discussions by the team of experts. They also have the use of relevant reference material that accompanies each Scientists in Action video. In the case of 'The Overturned Tanker,' these supplements include topographical maps, an official Emergency Response Guidebook, authentic television network news footage of a chemical spill, and materials for a 'hands-on' acid/base chemistry experiment. There is some degree of choice in how students may go about solving the problems, but their options are constrained by the material that is provided in the video scenes and in the accompanying reference material.

Most of the scaffolding of the students' inquiry occurs as a result of the simulated discussions between experts. The classroom teacher may also provide additional assistance by asking questions if students have not fully explored all the options or by structuring their activities.

Because the primary emphasis within Scientists in Action is on the process of students experiencing science and solving real-life problems, rather than on having a tangible artifact, the principal outcome is the students' answers to the video-posed problems. However, the developers of Scientists in Action have encouraged teachers to follow up on issues and content raised in the videos with student-generated projects and reports. Students may also write additional questions related to the scenes they have watched or even construct entirely new dilemma scenarios. In addition, CTGV are developing curricula to supplement some of the Scientists in Action scenarios that would involve students conducting investigations or experiments in their own community.

It is interesting to note that The Cognition and Technology Group at Vanderbilt have experimented with artifacts like contests in the Jasper videodisc series (Cognition and Technology Group at Vanderbilt, 1992b; Lamon, Secules, Petrosino, Hackett, Bransford, & Goldman, in press) but have not yet added this component to Scientists in Action. In these 'public performance challenges,' classes are linked via teleconferencing technology, and they compete with each other in a simulated game show format. Students simultaneously watch a video in which three self-claimed experts (actors with scripts) are given questions to answer that are similar to questions they have examined previously. Students must determine who is the true expert by identifying their correct and erroneous arguments. After watching the video students discuss their choice of who is the true expert, provide rationales for their decisions, and cast votes. Each class then has a representative send their answer, and they then learn which classes have won. This format allows for students to prepare for a public evaluation and receive feedback about their performance.

Project-Based Science

Many of the programs described here employ some form of project enhanced learning. Groups at the Technological Education Research Center (Roup, Gal, Drayton, & Pfister, 1992) and the University of Michigan (Blumenfeld, Soloway, Marx, Krajcik, Guzdial, & Palincsar, 1991; Krajcik et al., 1994) have focused on a theoretical base for project-based instruction along with developing pedagogy, curriculum, and technology. TERC was one of the first organizations to develop project-based approaches to learning in which technology, especially telecommunications, played a key role. Unlike other approaches described above, which are experimental and have been tried only in a few sites, numerous schools have participated in TERC's efforts. TERC has developed science units for upper elementary grades (Kidsnet) and for the middle and high school grades (Star Schools). Teachers receive a curriculum manual with suggestions for investigations and activities along with background readings and worksheets for students. The units are oriented around questions such as 'How does your body get the oxygen it needs?', 'What's in our water?' 'How can we light a house?' To answer these questions, students plan investigations and gather, interpret, and share data with others.

Collaboration via telecommunications is central to project-based learning. Classes from different locations are organized into research teams. The unit questions encourage long distance collaborative investigations which exploit regional variations (in, for example, weather patterns, water quality, or radon levels). For instance, students in agricultural, industrial, and residential areas might consider differences in levels of water pollution in their community and the influence of fertilizer use on these levels. Students work together in small groups to conduct their investigations and transmit their findings via telecommunication to other classes in their research team. As part of their investigations, they build artifacts; for instance, students build rain collectors as part of the water quality unit and model houses with solar panels as part of a solar energy unit. Locally collected data are transmitted to a central point where it is pooled, summarized, and distributed across sites for comparative analysis by scientists who are also available to answer questions.

The University of Michigan group has extended the TERC efforts by elaborating on the features of project-based science and by developing new technologies for students to use in data collection, analysis, and interpretation (Soloway, Guzdial, & Hay, 1994; Jackson, Stratford, Krajcik, & Soloway, in press). A unique aspect of the work is the focus on working with teachers (described in more detail in the section called Ramping Up). The investigators have studied challenges teachers face in enacting project-based instruction and ways to facilitate teacher learning, including the design and development of new technologies to help teachers learn about project-based science.

There are five essential components to project-based science as implemented by the Michigan group. It:

a) requires a question or problem that serves to organize and drive activities;

b) results in a series of artifacts, or products, that address the question/problem;

c) allows students to engage in authentic investigations;

d) involves communities of students, teachers, and members of society in discourse about the problem as well as collaborating together as a community of inquiry; and

e) promotes the use of cognitive tools.

Below, we amplify on each of these components.

Within this program, questions serve to organize and drive activities. Students, teachers or curriculum developers can create questions and activities. Regardless of the source of questions, they can not be so highly constrained that the outcomes are predetermined, leaving students with little room to develop their own approaches to answering the question. Good questions will be feasible (students can design and perform investigations to answer the question), worthwhile (contain rich science content, relate what scientists really do, and be broken down into smaller questions), contextualized (real world, non-trivial, and important), and meaningful (interesting and exciting to learners). As students pursue solutions to driving questions, they develop meaningful understanding of key scientific concepts. Questions include those developed by TERC on water and energy, as well as ones generated by teachers, such as 'How do I balance on my skateboard,? and 'Are there poisons in my home?'

Students produce artifacts or products which reflect emergent states of knowledge and understanding about solutions to the driving question. Because artifacts are concrete and explicit (e.g., a physical model, report, video-tape, or computer program), they are shareable and critiquable. This allows others (students, teachers, parents, and members of the community) to provide feedback and permits learners to reflect upon and extend their emergent knowledge and revise their artifacts. The creation and sharing of artifacts makes doing project-based science like doing real science and mirrors the performance of individuals in the work world.

Students carry out investigations; they ask questions, make predictions, design experiments, collect and analyze data and information, draw conclusions, and communicate their ideas and findings to others. Students collaborate with each other and their teachers. They also use telecommunication to access the wider community of knowledgeable individuals and students in different communities, as well as share data with other students and professional scientists.

Project-based science involves students and teachers in the use of a variety of technological tools such as telecommunication, microcomputer-based laboratories, microworlds, and graphing packages. Using technology in project-based science makes the environment more authentic to students because the computer can access real data, expand interaction and collaboration with others via networks, and emulate tools used by experts to produce artifacts. The multimodal and multimedia capabilities of technology not only enhance the physical accessibility of the information, they facilitate its intellectual accessibility as well. Technology also allows students to manipulate and construct their own representations and artifacts easily and to do so in several media.

Soloway and his colleagues in the Highly Interactive Computing Group (Hi-C) (Soloway et al., 1994; Jackson et al., 1996) have developed software based on a model called learner centred design for student use in project-based science classrooms. They have been working in a high school where the 9-11 grade curriculum has been redesigned as an enactment of project-based science so that different science disciplines (biology, chemistry, and earth science) are integrated into a three year program (Heubel-Drake, Finkel, Stern, & Mouradian, 1995). Work in each of the three years consists of a series of long term projects focused on different topics. The findings are presented to teachers, peers, and the community.

An important element of the new curriculum is that students explore science through construction of computationally based models that represent real world phenomena. Constructing, simulating, verifying, and validating models pose a serious challenge for students (Mandinach & Cline, 1989, 1994). Current procedures for teaching modelling in secondary schools are complex, requiring considerable prior knowledge and mathematical ability on the part of pupils. The HI-C group has taken on the challenge of making modelling accessible to pre-college students. They have created a computer application, Model-It, which requires minimal prior knowledge from other domains. By incorporating an advanced interface design, that does not require programming experience, students can rapidly construct simple models while at the same time developing more expert-like modelling capabilities. Model-It allows students who are unfamiliar with dynamic modelling procedures and mathematical or abstract symbol systems to model complex streamlike ecosystems (Jackson et al., 1996).

Model-It illustrates principles of learner centred design; it is based on a model of software scaffolding (Soloway, Krajcik, Blumenfeld & Marx, 1996) that represents information in a way that is familiar to learners but also helps to introduce them to more professional or symbolic representations. Using Model-It, students build models with objects ('things' in the system being modelled), factors (measurable or quantifiable aspects of objects), and relationships between those factors. All objects are represented in text and visually, with photo-realistic or graphical images. For instance, in building a model of the stream, the stream represents an object. Factors would include pH and other water quality indices. A relationship might be expressed qualitatively, such as – as the stream ph decreases below 6, water quality decreases. Once the model is built, Model-It allows real-time testing. It also allows smooth transitions between building and testing. The close linking of design and testing allows students to make connections between the configuration of relationships they designed into their model and the resultant representation of the model's behavior as shown on the meters and graphs.

Artifacts that students create in project-based science are authentic and relate to issues outside the school. For example, students have conducted investigations to determine water quality of a stream and have prepared slide presentations to communicate their conclusions to members of the local watershed council. They created exhibits to illustrate the geology of local parks for display at a museum. They also created HyperCard stacks to teach other students about evolution and natural selection.

ANALYSIS OF PROGRAMS

These programs differ considerably in their design, the theoretical elements of constructivist theory that are emphasized, and the application of these elements. Researchers interested in innovations of this type have examined student learning in terms for each program but have not systematically addressed the effect of these variations on large numbers of students. One reason is that the approaches are quite new and have not been implemented widely. A second is that most of the programs described can be characterized as 'design experiments' (Brown, 1992). Design experiments focus on a single or small set of classrooms. The goal is to engineer theoretically based interventions that work practically. Therefore, it is important to insure that the classroom and programs function smoothly as a learning environment in a small number of locations before they can be studied in other sites. Thus, program developers first seek to determine how and why the program works to foster learning and how to improve it, rather than to expand it quickly throughout school systems.

One of the premises of design experiments is that the intervention is integrated – it works as a whole. The elements are not orthogonal, and changing one element of the system affects all elements. Thus, one cannot decompose the program as if each element were an independent variable in a more conventional experimental design. As a result there is no attempt to separate variables to test their independent and interactive contributions to the instructional program as the basis for making recommendations for practice. In addition, comparison among the programs themselves is not likely to be attempted since they emphasize different points of the theory and are designed for somewhat different purposes. Instead, the research strategy is to modify the programs themselves based on evaluations and to track whether changes affect student learning. The idea is to obtain effects that are reliable and repeatable for the entire program so that eventually it can be disseminated with minimal support. Therefore, it is unlikely that enough information about each of the programs and their elements will be available so that a mix and match strategy of selecting and combining effective parts of each based on empirical findings could be used. It is interesting to note, however, that recently an attempt has been made to integrate various aspects of these efforts in a program called Schools for Thought (Lamon et al., in press).

Nevertheless, educators interested in adopting these approaches are likely to examine them to use particular features or to adapt an approach to their own students and contexts. At any rate, as we discussed earlier, constructivist theory is formulated in a way that does not lead to explicit prescriptions for action. Rather, it encourages adaptation and modification of programs as a way to enact the principles derived from theory. Likely concerns for enactment center on questions about instructional design and practice, student participation and motivation, technology, and individual differences. While these questions certainly are not different from ones that might be raised about innovations based on more traditional approaches, they are difficult to answer because of the philosophy of design experiments and, as we discuss below, because of the wide range of how features are defined and operationalized in programs. Collins (1995), in fact, recognizes this problem and argues for new approaches to design experiments in terms of design, implementation, and evaluation to allow for more systematic comparisons. Among the changes would be systematic variation within sites, using multiple sources of evaluation, and testing the effectiveness of different technologies.

Instructional Design

Questions about instructional design and practice are likely to include: What types of topics or problems and investigations are best suited to this approach? What constitutes authenticity? What is an effective balance of structure versus student choice? How can collaboration be established? How should learning be assessed?

With respect to focus of inquiry, generally there has not been enough experience with these types of programs to shed light on characteristics of questions that work well – that are conceptually rich, feasible and also motivating for students. The programs vary considerably in whether they center on topics, problems, or questions, whether these are predetermined, how structured they are, and how much choice students have in their determination. Some, like the Computer as Learning Partner, contain relatively structured instructional sequences and student materials for exploring a predesigned topic, like thermodynamics. Similarly, in Scientists in Action the sequence of questions, topics, and academic tasks are embedded within and predetermined by the video programs about a particular problem.

In contrast, teachers can introduce a topic or theme and have students initially identify questions or issues of interest to them and to refine them through the course of conducting investigations. For instance, students in the Communities of Learners programs have investigated endangered species and considered issues like interdependence, adaptation, predator/prey relations, and ecological balance. Students using CSILE have explored topics like fossil fuels and human evolution; students in the CoVis program examine topics related to weather, drawing from existing meteorological data, but pose their own questions. Project-based science employs a driving question rather than a topic or theme to organize inquiry; the question can be posed by either teachers or students, but like the other approaches, students raise issues for exploration related to the question.

How authenticity is achieved also varies by program. All appear to meet the criteria posited by Newmann and colleagues (Newmann & Archibald, 1992; Newmann & Wehlage, 1993) in that they potentially afford opportunities for higher-order thinking (manipulating and producing knowledge), development of deep knowledge (address central ideas of a subject), engagement in substantive conversations, and connectedness beyond the classroom. But how connectedness is achieved differs considerably. In some programs the questions posed are ones students may have heard about but not necessarily ones with which students are likely to have experience. For instance, Scientists in Action presents realistic problems such as the difficulties caused by an oil spill. Other programs use issues drawn from students' environments. CoVis uses questions about weather. Project-based science and TERC often focus on environmental questions about, for example, radon, water, and garbage in the students' communities. Still other programs such as CSILE and Communities of Learners use topics that are more school-like, such as adaptation, but uses examples students often find interesting, such as dinosaurs. Similarly, the Computer as Learning Partner examines thermodynamics but relates the information to student experience by using questions about keeping beverages like cocoa hot and soft drinks cold.

Obviously what constitutes topics varies from general areas to specific problems, questions and subquestions. We have little information about how large a set of ideas the problems/questions should encompass, about what constitutes optimal levels of disciplinary and interdisciplinary breadth, depth, and intellectual challenge so that students gain desired depth of conceptual and procedural understanding. Moreover, we know little about what problems students find valuable, interesting, or useful enough to work on for long periods.

The types of investigations in which students engage varies as well. Some of the programs require students to gather and interpret real-world data, such as TERC and Project-Based Science. The Computer as Learning Partner uses computer generated real time experiments for data. In CoVis students do not collect data themselves, but they analyze real data collected by the National Meteorological Center. Other programs do not necessarily require students to gather scientific data. For instance in CSILE students primarily use books and reference materials for investigations. In the videodisc programs, like Scientist in Action, students are provided with material in video sequences and have reference material. They do not collect data themselves.

Moreover, those programs differ in how much autonomy and choice students are given in determining how they go about posing questions, planning investigations, and reporting findings. The videodisc series afford low levels of decision making to students; there is a correct sequence of investigation and a correct answer at which the students must arrive. In the Communities of Learner programs students have a voice in the questions addressed and choose how they will gather information. However, structures and strategies are included to support and direct types of activities, including whole class benchmark lessons, reciprocal teaching, and cooperative jigsaw learning groups. In CoVis the topics focus on weather, but students can define the question and design the investigations themselves.

Another central aspect of program design that varies considerably is how collaboration is defined and organized. In some programs collaboration is relatively structured and is more like cooperative learning; for example Communities of Learners uses the Jigsaw method. Students also work in designated pairs in the Computer as Learning Partner program. Other programs use strategies and organization that are less clearly defined. In CSILE students engage in dialogue with their classmates to build a common database, whereas CoVis encourages students to work with peers in their own class and in other schools and also to draw upon experts outside the classroom via telecommunications. In both programs the technology is designed to support this interaction.

Technology

All the programs rely on technology; in fact, the uses of technology in these programs constitute one of their hallmarks. For some, like CoVis, CSILE, and Computers as Learning Partners, specially designed software is a centrepiece. Issues remain about how to design and exploit the benefits of technology. There is considerable evidence that instantiating and using technology in classrooms is problematic (Marx, 1993; Owen, 1992; Willis & Mehlinger, 1996). One problem is how to create programs that are learner centred so that the degree of scaffolding can be tailored depending on student needs (Soloway, Guzdial, & Hay, 1994). Another is to determine what constitutes effective scaffolding. Currently each program uses technology specially designed for its purposes. Customized scaffolding is provided at the macro level in terms of software organization and functionality and at the micro level through prompts. Some promote inquiry, such as those that ask students to make predictions; others aid collaboration via mutual visualization, common notebooks, or group databases; some help with interpretation and modelling. A third problem concerns making the technology user friendly; the cost of learning each application is often high, and students may need to learn several programs when functions are not integrated in order to collect, analyze, represent, and share data. Since each software application is tailored for the particular programmatic approach, all the features are not contained in any piece of software.

Although the instructional issues associated with these concerns are numerous, there are also many policy issues such as how to garner the financial resources needed to obtain a sufficient number computers, libraries of varied software packages, and access to telecommunication capabilities. Further, as we discuss in the section on Ramping Up, support is required for users and to maintain the technology once it is in place.

Assessment

Archibald and Newmann (1992) argue that assessment must provide an exhibition of mastery and represent disciplined inquiry, integrate prior knowledge with new learning, and have some value (aesthetic, utilitarian or personal) to the student beyond evaluative purposes. Wiggins (1993) argues, in addition, that assessment should be collaborative, public, and provide feedback to students.

Moreover, the assessment should occupy a central experience in student learning, allow for exploration of student thinking, and take multiple and varied forms. To meet these requirements, assessment tasks should reflect activities and challenges characteristic of the community of practice.

Many of the programs stipulate that assessment should focus on determining student understanding of key concepts and principles rather than retention and recall of facts. However, programs differ widely in the types of artifacts students create during learning for purposes of assessment. They also differ in the degree to which formal assessment is described and how closely these resemble the criteria for authentic assessment listed above. In some programs, like the videodisc based approaches, students create answers to problems but do not generate artifacts. In others, such as CoVis and Computer as Learning Partner, students generate scientific reports which contain graphs or maps. In CSILE students produce common databases and collaborative class generated text. The TERC curriculum packages contain suggestions for final projects that integrate what students have learned with respect to the question for the project. Whether and how these go beyond the classroom is less clear. Students engaged in Project-Based Science using Model-It and other software applications have given presentations about water quality to local groups and also developed museum exhibits.

Some approaches also include more traditional testing formats. Batteries of assessments are used to evaluate Scientists in Action. Communities of Learners uses class tests, constructed by students and teachers, that stress understanding and application. The tests are followed by whole class discussion and analysis as a way to provide feedback and promote learning. Program developers also use dynamic assessment. In individual interviews, they ask Socratic-like questions to determine how much students can do on their own and how much structuring or help they need to go further, in order to determine the student's zone of proximal development. Interviewers probe student understanding through explanations they offer and whether students can transfer the ideas by asking them to make predictions for novel scenarios. They also observe and evaluate students' scientific inquiry and computer skills.

Work on alternative assessment suggests the need for caution due to issues of validity and reliability. Shavelson, Baxter, and Gao (1993) compared different forms of performance assessment in science and math. They found that students performed differently on different tasks. A task that proved relatively easy for one student proved relatively difficult for another. Thus the authors recommend a large number of tasks with which to evaluate students. Moreover, teachers have difficulty helping students design and create artifacts that represent their understanding of content and process adequately and in judging the quality of students work.

Participation, Thoughtfulness, Motivation

These approaches to teaching for understanding represent a considerable departure from the type of classroom experience with which students are familiar. They require greater participation, more personal responsibility for learning, more self-direction, and more self-regulation. The approaches assume that students will be motivated to ask questions, join in discussion, and engage in sustained inquiry, critical analysis, and evaluation of their ideas. Whether students are willing to participate at this level is an open question. Program evaluations and writeups often do not discuss issues of participation as students engage in collaboration, investigations, and problem solving. Little is known about how actively students participate and whether the participation is widespread. Moreover, in contrast to older definitions which highlight on task behavior, the problem of examining participation is compounded by the fact that what constitutes participation itself and how it can be assessed is uncertain. For instance, Lave and Wenger (1991) postulate that students need not be active participants *per se*; they can also benefit from peripheral participation in which they observe and appropriate the language, ideas, and norms of the group. Thus, it is difficult to know how to determine whether students are involved.

Nevertheless, work in traditional classrooms provides some reason for caution. Research findings from previous innovations, like 'hands-on science,' suggests that there are a group of target students who dominate and help carry recitations and discussions (e.g., Tobin & Gallagher, 1987) and indicates that students are not always thoughtful, even they appear to be on task, so that they fail to reap the benefits of inquiry (Stake & Easley, 1978). Similarly, studies of cooperative groups report that participation varies by student gender, ability, and status unless deliberate attempts are made to minimize these differences (Bossert, 1988-89; Good, Mulryan, & McCaslin, 1992; Webb & Palincsar, 1996). However, it is not clear how applicable this work on instructional cooperation in traditional classrooms is to problems of how to encourage and promote true collaboration, where working with and engaging in dialogue with others is presumed to help students become members of a community of learners.

Scardamalia and Bereiter (1991) report unequal amounts of participation on CSILE, as students build a class data base; less able and less assertive students seem to be somewhat 'sidelined' from the action. Linn (1992) reports that students are often not respectful of each other – refuse to share computer keyboards or information – and groups developed status hierarchies and norms consistent with gender stereotypes. She found that real collaboration was rare; less dominant students tended to agree with more dominant ones; students would report a variety of perspectives rather than try to understand the merits of different points of view and come to some common understanding. One reason for the problems of getting students to collaborate fully is that they may not know how to do so productively. Palincsar, Anderson, and David (1993) have designed a program to help students learn scientific argumentation as a way to enhance the quality of dialogue and improve student learning.

In fact, reports from several of the programs attest to the challenge of eliciting thoughtfulness. Linn (1992) notes that students using Computers as Learning Partner experienced difficulties generalizing from the laboratory experiments to their everyday experiences and to other material they had not studied. Also, students tended to continue to respond to the questions with their intuitive ideas rather than with the scientific principles integral to the topic under study. Scardamalia and Bereiter (1991) found that students did not readily take advantage of the opportunity to ask each other questions and needed support in giving constructive rather than superficial feedback to others; they often incorporated commenting cues into the software to scaffold the process, such as 'one thing I didn't understand is ...' Also, there is some evidence that students who collaborate via networks do not necessarily engage in substantive conversations (e.g., Linn & Songer, 1988). Investigation of telecommunications in the TERC program found low occurrences of network conversations between sites beyond the initial 'send and receive' stage; there were also few instances of student to scientist communication despite the willingness of the scientists to be involved (Lenk, 1992).

It is also not clear whether the same types of techniques teachers can use to encourage active learning in more traditional classrooms (e.g., Blumenfeld, 1992; Winne & Marx, 1982) are compatible with more constructivist approaches. For example, while modelling and feedback are part of both the direct instruction, information processing and newer cognitive apprenticeship suggestions for instruction, ideas like the importance of holding students accountable for doing and understanding the work are not discussed in the newer approaches. Other techniques for insuring participation or attention during different participation structures – such as assigning roles in cooperative groups, or calling on students randomly, or asking students for a show of hands regarding agreement with a point during recitation – do not seem compatible with the newer approaches. Recent work that describes thought processes of students during scientific experiments holds some promise for helping teachers learn what to watch for as students work and how to encourage students via comments and questions (Roth, 1994; Schauble, Glaser, Duschl, Schulze, & John, 1995).

Issues of participation and thoughtfulness are closely linked to motivation. A fundamental goal of the new approaches is for students to take responsibility for and ownership of their own learning by inquiring, discussing, collecting, synthesizing, and analyzing and interpreting information. To work, the approaches require students to invest considerable mental effort and persist in the search for a solution to problems and adequate scientific explanation for phenomena. However, motivational elements are not always explicitly dealt with in these programs (see for instance Blumenfeld et al., 1991; Hickey, 1995; Young & Pintrich, in press). The presumption is that students will adopt learning rather than performance goals, where they attempt to understand the material rather than simply get good grades or appear smart. Learning goals are associated with increased effort, persistence, and use of learning and metacognitive strategies.

Basically it is assumed that students will be motivated to learn by the fact that they work with others, on authentic problems, using technological tools. It seems likely that while some youngsters might be exhilarated by these opportunities, it is also the case that students used to more traditional approaches may initially resist ones that are more demanding. As Pintrich, Marx and Boyle (1993) note, these types of intellectual endeavours require considerable self-efficacy on the part of students. They also rely on an epistemology which argues that knowledge development is not simply a function of memorizing and repeating correct answers; rather it is uncertain, changeable, and constructed. In addition, the approach assumes that students value knowledge as an object, are willing to challenge their preexisting assumptions and theories, and are committed to search for better and more complete explanations. Moreover, the authors of these programs assume that in addition to individual achievement motivation, social motivation is also likely to come into play. Social goals like responsibility, acceptance, and desire to impress others will affect whether students work well within the community of learners and contribute their share during collaboration, are willing to engage in public debate, and are able to risk being wrong as they express ideas and seek solutions to problems. There is some evidence that student attitudes improve in classrooms based on constructivist learning approaches (Hickey, 1995; Stratford & Finkel, 1995). However, to date there have been no studies of motivation in these classrooms in terms of student goals, use of learning strategies, and epistemologies.

Individual Differences

The various programs described above have been implemented at different grade levels. Some have been tried in elementary grades, like Communities of Learners and Scientists in Action; others, such as the Computer as Learning Partner, project based science, and CoVis have been implemented in middle and high schools. Program designers have not written about what alterations would be necessary if they were to be used in lower or higher grades. Obviously younger students are likely to need more help in using learning and metacognitive strategies. They will need assistance in thinking systematically, in organizing information, in designing studies, in gathering data methodically, and in drawing inferences. Moreover, for children of different ages, little is known about what types of questions or topics are conceptually rich but also appropriate, how to design and help students use tools to facilitate thinking, or how to help youngsters productively collaborate. Hints are available from the cognitive development and social development literature, and from previous work on cooperative learning, technology use, and strategy instruction. Nevertheless, much of this work was done in classrooms that emphasized transmission models; it was not done in classrooms that are premised on the newer constructivist approaches to instruction. The problems need to be considered specifically within the constructivist framework of teaching for understanding.

Issues of diversity also are likely to be of concern. While the programs have been tried in schools serving different types of communities and populations — from the affluent suburbs to inner city and blue collar communities — no systematic studies have been conducted about how students from varied backgrounds respond. We know little about what those attempting to design, tailor, or implement programs need to consider when designing programs for diverse groups. There are case studies that point to the fact that constructivist type programs can successfully involve poor, minority students (Rosebury, Warren, & Conant, 1989). However, in light of considerable evidence that children from varied backgrounds bring different participation styles, different discourse patterns, different ways of interacting socially, and different norms for language and number use, these are questions that deserve attention.

With respect to gender, there is an assumption that collaboration and authentic elements of these programs will increase girls' interest and achievement in science, but generally this assumption has not been tested. There is some evidence that in some cases boys dominate work groups and computer use (Linn, 1992). Videodisc programs have deliberately included women and minorities as scientists with the aim of increasing science interest in these groups (Cognition and Technology Group at Vanderbilt, 1992a). Nevertheless there is ample evidence that there are gender differences in interest in technology and in science that may influence how students respond to such programs (Eccles, 1993; Linn & Hyde, 1989).

RAMPING UP: DISSEMINATION WITHOUT PRESCRIPTION

Many of the programs that emphasize constructivist ideas about teaching for understanding have not been tried on a widespread basis. Thus, dissemination of these approaches so that they will be tried in a many classrooms is a challenge. Information from the literatures on teacher development, on past attempts to change instructional practice, and from studies of current attempts to 'reform' education can provide insight into the issues and problems that are likely to arise when teaching for understanding is attempted and which must be addressed in order for these innovations to be sustained.

Prior experience with innovation suggests that finding ways to support teachers is essential as they change practice from information transmission models to those which stress students' transformation of ideas (Fullan, 1993). The literature is unambiguous; change will not take root and innovation will not be sustained if one adopts traditional top down models of dissemination and enhancement which rely on single workshops, distribution of curriculum materials to be used exactly as prepared, and lists of prescribed practices to be implemented (Kaestle, 1993; Joyce & Showers, 1988). In fact, critics of current dissemination models assert that these models are frequently naive about complexities of teaching, are couched in abstract terms, are not situated in the reality of schools, and are limited in their follow-up help (Cohen & Ball, 1990). Cohen and Barnes (1993) note that policy makers have unrealistic ideas about what is necessary for change and that most enhancement efforts aimed at improving teaching for understanding do not follow their own precepts. On the one hand, teachers are told that they should shift from instruction which stresses transmission of information to practices that stress student transformation of ideas via dialogue, collaboration, investigations, and application of ideas in a variety of situations. On the other, enhancement efforts for teachers often continue to reflect transmission models in which information about expectations is distributed and lists and models of what to do are provided. In these efforts teachers are *not* seen as 'constructing' understanding. Such attempts to promote innovation often fail to account for difficulties new approaches pose for classroom management, the contextual factors that limit teachers' opportunities to make such changes, or for teachers' understanding and commitment to the innovation.

In contrast, current approaches stress the need for teachers to collaborate to try the innovative, to reflect and for the process to continue for extended periods of time (Krajcik et al., 1994; Marx, Freeman, Krajcik, & Blumenfeld, in press). The outcome of cycles of conversation, enactment, and reflection promotes vision of new possibilities, understanding of the basis for the innovation and its instructional features, and appreciation for and development of strategies to meet the challenges posed. The result is practice which is congruent with underlying theory but also tailored to individual contexts. Below we summarize aspects of collaboration, enactment, and reflection, then offer a detailed description of how teachers transitioned to one constructivist-based approach, Project Based Science.

Collaboration

Recent efforts to promote change points to the importance of providing opportunities for collaboration among teachers and between teachers and university personnel. Not surprisingly, it shows that teachers learn in much the same way that students do. They construct their knowledge through dialogue; they learn by integrating new information with prior knowledge and beliefs, applying ideas to practice, and evaluating and reflecting on the results. Reports describing the process of collaboration and its effects have been prepared in the field of reading (Richardson & Anders, 1994), mathematics (Bickel & Hattrup, 1995; Heaton & Lampert, 1993), science (Blumenfeld, Krajcik, Marx, & Soloway, 1994; Marx et al., 1994), and teacher expectations (Weinstein, Madison, & Kuklinski, 1995). They show that collaboration benefits teachers and researchers. During collaborative conversations, teachers and university personnel work to understand the basis for the innovation, assumptions underlying it, and implications for classroom practice. Researchers learn from teachers who provide knowledge of what does and does not work in classrooms. Teachers have opportunities to discuss ideas, to consider new instructional strategies, to try out new technologies, and to explore the meaning of subject matter concepts. As in classrooms based on constructivist ideas, the aim of the conversation is to develop common understanding and language, to share expertise, and to develop a community of practice.

It is important to note that such collaborations are time consuming, labour intensive, and take considerable commitment on the part of participants. A variety of ways to facilitate collaboration have been tried. For instance, prepared cases, case studies, teacher written case reports, and research articles have been used to promote conversation. We have found that sharing plans promotes productive conversations because it focuses the teacher directly on the innovation (Marx, Blumenfeld, Krajcik, Soloway, Cox, & Breen, 1995). Telecommunications also have been tried as a means to continue such conversations across the barriers of time and space (see Roup et al., 1992; Rud, 1995).

Enactment and Reflection

Although conversations serve as a stimulus for change, they are not enough to help teachers fully appreciate the innovation. Experience and accompanying reflection are essential. Teachers must try innovations in their classrooms before they understand their full implications. Teacher knowledge is anchored in classroom events and based on narrative, not on abstract principles or propositions (e.g., Carter, 1993). It is important to note, however, that during these enactments teachers are not merely applying a set of predefined prescriptions; rather, they are tailoring the innovation to fit their unique circumstances, encountering challenges and dilemmas, and devising strategies to deal with them. While conversations help expand declarative knowledge, enactment enhances what has been called 'practical knowledge' (Russell & Munby, 1992).

Reflection helps teachers extract from the experience the knowledge that leads to improved practice and understanding. By discussing their own or others' practice, teachers come to understand the innovation and of a variety of practices that are congruent with its premises. Such reflection can be fostered through use of cases, journals, and video-tapes. As they reflect, teachers analyze, evaluate, and change their practice as well as come to understand the innovation more fully. The result is that teachers develop a range of practice that matches with the premises of the innovation and with practical concerns.

Issues in Change

Studies of change point to the fact that it takes considerable time for teachers to understand and to become comfortable with 'teaching for understanding' (Ball & Rundquist, 1993; Heaton & Lampert, 1993; Wood, Cobb, & Yackel, 1990). For instance, case studies by researchers and case reports by teachers point to the challenges and dilemmas teachers face in transitioning to project-based science and how change is influenced by beliefs, knowledge of content, pedagogy, and context (Ladewski, Krajcik, & Harvey, 1994; Marx et al., 1994; Scott, 1994). We describe the process of teacher development in our program of research in some detail below because it closely mirrors what others have found.

Problems.

Most teaches faced similar types of problems in enacting project based science. One was time. Investigations and discussions often took longer than anticipated. Also, in-depth exploration of ideas took longer than the more familiar broad and superficial survey of concepts. A second related problem was how to incorporate meeting district curriculum guidelines while incorporating the new in-depth approaches. Teachers worried about not covering all the material stipulated. A third problem was management. Teachers needed to balance allowing students freedom and maintaining order so that students could work and converse productively. Also, some had difficulty organizing and monitoring situations where many tasks were simultaneously occurring and dealing with higher levels of activity and noise than they were used to. A fourth problem was control. Teachers often felt a need to control the flow of information based on concerns about learning. They assumed that students needed to master lower level materials and facts to understand the problems at hand, even though they also thought that students needed to build their own understanding. They wanted to direct lessons to insure that students got the right information. A fifth problem was support. Teachers had difficulty scaffolding experiences so that students could take responsibility for learning, often giving students too much independence without adequately modelling thinking processes, structuring the situation, or providing feedback. A sixth was technology use. Teachers who were not proficient users and had never experienced using technology as a tool had difficulty incorporating technology into the classroom. They used it to enhance their own instruction, such as for demonstrations, but it took considerable time before they helped students exploit its benefits as a tool. A seventh was assessment. Teachers had difficulty in designing assessments that would tap student understanding. The artifacts they asked students to produce often involved participating in a public performance or sharing reports. But students did not necessarily need to synthesize information or generate different conceptual representations in the production of these artifacts.

Progress.

Teachers tended first to explore aspects of the innovation related to their primary reasons for joining the effort, such as enhancing student motivation or becoming proficient with technology. Also their attempts to change practice often focused on one or two areas such as collaboration or investigation. Developing expertise in one area provided a base from which the teacher could venture to incorporate other features that were initially less compatible with their approaches and past experience. Moreover, teachers tended to concentrate and perfect a few strategies to meet challenges rather than to develop numerous ones. Their initial enactments were influenced by the teachers' incomplete understandings of project based science and the feature they were attempting to implement. It was also limited by lack of exposure to examples of instruction of this type. As a result, teachers modified their practices in idiosyncratic ways based on their prior experiences and their beliefs. This mapping of new onto old was sometimes problematic and unsuccessful, as when teachers tried to build collaboration but constrained discussion and sharing of ideas among students.

Moreover, initial attempts to change from a didactic model of instruction rendered teachers novices once more. As they tried unfamiliar instructional strategies or new arrangements for which their practical or event knowledge was limited, the results were choppy; teachers ran out of time, left activities unfinished, and did not respond to or return to student suggestions or questions. Also attempts to deal with one element often entailed problems with other features.

That is, teachers not only had difficulty with individual features of project based science; they had difficulty orchestrating among them.

How teachers dealt with student collaboration illustrates these points. Teachers who agreed to try project based science because they wanted to enhance student motivation tended to work first on issues of student collaboration and of fostering ownership and autonomy. Collaboration requires the exchanging of ideas and the negotiation of meaning. However, teachers' limited initial understanding of collaboration influenced enactment; the teachers often thought that simply working together, such as carrying out prescribed procedures for an experiment, constituted collaboration. They also presumed that any type of involvement equalled thoughtfulness (see Prawat, 1992). Moreover, they constrained opportunities for interaction; drawing on prior experience with the more structured cooperative learning approaches, they often overspecified tasks, assigning roles for students, and 'canned' problems with predetermined procedures and outcomes.

Teachers also faced dilemmas in reconciling conflicting priorities about the need for students to engage in conversation and the importance of students getting the right answers. It took considerable time for teachers to allow students the freedom to grapple with ideas and to meet the challenges of guiding students in generating problems and in engaging in productive conversations. The difficulties they encountered sometimes reaffirmed teachers' feeling that students were not mature enough for these endeavours, and thus some prematurely abandoned their efforts.

At the end of the first year of their work in project based science, each teacher's practices represented a profile of enactment, with some features adopted in a manner more congruent with the premises underlying the innovation than others. Overall, teacher progress was not linear; they moved back and forth between new and old ideas and practices. Generally, as Shulman (1987) suggests, development was 'dialectic.' Teachers advanced and retreated as they confronted dilemmas and attempted to meet challenges posed by the new approaches to teaching for understanding. In fact, it took almost three years for teachers to grasp the ideas underlying project based science and to become proficient enactors of the innovation.

Supporting Change: The Promise of Technology

Obviously the process of change to promote student construction and understanding is difficult. It is essential that we find ways to assist teachers so that they are willing to try new approaches and persist in their attempts. Supporting teachers as they collaborate, enact, and reflect is time consuming, labour intensive, and expensive. To accomplish widespread change we must find way to make the process more efficient. Harnessing the potential of the new technologies is one route being explored (Hunter, 1992; Lampert & Ball, 1990; Roup et al., 1992).

The new multimedia interactive technologies can be used to illustrate new instructional possibilities, to enhance understanding of premises underlying interventions, to demonstrate challenges of enacting the new approaches and strategies for meeting them, and to illustrate a range of practices congruent with the innovation. It also can extend the benefits of face to face meetings via telecommunication.

One example of the use of interactive multimedia technology for teachers is the Project Support Environment (PSE) developed at the University of Michigan to help teachers transition to project based science (Krajcik et al., 1994; Soloway et al., 1996). The PSE is designed to be used as an integral part of collaborative efforts along with interpersonal discussion (see Marx et al., 1997). It serves as a teacher's workbench. The components include:

a) planning software that assists teachers in designing, planning, and modifying projects using concept maps, graphical representations of the interrelation of project features (such as the driving question, investigations and artifacts), and textual fields for description of specific elements;

b) a video casebook of project practices that helps teachers learn the features of project based science and strategies for enactment via video based teacher cases, teacher and researcher written and verbal commentary, and suggested questions to promote reflection;

c) a personal multimedia casebook that supports reflection by allowing teachers to construct their own case book incorporating video from their own and others' enactments, their own and others' critiques, and personal notes; and

d) a telecommunications program that promotes collaboration and the sharing of documents such as PIViT plans and students' artifacts.

In the PSE, documents and applications are linked to each other in a seamless fashion providing teachers with a dynamic, nonlinear structure that allows them to move easily among the components. For instance, if a teacher is planning a project and has a question about investigations, she or he can easily bring up video cases of how other teachers helped students do investigations. The teacher can use the PSNet and ask colleagues questions via the PSNet. She or he can include video or text responses to the question in the personal journal for future reference.

The Student Learning Environment (SLE) was developed by Lampert and Ball (1990) and Lampert and Eshelman (1995) to help preserve teachers and teacher educators learn about teaching for understanding from the point of view of practice. They have experimented with technology to support efforts to use teaching practices as a context for teacher education and development. Multimedia materials, videos, teacher journals, and student notebooks were used to represent different perspectives on what occurred as teachers tried to teach for understanding in two mathematics classrooms over the course of a year. Users could ask questions such as 'what happens when third graders experiment with alternative representations for equivalent functions?'

In their work technological tools can be designed to aid in investigation of the question. Investigations involve finding documents, redefining and revising questions, collecting pertinent documents from various sources including the teacher journal, student notebook, and teaching videos and transcripts. The information collected can be examined simultaneously by the user and annotated to determine interconnections and to reflect on what they have found. Investigations may produce conclusions to be applied to teaching and/or stimulate further browsing.

Developers of such systems must confront unanswered questions related to design, use patterns, evaluation, and pedagogy if they are to capitalize on the potential of the new technologies (see Ball, 1994; Ladewski & Krajcik, 1995). With respect to design and pedagogy, for instance, there are similarities and differences in the PSE and the SLE. Obviously, both take advantage of technology and multimedia capabilities. The PSE illustrates new approaches to science education via selecting clips and organizing them into cases that depict challenges and dilemmas several inservice teachers in different contexts faced and solutions they devised. In contrast, the SLE illustrates the new approaches and teacher struggles using a large corpus of unselected information; the presentation of information is not organized for the user nor are predetermined issues identified. Nevertheless, the video in both systems displays actual teaching situations, thereby showing the complexity of real classroom practice. The video is neither staged nor of slick and polished professional quality. Both developers raise questions about what users learn from these realistic and complex depictions; that is, what types of images of teaching do they focus on?

In addition, there are questions about how to show change over time and what level of teacher proficiency to exhibit. Both systems use individual teachers to illustrate change in practice over time rather than contrasting teachers with differing levels of experience. However, the PSE uses experienced teachers who are novices with respect to project based science, whereas the SLE uses teachers who are also trained university researchers. Neither shows teachers implementing a predetermined set of practices. Thus both differ from most packaged video used for teacher development that shows expert teachers implementing prescribed programs which allow for little variation in implementation.

Other questions concern how to support learning. What types of structures and scaffolds are necessary? Both systems for instance offer written commentary by teachers in the video to help viewers interpret events and provide insight into the teachers' intents, reactions, and quandaries. They also provide work space for user writing. In the PSE teachers can create a personal journal which includes comments about cases, video imported from cases, or video of themselves and their own reactions. The SLE offers notebooks for users to store comments or impressions or analysis of evidence concerning the question under investigation. While there is considerable evidence that teachers can profit from the reflection that comes from writing about practice, how teachers use the functionality and how they benefit from it in hypermedia systems is not known.

Related questions concern how to design systems which are responsive to different levels of user proficiency. That is, what is necessary in order for systems to accommodate to increasing technological expertise? Also, how can such systems be helpful to users as their familiarity and experience with the innovation grows? Preliminary answers to these questions should be obtained from studies underway of how the systems are used and how that use changes over time.

Finally, the pedagogy surrounding use of such systems also requires attention. What are effective ways to introduce teachers to these tools? Many commercial software packages are designed to be used on a stand-alone basis. In contrast, it is interesting to note that both systems are not used in isolation but are part of a larger instructional effort. The PSE is embedded in a series of institutes as central parts of work sessions. The SLE has been used as part of a class in mathematics methods and as part of institutes for teacher educators. Moreover, to promote conversation both have groups of people working together on the systems.

Just as the teaching for understanding classroom programs described previously are in initial stages of evaluation, the technological attempts to help teachers learn to teach for understanding are in their infancy, and their effects just beginning to be examined. Much of the attention to date has focused on improving the features and functionality of the systems. More recently, questions about patterns of use of video and written materials and of personal work spaces have been addressed. Also, reports have appeared about how groups collaborate to create understanding and how understanding changes over time. In contrast, how such understanding translates into practice and how use of the system changes with increasing understanding are not known. Obviously, the findings from current work should add to more effective design of the technology and more effective pedagogy surrounding its use. Ultimately the result should be realization of a set of guidelines for creating and capitalizing on exciting new possibilities for helping teachers learn to teach for understanding.

CONCLUSIONS

Ideas about teaching for understanding have undergone profound changes. In the past, transmission approaches led to an emphasis on teacher behavior which structured the learning situation, sequenced the information presented, and shaped the learner's responses. With the rise of information processing approaches, emphasis shifted to a focus on student transformation. Teachers were to help the student to use memory, elaboration, and organizational strategies and to become more aware of the process of learning. Students were seen as active constructors of learning. Recent insight from studies of everyday learning have resulted in new emphases on social rather than individual influences on learning. They have highlighted the cultural and situated nature of knowledge and of learning. Newer social constructivist theories have asserted that understanding is contextualized and a function of social interaction with others, the tasks undertaken, the tools employed, and the immediate context which reflects the culture in which ideas are developed and used.

These approaches have not spawned a specific set of prescribed behaviors for teachers. Instead there are some general guidelines that can be derived; consequently, classroom enactments might vary considerably and still be commensurate with the theory. The teachers' role is like that of a master craftsman, creating a situation where the student apprentice is inducted into the ways of knowing in the discipline and to its important ideas. The teacher helps create an environment and selects areas of inquiry for students to engage while investigating, solving problems, and exploring ideas using technological tools as aids. The emphasis is on discourse and collaboration so that students can learn from each other and from others with greater expertise. The teacher scaffolds learning via modelling cognitive processes, coaching, providing feedback, breaking down tasks, and – as students gain proficiency – gradually releasing responsibility. The teacher assesses what students understand using alternatives to standardized short answer tests. The stress is on authenticity, on creating an environment where students must demonstrate mastery of concepts and of disciplinary ways of inquiry through various means such as public presentations or demonstrations which preferably have meaning beyond the confines of the classroom.

Programs described in this chapter that reflect constructivist principles in the teaching of science encompass many of the elements described above. They emphasize investigation of real problems, collaboration among students, use of tools (especially computers), the generation of artifacts where students represent understanding in a variety of different ways, and alternative forms of assessment. The programs vary widely in how they implement elements that stem from constructivist theory. They also differ with respect to the science content, grade level, and student population targeted. Consequently they are difficult to compare. Moreover, the programs are based on the notion of design experiments where the goal is to apply theory to practice and to use results of practice both to inform theory and to improve the program itself. The assumption is that instructional elements are inextricably bound; therefore, although student learning is examined, no attempts are made to vary different elements systematically or to analyze the contribution of different elements to student learning. While the programs are innovative and exciting as prototypes for the future, this approach to research means that educators hoping to adopt a program or incorporate some elements from each of them are not likely to find ready answers to likely questions about how to design programs effectively, use technology, motivate students, accommodate to individual differences, or assess learning.

Moreover, approaches to instruction derived from constructivist theories entail considerable changes for teachers. Such changes are not easily achieved. Thus, if new ideas about teaching for understanding are to gain acceptance, attention must be paid to ways to help teachers transition from familiar ways of working. New efforts in professional development demonstrate the importance of collaboration among teachers and researchers and the need for cycles of practice and reflection as a route to change in practice. Moreover, they suggest that teacher change takes considerable time and effort and requires a great deal of support. One source of support being explored is interactive multimedia technology. Two technological systems described are based on constructivist notions; teachers learn new ideas about teaching, learning, and the problems of practice these entail by raising questions and using a variety of sources, including video of students and teachers, and audio and written commentary to answer these questions. The systems are designed to be used collaboratively and include scaffolding for learning.

Like the instructional programs described, these technological experiments are quite new. Questions remain to be answered about how to design the systems, to use combinations of media, to scaffold learning, to develop pedagogies to facilitate their use, and to evaluate their impact. Both the programs and technology to support teacher change have potential for helping to create promising new occasions for teaching and learning in schools. Exploring their potential, their promise, and their limitations is the task that educators now face.

ENDNOTES

[1.]   This work was partially supported by a grant from the National Science Foundation (grant # TPE-9153759).

REFERENCES

Anderson, A. & Roth, K. (1989). Teaching for meaningful and self-regulated learning of science. In J. Brophy (Ed.), *Advances in research on teaching (Vol. 1). Teaching for meaningful understanding and self-regulated learning* (pp. 265-306). Greenwich, CT: JAI.

Archibald, D. A. & Newmann, F. M. (1992). Approaches to assessing academic achievement. In H. Berlak, F. M. Newmann, E. Adams, D. A. Archibald, T. Burgess, J. Raven, & Romberg, T. A. (Eds.), *Toward a new science of educational testing and assessment* (pp. 139-180). Albany, NY: SUNY Press.

Aronson, E., Blaney, E., Stephen, C., Sikes, J., & Snapp, M. (1978). *The jigsaw classroom.* Beverly Hills, CA: Sage.

Ausubel, D. P. (1960). The use of advanced organizers in the learning and retention of meaningful verbal material. *Journal of Educational Psychology, 51*, 267-272.

Ball, D. L. (1994, November). *Developing mathematics reform: What don't we know about teacher learning – but would make good working hypotheses?* Paper presented at Conference on Teacher Enhancement in Mathematics, Arlington, VA.

Ball, D. L. & Rundquist, S. S. (1993). Collaboration as a context for joining teacher learning with learning about teaching. In D. K. Cohen, M. W. McLaughlin, & J. E. Talbert (Eds.), *Teaching for understanding: Challenges for policy and practice* (pp. 13-42). San Francisco: Jossey-Bass.

Bartlett, F. C. (1932). Remembering: A study in experimental and social psychology. New York: Macmillan.

Bellack, A. A., Kliebard, H. M., Hyman, R. T., & Smith, F. L. (1966). *The language of the classroom.* New York: Teachers College Press.

Bereiter, C. & Engelmann, S. (1966). *Teaching disadvantaged children in the preschool.* Englewood Cliffs, NJ: Prentice-Hall.

Berliner, D. C. (1979). *Tempus educare.* In P. L. Peterson & H. J. Walberg (Eds.), *Research on teaching: Concepts, findings, and implications* (pp. 120-135). Berkeley, CA: McCutchan.

Bickel, W. E. & Hattrup, R. A. (1995). Teachers and researchers in collaboration: Reflections on the process. *American Educational Research Journal, 32*, 35-62.

Blumenfeld, P. C. (1992). The task and the teacher: Enhancing student thoughtfulness in science. In J. Brophy (Ed.), *Advances in research on teaching* (Vol. 3, pp. 81-114). Greenwich, CT: JAI Press.

Blumenfeld, P. C., Krajcik, J. S., Marx, R. W., & Soloway, E. (1994). Lessons learned: A collaborative model for helping teachers learn project-based instruction. *Elementary School Journal, 94*, 483-497.

Blumenfeld, P. C., Mergendoller, J., & Swarthout, D. (1987). Task as a heuristic for understanding student learning and motivation. *Journal of Curriculum Studies, 19*, 135-148.

Blumenfeld, P. C., Soloway, E., Marx, R. W., Krajcik, J. S., Guzdial, M., & Palincsar, A. (1991). Motivating project-based learning: Sustaining the doing, supporting the learning. *Educational Psychologist, 26*, 369-398.

Bransford, J. D. & Stein, B. S. (1984). *The IDEAL problem solver.* New York: Academic Press.

Bossert, S. T. (1988-1989). Cooperative activities in the classroom. *Review of Research in Education, 15*, 225-252.

Brophy, J. & Alleman, J. (1991). Activities as instructional tools: A framework for instructional analysis and evaluation. *Educational Researcher, 20*, 9-23.

Brophy, J. & Good, T. (1986). Teacher behavior and student achievement. In M. Wittrock (Ed.), *Handbook of research on teaching: Teacher behavior and student achievement* (pp. 328-375). New York: Macmillan.

Brown, A. L. (1992). Design experiments: Theoretical and methodological challenges in creating complex interventions in classroom settings. *Journal of the Learning Sciences, 2*, 141-178.

Brown, A. L. (1995). The advancement of learning. *Educational Researcher, 23*(8), 4-12.

Brown, A. L., Ash, D., Rutherford, M., Nakagawa, K., Gordon, A., & Campione, J. C. (1993). Distributed expertise in the classroom. In G. Salomon (Ed.), *Distributed cognitions* (pp. 188-228). New York: Cambridge University Press.

Brown, A. L. & Campione, J. C. (1994). Guided discovery in a community of learners. In K. McGilly (Ed.), *Classroom lessons: Integrating cognitive theory and classroom practice* (pp. 229-270). Cambridge, MA: MIT Press/Bradford Books.

Brown, A. L. & Campione, J. C. (in press). Psychological theory and the design of innovative learning environments: On procedures, principles, and systems. In L. Schauble & R. Glaser (Eds.), *Contributions of instructional innovation to understand learning.* Hillsdale, NJ: Lawrence Erlbaum.

Brown, J. S., Collins, A., & Duguid, P. (1989). Situated cognition and the culture of learning. *Educational Researcher, 18*(1), 32-42.

Bruer, J. (1995). Classroom problems, school culture, and cognitive research. In K. McGilly (Ed.), *Classroom lessons: Integrating cognitive theory and classroom practice* (pp. 273-290). Cambridge, MA: MIT Press.

Carter, K. (1993). The place of story in the study of teaching and teacher education. *Educational Researcher, 22*, 5-12, 18.

Clark, C. M., Gage, N. L., Marx, R. W., Peterson, P. L., Stayrook, N. G., & Winne, P. H. (1979). A factorial experiment on teacher structuring, soliciting, and reacting. *Journal of Educational Psychology, 71*, 534-552.

Cobb, P. (1994). Where is the mind? Constructivist and sociocultural perspectives on mathematical development. *Educational Researcher, 23*, 13-20.

Cognition and Technology Group at Vanderbilt (1990). Anchored instruction and its relationship to situated cognition. *Educational Researcher, 19*, 2-10.

Cognition and Technology Group at Vanderbilt (1992a). Anchored instruction in science education. In R. Duschal & R. Hamilton (Eds.), *Philosophy of science, cognitive psychology, and educational theory and practice* (pp. 245-273). New York: SUNY Press.

Cognition and Technology Group at Vanderbilt (1992b). The Jasper series as an example of anchored instruction: Theory, program description, and assessment data. *Educational Psychologist, 27*, 291-315.

Cognition and Technology Group at Vanderbilt (1993). *Experimental studies of a multimedia instructional environment in science classrooms.* Paper presented at the annual meeting of the American Educational Research Association, Atlanta, GA.

Cohen, D. K. & Ball, D. L. (1990). Policy and practice: An overview. *Educational Evaluation and Policy Analysis, 21*, 233-239.

Cohen, D. K. & Barnes, C. A. (1993). Pedagogy and policy. In D. K. Cohen, M. W. McLaughlin, & J. E. Talbert (Eds.), *Teaching for understanding: Challenges for policy and practice* (pp. 207-239). San Francisco: Jossey-Bass.

Collins, A., Brown, J. S., & Newman, S. G. (1989). Cognitive apprenticeship: Teaching the craft of reading, writing, and mathematics. In L. B. Resnick (Ed.), *Knowing, learning, and instruction: Essays in honor of Robert Glaser* (pp. 453-494). Hillsdale, NJ: Erlbaum.

Confrey, J. (1990). A review of the research on students' conceptions in mathematics, science, and programming. *Review of Research in Education, 16*, 3-56.

Cross, D. & Paris, S. (1988). Developmental and instructional analyses of children's meta-cognition and reading comprehension. *Journal of Educational Psychology, 80*, 131-142.

de Groot, A. D. (1965). *Thought and choice in chess.* The Hague: Mouton.

Denham, C. & Lieberman, A. (Eds.). (1980). *Time to learn.* Washington, DC: U.S. Department of Education.

Doyle, W. (1977). Paradigms for research on teacher effectiveness. In L. S. Shulman (Ed.), *Review of Research in Education* (Vol. 5, pp. 163-199). Itasca, IL: Peacock.

Doyle, W. (1983). Academic work. *Review of Educational Research, 53,* 159-199.

Driver, R. & Oldham, V. (1986). A constructivist approach to curriculum development in science. *Studies in Science Education, 13,* 105-122.

Driver, R., Asoko, H., Leach, J., Mortimer, E., & Scott, P. (1994). Constructing scientific knowledge in the classroom. *Educational Researcher, 23*(7), 5-12.

Duffy, G. (1993). Rethinking strategy instruction: Four teachers' development and their low-achievers' understandings. *Elementary School Journal, 93,* 231-247.

Duffy, G. G., & Roehler, L. R. (1987a). Improving reading instruction through the use of responsive elaboration. *Reading Teacher, 40,* 514-520.

Duffy, G. G. & Roehler, L. R. (1987b). Teaching reading skills as strategies. *Reading Teacher, 41,* 414-418.

Dunkin, M. J. & Biddle, B. J. (1974). *The study of teaching.* New York: Holt, Rinehart, & Winston.

Eccles, J. (1993, September). *User friendly science and mathematics: Can it interest girls and minorities in breaking through the middle school wall?* Paper presented at the Federation of Behavioral, Psychological and Cognitive Sciences, Science and Public Policy Seminars, Washington, DC.

Edelson, D. C. (in press). Realising authentic science learning through the adaptation of scientific practice. In K. Tobin & B. J. Fraser (Eds.), *International handbook of science education.* Netherlands: Kluwer.

Edelson, D. C. & O'Neill, K. (1994). The CoVis collaboratory notebook: Supporting collaborative scientific inquiry. In *Proceedings of NECC 94: National Educational Computing Conference* (pp. 146-152). Boston, MA: International Society for Technology in Education.

Ernest, P. (1995). The one and the many. In L. P. Steffe & J. Gale (Eds.), *Constructivism in education* (pp. 459-486). Hillsdale, NJ: Lawrence Erlbaum Associates.

Engelmann, S. & Brunner, E. (1984). *DISTAR reading.* Chicago: Science Research Associates.

Fennema, E., Carpenter, T., & Peterson, P. (1989). Learning mathematics with understanding. In J. Brophy (Ed.), *Advances in research on teaching: Vol. 1, Teaching for meaningful understanding and self-regulated learning* (pp. 195-221). Greenwich, CT: JAI.

Foley, B. (1995, April). *Using a knowledge integration approach to teach the physics of sound.* Paper presented at the National Association for Research on Science Teaching Annual Conference, San Francisco.

Fullan, M. (1993). *Change forces: Probing the depths of educational reform.* Bristol, PA: Falmer Press.

Gage, N. L. (1978). *The scientific basis of the art of teaching.* New York: Teachers College Press.

Gagné, R. (1985). *The conditions of learning* (4th ed.). New York: Holt, Rinehart, & Winston.

Gardner, H. (1983). *Frames of mind.* New York: Basic Books.

Gardner, H., Krechevsky, M., Sternberg, R. J., & Okagaki, L. (1994). Intelligence in context: Enhancing students' practical intelligence for school. In K. McGilly (Ed.), *Classroom lessons: Integrating cognitive theory* (pp. 105-127). Cambridge, MA: MIT Press.

Good, T. & Brophy, J. (1994). *Looking in classrooms* (6th ed.). New York: Harper Collins.

Good, T., Grouws, D., & Ebmeier, H. (1983). *Active mathematics teaching.* New York: Longman.

Good, T., Mulryan, C., & McCaslin, M. (1992). Grouping for instruction in mathematics: A call for programmatic research on small-group processes. In D. Grouws (Ed.), *Handbook of research on mathematics teaching and learning* (pp. 165-196). New York: Macmillan.

Gordin, D. N. & Pea, R. D. (1995). Prospects for scientific visualization as an educational technology. *Journal of the Learning Sciences, 4*, 249-279.

Gordin, D. N., Polman, J. L., & Pea, R. D. (1994). The climate visualizer: Sense-making through scientific visualization. *Journal of Science Education and Technology, 3*, 203-226.

Heaton, R. M. & Lampert, M. (1993). Learning to hear voices: Inventing a new pedagogy of teacher education. In D. K. Cohen, M. W. McLaughlin, & J. E. Talbert (Eds.), *Teaching for understanding: Challenges for policy and practice* (pp. 43-83). San Francisco: Jossey-Bass Publishers.

Heokter, J. & Ahlbrand, W. P. (1969). The persistence of recitation. *American Educational Research Journal, 6*, 145-167.

Heubel-Draube, M., Finkel, L., Stern, E., & Mouradian, M. (1995). Planning a course for success: Using an integrated curriculum to prepare students for the twenty-first century. *The Science Teacher, 62*(7), 18-21.

Hickey, D. T. (in press). Motivation's place in contemporary constructivist instructional perspectives. *Educational Psychologist.*

Hiebert, J. & Carpenter, T. (1992). Learning and teaching with understanding. In D. A. Grouws (Ed.), *Handbook of research on mathematics teaching and learning* (pp. 65-97). New York: Macmillan.

Hunter, B. (1992). Linking for learning: Computer-and-communications network support for nationwide innovation in education. *Journal of Science Education and Technology, 1*, 23-34.

Hunter, M. C. (1982). *Mastery teaching*. El Segundo, CA: TIP Publications.

Jackson, S. L., Stratford, S. J., Krajcik, J. S., & Soloway, E. (1996). Model-It: A case study of learner-centered design software for supporting model building. *Interactive Learning Environments*, 233-257.

Joyce, B. R. & Showers, B. (1988). *Student achievement through staff development*. New York: Longman.

Kaestle, C. R. (1993). The awful reputation of educational research. *Educational Researcher, 22*(1), 26-31.

Krajcik, J. S., Blumenfeld, P. C., Marx, R. W., & Soloway, E. (1994). A collaborative model for helping teachers learn project-based instruction. *Elementary School Journal, 94*, 483-497.

Ladewski, B. G. & Krajcik, J. S. (1995, April). *The iterative design and development process: Developing a technological partner that understands a teacher's world*. Paper presented at the annual meeting of the American Educational Research Association, San Francisco.

Ladewski, B. G., Krajcik, J. S., & Harvey, C. L. (1994). A middle grade science teacher's emerging understanding of project-based instruction. *Elementary School Journal, 94*, 483-497.

Lamon, M., Secules, T., Petrosino, A. J., Hackett, R., Bransford, J. D., & Goldman, S.R. (in press). Schools for thought: Overview of the project and lessons learned from one of the sites. In L. Schauble & R. Glaser (Eds.), *Contributions of instructional innovation to understanding learning*. Hillsdale, NJ: Lawrence Erlbaum.

Lampert, M. & Ball, D. L. (1990). Using hypermedia technology to support a new pedagogy of teacher education (Issue Paper 90-5). East Lansing: Michigan State University, National Center for Research on Teacher Education.

Lampert, M. & Eshelman, A. S. (1995, April). *Using technology to support effective and responsible teacher education: The case of interactive multimedia in mathematics methods courses*. Paper presented at the annual meeting of the American Educational Research Association, San Francisco.

Lave, J. & Wenger, E. (1991). *Situated learning: Legitimate peripheral participation*. Cambridge: Cambridge University Press.

Lenk, C. (1992). The network science experience: Learning from three major projects. In R. F. Tinker & P. M. Kapisovsky (Eds.), *Prospects for educational telecomputing: Selected readings* (pp. 51-60). Cambridge, MA: TERC.

Linn, M. C. (1992). The computer as learning partner: Can computer tools teach science? In K. Sheingold, L.G. Roberts, & S. M. Malcolm (Eds.), *This year in school science 1991: Technology for teaching and learning* (pp. 31-69). Washington, DC: American Association for the Advancement of Science.

Linn, M. C. (1997). Learning and instruction in science education: Taking advantage of technology. In D. Tobin & B.J. Fraser (Eds.), *International handbook of science education*. The Netherlands: Kluwer.

Linn, M. C. & Hyde, J. S. (1989), Gender, mathematics, and science. *Educational Researcher, 18*, 17-19, 22-27.

Linn, M. C. & Songer, N. B. (1988, April). *Curriculum reformulation: Incorporating technology into science instruction*. Paper presented at the annual meeting of the American Educational Research Association.

Linn, M. C., Songer, N. B., Lewis, E. L., & Stern, J. (1993). Using technology to teach thermodynamics: Achieving integrated understanding. In D. L. Ferguson (Ed.), *Advanced technologies in the teaching of mathematics and science* (Vol. 107, pp. 5-60). Berlin: Springer-Verlag.

Mager, R. F. (1975). *Preparing instructional objectives*. Belmont, CA: Fearon.

Mandinach, E. & Cline, H. (1989). Applications of simulation and modeling in precollege instruction. *Machine-mediated Learning, 3*, 189-205.

Mandinach, E. & Cline, H. (1994). *Classroom dynamics: Implementing a technology based learning environment*. Hillsdale, NJ: Lawrence Erlbaum.

Marx, R. W. (1993, March). *Integration of technology in the schools*. Testimony submitted to the House Subcommittee on Elementary, Secondary and Vocational Education.

Marx, R. W., Blumenfeld, P. C., Krajcik, J. S., Blunk, M., Crawford, B., Kelly, B., & Meyer, K. M. (1994). Enacting project-based science: Experiences of four middle grade teachers. *Elementary School Journal, 94*, 517-538.

Marx, R. W., Blumenfeld, P. C., Krajcik, J. S., Soloway, E., Cox, G., & Breen, T. (1995, April). *PIViT: Technology for the professional development of science teachers*. Paper presented at the annual meeting of the American Educational Research Association, San Francisco.

Marx, R. W., Freeman, J. G., Krajcik, J. S., & Blumenfeld, P. C. (1997). Professional development of science teachers. In D. Tobin & B. J. Fraser (Eds.), *International handbook of science education*. Netherlands: Kluwer.

Newell, A. & Simon, H. A. (1972). *Human problem solving*. Englewood Cliffs, NJ: Prentice-Hall.

Newman, D., Griffin, P., & Cole, M. (1989). *The construction zone: Working for cognitive change in school*. Cambridge: Cambridge University Press.

Newmann, F. M. (1993). Beyond common sense in educational restructuring: The issues of content and linkage. *Educational Researcher, 22*(4), 4-13, 22.

Newmann, F. M. & Archibald, D. A. (1992). Approaches to assessing academic achievement. In H. Berlak, F. M. Newmann, E. Adams, D. A. Archibald, T. Burgess, J. Raven, & Romberg, T. A. (Eds.), *Toward a new science of educational testing and assessment* (pp. 71-83). Albany, NY: SUNY Press.

Newmann, F. M. & Wehlage, G. G. (1993). Five standards for authentic instruction. *Educational Leadership, 50*, 8-12.

Owen, M. (1992). A teacher centered model of development in the educational use of computers. *Journal of Information Technology for Teacher Education, 1*(1), 127-138.

Palincsar, A. S., Anderson, C., & David, Y. M. (1993). Pursuing scientific literacy in the middle grades through collaborative problem solving. *Elementary School Journal, 93*, 643-658.

Palincsar, A. & Brown, A. (1984). Reciprocal teaching of comprehension fostering and comprehension monitoring activities. *Cognition and Instruction, 1*(2) 117-175.

Paris, S. G., Cross, D., & Lipson, M. (1984). Informal strategies for learning: A program to improve children's reading awareness and comprehension. *Journal of Educational Psychology, 76*, 1239-1252.

Pea, R. D. & Gomez, L. M. (1992). Distributed multimedia learning environments: Why and how? *Interactive Learning Environments, 2*(2), 73-109.

Perkins, D. (1992). *Smart schools: From training memories to educating minds.* New York: Free Press.

Perkins, D. N., Schwartz, J. L., West, M. M., & Wiske, M. S. (Eds.). (1995). *Software goes to school: Teaching for understanding with new technologies.* New York: Oxford University Press.

Perkins, D. N. & Unger, C. (1994). A new look in representations for mathematics and science learning. *Instructional Science, 2*, 1-37.

Peterson, P. & Walberg, H. J. (Eds.). (1979). *Research in teaching.* Berkeley, CA: McCutchan.

Peterson, P. L. (1979). Direct instruction reconsidered. In P. L. Peterson & H. J. Walberg (Eds.), *Research on teaching: Concepts, findings, and implications* (pp. 57-69). Berkeley, CA: McCutchan.

Petrosino, A. J., Sherwood, R. D., Bransford, J. D., & CTGV (in press). The use of cognitive tools to facilitate knowledge construction in macro context environments: Foundations, design issues, and the development of applications in applied settings. In S. Helgeson (Ed.), *Proceedings: Working conference on technology applications in the science classroom.* The National Center for Research in Science Teaching and Learning.

Phillips, D. C. (1995). The good, the bad, and the ugly: The many faces of constructivism. *Educational Researcher, 24*, 5-12.

Pintrich, P. R., Marx, R. W., & Boyle, R. A. (1993). Beyond cold conceptual change: The role of motivational beliefs and classroom contextual factors in the process of conceptual change. *Review of Educational Research, 63*, 167-199.

Posner, G. J., Strike, K. A., Hewson, P. W., & Gertzog, W. A. (1982). Accommodation of a scientific conception: Toward a theory of conceptual change. *Science Education, 66*, 211-227.

Prawat, R. S. (1989a). Promoting access to knowledge, strategy, and disposition in students: A research synthesis. *Review of Educational Research, 59*, 1-41.

Prawat, R. S. (1989b). The value of ideas: The immersion approach to the development of thinking. *Educational Researcher, 20*, 3-10, 30.

Prawat, R. S. (1992). Teachers' beliefs about teaching and learning: A constructivist perspective. *American Journal of Education, 100*, 354-395.

Pressley, M., El-Dinary, P., Gaskins, I., Schuder, T., Bergman, J., Almasi, J., & Brown, R. (1992). Beyond direct explanation: Transactional instruction of reading comprehension strategies. *Elementary School Journal, 92*, 513-555.

Pressley, M., Johnson, C., Symons, S., McGoldrick, J., & Kurita, J. (1989). Strategies that improve children's memory and comprehension of text. *Elementary School Journal, 90*, 3-32.

Resnick, L. B. (1987). Learning in school and out. *Educational Researcher, 16*(9), 13-20.

Richardson, V. & Anders, P. (1994). *A theory of teacher change and the practice of staff development.* New York: Teachers College Press.

Rosebury, A. S., Warren, B., & Conant, F. R. (1989). *Cheche Konnen: Science and literacy in language minority classrooms* (BBN Technical Report No. 7305). Cambridge, MA: BBN Laboratories, Inc.

Rosenshine, B. (1986). Synthesis of research on explicit teaching. *Educational Leadership, 43*, 60-69.

Rosenshine, B. & Furst, N. (1973). The use of direct observation to study teaching. In R. M. W. Travers (Ed.), *Second handbook of research on teaching* (pp. 122-183). Chicago: Rand McNally.

Rosenshine, B. & Stevens, R. (1986). Teaching functions. In M. C. Wittrock (Ed.), *Handbook of research on teaching* (3rd ed., pp. 376-391). New York: Macmillan.

Roth, W. M. (1994). Experimenting in a constructivist high school physics laboratory. *Journal of Research in Science Teaching, 31*, 197-223.

Roup, R. R., Gal, S., Drayton, B., & Pfister, M. (Eds.). (1992). *LabNet: Toward a community of practice*. Hillsdale, NJ: Erlbaum.

Rud, A. G. (1995, April). *The development of an on-line community of inquiry*. Paper presented at the annual meeting of the American Educational Research Association, San Francisco.

Russell, T. & Munby, H. (Eds.). (1992). *Teachers and teaching: From classroom to reflection*. London: Falmer Press.

Salomon, G. (1983). The differential investment of mental effort in learning from different sources. *Educational Psychologist, 18*, 42-50.

Salomon, G. & Perkins, D. N. (1989). Rocky roads to transfer: Rethinking mechanism of a neglected phenomenon. *Educational Psychologist, 24*, 113-142.

Salomon, G., Perkins, D. N., & Globerson, T. (1991). Partners in cognition: Extending human intelligence with intelligent technologies. *Educational Researcher, 20*(3), 2-9.

Scardamalia, M. & Bereiter, C. (1991). Higher levels of agency for children in knowledge building: A challenge for the design of new knowledge media. *Journal of the Learning Sciences, 1*, 37-68.

Scardamalia, M., Bereiter, C., & Lamon, M. (1994). The CSILE Project: Trying to bring the classroom into world 3. In K. McGilly (Ed.), *Classroom lessons: Integrating cognitive theory and classroom practice* (pp. 201-228). Cambridge, MA: MIT Press/Bradford Books.

Schauble, L., Glaser, R., Duschl, R. A., Schulze, S., & John, J. (1995). Students' understanding of the objectives and procedures of experimentation in the science classroom. *Journal of the Learning Sciences, 4*, 131-166.

Schuell, T. J. (1996). Teaching and learning in a classroom context. In D. C. Berliner & R. Calfee (Eds.), *Handbook on educational psychology* (pp. 726-764). New York: Macmillan.

Scott, C. A. (1994). Project-based science: Reflections of a middle school teacher. *Elementary School Journal, 95*, 75-94.

Shavelson, R. J., Baxter, G. P., & Gao, X. (1993). Sampling variability of performance assessments. *Journal of Educational Measurement, 30*, 215-232.

Shulman, L. (1987). Knowledge and teaching: Foundations of the new reform. *Harvard Educational Review, 57*, 1-22.

Slavin, R. E. (1990). *Cooperative learning: Theory, research, and practice*. Englewood Cliffs, NJ: Prentice-Hall.

Soloway, E., Guzdial, M., & Hay, K. E. (1994). Learner-centered design: The challenge for human computer interaction in the 21st century. *Interactions, 1*(2), 36-48.

Soloway, E., Krajcik, J. S., Blumenfeld, P., & Marx, R. (1996). Technological support for teachers transitioning to project-based science practices. In T. Koschmann (Ed.), *CSCL: Theory and practice of an emerging paradigm*. Hillsdale, NJ: Lawrence Erlbaum Associates.

Stake, R. E. & Easley, J. A. (1978). *Case studies in science education* (Vol. 2, No. 038-000-0037603). Washington, DC: U.S. Government Printing Office.

Sternberg, R. J. (1985). Beyond IQ: A triarchic theory of human intelligence. New York: Cambridge University Press.

Stodolsky, S. S. (1988). The subject matters: Classroom activity in math and social studies. Chicago: University of Chicago Press.

Stratford, S. & Finkel, E. (1995, May). *Impact of ScienceWare and foundations on student attitudes*. Paper presented annual meeting of National Association for Research on Science Teaching, San Francisco.

Suppes, P. (1966). The uses of computers in education. *Scientific American, 215*(3), 206-220.

Tharp, R. & Gallimore, R. (1988). *Rousing minds to life: Teaching, learning, and schooling in a social context*. Cambridge, MA: Cambridge University Press.

Tobin, K. & Gallagher, J. J. (1987). The role of target students in the science classroom. *Journal of Research in Science Teaching, 24*, 61-75.

Vygotsky, L. S. (1978). *Mind in society: The development of higher psychological processes* (M. Cole, V. John-Steiner, S. Scribner, & E. Sourberman, Eds. & Trans.). Cambridge, MA: Harvard University Press.

Webb, N. M. & Palincsar, A. S. (1996). Group processes in the classroom. In D. Berliner & R. Calfee (Eds.), *Handbook of research in educational psychology* (pp. 841-873). New York: Simon & Schuster.

Weinstein, R., Madison, S., & Kuklinski, M. (1995). Raising expectations in schooling: Obstacles and opportunities for change. *American Educational Research Journal, 32*, 121-159.

Weinstein, C. R. & Mayer, R. F. (1986). The teaching of learning strategies. In M. C. Wittrock (Ed.), *Handbook of research on teaching* (3rd ed., pp. 315-327). New York: Macmillan.

Wertsch, J. V. (1985). *Vygotsky and the social formation of mind*. Cambridge: Harvard University Press.

Wertsch, J. V. (1991). *Voices of the mind: A socio-cultural approach to mediated action*. Cambridge, MA: Harvard University Press.

Wiggins, G. (1993). Assessment: Authenticity, context, and validity. *Phi Delta Kappan, 74*, 201-214.

Willis, J. W. & Mehlinger, H. D. (1996). Information technology and teacher education. In J. Silcula, T. J. Buttery, & E. Guyton (Eds.), *Handbook of research on teacher education* (pp. 978-1029). New York: Macmillan.

Winne, P. H. & Marx, R. W. (1978). The best tool teachers have – their students' thinking. In D. C. Berliner & B. Rosenshine (Eds.), *Talks to teachers: A festshrift for N. L. Gage* (pp. 267-304). New York: Random House.

Winne, P. H. & Marx, R. W. (1982). Students' and teachers' views of thinking processes for classroom learning. *Elementary School Journal, 82*, 493-518.

Winne, P. H. & Marx, R. W. (1989). A cognitive-processing analysis of motivation with classroom tasks. In C. Ames & R. Ames (Eds.), *Research on motivation in education* (Vol. 3, pp. 223-257). New York: Academic Press.

Wood, T., Cobb, P., & Yackel, E. (1990). The contextual nature of teaching: Mathematics and reading instruction in one second-grade classroom. *Elementary School Journal, 90*, 497-513.

Young, A. J. & Pintrich, P. R. (in press). Three perspectives on the role of motivation in strategic learning. In C. E. Weinstein & B. L. McCombs (Eds.), *Strategic learning: Skill, will, and self-regulation*. Hillsdale, NJ: Erlbaum Associates.

Chapter 5: Peer Cultures and Their Challenge for Teaching

BARBARA J. BANK
University of Missouri-Columbia

In recent years, the term *peer group* has increasingly been replaced by the term *peer culture*. This chapter begins with a discussion of these two terms and the likely reasons for this change. Next, a typology of peer cultures is presented based on three different ways in which these culture can be created. The presentation of this typology is followed by a discussion of the diversity among peer cultures generated by background characteristics of peers such as social class, gender, age, and race-ethnicity. The chapter then assesses the claims that peer cultures of children and adolescents frequently conflict with teachers' goals and the official school culture that encompasses these goals. While not rejecting these claims, I argue that they are based on simplifying assumptions that ignore tensions and contradictions within official school cultures. In particular, I argue that it is useful to separate three strands of official school culture – academic goals, extracurricular activities, and school rules about deportment – and to show how each affects and is affected by the peer cultures students construct for themselves. Next, the influence of peer cultures on students' opinions and behaviours is assessed directly in a section of the chapter that reviews the literature concerned with the nature and strength of peer influence. The final section of the chapter assesses the implications of peer cultures for teaching by examining what school staffs have done and might do to affect peer group processes at different levels of schooling.

PEER GROUPS AND PEER CULTURES

The term *peers* is generally used to refer to persons who occupy equivalent positions in an organization or social network. These positions are usually designated by identity labels, and those with legitimate claims to the same label are said to be peers. Thus, students in a school are peers, as are teachers in a school, but students and teachers hold different positions and are not peers. Students in different schools may also be regarded as peers, especially when the students are at the same grade level. Students may also be regarded as the peers of those who drop out of school, but in such cases, a label other than student (e.g., adolescents, gang members, 16 year olds) will be used to identify the basis of their

B.J. Biddle et al. (eds.), International Handbook of Teachers and Teaching, 879-937

peer status. Although teachers or principals or school bus drivers or academics who judge one another's scholarship meet the definition of peers just as much as students do, the term is used in this chapter to refer to young people, especially children and adolescents.

Peer groups consist of two or more peers who are linked together by more than their common identity label. These linkages usually include contact, interaction, and positive, sociometric choices (who are your friends? whom do you like?). Peer groups vary in size and in closeness. Closeness is difficult to define precisely because it is based on multiple linkages, but increases in number of contacts, duration and variety of interactions, and reciprocated sociometric choices should all produce increased closeness in peer groups. Network theorists (Boissevain, 1974; Fischer, 1982) have also stressed the importance of density by which they mean the extent to which the members of a group are interconnected. The more of a person's friends who are friends of one another, the more dense his or her friendship network. Similarly, the higher the proportion of peers who identify themselves and one another as members of the same group, the more dense that group. Dense peer groups are likely to be perceived as not only closer but also more exclusive than peer groups that are less dense.

Peer groups may be important to their members even when the groups are not dense or particularly close (Granovetter, 1973). Peer groups may also serve as reference groups for people who do not belong to them. In such cases, people may identify with a group, seek to emulate it, and wish to join it, but they may have little, if any, contact and interaction with group members. Nor would such people be the target of positive, sociometric choices by group members. Indeed, group members may not even be aware of the people who use them as a reference group. This lack of awareness might be interpreted by others as snobbishness, and this interpretation might produce a 'cycle of popularity' like the one described by Eder (1985) in which a popular peer group is transformed from a positive reference group to the most disliked group in the school.

The behaviours of peer group members are interpreted not only by outsiders, but also by the members themselves. These interpretations give rise to a *peer culture* which consists of the descriptive and evaluative meanings that peer groups assign to behaviours and relationships. These meanings are never static, and the interactions among peer group members consist of talk and behaviours that construct, maintain, consolidate, challenge, or change these meanings. The interpretations peer groups construct for themselves and their own experiences are usually part of a broader process in which meanings are also assigned to other groups and individuals. This seems to be particularly true in school settings where peer groups often construct their identities in contrast to those of 'outsiders.' A classic example of this process is provided by 'the lads,' the group of rebellious, English, working class students studied by Willis (1977), whose conversations make abundantly clear that they define themselves and their experiences in opposition to attitudes and behaviours attributed to the conformist students they call 'the ear'oles.' The lads also construct their own efficacy and superiority through processes of interaction in which limited, sexualized identities are assigned to girls, and ethnic minorities are treated as 'smelly' interlopers.

Although peer cultures are constructed in interactions among peer group members, the descriptive and evaluative meanings that constitute these cultures do not necessarily originate in the peer group. It is more likely that the peer group will construct their meanings out of the beliefs, norms, preferences, and values they have learned at home, from the mass media, from teachers, and from the many other persons and groups to whose ideas they have been exposed. For example, Willis's analysis of racism in the English secondary school 'the lads' attended leads him to conclude that '(b)oth the lads and (teaching) staff do share, therefore, a sense in their different ways of resentment for the disconcerting intruder' (Willis, 1977, p. 49). What sets the lads and the teachers apart is not the core set of beliefs and feelings they direct toward minority groups, but the ways in which they express those beliefs and feelings. Unlike the teachers, the lads frequently use verbal violence, and sometimes use physical violence, to show their rejection of 'the wogs' and 'bastard Pakis.'

As this example suggests, what differentiates peer cultures from one another is not so much their unique beliefs, preferences, norms, or values, but the meanings and emphases given to these cultural elements in the behaviours of the peer group. It is also common for the same behaviours to be given different meanings in different peer cultures. A good example is alcohol use among adolescents. Several researchers (e.g., Everhart, 1983; Gordon, 1957; Hartup, 1983, p. 146; Wooden, 1995) have found that student athletes in junior and senior high schools in the United States frequently use and abuse alcohol and sometimes use illegal drugs as well. Despite their behaviours, these students tend to be defined by themselves and others as 'jocks,' 'the athletic crowd,' or 'sporties,' names that emphasize their interests and participation in sports and mask their substance abuse. In contrast to these peer cultures are those in which the core identity of both the group and its members is constructed around alcohol and drug abuse. Known around school as 'a group ... whose thing it is to go out and get drunk' (Cusick, 1973, p. 70), they tend to be called by such names as 'druggies' or 'burnouts.' Despite the sharp difference in nomenclature between these two peer cultures, it seems entirely possible that some of the 'burnouts' may actually engage in less substance abuse than some of the 'jocks.' What sets these peer cultures apart is the complex set of interpretations that surround specific behaviours. To jocks, drinking lots of beer may just be something everyone in their crowd does on week-ends, but to burnouts the same behaviour may signify maturity, or financial independence, or risk-taking, or rebellion against adult authority.

As this contrast between jocks and burnouts indicates, the term culture draws attention to the particular views that people develop about themselves, their behaviours, and the world around them. To analyze a culture it is necessary to ask not only what people are saying and doing, but what those activities mean to them. This concern with the ways in which people construct meaningful lives for themselves has a long history in social and behavioural sciences, and those who study children and adolescents have long been interested in the ways in which the beliefs, norms and values of these young people differ from, overlap, or are influenced by those of their teachers, parents, and other adults. Given these concerns, it is not surprising that the term peer culture has been a useful tool.

One reason this has become increasingly true is because the term group no longer seems to carry a strong cultural connotation. Of the eight definitions of this term with which Forsyth (1990) begins his text in group dynamics, only two incorporate cultural elements (e.g., 'a set of values and norms'). The rest of the definitions, all by famous group theorists, ignore culture in favour of an emphasis on interaction or interrelationships. Thus, the term group draws our attention to the ways in which people are linked to one another, but does not compel a search for the meanings and significance of those links. Perhaps this tendency to divorce group from culture reflects the laboratory-based, small-groups research tradition in which strangers whose beliefs or behaviours have been manipulated by experimenters are given little chance or encouragement to develop a group culture of their own.

The increased use of the term peer culture probably reflects not only the reduced utility of the group concept but also the popularity of two related terms, namely, subculture and youth culture. The former term is embedded in a long tradition of research and theory concerned with deviance and delinquency. The specific subcultures that have been studied range from gangs of youthful criminals in the United States (Cohen, 1955; Monti, 1994) to aggregates of young people in Britain, such as Punks or Skinheads, whose identities are based on such elements of style as appearance, demeanour, and argot (Brake, 1985; Hebdige, 1979). The term subculture draws attention to both the acceptance of some values from the dominant culture and to the development of oppositional norms and rebellious behaviours. Brake (1985, p. 8) suggests that the latter reflect the subordinate status of those who participate in the subculture:

> ... subcultures (are) meaning systems, modes of expressions or life styles developed by groups in subordinate structural positions in response to dominant meaning systems ... (A)n essential aspect of (a subculture's) existence is that it forms a constellation of behaviour, action, and values which have meaningful symbolism for the actors involved.

The parallels between this definition of subculture and the definition of peer culture presented earlier are obvious, and it is certainly the case that children and adolescents hold subordinate structural positions. Nevertheless, the term *sub*culture is rarely, if ever, used in the literature concerned with peers in schools. Perhaps, the term is too closely linked to extremely deviant behaviours to be considered a useful tool for analyses of most student behaviours in most school contexts. The term peer culture may be a better conceptual tool for calling attention to the possibility that peer groups may evolve interpretations and meaning systems that foster (some of) the official goals of the school. Whereas the term peer *sub*culture implies rebellion, the term peer culture leaves open the possibilities of compliance as well as resistance.

Unlike the term subculture, the term youth culture owes its existence and popularity as much to the mass media as to scholarly endeavours. It was most popular in the period from 1964 to about 1975 when it was thought that young people, particularly in Western countries, were developing a counter-cultural life style that both rejected and threatened the dominant culture. Cultural elements such as beliefs, preference, norms, and values were at the heart of the debates about the significance of the youth culture, and the established authorities felt strongly that they were battling against the youth culture to retain control of the hearts and minds of their constituents. In addition, the discussions of the youth culture called attention to the powerful effects of the mass media and of consumer goods aimed at the 'youth market.' Although some argued that media messages and consumer goods had simple, direct effects on the behaviours of youth, most recognized that youth often made unexpected uses and interpretations of what their society offered. Much was made of the fact that some clothing styles that originated in youth groups later came to be commercially produced and internationally marketed. Thus, youth were seen to be developing not only their own symbolic culture, but their own material culture as well.

Whereas the term subculture often references the culture of specific groups with specific identities, the term youth culture was loosely applied. Age seemed to be the major criterion for eligibility, and the slogan 'don't trust anyone over thirty' seemed to establish the upper limit. Following Keniston (1970), some argued that the youngest members of the youth culture should be older adolescents of high school age, a suggestion that makes the term unusable for students in junior high schools or below. Regardless of age limits, no one assumed that every member of the youth culture knew or had interacted with every other member, a fact that made it extremely unlikely that anyone would talk or write about 'the youth group.' Nevertheless, specific youth groups and networks often overlapped, and ritual gatherings, such as rock concerts or anti-war protests, provided opportunities for members of the youth culture from different regions and countries to affirm their cultural identity and to influence one another. As we shall see in the following section of this chapter, all of these characteristics of the youth culture have also been evidenced in the conceptualizations that some researchers have of the peer culture.

A TYPOLOGY OF PEER CULTURES

The literature on peer cultures in schools has yielded a colourful array of identity labels. In addition to the lads, ear'oles, jocks, sporties, burnouts, and druggies mentioned above, there are normals, freaks, politicos, rads, greasers, rah-rahs, crispies, grits, brains, trendies, grinds, hoods, populars, dweebs, workers, nerds, outcasts, musicians, preppies or preps, debaters, executioners, the power clique, and the leading crowd. This list does not exhaust all the names that appear in the existing literature, nor would an exhaustive list necessarily be a useful basis on which to construct a systematic typology of peer cultures. Some of the identity labels (e.g., crispies) appear in only one study, and others take on different meanings as one moves from school to school. In addition, many of the labels reflect the national context in which the research was done. It would be most surprising to find North American students calling one another ear'oles, and the lack of cheerleaders in British schools makes it unlikely that students in that country would form rah-rah cultures.

What seems more likely to be comparable across national and school contexts is information about the origins and originators of peer cultures. Three originating methods have appeared in the relevant literature: peer choice, reputational techniques, and school-initiation. Cultures based on peer choice are those in which children or adolescents choose one another to be group members and construct their own culture out of their interactions with other peer group members. In research, such cultures are often identified by using ethnographic techniques, but Gordon (1957) used formal sociometric techniques to identify peer groups ('cliques') in the high school he studied and used interviews, school records, and questionnaires to gain information about the cultures of those groups. Both the choices that students make and the cultural possibilities available to a chosen peer group are constrained by the contexts in which the peers find themselves. One of the most famous quotations from the writings of Karl Marx (1852/1963, p. 15) is an appropriate reminder of the fact that free choice is never entirely free:

> Men make their own history, but they do not make it just as they please; they do not make it under circumstances chosen by themselves, but under circumstances directly encountered, given and transmitted from the past.

Despite the constraints under which their choices are made, members of peer-initiated cultures will see themselves and one another as members of the same group who choose to be with one another. Sometimes the group will be given a name like those listed above, but sometimes the identity of the group will not be linked to a specific name ('It's my group of friends.' 'It's the guys I run around with.'). Personal claims to group membership will be validated by other members of the group and by the interaction patterns that exist among members. Sometimes group members would prefer to be in a different group than the one to which they belong, but it is membership claims and interaction patterns, rather than such preferences, that determine peer group membership and group culture. Nor do such preferences negate the fact that the peer group to which they belong is one that they have chosen. Their group membership is based on choice, but it may be a second or even a third choice.

Beyond the act of choosing peers which all cultures in this category share in common, the research suggests that there will be considerable variation across peer-initiated cultures in their beliefs, values, norms, and behaviours. In addition, chosen peer groups will vary in size, closeness, density, and duration. Generally, the groups will be small enough for face-to-face interaction to occur on a relatively frequent basis, but some members will usually play more active, initiating roles than others. An example of such differences among members was found by Everhart (1983) who studied the ways in which a group of junior high school students initiated and developed a peer culture:

> Don's group consisted of a nucleus of three boys together with three more peripheral members. The six spent most of their free time together in school and three of them interacted frequently outside the school … Don was the leader of this group. His opinions and perspectives, while not blindly followed, still set the pace for the group's activities both within and outside of school … While somewhat disparate, the group was bound together by a collectively shared understanding of school life. 'It's the people I hang out with' came to be *the* defining factor of life for Don and his friends throughout the two years that I knew them. Indeed, the most significant aspect of those two years revolved around what they did together, how they thought together, and what they shared together. (Everhart, 1983, pp. 92-95)

Whereas cultures based on peer choice are constructed out of the behaviours and interpretations of the peer group members themselves, cultures identified by reputational techniques are defined by outsiders. These outsiders may be other students, parents, teachers, school administrators, or researchers. Sometimes the peer cultures identified by outsiders actually exist as the cultural constructions of chosen peer groups. Cusick (1973) found this to be true of the jocks and a music-drama group identified by a student informant he calls Marilyn. He used ethnographic techniques to confirm the existence and cultural characteristics of the peer groups Marilyn described to him. Similarly, Gordon (1957) was able to confirm the existence of the 'cliques' students described to him by asking all of the students at Wabash High School to complete a sociometric test.

Not all of the peer cultures that are identified by reputational techniques also exist as the constructions of a peer group whose members have chosen one another. Many of the peer cultures identified by outsiders are cultural constructions by the outsiders. These constructions serve three major purposes. One purpose is to establish and elaborate the cultural identities of the outsiders. A good example of a peer culture constructed for this purpose is the ear'oles whose passivity and conformity were emphasized by Willis's (1977) lads as a means of asserting their own superior ability to create fun and excitement. Similarly, the students whom Eder observed at Woodview Middle School bolstered their own social standing by constructing a peer culture known as the grits (a reference to being tough and gritty):

> Students viewed as deviant by certain popular students were considered grits ... The 'grit' label generally implied the person was a loser in the struggle for social status. Certain boys might be feared because of their propensity toward violence, but they were not respected ... Many people who sat on the same side of the cafeteria as the most popular students viewed everyone on the other side of the cafeteria as being grits. People on the low-status side did not necessarily give themselves this label, however, and instead referred only to certain people as grits. For example, one girl told us that a grit was 'somebody who smokes marijuana and sleeps with just about any boy.' (Eder, 1995, p. 41)

A second major purpose of reputational peer groups is that they help to shape and direct interaction and relationships. Once people can label one another, they become more certain about the ways in which they can and should behave toward one another. So, even if the students at Woodview School could not agree on a precise definition of grits, they all knew that students who were grits were not desirable friends or associates. Similarly, Eckert (1989) found that students at Belton High School who were reputed to be Jocks were treated quite differently, and more favourably, by both peers and staff members than students reputed to be Burnouts. Recently, Brown, Mory, and Kinney (1994) have suggested three characteristics of reputational peer groups, or 'crowds,' that may affect the ways in which they channel interactions among adolescents in schools. These characteristics are reputational proximity (how similar are 'crowds' perceived to be?), permeability (how open or exclusive are 'crowds' perceived to be?) and desirability (how much prestige do 'crowds' have?). Following Eckert (1989), I would add to this list orientation to the official school culture. Such orientations are a characteristic of reputational (and chosen) peer cultures that have many implications for the interactions of students and staff, a point that will be discussed in more detail in later sections of this chapter.

Students and school staff are not the only ones to construct peer cultures to which they do not belong. Researchers do so, too. Their avowed purpose is to advance theories about adolescent or child cultures in school, national, or international contexts. A classic example may be found in the study of ten high schools by Coleman (1961). Although Coleman (1961, esp. pp. 173-219) presents considerable information about the peer groups that are *chosen* by the students he studied, the primary argument of his work is that an adolescent culture is emerging in industrial societies. Adolescents are becoming increasingly peer oriented, and they share values (e.g., prizing athletics above scholarship) that are contrary to the values of their parents and teachers. These trends are particularly evident in large urban schools (vs. smaller rural schools) and among the students who were reputed by their peers to be in 'the leading crowd' (vs. non-elite students). To support his arguments, Coleman (1961) presents a large amount of survey data.

Coleman's arguments parallel many of the arguments about the youth culture that were advanced in the decade following the publication of his book. Like the youth culture, Coleman's adolescent culture is a social construction and, as noted earlier, some social analysts (e.g., Keniston, 1970) argued that the latter culture was part of the former. When social constructions such as youth culture and adolescent culture become known to their supposed constituents, they can have important effects on peer cultures in many parts of the world. Connell, Ashenden, Kessler, and Dowsett (1982, p. 162) make the following observations about the Australian students whom they studied:

> One of the reasons why the kids can sustain a conflict with their parents' views on schooling is that youth now has a group identity ... (Their activities in school are) part of a larger complex of peer networks in and out of school, street life and beach life, and events in and around amusement parlours and the like, that is sometimes called 'youth culture.' The main interests in this complex are music, clothing, food, conversation, and sex; and it is crucial, both to the kids and to anyone dealing with them, that it is very largely outside adult control.

Like the reputational peer cultures identified by adolescents, those that are 'discovered' by researchers and popularized by journalists both affect and are affected by the interaction patterns and cultures adolescents choose to construct for themselves.

Unlike chosen peer cultures or reputational techniques for identifying peer cultures, school-initiated peer cultures are rooted in groups that are deliberately created by teachers or administrators to foster particular kinds of interpersonal relationships. Most instructional groupings in schools are not formed for these reasons. Instead they are formed to achieve academic goals, such as improved student motivation and performance. A common and controversial form of academic grouping is curricular tracking. Such tracking includes specialized programs for academic and vocational students, student placements in core subjects on the basis of ability, and elective courses for students with particular talents or interests. Although academic tracking is not designed to create peer groups, it does alter opportunities for peer interactions. Evidence for the effects of these opportunity structures has emerged from studies (e.g., Epstein, 1989; Epstein & Karweit, 1983; Hallinan & Sorensen, 1985; Hargreaves, 1967) showing that students are more likely to select friends from their own curricular track than from other tracks. These studies suggest that schools can shape peer relationships and peer cultures even when such effects are unintended.

Because the educationally relevant criteria used for tracking students are so highly correlated with their social background characteristics, tracking usually serves as a means for perpetuating segregation by age, gender, social class, race, and ethnicity. To counter this segregation and to foster better interpersonal relationships among students, particularly those of different race-ethnicities, a variety of dyadic and small-group instructional formats have been proposed. The starting point for the construction of these groupings is to bring together students of different race-ethnic backgrounds. Contact alone is rarely enough to reduce racial prejudices, however. To the contrary, some studies (Bank, Biddle, Keats, & Keats, 1977; Schofield, 1982) have shown that increased contact across racial lines is more likely to increase than to decrease both perceptions of racial dissimilarity and interracial antipathy. To prevent such outcomes, student dyads and small groups have been designed to foster not only contact among heterogeneous students but also interdependence and cooperation. According to a growing body of research (Aronson, 1978; Cohen, 1994; Johnson, 1980; Slavin, 1995), more positive interpersonal relationships, including improved race-ethnic relations, can be achieved in classrooms if students participate in instructional groupings that are deliberately and carefully structured to meet these goals. What is less certain are the effects that interdependent, cooperative peer groups initiated in school settings will have on the peer groups and cultures students choose for themselves (but see Stevens & Slavin, 1995).

DIVERSITY IN PEER CULTURES

Peer cultures vary not only in their originating method (chosen vs. reputed vs. school-initiated) but also according to the background characteristics of the students involved. These characteristics include social class, gender, age, and race-ethnicity, and a substantial literature has appeared concerned with the effects of each of them on peer cultures. Most of this literature is focused on chosen peer cultures, and the term friendship is often used as a synonym for what was defined above as a chosen peer group.

Internally, these peer groups are far more likely to consist of students who have the same background characteristics than of students with heterogeneous backgrounds. The reasons for this homogeneity are probably both structural and social psychological. Structural reasons include any features of school organization that promote segregation of students from different backgrounds. Age-grading has become an almost universal feature of schools worldwide. The kinds of curricular tracking mentioned above are also common, as are the tendencies to send students to schools in their own neighbourhoods or communities which are often homogeneous in social class and race-ethnic composition. Where they exist, private and parochial schools deliberately recruit students of particular social backgrounds. In addition, Epstein and her colleagues (1983, 1989) have identified a broad range of school characteristics that affect proximities among students and, therefore, possibilities for friendship formation. These school characteristics include architectural features of the school building and grounds, school size, equipment and supplies, the organization of extra-curricular activities, and the authority structures of the classroom and school.

Even when structural limits are taken into account, students still tend to choose friends who are similar to themselves. Two social psychological reasons seem to account for these tendencies. One of these is social pressure which has been found by some investigators to inhibit the development of friendships that cross age, gender, social class or racial-ethnic lines. Adults often intervene to make certain that children select 'appropriate' friends, and peers frequently do likewise. Everhart (1983) and Eder (1995) give vivid examples of the ways in which peer groups in junior high and middle schools demand conformity and reject anyone who deviates from the group norms for actions, interests, appearance, talk, attitudes toward school, or treatment of peers.

A more psychological reason for homophily in friendship selection is the set of assumptions people tend to make about those who are similar to them. Social psychologists (e.g., Aronson & Worchel, 1966; Condon & Crano, 1988) have found that most people make the assumption that similar others will like them more than dissimilar others. This assumption, coupled with the well-documented tendency of people to like those who like them, produces more reciprocal liking among those who are similar than among those who are not. Both assumed and actual reciprocity of liking, in turn, have been found by Byrne (1971), New-comb (1961), and other researchers (reviewed in Brehm, 1992) to be strong pre-dictors of friendship selection and stability.

If peer groups were less homogeneous internally, their cultures would prob-ably become more similar to one another. Instead, research completed in the last half-century suggests that the differences across peer cultures produced by dif-ferences in background characteristics continue to be large and socially signif-icant, and there is no indication that these differences are declining in size or importance. The sharpest and best substantiated of these differences are those produced by social class and gender. The differences produced by age are more debatable, despite the large literature concerned with peer relations among chil-dren of various ages. Surprisingly little research has appeared that directly con-trasts the peer cultures of different racial and ethnic groups, but interesting theoretical work has emerged suggesting some conditions that are likely to pro-duce race-ethnic, as well as national, differences in peer cultures.

Social Class

The major dimension for characterizing middle-class versus working-class (or lower-class) peer cultures is orientation toward schooling, and a large literature contrasts the positive orientation of middle-class groups with the negative ori-entation of those who come from working-class homes. The reasons given for these differences vary across researchers, depending on their theoretical pro-clivities. Cohen (1955), for example, draws on cultural deprivation theory to ar-gue that the cultural deficits of the working and lower classes limits their educational chances. The formation of delinquent peer cultures, which he calls sub-cultures, give working-class adolescents an opportunity to gain the social status that they cannot gain in school. Stinchcomb (1964) challenges the notion of an inadequate class culture by suggesting that school failure, regardless of so-cial class, prompts high school rebellion and expressive alienation by making schooling appear irrelevant to one's future.

Although they reject cultural deprivation theory, Marxist-oriented resistance theorists (e.g., McRobbie, 1991; Willis, 1977) agree with Cohen that working class students are more likely than their middle-class counterparts to form peer cultures that resist school authority. They also agree with Stinchcomb that one reason for this resistance is the perceived irrelevance of high school education for the kinds of jobs working-class students expect to obtain in the future. The behaviours of working-class peer cultures described by resistance theorists are not much different than those described by Cohen. They include confrontations with teachers, fights with 'outsider' students, truancy, substance abuse, vandal-ism, and other petty crimes. What sets sub-cultural theorists such as Cohen apart from resistance theorists, according to Davies (1995), is their evaluation of these working-class peer cultures. Whereas cultural deprivationists and sub-cultural theorists see these peer cultures as social problems, resistance theorists view them as expressions of proletarian culture with the potential to foster the revolutionary changes needed to eliminate the evils of capitalistic exploitation.

Davies (1995) is critical of this latter view, and he marshals considerable evidence to show that neo-Marxists have also 'vacillated from embracing the working class as the major agent of radical transformation.' Similarly, Corrigan (1979) has criticized the notion that youth are 'the vanguard of revolutionary change.' Despite their criticisms, neither of these writers argues against the proposition that working-class peer cultures are more likely than middle-class peer culture to reject the values of school authorities and to rebel against them. The form of this rebellion has varied across historical periods, however. Brake (1985) describes shifts in British youth subcultures during the postwar period as mods and rockers replaced teddy boys only to replaced, in turn, by skinheads and punks. He suggests these shifts occur when particular youth styles are adopted by younger and younger age groups for whom the style has little, if any, meaning.

A more structural reasons for changes in styles of rebellion has been suggested by Weis (1990) on the basis of her study of the students at Freeway High School. She notes that the deindustrialization of the American economy and the disappearance of well-paid working-class jobs is causing changes in the behaviours of working-class peer groups. Boys, in particular, realize that they will not be able to get the kinds of jobs their fathers got when they left high school. These boys accept the message that they must finish high school and get some post-secondary education or training in order to find steady employment and acceptable wages. As a result of these changes, the students at Freeway High engaged in less overt resistance against school authorities than was found in working-class peer cultures in earlier studies (e.g., Willis, 1977). Instead, Freeway students passively resisted the school authorities, thereby collaborating in the construction of limited futures for themselves:

> White working-class males resent institutional authority as in previous studies. However, the Freeway students attend school and adhere to the *form* of schooling to a seemingly greater degree than others have suggested. They do not, however, embrace its substance. They copy homework, elaborate the language of 'passing' (grades), reject the competitive and individualistic ethos of schooling by a willingness to be simply 'average,' and do not really pay attention in class, even though their expressed valuation of school meanings and culture is more positive than previous studies would have led one to expect. They want to go to college and see some value in education … (but the) fact is that

an adherence to form will *not* enable these students to pursue the type of college education that will be necessary for them to scale the class structure. (Weis, 1990, pp. 36-37)

Unlike working-class peer cultures, middle-class peer cultures help to perpetuate the educational system by embracing its central tenets, particularly competitive achievement. In their review of social class differences in peer cultures, Corsaro and Eder (1990) suggest that students from middle-class backgrounds, and especially those who are member of elite groups within their schools, tend to value social and academic competition and are more likely to base their friendships on interests and activities, often switching friends as their interests change. Larkin (1979) reports that the students at Utopia High School in affluent Pleasant Valley had superficial relationships with friends and other peers, and Wexler (1985) observes that students at Penbroke High, most of whom came from the professional middle-class, used peer life as 'a leisure relaxation and diversion from the boundless pressure to succeed.'

In contrast, Wexler (1985) reports that working-class white students at Grummitt High School tried to establish more caring and supportive relationships with peers. Similarly, Corsaro and Eder (1990) and Brantlinger (1993) report that students from working-class backgrounds exhibit more loyalty to their friends, often to the point of avoiding those activities in which their friends are uninvolved. Working-class adolescents are more likely than their middle-class counterparts to view their personal networks, including their chosen peer groups, as the continuous element in their lives. For the urban under-class, argues Wexler (1985, p. 142), the peer culture may be 'the place where basic self existence is validated.'

Gender

Although these findings about social class differences in competition versus loyalty to friends have been reported for both males and females, the literature concerned with subcultures and resistance has tended to focus on boys rather than girls. One reason for this tendency has been the fact that male researchers outnumbered female researchers until very recently, and male researchers probably found it easier to understand and establish rapport with boys. When Cusick (1973) learned about 'the power group,' an all-female peer culture, from his informant, Marilyn, he decided not to study them too closely even though

> ... I would like to have known more about this group, but a male adult, even if he is running a school-approved study, should not associate too closely with a group of teen-age girls. Also, some of these girls dated

athletes and I did not want to get between any of the boys and their girl friends.

Whatever one may make of Cusick's qualms, they are undoubtedly shared by other researchers. Interestingly, few male researchers seem to have adopted the strategy used by Eder (1995) who deliberately involved male collaborators in her study of Woodview Middle School in order to gain the same 'insider' access to the boys' peer cultures that she had achieved with the girls.

By using this strategy, Eder (1995) was able to document the ways in which the behaviours and speech patterns of the boys constructed aggressive relationships among peer groups and between boys and girls. Boys' cultures stressed a form of masculinity based on toughness and sexual domination, and those whose behaviours failed to be 'masculine' enough were declared to be homosexuals. Verbal, physical, and sexual aggression were also central to the British boys' cultures described by Brake (1985) who presents evidence to show that the celebration of tough masculinity is characteristic of middle-class, as well as working-class, youths. Fine (1981, p. 46) notes that the cruelty of the preadolescent boys he observed in the United States was 'almost always expressed in the presence of friends. Insults seem(ed) to be expressed as much for reasons of self-presentation to one's peers as to attack the target.' Similar observations were made by Connell and his colleagues (1982) of boys in Australian secondary schools who often had to fight with other boys to prove their masculinity to themselves and their mates. Even in elite, private schools in Australia, the dominant form of masculinity was focused on physical strength and aggression (Kessler, Ashenden, Connell, & Dowsett, 1985).

Given the centrality of 'masculine' aggression in the peer cultures of boys, it is hardly surprising that they tend to view girls as sexual objects and to treat them accordingly. Because many of the sexual comments and behaviours boys direct toward girls are *unwelcome*, they meet the standard definition of sexual harassment. Using this definition, a large number of studies (e.g., American Association of University Women Educational Foundation, 1993; Bogart & Stein, 1989; Eder, 1997; Larkin, 1994; Lees, 1993; Stein, 1993) have been able to document widespread sexual harassment in elementary and secondary schools. These studies reveal that girls are more likely to be the targets of sexual harassment than boys, and the harasser is much more likely to be a male student than a staff member. The acts of harassment discovered in these studies include unwanted sexual comments, labels, jokes, insults, propositions, touching, grabbing, pinching, voyeurism, kissing, disrobing, and physical assault. It is often difficult for girls to resist these forms of harassment effectively. Ignoring them or countering them with sexual comments or behaviours directed at their male harassers may only serve to intensify the attacks directed at the girls.

It is also difficult for girls (and boys) to know how to interpret some of the sexual comments and behaviours of the boys. Are these acts of unwanted sexual harassment or tokens of sexual and romantic interest? Popular cultural milieux that put so much emphasis on sex appeal and romantic relationships as the keys to self-fulfilment and happiness create contexts in which most girls would not want to ignore sexual and romantic overtures. In addition, the peer cultures girls construct for themselves often place a high value on attractiveness to the opposite sex (Eder, 1995; Schofield, 1982). Being popular with the boys or having a boyfriend who is admired by one's peers is a way of achieving status in school, just as finding a husband who will be admired by friends and family is important in later life.

The emphasis on sex appeal, romance, and boyfriends that is so often characteristic of the girl's peer cultures greatly strengthens the power that boys have over girls. Femininity comes to be defined as attractiveness to boys. Sexually aggressive behaviours by boys come to be seen as normal, even admirable. Similar behaviours among girls are deemed unacceptable and are likely to be sanctioned with derogatory terms, such as 'slut', 'slag,' and 'whore.' Lees (1993, p. 52) finds that these terms do not reference only sexual behaviours. They function to denounce and control 'any form of social behaviour by girls that would define them as autonomous from the attachment to and domination by boys.' Not only boys, but the girls themselves use these terms against one another. Acceptable girls come to be seen as those who are agreeable and passive. One 'good way' to protect themselves against sexist abuse is to get a steady boyfriend. Another is to escape into Teeny Bopper cultures in which girls organize their sexual fantasies and romantic behaviour around particular male recording stars (McRobbie & Garber, 1975).

Not all peer cultures are constructed around these styles of femininity and masculinity (Kessler et al., 1985), but considerable research has now emerged suggesting that these are dominant cultural constructions in male and female peer cultures, at least in the U.S., U.K., and Australia. Although these cultural constructions are undoubtedly more common among middle school and high school students than among younger students, Thorne (1993) reports that the elementary school boys whom she observed used sexual insults and approached relations with girls in a daring, aggressive manner. Generally, however, research on children younger than middle-school age tends to focus on gender differences that are less sexualized. This research (reviewed by Dickens & Perlman, 1981; Hartup, 1983; Winstead, 1986) reveals that the friendships of girls are intensively focused on one or a few friends and exhibit high levels of expressive intimacy, but boys both report and are observed to have more extensive friendship networks focused on activities, rather than 'just talking.'

As these findings suggest, researchers have also found a substantial amount of gender segregation in the peer groups of children This segregation is substantial even in preschools, and it tends to increase during the elementary and middle school years. High school peer groups seem to be somewhat less segregated by gender, but the data to support this claim are often sociometric choices that are subject to alternative interpretations. It is possible, for example, that high school students include dating partners among their best friends even though they and their partners are members of different, gender-homogenous peer groups. Conversely, it is possible that high rates of dating across certain groups in a school may lead to a merger of those groups as when male athletes and female cheerleaders join to become 'rah-rahs' or 'the leading crowd' (see also Dunphy, 1963).

Age

The possibility of alternative interpretations also plagues research findings concerned with age effects on peer cultures that are independent of gender. How should one explain, for example, the findings that adolescents are more peer oriented and more influenced by peers than younger children? Many have argued that these findings reflect developmental processes, especially the increased autonomy of adolescents who use the peer group as a means of becoming more independent from parents. It also seems possible, however, that differences between the size and structure of secondary schools compared to elementary schools may produce much of this difference. Some support for this possibility comes from Coleman's (1961) finding that, even among secondary schools, peer orientation and influence were greater in larger schools than in smaller ones. Perhaps the more complex academic, procedural, and social demands of larger secondary schools increases reliance on peers for information and support.

Even among developmental theorists, there is disagreement between those such as Selman (1976; Selman & Jacquette, 1977) who believe that children's friendships pass through an invariant sequence of stages related to the individual's cognitive development and those such as Rubin (1980) or Corsaro (1985) who take a more constructivist viewpoint. According to the stage theorists, children begin with a view of friendship as a momentary physical interaction and reach their highest level of development (usually in late childhood or early adolescence) when they can understand friendship as mutual sharing and intimacy. According to constructivists:

> ... children work out for themselves what social relationships are all about on the basis of their actual encounters with others ... Unlike walking, the development of social understanding depends on both developing intellectual skills, which may vary widely among

individuals, and on specific social experiences, which vary even more widely. As a result, we should be sure not to rely on chronological age as an unfailing index of children's social understanding. (Rubin, 1980, pp. 41-42)

Although these differences among developmental theorists have made it difficult to determine the importance of age differences, the developmental approach has stimulated a huge amount of research concerned with friendships and peer relations of children and adolescents. Much of this research provides only indirect information about age effects, and most of it uses individualistic research procedures. The strategy employed in many of these studies is to identify children who participate in reciprocal friendships and children who don't. The latter are sometimes further divided into those who are rejected and those who are social isolates. Sociometric techniques are often employed for these purposes, but interviews and observation have been used as well. Once children have been sorted into the two or three categories mentioned above, they can be compared on as many different measures as researchers can devise. From this research has emerged a huge literature (e.g., Ginsberg, Gottman, & Parker, 1986; Hartup, 1983, 1989; Laursen, 1993; Rubin, 1982; Shantz, 1983) documenting such positive correlates (usually claimed to be consequences) of friendship as high or improved self-esteem; mastery of symbolic expression; realistic assessments of one's abilities and achievements; acquisition of role-taking and communication skills; fulfilment of social needs; remediation of adjustment problems; development of self-identity and autonomy; self-validation; development of creative and critical thinking; and the learning of moral principles and social rules.

Even if one accepts the validity of all of these findings about the 'consequences' of friendship, the studies do not reveal *how* friendships produce these effects. In other words, the studies tend to ignore the interactions among friends (and non-friends) and the peer cultures these interactions produce. Unfortunately, the studies that have focused directly on friendship behaviours and on the ways in which peers construct cultures have usually studied only one age cohort. Researchers who observe the peer cultures of young children are not the same researchers who observe the peer cultures of adolescents. While specialization of this type is hardly surprising, given the labour-intensive nature of observational and ethnographic research, it is difficult if not impossible to make claims about age effects on the basis of different studies done at different times with different age groups for different purposes by different researchers. Even when researchers deliberately try to study age differences, they generally use cross-sectional designs in which different age groups are compared at the same point in time. Since these groups are likely to differ in other respects than age, it is hard to interpret any findings of differences in their peer cultures. Longitudinal studies of friendship behaviours among peers are rare. Hartup (1989) notes that there are some exceptions to this statement, but they are studies concerned with the limited topic of friendship stability, and even these studies tend to last for only one school year.

Nationality, Ethnicity, and Race

Only a few studies (Bank, 1994; Brake, 1985; Kandel & Lesser, 1972) have appeared examining the effects on peer cultures of nationality and national context, but Shlapentokh (1984) has used research into the role of friendship in the former Soviet Union as the basis for a theory about these effects. He begins by asserting that friendships often serve as a refuge for the individual against external threats, including threats from the state. He goes on to hypothesize that, all other things equal, the lower the sense of security among people and the weaker their confidence in the future, the more intense and vital are their interpersonal relationships. It is for these reasons, Shlapentokh (1984) argues, that the Soviet people attributed to friendship a more prominent place in their system of values that did their American contemporaries. It is also for these reasons, he suggests, that oppressed minorities have closer personal relations than those of the dominant majority.

Shlapentokh's (1984) theory may explain why some Western research, mentioned above, has found that working-class students tend to have closer, longer-lasting, and more loyal friendships than middle-class students. His theory may also explain the close bonds of 'fictive kinship' forged in African-American communities in the United States (Stack, 1974). Unfortunately, studies seem not to have appeared directly contrasting the peer cultures of students who come from different racial-ethnic backgrounds. Nor has there been systematic research to determine the conditions under which students in schools characterized by racial-ethnic diversity form peer groups that are also diverse, rather than peer groups that are racially and ethnically homogeneous.

Fordham (1988) has recently suggested that the bonds of fictive kinship may account for the low levels of academic achievement she found among many of the African-American students who participated in her ethnographic study of Capital High School. Departing from Stack's (1974) notion that the fictive kinship system is rooted in economic necessity and interdependence, Fordham (1988, p. 56) uses the term 'to denote a cultural mind set or world view that stresses group loyalty and a sense of peoplehood in opposition to White American social identity.' The ideology of American schools, with its emphasis on individualist, competitive achievement, conflicts with the collective ethos of the fictive kinship system. As a result, 'many Black adolescents are keenly aware of the stigma associated with being successful in school, since school is seen as an agent of the dominant society' (Fordham, 1988, p. 60). A specific example of these general processes could be found in her own study:

> At Capital High School there is not much support for students who adopt the individualistic ethos, because succeeding in school is invariably associated with movement away from the community and is seen as a sign of having been co-opted by the dominant society.

African-American students who do succeed are said to do so only by adopting a 'strategy of racelessness' (Fordham, 1988), and high-achieving females have 'the appearance of an erasable persona' (Fordham, 1993).

Undoubtedly, some of the conflict about achievement experienced by Fordham's (1988, 1993) students is similar to the conflicts students of all race-ethnicities experience when they are caught between the testing and grading systems of their school, on the one hand, and their peer culture's negative orientation toward schooling, on the other. The questions raised by Fordham's work are whether this conflict is greater for African Americans than other race-ethnic groups, and whether African Americans have to act 'raceless' and deny their fictive kinship in order to succeed. Systematic, direct evidence to answer these questions has not appeared (but see Ford,S Harris, Webb, & Jones, 1994), and evidence concerning the extent to which African-American students denigrate school achievement is mixed.

Like Fordham (1988), Kester (1994) found that African-American students at Sennett Middle School considered it 'white' to do well in school. Instead of attributing this perception to fictive kinship, however, Kester (1994) mentions students' desire for a 'cool' image and their consensual belief that 'people aren't used to black people doing well in school' (Kester, 1994, p. 71). These findings at Sennett Middle School and at Capital High School contrast sharply with those reported by Ford and her colleagues (1994). The majority of the 148 black fifth and sixth graders interviewed by Ford were unfamiliar with the concept of acting white, and those who had heard the term did not assign it negative meanings. The students also supported 'the achievement ideology' and 'the American dream – the efficacy of schooling, hard work, and effort' (Ford et al., 1994, p. 25).

Evidence showing support for achievement also emerged from Cauce's (1986) survey of poor, black adolescents attending a middle school in the eastern part of the United States. These students had a high regard for school achievement. Ninety-six percent rated being a good student as at least somewhat important among their friends. When asked what they would most like to be remembered for at their school, 70 per cent said best student, 16 per cent said most popular, and 14 per cent said best athlete.

Differences in the racial composition of the schools these students attended may explain some of the differences in research findings. White students attended both Capital High School, where they were a minority, and Sennett Middle School, where they were the majority. Almost all students at the school Cauce (1986) studied were African American, and the students interviewed by Ford (Ford et al., 1994) attended a school that was entirely black. Other differences across schools and samples may also have affected the findings. Cauce (1986, p. 612) reports that the middle school she studied 'had a reputation for being innovative in curriculum,' a comment that alerts us to the possibility that the schools differed in their official cultures. Perhaps, the ways in which African-American peer cultures orient themselves to achievement in schools has less to do with the communal ethos of African-American culture than with some of the characteristics of official school cultures that are discussed in the following section of this chapter.

CONFLICTS AND COMPROMISES BETWEEN OFFICIAL SCHOOL CULTURE AND PEER CULTURES

The image of official school culture that Fordham (1988) presents is a culture organized around 'the individualistic, competitive ideology of American schools.' The purpose of this individualistic competition is presumed to be high achievement, particularly in academic work but also in the non-academic activities sponsored by the school. Although school staff assume that not all students can achieve at the highest levels, all are expected to take achievement goals seriously. Seriousness can best be demonstrated by working hard, by respecting school staff, and by obeying school rules. This portrait of official school culture is not unique to the United States, and it seems reasonable to assume that most schools throughout the world expect students to make serious efforts to perform well.

Lack of seriousness (i.e., student resistance or rebellion) can be demonstrated in at least three different ways. First, students can reject the goal of academic achievement, fail to work hard, and underachieve. Second, students can reject the goal of achievement in non-academic activities sponsored by the school. The students might even refuse to participate in some or all of these activities. Third, regardless of their effort and achievement in academic and official non-academic programs, students might be disobedient and demonstrate disrespect for school staff. Much of the writing on peer cultures fails to make a distinction among these three ways in which student cultures and official school culture can clash. By analyzing each of them separately, however, it becomes possible to see some of the tensions and contradictions in official school culture that are exploited by peer groups, even by those that seem to take the official school culture seriously.

Getting Knowledge

One of the more surprising findings to emerge from many studies of peer cultures in schools is the relatively low emphasis those cultures give to anything associated with the academic life of the school. Everhart (1983, p. 232) concludes his study of peer cultures at a junior high school by noting that he rarely heard students discussing grades, assignments, or the subject matter that had been covered in class. Instead, students spent most of their time discussing after-school activities or the activities of their friends both in and out of school. Similar findings are reported by Cusick on the basis of his observations at a high school. After discussing the fact that a group of athletes spent so little time discussing their teachers, Cusick (1973, p. 97) observes:

> In the beginning of my study I thought that perhaps my presence was keeping the boys from revealing their true feelings about the teachers, but their behaviour was consistent over the entire semester. While occasionally a teacher would be mentioned by one member, the topic never became general. Nor were related topics of marks, grades, academic work, or assignments ever made topics of general conversation.

As Cusick's comments suggest, the low importance assigned to academic matters does not seem to result from characteristics of ethnographic research procedures.

This suggestion gains further support from studies using other research methods that have also found little emphasis among peer groups on academic matters. Csikszentmihalyi and Larson (1984), for example, asked a group of American teenagers to carry electronic pagers for one week and to fill out reports of their activities and feelings whenever they were paged. This sampling of student's time revealed that the majority of the time these adolescents spent with friends was spent in leisure activities or maintenance tasks, such as eating or doing errands. Only 3½ per cent of the sampled time with friends was spent studying or doing other school-related work. Reports of students' feelings indicated that they enjoyed studying with friends more than studying alone or in the presence of family members, but they admitted to having more difficulty concentrating on studies when friends were present than when they were not.

Supplementing these findings are results from surveys in which students were asked to describe and evaluate chosen or reputational peer cultures in their schools (e.g., Brown et al., 1994; Coleman, 1961; Gordon, 1957; Wooden, 1995; Youniss, McLellan, & Strouse, 1994). All of these studies report some negative associations with being in an academically oriented peer culture (usually called by such names as 'the brains' or 'scholars'), and none reports that such peer cultures received the highest evaluation given to various peer cultures. The negative associations with being 'a brain' include being 'a grind', lacking social skills and dating partners, being a teacher's pet, and being 'a nerd.' Some evidence has appeared from a study of two elementary schools suggesting that these prejudices against 'brains' begin quite early, especially among boys:

> Younger boys took pride in their work, loved school, and loved their teachers ... Yet sometime during the middle elementary years, by around third grade, boys began to change their collective attitudes about academics. This change in attitude coincided with a change in their orientation, away from surrounding adults and toward the peer group. The boys' shift in attitude involved the introduction of a potential stigma associated with doing too well in school. (Adler, Kless, & Adler, 1992, p. 177)

Although Adler and her colleagues did not find the same negative opinions about academics to be characteristic of girls, Elmen (1991) suggests that such opinions may emerge in adolescence among girls whose families or peers stress the importance of non-academic achievements. Such achievements may include physical attractiveness, popularity with boys, social skills, and traditional femininity. Just as negative opinions about 'the brains' and academic achievement are not limited by gender so, too, they are not limited to working-class peer cultures. The two elementary schools described by Adler and her colleagues (1992) drew most of their students from middle- and upper-middle class neighbourhoods in a large, mostly white university community. Many of the other schools and peer cultures that underemphasized academics and derogated 'the brains' were also composed of middle-class students. Sometimes even brainy peer cultures ignore academic matters. Eder (1995) notes, with surprise, that a peer group at Woodview Middle School which included four boys who were in advance-track classes never discussed academic achievements or interests during lunch.

Although the finding that peer cultures ignore academic matters or are hostile to high levels of academic achievement is a common finding, it is also contradicted by a substantial amount of research. As noted earlier, both Cauce (1986) and Ford (Ford et al., 1994) found that the African-American students whom they studied admired academic achievement and had high aspirations for themselves. Similar findings are reported for predominantly white student populations by several researchers. Berndt and Das (1987), for example, found that less popular and more rejected fourth- and eighth-graders were judged to be less able academically, and they cite other studies showing that popularity is positively associated with objective measures of achievement. Adler and her colleagues (1992) report that elementary-school students who struggled scholastically or had to be placed in remedial classrooms lost peer recognition. Purcell, Gable, and Caillard (1994) present data from a survey of high school students (grades 9-12) showing that they were more likely to give high-ability peers positive or neutral ('neither like nor dislike') ratings than negative ratings. Similarly, Brown and Steinberg (1991) report that most students in the nine high schools they studied believed that their friends encouraged academic achievement, at least to a moderate degree. Although he notes that 'it is rare to find an intellectual crowd in high schools, much less one that is accorded an elite status,' Larkin (1979, p. 72) reports that such a peer culture existed at Utopia High School. He describes them as a group of intellectuals who were reading Thomas Mann, T. S. Eliot, and Karl Marx for their own edification and who told him of their plans to study music, mathematics, philosophy, anthropology, literature, and sociology.

How can this information be reconciled with findings that peer cultures devalue academic achievement? Larkin (1979) attributes the presence of an identifiable crowd of intellectuals that are an elite at Utopia High School to two factors: the presence of a large Jewish minority and the academic emphasis of the school. Thus, the values of home and the official school culture have combined not only to foster intellectualism among (some) students but also to make it a respected activity throughout the school.

The importance of the official school culture in creating – or failing to create – such a climate of support and prestige for intellectual and artistic strivings is also evident in the writings of Cusick (1973) and Everhart (1983). As noted above, both found disinterest in academic matters and low levels of achievement in the peer cultures they studied. Both also found the classes in the schools they observed to be undemanding academically. Cusick (1973, p. 97) describes one of the teachers as someone who did little or no instructing. 'He would begin (class) with some topic and almost immediately relate it to his war experiences, his home town, his school days, or his brother-in-law and would just ramble on meaninglessly all period.' Although this teacher seems to be the worst of those whom Cusick observed, none of the others exhibited very high academic standards:

> It should be admitted that the school, on the whole, seemed to be very undemanding of students. One could easily see that those who were giving only bare compliance to the academic demands were not failing, nor were they being chastised by the teachers for non-achievement.

They simply were not expected to do very much and just about anyone who gave at least a little effort could and did succeed. (Cusick, 1973, pp. 60-61)

Ten years later, Everhart (1983, p. 84) made similar remarks about the low level of academic standards in the official school culture he observed:

... the modal form of instruction at Harold Spencer (Junior High School) does not demand much of the student's time in school. Over all, only slightly more than half of the time a student spends in school is occupied by instructional activities ... Nor did instructional tasks, on the average, seem to demand much in the way of intellectual effort from students. It was relatively easy, for example, for John and Steve to discuss intramural football games while, almost subconsciously, working on a social studies assignment, a practice indicative of the (low) intensity of intellectual work demanded of the students in the school.

Nor do low standards seem to have disappeared in the present decade. Like their students, the '(t)eachers (at Freeway High School) tend to adhere to the form rather than the substance of education,' writes Weis (1990, p. 81), with the result that 'knowledge distributed through the classes has nothing to do with either thinking or challenging.'

These studies support the conclusion that undemanding official school cultures are likely to be found in the same schools as peer cultures that are unconcerned about or hostile toward getting knowledge, and Larkin's (1979) study suggests that high academic demands may be a necessary, but not sufficient, condition for producing peer cultures that respect intellectualism. More research is needed to clarify the interaction processes by means of which a positive correlation is produced between the academic values (or lack thereof) of an official school culture and the values and behaviours of the peer cultures in that school. What is already clear from existing research is that many schools violate the popular image that they are places where an official culture that is focused on academic matters and is characterized by high achievement standards clashes with peer cultures that have failed to internalize the academic values of their schools. Instead, official school cultures often fail to develop themselves as contexts in which academic striving is expected, commonplace, and prized. Undoubtedly, there are many reasons for such failures (see, e.g., Powell, Farrar, & Cohen, 1985), but their likelihood is probably increased by the heavy emphasis in the official cultures of many schools, especially in the United States, on extracurricular activities that contribute little to the academic mission of the school, and may even undermine it.

Getting Involved

One of the best established findings in studies of peer cultures is the importance they assign to athletics. The emphasis on athletic participation as the best way for boys to demonstrate masculinity and to become popular with same-sex and cross-sex peers has been found as early as the third, fourth, and fifth grades of elementary school (Adler et al., 1992) where it seems to be correlated with a de-emphasis on academic interests. By middle school and junior high school, participation and interest in sports, although they are requirements for being thought masculine, are no longer enough for prestige. Instead, well-regarded boys become those who are members of school teams that compete with teams from other schools. Of these teams, the ones most likely to produce a good reputation around school are those, like football and basketball, that are highly visible to the student body (Eder, 1995). At the high school level, Coleman (1961) found that athletic success was the major source of prestige for young men in all ten of the schools he studied. Similar findings have been reported for other high schools by Connell and his colleagues (1982; Kessler et al., 1985), Cusick (1973), Eckert (1989), and Wooden (1995).

Coleman (1961, p. 172) explained the high prestige assigned to athletic success on the grounds that extracurricular activities, such as sports, are seen by adolescents to be 'activities of their own,' activities in which they can carry out positive actions on their own, in contrast to schoolwork, where they carry out assignments from teachers.' Coleman's explanation masks the extent to which extracurricular activities are part of the official school culture and the extent to which they can undermine the academic goals of the school. This latter problem is implicit in the comments of a teacher, interviewed by Cusick (1973, p. 30),

> ... who recalled with disgust the football rally at which, 'The whole student body stood up and cheered the captain of the football team for *five minutes*! And I know that Kid! He can't Read! But that's the way this place is.'

Although Cusick presents these comments to show the low regard in which students were held by teachers, the comments also reveal that the football rally was an official school function attended by everyone in the school.

At least in the United States, such rallies are commonplace. Schools that have only one convocation per year to present awards for academic excellence, artistic talent, and student leadership may have a football rally before every varsity game plus additional sports rallies during basketball and baseball seasons. School-sponsored squads of cheerleaders and pompon girls, along with special pep or spirit clubs, are often created to lead the rallies, and to insure an enthusiastic audience for sporting events. This heavy emphasis on athletics has implications for the ways in which students come to be viewed, not only by students, but also by teachers and school administrators:

> Although many feel that places on the teams are frequently won through favoritism, athletic ability itself cannot be awarded in exchange for docility or cooperation. The status of varsity athletics derives at least partly from its importance to the school image, and varsity athletes are thus seen as working in the interests of the school. (Eckert, 1989, p. 117)

While this reputation does not help athletes get academic knowledge, it may help them get better grades than they deserve (Gordon, 1957) and, as I will argue below, it helps them to 'get along' in the official school culture.

Within the student culture, male athletes often form peer cultures of their own (Cusick, 1973; Gordon, 1957; Wooden, 1995), sometimes in combination with cheerleaders (Larkin, 1979). For at least three reasons, these peer cultures are usually accorded elite status in the school. The first reason, alluded to above, is the high *visibility* of athletic teams even to students who never attend a game. Not only is school time devoted to sports rallies, but considerable space in the school paper and yearbook are devoted to athletic contests. Rare is the American high school, or junior high school, that does not have a glass-fronted cabinet in the hallway displaying athletic trophies. Also common are banners, posters, and other forms of decoration that publicize forthcoming games and announce support for the school team. Nor is this visibility limited to the school. In small and moderate-sized towns, local papers often cover high school athletics in considerable detail, and high school sporting contests attract sizable numbers of parents and other adults from the community. Even in major metropolitan areas, mass media coverage of city-wide high school athletic tournaments is commonplace, especially for football and basketball, and the media are also likely to take a keen interest in regional and statewide tournaments, especially if a local team is participating.

Two other, interrelated reasons why students accord elite status to athletes and their 'jock' peer cultures are the high *value* assigned to athletic talent and the *competition* that exists for positions on varsity teams. Undoubtedly, the high value assigned to athletics reflects the emphasis on them not only in the school, but also nationally and internationally. Undoubtedly, also, the value of team membership increases if there is a great deal of competition for positions. And both the value of and competition for positions are likely to increase if the team is winning. Even sports teams that are not usually very visible in schools, such as tennis or swimming, can become increasingly prestigious and attract increasing numbers of students to 'try-outs' if they have recently won a championship. As these comments indicate, the athletic programs of schools, far more than their academic programs, provide ample, public opportunities for male students to compete for success and to convert their successes into prestige for themselves personally and for their chosen peer group. Students who combine both athletic successes and academic achievement have also been found to gain high prestige in some schools (see Coleman, 1961; Rigsby & McDill, 1975) presumably because being an athlete neutralizes some of the negative stereotypes associated with being 'a brain.'

If these male athletes (or athlete-scholars) also want to be popular (i.e., well liked), they will probably have to possess or acquire social skills, especially the ability to be friendly to all and modest about their talents. Although research suggests that popularity is more a matter of being cheerful and sociable than of athletic or academic talent (Youniss et al., 1994), this finding comes from studies done in the United States where a concern with popularity is more evident than in other national contexts (but see Andersson, 1969, esp. pp. 92-98; Kandel & Lesser, 1972, esp. p. 17; Wheeler, 1961). Even in the United States, there seems to be a positive correlation between athleticism and popularity in many schools (Eder & Kinney, 1995), and it is rare to find a popular peer culture of males or mixed sexes in most schools that does not count some athletes among its members.

What about females? Despite legislation in many countries to prohibit gender discrimination and to foster gender equity, athletic programs for girls and women continue to lag behind those for boys and men. Even where inter-school competitions among girls' teams have been organized, they tend to attract less attention from students, school staff, and community members than boys athletics. Nor are girls' athletics elaborated in the official school culture, but this may be changing, and there have traditionally been some exceptions. In rural and small town high schools in the U.S. state of Iowa, girls' athletics have been an important, valued, and integral part of the extracurriculum. Perhaps this explains why Buhrmann and Jarvis (1971) found that girl athletes received consistently higher status ratings from their male and female peers and teachers than non-athletes. Similarly, Buhrmann and Bratton (1977) report that girls who participated in interscholastic athletics in six rural and small town high schools in Alberta (Canada) were more popular with (i.e., better liked by) female and male peers than girls who are not athletes. The Canadian female athletes were also more likely than non-athletes to be nominated as members of the leading crowd in their school by both peers and teachers.

Despite such findings, girls are still more likely to gain visibility in a U.S. school by attaching themselves to male athletes than by playing on a girls' team (Eder & Kinney, 1995). The most visible of these attachments in the United States is cheerleading, and many studies find a prominent peer culture consisting of cheerleaders or of cheerleaders and some male athletes (Eder, 1995; Gordon, 1959; Larkin, 1979; Wooden, 1995). Although some of these peer cultures form as a result of being selected for the cheerleading squad, some of them actually precede and promote selection. This is particularly true in schools where students, such as graduating cheerleaders or class officers, participate in the selection of next year's squad. Being a member of a prominent peer group that is known to and liked by these student judges is clearly an asset (see Eckert, 1989, p. 120).

Like athletes, cheerleaders hold positions that are highly visible in the school; they usually have to compete for these positions, and their activities help to promote a positive school image. Because they are chosen for their enthusiastic cheerfulness, friendliness, and physical attractiveness, they also have some of the characteristics that have been found to make students popular with their peers (Wheeler, 1961; Youniss et al., 1994). Nevertheless, they rarely attract the same amount of popularity as the varsity athletes in the school. The major reason for lower popularity seems to result from the fact that there are far fewer cheerleaders than male athletes in most schools. As a result of small numbers, cheerleaders are more likely to create closer, denser peer groups than the male athletes, especially if their peer cultures are single-sex. As noted at the beginning of this chapter, denser peer groups tend to be seen as more exclusive, and there is evidence that cheerleaders are more likely that athletes to be dismissed as 'snobs' (see Eder, 1985, 1995).

Aside from athletics, cheerleading, and the clubs that are organized to promote athletics, the most visible student organization across and within most U.S. schools is student government. Like athletics and cheerleading, there is often intense competition for positions in student government and, even more than athletes or cheerleaders, student governing bodies spend their time interacting with representatives of the official school culture. What is less certain as one moves across schools are the kinds of bonds student governments forge with the official school culture, on the one hand, and the kinds of relationships they have with peer cultures, on the other.

In some school settings, student government has been highly regarded by students, and election to student government has been a way for individuals to enhance their reputations as 'Big Wheels.' This is the situation Gordon (1957) found at Wabash High School where the official student governing body, known as the Student Assembly, was given the highest prestige ranking among fifty student organizations by the senior girls and the second-highest ranking (after varsity basketball) by the senior boys. Although the Assembly was a formal school organization rather than a peer culture, Gordon (1957) provides evidence to show that prominent cliques (i.e., chosen peer groups) in the school were composed of students who participated in Assembly, as well as athletics and other prestigious clubs and activities. The image that emerges from Gordon's work is one in which *many* students representing various peer cultures vie for positions in formal student organizations, especially in those, like Student Assembly that are visible and valued. Students who gain these positions, presumably on the basis of their perceived merits, gain school-wide prestige both for themselves personally and for their chosen peer cultures.

A different image emerges from Cusick's (1973) description of student governance at Horatio Gates High School. In the senior class of 364 members, observes Cusick (1973, p. 68), 'there were about fifteen to twenty students who seemed to get elected to whatever office happened to be available and who seemed to run whatever there was to run.' His investigations into the reasons for this fact led Cusick (1973, p. 68) to conclude that 'it was not ... just a matter of individual qualification, but a matter of group affiliation.' Specifically, Cusick discovered a peer culture constructed by young women known as 'the power group' who made it their business to nominate themselves or their friends for school offices and major committees.

When Cusick investigated the reasons why the power group was so successful in exercising control, he was often told that they took an interest in things and were willing to work for the school whereas other students were not. While this rhetoric seemed to contain some truth, Cusick also found that the power group and their male allies prevented other students from participating. They did this by dominating discussions during Student Council meetings and by ignoring anyone who was not part of their chosen peer group. When asked about their behaviours, however, members of the power group and their allies denied their own exclusivity and manipulation of the Council, suggesting instead that many students chose not to be more involved because they were introverted.

Eckert (1989, p. 121-122) presents another example of the ways in which peer cultures in a high school work to control the official student government, but the students Eckert observed were more willing to acknowledge their political strategies than those in Cusick's report:

> The choice of campaign manager for elections is the best example of conscious political alliance in the school and involves the choice of a person whose only formal function is to make a short introductory speech for the candidate at the campaign speech assembly. The real benefit is not in the speech itself but in the networks the manager can bring to the election. Campaign strategies, therefore, involve the careful choice of a manager who commands different networks from the candidate's. The managers, in turn, receive visibility from the post, as well as influence during the candidate's office if the campaign is successful.

In addition to the important role they played in campaigns for government offices, peer groups and alliances among them also provided a major basis on which class and student government officers made decisions about whom to select for the annual variety show, the pompon squad, and other positions over which they had some control.

In contrast to athletes, officers of student government often find it difficult to gain popularity in the school. To be popular, they need to exhibit an ability to get along well with everyone in the school, but the demands of their offices often require them to make choices among their peers. These choices leave student officers vulnerable to charges of bias and favouritism. In addition, where student government is controlled by one or a few peer groups, student leaders are likely to be perceived as an exclusive clique. The popularity of student leaders is further undercut in schools where they are thought to be supportive of administrative efforts to limit student autonomy and to deal harshly with misbehaviour (Eckert, 1989; Larkin, 1979).

At both the high school and the junior high school levels, school administrators have been found to intervene in the functioning of student governments. Sometimes they try to determine who gets elected (Cusick, 1973). More commonly, they set the agenda for discussion in student councils or assemblies, ignore or resist student proposals with which they disagree, and get student leaders to approve actions already planned or taken (Cusick, 1973; Eckert, 1989; Everhart, 1983; Larkin, 1979).

Student members of governing councils and other student leaders have been found to respond to these control tactics by administrators in at least three different ways. First, according to Everhart (1983), they may adopt an apathetic, cynical posture toward student government. No attempt is made to challenge school officials in a sustained or serious way, although many complaints and jokes are made about the decisions students are asked to make. This response seems likely to be more common at the middle school or junior high school level than at the high school level and among student leadership groups that are not very cohesive because they represent many different peer cultures in the school.

The second response student leaders may adopt toward administrative controls is to identify with their controllers. An example of this response is described by Larkin (1979) who uses the name 'politicos' to identify the distinct group of students at Utopia High School who held the student offices and were prominent in the committees that operated the student government. Unlike their predecessors in the previous decade of 1960s student activism, the politicos could no longer depend on the student body to engage in political action on its own behalf. As a result the politicos often felt that they were shouldering the responsibilities and work that the rest of the student body was too lazy and apathetic to assume. This disdain for their a-political peers made the politicos very 'vulnerable to the acceptance of adult definitions of the situation, and by implication (they) become agents of adult will' (Larkin, 1979, p. 140).

The third possible response student leaders can make to administrators is resistance or rebellion. Cusick (1973, p. 197) describes an example of resistance

by a committee of the Student Council at Horatio Gates Senior High School
against Mr. Rossi, the vice-principal for students:

> Dick, Jean, Tony, and Jack (four members of Council) formed a political
> committee to deal with what they considered to be some serious issues
> of student power. They even forced Rossi to stop harassing a student
> who had been threatened with suspension for wearing a moustache. In
> itself that must have been quite a shock for Mr. Rossi. Jean told me, 'He
> was really shook up. Seventeen times he told us it was none of our
> business. Seventeen times! 'Well, like I don't think that's any of your
> business.' And, 'Ah, I don't really think you should concern yourselves
> with it.' And, 'Well, what business is it of yours?' That's just the way
> he was. He was really shook up.'

The willingness of these students to confront Mr. Rossi was probably increased
by the fact that they all belonged to same chosen peer group. Because they were
friends, they trusted and supported one another more than they probably would
have done if they had been only political allies. It also seems likely that sustained acts of resistance by student leaders are more common in senior than junior high schools. Such actions also seem likely to occur when student leaders
and their student constituency perceive that they share an identity, values, and
interests distinct from those of school staff, as was the case in the 1960s (Larkin,
1979).

The fact that Mr. Rossi was 'really shook up' probably resulted both from his
fear of losing control of the Council, the student body, and the public image of
the school and from his surprise that the Student Council would oppose him. Indeed, such opposition is rare in most schools, not only because there is little support for student power in the broader culture at the present time, but also
because student leaders risk losing the privileges that they have gained by being
elected to positions in student government. These privileges include: being ex-
cused from class to attend meetings of the student governing body; being able
to wander around the school building more or less at will; receiving greater le-
niency from teachers and administrators than other students receive; and having
one's way paid to student leadership conferences.

Not only student leaders, but all who participate in extracurricular activities,
are likely to gain some privileges like these. In his discussion of the importance
of student organizations, Gordon (1957, pp. 47-48) notes that teachers tended
'to particularize with those (they) knew well in the distribution of rewards and
apply universalistic standards with greater affective neutrality in the distribution of rewards and punishments to least active, least-known students.' Which
students teachers come to know well and to favour depends partly on teachers'
own involvements in the extracurriculum and partly on the visibility of various

extracurricular activities and organizations to the teaching staff. Aside from varsity athletics, cheerleading, and student government, which seem to have high visibility in most American schools, the visibility and prestige of other activities seem to vary from school to school. For example, Eckert (1989, p. 117) reports that Belton High School had an excellent and well-known choir, but Gordon (1957, p. 61) reports that the choir at Wabash High School was accorded less prestige by student raters than the senior play cast or the junior prom committee.

As argued throughout this section of the chapter, the best predictors of which student organizations will gain the most prestige are likely to be their visibility, perceived value, and the amount of competition for positions in the organization. These virtues, in turn, depend on the prestige and popularity of the informal peer cultures that are active in the organization and on the extent to which it is seen as creating a positive, 'winning' image for the school. Regarding the latter, therefore, it is not surprising that Eckert (1989, p. 117) describes the well-regarded choir at Belton High School as one that had gained considerable prestige for the school through competitions and extensive tours.

Throughout the world, official school cultures honour certain kinds of student activities and achievements and try to ignore or punish other kinds of activities. The emphasis found in U.S. schools on 'getting involved,' having school spirit, and being a winner will not be found in all countries, but most schools will develop a dominant image of what a good student is and does. In some schools this image will be organized around academic achievement. In other schools, particularly in the U.K., the dominant image will be closely tied to social class background, with students from middle class or elite backgrounds assumed to be 'naturally' better students than those from the lower orders (Brake, 1985, esp. pp. 60-63; Corrigan, 1979; Downes, 1966; Lacey, 1970; Willis, 1977; see also Eckert, 1989). In schools that honour athletics and other types of non-academic behaviours, students can often gain major status rewards not only in the informal peer culture but also in the official school culture without having to be more than nominally interested in 'getting knowledge.' Such students enjoy successes and favours in school, and they may even make some effort to obtain the average or passing grades necessary for eligibility to continue their participation in the extracurriculum. They will be handicapped, however, if they do not acquire the skills, knowledge, and orientation necessary for educational and occupational success beyond the secondary level (Spady, 1970). To the extent that official school cultures elaborate and reward non-academic achievements, they may reinforce the anti-academic values and status hierarchy that are so characteristic of peer cultures in the school.

Getting Along

Most profiles of peer cultures in schools include at least one peer group that does not get along with school staff. Such groups are portrayed as disrespectful and disobedient, sometimes engaged in illegal behaviours in or out of school. Known to themselves and others by such names as the lads, the freaks, burnouts, greasers, toughs, punks, or druggies, these peer cultures are often portrayed as having little interest in academic matters and being uninvolved in the extracurriculum. Although they sometimes earn the admiration of their peers because of their rebelliousness against school authorities, they are also viewed with suspicion and sometimes fear because they are prone to make fun of students who conform to the official school culture. This fear is much greater in those school settings where peer groups of this kind are believed to have threatened, robbed, or assaulted other students in the schools.

This portrait of the more-or-less cohesive peer culture that can't or won't get along has received support from studies done in a variety of schools in different countries and in different decades of this century. Most of these studies have tried to suggest some reasons for the emergence and perpetuation of these cultures. Because these cultures exist in the same schools at the same time as peer cultures that can and do get along with school staff, the reasons cited are those that set the overtly rebellious students apart from their more cooperative peers. These reasons have included academic failure and alienation (Stinchcomb, 1964), identification with the 'shop floor culture' of the working class (Willis, 1977), dissociation from the official school culture (Downes, 1966), being placed in a lower academic track or stream (Hargreaves, 1967), limited economic means (Eckert, 1989), low self-esteem (Wooden, 1995), minority racial status (Larkin, 1973), and anti-establishment values (Eckert, 1989; Larkin, 1973).

Because the behaviours, and sometimes the appearance, of the most rebellious peer culture in a school are so noticeable and troublesome, they often become the focus of attention for school staff. Undoubtedly, this is appropriate behaviour on the part of staff if the peer culture in question actually threatens the survival not only of the official school culture, but of some of the staff and students as well. This seems to be the case in an urban high school described by Polite (1992) as a place in which 'the culture of the teenagers, particularly the drug subculture, had assumed ascendancy.' Most schools have not been taken over by criminal gangs, however, and most rebellious or resistant peer cultures are not serious threats to the survival of persons or institutions. Under these more usual circumstances, the emphasis on and vilification of a relatively small, distinctive peer culture of 'deviants' helps to mask four other problems that exist in many schools. For convenience, I will call these the problems of widespread rebellion, favouritism, school boundaries, and goal displacement.

I use the term *widespread rebellion* to call attention to the possibility that it is not just a small group of students who are disobedient and disrespectful. Nor is it only students with working class or minority backgrounds. Instead, students from all different social backgrounds and peer cultures, including the jocks and the so-called leading crowd, have been observed or have reported breaking school rules (Brantlinger, 1993; Cusick, 1973; Eckert, 1989; Wooden, 1995). Similarly, as noted early in this chapter, it is not just the toughs and burnouts who abuse alcohol and drugs, but also the athletes, the populars, and, again, the leading crowd. Corsaro and Eder (1990, p. 215) suggest that 'resistance to adult rules and authority provides children with a sense of control and autonomy, and for this reason may be a universal feature of peer culture.' Similar arguments have been advanced for adolescents by Coleman (1961) and Monti (1994, p. 162) whose study of gangs and drugs led him to the following conclusions:

> The subculture of gangs makes its presence felt in schools in much the same ways as the so-called 'peer culture' does. Youngsters generally work hard to subvert school routines, stretch school rules, and test the limits of their teachers' patience. This is immensely aggravating to adults, but it is an effective and safe way for young persons to learn how to manipulate a complex organization and to challenge, however symbolically, the influence of adult authority on their lives. The significance of the gang subculture is that it is an exaggerated, better organized, and meaner version of the 'peer culture' that operates in all schools to varying degrees.

If resistance and subversion are as common as the literature and personal observations suggest, then why are certain peer cultures singled out by school staff and students as the 'deviants'? One possibility is that the so-called deviants engage in more acts of disobedience and show more disrespect than other peer groups. This is a possibility that needs careful testing because it is also possible that the 'deviants' are the victims of a system of *favoritism* in which their behaviours are judged more harshly than comparable behaviours performed by students who are not regarded as troublemakers. Lacey (1970, pp. 178-179) describes the favouritism displayed by a British teacher he calls Mr. Bradley:

> Another time (Bradley) found that Macdonald, the top boy in the form made a mistake in setting out a problem, and remarked quietly, privately, reasonably, 'No, lad, you'll have to do it again.' When Priestly, an anti-group pupil (i.e., perceived troublemaker), made the same error (Bradley) declared for the whole class to hear, 'You know, it's amazing that you've been here three years. I gave you an example of how to set

it out, but you've done it differently. What's wrong with you, boy? Are
you too lazy to turn back one page?'

Studies of American schools are replete with examples of rule violations, and
even crimes, by varsity athletes and elected student leaders that went unpun-
ished even though school staff knew about them (see, e.g., Cusick, 1973; Eckert, 1989). A student at Grummitt High expressed the frustrations produced by
this kind of favouritism:

> For some reason, the jocks have got a way with teachers. If they need a
> pass for somewhere, fine. You can walk into a classroom behind a jock,
> and they'll say to me, 'Where's your pass?' It always happens ... It's
> like they don't want to help you. (Wexler, 1985, p. 52)

Similar complaints were voiced by some of the low-income students interviewed by Brantlinger (1993, p. 140):

> Karen complained: 'Some teachers are not really fair. They have
> favorites and let certain kids get away with stuff that others can't. A
> good teacher treats you equally. I think a lot of teachers like preps more
> than normal kids.' Thomas, who was not a 'trouble-maker' himself,
> observed: 'Some only help kids who have real good potential. Kids
> they've known for a while. Most favour preppies. At times – with grits
> – they are watched. Someone else could get away with the same things.
> Grits are assumed to be troublemakers.

Nor does this favouritism escape the notice of those who benefit from it. Interviews with the jocks and preppies suggest that they are well aware of the favours and forgiveness they can gain from school staff. More than half (56 per
cent) of the high-income adolescents interviewed by Brantlinger (1993, pp.
140-141) acknowledged a personal advantage in meting out of discipline:

> Libby concluded: 'They don't often punish those who are good in
> school.' Aaron believed: 'They're easy on jocks.' Hillary said: 'We're
> in a popular group. I think teachers kind of respect us. We don't get
> punished even when we get a little wild. Some teachers think it's funny.
> They don't care.'

Scholastic performance, extracurricular contributions, orientation toward
school, and peer group memberships emerge from the literature as major bases
for student reputations and for the treatments they can expect from teachers.
Other reasons for teacher favouritism include parental status (Brantlinger,

1993; Lesko, 1986) and the interpersonal skills of the students. Regarding the latter, Spencer-Hall (1981) provides evidence that some students become skilled at impression management by the fifth grade. They are able to hide their disruptive behaviours from the teachers and present themselves to the teachers as cooperative, well-behaved pupils. Such behaviours do not escape the notice of their peers, however. 'Preps lie about stuff so they look like little angels,' one student told Brantlinger (1993, p. 140), and another confessed: 'We get away with more. We're sneaky. We stick up for each other.' While it may be true, as Monti (1994) suggests, that such students are gaining valuable information about ways to manipulate complex organizations, it also seems likely that the perception of favouritism, whatever its reason, breeds increased disrespect for school staff both among students who are favoured and among those who are not.

The third problem that is masked by the vilification of a small group of rebellious students is the problem of *school boundaries*. How concerned should school staff be with the behaviours of students that occur away from the school and from school-sponsored activities? It seems likely that school staff and students may be able to construct more cooperative, academically oriented relationships if they are willing to ignore information about out-of-school activities that would discredit their identities. A good example of this process is described by Monti (1994) who studied the impact of drug-dealing gangs in a suburban school district called Fairview. Although what Monti (1994) calls the 'subculture of the gangs' has a great presence in the schools of Fairview, their presence was not known to some school staff and was ignored by others who were aware of its existence. Gang-related behaviours in school, such as fights, were explained by students as being personal in nature, and staff accepted these explanations. In general, staff dealt with unruly gang members the way they would deal with unruly students who were not gang members.

Monti (1994) suggests that the ability of school staff to carry on their routines without confronting the gangs as such was facilitated by the behaviours of gang members, particularly at the high school level. Many of them made the effort to blend in with their fellow students by doing passable and even outstanding academic work. Some participated in school-sponsored clubs or teams but not as a gang. They did not usually sell drugs during the school day, and they avoided wearing clothing that would identify themselves as gang members. Although Monti (1994, pp. 164ff.) acknowledges that these behaviours are different from those of gang members in inner-city schools, he notes that these behaviours allowed staff at Fairview High School to keep the official school culture intact and to maintain the appearance of having the school well under control. In addition, the gang members were able to earn the educational credentials that would allow them to move into more conventional work roles than those offered by the gangs.

Although Monti (1994) notes that ignoring gangs in school has disadvantages, as well as advantages, there are undoubtedly some student behaviours that should be considered beyond school boundaries but aren't. Cusick (1973) relates an outrageous incident in which a teacher who heard that a particular boy and girl were dating took it on himself to call the girl's mother, suggesting that she have her daughter checked for VD, and that she stop the relationship. Not only did the teacher earn the undying animosity of the male student, he apparently had little impact on the girl or her mother, and the dating relationship continued. In contrast, parents at Wexler Middle School sometimes enlisted school staff to prevent romantic relationships that crossed class and racial lines, a practice defended by the school principal because '(i)f these relationships develop and the parents get upset … it's very bad public relations for us' (Schofield, 1982, p. 145). Teachers at Wexler did not always wait for parental initiatives. They often reacted negatively to indications of interracial romance and sometimes talked to the girls about their concerns, occasionally even calling them at home.

Although systematic evidence is not available, it seems possible that the group in a school that is singled out for vilification as the 'deviants' are being judged as much for their peer group relations, including their dating behaviours, and for the reputations they bring with them to school as they are being judged for their behaviours within the physical and temporal boundaries of the school. In such cases, one would expect students to make trouble because, as Reynolds (1976, p. 135) found in the secondary schools he studied, 'the conflict between pupils and teachers is continually fuelled by the attempt of the staff to exercise control in areas of the pupils' lives where they expect autonomy, such as in their behaviour outside school.'

Like the problem of school boundaries, the problem of *goal displacement* calls attention to the fact that school staff may actually cause some of the troubles they attribute to the so-called deviants in their schools. My use of the term goal displacement follows that of Merton (1957) who defined it as the process whereby an instrumental value becomes a terminal value. In official school cultures, an important terminal value is high academic achievement levels of students. School rules concerning student deportment, appearance, attendance, and cooperativeness are examples of instrumental values that are usually justified as ways of making certain that the goal of academic achievement is reached. Goal displacement occurs when school staff (and students) become more concerned with adherence to the rules than with academic goals.

Several examples of this form of goal displacement have appeared in the literature (e.g., Cusick, 1973; Reynolds, 1976). An interesting approach is taken by Corrigan (1979) who suggests that students from working class backgrounds often view schools as a power structure in which subject matter is experienced as periphery, and the experience of schooling focuses on rules, sanctions and discipline. The teachers spend great amounts of class time trying to eliminate behaviours that would be considered normal outside of class:

> Violence is used (by teachers) to try to enforce a certain view of the sorts of activities which should take place in the classroom – that is, it is a place where there is silence, where boys pay attention to the teacher, where boys are not cheeking the teacher. It also represents a perception of the use of violence in creating the necessary conditions under which the teachers can teach discipline. It is interesting what violence is NOT used for. It isn't used to instill geography, history, maths or science; rather it is used to instil quiet and respect. (Corrigan, 1979, p. 63)

Even for teachers who never use violence, the focus of much class time may be on classroom discipline rather than academic matters.

Goal displacement by school staff creates a vicious circle in which student misbehaviour is met with rule enforcement, and rule enforcement – especially if it entails shouting, sarcasm, or violence – generates increased resentment and rebellion on the part of students. Goal displacement also interacts with teacher favouritism to affect student outcomes. As noted above, some students will have their initial misbehaviour overlooked, and some will be able to mask their resentment and rebellion. Both of these possibilities are unlikely for the students who are known participants in 'deviant' peer cultures. They, more than others, are likely to be locked into a circle of misbehaviour and sanctions with their teachers, and they, more than others, are likely to receive support for their rebellion from their chosen peer group. Because these 'deviant' students have so much trouble getting along, they also are less likely than other students to get academic knowledge or to get involved in official school activities.

THE INFLUENCE OF PEER CULTURES

No one can read the literature on peer cultures without concluding that there are sharp differences in the lives of children and adolescents who participate in different peer cultures. How are these differences produced? Obviously, some of them result from the direct influence of peer cultures on those who participate in them. Also, as the previous section of this chapter has demonstrated, the responses of school staff and peers to a particular student often depends on the peer culture with which that student is involved. In addition, parents sometimes influence the peer cultures in which their children participate either directly by controlling friendship choices (Connell et al., 1982) or indirectly by shaping behaviours which are significantly related to participation in certain peer cultures (Brown, Mounts, Lamborn, & Steinberg, 1993). Unfortunately, much of the research that has been centrally concerned with peer influence has ignored peer cultures in favour of an individualistic approach that examines the influence on students of their peers, classmates, or friends without determining whether those others and the students studied are part of a chosen peer group that has created a distinctive peer culture of the kind that is central to this chapter.

Because they usually ignore peer cultures, studies concerned with the influence of peers on one another probably underestimate the strength of peer influence. A similar suggestion has been made by Cohen (1983a, p. 164) whose review of relevant research leads him to conclude that 'peer emulation that involves no actual friendship selection results in little peer influence ... (M)ost influence stems from those who have been selected as close friends.' The overall strength of peer influence may also be underestimated in research that focuses on areas of life in which peers have little effect. According to Cohen (1983b), one of these is college aspirations. Even when peer influence was defined as the college aspirations of students' best friends, Cohen (1983b) found peer influence to have a weak effect on the college aspirations of those students.

Despite Cohen's warnings, much of the research concerned with peer influence has focused on educational aspirations and some of it has used measures of influence that did not necessarily focus on selected friends (e.g., belonging to clubs equals high exposure to peer influence). A quantitative synthesis of such studies done from 1966-1978, including some concerned with occupational aspirations and educational achievements, concluded that peer influence is 'a strong, consistent determinant of a wide range of educational outcomes for elementary and high school students' (Ide, Parkerson, Haertel, & Walberg, 1981, p. 483). Across all aspirations and achievements studied, the median correlation with peer influence was .24, and all but 5 of 110 correlations were positive. On the basis of these findings, Walberg (1986) has identified the peer group as one of nine influencers that appear to have consistent effects on student learning. (The other eight are age, ability, motivation, amount and quality of instruction, classroom and home environments, and mass media.)

Without doubting Walberg's (1986) conclusion, it should be noted that the size of the effect for peer influence reported by him and by Ide and her colleagues (1981) is questionable. On the one hand, as noted above, the measures used in most of the studies they reviewed and the failure of these studies to take account of peer cultures probably produced an underestimation of peer effects. On the other hand, the failure of most of these studies to control for teacher and parental influences may have led them to overestimate peer influence. As noted in the previous section of this chapter, official school cultures and some (but not all) peer cultures often influence students in the same direction. Similarly, parental and peer influences often overlap, and this overlap tends to be greater for school outcome variables of the type examined by Ide and her colleagues (1981) and by Walberg (1986) than for 'deviant' behaviours such as alcohol use (see Biddle, Bank, & Marlin, 1980a).

Another reason why the studies synthesized by Ide and her colleagues (1981) may have overestimated the amount of peer influence is their failure to control for peer selection. Similarity in aspirations and achievement levels may have preceded peer contacts and friendships. In a longitudinal study that controlled for selection, Kandel (1978) was able to show that only half of the similarity in educational aspirations between best friends could be due to their influence on each other. The remaining half of the correlation between their aspirations was due to the similarity in their aspirations before they became best friends. Kandel (1978) suggests that researchers have overestimated the influence of peers by 100 per cent because they have ignored that half of peer similarity that is due to selection. A direct test of Kandel's suggestion by Cohen (1983b) supported her conclusion.

Although controlling for peer selection reduces the effects of peer influence, these effects remain significant (Cohen, 1983b; Kandel, 1978), and they are stronger for drug use than for academic behaviours (Kandel, 1978). This finding from longitudinal research in which peer influences are measured separately from adolescents' behaviours calls into question the results of research in which adolescents are asked whether their friends influence them. Studies of this type done in England (Corrigan, 1979), Scotland (Smith, 1985), and the United States (Berndt, Miller, & Park, 1989) have found that adolescents often deny being influenced by their friends. This denial seems to be particularly likely when adolescents are given the opportunity to assert that they would 'make up their own mind' rather than being swayed by peer influence. Thus, it seems likely that denial of peer influence is part of an individualistic bias in impression management, rather than a valid report of whether peers are influential.

Although it is not possible at the present time to estimate with precision the strength of peer influence across students and school settings, studies have appeared suggesting that the strength of these effects may vary by age of students and by type of peer influence. Negligible differences in the strength of peer influence seem to be produced by gender (Biddle, Bank, & Marlin, 1980b; Cohen, 1983b; Coleman, 1980; Epstein, 1983), but Brown, Clasen, and Eicher (1986) report that 6th through 12th grade males were more willing than females to follow peers in antisocial behaviours, and Davies and Kandel (1981) found that peers had more influence on the educational aspirations of ninth and tenth grade girls than of comparable boys. As for age, most studies (for reviews, see Brown, 1990; Coleman, 1980; see also Biddle et al., 1980b) report that peer influences on behaviours increase during early adolescence and then decline after mid-adolescence (14-16 years of age).

At least two dimensions for characterizing types of peer influence have been identified. One of these distinguishes among different tactics that peers might use to influence one another. One such distinction proposed by Biddle and Bank (Biddle et al., 1980a, 1980b; Bank et al., 1985) contrasts modelling (what peers do) and normative influence (what peers think I should do). Their research in the United States found that peers influenced adolescents' alcohol use by modelling more than by their norms, but parents influenced adolescents' alcohol use more by their norms than by their behaviours. They were able to predict this pattern of results on the basis of findings from more than twenty American studies (reviewed in Biddle et al., 1980a) that had compared either the normative standards or the behaviours of parents and peers as predictors of adolescent behaviours. Although this finding seems to have validity in the United States, they could not replicate it in Australia, France, or Norway (but peer modelling was found to have significant effects on alcohol use in all three countries).

A second dimension for characterizing types of influence is the distinction between compliance and internalization (Kelman, 1958). Compliance refers to the tendency to do or say what the other does or says or wants you to say or do. Compliance is a response to influence which does not include psychological changes. One complies in speech or action, but one does not agree that this compliant behaviour is good or appropriate. Compliance is either automatic and thoughtless or is done for instrumental reasons. In contrast, internalization involves not only overt compliance but also psychological changes. The target of the influence attempt comes to accept the values, norms, or preferences of the influential other. As a result, the target person is likely to do what the other does or expects even when that other is absent.

In their research on alcohol use in four countries, Bank and her colleagues (1985) found that internalization was a more common form of influence among peers than compliance. For the topic of violence, however, Felson, Liska, South, and McNulty (1994) found that the violent behaviours of the U.S. adolescent boys whom they studied were directly affected by the values (favouring aggressive responses) prevalent among students in their high schools, independent of their own values (regarding aggressive responses). They label the process of compliance in which the values of the group predict individuals' behaviours, independent of the values of those individuals, a social control process. This social control process, more than individual values, affected not only the amount of violence in which a student engaged but also the amount of other forms of delinquency (theft, vandalism, truancy, cheating). They conclude that '(d)elinquency involves public compliance and impression management, rather than private acceptance or internalization of one's schoolmates' values' (Felson et al., 1994, p. 168).

More research is clearly needed to determine the types of influence that peers exert over different behaviours in different school settings. That research will be most useful if it uses longitudinal research designs that take account of peer cultures, of peer selection, of the influence strategies of peers, of the influences of parents and the official school culture, and of the age of the students studied.

IMPLICATIONS FOR TEACHING

The implications of peer cultures for teaching probably also vary depending on the age of the students. In particular, there seem to be substantial differences in the ways in which peer cultures are constituted at the three major levels of schooling: the elementary school level, the middle school and junior high school level, and the high school level. This section of the chapter examines each of these levels separately, looks at the ways in which school staff have (or have not) affected peer group processes at each level, and presents suggestions about new ways in which teachers at each level might respond to peer groups and cultures in their schools.

Peer Cultures in Elementary School

Although systematic evidence to support this proposition is not available, it seems to be true that school staff have more influence on the formation of peer groups and cultures at the elementary school level than at higher levels of education. This influence seems to take three forms. First, as noted earlier in this chapter, school staff influence the peer selection process by affecting proximity among students. Regardless of school level, any actions that sort and segregate students reduce the likelihood that they will form a peer group (see Epstein, 1989; Epstein & Karweit, 1983; Hallinan, 1992; Hallinan & Sorensen, 1985), and actions that foster interdependent cooperation increase the likelihood that students will become friends and create a common peer culture (Aronson, 1978; Cohen, 1994; Johnson, 1980; Schofield, 1982; Slavin, 1995).

The second way in which school staff influence the formation of peer groups and cultures is by affecting the status dimensions along which students learn to judge themselves and each other. Particularly at the elementary school level, teachers achieve these effects, not only through the systems of rewards and punishments that they employ in the classroom, but also through their own status. Popular teachers who consistently reward high academic achievement are likely to induce more admiration for high achievers among their students than are unpopular teachers using the same system of rewards. Indeed, the unpopular teacher may be dismissed as someone who practices favouritism, and the students she or he praises may be condemned by their peers as 'teacher's pets.' These predictions are consistent with the balance theory advocated by Aronson and Cope (1968) who present evidence to show that 'my friend's friend is my friend,' but 'my enemy's friend is my enemy.' In other words, students liked by popular teachers will also be admired by their peers, but students liked by unpopular teachers will not.

This same balance theory would also predict that the effects of teacher popularity would be reversed among teachers who give relatively low emphasis to academic performance and low rewards for academic achievement. Popular teachers who behave in this manner are likely to induce less admiration for high achievers among their students ('my friend's enemy is my enemy') than will less popular teachers ('my enemy's enemy is my friend'). This interaction between teacher popularity and teacher rewards may explain why some researchers (e.g., Berndt & Das, 1987) report that student popularity and achievement are positively correlated while other researchers (e.g., Adler et al., 1992) find that they are not. Presumably, the first set of findings occur primarily in classrooms in which popular teachers put a strong emphasis on academic achievement and praise those who do well. Such findings might also emerge when unpopular teachers fail to give high-achieving students the praise their peers think they deserve. The second set of findings would be likely to emerge in classes in which popular teachers place low emphasis on achievement levels and in those in which unpopular teachers praise high achievement. More research is needed to test these four possibilities in classroom settings, especially in the middle and upper grades where students are more likely than beginning pupils to make comparative judgements across teachers and across student achievements.

Academic achievement is not the only status dimension along which students can be encouraged to judge themselves and each other. Teachers may feel it necessary to give a great deal of attention to aggressive behaviours, thereby reinforcing them. Teachers may give a great deal of attention and praise to certain extracurricular activities or responsibilities, such as being a school crossing guard or a hall monitor. Or, teachers might collaborate with students in creating certain social types in the classroom, such as the court jester (Smith & Geoffrey, 1968) or helpers, enforcers, and go-betweens (Grant, 1994), that put a premium on social rather than academic skills. Teachers also might encourage students to create and consolidate their own hierarchies of skill, talent, or popularity by allowing them to pick teams for spelling bees or other contests, by allowing them to give Christmas or Valentine's cards to selected classmates, and by allowing them to organize their own work groups and study groups within the classroom context.

Finally, it should be noted that elementary school staff often influence peer group processes by the ways in which they define and deal with students whom they believe to be having problems with their peers. Commonly, these are students regarded as isolates or social rejects. Social skills training has become an increasingly popular and successful remedy for their problems. Berndt (1983) suggests that deficits in social skills are not the only source of unpopularity during childhood, and he notes that at least one study has found that a long-term tutoring program had more positive effects on academic achievement and sociometric status than did a social-skills training program. He also suggests that the popularity of isolated and rejected students could be improved by training programs that emphasize neatness, good grooming, and appropriate styles of dress. These suggestions are based on the assumptions that academic achievement and attractiveness increase popularity but, as noted above, this first proposition is not always true, and the second may not be either.

Literature seems not yet to have appeared in which the isolators and rejectors, rather than their targets, are considered to be the problems. Cohen (1994) hints at this definition of the problem when she describes the resistance to teacher-initiated groupwork that occurred in one of the sixth-grade classes she studied. The students felt the teachers were trying to force them to be friends with classmates assigned to their group. Cohen dealt with this problem by informing students that adult life often calls for working with people who are not close friends, and she encouraged the students to ask their parents if this is how adults worked. Although Cohen's tactics were effective in getting students to accept membership in teacher-initiated peer groups, their initial resistance raises questions not only about their lack of understanding of the adult world but also about their unwillingness to be friends with certain students.

By defining isolates and rejected students as problems that need solutions, well-intentioned teachers (and researchers) may be guilty of blaming the victims while defining their victimizers as successful, popular students. Thus, elementary school teachers may be helping students to lay the groundwork for the often vicious processes of exclusion and rejection that have been found in middle and junior high schools (see Eder, 1995; Everhart, 1983; Kinney, 1993). Perhaps elementary school staff should take a more active role in teaching students to be more accepting of those who are different from themselves. This is not just a matter of teaching about cultural diversity. It is also a matter of re-structuring interactions and reward structures in the classrooms.

At the least, elementary school staff need to decide what roles they should and shouldn't play with regard to peer group formation and the construction of peer cultures among their students. The evidence is overwhelming that actions by school staff affect these processes — by affecting proximity, status dimensions, and student identities — even when they are not intended to do so. Wouldn't it be better if teachers developed conscious values and goals to guide such actions?

Peer Cultures in Middle and Junior High Schools

Three major changes seem to occur in peer cultures when students move from elementary school to middle and junior high schools. First, the amount of influence of teachers on the formation of peer groups and construction of peer cultures seems to decrease. This decline probably results from the fact that students have several teachers rather than the single teacher (plus a few specialists) more characteristic of elementary schools. Multiple teachers will not necessarily emphasize the same status dimensions for judging students nor are they likely to attract the same intense liking (or disliking) that single teachers in traditional classrooms can elicit. Multiple teachers may disagree about which students are 'problems,' but even if they agree, they will not all behave toward those students in identical ways. Because the relationships between teachers and their students are of shorter duration (e.g., one hour every day or two hours thrice per week), they tend to be less intense, less authoritative, less supportive, and less influential.

The second major change affecting peer groups and cultures is the greater elaboration of the extracurriculum characteristic of middle and junior high schools. For some students these extracurricular activities become an important source of self-identity and peer group formation. To the extent that these extracurricular activities are highly visible and valued in the school, they are also likely to contribute to the prestige and popularity of these students. Unfortunately, the number of valued and visible positions in the extracurriculum is far fewer than the number of students, and the likelihood of obtaining these positions is particularly low for students in their first year of middle or junior high school. As a result, students who held relatively secure positions in their elementary school classrooms now find themselves 'outsiders' with little chance of obtaining the positions in their new schools that would give them a sense of importance and the opportunity to be popular.

The third major change from elementary to middle and junior high schools is the increased importance and influence of student-initiated and reputational peer groups. Although such groups often derive their prestige and popularity from their positions in the extracurriculum, this need not always be the case. Other visible and valued attributes, such as physical attractiveness, social skills, or evidences of wealth, can also make particular peer groups prominent and envied in their middle and junior high schools. Unfortunately, prestigious and popular groups are usually defined by themselves and others in opposition to outsiders who are not only seen as individual isolates and rejects (as they were in elementary school) but also as aggregates of 'nerds,' 'losers,' 'geeks,' 'grits,' 'dweebs,' etc. Such aggregates are rarely student-initiated peer groups with their own cultures. Instead they are reputational peer groups which fail to provide their 'members' with the friendship and social support necessary to withstand the imputation of such negative social identities. Indeed, the negative labels probably drive these students apart and prevent them from forming satisfactory relationships with one another.

Such aggregates of outsiders contrast sharply with the peer groups initiated by rebellious students who construct the resistant and oppositional peer cultures discussed earlier in this chapter. These groups also seem to emerge at the middle and junior high school level. Unlike the outsiders, however, rebellious peer cultures oppose both official school culture and the cultures of the prestigious, popular peer groups in their schools. Also, because they are part of a student-initiated group, they are likely to give each other support and loyalty. Thus, the image of middle and junior high schools that emerges from much of the literature is one in which a minority of students constitute themselves as the leading groups in the school; a second, smaller minority constitute themselves as the rebellious groups; and the large majority of students are reputed by others (especially by the leading groups) to be the 'social nobodies,' a reputation they are powerless to reject.

The three changes in the nature of peer group processes that occur between elementary schools and middle and junior high schools may explain why researchers have repeatedly found that students in junior high schools have lower self esteem than elementary school students (Simmons & Blyth, 1987). This finding is not simply due to age, because students who attend sixth, seventh, and eighth grades in elementary schools have been found to have significantly higher self esteem than students who attend those same grades in middle or junior high schools (Simmons, Blyth, VanCleave, & Bush, 1979). The rising importance of peer cultures, the development of a limited, exclusionary extracurriculum, and the decline in teacher influence over peer group processes seem to combine to create a context in which it is difficult for many students to gain the social supports necessary to feel good about themselves.

Another negative outcome that results from the three changes in the nature of peer group processes at the middle and junior high school levels is the intensification of traditional gender roles. As the extracurriculum becomes more elaborated in the official school culture, the varsity athlete and the cheerleader emerge as gender ideals among the students. The idealized athlete is not so much a sportsmanlike fair-player as he is a ruthless competitor, aggressor, womanizer, and winner. The cheerleader is appreciated for her enthusiasm, energy, attractiveness, and male-identification. As noted earlier, these prototypes of masculinity and femininity become the basis on which much cross-sex interaction becomes sexualized and abusive. Eder's (1995; 1997) observations of these processes have so alarmed her that she has suggested that schools should eliminate interscholastic athletics, particularly at the middle and junior high school levels where their effects on student behaviours are so negative and devastating.

Eder (1995) also suggests that school staff should attempt to reduce the sexual harassment and sexist insults that girls currently face in the public schools. As part of this effort, girls need to be helped by teachers and parent groups to develop more successful techniques for dealing with such behaviours. Eder's (1995, pp. 167-170) own experience with a group called KACTIS — Kids Against Cruel Treatment in School — leads her to suggest that humour of a light-hearted, playful kind is a particularly effective tool for girls to use not only to defend themselves but to gain admiration from their peers. As noted above, however, there is some danger in placing too much emphasis on skills training for victims.

Boys also need forums in which issues of masculinity and sexuality are discussed. Coaches need to stop the practice of berating boys who are not 'tough enough.' Eder (1995, p. 164) describes a physical education teacher who 're-quired nonathletes to do favors for the boys who were on the key athletic teams, setting up a system of male-to-male dominance and subservience.' School staff need to end such practices and develop ways in which all students are given opportunities to be publicly successful. In addition to the abolition of interscholastic sports, these changes could include more carefully structured groupwork in classrooms and more clubs, intramural sports, and non-athletic activities in the extracurriculum.

Peer Cultures in High Schools

Opportunities for success, especially academic success, also need to be expanded at the high school level. Without such expansion, it seems likely that efforts by school staff to emphasize the importance of academic achievement will have mixed success. On the one hand, such efforts may help to increase self-esteem among 'the brains' and may promote more academic effort and greater admiration for academic achievers throughout the school. On the other hand, such efforts might threaten average students (Powell et al., 1985) and might foster more rebellion among failing students (Felson et al., 1994; Stinchcomb, 1964). What is needed are instructional strategies in which *all* students benefit from a school-wide emphasis on academic success. Peer-learning techniques, such as peer tutoring, cooperative learning, and peer collaboration, seem to be strategies of this type; their benefits at various levels of schooling have been widely documented (for reviews, see Damon & Phelps, 1989; Hartup, 1983; Johnson, 1980; Slavin, 1995; for reservations, see McCaslin & Good, 1996).

Efforts by school staff to emphasize the importance of academic achievement should involve not only all the students, but all the staff as well. Just as academic standards for students vary across and within schools, so also do the standards and expectations for teachers. In many schools, some teachers try to create a trouble-free environment in which neither they nor their students have to work very hard. Classes focus on superficial learning rather than intellectual engagement; 'I think I get along fairly well with most of the kids,' admitted a Spanish teacher to Powell and his colleagues (1985, p. 76), 'but to be perfectly truthful I think I get along because I don't put a lot of pressure on them.' Teachers who demand 'too much' may be criticized not only by students but also by some parents and administrators. On the other hand, demanding teachers may be admired by those parents and colleagues who believe that 'students should be pushed' and who are critical of teachers who sacrifice academic standards for favourable student evaluations. As a result, all teachers become uncertain about what they can and should expect of themselves and their students. This uncertainty can breed hostility and resentment. Instead of engaging in a joint intellectual endeavour, teachers and students may collaborate in a mutual process of non-caring and withdrawal such as the one Wexler (1985) observed at Grummitt High.

Fortunately, some schools are effective in creating a climate in which students' scholastic efforts and achievements are expected, fostered, and rewarded. Rosenholtz (1989) describes such schools as those that are characterized by shared school goals, teacher collaboration, teacher learning, teacher certainty, and teacher commitment. Although a detailed discussion of Rosenholtz's findings and recommendations is beyond the scope of this chapter, her work makes clear that changing an official school culture in ways that put more emphasis on 'getting knowledge' may require extensive school re-organization. In particular, individualistic models of teachers and teaching may have to be replaced with more communal models in which teachers – perhaps by being organized into 'houses' or interdisciplinary teams (Little, 1995) – provide one another with the help and support necessary to promote academic successes among all students and to deal effectively with recalcitrant peer cultures.

Like their teachers, many students would also benefit from greater communalism among their high-school peers. To this end, older students might be encouraged to help orient new students by introducing them to other students, accompanying them during lunch hours, escorting them to school assemblies and extracurricular events, etc. Encouraging senior students to engage in such helpful actions might take the form of a big sister, big brother program comparable to those established at many U.S. colleges and universities. The goal would be to increase friendliness and tolerance among students, perhaps by making peer groups less dense and exclusive, but more likely by reducing animosity and opposition among them.

Even without such programs, high school students seem to be less likely to feel like 'social nobodies' and to suffer from low self-esteem than students in middle or junior high school. These positive changes seem to result from both developmental processes and the larger size of high schools. Larger size makes it possible for schools to sponsor more extracurricular activities and to provide expanded opportunities for students to form close, personal relationships (Kinney, 1993). Larger size and an expanded extracurriculum also makes it harder for a few, elite peer groups to dominate the entire social landscape of the school. The 'social nobodies' of junior high school have more opportunities in high school to gain social supports for a satisfactory sense of self (Kinney, 1993).

Despite these positive changes, interscholastic athletic programs continue to be highly visible and valued in the official school culture of most high schools, and they perpetuate the same traditional prototypes of masculinity and femininity that have been found to intensify in middle and junior high schools. Kessler and his colleagues (1985, p. 39) provide a particularly vivid description of the kind of masculinity constructed by the football program at Milton College, an elite secondary school in Australia:

> It celebrates toughness and endurance, relentlessly promotes competitiveness and fear of losing, and connects a sense of maleness with a taste for violence and confrontation. Moreover, because the game has an honoured place in this school, the kind of masculinity it promotes, the tough and macho kind, subordinates other kinds of masculinity. The boys who for reasons of physique, capacity, or preference have been relegated to study, nonviolent games, debating and the like are condemned by the football heroes to be known as 'the Cyrils,' a term indicating effeminacy.

In addition, interscholastic athletic programs have been found to reinforce the social class hierarchy in both the United States and the British Commonwealth. Hargreaves (1967, p. 187) reports that school staff in Lumley Secondary Modern School 'believed that it was the boys with superior academic performance – though they often referred to `ability' – who made the best sportsmen.' As a result, students in the upper streams (tracks) were encouraged to take part in sporting activities, and those in the lower streams were not. Not surprisingly, Hargreaves (1967) also finds that boys in the lower streams refused to take part in the extracurricular life of the school even when they had the talents and interests necessary to excel at particular activities. Similar findings are reported for working-class students by Brantlinger (1993), Corrigan (1979), Eckert (1989), and Willis (1977).

Despite the role played by varsity athletics in reproducing the gender and class hierarchies of high schools, it is unlikely that abolishing these sports is a viable option for most schools. A large proportion of school staffs are coaches who will undoubtedly resist losing their positions. Also, as noted above, sports play a central role in the public image of the school. Many parents are proud of their children's participation in the highly visible athletic program of the school.

Connell and his colleagues (1982, p. 52) make a somewhat cynical observation about paternal involvement in the independent (private) Australian schools they studied – 'Major fund-raising committees are likely to be run by men; and fathers who can't find the time for checking homework will often turn out to watch their sons play in school teams.' This connection is not unique to private schools, however. In the United States, parental and community support are essential for school funding through local financial initiatives, such as bond issues and local tax increases.

While the costs of abolishing varsity athletics may be unacceptable for many high schools, steps could be taken to decrease the importance of athletics in the official school culture. Fewer pep or spirit assemblies might be one place to start in American schools, but even this step might prove costly in the short run. Lesko's (1986) analysis of such assemblies at a Catholic high school led her to conclude that, by emphasizing communal values and 'fun,' such rituals help to mediate tensions in the school created by competitive individualism and the favouritism of teachers and coaches toward students who come from rich, influential families. In the long run, it might be possible to reduce competitive individualism and favouritism in high schools, thereby reducing the need to use athletic assemblies as a way of promoting students' cohesiveness and positive attitudes toward their school.

Reductions in the enactment and enforcement of school rules governing student deportment and appearance might also help to alleviate tensions among peer cultures and between students and school staff. Reynolds (1976) argues that many working class schools are like war zones in which students spend their time and energy resisting attempts by teachers to enforce rules about 'dress, manners, and morals' that students find inappropriate. One of the pupils in such a school had the following to say about such rules:

> The rules that I don't agree with are no smoking and no talking in class
> … And if they stop you talking in class – it's a load of rubbish. All boys
> will talk in class so is it worth bothering to keep this rule? Besides they
> can never stop you talking. You are punished for asking the boy you sit
> by what page is next in maths. (Reynolds, 1976, p. 136)

Reynolds argues that conflicts over rules of this sort produce a 'circular process of deviancy amplification' in which students' perceptions that teachers are using illegitimate authority make them less willing to defer to teachers' wishes in legitimate, academic areas of school life. Not only do students in such schools reject academic goals, they also express their resentment of school staff by means of relatively high rates of vandalism, truancy, and delinquency.

To remedy such problems, Reynolds (1976) suggests that teachers and students form a truce. The goal of the truce is to reduce the extent to which school lessons are the focus of conflict between teachers and students. In order to get on with lessons in a non-conflictful manner, Reynolds (1976, p. 133) suggests that teachers reduce their efforts to get students to comply with 'expressive, non-pedagogic or character moulding goals' that only increase student rebellion. As students begin to realize that teachers are willing to ignore the rules that students consider to be illegitimate, they become more willing to cooperate with teachers' efforts to achieve legitimate pedagogical goals. Such a truce makes life easier for both teachers and students, thereby encouraging all of them to abide by the truce and to encourage their peers to do likewise. As a result, '(i)n schools where a truce exists, social status within the informal pupil subculture will not necessarily be gained by a pupil's doing things which the school and its teachers believe to be wrong' (Reynolds, 1976, p. 134).

CONCLUSIONS

With the exception of peer learning strategies, most of the suggestions for school staff made in the previous section of the chapter have not received much testing or research. This is because many of these suggestions go beyond the traditional concerns of teachers such as the curriculum and the academic achievements of their students. What this chapter has tried to show, however, is that these traditional, teacher-initiated activities are not and probably cannot be separated from either the school-sponsored extracurriculum or the student-initiated peer groups and cultures.

Teachers may try to ignore these other components of the school system in order to 'focus on learning,' but they need to realize that the social system of the school is not only a context for classroom learning, it is part of what every student learns. For some students, this learning is a painful composite of isolation, rejection, verbal abuse, and social failure. For others, this learning induces cynicism about teacher favouritism and the (illegitimate) authority exercised by school staff. Still others learn how to ingratiate themselves to teachers without working too hard. And, there are some who learn to excel at self-promotion among school elites and at aggression against students they don't like.

It is inconceivable that what is learned outside the classroom would fail to affect the ways in which students interpret what they are taught in class. What do classroom lessons about cultural diversity mean to students whose peer groups are racially exclusive and whose peer cultures elaborate racist themes? How effective can in-class lessons about citizen rights and responsibilities be to students whose elected student government is expected to rubber-stamp administrative decisions over which they have no control? Can students be convinced that academic achievement in any subject is important when the elite students in their school are more likely to excel on the sports field than in the classroom?

What do teacher requests for cooperation and mutual helping in the classroom mean to students who are praised and prized for their ability to win school-sponsored competitions against students from other schools?

As these questions suggest, the learnings that students bring into the classroom are neither idiosyncratic nor the result of 'family background.' They are lessons learned from observing and participating in the official culture and peer cultures that constitute the social system of the school. Teachers can try to create classroom cultures that ignore this broader context, but they should not be surprised if their efforts fail. Indeed, if the contrast between what goes on inside and outside the classroom is too great, students may simply conclude that teacher-initiated activities in the classroom are irrelevant to what school (and life) is really all about. Teachers interested in avoiding this outcome will benefit from more efforts to take peer cultures into account. Whether they should also make efforts to change peer cultures by working directly with students or by changing the extracurriculum and the official school culture will require extensive discussions among school staff. Central to such discussions must be questions about the kinds of student learning the school seeks to promote, the kinds of student learning the school would like to prevent or challenge, and the kinds of school and peer cultures that would promote these goals.

REFERENCES

Adler, P. A., Kless, S. J., & Adler, P. (1992). Socialization to gender roles: Popularity among elementary school boys and girls. *Sociology of Education, 65*, 169-187.

American Association of University Women Educational Foundation. (1993). *Hostile hallways: The AAUW survey on sexual harassment in American's schools.* Washington, DC: AAUW Educational Foundation.

Andersson, B-E. (1969). *Studies in adolescent behaviour.* Uppsala, Sweden: Almqvist & Wiksells Boktryckeri.

Aronson, E. (1978). *The jigsaw classroom.* Beverly Hills, CA: Sage.

Aronson, E. & Cope, V. (1968). My enemy's enemy is my friend. *Journal of Personality and Social Psychology, 8*, 8-12.

Aronson, E. & Worchel, S. (1966). Similarity versus liking as determinants of interpersonal attractiveness. *Psychonomic Science, 5*, 157-158.

Bank, B. J. (1994). Effects of national and school contexts on friendships among adolescents in Australia and the United States. *Youth & Society, 25*, 435-456.

Bank, B. J., Biddle, B. J., Keats, D. M., & Keats, J. A. (1977). Normative, preferential and belief modes in adolescent prejudice. *The Sociological Quarterly, 18*, 574-588.

Bank, B. J., Biddle, B. J., Anderson, D. S., Hauge, R., Keats, D. M., Keats, J. A., Marlin, M. M., & Valantin, S. (1985). Comparative research on the social determinants of adolescent drinking. *Social Psychology Quarterly, 48*, 164-177.

Berndt, T. J. (1983). Correlates and causes of sociometric status in childhood: A commentary on six current studies of popular, rejected, and neglected children. *Merrill-Palmer Quarterly, 29*, 439-448.

Berndt, T. J. & Das, R. (1987). Effects of popularity and social behavior of peers. *Journal of Early Adolescence, 7*, 429-439.

Berndt, T. J., Miller, K. L., & Park, K. (1989). Adolescents' perceptions of friends' and parents' influence on aspects of their school adjustment. *Journal of Early Adolescence, 9*, 419-435.

Biddle, B. J., Bank, B. J., & Marlin, M. M. (1980a). Parental and peer influence on adolescents. *Social Forces, 58*, 1057-1079.

Biddle, B. J., Bank, B. J., & Marlin, M. M. (1980b). Social determinants of adolescent drinking: What they think, what they do and what I think and do. *Journal of Studies on Alcohol, 41*, 215-241.

Bogart, K. & Stein, N. (1989). Breaking the silence: Sexual harassment in education. *Peabody Journal of Education, 64*, 146-163.

Boissevain, J. (1974). *Friends of friends: Networks, manipulators and coalitions*. Oxford: Basil Blackwell.

Brake, M. (1985). *Comparative youth culture: The sociology of youth cultures and youth subcultures in America, Britain and Canada*. London and New York: Routledge.

Brantlinger, E. A. (1993). *The politics of social class in secondary school: Views of affluent and impoverished youth*. New York: Teachers College Press.

Brehm, S. S. (1992). *Intimate relationships* (2nd ed.). New York: McGraw-Hill.

Brown, B. B. (1990). Peer groups and peer cultures. In S. S. Feldman & G. R. Elliott (Eds.), *At the threshold: The developing adolescent* (pp. 171-196). Cambridge, MA: Harvard University Press.

Brown, B. B., Clasen, D. R., & Eicher, S. A. (1986). Perceptions of peer pressure, peer conformity dispositions, and self-reported behavior among adolescents. *Developmental Psychology, 22*, 521-530.

Brown, B. B., Mory, M. S., & Kinney, D. (1994). Casting adolescent crowds in a relational perspective: Caricature, channel, and context. In R. Montemayor, G. R. Adams, & T. P. Gullotta (Eds.), *Personal relationships during adolescence* (pp. 123-167). Thousand Oaks, CA: Sage Publications.

Brown, B. B., Mounts, N, Lamborn, S. D., & Steinberg, L. (1993). Parenting practices and peer group affiliation. *Child Development, 64*, 467-482.

Brown, B. B. & Steinberg, L. (1991). Noninstructional influences on adolescent engagement and achievement (Final Report: Project 2). Madison, WI: National Center on Effective Secondary Schools. (From ERIC, Abstract No. ED340641)

Buhrmann, H. G. & Bratton, R. D. (1977). Athletic participation and status of Alberta high school girls. *International Review of Sport Sociology, 12*, 57-67.

Buhrmann, H. G. & Jarvis, M. S. (1971). Athletics and status: An examination of the relationship between athletic participation and various status measures of high school girls. *Canadian Association of Health, Physical Education, and Recreation Journal, 37*, 14-17.

Byrne, D. (1971). *The attraction paradigm*. New York: Academic Press.

Cauce, A. M. (1986). Social networks and social competence: Exploring the effects of early adolescent friendships. *American Journal of Community Psychology, 14*, 607-628.

Cohen, A. (1955). *Delinquent boys: The culture of the gang*. New York: Free Press.

Cohen, E. G. (1994). *Designing groupwork: Strategies for the heterogeneous classroom* (2nd ed.). New York: Teachers College Press.

Cohen, J. (1983a). Commentary: The relationship between friendship selection and peer influence. In J. L. Epstein & N. Karweit (Eds.), *Friends in school: Patterns of selection and influence in secondary schools* (pp. 163-174). New York: Academic Press.

Cohen, J. (1983b). Peer influence on college aspirations with initial aspirations controlled. *American Sociological Review, 48*, 728-734.

Coleman, J. C. (1980). *The nature of adolescence*. New York: Methuen.

Coleman, J. S. (1961). *The adolescent society: The social life of the teenager and its impact on education*. New York: The Free Press of Glencoe.

Condon, J. W. & Crano, W. D. (1988). Inferred evaluation and the relation between attitude similarity and interpersonal attraction. *Journal of Personality and Social Psychology, 54*, 789-797.

Connell, R. W., Ashenden, D. J., Kessler, S., & Dowsett, G. W. (1982). *Making the difference: Schools, families and social division*. Sydney, Australia: George Allen & Unwin.

Corrigan, P. (1979). *Schooling the Smash Street kids*. London: Macmillan.

Corsaro, W. A. (1985). *Friendship and peer culture in the early years*. Norwood, NJ: Ablex Publishing Co.

Corsaro, W. A. & Eder, D. (1990). Children's peer cultures. *Annual Review of Sociology, 16*, 197-220.

Csikszentmihalyi, M. & Larson, R. (1984). *Being adolescent: Conflict and growth in the teenage years*. New York: Basic Books.

Cusick, P. A. (1973). *Inside high school: The student's world*. New York: Holt, Rinehart & Winston, Inc.

Damon, W. & Phelps, E. (1989). Strategic uses of peer learning in children's education. In T. J. Berndt & G. W. Ladd (Eds.), *Peer relationships in child development* (pp. 135-157). New York: Wiley.

Davies, M. & Kandel, D. B. (1981). Parental and peer influences on adolescents' educational plans: Some further evidence. *American Journal of Sociology, 87*, 363-387.

Davies, S. (1995). Leaps of faith: Shifting currents in critical sociology of education. *American Journal of Sociology, 100*, 1448-1478.

Dickens, W. J. & Perlman, D. (1981). Friendship over the life-cycle. In S. Duck & R. Gilmour (Eds.), *Personal relationships 2: Developing personal relationships* (pp. 91-122). New York: Academic Press.

Downes, D. M. (1966). *The delinquent solution: A study in subcultural theory*. New York: Free Press.

Dunphy, D. (1963). The social structure of urban adolescent peer groups. *Sociometry, 26*, 230-246.

Eckert, P. (1989). *Jocks & burnouts: Social categories and identity in the high school*. New York: Teachers College Press.

Eder, D. (1985). The cycle of popularity: Interpersonal relations among female adolescents. *Sociology of Education, 58*, 154-165.

Eder, D. (1997). Sexual aggression within the school culture. In B. J. Bank & P. M. Hall (Eds.), *Gender, equity, and schooling*. New York: Garland Publishing Co.

Eder, D. with Evans, C. C. & Parker, S. (1995). *School talk: Gender and adolescent culture*. New Brunswick, NJ: Rutgers University Press.

Eder, D. & Kinney, D. A. (1995). The effects of middle school extracurricular activities on adolescents' popularity and peer status. *Youth & Society, 26*, 298-324.

Elmen, J. (1991). Achievement orientation in early adolescence: Developmental patterns and social correlates. *Journal of Early Adolescence, 11*, 125-151.

Epstein, J. L. (1983). The influence of friends on achievement and affective outcomes. In J. L. Epstein & N. Karweit (Eds.), *Friends in school: Patterns of selection and influence in secondary schools* (pp. 177-200). New York: Academic Press.

Epstein, J. L. (1989). The selection of friends: Changes across the grades and in different school environments. In T. J. Berndt & G. W. Ladd (Eds.), *Peer relationships in child development* (pp. 158-187). New York: Wiley.

Epstein, J. L. & Karweit, N. (Eds.). (1983). *Friends in school: Patterns of selection and influence in secondary schools*. New York: Academic Press.

Everhart, R. B. (1983). *Reading, writing and resistance: Adolescence and labor in a junior high school*. Boston: Routledge & Kegan Paul.

Felson, R. B., Liska, A. E., South, S. J., & McNulty, T. L. (1994). The subculture of violence and delinquency: Individual vs. school context effects. *Social Forces, 73*, 155-173.

Fine, G. A. (1981). Friends, impression management, and preadolescent behavior. In S. R. Asher & J. M. Gottman (Eds.), *The development of children's friendships* (pp. 29-52). Cambridge, England: Cambridge University Press.

Fischer, C. S. (1982). *To dwell among friends: Personal networks in town and city*. Chicago: University of Chicago Press.

Ford, D. Y., Harris III, J. J., Webb, K. S., & Jones, D. L. (1994). Rejection or confirmation of racial identity: A dilemma for high-achieving Blacks? *The Journal of Educational Thought, 28*, 7-33.

Fordham, S. (1988). Racelessness as a factor in black students' school success: Pragmatic strategy or pyrrhic victory? *Harvard Educational Review, 58*, 54-84.

Fordham, S. (1993). 'Those loud black girls': (Black) women, silence, and gender 'passing' in the academy. *Anthropology & Education Quarterly, 24*, 3-32.

Forsyth, D. R. (1990). *Group dynamics* (2nd ed.). Pacific Grove, CA: Brooks/Cole Publishing Co.

Ginsberg, D., Gottman, J., & Parker, J. (1986). The importance of friendship. In J. M. Gottman & J. G. Parker (Eds.), *Conversations of friends: Speculations on affective development* (pp. 3-48). Cambridge: Cambridge University Press.

Gordon, C. W. (1957). *The social system of the high school: A study in the sociology of adolescence*. Glencoe, IL: Free Press.

Granovetter, M. S. (1973). The strength of weak ties. *American Journal of Sociology, 78*, 1360-1380.

Grant, L. (1994). Helpers, enforcers, and go-betweens: Black girls in elementary schools. In M. B. Zinn & B. T. Dill (Eds.), *Women of color in America* (pp. 43-63). Philadelphia: Temple University Press.

Hallinan, M. T. (1992). Determinants of students' friendship choices. *Advances in Group Processes, 9*, 163-183.

Hallinan, M. T. & Sorensen, A. B. (1985). Ability grouping and student friendships. *American Educational Research Journal, 22*, 485-499.

Hargreaves, D. H. (1967). *Social relations in a secondary school*. London: Routledge & Kegan Paul.

Hartup, W. W. (1983). Peer relations. In P. H. Mussen (Ed.), *Handbook of child psychology* (4th ed., pp. 103-196). New York: John Wiley & Sons.

Hartup, W. W. (1989). Behavioral manifestations of children's friendships. In T. J. Berndt & G. W. Ladd (Eds.), *Peer relationships in child development* (pp. 47-70). New York: Wiley.

Hebdige, D. (1979). *Subculture: The meaning of style*. London: Methuen.

Ide, J. K., Parkerson, J., Haertel, G. D., & Walberg, H. J. (1981). Peer group influence on educational outcomes: A quantitative synthesis. *Journal of Educational Psychology, 73*, 472-484.

Johnson, D. W. (1980). Group processes: Influences of student-student interaction on school outcomes. In J. H. McMillan (Ed.), *The social psychology of school learning* (pp. 123-168). New York: Academic Press.

Kandel, D. B. (1978). Homophily, selection, and socialization in adolescent friendship. *American Journal of Sociology, 84*, 427-436.

Kandel, D. B. & Lesser, G. S. (1972). *Youth in two worlds*. San Francisco: Jossey-Bass.

Kelman, H. (1958). Compliance, identification, and internalization: Three processes of attitude change. *Journal of Conflict Resolution, 2*, 51-60.

Keniston, K. (1970). Youth: A 'new stage' of life. *The American Scholar, 39*, 631-654.

Kessler, S., Ashenden, D. J., Connell, R. W., & Dowsett, G. W. (1985). Gender relations in secondary schooling. *Sociology of Education, 58*, 34-48.

Kester, V. M. (1994). Factors that affect African-American students' bonding to middle school. *Elementary School Journal, 95*, 63-73.

Kinney, D. A. (1993). From Nerds to Normals: The recovery of identity among adolescents from middle school to high school. *Sociology of Education, 66*, 21-40.

Lacey, C. (1970). *Hightown Grammar: The school as a social system*. Manchester, England: Manchester University Press.

Larkin, J. (1994). Walking through walls: The sexual harassment of high school girls. *Gender and Education, 6*, 263-280.

Larkin, R. W. (1979). *Suburban youth in cultural crisis*. New York: Oxford University Press.

Laursen, B. (Ed.). (1993). *Close friendships in adolescence*. San Francisco: Jossey-Bass Publishers.

Lees, S. (1993). *Sugar and spice: Sexuality and adolescent girls*. London: Penguin Books.

Lesko, N. (1986). Individualism and community: Ritual discourse in a parochial high school. *Anthropology & Education Quarterly, 17*, 25-39.

Little, J. W. (1995). Contested ground: The basis of teacher leadership in two restructuring high schools. *Elementary School Journal, 96*, 47-63.

Marx, K. (1852/1963). *The 18th Brumaire of Louis Bonaparte*. New York: New World Paperbacks.

McCaslin, M. & Good, T. L. (1996). The informal curriculum. In D. Berliner & R. Calfee (Eds.), *The handbook of educational psychology* (pp. 622-670). New York: Macmillan.

McRobbie, A. (1991). *Feminism and youth culture: From Jackie to just seventeen*. Boston: Unwin Hyman.

McRobbie, A. & Garber, J. (1975). Girls and subcultures. In S. Hall & T. Jefferson (Eds.), *Resistance through rituals: Youth subcultures in post-war Britain* (pp. 209-222). New York: Holmes & Meier Publishers, Inc.

Merton, R. K. (1957). *Social theory and social structure* (rev. ed.). Glencoe, IL: Free Press of Glencoe.

Monti, D. J. (1994). *Wannabe: Gangs in suburbs and schools*. Oxford, UK and Cambridge, MA: Blackwell.

Newcomb, T. M. (1961). *The acquaintance process*. New York: Holt, Rinehart & Winston.

Polite, V. C. (1992). *All dressed up with no place to go: An ethnography of the African-American male students in an urban high school*. Abstract of paper presented at the annual meeting of the American Educational Research Association (From ERIC Abstract No. ED344971)

Powell, A. G., Farrar, E., & Cohen, D. K. (1985). *The shopping mall high school: Winners and losers in the educational marketplace*. Boston: Houghton Mifflin.

Purcell, J. H., Gable, R. K., & Caillard, F. (1994). Attitudes of suburban high school students toward behaviors associated with high-achieving peers: Development and validation of the peer assessment scale. *Educational and Psychological Measurement, 54*, 383-393.

Reynolds, D. (1976). When pupils and teachers refuse a truce: The secondary school and the creation of delinquency. In G. Mungham & G. Pearson (Eds.), *Working class youth culture* (pp. 124-137). London: Routledge & Kegan Paul.

Rigsby, L. C. & McDill, E. L. (1975). Value orientations of high school students. In H. R. Stub (Ed.), *The sociology of education: A sourcebook* (pp. 53-75). Homewood, IL: Dorsey Press.

Rosenholtz, S. J. (1989). *Teachers' workplace: The social organization of schools*. New York: Longman.

Rubin, K. H. (1982). Social and social-cognitive developmental characteristics of young isolate, normal, and sociable children. In K. H. Rubin & H. S. Ross (Eds.), *Peer relationships and social skills in childhood* (pp. 353-374). New York: Springer-Verlag.

Rubin, Z. (1980). *Children's friendships*. Cambridge, MA: Harvard University Press.

Schofield, J. W. (1982). *Black and white in school: Trust, tension, or tolerance?* New York: Praeger.

Selman, R. (1976). Toward a structural analysis of developing interpersonal relations concepts: Research with normal and disturbed preadolescent boys. In A. Pick (Ed.), *Minnesota symposium on child development* (Vol. 10). Minneapolis, MN: University of Minnesota Press.

Selman, R. L. & Jacquette, D. (1977). Stability and oscillation in interpersonal awareness: A clinical developmental analysis. In C. B. Keasey (Ed.), *Nebraska symposium on motivation* (Vol. 25, pp. 261-304). Lincoln: University of Nebraska Press.

Shantz, C. U. (Ed.). (1983). Popular, rejected, and neglected children: Their social behavior and social reasoning (Special issue). *Merrill-Palmer Quarterly, 29*(3).

Shlapentokh, V. (1984). *Love, marriage, and friendship in the Soviet Union: Ideals and practices*. New York: Praeger.

Simmons, R. G. & Blyth, D. A. (1987). *Moving into adolescence: The impact of pubertal change and school context*. New York: Aldine.

Simmons, R. G., Blyth, D. A., VanCleave, E. F., & Bush, D. M. (1979). Entry into early adolescence: The impact of school structure, puberty, and early dating on self-esteem. *American Sociological Review, 38*, 553-568.

Slavin, R. E. (1995). *Cooperative learning* (2nd ed.). Needham Heights, MA: Allyn and Bacon.

Smith, D. M. (1985). Perceived peer and parental influences on youths' social world. *Youth & Society, 17*, 131-156.

Smith, L. M. & Geoffrey, W. (1968). *The complexities of an urban classroom: An analysis toward a general theory of teaching*. New York: Holt, Rinehart & Winston.

Spady, W. G. (1970). Lament for the letterman: Effects of peer status and extracurricular activities on goals and achievement. *American Journal of Sociology, 75*, 680-702.

Spencer-Hall, D. A. (1981). Looking behind the teacher's back. *Elementary School Journal, 81*, 281-289.

Stack, C. (1974). *All our kin*. New York: Harper & Row.

Stein, Nan D. (1993). It happens here, too: Sexual harassment and child sexual abuse in elementary and secondary schools. In S. K. Biklen & D. Pollard (Eds.), *Gender and education* (pp. 191-203). Chicago: University of Chicago Press.

Stevens, R. J. & Slavin, R. E. (1995). The cooperative elementary school: Effects on students' achievement, attitudes, and social relations. *American Educational Research Journal, 32*, 321-351.

Stinchcomb, A. L. (1964). *Rebellion in a high school*. Chicago: Quadrangle Books.

Thorne, B. (1993). *Gender play: Boys and girls in school*. New Brunswick: Rutgers University Press.

Walberg, H. J. (1986). Syntheses of research on teaching. In M. C. Wittrock (Ed.), *Handbook of research on teaching* (3rd ed., pp. 214-229). New York: Macmillan Publishing Company.

Weis, L. (1990). *Working class without work: High school students in a deindustrializing economy*. New York: Routledge.

Wexler, P. with assistance of Crichlow, W., Kern, J., & Martuswicz, R. (1985). *Becoming somebody: Toward a social psychology of school*. London: Falmer.

Wheeler, D. K. (1961). Popularity among adolescents in Western Australia and in the United States of America. *The School Review, 49*, 67-81.

Willis, P. (1977). *Learning to labor: How working class kids get working class jobs*. New York: Columbia University Press.

Winstead, B. A. (1986). Sex differences in same-sex friendships. In V. J. Derlega & B. A. Winstead (Eds.), *Friendship and social interaction* (pp. 81-99). New York: Springer-Verlag.

Wooden, W. S. (1995). *Renegade kids, suburban outlaws: From youth culture to delinquency*. Belmont, CA: Wadsworth Publishing Co.

Youniss, J., McLellan, J. A., & Strouse, D. (1994). 'We're popular, but we're not snobs': Adolescents describe their crowds. In R. Montemayor, G. R. Adams, & T. P. Gullotta (Eds.), *Personal relationships during adolescence* (pp. 101-122). Thousand Oaks, CA: Sage Publications.

Chapter 6: The Micropolitics of Teaching

JOSEPH BLASE
The University of Georgia

During the last two decades, research on teachers and teaching has produced significant findings on the social and cultural aspects of work. What is loosely referred to as teacher work-life literature provides valuable insights into the structural and experiential dimensions of teachers' work. Studies of cultural norms, satisfaction, commitment, gender, professionalism, career, socialization, induction, purposes, and sentiments have appeared in this literature. For example, substantial work on teachers' lives has been completed using life history and narrative methods (Goodson, 1992; Schubert & Ayers, 1992). In fact, research on teachers' worklives has produced substantial data relevant to understanding the micropolitics of teaching; that is, how teachers use formal and informal power to achieve their ends in school organizations. However, because these data have not been interpreted from a micropolitical perspective, their significance along these lines has not been apparent. And although some theoretical attention has been given to the political aspects of teachers' work by feminists (Grumet, 1988; Lather, 1991) and critical theorists (e.g., Apple, 1986), little empirical work on the everyday micropolitics of teaching has been completed until recently.

The micropolitics of teaching is an important subset of the micropolitics of education. The purpose of this chapter is to examine this exciting and rapidly emerging area of inquiry. Specifically, this chapter provides a comprehensive review of micropolitical studies of teachers and their work as well as other studies that have produced data about the micropolitics of teaching. In addition, because of the limited amount of research completed thus far, teacher work-life studies with implicit micropolitical content are also included in this review.

Section 1 of this chapter presents a brief overview of several conceptual and theoretical approaches to micropolitics. The second section – divided into the four subsections of teachers' political relationships with principals, other faculty, students, and parents – examines micropolitical studies of teaching and work-life studies with politically relevant findings. Because the micropolitics of teaching is a nascent area of inquiry that may be unfamiliar to many readers, relatively comprehensive descriptions of individual studies are presented. A summary of research perspectives, methods, and procedures used in micropolitical studies of teachers appears in Section 3. Section 4 of the chapter offers a the-

B.J. Biddle et al. (eds.), International Handbook of Teachers and Teaching, 939-970
© *1997 Kluwer Academic Publishers, Printed in the Netherands*

matic analysis of the emerging micropolitics of teaching knowledge base. Ideas central to understanding teacher politics appearing across the extant literature (e.g., vulnerability, strategies, exchange) are discussed. Section 5 provides a general framework for advancing future micropolitical research on teachers, and the final section briefly discusses implications of micropolitics for preservice and inservice teacher training.

SECTION 1: THE MICROPOLITICAL PERSPECTIVE

Traditional theories of school organization and descriptions of behavior fail to capture the complex and dynamic nature of life in schools. Consequently, such theories do not address the realities of school life as people experience it. The micropolitical perspective provides a valuable and potent approach to understanding the complexity of everyday life in schools:

> This perspective highlights the fundamentals of human behavior and purpose. Micropolitics is about power and how people use it to influence others and to protect themselves. It is about conflict and how people compete with each other to get what they want. It is about cooperation and how people build support among themselves to achieve their ends. It is about what people in social settings think about and have strong feelings about, but what is so often unspoken and not so easily observed. (Blase, 1991c, p. 1)

During the 1960s micropolitics (organizational politics) began to draw increasing attention in the United States. Early micropolitical writers challenged traditional-rational models of organization discussed by Weber (1947), Taylor (1947), and Fayol (1949). The importance of factors such as span of control, division of labor, roles, and authority and the assumption that these factors determine the behavior of individuals and groups in organization were seriously questioned (Bacharach & Mitchell, 1987; Mangham, 1979). Also challenged were assumptions of rational efficiency and effectiveness in decision making and problem solving (Hardy, 1987; Pfeffer, 1981), as well as the assumptions of value and goal consensus in open systems models of organization (Bolman & Deal, 1984; Miles, 1980). Generally, it has been argued that neither rational nor systems models of organization account for complexity, instability, conflict, and consensus in organizational settings. These models also fail to explain individual differences related to ideologies, values, goals, interests, expertise, history, and motivation (Bacharach & Lawler, 1980; Ball, 1987; Blase, 1989; Gronn, 1986; Hoyle, 1986; Morgan, 1986; Pfeffer, 1981).

During the 1960s and 1970s, valuable theoretical and empirical work was done in micropolitics, particularly in the fields of public administration and management. Burns (1961), Strauss (1962), Cyert and March (1963), and Wamsley and Zald (1973) made seminal contributions to the study of micropolitics. In the field of management, significant early work was completed by writers such as Bacharach and Lawler (1980), Pfeffer (1981), Mangham (1979), Mayes and Allen (1977), and Schein (1977).

Without exception, all perspectives on micropolitics have underscored the considerable role of power in the organization. Bacharach and Lawler (1980) define politics in organizations as 'the tactical use of power to retain or obtain control of real or symbolic resources' (p. 1). They describe a political model of organization that emphasizes the power and conflict dynamics of coalitions within a framework of bargaining relationships and bargaining tactics. More broadly, Pfeffer (1981) defines organizational politics as 'activities taken within organizations to acquire, develop, and use power and other resources to obtain preferred outcomes in a situation in which there is uncertainty or dissensus about choices' (p. 7). Accordingly, for Pfeffer the concept of organizational politics refers both to the exercise of power by individuals and groups to achieve goals and to the activities employed to expand power or the extent of its effect.

Iannaccone (1975), one of the early theorists to discuss the applicability of the micropolitical perspective on public education in the United States, focused on the interaction of administrator, teacher, and student subsystems within the school building and lay and professional subsystems at the school-building level. Of particular interest are Iannaccone's insights about teacher autonomy as a political ideology. But it was not until the 1980s that several American and British writers began significant work on the now growing empirical, conceptual, and theoretical knowledge base on the micropolitics of education. Although each writer has emphasized different political subject matter (e.g., formal versus informal processes and structures, decision making versus other types of political behavior, and the inclusion of conflictive versus cooperative/consensual interactions), all share a focus on how individuals and groups use power and influence to achieve their interests in organizational settings.

Hoyle's (1986) formulation of micropolitics emphasizes the strategies employed by organizational participants to use authority and influence to achieve their interests. In his groundbreaking book, *The Micropolitics of the School*, Ball (1987) offers a comprehensive political theory of school organization that centers on group-level analysis and conflictive interactions and focuses on the interests of actors. Ball discusses the maintenance of administrative control, particularly through the leadership of school heads (principals), as well as policy conflicts. Ball writes:

> I take schools, in common with virtually all other social organizations, to be arenas of struggle; to be riven with actual and potential conflict between members; to be poorly coordinated; to be ideologically diverse. I take it to be essential that if we are to understand the nature of schools as organizations, we must achieve some understanding of these conflicts. (p. 19)

Despite the importance of Ball's early contribution to the micropolitics of education, his approach has certain limitations. His emphasis on conflictive 'dark-side' politics ignores cooperative/consensual political dynamics (óBlase, 1991c; Burlingame, 1988; Townsend, 1990). A focus on meso-level (group-level) political interactions understates the individuals' political interactions with the organization (Burlingame, 1988).

To address these and other limitations apparent in the theoretical literature, Blase (1991c) constructed a broad-based, inclusive definition of micropolitics from a comprehensive review of the extant literature:

> Micropolitics refers to the use of formal and informal power by individuals and groups to achieve their goals in organizations. In large part political actions result from perceived differences between individuals and groups, coupled with the motivation to use power to influence and/or protect. Although such actions are consciously motivated, any action, consciously or unconsciously motivated, may have political 'significance' in a given situation. Both cooperative and conflictive actions and processes are part of the realm of micropolitics. (p. 11)

This definition of micropolitics includes both legitimate and illegitimate forms of power; goals may be interests, preferences, or purposes; and differences may be related to needs, values, and ideologies. Consciously motivated actions are intended, calculated, or strategic. Unconsciously motivated actions may be routine, nondecision making, habitual actions that result from socialization and actions that limit others' influence. Political significance may refer to the consequences or the meaning that actions have for others. Political action includes both conflictive and cooperative-consensual processes and may emerge through individual and group behavior as well as organizational structure. Hierarchical authority, policy, and cultural norms, for example, can be political factors consciously used by administrators to control or influence subordinates, but they are also factors that may control or influence subordinates regardless of their use or lack of use by organizational participants.

The definition of micropolitics discussed above is not limited to informal organizational processes, formal decision making, conflictive interactions and structures, and conscious (purposive) action. Limitations of this kind at this early stage of development would artificially restrict conceptual and empirical work on the micropolitics of education and would ignore many critical aspects of life in schools. (See Blase, 1991c, for a detailed discussion of this perspective on micropolitics.)

SECTION 2: RESEARCH ON THE MICROPOLITICS OF TEACHING

In each of the four subsections that follows, micropolitical studies and teacher work-life studies are reviewed in terms of teachers' relationships with school principals, faculty, students, and parents.

The Teacher-Principal Relationship

Micropolitical studies examining the teacher-principal relationship have stressed principals' political perspectives, although some studies have focused on teachers. This section integrates findings from both lines of political inquiry as well as political findings contained in studies of teachers' work lives.

Blase conducted two studies of teachers' political orientations toward open principals: one used a wide sample of teachers (1989), and the other was based on a case study of one high school (1988c). Blase found that 'open' political approaches by school principals (e.g., based on honesty, collegiality, nonmanipulation, supportiveness, communicativeness, and participation) precipitated relatively 'open' political responses from teachers who relied on strategies such as diplomacy, conformity, extra work, and visibility. Diplomacy, the strategy teachers reported most frequently in working with open principals, was defined as a positive and proactive approach to influence, although protective considerations (e.g., avoidance of conflict) were also identified with this strategy. Presenting oneself as composed and honest and relying on 'rational' problem solving methods were central to diplomacy. In addition, Blase learned that exchange processes provided the infrastructure for political interaction with open school principals. To maximize benefits, teachers exchanged tangible (e.g., extra work) and intangible (e.g., loyalty) goods for principal support and less frequently for job security and advancement. To reduce the costs of political interaction, teachers engaged in conformity, avoidance, and other predominantly protective strategies.

In two studies of teachers' perspectives, Blase described micropolitical relationships between teachers and

a) 'closed' school principals (e.g., those defined as authoritarian, inaccessible, inflexible) (1991b) versus

b) manipulative, control-oriented principals (e.g., those defined as self-serving and dominating) (1990).

Blase (1991b) demonstrated that closedness in principals provoked accommodative, reactive, and protective political responses from teachers and the use of strategies such as avoidance, rationality, and ingratiation. A manipulative-control orientation in principals – expressed through the use of sanctions, harassment, and the management of personal access – was linked to strong negative outcomes in teachers, including feelings of anger, depression, and a sense of resignation (Blase, 1990).

From these studies, Blase (1991b, 1990) concluded that teachers' political responses to 'open' principals (in comparison with closed and manipulative principals) reflect greater proactivity, two-way (bilateral) communication and influence, and complexity. Teachers' political responses to closed and manipulative principals were described as more covert and indirect as well as less effective compared with those used with open principals. Blase found little evidence of collective action or resistance by teachers to principals in any of the studies cited above; teachers' political responses to principals tended to be highly individualized, privatized, and reactive. In both cases, principals' leadership orientations appeared to be more influential than teachers' political orientations in defining the nature of micropolitical interaction.

Blase (1989, 1988c) also concluded that teachers develop relatively 'conservative' (passive) political orientations toward closed and manipulative principals, orientations that emphasize survival considerations. The actions of both types of principals (even though they did not exceed the limits of positional authority) had devastating effects because these actions violated teachers' professional values and norms. This latter point was highlighted further in another study of the micropolitics of favoritism. Blase (1988b) found that when school principals and other school officials engaged in practices that violated norms of equity and fairness, severely negative political consequences resulted for teachers. Sense of control, willingness to collaborate with others, and participation in decision-making opportunities were dramatically depressed. Under these circumstances, protective and reactive forms of political behavior, particularly acquiescence and ingratiation, were salient.

The control orientation appears to be prevalent even among 'effective' (traditional) principals; however, a comparison of principals' strategies and their impacts on teachers for both effective and ineffective principals yields startling differences. In a large-sample study of teachers, Blase and Roberts (1994) found that effective principals relied heavily on the use of powerful forms of normative control (e.g., giving praise, defining expectations, and seeking input). Blase and Roberts reported that this type of control orientation resulted largely in 'good subordination' and followership by teachers based on

a) internalization of principals' goals and expectations, and
b) exchange processes initiated and sustained by principals over time.

Although one strategy used by effective principals — involvement in decision making — enhanced teachers' political efficacy, expression or voice, and involvement in decision making, the researchers noted that teachers seldom exhibited noteworthy levels of empowerment. Teachers' role in decision making was typically advisory, and it was limited to giving opinions on a narrow range of issues defined by principals. In another article drawn from the same study Blase (1993) found that despite their ability to use positive political strategies, effective principals were fundamentally control-oriented; they 'articulate their visions, set their goals, explain their expectations ... [and] teachers are normatively influenced to buy into the principal's agenda' (p. 158).

Ball's (1987) earlier studies of British school heads (principals) yielded similar findings about school principals; he found no evidence of democratic empowering leadership among school heads. Ball describes the range of 'control' styles — interpersonal, managerial, authoritarian, adversarial — employed by school heads and their impact on teachers' political behavior. To illustrate, the interpersonal style — based on personal relations, face-to-face contact, and high visibility — resulted in confusion and contradiction for teachers; the 'sinews of power' (p. 92) were invisible; decision making was not public; and there were no formal decision-making structures and procedures. The elusive nature of decision making provoked a highly individualistic political orientation in teachers that emphasized private negotiations and compromise. Ball argues that all of the control styles noted above drastically limit teacher autonomy and participation, and in general, that teachers are 'manipulated' and 'excluded' from decision making by school heads even in those schools in which they are routinely 'consulted.'

Anderson's (1991) research on how school principals (in one suburban school) manipulated teachers through 'cognitive politics' (i.e., the manipulation of language) underscores what others have identified as an emerging trend in school administration (Bates, 1986); that is, the increasing use of subtle forms of control. Anderson found that to control teachers, principals manipulated language and meaning to create an illusion of harmony and consensus in their schools. He concludes that this approach to mediating conflict, particularly the use of pejorative labelling, produces safe decisions; teachers who hold dissenting views on issues are marginalized and effectively silenced.

Ball and Bowe's (1991) exploration of the changes precipitated by the 1988 Education Reform Act in one British school demonstrates how a head's control of the School Management Team undermined democratic processes in the school and exacerbated conflicts with teachers. These researchers describe how the head and management team, influenced by externally imposed marketing and financial concerns, circumvented teachers' political influence in decision making and, consequently, their ability to advance educational and student interests.

Other American, British, and Canadian micropolitical studies provide additional evidence of the direct and indirect means used by school principals (and heads) to control teachers and how such control significantly restricts the political efficacy of teachers (Hargreaves, 1991; Radnor, 1990; Schempp, Sparkes, & Templin, 1993; Spaulding, 1994). Hargreaves's (1990) theoretical analysis of planning time based on data collected from elementary principals and teachers in Canada further illustrates an administrative control orientation. Hargreaves suggests that political conflicts between teachers and administrators occur, in part, because the latter view time 'monochronically' (i.e., with low sensitivity to classroom context) and because they attempt to 'colonize' (i.e., fill) teachers' planning time with their purposes.

Other studies provide additional findings about political relationships between teachers and school principals. Corbett (1991) researched the effects of parental influence on one high school's discipline policy and how its principal's attempts to pre-empt such influence undermined the foundations of teachers' micropolitical power with students. Corbett concludes that although inconsistent enforcement of student discipline policy by the principal was a means of avoiding confrontations with parents, this approach inadvertently eroded teachers' authority and influence over students in the classroom, thus the new discipline policy redistributed power away from teachers toward students and parents. Corbett's study makes apparent some of the stark differences between the micropolitical world of teachers and that of administrators.

To study the power dynamics and strategic orientations of a varied sample of 20 principal-teacher dyads engaged in postobservation instructional (feedback) conferences, Blase and Blase (1995) used a discourse analysis approach. The researchers determined differences in micropolitical interaction between successful (e.g., perceived by both participants as both non-threatening and conducive to professional growth) and less successful instructional conferences. Analysis of data produced four major micropolitical strategies (personal orientations, conversational congruence, formal authority, and situational variables) which facilitated or constrained instructional conferences. For example, the strategies of personal orientations and conversational congruence (i.e., congruence between participants' affective and cognitive frameworks, semantic congruence, and personal expectations of self and others) were employed to facilitate and constrain interaction in successful conferences. Teachers also relied on the strategies of mutual agendas and credibility, shared meanings and assumptions, and role expectations to equalize and balance power, to build trust, and to foster openness. Blase and Blase also learned that successful conferences produced higher levels of reflection and equitable exchange by comparison with less successful conferences.

One study of reform programs in the 1980s specifically illustrates the strong impact of micropolitics on school-level change. Noblit, Berry, and Dempsey (1991) describe how faculties in two schools working with different types of principals used district-level reform initiatives to gain political power. For example, in one school, the formation of a school-level committee allowed teachers to discover their collective interests, to raise issues for public discussion formerly defined by the school principal, and to transform informal power into political authority.

The second wave of educational reform in the United States has been identified strongly with the goal of restructuring schools along democratic lines. Terms such as site-based management, shared governance, participatory decision making, decentralization, and empowerment are used to denote a move away from top-down control to a redistribution of political power and authority at the school-building level (Glickman, 1993; Lightfoot, 1986; Maeroff, 1988). Surprisingly, only a few studies have examined these innovative relationships and newly initiated governance structures and processes in schools from a micropolitical perspective.

Smylie and Brownlee-Conyers (1990) studied newly developed collaborative relationships between seven teacher leaders and seven principals in one school district. Their research demonstrates that innovative working relationships resulted from intentional political strategies used by teacher-leaders and principals to protect and/or advance their respective self-interests. Teacher leaders, for example, acknowledged principals' prerogatives in order to secure their support and avoid conflict and disfavor; their strategies included 'planting' ideas and giving compliments. Although Smylie and Brownlee-Conyers did not find that the political behavior of teacher-leaders and principals departed substantially from traditional expectations and norms, they did find that collaborative relationships with principals involved more exchange, negotiation, and accommodation than competition, and over time, greater openness, informality, and trust developed in their relationships.

Micropolitical studies of facilitative-empowering principals in restructured schools have also produced some interesting findings about teachers' political behavior (e.g., Allen, 1993; Blase & Blase, 1994; Blase, Blase, Anderson, & Dungan, 1995). In contrast to Smylee and Brownlee-Conyers (1990), for example, Blase and Blase (1994) found that the use of facilitative strategies by shared governance principals (e.g., building trust, developing democratic decision-making structures, encouraging autonomy, encouraging innovation and risk taking) contributed significantly to teachers' sense of empowerment in schools affiliated with Glickman's (1993) League of Professional Schools. Facilitative principal leadership was linked to substantial increases in teachers' involvement in decision making, expression and voice, commitment to democratically derived decisions, and efficacy.

Many teacher work-life studies have generated politically relevant findings about the teacher-principal relationship. Among other things, these studies, discussed below, confirm the predominance of a control orientation in principals and its adverse political effects on teachers.

The role of the school principal (or head) in shaping political relationships with teachers is discussed throughout the work-life literature. For instance, Lieberman and Miller (1984) write: 'The principal (especially in the elementary school) makes it known what is important, what will not be tolerated, and in a strange way, sets the tone for tension, worth, openness, and fear' (p. 28). Sikes, Measor, and Woods (1985) recognize that school heads in Britain have substantial freedom in organizing their schools and that variation in their leadership — that is, their philosophies, values, and personalities — has a considerable impact on teachers.

In fact, Lortie (1963) and Dreeben (1970) maintain that although the school principal's formal authority over teachers is limited by the cellular structure of the school and the value teachers place on attaining intrinsic rewards with students, 'control over teachers is accomplished through selection-socialization and subtle mechanisms which refine bureaucratic rule' (Lortie, p. 10). Lortie also emphasizes that principals are the ultimate authority on student discipline and make decisions about the allocation of space, materials, and equipment — decisions that strongly influence teachers' working conditions.

Studies of purportedly 'participatory' relationships between teachers and principals provide additional evidence of principal control. Connell (1985) found that although Australian principals have been expected to use 'more consensual,' 'open textured' methods in working with teachers, frequently the result is a pseudo-democratic stance. Administrators maintain control by chairing committees, controlling agendas, and avoiding contentious issues.

Hunter (1979) also demonstrated how a school head maintained control of decisional processes through indirect means, despite the existence of democratic governance structures. Hunter found that the consultative structures designed to facilitate faculty participation also 'keep the head informed' (p. 129) and actually increased his control and substantiated his claim that he alone had a global view of the school. Hunter's work underscores the significance of taken-for-granted assumptions that make up the political culture of the school (for example, the staff's acceptance of an advisory rather than power-sharing role in decision making) in explaining the head's control. Not uncommonly, studies of 'restructured' schools in the United States demonstrate the salience of a control orientation in principals (e.g., Malen & Ogawa, 1988).

Teachers' work-life literature has also documented the devastating effects on teachers of unfair and ineffective leadership by principals. Sikes, Measor, and Woods (1985) reported that in some British schools unfair use of appointments and promotions by school heads leads to the development of 'latent status hierarchies' among teachers in support of heads. Blase (1987b) found that characteristics of closed and ineffective principals — inaccessibility, indecisiveness, lack of direction, lack of follow-through, authoritarianism, and nonsupportiveness — correlated strongly with increases in teachers' feelings of frustration, anger, insecurity, confusion, and apathy. Fuchs (1967) described actions by principals that routinely violate professional and interpersonal norms (e.g., overloading teachers with extra responsibilities) and lead to feelings of exploitation and alienation among teachers.

In a seminal study of freedom in teaching, Beale (1936) concluded that the rights of American teachers are systematically violated by school principals:

> The principal's power over the teacher and the importance of a good standing with him leads to submissiveness to his will ... the general climate of schools and the undemocratic rules under which they are administered tend to make principals autocrats and teachers yes men. (p. 602)

Questions about the loyalty or character of teachers usually lead to dismissal. Beale suggested that a 'liberal minded principal may be the best friend that freedom in teaching has' (p. 605).

Clearly, the literature referred to above indicates that school principals wield considerable political power over teachers and that such power has significant effects on teachers. However, evidence from this literature also points out that some school principals use leadership styles that depart from strict control, domination, and subordination of teachers, even in traditional schools. The resulting teacher behavior contradicts portrayals of teachers as politically compliant and submissive (e.g., Lightfoot, 1983). In fact, Lortie (1963) argues that control of teachers is not possible (for reasons identified above) and contends that 'exchange' processes rather than domination frequently drive teacher-principal relationships. Little (1982) discovered that in successful and adaptable schools, 'reciprocation' (defined as equality of effort and equal humility) is an important property of teacher-administrator interaction. Blase (1988c, 1987a) found that those principals whom teachers defined as 'open and effective' (e.g., accessible, consistent, knowledgeable, decisive, problem oriented, supportive, participatory and consultative, fair) promote the development of relatively open political relationships based largely on exchange and reciprocation.

Hanson's (1976) work further indicated that bureaucratic authority and control do not fully explain the political dynamics between school principals and teachers in traditional schools. Hanson discovered that administrators and teachers control different 'spheres of influence,' or decision zones, in schools and that each sphere retains relative degrees of power, autonomy, decisional discretion, and legitimacy. Hanson also found that administrators and teachers develop informal tactics to influence one another even in their own sphere of influence. Teachers, for example, formed coalitions with colleagues and took stands on issues at faculty meetings; principals tried to control teachers by manipulating their concept of 'professional' behavior.

Additional evidence of the variability of teachers' political responses to school principals is apparent in work-life studies. Biklen (1988) described several ways teachers react to administrators, including unhappy compliance, the standoff, silent noncooperation, and the open challenge. Brieschke's (1983) typology of teacher role enactment described three major orientations – elite, reinforcement, fringe – to school principals. Other researchers have emphasized the subtle ways teachers resist administrative control of their work (Apple, 1986; Becker, 1980; McNeil, 1983; Zeichner & Tabachnick, 1984). Bridges (1970) theorized that teachers typically use strategic tactics to influence administrators, including exchange, bargaining, threats, bluff, flattery, exercising influence through significant others, providing biased information, and dramatizing involvement.

Other work-life studies describe additional facets of teachers' micropolitical relationships with school principals. Several writers have demonstrated the importance of principals' 'buffering' from a range of organizational and external intrusions (Becker, 1980; McPherson, 1972; Rosenholtz & Simpson, 1990). Rosenholtz and Simpson (1990) found that buffering by principals is related strongly to new teachers' work commitment. In essence, teachers expect principals to use their authority to support them in conflicts with students and parents; teachers lose respect for those who fail to support them and in some cases view them as 'cowardly' (Becker, 1980; Cusick, 1983; McPherson, 1972). Cusick (1983) reported that a failure on the part of administrators to support teachers in dealing with student discipline undermined significantly the academic programs of three high schools. In general, the work-life literature suggests that teachers are willing to extend loyalty to principals who use a 'light rein' with them (Lortie, 1975, p. 200) and who make their authority available to protect and help teachers achieve instructional goals and rewards (Blase, 1987a; Lortie, 1975).

Taken together, the studies discussed in this section reveal that teachers' micropolitical orientation varies in relation to the political orientation of principals. Interactions with open principals tend to provoke an open and diplomatic political stance in teachers (Blase, 1989, 1988c), and interactions with closed and/or manipulative principals tend to result in a protective stance based on avoidance and ingratiation (Blase, 1990, 1991b). In addition, this relationship appears to influence teachers' political relationships with other faculty, students, and parents (Blase, 1988c, 1990, 1991b, 1991c). Micropolitical studies of teachers also point out that principals working in traditional school organizations tend to be control-oriented; however, such principals use a range of direct, overt, and even blatant strategies as well as indirect and subtle strategies (e.g., Anderson, 1991; Ball, 1987; Blase, 1991b, 1993; Hargreaves, 1991; Noblit et al., 1991). Congruence between open and effective principals' strategies and purposes and the professional norms and values of teachers tends to result in deeper levels of teacher motivation and commitment to work (Blase, 1993).

In open political relationships with principals, interactions with teachers are based largely on equitable and reciprocal (i.e., bilateral) exchanges. Such exchanges, however, do not seem to eliminate the teachers' sense of vulnerability to principals. It seems that truly empowering, democratic, and facilitative forms of principal leadership are required to enhance teachers' trust, voice, involvement in decision making, and efficacy (Blase & Blase, 1994).

The teacher work-life literature confirms the salience of a control orientation in school principals. (It has been argued elsewhere that ideological forms of control have, to some degree, replaced openly authoritarian and coercive approaches to school leadership, see Bates, 1986). Moreover, this literature indicates that some school principals routinely violate the rights and professional norms of teachers, and this usually results in stress, alienation, and role conflict. There is some evidence that teachers successfully resist adverse actions by principals, also through subtle means. However, the work-life studies, perhaps more directly than the political studies discussed above, also point out that principals and teachers (as a group) have spheres of influence in the school, and that much micropolitical interaction is based on negotiation, reciprocation, and exchange (Hanson, 1976). This is not to say that democratic values and procedures govern such teacher-principal interaction; to the contrary, there is often a stark discrepancy between school principals' espoused commitment to democratic structures and processes, and their willingness and/or ability to implement such structures and processes. Consequently, efforts to restructure schools often result in a facade of democracy with little if any positive effect on teachers' individual or collective political power in the school (Blase, 1993; Connell, 1985; Hunter, 1979; Malen & Ogawa, 1988).

The Teacher-Teacher Relationship

Several studies have produced valuable findings about the micropolitics of the teacher-teacher relationship. Ball (1987), for example, showed how various factions of teachers in British schools, ascribing to contrasting ideologies and interests, oriented themselves to proposals to introduce mixed-ability grouping.

Ball's descriptions of ensuing conflicts among factions of teachers illustrate how political considerations shape efforts at innovation at the school level.

Ball's (1987) analysis of school staffrooms provided additional insight into the micropolitics of teaching. He writes,

> The social relations of the staffroom are often a near direct reflection of the micropolitical structure of the institution. Furthermore, these social relations will almost inevitably bear the marks of the particular political history of the institution – battles lost, ambitions frustrated, alliances which crumbled and trusts betrayed. This history will continue to have its impact in the interpretation of new events and the taking of sides in fresh disputes. (p. 213)

Ball (1987) also offered an incisive analysis of the micropolitical functions of gossip, rumor, and humor among teachers. He argues, for example, that gossip is used to undermine others' credibility and reputation, to test ideas, and to stimulate debate. In addition, Ball refers to staff meetings as opportunities for school administrators to reinforce official definitions that cast teachers into a passive political role as recipients of information: 'The teachers are not so much participants in, as subject of, the meeting. The meeting is a camouflage, a diversion. The ritual of information giving and consultation is asserted over any substantive involvement in decision making' (pp. 239-240).

Sparkes (1990) conducted a three-year case study of department head-initiated curriculum change in a physical education department in a British school. Sparkes examined what Anderson (1991) called 'cognitive politics,' in this case, the use of 'contrastic rhetoric' (i.e., usual practices are contrasted with alternative practices, which are discussed in trivialized and pejorative terms) to undermine faculty who held different views of physical education. Sparkes presents an intriguing account of how the department head dominated the direction, content, and outcome of meetings by using contrastic rhetoric and other political strategies and how this led to stress, confusion, and alienation among some staff.

In another publication derived from the same study, Sparkes (1988) discussed the physical education department's political manoeuvring within the school, particularly with the senior management team. Here, Sparkes describes how another cognitive strategy, 'rhetorical justification' (the use of stylized language, for example, 'developing the whole child' and 'individualized learning styles'), was employed, in this instance, by department members to enhance the status of physical education in the school. The researcher posited that department faculty frequently employed rhetorical justification to create the 'illusion' of innovative change in subject pedagogy in the classroom.

In a micropolitical study of one public elementary school in Zuni, New Mexico, Osborne (1989) found that 'status' differences and power struggles between Anglo and Zuni prevented some teachers from making cultural adjustments essential to responsive classroom teaching. Osborne discovered that by 'playing along' with one another, Anglo and Zuni teachers reinforced 'insider' and 'outsider' roles, preserved cultural borders by impeding the exchange of relevant cultural information, and, in effect, colluded in maintaining the sociopolitical status quo at the expense of children. Osborne writes, 'To play at `insiders and outsiders' not only maintains an Anglo power base, it also deprives the Zuni children of Anglo teachers' increased sensitivity to ways they can be best taught' (p. 211).

Schempp, Sparkes, and Templin (1993) employed a life history method to investigate the micropolitics of induction of three teachers in three schools. These researchers found that induction is largely a process of learning about who holds power and about the roles and expectations of others, as well as a process of developing strategies to gain political influence. Not surprisingly, Schempp et al. state that 'fitting in' and, in particular, 'silence' (i.e., an unwillingness to express controversial opinions to peers) was the primary strategy used by new teachers to survive in their schools. They also discovered that colleagues were not powerful in influencing pedagogical beliefs or practice; the authors characterized such relationships as 'supportive' but 'independent.'

Blase (1987c) used a variety of qualitative methods to study variations in political interaction among teachers working with different principals in one high school over time. He found that the actions of effective principals (e.g., fairness of treatment, clear goals, and rational policies) were linked to the development of positive political practices among teachers. These practices were defined as diplomatic, supportive, collaborative, integrative, and reciprocal. The actions of ineffective principals (e.g., favoritism, inconsistent implementation of policy), in contrast, were associated with nonsupportive, noncollaborative, fragmented, and self-serving political interactions among teachers. Ingratiation, flaunting, spying, criticism, gossip, and aloofness were reported for this type of political interaction.

Greenfield's (1991) case study of an elementary school principal and teachers illustrated how a common moral commitment to serving children can provide the basis for developing a cooperative political culture among teachers. According to Greenfield, teachers assumed leadership roles and exercised political influence with one another primarily by 'sharing' compliments, questions, teaching strategies, and techniques.

From a study of collegiality conducted in elementary schools in one school board (i.e., district) in Ontario, Canada, Hargreaves (1991) learned that district-level mandated and regulated teacher collegiality frequently led to 'contrived collegiality,' which Hargreaves concluded was inefficient, inflexible, and actually politically disempowering.

The work-life literature further extends the knowledge base cited above by discussing the critical role of classroom autonomy and noninterference norms to micropolitical interaction among teachers (Becker, 1980; Cusick, 1983; Lortie, 1975; McPherson, 1972; Nias, 1989; Rosenholtz & Simpson, 1990). Other norms discussed in this literature relate to friendliness, sociability, support (i.e., responding to requests for assistance), sharing (e.g., ideas, work supplies, and materials), and meeting school-wide obligations (Lortie, 1975).

Several studies point to the salience of faculty loyalty and solidarity norms to intrafaculty politics. For example, Becker (1980) describes such norms in terms of dealing with discipline, the amount of work that should be accomplished, and attitudes about school principals. Cusick (1983) reports that teachers often unify and exhibit open hostility in the face of attempts by others to elicit their support or modify their behavior. Cusick also describes teachers' attempts to build support to advance their personal curricular and extracurricular interests. Nias (1983) found that teachers engage in impression management to build support among their colleagues. Pollard (1985) describes how teachers use humor among themselves to reduce the impact of external threats to the classroom. Beale (1936) discusses how teacher ostracism was used to elicit compliance from unconventional teachers: 'Few like to get the reputation of being a crank' (p. 599).

The studies discussed in this section indicate that intrafaculty relations are most frequently enacted between and among individuals; however, informal and formal groups are also used to advance teachers' political interests. The negative impacts of a manipulative department head on relationships among teachers (Sparkes, 1988, 1990) and problems identified with 'contrived collegiality' have been described (Hargreaves, 1991). The actions of open and closed principals have been linked to the development of collaborative and reciprocal relationships and noncollaborative and fragmented political relationships among teachers, respectively (Blase, 1987c). The work-life literature has emphasized the political significance of faculty loyalty and solidarity norms, especially in the face of external threats (e.g., Cusick, 1983).

The Teacher-Student Relationship

Only a few micropolitical studies have dealt with the teacher's relationship with students. Bloome and Willet (1991) offered a comprehensive micropolitical perspective on teacher-student political interaction in the classroom that addresses structural issues (how classroom interaction is organized), substantive issues (the meanings constructed through classroom interaction), and historical issues (teachers' and students' classroom experiences over time). Building on classroom interaction research, Bloome and Willett argue that what counts as teaching and learning is, in large part, determined through a political process: Political struggles occur between teachers and students to define what is happening and its meaning, and who will have particular rights, responsibilities, and privileges. The authors used data from a four-year ethnographic study, part of which investigated a first grade classroom over a period of one year, to illustrate how the teacher's choice of phonics disempowered students, constrained access to academic education for nondominant ethnic and linguistic groups, and created competition among students for status rather than text meaning.

Spaulding (1994) described the complex nature of micropolitical interaction that occurred even in the elementary classroom and the range of everyday strategies (and related tactics) used by a teacher and her students. The teacher's use of support strategies was associated with positive impacts on students, whereas her excessive use of control strategies was linked to negative consequences for students (e.g., apathy, anger, decreases in work effort and achievement, fatigue, fear). Similarly, excessive use of resistance strategies by students (designed to delay, distract, modify, or prevent teacher- initiated actions) was related to negative effects on the teacher. Spaulding's study reveals the possibility of developing mutually beneficial reciprocal political relationships in the classroom based on positive cycles of teacher-student influence and response.

Blase's (1991a) case study of high school teachers presented a concrete description of how routine classroom problems (e.g., instruction, student discipline), extracurricular involvements, and personal factors contribute to the development of a political orientation in teachers toward students. Blase reports that teachers tended to develop a diplomatic political orientation toward students based on introspection, friendliness, and tactfulness. This orientation allowed teachers to balance two primary political considerations: an inclination to be responsive to student's individual needs and an inclination to protect themselves from criticism and attack from students and their parents. Blase also learned that political considerations often led teachers to emphasize control of students over educational concerns and standards. Similarly, Schempp, Sparkes, and Templin (1993) found that although knowledge of teaching and subject were associated with increases in new teachers' classroom status, status was used primarily for political purposes, to establish classroom authority and control rather than to advance the education of students.

Like the micropolitical studies discussed above, teacher work-life studies consistently suggest that problems related to academic instruction and social control provoke political interactions between teachers and students (Becker, 1980; Cohen & Kottkamp, 1993; Connell, 1985; Dreeben, 1970; Fuchs, 1967; Gitlin, 1983; Jackson, 1968; Lieberman & Miller, 1984; Lightfoot, 1983; Metz, 1978; Nias, 1989; Pauly, 1992; Powell, Farrar, & Cohen, 1985; Sarason, 1982;

Sedlak, Wheller, Pullin, & Cusick, 1986; Veenan, 1984; Wilson, 1962). Lortie (1975) is one of many researchers who has pointed to the importance of achieving social and moral outcomes with students. Others have reported that control of students is frequently more important to teachers (and administrators) than the achievement of academic goals (Willower, Eidell, & Hoy, 1967). For example, Cusick (1983) found that student control in the high schools he studied was so problematic that maintaining 'good relationships' (i.e., 'cordial' relationships) with students was more highly valued than academic instruction or adhering to policies and procedures. Similarly, according to McNeil's (1983, 1986) research on high schools, faculties' and administrators' inordinate concern about controlling students adversely affected teaching and learning in the classroom.

Other studies parallel what is hinted at in micropolitical literature by presenting graphic examples of the dynamic and 'negotiated' nature of teacher-student interaction in classrooms (Pauly, 1992; Sedlak et al., 1986). Pauly states that 'education is the result of working agreements that are hammered out by the people in each classroom, who determine the rules, the power relationships, and the kinds of teaching and learning that will take place there' (pp. 13-14). Such agreements, he found, develop through a process of 'reciprocal power' (in contrast to domination) wherein teachers and students 'negotiate' the nature of teaching and learning in the classroom. Like others, Sedlak et al. argue that in high schools, in particular, negotiate classroom agreements that are designed to 'avoid sustained, rigorous, academic inquiry. A bargain of sorts is struck that demands little academically of either teachers or students' (p. 5).

The work-life literature also indicates that teachers employ a host of strategies to influence students to achieve instructional and social goals. For instance, Pollard (1985) argued that 'good' teaching is fundamentally manipulative; teachers strive to get students to internalize and pursue goals defined by teachers. Acting ability, communication skills, ability to give praise, and other such factors are associated with good teaching. Pollard delineates four major strategies (open negotiation, routinization, manipulation, domination) that teachers use to control students.

Waller (1932) examined such techniques as punishment, command, manipulation of interpersonal and group relationships, appeal, and 'controlled anger' used by teachers to maintain classroom control and discipline. McPherson (1972) described teacher control strategies including blame, praise, labelling, competition, and standardized classroom procedures. Hargreaves (1979) discussed teachers' use of policing as a strategy (e.g., articulation of rules and display of hierarchical relations) for control of students in the middle school.

Woods (1990) observed that teachers devised several 'survival' strategies – socialization, domination, negotiation, fraternization, absence or removal, ritual and routine, occupational therapy, and morale boosting – to control incidents and to 'avoid,' 'mask/disguise,' 'weather,' and 'neutralize' classroom incidents. McNeil (1986) described several defensive teaching strategies, for example, mystification, omission, and simplification, which teachers employ to control students.

The micropolitical and work-life studies discussed in this section describe the issues that provoke political interactions between teachers and students, the 'negotiated and reciprocal nature of power in classrooms, and a range of strategies that teachers employ to influence and protect themselves from students.'

The Teacher-Parent Relationship

Only Blase (1987d) has explicitly examined the micropolitics of the teacher-parent relationship. He found that high school teachers are especially vulnerable to parents, and in general, their vulnerability is related to academic and social issues that emerge through classroom interaction and teachers' extra-curricular involvements. Blase also learned that personal-life factors contribute to teachers' sense of vulnerability; teachers who lived in the same community where they taught compared being a teacher to 'living in a fishbowl.' Consequently, they made compromises related to dress, hairstyle, and language. Moreover, teachers were careful about drinking and dancing at establishments in the community; some participated in community activities and even attended church because of parental expectations. Many reported not sharing information about their personal lives with students because of the possibility of distortion and criticism from parents. Blase concludes that although micropolitical interactions with parents produce some positive outcomes, overall the quality of teaching and learning in classrooms is depressed.

A few teacher work-life studies have also yielded findings relevant to an understanding of micropolitical conflict between teachers and parents. These studies disclose that teachers typically define relationships with parents as distant, distrustful, and hostile and that such relationships result, in part, from the conflicting perspectives of teachers and parents regarding the student, as well as overlapping and unclear lines of authority (Becker, 1980; Dreeben, 1968; Lortie, 1975; McPherson, 1972; Waller, 1932). With regard to differing perspectives, Waller (1932) wrote that teachers and parents 'wish [the student] well according to different standards of well-being, parents and teachers want to do different things with the child' (p. 68). Relatedly, #Lortie (1975) and McPherson (1972) argued that teacher-parent enmity results from conflict between universalistic expectations (required for group life) and particularistic expectations (related to individual needs). Teacher-parent conflicts are considered inevitable because they stem from differences linked to primary (e.g., intimate) and secondary (e.g., impersonal) group affiliations (Bates & Babchuk, 1961).

Waller (1932) reported that conflicts between teachers and parents can be exacerbated when parents' 'own ego feelings, or their own projected ambitions' (p. 68) become involved in responding to a child's progress in school. Teachers' knowledge of the 'guilty secrets' of the families of their students (Naegle, 1956) and teachers' judgments about grades and the values they choose to emphasize in socializing children may strain political relationships with parents (Lortie, 1975).

The research cited above also links teacher-parent political interactions to academic instruction and student discipline. Work-life studies reveal that parents attempt to elicit special favors for their children in each of these areas. The parents' inclination to 'interfere,' to challenge the teacher's authority, and to do so in ways that violate interpersonal and professional norms for reasonable, productive, and supportive interaction, further exacerbates political conflicts (Becker, 1980; Connell, 1985; Lortie, 1975; McPherson, 1972).

As a result, teachers develop politically cautious strategies to deal with parents. Connell (1985) found that teachers seldom respond to parental pressure through genuine power sharing. Generally, teachers responded defensively; they often created 'tokenistic' ways of involving parents in the school (i.e., a 'public relations exercise') or worked to minimize contact with parents. McPherson (1972) and Becker (1980) have described teachers' attempts to establish common bonds of parenthood and invoke bureaucratic rules to deal with obtrusive parents. McPherson identified other strategies such as politeness, avoidance, conferencing, and forming coalitions with students in response to parental challenges to decisions about student promotions, group placement, instructional materials, and practices that departed from the 'tried and true.' Waller (1932) remarked on the efficacy of projecting a stable, friendly, and judicial disposition to disarm 'irate' parents. Lortie (1963) and McPherson (1972) noted that teachers often develop coalitions with school principals to protect themselves from intrusions by parents.

The micropolitical and work-life studies discussed in this section suggest that teachers' vulnerability to parents and their tendency to act conservatively, even in their personal lives, is central to the teachers' political orientation toward parents (Blase, 1987d). In addition, both political and work-life studies point to several sources of political conflict between teachers and parents (Becker, 1980; Connell, 1985; Lortie, 1975; Naegle, 1956; Waller, 1932) and a host of political strategies teachers use to deal with parents.

SECTION 3: RESEARCH PERSPECTIVES, METHODS, AND PROCEDURES

Most of the empirical research on the micropolitics of education and specifically the micropolitics of teaching seems to have been produced in the United

States, Great Britain, and Canada.Without exception, micropolitical studies of teaching have employed qualitative research approaches, including grounded theory (e.g., Ball, 1987; Blase, 1993; Spaulding, 1994), ethnography (e.g., Anderson, 1991; Bloome & Willett, 1991; Osborne, 1989) and discourse-linguistic analysis (Blase & Blase, 1995).

One researcher has made extensive use of wide samples of teachers (e.g., Blase, 1988b, 1990, 1993); another has used data drawn from 11 case studies (Ball, 1987). However, most research on the micropolitics of teaching has relied on studies of single schools (e.g., Blase, 1991a; Corbett, 1991; Greenfield, 1991; Noblit et al., 1991), and only two studies have examined the micropolitics of the classroom (Bloome & Willett, 1991; Spaulding, 1994). Case studies have employed a variety of qualitative procedures, including interviews, observations, document analysis, and open-ended questionnaires (e.g., Anderson, 1991; Ball, 1987; Blase, 1987c, 1988b, 1989; Blase & Blase, 1995; Bloome & Willett, 1991).

Case studies of high schools in suburban and urban areas have appeared most frequently in the literature, followed by studies of elementary schools (e.g., Bloome & Willett, 1991). Few micropolitical studies have investigated teachers in middle or junior high schools.

Conflict theory, power theory, socialization theory, symbolic interaction theory, leadership theory, and compliance theory have been frequently used to frame studies of the micropolitics of teaching or to interpret data generated by such studies.

Some micropolitical studies of teaching have drawn solely from samples of teachers (e.g., Blase, 1987c, 1988c, 1990, 1993); however, both teachers and principals have participated in most case studies (e.g., Ball, 1987; Corbett, 1991; Greenfield, 1991; Osborne, 1989; Smylie & Brownlee-Conyers, 1990). Some studies have included students; however, parents were not participants in any of the studies discussed in this chapter.

Classroom teachers have been the target of most micropolitical studies of teaching, although relationships between teacher-leaders and principals (Smylie & Brownlee-Conyers, 1990) and teachers' participation in school councils (Noblit et al., 1991) have also been the subject of study. Typically, studies have emphasized political relationships with principals and less frequently political relationships with other faculty. Few micropolitical studies have examined teachers' relationships with students (e.g., Spaulding, 1994) or parents.

Explicitly and implicitly, most micropolitical studies of teaching have focused on the strategies teachers use to influence or protect themselves from others as well as teachers' cognitive and affective responses to others, especially school principals. Topics of inquiry have included, among others, the micropolitics of socialization (e.g., Blase, 1988a; Schempp, Sparkes, & Templin, 1993), innovation (e.g., Ball & Bowe, 1991; Corbett, 1991; Smylie & Brownlee-Conyers, 1990), participation (e.g., Blase & Blase, 1994; Smylie & Brownlee-Conyers, 1990), and domination (e.g., Ball, 1987; Blase, 1988b, 1990, 1991b).

Most micropolitical studies of teaching were completed during the 1980s and early 1990s. In effect, micropolitical research has investigated teachers working in relatively traditional school organizations and has tended to address conflictive political dynamics. Micropolitical investigations of teachers in restructured schools, although very limited, have produced some interesting findings about cooperative or consensual relationships between teachers and principals (e.g., Blase & Blase, 1994).

SECTION 4: A THEMATIC ANALYSIS OF THE MICROPOLITICS OF TEACHING

The purpose of this chapter has been to review the emerging theoretical and empirical literature on the micropolitics of teaching and the teachers' work-life literature containing micropolitical content. Although beyond the scope of this chapter, other areas of inquiry such as school restructuring, critical theory (e.g., Apple, 1986; Giroux, 1992), and feminist studies (e.g., Grumet, 1988) should be considered valuable additional sources of concepts, theory, and empirical findings relevant to the micropolitics of teaching. Despite the limited nature of the current knowledge base on the micropolitics of teaching, it is possible to identify several themes that offer a beginning characterization of this important emerging area of inquiry.

Studies reviewed in this chapter suggest that the micropolitics of teaching are shaped by extraorganizational factors (e.g., legislation, community norms), organizational factors (e.g., superintendents' actions), and building-level organizational factors (e.g., policies, programs, innovations, principal leadership). Both negative and positive effects on the political behavior and purposes of teachers appear to result from such factors. However, studies completed thus far have tended to emphasize negative political dynamics and negative effects on, for example, teacher esteem, relationships with parents, and the quality of teaching and learning in the classroom. This has occurred, in part, because micropolitical studies have tended to focus on conflictive ('darkside') interaction in contrast to consensual or nonadversarial ('brightside') democratic interaction.

At the school level, variations in principals' political stance toward teachers, perhaps more than any other single set of factors, tend to provoke significant positive and negative variations in teachers' political behavior and purposes. Whether teachers substantially affect principals is not evident in the micropolitical literature. There is, however, strong evidence of the interactive and reciprocal nature of teachers' relationships with students, when teacher work-life studies are considered in conjunction with micropolitical studies. Micropolitical research completed thus far generally suggests that teachers are highly strategic in their interactions with others and employ a variety of influence and protectionist strategies to secure their interests. Micropolitical power seems to be derived primarily from personal factors (e.g., experience, knowledge, interpersonal skills), as well as knowledge/information (Bacharach & Lawler, 1980). Positional authority does not appear to be a dominant source of political power, even in relationships with students.

Protectionist strategies seem to be employed by teachers most frequently with those who attempt to control them, especially with individuals who have greater authority and/or the capacity to harm teachers. Teachers appear to be extremely vulnerable to such individuals and groups and, at least overtly, tend to comply with their demands or expectations. There is evidence that teachers, individually or in groups, seldom confront powerful others with whom they interact; at best teachers use diplomatic tactics and passive (and often private) forms of resistance in such interactions. At the same time, teachers' everyday political stance consists of a complex array of strategies and tactics designed to achieve influence and to protect their interests.

Micropolitical research on teaching also suggests that external and internal political actors and the structures, processes, policies, and practices they employ are demonstrably control-oriented and reflect a strong 'power over' approach to teachers, in contrast to a 'power with' approach (Kreisberg, 1992). Relatedly, there is some evidence of an increase in the use of subtle and manipulative strategies by school administrators to control teachers. The management of language, organizational meanings, and school culture, in contrast to the use of formal authority and coercive power, has been described by researchers in recent years.

Moreover, open and participatory principal leadership in traditional schools and facilitative-democratic leadership in purportedly restructured schools are forms that frequently exemplify subtle administrative control and manipulation. In both cases, control and manipulation of teachers tend to occur within a dynamic process of exchange and reciprocation of both tangible and intangible goods. Equitable exchanges between teachers and others occur in traditional bureaucratic schools as well as in restructured schools. In the former, however, teachers' political efficacy is severely restricted, whereas in the latter, political efficacy is transformed significantly in both degree and kind. That is, where school restructuring is promoted along democratic lines, increased levels of risk taking, involvement in decision making, authentic expression, and commitment by teachers can be expected.

Interestingly, the teachers' traditional subordinate political role in schools – the legacy of a long history of domination by societal and school organizational factors – is partly responsible for the failure of many efforts to restructure school governance along democratic lines. Teachers' traditional expectations for principals, their need to 'please the principal' and maintain working relationships, norms of propriety and civility, and fear of reprisals undoubtedly contribute to a form of collusion, inadvertent in part, that reinforces the structures of domination and works to maintain the micropolitical status quo in schools.

SECTION 5: DIRECTIONS FOR FUTURE RESEARCH

The micropolitics of education and the micropolitics of teaching in particular are new and exciting areas of educational research that have the potential to produce valuable knowledge. Among other things, micropolitics is about how individuals and groups use power to protect themselves and to advance their interests in conflictive, cooperative, collegial, and democratic relationships. To be sure, micropolitics is a fundamental dimension of life in schools, one that is central to work processes. Micropolitical research focuses on the strategies, interests, values, ideologies, influence and authority, decision making, and status of individuals and groups in organizations.

This chapter has reviewed some of the different theoretical perspectives in the field of micropolitics. The emphasis has been on micropolitical studies of teachers and teacher work-life studies with political content. Although significant work has been produced about relationships with principals, the micropolitics of teaching remains a nascent area of inquiry, and much more research needs to be done in the areas of teachers' relationships with other faculty, students, and parents, as well as with principals.

A framework for future research includes the study of relationships, roles, events, structures, and processes. Research focusing on *relationships* might include interactions between individual teachers, informal and formal groups (e.g., teachers' unions) and support personnel (e.g., secretaries, custodians, cafeteria workers), school boards, central office, administrative teams, and community organizations. Future research may also target the formal *roles* teachers play, including coaching, advising, teaching, disciplining, planning, and evaluating, as well as informal *roles*, including counselling, mentoring, parenting, and policing. Research on the politics of teaching with regard to school *events* has great potential and could include graduation, band and athletic contests, plays, fairs, performances, and statewide activities. Another direction for future research centers on organizational *structures* – hierarchy, time, advancement, governance, policy, programs – and their impacts on the politics of teaching.

Finally, studies are needed that examine organizational *processes* and teacher politics, including education, socialization, participation, domination, innovation, collegiality, autonomy, empowerment, and restructuring. For example, research on the micropolitics of teacher empowerment and school restructuring would be especially valuable at this point in time. By and large, micropolitical studies of teachers have been conducted in traditional school organizations. In general, these studies suggest that teachers are quite vulnerable to others, and their political stance tends to be rather conservative and frequently submissive, especially in relationships with closed or manipulative school principals.

At the same time, future research might seek to clarify the sometimes contradictory findings of studies of teacher empowerment and restructuring. Such studies frequently demonstrate that empowerment and democratic structure are more illusion than reality: There is often a substantial discrepancy between the expected and actual political role of teachers in restructured schools. Principals' traditional expectations for self and others and teachers' professional norms of propriety and civility frequently undermine democratic processes and teachers' involvement in decision making (Malen & Ogawa, 1988; Reitzug & Cross, 1994; Robertson & Briggs, 1994; Wohlstetter, Smyer, & Mohrman, 1994). However, other studies of school restructuring point to positive impacts on teachers' political role in schools, specifically with regard to decision making, voice/expression, ownership, autonomy, risktaking, status, and collaboration (Allen, 1993; Blase & Blase, 1994; Bredeson, 1989; Kirby & Colbert, 1992; Melenyzer, 1990; Reitzug, 1994).

Research on the micropolitics of teaching has been dominated by qualitative methods, yet there exist no comprehensive case studies of the micropolitics of teaching. Such studies could explore many facets of teacher politics simultaneously in one setting and would therefore be especially valuable in developing conceptual and theoretical understandings about the micropolitics of teaching in the context of organizational and extraorganizational factors.

Qualitative research methods appear to be particularly valuable in producing the rich descriptive and theoretically grounded knowledge essential to this emergent area of scholarly inquiry. There may be good reason for this. The micropolitical perspective is, after all, an alternative approach to understanding life in organizational settings. This perspective acknowledges and emphasizes the subjective, dynamic, complex, and multifaceted nature of organizational life. As such, qualitative research methods are particularly powerful in assessing organizational phenomena.

SECTION 6: IMPLICATIONS FOR TEACHER EDUCATION

In the introduction to this chapter, it is noted that although teacher education programs may give some attention to the cultural and social dimensions of teaching, the micropolitics of teaching has been virtually ignored. This point is particularly significant, since micropolitics is pervasive in the classroom, the school, and the community. More than ever, teachers are forced to deal with internal and external constituencies. Issues related to community and parents – school choice, racial equity, and ability grouping – are fundamentally micropolitical in nature. In addition, with the advent of school restructuring (e.g., shared governance, site-based management, participatory decision making), with greater stress on collegiality and participation (rather than autonomy and isolation), the micropolitical dimensions of teaching have become more complex, dynamic, and unpredictable.

Consequently, more than ever before, teachers will be required to understand and use power and authority in the interest of student learning. Teachers will need to be active political participants, to work as individuals and in groups, to create dynamic school organizations to improve student achievement. Indeed, until micropolitics is acknowledged and systematically pursued in preservice and inservice teacher training, programs like restructuring will most likely have little direct relevance and attraction for teachers.

In the previous sections a framework for future research that includes relationships, roles, events, structures, and processes has been laid out. This same framework can be used to organize the micropolitical knowledge base for preservice and inservice teacher training programs.

The goal for preservice training might be to develop greater sensitivity and awareness of the micropolitics of teaching, to demonstrate the importance of micropolitics to teaching and how it affects teaching and learning in the classroom. The first three dimensions of the framework described above – relationships, roles, and events – could be emphasized during preservice training. These dimensions are directly and dramatically related to teaching and learning in the classroom. Throughout preservice training, micropolitics could be introduced in courses, special seminars, and, perhaps most important, field experiences (in which students explore micropolitics, for example, through observation and interviewing with teachers, administrators, and students). During the first year of training, a foundations course could be used to introduce the micropolitical knowledge base. Additional micropolitical content could be incorporated into methods courses and special seminars in subsequent years. Student teaching would be an opportunity for students to pursue the micropolitics of teaching through the use of qualitative research methods in the classroom and in the school.

The goal in inservice training would be the development of deeper micropolitical understandings and application of related knowledge. Again, the micropolitics of relationships, roles, and events might form an initial focus. For example, micropolitical content could easily be integrated into a course on classroom management in which teachers are directly confronted with issues of control, power, and authority. Courses that deal with parents and family involvement would be significantly strengthened through the study of micropolitics. In addition, the micropolitics of school structures and processes could be introduced during inservice training. As suggested above, understanding and skill in dealing with organizational and extraorganizational factors that affect teaching and learning could be pursued.

REFERENCES

Allen, L. R. (1993). *The role of voice in shared governance: A case study of a primary school.* Unpublished doctoral dissertation, University of Georgia.

Anderson, G. (1991). Cognitive politics of principals and teachers: Ideological control in an elementary school. In J. Blase (Ed.), *The politics of life in schools: Power, conflict, and cooperation* (pp. 120-130). Newbury Park, CA: Sage.

Apple, M. W. (1986). *Teachers and texts.* New York: Routledge & Kegan Paul.

Bacharach, S. B. & Lawler, E. J. (1980). *Power and politics in organizations: The social psychology of conflict, coalitions, and bargaining.* San Francisco: Jossey-Bass.

Bacharach, S. B. & Mitchell, S. M. (1987). The generation of practical theory: Schools as political organizations. In J. W. Lorsch (Ed.), *Handbook of organizational behavior* (pp. 405-418). Englewood Cliffs, NJ: Prentice Hall.

Ball, S. J. (1987). *The micro-politics of the school: Towards a theory of school organization.* London: Methuen.

Ball, S. J. & Bowe, R. (1991). Micropolitics of radical change: Budgets, management, and control in British schools. In J. Blase (Ed.), *The politics of life in schools: Power, conflict, and cooperation* (pp. 19-45). Newbury Park, CA: Sage.

Bates, R. (1986, April). *The culture of administration, the process of schooling and the politics of culture.* Paper presented at the annual meeting of the American Educational Research Association, San Francisco.

Bates, A. P. & Babchuk, N. (1961). The primary group: A reappraisal. *Sociological Quarterly, 2,* 181-192.

Beale, H. K. (1936). *Are American teachers free? An analysis of restraints upon the freedom of teaching in American schools.* New York: Scribner.

Becker, H. (1980). *Role of the Chicago public school teacher.* New York: ARNO Press.

Biklen, S. D. (1988, April). *Teachers in conflict: A case study.* Paper presented at the annual meeting of the American Educational Research Association, New Orleans.

Blase, J. (1987a). Dimensions of effective school leadership: The teachers' perspective. *American Educational Research Journal, 24*(4), 598-610.

Blase, J. (1987b). Dimensions of ineffective school leadership: The teacher's perspective. *The Journal of Educational Administration, 24*(2), 193-213.

Blase, J. (1987c). Political interaction among teachers: Sociocultural contexts in the schools. *Urban Education, 22*(3), 286-309.

Blase, J. (1987d). The politics of teaching: The teacher-parent relationship and the dynamics of diplomacy. *Journal of Teacher Education, 38*(2), 53-60.

Blase, J. (1988a). The everyday political perspectives of teachers: Vulnerability and conservatism. *Qualitative Studies in Education, 1*(2), 125-142.

Blase, J. (1988b). The politics of favoritism: A qualitative analysis of the teachers' perspective. *Educational Administration Quarterly, 24*(2), 152-177.

Blase, J. (1988c). The teachers' political orientation vis-à-vis the principal: The micropolitics of the school. In J. Hannaway & R. Crowson (Eds.), *The politics of reforming school administration: The 1988 yearbook of the politics of education association* (pp. 113-126). New York: Falmer Press.

Blase, J. (1989). The micropolitics of the school: The everyday political perspective of teachers toward open school principals. *Educational Administration Quarterly, 25*(4), 377-407.

Blase, J. (1990). Some negative effects of principals' control-oriented and protective political behavior. *American Educational Research Journal, 27*, 727-753.

Blase, J. (1991a). Everyday political perspectives of teachers toward students: The dynamics of diplomacy. In J. Blase (Ed.), *The politics of life in schools: Power, conflict, and cooperation* (pp. 185-206). Newbury Park, CA: Sage.

Blase, J. (1991b). The micropolitical orientation of teachers toward closed school principals. *Education and Urban Society, 23*(4), 356-378.

Blase, J. (1991c). *The politics of life in schools: Power, conflict, and cooperation.* Newbury Park, CA: Sage.

Blase, J. (1993). The micropolitics of effective school-based leadership: Teachers' perspectives. *Educational Administration Quarterly, 29*(2), 142-163.

Blase, J. & Blase, J. R. (1994). *Empowering teachers: What successful principals do.* Newbury Park, CA: Corwin.

Blase, J., Blase, J., Anderson, G., & Dungan, S. (1995). *Democratic principals in action: Eight pioneers.* Thousand Oaks, CA: Corwin Press.

Blase, J. & Roberts, J. (1994). The micropolitics of teacher work involvement: Effective principals' impacts on teachers. *The Alberta Journal of Educational Research 40*(1), 67-94.

Blase, J. R. & Blase, J. (1995). The micropolitics of successful supervisor-teacher interaction in instructional conferences. In D. Corson & A. Hargreaves (Eds.), *Discourse and power in educational organizations.* Cresskill, NJ: Hampton Press.

Bloome, D. & Willett, J. (1991). Toward a micropolitics of classroom interaction. In J.

Blase (Ed.), *The politics of life in schools: Power, conflict, and cooperation* (pp. 207-236). Newbury Park, CA: Sage.

Bolman, L. G. & Deal, T. E. (1984). *Modern approaches to understanding and managing organizations.* San Francisco: Jossey Bass.

Bredeson, P. V. (1989). Redefining leadership and the roles of school principals: Responses to changes in the professional work-life of teachers. *The High School Journal, 23*(1), 9-20.

Bridges, E. M. (1970). Administrative man: Origin or pawn in decision making? *Educational Administration Quarterly, 6*(1), 7-24.

Brieschke, P. A. (1983). A case study of teacher role enactment in an urban elementary school. *Educational Administration Quarterly, 19*(4), 59-83.

Burlingame, M. (1988). [Review of *The micro-politics of the school: Towards a theory of school organization*]. *Journal of Curriculum Studies, 20*(3), 281-283.

Burns, T. (1961). Micropolitics: Mechanisms of institutional change. *Administration Science Quarterly, 6*, 257-281.

Cohen, M. M. & Kottkamp, R. B. (1993). *Teachers: The missing voice in education.* Albany, NY: State University of New York Press.

Connell, R. W. (1985). *Teacher's work.* Sydney: George Allen & Unwin.

Corbett, H. D. (1991). Community influence on school micropolitics: A case example. In J. Blase (Ed.), *The politics of life in schools: Power, conflict, and cooperation* (pp. 73-95). Newbury Park, CA: Sage.

Cusick, P. A. (1983). *The egalitarian ideal and the American high school: Studies of three schools.* New York: Longman.

Cyert, R. M. & March, J. G. (1963). *A behavioral theory of the firm.* Englewood Cliffs, NJ: Prentice Hall.

Dreeben, R. (1968). *On what is learned in school.* Reading, MA: Addison-Wesley.

Dreeben, R. (1970). *The nature of teaching.* Glenview, IL: Scott Foresman.

Fayol, H. (1949). *General and industrial management.* Constance Starrs, London: Sir Isaac Pitman.

Fuchs, E. (1967). *Teachers talk: Views from inside city schools.* New York: Anchor Books.

Giroux, H. (1992). Educational leadership and the crisis of democratic government. *Educational Researcher, 21*(4), 4-11.

Gitlin, A. (1983). School structure and teachers' work. In M. Apple & L. Weis (Eds.), *Ideology and practice in schooling* (pp. 193-212). Philadelphia: Temple University Press.

Glickman, C. D. (1993). *Renewing America's schools: A guide for school-based action.* San Francisco: Jossey-Bass.

Goodson, I. F. (1992). *Studying teachers lives.* New York: Teachers College Press.

Greenfield, W. D. (1991). The micropolitics of leadership in an urban elementary school. In J. Blase (Ed.), *The politics of life in schools: Power, conflict, and cooperation* (pp. 161-184). Newbury Park, CA: Sage.

Gronn, P. (1986). Politics, power and the management of schools. In E. Hoyle (Ed.), *The world yearbook of education 1986: The management of schools* (pp. 45-54). London: Kogan Page.

Grumet, M. (1988). *Bitter milk: Women and teaching.* Amherst: University of Massachusetts Press.

Hanson, M. (1976). Beyond the bureaucratic model: A study of power and autonomy in educational decision making. *Interchange, 7*(1), 27-38.

Hardy, C. (1987). The contribution of political science to organizational behavior. In J. W. Lorsch (Ed.), *Handbook of organizational behavior* (pp. 96-108). Englewood Cliffs, NJ: Prentice Hall.

Hargreaves, A. (1979). Strategies, decision, and control: Interaction in a middle school classroom. In J. Eggleston (Ed.), *Teacher decision-making in the classroom* (pp. 137-179). London: Routledge & Kegan Paul.

Hargreaves, A. (1990). Teachers' work and the politics of time and space. *Qualitative Studies in Education, 3*(4), 303-320.

Hargreaves, A. (1991). Contrived collegiality: The micropolitics of teacher collaboration. In J. Blase (Ed.), *The politics of life in schools: Power, conflict, and cooperation* (pp. 46-72). Newbury Park, CA: Sage.

Hoyle, E. (1986). *The politics of school management.* London: Hodder and Stoughton.

Hunter, C. (1979). Control in the comprehensive system. In J. Eggleston (Ed.), *Teacher decision-making in the classroom: A collection of papers* (pp. 118-133). London: Routledge & Kegan Paul.

Iannaccone, L. (1975). *Education policy systems: A study guide for educational administrators.* Fort Lauderdale, FL: Nova University.

Jackson, P. (1968). *Life in classrooms.* New York: Holt, Rinehart & Winston.

Kirby, P. C. & Colbert, R. (1992, April). *Principals who empower teachers.* Paper presented at the annual meeting of the American Educational Research Association, San Francisco.

Kreisberg, S. (1992). *Transforming power: Domination, empowerment and education.* Albany, NY: State University of New York Press.

Lather, P. (1991). *Getting smart: Feminist research and pedagogy within the postmodern.* New York: Routledge.

Lieberman, A. & Miller, L. (1984). *Teachers, their world and their work.* Alexandria, VA: Association for Supervision and Curriculum Development.

Lightfoot, S. L. (1983). *The good high school: Portraits of character and culture.* New York: Basic Books.

Lightfoot, S. L. (1986). On goodness in schools: Themes of empowerment. *Peabody Journal of Education, 63*(3), 9-28.

Little, J. W. (1982). Norms of collegiality and experimentation: Workplace conditions of school success. *American Educational Research Journal, 19*(3), 325-340.

Lortie, D. C. (1963). The balance of control and autonomy. In A. Etzioni (Ed.), *The semi-professions and their organization* (pp. 1-53). New York: Free Press.

Lortie, D. C. (1975). *Schoolteacher: A sociological study.* Chicago: University of Chicago Press.

Maeroff, G. I. (1988). A blueprint for empowering teachers. *Phi Delta Kappan, 69*(7), 473-477.

Malen, B. & Ogawa, R. (1988). Professional-patron influence on site-based governance councils: A confounding case study. *Educational Evaluation and Policy Analysis, 10*(4), 251-270.

Mangham, I. (1979). *The politics of organizational change.* Westport, CT: Greenwood Press.

Mayes, B. T. & Allen, R. W. (1977). Toward a definition of organizational politics. *Academy of Management Review, 2,* 672-678.

McNeil, L. (1983). Defensive teaching and classroom control. In M. Apple & L. Weis (Eds.), *Ideology and practice in schooling* (pp. 114-142). Philadelphia: Temple University Press.

McNeil, L. (1986). *Contradictions of control: School structure and school knowledge.* New York: Routledge & Kegan Paul.

McPherson, G. H. (1972). *Small town teachers.* Cambridge, MA: Harvard University Press.

Melenyzer, B. J. (1990, November). *Teacher empowerment: The discourse, meanings and social actions of teachers.* Paper presented at the National Council of States on Inservice Education, Orlando.

Metz, M. H. (1978). *Classrooms and corridors: The crisis of authority in desegregated secondary schools.* Berkeley: University of California Press.

Miles, R. H. (1980). *Macro organizational behavior.* Santa Monica, CA: Goodyear.

Morgan, G. (1986). *Images of organizations.* Beverly Hills, CA: Sage.

Naegle, K. D. (1956). Clergymen, teachers, and psychiatrists. *Canadian Journal of Economics and Political Science, 22,*46-62.

Nias, J. (1983). *The definition and maintenance of self in primary teaching: Values and reference groups.* Unpublished manuscript, Cambridge Institute of Technology, Cambridge, England.

Nias, J. (1989). *Primary teachers talking: A study of teaching as work.* London: Routledge.

Noblit, G., Berry, B., & Dempsey, V. (1991). Political responses to reform: A comparative case study. *Education and Urban Society, 23*(4), 379-395.

Osborne, A. B. (1989). Insiders and outsiders: Cultural membership and the micropolitics of education among the Zuni. *Anthropology and Education Quarterly, 20,* 196-215.

Pauly, E. (1992). *The classroom crucible: What really works, what doesn't, and why.* New York: Basic Books.

Pfeffer, J. (1981). *Power in organizations.* Marshfield, MA: Pitman.

Pollard, A. (1985). *The social world of the primary school.* London: Holt, Rinehart & Winston.

Powell, G., Farrar, E., & Cohen, D. K. (1985). *The shopping mall high school: Winners and losers in the educational marketplace.* Boston: Houghton Mifflin.

Radnor, H. A. (1990, April). *Complexities and compromises: The new era at Parkview School.* Paper presented at the annual meeting of the American Educational Research Association, Boston.

Reitzug, U. C. (1994). A case study of empowering principal behavior. *American Educational Research Journal, 31*(2), 283-307.

Reitzug, U. C. & Cross, B. E. (1994, April). *A multi-site case study of site-based management in urban schools.* Paper presented at the annual conference of the American Educational Research Association, New Orleans.

Robertson, P. J. & Briggs, K. L. (1994, April). *Managing change through school-based management*. Paper presented at the annual meeting of the American Educational Research Association, New Orleans.

Rosenholtz, S. J. & Simpson, C. (1990). Workplace conditions and the rise and fall of teachers' commitment. *Sociology of Education, 63*(4), 241-257.

Sarason, S. B. (1982). *The culture of the school and the problem of change* (2nd ed.). Boston: Allyn & Bacon.

Schein, V. E. (1977). Individual power and political behaviors in organizations: An inadequately explored reality. *Academy of Management Review, 2*(1), 64-72.

Schempp, P. G., Sparkes, A. C., & Templin, T. J. (1993). The micropolitics of teacher induction. *American Educational Research Journal, 30*(3), 447-472.

Schubert, W. H. & Ayers, W. C. (1992). *Teacher lore: Learning from our own experience*. New York: Longman.

Sedlak, M. W., Wheller, C. W., Pullin, D. C., & Cusick, P. A. (1986). *Selling students short: Classroom bargains and academic reform in the American high school*. New York: Teachers College Press.

Sikes, P. J., Measor, L., & Woods, P. (1985). *Teacher careers: Crisis and continuities*. London: Falmer Press.

Smylie, M. A. & Brownlee-Conyers, J. (1990, April). *Teacher leaders and their principals: Exploring new working relationships from a micropolitical perspective*. Paper presented at the annual meeting of the American Educational Research Association, Boston.

Sparkes, A. C. (1988). The micropolitics of innovation in the physical education curriculum. In J. Evans (Ed.), *Teacher, teaching and control in physical education* (pp. 157-177). Lewes, England: Falmer Press.

Sparkes, A. C. (1990). Power, domination and resistance in the process of teacher-initiated innovation. *Research Papers in Education, 5*(2), 153-178.

Spaulding, A. (1994). *The micropolitics of the elementary classroom*. Unpublished doctoral dissertation, Texas Tech University, Lubbock.

Strauss, G. (1962). Tactics of lateral relationship: The purchasing agent. *Administrative Science Quarterly, 7*(2), 161-186.

Taylor, F. W. (1947). *Scientific management*. New York: Harper.

Townsend, R. G. (1990). Toward a broader micropolitics of schools. *Curriculum Inquiry, 20*(2), 205-224.

Veenan, S. (1984). Perceived problems of beginning teachers. *Review of Educational Research, 54*(2), 143-178.

Waller, W. (1932). *The sociology of teaching*. New York: John Wiley.

Wamsley, G. L. & Zald, M. N. (1973). *The political economy of public organizations: A critique and approach to the study of public organizations*. Lexington, MA: Lexington Books.

Weber, M. (1947). *The theory of social and economic organization*. New York: Free Press.

Willower, D. J., Eidell, T. L., & Hoy, W. K. (1967). *The school and pupil control ideology* (Monograph No. 24). University Park: Pennsylvania State University.

Wilson, B. (1962). The teacher's role – A sociological analysis. *British Journal of Sociology, 13*, 15-32.

Wohlstetter, P., Smyer, R., & Mohrman, S. A. (1994, April). *New boundaries for school-based management: The high involvement model*. Paper presented at the annual meeting of the American Educational Research Association, New Orleans.

Woods, P. (1990). *Teacher skills and strategies*. London: Falmer Press.

Zeichner, K. M. & Tabachnick, B. R. (1984, April). *Social strategies and institutional control in the socialization of beginning teachers*. Paper presented at the annual meeting of the American Educational Research Association, New Orleans.

Chapter 7: The New Politics of Teaching

PETER W. COOKSON, JR. AND CHARLOTTE SHUBE LUCKS
Teachers College, Columbia University, Adelphi University

We can change teachers only by changing the environment in which teaching takes place. Teaching can be changed only by reinventing the institution where teaching takes place – schools.

Deborah Meier
(Sadovnik, Cookson, & Semel, 1994, p. 549)

If teachers are not critically conscious, if they are not awake to their own values and commitments (and the conditions working upon them), if they are not personally engaged with their subject matter and with the world around, I do not see how they can initiate the young into critical questioning or a normal life.

Maxine Green
(Sadovnik et al., 1994, p. 225)

Teaching is a Dangerous Activity

When Socrates was condemned to death his alleged crime was corruption of the youth. His accusers were at once completely wrong, yet at a deeper, more sinister level, completely correct. The quest for truth does corrupt a sense of complacency, does undermine a willingness to watch others suffer and challenges the passive acceptance of those polite lies upon which the status quo is built. By asking questions such as: What do we mean by 'the good,' 'justice,' and 'love,' Socrates and other teachers have suffered exile, rejection, and sometimes death. Historically, teaching has been a dangerous activity because the transmission of ideas and the acquisition of literacy invites critical reflection. Whatever the dailiness of teaching, its underlying purpose remains quietly revolutionary, although few teachers think of themselves as change agents. The evolution of the teaching profession is the story of the dynamic tension between the conservation of culture and the development of critical consciousness (Giroux, 1990).

Because teaching and learning is a core human activity, it is difficult to define when the 'politics' of teaching originated. After all, teaching has never been the exclusive property of one particular group or caste; teaching and learn-

B.J. Biddle et al. (eds.), International Handbook of Teachers and Teaching, 971-984
© *1997 Kluwer Academic Publishers, Printed in the Netherlands*

ing are woven into social life through culture, economics, religion, and politics – parents are teachers, peers are teachers, villagers are teachers, priests are teachers, soldiers are teachers, artists are teachers, and employers are teachers. To write a comprehensive history of the politics of teaching would not only require a definition of teaching, but an encyclopedic knowledge of how teaching has evolved in different parts of the globe. Our task is far more modest. We focus our attention on the contemporary American elementary and secondary education landscape.

By the 'new' politics of teaching we refer to the rapidly changing conditions of employment for teachers, the political context of teaching, and the larger political environment that generally shapes the definition of schooling and the condition of children (Lieberman, 1992). One of the underlying issues that structures the politics of teaching is the struggle by educators for professional, personal, and intellectual autonomy (Darling-Hammond & Snyder, 1992). The history of teaching, as in the case of Socrates, is a history of struggle for independence. Unlike most other professions, teachers have never been able to assume their autonomy; autonomy is the result of organizational and political struggle. In our opinion, the current political and economic climate poses a real threat to the classroom autonomy of teachers. Privatization, 'teacher proof' curricula, poorly organized schools, and a general tendency to scapegoat teachers for society's problems are indicative of a larger political climate where teachers often find themselves losing their professional status (Sadovnik et al., 1994). The new politics of teaching is also shaped by a cultural environment where traditional American anti-intellectualism has been reinforced by a popular culture that has in many ways obliterated the traditional beliefs in learning and a reverence for the life of the mind (Hofstadter, 1964; Postman, 1985). This cultural assault on the core values of education is reflected in the intense struggle over curricula and standards. Today, teaching cannot escape the politics of cultural struggle as the writers of curriculum try to create new social narratives that include the aspirations and backgrounds of 'new' students whose families are increasingly likely to have immigrated from Latin America, Asia, and Africa, rather than Europe (Cibulka, Mawhinney, & Paquette, 1995; New York State Education Department, 1994).

Additionally, Bill Clinton's election to the presidency in 1992 took the Federal government in a new direction in terms of educational reform. Based on the policy principles of 'systemic reform,' the Clinton administration successfully negotiated a number of reform bills through Congress including the 'Goals 2000, Educate America Act.' This law provides a comprehensive approach to educational reform that could deeply influence how teachers teach, how they are evaluated, and how professional standards are set (Riley, 1995; Smith & Scoll, 1995). Goals 2000 is the core of the 'new federalism' in educational reform, a topic which will be discussed later in this chapter (Cookson, 1995b). As of this writing, the 104th Congress is 'revisiting' the Goals Act because many Republicans believe that the Act creates a 'national' school board, an intrusion they find repellent because it violates local control. The central argument of this chapter is that teaching is undergoing a rapid redefinition and that the very status of public school elementary and secondary teaching is on the verge of devaluation. The evidence for this argument is drawn from a variety of sources including the current literature concerning teaching, secondary analyses of the conditions of teaching, and first-hand observations.

The Social, Cultural, and Economic Context of Teaching

The professional and political ideology of public school teaching has been shaped by the organizational models of schooling adopted during the late nineteenth century (Spring, 1972). During this period the concept of mass schooling was introduced. Fueled by progressive notions of social progress and social engineering, public schools sought to 'Americanize' new immigrants. During the late nineteenth century and for most of the twentieth century, schools have been considered to be critical to society's democratic development (Cremin, 1977; Popkewitz, 1991). From this perspective the purpose of education is to prepare good citizens and consequently teachers are to introduce students to conventional and conservative notions of citizenship and patriotism. The tensions associated with class and racial conflict, technological innovation, and immigration has done little to change the focus of teaching, although in the 1960s and 1970s 'open' schooling and other reforms attempted to liberate teachers and students from the constraints of the industrial model of education. However, most schools today remain firmly in the nineteenth century factory mode of organization, complete with an emphasis on standardized products, bureaucracy, and a sharp division between management and labor (Cibulka et al., 1995).

Because teachers increasingly became civil servants in the late nineteenth century and early twentieth century, the 'art' of teaching became increasingly defined as 'craft' or a 'semi' profession (Cremin, 1977; Lortie, 1975). This new semi-profession called out for training. Part of this training impulse came from 'Taylorism' and the 'cult of efficiency,' but there was also a perceived need to raise the status of teaching through scientific pedagogy (Callahan, 1962). The state began to mandate qualifications required for teaching in public schools. Since the 1970s, certification requirements for teachers have increased rapidly as a response to the public perception that teachers are not highly qualified and have failed to raise student achievement. It is argued that restructuring teacher education and demanding higher certification standards will have a direct effect on student achievement (Darling-Hammond & Snyder, 1992). The demand for further credentials is reflected in the marked increase in the number of teachers with post-baccalaureate degrees.

Historically, the politics of teaching has been influenced by the social relations of a particular era. The definition of social relations includes not only the economic connections between dominant and subordinate classes but the political and cultural expression of these connections in terms of ideology, values, and aspirations (Bourdieu & Passeron, 1977). Whether individual scholars are paid directly by their students, as in ancient days, or are clerics teaching under the supervision of a church hierarchy, or are civil servants, the conditions of labor for teachers are shaped by power relations outside the classroom. In the period of late capitalism, teachers are essentially members of the service sector of the economy; the 'goods' they produce are symbolic and credentializing (Goodson, 1992). Public school teachers are agents of the state, largely regulated by the state, and paid through tax levied dollars. States are unforgiving masters; it is generally assumed that teachers will support the goals of the state, no matter how loosely defined or unclearly articulated. Because of the decentralization of American education, each state has responsibility for its own school system, and most states attempt to reach down into individual classrooms by controlling who shall teach, the conditions of teaching and what will be taught. Most teachers have little control of basic pedagogic and curricular decisions associated with classical definitions of teaching (Louis, 1992). Private school teachers relate to the state differently; their salary is derived mostly from privately paid tuition, and their conditions of employment more resemble a craft than a profession (Cookson & Persell, 1985). In this chapter we will concentrate on the politics of public school teaching.

Notwithstanding the power of the state, the regulation of public school teaching can do little to control the classroom experience, because students, especially American students, bring to the learning environment their own culture. Schools are modern; students are post-modern. In addition to the learning obstacles posed by violence and drugs, many students lack the 'cultural capital' to participate fully in the life of the school. Teenagers who are using drugs or are involved in gangs seldom succeed academically. Teenage pregnancy causes many girls to have poor attendance and eventually drop out (New York State Education Department, 1994). To add to these conditions, post-modern students often seem to have a short attention span. In many schools respect for authority and tradition has withered in the face of a popular culture where children learn about life through MTV, movies, and an electronic blanket of continuous media (Postman, 1985). The media play a major role in the apparently growing anti-intellectualism and voracious consumerism that marks late twentieth century American life; commercial television, video, and film have taken the place of literature for many children as well as adults. News reports sensationalize events and give substantial significance to issues that sell but may be of trivial importance (Bennett, 1988; Pines & Lamar, 1994).

In this environment the very basis of democracy becomes threatened as the individual becomes narcissistically aggrandized but simultaneously diminished as a citizen (Ignatief, 1995). Political activism seems to have become an area of expertise and professionalism rather that a statement of personal commitment. This breakdown of traditional notions of citizenry coupled with a popular culture which appears to glorify power and even violence creates a culture that is without boundaries for the individual, yet at the same time, sociologically shallow and spiritually constrained (Shorris, 1994). The 'post-modern mind' – a much discussed phenomena – is noted for its fragmentation and lack of commitment (Foucault, 1988). One might even go so far to say that the drama of the post-modern mind is acted out with imaginary players randomly and sometimes chaotically drawn from the world of media, politics, and sports rather that family, church, and community. The consequence of this cultural fragmentation is that students have few intellectual or moral anchors that can act as guides to behavior and thought. From a pedagogic point of view, the very definition of teaching and learning becomes radically altered. A modern day Socrates has many teaching challenges because the very meaning of education – 'to draw out' – no longer seems applicable to minds that are innocent of logic, firm belief, and attention to linguistic detail. In selling the 'products' of education, the very essence of education is lost and its purpose forgotten. As Arthur Powell and his colleagues so astutely detailed in their book *The Shopping Mall High School*, many American high schools are like shopping centers where 'learning is voluntary; it is one among many things for sale' (Powell, Farrar, & Cohen, 1985).

To counter these trends, many states have pressed for higher standards. In New York, for example, mandatory Regents Diplomas have been instituted (New York State Education Department, 1991). As of September 1994, all incoming high school students are required to complete a specific number of courses in various disciplines and take the corresponding standardized tests. Although admirable, the idea of forcing all students to take difficult math and science courses may prove to be counter-productive. Many students are ill prepared to handle the rigor of such courses, some may not be capable, and still others may not understand the purpose since they are not planning to attend college. The difficulties these students encounter may increase a sense of failure instead of bolstering self-esteem. To raise standards without providing effective remediation and guidance is likely to result in more drop-outs, not more degrees.

Although characteristics of the student population have changed in the last twenty years, the demographic characteristics of teachers has not. Of the three million teachers in America today, over 70 per cent are women, and 80 per cent are from families of European origin. Most teachers have middle class backgrounds. The largest percentage of teachers are between the ages of 40 and 50, and the median years of experience is fifteen. Controlling for inflation, teachers' salaries have not increased significantly since the 1960s; the mean salary of today's teachers is $30,000 (United States Department of Education, 1993). The professional rewards of teaching have been somewhat tarnished by an overall decline in job satisfaction (óCohn, 1992). One of the primary reasons that teachers leave the profession is lack of support from parents and students (United States Department of Education, 1993). Although there has been a slight decline in class size since the 1970s, many public school classrooms are still overcrowded. Many teachers complain about excessive paperwork that often has little to do with pedagogy. In many schools violence has become a major issue; in New York City high schools, for example, metal detectors and security personnel have become a necessity. In some schools the administrative personnel are overburdened by serious offenders, such as students who carry guns, destroy property, and rob fellow students and teachers. Minor infractions, such as lateness or disruptive behavior are often overlooked. As the late President of the American Federation of Teachers, Albert Shanker, recently wrote, 'There seems to be a high level of tolerance for this behavior where there should be none. We teach kids a bad lesson that nothing will happen if they break the rules' (1995, p. E-7).

The learning environment of many schools is highly controlled by regulation and a lack of educational vision. There is a strong pressure to remain within the boundaries of curricular guidelines, and teachers who deviate tend to be criticized by supervisors. Moreover, these teachers are often ostracized by peers who are more comfortable with the status quo. In this way, the lack of teacher autonomy is internalized and even promoted by faculty themselves. Professional autonomy is a controversial issue. The public insists that schools produce literate and numerate young citizens; administrators and teachers try to ensure that the school's pedagogic practices have a positive effect on academic success and that curricula meet acceptable standards. The pressure on teachers to conform can be intense. In fact, a 'teacher-proof' curriculum, which was once frowned upon, is now welcomed by administrators who view it as a safety net. While some teachers consider such a curriculum a convenience, most would prefer to make their own decisions about how and what they should teach. Most creative teaching is finding subtle ways of subverting standardized curricula (Wigginton, 1988).

Often the desires of teachers and the goals of administrators are in conflict, creating a rift between them. Teachers complain that administrators do not understand or care about work conditions. Tensions exist between long time teachers and newer administrators whose ideas are often opposed. Although not common in practice, there is the potential for principals to abuse their power.

Poor evaluations, for example, can result in ostracizing or firing teachers who are not meeting expected standards. Teacher unions act to protect teacher benefits, security, and rights. As an outgrowth of this 'meat and potatoes' stance, administrators treat teachers as employees – often following strict procedures prior to every action – thus stifling innovation and spontaneity. Union leaders walk the thin line between the ethos of professionalism, which emphasizes autonomy, and the 'ethos of employment,' which emphasizes security. The dual status of public school teachers – employees and professionals – has yet to be resolved. In sum, the struggle of teachers to achieve professional status is much in doubt; teachers believe themselves to be professionals, yet they are civil servants who are protected by a union. In sociological terms, there is a certain status incongruity in these competing vocational identities. Perhaps this is why the teaching profession is particularly vulnerable to downward mobility; the very ambivalence of roles make teachers potential political targets in a society that is quickly deunionizing and has lost faith with public institutions.

Conservative Populism and the Coming Deregulation of Public Education

As the United States prepares to enter the twenty-first century, virtually every aspect of public and personal life is in question. In the public realm, state schools have been attacked by conservatives and libertarians who claim that public schools are universally inefficient and mediocre, and rob students and families of the fundamental right to attend a school of their choice. This confederation of influential people and interest groups might be called 'conservative populism' (Cookson, 1994; Henig, 1994). Not withstanding the differences that exist between these groups, they share a general sense that public institutions pose a threat to individual liberty and economic prosperity. This coalition has become extremely powerful politically in the last fifteen years, and there is good reason to believe that through political and ideological mobilization the organizations which compose this new populism will seek an ever wider role in public affairs. This growing power is enhanced by support from the corporate sector which has acquired an unprecedented amount of control over the media and other cultural institutions such as publishing houses and university based think-tanks (Parenti, 1995).

To some degree this conservative restoration has created an increasing sense of cultural disunity and even rancour. The pollster Daniel Yankelovich (1994, pp. 2-3) refers to the 'foul public mood.' He believes that the current environment can harden into 'class warfare, generational warfare, exacerbated racial tensions, polarization and political extremism, demagogy and instability as we careen from one overly simplistic solution to another.' He cites three trends as responsible for this new nastiness: first, the majority of Americans are failing to participate in the benefits of economic growth; second, some of the most important core values Americans share in common are growing weaker; and third, there is a serious and growing disconnection between America's leaders and the citizenry. To support these assertions, he points to some basic facts: the median family income has declined every year since 1991; controlling for inflation, hourly wages have stagnated for more than twenty years; and while the total economy grew last year, the main beneficiaries were the top 20 per cent of the work force.

In terms of the weakening of core values, he points to current crime rates and violence, the decline in community participation by most citizens, and the high levels of child abuse reported nationally. Given this situation, it is not surprising that the most important concern that Americans express about public education is safety and order, not standards and achievement. As for the growing disconnection between leaders and the public, Yankelovich (1994, p. 12) writes,

> It is almost as if the public were living in one world and the politician and economists and journalists and other experts in another. The one percent elite of political, business, scientific and professional experts do seem to live in one world and the 99 per cent majority in another.

These trends bear directly on a general understanding of the new politics of teaching. Public school teaching for most of this century was a public service. Based on public support for equal educational opportunity and individual mobility, a high quality and fair public school system has been a corner stone for both legitimizing and reinforcing democracy. Historically, public institutions developed as a strategy for partially undoing some of the harmful effects of capitalism on the economically vulnerable. Market economies are cyclical and profit-driven. During a depression or recession, those in the weakest market positions suffer downward mobility, particularly in comparison with those who are more securely located in the economic structure. To protect the economically weak, the government created, through popular representation, a set of public institutions that aim to mitigate the effects of market fluctuations. The result was (and is) a very weak welfare state. Most welfare policies, in fact, are monetary transfers within the middle class rather than transfers from the rich to the poor (Parenti, 1995).

The American underclass is extremely poor and economically marginalized, while the American upper class has created elite institutions which allow them to control the commanding heights of the economy while camouflaging their dominant position (Harrington, 1962; Phillips, 1990). The very weak American welfare state has become a target of the populists who claim that welfare programs, such as Aid-to-Dependent-Children, contribute significantly to the federal government's debt. In reality, the major contributors to the federal debt are defense expenditures, subsidies to industries, and service on the debt itself. This environment of denigrating public institutions and the welfare state has placed public education in a dangerous situation. Public education relies on public support – financially, culturally, and ideologically. Moreover, public schools have become the key institution in trying to resolve the deep social problems that emerge when a society and an economy produce increasing tension and inequality.

In the classrooms of America the culture wars engendered by these deep inequalities are acted out on a daily basis; teachers often try to negotiate and integrate social problems into curriculum and teaching. As an example of how politicized the intersection between social change and classroom practices has become, one need only to refer to the heated debate that accompanied former New York City School Chancellor Joseph Fernandez's attempt to expand the elementary school curriculum by the introduction of unconventional lifestyles through a 'Children of the Rainbow' curriculum. In the end, the controversy surrounding the rainbow curriculum was part of the reason Fernandez resigned. Moreover, other examples of how public education has lost its aura of innocence may be cited: the Christian right has successfully managed to gain positions of power on school boards in San Diego and other cities; the entire issue of sex education remains unresolved; and the content of textbooks still arouses public passions.

As though to highlight the comments above, the elections of November 1994 altered the contours of the United States Congress by bringing to power a Republican majority in both houses. The majority is deeply conservative, and – as the 'Contract with America' demonstrates – the new Republican majority is convinced that the heavy hand of government and corrupt and inefficient public institutions are the sources of the country's economic and social problems. In terms of education, this challenge is reflected in the increasing popularity of legislation proposing educational vouchers. The political battle over vouchers in Pennsylvania, Colorado, and California indicate how strong the voucher movement is nationally (Cookson, 1996). Many states are seriously investigating the possibility of creating a system of charter schools which would operate as publicly funded private schools. Throughout the United States there is a general movement to slash educational budgets, eliminate programs, and a deep skepticism about the benefits of increasing teachers' salaries.

At the national level, the new mood is manifested by significant cuts in educational programs. In the spring of 1995 the House Appropriation Subcommittee suggested a very large rescissions bill which would roll back $1.7 billion in already appropriated 1995 education funds. The United States Department of Education suffered a disproportional share of proposed funding cuts, exceeded only by the Department of Housing and Urban Development. The Economic and Educational Opportunities Committee established by the new Congress was instrumental in abolishing school food programs in favor of a new school-based nutrition block grant. Even the Federal government's commitment to 'Goals 2000: Educate America Act' is questionable given that the 1995 appropriation of over 400 million dollars which was targeted for a reduction to under 175 million dollars (Council of the Great City Schools, 1995). Even though the Federal government's financial commitment to public education has always been small relative to states and local communities, this share declined in the 1980s and will likely decrease even further (Cookson, 1995a).

Clearly, the politics of teaching reflects this larger context. It is no longer business as usual for public school educators. Their financial base is being under-cut, and society's unquestioned commitment to the values of public education is wavering. Nowhere is this lack of commitment to public education more pronounced than in the voucher and privatization movement (Arons, 1983; Henig, 1995; Lieberman, 1993). The implications of large scale voucher plans for the social organization of teachers' work are immense. Vouchers would undermine and eventually erode support for unions because private schools, with rare exceptions, have never engaged in collective bargaining with their teachers (Cookson, 1996). If teachers are no longer able to bargain collectively with school boards, their market power is significantly diminished. The same principle applies to the privatization movement. Privatization is a term that covers a wide variety of practices from 'for-profit' schools to the out-sourcing of particular programs and services. Prior to the 1980s, almost all public schools were self-contained, and school services were provided by school personnel. Certainly private schools existed, but because of the baby boom there was little competition between public and private schools. Moreover, private schools tended to cater to specific segments of the population leaving the public sector schools little competition in attracting the children of the middle class. All this has changed considerably. There has been a growth of religious schools and the middle class largely has left the city for the suburbs. Thus, most non-suburban public schools find themselves educating students who are economically disadvantaged and quite often come from family backgrounds were the opportunities for education are slim if non-existent (Cookson & Lucks, 1995). As a consequence of these cultural and demographic shifts, there is a perception that public education is inadequate to meet the challenges of a changing economy and society.

This sense of failure has provided a window of opportunity for a wide variety of educational entrepreneurs who claim that they can provide better educational services at lower costs. Perhaps the most visible example of the privatization movement is the Edison Project, which was founded by the entrepreneur Christopher Whittle. The Edison Project originally sought to establish one thousand private schools to compete with public schools. The Edison Project was portrayed by its promoters as being on the cutting edge of reform by planning

schools that are small, attentive to the needs of students, flexible and accountable to families (Schmidt, 1994). As of the writing of this chapter, the Edison
Project has substantially scaled down its ambitions, and there is some question
as to whether or not the Project will remain solvent (Cookson, 1996). Other private firms have taken over school systems in Baltimore, Maryland, and West
Hartford, Connecticut, although their efforts have received mixed reviews.
Many public school administrators continue to reach out to businesses, foundations, and other philanthropic organizations for funding (Rosenberg, 1995).
This trend has been accelerated by the slashing of such school programs as student lunches, sports, extracurricular activities, and special education. This in-
solvency has left some school systems, such as that in Orange County,
California, in a state of near bankruptcy (Lindsay, 1995).

The implications of these trends for teachers are critical. The days in which
a young teacher could expect lifetime employment in a school district are virtually over. Between the politics of educational reform, demographic shifts, and
the market challenge to public education, there is little expectation that elementary and secondary education will remain as it is in the future. Competition
among teachers for the best jobs may well result in the deregulation of the teaching profession. The likely result will be lower pay, less control over the working
environment, less control over the intellectual content of teaching, and greater
vocational marginalization. The decline of the middle class in terms of its economic and political strength has been well documented (Lardner, 1993). As
members of the middle class teachers are also in a state of decline economically
if not socially. The implications of this decline for the politics of teaching are
unclear. One can foresee a scenario where teacher lose their collective authority, but there is also the possibility that the objective conditions influencing the
teaching profession may draw teachers together. In any case, there is little likelihood that the teaching profession will remain the same in terms of its organization and social authority even into the twenty-first century.

Conclusion: Teachers As Moral Agents and Political Actors

As we have seen, the profession and vocation of teaching is in a state of suspended social animation; who really knows how teaching will be organized in
twenty years? Certainly, it will be different than it is today and the changes that
will take place will be the result of the political environment in which schools
operate. If the country continues to apply market solutions to public policy,
there is every reason to expect that public education as an unifying social and
institutional force will be diluted, perhaps even disappear. In such a situation
teaching, as a profession, is likely to lose its political power as individual teachers will have to compete against other teachers in a free-wheeling market-place

where traditional professional credentials will have little force. Teaching could return to its 'amateur' status, where the individual 'teacher-worker' will only be as valuable as her or his marketplace skill.

Even further, it doesn't require a great imagination to guess that teaching as we know it, may disappear. Machines, most notably computers, can and do 'teach.' What could be required will be technical facilitators who can make sure that the 'interface' between students and machines is efficient. The role of teachers as shapers of youth may become antiquated. In a world dominated by technology the very concepts of social commitment, empathy, and bettering group life might be the subject of historical software. In the brave new world of machine efficiency, 'oughtness and isness' may be hard to distinguish.

Is this scenario an unreasonable leap of the imagination? Unfortunately, no. Naturally, we hope that in twenty years the profession of teaching is neither destroyed by market forces or reduced to intellectual and moral poverty through technological efficiency. On the contrary, we would like to see a wholly different politics of teaching. In our preferred scenario, teachers remain active shapers of public life by rousing children's minds to life and creating schools where children and adults participate in the excitement of learning and the satisfaction that come from being a positive member of a community.

Earlier in this essay we argued that teacher autonomy was the key to creating a profession that was capable of transforming schools and recreating a culture of learning. To our way of thinking, professional autonomy can best be achieved by setting higher standards for those who enter and remain in the profession. In order to gain the respect that is a prerequisite to professional status, teachers must demand more of themselves and take a role in reforming schools; without vibrant, strong teachers, surely the future of the United States is likely to be less optimistic, less productive, and less just.

REFERENCES

Arons, S. C. (1983). *Compelling belief: The culture of American schooling.* New York: McGraw-Hill.

Bennett, L. W. (1988). *News: The politics of illusion.* New York: Longman.

Bourdieu, P. & Passeron, J. (1977). *Reproduction: In education, society and culture.* Beverly Hills, CA: Sage.

Callahan, R. (1962). *Education and the culture of efficiency: A study of the social forces that have shaped the administration of public schools.* Chicago: University of Chicago Press.

Cibulka, J. G., Mawhinney, H. B., & Paquette, J. (1995). Administrative leadership and the crisis in the study of educational administration: Technical rationality and its aftermath. In P. W. Cookson, Jr. & B. Schneider (Eds.), *Transforming schools* (pp. 489-532). New York: Garland.

Cohn, M. M. (1992). How teachers perceive teaching: Change over the decades, 1964-1984. In A. Lieberman (Ed.), *The changing contexts of teaching* (pp. 110-137). Chicago: University of Chicago Press.

Cookson, P. W., Jr. (1994). *School choice, the struggle for the soul of American education* New Haven: Yale University Press.

Cookson, P. W., Jr. (1995a). The federal commitment to educational reform 1979-1993: From self-help to systemic reform in continuity and contradiction. In W. T. Pink & G. W. Noblit (Eds.), *The future of sociology of education* (pp. 239-254). New Jersey: Hampton Press.

Cookson, P. W., Jr. (1995b.) Goals 2000: Framework for the new educational federalism. *Teachers College Record, 96*(3), 405-417.

Cookson, P. W., Jr. (1996). There is no escape clause in the social contract: The case against educational vouchers. In J. Hanus & P. W. Cookson, Jr. (Eds.), *Choosing schools: Vouchers and American education.* Washington, DC: American University Press.

Cookson, P. W., Jr. & Persell, C. H. (1985). *Preparing for power: America's elite boarding schools.* New York: Basic Books.

Cookson, P. W., Jr. & Lucks, C. S. (1995). School choice in New York City: Preliminary observations. In M. Hallinan (Ed.), *Restructuring schools: Promising practices and policies* (pp. 99-110). New York: Plenum Press.

Council of the Great City Schools. (1995). *Urban legislator.* Washington, DC: Author.

Cremin, L. A. (1977). *Traditions of American education.* New York: Basic Books.

Darling-Hammond, L. & Snyder, J. (1992). Reforming accountability: Creating learner-centered schools. In A. Lieberman (Ed.), *The changing contexts of teaching* (pp. 11-36). Chicago: University of Chicago Press.

Foucault, M. (1988). The political technology of individuals. In L. Martin, H. Gutman, & P. Huttan (Eds.), *Technologies of the self: A seminar with Michel Foucault* (pp. 145-162). Amherst: University of Massachusetts Press.

Giroux, H. A. (1990). Rethinking the boundaries of educational discourse: Modernism, post modernism, and feminism. *College Literature, 17*(213), 1-50.

Goodson, I. F. (1992). On curriculum form: Notes toward a theory of curriculum. *Sociology of Education, 65*(1), 66-75.

Harrington, M. (1962). *The other America.* New York: Macmillan.

Henig, J. R. (1994). *Rethinking school choice: Limits of the market metaphor.* Princeton, NJ: Princeton University Press.

Hofstadter, R. (1964). *Anti-intellectualism in American life.* New York: Alfred A. Knopf.

Ignatief, M. (1995). On civil society. *Foreign Affairs* (March/April).

Johnson, J. & Immerwahr, J. (1994). *First things first — What Americans expect from the public schools.* New York, NY: Public Agenda.

Lardner, J. (1993). The declining middle. *New Yorker, 19*, 108-114.

Lieberman, A. (1992). *The changing contexts of teaching: Ninety-first yearbook of the National Society for the Study of Education.* Chicago, IL: University of Chicago Press.

Lieberman, M. (1993). *Public education: An autopsy.* Cambridge, MA: Harvard University Press.

Lindsay, D. (1995, January 11). Uncertainty over bankruptcy in California leaves schools dangling. *Education Week,* p. 8.

Lortie, D. (1975). *School teacher: A sociological study.* Chicago: University of Chicago Press.

Louis, K. S. (1992). Restructuring and the problem of teachers' work. In A. Lieberman (Ed.), *The changing context of teaching* (pp. 138-156). Chicago: University of Chicago Press.

New York State Education Department. (1991, November). *A new compact for learning: Improving public elementary, middle and secondary education results in the 1990s.* Albany, NY: University of the State of New York, State Education Department.

New York State Education Department (1994, February). *The state of learning — A report to the governor and the legislature on the educational status of the state's schools.* Albany, NY: University of the State of New York.

Parenti, M. (1995). *Democracy for the few*. New York: St. Martins Press.

Phillips, K. (1990). *The politics of rich and poor*. New York: Random House.

Pines, B. Y. with Lamar, T. W. (1994). *Out of focus: Network television and the American economy*. Washington DC: Regnery Publishing.

Popkewitz, T. S. (1991). *A political sociology of educational reform*. NY: Teachers College Press, Columbia University.

Postman, N. (1985). *Amusing ourselves to death: Public discourse in the age of show business*. New York: Penguin Books.

Powell, A. G., Farrar, E., & Cohen, D. K. (1985). *The shopping mall high school*. Boston: Houghton Mifflin.

Riley, R. W. (1995). Reflections on goals 2000. *Teachers College Record, 96*(3), 380-388.

Rosenberg, M. (1995, March 5). Schools relying on foundations. *The New York Times*, p. 1, section 13.

Sadovnik, A., Cookson, P. W., Jr., & Semel, S. (1994). *Exploring education*. New York: Allyn & Bacon.

Schmidt, B. C., Jr. (1994). *The Edison project – An invitation to public partnership: Executive summary*. New York: Author.

Shanker, A. (1995, February 15). Where we stand. *New York Times Week in Review*.

Shorris, E. (1994). *A nation of salesmen: The tyranny of the market and the subversion of culture*. New York: W. W. Norton and Co.

Smith, M. S. & Scoll, B. W. (1995). The Clinton Human Capital Agenda. *Teachers College Record, 96*(3), 389-404.

Spring, J. H. (1972). *Education and the rise of the corporate state*. Boston: Beacon Press.

United States Department of Education, Office of Educational Research and Improvement. (1993). *Digest of educational statistics*. Washington DC: Author.

Wigginton, E. (1988). *Sometimes a shining moment: The foxfire experience*. New York: Doubleday.

Yankelovich, D. (1994). *Three destructive trends: Can they be reversed?* Speech to the National Civic League's 100th National Conference On Governance. New York: Public Agenda.

Chapter 8: The Changing Social Context of Teaching in Western Europe

J.H.C. VONK
Instituut voor Didactiek en Onderwijspraktijk

INTRODUCTION AND CONCEPTUAL FRAMEWORK

Introduction

If one studies education documents that have been published by both the national governments and the various bodies of the European cooperation structures[1] during the last decades, it is easy to establish that the conditions for teaching are changing rapidly. Sometimes it seems that time is accelerating.

Not only the process of the unification of Europe (which has led to the European Union) but also the struggle to keep abreast of economic and industrial developments elsewhere in the world have had a fundamental influence on the changes that are taking place in European societies and their education systems in particular. Europe is no longer the cultural and industrial centre of this world. As a consequence, it has to redefine its place in this world: by reassessing the essence of its social and cultural heritage and values, by revaluing the aims and objectives of its education in perspective of the coming Information Society, and by regaining a proper balance between the aims and contents of education and the demands of the world of work.

Apart from this, the leading intellectual traditions (e.g., religion and social ideologies) have lost their socially directing influence in the current post-modern era, and together with them many educational ideals that had their basis in those traditions have been removed from active political agendas. The ideals that remain are more a matter of rhetoric than a concrete basis for political action.

In this chapter education systems are considered as open systems.[2] The relation between teaching, as it takes place in the context of education systems and their social contexts is rather complex, in particular in Europe where one is confronted with a variety of education systems and differing social contexts. Nearly every country has its own education system, its own culturally defined teaching tradition, and its own particular social context including differences in the relation between the state and in relations between the various other social institutions with respect to the education system. This diversity is a prominent

B.J. Biddle et al. (eds.), International Handbook of Teachers and Teaching, 985-1051
© *1997 Kluwer Academic Publishers, Printed in the Netherlands*

hallmark of education in Europe and has to be taken into consideration if one studies the process of the unification of Europe and its implications for teaching. As a consequence, it is impossible to go into much detail in this chapter, and, therefore, I will restrict myself to the analysis of some major trends. The rationale of this chapter is an analysis of current trends and how these trends affect both the shape, conditions, and content of teaching in current Western Europe (i.e., the European Union).

As a consequence of the developments mentioned above, the following issues have become the subject of continuous and intensive political debate: the education system, its role in society, its aims, its curricula, teaching methods, the role and position of teachers, and the structure of schools. Since 1945 the education systems seem to have been in a permanent state of reform in a growing number of European countries. The challenges Europe and its nations are facing originate from a number of developments in European societies which put high demands on their educational systems and as a consequence on their teaching force. Those developments include:

1. Changes in the world of schooling (Council of Europe, 1987b).

- The transition from elite education to education for all affects the basic aims of education (i.e., the change from becoming 'educated persons' – which was the traditional aim of education in continental Europe during the last century – into 'equipping pupils with basic skills which enable them to participate effectively in current society' resulting in the adoption of the comprehensive school).
- The extension of compulsory education, higher retention rates, increasing cultural diversity, changes in family structure, and the trend toward the integration of children with special needs into main-stream education – all result in a wider variety in the school population. This challenges teachers to apply differentiated teaching strategies and forces them to cope with educational and counselling problems.
- The introduction of new technologies at school will increasingly affect the teaching and learning process in ways no teacher can afford to ignore, and this will challenge teachers to develop different classroom management skills (moving from teacher-centred to more pupil-centred strategies).
- The opening up of the school to the outside world is another step forward in the development of broadened education for all. Different groups in society will try to reinforce their influence on education. As a consequence, teachers will be faced with a wide variety of expectations,

and the results of their work will increasingly become subject to conflicting judgments.

2. The technicalization of the world of work.

This results in a shift from the need for semi- and unskilled personnel to an extensive need for highly skilled personnel. Particularly in business, industry, and the services, the demand for engineers, technicians, liberal professions, and managers is expected to increase considerably, and the need for semi- and unskilled labour is expected to decrease. As a consequence, governments see a need to raise the general level of qualification and to reduce the numbers of early school leavers (drop-outs) by means of the renewal of the school curriculum regarding both content (i.e., new tracks should be developed and/or existing tracks be changed) and methods.

3. The technicalization and consequently the rationalization of the education sector.

This also has sweeping consequences for the conditions of teaching. This trend has gained momentum in mechanisms that are used to ensure that particular types of curricula will be implemented, monitored, and safeguarded at the direction of the (central) government. In practice this means a reduction of costs per student by increasing the efficiency of the system (for example, through reducing study time, introducing quality control systems for both student achievements and teaching staff, improving educational management, and increasing the scale of educational institutes in order to be able to use the available means more cost effectively). This process of technicalization can be referred to as 'the industrialization of education.' It tends to lead to an industrial way of producing educated people who are well prepared for entering the labour market, and in which input and output rates, standardization, efficiency, and economy are becoming the leading principles. In such an environment pupils become objects liable to a standardized process called 'education.' Teachers in turn tend to be regarded as technicians who execute a prescribed curriculum in a prescribed way. The latter development is emphasized by a new political jargon in which policy makers talk about 'educational workers' instead of teachers.

4. The growing governmental attention for value education.

In particular, where it concerns education on democracy, human rights, and tolerance. For example, during a session of the Standing Conference of European

Ministers of Education there was an in-depth discussion of the methods to be used to teach young people to fight for democratic values. Also on the national level there is increasing attention for value education.

5. The internationalization of education and training in Europe.

This means that individuals are no longer educated and trained to work exclusively in their own country; the future generation has to be prepared for work anywhere in Europe.

All European governments are convinced that meeting these challenges is a prerequisite to ensure the further development of Europe and its nations. In this context, there is increasing governmental attention for continuous improvement of the quality of education at all levels, particularly in being more adapted to working life, more effective, and more efficient.

This chapter is based on the study of recent reviews of developments in education, in particular those focusing on teaching, teachers, and their education (Lundgren, 1987, 1989; Naeve, 1987, 1991, 1992; Organisation for Economic Cooperation and Development [OECD], 1988a, 1990b, 1990c, 1991, 1992a, 1992c, 1993b, 1993c, 1995; Vonk, 1990, 1991, 1994, 1995), on overviews of the structures of educational systems in the various countries (Brock & Tulasiewicz, 1994; Buchberger, 1992; European Community, 1991; Vaniscotte, 1989), on data taken from recent national documents concerning education (e.g., OECD National Reviews), and, to the extent available, on journal articles which most often provide detailed critical discussions of governments' views as they are expressed in 'green' and 'white' papers.[3]

Relations Between Social Context and Teaching: A Conceptual Framework

The structure of contemporary societies is often referred to as being 'functionally differentiated' (i.e., it constitutes a social system consisting of a number of *relative autonomous* sectors or (sub)systems in the context of which specialized activities are taking place). *Autonomous*, because each (sub)system defines its own principles, logic, and procedures on the basis of which it functions. Modern system-theorists suggest that (sub)systems are self-referential (autopoietic) and closed at the operational level, and cannot be easily influenced by their environment (Teubner, 1993). (Sub)systems do not speak each other's languages. *Relative autonomous*, because each (sub)system remains dependent on the provisions of other (sub)systems. However, the process of influencing is not a direct one but rather the result of a more reflexive approach. Systems draw information from the constant flow of informational noise produced by their environment and process this information in their internal networks in accordance with their own principles, logic and procedures. However, each (sub)system has equal rights to maintain its own autonomy, which does not exclude that a certain (sub)system may dominate during a certain period.

To map out the relations between social context and teaching, first some basic concepts have to be clarified. In this chapter, *teaching* is defined as 'the constant flow of teacher actions[4] aimed at educating[5] pupils.' Teaching takes place in organized institutions called schools which are part of the education system. I regard every school as a separate entity with its own internal culture and rule-system (i.e., its own identity). The *education (sub)system* comprises the various types of schools, support structures, and local and national policy-making apparatus and administration (i.e., the ministry, the inspectorate, local authorities, and the like). This system also has its own internal culture, tradition, and rule-system. The relation between the school and education system can be characterized as hierarchical in nature, although the latter cannot fully prescribe what is to happen in schools but rather defines the operation space of schools. Within the context of that space, schools have a certain amount of autonomy. The same is true for the relation between the education system and its social context. The social context sets the boundaries for and gives direction to developments in the education system, but it does not fully determine the system.

In this chapter the education system is regarded as a relative autonomous and open system which is influenced by the environment in which it operates. This environment, or *social context*, which affects the developments in the education system, co-defines the conditions and the nature of teaching and puts social demands on the education system as a whole which may lead to changes or innovations in education. To map out the relation and influence of this social context to or on the education system, I distinguish between a number of *social forces*. Social forces are regarded as the result of developments in other sectors of society (e.g., changes in social beliefs and values, the economic state of affairs, demographic developments, developments in the social system, developments in science and technology, or political developments). Although social forces represent micro (local level) and macro (national or regional level) elements, they are largely determined by developments on a global scale which not only affect the various national societies but also European society as a whole. These forces are largely autonomous and can therefore hardly be controlled on the national or the European level. Educational politicians and their bureaucracy translate the demands made on the education system by its social context into educational aims, goals, and objectives which are subsequently implemented in curricula. At school level, management and teachers translate these curricula into concrete acts of teaching.

With respect to the changes in the social context, the education system as such functions as a filter for schools. However, the influence is not unilateral (i.e., top-down) but reflexive in nature. Regarding the pace and the nature of changes in the various elements of the social context, it can easily be observed that social forces are most open to change, whereas the school system – because of its culture and traditions – is more oriented to conservation, and finally that changes in society become noticeable in educational regulations only after a couple of years and that their implementation in teaching takes even more time.

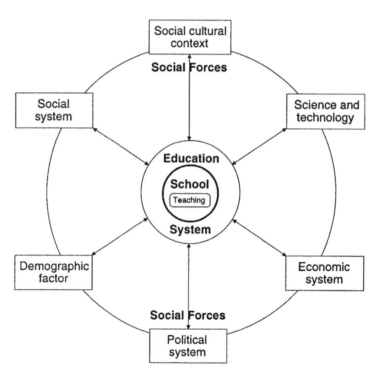

Figure 1: Factors in the social context of teaching

Since this chapter is aimed at creating insight into those relations and into the way changes in the social context affect teaching, I have developed a model (Figure 1) by which those relations will be described. It is a modification of the model originally developed by Idenburg (1971) for an in-depth analysis of Dutch educational policies. It is meant as a classification of materials available and is therefore heuristic in nature. The outer circle of social forces refers to the broader social context in which the education system is embedded. The inner circle represents the education system which, in turn, consists of the educational administration – national and local, the educational support structure, and the schools. The implementation of any change in any factor is largely culturally defined. Because social contexts and education systems in Europe are very diverse, I consider an education system to be the expression of a nation's culture. As a consequence, different nations may come up with different solutions for similar problems (Brock & Tulasiewicz, 1994, p. 5). The model is meant to picture relations between changes in the various areas of society (i.e., social forces and social institutions) and the education system. The arrows suggest reciprocity between the outer circle and the inner area. In order not to make the figure too complex, the arcs of the circle connecting the social forces should be read as bi-directional arrows which means that all factors are reciprocally related. The model, however, does not provide information about the intensity or the weight of these relations. I consider this to be beyond the scope of this chapter and will restrict myself to using it as a framework for description.

In this model the emphasis is on external relations. This might give the impression that what happens in the education system (i.e., in schools and in teaching) is mainly determined by external factors. However, the failure of many innovations during the last few decades has shown that existing structures with their own cultures and traditions are difficult to influence; indeed, sometimes they even seem to be change-resistant or at least tenacious. Consider for instance the existing experience and quality of the standing teaching force, school management, the existing curricula, teaching practices, the internal organization of the system with its own interests and modes of decision making, and the like. Apart from the many innovations that have only touched the surface of these social forms, many such innovations have been perceived as being 'radical' and have hardly met their aims, a judgment illustrated by Leschinsky and Mayer (1990) in their in-depth study, *The Comprehensive School Experiment Revisited: Evidence from Western Europe*. However, the conclusion that education systems are static in nature is not justified, although the different interests of the parties concerned make it a slow changing structure. This is not only true on the various national levels but also on the level of Europe as a whole.

In the next section of this chapter changes in various social forces and their impact on education in Europe are analysed, paying special attention to the situation in the Netherlands. In the section that follows, the impact of these changes on curriculum, teachers and teaching are analysed in more detail. Finally, in the last section some conclusions are drawn.

SOCIAL FORCES

At present Europe is at a stage of transition involving social, cultural, and economic changes. It is gradually moving from *modernity* to *post-modernity*, from an *industrial* to an *information* society, and most of its member states are changing from *welfare states* into *liberal market economies*. The effectiveness of Europe's economic principles – which have heretofore involved a moderate social market economy combined with an elaborate welfare system – is now strongly questioned, the value of its cultural heritage is an issue of discussion, and traditional norms and values are no longer shared by the masses but tend to become increasingly individualized. As expressed in various 'white' papers, for many governments economic concerns and concerns for international competitiveness lead to policies in which the development of economically effective individuals is strongly emphasized. More than before, children and young people in school may be seen as instruments for the promotion of the national economy rather than individuals whose growth potential as human beings should be developed in its own right (Eide, 1992, p. 12).

As a consequence of this shift, the role of education (including its aims and objectives) has to be redefined, and new perspectives have to be developed on the curriculum, teaching, and the role of teachers. At this moment the educational systems in Europe represent a mosaic. Although these systems and their practices differ on numerous points, it is wise to bear in mind that they are the result of centuries of parallel experiences. At times joint efforts have been made to provide educational responses to social, cultural, religious, political, and economic developments of a broadly comparable though asynchronous nature. This common European tradition can only be discovered in the broadly similar basic sequence and structure of schooling (from nursery to university education), the distinction between academic and vocational education, control of access, and the scope of school leaving certificates (Brock & Tulasiewicz, 1994, p. 5).

In this section I make a detailed analysis of the changes in the various social forces and the consequences thereof for education. Although developments in the various countries, illustrated in several tables, are taken as starting point, the aim of this section is to describe the general patterns of development in Europe. Therefore I do not discuss the impact of country specific problems – such as the high crime rate and the massive youth unemployment in Southern Italy or the unification of Germany and the like – on education in the various European countries.

The Social-Cultural Context of Teaching in Post-Modern Europe

Although most European societies are in transition from modern to post-modern societies, they still have major modernist traits. Modernist thinking involves the idea that 'To influence for better human condition' is the ultimate purpose of knowledge acquisition, and this implies the constant pursuit of the improvement of progress. Modernity is characterized by three aspects, as suggested in a recent *Social Studies Review* article (1990):

- *Economically*, modernity involves capitalist practices of a market economy. It involves the growth production for profit, wage labour as the principle form of employment, the development of industrial technology, and the extension of the division of labour.
- *Politically*, modernity involves the consolidation of the centralised nation state and the extension of bureaucratic forms of surveillance, and democratic political party system.
- *Culturally*, modernity involves a challenge to 'tradition' in the name of 'rationality' and a stress on the virtues of scientific and technical knowledge. (Jones, 1993, p. 21)

Modernist thinking is based on belief in the power of human reasoning which can be used to achieve progress and on the belief that *true* knowledge is not culture related. This way of thought produced shared values, theories, and 'basic' principles such as, Human Rights, Western type democracies as the ideal type of governance, scientific theories as representing *the* truth and *the* nature of reality (Van der Pot, 1985). The project of modernity declared Europe's culture with its mode of reasoning and its (secularized) Christian norms and values superior to all other cultures. At present, however, this superiority is being questioned at all levels (Carrithers, 1992; Lemaire, 1990; Lyotard, 1986). The consequence of the loss of concepts as universal values is that most values of European culture have become void and are replaced by individual values (Finkielkraut, 1987) which are highly influenced by the instant culture as is produced by the world of advertisement (Ellul, 1990).

For education this transition has far-reaching consequences. In modernist thinking, according to the famous French sociologist Emile Durkheim (1858-1917), the socialization or integration of individuals into the social structure is an important function of education because it helps them to develop common perceptions about the world and how to act in it. Social-cultural environments pass on to the next generation the stories, myths, ideologies, and rituals through which these perceptions are expressed, actualized, and revived. In this context the attribution of meaning to human actions and events is central and it creates a 'meaningful order' which has both a *guiding* and a *normative* aspect. A *guiding* aspect, in that it creates an orderly world, in which people can situate themselves and their vicissitudes, and which provides aims and guidance to human life (a world view). This is not only true for individual lives but also for the way people together structure society as a whole. A *normative* aspect, in that this meaningful order always provides directives for human and social actions. Apart from home education, formal education is expected to play an important part in this process. However, to fulfil this function, education (i.e., teachers, parents, and governing authorities) need a shared perspective of the society it serves which is only possible if that society has a clear perspective on itself. In post-war Europe this perspective is rather fragmented. Marxist, neo-marxist, social democratic, Christian democratic, neo-liberal, and neo-conservative world views have competed for dominance. Most of these world views have had (some) guiding influence either on the thinking of scholars and policy makers about education as a whole, or on their thinking about the function of education – elite versus mass education, a curriculum directed at personal development versus another designed to prepare economically effective individuals. In most countries where a socialist oriented world view dominated in the third quarter of this century, such as the Scandinavian countries, the U.K., the Netherlands, and, to some extent, Germany, comprehensive schools have become the norm. In many Western European countries, however, 'the reformers brimmed over with plans for enhancing compulsory education, reforming structures, content, evaluative processes, but there was little thought about the reason for this extended stage of education, save in materialistic and pragmatic terms' (Halls, 1994, p. 28).

In contrast, within contemporary post-modern individualistic society, the belief in such guiding principles is no longer self-evident. In his analysis of post-modern society Lyotard (1979) argues that nowadays the great narratives, myths, and ideologies (Les grands récits), that functioned as a universal touchstone for both the guiding and normative aspect, have lost their validity. A world in which such constructs could be put into practice directly and in a controllable way no longer exist. Our reality consists of a conglomerate of competing and contradictory forces and perspectives. In that context everybody creates his or her own interpretation of meaning, and the consequence of this fragmentation is that the sense of being part of a totality fades away.

The picture of the social systems in Western European countries is a fragmented one. It is made up of a collection of relative autonomous (sub)systems or sectors, which often compete for dominance. All actions within these (sub)systems are guided by their own ruling principles and logic. At first sight, universal coordinating principle(s) and logic, which function as a touchstone for the rules, logic, and principles of all the (sub)systems, no longer exist. In each (sub)system meaning is attributed to specific actions as they are related to the principles of the (sub)system in question (e.g., in the context of the economic sector, 'production' only has meaning as far as it is related to 'profit'; in the 'science and technology' sector, research only has meaning as far as it directed at finding 'scientific truth,' and technology aims for 'efficiency'; in the political sector, actions only have meaning as far as they aim for practicability. So, the outcomes of scientific research (scientific truth), as such, have little meaning for a politician. They have meaning for politicians insofar as they facilitate practicable policies.

However, a closer look at the way of thinking which is characteristic in the various sectors for planning, structuring its organization, decision making, and defining what is valuable knowledge and what not, leads to the conclusion that the principles of the technological domain are dominant. This way of thinking is often referred to as 'instrumental rationality,' 'functional rationality,' or 'goal oriented rationality.' As a consequence, the statement that the process of continuous differentiation and pluralization of society has made the principles which guided the attribution of meaning disappear has to be amended.[6] Nowadays, those guiding principles are in the hands of what I referred to as the 'instrumental rationality.' There is a strong emphasis on the means-objective orientation which stresses thinking in terms of usefulness, efficiency, and effectiveness. From this perspective, only usefulness can attribute meaning to objects, events, and phenomena.[7]

If one says that we live in a technological society, one is inclined to think of the great developments in science and technology, of the production of goods, of information processing and distribution, and the like. Ellul (1964) in his profound analysis of the technological society sees it in a broader context. He defines technique as 'the totality of methods rationally arrived at and having absolute efficiency (for a given state of development) in every field of human activity.' Technique is the translation into action of human concerns to master things by means of reason, to account for what is subconscious, make quantitative what is qualitative, make clear and precise the outlines of nature, take hold of chaos and put order into it (p. 43). Technique refers to any complex of standardized means for attaining a predetermined result. Thus it converts spontaneous and unreflective behaviour into behaviour that is deliberate and rationalized. Above all, the 'technical man' (or woman) is committed to the never ending search for 'the one best way' to achieve any designated objective. But when technique enters into every area of life (including human life), it ceases to be external to human beings and becomes their very substance. It is no longer face to face with them but is integrated with them and progressively absorbs them. Technical activity automatically eliminates every non-technical activity or transforms it into technical activity. What we are witnessing at present is the rearrangement of our world at an intermediate stage. This is not a change in the use of natural forces but in the application of 'technique' in all spheres of life. This transformation, so obvious in modern society, is the result of the fact that technique has become autonomous. Ellul distinguishes three important areas in modern techniques: economic techniques – ranging from the organization of labour to economical planning; organization techniques – referring to business and industry but also to the state, administration, and so forth; and techniques of which the human being himself is the object – ranging from medical techniques, genetic engineering to propaganda, education, and the like. Education was one of the last areas that still had to be colonized, and that is happening today in Western Europe as can be observed from the rationalization of both the curriculum and the school organization.

An increase in the extent of instrumental rationality as it is experienced today is inevitably accompanied by a decrease in 'substantial rationality' (i.e., the rationality in which the justification of purpose is fundamental – what are the purposes of production, economic growth, and making profit; what is the purpose of developing new knowledge; what is the rationale for the process of schooling?). Such questions, however, can only be answered from a broad perspective on society as a whole, in particular with respect to continuity in the history of human beings in the process of humanization. This, however, presupposes a shared idea about the 'meaning' of being. Ideas about the meaning of human existence and the aims of society have to be considered as human constructs, as they can be found in religion (transcendental) or in social ideologies. Halls (1994) observes that: 'today the institutions of (upper) secondary education function in an ethical void' (p. 29). Except in materialistic and pragmatic terms, most education reforms in Western Europe have hardly been guided by thoughts about the reason for the reforms concerned. Hannah Arendt (1993), in analysing the essence of the crisis in education, argues:

> The difficulty in modern education lies in the fact that, despite all the fashionable talk about new conservatism, even that minimum of conservation and the conserving attitude without which education is simply not possible is in our time extraordinarily hard to achieve. The crisis of authority in education is most closely connected with the crisis of tradition, that is with the crisis in our attitude toward the realm of the past. (p. 193)

However, according to Ellul (1990), it is the principle of *efficiency* that defines, independent of human choices or ethical values, how the system has to develop. In technical actions it is not the end that justifies the means, but the driving force behind the dynamics of modern society is efficiency. In this context Ellul argues that in technical developments it is always a matter of finding 'the best way,' and since technology cannot learn anything from the past it is only in looking forward that it makes progress. As a consequence, history and tradition are losing their meaning. One finds clear examples of this in France where there was a recent discussion on removing the systematic study of great French literature from the secondary school curriculum, and in the U.K. where proposals were launched to remove the study of Shakespeare from the comprehensive school curriculum. Such proposals fall under the heading of: What is the significance of this type of knowledge for ordinary people? Lemaire (1990), speaks of the 'barbarism of technocracy' (i.e., the ruling of technique with its unidirectional development of the 'area of means' and simultaneously its withdrawal from and impotence in the 'area of ends'). An explanation for all of this can be found in the profound influence of the continuing technologization of all aspects of human life on the meaning and use of 'knowledge' (Solway, 1989, pp. 71-85).

The late fifties in European history can be earmarked as the period of transition from the industrialized to the post-industrialized era, with the introduction of information technologies as its main characteristic. The pace of this transition differed considerably from country to country which makes it impossible to provide a condensed overview here. Nevertheless, both information and communication technologies have had a profound influence on the production of knowledge, on the definition what is valuable knowledge and what is not, and on the ways knowledge is used and distributed today (i.e., through research and the transmission of knowledge). What is highly valued in particular, is knowledge that enables people to control technical society. The OECD indicators of education systems confirm this conclusion. They show that of all respondents in the European Community (EC) countries who were asked to rate the importance of secondary school subjects, 86.4 per cent valued mother tongue 'essential' or 'very important,' 83.5 per cent mathematics, 81.3 per cent foreign languages, 70.2 per cent information technologies, and 62.2 per cent sciences. All other subjects scored at lower levels (Organisation for Economic Cooperation and Development, 1995).

The extensive introduction and normalization of computing machinery (PCs) and peripherals has also affected the nature of knowledge strongly, because knowledge can only make use of these new acquisitions and become operational if it can be translated into 'information units' (i.e., can be translated into languages that can be read by information processing apparatus). This means that knowledge now follows the logic of information technology (i.e., a set of directions or rules regarding the nature of statements which are accepted as being 'knowledge'). As a consequence, all traditional knowledge that cannot be translated into such units will henceforth be neglected, and all future knowledge development will be subject to the condition that its results can be translated into such units.

Related to this development, I observe that the relation between the 'knower' and 'knowledge' is changing radically. Knowledge becomes increasingly independent of persons, regardless of the knower's stage in the knowledge process. The traditional principles of obtaining knowledge, reflecting *The Enlightenment*, still underlie most of the contemporary European school systems. They are inextricably linked with the education of the mind and the person ('Bildung' in continental Europe, or the idea of the 'educated person' in the Anglophone countries). Nowadays they tend to become more and more outdated, for knowledge now increasingly exists separate from the individual human being. It has become depersonalised, and the mastery of manipulating knowledge has become more important than the acquisition of knowledge. Consequently, the new generation must be trained in cognitive strategies to access knowledge as it is stored in knowledge databases, problem solving strategies, and communication approaches, rather than in acquiring a breadth and depth of knowledge itself.

The production of knowledge has become an industrial process in which consumers and producers perceive knowledge as merchandise. Knowledge is increasingly produced to be sold and consumed. A good example of this development is the concept of the 'Entrepreneurial University' which is quite popular amongst politicians and managers in the U.K. and the Netherlands. Resulting from the commercialization of knowledge, its production has increased steadily. Although every ten years the total amount of knowledge doubles, new knowledge tends to become obsolete very quickly, in particular in areas such as information technology. This development makes the traditional approaches to knowledge acquisition inappropriate for education today. If I go back to one basis of modernist thinking – 'To influence for better human condition' – it becomes obvious that one can no longer argue that at present progress is determined by an economic or a social condition, or education, or any other human factor. Essentially the preceding technical situation alone is determinative (Ellul, 1964, p. 90). However, in post-industrial Europe, the production of knowledge has become an important economic power, and the extent to which Europe will be able to play a role in the world depends on its success in producing marketable knowledge.

The Impact of Changes in the Social System on Education

Many aspects in social life are subject to change in Western European countries. The most obvious developments which have strong implications for education are changes in traditional family life, the disintegration of a centrally organised social support and welfare system, and the change from a mono-cultural to a multi-cultural society.

Changes in family and community life.

It is easy to see that the relation of the individual to society has become unstable in contemporary society. This becomes apparent if one takes a closer look at the dissolution of the influence of the socio-cultural environment – the family, community life in villages and neighbourhoods, the school and the church – on individuals in general and the younger generation in particular. This influence has been strongly reduced over the last three decades. Within families, for instance, the continuity in the transfer of ideas, norms, and values has greatly decreased as a consequence of evolving individualization. However, individuals not only wish to safeguard their material existence, they also want to experience 'meaning' in their lives. This has become even more complex because their participation in a number of (sub)systems is of a temporary nature, which confronts them with competing interests, principles, values and the like. Because of the absence of a generally accepted system for attributing meaning, individuals themselves have to integrate those competing principles and values, they are expected to function according to their own private principles. All this makes it difficult for the younger generation to develop a stable identity. In this I agree with Maslow (1970) when he argues that a feeling of security, the feeling of being part of a greater more or less stable community, is a basic need for identity development. In addition, increasing individualization makes experiences of 'community' rare. As a result of the dissolution of social coherence, one can observe in some groups of youngsters the development of a so-called 'instant identity' (i.e., an identity that is strongly determined by superficial phenomena such as fashion and dress, which interferes with the development of long lasting social commitments).

The weakening of a meaningful order with its guiding and normative functions has tremendous implications – positive and negative – for both the individual lives of people as well as for the development of society as a whole. A positive aspect is that the social differentiation and pluralization has resulted in more opportunities for individual development, a greater freedom to choose, more equal opportunities for all, a greater social and political awareness, and the like. A negative side of this development is that through the great variety of options about how to give shape to one's own life, individuals are increasingly confronted with the contingency of life; every choice made could also have been another one, and one never knows whether the alternate choice would have been better or whether the choice made is the wrong one. Because of the decreasing influence of the existing regulating powers (religion, ideologies) in contemporary Western European societies to which failures could be attributed, every individual has to face his or her own failures and to take responsibility for them. This makes high demands on individuals.

Changes in family life, such as the steady increase of single-parent families, are clear examples of how changes in the social structure result in the disintegration of the traditional support networks for children. At present, single-parent families constitute 10 to 15 per cent of all families in the European OECD countries. (Exceptions should be noted for Spain and Ireland with percentages under ten – see Organisation for Economic Cooperation and Development, 1990a). One may expect an increase in the numbers of single-parent families in the coming decades. Combined with the expectation that the participation of women in working life will increase, this development will have far-reaching consequences for the emotional and learning environment of children. It places important responsibilities on pre-schooling and primary schools with respect to child-care and socialization. As a consequence, in view of the more varied and complex configurations that typify modern social life, the more traditional views of families and the community as support structures have to be revised. It has become obvious that education can no longer rely on traditionally power-ful socialization agents such as family and the community. As a result, schools are left holding the baby, when it comes to child-care, socialization, and welfare (Organisation for Economic Cooperation and Development, 1990d, chapter 5). This marks a radical departure from traditional views of education.

From a welfare state to a market driven economy.

The economic decline which started in the late seventies resulted in intensive criticism of the fundamentals of the European welfare state which had devel-oped on the basis of the unwritten post-war social contract. The criticism ranged from the height of the unemployment benefit, child allowance, and disability pensions, to the extent of governments' financial responsibilities for post-com-pulsory education. So many people depended on the welfare state that, econom-ically speaking, the financial burden became too heavy for most states. As a consequence, the tenor of political debate changed. The European model of the welfare state was declared no longer able to fulfil its social function as safety net; on the contrary, it was argued that because people could make use of it so easily, they were no longer stimulated to achieve and thus impeded economic growth. Where previously social need had begun to establish its own impera-tives against the laws of the market-forces, now matters of 'value for money,' the private right to dispose one's own wealth, and the equation of freedom and the free-market became the terms of the trade. Margaret Thatcher, former Prime Minister of the U.K., is often regarded as the personification of this critical movement.

Not only in political debate are market values stressed, but they appear also in everyday thought and language as the birth of the 'calculating citizen.' As a result, a redefinition of values can be observed; the aura that used to be attached to the value of public welfare (i.e., the common good) has been replaced by an-ything that is private or can be privatized (Apple, 1989). It may seem paradox-ical that, on the one hand, societies should acknowledge the critical importance of developing human resources to their fullest potential and, on the other, to oblige education to seek other than public funds as though it were operating in the market place. Nevertheless, the market orientation is real and for the time being seemingly irreversible, notably at post-secondary level (Lowe, 1992, p. 585). In the course of the eighties and the early nineties, many governments de-veloped a conservative (i.e., more market-oriented) philosophy of governance in which individualization, decentralization, rationalization and cost effectiveness were the central issues. At the labour market level in the Netherlands and the U.K., for example, this has resulted in a shift from permanent appointments to contracts for a limited number of years, and this has generated an increase in the use of temporary employees.

This way of thinking also affected the mode of governance in education, in that the concept of decentralization came under discussion, procedures were developed to safeguard quality in education, and ideas for teacher assessment were launched. For students this development has three consequences. First, some countries are gradually discontinuing the centrally organised granting system for post-compulsory education. The result is that those who profit will have to pay (known as 'the direct benefit principle'). If they cannot afford the resulting fees, they can borrow money from the state at regular market interest. Second, in a number of countries, such as the Netherlands and the U.K., study time has been reduced for all tertiary studies (university and non-university higher education) from five years of study to four years, and a further reduction is under discussion. Third, a number of countries have implemented a stricter study-progress control system in order to keep students on study track. Besides, the social relevance of a number of topics for study (i.e., their relation to the labour market) is more often questioned; as a consequence, access to those topics that are deemed to have little social relevance in the contemporary societies may be limited. All in all, this means that the principle of 'Education for all' as it was implemented during the sixties and the seventies – i.e., one should have the opportunity to study whatever one wished, provided that one had appropriate abilities – is under fire, and a new definition of education is emerging. Recent discussions on what falls under the financial duties of the state with respect to education tend in the direction of providing a free, basic, compulsory education which prepares for participation in future society, whereas those who wish to study further will have to make a substantial financial contribution. Access to education will remain guaranteed, but the user will have to invest in his or her own further development.

With respect to teachers, the consequences are sweeping. The 1991 conference on 'The Teaching Profession' (European Commission, 1991) focused on quality in teaching, on teachers' careers, and on the system of permanent appointments. In a number of countries the first issue started or intensified the discussion on teaching as a profession, teachers' professional profile, teacher task profiles, accountability, and assessment. The second issue is related to these trends; since most teachers in Europe have a permanent appointment (civil servant or an equal position) and cannot now make a career in teaching, there are few instruments to correct those who perform poorly or frustrate the implementation of innovations. Many governments consider this an obstacle for quality improvement in education. As a consequence, the position of teachers is under discussion in a number of countries, and one may expect this to be but a first step in the redefinition of their position in a European context.

From a mono-cultural to a multi-cultural society.

A second change in the social structures of many European countries which affects education concerns the changing composition of the population. The influx of citizens from former colonies as a result of the decolonization process together with a considerable influx of migrant labourers from Turkey and Northern Africa have, in combination with the free movement of labour, coloured most societies. The first group, in general familiar with the culture and the language of the country, was expected to stay permanently, whereas the second group of people were considered temporary labourers who would go back to their home countries when their contracts expired. For that reason, little attention was paid to the education of the second group. However, many migrant labourers stayed permanently and brought their families to Western Europe after some time. As a consequence, a general lack of language skills in this group can be observed which leads to problems with participating in the societies effected. Amongst politicians in Europe, however, awareness is growing that Europe only has a future if it changes from a mono-cultural to a multi-cultural society. In a multi-cultural society ethnicity does not determine access to and participation in the rights and responsibility of that society. Multi-culturalism is aimed at creating a nation rich in diversity, with citizens who are able and willing to contribute to the common good (Leurin, 1989).

Table 1
Percentages of 9 year-old and 14 year-old pupils for whom school language and home language are the same and of those who speak an other language at home

		B*	DK	SF	F	D	GR	IRL	I	NL	N	P	E	S
9 year-olds	Other	11	5	1	9	10	6	3	27	12	4	3	13	9
	School	89	95	99	91	90	94	97	73	88	96	97	87	91
14 year-olds	Other	9	2	1	4	8	3	1	26	9	2	2	11	5
	School	91	98	99	96	92	97	99	74	91	98	98	89	95

Source: *Education at a Glance* (OECD, 1993b, p.42)

*B=Belgium (French Community); DK=Denmark; SF=Finland; F=France; D=Germany; GR=Greece; IRL=Ireland; I=Italy; NL=Netherlands; N=Norway; P=Portugal; E=Spain; S=Sweden. In Finland schools with Swedish as communication language are not included, in Belgium (French speaking community) not the Flemish and German speaking schools; in Italy no clear distinction is made between Italian and the variety of dialects, and in Spain the autonomous areas have their own language (Bask, Catelan, and the like).

Education plays an important part in the realization of these goals (i.e., in language acquisition, in creating multi-cultural understanding, in the promotion of equal opportunities, and the like). To gain some insight into the problems education is facing with respect to languages, I cite a report from 1991 on Home and School language in the EU-countries (Table I). The results of this table are based on the opinions of the pupils about their language situation. It is well-known that in situations where school language and home language differ, difficulties in learning at school can occur. Countries with a high presence of migrant populations, such as B*, F, D, NL, and S, have pupils with a variety of mother tongues. To tackle that problem different approaches are used ranging from special language training programmes to instruction in both the mother tongue and the main language of instruction in the school.

Nevertheless, in spite of all efforts to cope with multi-culturalism and all policies to fight the segregation of the non-native citizens, concentrations of ethnic groups can be found within or close to the bigger cities and industrial centres of many countries. As a consequence, the urban areas in Western Europe are becoming increasingly multi-cultural. Think of the Kreuzberg quarter in Berlin, or the northern suburbs of Paris, or the prognosis for Amsterdam that about 70 per cent of the school population will be non-native in 2005. The ensuing confrontation with this variety of cultural backgrounds and mother tongues makes heavy demands on education systems and on teachers and the curriculum in particular (Organisation for Economic Cooperation and Development/CERI, 1989; Organisation for Economic Cooperation and Development, 1987). In such contexts two types of schools tend to develop, white and coloured schools. The coloured schools are designed for non-native pupils, many of whom have language deficiencies, lower achievements in other subjects, and as a consequence, less chances on the labour market. Nowadays, the urban school population in most European countries is not only characterized by an increasingly diverse ethnic and linguistic background, but also by pupils who, in increasing numbers, come to school with many other physical, emotional, and social problems which cause them to be far from ready to learn. Although pupils with these type of problems have always been a challenge to teachers – in that they need highly personalized and individualized attention, emotional sustenance, and often specialized learning tasks – some of the problems teachers are confronted with today are so new that they have yet to be described, much less diagnosed for possible solutions. For this and other reasons, many schools in urban areas have not been able to stem the rising tide of dropouts, many leaving at earlier ages (Lieberman, 1992, p. 3).

Implications for education.

The developments as outlined above have strong implications for schools, teachers, and teaching. First, progressive individualization, the weakening of the influence of family education on the development of generally accepted norms and values, and the increasing multi-cultural composition of the school population place heavy burdens on teachers with respect to their educational tasks. It is no longer self-evident that pupils and their families regard the school as the place where the new generation is prepared for future life. Many pupils see school rather as a social environment where they meet their peers, and teachers are expected to create a pleasant and entertaining learning climate which does not put too heavy a burden on their shoulders. For many pupils real life starts after school; they want to have time for a part-time job so they can earn money for the things that are important to them. The reducing impact of social environments has as its consequence that pupils have to develop their own values, standards, and perspective on their lives. Schools and teachers are confronted with these phenomena and are expected to deal with them. More and more schools have to take over tasks which formerly belonged to the area of family education. This becomes apparent if one looks at the outcomes of the OECD investigations with respect to the 'importance of qualities/aptitudes' to be developed and 'priorities in school practice' in secondary education. With respect to the development of qualities/aptitudes, 'self-confidence' was scored *essential* or *very important* by 88.3 per cent of respondents, 'how to live with people from different backgrounds' was so scored by 81.2 per cent, 'a lifestyle which promotes good health' earned 75 per cent, while 'being a good citizen' achieved 73.9 per cent. With respect to indicators for 'priorities in school practice,' 'helping with learning difficulties' is regarded as 'essential' or 'very important' for practices in schools in order to achieve their goals by 86.5 per cent of the general public in Europe (Organisation for Economic Cooperation and Development, 1995). Next to that, most European governments have great concerns about the fading away of public morale in general, and of the impact of ideas which are basic to the European democracies, such as equality, solidarity, tolerance, and respect for being different and cultural differences, in particular (Vonk, 1993, p. 156).

Science, Technology and Education

In all fields of contemporary society the effects of the developments in science and technology are palpable. As a consequence of the continuing rationalization (e.g., automatization and robotization) at all levels of human labour, everyday working life has changed drastically. Whereas agriculture and industrial labour were the main types of labour in the industrial era, the service industry is today. In many countries about 70 per cent of the labour force is working in the service field. However, the excessive automatization of this industry – from banking and insurance companies to the whole recreation industry – results in an increase in unemployment on the one hand and is expected to create new jobs on the other. It is questionable whether the number of new jobs will be sufficient (Kennedy, 1994). The job question is one of the issues most young people are very concerned about, and which to a large extent determines their motivation, in particular for pupils from a socially deprived background and those from minority groups. But it even determines the motivation of students in secondary and higher education. If one takes a look at youth unemployment in the European Union (state of affairs, 1992), one sees that among the age group 15-24 years of age, on average 8.2 per cent was unemployed, Italy and Spain were extremes with over 14 per cent, and Germany, Luxembourg, and Austria were under 5 per cent. An average of 53 per cent had a job, either full-time or part-time, with as extremes Denmark, the U.K. and Sweden with over 68 per cent, and France and Belgium with less than 40 per cent (Organisation for Economic Cooperation and Development, 1995, p. 42). One has to apply these figures with caution because school leaving ages differ in the various countries, but nevertheless they give a good impression of the current situation. In contrast with the students of the sixties who went for further education and who, whatever they studied, knew themselves assured of a lifelong job afterwards, it is difficult today to select a study that more or less guarantees a job afterwards, and if one has selected a particular study it often does not prepare well for functioning in contemporary society.

Until recently, developments in science and technology had, in contrast with the changes in society at large, little impact on teachers and teaching apart from changes in the school curriculum. In spite of sweeping reforms in education during the last decades, teaching in many schools is still rather traditional. In his review of research on (teacher) education in Germany, Klinzing (1990) concludes: '... the knowledge obtained from research has very little impact on the organization and content of (teacher) education' (p. 99). This conclusion was endorsed by the chairman of the conference on the 'Teaching Profession in Europe' (European Commission, 1991), the then minister of education of the Netherlands. Unfortunately, apart from equality and gender issues, the same seems to be more or less true for education at large and for teaching in particular. At present, most educational research is devoted to enhance the efficiency of the various systems (i.e., the search for the effective school). In contrast with the U.S., within most European countries the impact of research generated knowledge on teachers' every day life is rather limited. However, in most countries the development of the comprehensive school has led to extensive curriculum research, which involved developmental studies by nature. This research was mainly executed by institutes for curriculum development which have been established and subsidized by the government.

In contrast, people are gradually becoming aware of the need to prepare the new generation for the 'Information Society' – totally different from the contemporary post-industrial society – which requires a radically different way of thinking about the curriculum, the school as central learning organization, teaching, and teachers' role in education. The European Commission's white paper on 'Growth, Competitiveness, Employment' gives a good idea of the new demands made on the coming generation by the Information Society (Eraut, 1989).

> The basic skills which are essential for integration into society and working life include a mastery of basic knowledge … and skills of a technological and social nature, that is to say, the ability to develop and act in a complex and highly technological environment, characterized, in particular, by the importance of information technologies; the ability to communicate, make contacts and organize etcetera. These skills include, in particular, the fundamental ability to acquire new knowledge and new skills – 'to learn how to learn' throughout one's life. People's careers will develop on the basis of the progressive extension of skills. (European Commission, 1995, p. I)

To implement these new demands will surely be a *major* challenge for the schools in Europe.

Apart from that, in the context of enhancing the efficiency of teaching, one may expect a greater role for computers in education. Everything that can be learned with the help of a computer will be automated. This refers in particular to elements in a teacher's job that are routine activities (i.e., pupil learning activities aimed at acquiring algorithmic knowledge, such as basic language skills, fact learning, basic calculus skills, and the like; as well as teacher activities aimed at monitoring and registering pupil progress, etc.). That this is not yet the case has mainly to do with three facts: first, software industries can more easily earn a lot of money with office software; second, cooperation between software developers and education specialists has been rare; and third, a considerable number of the current teaching staff is still computer illiterate and do not believe that a lot of their teaching and monitoring tasks can be carried out more effectively and more efficiently with the assistance of computers. Apart from that, up until now most education programmes have been either amateurish or too inflexible to meet the learning needs of pupils. Besides, only few schools have the proper equipment and space for computer facilities. Nevertheless, a number of good education programmes exist, and the majority of pupils like to use them. The introduction of graphic interfaces, high speed computers at a reasonable price, network facilities, CD-Roms, and multi-media approaches have created completely new opportunities for education software with which interactive learning can become possible.

However, the development of adequate software that offers a variety of opportunities for learning requires a solid cooperation between software developers, curriculum designers, and teachers. The participation of this last group is particularly important because all innovations in the use of computers will fail unless teachers are convinced that such innovations are worthwhile. Their judgement is based on whether they have a feeling of ownership and commitment, whether they are convinced that the innovation will help pupils to make progress, and that it will decrease their workload (Fullan, 1991). Although education is just on the brink of the era of the computerization of a number of teacher tasks, one may expect the computer to play an important role in pupils' learning at school in the decades ahead.

Another development in the education arena has to do with education outside the school. As technology becomes more complex and conditions of work change, so the functions of schooling, training, and education move beyond the traditional formal structures as developed in the various countries. Access to knowledge is no longer limited to schools or universities as one finds in 'Open Learning,' distance learning, company classrooms, and knowledge networks which are accessible through the mass media (Naeve, 1991, p. 1). Rapid changing job contents require life long learning for all. In such learning, mainly directed at adults, networking and video conferencing will play an important role, as is already the case in Norway, Sweden, and Finland where people in remote areas – sometimes 1,000 kilometres from the education institute – are taught interactively by systems based on a combination of video and computer. Although it is still true that all initial education and training aimed at developing the basic skills which largely determine an individual's access to further knowledge is mainly imparted in systems of formal schooling, it is not unthinkable that the role of 'the place called school' will change radically in the near future as a consequence of developments in the information and communication technology.

Some Facts About Pupil and Teacher Demography

In this section I discuss two important demographic developments that strongly affect teaching conditions: first, the evolution of births which determines the size of the school population; and second, the evolution of supply and demand of teachers, and in particular the influence of the greying of the profession.

Evolutions in the size of the school population.

As Table 2 indicates, the evolution of birthrates reveals a clear dichotomy between Northern and Southern European countries. All countries marked with an
asterisk in the table have shown an increase since 1985 after a steady decrease
in births between 1960 and 1985, while in all other countries the number of
births is still declining. Nevertheless, if one takes the whole 1965-1990 period
into consideration, it becomes obvious that, apart from Sweden, a significant
fall in births can be observed.

Table 2
Evolution of births in Western Europe 1960-1990 (in 1000s)

Country	1960	1965	1970	1975	1980	1985	1990	% change 1960-1990
Austria	126	130	112	94	91	87	90	- 28
Belgium*	156	155	141	119	125	114	124	- 20
Denmark*	76	86	71	72	57	54	63	- 17
Finland*	82	78	65	66	63	63	66	- 20
France	816	862	850	745	800	768	762	- 6
Germany*	969	1.044	811	601	621	813	905	- 6
Greece	157	151	145	142	148	116	102	- 35
Ireland	61	63	64	68	74	62	53	- 13
Italy	923	1.108	917	842	658	577	554	- 39
Luxembourg*	50	53	44	40	42	41	49	- 2
Netherlands*	239	245	239	178	181	178	198	- 17
Norway*	62	66	65	56	51	51	61	- 2
Portugal	214	210	181	180	161	130	116	- 45
Spain	655	668	656	669	566	456	401	- 38
Sweden*	102	123	110	104	97	98	124	+ 21
United Kingdom*	918	997	904	698	754	750	798	- 13

Source: Eurostat, *Demographic Statistics 1993*

Table 3 gives a closer analysis of the evolution of the school population in various age groups (i.e., primary education, junior and senior secondary education). If one considers the developments in the compulsory school age
population, one can learn from Table 3 that the age group 5-9 year olds showed
a sharp increase in all European countries between 1960 and 1970 except for
Greece. From 1970 until 1990 this was followed by a general decrease. (Only
Germany shows a deviating pattern.) For junior secondary education the picture
is about the same, albeit most things happen ten years later (i.e., an overall
growth pattern until 1980 followed by a decrease in the 1980-1990 period). If
one now takes a look at Table 4 with prognoses for the compulsory school age
population based on the birthrates estimations made by the United Nations, it is
easy to observe a slightly different picture for the decades ahead. One may expect a considerable increase in the primary school population in Denmark, the
Netherlands, Norway, and Sweden from 1990 onwards; a moderate increase in
Luxembourg and the U.K.; a certain stabilization in Austria, Belgium, Finland,
France, and Germany; while in Greece, Ireland, Italy, Portugal, and Spain the
decrease will continue until the year 2000.

Table 3
Numbers of young people (in hundred thousands) in the various age-groups in the EU 1960-1990

Country	Age-group 5-9				Age-group 10-14				Age-group 15-19			
	1960	1970	1980	1990	1960	1970	1980	1990	1960	1970	1980	1990
Austria	4.8	6.4	5.0	4.6	5.0	5.7	6.1	4.5	5.9	4.8	6.5	5.2
Belgium	7.1	7.9	6.4	6.0	6.9	7.7	7.2	6.1	5.4	7.3	7.9	6.5
Denmark	3.7	3.9	3.6	2.7	4.2	3.7	3.9	3.1	3.8	3.7	4.0	3.7
Finland	4.4	3.8	3.0	3.2	4.9	4.0	3.5	3.2	3.7	4.3	3.8	3.0
France	40.1	42.6	41.1	38.5	40.3	41.7	41.7	37.8	27.8	41.6	42.9	42.2
Germany	38.3	49.9	33.9	42.9	34.8	43.5	48.7	41.5	39.0	40.0	52.2	43.7
Greece	7.1	7.0	7.0	6.5	7.2	7.1	7.8	7.2	6.3	6.6	7.2	7.0
Ireland	2.9	3.1	3.5	3.2	2.9	2.9	3.9	3.5	2.3	2.8	3.2	3.4
Italy	40.3	45.5	43.2	30.2	43.0	40.8	45.7	35.4	38.1	38.6	45.8	43.7
Luxembourg	--	0.2*	0.2	0.2	--	0.3*	0.3	0.2	--	0.3*	0.3	0.2
Netherlands	11.0	12.1	10.5	8.9	11.7	11.6	12.2	9.0	9.1	11.1	12.5	10.5
Norway	3.0	3.1	3.1	2.6	3.2	3.1	3.3	2.6	2.6	3.1	3.1	3.1
Portugal	8.5	--	8.3	6.9	8.3	--	8.6	7.9	7.5	--	8.4	8.2
Spain	26.9	31.7	32.7	24.2	26.2	30.2	32.3	30.5	24.1	26.9	31.8	32.8
Sweden	5.4	5.6	5.6	4.9	6.2	5.3	5.8	4.9	5.7	5.5	5.7	5.6
United Kingdom	38.0	46.8	38.9	36.6	42.6	41.1	45.3	34.6	35.7	38.5	47.0	38.2

Source: Eurostat, *Demographic Statistics 1993*
* =1974

For the decade immediately ahead it is easy to learn from Table 4 that the school population for junior secondary education will continue to decrease in Greece, Ireland, Italy, Portugal, and Spain (with the latter as the extreme with a decrease of 36 per cent); stabilize in Belgium and France; increase slightly in Austria and Denmark; while a considerable increase will take place in Germany, Luxembourg, the Netherlands, Norway, and Sweden (with the latter as the extreme with an increase of 24 per cent). Finally, it is easy to conclude that a dichotomy exists between the developments in Southern and Northern Europe, which may have serious consequences for the recruitment of teachers.

Table 4
Prognoses for the developments in the compulsory school age population between 1990 - 2005 (in percentages)
(based on the 'medium variant', 1990 = 100%)

Country		5-9 year olds			10-14 year olds		
	1990	1995	2000	2005	1995	2000	2005
Austria	100	98	100	99	107	104	106
Belgium	100	100	100	98	98	98	98
Denmark	100	108	119	122	84	89	100
Finland	100	95	97	99	100	94	97
France	100	98	99	98	99	98	99
Germany	100	103	102	102	112	113	112
Greece	100	80	76	77	97	78	74
Ireland	100	84	73	73	96	81	71
Italy	100	91	92	96	80	73	73
Luxembourg	100	105	109	109	105	111	115
Netherlands	100	105	119	128	99	102	116
Norway	100	108	124	132	97	105	120
Portugal	100	84	82	84	87	74	71
Spain	100	85	85	89	80	68	68
Sweden	100	114	126	131	98	111	122
United Kingdom	100	105	108	106	107	113	116

Source: United Nations, *World Population Prospects: The 1992 Revision*

In a number of Northern European countries (e.g., Denmark, the Netherlands, Norway, and Sweden) the demand for primary school teachers will increase in the decade ahead, in part because large numbers of primary school teachers will retire in that decade, while in Southern European countries an oversupply of teachers will develop. The same increase in demand will exist for Junior Secondary in Germany, Luxembourg, the Netherlands, Norway, Sweden, and the U.K., while an oversupply may be predicted for Ireland, Italy, Portugal, and Spain.

Teacher supply and demand.

A second issue that has become an urgent matter for the profession is that of teacher supply and demand. Due to the demographic decline which became visible in the late seventies (see Table 5), primary school enrolment decreased by 20 per cent – and junior secondary school enrolment by 10 per cent – between 1975 and 1985 whereas in the same period senior secondary school enrolment increased by 20 per cent. The general demand for extra teachers during the sixties and early seventies turned into a surplus in a few years – a trend which started in primary education and now affects the universities.

Table 5
Evolution of the number of full-time primary and secondary school teachers in the countries of the EU 1975-1991 (numbers of 1975/76=100%)

Country	Primary School Teachers				Secondary School Teachers			
	1975/76	1979/80	1985/86	1989/90	1975/76	1979/80	1985/86	1991/92
	in 000s	perc.	perc.	perc.	in 000s	perc.	perc.	perc.
Denmark*	37	117.1	125.1	106.5	6	119.6	141.1[e]	.
France	258	110.7[c]	116.6	86.4	225	121.7[c]	134.4	155.1
Germany	240	101.1	91.5	59.7	232	118.0	126.4	151.5
Greece	33[b]	115.5	127.1	143.9	21	138.0	177.9	276.6
Ireland	13	110.7	124.9	90.6	15	116.6	127.8	130.6
Italy	255	107.9	111.6	100.8	400	118.8[d]	121.3	-
Luxembourg	2[b]	112.5	--	--	2	93.3[c]	107.0	135.0
Netherlands	60	107.7	--	97.01	80	127.5	--	113.1
Portugal	33[a]	--	127.4[f]	--	26[a]	144.5[d]	147.7[f]	-
Spain	169	109.0	114.6	69.2	77	127.1	163.4	-
United Kingdom	261	91.3[d]	81.0	84.8	264	106.6[d]	101.4	118.6

Sources: Eurostat: Demographic Statistics, 1993**; Key data on education in the EU (1995) for the 1991/92 data

a=1973/74; b=1976/77; c=1977/78; d=1980/81; e=1983/84; f=1984/85
* Including the Folkskola (lower secondary).
** This survey did not include data from Austria, Belgium, Finland , Norway and Sweden.

Because many of the teachers who were appointed in massive numbers during the educational boost of the sixties and early seventies are still in service, the age structure of the profession is a matter of concern for all European countries (Neave, 1992). In this respect two issues are of importance. First, the demographic decline resulted in a considerable surplus of teachers for a large number of school subjects resulting in few new entrances into the profession. Second, because of the legal status of teachers in most countries – civil servant or a similar status, combined with the principle of 'first in last out,' the age group 35-45 is now over-represented in many countries (see Table 6), while the age group under thirty is under-represented, so that the governments in Northern Europe will face the problem of an ageing profession in the coming decade. In the Netherlands, for example, the average age of the teaching force in secondary education is about 46 years, augmenting by one year every year, whereas one can hardly find an active teacher of over 55 years of age (Organisation for Economic Cooperation and Development, 1995, pp. 194-196).

Table 6
The age distribution of teachers: The proportion over 40 or 45 Years

Country	Year	Primary Ed.	Junior Sec. Ed.	Senior Sec. Ed.	Vocational Ed.
Austria*	88/89	28.0		34.8	52.7
Denmark	89/90	44.0		43.0	--
Finland	89	52.0		65.0	32.0
France	88/89	29.9	31.8		--
Germany	89	43.1			39.4
Greece	86/87	27.2	17.7		--
Ireland	87	28.9	27.9		29.2
Luxembourg	88	32.1	12.9		--
Netherlands	90	20.0	31.6		38.0
Norway*	88	42.0		67.0	--
Portugal	86/87	24.7			--
Spain	89/90	54.0		23.0	23.0
Sweden*	89	71.0		82.0	--
United Kingdom	86/87	38.2	28.1		--

Source: OECD, 1992a**

*   Countries marked with an * have adopted an age classification with 40 instead of 45.
**   This survey did not include data from Belgium and Italy.

Many national governments met these issues by restricting access to the profession; i.e., by closing down colleges of education and/or limiting the number of entrances (e.g., in the Netherlands no more than 1,000 new teachers for senior secondary level may be educated, each year, for all subjects). All of this, enhanced by decreasing salaries in some countries, makes the teaching profession unattractive to the new generation. Another problem may appear in the near future in that many tenured teachers will simultaneously leave the profession, which may result in recruitment problems. At present, a number of countries have reached a balance between supply and demand (e.g., Denmark and Ireland), while other countries face a teacher shortage only in a number of subjects, in particular mathematics, economics, and the sciences (e.g., Belgium, The Netherlands, the Scandinavian countries, and Germany). In the long term, all countries will face the problems mentioned above. It is expected that due to the retirement of tenured teachers in the second half of the nineties and the first decade of the twenty-first century, the demand for teachers at all levels will grow.

France is a special case because the problem of massive simultaneous retirement has arisen sooner than in other countries. This country currently faces a recruitment crisis. The massive retirement of tenured teachers – between 1988 and 2000 about 100,000 primary school teachers will leave the profession, whereas in secondary education about 35 per cent of the tenured teachers, again about 100,000, will retire – and changes in the secondary school system have compelled the government to launch an extensive recruitment campaign. Until about the year 2010, for both the primary and the secondary level, 10,000 new teachers need to be trained annually (Ministère de l'Education Nationale, 1988). The U.K. is also engaged in a massive recruitment programme. In contrast with France which faces both short and medium term shortages, the U.K. primarily has a short term need of qualified teachers, particularly in a number of secondary and vocational curriculum areas and in the primary sector for unattractive inner city posts (Organisation for Economic Cooperation and Development, 1988b). To fill the empty places, apart from new training schemes (licensed and articled teachers), teachers are to be recruited from abroad, in particular from Ireland as the traditional resource, but also from France, Germany, and Spain for foreign language teaching. To fill the inner city posts in the primary sector, the British Government has experimented with hiring primary school teachers from all over Europe since 1990, in particular from Denmark and the Netherlands, since these teachers are well-trained to teach in a multicultural environment. In Southern Europe, where the expansion of the school system started later, the demand for teachers is declining now (Spain), and the average age in the profession is still rather low (Portugal). For the medium range, one may expect the same situation as in Northern Europe.

One of the major problems governments face when recruiting new teachers is the fact that during the last decades a steady decrease in status of the profession can be observed in nearly all countries. This is due to a number of factors including relatively low incentives, the lack of career opportunities, an increase in job load, and a situation of nearly continuous changes in education. The OECD-indicator 'Respect for secondary teachers' largely confirms the not very high status of the profession in most countries (Organisation for Economic Cooperation and Development, 1995). Teaching has become less attractive to the new generation, in particular for the brighter students. Governments are considering measures to make the profession attractive again (European Commission, 1991), but budgetary constraints make it difficult to find solutions.

Education and Economy

The conviction, originating from the fifties and sixties, that education contributes both to economic growth and to the equitable distribution of knowledge,

political power, and income – resulting in increasing investments in human capital – still influenced educational expenditures in most European countries at the
beginning of the seventies. Both state and parents had good confidence in the
value of education for the coming generation. This conviction, accompanied by
free access for all, boosted the demand for education at all levels, and governments strove to meet these demands. As a consequence, decision making was
in this respect guided by social demands rather than solely by economic development concerns. In addition, the strong economic developments in these decades (see Table 7) enabled public budgets to increase rapidly. The excellent
employment situation created conditions for numerous jobs requiring new qualifications.[8] In the early seventies, however, after the 1973 oil crisis, economic
development started to decline in the Western European countries.

Table 7
Average annual growth rates of real GDP 1960-1988

Country	A	B	SF	F	D	GR	IRL	I	NL	N	P	S	GB
1960-1973	4.9	5.0	5.0	5.4	4.4	7.7	4.4	5.3	4.8	4.3	6.9	4.1	3.2
1974-1982	2.3	2.1	2.7	2.4	1.6	2.7	4.3	3.1	1.6	3.8	2.8	1.5	0.8
1983-1988	2.2	2.3	3.6	2.2	2.5	2.2	2.9	3.1	2.2	3.4	2.8	2.7	3.8

Source: OECD, 1992b*

A=Austria; B=Belgium; SF=Finland; F=France; D=Germany; GR=Greece; IRL=Ireland; I=Italy; NL=Netherlands;
N=Norway; P=Portugal; S=Sweden; GB=United Kingdom.
* Denmark, Luxembourg, and Spain are left out because no data were available from the OECD statistics.

Due to the pressure on public budgets rising from new social needs in a shrinking economy and high unemployment, the sensitivity of many governments to
the cost-effectiveness of educational policies increased rapidly. As a consequence, governments suggested a reduction in public funds and a reform of the
behaviour of spending agencies. In addition, a number of evaluation studies
concerning the results of education indicated that education did not contribute
as expected in eradicating social inequality. Surveying the developments in education during the sixties and early seventies, it was concluded that two important social phenomena had outshone the educational reforms that were taking
place (Council of Europe, 1987a).

The first was the growth of youth unemployment all over Europe, in particular among low-skilled youngsters, mostly originating from socially deprived
families and minority groups. The persistence of social inequalities, which appeared to be deeply rooted in various national social systems and which educational reform was apparently unable to eradicate,[9] created a new political
climate in which questions could be raised such as: How much should a society
invest in education? What kind of education should be provided? Who should
pay for it, and how should the expenditures be distributed over the various population groups? As a result of these trends, political and social confidence in the
results of educational change were reversed very rapidly. Doubts were cast on

the efficiency of education, and as a consequence, educational expenditures came under scrutiny.

The second phenomenon was the accumulation of evidence of demographic decline, which at first did not result in budget reductions, and of the ongoing decrease in the need for labour in industry and agriculture. All these developments strongly contributed to a fundamental reappraisal of the value of education and the effectiveness of educational expenditures. Nevertheless, based on my study of documents on educational policies, I support Lowe's (1992) observation that:

> Many European countries perceive (i) a causal relationship between the quality and level of their education and training provision and the efficiency of their economies; (ii) the necessity of competing with Japan, the United States, and the newly industrialised countries in Asia and Latin America by ensuring that such provision is geared to the needs of modern societies. They are interested, therefore, in any kind of European co-operation designed to exploit human-resources to the full and, explicitly, to facilitate the transition of young people from education to paid employment. In this respect the acid test of education systems and schools is not how they are modelled but what they achieve. (p. 584)

Table 8
Real public educational expenditure (primary, secondary and higher education)

Country	8a. Real public educational expenditure as a percentage of real GDP (1970-1989)					8b. Real public educ. exp. per pupil/student as perc. of real public outlays per capita (1975-1988)			
	1970	1975	1980	1985	1989	1975	1980	1985	1988
Austria	5.6	6.1	5.6	5.8	5.5	62.7	58.7	61.6	62.0
Belgium	--	5.9	5.7	5.6	5.1	--	51.1	46.6	44.5[3]
Finland	--	--	5.8	5.7	5.2	--	72.9	69.2	71.3
France	--	5.6	5.1	5.7	5.3	48.1	45.0	45.5	43.6
Germany	4.2	5.2	4.6	4.1	4.0	45.4	42.8	42.1	42.7
Greece	2.8	3.4	3.5	4.0	2.7[1]	51.4	47.4	44.6	36.3
Ireland	6.2	6.5	6.4	6.0	5.1	49.3	47.6	40.1	43.3
Italy	5.0	4.8	4.5	5.0	4.1	--	46.6	47.1	--
Netherlands	7.5	7.4	7.1	6.6	6.2	58.6	55.5	49.4	53.9[3]
Norway	--	6.4	5.8	5.6	7.4	79.4	57.4	57.2	57.3
Portugal	--	3.3	3.7	4.0	4.8	--	48.3[2]	42.3	--
Sweden	7.9	7.1	8.5	7.0	7.1	--	70.9	53.8	53.6
United Kingdom	6.2	6.8	5.7	4.9	4.7	67.9	61.8	56.3[2]	54.2[3]

Source: OECD statistics 1992b, 1993a.

[1] =1988; [2] =1979; [3] =1987

The reduction in public funding for education in a number of European countries coincided with a decrease in enrolment due to declining births rates since 1960. To demonstrate the decrease in educational expenditures, I will make use of two indicators: first, the *real public educational expenditure as a percentage of the real GDP* (Gross Domestic Product) (Table 8a) and second, the *real pub-lic educational expenditure per pupil/student as percentage of the real public outlays per capita* (Table 8b). The share of GDP declined between 1980 and 1989 in almost all EU countries, except for France and Portugal (Table 8a). The decline in educational expenditures under the 6 per cent barrier was accompanied by a decline in enrolment in a number of countries (Table 2), and it still continues even in those countries that face an increase in enrolment. However, this does not fully explain that decline. If one looks at trends in the share of real total outlays per capita spent per pupil (see Table 8b), it become apparent that, though subject to fluctuations, this share has declined constantly over time.

Table 9
The share of each level of education in total public expenditure on education

Year	1975				1980				1985				1989			
Level of Educ.	PP	P	S	T	PP	P	S	T	PP	P	S	T	PP	P	S	T
Austria	1.1	22.2	50.5	14.9	6.1	17.3	54.3	14.5	5.9	16.9	47.5	17.1	5.9	17.3	46.6	19.8
Belgium*	--	23.4	43.3	17.1	--	25.0	46.3	17.9	--	24.9	47.0	17.2	--	24.2	44.6	17.4
Finland*	--	--	--	--	--	31.6	40.8	19.5	--	29.9	42.1	19.4	--	29.2	40.4	22.0
France	8.2	22.8	39.4	12.9	8.6	22.0	40.2	17.1	9.9	19.8	40.7	12.3	9.7	18.6	40.6	14.3
Germany	3.2	17.6	51.0	17.7	3.4	15.4	54.4	15.0	4.2	15.0	52.9	14.7	2.8	14.1	46.9	23.9
Greece*	--	38.9	29.5	21.0	--	37.9	33.7	18.2	--	35.1	35.5	20.2	5.5	27.1	42.7	24.0
Ireland*	--	36.1	36.4	17.7	--	34.0	39.8	18.3	--	39.1	40.3	17.6	8.8	29.0	40.9	19.6
Italy	5.1	29.3	40.9	13.1	6.5	29.0	46.5	9.1	6.7	21.9	34.0	14.6	4.6	20.7	49.7	18.3
Netherlands**	--	26.7	35.0	27.5	--	23.8	32.1	27.0	--	22.5	33.4	26.5	--	22.5	29.8	27.7
Norway***	--	46.7	22.5	12.8	--	49.8	24.6	14.1	--	46.9	27.7	11.0	--	43.4	23.0	15.6
Portugal	--	54.0	27.1	10.6	--	53.8	28.0	11.8	--	50.4	30.8	14.1	2.0	40.9	32.7	17.8
Sweden***	--	--	65.9	12.0	--	--	57.9	9.4	--	--	64.7	12.5	--	43.2	23.0	15.6
United Kingdom*	--	24.9	37.0	21.1	0.4	26.0	39.9	22.9	3.0	23.6	45.9	20.1	3.4	25.5	44.8	19.5
Mean	4.4	31.2	39.9	16.5	5.0	30.5	41.4	16.5	5.9	28.8	41.7	16.7	5.3	27.4	42.2	19.7

Source: OECD, 1992b, 1993a

PP=Pre-Primary Education; P=Primary education; S=Secondary Education; T=Tertiary Education. THe share of expen-ditures for Adult Education, Special Education, other types of education and the expenditure which are not devoted to a certain level - undistributed, is left out. In most countries that share is below 5%, except for Finland 21%, France 17%, Italy 23% and Sweden 23%.
*   Pre-primary education is provided on a full-time or a part-time basis in nursery schools, kindergartens or similar in-stitutions or in sections attached to primary schools. Except for the Netherlands and Greece it does not belong to com-pulsory education. In the Netherlands compulsory education starts at the age of 5, in Greece at 5.5, in Norway and Sweden at 7, and in most other countries at 6 years of age.
** In the Netherlands pre-primary had a long standing tradition but in 1985 it was amalgamated with primary educa-tion. Also the teacher training institutes for pre-primary education were integrated with those for the training of pri-mary school teachers.
***In Sweden and Norway basic education ranges from 7 till 16 years. As a consequence, the category secondary edu-cation comprises primary education and both junior and senior level secondary education. The 1989 OECD statistics distinguish second level, first stage (primary and junior secondary) and second stage (senior secondary).

A closer study of the share of educational expenditures per level of schooling (see Table 9) leads to the conclusion that pre-primary education (4-6 years) is, in most countries – with the exception of Belgium (3, 4, and 5 years, 98 per cent), France (3, 4, and 5 years, 99 per cent), the Netherlands (4 and 5 years, 98 per cent), and Spain (4 and 5 years, 99 per cent) – the least developed field in the education arena. Nevertheless, enrolment in pre-primary education has in-creased considerably in all EU countries. These enrolment rates were not strongly influenced by falling birthrates but rather responded to the increasing social demands. This development has lead to growing attention for the training of early childhood teachers (Pascal, Bertram, & Heaslip, 1991).

If one combines the results of Tables 3, 4, and 9, it is easy to conclude that, from 1970 onwards, more or less following demographic decline, the share of primary education has decreased, with fluctuations, in a vast majority of EU countries – as in Austria, France, Germany, Greece, Italy, the Netherlands, Norway, Portugal, and Sweden – while in Belgium, Ireland, Finland, and the United Kingdom it has remained relatively stable. One may expect that in view of the increasing birthrates in a number of countries (see Table 4) after the steady decline in the years before 1985, the share of primary education will shortly rise considerably in Denmark, Luxembourg, the Netherlands, Norway, and Sweden. In most other countries the decline will continue.

In the field of secondary education the situation is more complex; a distinction has to be made between the junior and senior levels and between secondary general and vocational education (comprising technical, vocational, and apprenticeship schemes). That the junior level (10-14 years in Table 4) is part of compulsory education mainly concerns secondary general education, except in Belgium, Greece, and Luxembourg where the vocational option is available at the age of 12 and in France at the age of 13. One may expect that, as a consequence of the increase in numbers of 10-14 year olds (see Table 4), the share of junior secondary education will increase considerably in Germany, Luxembourg, the Netherlands, Norway, Sweden, and in U.K. in the decades to come.

As Table 10 suggests, senior secondary is often divided into senior secondary-general – preparing for university or other forms of post-secondary education, and secondary-technical and/or vocational education which start at the age of 14 in Austria, Italy, and Spain, while in all other European countries this option is not available before either 15 or 16 years of age (De Vries, 1994). One of the major problems in senior secondary-general education is that there is no agreement as to the basis for senior secondary-general education curricula; What should be the number of subjects studied, and what should their content be? In England and Ireland the curriculum is mainly determined by examining boards for which specialization in three or four subjects is the criterion.

Table 10
Participation in senior secondary general and vocational Education, 1991

Country	A	B	DK	SF	F	D	IRL	I	NL	N	P	E	S	GB
Perc. Sec. Gen. Ed	23.7	41.5	33.4	45.5	46.0	19.9	77.6	29.4	29.9	39.8	83.2	63.5	26.6	79.7
Perc. Voc. Ed	76.3	58.5	66.6	54.5	54.0	80.1	22.4	70.6	70.4	60.2	16.8	36.5	73.4	20.3

Source: OECD 1993b*

A=Austria; B=Belgium; DK=Denmark; SF=Finland; F=France; D=Germany; IRL=Ireland; I=Italy; NL=Netherlands; N=Norway; P=Portugal; E=Spain; S=Sweden; GB=United Kingdom.

France, Belgium, Spain, Italy, and Greece still opt for a broad range of subjects. In Germany, Austria, and to a lesser extent the Netherlands a rather lengthy canon of subjects is prescribed that should lead to the production of all-round general education (Halls, 1994).

The growth of the 'non-academic' senior secondary population also requires the development of alternative programmes. Technical and vocational education, previously held in low esteem, revives in particular in those countries with a long standing tradition in vocational education, such as the Scandinavian countries, Germany, Austria, The Netherlands, and France. In the other European countries, results are mixed. In the U.K., apprenticeship schemes are still favoured, and the same is true for Italy. This means training on the job, which often results in reproductive instead of productive learning. In Spain and Portugal, recent reforms are focused on the improvement of the quality of vocational education.

The percentages of the various age groups attending senior secondary education in 1991 were 85.2 per cent for 16 year olds, 76.9 per cent for 17 year olds, and 52.7 per cent for 18 year olds. The last figure is low in comparison with the two preceding ones, and this is due to the fact that in a number of countries senior secondary education ends at the age of 17. The balance between participation in secondary-general and vocational education at senior secondary level is shown in Table 10. However, the standard for and organisation of vocational education for 16 year olds and over differs widely in the various countries of the EU. The Scandinavian countries, the Netherlands, Belgium, Germany, Austria, and France have a long standing tradition in this respect, while many countries from Southern Europe have just begun to build up a system for vocational education. A special case is Germany with its 'dual system.' The 'duad' upon which the Dual System is based refers to a partnership between the school sector and the business sector, the latter assuming a predominant role. The trainee serves an apprenticeship in a firm and is taught vocational and general subjects in a vocationally oriented school. Jobs for which apprentices can train have clear specifications and precise designations (Pritchard, 1992, p. 131). The existence of the dual system has contributed considerably to the German 'Wirtschaftswunder.' However, the lack of firms which can receive apprentices is one of the major problems for the implementation of a similar system in the former Eastern Germany (Mitter, 1992, p. 50).

European nations can be divided into three groups when it comes to the share of higher education in public educational expenditures: first, those countries where the share of expenditures for higher education remained relatively stable between 1975 and 1990, such as Belgium, Ireland, and the Netherlands; second, countries where the share has increased over time, as in Austria, Finland, Italy, Norway, Portugal, and Sweden and those countries where the share remained stable between 1970 and 1985 but has increased from 1985 onwards, such as

France, Germany, Greece, and Italy; and third, countries that show a constant decline in this share, such as the U.K.

Although developments in the current and capital expenditures in education in the 1970-1989 period demonstrate an overall growth, a decrease in the share of total public expenditures can be observed, which leads to the conclusion that from a budgetary point of view education has been given a less prominent place in the public policy agenda. Alternatively, if one assumes that quality has not declined, one could conclude that a considerable increase in efficiency has taken place in education during the eighties.

European Education Policies

The rush for more extensive schooling for all is a relatively recent historical phenomenon in most European nation-states, generally not having started before 1945. Since then, starting with the countries in Northern Europe, governments, groups, and individuals have begun to act as if education were an inevitable system of socialization, certification, and legitimation without which social life itself would not be possible (Altbach, Arnove, & Kelly, 1982). Nevertheless, the role of state leadership in contemporary European social systems contains a powerful dialectic whose poles are continuously undergoing elaboration in the various national societies. One pole is an ideology that regards the state as the centre of social organization and the vehicle for social development, the other is the ideology of the individual as the basic unit of social action, the ultimate source of value and the locus of social meaning (Rubinson, 1981). These poles are united in an ideology of citizenship, in which the individual is seen as both a contributor to the national development project and a beneficiary of state organizational action. Education is the means to achieve two purposes: first, to integrate individuals into the social structure; and second, to provide individuals with the means to carry out their own, self-directed personal development.

Depending on culture, tradition, and national history, different outcomes can be observed with respect to this dialectic in the conglomerate of European nations, reflecting more or less governmental dominance in educational decision making. To give an example, during the sixties and seventies self-directed personal development was emphasized in most Northern European countries (e.g., Sweden, Norway, Denmark, Finland, West Germany, the Netherlands, the U.K.) resulting in rather open curricula. Nowadays, a shift is made towards stressing the importance of the 'core curriculum' as can be observed in the U.K. (the National curriculum) and in the Netherlands (minimum objectives for all pupils in Junior Secondary education). As a contrast, consider France with its highly centralized educational system with a strong emphasis on the integration of individuals into the social structure. However, in all cases an underlying pattern of *state-directed* and *formalized* education may be detected. In this connection, the question can be raised – why cannot parents themselves provide the right sort of education for their children? Here the *ideology of the state* clearly plays a role; children are not to be initiated only into society but rather into the twentieth century world (i.e., the 'national' society and/or the 'European' society). In this view, the state dominates in organizing society, and therefore, if the social structure is to function properly, individuals are expected to behave as active agents of the state. In order to ensure the success of state action, they must become citizens who identify themselves with national and/or European symbols and programmes. At the European level (European Commission, 1988b), a campaign has been started to promote the development of the 'European Dimension in Education and Teacher Training' which is aimed at developing a better understanding among Europe's nations and at the development of a European awareness (i.e., the education of the European citizen). The underlying objective of this campaign, however, is to support European policies in creating the 'European labour market' and the free mobility of labour force (Single European Act of 1988, which came into force in 1992). Two elements dominate these policies: the mutual recognition of diplomas – which will lead to the mutual attuning of education; and training structures in order to prepare the future generation better for that labour market and the contribution of education to the development of the European citizen.

All of this takes place in a European society which is becoming more and more technocratic in nature and is dedicated to 'the myth of progress' – the latter being criticized fundamentally by Ellul (1990). In Europe many governments have taken over the responsibility for the organization of national development, with varying success. The doctrine of progress declares that only the state can be counted on to bring about the equality of individuals and to ensure basic integrity of each social member. Moreover, in order to ensure orderly economic growth, rising per capita income, health care, pensions and the like, the technical necessity of state control, and the coordination of the national economy and polity are universally accepted across a wide range of domains. All these elements are the very essence of 'progress' in the contemporary European world. At present, however, it is easy to observe that since the mid-eighties the doctrine of state-leadership has eroded and, in many domains, has been gradually replaced by the ideology of the 'free-market' and by greater responsibility for the individual.

However, the myth of *state-directed progress* still defines the relationship between state and education to a large extent. The intermediate class still sees education as a major source of value in that it creates *cultural capital*[10] which can be used by individuals for further personal development, but also which contributes to more general (social) progress, such as literacy, environmental awareness, racial tolerance, self-actualization and so on. State-leadership with respect to social progress includes planning and guiding the state with respect to education and teacher education.[11] The consequence of this doctrine has been and will continue to be a growing influence of the state on education, resulting in continuous tension between the interests of individuals in self-directed personal development and those of the state in educating economically effective citizens.[12] According to Eide (1992), the latter issue will be the main thread for the 'Nordic' model of education which is committed in first instance to a universalistic version of welfare policy (p. 9).

Since all European nation-states have developed their own culturally defined strategy for state-directed progress, and since education plays a crucial part in those strategies, it will be obvious that the development of a European policy of education will always be kept within narrow bounds: on the one hand, because it is not possible to define Europe clearly due to the existing structures; on the other, because neither the European Council nor the European Union have the authority 'to lay down binding regulations for the school and the university system by way of majority decision' within these structures. In particular, the Federal Republic of Germany emphasizes this point because it also concerns the typically German experience and approval of a federal constitution which says that 'culture and education are not part of those state matters requiring central control and uniformity.' In Germany this has resulted in a politico-educational concept according to which European integration is to be understood as agreement and cooperation rather than standardization. Moreover, the point must be made that in the course of the history of the creation of a united Europe (as an economic, monetary, and cultural union) – altogether more than 30 years – the areas of culture and education were on the whole of marginal importance. For, in the past, the economic aspects of the European integration clearly dominated, and from this economic point of view it was not possible for citizens to recognize the significance of the unification of Europe. This has gradually changed since the middle of the seventies. It was not until 1984/85 that the significance of general and professional education was acknowledged following the decision to realize the internal market in 1992. The *Medium-term Perspectives: 1989-1992*, a communication of the Commission of the European Community to the Council of 2 June 1989, mentions teachers and teacher education on the side only, in the context of evaluation of the transfer of credits for academic diplomas and degrees as well as the promotion of the freedom of movement for people looking for employment. In the course of 1990, the *Perspectives* were to be followed by an information brochure 'giving information about the recruitment and employment laws and regulations to give teachers a better idea of the available possibilities and the currently valid regulations.' However important it may be to solve these questions and problems by way of mutually agreed regulations, the latter will hardly give impulses for an increased interest in the European Community and the promotion of the process of European integration. However, it appears that the objectives of a European education policy should be preceded by certain principles which set narrow bounds for any policy trying to realize the objectives by way of central decision making. The two most important principles are: *respect for the diversity of cultures and educational traditions*; and *subsidiarity*, i.e., giving additional support to the self-responsibility of small communities. In this connection, the communication (of 2 June 1989) from the Commission to the Council reads:

> Preserving and respecting the rich diversity of educational traditions in the Community is imperative; however, optimal use is to be made of this joint heritage in order to achieve higher standards in the future. Any undifferentiated harmonization or standardization of the education systems is to be totally rejected; it cannot be an objective for the Committee in this area.

And with regard to the principle of subsidiarity, the text reads:

> In the development of new forms of cooperation at Community level the Commission absolutely acknowledges the importance of clearly differentiating between measures to be taken by and implemented in the Member States and those tasks the Commission can fulfil itself due to its specific function as a catalyst and coordinator and due to the increased value it thereby adds to the efforts of the Member States.

For the further development of educational policies in Europe, three issues or barriers are of importance: differences in the nature of educational governance in the various countries; differences in the nature of school knowledge traditions; and the internationalization of education and teacher training from an European perspective.

Governance in education: De-centralization and de-regulation.

The last few decades have demonstrated that state-initiated and controlled actions are not adequate to achieve the desired improvement of quality of education and teaching. The recent trend towards the rationalization of education has resulted in decentralization and deregulation (i.e., power over and responsibility for the functioning of the educational enterprise is now delegated – see Table 11). All this under the supervision of the state in the form of 'meta-control.'

Table 11
Decision-making processes for junior secondary education**: Locus, domains and modes of decision-making

	I. Locus of decision-making				II. Decisions taken at school level Decision domains				III. Modes of decision-making at country level		
	School	Interme-diate 1	Interme-diate 2	Country	Resour-ces	Person-nel	Structu-res	Org. of instruc-tion	Autono-mous	Consult-ation	Stipula-ted
Countries with a centralized education system											
Austria	44	8	26	23	11	0	8	25	23	0	31
France	35	0	35	30	7	4	3	20	27	3	21
Italy	29	11	2	57	0	0	3	26	26	0	3
Portugal	42	0	3	55	7	10	6	19	52	3	33
Spain	28	26	14	32	2	10	19	26	28	4	24
Countries with a decentralized education system											
Belgium*	26	50	24	0	2	0	6	18	--	--	--
Ireland*	74	8	0	18	17	17	18	22	13	5	54
Germany*	32	44	17	7	4	0	6	22	7	0	0
Countries with an education system in transition											
Denmark	39	48	0	14	4	5	9	22	14	0	14
Finland	38	50	0	13	4	6	13	16	13	0	48
Netherlands	46	28	0	26	0	0	20	26	22	2	22
Norway	31	45	0	24	7	0	6	18	24	0	17
Sweden	47	47	0	6	7	8	9	22	6	0	31

Source: OECD statistics 1992,1993

Explanation of the table

This table only regards decision-making at junior secondary education. However, there is no reason to suppose that similar processes at other levels of education will substantially deviate from the table above.

I. Level of decision-making (as percentage of all decisions
- — School: decisions taken by the governing board; principal/head of a school; teachers; parents; pupils/students.
- — Intermediate 1: decision makers closest to the school; e.g. local educational authorities (UK); district (DK); municipal authorities (F); province (E).
- — Intermediate 2: decision makers closest to the government, e.g. county (DK); regional education authorities (P); autonomous community (E).
- — Country level: central government

II. Decisions at school level: Domains of decision-making (as percentage of all decisions)
- — Decisions about the allocation of resources, e.g. staff, capital expenditures, operating expenditures.
- — Decisions about personnel management, e.g. hiring and firing, fixing salary levels of staff, career of staff.
- — Decisions about planning and structure, e.g. cr4eating and /or closure of a school, designing programmes, choosing subjects to be taught, setting qualifying examinations.
- — Decisions about the organization of instruction, e.g. number of period for instruction, grouping, grading, assessment, teaching methods, choice of textbooks, (syllabuses), setting admission requirements.

III. Modes of decision-making at country level (as percentage of all decisions)
- — Autonomous decisions taken without consultation of other levels and only subjected to constraints of legislation which is external to the education system of very general.
- — Consultation: decision-making after consultation with other levels.
- — Stipulated: decisions which result in creating a framewrok within which other levels can take decisions, i.e. binding legislation, regulations or finite options, budget and the like.

  * Belgium and Germany are federal states, which explains the low level of country level iunfluence. However, we may expect that the decision-makers at the regional elvel, e.g. Länder (D), Ministries of the Communities (B) have taken over the role of the central government. Ireland follows the English tradition of great autonomy for schools.

  ** The OECD survey did not include data from Greece, Luxembourg and the UK.

How this trend towards decentralization and deregulation is, or will be, implemented in the various European countries strongly depends on the nature of their national cultures in education management. With respect to that management various decision-making structures can be distinguished in Europe, *centralization* and *decentralization* being its extremes. In a centralized system, the demands for change must be accumulated, aggregated, and articulated at the political centre. They must be negotiated in the central political arena, and, once accepted, they are transmitted top-down to educational institutions as policy-directed changes. Changes are evident and documented at the political centre in laws, decrees, and rules (Archer, 1979). Changes brought about in this way are general and national in their application rather than specific and local. As a consequence, sometimes only very little changes in a centralized system. In contrast, within a decentralized system, not all demands have to be passed upward to the political centre. Some can be negotiated autonomously within educational institutions, and others can be transacted independently by external interest groups. Consequently, everything is in a constant state of change, changes are continuously initiated, imitated, modified, reversed, and counteracted at the level of the institution, the community, and the nation. Likewise, these changes are usually undramatic, frequently indefinite, and usually specific and local in their application.

To gain some insight into the extent to which countries have a more centralized or decentralized education system, I make use of the experimental OECD indicator on educational decision making. This indicator distinguishes four levels of decision making: the school, intermediate 1 (closest to the school), intermediate 2 (closest to the national level, most often the regional level), and finally the national level (government). Decisions taken into account at these levels include only the primary decision makers and do not include consultation with other levels during the decision-making process or whether decisions are taken within a framework stipulated by another decision-making level. This last issue, however, makes the value of the indicator questionable. If a higher level stipulates only a very narrow framework for decision making, this will influence the decisions taken on a lower level, and the OECD indicator neglects this influence. A good example appears in the U.K. which is judged to have a decentralized system, but the government largely determines what happens in the classroom through narrow prescriptions about the curriculum, standards, and reporting. Therefore, in Table 11 I have also used data concerning the mode of decision making at the country level.

If one looks at the locus of decision making displayed in that table, one sees that in Denmark, Finland, the Netherlands, Norway, and Sweden 75 per cent of all decisions are taken at school level or intermediate 1 level. In Ireland the school level is the predominant decision-making platform. In Austria, France, and Spain the intermediate levels together with the country level have a sizable role. In Belgium and Germany the intermediate 1 level is very powerful, while in Italy and Portugal the country level dominates in the decision-making process. However, the extremes in the decision-making structure are not absolute. In many countries, such as the Scandinavian countries, the Netherlands, and Belgium a certain mixture of these extremes exists. Over a certain period of time changes in the structure may occur. For example, in the U.K., a country with a traditionally and formally decentralized structure of decision making, at present two trends are appearing: on the one hand, a distinct tendency favouring centralization; while on the other, the development of more autonomy for schools with respect to curriculum implementation, staff-policies, and quality control – all to be based on free-market principles that are client-centred, market-oriented, and competitive – is a hot item. Examples of these centralizing tendencies are *The National Curriculum* (Department of Education and Science, 1989a) and the circular of the DES on *Initial Teacher Education: Approval of Courses* (Department of Education and Science, 1989b). The same is more or less true for the Netherlands. In contrast to this development, in some countries with a traditionally centralized system, such as Italy, Spain and France, a strong tendency to decentralize has appeared. In Spain, for example, one can observe a regionalization of the responsibility for education and teacher education, while in France educational policies are now tending to transfer part of the responsibility for the curriculum to the local level (Council of Europe, 1988).

In the Scandinavian countries, however, decentralization seems to mean more active participation of all interested parties in the educative enterprise (e.g., parents, business and industry, local authorities). If one looks at the decision domains at school level, it becomes obvious that most decisions taken at this level concern the organization of instruction. In seven countries, schools have no say in personnel management, while only in two countries do schools have a firm say in decisions with respect to the allocation of resources. Looking at the mode of decision making at country level, it is easy to conclude that in most countries decisions are taken without consultation of other decision-making levels. In Finland, Ireland, and Sweden the decisions are predominantly aimed at creating a framework within which other levels can take their own decisions, while in Portugal and Italy the autonomous decision-making role of the central government becomes obvious. In all other countries there is a balance between what the central level prescribes and for what it only creates a framework.

Education and teacher education from a European perspective.

The 'Treaty of Rome,' the founding treaty of the European Union, did not regulate anything with respect to education, which certainly does not simplify making EU educational policies or efforts in that direction. In order to give the EU a more humane character, education became part of the EU Human Resources policies in 1980 and was placed in DG-V of the European Commission. That EU policies with respect to education are a touchy subject is shown by the re-endorsement of the autonomy of all European nation-states with respect to all matters that concern culture – including education – in the *Medium-Term Perspectives, 1988-1992* (European Commission, 1988a) which dealt with the 'European dimension in education,' thus *preserving and respecting the rich diversity of educational traditions in the Community is imperative.*

It may in fact be possible to come to certain agreements with respect to the structure and organization of European education systems over a period of time, but I foresee great problems with respect to differences in 'school knowledge traditions' and the nature of 'educational administration' in the various countries. These two aspects are strongly culturally defined. With respect to 'school knowledge traditions,' McLean (1990) distinguishes three forms (i.e., Encyclopedism, Humanism, and Naturalism). Encyclopedism with its main principles of universality, rationality, and utility is typical for French education and to a lesser extent for Italy, Belgium, Luxembourg, Spain, and Portugal. Humanism with its emphasis on morality, individualism, and specialism is typical for the British, Irish, and Greek educational systems. Naturalism, which combines a number of characteristics of both Encyclopedism and Humanism and emphasizes the moral and intellectual development of pupils, individualism, and creativity, is typical for the Netherlands, Austria, Switzerland, Germany, and the Scandinavian countries. While these descriptions say more about the goals and the aspirations of the education systems than about everyday practice, they clearly illustrate the variety in cultural traditions. Teachers, parents, and pupils are – by way of the education they give or have received – embodiments of these cultural concepts. As a consequence, different societies expect different things from their teachers (European Commission, 1991).

a) When the system has for first objective the development of the child as is common in Anglo-Saxon countries, personal qualities are expected first of all from teachers. Attention is paid to the interactive quality in teacher-student relationships, to a differentiated pedagogy, and to aptitude for the tutor relationship.

b) When the education system has as its first objective the acquisition of knowledge – as is common in France, Spain, Portugal, and Italy – it is normal that the act of teaching tends to be more academic.

c) When social and professional insertion are the first objectives of a school system, teachers pay more attention to the orientation procedures – as is the case in Germany, the Netherlands, Austria, and the Scandinavian countries. Teaching will then be differentiated according to an educational hierarchy, and teachers will be trained accordingly (p. 20).

Conclusions of a study on mobility problems in teacher education by Bruce (1991) suggest that teacher education is often too much nation oriented (i.e., it only works for the local market), there is a lack of tradition in international co-operation, the staff often have language problems and little knowledge of education and teacher education in other countries, and differences in structure and curriculum orientation do not facilitate student mobility. Interesting in this respect is the so-called IBM-study from Hofstede (1994) in which he analyses cultural differences within the IBM organization in 53 countries. In his book, *Culture and Organizations*, Hofstede describes four dimensions basic to the cultural value systems. These dimensions concern:

i)   the relations to authority, expressed in 'power distance' (PD);
ii) the relations between the individual and the group, expressed in 'individualism versus collectivism';
iii) the social implications of being born a boy or girl, expressed in 'masculine versus feminine';
iv) the ways of dealing with uncertainty, relating to control of aggression and the expression of emotions, expressed as 'uncertainty avoidance.' (UA, p. 14)

A number of differences in the culture of education were explored through these dimensions.

An illustrative example of the confusion that can be caused by the cultural differences comes from a report written by French and English students who participated in an exchange programme. The English students, while studying in Paris, were expected to attend lectures during the whole week. Independent work was minimized to studying prescribed textbooks. The French students, while studying at a London institute, only had to follow a number of introductory lectures which provided a general overview of the subject under study. The hard core of their study was, however, independent work (i.e., going to the library, searching for appropriate study materials and books and making sense of it themselves). Both groups returned to their home base with feelings of dissatisfaction. Discussion afterwards led to the conclusion that neither the exchange students nor their professors had understood the differences in tradition of acquiring knowledge. (Bruce, 1990)

Hofstede's study offers a good framework for explaining such problems. The English score low on PD (little hierarchy), while the French score high (professors have a lot of authority and are difficult to contact). In contrast, the English score low on UA (they can easily cope with uncertainty which results in a preference for independent work), while the French score high on UA (they want to know exactly what they are supposed to do). Internationalization cannot sidestep these differences in culture, traditions and the problems that arise from it (Peters, 1992).

However, as of 1992, the unification of Europe is progressing again (via The Maastricht Treaty), and increasing internationalization of both education and teacher education will result in standards for both education and teacher education becoming more similar in all European countries. Thus, the further unification of Europe will result in an increasing internationalization of both education and teacher education. The so-called Single Europe Act of 1988, which came into force in 1992, guarantees the free movement of labour in the EU. Among other things, this means that school diplomas and professional diplomas have to be mutually recognized. Apart from that, the OECD (1993b, Part III) and the IEA[13] have carried out world-wide comparative studies on 'Results of Education.' In the long term, the outcomes of these studies will definitely influence European curricula, particularly those in science and mathematics. As a consequence, standards for (teacher) education in the European countries will gradually become more alike, as will qualifications.

Recent comparisons of developments in teacher education in the various European countries show that, in spite of many cultural differences, the systems are developing more or less along the same lines. All in all, the solutions for the problems in education and teacher education provided by most nations are tending to become similar. In addition, there is a strong emphasis on (student) teacher mobility as a consequence of the Single Europe Act of 1988 (i.e., student teachers are encouraged to study abroad for at least half a year by participating in programmes such as ERASMUS, the exchange programmes of the Nordic Council, or the various exchange programmes within the framework of bi-lateral treaties between Eastern and Western European countries). However, in terms of the number of student-teachers who spend part of their studies abroad, these exchange programmes are not very successful. In some countries with an accreditation system, such as the U.K., various parts of the professional preparation acquired abroad are not even recognized because they are not validated by the accreditation committee (Bruce, 1990). For teachers, opportunities have become available to teach abroad for a certain period. The internationalization of (teacher) education, however, makes new demands on the existing programmes. First of all, the structures of most teacher education programmes will have to change. A modular curriculum, for example, is more flexible and therefore offers better opportunities for international student exchange. Furthermore, a certain harmonization between programmes in their respective countries must be reached with respect to the content and the duration of the various elements of the programmes, such as teaching practice and professional, educational, and subject studies. Another issue in this connection, which will strongly influence teacher education in the decade to come, is the long-term goal of bringing the teacher qualifications in the various European countries more into line. To this effect, it is necessary to improve the set-up of programmes for teacher education, in particular if one considers the high demand for teachers in the north of Europe in the near future and the growing oversupply in the south. However, if one takes into consideration both the (new) demands made on present teacher education programmes and the need to improve the quality of teacher educators and their practices, it is reasonable to conclude that more in-service training for teacher educators is imperative. Elsewhere (Vonk, 1992), I have emphasized the necessity to develop a European curriculum for the education and training of teachers. However, this will be a very complex operation, as culture and education are very sensitive issues.

The European dimension in education and teacher education.

In developing the European Community in a wider sense (i.e., not only in terms of a common market, but also promoting a real 'unity in cultural diversity'), Europe has to be relocated in the human adventure.

In the *Resolution of the Council and the Ministers of Education meeting within the Council* of 24 May 1988 on the European dimension in Education (European Commission, 1988b) the following objectives were adopted:

- to strengthen in young people a sense of European identity and make clear to them the value of European civilization and of the foundations on which the European peoples intend to base their developments today, that is in particular safeguarding the principles of democracy, social justice and respect for human rights;
- to prepare young people to take part in the economic and social development of the Community and in making concrete progress towards European Union, as stipulated in the Single Act;
- to make them aware of the advantages which the Community represents, but also of the challenges it involves, in opening up an enlarged economic and social area to them;
- to improve their knowledge of the Community and its Member States in their historical, cultural, economic and social aspects and bring home to them the significance of the Member States of the EU with other countries in Europe and the world.

All countries undertook to initiate measures to ensure the introduction of the European dimension at all levels and to coordinate actions in their respective countries (i.e., to take curriculum initiatives, to disseminate information on education systems in Europe, to organize seminars for teachers, and to give greater attention to these issues in teachers' initial and in-service training). The following measures that can contribute to the latter were suggested:

- to develop suitable teaching material;
- to give access to documentation on the Community and its policies;
- to provide basic information on the educational systems of the Member States;
- to cooperate with teacher education institutes in other Member States, particularly by developing joint programmes for student and teacher mobility;
- to make provisions in the framework of in-service training for specific activities to enhance serving teachers' awareness of the European dimension in education and give them the opportunity to keep up-to-date with Community developments. (Association for Teacher Education in Europe, 1990)

As a result, a number of descriptions of educational systems including teacher education have become available in the Community languages; and (inter)national networks of teacher education institutes have become involved in the development of curriculum modules for the European dimension in (teacher) education. Apart from that, the foreign language component has become extremely important. (Interestingly, 86.5 per cent of the respondents from continental Europe rating the OECD indicator 'Importance of school subjects' judged foreign languages as 'essential' or 'very important,' whereas only 56 per cent of the respondents of the U.K. gave this judgment). In this respect the European Commission's review of the state of affairs of foreign language teaching in Europe is also of interest (European Commission, 1995, pp. 65-85). The mastery of one or more foreign languages by all European citizens is certainly a condition for the further integration of Europe. As a consequence, all over Europe foreign language teaching has intensified considerably.

The realization of a greater awareness of Europe as an economic and cultural union is also crucial for the further development of the EU. However, a number of nation-states tend to emphasize diversity by promoting their own culture and language rather than emphasizing unity (i.e., the common cultural base). This seems to be the case in France, for example, where in 1994 the then minister of education proposed a bill which would force the removal of all 'loan words,' in particular English ones, from school books, official governmental documents, public advertisement, and the like, to be replaced by French words or expressions. After a heated debate in the French parliament, the bill was accepted for education and governmental publications only. This type of language purism is aimed at preserving and strengthening the influence of French culture in Europe. But it is not only the French who are concerned about the prospects of their culture and language in a united Europe. Similar reactions can be found in the U.K., although without governmental support, where publications appear regularly which protest against the erosion of the British English language through a dominating influence of American English on the younger generation. A real European Union cannot develop unless cultural cooperation on all levels of society is intensified.

Concluding Remarks Regarding Social Forces

In this section on social forces and their implications for education, I have outlined, using data from the various European states, some general trends of development in the social context of teaching in Europe as a whole. An important element in this process of change is the tendency to opt for neo-liberal or neo-conservative ideas in the political arena all over Europe, in which the 'free market' is the dominating regulating factor. Even in education, governments tend to restrict themselves to regulating the education market, rather than to work on developing a clear view on education for the decades ahead. In Europe there is still much confusion about the redefinition of the aims of schooling for the first decades of next century.

However, if one considers current developments in their social contexts, it becomes apparent that these developments will result in major changes in education in nearly all European countries.

- One may expect an increase in the technicalization and rationalization of education.
- Education will increasingly become involved in matters which previously belonged to family education.
- Economic pressure will cause a reduction in available study time, which will require students to use time more efficiently.
- One may expect an increasing pressure on both vocational and secondary general education to prepare pupils for more effective participation in the labour market.
- As a consequence of the differences in the development of the school population between Northern and Southern Europe and the differences in teacher supply and demand in the various parts of Europe, one may expect an increase in teacher mobility.

— The 'European' focus of education will be reinforced, in particular with respect to foreign language teaching and learning.

From the data presented in this section, it is easy to conclude that substantial differences exist between developments in education in Northern and Southern Europe nowadays. Some of these differences find their origin in differences in culture and tradition, while other differences originate from economically created differences in speed of development, as becomes apparent from the recent development plans for education in Spain and Italy.

Although many different cultures and traditions exist with respect to education in Europe, I strongly believe that developments such as the increasing economic cooperation, the establishment of a European currency, the increasing mobility of labour, the intensification of student and teacher exchanges, the growing cooperation in education and teacher training, and the like, in the long run, will help to amalgamate the various national educational systems and their contents into mutually agreed European standards.

IMPLICATIONS FOR TEACHERS AND TEACHING

The profound changes in the social context of education in Europe, as outlined in the previous section, make new demands on education and on the teaching profession in particular and place them on the threshold of a new era. Although today the old forms are still alive, in the long term they will not hold under the pressure of fundamental changes in the nature of school knowledge, changes in school population, economic demands, progress in technology, and changes in everyday working life. One may expect sweeping changes in the decades ahead in the nature of school learning, teaching, the role of teachers, and finally in the organization of schools.

I start however with an outline of the present situation of teachers and teaching as it emerges from a broad range of recent official documents concerning teachers and their teaching, beginning with the statement of the Standing Conference of European Ministers of Education in Helsinki (1987). All these documents, however, contain a confusing dichotomy with respect to the teacher's role. On the one hand, the social significance of the teacher's role is emphasized, as expressed by governmental efforts to raise the status of the profession, but on the other, continuous criticism of teachers and their teaching appears which undermines the authority of teachers as professionals. Representative for the first pole of this dichotomy is a statement made by Naeve (1991).

Few groups in society have a weightier responsibility for the development of the European Community than the teaching profession.

And whilst it is far from being alone in this task, it is, ultimately, the main channel through which decisions taken elsewhere – be the domains as diverse as industrial policy, economic practice, technological change, as too the most delicate of all, how citizens and future citizens of Europe view their Community – are transmitted, take root and assume substance in the form of skills, knowledge, the will to apply them, and no less important, the readiness of individual citizens to adapt them to changing circumstances. (p. 1)

With regard to the second pole, almost all official documents – be it between the lines – have two subjects in common: first, they express criticism of the developments in education during the sixties and seventies, emphasizing the failure of most innovations and to a large extent blaming teachers for this; and second, they emphasize the need to improve the quality of teaching, teacher assessment, and teacher accountability in such a way that they seem to suggest a complete lack of faith in the quality and commitment of teachers.

The solution most often proposed is aimed at 'raising standards' by emphasizing the need to mandate competencies for both teachers and students, basic curricular goals, and knowledge, thereby centralizing the control of teaching and curricula at the governmental level. Developments in this direction can be observed in many European countries, led by the U.K.[14] and the Netherlands.[15] During the conference, *The teaching profession in Europe* (European Commission, 1991), however, the following was concluded about the teacher as a professional:

Being a teacher today means doing a job in the sense of an activity which is organized and programmed by a central power, it means carrying out a trade by implementing learned techniques and know-how. It is a profession and by that must be understood:

– the exercise of an intellectual and responsible activity;
– the exercise of a scientific, non-repetitive activity;
– the fact that for this purpose a long and thorough training has been followed;
– the exercising of activities which renders a service to society, therefore possessing a whole series of personal qualities that enable the transfer of knowledge and values. (p. 20)

As a consequence, becoming a teacher in general no longer corresponds to the long sustained idea of a vocation – however, many testimonies to the contrary may have been offered. At first, professionalism seems to be opposed to the idea of vocation, but in the longer term it replaces vocation. The above statement about teacher professionalism refers to teaching as a 'technique' in the sense as defined earlier in this chapter. From most official publications about 'raising the status of the teaching profession' and 'the improvement of quality in education,' one learns that, in the eyes of governments, a teacher is regarded as a 'technical man,' who converts his or her spontaneous and unreflective behaviour into behaviours that are deliberate and rationalized and who is committed to the never ending search for the 'one best way' to achieve externally designated objectives. All personal elements are translated into technical ones, and those elements that cannot be translated are declared non-existent. All this has made teaching a technical act.

The Industrialization of the Education Sector

The renewed political attention for the teaching profession and teacher education since the mid-eighties must be understood in the context of the expected demand for teachers in the near future, the budgetary problems faced by governments all over Europe, and the development of the European Union which entails the need to harmonize education. As a consequence, teacher recruitment, together with provisions for the quality control of education and teacher education, the control of expenditures, and the internationalization of education, have become key issues in an educational policy which has 'human resources development' as its main focus. In this context, issues such as rationalization, formalization, quality control, improvement of efficiency, and thus standardization have become topical. This purely technical approach to problems in education has resulted in the *industrialization* of the educational sector. This means that schools are increasingly becoming production oriented organizations with a hierarchical structure (top-down model) in which the management defines the goals and distributes the means. The output is submitted to standardized quality control, and the efforts and qualities of the workers in these organizations (teachers) are continuously assessed. In that respect, the assessment of the educational system in terms of production results (e.g., the OECD quality indicators which are based on student achievement) is a hot item in the current education debate. From this point of view, policy makers in Europe tend to discuss education in terms of input, output, throughput, efficiency, and effectiveness. Under the pressure of economic decline this process has even intensified during the last ten years. Sometimes one gets the impression that pupils, students, and teachers are no longer regarded as unique human beings in educational policy but rather as objects liable to an industrial process called 'education' in which costs, benefits, efficiency, labour market orientation, and production rates play a decisive role. The traditional kernel of education – to 'educate' the new generation, in continental Western Europe often referred to

with the term pedagogy (see endnote 5) – has disappeared from nearly all official documents. Educational problems, even problems which concern norms
and values, are translated into 'technical problems' and are solved in a technical
way. At present, on many occasions, management jargon is used to describe
(quality) problems in education, and management techniques are introduced to
solve them.

Quality in education.

The same thing is happening to the 'quality' discussion. All education documents that have appeared since 1986 discuss the 'quality of education' and strategies to improve that quality. This is, however, a highly 'technical' debate in
which efficiency and effectiveness seem to be the only criteria (e.g., in the Netherlands a discussion has developed about the introduction of ISO-standards for
education and teacher education). From an economic point of view, governmental concern with the quality of education is understandable; governments
regard it as highly significant for the social and economic development of any
high-tech society, maybe even a condition for survival in the current free-market oriented world. The present slogan of many neo-liberal or neo-conservative
governments is 'Quality Education for All.' But in contrast to the sixties and
seventies, the emphasis is on 'quality' rather than on 'all.' A definition of the
concept 'quality,' however, is as problematic as that of the concept 'health' in
that the definition of quality is in the eye of the beholder. In current debates
about quality in the EU, the ideology of the neo-liberals or neo-conservatives –
the 'New Right' (Elliot, 1993) who emphasize narrowly conceived economic
(efficiency, cost-effectiveness, market forces) and administrative (deregulation,
strong management, output control) dimensions – is clearly present (Buchberger & Byrne, 1995, p. 10). As a consequence of this way of thinking, many reforms in education are currently designed to exploit human resources to the full
and so to train economically effective individuals in the shortest time possible.
In many countries the concern for quality is expressed by a determination to
identify practical and measurable ways and means of making schools more effective (Lowe, 1992, p. 585). The risk now is that these countries will equate
quality only with academic standards and tacitly abandon their search for social
justice. In many education documents today 'quality of education' is more or
less defined by the following three parameters:

— the level of the minimum standards of education outcomes for all (basic
    education: age 6-16), in particular with respect to languages,
    mathematics, and science (and see, for example, various indicators

appearing in Organisation for Economic Cooperation and Development, 1993b, 1995);
- the percentage of pupils who achieve those standards in the minimum amount of time (with the reduction of school staying-on time as an economic target); and
- the extent to which high-achievers can reach 'excellence.'

European governments have agreed that in order to achieve and maintain quality in education as indicated above, the quality of teaching has to be improved. In such a context, two issues are regarded as of highest importance. First, the necessity to prepare a new generation of teachers adequately for the challenges and demands that will be made on them in the near future, which implies a stronger central grip on initial teacher education. Second, the improvement of the in-service training of teachers. These steps should be taken with the expectation that the improvement of quality in teaching (i.e., raising the standards of the profession) is crucial for the efforts to raise the quality of education as a whole and of the status of the teaching profession in particular.

The current technicalization of the education sector, together with the governmental desire to control education, leads however, to a bureaucratic-managerial mode of governance of education in which topics such as the role of school management, quality control, efforts to formulate a precise description of teacher tasks and responsibilities, measurability of student achievement and the like are the central issues. As a consequence, the debate about the improvement of the quality of teaching focuses on issues such as, teacher professional profiles, teacher tasks, teacher competencies and skills, and on how to monitor these effectively. Apart from that, one observes a tendency to introduce competition between schools as a means to enhance quality, as in the U.K. where in the context of the supposed accountability of schools to the community and parents, schools have to make public their annual examination results based on national tests. The British government also proposes to improve financial support for schools with good test results and to lower the subsidy for low-achieving schools. In view of this policy, the government expects that in the medium term low-achieving schools will be weeded out. A similar development can be observed in the Netherlands. Whether the less able pupils will profit from this approach is highly questionable. However, in view of the decreasing numbers in the compulsory school age population, this approach can no longer be regarded as fiction in many countries.

As a consequence of the demand for an improvement in the quality of education and the challenges ensuing from socio-economic and political changes, teachers are confronted with inherent contradictions and multiple pressures. The quality debate, for example, supports the centrality of a properly planned and implemented *core curriculum* and the standardization of teaching methodologies. Even in countries that have adopted a greater autonomy for schools and other educational institutes, such as the Scandinavian countries, the Netherlands, and the U.K., one observes, on the one hand, an apparent freedom with respect to curriculum implementation (i.e., given a number of broad, centrally defined aims and objectives, the implementation of the curriculum contents is mainly placed in the hands of management, teachers, and professional educators who are responsible for the school), but on the other, stricter quality control mechanisms which tend to annul that freedom for the large part. As a consequence of the industrialization of education, third parties and bodies (i.e., the government as facilitator and financier, and parents, the community, business, and industry as the clients and interested parties) will tighten their grip on education. In a number of countries, for example, employers, community representatives, and others are already having a more direct say in vocational education policies regarding curriculum objectives, assessment, and the reporting of student achievement (i.e., qualification). There is also an intensive pressure on secondary general education to prepare pupils more adequately for working life — which means economical effective individuals. An example of this development can be found in the Netherlands where all members of the governmental advisory commission on the 'teaching profession' came from outside the pedagogical province (i.e., politicians and clients of education). In these circumstances teachers are likely to have little influence on the shaping of their professional activities or content of the curriculum they teach.

Management in education.

How technique, as it was defined earlier, affects teachers and teaching becomes obvious if one takes a closer look at recent developments in the 'school as organization.' In spite of all rhetoric about teacher empowerment, it can be observed that buzzwords such as 'standards,' 'professional competence,' 'accountability,' and 'appraisal' are used to define the problem of quality improvement and so to promote solutions in terms of management. As a result, schools as organizations are increasingly aimed at assigning appropriate tasks to individual teachers or groups of teachers in order to attain the objectives imposed by governments, in an efficient and economic way, and by coordinating and combining all their activities. In this technical approach, problems are identified in terms of organization rather than in terms of content (e.g., teacher burnout is attributed to the lack of career perspectives rather than to the content of the profession or to the lack of recognition and respect), and effective teaching is considered to be a matter of classroom management for which research outcomes provide good guidelines, and the like. In the Netherlands, for example, scaling-up the size of educational institutions is seen as an important instrument for the improvement of the quality of education: in primary education, schools with less that 250 pupils are doomed to disappear; in secondary education, the number of schools is to be reduced by 50 per cent; and in tertiary and vocational education, the number of centres has been reduced from over 100 to 16 mammoth institutes during the last decade. Bigger schools offer students more opportunities to choose their own subjects, a greater versatility of teachers, and a more efficient use of capital expenditures in education, it is argued. In practice, however, the opposite is true; the government constantly tries to reduce that freedom of choice for budgetary reasons.

This instrumental way of thinking leads to the standardization and rationalization of life in schools for both teachers and pupils. In this context, standardization means resolving all the problems that might possibly interfere with the functioning of the organization in advance. It is no longer left to inspiration, ingenuity, or even to intelligence to find a solution for a problem when it actually arises; problem and resolution are anticipated in advance. In this context the act of teaching becomes a more and more planned and externally controlled action. As a consequence, standardization creates impersonality, in the sense that organization relies more on methods and instructions than on individuals, and organization in education has become a technique.

Another result of this technical approach is the discussion about making the teaching profession more attractive. National and international commissions studying the problems of the teaching profession have adopted the idea to break through the present concept of a teacher's career (European Commission, 1991; Organisation for Economic Cooperation and Development, 1990b). Proposals for the differentiation of teachers' careers, thus creating status-differentiated patterns such as the sequence of junior teacher, teacher, and senior or expert teacher, are argued to create career opportunities. Needless to say, the junior status would be for novice teachers whose only duty is teaching. Major competencies for such teachers are instructional competencies and classroom management knowledge and skills. The content of initial teacher education is exclusively devoted to acquiring these competencies. Once a junior has decided to stay in the profession, and after passage of a certain period of time, and if he or she has met a number of well-defined criteria, the way would be open for further training and specialization, for example in: student guidance, middle management functions, curriculum development at the school level, or mentoring. After successful completion of the additional studies he or she would then be appointed 'teacher.' Such teachers would be regarded as professionals. For those who excel in teaching and participate successfully in a wide range of school activities – the truly high-level professionals – there would be, after additional training, a third career opportunity, such as teacher trainer, mentor for junior teachers, curriculum developer, or even participant in research programmes. These teachers could be designated 'expert teacher.'

It should be emphasized that this type of career path, based on the principle of task and role differentiation, would require a totally different approach to the role of the teacher and his or her education. One would have to move away from the principle that a teacher's initial education is sufficient for his or her whole career, a teacher would have to continue developing throughout his or her career. In this view, teacher professional development is conceived a lifelong enterprise, and initial education only prepares for the entry into the profession. Furthermore, in-service training is in this view inextricably linked with teacher professionalism; upgrading the knowledge and skills related to one's current position is no longer regarded as a voluntary activity but as an obligation for every teacher. Apart from that, in-service training must offer opportunities for further study which will lead to new career perspectives. The latter scheme is well known in a number of countries, for example in the U.K., Sweden, and West Germany. In a number of other countries, training routes to the various parts of the educational system differ so much that it is nearly impossible to switch among them (Vonk, 1995).

The teachers' role: The delivery model of teaching.

In nearly all countries the process of professionalization has triggered a debate about the role of the teacher in education, focusing on the issue of teacher professionalism. In that debate various models of the teacher's role are under discussion (Organisation for Economic Cooperation and Development, 1990b). The model which fits best into the industrial approach of education and which offers major opportunities for bureaucratic control mechanisms can best be described as the *minimum competency model*. It basically considers education as an arbitrary, imposed, pedagogically designed and bureaucratically structured 'delivery system' which is the result of political and economic debates rather than dialogues between interested parties about educational policies and practices. In this model, also called the bureaucratic-managerial approach to education, the teacher is regarded as a technician, as someone who is able to implement the curriculum that has been defined by external bodies. Decisions about what will be taught and how it has to be taught are made by management, over the heads of the classroom and the school. The teacher's job is regarded as delivering the curriculum to the pupils as effectively and efficiently as possible. In this context it is easy to assess teachers by judging how well they do this. Teacher education can be organized in such a way that deficiencies can be remedied. This minimum competency model requires initial education to instill a high degree of subject-knowledge and instructional competence. Regular in-service education and training are deemed appropriate to update this knowledge and competence and to provide remedial action for those falling short of acceptable norms. The reasoning for this approach can be characterized by the values of immediacy, practicality, relevance, and utility – all of which are expected to lead to student success and achievement – but whether they also lead to job satisfaction is questionable. Teaching quality will not be assessed on the basis of criteria which serve to enhance teaching as an educational process, but rather by using criteria that enhance the effectiveness of teaching as a means to an end which is not itself examined from an educational point of view. This approach transforms the process of 'educating' teachers into a process of 'training' teachers, and teacher education institutes will increasingly be regarded as skills centres. In that context teachers are no longer teachers but 'educational workers' who have lost their central position in education and who simply play their part in the production process called 'schooling.'

In the context of a mainly technical approach to teaching, the problem of teacher supply and demand can be solved in a technical way. If one makes teaching more extensive through modularization of the curriculum, the promotion of independent learning, and by computerizing the routine aspects of a teacher's job, teachers could take up more pupils. Apart from the supply and demand issue, this strategy may also result in a decrease of expenditures for education; on average 70-80 per cent of the education budget is spent on salaries in Europe. In particular if one considers the new developments in the field of information technology, this perspective is not unrealistic. The current trend towards the normalization and standardization of teaching, which is the ultimate consequence of the technicalization of the 'pedagogical province,' might lead to a mode of teaching in which a number of teaching tasks can easily be taken over by computers. This would make the teaching profession even less attractive. For everybody who considers this to be hypothetical, I refer to discussions about the automatization of office work in the early eighties. Look around you today! Thus, there appears to be little future for such an instrumental approach to teaching. The changing social and cultural demands made on education, and on teachers in particular, require a new definition of the teacher's role in the education process which is more pedagogic and less technocratic.

Perspectives

If one abandons the view that teaching is a technical activity taking place in an externally defined learning environment, and place pupils or students and their learning at the centre of the educational adventure, different criteria for quality in teaching emerge. It is not the level of measurable output, or the extent to which pupils are prepared to function as economically effective individuals, but the social and emotional well-being of the pupils that become important – in particular if one takes into consideration the changes in the social context of education as discussed earlier, changes in the nature of school knowledge, and the new opportunities for the use of computers as teaching aids. In this context teaching should not be standardized but rather attuned to the social and learning needs of pupils – even more so, if one takes into consideration that continuing automatization will inevitably reduce the amount of paid work. Consequently, full employment, or at least long working weeks, months, years, or careers will become rare in the decades ahead. In the near future, education can no longer be exclusively devoted to the preparation of economically effective individuals; it should also prepare pupils for leisure and the like. I have observed that this subject has also become an issue in the debate about the role of education in the Information Society.

Changes in school knowledge.

The change in the nature of school knowledge and school learning – from factual knowledge to more procedural knowledge, and from reproductive learning, to productive learning – requires a radically different approach to teaching, pupil learning, and the curriculum. Traditionally, education was aimed at transferring the cultural heritage as it had crystallized in the various disciplines to pupils – the encyclopedic approach. Teachers were regarded as experts in their respective fields. Knowledge development was considered an individual act, and, as a consequence, knowledge and expertise were an individual property, and thus teachers found themselves at the centre of the education process. Teachers were regarded as ultimately responsible for pupils' learning successes or failures. Today, however, as a result of changes in the meaning of knowledge, there is a strong emphasis on the development of meta-cognitive skills, such as 'learning to learn,' and 'managing one's own learning processes' (i.e., gaining insight into the conceptual structure of a discipline, into its strategies to develop new knowledge, and insight into strategies to retrieve information, to solve problems, and to develop procedures for self-correction).

Knowledge development has become a 'planned' and carefully 'monitored' act of a group of individuals, and knowledge and expertise belong to the knowledge production institute. In this context the nature of knowledge tends to become procedural rather than factual, and consequently pupils' learning processes are at the centre of education, and the role of teachers has become a guiding one. For teachers this means a shift in their professional knowledge; they have to become less focused on transition and more learning oriented. Apart from being subject experts, they have to act as:

- *examples* (i.e., showing interest and enjoyment in the subject they teach, demonstrating subject specific modes of thinking and acting, stimulating curiosity, emphasizing learning);
- *cognitive guides* (i.e., stimulating pupils to reflect on their own thinking process, promoting self-control, giving feedback about modes of self-control and learning, stimulating the acquisition of self-motivation strategies);
- *monitors of pupils' learning processes* (i.e., monitoring learning activities, clarifying relations among objectives and learning activities, demonstrating control and repair strategies, inviting pupils to explain why they follow a distinct mode of work); and
- *educators* (i.e., helping pupils to grow from being dependent on the teacher to independence by gradually transferring the responsibility for the learning process from teacher to pupil and by transforming external monitoring into internal monitoring).

Teaching pupils to 'learn to learn' and to 'manage their own learning process' requires a different teaching repertoire from teachers and calls for more adaptive individuals than those simply trained in narrow domain-specific knowledge. Training such teachers is the great challenge for teacher education in the decades ahead. It will be obvious that it is vital for the prosperity of this undertaking that teacher education institutes manage to attract the brighter students.

The teacher's role redefined.

The mode of teaching as described above makes heavy demands on the teacher as a person. Qualities such as enthusiasm, a high degree of motivation, commitment, expertise, enjoyment in teaching a subject, and an inclination to social relations and dialogue are required. Because a teacher uses him or herself as an instrument while teaching, he or she needs a high degree of autonomy to be able to fulfil this function adequately under the conditions indicated above. This leads to a second model identified by the OECD, indicated as *open professionalism*. This model regards teachers as self-affirming adults who perceive their initial and in-service education and training as a vital part of their professional development (Bernier & McClelland, 1989), and is designed for lifelong learning. It emphasizes the importance of participant involved planning, collaborative efforts, shared authority, and responsibility among the various educational bodies and the public as prerequisites for meaningful developments in education. In this approach teachers have a central decision-making role. Governments who support this model regard teaching as a profession and teachers as carrying out their professional responsibilities within a framework of self-determination and commitment to education. In this context governments seek to improve the material conditions of class size, teacher contact time, and in-service education provisions. Sergiovanni and Starratt (1993) argue that: 'Being a professional has to do with something else besides being competent. One might refer to this 'something else' as professional virtue' (p. 48). They distinguish four dimensions of professional virtue:

- A commitment to practice in an exemplary way;
- A commitment to practice toward valued social ends;
- A commitment not only to one's own practice but to practice itself; and
- A commitment to the ethic of caring. (p. 48)

The first dimension refers to teachers' professional obligation to reflect, improve, and to stay informed about research in practice. The second dimension represents a commitment to place oneself in the service of pupils, parents, and agreed-upon school values and goals. The third dimension forces teachers to broaden their outlook (i.e., to develop into an 'extended' professional). Hoyle (1989) distinguishes between restricted professionals, who perceive their work in terms of classroom activities mainly based on experience and intuition, and extended professionals, who have a more extended view on their work. The latter perceive the interaction between theory and their practical experiences as valuable, adopt a broader social context of education, and see activities outside the classroom as an essential part of their work (p. 419). The last dimension shifts the emphasis from viewing teaching as a technical activity towards viewing teaching as a professional activity involving concern for the whole person.

In contrast to regarding teaching as a technical activity, the model of open professionalism regards professional knowledge as the result of deliberate reflection. That knowledge is considered relativistic, dependent on context, and is used to inform and not to direct practice (Calderhead, 1988; Grimmett, MacKinnon, Erickson, & Riecken, 1990; Kremer-Hayon, Vonk, & Fessler, 1993). In this model, accountability and responsibility are conceived as operating in mutual trust and partnership between the interested parties in the education venture.[16] This approach to teaching places the teacher at the centre of the process of improving the quality of education. Teachers, individually as well as in groups, are responsible for analysing the needs of the school. They are regarded as being able and willing to discuss possible solutions or developments in open debate, not only among themselves, but also with other legitimate and interested parties, and, if necessary, they are prepared to take decisions about what is to be done and to ensure its implementation. Teacher evaluation in this context is regarded as 'horizontal evaluation' (Gitlin & Smyth, 1989) which is supposed to change teachers' basic understanding of themselves and their teaching world (p. 62). Teachers are seen as self-improving innovative leaders who are capable of analysing their own actions, identifying pupils' needs and reacting to them and evaluating the outcomes of those interventions.[17] Teachers, just like all human beings, have the need to give meaning to their professional lives, to experience a sense of their own worth and dignity (Fukuyama, 1992, p. 198). They wish to be recognized, respected, and valued. Job satisfaction is not only defined by status, career opportunities, or salaries; an important aspect of satisfaction for teachers is the conviction that they are doing an important job in which they can find fulfilment and that they have a real say in giving shape to that job. The 'open professionalism' approach, which recognizes teachers as responsible professionals, may give teachers greater satisfaction which results in a reduction in early job leaving and burn-out.

However, here we hit upon a major dilemma for education reform. The majority of the contemporary teaching force is educated and trained in a different tradition. Apart from that, evaluations of teacher empowerment efforts show meagre effects, teachers hesitate to 'take the new responsibility,' and too many members of today's teaching force see themselves as restricted professionals rather than extended professionals. As a consequence, beginning teachers, who may have acquired a different perception of their profession during training, are not encouraged by their colleagues to develop in such a way that they will be able to meet the challenges that lie ahead, and because they do not really have a choice they simply become part of the existing tradition. In these circumstances, the deployment of well-trained mentors could pay off (Vonk, 1995). This is a serious problem for more school-based teacher education, such as in the U.K. and the Netherlands. Nevertheless, I strongly believe that the pursuit of a high-quality teaching force only has a future when teachers and the teaching profession adopt the view of teachers as 'open professionals.' However, we still have a long way to go to achieve this goal. The profession has to ensure that in-service education and training are not only concerned with upgrading the knowledge and skills of teachers but also with issues such as teachers' perceptions of teaching, pedagogy, professional ethics, professional responsibility towards society, and the like. Apart from that, it is high time to start with the training of trainers, both inside (mentors) and outside the school (teacher educators). These two ends are to be met if one really wants a more school-based initial teacher training that can contribute to the pursuit of improving the quality of education.

CONCLUSIONS

In Europe many issues, such as policies regarding the economy, welfare, social security, and the labour market, are no longer the exclusive domain of the individual nation-states but tend to be implemented at the European or, even at a global level. So far education is one of the last domains that seem to be exclusively the concern of the national states, but developments in Europe and abroad show that education too has become an international issue. For Europe's future it is crucial to find a solution for the cultural dilemma of 'uniformity versus diversity.' This is not only a European dilemma but, because of the development of the 'global village,' rather a universal one. Elsewhere (Vonk, 1992) I have advocated the principle of 'uniformity in diversity,' which means that we recognize and honour cultural differences but strive to find a common basis for cooperation. No culture has the right to dominate; national, regional, ethnic, and religious identities should be respected. Knowledge and understanding of the differences in culture, history, the structures of the various societies, and the habits in everyday life in various countries is a condition for peaceful coexistence. One may, however, expect teachers to represent certain values that are basic for Western European societies, such as democracy, equality, solidarity, tolerance, and respect for cultural identities, and to practice these in every day school life.

Apart from promoting European unity in education, the major concern of most European governments is to provide high-quality teaching and so to ensure the maintenance of high standards throughout teachers' careers. However, it is my impression that standards, professional competence, accreditation, accountability, and appraisal are part of the rhetoric employed 'to define' the problem of teaching quality and to promote certain technical proposals to solve that problem. The nature of these proposals is mainly bureaucratic and management-oriented. In contemporary society, technocrats and bureaucrats define many social, educational, and other problems in terms of management instead of content (Carr, 1989). At present, management seems to have the status of a 'panacea' for all problems in education. If one considers the constant tension resulting from the dialectic between governmental responsibilities towards education, on the one hand, and teachers' responsibilities, on the other, I observe that in a number of countries legislation has provided the governing bodies with the power to impose their opinion about curriculum and sometimes even teaching methodologies on teachers. This is a clear example of the 'management of teachers' approach and illustrates that teachers are losing out in the curriculum power struggle. Trends in the U.K. and a number of other countries in Europe suggest that the work of a teacher is becoming more strictly defined, more fragmented, more often supervised, and more thoroughly assessed. If pursued further, this 'delivery model' of the teacher's role would lead to the (further) deprofessionalization of teaching in the long term.

In view of changes in the social context currently taking place, and consequently the new demands that will be put on education in the decades ahead, it is obvious that both the content and the nature of the teacher's role will change. If one places the teacher at the heart of the process of education reform, this reform can only lead to maintaining or increasing the quality of education if teachers feel a strong commitment to their duty and experience a feeling of ownership with respect to the process of change. However, if teachers really want to see themselves as professionals and to be recognized as such by the governing bodies, they will have to regain at least partial control over the decisions concerning their work and the curriculum. In this respect I fully agree with Darling-Hammond (1985) who argues:

> Professionalization involves not only the status and compensation accorded to the members of an occupation; it also involves the extent to which members of that occupation maintain control over the content of their work and the degree to which society values the work of that occupation. (p. 205)

This view corresponds to a great extent with the attributes of what I described as open professionalism.

ENDNOTES

1. The European Commission (EC), the executive committee of the European Union, DG-V (the Task Force: Human Resources, Training and Youth of the EU), the Council of Europe, and the UNESCO and the OECD as far as they have published about education in Europe.
2. An *open system* is a system that interacts with other social systems, external organizations and the like (i.e., the social context). This interaction concerns the exchange of particular types of information and the reception of certain resources.
3. The reference date of the consulted documents is 1 May 1995.
4. *Action* is defined as: A purposive change in the world of objects with which an individual is confronted. This is Vygotsky's original definition (Leont'ev, 1989, p. 27). In modern action-theory it is defined as: A special category of behaviour: it is intentional and controlled by thought processes. Actions are considered as interpreted patterns of behaviour which are hierarchical in nature (Hofer, 1986).
5. In continental European languages the term 'pedagogy' is often used in connection with education. In contrast with the English definition of the concept: *the study of the methods and principles of teaching* (Collins, Hanks, Fox, Moon, & Stock, 1987), 'pedagogy' has a different meaning in continental European languages. Education includes both instructional and pedagogical actions (i.e., the latter are used by teachers to empower pupils to give shape to their life's contingencies actively). Pedagogic actions are situational, practical, normative, relational and self-reflective (Van Manen, 1991).
6. Critics of this development are Habermas – an exponent of the Frankfurt School (Ewert, 1991) – and the members of the 'Critical Theory' movement (Davies, 1995).
7. Habermas (1962) argues that stability and growth in an economic system is only possible when the population is de-politicized. In order to ensure the loyalty of the masses political neutralization has to be justified. This is done by means of the technocratic ideology which emphasizes concepts such as 'effectiveness,' 'efficiency,' 'technical control,' and 'objective rationality,' all in all, these concepts are borrowed from the world of scientific-technical progress. A consequence of this development is that discussions on practical questions about

norms and values for human social life are banned. Those practical questions are treated as or translated into technical problems, which has the advantage that they can be solved separate from public discussions.

8. Apple (1989), gives an analysis of the developments with respect to education in the U.S. since World War II, and particularly of the shift from the social democratic oriented to the conservative oriented Social Accord. In a number of European countries a similar development is taking place.

9. Shavit and Blossfeld (1993) concluded from their studies that during the last half century in 11 of the 13 countries studied there was little evidence of change in the link between peoples' social origin and their access to higher education. Exceptions are the Netherlands and Sweden, where due to advanced social welfare policies, the correlations between social class and educational achievement declined and remained lower than in other the countries.

10. The *cultural capital* thesis was introduced by Bourdieu and Passeron (1970, pp. 230-253). They assume that education has only a relative autonomy and that it has to adapt to the competing needs of a socially divided society: elite, intermediate, and lower class. They argue that what is identified in society as 'valid knowledge,' is the condensation of the world view of the ruling elite, and the validity of that knowledge depends on the extent to which the elite succeeds in having it reproduced through education. Cultural capital exists of language competence and cultural competence. These competencies are present in the ruling elite. Based on a closer look at the study of Shavit and Blossfeld (1993) it is easy to conclude that in most European countries milieu-specific school-success still increases when pupils move through the system from primary to university education. Adhesion of the middle class to education stems from the expectation that education is still the basis for social opportunities. If one interprets this thesis as less static than was originally meant by the authors (i.e., cultural capital is liable to change as result of competition between rivalling elites), then it is a useful guide for a sociological analysis of education.

11. A good example of state leadership in education is the 1985 policy plan for the reconstruction of French secondary education by the then Secretary of State Chevènement, aiming at a baccalauréat for 80 per cent of each pupil cohort in the year 2000 (Rochex, 1991).

12. A discussion on the issue of 'hegemony vs. counter-hegemony' is found in Kyle (1991).

13. *International Mathematics and Science Studies*, which are being undertaken under the auspices of the IEA (International Association for the Evaluation of Educational Achievement). See, for example, Postlethwaite and Wiley, 1991.

14. Examples are publications of the Department of Education and Science (DES), such as: *Teaching Quality*, 1983; *The National Curriculum*, 1989a; *Initial Teacher Education: The Approval of Courses*, 1989a.

15. An example is a recent publication of the Dutch Ministry of Education and Science (1993): *Een beroep met perspectief* (The Teaching Profession, A Profession with a Future), in which teachers' professional profiles play an important part.

16. A similar approach is observed in the *Teacher Empowerment* movement in the U.S. (e.g., Lichtenstein, McLaughlin, & Knudsen, 1992).

17. An enlightening article on this topic is Strike (1993), *Professionalism, Democracy and Discursive Communities*.

REFERENCES

Altbach, P. G., Arnove, R., & Kelly, G. (Eds.). (1982). *Comparative education*. New York: Macmillan.

Apple, M. W. (1989). The politics of common sense: Schooling, populism, and the New Right. In H. A. Giroux & P. McLaren (Eds.), *Critical pedagogy, the State, and cultural struggle* (pp. 32-50). New York: SUNY.

Archer, M. S. (1979). *Social origins of educational systems*. London: Sage.

Arendt, H. (1993). *Between past and future* (pp. 173-197). New York: Penguin Books Inc.

Association for Teacher Education in Europe (1990, September). *ATEE-News* (No. 29). Brussels: Author.

Bernier, R. & McClelland, A. F. (1989). Contexts of professional development. In M. L. Holly & C. McLoughlin (Eds.), *Perspectives on teacher professional development* (pp. 19-55). London: Falmer Press.

Bourdieu, P. & Passeron, J. C. (1970). *La réproduction: Element pour une theorie du système d'enseignement*. Paris: Editions Minuit.

Brock, C. & Tulasiewicz, W. (Eds.). (1994). *Education in a single Europe*. London: Routledge.

Bruce, M. (1990). *Teacher education and the ERASMUS programme*. Brussels: Association for Teacher Education in Europe.

Bruce, M. (1991). Internationalizing teacher education. *British Journal of Educational Studies, XXXIX*(2), 163-173.

Buchberger, F. (Ed.). (1992). *ATEE-guide to institutions of teacher education in Europe (AGITE)*. Brussels: Association for Teacher Education in Europe.

Buchberger, F. & Byrne, K. (1995). Quality in teacher education: A supressed theme? *European Journal of Teacher Education, 18*(1), 9-23.

Calderhead, J. (Ed.). (1988). *Teachers' professional learning*. London: Falmer Press.

Carr, W. (Ed.). (1989). *Quality in teaching: Arguments for a reflective profession*. London: Falmer Press.

Carrithers, M. (1992). *Why humans have cultures: Explaining anthropology and diversity*. Oxford: Oxford University Press.

Collins, J., Hanks, P., Fox, G., Moon, R., & Stock, P. (Eds). (1987). *Collins cobuild dictionary of English language*. London: Harper Collins Publishers.

Council of Europe (1987a). *The quality and effectiveness of school teaching* (Document #5670-A). Strasbourg: Author.

Council of Europe (1987b). *Documents of the fifteenth session of the standing conference of the European ministers of education, Helsinki, 1986*. Strasbourg: Author.

Council of Europe (1988). *Innovation in primary education: Final report of Project No. 8 of the CDCC*. Strasbourg: Author.

Darling-Hammond, L. (1985). Valuing teachers: The making of a profession. *Teachers College Record, 87*(2), 205-218.

Davies, S. (1995). Leaps of faith: Shifting in currents in critical sociology of education. *American Journal of Sociology, 100*(6), 1448-1479.

Department of Education and Science (1983). *Teaching quality*. London: HMSO.

Department of Education and Science (1989a). *The national curriculum*. London: HMSO.

Department of Education and Science (1989b). *Initial teacher training: Approval of courses* (Circular No. 24/89). London: HMSO.

De Vries, M. J. (1994). Teacher education for technology education. In M. Galton & B. Moon (Eds.), *Handbook of teacher training in Europe* (pp. 153-165). London/Strasbourg: David Foulton Publishers/Council of Europe.

Dutch Ministry of Education and Science (1993). *Een beroep met perspectief*. The Hague, NL: Commissie Toekomst Leraarschap.

Eide, K. (1992). The future of European education as seen from the North. *Comparative Education, 28*(1), 9-17.

Elliot, J. (1993). *Reconstructing teacher education*. London: Falmer Press.

Ellul, J. (1964). *The technological society*. New York: Vintage Books.

Ellul, J. (1990). *The technological bluff*. Grand Rapids, MI: Eerdmans Publication.

Eraut, M. (1989). *The information society – A challenge for education policies?* (Background document for the Standing Conference of Ministers of Education, 16th Session, Istanbul). Strasbourg: Council of Europe.

European Commission (1988a). *Education in the European community, medium-term perspectives, 1988-1992* (Vol. 1988, p. 280 et seq.). Brussels: Author.

European Commission (1988b). *Resolution of the Council and the ministers of education within the Council on the European dimension in education of 24 May 1988*. Brussels: Author.

European Commission (1991, October). *Final report of the EC conference on 'The teaching profession in Europe', Noordwijkerhout, The Netherlands*. The Hague, NL: Ministry of Education and Science.

European Commission 1995). *Key data on education in the European Union*. Luxembourg: Office for Official Publications of the European Communities.

European Community 1991). *Structures of the education and initial training systems in the member states of the EC*. Luxembourg: Officer for Official Publications of the European Community.

Eurostat 1993). *Demographic statistics*. Luxembourg: Statistical Office of the European Community.

Ewert, G. D. (1991). Habermas and education: A comprehensive overview of the influence of Habermas in educational literature. *Review of Educational Research, 61*(2), 345-378.

Finkielkraut, A. (1987). *La défaite de la pensée*. Paris: Gallimard.

Fukuyama, F. (1992). *The end of history and the last man*. New York: Penguin Books.

Fullan, M. G. (1991). *The new meaning of educational change*. New York: Teachers College Press.

Gitlin, A. & Smyth, J. (1989). *Teacher evaluation: Educative alternatives*. London: Falmer Press.

Grimmett, P., MacKinnon, A., Erickson, G. & Riecken, T. (1990), Reflective practice in teacher education. In R. T. Clift, W. R. Houston, & M. Pugach (Eds.), *Encouraging reflective practice: An analysis of issues and programs* (pp. 212-233). New York: Teachers College Press.

Habermas, J. (1962). *Stukturwandel der Öffentlichkeit*. Berlin: Neuwied.

Halls, W. D. (1994). 16-19: Some reflections on Europe and the reforms. *Comparative Education, 30*(1), 25-29.

Hofer, M. (1986). *Sozialpsychologie erzieherischen Handelns*. Göttingen: Verlag für Psychologie.

Hofstede, G. (1994). *Cultures and organizations: Intercultural cooperation and its importance for survival*. London: Harper Collins Publishers.

Hoyle, E. (1989). The primary school teacher as professional. In M. Galton & A. Blyth (Eds.), *Handbook of primary education in Europe* (pp. 415-433). London: David Foulton Publishers/ Council of Europe.

Idenburg, P. J. (1971). *Theorie van het onderwijsbeleid*. Groningen: Wolters-Noordhoff.

Jones, P. (1993). *Studying society: Sociological theories and research practices*. London: Collins Educational.

Kennedy, P. (1994). *Preparing for the 21st century*. New York: Random House.

Klinzing, H. G. (1990). Research on teacher education in West Germany. In R. P. Tisher & M. F. Wideen (Eds.), *Research in teacher education: International perspectives* (pp. 89-105). London: Falmer Press.

Kremer-Hayon, L., Vonk, J.H.C., & Fessler, R. (Eds.). (1993). *Teacher professional development: A multiple perspective approach*. Amsterdam/Berwyn, PA: Swets & Zeitlinger.

Kyle, W. C., Jr. (1991). The reform agenda and science education: Hegomonic control versus counterhegomony. *Science Education, 75*, 403-411.

Lemaire, T. (1990). *Twijfel aan Europa*. Baarn: Ambo.

Leont'ev, A. N. (1989). The problem of activity in the history of Soviet psychology. *Soviet Psychology, 27*, 22-39.

Leschinsky, A. & Mayer, K. U. (1990). *The comprehensive school experiment revisited: Evidence from Western Europe*. Frankfurt am Main: Peter Lang.

Leurin, M. (1989). Multi-cultural education within European traditions. In M. Galton & A. Blyth (Eds.), *Handbook of primary education in Europe* (pp. 354-369). London: David Foulton Publishers/Council of Europe.

Lichtenstein, G., McLaughlin, M. W., & Knudsen, J. (1992). Teacher empowerment and professional knowledge. In A. Lieberman (Ed.), *The changing contexts of teaching* (Ninety-first yearbook of the National Society for Studies in Education, pp. 37-59). Chicago: University of Chicago Press.

Lieberman, A. (Ed.). (1992). *The changing contexts of teaching* (Ninety-first yearbook of the National Society for Studies in Education). Chicago: University of Chicago Press.

Lowe, J. (1992). Education and European integration. *International Review of Education, 38*(6), 579-590.

Lundgren, U. P. (1987). *New challenges for the teachers and their education* (M-ED-15-4). Strasbourg: Council of Europe.

Lundgren, S. (1989). *Teacher training for basic education: The teacher education reform*. Stockholm: National Board of Universities and Colleges.

Lyotard, J. F. (1979). *La condition postmoderne: Rapport sur le savoir*. Paris: Editions Minuit (Translation: The post-modern condition. In *Theory and history of literature series, 10*, 1984. Minneapolis: University of Minnesota Press.)

Lyotard, J. F. (1986). *Le postmodernisme expliqué aux enfents* (Chapter 3). Paris: Éditions Galilée.

Maslow, A. H. (1970). *Motivation and personality*. New York: Harper.

McLean, M. (1990). *Britain and a single market Europe: Prospects for a common school curriculum*. London: Kogan Page.

Ministère de l'Education Nationale (1988). Les besoins de recrutement en personnels enseignants des collèges et lycées publics entre 1988 et 2000. *Note d'Information*, No. 88-12. Paris: Author.

Mitter, W. (1992). Educational adjustments and perspectives in a united Germany. *Comparative Education, 28*(1), 45-52.

Naeve, G. (1987). Challenges met – Trends in teacher education 1975-1985. *News-Letter 4/87* (pp. 19-38). Strasbourg: Council of Europe.

Naeve, G. (1991, October). *Change and challenge: The mobilization of Europe's teachers*. Document prepared for the conference on 'The Teaching Profession in Europe,' Noordwijkerhout, The Netherlands.

Naeve, G. (1992). *The teaching nation: Prospects for teachers in the European community*. Oxford: Pergamon Press.

Organisation for Economic Cooperation and Development (1987). *Multicultural education*. Paris: Author.

Organisation for Economic Cooperation and Development (1988a, October). Documentation for the conference on *'Teacher training for basic education'*, Novi Sad (Y).

Organisation for Economic Cooperation and Development (1988b). *Teachers in the United Kingdom: Teacher supply in England and Wales in an age of educational change* (SME/ET88.21). Paris: Author.

Organisation for Economic Cooperation and Development (1990a). *Lone parent families: The economic challenge*. Paris: Author.

Organisation for Economic Cooperation and Development (1990b). *The teacher today: Tasks, conditions, policies*. Paris: Author.

Organisation for Economic Cooperation and Development (1990c). *Reviews of national policies for education: Norway*. Paris: Author.

Organisation for Economic Cooperation and Development (1990d). Childcare in OECD countries. In *Employment outlook* (Chapter. 5). Paris: Author.

Organisation for Economic Cooperation and Development (1991). *Reviews of national policies for education: Ireland*. Paris: Author.

Organisation for Economic Cooperation and Development (1992a). *High-quality education and training for all*. Paris: Author.

Organisation for Economic Cooperation and Development (1992b). *Public educational expenditure, costs and financing: An analysis of trends 1970-1988*. Paris: Author.

Organisation for Economic Cooperation and Development (1992c). *Reviews of national policies for education: Netherlands*. Paris: Author.

Organisation for Economic Cooperation and Development (1992d). *Education at a glance: OECD indicators*. Paris: Author.

Organisation for Economic Cooperation and Development (1993a). *Education in OECD countries 88/89 and 89/90: Compendium for statistical information*. Paris: Author.

Organisation for Economic Cooperation and Development (1993b). *Education at a glance: OECD indicators*. Paris: Author.

Organisation for Economic Cooperation and Development (1993c). *Reviews of national policies for education: Belgium*. Paris: Author.

Organisation for Economic Cooperation and Development (1995). *Education at a glance: OECD indicators*. Paris: Author.

Organisation for Economic Cooperation and Development/CERI (1989). *One school, many cultures*. Paris: CERI.

Pascal, C., Bertram, T., & Heaslip, P. (1991). *Comparative directory of initial training for early years teachers*. Harwick Grove/Brussels: Worchester College of Education/ATEE.

Peters, J. J. (1992). The European dimension in teacher education. In J.H.C. Vonk, J.H.G.I. Giesbers, J. J. Peters, & T. Wubbels (Eds.), *New prospects for teacher education in Europe II* (pp. 89-98). Amsterdam/Brussels: Vrije Universiteit, Teacher Education Department.

Postlethwaite, T. N. & Wiley, D. E. (Eds.). (1991). *The second IEA science study II: Science achievements in twenty-three countries*. Oxford: Pergamon Press.

Pritchard, R.M.O. (1992). The German dual system: Educational utopia? *Comparative Education* 28(2), 131-143.

Rochex, J. Y. (1991). France: Crisis in the schools. *Contemporary European Affairs, 3*(4), 73-86.

Rubinson, R. (Ed.). (1981). *The dynamics of world development*. Beverly Hills: Sage Publications.

Sergiovanni, T. J. & Starratt, R. J. (1993). *Supervision a redefinition* (5th ed.). New York: McGraw-Hill.

Shavit, Y. & H. P. Blossfeld (1993). *Persistent inequalities: A comparative study of educational attainment in thirteen countries*. Boulder, CO: Westview Press.

Social Studies Review, (September 1990). Oxford: Philip Allan Publishers.

Solway, D. (1989). *Education lost. Reflections on contemporary pedagogical practice*. Toronto: OISE Press.

Strike, K. A. (1993). Professionalism, democracy, and discursive communities: Normative reflections on restructuring. *American Educational Research Journal, 30*(2), 255-275.

Teubner, G. (1993). *Law as an autopoietic system*. Oxford: Blackwell.

United Nations (1993). World population prospects: The 1992 revision. New York: UNESCO.

Van der Pot, J.H.J. (1985). *Die Bewertung des technischen Fortschritts: Ein systematisches Ubersicht der Theorien*. Assen: Van Gorcum.

Vaniscotte, F. (1989). *70 Millions d'élèves: L'Europe de l'éducation*. Paris: Hatier.

Van Manen, M. (1991). *The tact of teaching: The meaning of pedagogical thoughtfulness.* Ontario: Althous Press/SUNY.

Vonk, J.H.C. (1990). Professional preparation and development of teachers in Europe: Regional report on the pre- and in-service training of teachers in Europe. In F. Klassen (Ed.), *Standards of excellence* (Report of the ICET/UNESCO Interregional Seminar, Cairo 1989, Chapter 4). Arlington: UNESCO/ICET.

Vonk, J.H.C. (1991). Trends and the development of curriculum for the professional preparation of teachers in Europe. *British Journal of Educational Studies, XXXIX*(2), 117-138.

Vonk, J.H.C. (1992). New prospects for teacher education in Europe. In J.H.C. Vonk & H. J. van Helden (Eds.), New prospects for teacher education in Europe I (Symposium proceedings of the 16th annual conference of ATEE, pp. 43-57). Amsterdam/Brussels: IDO-VU/ATEE.

Vonk, J.H.C. (1993). Konzequenzen und Vorschläge für die Lehrerausbildung unter Berücksichtigung der europäischen Dimension. *Pädagogik und Schule in Ost und West, 41*(3), 150-160.

Vonk, J.H.C. (1994). Teacher induction: The great omission in education. In M. Galton & B. Moon (Eds.), *Handbook of teacher education in Europe* (pp. 85-109). London: David Foulton Publishers/Council of Europe.

Vonk, J.H.C. (1995). Teacher education and reform in Western Europe. In N. K. Shimahara & I. Z. Holowinsky (Eds.), *Teacher education in industrialized nations* (pp. 255-319). New York: Garland Publishing, Inc.

Chapter 9: The Changing Social Context of Teaching in the United States

LINDA DARLING-HAMMOND WITH THE ASSISTANCE OF
MARCELLA L. BULLMASTER
Columbia University

As the twenty-first century nears, most nations around the world are undertaking major transformations of their governmental and education systems to respond to changing economic, demographic, political, and social imperatives. Nearly all countries are engaged in serious discussion of school reform to address demands for much higher levels of education for much greater numbers of citizens – demands created by a new information age, major economic shifts, and a resurgence and redefinition of democracy around the globe. These demands are being imposed upon educational institutions designed a century ago for a different time. In the United States as elsewhere, the need to prepare future citizens and workers who can cope with complexity, use new technologies, and work cooperatively to frame and solve novel problems – and the need to do this for a much more diverse and inclusive group of learners – has stimulated efforts to rethink school goals and curriculum, to better prepare teachers, and to redesign school organizations.

The challenges that face the U.S. are not unique. As the global economy becomes more interdependent and as the pace of technological change continues to increase exponentially, other nations, too, are examining the relationships between education and economic well-being. With the birth of new democracies in Africa, Eastern Europe, and South America, schools there are assuming the weighty task of preparing new citizens for educated decision making and democratic life. With burgeoning migration and immigration worldwide, virtually all societies are seeking simultaneously to educate a more diverse population and to extend schooling so as to ensure higher levels of more complex skills.

This is a new agenda for most countries. In agrarian and industrial societies, economic growth did not require high levels of education for most citizens: Economies were dominated by low- or unskilled work in factories or on farms. One could argue then, as many have, that too much education would have reduced the supply of willing workers and made them too independently thoughtful to sustain the routines essential to factory line organizations. As industrialized societies move into the information age, most new jobs require

B.J. Biddle et al. (eds.), International Handbook of Teachers and Teaching, 1053-1079

high levels of knowledge and skill, while managing life as a citizen also requires increasingly complex skills (Drucker, 1989).

In addition, until the last twenty years, a minority of countries tried to operate democratic forms of government. For governments run by small elites without popular involvement, broadly available education was neither necessary nor desirable. The many countries that have recently become democracies must now contend with the fact that low levels of education for many citizens pose a threat to peaceful, thoughtful political decision making. Thus, nations that are leading the world into a technological age managed through democratic governance are experiencing a convergence of political and economic demands for high levels of education that is relatively new in our history.

At the same time, of course, each nation has its own individual history and tradition that frame its current context and response to these challenges. In the United States, born a democracy and always a nation of diverse peoples, these historical influences include a vast industrial engine that generated growth and offered prototypes for social and educational organization, an ethic of competition and individualism that has encouraged entrepreneurship as well as dramatic inequality in access to education, and a mixed view of education as both the 'great equalizer' and the primary vehicle for sorting individuals into their 'rightful' societal slots. These influences have shaped the current system of education in important ways over the last century. The changing social context of teaching today must be understood in relation to the industrial revolution and associated major reforms of education that occurred a century ago.

THE TWENTIETH CENTURY CONTEXT

One hundred years ago, at the dawn of a massive economic transformation from an agricultural to a manufacturing society, a sense of urgency like today's characterized school reform efforts. John Dewey (1900) described the situation in this startlingly contemporary manner:

> One can hardly believe there has been a revolution in all history so rapid, so extensive, so complete.... The face of the earth is making over; political boundaries are wiped out and moved about, as if they were indeed only lines on a paper map; population is hurriedly gathered into cities from the ends of the earth; habits of living are altered with startling abruptness and thoroughness; the search for the truths of nature is infinitely stimulated and facilitated, and their application to life made not only practicable, but commercially necessary.... That this revolution should not affect education in some other than a formal and superficial fashion is inconceivable. (p. 9)

The Adoption of the Factory Model

Progressive educators like Dewey advocated that school leaders respond to this evolving social climate by structuring schools as communities of learners where teachers and students could engage in meaningful work connected to real-life tasks. However, the prevailing model of school reform that took hold in the United States mimicked the then-popular factory line managed by centralized bureaucracy. Like manufacturing industries and twentieth-century businesses, schools developed as increasingly specialized organizations run by carefully specified procedures engineered to yield standard products. Based on faith in rationalistic organizational behavior, in the power of rules to direct human behavior, and in the ability of administrators to discover and implement the common procedures that would produce desired outcomes, twentieth-century education policy has assumed that continually improving the design specifications for schoolwork – required courses, textbooks, testing instruments, and management systems – will lead to student learning.

The twentieth-century search for a bureaucratic route to the 'one best system' of education (Tyack, 1974) was based on the assumptions that students are standardized and that educational treatments can be prescribed. Because most major teaching decisions were handed down through administrative channels and encapsulated in packaged teaching materials, teachers were viewed as needing little knowledge or expertise (Darling-Hammond, 1990c). In the model bureaucracy where students learn according to plan and centralized procedures outline decisions for every circumstance, there are no problems of practice; there are only problems of implementation. Because decisions are made at the top of the educational hierarchy, there is no rationale in this kind of organization for substantial teacher preparation or professional development, aside from 'in-servicing' designed to ensure more exact implementation of prescribed teaching procedures. The presumption of regularity and the faith in routine meant that schools were designed to function without major investments in teachers' professional knowledge and without time for collegial consultation and planning.

Factory model schooling led to a lack of investment in teacher knowledge, as it invested (both in businesses and in 'modern' school systems) in an extensive administrative apparatus to design, monitor, and inspect work rather than investing in the knowledge of the people doing the work. Over time, the bureaucratic approach to schooling has led to a reduction in resources devoted to the actual activities of teaching and learning due to the perceived need to maintain a large cadre of supervisors and specialists to manage practice and to administer a wide array of special programs. From 1950 to 1980, the number of administrative staff grew at more than twice the rate of the number of teachers in American schools. The U.S. Department of Labor (1986) reported that in 1986 school systems employed approximately one administrative staff person for every two-

and-one-half teachers. By 1991, the proportion of public school staff who were classified as classroom teachers had declined to only 53 per cent from over 70 per cent in 1950. Even fewer of those classified as teachers actually teach as their primary duty (National Center for Education Statistics [NCES], 1993a).

While less than half of all public education employees in the U.S. are teachers, teaching staff comprise more than three fourths of all public education employees in Australia and Japan, and more than 80 per cent in Belgium, Germany, the Netherlands, and Spain (Organization for Economic Co-operation and Development [OECD], 1992). These teachers have broader responsibilities for teaching and counselling students; more extensive involvement in developing curriculum and assessments; and more time for collaborative work, professional development, and one-on-one meetings with parents and students.

Teachers in these countries generally teach large groups of students only about 15 to 20 hours out of a 40- to 45-hour work week (Darling-Hammond, 1990b; Nelson & O'Brien, 1993). The remaining time is spent developing lessons with colleagues, observing other classrooms, and engaging in study groups and other forms of professional development. These nations assume that teachers must continually learn and consult with each other to make instructional decisions, rather than stamping students with formulaic lessons as they pass by, conveyor-belt style, in five or six batches of 30 each day.

Despite a shorter school year (averaging 185 days per year), teachers in the United States teach more hours per day and year than those in any other country (Nelson & O'Brien, 1993). Teaching consists primarily of instructing large groups of students, in isolation from colleagues, for most of the day. Almost everything else a teacher does is considered 'released time' or 'homework.' Time for preparation, planning, working with other colleagues, meeting individually with students or parents, or working on the development of curriculum or assessment is rarely available and not considered part of the teacher's main job. Most U.S. elementary teachers have three or fewer hours for preparation per week (only 8.3 minutes for every hour in the classroom), while secondary teachers generally have five preparation periods per week (13 minutes per hour of classroom instruction). Of course, most teachers are accustomed to working long hours outside of school. On average, teachers work on teaching-related tasks an additional 10 to 15 hours per week outside of school hours (National Education Association [NEA], 1992).

Countries that organize their schools around a greater number of well-supported teachers invest more of their resources in supporting the efforts of 'front line workers' than in trying to inspect, monitor, and control that work. Roles for educators are more fluid and less rigidly taylorized: Rather than hiring some people to 'do' teaching and others to plan and administer it, virtually everyone teaches, and virtually everyone plans and manages the work of the school. The result is more collective practice and more shared knowledge, as teachers have more time to work together. If U.S. schools were to debureaucratize roles and involve all professional staff in teaching at least some of the time, they, too, could make more productive use of professional staff in schools and provide more time for teacher learning.

From a student's point of view, the factory model school has other shortcomings. We now know that effective teachers have substantial knowledge of learning, development, subject matter, and teaching, and they accommodate a variety of cognitive styles and learning rates with activities that broaden rather than reduce the range of possibilities for learning. Yet, the factory model assumed that students were standardized, learning goals were simple and nonvariable, and teaching could be prescribed from far beyond the classroom. If teachers followed the detailed guidance they were given for marching through subjects and texts, it was believed, students would invariably learn.

We have since learned that this view of learning – and its translation into assembly line technologies for sequencing learning tasks – was fundamentally flawed. Students learn in very different ways, and effective teachers must take hundreds of curricular goals and student needs into account in fashioning learning experiences (Darling-Hammond, 1990a; Shulman, 1983). By its very nature, conventional bureaucratic management is incapable of providing appropriate education for students who do not fit the mold upon which the prescriptions for practice are based.

Impersonal school structures and the fragmentation of curriculum, programs, and services work against teachers' abilities to adapt instruction to individual students' needs. Within each of these separate arenas, the narrowly prescriptive curriculum mandates levied by many states and districts reduce teacher effectiveness. Because they cannot meet the non-standardized learning requirements of students, they limit the efficacy of teachers' work and widen the 'cracks' into which students can fall and be lost.

Changing Demands of Education

This kind of schooling system worked reasonably well many decades ago for the purposes for which it was designed: the acquisition of minimal basic skills and preparation for routine work for most students, and the development of higher order thinking and performance skills for only a few. Despite high drop-out rates – only 2 per cent of students graduated at the beginning of the twentieth century, and only about 50 per cent by the 1950s (Cremin, 1989) – there were decent jobs on the farm or in the factory to accommodate those for whom schooling was not a success.

However, these circumstances have changed. Whereas in 1900 about half the nation's jobs required low or unskilled labor, today fewer than 10 per cent do.

And while fewer than 10 per cent of jobs at the beginning of the century were professional or technical positions requiring higher education, more than half of the new employment opportunities created in this decade will require education beyond high school, and fully 90 per cent will require at least a high school education (Hudson Institute, 1987). The technological explosion has hastened new methods of organization for business and industry which demand better-educated, more thoughtful workers for virtually all kinds of jobs (Drucker, 1986).

There is little room in today's society for those who cannot manage complexity, find and use resources, and continually learn new technologies, approaches, and occupations. In contrast to low-skilled work on assembly lines, which was designed from above and implemented by means of routine procedures applied below, today's work sites require employees to frame problems, design their own tasks, plan, construct, evaluate outcomes, and cooperate in finding novel solutions to complicated problems (Drucker, 1986). Increasing social complexity also demands citizens who can understand and evaluate multidimensional problems and alternatives and who can maneuvre ever more intricate social systems.

Thus, life chances grow increasingly dim for students whom schools have failed. A male high school dropout in 1986, for example, had only one chance in three of being employed full-time – half the odds of twenty years earlier. If employed, he earned only $6,700 a year, about half of what a high school dropout earned in 1973 (Commission on Youth and America's Future, 1988). Lack of education is also linked to crime and delinquency. More than half the adult prison population is functionally illiterate, and nearly 40 per cent of adjudicated juvenile delinquents have treatable learning disabilities that were not diagnosed in the schools.

In addition, the population of the United States is aging, placing greater demands on worker productivity. In the 1950s the ratio of active workers to Social Security beneficiaries was 10 to 1. By 2020 that ratio will be 3 to 1. Unless all of these workers are employable, a growing class of permanently impoverished Americans will deplete the nation's resources and make it impossible to honor the social contract that supports promises to older generations of Americans.

In sum, there is a growing consensus that the United States cannot maintain its democratic foundations or its standard of living unless all students are much better educated. Students who have traditionally been allowed to fail must be helped to succeed; many more must become not just minimally schooled but highly proficient and inventive. This consensus signals a new mission for schools and entirely new approaches to learning and teaching. Schools in the twenty-first century will be required not merely to 'deliver' instructional services but to ensure that all students are engaged in learning at high levels. In turn, the teacher's job is no longer to 'cover' the curriculum but to enable diverse learners to construct their own knowledge and to develop their talents in effective and powerful ways.

The new mission for education clearly requires substantially more knowledge and radically different skills for teachers, as well as changes in the ways in which schools operate. The kind of teaching required to meet these demands for more thoughtful learning cannot be produced through teacher-proof materials or regulated curriculum. In order to create bridges between common, challenging curriculum goals and individual learners' experiences and needs, teachers must understand cognition and the many different pathways to learning. They must understand child development and pedagogy as well as the structures of subject areas and a variety of alternatives for assessing learning. And they must have a base of knowledge for making decisions about curriculum, assessment, and school design traditionally reserved for others in the educational hierarchy (Darling-Hammond, 1990c; Shulman, 1987).

There is another challenge, as well, that requires a more knowledgeable and highly skilled teaching force – the social setting for teaching is more demanding than ever before. Teachers are currently striving to address the needs of a growing number of low-income children – one in four American children now lives in poverty (Carnegie Corporation of New York, 1994) – and are working with the largest wave of immigrants since the turn of the last century. Children who encounter a wide variety of stresses in their families and communities are present in virtually every classroom. Half a million are homeless, and at least that many again are born carrying the scars of drug dependency in ways that affect their learning. Furthermore, educators are striving to attain more ambitious goals at a time when schools are more inclusive than they have ever been before. More students stay in school longer, and more students with special needs – many of them unserved several decades ago – are served in more mainstreamed settings.

The need to match learning opportunities to the needs of individual children defies the single, formulaic approach to delivering lessons that has characterized much regulation of teaching in the past. If all children are to be effectively taught, teachers must be prepared to address the substantial diversity in experiences that children bring with them to school – the wide range of languages, cultures, learning styles, talents, and intelligences that require in turn an equally rich and varied repertoire of teaching strategies. In addition, teaching for universal learning demands a highly developed ability to discover what children know and can do, how they think and how they learn, and to match learning and performance opportunities to the needs of individual children.

This altered charge for education requires legislators, policy makers, and school leaders to shift their efforts from designing controls for an out-dated bureaucratic model of school management to initiatives that will develop the capacities of schools and teachers to be responsible for student learning and responsive to student and community needs, interests, and concerns. Capacity-building requires different policy tools and different approaches to producing, sharing, and using knowledge than those traditionally used throughout this century.

THE NEW SOCIAL CONTEXT FOR TEACHING

The 1980s saw the emergence of the most sustained and far-reaching set of efforts to 'reform' American elementary and secondary education since the formation of the common school nearly a century earlier. Spurred by a widely held consensus on the part of school reformers that public schools designed for the needs of the nineteenth century will not meet the demands of the twenty-first, initiatives to reinvent schooling and to fashion more responsive and responsible roles for teachers are proceeding on national, state, district, and local levels in the 1990s.

In 1983, the National Commission on Excellence in Education's report, *A Nation at Risk*, brought a score of concerns regarding the nation's educational system to the forefront. This report and a barrage of others that followed focused on perceptions of declining student achievement in an era requiring greater levels of educational success for all students. The educational reform imperative was pursued in the next several years through greater state control of educational processes and mandates for higher educational standards.

In 1986, a 'second wave' of educational reform followed, with reports from the National Governor's Association (1986), the Education Commission of the States (Thompson, 1986), the Carnegie Forum on Education and the Economy (1986), the Holmes Group (1986, 1990), and others. These reports affirmed the need to improve education by emphasizing the need to professionalize teaching (Darling-Hammond & Berry, 1988). Reforms aimed at building the capacity of teachers differ from past educational change efforts that mandated new programs, courses, tests, curricula, and management systems by acknowledging the importance of teachers' knowledge and the nature of the school environments in which they work. The recruitment, preparation, and renewal of a competent teaching force are now widely recognized as among the central policy issues facing the United States in its educational reform efforts.

These endeavors to fundamentally rethink American education are being carried out with a sense of urgency born of the convergence of a number of other trends, which signal further profound changes in the social fabric of the nation. These economic, technological, demographic, political, and educational developments include: successive waves of immigration from Eastern Europe and the former Soviet Union, Central and South America, Africa, Southeast Asia, and the Caribbean; internal migrations from country to city and from city to suburb, as well as from the Midwest to the coasts and from the Rust Belt to the Sun Belt; major breakthroughs in communications and other forms of technology; and the emergence of a global, transnational economy (Cremin, 1989; Drucker, 1989). Other major factors impacting upon teaching include the profound alterations throughout society in child-rearing and family patterns (Cremin, 1989). In the following sections, we examine some of these evolving contexts as they relate to American education.

The Economic Context

Until 150 years ago, the vast majority of U.S. citizens, like their counterparts around the globe, lived basically according to their needs and did not heavily tax the natural resources of the environment. Since then, the pace and effects of change have been stunning. In 1920, the number of Americans employed in manufacturing jobs exceeded, for the first time, the number engaged in agriculture (Cremin, 1989). The brisk development of automated means of mass production of goods spawned new notions of efficiency and specialized divisions of labor, creating entirely different kinds of jobs; for most, the new employment meant repetitive kinds of highly structured, semi-skilled work. The 'Taylor system,' widely adopted around in the decade after 1910, provided techniques for using rules and routines to manage the work of people assigned to discrete, specific tasks requiring limited knowledge or authority. 'Scientific management' brought with it a distinct division of responsibility between a new class of managers, who did all the thinking, and the workers, who followed procedures developed by the managers. As Taylor (1911) put it, 'One type of man is needed to plan ahead and an entirely different type to execute the work' (Callahan, 1962, pp. 37-38). Schools stressed compliance and the capacity for repetitive, rote tasks in response to the demands from industry (Tyack, 1974).

However, continued economic changes required a greater number of 'thinking workers.' The number of 'white-collar' workers first surpassed the number of 'blue-collar' workers in 1956 (Cremin, 1989). The concept of a 'knowledge economy' was introduced in the early 1960s, followed a few years later by the notion of a 'post-industrial society.' Now, as communications and information technologies have continued to develop in ever more sophisticated forms, and as more competitors vie for a shrinking resource pool, a transnational economy based on the exchange of services and information has emerged. In the new 'information society,' roughly half of the American work force

> ... is occupied with what might be called the processing of knowledge — a phrase that would include people involved in education, entertainment, science, and culture, and who draw upon materials as

different as musical tapes, industrial and commercial computer
programs, and scientific data bases. (Cremin, 1989, pp. 57-58)

By the year 2000, blue-collar jobs of the sort that once provided high wages for
relatively low levels of skill are expected to dwindle to only 10 per cent of the
workforce in the United States (Drucker, 1994).

This rapidly changing industrial base and the prospective loss of U.S. economic dominance in international markets have stimulated political concerns as
well as rapid job changes, industrial restructuring, and the need for many workers to learn new occupations and new roles. Manufacturing industries can no
longer pay high wages for low-skilled work. High wages and corporate growth
characterize industries that rely on high levels of skill, complex technologies,
and new knowledge and information. Because today's corporations are eliminating layers of rigid hierarchy in their management systems in order to become
more flexible and adaptive to the ever-changing demands of the global marketplace, their employees will need to be prepared for this more fluid form of organizing work and resources. 'An economy in which knowledge is becoming
the true capital and the premier wealth-producing resource' means that 'once
again we will have to think through what an educated person is' (Drucker, 1989,
p. 232). The changes demanded of workers and of educational institutions are
striking:

> The great majority of the new jobs require qualifications the industrial
> worker does not possess and is poorly equipped to acquire. They require
> a good deal of formal education and the ability to acquire and to apply
> theoretical and analytical knowledge. They require a different approach
> to work and a different mind-set. Above all, they require a habit of
> continuous learning. Displaced industrial workers thus cannot simply
> move into knowledge work or services the way displaced farmers and
> domestic workers moved into industrial work (at the turn of the last
> century). At the very least, they have to change their basic attitudes,
> values, and beliefs. (Drucker, 1994, p. 62)

Many recent reports have described a growing 'overclass' – an expanding group
of well-educated Americans who are leading the knowledge society – counterposed by a growing 'underclass' – an also expanding group of inadequately educated Americans who are being squeezed out of their chances to participate
fully in that society. This lower tier of an increasingly bimodal society includes
not only seriously disadvantaged children and young people who live in high-
poverty communities and attend low-quality, underfunded schools – a description that characterizes at least 20 per cent of the population. It also includes
working class youth and adults who have not been prepared for the demands of

today's society, whose levels of education and skills were sufficient to the jobs of the 1970s but are inadequate to those of today and tomorrow. This group probably includes another 30 per cent or more of the population. This is just one of the factors compelling the redesign of teaching and schooling.

Technological Contexts

Technology has not only transformed workplaces; it has also begun to transform learning and its relationship to persons and places. Although schools are seen as repositories of knowledge – as the premier locations where learning and teaching take place – the very nature of information access and transfer has changed. Today's technologies have rendered information retrieval and on-line learning so quick and accessible that schools structured according to the old model may well be the places where a student's learning slows down. As far back as 1967 Marshall MacLuhan characterized this emerging state of affairs as a challenge to schooling as we have known it:

> The electronic environment makes an information level outside the schoolroom that is far higher than the information level inside the schoolroom. In the nineteenth century the knowledge inside the schoolroom was higher than knowledge outside the schoolroom. Today it is reversed. The child knows that in going to school [he] is in a sense interrupting [his] education. (cited in Cremin, 1989, p. 51)

In 1950, roughly 10 per cent of American homes had a television set. By the early 1980s, 98 per cent of American homes had television sets (frequently two, three, or four of them), and surveys indicate that viewing patterns average seven hours per day, mostly by the very young, the very old, and the very poor (Cremin, 1989). By 1989, over 20 per cent of homes had computers, a proportion undoubtedly much higher today. Here, as elsewhere, however, access is unequal both in and out of school. Only about 7 per cent of African American and Hispanic students as compared to 23 per cent of white students had access to computers at home, and about one third of African American and Hispanic students used computers at school, as compared to 46 per cent of white students (U.S. Department of Commerce, 1989).

Cable television, electronic communication networks of all types, and other interactive computerized devices are breaking open access routes to information with explosive force and shaping the discourse of the nation in very new ways. For all their potential benefits, some fear that differential access to and use of these technologies and the information they carry also creates dangers for both social cohesiveness and equality (Apple, 1987). To offset these dangers, schools will need to provide common access, on the one hand, and intellectual tools for critical use, analysis, and synthesis of diverse sources, on the other.

While electronic media in all its forms undoubtedly provide today's young person with more information at greater speed than does the school, Peter Drucker (1989) asserts that 'only through the school – through organized, systematic, purposeful learning – can this information be converted into knowledge and become the individual's possession and tool' (p. 233). A crucial aspect of twenty-first-century teachers' work will be to take an active part, along with their students, in the new electronic discourse. The sheer volume of available information and the unprecedented speed with which it is attainable, combined with the fact that Americans are insatiably enamored with the new and the instant, profoundly affects every aspect of life in the United States and calls for radical reconfigurations of the work of teaching and the role of schools.

Demographic Contexts

Alongside changes in the economy and technology, the U.S. is experiencing major demographic shifts, including significant patterns of immigration and migration. As populations have become more mobile, American classrooms are reflecting an ever greater diversity in students' home circumstances, language backgrounds, and ethnic and cultural backgrounds. Teachers must be prepared to teach students who have had widely varying experiences, previous levels of education, linguistic needs, and approaches to learning. Sophisticated skills for diagnosing and addressing diverse student needs as well as commitments to equity are increasingly crucial aspects of teachers' work.

Our current school system was designed for much greater homogeneity, not only in the cultural characteristics of the population, but also in the basic shape of the American family, which has altered significantly in recent years. Today one in four children lives in a single-parent family, and 90 per cent of these households are headed by women. The number of children living with a divorced mother more than doubled between 1970 and 1986, while births to unmarried women increased by a factor of six (William T. Grant Foundation, 1988). In 1991, an estimated 429,000 children were in foster homes, group homes, or institutional settings in the child welfare system – over 50 per cent more than five years earlier; if the same trends have continued since, close to 900,000 children live away from their families in 1995.

Family earning patterns have also changed. In 1991, 67 per cent of mothers with children younger than 18 were in the civilian labor force – up from 47 per cent in 1975 (Children's Defense Fund, 1992). All of these trends have contributed to a growing number of 'latch key' children who are home alone or unsupervised for many hours at a time (Martin, 1995).

There has also been a substantial growth in the population over age 65 – a population that will need to be supported by a shrinking number of young people currently entering the work force, more of whom are the children of immigrants, poor families, and minorities (Gill, Glazer, & Thernstrom, 1992). These complexities are compounded by the continuing underperformance of the educational system for these same young people, who by the end of the 1990s will comprise 40 per cent of the public school population and over a third of the entering workforce. Widespread inequality in access to high quality educational opportunities for low-income and 'minority' children is a major source of economic as well as social danger for U.S. society.

Educational and Political Contexts

Because teachers work directly with young people in profoundly influential ways, teaching is fundamentally political work, carried out under conditions molded by a host of societal factors that alternately impel, constrain, or shape the success of the work. These forces include the public and policy environment that places academic and social expectations and limits on teachers' work and the distribution of learning resources to both students and teachers.

Academic and social expectations.

The outcomes of the U.S. educational system are now widely viewed as disappointing, a circumstance that affects public views of education, and creates pressures for reform. To be sure, schools are embedded 'in a larger ecology of education that includes what families, television broadcasters, workplaces, and a host of other institutions are contributing at any given time' (Cremin, 1989, p. viii). However, schools are typically singled out for blame when student learning is less than what society demands.

The problem is not that America's schools are doing worse than they were in the 'good old days.' In fact, they are on most counts doing as well as they ever did for a greater number of students: graduation rates have risen dramatically throughout the century in both numerical terms and as a share of the total school-age population; basic literacy rates have risen; more students are participating in a greater range of educational opportunities at the secondary and post-secondary levels than they were several decades ago (Berliner & Biddle, 1995). Furthermore, schools are much more diverse and inclusive places than they were 50 years ago, when nearly half of all high school students dropped out. Most of the students who are the focus of special programs in today's schools were not in school at all at that time. Handicapped students were largely excluded from schooling; students who did not speak English coped on their own or left. In addition, large numbers of African American, Latino, and Native American students were relegated to poorly funded segregated systems or denied access entirely. Although a small share of students did well academically, their successes were modest in light of current demands for knowledge and skill.

Although, arguably, schools are doing as well as they ever have for a greater number and a more diverse group of students, the signs are many that the current educational system is not capable of responding to contemporary needs without major overhaul. Most critical is the need to move from the kinds of rote learning favored by earlier behaviorist learning theory and useful for mid-century factory jobs to more complex kinds of thinking and performance.

Over more than a decade, the National Assessment of Educational Progress tests have found stable or increasing performance on basic skills tasks at low levels of cognitive functioning but declining performance on tasks requiring critical thinking or problem-solving abilities. These declines in students' thinking and performance abilities have been steady and unreversed since the early 1970s and are particularly noticeable at the high school level. A recent NAEP report summarized the status of high school students' performance as follows:

> Sixty-one percent of the 17-year-old students could not read or understand relatively complicated material, such as that typically presented at the high school level. Nearly one half appear to have limited mathematics skills and abilities that go little beyond adding, subtracting, and multiplying with whole numbers. More than one half could not evaluate the procedures or results of a scientific study, and few included enough information in their written pieces to communicate their ideas effectively. Additionally, assessment results in other curriculum areas indicate that high school juniors have little sense of historical chronology, have not read much literature, and tend to be unfamiliar with the uses and potential applications of computers. (Educational Testing Service [ETS], 1989, p. 26)

At the levels of achievement needed to fill the 30 per cent of jobs in our new economy that are professional and technical jobs, the picture is even more grim. Only 5 per cent of 17-year-olds can synthesize and learn from specialized reading materials. Only 6 per cent can use basic algebra and solve mathematical problems with more than one step. Only 7 per cent can draw conclusions using detailed scientific knowledge (ETS, 1989).

Furthermore, this level of performance includes only those students who are still in school at the age of 17, thus it overestimates the level of performance of all 17-year-olds. Compared to most other industrialized countries, the U.S. is behind in terms of the proportion of students still in school at 17 (just over 75 per cent), the proportion taking advanced level courses, and their achievement. Generally, the disparities grow greater as students grow older: American 5th graders score near the median among countries represented in international assessments; 8th graders slip behind; and 12th graders score near the bottom of the distribution (ETS, 1989).

In the second International Science and Mathematics Studies, for example, U.S. 8th graders ranked 16th out of 20 in Geometry, just above Nigeria, Swaziland, and Israel; and 12th graders were next to the bottom in Advanced Algebra, just above Thailand. The average Japanese student scores higher than the top 5 per cent of American students in advanced mathematics courses, and more of them are in school and taking these subjects (McKnight, Crosswhite, Dossey, Kifer, Swafford, Travers, & Cooney, 1987). Similarly, the most advanced U.S. 12th graders ranked 9th out of 13 countries in physics, 11th in chemistry, and 13th in biology.

One reason for the low participation rate in certain advanced courses in American schools is that, traditionally, U.S. schools have rationed curricular opportunities to a relatively small number of students presumed to be headed for intellectual pursuits. Now, however, there is a steady increase in demand for college-educated workers, with high demand projected in most professional and technical occupations. Meanwhile, the proportion of American 18-to-24-year-olds enrolled in U.S. colleges is under 25 per cent, having declined between 1976 and 1982 and having increased only erratically since. At the same time, the proportion of foreign students enrolled in U.S. colleges has steadily increased throughout the 1980s, especially in the sciences and engineering (National Center for Education Statistics, 1988), accounting for virtually all the gains in degrees earned.

A wide variety of factors are blamed for this state of affairs, including an anemic curriculum; tracking policies that water down the offerings most students experience; and texts, tests, and pedagogy focused on lower level cognitive skills like memorization and recall rather than powerful thinking and performance skills like analysis and production (Darling-Hammond, 1990a; Resnick, 1987). These concerns create pressure for public school reform, on the one hand, and for privatization and vouchers, on the other.

In addition to what they expect from schools in terms of student academic achievement, Americans also tend to look to the public schools to solve a wide range of social problems (Popkewitz, 1987). The politics of American education are such that schools operate under relentless pressure from a host of interest groups, each of which seeks to assign to them yet another aspect of responsibility for nurturing the young. In the view of various segments of the public, teachers are charged with imparting fundamental academic and social skills, nurturing critical thinking abilities, developing moral character and the rudiments of good citizenship, transmitting cultural literacy, and dealing with issues related to health and wellness, including warning about the dangers of drugs and sexually transmitted diseases (Cremin, 1989). In this context, teachers have increasingly had to attend to the health, nutritional, housing, and welfare needs of their students. Though teachers are asked to take on these charges, neither their preparation nor the organizational structures within which they work support them well in doing so.

Inequality in access to resources for learning.

This picture is further complicated by the fact that America's public schools also reflect the stratification along socioeconomic class lines of the society as a whole. Therefore, issues of equity of access to quality schooling, by all social classes and racial and ethnic communities, including the mainstreaming and inclusion of special education students, are formative forces in relation to the social context of teaching.

While much has been made of the low performance of U.S. students on international assessments, still more striking is the finding from the Second International Mathematics Study that inequalities in measured resources and opportunities to learn are many times greater in the U.S. than in other industrialized countries, and are comparable to the disparities found in developing nations that do not yet provide universal access to education (McKnight et al., 1987). Unlike many other nations, the U.S. does not fund schools centrally and equally, nor do U.S. schools typically organize students for a common, non-tracked curriculum until high school as many other countries do.

As a consequence of structural inequalities in access to knowledge and resources, low-income students and students from racial and ethnic 'minority' groups in the United States face persistent and profound barriers to educational opportunity. As a function of disparities in local and state funding that allow the richest districts to spend as much as 10 times the amount that poorer districts can spend, students encounter dramatically different levels of education across every dimension of schooling. Traditionally disadvantaged students in cities and poor rural areas have much less access to qualified teachers, high quality curriculum, small class sizes, adequate facilities, computers and science labs, or books, materials, and supplies (Darling-Hammond, 1995; Kozol, 1991; Oakes, 1990). Because most minority students still attend predominantly minority schools, which are also generally underfunded, they receive an education that is distinctively different from that of their more affluent peers.

Jonathan Kozol's (1991) *Savage Inequalities* describes the striking differences between public schools in urban settings – schools whose population is between 95 and 99 per cent non-white – and their suburban counterparts: for example, MacKenzie High School in Detroit where word processing courses are taught without word processors because the school cannot afford them (p. 198), Public School 261 in New York City which has no windows in many class-rooms and where recess is not possible because there is no playground (pp. 85-87), or East St. Louis Senior High School whose biology lab has no laboratory tables or usable dissecting kits (p. 28). Meanwhile, children in neighboring sub-urban schools enjoy features like a 27-acre campus (p. 65), an athletic program featuring golf, fencing, ice hockey, and lacrosse (p. 157), and a computer hookup to Dow Jones to study stock transactions (p. 158).

Teachers are among the most inequitably distributed of all educational re-sources. Recurring shortages of teachers caused by below-market wages and distributional problems have characterized the U.S. labor market for most of the twentieth century, with the exception of a brief period of declining student en-rollments during the late 1970s and early 1980s (Sedlak & Schlossman, 1986). Currently, shortages are most pronounced in areas like bilingual education, spe-cial education, physics, chemistry, mathematics, computer science, and tech-nology education, in geographic areas of growing enrollment like the South and West, and in central cities (Akin, 1989; National Center for Education Statistics, 1993b, p. 132). In 1991, nearly 10 per cent of all teachers and one fourth of new-ly hired teachers were not licensed in their fields; however, the proportions were more than twice as high in central cities. Disparities in salaries and working conditions left nearly one-fourth of central city schools unable to fill vacancies with a qualified teacher in 1991 (National Center for Education Statistics, 1993b) and more than 20 per cent of teachers in these schools working in jobs for which they were not prepared (National Center for Education Statistics, 1994; National Data Research Center [NDRC], 1993).

For a variety of reasons, most states and districts continue to respond to shortages by lowering standards rather than by creating incentives that will at-tract an adequate supply of teachers. As a consequence, this era is developing an even more sharply bi-modal teaching force than ever before. While more ad-vantaged children are gaining access to teachers who are more qualified and better-prepared than ever before (Darling-Hammond, 1997), a growing number of poor and minority children are being taught by teachers who are sorely un-prepared for the task they face. This creates heightened inequality in opportuni-ties to learn and in the outcomes of schooling – with all of the social dangers that implies – at the very time when schools most need to prepare all students more effectively for the greater challenges they face.

IMPLICATIONS FOR LEARNING AND TEACHING

The role of teachers in twenty-first-century schools will be to ensure that stu-dents learn how to learn. Students in the twenty-first century will need to be much more inventive and flexible as learners and performers than were their predecessors. The continuing explosion of knowledge and the fast pace of changing social conditions means that there is no single, limited body of facts to be committed to memory that will suffice for modern living. Teachers cannot prepare their students for a predictable occupation with a contained set of skills; what they must do is prepare them to manage change and to maneuvre information systems. These abilities are much more important in today's world than the mastery of specific, discrete facts and isolated bits of knowledge.

Today's literacy includes technological skills and wide-ranging problem solving and inventive abilities needed by the 'knowledge industry' sector. Consequently, rigid boundaries between traditional subject area disciplines and the ways in which they have been fragmented and organized in schools are becoming outdated (Drucker, 1989) as students require more flexible, integrated, and portable skills.

In order to promote the development of inquiry and problem solving abilities, schools will need to organize and use knowledge in cross-disciplinary ways that allow for more ambitious applications of knowledge and skills. This may mean the creation of interdisciplinary courses in areas like mathematics and the physical sciences or the arts and humanities. It may mean such configurations as the study of applied social sciences connected to study of statistics, on the one hand, or the study of human development on the other. It may mean the development of social problem solving skills in new subjects like social communication and participation.

Some of these goals may also be attained through the use of projects or portfolios that enable students to connect and apply their learning across more traditionally discipline-based courses. For example, some schools are beginning to develop major projects that combine an exhibition of an area of skill tied to the development of a paper and presentation that draw on language arts and historical, scientific, or social science research skills. Others are developing portfolios that allow students to assemble evidence of their learning that is both discipline-based and problem-oriented across many fields, and that includes both collaborative and independent work (Darling-Hammond, Ancess, & Falk, 1995).

Success in the workplace and the society will be better supported by the ability to marshall and integrate knowledge from diverse domains than to recall discrete domain-specific facts or algorithms on cue. People will also need to be proactively engaged in more inventive, wide-ranging tasks that require greater planning, perseverance, and self-assessment than simple assembly line tasks once demanded. Thus, one clear need in the curriculum of the future is the opportunity for in-depth study of ideas and development of proficient performances, in lieu of superficial encounters with a bevy of unused facts (Darling-Hammond, 1997). Gardner, Torff, and Hatch (in press) argue that in the ongoing battle between 'breadth' and 'depth,' a clear advantage should be given to the latter:

> Once the basic literacies have been acquired, once individuals are comfortable in the crucial symbol systems of reading, writing, and reckoning, we discern no necessity to place a special premium on one subject as opposed to another (biology vs. chemistry; American history vs. world history), let alone particular topics (light vs. gravity) or books (Homer vs. Hamlet). Far more important, in our view, is the experience of approaching with depth *some* key topics or themes in the broadest disciplinary areas – math and science, history and philosophy, literature and the arts. Students need to learn how to learn and how to probe deeply into one or another topic. Once they have achieved these precious insights, they can continue their own education indefinitely. And if they have not mastered these lessons, all the facts, factoids, and mandated tests will not save their souls. (p. 39)

Developing a capacity for understanding requires both the time for this kind of extended, indepth learning, and the skillful guidance of teachers who can scaffold key ideas, anticipate misconceptions or stereotypes, and create learning experiences that build on students own thinking and reflect the standards for inquiry in the discipline. 'A combination of exposure to models of understanding, on the one hand, and regular opportunities to work out the consequences of one's own beliefs and conceptions, on the other, seem necessary prerequisites for a deeper understanding' (Garnder, Torff, & Hatch, in press, p. 37).

In order to 'teach for understanding' (Cohen, McLaughlin, & Talbert, 1993), teachers must understand the structures of the disciplines they teach as well as the many different ways in which children learn (Darling-Hammond, 1990c; Shulman, 1987). As McLaughlin and Talbert (1993) note:

> Teaching for understanding ... requires change not only in what is taught but also in how it is taught.... Teaching for understanding requires teachers to have comprehensive and in-depth knowledge of subject matter, competence in representation and manipulation of this knowledge in instructional activities, and skill in managing classroom processes in a way that enables active student learning. (pp. 2-3)

In order to foster meaningful learning, teachers must design experiences that allow students to confront powerful ideas whole. They must create bridges between the very different experiences of individual learners and the common curriculum goals, and they must use a variety of approaches to build on the conceptions, cultures, interests, motivations, and learning modes of their students.

Teachers also must understand how their students think as well as what they know. This more complex approach to teaching requires that teachers combine deep knowledge of subject matter and a wide repertoire of teaching strategies with intimate knowledge of students' growth, experience, and development (Darling-Hammond, 1993; Shulman, 1987).

Today's social, economic, and political climate demands this more complex kind of adaptive teaching – teaching that is reciprocal, responsive, and attentive to the needs of learners, as well as teaching that is prepared to accommodate more challenging learning goals. If schools are to be responsive to the different needs and talents of diverse learners, they must be organized to allow for variability rather than to assume uniformity. Teachers must diversify their practice so that they can engage each of their students in whatever ways are necessary to encourage learning.

This kind of practice requires changes in teaching and schooling that cannot be 'teacher-proofed' through new textbooks, curriculum mandates, or tests. As state after state has sought to re-create schools so that they can meet twenty-first-century demands, it has become apparent that their success depends fundamentally on teachers: What teachers know and can do is the most important influence on what students can learn (Darling-Hammond, 1997).

Thus, an important implication of the changing social context of teaching for the twenty-first century is the need to enhance the quality of teaching as a profession. A well-prepared profession of teaching is an important prerequisite for creating knowledge-based schools – schools that are organized to build on what is known about teaching, learning, curriculum, and human development. Efforts to produce effective schools – primarily by teacher-proofing education, by enacting more and more specific and prescriptive regulations which aim to tell teachers what to do and how to do it – have failed. One of the things that we have learned from these efforts is that regulations do not transform schools. Only teachers can do that, in concert with parents, students, administrators, and the wider community. The task of actually reaching every student rather than covering the curriculum, of connecting to all learners rather then merely offering education, is the task that teachers have ahead of them for the schools of the twenty-first century.

IMPLICATIONS FOR SCHOOL REFORM

Current education reform efforts in the U.S. are addressing every aspect of schooling: curriculum, instruction, assessment, school organization, governance, management, funding, and policy. All of these have important implications for teaching.

Professional standards-setting initiatives undertaken by national professional associations as well as state and local education agencies are rethinking the goals of education. The National Council of Teachers of Mathematics, the National Science Teachers Association, the National Council of Teachers of English, and many other professional groups are working alongside federal and state government agencies to redefine standards for teaching and for student learning. These are linked, in turn, to the creation of curriculum frameworks and new forms of performance-based testing in many states, and exhortations for more constructivist approaches to teaching. Nearly all states are now engaged in curriculum and assessment reforms aimed at encouraging higher order thinking and performance abilities; the recent enactment of the 'Goals 2000' legislation at the federal level creates an additional stimulus for this work as it provides funds for states to engage these curriculum and assessment reforms linked to voluntary national standards. Encouragements for tying these learning goals to opportunity-to-learn standards that could begin to equalize educational access are also a part of the federal legislation. These may ultimately include resource standards that help to create a more level playing field for students, as well as standards of practice that point to school and teaching practices likely to help students achieve more challenging kinds of learning (Darling-Hammond, 1992).

The implications for teacher education are many: Teachers will need to be prepared to teach in the ways these new standards demand, with deeper understandings of their disciplines, of interdisciplinary connections, and of inquiry-based learning. They will need skills for creating learning experiences that enable students to construct their own knowledge in powerful ways. In addition, teachers will need to understand and use a variety of more authentic and performance-based means for assessing students' knowledge and understanding, as well as evaluating students' approaches to learning and their prior experiences and conceptions. These kinds of assessments will require keen observation conducted in the context of a highly developed understanding of how children learn, develop, and demonstrate their knowledge. They will rely on teachers' capacities to invent their own means for looking carefully and deeply at student learning processes and products as well as to use – and teach for – much more sophisticated performance assessments developed by others.

Changes in school organization are also occurring. Like current restructuring initiatives in business, efforts to restructure schools are seeking to reduce long hierarchies, push decision making closer to the school and classroom, and reshape roles for teachers so that they can be more fully accountable for students. These initiatives also have implications for teacher preparation. Teachers and other educators will need to know a great deal about learning and instruction, about research and theory as well as classroom practice, and about areas of curriculum and assessment development previously reserved to 'specialists' at the top of the educational hierarchy or to 'outside experts.'

In addition to the increasingly widespread use of school-based management approaches, there are many proposals to restructure schools, to break up what is viewed as a gridlock in public bureaucracies that manage schooling, to introduce market mechanisms and other new approaches ranging from public school choice to charters, vouchers, and private management of public schools. In some communities, substantial reform energy is going into the creation of new schools, and in many schools and districts, policy makers are introducing results-based strategies for regulating education. All of these initiatives are aimed at opening up schools to greater client input and participation in decision making, and they focus on the results of schooling rather than the continued regulation of schooling processes. Not all of these approaches would have equally beneficial outcomes for educational quality and equality. However, their emergence from a deep well of public frustration with the regulation of public schools must be acknowledged.

However the tussle over these various strategies for stimulating school reform turns out, they have some common implications for teaching and teacher education. They all require deeper knowledge and greater responsibility for teachers, and to the extent that radical changes in governance and regulation are pursued, the reliance on increased professional accountability grows. Professional accountability starts from the presumption that the basis for quality teaching is knowledgeable and committed teachers. If regulatory accountability mechanisms that define teaching procedures and practices are swept aside, it is more important than ever that educators can be trusted to have the knowledge upon which to base responsible decisions. As Shulman (1983) notes:

> The teacher remains the key. The literature on effective schools is meaningless, debates over educational policy are moot, if the primary agents of instruction are incapable of performing their functions well. No microcomputer will replace them, no television system will clone and distribute them, no scripted lessons will direct and control them, no voucher system will bypass them. (p. 504)

Efforts to strengthen professional accountability assume that, since decisions about different clients' needs are too complex and individualistic to be prescribed from afar, practitioners must be educated so that they will be able to make those decisions appropriately. Professional accountability aims to ensure competence through rigorous preparation, certification, selection and evaluation of practitioners, as well as continuous peer review. It requires that educators make decisions on the basis of the best available professional knowledge; it also requires that they pledge their first commitment to the welfare of the client. Thus, rather than encouraging teaching that is procedure-oriented and rule-based, professional accountability seeks to create practices that are *client-oriented* and *knowledge-based*. In addition, professional accountability requires that members of the profession take collective responsibility for defining, transmitting, and enforcing standards of professional practice so that clients are well-served.

Reforms that rely on the transformative power of individuals to rethink their practice and to redesign their institutions can be accomplished only by investing in individual and organizational learning, in the human capital of the educational enterprise – the knowledge, skills, and dispositions of teachers and administrators, as well as those of parents and community members. The new reforms also demand attention to equity in the distribution of those educational resources that build school capacity, including well-qualified teachers supported by adequate materials and decent conditions for teaching and learning. The dramatic inequalities that currently exist in American schools cannot be addressed by pretending that mandating and measuring are the same thing as improving schools for all children.

If today's educational reforms are to succeed, they will require highly educated and well-prepared teachers who can make sound decisions about curriculum, teaching, and school policy. Indeed, all the solutions to the problems cited by contemporary education critics are constrained by the availability of talented teachers, by the knowledge and capacities those teachers possess, and by the school conditions that define how that knowledge can be used. Raising graduation requirements in mathematics, science, and foreign language, for example, is of little use if we do not have an adequate number of qualified teachers to teach those subjects. Exhortations to improve students' higher-order thinking will accomplish little without able teachers who know how to engender such thinking and who teach in an environment that supports rather than undermines such learning. Concerns about 'at-risk' children – those who drop out, tune out, and fall behind – cannot be addressed without teachers who are prepared to understand and meet the needs of students who come to school with varying learning styles, from diverse family situations, and with differing beliefs about themselves and about what school means for them.

Growing awareness of the importance of teacher knowledge has led to major changes in teacher preparation programs across the country (Darling-Hammond, 1994; Darling-Hammond & Cobb, 1995). Approaches to accreditation, licensing, and induction are being reconsidered (Darling-Hammond, Wise, & Klein, 1995); and a new National Board for Professional Teaching Standards is beginning to offer recognition to highly accomplished teachers. These changes are evidence of a deepening commitment to professionalism in teaching as a means to improve education. There is increasing recognition that the capacities teachers need in order to succeed at the twenty-first-century agenda for education can only be widely acquired throughout the teaching force by major reforms of teacher preparation and major restructuring of the systems by which states and school districts license, hire, induct, support, and provide for the continual learning of teachers.

Reforms aimed at building the capacity of teachers differ from past efforts at educational change which mandated new courses, tests, curricula, and management systems, but did not worry about how they would make it from the statehouse to the schoolhouse. However, in contrast to teaching in other industrialized countries, supports for teachers and teacher learning in this country are meagre. Not only are U.S. teachers typically paid less than other college-educated workers; they have lower levels of investment in their knowledge, have less time to work with and learn from each other, and are given less decision-making authority (Darling-Hammond & Cobb, 1995). Policy makers and practitioners need to find ways to support collegial discourse and inquiry in schools. Teachers will need opportunities to engage in peer coaching, team planning and teaching, and collaborative research that enables them to construct new means for inquiring into their practice.

The juxtaposition of the nation's need for substantially more successful schools and current problems in staffing them with enough well-prepared teachers raises many questions: What do teachers need to know and be able to do to succeed at the challenging goals posed by current school reforms? How can teacher preparation be strengthened to ensure that teachers know how to teach their subjects and all students well? How can schools be organized to better support student and teacher learning? What steps are needed to recruit and hire well-prepared teachers in all communities, and to keep them in the profession? These questions are at the heart of current efforts to redesign education in order to develop the capacity to recruit, prepare, and support a teaching force capable of teaching all children to high standards in all communities.

CONCLUSION

The panoramic scope and breathless rate of continued, pervasive societal change may render it impossible for today's teachers to imagine life in the twenty-first century. Michael Fullan (1991) reminds us that:

> We have become so accustomed to the presence of change that we rarely stop to think what change really means as we are experiencing it at the personal level. More important, we almost never stop to think what it means for others around us who might be in change situations. The crux of change is how individuals come to grips with this reality ... *all* real change involves loss, anxiety, and struggle. (p. 30)

Clearly, educators and policy makers in the United States must work together to come to grips with the enormous task of fundamentally restructuring the mission of schools and the work of teaching in order that all children not just some will be educated as life-long learners who can cope successfully with a future in which the only thing certain is change.

REFERENCES

Akin, J. N. (1989). *Teacher supply and demand in the United States: 1989 report.* Addison, IL: Association for School, College, and University Staffing.

Apple, M. (1987). Will the social context allow a tomorrow for tomorrow's teachers? *Teachers College Record, 88*(3), 330-337.

Berliner, D. C. & Biddle, B. J. (1995). *The manufactured crisis.* NY: Addison-Wesley.

Callahan, R. E. (1962). *Education and the cult of efficiency.* Chicago: University of Chicago Press.

Carnegie Corporation of New York (1994). *Starting points: Meeting the needs of our youngest children.* New York: Author.

Carnegie Forum on Education and the Economy (1986). *A nation prepared: Teachers for the 21st century.* New York: Carnegie.

Children's Defense Fund (1992). *The state of America's children, 1992.* Washington, DC: Author.

Cohen, D. K., McLaughlin, M. W., & Talbert, J. E. (1993). *Teaching for understanding: Challenges for policy and practice.* San Francisco: Jossey-Bass.

Commission on Youth and America's Future (1988). *The forgotten half: Non-college-bound youth in America.* Washington, DC: William T. Grant Foundation.

Cremin, L. A. (1989). *Popular education and its discontents.* New York: Harper & Row.

Darling-Hammond, L. (1990a). Achieving our goals: Superficial or structural reforms? *Phi Delta Kappan, 72*(4), 286-295.

Darling-Hammond, L. (1990b). Teachers and teaching: Signs of a changing profession. In R. Houston, M. Haberman, & J. Sikula (Eds.) *Handbook of research on teacher education* (pp. 267-290). New York: Macmillan.

Darling-Hammond, L. (1990c). Teacher professionalism: Why and how? In A. Lieberman (Ed.), *Schools as collaborative cultures: Creating the future now* (pp. 25-50). New York: The Falmer Press.

Darling-Hammond, L. (1992). *Standards of practice for learning-centered schools.* New York: National Center for Restructuring Education, Schools, and Teaching.

Darling-Hammond, L. (1993). Reframing the school reform agenda: Developing capacity for school transformation. *Phi Delta Kappan, 74*(10), 253-261.

Darling-Hammond, L. (Ed.). (1994). *Professional development schools: Schools for developing a profession.* New York: Teachers College Press.

Darling-Hammond, L. (1995). Inequality and access to knowledge. In J. A. Banks (Ed.), *Handbook of multicultural education* (pp. 465-483). New York: Macmillan.

Darling-Hammond, L. (1997). *The right to learn.* San Francisco: Jossey-Bass.

Darling-Hammond, L., Ancess, J., & Falk, B. (1995). *Authentic assessment in action: Studies of schools and students at work.* New York: Teachers College Press.

Darling-Hammond, L. & Berry, B. (1988). *The evolution of teacher policy.* Santa Monica, CA: The RAND Corporation.

Darling-Hammond, L. & Cobb, V. (1995). The changing context of teacher education. In *Knowledge base for the beginning teacher* (pp. 14-16). Washington, DC: American Association of Colleges of Teacher Education.

Darling-Hammond, L., Wise, A. E., & Klein, S. (1995). *A license to teach: Building a profession for 21st century schools*. Boulder, CO: Westview Press.

Dewey, J. (1900/1990). *The school and society*. Chicago: University of Chicago Press.

Drucker, P. F. (1986). *The frontiers of management*. New York: Harper & Row.

Drucker, P. F. (1989). *The new realities*. New York: Harper & Row.

Drucker, P. F. (1994). The age of social transformation. *The Atlantic Monthly, 62*, 53-80.

Educational Testing Service (1989). *Crossroads in American education*. Princeton, NJ: Author.

Fullan, M. G. with Stiegelbauer, S. (1991). *The new meaning of educational change*. New York: Teachers College Press.

Gardner, H., Torff, B., & Hatch, T. (in press). The age of innocence reconsidered: Preserving the best of the progressive tradition in psychology and education. In D. Olson & N. Torrance (Eds.), *Handbook of psychology in education: New models of learning, thinking, and teaching* (pp. 28-55). Cambridge, MA: Basil Blackwell.

Gill, R. T., Glazer, N., & Thernstrom, S. A. (1992). *Our changing population*. Englewood Cliffs, NJ: Prentice Hall.

Holmes Group (1986). *Tomorrow's teachers: A report of the Holmes Group*. East Lansing, MI: Author.

Holmes Group (1990). *Tomorrow's schools: A report of the Holmes Group*. East Lansing, MI: Author.

Hudson Institute (1987). *Workforce 2000: Work and workers for the 21st century*. Indianapolis, IN: Author.

Kozol, J. (1991). *Savage inequalities*. New York: Crown.

Martin, J. R. (1995). A philosophy of education for the year 2000. *Phi Delta Kappan, 76*(5), 355-359.

McKnight, C., Crosswhite, F. J., Dossey, J. A., Kifer, E., Swafford, S. O., Travers, K. J., & Cooney, T. J. (1987). *The underachieving curriculum: Assessing U.S. school mathematics from an international perspective*. Champaign, IL: Stipes Publishing.

McLaughlin, M. W. & Talbert, J. E. (1993). New visions of teaching. In D. K. Cohen, M. W. McLaughlin, & J. E. Talbert (Eds.), *Teaching for understanding: Challenges for policy and practice* (pp. 1-10). San Francisco: Jossey-Bass.

National Center for Education Statistics (1988). *Education indicators, 1988*. Washington, DC: U.S. Department of Education.

National Center for Education Statistics (1993a). *The condition of education, 1993*. Washington, DC: U.S. Department of Education.

National Center for Education Statistics (1993b). *Schools and staffing in the United States: A statistical profile, 1990-91*. Washington, DC: U.S. Department of Education.

National Center for Education Statistics (1994). *The condition of education 1994*. Washington, DC: U.S. Department of Education.

National Commission on Excellence in Education (1983). *A nation at risk: The imperative for educational reform*. Washington, DC: Author.

National Data Research Center (1993). [Schools and staffing surveys, 1991]. Unpublished data.

National Education Association (1992). *Status of the American public school teacher, 1990-91*. Washington, DC: Author.

National Governor's Association (1986). *Time for results: The governor's 1991 report on education*. Washington, DC: Author.

Nelson, F. H. & O'Brien, T. (1993). *How U.S. teachers measure up internationally: A comparative study of teacher pay, training, and conditions of service.* Washington, DC: American Federation of Teachers.

Oakes, J. (1990). *Multiplying inequalities: The effects of race, social class, and tracking on opportunities to learn mathematics and science.* Santa Monica, CA: The RAND Corporation.

Organization for Economic Co-operation and Development (1992). *Education at a glance.* Paris: Author.

Popkewitz, T. S. (Ed.). (1987). *Critical studies in teacher education: Its folklore, theory, and practice.* New York: The Falmer Press.

Resnick, L. B. (1987). *Education and learning to think.* Washington, DC: National Academy Press.

Sedlak, M. & Schlossman, S. (1986). *Who will teach?* Santa Monica, CA: The RAND Corporation.

Shulman, L. S. (1983). Autonomy and obligation: The remote control of teaching. In L. S. Shulman & G. Sykes (Eds.) *Handbook of teaching and policy* (pp. 484-504). New York: Longman.

Shulman, L. S. (1987). Knowledge and teaching: Foundations of the new reform. *Harvard Educational Review, 57*(1), 1-22.

Taylor, F. W. (1911). *The principles of scientific management.* New York: Harper.

Thompson, J. A. (1986). *The second wave of educational reform: Implications for school leadership, administration, and organization.* Denver, CO: Education Commission of the States.

Tyack, D. B. (1974). *The one best system: A history of American urban education.* Cambridge, MA: Harvard University Press.

U.S. Department of Commerce (1989). *Current population survey, October, 1989.* Washington, DC: Bureau of the Census.

U.S. Department of Labor (1986). [Current population survey, 1986, 1987]. Unpublished data.

William T. Grant Foundation Commission on Work, Family, and Community (1988). *The forgotten half: Pathways to success for America's youth and young families.* Washington, DC: Author.

Chapter 10: Teaching and Social Policy: Images of Teaching for Democratic Change[1]

JOHN SMYTH

INTRODUCTION

The term 'social policy' is not one we normally expect to find associated with discussions about matters instructional and pedagogical. In normal parlance, social policy refers to actions that are more likely to be associated with actions of the state or related to matters of the wider well-being of the population at large. In a recent book on this topic in Australia, Paul Smyth (1994) argued that the term social policy has become a 'political catchword' (p. 1) for a range of activities. Originally, it was a term popularised in the post World War II years as a way of referring to the mechanisms for 'protecting citizens from market forces' (p. 1) and ensuring that struggling industries and the wider community were shielded from the worst rigours of economic competition. Such government intervention was regarded as important for those least advantaged, like working class people, and other sections of the community ill-equipped to engage in muscular cut-and-thrust activity. In other words, it was a way of government ensuring protection for weaker sections of society, while at the same time ensuring a certain degree of social cohesion through public ownership of resources – if you will, a kind of 'mixed' economy with both market and government control. On occasions, it meant considerably more than this as the state moved beyond 'mere[ly] protect[ing] people from markets' (p. 3) and actively participating in planning the way in which social and economic welfare was to be achieved. The post-war years have seen an increasingly affluent society narrow the social policy debate considerably '... to the margins of welfare and public finance. '[The effect has been that] the state's social policy or 'nation building' role was increasingly defined in terms of social welfare and ... [its] political character was forgotten' (Smyth, 1994, p. 4).

What we have had occurring, therefore, is a gradual narrowing of the notion of social policy to issues of welfare, accompanied at the same time by a turn to market-based approaches. It is an interesting question as to where schooling, and teaching in particular, fits in this. Publicly provided comprehensive education has historically fallen squarely within the wider interpretation of social policy, based largely on the view that schooling was about the wider processes of nation-building in a context of creating a democratic and informed citizenry –

B.J. Biddle et al. (eds.), International Handbook of Teachers and Teaching, 1081–1144
© *1997 Kluwer Academic Publishers, Printed in the Netherlands*

a notion that has been the centerpiece of public education in the U.S. for most of this century. According to Wraga (1992), in this country, there has been 'a steady decline in commitment and a concomitant rise of opposition to the model [at least as applied to the comprehensive high school] since mid-century' (p. 28). When considered at all, education (and by implication, teaching) is invariably regarded as a residual item in the social policy arena. As Halsey (1972) aptly put it:

> Education is seen as a wastepaper basket of social policy – a repository for dealing with social problems where solutions are uncertain or where there is a disinclination to wrestle with them seriously. Such problems are prone to be dubbed 'educational' and turned over to the schools to solve. (p. 8)

This residual approach has, in recent times, been converted into a turn to a decidedly market-based approach to schooling, which takes its most potent expression in the work of Chubb and Moe (1990) in their *Politics, Markets and School Choice*, where it is argued that 'public schools can improve only if a market system of educational choice replaces the existing form of democratic control' (Wraga, 1992, p. 34). The major argument of Chubb and Moe (1990) is that schools work best if they operate more like private enterprises, driven by consumer choice, in a context where 'as far as possible, all higher-level authority must be eliminated' (p. 219) and schools are controlled 'by the market ... free to organize any way they want ... [so as] to please their clientele' (p. 190). It is this 'anything goes' mentality (Wraga, 1992, p. 38) that is supposed to produce alleged diversity through the choices available to individuals. Critics, however, counter-claim that what this amounts to is a 'dismantling [of] the comprehensive ideal' – the notion that schools exist not only for private gratification and gain, and that what is produced as a consequence, is 'aggravated fragmentation along a variety of lines' (Wraga, 1992, p. 39) as students are provided with 'limited access to peers of different background, abilities and aspirations' (p. 39). Thus, the ultimate effect of the marketing of schooling is that society becomes even more stratified, fractured and fragmented than it is at the present. As Wraga (1992) says, 'during a time of seething racial tensions, a rash of bias crimes, political exploitation of racial anxieties, and evidence of lingering and widespread school segregation, choice advocates would foist upon our public education system an inherently separatist organization' (p. 40).

The largely unsubstantiated claim that schools need to be reformed (and, indeed, can *only* be reformed) through the artificial creation of a marketplace in education reflects the flawed economic ideas of Milton Friedman who argued for a pervasive free-market basis for society. It fails largely on the grounds that it actually violates the possibility of unity within a broader and wider view of diversity. The view that a reduction in inefficient bureaucracy (a not unreasonable request in and of itself), can be brought about through a single model of decentralisation, is a leap of logic that has certainly not been validated, although it has yet to be thoroughly challenged and dismissed. Providing further grounds for enforced segregation and separation of students based on so-called educational choice, according to ability, aspiration, and socio-economic background, is hardly likely to be a recipe for producing a more tolerant, informed, understanding, and socially cohesive society. On the contrary, I argue here that teaching is more than didactically imparting preformulated knowledge to passive cohorts of students – it is and must be an active process working to produce discursive and critically informed communities, with habits of mind that are simultaneously more just, humane, and equitable. This is a view of teaching that involves being open to argument, disputation, debate, and contestation about how ideas, ideologies, and practices are formed, whose interests they represent, and how they might be changed to produce greater inclusivity. In other words, teaching is about engagement with 'big' issues that are inconclusive, that are highly tentative (in the sense that they need to be continually justified on the basis of argument), and redefined in more inclusive ways. There is something inherently argumentative about the real world of teaching as questions about what's worth teaching, who and what is marginalised, and what ought not be taken-for-granted are worked through and struggled over in classrooms.

In the next section I sketch out how the vocational debate has surfaced in the contemporary educational discussion of what schooling is for, and by implication, how teaching ought to proceed. I further connect this to two conceptions of teaching – one as teaching *is* commonly conceived, and the other as it *might be*. But, before I do these I should disclose my basic orientation.

I should say, at the outset, that the line of argument I shall be taking here is not one that regards vocationalism, and its concomitant instrumental teaching, as in any way obliterating the social policy effects of teaching. On the contrary, I maintain that there has been considerable resistance by teacher activists and academics in the direction of sustaining a more democratic alternative, rather than acquiescing to domesticating forms of education. There is clearly an important point to be made here in terms of the battle over the discourse of teaching, and it is important not to conceal the nature of the struggle for to do so would be to deny the significant advances made daily (albeit sometimes sporadically) by many teachers in classrooms across the nation and around the world. I am less inclined to the view expressed by Neave (1988) that 'education is less part of social policy, but is increasingly viewed as a subsector of economic policy' (p. 274) even though it may sometimes appear and feel that way. Education, and necessarily teaching, do need to engage constantly with questions like 'What sort of society do we have?' and 'What sort of society do we want to have?', and unless we are prepared to struggle with the 'means/end reversal'

that Neave (1988) refers to, then we will have leaner and economically fitter societies, but we will have lost the capacity to ask questions like 'Fitter to do
what?'; 'Will the quality of life be changed?'; and 'To whose benefit?' These
are crucial questions that ought to underpin teaching, and we have seen recently
through the alleged activities of the AUM sect in Japan, and the way in which
forms of rote teaching and learning considerably diminish the capacity for critical judgement, where we can finish up as a society. The question is not whether
teaching should be critical or not but rather 'critical to what end?' (Warham,
1993, p. 210).

SCHOOLING AND THE 'NEW' INDUSTRIAL EFFICIENCY MOVEMENT

The genesis of the ideas I explore in this section (as a prelude to addressing the
broader question of 'What then is to be done?') have their origins in the 'social
efficiency movement' early this century in the U.S. According to Knoll (1988),
analyses of this type became popular when Edward Krug (1964) wrote about the
origins of social efficiency in his *The Shaping of the American High School
1880-1920*:

> According to Krug, the social efficiency movement derived from two
> major groups: one led by Edward A. Ross and David S. Snedden,
> favoured an education for 'social control' and the other led by Samuel
> T. Dutton and John Dewey, favoured education for 'social service.'
> Integrating both groups, social efficiency became the educational aim
> between 1905 and 1915. (p. 1)

But, as Knoll (1988) points out, the term 'social efficiency' did not necessarily
always have the connotation of 'social control' that it tends to conjure up today:
'The social efficiency movement did not have just one branch, it was as broad
and differentiated as progressive education itself' (p. 14). Indeed, it appears that
educationists who eventually popularised the term in the U.S. in the first two
decades of this century (like Bagley, Snedden, Bobbitt, and Charters) were
heavily influenced (although they didn't always acknowledge it) by Benjamin
Kidd who first wrote about the notion of 'social efficiency' in *Social Evolution*
in 1894. Summarizing Kidd's view of social efficiency, Knoll (1988) wrote:

> For Kidd as for Darwin and Spencer, competition was indispensable in
> ensuring human progress ... (p. 3). Society profited when every
> individual had a chance to develop his capabilities and compete. By
> intensifying competition, Kidd argued, democracy provided the most
> efficient system for human progress (p. 4) ... The idea of efficiency

figured prominently in *Social Evolution*. In fact, 'social efficiency' was the cause of progress; it was the aim of evolution; and it was the means of measuring the development of an individual or a nation (p. 4).... 'The most vigorous social systems,' he wrote, 'are those in which are combined the most effective subordination of the individual to the interest of the social organism with the highest development of his own personality. Apparently, two principles had to be reconciled: social control and 'equality of opportunity.' ... Education for social efficiency, Kidd could have said, is less than the training of intellect but primarily the development of character, strength and discipline. (Knoll, 1988, p. 5)

With the benefit of hindsight, it seems that Benjamin Kidd may have been dealt with somewhat unfairly in not receiving full credit for coining the term 'equality of opportunity' (Knoll, 1988, p. 6). None of this is to suggest, of course, that social efficiency was without its quite strident critics. As Knoll (1988) notes:

John A. Hobson, the political economist from England ... criticized Kidd for defining progress and 'social efficiency' quantitatively ... A society, Hobson said, could only become socially efficient when 'the bonds between individual and individual [were] numerous and strong.' Cooperation, as democracy, was not an instrument of competition but an expression of the reason and dignity of man. (pp. 7-8)

It was out of these origins that educators such as Dewey 'began to discover the usefulness of 'social efficiency'' (p. 9); for example, James Seth of Cornell University asserted, 'The social estimate of education ... is based upon the contribution which it makes to the social efficiency of the individual (p. 9), while for educational sociologist from the University of Chicago, Ira W. Howerth, 'The primary task of education is that of assisting nature in developing the social, and eliminating the unsocial impulses' (Knoll, 1988, p. 10). So, what we had emerging was a much more 'qualitative' notion of social efficiency that, while it was more vocational, was oriented towards strengthening individuals and enabling them to contribute more fully to life and the progress of society. As Charles R. Richards of the manual training department at Teachers College Columbia University said, 'The real thing ... is to connect with life, to connect with the healthy instincts that make for mental, moral, physical growth in such a way that every step tends to strengthen the sense of self-fulfilment and the powers of social effectiveness' (Knoll, 1988, p. 11).

This was occurring at the same time as David Snedden of Stanford University was lecturing about social efficiency from a 'utilitarian' point of view (Drost, 1967) – postulating schools for 'the rank and file,' using schools to prepare young people for work (Knoll, 1988, p. 11). In a passage that has a remarkable ring of the contemporary about it, he believed that:

> ... only by developing 'the greatest degree of efficiency' at all levels of education would America be able to compete successfully in the world market. (p. 12)

Dewey's major contribution to this debate was his insistence on the need to clarify the intent behind the notion of social efficiency in education:

> In the former [narrow sense] social efficiency is supposed to be measured on the basis of definite output of overt acts and external products.... In the truer and more generous sense, social efficiency means ... the increase of ability to share in the appreciation and enjoyment of all values of social intercourse and thus necessarily includes the enriching of conscious experience (p. 13).... Social efficiency ... is nothing less than the socializing of *mind* which is actively concerned in making experiences more communicable, in breaking down barriers of social stratification which make individuals impervious to the interests of others. When social efficiency is confined to the service rendered by overt acts, its chief constituent is omitted – intelligent sympathy and good will. (p. 13)

The 'scientific management' of Frederick Taylor was not unconnected to the way in which some educators were seeking to advance the ideas of social efficiency in curriculum. As Knoll (1988) put it:

> Snedden, Bobbitt and Charters spoke of the school as 'plant' and the student as a 'product.' Like Taylor, they were concerned with measurement and the 'elimination of waste.' ... [T]hey had read Kidd's *Social Evolution* and had developed a social efficiency curriculum one decade before Taylor had published his *Principles of Scientific Management* in 1911.... Taylorism increased but did not create the 'orgy' of social efficiency that swept the curriculum field in the progressive era. (Knoll, 1988, p. 15)

What is interesting about this is the sometimes misconceived contemporary view that scientific management was imposed on schools from industry – if anything, it was the reverse, as Callahan (1962) so cogently argued.

In many respects, Bowles and Gintis (1976) (see also Cole, 1988) carried many of these arguments forward in their *Schooling in Capitalist America*.

They argued, in essence, that there were three criteria for an adequate education system in a democratic society:

> First, education should foster the personal development of each member of society. Personal development … is not limited to the acquisition of knowledge and cognitive skills. Equally important … are those affective and interpersonal skills which allow individuals to control their lives, and foster the self-esteem and sense of personal dignity which lead them to demand the resources to exercise such control. Second, education should act as an equalizing force, removing obstacles to substantive social equality and tempering the tendency for social privilege, and more importantly social deprivation, to be transmitted from generation to generation.

> Finally, education should be a stabilizing force in the good society, fostering what John Dewey called the social 'continuity of life,' by training youth to accept and affirm dominant culture and its institutional expression. Indeed we might judge a good society by the extent to which the success of its educational system in assuring the social continuity of life would simultaneously promote the personal developmental and egalitarian objectives of schooling. (pp. 235-236)

In their original work, and again in their revision of it a decade later (Cole, 1988), Bowles and Gintis argued that 'Educational systems of advanced capitalist society fail to perform their developmental and egalitarian functions …. This failure … lies not so much in schools themselves as in the type of society in which these schools are embedded' (p. 236). They say that only in a democratic society do the circumstances exist where the personal development of individuals can be promoted at the same time as crucial social institutions affirmed:

> … capitalist societies … fail to be democratic in the strict sense that their economies are systems in which decisions makers (the owners and controllers of wealth) remain *unaccountable* to the individuals who implement, and are affected by, their actions. (Bowles & Gintis, 1988, p. 236)

While acknowledging that their stance had 'often been subjected to the criticism of economism and reductivism, on the grounds of ignoring racism, sexism and other non-class forms of oppression … [they argued that] the major conclusions of *Schooling in Capitalist America* have not been subjected to what we consider damaging criticism, and hence we continue to hold that they are correct' (p.

236). While their explanation of capitalist relations is sometimes disparagingly labelled in terms of the so-called 'correspondence principle,' Bowles and Gintis (1988) argued that they had never portrayed the education system as a 'system of uncontested domination ... [but rather that their] own framework was grounded in a quite divergent framework stressing that the organization of production was, and is, the product not of class *domination*, but rather of class *struggle*' (p. 237).

None of this has been without its substantial number of critics (see Davies, 1995, for an expanded critique), but as Davies (1995) notes, what marks out the claims of reproduction theorists from their more recent 'resistance theorist' counterparts (see Willis, 1977), is the way in which the latter has evolved out of the former with a more positive spin. From a circumstance in which the trajectory of reproduction theory (i.e., how schools work through the social relations of classrooms to replicate the social relations of wider capitalist production) was argued as being too limited 'deterministic, mechanical and simplistic' (Bowles & Gintis, 1988, p. 238), reproduction theory 'gradually evolved into resistance theory ... [where] school opposition [was regarded] as a youthful expression of a proletarian culture' (Davies, 1995, p. 1455). According to Davies (1995), the determinism of reproduction theory was resolved through the notion of 'reproduction through resistance ... working-class students ... condemn[ing] themselves to working-class futures by affirming their autonomous culture' (p. 1456). He extensively cites Willis' (1977) *Learning to Labor* as the archtypical example. It should be noted in all of this that Davies' (1995) own position is one that takes a less overtly political 'subcultural theory' stance in which 'school rebellion [is portrayed] as a youthful expression of disappointment over thwarted goals ...' (p. 1458). He says:

> Resistance theorists thus transform many of the same student traits identified by the cultural deprivationists into favourable attributes. Whereas the deprivationists traced these traits to the strain of unequal opportunity, resistance theorists link them to the exigencies of capitalist production and see them as expressions of proletarian culture. (p. 1459)

That schools in the current economic climate ought to be considered appendages to industry, is therefore far from a novel idea. Almost since organized forms of schooling and education have existed, there has been an expectation, to varying degrees, that schools provide for the labor power needs of industry. Such demands have tended to be somewhat more muted (but they never totally disappear) at certain historical junctures (namely, in buoyant economic times rather than in times of economic and social uncertainty, when capitalist economies are undergoing the kind of fundamental restructurings they are experiencing at the moment due to the emergence of strident, newly developing economies in

Asia and South America). Periods of economic turmoil, uncertainty, and unpredictability have inherent within them demands for at least the outward appearance of certainty. Schools as social institutions are sufficiently familiar to large sections of the population to be convenient institutions required to carry a major portion of the consequences of these kinds of social dislocations. It sounds a reasonable proposition to expect that schools ought to serve the interests of industry and be compliant agents in assisting in the wider restructuring. But, in order to make the argument stick with the kind of veracity necessary for it to have an impact, schools have to be simultaneously blamed for the crisis (i.e., be ascribed as the 'cause' of the problem) while also being held out as the path by which restitution might be affected (i.e., as the 'solution' to the problem). We have the larger crisis, so we are told, because we have erred by allowing ill-advised egalitarian teaching and learning practices to prevail. Standards in schools have slipped because of inadequate attention to discipline, competencies, rigour, appraisal, and testing. Widespread and largely unsubstantiated claims, backed by prestigious commissions of inquiry derived exclusively from industry and business, put the view that learning and teaching need to return to modes of the past if we are to have a chance of ever experiencing the hoped-for economic recovery. Schools are exhorted to dutifully deliver literate, numerate, compliant (but not socially critical) skilled workers able to engage in economic restoration. Noticeable in this view of education are perspectives on schooling that largely prevailed in the past – namely, a view of schooling that is about drilling and training. Even worse, this is a kind of cargo cult mentality that says we have risen to earlier forms of economic pre-eminence because of instrumental and utilitarian modes of schooling. The fact that earlier periods of economic ascendancy were almost completely due to the annihilation and colonisation of one part of the world (largely Afro and Asian) by another (largely European), at the expense and degradation of the former seems largely to escape attention. To put it another way, mooted changes to education and schooling (and teaching and learning in particular) are being predicated upon a set of views that are informed and framed by a set of conditions that are no longer with us, if they ever did have much efficacy as explanations anyway.

To put this yet another way, the 'solutions' that are being arrived at as the way to resolve current perplexities are solutions to do with rigour, relevance, quality, discipline, standards, forms of assessment, and competencies that purportedly prevailed during some romanticised golden era when life was good, children listened to their elders, and we all lived prosperously. This is a style of policy making that is metaphorically akin to driving a car by means of looking in the rear-vision mirror. The fact that reaching back to the perceived comfort and certainties of the past for ways of explaining and resolving present difficulties is inadequate as an explanation seems to go largely uncontested by the majority of the community. For those who craft such inaccurate ways of resolving difficulties, what is most astounding and disturbing is that they actually seem to believe in the correctness and rightness of what they offer as solutions in areas like education. Part of the problem here lies with the apparently commonsense nature of much of what passes as schooling – we have all, after all been students of one sort or another, and the process of teaching did not appear to us to be *that* complicated or mysterious. But if one looks carefully at the agenda being created for schools by avid reformers outside of schools, what is most uniformly striking about it is its apparent 'naturalness.' There is something appealing about the notion that western capitalism is in trouble because schools are failing to deliver the requisite kind of skilled labor, and what is need as a consequence are ways of whipping schools and teachers into shape. This ideology is so pervasive and compellingly self-evident as to be almost an unquestionable axiom in western capitalist countries. Arguments abound as to how to proceed to make schools more like industry, with heavy doses of effective, clearly focused, narrowly utilitarian objectives, pursued in a context thoroughly committed to adding value to educational raw material in order to produce the highest quality and most saleable product.

The logic of positions like that just sketched out break down because the 'causation' (bad schools) has not been anywhere near substantiated, nor its corollary that industrial models of administration, organization, and management are necessarily any better 'solutions' than the modes of operation that they seek to so readily supplant in schools. The unfortunate consequence is that schools are being driven to follow modes of operation that are informed by a largely bankrupt set of ideologies and paradigms from a quarter in which they have proven demonstrably ineffectual. We only need a cursory glance around the littered landscape of the 1980s to see the rate at which the industrial model of management failed dismally. Rather than a carefully considered approach to 'What's wrong with our schools?' (if anything), what we are tending to experience instead are a set of ideologically driven solutions to as yet only partly (or poorly) articulated or even misconstrued problems – hardly an edifying spectacle for so-called educated and civilised societies.

In this section I have attempted to summarize, in so far as it is possible to do that for global trends, what is happening to education in advanced capitalist countries. There is inevitably a risk in doing that because of local variations in terms of history and evolution of education, not to mention regional variations in the nature of the way capitalism is being redesigned (see Keegan, 1992, for examples of this). However, there is mounting evidence (Smyth, 1995a) to suggest some quite remarkable similarities (beyond what could be construed as mere coincidence) in what is happening to educational reform worldwide. I say this as one who lives in Australia, who closely observes what is happening in New Zealand, and constantly studies developments in the U.K. and the U.S. Notwithstanding, more detail about a particular instance may serve to illustrate the more general point. Berliner and Biddle (1995) in their insightful book, *The Manufactured Crisis: Myths, Fraud, and the Attack on America's Public Schools*, provide a detailed and well argued case of how the last decade has seen unprecedented attacks on the credibility and veracity of public schools in America. The argument and evidence they provide is of an extensive, persistent, and orchestrated campaign of misinformation, deceit, half-truths, misrepresentations, myths, and outright lies (p. 4). They label this as collectively amounting to a 'manufactured crisis' about the true nature of contemporary American schooling. To their considerable credit these authors take on the difficult and complex task of presenting the evidence necessary to counter arguments about the supposed crisis in teaching and schooling in the U.S. What they present is a carefully considered body of research that, far from showing any crisis of competence in U.S. schools as maintained by narrow sectional interest groups, reveals instead an agenda that 'diverts attention away from the real problems faced by American education ...' (p. 4), which are about a significant loss of public confidence and dramatically declining public resources for education. Berliner and Biddle (1995) conclude that:

1) on the whole, the American school system is in far better shape than the critics would have us believe;
2) where American schools fail, those failures are largely caused by problems that are imposed on those schools, problems that the critics have been only too happy to ignore. (p. 12)

While it is not possible to cite the extensive body of evidence here, the particular myths that are exploded are:

- Student achievement in American primary schools has recently declined.
- The performance of American college students has also fallen recently.
- The intellectual abilities and abstract problem-solving skills of America's young people have declined, although – paradoxically – it is also believed that their intelligence and the skills that indicate 'giftedness' are fixed and identifiable at an early age.
- America's school have always come up short when compared with schools in other countries, indicating that our educational procedures are deficient and that our educators are feckless ...
- America spends a lot more money on its schools than other nations do.
- Investing in the schools has not brought success – indeed, money is unrelated to school performance.
- Recent increases in expenditures for education have been wasted or have gone merely to unneeded raises for teachers and administrators.

- The productivity of American workers is deficient, and this reflects the inadequate training they receive in American schools.
- America produces far too few scientists, mathematicians, and engineers; as a result, the country is losing its industrial leadership.
- Our schools are not staffed by qualified teachers, the textbooks they use promote immorality, and most American parents are dissatisfied with their local schools.
- Because they are subject to market forces, private schools are inherently better than public schools. (pp. 5-6)

While the history of these mischievous misconstruals is interesting in itself, it is not the topic I want to pursue here. I am more interested in why this is the case, who is working in schools to expose it, how, and what alternatives are being constructed. Suffice to say at this point, that Berliner and Biddle (1995) have taken on directly the critics of U.S. education in a courageous, well-informed, and cogent rebuttal of these widespread and largely unfounded criticisms. Their conclusion is most apt:

> … recent criticisms of American schools have often been bolstered by impressive claims of evidence that appeared, on first glance, to support arguments about our 'troubled' schools. On closer examination, however, many of these claims have turned out to be garbage…. People who are sincerely interested in improving American education must be alerted to such chicanery. (p. 171)

While it is clearly difficult and dangerous to engage in widespread generalization about the extent to which such campaigns of public misinformation have been engaged in other countries, there is evidence that many of the ill-informed ideas (often glamorised with the label of 'reforms'), have spread to other parts of the world through the ideology of the New Right. An example of this can be found in 'Something borrowed, something blue? A study of the Thatcher Government's appropriation of America's education and training policy' (Finegold, McFarland, & Richardson, 1992, 1993).

The reason the American case just cited is so important is that if the level of hysteria generated by the misinformation campaigns of the past decade are in any way representative of what has likely occurred in other countries, and knowing what we do about the extraordinary capacity of American culture to shape global thinking, then recent policies that reflect New Right 'solutions' in other countries could well have all of the same shortcomings outlined by Berliner and Biddle. There seems to be little doubt as to the ideological lineage of calls for educational reform worldwide, despite quite different educational, political and social histories. For example, current moves to 'devolve' school administration are occurring simultaneously in all western countries even though the U.S. has a history of local school boards, the U.K. a mediated structure of Local Educational Authorities, and Australia and New Zealand much more centralized systems. All are actively pursuing policies of dismantling and privatizing education by means of 'consumer choice,' generally disguised behind labels like school-based management, the self-managing school, site-based management, and locally managed schools.

In the next section I explore two somewhat artificial and dichotomous views of teaching. While such portrayals have obvious limitations as categories, or even as orientations, they nevertheless serve usefully to begin to mark out what it might mean to see teaching through a social policy lens that is more complex than prevails at the moment. In addition, it is also useful to point to the ways in which teaching is a more problematic activity than is generally acknowledged. (None of this should be taken as precluding or denying other construals of teaching, however. Indeed, I have alluded to others elsewhere, such as teachers viewed as professionals, managers, artisans, or crafts persons – see Smyth, 1992).

CONFLICTING CONSTRUALS OF TEACHING

This section focuses on the kind of society we have, the nature and quality of the relationships between society and schools, how that society regards teachers, and the kind of construals it places on their work.

There have been extensive discussions recently (Putnam, 1993, 1995, 1996) regarding the disappearance of 'civic culture' in America as well as in other western societies like Australia (Cox, 1995). By whatever terms we choose to describe it, there has been a marked diminution in 'social capital,' 'social connectedness,' or 'civic engagement' which is to say, 'those features of social life, networks, norms and trust, that enable participants to act together more effectively to pursue shared objectives' (Putnam, 1996, p. 1). Putnam (1995) cites extensive evidence which shows, on a range of indicators, that Americans are 'disengaging psychologically from politics and government,' and 'by almost every measure, Americans' direct engagement in politics and government has fallen steadily and sharply over the last generation' (p. 68). This has been accompanied, he says, by an across the board decline in forms of associational membership:

> The most whimsical yet discomforting bit of evidence of social disengagement in contemporary America that I have discovered is this: more Americans are bowling today than ever before, but bowling in organized leagues has plummeted in the last decade or so. (p. 70)

Trends in 'social connectedness' are clearly heading downwards, and evidence across 35 countries show that there is a strong correlational relationship between social trust and civic engagement:

> ... the greater the density of associational membership in a society, the more trusting its citizens. Trust and engagement are two facets of the same underlying factor – social capital .... The trends of the past decade have apparently moved the United States significantly lower in the international rankings of social capital. (pp. 73-74)

The point behind all of this is the need to better understand the problem:

> We must sort out the dimensions of social capital .... What types of organizations and networks most effectively embody – or generate social capital, in the sense of collective action, and the broadening of social identities? ... [H]orizontal ties are more productive of social capital than vertical ties. (p. 76)

According to Cox (1995) while Putnam's research is useful 'his view points are still too narrow' (p. 11). She argues that in order to reverse the depletion of social capital we need to concentrate, not only on forms of community association, but on how to foster egalitarian relationships in the culture of the workplace. This has considerable import for teaching because the nature of teaching as work informs the manner in which we inculcate our children in the formal context of schooling. If the work of teaching is driven by a competitive rather than a cooperative ethos, if there is a lack of generosity of spirit towards the views of others, and if the purpose of education is narrowly conceived as being to satisfy the dictates of the economy, then social capital will be eroded and the capacity of schools to enhance that will diminish. The discussion that follows will, therefore, focus on various competing conceptions of teachers – as technicians or civil servants, and intellectuals or political actors. The attempt is to try and extend our thinking about how teaching figures in the production or loss of future social capital.

Teachers as Technicians or Civil Servants

Over the years it has been fashionable to portray teachers (and indeed to treat them) as compliant workers. It was Scheffler (1968) who argued 30 years ago that teachers' work was becoming construed as that of:

... a minor technician within an industrial process, the overall goals of which are to be set in advance in terms of national needs, the curricular materials prepackaged by disciplinary experts, the methods developed by educational engineers – and the teachers' job ... just to supervise the last operational stage, the methodical insertion of ordered facts into the students mind. (pp. 5-6)

This is just as true today as we grapple with moves to reintroduce technical and rational ways of construing the work of teachers. Scheffler's (1968) argument is that to trivialise the work of teachers in this way is to deny its complexity. The teacher is more than a technician; he or she should be an active force shaping and determining the educational process. Scheffler's problem with the industrial analogy is that it flies in the face of what goes on in schools. Technicians do things to materials according to certain rules and procedures. These materials, in return, are shaped by what he or she does; but those materials are not responsive, there is no communication with them. Neither is there any questioning of 'judgements ... beliefs ... perspectives and purposes [nor do] they present him [/her] with ... new centers of personal experience [with] which his [/her] own meanings may be engaged or transformed' (p. 6). According to Scheffler (1968), teachers' work is vastly different on several counts: students *are not* inert materials to be worked on; teachers *do* enter into communications with their students and they *do* share varying degrees of a common culture; and there *is* a dual process at work of refining students' outlooks while enabling the teacher to broaden his or her understanding. Students, on the other hand, are not passive, either – they 'question,' 'explore,' 'doubt,' and 'evaluate' as they respond, not only to the content of what they are taught, but also how it is taught, to the orientations and convictions thus reflected, and to the 'larger rationale that underlies them' (p. 6). Teaching is thus a complex process of risk taking in which disclosure is a key element in understanding the judgemental basis of the work of teaching. As Scheffler puts it, it is only when teachers embrace this risk that they are 'forced to a heightened self-awareness, and a more reflective attitude towards [their] own presuppositions ...' (p. 6). The notion of reducing teachers' work to purely operational terms, is, therefore, fallacious in the extreme. We can see this in the obvious and very public failure of several attempts over the years to treat teachers as if they were technicians. The reason why innovations like 'competency-based instruction, mastery learning, teacher proof materials, performance contracting, accountability testing, and programmed instruction' (Hlebowitsh, 1990, p. 147) have so demonstrably failed, is because of the way they have ignored the realities of teaching and tried to segment teachers' work in ways that make them operatives in somebody else's processes.

If teachers are not simply the purveyors of unproblematic received bodies of knowledge to compliant students, then their concerns and interests must go considerably beyond the classroom into the larger setting of the school involving an active responsibility for setting goals towards which they will work. Unless they do this, Hartnett and Naish (1980) argue, then teachers will develop a pre-occupation with 'means and [an] indifference to ends [that] is at best immoral' (p. 265). Specifying what teachers do through national curricula, statewide testing, and curriculum guidelines and frameworks, is to force them into the educational cul-de-sac of being technical operatives. While this may appear to be an attractive administrative or bureaucratic solution to the relationship between schooling and the economy, and may seem to enable reskilling to meet the new requirements for international competitiveness, it actually fails to acknowledge that educational ends are highly contentious, contested, negotiated, constructed, and resisted.

The teacher-as-civil-servant analogy is another closely related notion. Bullough, Gitlin, and Goldstein (1984) point out that the classical notion of the public servant comes from Plato's *Republic* in which stipulations were made as to how a particular class of people (civil servants) were expected to suppress their individuality in order to serve the state. The basis of this was described as 'objective necessity'; that is to say, acting in the interests of the nation, for the betterment of the majority, or according to God's will. Bullough et al. (1984) also note that Hegel extended this to refer to a class who would have 'no political interests beyond the efficient administration of the state' (p. 344) and who would be unquestioningly obedient to wise rulers. Responding to this model, the ideal teacher for most of the twentieth century has often been portrayed as having the qualities of a public servant. For example, in America this can be clearly seen in the early advocates of scientific management such as Bagley (1907), Bobbitt (1924), and Cubberley (1922) in which teachers had a duty of 'unquestioned obedience' to technocratic forms of rationality. Teachers' work in America is still largely characterized by features that are consistent with this servile attitude: 'a rapid work pace, little, if any, involvement in establishing aims, impersonal student-teacher relations, and much time spent in doing 'necessary' clerking and management tasks' (Bullough et al., 1984, p. 346). When teaching is driven by this kind of metaphor, teachers are excluded from curriculum decisions, are denied the opportunity to participate in the ends towards which they work, and have neither the time nor the inclination to question what they do. Goodlad's (1984) research shows this to be pretty much the state of affairs in the U.S. today.

In Britain, White (1979) has also canvassed the prospect of teachers (at least, primary teachers) as civil servants. He asks whether the teacher should be 'reduced to no more than a functionary, an obedient executive of political decisions taken elsewhere' (p. 19). His argument is that the conceptualisation of the teacher as civil servant need not be as restrictive as it might first appear. There are, he argues, varying degrees of autonomy for civil servants (at least in Britain) – 'from the tightly circumscribed work of a clerical officer to the very broad scope work of [senior civil servants] in interpreting government policy' (p. 19). He claims that teachers as civil servants need not be in this more restricted class. In other words, he sees teachers operating more as 'senior' rather than 'junior' civil servants. The teacher would thus be 'a person of wide horizons ... [capable] of understand[ing] the aims of the whole education system as democratically laid down ... need[ing] to reflect on how to fit her own teaching into this framework ensuring at the same time that it meshes with what her colleagues are doing in other institutions' (p. 20). The kind of civil servant status White (1979) envisages, which has yet to come about, is one who is politically aware and more knowledgeable and reflective about society generally and of the place of schooling in it (p. 20). What White (1979) really describes is a teacher who is a political activist capable of bringing 'pressure to bear to ensure that official aims are the aims that she can practically, logically and morally, teach to. She is not to be a passive recipient of aims from above, but plays an active role in helping to improve them' (p. 22).

Lawn (1987) has taken a slightly different tack in his historical study of British teachers called *Servants of the State: The Contested Control of Teaching*. He argues that in Britain there has been a strong tradition of the 'serving teacher' – one who has existed very much in a master – servant relationship, which is not to suggest that teachers have not struggled for better working conditions, for they clearly have. At root, he see the struggle over 'the kind of work teaching should be and the responsibilities of society for its education which were deployed in ideas of a loyal servant [and] an apolitical policy ... (p. xi). Treated in the ways they were, it was not surprising to find teachers seeing themselves as 'workers' who, if treated as servants, were prepared to fight to better their conditions.

The metaphor of teachers acting as servants of the state produces some interesting kinds of relationships (Smyth, 1991a). What we are witnessing at the moment is a resurgence of the idea that to act professionally, teachers must be prepared to enter a *partnership* with the State in return for varying degrees of 'limited or licensed professionalism' (Lawn & Ozga, 1986, p. 225). This 'mock partnership' in which 'teamwork' (Lawn, 1988, p. 164) and 'cooperation' (Lawn, 1988, p. 162) are becoming central expressions of the new work relations, amount in effect, to an ideological form of control over how teachers relate to others in the course of their work. To display 'collegiality' means to be able to work as 'part of groups and teams' in the policy and decision-making process in schools and amounts to a form of 'indirect rule' that is increasingly coming to characterise discussion about the management of schools. Lawn and Ozga (1986) borrow the term 'indirect rule' from the notion of British colonial administration in which:

> ... [there] was the appearance of decentralisation and devolution, with
> a quasi-autonomous role for the 'natives' which ensured their co-option,
> while the major powers of government remained firmly in British hands.
> (p. 226)

Within education this has meant a gradual 'rejection of direct prescriptive controls' (p. 226) and accepting in its place a process that is much more reliant on engineering broad forms of consensus. Lawn and Ozga (1988) note that, as with the colonial experience, emancipation is only for parts of the system – it does not mean endangering 'real tactical control' (p. 88) but rather dispensing with some of the more burdensome aspects of unnecessary central power.

By way of summary then, the notion of teachers as obedient operatives dutifully carrying out the instructions of others is antithetical to the notion of teachers who have a collective and expansive view of their role as teachers as well as the place of schooling in society. Sadly, conceiving teachers as individual technicians is a viewpoint that has widespread currency in schools and the community, and it will continue to receive endorsement as long as schools are regarded as legitimately constituting an extended arm of industry, can be welded onto the economy, and are thought to serve only the national interest (usually narrowly defined).

Teachers as Intellectuals and Political Actors

Argument in this section was foreshadowed in a comment by Warham (1993):

> ... no matter how hard teachers or researchers try to escape from the
> fact, the very nature of teaching is political. It is political both within
> the classroom and influenced by political factors outside the classroom.
> Any theory which attempts to describe teacher behaviour cannot fail to
> take this into account. (p. 210)

Probably more than any other contemporary educator, Henry Giroux (1988) has championed the cause of teachers as intellectuals and what that means politically. Giroux's extensive writings have occurred against a backdrop of 'educational reforms' that have aimed at reducing teachers to 'the status of low-level employees or civil servants whose main function seems to be to implement reforms decided by experts in the upper levels of state and educational bureaucracies' (Giroux, 1985a, p. 20). The consequence, Giroux argues, is that the search and the push for technical or administrative solutions to the complex economy-society-education linkage, has produced a growing gulf between those who decide on technical and methodological grounds what is best for schools, and the schools and teachers who must deal with students, curricula, and pedagogy on a daily basis. He argues that there is a process of subjugation of intellectual labor at work here that in many cases reduces teachers to the status of 'high level clerks implementing the orders of others ... or to the status of specialised technicians' (p. 21). This dominance of technocratic rationality has had the effect of producing a form of proletarianization of teachers' work, not dissimilar to what happened to factory workers in the nineteenth century as the control of what had previously been highly independent craftsman came increasingly under corporate and factory control. But, as Giroux argues, what has occurred in schooling is more than just an elevation of the importance of the technical and the economic in the everyday life of schools.

> Underlying this technical rationality and its accompanying rationalisation of reason and nature [has been] a call for the separation of conception from execution, the standardisation of knowledge in the interests of managing and controlling it, and the devaluation of critical intellectual work for the primacy of practical considerations. (p. 23)

In a similar vein, teacher education has, Giroux says, all too often been reduced to questions of 'what works' (see U.S. Department of Education, 1986; and Berliner & Biddle, 1995, for a critique); and issues concerned with what counts as knowledge, what is worth teaching, and how one judges the purpose and nature of teaching become submerged (or even obliterated) in the press for routinisation and standardisation through 'management pedagogies.'

Giroux's claim is that one way of rethinking and restructuring teachers' work is to view teachers as intellectuals and to see what teachers do as a form of intellectual labor. The argument here is that if we regard teachers in this light, then we can begin to 'illuminate and recover the rather general notion that all human activity involves some form of thinking, [and] no activity, regardless of how routinised it might become, is abstracted from the functioning of the mind in some capacity' (Giroux, 1985a, p. 27). When applied to teaching, Kohl (1983) put it this way:

> I believe a teacher must be an intellectual as well as a practitioner .... I don't mean an intellectual in the sense of being a university professor or having a PhD .... I am talking about activities of the mind. We must think about children, and create many philosophies of life in the classroom .... An intellectual is someone who knows about his or her field, has a wide breadth of knowledge about other aspects of the world, who uses experience to develop theory and questions theory on the basis of further experience. An intellectual is also someone who has the

courage to question authority and who refuses to act counter to his/her experience and judgement. (p. 30)

Equally important, Kohl (1983) argued that unless teachers

> ... assume the responsibility for theory making and testing, then theories will be made for us by ... the academic researchers and many other groups that are simply filling the vacuum that teachers have created by bargaining away their education power and giving up their responsibility as intellectuals. (p. 30)

Harris (1990) expressed similar thoughts.

> To teach is always to impose, to some extent, even if only by expressing a powerful voice in setting the agenda. The issue, at the school level ... is not to avoid or diminish teacher intervention in the lives of the young: it is not to look beyond teachers for setting the curriculum agenda, either by placing it in the province of government or by having it negotiated with pupils through intercultural articulation. It is, rather, to produce knowledgeable teachers committed to improving the human condition, who can provide informed reasoned justification for both their stance and for the substantive content they guard, further and profess ... (p. 181)

Giroux finds it useful to draw on the work of Antonio Gramsci in articulating what it might mean if we used the analogy of teachers as intellectuals. The essence of the argument is that 'all men and women are intellectuals, but not all of them function in society as intellectuals' (Giroux, 1985b, p. 84). What he underscores is the political nature of the role and function of an intellectual in society. Specifically, he says, this means 'inserting education into the political sphere by arguing that schooling represents both a struggle for meaning *and* a struggle over power relations' (p. 87). Viewed in this way, schooling becomes a project of helping students to see injustices, assisting them to locate themselves in relation to such issues, and learning how society is structured in ways that both sustain and maintain those inequities. This necessarily involves working with students in ways that enable them to see, through their own pedagogical work in classrooms, that knowledge and power are inextricably linked and that students need to see themselves as 'critical agents, problematizing knowledge, utilising dialogue, and making knowledge meaningful so as to make it critical in order to make it emancipatory' (p. 87). The kinds of questions Giroux suggests are necessary if teachers are to interrogate their work in the way he is suggesting so as to become intellectuals, include:

What counts as school knowledge?
How is such knowledge selected and organized?
What are the underlying interests that structure the form and content of
school knowledge?
How is what counts as school knowledge transmitted?
How is access to such knowledge determined?
What cultural values and formations are legitimated by dominant forms
of school knowledge?
What cultural formations are disorganized and delegitimated by
dominant forms of school knowledge? (p. 91)

Writers like Ginsburg (1988, 1994), White and White (1987), Carlson (1987),
and Stevens (1987) have all documented both the argument as well as evidence
on the need for teachers to be political actors in their educational settings; that
is to say, to be clear about the different ways in which they experience their
work – how they encounter it, how they understand it, and how they feel about
it (Ginsburg, 1988, p. 363). Adopting a political stance to one's work does not
mean being partisan political; it involves what Popkewitz (1987) describes as
'critical intellectual work,' where

> … 'critical' means moving outside the assumptions and practices of the
> existing order. It is a struggle … [to make] categories, assumptions, and
> practices of everyday life … problematic. (p. 350)

But, as Ginsburg (1988) argues, it is more than just problematizing the work of
teaching because it involves 'struggle to challenge and transform the structural
and cultural features we … come to understand as oppressive and anti-demo-
cratic' (pp. 363-365). Ginsburg's point hinges upon the need for teachers to see
themselves as actively participating in progressive movements committed to
bringing about fundamental social change. According to this view, the image of
the teacher as a compliant, passive, and easily moulded worker is replaced by a
view of the teacher 'as an active agent, constructing perspectives and choosing
actions' (Feiman-Nemser & Floden, 1986, p. 523).

    To summarize: the viewpoint that conceives teachers as intellectual and po-
litical actors is one that positions the work of teaching as a form of intellectual
labor, and to that extent, is concerned with teaching as a form of debate or struggle over important ideas and ideals. Teachers' own classrooms and schools thus
become sites of serious inquiry, and questions are asked and answered as to
what schooling is about, how it works for some, and what conditions act to exclude others. This is a construal of teaching that is decidedly political in the
sense that teachers do not take the nature of their work for granted – they are

prepared to question how it came to be that way and what sustains and maintains the tasks they are called on to do.

PROBLEMATIZING AND PROBLEM-POSING APPROACHES TO TEACHING

To view teaching in ways that are informed and shaped by the lives, histories, theories, and practices of teachers and how they experience the work of teaching is what a 'problematizing' approach to teaching is about. Such an approach challenges the habitualness and the taken-for-grantedness that often attaches to being a teacher. To problematize teaching involves a willingness to call into question one's most fundamental and cherished assumptions. This usually occurs through a collective and collaborative process of teachers working with one another, interrogating their teaching with probing questions such as:

> What is happening here?
> Who says this is the way things ought to happen?
> Who is it that is defining the work of teaching?
> How is that definitions are being fought over and resisted in various ways?
> What concessions and accommodations are being made?
> How are issues of skill, competency, professionalism and autonomy being
> expressed in the social relations of teaching?
> Whose interests are being served in the change process?
> What new forms of power are being used to focus power relations in teaching?
> How are the redefined labor relations of teaching being played out? (Smyth, 1995b, p. 85)

And:

> What overall purposes are being served?
> Whose vision is it anyway?
> Whose interests are being served?
> Whose needs are being met?
> Whose voices are being excluded, silenced, denied?
> How come some viewpoints always get heard?
> Why is this particular initiative occurring now?
> What alternatives have or should have been considered?
> What kind of feasible and prudent action can we adopt?
> Who can we enlist to support us?

How can we start now?

How are we going to know when we make a difference? (Smyth, 1996, p.117)

What is significant about this approach to questioning the fundamentals of teaching, curriculum, pedagogy, and assessment is that it moves significantly beyond examining teaching as conceived in limited, individualistic frameworks or exclusively in terms of the personal deficits (of teachers or students). Causation is often pursued in terms of political and ideological structures that are examined against a wider social canvass. While the starting point of discussion might still be instances of classroom activity that are perplexing, confusing, or troublesome, the intention is to locate or situate them in relation to wider change forces. A concerted attempt is made not to move into premature 'problem solving' before adequate explorations are made of the wider and deeper sources causing concern within teaching and learning. In other words, the emphasis is upon forces making teaching the way it is, and how these forces act to reproduce, sustain, and maintain what often amount to the alienating status quo.

When teachers are treated in ways that enable them to operate reflectively so as to theorize about their teaching, the trajectory of their life histories, and their work lives generally, then they have a measure of empowerment that makes their work qualitatively different from those situations in which teachers are expected to respond unquestioningly to agenda and reforms developed by others, usually at some distance from the classroom. The difference is one of teaching being construed as an intellectual process (or an intellectual struggle) in which the elements are argument, debate, and contestation of ideas and practices, compared with the implementation of a set of technical or mechanical procedures to be dutifully administered by teachers. In the case of the former, significant and mature judgements are being made by people who are close to the work of teaching, who have the freedom (with their students) to develop what they consider to be defensible standards and make decisions about what is likely to work, informed by local conditions.

As long as attempts to improve teaching continue to be couched solely in terms of perceived individual deficits within teacher's pedagogical repertoires and styles (or the concomitant learning styles of their students), then the process of improving teaching will fail to grapple systematically with historical and structural factors that have come to make teaching (and learning) the way it is. For example, arguing that teaching must improve in order to enhance national economic performance is to mask the wider social forces that make it difficult (if not impossible) for some groups in schools to embrace middle class curricula or approaches that are blatantly class, race, and gender blind. Constructing the problem in this way also obscures the ways in which collective forms of resistance from particular groups have been exercised so as to supplant what amount to racist or gendered curricula. It amounts to circumventing the process of wider understanding as to how power gets exercised in and through schools, and whose knowledge is celebrated, counted, and acknowledged.

Another way of expressing a problematizing approach involves adopting a 'critical' approach to teaching – which is not to imply an excessively negative or carping outlook. Rather, to adopt a critical stance to teaching (or indeed to the wider process of how adults learn, generally) is to adopt the posture of 'a certain scepticism, or suspension of assent, towards [an] ... established norm or mode of doing things' (McPeck, 1981, p. 6). As Garrison (1991) put it:

> Scepticism implies not taking things for granted but, more importantly, allowing for alternative possibilities. In this sense critical means not only a questioning but a more proactive [stance as well in a] ... search for a more satisfactory insight or resolution of a troubling situation. (p. 289)

Cox (1980) put it most succinctly of all: 'It is critical in the sense that it stands apart from the prevailing order of the world and asks how that order came to be' (p. 230).

According to Brookfield (1987), adopting a critical perspective involves more than an indiscriminate questioning of ideas and activities but also a constructive process of gaining insights in order to bring about informed social change. He proposed two core activities:

1) 'identifying and challenging assumptions; and
2) exploring and imagining alternatives' (p. 15).

In other words, being critical is a process of analysis, questioning, inquiry, criticism, *and* acting, that is guided and shaped by reason.

Paul (1990) carries this further by arguing that it is possible to conceive of being or becoming critical on two broad levels: one is 'atomistic' (which is being critical in a 'weak sense'), and the other is 'global' or holistic (which is a 'strong sense'). There is a major qualitative difference between the two, he says, based on narrow reasoning, micro-skills, and technical reasoning in the case of the former, and integrated, macro-skills, and a holistic approach in the latter, 'concerned with insight and the development of emancipatory reason' (Garrison, 1991, p. 290).

There are close parallels, too, between being critical in the strong sense, and Dewey's (1933) notion of operating 'reflectively.' Being critical (or reflective) is regarded as a natural precursor to 'action' (or testing). Summarising Dewey, Garrison (1991) put it that operating critically is similar, if not synonymous, with the term reflective, where 'reflective thinking originates in a state of doubt and requires an act of inquiry to settle the doubt' (p. 290).

The process of acting critically or reflectively follows a sequence that goes broadly like this: It begins with

Problem Identification or Definition – which occurs when some disorienting or 'triggering event' creates a situation of 'personal dissonance' or unexpected happening that 'prompts a sense of inner discomfort and perplexity' (Brookfield, 1987, p. 26). This is followed by a process of 'deliberation and information gathering' (Garrison, 1991, p. 294) when the individual or group seeks to 'redefine the issue or dilemma' (p. 294) to obtain a better understanding or what was initially an ill-defined or uncertain situation. This is followed by an

Exploration Phase – in which alternative explanations to the dilemma or problem are canvassed and, as Garrison (1991) puts it, one moves from 'the world of facts to the world of ideas ... [never being] entirely sure where our insights and ideas originate [from]' (p. 294). In turn, this leads to

Applicability – which comes when we move beyond abstract thought and begin to pose ideas for 'resolving the dilemma' (Garrison, 1991, p. 294). Of necessity, this step involves critical analyses of the alternative options available for action. Which leads to

Integration – involving 'a test of the applicability of the idea and a return to the concrete world' (Garrison, 1991, p. 294) as one engages in a process of 'confirming' and then 'adopting' an idea into one's life.

The challenge here, in Razack's (1993) terms, is how to 'build critical thinking in the activist classroom without recourse to alienating and abstract theoretical notions ...' (p. 44). The starting point, she says, has to be with a clear definition of what it means to act critically with a passionate commitment to '... understand how societal structures hinder and impede the fullest development of humankind's collective potential to be self-reflective and self-determining historical actors' (Welton, 1991, p. 24).

To summarize teaching from the vantage point of seeing it problematically, Tom (1985) suggested that:

> To make teaching problematic is to raise doubts about what, under ordinary circumstances, appears to be effective or wise practice. The object of our doubts might be accepted principles of good pedagogy, typical ways teachers respond to classroom management issues, customary beliefs about relationships of schooling and society, or ordinary definitions of teacher authority – both in the classroom and in the broader school context. (p. 37)

TEACHERS AS SOCIAL AND POLITICAL ACTIVISTS

My arguments about how teachers might position themselves critically or reflectively imply that some teachers may be unsatisfied with the status quo. Indeed, I would argue that this is the case for many teachers, not just in terms of
their classroom practices, but also when they think about the wider structures
that are shaping both their work and the learning possibilities of their students,
especially in relation to the inequitable and unjust outcomes for some groups of
children.

The notion of teachers as activists is understandably not one that has (or is
likely to acquire) widespread currency, mainly because it conjures up images of
conflict, troublemakers, and people who generally want to upset existing arrangements of privilege and power. In a sense, this is indeed correct. But, on the
other hand, it can be argued that schooling is never value neutral, and that whatever schools and classrooms do is always infused with perspectives and choices
as to who or what is to be advantaged, and concomitantly, who is to be disadvantaged, excluded, or marginalised. In other words, schooling is never innocent in the sense that it is socially detached or value-free. Some may try to
portray it in such a fashion, but this is a false image. Schooling always involves
undisclosed agenda and interests, most noticeably: whose language, cultures,
customs, and practices are allowed to prevail; whose version of history is portrayed in curricula and textbooks; who gets relegated to particular ability groups
and streams; and who fails tests that are framed in ways that acknowledge the
perspectives and lived experiences of some groups while denying others.

As a teacher-educator, I often meet with teachers who come to me with vague
feelings of unease. I try to engage those persons as critical activists of their own
teaching and the contexts within which it occurs by having them explore their
teaching using questions such as:

- Who talks in this classroom?
- Who gets the teacher's time?
- How is ability identified and attended to here, and what's the rationale?
- How are the unequal starting points of students dealt with here?
- How are instances of disruptive behaviour explained and handled?
- Is there a competitive or a cooperative ethos in this classroom?
- Who helps who here?
- Who's ideas are the most important or count most?
- How do we know that learning is occurring here?
- Are answers or question more important in this classroom?
- How are decisions made here?
- How does the arrangement of the room help or hinder learning?
- Who benefits and who is disadvantaged in this classroom?

- — How is conflict resolved?
- — How are rules determined?
- — How are inequalities recognised and dealt with?
- — Where do learning materials come from?
- — By what means are resources distributed?
- — What career aspirations do students have, and how is that manifested?
- — Who determines standards, and how are they arrived at?
- — How is failure defined, and to what is it ascribed?. Who or what fails?
- — Whose language prevails in the classroom?
- — How does the teacher monitor his or her agenda?
- — How does the teacher work to change oppressive structures in the classroom?
- — What is it that is being measured and assessed in this classroom?
- — Who do teachers choose to work with collaboratively, on what, and under what circumstances? (Smyth, 1995c)

Schooling, and by implication, teaching, is therefore always about social change (or its inverse, social inertia), and to a greater or lesser extent it ought to be inextricably connected to 'restructuring social arrangements along more equitable, just and humane lines' (Little, 1991, p. 13).

Posing such questions with groups of teachers who are receptive because of general feelings of unease and who are looking for assistance is one way to interrupt the social and cultural frameworks of teaching in schools. Despite frequent claims about 'lack of time to reflect,' teachers need assistance with ways of 'puncturing the images of normality' (Thompson & McHugh, 1990, p. 357) and developing 'extraordinarily re-experiencing the ordinary' (Shor, 1980, p. 37). Razack (1993) makes the same point in terms of how teachers for social change can explore 'such seemingly mundane questions ... as 'Why are we doing this?' and 'Where will it get us?'' as an important starting point. For Razack (1993), this is only possible through participant-centered collective reflection on how schools need to be 'described, analysed and confronted' (p. 46). It might also involve disturbing and uncovering 'deep[ly] entrenched systems of domination in our daily lives ... [and becoming increasingly vigilant and] self-conscious about our multiple and sometimes contradictory locations' (p. 47).

To take a particular concrete case,

Connell (1994) has provided evidence indicating that 'Australian schools deliver massive advantages to the children of the well-off and well-educated parents, and massive disadvantages to children of the poor and the poorly educated' (p. 1). Furthermore, with schools operating to produce and reproduce these effects for over half a century, such circumstances 'are not accidental, and they cannot be eliminated by minor tinkering with the system. It is clear that [the Australian] education system is designed in a way that delivers success along lines of social and economic privilege. The way school knowledge is defined, and school learning is organized, has this effect' (p. 1). The overall consequence, as Connell (1994) perceives it, is that where education produces success for the privileged, education overall as a social institution fails – because the moral nature of the enterprise converts teachers into 'gatekeepers of privilege' implementing curriculum that 'narrows the immense possibilities of learning' (p. 1). This tendency is further exacerbated by the already well advanced moves towards privatising public education, brought on by the exhortation to teachers, students, and schools to compete against one another. This is a recipe that, to date, has produce social stratification, segmentation and alienation.

Connell (1994) argues against rectifying this through forms of *negative social justice* thinking based on compensatory approaches for targeted groups as enshrined in Equity and Social Justice Action Plans. He argues instead for *positive social justice* thinking based on teacher activism at the grassroots level, through posing questions such as:

— What way of organising learning and teaching will most benefit the least advantaged?
— What concept of teacher professionalism will most benefit the least advantaged?
— How can we democratise the relationship between public schools and working-class communities?
— How can we redefine the relationships between schools and other public and cultural institutions? (p. 2)

Connell's position is similar to the one I have been developing so far in this paper – namely, that social change in schooling will come about at the level of the curriculum when teachers adopt the view that 'we cannot afford to keep curriculum debate a professional monopoly' and that the 'content of learning, the way school knowledge is organized ... [must become] public issues' (p. 2).

One of the most significant issues teachers who want to become social activists have to grapple with is the transition from thinking exclusively about individual students, to thinking about the social group from which they come. This requires confronting the oppressive nature of individualism in our society (which is really diversionary – see Berliner and Biddle, 1995, pp. 152-158 for discussion about why Americans embrace the myth of individual efficacy) and seeing that students actually come from social groups. Schools and classrooms are deeply entrenched in a pervasive liberal ideology of individualism which frames modes of thinking and acting when it comes to measurement and assessment, school discipline and behaviour management, social justice and disadvantage, competencies and standards, and the like. According to Razack (1993), socially activist teachers are able to uncover the dominant fallacy that 'individuals are autonomous and [therefore] responsible for making their own way,' and that failure is something that can, therefore, be 'attributed to personal not social causation.' In fact, the individual rights model does not give us any conceptual tools for understanding oppression and the systems that constrain individual choice (p. 49). The model for positive social justice, in contrast, shifts the focus to the systemic processes that block opportunities for groups and exposes the inadequacy of the individual rights model as an explanation for what is occurring in classrooms. The social justice model thus makes the invisible visible.

To summarize, teachers should be encouraged to become self-conscious social activists. This should not be taken to mean that teachers ought to incite revolution, or act in ways likely to jeopardise their employment. This might be more likely if they were being urged to act militantly, but that is *not* what is being suggested here. Rather, the attempt is to have teachers work in ways that challenge the taken-for-granted in their teaching and operate from the position that there may be other more just, inclusive, and democratic ways of working that help to overcome various forms of classroom disadvantage. These may not always be self-evident to teachers, and making progress will require close interrogation of particular classroom contexts. To say that teachers cannot (or should not) engage in these forms of analysis because they work within bureaucratic systems that may find them threatening is to fall barely short of adopting a position that is morally reprehensible. As Rudduck (1984) put it:

> ... good teaching is essentially experimental, and experiment entails rescuing at least part of one's work from the predictability of routine ... Indeed, one could argue that it is the child in the everyday world of the classroom, where the pattern of teaching and learning remains unexamined, that is at risk because he or she is subject to constant unmonitored and unreflected-upon action. *Not* to examine one's practice is irresponsible: to regard teaching as an experiment and to monitor one's performance is a responsible professional act. (p. 6)

Some examples of how the reforms spoken about so far in this chapter might further be acted upon, are provided in the following section. These are not recipe approaches for the obvious reason that such matters are inherently complex, but they are pointers in the right direction. Writings (either by teachers who have adopted these approaches, or ghost-writing by others on teachers' experiences) are too numerous to cite here, but representative examples include: Boston Women's Teachers Group (1986); Shor (1980); McLaren (1989); Kemmis and McTaggart (1988); Lampert (1985); Berlak and Berlak (1981); Goodman (1992); Schubert and Ayres (1992); Ayres (1993); Warham (1993); Miller (1990); McDonald (1992); Weber and Mitchell (1995); Raphael (1985); Perl and Wilson (1986); Strieb (1985); and Traugh et al. (1986). All of these examples indicate a preparedness on the part of teachers to challenge the status quo, and while the outcomes in all cases might not have been as salutary as expected, the experience was both chastening and professionally enhancing.

TEACHING FOR RESISTANCE AND EMPOWERMENT

The term teaching for resistance or empowerment is an umbrella term that is a convenient way of describing what is coming to be a constellation of approaches to teaching that share certain features. Essentially what they share with one another is being able to 'make a difference' in terms of teaching in ways that interrupt and supplant the educational status quo. Viewed from this vantage point, teaching becomes a counter-hegemonic activity committed to changing the life chances and expectations for children whose options might otherwise have been severely circumscribed because of language, culture, race, gender, socio-economic background, or simply because their life experiences are at variance from those of the dominant group in society. Teaching for resistance and empowerment has many variants and descriptors, but by whatever name it is known, it amounts to teachers working in ways that break the bonds of power so as to acknowledge diversity and celebrate difference and living out values that challenge entrenched and habitual norms.

Below are some brief glimpses into a few of the major contributors who fall under this heading, and whose work reflects a concern with teaching as social policy.

Teaching for Social Responsibility, Cultural Diversity, and Against the Grain

Seth Kriesberg's (1992) ideas are encapsulated in his *Transforming Power: Domination, Empowerment and Education* and can best be summed up as having a fundamental commitment to teachers working in classrooms in ways in which they continually struggle with the central issue of how to convert the 'power of position' into the 'expertise of authority.' The kind of questions that infused his approach, included:

> What would an education based on dialogue and empowerment look like across cultures with their various ways of engaging in talk and learning? What would it mean to take democracy seriously in our daily lives? What kinds of relationships must exist among teachers so that they can respond directly and forcefully to racism, sexism and other forms of fascism, and the violence they bring, without simultaneously

disempowering others? What are the possibilities for dialogue in a society that seems to value 'talking at' more than 'talking with?' (p. 212)

For Kriesberg (1992), the major obstacle to overcome is the 'coercive character of schooling, and in particular the traditional power of the teacher' (p. 154) which he regards as the major blockage to student empowerment. He sees relationships of domination as saturating all aspects of what occurs in schools, and the greatest challenge confronting teachers is the development of their capacity to enter into 'power-with relationships' with their students. He is under no delusions about the difficulties involved:

> The obstacles to creating such relationships [are] situated in many places, not the least being within the teachers themselves. Relationships of domination not only saturate the structures and norms of schools and the experiences and expectations of students and administrators, but they also lie deep within teachers. The struggle to move beyond relationships of domination is not solely with external forces, it is an internal struggle as well. It means wrestling with our commonsense assumptions about teaching and shaking our taken-for-granted patterns of acting and relating in classrooms. (p. 154)

An example may serve to reinforce the continuing shifting relationship between hegemonic forms of teaching and views that are counter-hegemonic, and how these are used to frame models of teaching competency. Within a dominant model, Warham (1993) argues that teachers are employing dominant strategies when we see them:

- using ritual language;
- using routines to control large groups;
- using contrasts in the loudness and softness of their voices;
- using dominant rising tones;
- using nonverbal communication to control attempts at contesting the power outcome;
- using strategies of disengagement; and
- manipulating the structure of the discourse to inhibit interruption. (p. 214)

When teachers use less dominant strategies, we see them:

- drawing on peer group pressure;
- encouraging;
- establishing long eye contact;

- manipulating the discourse to support the children;
- encouraging positive thinking;
- asking favours;
- establishing group coherence;
- restating the children's position when they lose track of the discourse;
- keeping quiet and allowing the children to take responsibility for a discussion;
- acts of politeness;
- making suggestions;
- praising and being complimentary; and
- enjoying humour. (p. 214)

But, classroom power is never unidirectional; it is always two-way and dialectical with forms of resistance (in varying degrees) from and by students. When children exercise dominant power strategies upon their teachers, they:

- do not pay attention;
- yawn and show disinterest;
- demand attention;
- do not listen to their teacher;
- fiddle and distract other children;
- shuffle and become restless; and
- disobey the teacher's instructions. (p. 215)

When children exercise less dominant power strategies on the teacher, they:

- establish long eye contact;
- smile;
- enjoy humour;
- cooperate;
- listen carefully; and
- obey instructions. (p. 215)

Within and between the kind of spaces alluded to above that exist within classrooms, it becomes clear that learning is not what the teacher or school or system requires that students do so much as a negotiated process 'of what the children will allow the teacher to do' (Warham, 1993, p. 215)

Ken Zeichner is well known for the approach he adopts towards (in the apt title of a recent paper) 'Connecting genuine teacher development to the struggle for social justice' (Zeichner, 1992). Zeichner's claim is that there is much in the educational literature at the moment that trumpets the virtues of teachers taking more control of their own professional development (under such banners as 'reflective approaches to teaching') but in a context in which 'teachers often remain under tight control and limited in the scope of their power to influence the conditions of their work' (p. 3). While there is much, he says, that amounts to 'bogus teacher development' (p. 3), even when teacher development is 'not a charade,' teacher development often becomes an end in itself largely because many teachers are insulated from asking 'questions related to the broader purpose of education in a democratic society' (p. 3). When teachers aim to use reflective approaches to replicate what university researchers deem to be effective teaching, or where teachers merely share their individual experiences with one another, Zeichner (1992) argues that this is symptomatic of teachers being trapped within a 'social efficiency tradition' of teaching. Continuing to perpetuate a circumstance of 'isolation of individual teachers and the lack of attention to the social context of teaching' (p. 9) means that this 'individualist bias makes it less likely that teachers will be able to confront and transform those structural aspects of their work that hinder the accomplishment of their educational mission' (p. 8). Zeichner's approach is one that seeks to engage teachers with questions about how their 'everyday actions challenge or support various oppressions and injustices related to social class, race, gender, sexual preference, religion, and numerous other factors ...' (p. 12). His central point is that we cannot assume teachers' willingness to educate everyone's children, and unless teachers, even innovative ones, develop a commitment 'to the quality of relationships' and work to ensure that 'everybody's knowledge and cultural heritage is represented,' then 'many students will continue to be bypassed by innovative school practices and continue to be denied, with the complicity of the school, access to decent and fulfilling lives' (p. 12). While it is unacceptable, he says, that teaching be reduced to 'only its political elements' (p. 14), it is equally unacceptable that issues of equity and social justice be relegated to the category of being other people's problems outside of the classroom.

Working from two slightly different traditions, Cochran-Smith (1991) and Simon (1992) have come up with the not dissimilar idea that in order to bring about change through teaching, it is necessary that teachers place themselves in situations in which they work against and challenge established norms. For Simon (1992), in his *Teaching Against the Grain: Texts for a Pedagogy of Possibility*, the essence lies in trying not to succumb to pressures to encase notions like 'critical pedagogy' within rigid definitions or procedures, but rather to see its utility as being a reference point for 'an ongoing project and certainly not a prescriptive set of practices' (p. xvi). Simon starts from the presumption that 'teachers are cultural [and political] workers' and, as such, they are continually engaging in a process of helping students by 'challeng[ing] and assess[ing] existing social conventions, modes of thought, and relations of power' (p. 35), and seeking insights about how situations came to be the way they are. He, therefore, admits to having a political vision that structures his work that embraces questions such as:

> How is experience to be understood? What information and experience do I have access to that is important and possibly helpful to others? In what way does the form and substance of the knowledge engaged in teaching situations enable/constrain personal and social possibilities? How do I understand learning and the relationship teaching has to it? What is my view of a 'person?' How do emotions, desires, and psychic investments influence teaching situations? How do the oppressive forms of power in my community manifest themselves in classrooms, and how do I situate myself in relation to such forms? And finally, how do I define my responsibilities as a teacher – to what should my students be held accountable, and to what should I be held accountable? (p. xvi)

Simon pursues his project by locating himself 'in the picture' and then seeking to offer 'a critical yet constructive way of reconstituting educational practice' (p. 5) while keeping in mind, in the best tradition of self-reflection, that his own experiences as a teacher are continually 'knotted together in such a way that they rub against the grain of [his] participation in existing relations of domination … [but if he] can highlight the rough spots, the points of [his] own contradictions … [then he can come to] know where there is work yet to be done' (p. 6). It is this articulation of a moral vision for schooling, based solidly in a thorough commitment to his own self-reflexivity, that gives Simon such a sound basis from within which to develop and continually critique, analyse, assess, and then reconstruct a pedagogy that enables him to pursue a progressive agenda within schools. More importantly, conceived of in this way, Simon is able to fulfil his own larger agenda for the teacher as a cultural worker by contesting the paralysing view that nothing is possible or that social change is impossible in schools. His argument is that when students are given opportunities to experience the world of work, it is insufficient for them merely to have experienced it. Rather, 'while speaking or writing one's experience can be both empowering and a mode of resistance to silencing social forms, experience is not an unproblematic notion. We must avoid the conservatism inherent in confirming that which people already know' (p. 124). It is equally important to not only recognise and legitimate such student experiences, but 'at the same time working to challenge such experiences' (p. 135).

Schools committed to the kind of core values represented in the orientations alluded to above depart markedly from the traditional view of how teaching occurs. Teachers engage with the social, intellectual, ethical, and political aspects of what it means to teach. Cochran-Smith (1991) in her 'Learning to teach against the grain' claims that what distinguishes truly effective schools and

teachers from others is that they have a strong commitment to interrupting conservative influences and to developing the kind of structures that produce 'critical dissonance' and 'collaborative resonance' (p. 304). That is to say, they
generate 'intensification of opportunities to learn from teaching through the co-
labor of communities' (p. 304) that focus on how school participants themselves
might begin to 'bear upon the institutional and instructional arrangements of
schooling' (p. 282). The process of collaborative resonance involves, she says,
participants in 'critiqu[ing] the cultures of teaching and schooling, research[ing] their own practices, articulat[ing] their own expertise, and call[ing]
into question the policies and language of schooling that are taken for granted'
(p. 283).

Summarizing the main issues when teachers teach for social responsibility:
writers like Kriesberg, Zeichner, and Simon – who see teaching in terms of social responsibility, cultural diversity, and as working against the grain – portray
the critical issues as those of:

- converting positional power into expertise of authority;
- teachers working through dialogue with students;
- teachers fostering forms of teaching that transcend dominance;
- asking questions about the broader purpose of teaching;
- moving outside of isolated teaching arrangements;
- engaging with questions about how everyday teaching supports
  injustices and oppression;
- assisting students to challenge existing social conventions and
  arrangements; and
- above all, having a moral vision for schooling.

Critical Teaching and Critical Pedagogy in the Classroom

Ira Shor's (1980) *Critical Teaching and Everyday Life* is one of the most read-
able works on how teachers can take mundane and everyday occurrences in
schools and classrooms and render them problematic through asking questions
about how things might be done differently in ways that are more inclusive of
the life experiences of students. Drawing on his own attempts to create a curriculum for students of working-class background in a community college, Shor
suggests creative ways for democratising social relations in the classroom
through dialogue. His continual use of colourful metaphor and excursions behind the normalising facade of what counts as mass education gives us a pene-
trating analysis of teaching practices that normally go unacknowledged as well
as modes of analysis by which the processes of schooling might be different. He
not only shows the sources within our culture that interfere with critical thought,

but he works the reader through countless examples of how a critical orientation to the everyday life of teaching might feasibly occur. His starting point is schooling as a social practice, where 'dialogue is a democratic model of social relations, used to problematise the undemocratic quality of social life' (p. 95). To take one particularly colourful incident, he started his students with:

> ... [a] representation of an ordinary piece of reality abstracted from its habitual place in society. We studied each object or situation structurally, using writing, reading, speaking and analysis to unveil the meaning of this event in our lives and in the totality of social life. In the case of the hamburger we recreated the largely invisible commodity relations which deliver a fried piece of dead beef to our palates. (p. 106)

In various papers, notably 'The Challenge of Critical Education,' 'Towards a Critical Teaching Practice, 'Notes for the Teacher Educator,' and 'What's Keeping Them Back: Life Choices and Life Chances,' Ronald Sultana (1989, 1990, 1991) provides a mode of analysis and a way of thinking and operating that enables one to see schools as institutions that cannot be divorced from the wider social order. He says:

> Whatever we do in the classroom, even when we are not conscious of it, reflects a particular theory or set of beliefs about teaching. We are never neutral, but are constantly making choices in favour of presenting and promoting one world view instead of another. (p. 21)

To make his point, he presents an extensive array of questions (Sultana, 1990) with which he engages teachers in dialogue about what they do in their classes. These are used as a method for assisting teachers to probe the often unexamined depths of their teaching across such areas as lesson preparation, social relationships in the classroom, pedagogy and teaching strategies, classroom behaviour and control issues, and modes of assessment. He says that 'the fact that individual schools and teachers *can* have a real and positive effect on their students' lives is of paramount importance.... The fact that we can make a difference implies the confrontation of a challenge, that of increasing our awareness of the symbolic violence we – surely unwittingly and unwillingly – inflict on specific groups of students' (Sultana, 1989, p. 4).

   Deborah Britzman (1991), in her *Practice Makes Practice: A Critical Study of Learning to Teach*, provides an ethnographic account of the experiences of a group of students learning to teach in secondary schools, and of how teachers who are in the process of becoming handle the unequal distribution of power in the oppressive structures of schooling. The study addresses several kinds of critical questions:

> How do student teachers see themselves as resisting cultural hegemony?
> How can student teachers come to take up discursive practices that both
> challenge the taken-for-granted passivity presently dominating learning
> and teaching, and fashion activist styles of knowing and being? (p. 11)

One of Britzman's major claims is that teaching is consistently represented inside schools, as well as portrayed in the wider community, according to misleading stereotypes (for example, that teaching is a self-sacrificing occupation,
and that teachers are unlimited reservoirs of patience):

> Such images tend to subvert a critical discourse about the lived
> contradictions of teaching and the actual struggles of teachers and
> students. Stereotypes engender a static and hence repressed notion of
> identity as something already out there, a stability that can be assumed.
> (p. 5)

But even here, the nature of what is being investigated, the search for meaning,
and the material location of Briizman in the account are never far from the surface. According to her, 'such a search is interpretive, constructivist, and critical,
moving back and forth between the story, its telling, and the contingencies of
the perspectival borders …. [As a rendered account] although experience cannot be recovered, it can be narrated [but always with the qualifications that]
meaning is historically contingent, contextually bound, socially constructed,
and always problematic' (p. 14).

Alan Reid (1992), in a paper entitled 'Critical Teaching,' advocates a series
of systematic and practical steps which he believes provide teachers with a way
forward in what is a fairly confusing and largely impenetrable area of dense theorising. The precursor is a mind set that regards teaching as being essentially a
democratic process, which is to say, 'more than simply giving students a say ….
In critical teaching, teachers and students operate as co-learners, each learning
from the other, each engaging in systematic analysis of the everyday, and each
collaboratively searching for strategies capable of contributing to social transformation' (p. 11). The second phase, is a 'stepping outside' of normal everyday
routines in order to:

— reconstruct them …
— locate them systematically in larger and larger systems of social
  relations …
— review their own attitudes to the everyday routines in the light of this
  analysis … and to ascertain [how] they work against their own interests
  …

- theorize the causes of systematic oppression and the process of
  hegemony [and]
- identify and evaluate various resistance strategies to the forms of
  oppression which are embodied in the everyday routines. (p. 11)

In his *Critical Incidents in Teaching: Developing Professional Judgement*,
David Tripp (1993) presents a cogent representation and analysis of how teachers might capture and transcend issues from their own teaching that are worthy
of analysis. Through actual examples, Tripp shows how teachers can create and
analyse in a practical way what start out as non-problematic aspects of their
teaching, and how they can come to a realisation of the way in which human
interests cloud the analysis of judgement. His position is well stated in the following:

> At first sight, all analysis of practice by teachers might appear to be
> socially critical in that it tends to empower individual teachers by
> increasing their understanding and thereby increasing the possibility of
> the development of radical different practices in a professional
> community that is likely to challenge the existing order. But it is
> important not to confuse such side effects of critical incident analysis
> with an intentionally socially critical project. Teachers' professional
> judgements become socially critical when they become aware of the
> social implications of their practice and begin to work on those ...
> Socially critical practice does not, therefore, necessitate a totally
> different kind of project to reflective practice at the outset, but it is more
> a matter of incorporating into practice, diagnosis, and reflection an
> understanding of social context and social effects, and acting upon that
> context and those effects to facilitate forms of consciousness and
> practice which would not have been available within the initial situation
> or practice (p. 116) .... Socially critical practices therefore depend first
> on a critique of our existing practice in terms of the extent to which it
> meets our criteria of social justice, and second on our imaging how we
> could in future improve the match between the two. (p. 117)

Bill Bigelow (1990, 1992), a classroom teacher in Portland, Oregon, pursues a
broadly similar agenda in that what he is trying to do is create a way of working
in which his classroom becomes 'part of a protracted argument for the viability
of a critical and participatory democracy' (1992, p. 19). What Bigelow is attempting flies in the face of a society that is bent on reproducing manifest inequality. He knows this, but not withstanding, his agenda is one of 'How can
classroom teachers move decisively away from a model of teaching which
merely reproduces and legitimates inequality?' (p. 19). He does this through a

'dialogical' approach to teaching which is about more than involving students in more classroom discussion.

> In my construction a dialogical classroom means inviting students to critique the larger society through sharing their lives. As a teacher I help students locate their experiences socially; I involve students in probing the social factors that make and limit who they are and I try to help them reflect on who they *could* be. (pp. 19-20)

Bigelow is also concerned about having teachers and students question their own role in maintaining the status quo (1992, p. 22). In effect, he asks that they question the dynamics of power and the role of resistance – in other words, that they learn about the 'causes for their own insubordination, [and] the role they could play ... in resisting it' (p. 22). Through the way in which he works with his students, Bigelow concludes that his students are 'excited by this sociological detective work' (1992, p. 22) and that 'whether or not we want to be, all teachers are political agents because we help shape students' perceptions of the larger society' (p. 24)

My own not dissimilar approaches, especially in *Teachers as Collaborative Learners: Challenging Dominant Forms of Supervision* (Smyth, 1991b), have expressed a set of views and practices that seek to engage teachers in recognising and extirpating inappropriate pedagogies and ideologies so as to engage teachers systematically in reclaiming what is rightfully theirs. We need to expel the toxic waste of the values of the corporate sector that we have allowed to seep into our schools in recent times and produce forms of distortion and disfigurement. What we need in their stead are coherent theories about teaching crafted by teachers themselves on their terms and on their turf. I have actually been working at this project for more than a decade. As I conceive it, the goal involves several different tasks (see Smyth, 1993):

1. Describing.

Before teachers can do anything, they need to be clear about *what it is they do.* If they are to celebrate the virtues of their work, as well as convince others of its efficacy, then the starting point clearly has to lie in fleshing out (in concrete terms) the situational specifics of their teaching. In this I am heartened by teacher research that is currently underway involving autobiographical, life history, teacher narrative, and story telling methods. But, this kind of work is not sufficient. Teachers need assistance in looking for similarities within difference, and for the regularities, discontinuities, contradictions, and ruptures in what they do.

In a word, they need assistance in becoming 'informed' and seeing the *theories in their teaching.*

2. Informing.

Teachers have a long history of having been prevailed upon in all kinds of ways, particularly in respect of how they ought to do their teaching. In the 'business' of teaching, everyone in the community is an expert. Sometimes this comes in the guise of scientific evidence of what supposedly works best in teaching. Education is a good example of where other people's theories are often foisted onto teachers. Experience tells me that when teachers are given the opportunity of explaining the meaning that lies behind their teaching, they are fairly perceptive at unravelling the complexity of classrooms. They seem to have robust ways of untying the text of their teaching in ways that exemplify the idea of local theories. Such theories might not be generalisable and might be limited to explaining why things work in particular contexts, but they are nevertheless theoretical accounts in the sense that they help teachers explain the nature of their work and make sense of what they do.

Once teachers can begin to see that they can (and indeed do) have theories, then they are well along the way to gaining a measure of independence. They are no longer exclusively dependent upon other people's theories that have to be imported from outside. In theorising about their work, teachers also confront who it is that defines, articulates, and legitimates knowledge about teaching – indeed, the whole question of who has the right to do these things is confronted and contested.

3. Confronting.

Questioning the legitimacy of what counts as teaching amounts to teachers 'confronting' their teaching. Questions about 'How things came to be this way?' and what broader forces operate to make them like this are crucial matters. I try to assist teachers to confront their local theories biographically as well as professionally by prompting them to ask and answer questions such as:

- What do my teaching practices say about my assumptions, values, and beliefs about teaching?
- What social practices are expressed in these ideas?
- What is it that causes me to maintain my theories?
- What is it that acts to constrain my views of what is possible in teaching?

By the time teachers have begun to grapple with questions such as these and to get at some of the bigger forces that inform what they do, they are starting to think about how they might act in different ways — ways that are informed by evidence. In other words, they are beginning to move towards *reconstructing* parts of their teaching and the contexts and structures within which they do it.

Drawing together the key thematic issues in this section as they have focused on critical approaches to teaching and classroom pedagogy, one finds that the following have become apparent:

- the asking of critical questions is the major method by which teachers probe the unexamined depths of their teaching;
- challenging passivity is an important place to start;
- the search is for a continually moving set of interrelationships between narrated, storied accounts of teaching, and the deeper, sedimented meanings they contain;
- critiquing the everyday practice of teaching, as well as envisaging what alternatives might look like, is crucial;
- asking how teaching becomes unwittingly implicated in maintaining the status quo is an important part of the detective work;
- finally, this all involves a number of moments or phases as discrete as: describing, informing, confronting, and reconstructing.

Teaching for Democracy

Engaging students with the big questions that fire the imagination and the forces that shape their lives is what George Wood (1990) of the Institute for Democracy in Education at Ohio University regards as the hallmark of a socially critical teacher. For example, in areas of high unemployment, teachers 'as curriculum workers' should have their students pursue questions such as: 'What work is here? Why are there no industries? How can we get higher unemployment benefits?' While questions such as these do not have ready answers, they are at least a starting point for students to go considerably beyond the mere attribution of individual victim-blaming responses to what is occurring. Or, to suggest another example, concern about the discharge of industrial waste into the environment, when tackled as an issue, can lead to students working in ways so as to test and monitor the quality of water in local rivers and streams as well as to discuss what might be done to improve it (Wood, 1990, p. 98). Part of Wood's agenda is to have teachers develop critical forms of literacy which involve students in 'the ability to evaluate what is read or heard with respect to the interest being served or the positions taken' (Wood, 1988, p. 178). It also involves enhancing 'the ability [as a consequence] to mould one's own world through naming and constructing models of preferred social and personal life' (p. 178). More specifically, 'critical literacy involves building reading skills around students' own reading agendas. Having them read about things in which they have an interest and helping them write their own reading material are key components in this process' (p. 178). Viewed in this way, Wood (1990) argues that curriculum becomes 'a shared process – not ... something that teachers dispense the way physicians prescribe medicine. Curriculum is a process in which teachers and students engage to order and make sense of the world' (p. 107). As such, he says, 'the genuine, shared problems of classroom teachers become the curriculum of my classes. We trace the roots of these problems and find that they come from choices made, not inevitabilities. Things can be different – and often should be – if we take seriously the democratic mission of schools' (p. 108).

Jesse Goodman (1992), in his *Elementary Schooling for Critical Democracy*, provides an antidote to the current worldwide neo-conservative restoration currently strangling our schools. Through the practices of 'Harmony School,' Goodman highlights how the experiences at 'Harmony' represent three-dimensional characters continually engaging in the redefinition of the tension between 'individuality' and 'community' as they seek to rework what is meant in structural terms by the notion of critical democracy. What the experiences of 'Harmony' show is the importance of not pursuing the idea of schools as asymmetrical organizations per se, but rather the rituals and practices necessary to enable students to acquire an informed perspective towards power that is tied to 'increasing their sense of social responsibility.' Goodman argues that it is the reciprocity that comes with understanding power that is crucial to its democratic enactment. The struggle as he described it is really between those who come from a society which is enamoured with an ethos of competitive individualism, and a school that is trying to develop a collective sense of caring and a commitment to shared responsibility. Goodman's 'connectionist' view of power rests upon the claim that at essence students must be given genuine opportunities to negotiate successfully with their teachers, and that in such a process teachers themselves must be put 'at the center of the curriculum.' This is a far cry from worldwide moves at the moment to recentralise control over schools, to colonise the curriculum, to narrow the curriculum through uniformity, and to turn schools into institutions preoccupied with cultural production and mindless vocational training of the worst kind.

One of the central organising images that comes through in the actions of the teachers and students Goodman describes is the importance of the notion of 'community' in schooling, as distinct from forms of 'individualism' that are so rampant in schools. It is not, as Goodman argues, that we should strive for one without the other, because this would be to endorse either an atomistic society, on the one hand, or a society characterized by social conformity, on the other.

It is the 'dialectical tension' between these and the tendency for them to get out of balance that we should be especially mindful of. Goodman's laying out of how the tendency towards individualism reaches deep into American culture makes it easier to comprehend the profound significance of the attempt by teachers, administrators, parents, and students at 'Harmony' to work 'against the grain.'

While Goodman provides descriptions that are solidly rooted in concrete practices, he does not provide a way of mimicking 'how to do it.' His agenda is more subtle and more complex than that – he seeks to raise to our consciousness, the language and the process of critical democratic imagery. Through his portrayal of imagery and of the way things were in one particular school, he skilfully steers himself (and us as readers) away from 'recipe' and 'cookbook' approaches that have no place in a critical democracy for schooling. Through the incidents, the characters, and the imagery he portrays, he provides us with a way of learning from images that amount in effect to 'apply[ing] what is vicariously experienced to one's own particular situations and limitations.' One of the themes coming through Goodman's book is that while teachers at 'Harmony' mostly had a well developed sense of caring and social responsibility in the way they worked with their students, they had been largely untouched by the forms of critical theorising emanating from the academy. This is both understandable and explainable in terms of the genre and the arena upon which the largely academic debate has occurred. If Goodman sees a difficulty at all in schools like 'Harmony,' it resides in the lack of connectedness to wider arenas of struggle outside of schools – despite the fact that he cites several illustrations in which 'Harmony' was apparently doing this. His point, I suspect, is not so much that schools are deficient in doing this (although that may be true) but rather that those of us outside of schools (especially in institutions of higher learning who are avowedly committed to the ideals of critical pedagogy) need better ways of 'adopting' practitioners in schools and working with them to more effectively theorize about the essence of what is occurring in schools. Goodman provides those committed to challenging the dominant and oppressive modes of instrumentalism currently gripping public schools with a beacon to work towards. While the opposing impositional agenda might be writ somewhat larger in public schooling than it is in independent schools like 'Harmony,' the point nevertheless is that notions of democratic schooling are not forms of dogma to be blindly followed or transferred from one setting to another. Rather, they are social, cultural and political constructions that reflect the way in which people inside schools choose to live their lives as students, teachers, administrators, and parents.

In another illustration of how this might work in practice, David Hursh (1994) in his notion of 'working both ends' explores how the preparation and development of teachers might be used as a basis upon which to build a different set of theories that have political consequences not only in schools but in the practices of universities. His argument is based on a reconstrual of the relationship between theory and practice. He sees three elements:

1) a situation in which teachers locate their work in 'social and political questions of how schools as social institutions can either alleviate, produce, or reproduce both particular ways of acting in and making sense of the world, and race, gender and class inequalities' (p. 2);

2) how the theory and practice of teaching are 'mutually constitutive,' for example, in the way particular approaches to literacy are based on ethical and political goals of 'respecting students and their own literacy, even when their literacy deviates from standard English' (p. 3); and, how universities and schools need to move closer to inhabiting the world of the other, through mutually examining their own (and one another's) understandings. According to Hursh (1994), this occurs by developing

> ... within each school and across sites, including between the schools and university, a community of learners who are engaged in developing, documenting, evaluating and disseminating their efforts to rethink and reform schooling and teaching. We are aiming to analyse and change not only classroom practices but the way we talk about schooling and the way schools are organized (p. 25) ... At the university level [this means] restructuring programs so that seminars led by faculty from both institutions can occur in schools. (p. 26)

It is easy in volumes like this, even in sections that are ostensibly oriented to providing teachers with more power over their work, to grant privilege to the voices of those outside of classrooms who claim to speak for and on behalf of teachers. How often have we heard reviewers of works such as this complain '... and, there was not a single piece written by a classroom teacher?' To make matters worse, I am not even sure how we can proceed to change that situation either, given the vastly different aspirations, values, and modus operandi of the two groups. The written culture of the academic community and the largely oral culture of teaching seem to be decidedly at odds with one another. To require or even suggest that teachers write more about their classroom experiences seems to be no less impositional than having others write those accounts for and on behalf of teachers. There is an impasse here that has yet to be seriously grappled with – on the one hand, the academy's persistent preoccupation with written portrayals, and on the other, teachers' largely ephemeral stories that insist on remaining trapped within the private experiential granary of teachers' work. The dearth of accounts by teachers may be as much an artifact of the manner in which the academy has worked, as it is a reflection of how best to make public accounts of teachers' work. It may even be the case that the medium is wrong headed.

One illustration of the above point (among a number of possibilities) as to how this might be done differently is the initiative of the 'Re-Thinking Schools' group operating out of Milwaukee. For several years this cooperative of classroom teachers has worked to capture in largely journalistic and accessible format the progressive issues with which teachers are struggling, while at the same time providing a networking function through which teachers can feel free to contact and support one another. 'Re-Thinking Schools' has fulfilled an important clearinghouse function for teachers involved in socially democratic reform using a model that appears to be considerably more 'user friendly' than traditional modes of academic discourse which teachers understandably shy away from.

Thematically, the issues that have arisen in this section about 'teaching for democracy' can be summarized thus:

- the task is concerned with teachers engaging students with questions that spillover beyond the classroom;
- it involves engaging students in ways that try to get behind what is normally presented to them;
- schools and teachers need to work in other than individual and competitive ways and to create forms of shared responsibility and community;
- this is difficult work that has much to do with the changing of 'mindsets' and orientations, and little to do with 'how-to-do-it' recipes;
- the voices to be heard are those that originate from within classrooms, and because they do not by and large come out of a written culture, this generates difficulties in breaking out of the oral tradition;
- more 'teacher friendly' formats are available, but they have to be persisted with if they are to work effectively.

Feminist Pedagogy

The issues for writers who actively implement notions of 'feminist pedagogy' are not a long way removed from matters already discussed. These classroom activists provide valuable insights 'grounded in a vision of social change' (Weiler, 1991, p. 456) through experiences derived largely from practices in women's studies programs in universities. Kathleen Weiler (1991) has captured the epistemological history of this element of the feminist movement and shows how there are three basic elements: '... its questioning of the role and authority of the teacher; ... its recognition of the importance of personal experience as a source of knowledge; and … its exploration of the perspectives of people of different races, classes, and cultures' (p. 449). At the level of the classroom, Weiler (1991) argues that this necessitates a focus on 'collective political change rather than on individual therapy,' or to put it another way, forms of consciousness raising that 'demand fundamental changes in society' (p. 457). Added to this, 'reliance on experience and feeling' (p. 457) is also another important facet of feminist pedagogy, with the role of the teacher being that of 'making students themselves theorists of their own lives by interrogating and analysing their own experience' so as to arrive at a critical and collective understanding 'of the forces that have shaped that experience' (p. 462).

Nancy Schniedewind (1987), again from a women's studies program, works in ways that examine educational practices from a vantage point that acknowledges 'certain feminist principles': the development of an atmosphere of mutual respect, trust and community in the classroom; shared notions of leadership in the classroom; a cooperative classroom structure that moves students beyond forms of individualism; the integration of cognitive and affective learning so as to 'strengthen women's intellectual activities so long suppressed by … [the] sexist norms [of] institutions' (p. 176); and a commitment to take 'action to transform institutions and values' (p. 178). The intent behind processes of this kind is to not only promote democratic feminist principles within the classroom, but also to 'critically analyse social relations outside of the classroom for their hidden underlying sexist values' (p. 179). Jo Anne Pagano (1990), in the women's stories she provides in her *Exiles and Communities: Teaching in a Patriarchal Wilderness*, provides further illustration of how such processes might work. Magda Lewis (Lewis & Simon, 1986) shows how silencing occurs in classrooms through the way in which relationships are actively constructed and contested through power and language. For Lewis, the poignancy of this occurred when she and her colleagues confronted the largely unarticulated but silencing patriarchal power of a graduate class and how for the women involved 'what could never have been accomplished individually became possible for us as a group. We disrupted the male agenda and appropriated our space' (p. 467). Ellsworth (1989) in her provocative article 'Why doesn't this feel empowering?' makes the same point.

To summarize the issues for teachers committed to feminist pedagogy:

- personal experience is an important starting point and source of knowledge;
- the authority role of the teacher as the sole source of knowledge is questioned;
- students themselves become important alternative sources of theorizing about learning;

- focusing on how power is reproduced through structures and forms of language is a prominent aspect;
- encouraging the translation of democratic processes pursued inside the classroom into venues outside are seen as important.

Storied Accounts of Teachers Reclaiming Teaching

The range and depth of other activist educators similarly engaged in 'creating the spaces and finding the voices' (Miller, 1990) within which teachers can do the kind of political and collaborative work (Shannon, 1992) envisaged in this paper is very impressive indeed. Peter McLaren (1989), for example, provides a searing account – through the five years he kept a journal – as a classroom teacher on what he termed 'the frontiers of despair ... [and] the invisible epidemic' in his books *Cries from the Corridor* and *Life in Schools* (McLaren, 1980, 1989). Joseph McDonald (1986) showed how a group of teachers worked over an extended period to overcome 'silences [that were] enforced by teachers' subordinate roles and ... isolation [in] the classrooms in which they work' (p. 355). Through the story of how a group of high school teachers established a collective through which to examine their practical knowledge as teachers, McDonald was able to show how these teachers were able to stay in charge while at the same time 'bring theory into their conversation on their own terms' (p. 355). His 'Raising the teacher's voice and the ironic role of theory' (McDonald, 1986) is fine testimony to what can happen when teachers move beyond the isolation of their own classrooms to explore together 'the insights, uncertainties, and paradoxes that arise from their teaching work' (p. 355). It was 'ironic' in the sense that here was an instance in which teachers were engaging in theorising when 'theorists of teaching have long been intimately associated with the suppression of the teacher's voice' (p. 355).

Ross, Cornett, and McCutcheon (1992) and their contributors provide another account of what *Teacher Personal Theorizing* might look like in their edited collection. In particular they:

i)   eschew the merely technical in teaching;
ii) show the problematic nature of teaching and curriculum;
iii) demonstrate that being a professional in teaching means theorizing about one's teaching;
iv) show that to theorize adequately about teaching requires involving others as collaborators in establishing a 'community of reflective practitioners';
v)   show that not only is theorizing about teaching a legitimate thing to do by practitioners, but that there is a substantial literature on teachers

doing this across varied areas, drawing upon a quite sophisticated methodological literature;

vi) suggest that none of this is to deny that there are not formidable (even awesome) forces operating to frustrate the notion of teachers being theorizers of their own work.

Sadly, teaching is inextricably caught up in what Beyer (1992) calls an 'applicative' view of the teaching process – that is to say, in applying the 'ideas, perspectives, and theoretical frameworks of others.' Teachers become 'applicative technicians' implementing other people's agenda.

Ross et al. argue the need to move teacher theorizing beyond the localised or private domain, which is to say, outside of personal histories and immediate classroom contexts and into the broader social-historical contexts of interpretive or critical communities. As Beyer (1992) puts it, we need to view the personal and the political as continuous rather than dichotomous. The concern of these activists is to move beyond the 'what is' (a descriptive view of teaching), to a concern with 'what ought to be' (or a normative view of teaching). Their concern is with a relational consideration of the valued social purposes of teaching and issues of power and ideology that are inevitably implicated in it.

A good illustration of how this might occur is contained in The Boston Women's Teachers' Group (Freedman, Jackson, & Boles, 1983) paper 'Teaching: An Imperilled 'Profession.'' This is a report by a group of elementary teachers who describe the alienation and frustration of being a largely female teaching force organized, administered and evaluated largely by males. They make the compelling case, and give illustrative evidence, of the need to move the emphasis away from victim-blaming approaches in which the problems of schooling are attributed to the personal and technical inadequacies of teachers to a focus on the way the structure of schooling controls and deeply affects the nature of the relationships between teachers, students, and their families.

The works of Ayres (1993) and Schubert and Ayres (1992) provide yet further evidence of what it means for teachers to produce theorized and political auto-biographical accounts in ways that are accessible to other teachers. The writings of these academics describes how some teachers have transcended the oral tradition of teaching and begun to move out from underneath the 'intellectual claustrophobia' and sterility imposed on it by outsiders. What Ayres and Schubert do is provide the much needed antidote to the uninspiring and apolitical analyses that abound of teaching by people outside of classrooms. Their approaches do not so much criticise or confront dominant approaches so much as ignore them for their irrelevance. While teaching is portrayed as a deeply personal experience, it is shown as still being at heart a profoundly social and political process as well.

Thematically, the issues raised in this section on storied accounts of teachers' work involve:

— finding the 'spaces' in which voices can be expressed;
— teachers working through what is possible collectively and sharing knowledge about their work;
— teachers bringing their own theories into the conversations and moving beyond an 'applicative' view of teaching;
— teachers proclaiming that while teaching has a technical dimension not to be ignored, it is also about a lot more as well;
— teachers regarding theorizing as a respectable and worthwhile thing to do in relation to teaching;
— introducing into discussions aspects of how broader social structures and institutions impede the work of teaching.

Teaching for Social Justice and Emancipation

Two Australian orientations stand out as being particularly exemplary in having a strong socio-political orientation to the role of the teacher as a facilitator of students engaging with social justice issues in schools. The more recent of these is associated with Basil Moore, Karen Starr, and the 'Social Justice Research Project' at University of South Australia. The earlier is the work of Stephen Kemmis and the action research group at Deakin University which has been widely reported in education literature since the early 1980s.

The approach of Karen Starr and Basil Moore (Starr & Moore, 1994) and their associates (Education for Social Justice Research Group, 1994), involves university faculty working with teachers and students in school settings against sexism, racism, and poverty. Their central construct is the notion of 'teaching for resistance' which involves:

a) consciousness raising — becoming aware of injustice and other particular ideological, attitudinal, and behavioural formations;
b) establishing contact with wider social movements beyond schools involved in organising and pursuing strategic action; and
c) taking steps to become involved in resistance actions (Starr & Moore, 1994).

Participants develop and interrogate 'resistance narratives' which they use as a basis for making judgements about what might constitute feasible and prudent forms of social action. While this strategy may give the appearances of being a research approach, in point of fact it is a way of teaching *for* something – most noticeably, the overcoming of oppression as defined by the participants. This might include the right of all groups to be equitably involved in an education, an attempt to redistribute educational resources, provision of safe learning environments, a common curriculum for all students, or how to educate students *for* social justice rather than *about* it.

The work of Stephen Kemmis and colleagues is best known because of the 'emancipatory' orientation they have teachers adopt through action research on issues such as: curriculum theorizing, curriculum development, teacher in-service education, and the work of teaching – which they envisage as 'a form of critical social science' (Carr & Kemmis, 1986, p. 2). Put another way, the process they describe concerns a form of 'self-reflective inquiry undertaken by participants in social situations in order to improve the rationality and justice of their own social or educational practices as well as their understanding of the situations in which these practices are carried out' (Henry & Kemmis, 1985, p. 1). The focus can be on issues such as: school or classroom policies and rules; non-competitive assessment; school improvement programs; classroom management; classroom talk; or engagement with controversial issues.

Although Barry Kanpol (1992) makes no particular claim to provide a strategy for social action like some of the other contributors referenced so far, his work on 'cultural political resistance' is relevant to teachers and students attempting to develop a more defensible classroom praxis. Kanpol shows how teacher narratives can be used by teachers to begin to locate themselves in personal histories and as a starting point in examining and integrating meta and micro aspects of wider classroom narratives.

The work of Hattam, Kerkham, and Wooldridge (1994) on 'critical literacy' builds on Lankshear and McLaren (1993), Shannon (1992), and the considerable theoretical contributions of Henry Giroux in his many writings. What these particular authors contribute is a process that provides teachers and students with the tools with which to interrogate texts for meaning that are essentially obscured. The process they proffer involves students being taught 'not only to question the content of texts, but also the way in which texts position them [as students]' (Hattam, Kerkham, & Wooldridge, 1994, p. 10). Their toolkit incorporates elements such as:

1) acknowledging the socially constructed nature of knowledge based on the explicit exercise of choices;
2) engaging students so as to regard reading as more than sifting meaning but in ways that challenge the reader to uncover implicit assumptions, the ways in which views are imposed as to how readers should feel, and the blurring of facts and values;

3) finding and celebrating ways in which students can burst through into the real text or curriculum, rather than simply engage at the level of the espoused agenda;

4) and, providing models of leadership by which students can engage in 'meaningful and authentic action' (p. 9) that connects to the wider public sphere.

Bob Connell (1993) has provided cogent argument and evidence on the manner in which schooling is structured in ways that privileges the education one group of children receives in contrast to another. He claims that when this occurs (as it invariably does through ability streaming, inappropriate modes of testing and assessment, the imposition of competencies and standards, and the like), then education becomes 'degraded.' Doing something about this 'corrupted education,' Connell argues, requires a process of 'whole school change' – a deliberate process of planning according to democratic principles. As Connell, White, and Johnston (1990) put it, '[This] implies participation of the whole staff and parent groups in planning, which challenges the conventional authority relations in schools and has significant costs of time and effort' (p. 10). Hattam (1994) argues that whole school change is inextricably connected to conceiving of what it means to work in socially just ways:

> Whole school change in response to educational disadvantage has been an attempt to generate more democratic structures and processes in schools. It is difficult to imagine how a school can improve the lack of power of certain groups in society without implementing measures to 'empower.' The term whole school change implies that the whole school community is involved in the process of deciding what is an appropriate curriculum. More than that, whole school change is about ensuring the curriculum reflects the concerns, life experience and aspirations of the whole school community. In essence whole school change is a process or a struggle to actively involve the whole school community in the curriculum process, to ensure all students are actively engaged and being successful, that the school actively works to include groups that have been traditionally marginalised or silenced. (p. 4)

Kretovics, Farber, and Armaline (1991) provide further practical detail on what such communities might look like. Described as 'reform from the bottom up that aims to empower teachers to transform schools,' the process they describe involved three key features in a high school they worked in Toledo, Ohio:

i) creating a sense of family – which amounted to structuring 'the school day to keep students and teachers in the program for a continuous block of time' (p. 296);

ii) facilitating collaboration between teachers – through providing them with a 'common work period each day' (p. 296);

iii) establishing an extensive program of professional development – this was an opportunity for teachers 'to examine research in a collegial atmosphere and to develop strategies appropriate to the students with whom they would be working.' (p. 296)

To summarize, pursuing emancipatory interests in teaching involves:

– engaging teachers and the wider school community in matters of social justice;

– producing narratives of teaching as a basis for analysis and action within and beyond the school;

– focusing on matters that can be as diverse as classroom policies and rules, forms of student assessment, school improvement, classroom management, and classroom talk;

– examining the content of what is contained in texts, particularly in the way texts locate the readers in relation to them; and

– acting in concert with others to pursue 'whole school change' so that more democratic structures can be achieved.

SCHOOLS AS CRITICAL AND DISCURSIVE COMMUNITIES

Teachers who make the deliberate, overt, and public choice to pursue the kind of agenda outlined above that privileges the morality, the ethics, and the politics of their work have clearly entered into a conscious commitment to struggle with 'explicitly political questions' (Shannon, 1992, p. 5), in addition to the peda-gogical questions they were already asking as they seek to develop a critical the-ory of teaching. In other words, they have made a choice to regard their work of teaching as liberating rather then dominating, which in practice means blurring the boundaries between teachers and those taught and dismantling hierarchies of organization, authority, gender, race, and class which can operate to make teaching and learning such unsatisfying activities. Shannon (1992) makes the point well:

Even apparently innocuous decisions about setting goals for programs and lessons, selecting materials, and deciding how to interact with students during lessons are actually negotiations over whose values, interests, and beliefs will be validated at school. Sometimes these negotiations are explicit and loud, as when a parent attempts to remove a book from a class reading list or a library shelf. More often, though, negotiations are implicit and silent, as when textbook authors and publishers make decisions about goals, materials, and instruction and embed them in the language of a teacher's manual and the lesson procedures for teachers and students to follow. (p. 2)

Shannon (1992) points to the well documented, sizeable, and growing body of evidence revealing the detrimental effects of dominating practices in schools on racial and ethnic minorities, the restrictions placed on females in terms of access to certain forms of scientific literacy, the relegation of the poor to vocational forms of literacy, and the extent of teacher burnout in classrooms. Yet, despite these alarming consequences, Shannon (1992) says:

> ... few practicing teachers recognise the political facts of school life .... Rather, they consider themselves apolitical in their work – lamenting the politics they do recognise in 'the system,' defining their role as delivering already determined content in traditional ways, and abdicating their rightful place in the decision making that influences their students' and their lives in and out of school. However, teachers' denial does not mean that they stand apart from the politics of ... education. Their inattention and lack of action perpetuates the status quo ... All teachers are political, whether they are conscious of it or not .... The process [of becoming political] begins by asking questions: why are the dominating sides of ... teaching and schooling more often practiced than the liberating sides? Why is it that despite the rhetoric that education is the backbone of democracy the participants in schooling have so little voice in matters of consequence in the classroom? Why are they so unfree? Who is served by the current organization and practice of schools? .... Asking questions is a constructive act because it makes change possible. (p. 2)

None of this is in any sense to underestimate the manifold complexity or diffi-culty of teachers acting politically as social theorists and political actors in re-spect of the work of teaching. But as Phelan and Lalik (1993) note, to act in the ways being suggested is a task that is more honoured in the breach than in real-ity. In their opinion, the notion of teacher as 'transformative intellectual,' often advocated, relies too 'heavily on abstract and highly rationalistic constructions of 'empowerment' and 'dialogue' as transformative strategies' (p. 155). To be transformative, in Phelan and Lalik's view, has less to do with the characteris-tics of an individual teacher and more to do with 'relationships between individuals in a group' (p. 156). This is where the notion of teachers being part of discursive communities comes in.

The one indispensable requirement for schools to operate in ways that are informed by notions of social justice and teachers who operate in ways to create social policy as distinct from receiving it, is what Strike (1993) describes as 'local deliberative or discursive communities' (p. 226). His argument is that we need to understand schools as democratic institutions is based on the nature of collective deliberations that ensue within them rather than according to the way they represent the interests of particular citizens. The basis of Strike's (1993) claim is a Habermasian view of the ideal speech community 'in which practical arguments are made and in which all relevant considerations can be aired, and all competent speakers are heard' (p. 263). The consequence is a process of discursive redemption of social norms through consensus and open 'undominated discourses' in an 'ideal speech community' (p. 263). As far as schools are concerned, Strike (1993) claims that:

> These aspirations might be pursued in schools by transforming them into local deliberative communities [where] the social relations between members of the community will have to be characterized by equality, autonomy, reciprocity, and a high level of respect for the construction of rational consensus. Discursive communities require a supportive culture. (p. 266)

Corson (1993) carries this notion of 'communicative action' in 'discursive communities' considerably further, particularly as it relates to issues of how power is exercised dialogically in sociocultural settings. Drawing upon Habermas's insights, Corson (1993) argues that institutions tend to have a certain in-built pathological, distorted, even dysfunctional quality about them when it comes to the norms of most communicative situations, and it is this which makes them inherently unjust. It is when people within institutions, schools included, strive towards the ideal of 'sort[ing] out their real interests from their illusory ones' (Corson, 1993, p. 36), that the possibility of pursuing discursive communities begins to become a reality – especially in the ways incompatible interests 'are resolved through compromise' (p. 39). Without pursuing this in excessive detail, Corson (1993) argues that the 'ideal speech situation' is central to discussion, from which can emerge 'the true interests of the participants' (p. 156) and hence a 'critical measure' of the quality and extent of interaction that informs democratic public discussion (p. 157). Having as a starting point a well-rounded understanding and appreciation of the nature of society, its character, and its materiality, is regarded by Young (1981) as a crucial knowledge prerequisite for any such discursive community.

In summary, the features of such discursive communities, are that:

- the work of teachers and administrators is characterized by team work;
- scale requirements are such that they allow for formations that permit the kind of face-to-face discourse that characterizes and permits intense dialogue;
- parents are included as integral members of the community and are not conceptualized as 'clients';
- no relevant argument in such decision-making communities is barred, and no competent and interested speaker is excluded;
- everyone acknowledges that decisions are the property of the community as a whole and proposals for change are publicly discussed;
- the burden of justification is not met until a reasoned consensus has been achieved;
- the question of 'who (or what) is the community?' is still open to debate because 'school communities have vague boundaries' (p. 276);
- the role of teachers is characterized as 'first among equals' (p. 267) and;
- 'educational authorities' enact a role of 'sovereign of last resort' in a context where the 'primary deliberative forum' is the school as a whole.

In sum, what Strike is saying is that schools need to be restructured along lines that decentralize and debureaucratize decision making (adapted from Strike, 1993, pp. 206-267).

Curriculum issues provide a particular illustration of what local deliberation and discursive community might mean in terms of the management of knowledge and culture. Ashenden, Blackburn, Hannan, and White (1984) express this as a 'Manifesto for a Democratic Curriculum' where the touchstones are principles of equality, commonality, and making the curriculum public. They propose the following hallmarks of the curriculum as being consistent with the nature of knowledge and learning in a socially just, self-managing school:

- It should be common, in that all students are able to progress consistently through all areas of the course. Choices or groupings within major areas should not impede this progress or close off other options irrevocably.
- It should be premised on cooperation rather than competition, and on success rather than failure.
- It should be worthwhile, in that it offers something of enduring relevance to the learners.
- It should be coherent in that its structure shows how human knowledge grows and builds on itself.
- It should be systematic in the way that student growth and autonomy is steady and widespread, rather than haphazard and limited to the few.
- It should be reflective in that knowledge is open to question, and its application to one's framework of meaning is actively explored.

- It should be moral rather then neutral, and is critical in the way it addresses conceptions of right and wrong, truth, compassion and justice.
- It should be inclusive in its coverage of the everyday experience of all of its students, and reflects the diverse character of its community.
- It should be practical in the way it combines doing and reflecting, so as to make learning accessible to the largest possible range of students.
- It should be doable and structured in a way that is not a mechanism for selecting or spotting students (p. 16).

CONCLUSION

To return to one of the central points I made at the beginning of this chapter, the argument I have been making under the general heading of teaching and social policy is that when teaching is enacted for social responsibility or in socially critical ways, it becomes an important ingredient in the restoration of social capital within society. Schools may be one of the few remaining social institutions that still have a capacity to enculturate the young in ways of organizing that celebrate social relationships. Teachers thus become significant creators of social capital in the sense that they 'recognize the importance of concrete personal relations and networks of relations – what [Granovetter, 1985] calls 'embeddeness' – in generating trust, in establishing expectations, in creating and enforcing norms' (Coleman, 1988, p.s. 97). Restoring the willingness and ability to ask unmasking questions about the nature of the work of teaching and the sets of interests served or denied in a context that celebrates interpersonal relationships means that:

> ... a group within which there is extensive trustworthiness and extensive trust is able to accomplish more than a comparable group without that trustworthiness and trust. (Coleman, 1988, p.s. 101)

This chapter has explored an issue that rarely receives coverage in volumes about teachers, teaching, and teachers' work – namely, that teachers can and should be social theorists and political actors. The broader purpose of this chapter has been to illustrate how teaching might be construed so as to assist in the reclamation of social capital, cooperatively engaging teachers in investigating the practise, meaning, and intent of what lies behind schooling. The central argument has been that for too long teachers have been treated in ways that deny the importance of teaching as a social practice. Teachers' work has always been an avowedly political process, despite claims to the contrary that it should be objectivist and value neutral. The work of teaching has long been characterized by decisions about what knowledge gets taught and what gets omitted; whose view of the world is privileged and whose is denied; what forms of pedagogy are inclusive and which are exclusive; and, whose interests are served, and whose are marginalised and excluded. These are no longer matters that should be spoken about in hushed tones, for it is clear that if teachers are not political about their work (in the sense of being critically reflective about it, and the implications that has for the life chances of children), then they are the only group affiliated with teaching who operate in such allegedly detached ways.

These issues have been dealt with in this chapter by giving something of a flavour (but nothing like a comprehensive account) of some of the similarities and differences among the many views of teaching as a form of social policy. The focus has been upon the forces working to shape teachers' work, how teachers are (or might be) assisted in responding, and what this is likely to mean. The emphasis has been upon questions such as the following:

- What's happening to teachers' work?
- Who is reconfiguring what passes as teaching?
- How are or might teachers reposition themselves to reclaim teaching?
- What are the likely effects of this on how teachers regard themselves and their work?

The perspective adopted has been one that embraces the view that teachers are influenced by, at the same time as they shape, social policy. They are not the passive receptacles of educational edicts developed at a distance from classrooms but are actively engaged in reading and co-authoring those texts (to use Stephen Ball's analogy). In resisting, accommodating, contesting, and reconstruing policies, teachers are continually exercising professional judgement in all kinds of matters. As Rachael Sharp (1994) put it recently, it seems unlikely that, as a consequence of recent reforms aimed at restructuring the work of teaching, teachers are going to be able to return to former nonthoughtful states, and that it would be futile for them to emulate King Canute in his pathetic attempt to reverse the tide. Much better she says, that they 'dance in the spaces that the ebb and flow of the waves make available.'

ENDNOTE

1. Publication of this paper was made possible through a grant from the Australian Research Council.

REFERENCES

Ashenden, D., Blackburn, J., Hannan, B., & White, D. (1984). A manifesto for a democratic curriculum. *Australian Teacher, 7*, 14-20.
Ayres, W. (1993). *To teach: The journey of a teacher.* New York: Teachers College Press.
Bagley, W. (1907). *Classroom management: Its principles and techniques.* New York: Macmillan.
Berlak, A. & Berlak, H. (198). *Dilemmas of schooling: Teaching and social change.* London: Methuen.
Berliner, D. C. & Biddle, B. J. (1995). *The manufactured crisis: Myths, fraud and the attack on America's public schools.* Reading, MA: Addison-Wesley.
Beyer, L. (1992). The personal and the social in education. In W. Ross, J. Cornett, & G. McCutcheon (Eds.), *Teacher personal theorizing: Connecting curriculum practice, theory, and Research* (pp. 239-256). Albany: State University of New York Press.
Bigelow, W. (1990). Inside the classroom: Social vision and critical pedagogy. *Teachers College Record, 9*(3), 437-448.
Bigelow, W. (1992). Inside the classroom: Social vision and critical pedagogy. *Education Links, 43*, 19-24.
Bobbitt, F. (1924). *How to make a curriculum.* Boston: Houghton Mifflin.
Boston Women's Teachers' Group (1986). *The effect of teaching on teachers.* Grand Forks: University of North Dakota, Centre for Teaching and Learning.
Bowles, S. & Gintis, H. (1976). *Schooling in capitalist America: Educational reform and the contradictions of economic life.* New York: Basic Books.
Bowles, S. & Gintis, H. (1988). Schooling in capitalist America: A reply to our critics. In M. Cole (Ed.), *Bowles and Gintis revisited: Correspondence and contradiction in educational theory* (pp. 235-245). London & New York: Falmer Press.
Britzman, D. (1991). *Practice makes practice: A critical study of learning to teach.* Albany: State University of New York Press.
Brookfield, S. (1987). *Developing critical thinkers: Challenging adults to explore alternative ways of thinking and acting.* Milton Keynes: Open University Press.
Bullough, R., Gitlin, A., & Goldstein, S. (1984). Ideology, teacher role, and resistance. *Teachers College Record, 86*(2), 339-358.
Callahan, R. (1962). *Education and the cult of efficiency.* Chicago: University of Chicago Press.
Carlson, D. (1987). Teachers as political actors. *Harvard Educational Review, 57*(3), 283-306.
Carr, W. & Kemmis, S. (1986). *Becoming critical: Education, knowledge and action research.* Geelong, Australia: Deakin University Press.
Chubb, J. & Moe, T. (1990). *Politics, markets and America's schools.* Washington, DC: Brookings Institute.
Cochran-Smith, M. (1991). Learning to teach against the grain. *Harvard Educational Review, 61*(3), 279-310.
Cole, M. (Ed.). (1988). *Bowles and Gintis Revisited: Correspondence and contradiction in education theory.* London: Falmer Press.
Coleman, J. (1988). Social capital in the creation of human capital. *American Journal of Sociology* (Supplement), *94*, S95-S120.
Connell, B. (1993). *Schools and social justice.* Toronto: Our Schools/Our Selves Education Foundation.
Connell, R. (1994). *Equity through education – directions for action.* Address to the Australian Centre for Equity through Education Conference, Canberra, Australia.
Connell, R., White, V., & Johnston, K. (1990). *Poverty, education and the disadvantaged schools program (DSP).* Sydney: Macquarie.

Corson, D. (1993). *Language, minority education and gender: Linking social justice and power.* Clevedon: Multilingual Matters.

Cox, E. (1995). *A truly civil society.* Sydney: Australian Broadcasting Commission.

Cox, R. (1980). Social forces, states and world orders' millenium. *Millenium: Journal of International Studies, 10*(2), 126-155.

Cubberley, E. (1922). *Public school administration.* New York: Houghton Mifflin.

Davies, S. (1995). Leaps of faith: Shifting currents in critical sociology of education. *American Journal of Sociology, 100*(6), 1448-1478.

Dewey, J. (1933). *How to think: A restatement of the relation of reflective thinking to the educative process.* Chicago: Henry Regnery.

Drost, W. (1967). *David Snedden and education for social efficiency.* Madison: University of Wisconsin Press.

Education for Social Justice Research Group (1994). *Teaching for resistance.* Adelaide: University of South Australia, Center for Studies in Educational Leadership.

Ellsworth, E. (1989). Why doesn't this feel empowering? Walking through the repressive myths of critical pedagogy. *Harvard Educational Review, 59*(3), 297-324.

Feiman-Nemser, S. & Floden, R. (1986). The cultures of teaching. In M. Wittrock (Ed.), *Third handbook of research on teaching.* New York: Collier-Macmillan.

Finegold, D., McFarland, L., & Richardson, W. (1992/1993). Something borrowed, something blue? A study of the Thatchers government's appropriation of American education and training policy Part 1 and 2. *Oxford Studies in Comparative Education, 2 & 3* (2 & 1).

Freedman, S., Jackson, J., & Boles, K. (1983). Teaching: An imperilled 'profession.' In L. Shulman & G. Sykes (Eds.), *Handbook of teaching and policy* (261-299). New York: Longman.

Garrison, D. (1991). Critical thinking and adult education: A conceptual model for developing critical thinking in adult learners. *International Journal of Lifelong Education, 10*(4), 287-303.

Ginsburg, M. (1988). Educators as workers and political actors in Britain and North America. *British Journal of Sociology of Education, 9*(3), 359-367.

Ginsburg, M. (Ed.). (1994). *The politics of educators' work and lives.* New York: Garland Press.

Giroux, H. (1985a). Intellectual labor and pedagogical work: Re-thinking the role of the teacher as intellectual. *Phenomenology and Pedagogy, 3*(1), 20-32.

Giroux, H. (1985b). Critical pedagogy and the resisting intellectual, part II. *Phenomenology and Pedagogy, 3*(2), 84-97.

Giroux, H. (1988). *Teachers-as-intellectuals: Toward a critical pedagogy of learning.* South Hadley, MA: Bergin and Garvey.

Goodlad, J. (1984). *A place called school.* New York: McGraw-Hill.

Goodman, J. (1992). *Elementary schooling for critical democracy.* Albany: State University of New York Press.

Granovetter, M. (1985). Economic action, social structure and embeddedness. *American Journal of Sociology, 91*, 481-510.

Halsey, A. H. (1972). Political ends and educational means. In A. H. Halsey (Ed.), *Education priority* (Vol. 1, pp. 3-12). London: HMSO.

Harris, K. (1990). Empowering teachers: Towards a justification for intervention. *Journal of Philosophy of Education, 24*(2), 171-183.

Hartnett, A. & Naish, M. (1980). Technicians or social bandits? Some moral and political issues in the education of teachers. In P. Woods (Ed.), *Teacher strategies: Explorations in the sociology of the school* (pp. 254-274). London: Croom Helm.

Hattam, R. (1994). *The socially just school in the 90s: Where is it and what does it look like?* (Discussion paper). Adelaide: Flinders Institute for the Study of Teaching.

Hattam, R., Kerkham, L., & Wooldridge, N. (1994). Critical literacy: Against consent. *Critical Pedagogy Networker, 7*(1), 1-11.

Henry, C. & Kemmis, S. (1985). A point-by-point guide to action research for teachers. *The Australian Administrator, 6*(4), 1-4.

Hlebowitsh, P. (1990). The teacher technician: Causes and consequences. *Journal of Educational Thought, 24*(3), 147-160.

Hursh, D. (1994). Developing discourses and structure to support action research for educational reform: Working both ends. In S. Noffke & R. Stevenson (Eds.), *An invitation to teacher research in education: Practically critical.* Albany: State University of New York Press.

Kanpol, B. (1992). *Towards a theory and practice of teacher cultural politics: Continuing the postmodern debate.* Norwood, NJ: Ablex.

Keegan, W. (1992). *The spectre of capitalism: The future of the world economy after the fall of communism.* London: Radius.

Kemmis, S. & McTaggart, R. (Eds.). (1988). *The action research planner* (3rd ed.). Geelong: Deakin University Press.

Krug, E. (1964). *The shaping of the American high school 1880-1920.* Madison: University of Wisconsin Press.

Knoll, M. (1988, April). *The origin of 'social efficiency' – a research note.* Paper presented at the annual meeting of the Society for the Study of Curriculum History, New Orleans.

Kohl, H. (1983). Examining closely what we do. *Learning, 12*(1), 28-30.

Kreisberg, S. (1992). *Transforming power: Domination, empowerment and education.* Albany: State University of New York Press.

Kretovics, J., Farber, K., & Armaline, W. (1991). Reform from the bottom up: Empowering teachers to transform schools. *Phi Delta Kappan* (December), 295-299.

Lampert, M. (1985). How do teachers manage to teach? Perspectives on problems in practice. *Harvard Educational Review, 55*(2), 178-194.

Lankshear, C. & McLaren, P. (Eds.). (1993). *Critical literacy: Politics, praxis and the postmodern.* Albany: State University of New York Press.

Lawn, M. (1987). *Servants of the state: The contested control of teaching 1900-30.* Lewes: Falmer Press.

Lawn, M. (1988). Skill in schoolwork: Work relations in the primary school. In J. Ozga (Ed.), *Schoolwork: Approaches to the labor process of teaching* (pp. 161-176). Milton Keynes: Open University Press.

Lawn, M. & Ozga, J. (1986). Unequal partners: Teachers under indirect rule. *British Journal of Sociology of Education, 7*(2), 225-238.

Lawn, M. & Ozga, J. (1988). The educational worker? A reassessment of teachers. In J. Ozga (Ed.), *Schoolwork: Approaches to the labor process of teaching* (pp. 81-98). Milton Keynes: Open University Press.

Lewis, M. & Simon, R. (1986). A discourse not intended for her: Learning and teaching within patriarchy. *Harvard Educational Review, 56*(4), 457-472.

Little, D. (1991). Critical adult education: A response to contemporary social crisis. *Canadian Journal for the Study of Adult Education* (Winter).

McDonald, J. (1986). Raising the teacher's voice and the ironic role of theory. *Harvard Educational Review, 56*(4), 355-378.

McDonald, J. (1992). *Teaching: Making sense of an uncertain craft.* New York: Teachers College Press.

McLaren, P. (1980). *Cries from the corridor: The new suburban ghettos.* Toronto: Methuen.

McLaren, P. (1989). *Life in schools: An introduction to critical pedagogy in the foundations of education.* New York: Longman.

McPeck, J. (1981). *Critical thinking in education.* Oxford: Martin Robertson.

Miller, J. (1990). *Creating spaces and finding voices: Teachers collaborating for empowerment.* Albany: State University of New York Press.

Neave, G. (1988). Education and social policy: Demise of an ethic or change of values? *Oxford Review of Education, 14*(3), 273- 283.

Pagano, J. (1990). *Exiles and communities: Teaching in the patriarchical wilderness.* Albany: State University of New York Press.

Paul, R. (1990). *Critical thinking: What every person needs to survive in a rapidly changing world.* Rohnert Park, CA: Sonoma State University.

Perl, S. & WIlson, N. (1986). *Through teachers' eyes.* Portsmouth, NH: Heinemann.

Phelan, A. & Lalik, R. (1993). An examination of teaching as a practical political activity. *Curriculum Inquiry, 23*(2), 155-174.

Popkewitz, T. (1987). *Critical studies in teacher education: Its folklore, theory and practice.* London and Philadelphia: Falmer Press.

Putnam, R. (1993). *Making democracy work: Civic traditions in modern Italy.* Princeton, NJ: Princeton University Press.

Putnam, R. (1995). Bowling alone: America's declining social capital. *Journal of Democracy, 6*(1), 65-78.

Putnam, R. (1996). The strange disappearance of civic America. *The American Prospect [http:// epn.org/prospect/24/24putn.htmll, No. 24* (Winter).

Raphael, R. (1985). *The teachers' voice.* Portsmouth, NH: Heinemann Educational Books.

Razack, S. (1993). Teaching activists for social change: Coming to grips with questions of subjectivity and domination. *Canadian Journal for the Study of Adult Education, 7*(2), 43-56.

Reid, A. (1992). Critical thinking. *Education Links, 43,* 9-12.

Ross, W., Cornett, J., & McCutcheon, G. (1992). *Teacher personal theorizing: Connecting curriculum practice, theory and research.* Albany: State University of New York.

Ruddick, J. (1984). *Teaching as an art, teacher research and research-based teacher education.* Paper presented at the Second Annual Lawrence Stenhouse Memorial Lecture, University of East Anglia.

Scheffler, I. (1968). University scholarship and the education of teachers. *Teachers College Record, 70*(1), 1-12.

Schniedewind, N. (1987). Feminist values: Guidelines for teaching methodology in women's studies. In I. Shor (Ed.), *Freire for the classroom: A sourcebook for liberatory teaching* (pp. 180-203). Portsmouth, NH: Boynton/Cook.

Schubert, W. & Ayres, W. (Eds.). (1992). *Teacher lore: Learning from our own experience.* White Plains, NY: Longman.

Shannon, P. (1992). *Becoming political: Readings and writings in the politics of literacy education.* Portsmouth, NH: Heinemann.

Sharp, R. (1994). Lesson for the market. *Campus Review* (May 26-June 1), 19.

Shor, I. (1980). *Critical teaching and everyday life.* Montreal: Black Rose Press.

Simon, R. (1992). *Teaching against the grain: Texts for a pedagogy of possibility.* Amherst: Bergin and Garvey.

Smyth, J. (1991a). International perspectives on teacher collegiality: A labor process discussion based on teachers' work. *British Journal of Sociology of Education, 12*(4), 323-346.

Smyth, J. (1991b). *Teachers as collaborative learners: Challenging dominant forms of supervision.* London: Open University Press.

Smyth, J. (1992). *Conflicting conceptualizations of teaching and teachers' work: Implications for professional development*. Paper presented to the Seven Oaks School Division Symposium Series, Winnipeg, Manitoba, Canada.

Smyth, J. (1993). *Becoming political about teachers thinking politically about their work: Interactive action planning session*. Paper presented to the annual meeting of the American Educational Research Association, Atlanta. GA.

Smyth, J. (1995a). Devolution and teachers' work: The underside of a complex phenomenon. *Educational Administration and Management, 23*(3), 168-175.

Smyth, J. (1995b). Teachers' work and the labor process of teaching: Central problematics in professional development. In T. Guskey & M. Huberman (Eds.), *Professional development in education: New paradigms and practices* (pp. 69-91). New York: Teachers College Press.

Smyth, J. (1995c). Some possible candidates for classroom observation by socially critical teachers and colleagues (Unpublished paper, Schools as Critical Collaborative Communities Project). Adelaide: Flinders Institute for the Study of Teaching.

Smyth, J. (1996). The socially just alternative to the 'self-managing school.' In K. Leithwood, J. Chapman, D. Corson, P. Hallinger, & A. Hart (Eds.), *International handbook of educational leadership and administration, Part 2* (pp. 1097-1131). Dordrecht/Boston/London: Kluwer Academic Publishers.

Smyth, P. (1994). *Australian social policy: The keynesian chapter*. Sydney: University of New South Wales Press.

Starr, K. & Moore, B. (1994). Education for social justice research project. *Critical Pedagogy Networker, 7*(4), 1-9.

Stevens, P. (1987). Political education and political teachers. *Journal of Philosophy of Education, 21*(1), 75-83.

Streib, L. (1985). *A (Philadelphia) teachers's journal*. Grand Forks, ND: North Dakota Study Group on Evaluation.

Strike, K. (1993). Professionalism, democracy, and discursive communities: Normative reflections on restructuring. *American Educational Research Journal, 30*(2), 255-275.

Sultana, R. (1989). What's keeping them back? Life choices and life chances. *Set, 1*, 1-4.

Sultana, R. (1990). Towards a critical teaching practice: Notes for the teacher educator. *Journal of Further and Higher Education, 14*(1), 14-30.

Sultana, R. (1991). The challenge of critical education. *McGill Journal of Education, 26*(2), 115-128.

Thompson, P. & McHugh, D. (1990). *Work organizations: A critical introduction*. London: Macmillan.

Tom, A. (1958). Inquiring into inquiry-oriented teacher education. *Journal of Teacher Education* (Sept-Oct), 35-44.

Traugh, C., Kanevsky, R., Martin, A., Seletsky, A., Woolf, K., & Strieb, L. (1986). *What works: Research about teaching and learning*. Washington, DC: U.S. Department of Education.

Tripp, D. (1993). *Critical incidents in teaching: Developing professional judgement*. London: Routledge.

U.S. Department of Education (1986). *What works: Research about teaching and learning*. Washington, DC: U.S. Department of Education.

Warham, S. (1993). Reflection on hegemony: Towards a model of teacher competence. *Educational studies, 19*(2), 205-217.

Weber, S. & Mitchell, C. (1995). *That's funny you don't look like a teacher: Interrogating images, identity and popular culture*. London: Falmer Press.

Weiler, K. (1991). Freire and a feminist pedagogy of difference. *Harvard Educational Review, 61*(4), 449-474.

Welton, M. (1991). Shaking the foundation: The critical turn in adult education theory. *Canadian Journal for the Study of Adult Education, 5*, 21-42.

White, J. (1979). The primary teacher as servants of the state. *Education, 3*(13), 18-23.

White, J. & White, P. (1987). Teachers as political activists. In A. Hartnett & M. Naish (Eds.), *Education and society today* (pp. 171-182). London: Falmer.

Willis, P. (1977). *Learning to labour: How working class kids get working class jobs.* Westmead, England: Gower.

Wood, G. (1988). Democracy and the curriculum. In L. Beyer & M. Apple (Eds.), *The curriculum: Problems, politics and possibilities* (pp. 166-190). Albany: State University of New York Press.

Wood, G. (1990). Teachers as curriculum workers. In J. Sears & D. Marshall (Eds.), *Teaching and thinking about curriculum* (pp. 97-110). New York: Teachers College Press.

Wraga, W. (1992). School choice and the comprehensive ideal. *Journal of Curriculum and Supervision, 8*(1), 28-42.

Young, I. (1981). Towards a critical theory of justice. *Social Theory and Practice, 7*, 279-302.

Zeichner, K. (1992). Connecting genuine teacher development to the struggle for social justice (Issue Paper 92-1). East Lansing: Michigan State University, National Center for Research on Teacher Learning.

Chapter 11: Teaching in Context: From Socialization to Redemption[1]

PHILIP WEXLER

University of Rochester

INTRODUCTION

I don't know how anyone can begin with the question of teaching. It is so profound a question that it must be an end point, a destination that one arrives at from somewhere else.

My way into this daunting topic of teaching is by understanding education socially, both as a practice and as a theory; I come to the question of teaching from a reflexive sociology of education, from a social, historical study of education, and from the view that social understandings of education *themselves* are within culture and change historically along with the evolution of culture.

First, I want to briefly trace this evolving path in the social understanding of education and show how it has been intertwined with broader cultural movements. Only after arriving at the unlikely and unforeseen place of what I understand as a religious reversal of historic secularization of culture and society do I dare to offer some interpretation of teaching. Finally, I return to understanding education in its social context with the transformative social interest from which the new sociology of education began; but perhaps in a different way.

NEW SOCIOLOGY OF EDUCATION

The starting point in the recent history of social interpretation of education is ideological critique applied in the field of education, as it was across the social sciences as part of a cultural movement that I think we may now call the 'cultural revolution of the sixties.' In this movement of mass and academic culture, social institutions and discourses were debunked as impostors of objectivity and neutrality through political, socially interested critiques of power and its falsely neutralized, legitimating representations (Blackburn, 1972; Gouldner, 1970).

This movement assaulted the functionalist position in sociological thought with its social functions of the classroom analyses of teaching and learning (Dreeben, 1968; Parsons, 1953) and the view of education as a process of socialization into shared social values and appropriate, role-prescribed behaviors.

B.J. Biddle et al. (eds.), International Handbook of Teachers and Teaching, 1145-1161
© 1997 Kluwer Academic Publishers, Printed in the Netherlands

The new sociology brought awareness of class conflict and domination into the school, as in the society. It substituted conflict for integration and concepts of reproduction and resistance in education for those of a smoothly internalized 'socialization' into the status quo (Parsons, 1955).

The glow of the new sociology of education that shone from England to North America and enabled an occasional blurring of boundaries between curriculum and sociology (Wexler, 1987) was reflected, most popularly, in the work of Apple (1979, 1982) and Giroux (1983, 1985). This work continues in contemporary applications to postmodernism and feminism and in uses of later continental theories of difference and domination for purposes of social-educational critique (Apple, 1993; Aronowitz & Giroux, 1985, 1991).

One obvious implication of the new sociology of education for teaching was the effort to work from social criticism to an alternative educational practice embodying this criticism, a view best captured by the term 'critical pedagogy.' Of this implication, McLaren writes (1995):

> At the same time, many current trends in critical pedagogy are embedded in the endemic weaknesses of a theoretical project overly concerned with developing a language of critique. Critical pedagogy is steeped in a posture of moral indignation toward the injustices reproduced in American public schools. (p. 32)

Jay and Graff (1993) excoriate critical or 'radical' pedagogy more directly and more saliently to the question of teaching:

> What worries us is the way that efforts by teachers to empower students often end up reinforcing the inequalities of the classroom. This is clearest when teachers directly promote progressive doctrines in their courses, merely inverting the traditional practice of HANDING knowledge DOWN to passive students who dutifully copy it into their notebooks. (p. 1)

Of the guru of critical pedagogy, Paulo Freire, they write:

> In picturing the classroom, Freire and other proponents of critical pedagogy seemingly envisage a teacher who is already committed to social transformation and simply lacks the lesson plan for translating the commitment into practice.

It means that critical pedagogy is usually a business of preaching to the converted, leaving the unpersuaded overlooked, alienated, and receptive to the counter-propaganda of conservatives. (p. 15)

Complementary to 'critical pedagogy,' the new sociology encouraged a wave of what Anderson (1989) called 'critical ethnography' in education. Against the variable analysis which defined the pre-revolutionary movement of the sixties and continued to characterize American sociology of education, there was a great wave of research offering socially critical descriptions of school life. Understood as a social and cultural phenomenon itself, critical ethnography may have represented still another incipient and incorporated attempt to overcome more general, as well as social science research performance, alienation. Yet, perhaps like broader individuated and collective strategies of escape from alienation, domination, and inequality, critical ethnography, like critical pedagogy, was drawn back into a powerful hegemony of administrative logic that pervades schooling no less than research or everyday social life (Hunter, 1994).

CRITICAL ETHNOGRAPHY: EMPTYING SOCIETY AND EDUCATION

The new sociology of education was part of the larger academic and cultural revolt against inequalities and alienation in the administered, culturally complacent society. The cultural movement of postmodernism which followed it offered new languages and new fuel for cultural criticism (Smith & Wexler, 1995). But both in education and more broadly in the society, it did not stem the individual and institutional effects of deepening inequality, administrative rationalization, and self-alienation. Behind the critical front of postmodern discourse, there took place, I suggest, in social and educational life, a pervasive process of social emptying.

My empirical studies of social-class differentiated American high schools reported in *Becoming Somebody* (Wexler, 1992) describe the emptying and fragmentation of different aspects of the social core of the teenaged self.

Articulations of identity in a postmodern world presume the triumph of consumption as the leading social activity. Instead, we have studied everyday school life in different social strata and have tried to describe not a textual, but an institutional postmodernism in which there are class differentiated 'lacks.' These absences are experienced by youths, who struggle with and against them in their efforts to establish distinguishable identities — 'to become somebody.'

In each school and class, a basic constituent aspect of social relations is being destroyed. In the working class it is interaction. For the professional middle class it is no longer, as Horkheimer and Adorno wrote (1972), that everyone is belabored by the social whole or totality. Rather, they are belabored by the absence of the social whole. Here it is society that is missing at the center of school and class social relations. For the urban 'underclass' of mostly African-American and Hispanic youths, virtually pre-school moral stigma and inferiorization makes society's constituent antipode — the self — tenuous and, if not absent, then certainly under attack and acting to defend itself against an imminent absence. Interaction, society, and self are basic elements of social relations that are differentially expressed in each school and class but not by their realization or fullness. Instead, it is the emptying and putative lack of these practices and their representations which appears to stand, lacking and absent, at the center of what we my still call social life.

The emptying process is unintended and overdetermined in each case. In the working class school, attenuation of dyadic interaction is a by-product of distrust created by a school administration, in harmony with its community, as it strives for order and respect. The direct effect, of course, is social selection, stratification, and the polarization of student peer groups. The resultant atmosphere is one of containment and suppression.

The emptying of society is less perceptible and can occur without projecting blame in the professional middle class school. Students complain about the 'apathy' and lack of school spirit. These understandings appear as qualifications, addenda to a struggle for identity built within a limited range of acceptable personal achievements, that ultimately pushes society out of the center of school and class – only then to complain about the corrosive effects of its absence.

In the urban school, students fight against the institutionalized process of emptying because their selves are openly at stake. Emptying here is of the self, and it occurs less behind the backs of the students than against their will, imposed forcibly and out of fear by their teachers and guards. The quest for control is not so much to restore respect for authorities. Rather, it is the control of population management, an apparently logistical problem that presents itself as an issue of attendance. Dittoed in-class quiet assignments avoid the pedagogical encounter, while 'attacks' mounted by deans and guards usually prevent any unmanageable forms of collective self-expression. Such a process presents problems for population management and gives cues of fear-inspiring uncontrollability when students are overly self-expressive outside the decaying forms of the old bureaucratic fortress of school. This vibrant self is not harnessed and elevated but rather pressed into corners and locked out by the steel doors of school time. Where the internal apparatus of control fails, the therapeutic and legal ministries reach beyond the school to the city's welfare management system.

The process of self-formation, or identity as compensation for a social relational lack, is a defense against a social structuring absence at the center of school life. It is an important part of the story we see enacted as high school youths struggle to become somebody. In my case studies, we see how much identity is created as a defensive compensation to a failure in modern social relations, how the compensatory defensive processes operate as self-formative.

The emptying of social relations induces a set of defensive self-processes as compensation to the lack. The absence of reciprocal interaction in the working class school eventuates in a series of divisions or 'splits' that protects against a vulnerability created by an absence of caring interaction and completed identification with adult authority. 'Rads' and 'jocks,' 'good kids and losers,' disciplinary and therapeutic locales, exaggerations of male and female – all are some of the divisions that occur in the absence of a consistent positive identification with a listening though powerful adult.

Division is the first line of defense, underlined and secured by the exaggeration of differences. But the final victor is alienated identity formation in which, not a self, but an image of self emerges. The mirror replaces the subject.

For the professional middle class students, through a combination of ironic humor and depression, limitless performance expectations (which are themselves integral to student identity) are put under control by dampening commitment to them. Performance, which is the medium and goal of self-affirmation, is also a threatening enemy of the self. Its never-ending character – through college that is beyond high school, and career demands beyond college, and social conscience and economic status beyond career – instigates strategies of dampening, depression, and distance.

The school as a whole – society – has, as the students say, become 'nothing.' Socially created performance pressures carry along with them built-in defenses against limitlessness itself. Society is a threat to the self, as a channel of boundarylessness, uncontrollable demand, unpredictability, and finally, self-surrender. 'Mellowing out' or getting 'psyched down' is a means of self-defense against society's limitless performance demands.

There is a difference between the interactional and societal lack in working class and professional middle class schools and a more basic lack of self-affirmation in the urban, poor, minority, or so-called 'underclass' school. Self-establishment has to be repeatedly accomplished before any other direction or shaping takes place. The compensatory process is more direct. Where the lack of self-affirmation is the basic social absence, the socially patterned defensive self-formation occurs at the first, basic line of self-defense: self-existence.

From the first hello that says, 'we are not who you have heard we are,' to the last goodbye's pleading to remind the world that 'we have value as human beings,' the students work to create and display a visible, differentiated, and reputable self. The moral language of being 'good' or 'decent' is the way that the social comes to be represented in demarginalizing self-existence. Whatever they may have to prove about their self-value at the outset of their school career is exaggerated by the school's organization around the assumption that what is lacking among the students is a decent, moral self. Morality here is not the neat, the clean concern of the upwardly mobile working class teacher, but again a more basic placing in question of the student's integrity. From the first early morning meetings of the administrative staff to the close of the school day, the students are managed, at worst as a potentially dangerous population and at best as a deficit self, to be classified, guided, or uplifted.

Taken together, these defensive processes of a self formed within institutions characterized by social practices of emptying core elements of social relations are, I think, more revealing of what postmodern society means practically than general, textualists' talk about a 'decentered,' postmodern self.

The defensive formation and emptying of the class differentiated self neglected by high status postmodern talk in education is complemented by a parallel process of institutional- rather than self-emptying, as part of what Weber referred to as the 'universal rationalization of culture.' I mean the institutional process that I have referred to as 'educational corporatism' (Wexler, 1993/94). 'Critical ethnographies,' including my own, have not operated to halt or in any way alter the larger secretal process of rationalization that is represented by school restructuring.

RESTRUCTURING: INSTITUTIONAL RATIONALIZATION

The ideal 'new American school' is a 'Toyota school.' (Schmoker, 1992). It is a 'high performance' school run by 'new collar' leaders, who 'design' 'hands on,' 'real life,' team-organized learning of new skills for a 'restructured' workplace.

There is no longer any pretense of an organized public institutional mediation between education and economic production. From 'the school to work transition,' to the redefinition of educational knowledge, and, finally, the subject of schooling the student, education is to be restructured. New corporatism is simultaneously the vehicle and the expression of an increasingly elite-organized, mass-mobilized, national social movement to create a post-Fordist educational apparatus that matches the economic shift to 'postindustrialism,' or to a new regime of 'capital accumulation.'

The language of education is the language of restructured, post-Fordist, postindustrial work. Individual schools, school systems, states, and the nation ('America 2000') need 'vision statements.' The 'crisis of productivity' (Ray & Mickelson, 1989) and global economic competition, which induce the creation of 'the restructured workplace' (and as a corollary, the 'restructured school'), requires 'benchmarking' and the innovative but nationally standardized and eventually computer networked assessment of the products of 'this new model of work, organization, and management.' Educational leaders and teachers are 'team leaders' and 'vendors of schooling as a client driven, worklife derived commodity.' The crisis of education is recast as a 'design problem.'

Corporatist social forms include not only the elite functional representation that appears in the emergent national educational restructuring networks but also mass mobilization. Increasingly, entire 'communities' are encouraged to join expanded coalitions. Parents are organized to work for reform under the slogan of 'parental involvement.' Full community mobilization to restructure public schooling to the new model is an essential and a growing part of the new corporatism in education.

The reorganization of educational control through the establishment of interlocking networks may increase the centralization of the 'design' function at the same time that the design itself calls for a greater degree of 'innovative,' customized, and, above all, 'flexible' social organization and school culture within the controlled network of design. Even the standardization, which the main restructuring networks propose, test, and implement, is justified on the ground that it will provide 'flexibility.'

The precise content of the flexible, anti-assembly-line knowledge in schools is not however easily agreed upon. The most widely discussed new curriculum is the Labor Department's commission report of the Secretary's Commission on Achieving Necessary Skills, SCANS. The report, 'Learning a Living: A Blueprint for High Performance,' calls for an approach that sounds like the 'Toyota school': teamwork, collaborative learning, and a set of changes in teacher education and professional development.

The main point of the report is that there be a 'translation' of work skills into the academic curriculum – a redefinition of the curriculum as high performance workplace relevant skills which are taught in 'the context of real life situations and real problems.'

The new knowledge or culture is, in the educational sector, expressly tied to the newly restructured workplace as a 'translation' of 'real life' skills to academic curriculum. It represents a shift 'from an academic to a real world focus.' For those worried about the excessive narrowing of school knowledge to new workplace skills, there is reassurance that traditional disciplines such as history will also be included. Yet all social studies or sciences are absent from such a curriculum, represented only by history, 'the human record.'

The key to the new knowledge, and the subject or person it helps to position and construct is that it redefines meaning and subjectivity. The new knowledge is an intentional superfluity. It removes both the cultural resources and the practice of any depth, distanced, or reflexive knowledge when the standard is neither skill- nor task-related but is instead autonomous, different, decontextualized, and critical. What is further important about this one-dimensionalizing or desocializing of knowledge and culture is precisely that it is not rooted in the spectacular culture of mass consumption. Instead, it displays how the redefinition of culture is mediated institutionally in the educational sector.

ENERGY IN THE NEW AGE

Societal and institutional rationalization and emptying, with individual effects that Weber termed, more than half century ago, 'mechanical petrification,' was the main, but not the sole, social tendency within broad-scale cultural change. Increasingly, counter-tendencies also developed.

These were disparate cultural expressions which shared, however, efforts to reconstitute self and meaning in the wake of both rationalization and postmodernism. Reacting against 'emptying' as an individual and collective process, there began searches for refilling, for 'fulfilment,' or, in the language of new age cultural movements, for 'energy' and for 're-energizing.' Both the new age interest in energy and the subsequent mass tendency toward 'resacralization' were represented in social understanding and in education which are part of these larger patterns of cultural and social movements for revitalization and renewal. To underline, my view is that any effort to grasp the trajectory of teaching has to be nested within a *context* of cultural movement and societal evolution.

I have called the social understanding that emerges during this counter-revolution against both rationalization and postmodernity as a sociology of presence, or a new age sociology.

Talk of a new cultural age is very general, hypothetical, and removed from the traditions of empirical social science. What is, I think, interesting, is the extent to which survey analyses of the hegemonic, so-called 'baby-boom,' generation reveal at the concrete level of individual lives and opinions the same sort of cultural, new-age shift in assumptions. Wade Roof (1993) reports survey results on what he refers to as a 'generation of seekers.' According to Roof:

> They are still exploring, as they did in their years growing up; but now they are exploring in new, and, we think, more profound ways. Religious and spiritual themes are surfacing in a rich variety of ways – in Eastern religions, in evangelical and fundamentalist teachings, in mysticism and new age movements, in Goddess worship and other ancient religious rituals, in the mainline churches and synagogues, in Twelve Step recovery groups, in concern about the environment, in holistic health, and in personal and social transformation. [And further,] ... baby boomers have found that they have to discover for themselves what gives their lives meaning, what values to live by. (pp. 4-5)

What Roof foresees for the nineties is a 're-emergence of spirituality.' Indeed, against the conventional wisdom of this as the political, radical generation, he observes:

The generation may well be remembered, in fact, as one that grappled hard in search of a holistic, all-encompassing vision of life and as a spiritually creative generation. (p. 243)

While there is a postmodernism in this 'pastiche-style of spirituality,' it is also a search for post-material values, although the commitment to the search is through an emphasis on self. Indeed, like Norman O. Brown (1959), Roof raises the possibility of a two-sided narcissism, in which baby-boomer narcissism is

... compatible with the positive, reinforcing role of religion: a person's need for affirmation, for encouragement, for support, for expressiveness ...

He continues

... a transformed narcissism is not only compatible with a religious orientation but may well be crucial to the continuing role of the sacred in a secular society. (p. 258)

Roof's analysis leads to the view that a new vision has (p. 260) a vital balance of spirituality and social action, creating new community's through a 'far quieter rhetoric- that of the soul' has emerged. Additional support for these surveys is in the best seller lists in which the traditional self-help literature now has as a best seller, a book on spiritual practices that calls for 'the care of the soul' (Moore, 1992). At the same time, phenomenological psychologists, such as Eugene Gendlin, also see narcissism's value in self and social transformation. As Gendlin asks (1987, p. 251): 'Has experience now become a possible source of social criticism?'

Education in the new age is first and foremost necessarily self-centered. Any transformatively interested education for a new age will be about the body. New age body education is about 'energy' and the recovery and stimulation of life energy that has, like Weber's 'mechanical petrification,' become inert. This education is about wakening the body – the energy streamings, as Reich (1949, 1961) would have had it – from their bounded death in life. Of course, the new age therapeutic apparatus is importantly about this project. From a social psychological vantagepoint, such a new 'triumph of the therapeutic' is a response to the need for an effective agency of human beings which has been so far repressed interpersonally, culturally, and macrosocially, that only at the bio-feedback level can the alienated self re-experience itself.

Body education is already a simultaneous sign of defeat and the stirring of a counter-force, energy. But the dialectic of body education for the awakening and release of bio-energies is that it is an energy regeneration for residual self-effectivity that has merely the consequence of producing more individual energy for incorporation and use by the petrified and petrifying social apparatus. Incorporation occurs not only into the apparatus but also into unthinking cults of the new age. What begins as a stirring of bioenergy for self and social effectivity – which, of course, in actuality goes beyond the minimal, biological level – becomes reassimilated into cultural programs as diverse as twelve-step methods, evangelical, fundamentalist religion, and mass amalgamated reductions of psychoanalysis which use the apparatus to manipulate the 'unconscious' electronically rather than either mechanically or interpersonally.

What Weber understood for his own day was that while such activity may be enjoyable, the transformative possibility – which he called 'revolutionary' – is only realized when the release of energies (to use current terms) is poured into the work of intellectualization. Without intellectualization, 'experience,' however altered, remains enjoyment, working in the unintended service of incorporation into the uncritical, prevailing social apparatus and its new age counterposed cultures. My point is that a social-theory based education in a new age recognizes the need for the reintellectualization of released energies. It so becomes necessarily an education of the mind and not only for the body. What the new age cultural shift can offer, however, is the opening of alternative cultural resources for learning and thinking.

Re-collection of the body for an energic, life awakening in new age education can only resist feeding the electronic apparatus which now regulates the unconscious imagically by re-intellectualizing the life of the mind. Given the medium of religiosity, both in the contemporary cultural transformation and in the emergence of a social theory with practical implications for education, re-minding will occur in the thrall of states of being such as those that moved William James, Whitman, and Emerson in American culture. Re-intellectualization motivated by experienced values through religious states of being unavoidably recalls the language of spirit and soul.

The practical, educational effects of the cultural transformation that I am indicating – one well outside and beyond the contemporary main trends of the economist, corporatist, and culturalist character of education programs – are now institutionalized only in the most fragmentary forms. Both economic and cultural interests are forging educational change through a successful mobilization of broad scale networks, while new age movements have so far been most successfully networked only in the most commodified, commercial forms. Thus, the transformative aspect of this new educational movement remains local, body-centered, and eclectic. It can, I believe, provide a real alternative to the dominant contemporary pair of work and character, although it is still diffuse and uncrystallized.

RESACRALIZATION: FROM NEW AGE TO RELIGION

Yet, as new age movements reveal their cultural foundations in classical religions, and as religious discourse becomes more publicly pervasive, there is an inevitable exploration of the value of religious understanding as social understanding. The translation – or recontextualization (Bernstein, 1990) of religious to secular language – is now being saliently reversed, in a change in everyday culture that Wuthnow (1992) terms the 'rediscovery of the sacred' and Thompson (1990) refers to simply as 'resacralization.' The implication of this religious turn for social understanding has not yet been very much explored, at least not by specialists in social interpretation.

A rare exception (importantly, see also, for literary theory, Handelman, 1991) is Michawel Lowy's (1992) history of the 'elective affinities' between libertarian and messianic thought in central Europe. He puts this preface to using traditionally religious categories as instruments of social understanding as follows:

> A century after August Comte, sociology continues to borrow its conceptual terminology from physics or biology. Is it not time to break away from this positivist tradition and to draw upon a spiritual and cultural heritage that is broader, richer in meaning and closer to the very texture of social facts? Why not use the vast semantic field of religions, myths, literature and even esoteric traditions to enrich the language of the social sciences? Did not Max Weber borrow the concept of 'charisma' from Christian theology, and Karl Mannheim that of 'constellation' from classical astrology? (p. 6)

In the writings of Martin Buber, Franz Rosenzweig, and Gershom Scholem, there is already, despite their significant differences, in Geertz' term, a shared 'blurring of genres,' between the religious, social interpretation and individual and collective commitment and transformation that Lowy calls for. The later writings of the French philosopher, Emmanuel Levinas, also reflect this interest in a 'movement from the dialectic to the dialogical' (Smith, in Levinas, 1994). Further, there is a transformative model in their representations of both Jewish exoteric and esoteric traditions that, while it may bear more than a passing resemblance to dialectics, opens new possibilities for social interpretation and fruitfully maps recent and historical self and educational processes.

TEACHING AS REDEMPTION

I believe that it is precisely this complex series of cultural movements in social theory and social practice that now makes possible a more deeply alternative approach to teaching, one that pits it directly against the instrumentalizing rationalization of current pedagogic emphasis on 'performance' – what I have called teaching for the 'Toyota School.'

The current religious turn in culture can have the same incorporative result as commodified new ageism and authoritarian critical pedagogy. What makes the deeper alternative now culturally possible is a conjuncture of interest in energy, religion, and everyday social interaction.

In the first instance, teaching is, to use Csikszentmihalyi's (1993) application of the interest in energy to cognitive psychology, the opposite of entropy or energy loss. It is 'negentropy':

> But entropy is not the only law operating in the world. There are also processes that move in the opposite direction: creation and growth are just as much part of the story as decay and death. Beautifully ordered crystals take shape, new life-forms develop, increasingly improbable methods of exploiting energy emerge. Whenever order in a system increases instead of breaking down we may say that negentropy is at work. (p. 20)

Buber (1965) says the same, in the language of Existentialism:

> In every hour the human race begins. We forget this too easily in the face of the massive fact of past life, of so-called world history ... *in spite of everything* (my emphasis), in this as in every hour, what has not been invades the structure of what is ... a creative event if ever there was one, newness rising up, primal potential might. This potentiality, streaming unconquered, however much of it is squandered, is the reality *child*: this phenomenon of uniqueness, which is more than just begetting and birth, this grace of beginning again and ever again. (p. 83)

The desire for negentropy that is so evident in new age culture leads, as I have suggested, at first to narcissism. But narcissism is insufficient to the task of re-subjectification. It moves outward, to the environment, to whole energy, to 'have' (Fromm, 1976), and to grasp. Our environment increasingly responds virtually with the condensed consumption of the automatic images of television. This voyeurism is like narcissism, like environmental dependency and addiction, in its greed for energy by 'having' the image of the other, the image of the object. Both the narcissism of commodified new age fetishism and the voyeurism of imaginary, virtual, information culture de-mediate interaction and relationality (Gergen, 1994) – depriving rather than nourishing the microsocial interactional conditions of teaching and learning as creativity and growth, as resubjectification and resymbolization, the essence of teaching as redemption.

Under these socio-psycho-cultural conditions, what makes redemptive teaching possible? My view is that the cultural trajectory I have outlined, and which is now in a mass resacralization of self and culture, sets the stage for teaching as negentropy and as the kind of historically redemptive interaction or relational intersubjectivity which Martin Buber envisioned (1992). This becomes culturally and interactionally possible to the extent that the religious turn in contemporary culture – especially the renewal of esoteric traditions in all the classical world religions (Merkur, 1993) – functions *collectively* as well as individually as a useful cultural 'regression.'

The term 'regression' reflects psychoanalytic understanding, with the added qualification of 'regression in the service of the ego'; in other words, developmentally healthy and indeed, creative regression (see also Appel's 1992 application of psychoanalysis to sociology of education). Fauteux (1994) describes the traditional psychoanalytic view, with Kris' revision of an adaptive value for regression, particularly as seen in the creative process of artists. What Fauteux adds is an understanding of religious experience – following Freud – as emotionally and symbolically regressive. However, in Fauteux's view, religious experience (here following William James), can provide the same adaptive regression as art or other individual forms of ego regression.

What is especially relevant for our cultural, historical, or 'contextual' social understanding of teaching is the interpretation of the regressive process itself as one that enables expression and experience of the sense of 'communion' (and its relational attendant 'basic trust' – see Erickson, 1963) which gets suppressed in the individuating, agentic path of autonomous ego development. This trusting communion has, in the creative regression view, the effect of fostering creative insight and growth, and when re-assimilated to the ego, it enables symbolic elaboration, which is a communication – or teaching – of the re-experienced trust, communion, and receptivies of unitive experience.

This is, of course, the best of art and mysticism in its elaborative, expressive, and returning to the world of others aspect. Fauteux (1994) observes:

> Religious experience restores the communion structures that existed prior to the anxious development of a separate self and hence prior to the fears, conflicts, and basic fault that formed out of the infant's earliest unitive state. (p. 154)

What is described here is twofold: first, a psychological process of regression is understood in its adaptive, elaborative, and creative aspect; second, that religious experience is one channel or medium of this creative regressive psychological state. In a sense, religion may function as 'a transference' for primary object relations and regressively restore the basic trust and communion of interactional unity in a symbolic mode.

From the vantage point of our cultural and pedagogic interest, there are a number of implications in such a model. As Weber (1946) hoped, I believe religion, with all the dangers that he perceived as strongly as Freud did, can be an antidote – in culture and interaction – to the 'mechanical petrification' of the industrial, administrative apparatus that has been the unintended heir of our ascetic, historical, religious tendency. The unitive emphasis helps explain the particular appeal of the esoteric and mystical spiritual interests in the lives of the baby boomers Roof studied.

This circuitous cultural path, through what I am calling 'the religious transference,' reopens intersubjectivity that has been socially 'emptied' in the institutional rationalization process 'managed' by class differentiated, defensive selves. The religious transference facilitates trust, and therefore social interaction or intersubjectivity. In a view of teaching that is not limited to skill transmission, but rather aims at growth, transformation, and creativity, these are the cultural, then interactional, conditions of possibility. What the 'religious transference' does (since, as we have argued, the religious turn is part of a mass cultural as well as theoretic reversal) is to create these conditions for creative regression – in a symbolic transference of religion – as an individuated but widely shared collective process.

Redemptive teaching then does not mean teaching religion. What it does mean is that cultural conditions exist that facilitate the sort of intersubjectivity or relationality – or, simply, 'social interaction' – that are simultaneously part of a collective process of sociocultural renewal ('resymbolization') and an education that promotes individual transformation and development ('resubjectification'). These interactional, relational possibilities are described in Benjamin's (1988) feminist-psychoanalytic approach to domination, and to its opposite, which she terms 'mutual recognition':

> What I call *mutual recognition* includes a number of experiences commonly described in the research on mother-infant interaction: emotional attunement, mutual influence, affective mutuality, sharing states of mind. The idea of mutual recognition seems to me an ever more crucial category of early experience. (p. 16)

Benjamin underlines the simultaneous duality of interaction – between assertion and recognition – and argues that contemporary culture overemphasizes assertion and individuation at the cost of sacrificing communion and valuing domination and submission, so that 'the image of the other that predominates in

Western thought is not that of a vitally real presence but a cognitively perceived object' (1988, p. 78).

Intersubjective mutuality is negentropy and supplants narcissism and voyeurism as prevailing forms of 'social' interaction. Redemptive teaching is the strong form of this mode of interaction. In Buber's formulation, there is an 'experience of inclusion of the other side' (1965, p. 97). In teaching, there is '... that subterranean dialogic, that steady potential presence of the one to the other is established and endures. Then there is reality *between* them, there is mutuality' (1965, p. 98). Buber's pedagogic language in his 1926 speech foreshadows contemporary feminist psychoanalytic and humanist relational models in his understandings of trust ('the silver mail' of the child), communion, and communication ('The relation of education is one of pure dialogue.')

My interest in 'the context' is, I hope, a way of avoiding pedagogic idealism. I offer Buber's dialogic model as an example, not simply of an ideal of teaching, but as an interactional possibility brought to the fore by social and cultural changes. Whether such examples are transhistorical ideals, I do not know. But, I do think that our ability to reach toward such an ideal now is the effect of our current location in the recent trajectory of cultural evolution.

What such an ideal suggests, beyond the strong, pedagogic, interactional model, is that it is the vital 'presence' of the teacher that needs to be addressed, a teacher who 'concentrates' the social world and its possibilities in her presence, rather than providing mere skill training in assessment or organizational effectiveness. This would mean an entirely different repertoire for teacher education, an education for being and meaning and for the capacity to creatively include the other side.

ENDNOTES

[1.]   Parts of this essay appear in Philip Wexler, *Holy sparks: Social theory, education and religion*, 1996, New York, St. Martins Press.

REFERENCES

Anderson, G. (1989). Critical ethnography in education: Origins, current status and new directions. *Review of Educational Research, 59*(3), 249-70.

Appel, S. (1992). *Psychoanalysis and 'new' sociology of education: Positioning subjects.* Unpublished doctoral dissertation, University of Rochester, Rochester, NY.

Apple, M. (1979). *Ideology and curriculum.* London and Boston: Routledge & Kegan Paul.

Apple, M. (1982). *Economic and cultural reproduction in education.* London and Boston: Routledge & Kegan Paul.

Apple, M. (1993). *Official knowledge: Democratic education in a conservative age.* New York: Routledge.

Aronowitz, S. & Giroux, H. (1985). *Education under siege*. South Hadley, MA: Bergin & Garvey.

Aronowitz, S. & Giroux, H. (1991). *Postmodern education*. Minneapolis: University of Minnesota Press.

Benjamin, J. (1988). *The bonds of love*. New York: Pantheon Books.

Bernstein, B. (1990). *The structuring of pedagogic discourse*. London and New York: Routledge.

Blackburn, R. (1972). *Ideology in social science: Readings in critical social theory*. New York: Pantheon Books.

Bloom, H. (1975). *Kabbalah and criticism*. New York: Seabury Press.

Brown, N. (1959/85). *Life against death*. Middletown, CT: Wesleyan University Press.

Buber, M. (1925/65). Education: The development of the creative powers in the child. An address to the Third International Educational Conference, Heidelberg. In M. Buber, *Between man and man* (pp. 83-103). New York: Collier Books; Macmillan.

Buber, M. (1939/65). The education of character. Address given to the National Conference of Palestinian teachers. In M. Buber, *Between man and man* (pp. 104-117). New York: Collier Books; Macmillan.

Buber, M. (1963). *Israel and the world: Essays in a time of crisis*. New York: Schocken Books.

Buber, M. (1965). *Between man and man*. New York: Collier Books.

Buber, M. (1992). *On intersubjectivity and cultural creativity*. Chicago and London: University of Chicago Press.

Csikszentmihalyi, M. (1993). *The evolving self: A psychology for the third millennium*. New York: Harper Collins.

Dreeben, R. (1968). *On what is learned in school*. Reading, MA; Menlo Park, CA; and London; Ontario: Addison-Wesley.

Erikson, E. (1963). *Childhood and society*. New York: Norton.

Fauteux, K. (1994). *The recovery of self: Regression and redemption in religious experience*. New York; Mahwah, NJ: Paulist Press.

Fromm, E. (1976). *To have or to be*. New York: Bantam Books.

Gergen, K. (1994). *Realities and relationships: Soundings in social construction*. Cambridge, MA; London: Harvard University Press.

Gendlin, E. T. (1987). A philosophical critique of the concept of narcissism: The significance of the awareness movement. In D. M. Levin (Ed.), *Pathologies of the modern self: Postmodern studies on narcissism, schizophrenia, and depression*. New York: New York University Press.

Giroux, H. (1983). *Theory and resistance in education*. South Hadley, MA: Bergin & Garvey.

Gouldner, A. (1970). *The coming crisis of western sociology*. New York and London: Basic Books.

Handelman, S. (1991). *Fragments of redemption: Jewish thought and literary theory in Benjamin, Scholem, and Levinas*. Bloomington: Indiana University Press.

Horkheimer, M. & Adorno, T. W. (1972). *Dialectic of enlightenment*. New York: Herder and Herder.

Hunter, I. (1994). *Rethinking the school: Subjectivity, bureaucracy, criticism*. New York: St. Martin's Press.

Jay, G. & Graff, G. (1993). Some questions about critical pedagogy. *Newsletter of Teachers for a Democratic Culture, 3*(2), 2.

Levinas, E. (1994). *Outside the subject*. Stanford: Stanford University Press.

Lowy, M. (1992). *Redemption and utopia: Jewish libertarian thought in Central Europe*. Stanford: Stanford University Press.

McLaren, P. (1995). *Critical pedagogy and predatory culture*. London and New York: Routledge.

Merkur, D. (1993). *Gnosis: An esoteric tradition of mystical visions and unions*. Albany, NY: State University of New York Press.

Moore, T. (1992). *Care of the soul*. New York: Harper Collins.

Nemiroff, G. (1992). *Reconstructing education: Toward a pedagogy of critical humanism.* Toronto: OISE Press.

Parsons, T. (1953). *Working papers in the theory of action.* New York: Free Press.

Parsons, T. (1955). *Family, socialization, and interaction process.* Glencoe, IL: Free Press.

Ray, B. & Mickelson, R. (Eds.). (1989). Business leaders and the politics of school reforms. *Yearbook of the Politics of Education Association* (p. 120). New York: Falmer Press.

Reich, W. (1949). *Character analysis.* New York: Farrar, Straus, & Giroux.

Reich, W. (1961). *The function of the orgasm.* New York: Farrar, Straus, & Giroux.

Roof, W. C. (1993). *A generation of seekers: The spiritual journeys of the baby boom generation.* New York: Harper Collins.

Schmoker, M. (1992). What schools can learn from Toyota America. *Education Week, XI*(34), 23.

Smith, R. & Wexler, P. (1995). *After postmodernism: Education, politics and identity.* Washington, DC and London: Falmer Press.

Thompson, K. (1990). Secularization and sacralization. In J. C. Alexander & P. Sztompka (Eds.), *Rethinking progress: Movements, forces, and ideas at the end of the 20th century.* Boston, London, Sydney, Wellington: Unwin Hyman.

Weber, M. (1946). *From Max Weber: Essays in sociology* (H. H. Gerth & C. W. Mills, Trans.). New York: Oxford University Press.

Wexler, P. (1987). *Social analysis of education: After the new sociology.* London and New York: Routledge & Kegan Paul.

Wexler, P. (1992). *Becoming Somebody: Toward a Social psychology of school.* Washington, DC and London: Falmer Press.

Wexler, P. (1993/94). Educational corporatism and its counterposes. *Arena Journal, 8*(2), 175-194.

Wuthnow, R. (1992). *Rediscovering the sacred.* Michigan: William B. Michigan Eerdmans Publishing.

Chapter 12: Teachers As Innovators

JUDI RANDI, LYN CORNO[1]
Teachers College, Columbia University

The study of innovation has a history extending back to Plato:

> I notice endless innovation, constant change, inspired not by the laws but by a sort of unregulated taste which is so far from being fixed and permanent, that it never shows any constancy. (Laws: 2.660b)

To Plato, innovation was dangerous; practitioners at that time, particularly in education and the arts, were forbidden to innovate. Etymologically, the word, 'innovation' is derived from the Latin, *innovare* – to change something into something new. On the one hand, history has viewed innovation as a destructive force that disrupts the status quo. While on the other, innovation has been valued historically as a means toward progress and modernization (House, 1979).

Today, the study of innovation is world-wide. Rogers (1983), for example, chronicled numerous studies of the diffusion of innovations in the developing nations of Latin America, Africa, and Asia since the 1960s. Drawing on diffusion research in such diverse fields as anthropology, communication, economics, industrial engineering, medical sociology, public administration, and psychology as well as education, Rogers shows how these fields have construed innovations as specific products to be disseminated. In the adoption of new agricultural practices by farmers, for example, innovation was defined as 'an idea, practice, or object that is perceived as new by an individual or another unit of adoption' (1983, p. xviii). Further, the explicit purpose of these innovations was change, although not necessarily in response to a demonstrated need. Rogers also wrote: 'It matters little whether or not an innovation has a great degree of advantage over the idea it is replacing. What does matter is whether the individual perceives the relative advantage of the innovation' (1983, p. 24).

Business, in contrast, has viewed innovation as 'the specific tool of entrepreneurs, the means by which they exploit change as an opportunity for a different business or a different service' (Drucker, 1985, p. 19). The business world defined innovation in two ways:

a) something that has never been done before, and

B.J. Biddle et al. (eds.), International Handbook of Teachers and Teaching, 1163-1221
© *1997 Kluwer Academic Publishers, Printed in the Netherlands*

b) something that has never been done before by a particular company or industry now doing it (Levitt, 1983, pp. 200-201).

Levitt distinguished innovators from imitators of innovations. In the business world, Levitt argued, there was a place for 'creative imitation' as well as innovation. Drucker (1985) expanded on Levitt's concept of 'creative imitation.' Creative imitators improve and perfect the original innovation, as entrepreneurs, creative imitators, capitalize on existing markets rather than create new ones.

In education as in business and in other fields there has been considerable interest in innovation. The number and variety of studies focusing on innovation in education over the past three decades suggests that innovation has maintained prominence among those concerned with school improvement (Berman & McLaughlin, 1975, 1976; Crandall & Loucks, 1983; Goodlad, 1975; Gross, Giacquinta, & Bernstein, 1971; Huberman & Miles, 1984; McLaughlin, 1976; Smith, Dwyer, Prunty, & Kleine, 1988; Smith, Kleine, Prunty, & Dwyer, 1986; Smith, Prunty, Dwyer, & Kleine, 1987). During the 1970s, educational reform was characterized by the temporary adoption of a steady stream of externally developed innovations, sometimes politically motivated (Fullan & Miles, 1992). During the 1980s, educational reform placed greater emphasis on restructuring at the school site and the simultaneous implementation of multiple innovations (Fullan, 1993). Large-scale studies of school improvement documented adaptations of particular innovations during the process of implementation (Crandall & Loucks, 1983; Huberman & Miles, 1984). The replication of innovations, in theory, was expected to drive changes in practice; yet adaptation, not replication, was evidenced in practice (Bird, 1986; McLaughlin, 1976; McLaughlin & Marsh, 1978; Popkewitz, Tabachnick, & Wehlage, 1982).

At the classroom level, teachers' adaptations of instructional innovations have been studied from fundamentally contradictory perspectives. Those who see teaching as a set of routine procedures, and teachers as line workers whose efforts are to be planned and constrained, assume that instructional innovations can be uniformly implemented and that faithful implementation will result in improved teaching and learning. Those who view teaching as a complex task that takes into account students' needs and differences, and teachers as professionals who should be trusted to do their best for their 'clients,' see teachers' adaptations in a more favorable light (Fullan, Bennett, & Rolheiser-Bennett, 1990; Lieberman & Miller, 1986). This ambivalence about the role of the teacher in the implementation of curricular and instructional innovations pervades the education literature, and models for education reform have often reflected this contradiction.

Research is equally ambivalent about whether or not educational innovation improves teaching and learning. The diffusion of innovations as a vehicle for effecting change in education has been the focus of much research. Despite substantial investments in human and material resources, some research has found little evidence that the implementation of externally developed innovations actually improves schools (Cuban, 1990, 1993; Goodlad, 1984; McLaughlin, 1987). Berliner and Biddle (1995) argued that many reforms fail simply because they 'don't work.' In their review of reform ideas, these authors found few externally generated innovations based on research findings (see also Anderson & Biddle, 1991). On the other hand, schools and teachers are continually changing (Little & McLaughlin, 1993; Richardson, 1990). Lieberman and Miller (1986), for example, assign responsibility for the continuous improvement of schools to those closest to teaching and learning.

Another fundamental contradiction that has surfaced in the literature is a tension between institutionalization of particular innovations and the continuous improvement of schools. The tension between the implementation of specific innovations and the dynamics of change has been observed by several researchers concerned with educational change (Fullan et al., 1990; Miles, 1983). Lieberman and Miller (1986) cautioned, 'innovations cannot be sold as recipes' (p. 98). Change is not simply a matter of implementing innovations.

ORGANIZATION OF THE CHAPTER

This chapter explores these tensions between implementation and innovation through a critical review of selected literature. Our review identifies conflicts between implementing new ideas and crafting new ideas, between directed change and the endless possibilities for change. In the end we find the process of implementation of research-based innovations raises several important questions of interest to both researchers and practitioners: How have researchers documented and evaluated practitioners' adaptations and transformations of instructional innovations during the process of implementation? Has the press to 'measure' implementation constrained teachers as innovators? What have practitioners' adaptations revealed about researchers' and teachers' perceptions of the need for change? What has been the nature of the changes brought about by the diffusion of instructional innovations? When re-examined through the lens of innovation, what can practitioners' adaptations of instructional innovations reveal about how teachers learn?

To help address these questions, we bring together research from four distinct yet related bodies of literature: research on teacher implementation of innovations; studies of the diffusion of innovations as a teacher-change strategy; curriculum implementation research; and, research on teachers' knowledge and learning. In each of these areas, there has been a growing interest in how teachers change, learn, and bring new ideas to bear in their work with students. Taken together, these four bodies of literature serve to deepen our understanding, not only of how new knowledge is acquired and synthesized by teachers, but also how new instructional practices are invented by teachers in classrooms. It is not uncommon for researchers to hear parents or even students say 'the best teachers are creative.' Yet remarkably little systematic research has been done on creativity in teaching. In searching for such research, accordingly, we have had to review selected studies of implementation addressing practitioners' use of instructional innovations introduced in inservice programs.

In our section on teachers as innovators, we argue that what have often been documented as teachers' adaptations of innovations may have been teachers' innovations created in response to the contexts in which they work. We suggest that part of what teachers learn as they teach is to synthesize new ideas from instructional models they imitate. That is, teachers infer new knowledge and invent new practices based on instructional models introduced by researchers and others. Classroom innovations are thus co-constructed and socially derived. Our chapter concludes with teacher education and methodological considerations pertinent to our discussion of teachers as innovators.

IMPLEMENTATION PERSPECTIVES IN EDUCATIONAL RESEARCH

Our first body of literature focuses on the implementation and institutionalization of innovative practices. Early work generally defined implementation as a process relating to 'the extent to which organizational members have changed their behavior so that it is congruent with the behavior patterns required by the innovation' (Gross et al., 1971, p. 16). Implementation (from the Latin, *implere* – to use) also typically involves the use of an instructional innovation developed by someone other than the end-user.

Measuring Fidelity

In efforts to effect school change, the research-development-diffusion (RD&D) model has been used extensively. This model is highly prescriptive and assumes that teachers are passive consumers of the products of educational research (Havelock, in House, 1979). Studies of implementation using this model generally measured the degree of fidelity (i.e., the extent to which the user implemented the innovation as planned by the developer) as well as the processes of implementation (i.e., the organizational changes and supports that account for the degree of implementation) (Scheirer & Rezmovic, 1983).

One major study supporting this view of implementation examined how well educational models introduced through staff development had been implemented (Stallings, 1979). Seven educational models were studied, each representing an innovative educational theory or program. The models were disseminated in Project Follow-Through, a field-based inservice teacher training program. To assess implementation, data were collected from classroom observations of some 271 teachers and self-reports of 231 teachers. A detailed low-inference Classroom Observation Instrument was developed to record information about the physical environment of the classroom, groupings of children and staff, and teacher-student interactions. Stallings concluded that the models were generally well-implemented and that, therefore, Project Follow-Through was an effective vehicle for teacher training. The effectiveness of the training was directly related to the teachers' degree of 'consistency with the goals of the model within which they worked' (p. 165). Fidelity to a particular model was described by Stallings as 'a great tribute to the sponsors who had set out to train teachers in diverse locations to behave in some very specific ways' (p. 165). This research perspective was consistent with teacher effectiveness research of the 1970s that focused on changing teacher behavior through the acquisition of specific skills. However, other research on teacher effectiveness conducted during this period found that teachers did not maintain fidelity to treatments, even in the context of controlled experiments (Crawford et al., 1978).

One study suggested that teachers may have been reluctant to implement treatments they considered inappropriate for their particular students. Anderson, C.Everston, and Brophy (1979) studied the relationship between implementation of effective practices and student outcomes and demonstrated the importance of teacher judgment in implementing principles of effective instruction. In this experimental study, the researchers provided 17 first grade teachers with instruction in 22 principles believed to promote effective instruction in small groups. Ten other teachers served as a control group. Teachers were observed weekly for six months, and student achievement data were collected using standardized measures of reading comprehension in a pre-post design. The treatment did not prescribe specific behavior but rather instructed teachers in general principles of effective instruction and the underlying rationale:

> In this study teacher behaviors were examined in a more natural way, because the study used the materials, the schedules, the lessons, and the settings that already existed in the schools. The teachers who served in the treatment group were asked to follow certain principles of instruction, but no attempt was made to determine exactly what the teacher was to say or do at any given time. (p. 194)

The study found poor implementation of several principles by the treatment group as well as low natural use by the control group. In explaining this finding, the authors suggested that the techniques prescribed in this study may not be ap-

propriate for first grade instruction. The study documented teachers' application of general principles of effective teaching to a specific context. No
interviews were conducted to determine teachers' reasons for non-implementa-
tion or whether or not teachers found discussion of the rationale helpful for
making decisions about use of the principles. Nonetheless, the study demonstrated that 'the process of translation and implementation is as worthy of investigation as the original research on effective teaching' (Anderson et al., 1979,
p. 194).

Measures of implementation have evaluated, and by extrapolation valued,
the replication of innovations, not innovation itself. Although measures of fidelity may be appropriate for evaluating the implementation of specific innovations, such measures are not appropriate for investigating how and why teachers
applied (or chose not to apply) particular innovations in their classrooms (Fullan, 1983). As of the early 1980s, there was little understanding of teachers'
points of view.

Practitioners' Perspectives

The success of the RD&D model depended on the willingness of practitioners
to replicate innovations in their classrooms. Teachers' attitudes toward the implementation of innovations thus became one focus of implementation research.
Doyle and Ponder (1977) conceptualized teachers' decision-making in the implementation of innovations and established the need for considering the role of
teacher decision-making in the adoption of innovations. The work also recognized that the implementation process, and in particular the evaluation component, generated a 'set of control mechanisms which are typically absent from
the normal teaching environment' and that 'such mechanisms increase teacher
passivity and suspend normal teacher reactions to improvement directions' (p.
3). Based on these assumptions, Doyle and Ponder suggested that teachers responded to innovations favorably or not based on consideration of three factors.
These they labelled instrumentality, congruence, and cost. First, teachers decided on the practicality of the innovation, considering whether the innovation allowed for classroom contingencies. Second, teachers decided whether the
innovation was congruent with their current educational philosophy and practices. Third, teachers weighed the costs of implementation and decided whether
the extra time and effort would benefit their students.

Doyle and Ponder's work provided a framework for subsequent studies of
teachers' attitudes toward implementation of innovations. Mohlman, Coladarci,
and Gage (1982) reviewed the results of five experimental studies of teacher effectiveness and interpreted them in light of Doyle and Ponder's thesis. Their
goal was to 'discover not only which teacher behaviors are most effective but

also why teachers do or do not adopt recommended teaching practices' (p. 31). The authors concluded that congruence, instrumentality, and cost did influence teachers' implementation practices.

Guskey (1988) also investigated teachers' attitudes toward instructional innovations. In a correlational study, Guskey administered a questionnaire to 120 elementary and secondary teachers participating in a staff development program on mastery learning instructional strategies. Guskey found that effective teachers were more receptive to innovations and that teacher efficacy and self-confidence were related to teachers' attitudes in regard to the instrumentality, congruence, and cost of implementing the recommended practice. Building on attitude change theory, Guskey hypothesized that effective teachers may find a particular program congruent because they are most likely incorporating aspects of the innovation into their current teaching practices. Guskey's study illustrated the importance of differentiating outcomes produced by the innovation from outcomes produced by effective teachers, as well as the role of teacher judgment in deciding whether or not to use an innovation.

The teachers' attitude toward innovations was a person variable that affected implementation; the design of inservice activities was an aspect of the environment likely to have both independent and interactive effects. Sparks (1986) studied the relationship between types of inservice activities and changes in teaching behavior. In a quasi-experimental study, Sparks provided inservice in effective teaching strategies to three groups of junior high teachers. One group attended only inservice workshops. Another group also participated in peer observations, and a third group received coaching from the trainer in addition to the workshops. The 19 participating teachers studied were observed using a measure of academic interactions before and after the treatment. Quantitative measures were supplemented by the collection of qualitative data through interviews, observation logs, and anecdotal records. The study found that four of the six teachers needing improvement in the peer observation group reached the criterion set for effectiveness, and two improved to slightly below the criterion. Sparks concluded that the peer observation training activities appeared to be more powerful than coaching or workshop sessions alone. Sparks cautioned, however, that these results might have occurred not because of differences in training alone. It is likely that other differences (such person variables as the age or attitudes of the teachers) exert combined effects with treatments that quasi-experimental designs do not control.

One important factor in this study was the use of qualitative data to inform the quantitative results. Qualitative data enabled the researcher to explain variations in teachers' interaction patterns. For example, 'seatwork' lessons naturally had low interaction levels. Sparks, therefore, concluded that quantitative measures of implementation were insufficient to determine the extent of implementation by particular teachers. Sparks maintained that 'close examination of observation data in light of qualitative data yields insights into the measurement and interpretation of teaching behavior.... Merely examining averages of three observation occasions may hide rich information about teachers' daily activities' (p. 220-221). This study was another indication that measures of implementation typically used in teacher effectiveness research were inadequate for assessing the appropriate use of the innovation in classrooms.

Recognizing Adaptation as a Goal

The replication of innovations was, in theory, intended to change practice. Adaptation of innovations, however, proved more likely to occur (Berman & McLaughlin, 1976). The increasing numbers of studies of educational change documenting the adaptation of innovations have led researchers to question the necessity, desirability, and feasibility of fidelity of implementation as a goal. The adaptation perspective, however, has proven no less problematic than the fidelity perspective. Researchers differ in their conclusions about the role of adaptation in the change process (Loucks, 1983). In their RAND-sponsored study of the implementation of federally mandated programs, Berman and McLaughlin (1976) argued that mutual adaptation by users (i.e., adaptation of both the innovation and the organizational setting) was not only necessary but desirable: 'To implement significant innovations, there must be a process of mutual adaptation' (p. 349). McLaughlin (1976) also maintained that local adaptation was critical to the implementation process. Other researchers cautioned that 'fiddling with a project to improve the fit between the school and the innovation can often trivialize results' (Huberman & Miles, 1986, p. 76).

Some researchers found that practitioners' adaptations often resembled existing practices. Popkewitz et al. (1982) reported on the process of adaptation in six schools implementing Individually Guided Education, a curriculum that was responsive to student individual differences. Their descriptive research found that reforms in some schools were 'illusory' because schools had adapted the new practices to conform to existing norms and therefore conserved the practices that the reforms were intended to change.

Bird (1986) described a process of mutual adaptation in which both the innovation and the adopting organization underwent transformation. Bird described the implementation of the Delinquency Prevention Research and Development Program as a case of 'mutual adaptation.' In that program, schools were created within schools to alter teaching practices, increase school success, reduce anonymity, and involve parents. Although Bird recognized that mutual adaptation sometimes resulted in 'a reduction in the integrity of the innovation and perhaps in the integrity of the host school as well' (p. 47), the situation differed when mutual adaptation resulted in improvement in both the innovation and the school:

> There is a limit to adaptation beyond which little good, particularly little replicable good, can be expected. What is required is a solution, an organization of the innovation and the school, in which the essential requirements of both are met. This is not likely to be a simple graft or attrition of the two. It is likely to be a third, new creation. (p. 47)

In this view, mutual adaptation led to creation of new practices. This perspective suggested that teachers engaged in the thoughtful practice of adaptation might become originators of new practices.

Measuring Adaptation

The study of the educational change process has also contributed to the planning and evaluation of educational innovations. Fullan (1983) maintained that the process of implementation compelled developers to be more precise in defining and operationalizing components of their programs. Fullan argued that the degree of adaptation required at the adoption site was a measure of the program's worth; 'modifications in use may reflect or signal needed improvements in the program itself' (p. 221). This perspective contributes to the conception of teacher as innovator in assigning the practitioner a part in evaluating and redesigning the innovation. Measures of implementation, however, generally continued to focus on the degree of implementation.

Recognizing that teachers adapted innovations in classroom practice, the Research and Development Center for Teacher Education at the University of Texas in Austin (Hord & Hall, 1986) developed the Concerns-Based Adoption Model (CBAM) as an instrument to monitor changes in teachers' attitudes toward innovation as well as teachers' level of use of the innovation. The CBAM instruments included the Stages of Concern, Levels of Use, and Practice Profiles. These instruments were and continue to be widely used in the evaluation of teacher inservice programs (Loucks-Horsley & Steigelbauer, 1991).

The Practice Profile, originally the Innovation Configuration, was developed to fill the need for a standardized instrument for comparing components of one practice to another (Loucks & Crandall, 1982). The instrument operationally defined each component of an innovation as well as variations of the components. That is, 'Practice Profiles' were developed for particular innovations and were used to describe the various forms of an innovation that resulted when the innovation was practiced by users in their individual situations (Hord & Hall, 1986). The instrument recognized that teachers modified innovations in practice but implied that fidelity to the innovation was the 'ideal' practice. The instrument was designed to categorize three types of implementation practices: 'ideal' use of the innovation, 'acceptable' variations, and 'unacceptable' practices. The Practice Profile was developed during a process of negotiation between the innovation's developer and practitioners who used the innovation. 'Acceptable' variations were negotiated with the program's developer (Hord, 1986).

The Levels of Use Chart (LoU) measured implementation of innovations at the individual user level (Hall & Loucks, 1977). Unlike the Practice Profile that defined the innovation, the LoU instrument defined the behavior of users as they became more adept at using the innovation. The LoU Chart represented a developmental growth continuum; levels of use ranged from 'non-use' to 're-newal' (Hall, Loucks, Rutherford, & Newlove, 1975). Implicit in the continuum was a hierarchy of professional growth that culminated in a practitioner's demonstrated ability to reconceptualize an innovation in response to the needs of clients.

Researchers provided an example of a teacher using an innovation at the re-newal level (Hord, Rutherford, Huling-Austin, & Hall, 1987). The teacher was described as exploring the possibility of borrowing some ideas from the innovation and using them in 'combination with the traditional as a synthesis of the old and new' (Hord et al., 1987, p. 62). Such teachers were recognized as a 'positive force' but were not encouraged to replace or significantly modify the original innovation. In the RD&D model, such practices tended to be 'disruptive to the efforts of the facilitator who is attempting to help users attain maximum effective use of the innovation' (p. 69). Inherent in the instrument was the recognition that some teachers invented new practices by synthesizing new and old, but these teachers did so with little support for innovation.

Teachers' Adaptations

Thus researchers (McLaughlin, 1976; McLaughlin & Marsh, 1978) began to re-define implementation as a process in which practitioners actively engaged in adapting instructional innovations to their particular classroom settings and to the 'day-to-day realities of the school and classroom' (McLaughlin & Marsh, 1978, p. 77). Since that point there has been a proliferation of studies investigating the individual teacher's role in the implementation of innovations. Although researchers differ in their conclusions about why teachers adapt innovations, the number and diversity of explanations reflects a growing concern for the complex and dynamic environments in which teachers work. Viewed through the lens of innovation, these studies also offer insight into factors that may constrain or encourage innovative teachers.

For those who see teaching as a complex task responsive to the dynamic contexts of classrooms, change involves more than just the replication of others' innovations. Guskey (1990) encouraged educators to broaden the definition of implementation to include the synthesis of innovative strategies. He assigned the task of integration to practitioners, including making decisions about which innovations to use, understanding how to integrate them, and translating synthesis into classroom practice. Guskey implied that integration is a form of innovation when practitioners are individually challenged to determine 'optimal combinations for particular settings' (p. 14). Integration and synthesis required an understanding of the principles of teaching and learning as well as knowledge about the design process. In emphasizing the replication and application of particular instructional models, traditional forms of staff development have tended to neglect the general theories of teaching and learning that undergird more than one model and left teachers to infer theory from practice.

One study differentiated teachers with only procedural knowledge about the innovation from teachers with theoretical knowledge (Amarel & Chittenden, 1982). In this study, the authors viewed teachers' adaptations as indications of responsive teaching. The researchers studied the relationship between school organizational practices and teachers' knowledge use in the implementation of a reading program in four urban schools. School sites were purposively selected to include schools that differed in the degree of authority of the central board. In their descriptive study, Amarel and Chittenden interviewed teachers and school officials, observed teachers in informal classroom visits, observed faculty meetings related to program implementation, and collected documents. Additionally, three teachers and three reading specialists were asked to respond to tape-recorded samples of children reading aloud. In this performance task simulating in-class activities, the researchers asked teachers what they gained from the sample and how that information was or was not relevant to their practice.

The researchers found that differences in the organizational structure of the school district paralleled differences in implementation. The researchers analyzed differences in the ways teachers implemented curriculum, including interactions between school factors and fundamental differences in teachers' knowledge base. In centrally controlled schools, teachers were observed implementing programs procedurally (i.e., as planned by the developers). When these teachers did alter the program, the modifications were within guidelines acceptable to program originators. These teachers became 'boxed in' by the rules and procedures of the program and did not bypass procedural requirements of the program, even when students had difficulty. For example, one such teacher required students, despite apparent difficulty, to continue to identify sounds before proceeding to the phonetic program. Teachers judged to have theoretical knowledge, on the other hand, were found in more autonomous schools. Referring to principles of teaching and learning, these teachers used student feedback and classroom interactions to modify curriculum and respond to student needs. One such teacher, for example, moved students into other reading materials when she observed they were spending too much time trying to sound out words. She explained that she did this to regain students' interest and focus their attention on meaning.

Amarel and Chittenden concluded that prescriptive programs characterized by centrally controlled decision making minimized the role of teachers' theoretical knowledge and discouraged interactive teaching. Emphasis on replication of procedures, the researchers pointed out, raised concerns about the consequences of prescription for the development of competent teachers.

Other studies viewed teachers' adaptations less favorably. Olson (1981) described teachers' adaptations of innovations as attempts to 'translate' the innovation into more familiar terms and maintain control over the curriculum. Olson interviewed eight teachers implementing an integrated, 'discovery approach' science curriculum in three different schools. Teachers were asked to discuss what they thought about the curriculum project and how they coped with problems encountered as they implemented the curriculum. The assumption underlying Olson's study was that teachers faced dilemmas in attempting to implement innovative practices, and the teachers' language was analyzed for evidence of such dilemmas.

Olson concluded that teachers modified the new curriculum because they were uncomfortable with a curriculum that afforded teachers 'low influence' over curriculum and instruction. The innovative science curriculum was termed 'low influence' because of its emphasis on student-centered discovery learning. This style of teaching contrasted with 'high influence,' teacher-centered instruction that was more familiar to the teachers. Olson found that the teachers lacked a clear language and models for low influence teaching. Teachers, therefore, 'domesticated' the new curriculum to make it more congruent with their usual practices. This research may speak to the importance of models in influencing teachers' instructional practices, whether the models are found in current familiar practices or introduced as new ideas.

Thus, incongruities between the familiar and the new were offered as reasons for teachers' adaptations. Like Doyle and Ponder (1977) and Guskey (1988), Olson found teachers less likely to implement innovations that are significantly different from their current practices. But Olson (1980) also presented a view of teachers trying to adapt innovations to accomplish purposes other than those intended by the developer. Although Olson drew a sharp distinction between teacher and innovator, the teacher essentially became the innovator during the process of adaptation:

An innovation is in the eye of the beholder. What the innovator makes of the innovation simply isn't what the user will make of it. How teachers do their work is usually well-related to what the teacher thinks is important in that work. The use of innovative ideas will be appraised in relation to the existing goals and techniques of the teacher. (pp. 3-4)

Olson (1980) reviewed Doyle and Ponder's (1977) typology that drew our attention to the importance of teachers' attitudes in the implementation of instructional innovations. Olson found a number of difficulties in their perspective: First, innovations were often presented as 'things ready to elicit types of adoption behaviour' rather than as new ideas (p. 3). Second, problems in implementation were attributed to lack of instruction about how to make the innovation work. This view assumes that innovators and teachers construe instructional practice in the same way. Third, teachers were viewed as resisting change – a view that implies that teachers need to change. Teachers saw the innovation as a tool to accomplish their goals; innovators saw the innovation as a means to change teachers' practice. To change teachers' practices, rather than focusing on specific behaviors, Olson recommended focusing on teachers' beliefs and what teachers understand the idea of the innovation to be. Olson's research also demonstrated that the developer's innovations often do not serve the purposes practitioners have in mind. Although Olson recommended changing teachers' beliefs, his emphasis remained on changing the teachers' beliefs to conform to someone else's idea of what instruction should be.

In more recent studies, teachers continued to adapt the instructional practices they were asked to implement, and researchers continued to ask why. Wilson (1990) studied one teacher implementing the California Mathematics Curriculum Framework (CMCF). Through classroom observations and interviews, Wilson documented how that teacher transformed the innovative math curriculum into the traditional math curriculum that was more familiar to him. Like Olson (1980), Wilson also interpreted the teacher's adaptations as responses to the incongruity between new and old teaching practices. In Wilson's case study, the teacher's understanding of mathematics as a set of procedures was incongruent with the philosophy of the framework that focused on teaching for understanding.

Unlike Olson (1980), Wilson, however, uncovered other reasons for the teacher's adaptations. Wilson suggested that the teacher adapted materials because of lack of time, the press to prepare students for state-mandated tests that were not yet aligned with the new framework, the teacher's own limited knowledge of the framework, and the instructional strategies supportive of teaching for understanding. The teacher, according to Wilson, sincerely believed he was following the CMCF text but he was not implementing the spirit of the framework. This interpretation suggested that the teacher was imitating the model without understanding it.

Incongruity between beliefs and new practices was one explanation research offered for teachers' adaptations. Hearing mixed messages was another. McTaggart (1989) conducted a case study in one school district implementing an Aesthetics Project. The intent of the study was to 'portray the ways in which the commitment to privacy functioned to inhibit teachers' learning from each other, and to confound the diffusion of a curriculum innovation' (p. 347). McTaggart interviewed two teachers who served as resources to their colleagues in the implementation of an aesthetics curriculum supported by the administration but funded by a local benefactor. McTaggart then analyzed conditions in the school district and suggested that factors implicit in the teachers' working conditions served as obstacles to teachers' learning from each other.

McTaggart found that, despite the expertise and commitment of the two teachers who had been trained as project advocates, few teachers used the teacher-advocates as resources. The study concluded that the district administration, despite overt support for the new curriculum, sent covert messages to teachers that impeded the implementation of the aesthetics project. Aesthetics achievement, for example, was not measured in curriculum evaluation processes; rather, teachers were accountable for student achievement in the 'basics.'

The district sent other messages to the teachers as well. In this district, teachers participated in the selection of curriculum materials, but then – once materials were selected – teachers were required to implement the curriculum uniformly across schools. McTaggart interpreted teachers' participation in curriculum efforts as a form of bureaucratic control that devalued the knowledge of teachers: 'Reliable knowledge in the Brenton School district was knowledge which facilitated centralized control. That knowledge came from the trusted technologies of positivistic science' (p. 359).

In a district where 'teachers' knowledge claims were considered spurious and indefensible' (p. 359), teachers' individual instructional practices, including action research, risked coming into conflict with established practices and shared district traditions. McTaggart found few action research efforts and these were individualistic. According to McTaggart, teachers retreated to the privacy of their classrooms to engage in teacher research and innovation – practices that were not valued in the settings in which they worked. But McTaggart cautioned,

> It is obviously difficult to establish causal links between the conditions outlined above and the paucity of action research, the limited momentum of aesthetic education, a commitment to privatism, or teachers' deference to other knowledge authorities. (p. 359)

This warning about the limitations of qualitative research for informing statements about causality too often goes unheeded. We shall return to a discussion of methodology later in this chapter. Nevertheless, McTaggart's case study underscores the need for research on organizational factors that may constrain or support innovative teaching.

The Role of Practitioners in the Change Process

Innovation has occupied a central role in the change process. Yet, seldom have teachers been encouraged to innovate. Instead, teachers have been expected to implement others' ideas in practice. The view of teachers as technicians (Mitchell & Kirchner, 1983) assigned to researchers the task of generating new instructional practices and to teachers the task of implementing them. This sharp distinction between research and practice left the educational marketplace open for innovators outside the classroom. Consequently, educational reform has been characterized by consumerism (Little, 1993) and the temporary adoption by practitioners of a steady stream of externally generated innovations (Fullan & Miles, 1992).

Taking innovation out of the hands of practitioners has done little to stem the tide of unregulated change. On the contrary, John Dewey (1904) implied 90 years ago that the contributions of teachers themselves might replace the constant stream of externally generated innovations.

> The tendency of educational development to proceed by reaction from one thing to another, to adopt for one year, or for a term of seven years, this or that new study or method of teaching, and then as abruptly to swing over to some new educational gospel, is a result which would be impossible if teachers were adequately moved by their own independent intelligence.... If teachers were possessed by the spirit of an abiding student of education, this spirit would find some way of breaking through the mesh and coil of circumstance and would find expression for itself. (p. 16)

Teachers have had little support for 'breaking through the mesh and coil of circumstance.' The hierarchical transmission model discouraged 'the exercise of critical intelligence' by teachers (Berlak & Berlak, 1981, p. 234). In general, the widespread use of generic programs developed by outside experts (Little, 1989) together with the persistent use of measures of implementation has targeted teachers as passive consumers, focusing teachers' attention on learning to use specific strategies rather than solving complex and chronic problems (Fullan & Miles, 1992), contributing to simple applications of research findings, and discouraging innovation at the classroom level.

Preparing Teachers to Implement Innovations

Not surprisingly, the content and design of staff development paralleled the changing perspectives in implementation research. The educational change process introduced a new role for staff development (McLaughlin & Marsh, 1978; Zumwalt, 1986). In this role, staff development was not a means of correcting deficiencies. Rather, the adaptation process itself was a learning experience as staff adjusted the innovation to local needs. Staff development, according to McLaughlin and Marsh (1978), played an important role in facilitating the change process through the provision of specific skill training and ongoing support from consultants during the implementation stage.

Despite the growing interest in teaching as reflective practice (Schon, 1983) and calls for reform at the individual classroom level, however, staff development has seldom supported teachers in becoming critical readers of research. Nor has staff development acknowledged teachers' contributions to the knowledge base of teaching (Lieberman & Miller, 1992). Little (1993) noted that 'an invitation to teachers to act not only as consumers of research but also as critics of research and producers of research' was missing from professional development programs (p. 16). Staff development has supported teachers in learning to implement innovations, but few staff development programs have assisted teachers in learning to innovate.

Consistent with the view of teachers as passive consumers of research, transfer of training became a goal of inservice programs. The content of staff development focused almost exclusively on the dissemination of the products of educational research (Little, 1989). Moreover, the training design facilitated replication of specific teaching behaviors. The 'theory, demonstration, and practice' training design has dominated staff development programs for more than a decade (Joyce & Showers, 1980). Measures of implementation became increasingly important as measures of the effectiveness of staff development programs (Castle, 1988; Marshall, 1988; Patton, 1982).

But the transfer of training from workshop to classroom proved difficult to accomplish, and implementation did not guarantee improved student outcomes (Gage, 1984). Research on teaching and learning contributed to new understandings of professional development. In 1991, McLaughlin, for example, revisited her earlier assumptions about staff development and the change process. Recognizing that teaching and learning are embedded in classroom and school contexts and that teachers and students co-construct the curriculum, McLaughlin concluded that 'narrowly focused special projects ... are incompatible with the daily realities confronting teachers and administrators' (p. 69). The differing contexts of teaching and the skill of the teacher became important considerations: 'Educators should not go about blindly doing what research says' (Sparks & Simmons, 1989, p. 126). Teachers need to know how and when to apply the research (Sparks & Simmons, 1989). Neither the content nor the deductive training design has assisted teachers in acquiring a deep understanding of the research to enable them to apply the strategies appropriately without additional support.

The Role of Coaching

Coaching has played a significant role in staff development training, not only because it has encouraged implementation of newly learned strategies, but more importantly because it has assisted practitioners in applying specific innovations appropriately. According to Glathorn (1987), one function of coaching is to assist the practitioner to adapt new strategies to the needs of individual students and settings. Implementation of new strategies requires teachers to analyze the effects of innovations and adjust teaching accordingly (Wu, 1988). Thus, coaching has become a critical component in the design of many staff development programs (Joyce & Showers, 1981, 1982, 1988; Showers, 1984).

Generally, models and examples presented in training sessions – workshops – demonstrated the use of the strategy (procedural knowledge) but were seldom accompanied by explicit instruction in when and why to implement the strategy (conditional knowledge) (Zumwalt, 1986). Coaching contributed to a deeper understanding of the theory and appropriate uses of the research-based instructional strategies modelled in the workshops (Joyce & Showers, 1988). A study by Pasch and Harberts (1992) assessed the impact of one district's staff development program over a two-year period. Twelve 'high need' elementary schools were chosen on the basis of low student achievement on standardized test scores. From these 12 schools, two were selected based on the proportion of teachers who agreed to participate in the evaluation. In addition to data collected from classroom observations, interviews were conducted with 15 randomly selected teachers from participating schools four times during the two-year study. Based on the Taxonomy of Teacher Reflective Thought (Sparks-Langer, Simmons, Pasch, Colton, & Starko, 1990), the interviews did indeed measure teachers' reflective thinking.

These researchers found that increases in teachers' levels of reflective thinking occurred only after the teachers were observed and coached in the classroom. They also reported gains in student achievement on standardized tests in both language arts and math exceeding the district average. Student achievement gains cannot be attributed to the staff development program in this study, however, because staff development was one of several initiatives (e.g., business partnerships, school improvement plans) in each school designed to improve student achievement.

The researchers concluded that coaching encouraged a deeper level of analysis and that 'when internalization and problem-solving opportunities are absent, behavior changes by teachers in the classroom cannot be expected' (Pasch & Harberts, 1992, p. 44). In contrast to the training design, coaching provided an inductive thinking model. Teachers were encouraged to analyze teaching episodes, isolate critical attributes of the new strategy, and identify what worked, why, and under what conditions. In essence, coached teachers reconstructed for themselves the theory underlying the newly acquired strategy. Such actions are not unlike the tasks of qualitative researchers discovering theory (Duckworth, 1986) or other examples of discovery learning (Cronbach & Snow, 1977).

Summary

Gradually, the focus of research on teacher implementation of innovations has shifted from measuring fidelity to investigating teachers' implementation practices. Whether approached from the fidelity or adaptation perspective, the RD&D model or diffusion paradigm directed change toward the use of particular innovations. Change is narrowly defined and measured in terms of the targeted innovation, and – regardless of the perspective – teachers have still been expected to change their practices to conform to the ideas of external change agents.

THE DIFFUSION PARADIGM AND TEACHER CHANGE

In retrospect, the diffusion of innovations as an approach to change has been the focus of much debate. We take this up here in our second body of literature. On the one hand, the replication of specific innovations has done little to change practice (Bussis, Chittenden, & Amarel, 1976; Popkewitz et al., 1982). On the other, the diffusion paradigm has been responsible for endless change. The last three decades have been characterized by a series of recurring educational reforms (Cuban, 1990).

Advocating change, reformers called for the institutionalization of innovations. But this was a Holy Grail. For each new innovation replaced a previously established one. Institutionalization implies maintenance of an established custom, not continuous change in response to identified needs. Institutionalizing one innovation after another was not consistent with norms of continual improvement (Miles, 1983). More than a decade after the RAND Change Agent Study, McLaughlin (1990) reinterpreted the results of that effort. She concluded that 'single-focus assumptions implicit in special projects are inconsistent with schools and classrooms' (p. 15). The implementation of specific innovations could actually diminish an organization's effectiveness when innovations become ends in themselves and serve as diversions from goals of continuous improvement.

McLaughlin's conclusion raises questions fundamental to the nature of innovation itself. The history of educational innovation has demonstrated that innovations quickly become old ideas replaced by 'new' innovations; and, 'innovations' that have withstood the test of time are no longer 'innovations.' McGuffey's readers, for example, were once considered innovative.

Further, whether or not a particular innovation should last is often an issue of values rather than the effectiveness of the innovation itself. In a long-term ethnographic study of the Milford School District, Smith et al. (1971, 1986, 1987, 1988) studied innovation within the context of one school district, in one particular school. The authors defined innovation as 'specific, planned, improved change' (Smith et al., 1988, p. 337). 'Improved' implied a theory of values, and innovations tended to be treated as 'all good' or 'all bad.'

> The all good group tend to be true believers with the one right way which they are currently advocating. The all bad group tends [sic] to be those with minimal power, frequently teachers, who are having the innovation done to or on them, with or without their consent. (p. 336)

Through interviews with staff members and analyses of Board of Education minutes, the authors traced the sixty-five year history of the Milford School District. Founded as an 'innovative' school in 1964-65, Kensington School flourished under the leadership of an 'innovative' principal and superintendent. The early days of Kensington were characterized by open classrooms, team teaching, and independent learning in classroom environments supplied with a variety of instructional resources and new technologies. As the original leaders left and community demographics changed, however, Kensington reverted to the conservative ideals of the old Milford type – ideals that the 'innovative' Kensington had once replaced. Walls were constructed to create more traditional classroom spaces; textbooks, workbooks, and direct instruction replaced the enriched learning environments of the original Kensington.

Apparently, competing ideologies and changing circumstances have accounted for much of the recurring reforms in American education. Cuban (1993) charted 90 years of educational reform in America. Throughout this time, two opposing educational philosophies, one teacher-centered, the other student-centered, vied for attention in the educational arena. Cuban offered six explanations for the persistence of teacher-centered practices despite efforts to implement more student-centered practices:

1) Beliefs about the nature of knowledge, how teaching should occur, and how children should learn are embedded in our culture; these beliefs influence policy makers, practitioners, parents, and citizens toward certain forms of instruction.

2) The organization and practice of schools tend to sort students into various socioeconomic levels.

3) Educational policy makers, at times, ineffectively implemented reforms aimed at changing teachers instructional practices.

4) The organizational structure of schools shaped teachers' instructional practices.

5) The cultures of teaching tend toward stability in instructional patterns.

6) Teachers' knowledge of subject matter and their personal and professional beliefs influence their instructional practices

Although teacher-centered practices have persisted, Cuban cited some instances where, despite bureaucratic controls, many teachers found ways to make structural changes in their classrooms and move gradually toward more student-centered practices. Cuban called these 'hybrid versions' of the two educational traditions:

> These teacher-invented mixtures of teacher-centeredness and student-centeredness varied from classroom, from subject to subject, from school to school, and from district to district. Such mixtures seldom satisfied ardent reformers fighting for student-centered instruction. Slight modifications in routine practices appeared as failures to these reformers. (p. 277)

As Cuban suggested, the definition of change often escaped researchers and policy makers. Policy makers had difficulty determining whether change had actually occurred when externally developed innovations were modified by practitioners. And, thus far, 'the researcher's view of change counts far more among policy makers than the teacher's view' (p. 287).

Despite the introduction of externally developed innovations and externally imposed controls, the classroom teacher has always played an active role in designing curriculum (Connelly & Ben-Peretz, 1980; Corno, 1977); the improvement of teaching and learning depends on teachers (Lieberman & Miller, 1986). But, as Smith et al. (1988) have demonstrated, what constitutes 'improved instruction' is a matter of value and which innovation prevails is often a matter of power. Despite the efforts of some teachers to create learner-centered classrooms where curriculum grows out of students' interests, conservative policy-makers with a different view of 'improved instruction' continue to impose more control over teachers and teaching through the institution of the national and state curriculum, national standards, and assessments that hold teachers and students accountable. These too are 'innovations' that teachers have been 'encouraged' to implement.

Cohen (1988) also reviewed the history of failed educational reforms and found competing ideologies at the heart of the problem. Failed reforms, Cohen argued, could not be attributed to the organizational structures of schools or the conditions of teaching. Innovative practices were no more abundant in private schools that, for the most part, freed teachers from bureaucratic constraints. Instead, Cohen looked to teaching from a perspective of practice to account for repeated failures of school reform.

From the perspective of practice, Cohen found teaching essentially a practice of human improvement characterized by dependent clients and uncertain results. Unlike in other practices of human improvement, however, teachers do not select their clients, making it more difficult and risky for teachers 'to press their clients for serious improvement' (p. 50). In organizations where clients are selected for their willingness to work or the likelihood of success, practitioners depend less on their own personal resources. Teachers, on the other hand, cope every day with insoluble problems with few organizational supports and many risks.

Current reforms calling for more adventurous teaching reflect, as Cohen argues, the continuing struggle between traditional and innovative modes of instruction. Changing traditional instructional practice is not only difficult for teachers; many parents and students cling to traditional notions of teaching and learning as well. To change teaching requires an understanding of both research and practice. Reformers must understand the implications of change for practice, and teachers need to be aware of the demands that reform would make on practice. Like Cuban, Cohen also implied that meaningful change involved a blend of two traditions. Researchers and practitioners would need to arrive at a mutually agreed upon definition of change.

Reviewing the research on teacher change and learning to teach, Richardson (1990) asked three questions: 'Who is in control of change? What is the focus of change? What is significant and worthwhile practice?' Richardson concluded that the content of change should emanate both from the practical knowledge held by teachers and empirical knowledge derived from research. Richardson (1990, 1991) argued that teachers were not resistant to change but to externally imposed innovations, many of which they could not justify in light of the demands of practice. Teachers continually and voluntarily changed their practice in response to the contexts in which they worked. Acknowledging the role of teachers' knowledge and beliefs in learning new practices, Richardson (1990) affirmed that experience 'is an extremely potent teacher' (p. 12).

Describing the University of Arizona Reading Instruction Study (Richardson & Anders, 1990), Richardson concluded that teachers often based their decisions to try new practices on 'what works.' Richardson (1990) explained, 'Working for the teachers in our study meant that the activities did not violate the teachers' beliefs about teaching and learning' (p. 14). Richardson described teachers' knowledge as highly contextualized and resembling no single theory of reading comprehension. Likewise, decontextualized and theoretical descriptions of practices made no sense to the teachers Richardson studied. Richardson concluded that research should provide teachers, not just with specific activities and behaviors that work, but with empirical knowledge related to teaching and learning that, in turn, becomes a context for re-examining their own theoretical frameworks.

Richardson (1992) described one such staff development program that provided teachers with opportunities for examining their own practice. Richardson studied changes in teachers' beliefs before, during, and after teachers participated in that staff development program. The study was part of the Reading Instruction Study, a three-year study that investigated teachers' use of research-based practices in reading comprehension (Richardson & Anders, 1990). From the six schools participating in the Reading Instruction Study, two school sites were selected on the basis of their reputation for their willingness to change, and all grade 4-6 teachers in those schools participated in the study. In one school, six teachers were involved; in the other, five teachers and the curriculum coordinator participated in the staff development program. The researchers served as the two primary staff developers. Videotapes of the group staff development sessions as well as materials handed out at the sessions comprised the data for the study. Data were analyzed to determine the nature of the conversations, who initiated them, and the participation level. The researchers reported five categories of presentation modes:

1) Sharing: Both staff developers and teachers shared instructional practices spontaneously when the discussion reminded them of something they had done in the past.
2) Show and Tell: Participants prepared to talk about something they had done during the week.
3) Lecture 1: The staff developers prepared in advance a presentation of an activity from the literature or observation
4) Lecture 2: The staff developers delivered a formal presentation spontaneously; the presentation grew out of the discussion and was not prepared in advance.
5) New Suggestion: Participants learned a 'new' practice emerging out of the conversation.

The study described the teachers' gradual progress in sharing instructional practices and constructing their own knowledge. After a while, teachers became more willing to share their instructional practices with the group. In the end, teachers presented twice as many practices as the staff developers. As staff developers, Richardson and her colleague inquired into their own practice; they engaged in the process that teachers use to acquire and construct practical knowledge.

Summary

Whether or not change occurred and what motivated teachers to implement and adapt new instructional practices were important questions for researchers concerned with educational change. Given the nature of change and the complexity of teaching, such questions were not easily answered. Nonetheless, some researchers agreed that at least some change had occurred (Cuban, 1993; Richardson, 1990) and the teacher was an important and active figure in the change process.

From the perspectives of fidelity and adaptation, however, where change was externally defined, not much change had occurred. From the outside, schools appeared to be running business as usual. Yet, within classrooms, some teachers were gradually and tentatively changing their instructional practices, blending the new with the old, and balancing the immediate realities of practice with visions of the ideal.

NEW PERSPECTIVES FROM CURRICULUM RESEARCH

Although the diffusion paradigm as a change strategy apparently produced few long-term effects, curriculum research offers a third perspective on innovation. The teacher's active role in curriculum development supports the concept of teacher as innovator. Despite decades of 'teacher-proof' curriculum, there is evidence that the teacher has always played an active role in the design of curriculum (Corno, 1977). Connelly and Ben-Peretz (1980) described three ways in which research has portrayed teachers' roles:

a)   as implementers of teacher-proof curricula;
b)   as active implementers; and
c)   as adapters and developers of alternative versions.

In the first view, teachers are treated as transmitters of others' ideas. The second perspective assumes teachers play an active role in curriculum implementation through action research that helps teachers understand curricular innovations. In the third perspective, teachers are assumed to be adapters and developers of curriculum, engaging in the transformation of materials and inventing new alternatives. Thus, the active role of the teacher in curriculum design has been acknowledged. The curriculum implementation literature provides several examples of teachers as innovators.

In a review of the literature on curriculum implementation, Snyder, Bolin, and Zumwalt (1992) documented three perspectives in curriculum implementation research. In addition to the fidelity and adaptation perspectives previously described, these authors described the 'enactment' perspective. According to these authors, the 'enacted curriculum' consists of 'educational experiences jointly created by teacher and student' (p. 418). Externally developed curriculum materials are perceived only as tools for teachers and students to use as they 'enact' curriculum. In their review, these authors included only three studies that approached implementation from this enactment perspective, (viz., Aiken, 1942; Bussis et al., 1976; Paris, 1989). And yet, this 'curriculum enactment' perspective, although rarely studied, is not new.

The Teacher As Curriculum Maker

From curriculum studies, we have learned that teachers have accepted the responsibility of creating curriculum for some time and that experimental schools often produced improved student outcomes (Aiken, 1942). We have also learned that curriculum implementation may be more difficult to achieve than curriculum development. Just as competing ideologies may have accounted for the steady stream of different innovations introduced into schools, so too conflicting priorities may account for failed attempts to implement curriculum. As Smith et al. (1986) demonstrated, 'innovation' is value-laden, and implementation attempts raise questions about what constitutes improvement and who decides what constitutes improved instruction. Bolin (1987) attributed failures in curriculum implementation to misaligned perspectives between developers and teachers. For example, a teacher who views curriculum as an outgrowth of students' interests encounters conflicting priorities when asked to implement a curriculum developed outside his or her classroom. Bolin explains:

> The teacher is the key factor, closest to the intentions of students who have their own ideas about the curriculum. It is the teacher who is representative of society's interest in the education of its youth. To separate the teacher from the curriculum development process is not only to make the teacher an instrument rather than a decision maker, but to separate curriculum and instruction, leaving curriculum development as intellectual reflection and instruction as activism. (p. 101)

Bussis et al. (1976) demonstrated how difficult curriculum implementation can be. In their interview study of 60 teachers, Bussis et al. (1976) investigated teachers' conceptions of open education. The researchers found that a commitment on the part of individual teachers to the educational philosophy underpinning innovations was necessary for implementation. Further, few teachers, including those committed to the philosophy of open education, acquired a deep level understanding of innovations without the support of consultants or coaches. The authors' stated purpose was to demonstrate the importance of the teacher's role as curriculum developer. The study, therefore, probed the thinking of individual teachers and investigated teachers' reported reasons for assumptions and decisions with regard to curriculum implementation. Justification for the teacher's role as curriculum maker, and by extrapolation as innovator, was predicated on the assumption that 'unless the teacher engages in the thinking from which new policies eventuate, he [sic: or she] can only be what he has so long been – at best, an artisan who can work only according to definite specifications and under close supervision' (Jesse Newlon in Snyder et al., 1992, p. 419).

Curriculum Enactment

One study in the area of curriculum enactment (Paris, 1993) was intended to challenge traditional conceptions of curriculum as scientific products created by experts, independent of classroom contexts, and delivered to teachers for implementation. This study not only documents teachers' work in developing a word processing curriculum but also describes these same teachers implementing a prescribed writing process curriculum. We describe Paris' research in some detail because it also raises several important issues suggested by other researchers concerned with the process of implementation and change, namely the tension between: collaboration and artisanship (Hargreaves, 1993); institutional authority and the use of research findings (Hargreaves & Dawe, 1990; Little, 1993); and conflicting messages from school contexts (McTaggart, 1989).

Paris studied four elementary teachers as they learned to use word processing and subsequently designed their own curriculum for teaching children to use word processing in a writing program. According to an agreement with a university research team, the teachers were given word processing hardware and software, instruction in the use of the word processing systems, and a university-student teaching assistant. Teachers were free to decide what word processing skills to teach and how; in essence, they were given the tools and the license to create curriculum. Selected teachers were invited to participate in the research study by their building principal who saw the research project as an opportunity to integrate computers into the curriculum.

An explicit constructivist and interpretive perspective led the researcher to select long-term participant observation and ethnographic interviewing as the primary sources for data collection. Participants were also asked to keep journals, but the task of writing weekly journal entries proved, not surprisingly from a teacher's perspective, too time-consuming for participants. In addition to weekly classroom observations and interviews conducted throughout the two-year study, teachers attended summer workshops and group discussions. Although long-term observation is characteristic of ethnographic research conducted in a natural setting, given the nature of classroom life, it is not surprising that the researcher found that the research process itself – which had been intended to support the teachers' curriculum work – was often obtrusive and constraining. On the other hand, these teachers were supplied with computer hardware and software as well as a teaching assistant. Such resources were not typically available to these teachers. Thus, the collaborative research process both constrained and supported teacher agency.

This study placed the researchers and participants in continually juxtaposed roles of teacher and learner. The researchers, for example, learned to negotiate with the teachers about the content of the inservice workshops and group discussions. (In designing their inservice program, the researchers had not acknowledged the teachers' prior experience with computers and the writing process.) Paris noted the contradiction between the researchers' stated plan to give the teachers license to create and their actions that failed to acknowledge the teachers' prior knowledge. 'This contradiction was not lost on the teachers,' Paris observed (p. 101). Subsequent workshops were redesigned based on what researchers had learned from participants. The researchers also identified the teachers' frustrations in working with the equipment and software which, although it was made readily available to them, they had no part in selecting.

Paris found that teachers initially requested prescriptions from the research team about the use of the word processors. Paris interpreted these requests as 'requests for parameters' (which teachers' prior experience with received materials had led them to expect). If this interpretation is accurate, it speaks to the power of expectations in the collective experience of teachers and may point to a self-fulfilling prophecy of teachers as consumers of curriculum. Furthermore, conflicting messages, similar to those documented by McTaggart (1989), may have influenced the teachers' behavior in the Paris study (1993). For example, the contradiction between the researchers' stated intentions and their actions that led teachers to resist the workshops might also have led them to expect that these researchers had a prescriptive list of curriculum activities for them despite their stated intentions.

The real (scheduling constraints and pre-selected materials) and perceived parameters that this study disclosed raises an important question to consider for any emerging model of university-school collaboration. Can there be collaboration without imposing real or perceived constraints? Hargreaves (1993) argued that the power to exercise independent judgment was closely linked to competence since teachers viewed the right to exercise professional autonomy as evidence that their principals had confidence in their abilities as teachers. Hargreaves also argued that creative individuals require solitude and independence, and decried schools which are 'prepared to punish excellence in pursuit of the collegial norm' (p. 73). This tension between artisanship and collaboration merits further study. Research conducted from teachers' perspectives may uncover other constraints perceived by teachers engaged in innovative practices.

Although the teachers' agency in developing a word processing curriculum was the focus of the Paris study (1993), this research also provided valuable insights into the way the teachers dealt with mandated curricula. These teachers had been directed to implement a district-wide standardized writing curriculum. The study revealed that the teachers found ways to improvise and adapt this curriculum to their needs with the full support of the principal whom Paris characterized as balancing district mandates with school-wide support for experimentation. Little (1993) argued that implementation of research findings is often a way of exercising institutional authority. Similarly, Hargreaves and Dawe (1990) cautioned that district mandates often disguised as collaboration and coaching may be 'forms of contrived collegiality ... administratively designed to smooth the path of externally imposed innovation' (p. 230). In the Paris study (1993), the principal's encouragement of the teachers' work did appear to move forward the principal's own agenda of computer integration.

Nonetheless, the study contributed to an understanding of the way in which teachers shape curriculum by suggesting a cyclical model of observing, questioning, and altering existing curriculum practices. Paris suggested that the concept of teacher agency required further elucidation and refinement. Again, the teachers in this study, although they were given the tools and license to create, were constrained from exercising a full range of agency by the conflicting contexts in which they worked, by the nature of the research process itself, and to some degree, by the contradictions they perceived in the researchers' intentions and actions. Although teachers assumed some agency in curriculum making, they participated minimally in articulating the motivations or thinking underlying their agency. This study, together with the findings of other researchers (Hargreaves, 1993; Little, 1993; McTaggart, 1989), suggest the need for more research to illuminate constraints against real agency from teachers' perspectives.

Studies of Curricular Choices

Research on teacher decision making has generally supported the view that teachers play an active role in deciding what and how to teach (Borko, Cone, Russo, & Shavelson, 1979; Shavelson & Stern, 1981). This research has also demonstrated that context plays an important role in informing teachers' decisions (McLaughlin & Talbert, 1993; McLaughlin, Talbert, & Bascia, 1990). Curricular choices and instructional decisions are influenced by student characteristics (Merryfield, 1993; Metz, 1993), teachers' beliefs and values (Gudmundsdottir, 1990; Hawthorne, 1992; Munby, 1984), practical theories or principles derived from practice that guide teachers' beliefs, actions, and decisions (Cornett, 1990; Sanders & McCutcheon, 1988), the nature of the curriculum content (Grossman, 1992; Stodolsky, 1988, 1993), and teachers' knowledge of the subject area (Hawthorne, 1992; Reynolds, Haymore, Ringstaff, & Grossman, 1988).

Hawthorne's (1992) study of curricular choices contributes to an understanding of the teacher's active role in shaping curriculum at the individual classroom level and highlights the teacher's individual quest for innovation at the classroom level. The study explored the tension between teachers' desire for autonomy and the organizational obligations that accompany curriculum implementation mandates. Hawthorne's research intended to learn whether top-down mandates changed teachers' curricular decisions.

Four middle-school, English teachers in two different schools participated. The school sites were purposefully selected to represent schools with varying degrees of curriculum prescription. Anticipating that teachers might place themselves at risk in revealing how they sometimes thwarted organizational directives, the researcher relied on volunteers. Interviews, observations, and stimulated recall exercises were the primary sources of data. Inquiries focused on sources of curriculum materials, the teachers' opinions of the materials, and reasons for using particular materials or instructional strategies. Interviews with secondary informants and document analysis assisted in comparing differing perceptions and discovering discrepancies between classroom practice and organizational policy. Additionally, the researcher shared drafts of interpretations with teachers and conducted a cross-case analysis to identify common themes and influences.

Teachers' curricular choices were found to be influenced by their professional knowledge, their knowledge of clients, and their values and experiences. The study also confirmed that organizational factors influenced teachers' choices about curriculum and that teachers were often faced competing demands from organization, clients, and personal values. Organizational press came, as Hawthorne found, not only in forms of prescription, but also in forms of omission, where teachers were constrained by a teaching load that left no time for real curriculum work and placed a higher value on management than on instruction. Hawthorne found that teachers were continually balancing organizational demands with curriculum needs.

Perhaps most interesting was the finding that teachers often engage in what they consider 'subversive' activities to maintain professional autonomy. For example, one teacher in a school with a highly standardized curriculum accepted a position as department chair to ensure her influence in curriculum development. Hawthorne described another teacher who had devised a strategy of 'staggering curricula' to balance his paper load. He assigned writing assignments to each of his five classes at different times during the year; 'I try to stagger my curriculum out of self-defense. I can't bear to read the same set of compositions at the same time for all my classes' (p. 24). This strategy enabled him to read student papers himself rather than use the readers provided by department funds. He did this because he considered it important to provide students feedback about their work. This teacher disclosed to Hawthorne that 'one of the best things about the teaching profession is that you can be creative. It's so important to be able to feel like you can create something' (p. 35). According to Hawthorne, this particular teacher's creativity manifested itself, not in innovative instructional strategies, but in subversive 'self-defense' strategies that enabled the teacher to cope with organizational demands. Hawthorne's interpretation implies that teachers 'go underground' to find opportunities to create, opportunities that are seldom legitimately within the purview of teachers. Hawthorne's study of curricular choice supports Hargreaves' (1993) view that autonomy and innovation are interrelated.

Hawthorne's study also acknowledged the significance of individual variations among teachers. Hawthorne concluded that 'levels of support, incentives, and degrees of autonomy must vary in response to individual teachers' needs and capabilities' (p. 131). Despite the small sample and non-experimental design of this study, it provides insight into the power of teacher classroom decision-making and demonstrates that universal mandates are not always effective in bringing about improvement at the level of the classroom and individual teacher.

Although Hawthorne's study documented variations among English teachers, Grossman (1992) suggested that English as subject matter may afford teachers more latitude in curriculum design and delivery than other subject areas do. There is increased communication among teachers who teach subject areas with hierarchical course sequences, such as math, and there is a tendency toward more uniformity as well (Stodolsky, 1993). Math and social studies lessons apparently differ even when the same teachers teach both subject areas (Stodolsky, 1988). These studies raise questions about the relationship between subject area and innovation as well as the relationship between collaboration (Hargreaves, 1993) and innovation. These findings also challenge researchers to study innovative teachers who teach hierarchical course sequences to learn, for example, whether these teachers incorporate lesson structures and ideas from other disciplines or whether they collaborate with teachers in other subject areas.

Summary

Although teachers have played an active role in designing curriculum, the development of new curriculum by teachers has seldom been characterized as innovation. Many teachers have designed curriculum in their own classrooms, but their solitary work has often gone unrecognized. Stenhouse (1985) described teachers working together 'on defined problems and tasks until they begin to develop a new tradition' (p. 64). Stenhouse encouraged these teachers to transmit their experiences to colleagues; in essence, he advocated the diffusion of teachers' curricular innovations.

Rogers (1983) has usefully distinguished invention from innovation. He defined invention as 'the process by which a new idea is discovered or created' (p. 138). Drawing on the definition of innovation popularized by the diffusion paradigm, he defined innovation, on the other hand, as the adoption of a new idea. By this definition, curriculum growing from the unique contexts of individual classrooms and hence not readily adoptable can never be characterized as 'innovative' unless innovation is viewed as a process as well as a product.

RESEARCH ON TEACHERS' KNOWLEDGE AND LEARNING

While the pursuit of curricular and instructional innovations occupied the attention of some researchers, others followed the journey of the teacher from imitator to inventor. This work encompasses our fourth body of literature. Studies in the area of teacher thinking have demonstrated the complexity of teaching (Clark & Peterson, 1986). As Calderhead (1987) maintained:

> ... how unrealistic it is to conceive of innovation as a set of preformulated ideas or principles to be implemented by teachers. Innovative ideas are interpreted and reinterpreted by teachers over a period of time and translated into practice in a process that involves teachers drawing upon several different knowledge bases and interpreting and manipulating various interests. (p. 17)

How teachers learn new instructional practices and acquire new ideas has become an important area of research. Studies of teacher thinking have contributed to an understanding of why the diffusion of externally generated innovations as an approach to change oversimplifies what it takes to improve schools.

Learning through Implementation

Considering the long history of the diffusion paradigm as an educational change strategy together with research in the area of curriculum development and enactment by teachers, we suggest that teachers may have learned to innovate through imitation of innovations. Experience may be one source of knowledge for teachers, but the models teachers are encouraged to implement may be another potent source of learning. Studies of implementation have traditionally viewed teachers as imitators of innovations. Crandall (1983), in describing the teacher's role in school improvement, identified teachers as 'natural emulators (who) seldom have the opportunity to be innovative' (p. 8). Crandall described classroom improvement as a cycle of emulation, implementation, and replication. From this perspective, the imitation or replication of externally developed and research-validated exemplary practices was synonymous with successful change. Further, imitation and innovation were seen as disparate and opposing constructs.

Imitation, however, may be one building block of innovative teaching. Yinger (1987) investigated the role of models in teaching and suggested that teaching was an improvisational performance aided by patterns or models in a teacher's repertoire. Citing the patterned language and formulae that poets used to construct poetry in the oral tradition, Yinger argued that teachers construct classroom discourse in similar patterned ways. Grounding his theory in a qualitative description of one eighth grade math teacher, Yinger demonstrated how that teacher composed classroom interactions on the spot by drawing from models of previous classroom interactions. For example, to help students solve math problems, the teacher selected from his repertoire of previously established routines such as thinking aloud, explicating knowledge, or debugging mistakes. These routines, Yinger argued, enabled the teacher to improvise or compose during and in response to the dynamics of classroom action. 'Teachers and students follow previously learned, culturally normative 'rules' and also innovate by making new kinds of sense together in adapting to the fortuitive circumstances of the moment' (Erickson in Yinger, 1987, p. 23).

Imitation plays an important role in constructing new knowledge and in learning. Building on social learning theory and social constructivist concepts, Eisner (1994), for example, has argued that multiple forms of representation (models) and a context that supports their imaginative use are integral to effective education. Duckworth (1987), citing Piaget, explained that children first learn new behaviors by internalizing imitations. Imitation also plays a role in the development of new ideas: 'The more ideas about something people already have at their disposal, the more new ideas occur and the more they can coordinate to build up still more complicated schemes' (p. 14).

A similar process may occur when teachers imitate innovations. Some researchers have suggested that teachers appropriate innovations for purposes other than the developer intended (Connelly & Clandinin, 1988; Richardson, 1991). Although teachers may not precisely replicate the innovations, they may imitate portions of the modelled instructional strategies or take ideas from the innovation and develop new instructional practices to meet the needs of their particular students. Darling-Hammond (1990) explained teachers' adaptations in terms of a synthesis of new and old:

> Interpreting the new through the lens of the familiar is, as cognitive science now tells us, how all of us construct meaning from the information we process using our existing schema. There is no reason why teachers should behave any differently. (p. 236)

Most staff development programs are designed on just that principle. For more than a decade, staff development programs have relied on theory, demonstration, and practice to introduce new teaching practices (Joyce & Showers, 1980). The ancient Greeks and Romans employed a similar pedagogical model of *ars*, *imitatio*, and *exercitatio* (theory, imitation, and practice) to train orators and writers. Placed strategically between theory and practice in the classical triad, imitation was the stage in which students analyzed the model and evaluated how closely the particular model resembled existing theory. In classical pedagogy, imitation was a synthesis of research and practice. In the practice stage or *genesis* (emphasis added), students attempted to produce something like the model (Sullivan, 1989). Imitation led to invention.

Until the Renaissance, imitation was associated with production. Aristotle associated imitation with the creative arts. For Aristotle, imitation engendered creation: 'Imitation, then, is one instinct of our nature.... Persons, therefore, starting with this natural gift, developed by degrees their special aptitudes, till their rude improvisations gave birth to poetry' (Poetics: IV).

Plato also associated imitation or *mimesis* with the arts. Plato, however, distinguished the 'versatile imitator,' who was only capable of imitating the works of craftsmen from the true imitator who engaged in the work of different kinds of craftsmen. The 'versatile imitator' was ignorant about what he imitated, and that distinguished him from the craftsman (Belfiore, 1984). Plato's true imitator did not merely imitate models; the true imitator emulated the process of design.

From ancient times through the Renaissance, the imitation of classical models was an accepted form of composition. Imitation, however, was not mere replication of a model: 'The chief aim was to produce something original.

Whatever they took from the classics, they used simply as materials — like the materials they acquired from other sources, from their observations of life, their own fancies, ... or contemporary journalism' (Highet, 1967, p. 86; see also Bandura, 1986).

In ancient times, as we have seen, imitation was the principle underlying the apprenticeship model. Likewise, social learning theory views imitation of models as a means of learning new ways of thinking and behaving (Bandura, 1977). But learning to teach, as Feiman-Nemser and Buchman (1985) demonstrated, involves more than just 'unreflective imitation.' Dewey (1904) argued that observation was an important part of learning to teach, but he cautioned teachers to consider how and why particular instructional practices worked. Otherwise, Dewey maintained, the principle of imitation could play an exaggerated part in learning to teach. Collins, Brown, and Newman (1989) proposed a model of 'cognitive apprenticeship' that makes expert thinking as well as behavior visible to apprentice learners. The model rests on the assumption that expertise depends on the integration of a complex array of cognitive strategies that are difficult to articulate. In this model, it appears that imitating the process of innovation is more important than imitating the model. That is, instead of imitating observed instructional behavior, teachers imitate the coordinated thinking that leads to innovative instructional behavior and practice.

Kagan (1988) traced the history of research on teacher cognition and demonstrated a shift from providing models of classroom teaching based on a medical model of diagnosis and treatment to newer, hierarchical models of problem solving that moved teaching closer to an art form. The new models were described as multidimensional and flexible, and the goal of the model was for the teacher to 'create meaning from a large amount of data and to transmit that meaning to the clients (students)' (p. 495). For Kagan, like Schon (1983), teaching was a synthesis, 'a weaving together of meanings,' an act of creation or innovation. Kagan examined the implications of this new model in terms of preservice and inservice education. Because current evaluations of teacher development were inadequate in measuring the complex and varied thinking skills that underpin the hierarchical model, Kagan called for the development of nontraditional assessments of teachers' thinking and new models of teacher development 'based on naturalistic studies that chart the course of cognitive development among teachers as they mature in the profession' (p. 499). Thus we turn our attention to studies of the development of teachers' knowledge.

Teachers' Knowledge: Inferring Theory from Practice

Studies of teachers' knowledge aim to 'make explicit the implicit knowledge that teachers use in responding as they do in classrooms' (Carter & Doyle, 1987,

p. 147). In addition to the formal content of teacher education programs, teachers possess a specialized knowledge base acquired only through teaching (Grossman & Richert, 1986; Shulman, 1986; Wilson, Shulman, & Richert, 1987). Shulman (1987) described teachers' 'practical pedagogical wisdom' as a highly contextualized or situational knowledge acquired through experience. Shulman's model of pedagogical reasoning includes the critical interpretation and transformation of content and materials in response to the needs of learners. In this model, the teachers' knowledge base is dynamic and grows through reflection and new comprehensions of subject matter, students, and teaching.

Studies of teachers' pedagogical content knowledge (Grossman, 1990; Gudmunsdottir, 1987; Hashweh, 1987; Leinhardt & Smith, 1985) have contributed to our understanding of the ways in which experienced teachers acquire new ideas. Gudmundsdottir (1987) studied the pedagogical content knowledge of two secondary English teachers who had each been teaching more than 25 years. The researcher was interested in learning how these teachers characterized their knowledge about their discipline and how they restructured that knowledge for the purpose of teaching it. Classroom observations and field notes yielded the data for this descriptive study. Additionally, three interviews were conducted with each teacher at the beginning, middle, and end of a 3-month period. From these data, Gudmundsdottir concluded that 'there is no indication that (the teachers) were taught to organize their content knowledge in that way. Instead, they invented those models themselves' (Gudmunsdottir, 1987, p. 17).

Several studies have identified experienced teachers' practical knowledge (Clandinin, 1985; Elbaz, 1981, 1983) or situational knowledge (Leinhardt, 1988) that is learned through classroom interactions. Other studies (Connelly & Clandinin, 1988; Janesick, 1982; Lampert, 1985) have characterized teachers' knowledge as personal and experiential, based in episodic memories and stories of particular cases or instances. Teachers may also acquire new ideas from colleagues, from students, and from commercially prepared instructional materials as well as from instructional innovations they have been encouraged to implement (Randi, 1996).

Context plays an important role in informing teachers' decisions; it may also play a critical role in building teachers' knowledge. Drawing upon their research conducted under the auspices of the Center for Research on the Context of Teaching (reviewed later in this chapter), Talbert, McLaughlin, and Rowan (1993) explained the role of context in teachers' construction of knowledge. These authors distinguished contextual decision making (influenced by factors in specific instructional settings) from teachers' decision making informed by a knowledge base. They observed that teachers with a knowledge base vary their teaching goals, strategies, and techniques during the course of a day or week. They argued that context differences explained the observed variability of knowledgeable teachers' decisions and practices. That is, 'a teacher's choice about classroom practices at any point in time is not simply a product of knowledge ... but depends also upon assessments of the feasibility and desirability of particular practices in specific instructional settings' (p. 49). These authors argued that varying teaching contexts afford teachers opportunities to learn as they make judgments about when to apply (or not apply) particular teaching strategies in different contexts.

Thus contextual decision making and decision making informed by a knowledge base may not be incompatible. For teachers' craft knowledge is knowledge that has been generalized from particular contextual experiences. Cronbach (1975) argued twenty years ago that more attention should be given to unique cases. Similarly, Sockett (1989) contended that, although teachers have been criticized for their interest in specific techniques, there is a need to pay more attention to the ways in which teachers use their knowledge of the specific to inform their practice.

Teachers' practical knowledge.

Elbaz (1981, 1983) studied how one teacher used knowledge in practice. This study explicitly linked teacher knowledge and instructional design and aimed to validate the teacher's role in curriculum development. Elbaz believed that 'the single factor which seems to have the greatest power to carry forward our understanding of the teacher's role is the idea of teacher's knowledge' (Elbaz, 1983, p. 11). Underlying this belief was the assumption that possession of a knowledge base would enhance the status of teachers in the eyes of laymen (Lortie, in Elbaz, 1981).

Elbaz studied the thinking of one high school English teacher as the teacher developed a course on learning skills. Through a series of five informal interviews with 'Sarah,' a veteran English teacher, and two classroom observations that served as catalysts for discussion during the interviews, Elbaz guided the teacher in articulating her knowledge. Elbaz, by sharing with Sarah her own assumptions and research agenda, included Sarah as a participant in the research. In fact, Elbaz' research questions were directly posed to Sarah in the interviews: 'I'm interested in ... what kind of knowledge you used and how you used it in order to work through the thing (the development of the Learning Course)' (1983, p. 177).

It is probable that this collaboration facilitated Sarah's articulation of her knowledge base. It is also probable that Sarah herself contributed to the success of this study. Sarah may not have been a typical teacher in the sense that she had at least two direct experiences with curriculum development. Although this case study yielded an interpretive understanding of only one teacher's knowledge, and even if that teacher were an atypical case, the case provided, as the research-er hoped, 'a critical understanding of how that knowledge functions in a social context' (Elbaz, 1983, p. 168). Unlike Hawthorne (1992) and Paris (1993), El-baz focused on an analysis of one teacher's thinking, rather than behavior, and purposefully adopted what she termed an 'uncritical' perspective. Consequent-ly, the study yielded findings authenticated by the teacher's own perspective.

Data comprising the teacher's knowledge base were analyzed by Elbaz with three categories of practical knowledge: content, orientation, and structure. She found that practical knowledge was structured by rules of practice, practical principles, and images. A rule of practice was defined as 'a clearly formulated statement of what to do or how to do it in a particular situation frequently en-countered in practice' (1983, p. 132). Practical principles were defined as gen-eral constructs that may be acquired from theoretical viewpoints or intuitively out of experience. And, images were defined as personal pictures or visions of what teaching should be. Images are constructed from teachers' personal beliefs and experiences, theoretical knowledge, and school contexts. This conception of the structure of teachers' practical knowledge provides one framework for studying teachers' thinking as they implement instructional innovations. For example, the application of an instructional innovation may provide an experi-ence from which a teacher inductively acquires a practical principle.

Elbaz was convinced that expert teachers, like Sarah, could articulate their own knowledge. Other researchers have argued that teachers hold 'tacit' knowl-edge or knowledge that is not easily articulated (Schon, 1983) and experts who have achieved automaticity are often unable to articulate the basis for their ac-tions (Berliner, 1987). Elbaz maintained that the research process itself, con-ducted from an 'uncritical stance' (1983, p. 165), fostered professional growth, enhanced the teacher's self-understanding, and contributed to the articulation of her knowledge base. Conversely, Elbaz' study suggests that the articulation of teachers' knowledge may be discouraged by covert messages (McTaggart, 1989) that often devalue teachers' competence and knowledge. Elbaz' study stands in marked contrast to the work of Paris (1993) whose research process may have constrained the same teacher agency that the study intended to docu-ment. Further research is needed to explore the relationships among 'tacit' knowledge, innovation, and the overt and covert messages of school contexts.

Building on Elbaz' conception of teachers' practical knowledge, and in par-ticular, the concept of image in teaching, Clandinin (1985) studied two primary teachers for two years through observations and interviews. Clandinin found evidence of one teacher's image of the 'classroom as home' and one teacher's image of 'language is the key.' Clandinin described teachers' 'personal practi-cal knowledge' as it was found in practice and included images that embodied emotions, morality, and aesthetics. Clandinin highlighted the importance of her study by arguing that 'failure to understand the teacher as an active holder and user of personal practical knowledge helps explain the limited success of curriculum implementation' (p. 364) where teachers are expected to implement someone else's innovation. Clandinin concluded with a recommendation that school improvement efforts should build on teachers' personal practical knowledge by working with teachers rather than against them.

Summary

Elbaz (1981, 1983) and Clandinin (1985) described teachers' personal and practical knowledge acquired, not from formal coursework or staff development workshops, but inferred from practice. These studies are significant in that they connect teachers' knowledge with the development of curriculum. Taken together with the research of Hawthorne (1992) and Paris (1993), this body of work demonstrates that teachers are capable of designing curriculum and instruction. These studies also reveal a great deal about the instructional design process practiced by experienced teachers when they adapt instructional innovations and research findings to their particular classrooms.

Unlike Elbaz's Sarah who had direct experience in curriculum development and Paris's teachers who were given the license and tools to develop curriculum, most teachers have few legitimate opportunities to construct curriculum. Like Hawthorne's teachers, most teachers are left to balance the demands of the organization with their responsibility for developing effective learning experiences for their students. As a result, the position of the teacher as innovator is compromised. The process of implementation of instructional innovations often places teachers in a visible yet precarious position of balancing implementation with innovation.

TOWARD A CONCEPTION OF THE TEACHER AS INNOVATOR

Given these four bodies of distinct yet related literature, we can begin to formulate a conception of the teacher as innovator. One early conception of the teacher as innovator was offered by Joyce and Weil (1973) and became the foundation of their later work (Joyce & Weil, 1986). These authors are noted for having defined a repertoire of 'models of teaching.' Their conception of teacher as innovator involved the acquisition and synthesis of a range of models of teaching. Their stated goal was innovation: 'To prepare the teacher to innovate is our quest. Our goal is not to indoctrinate him [sic: or her] in a single method of teaching or one au courant educational philosophy' (Joyce & Weil, 1973, p. 47). Yet their view of teacher education was grounded in a technological orientation and the belief that 'we can design an effective technology of teacher education – one offering teacher trainees the chance to master a wide range of approaches to their work' (p. 58). The models of teaching approach differs from specific skill training, however, because it encourages teachers to reflect on their behavior and to select from a repertoire the instructional strategies most likely to increase their effectiveness.

Teaching as an Art Form

The more recent recurrent theme of design in the literature on teaching and learning (Bennett & Rolheiser-Bennett, 1992; Kagan, 1988; Perkins, 1986; Schon, 1983, 1987) associates teaching with the creative arts and focuses attention on instruction as a dynamic, innovative process responsive to the contexts of teaching. In 1983, Schon compared teaching with the process of design. Schon's epistemology identified teaching as a kind of reflection-in-action or experimenting in a highly contextual context. Schon's conceptualization of professional practice as design identified teaching as a creative process generated within the contexts of teaching.

The artistry of teaching has been recognized and described as innovative, intuitive, spontaneous, and imaginative (Rubin, 1983, 1985). Rubin (1985) argued that these capacities are so integral to teaching that teachers should receive 'systematic practice in developing their capacities for innovation, spontaneity, perception, and intuition' (p. 165). Rubin suggested that teachers acquired these skills through constant experimentation with new practices and posited invention as a necessary condition for teaching. He argued that inventiveness was essential to effective teaching because ready-made solutions were not available for all the problems of teaching and learning. Rubin described two types of inventiveness in teaching. In its simple form, invention involves adapting lessons to particular classrooms and students. In its complex form, invention involves devising ways to solve instructional problems. Rubin described artist teachers as self-directed teachers open to new possibilities:

> Artist teachers are self-directed. They obey an inner instinct which makes them independent and autonomous. Ever open to new possibilities, they constantly look for a better way – for an unsuspected bonanza or a novel solution to a difficulty. They like to invent, first because invention creates alternatives, and second, because it makes teaching far more interesting. (1985, p. 33)

Invention characterizes the arts: 'What the arts make possible … is an invitation to invent novel ways to combine elements' (Eisner, 1994, p. 56). Eisner (1985) views teaching as an art practiced in a complex and uncertain environment. Although teachers need to draw on available repertoires, Eisner's 'teacher must function in an innovative way in order to cope with ... contingencies' (p. 176) that the uncertainties of the classroom environment present. Eisner identified teaching as an art in the sense that ends are often created in the process of teaching. For Eisner, artistry is a playful and risky process that equates synthesis with creation. 'To be able to play with ideas is to feel free to throw them into new combinations, to experiment, and even to fail' (p. 183).

Creativity and invention have been continually associated with innovation. Perkins (1981) investigated the essence of invention: 'The essence of invention isn't process but purpose. Purpose is what organizes the diverse means of the mind to creative ends' (p. 100). Further, Perkins contended that invention occurred not because a person tried to be original but because that person attempted to do something difficult. In other words, the more complex the problem, the more the problem demanded an unconventional solution. If complexity begets invention, then nowhere is invention more at home than in teaching.

Bennett and Rolheiser-Bennett (1992), citing Perkins' *Knowledge as Design* (1986), underscored the importance of teachers' conceptual understanding of the design process. They found that when teachers failed to understand the design of the innovations they were attempting to use, they were less likely to implement them effectively. The solution, according to these researchers, was to provide teachers with the opportunity to think critically about innovations and to make explicit connections between the various curricular and instructional concepts during inservice teacher education.

Teaching As Research

The process in which teachers engage as they learn from practice is, in many ways, similar to research. That process, however, is also similar to an art form. Stenhouse (1985) argued that teachers develop understanding expressed in performance:

> The artist is the researcher whose enquiry expresses itself in performance of his (sic) art ... there is in education no absolute and unperformed knowledge. Educational knowledge exists in, and is verified or falsified in, its performance. (p. 110)

Other writers have also viewed teaching as both an art and a science. Gage (1984) revisited his earlier work, *The Scientific Basis of the Art of Teaching* (1978), and reminded us of the complexity of teaching:

As an instrumental art, teaching departs from recipes, formulas, and algorithms. It requires improvisation, spontaneity, the handling of a vast array of considerations of form, style, pace, rhythm, and appropriateness in ways so complex that even computers must lose the way, just as what a mother does with a 5-year-old. (p. 88)

The practice of teaching as research or inquiry has been described as 'a process of engaging learners in trying to make sense' (Duckworth, 1986). Duckworth conceptualized teaching as the construction of knowledge and envisioned teacher education as a process in which teachers observed teaching, engaged in inquiry about teaching and learning, and experienced learning themselves. Through journal writing and reflection, Duckworth engaged her students in the process of learning about teaching and learning. Duckworth's own experience in preparing educators to teach provides a model for staff development that promises to lay the theoretical foundation required for reflective practice and in-novation.

The growing interest in teaching as research promises to legitimate the role of teacher as researcher as well as reveal what teachers learn from practice. Descriptions of teacher research have highlighted the teacher's role as generator of knowledge about teaching and learning. Cochran-Smith and Lytle (1992) viewed teacher research as a powerful tool for change because it 'makes visible the ways that teachers and students co-construct knowledge and the curriculum' (p. xiv). Recognizing that efforts to regulate classroom instruction by outside agents have often failed, Cochran-Smith and Lytle sought to develop teachers' potential as 'architects of teaching and learning' (p. 101) through inquiry. Defining teacher research as 'systematic and intentional inquiry about teaching, learning, and school carried out by teachers in their own schools and classroom settings' (pp. 23-24), Cochran-Smith and Lytle identified four types of teacher research: journals or teachers' accounts of classroom life; oral inquiries or teachers' oral examinations of classroom contexts and experiences; classroom or school-based studies or teachers' explorations of practices using data collected from observation, interviews, and artifacts; and, essays or teachers' interpretations of the assumptions and characteristics of school or classroom life. Teacher research appears closely aligned with the practice of innovation in its assumption that teachers are generators of knowledge and constructors of meaning.

Studies of Innovative Teachers

Little research has focused on innovative teachers and attempted to describe their particular methods. Documentaries have been produced on famous innovative teachers, such as Marva Collins and Jaime Escalante, but structured research studies are rare. One investigation by Jagla (1989) examined the practical knowledge of eight teachers recognized for excellence through awards and recommendations. One purpose of the phenomonological study was to attach meaning to the terms 'imagination' and 'intuition' as they apply to teaching. Phenomonological studies in education attempt to understand common but abstract terms, such as excellence and artistry, by exploring what meanings individuals attach to those terms as they are embodied in common classroom occurrences. Teachers and the researcher together reviewed and interpreted transcripts of their conversations and pre-arranged classroom visits. The purpose of the classroom observations was to provide the researcher and teachers common phenomena upon which to reflect as they explored the meaning of 'imagination' and 'intuition.' All eight teachers reported they valued the use of 'imagination' and 'intuition' as essential in teaching. The participants also felt that modelling by experts was one important way to promote such qualities in teaching. Another way was through the sharing of instructional techniques among teachers.

Noddings and Shore (1984) defined intuition as 'the mental capacity that receives and creates representations' (p. 141). These authors associated intuitive capacity with creativity and argued that creation 'is never a pure act of the human creator, since what-is-there plays a substantial part in contributing to the creation' (p. 141). In her attempt to characterize intuition in teaching, Jagla (1989) also noted that teachers in her study called upon internal as well as external resources. External resources included such materials as books or equipment; internal resources included the ideas teachers 'conjured up' within themselves (p. 262). Jagla contended that intuition is fostered when teachers combine internal and external resources to internalize new ideas.

Citing Greene (1988), Jagla defined imaginative teaching in terms of possibilities. Similarly, teachers in Jagla's study also associated 'imagination' with possibilities. One teacher defined 'imagination' as 'a cluster of ideas around a concept' (p. 71). Several teachers in Jagla's study associated imagination, like intuition, with creativity, and they considered imaginative teachers innovative. One teacher stated: 'Imaginative instruction would imply teaching that is creative ... probably conjuring up something that is either new to you or new to others' (Jagla, 1989, p. 72). Studies like Jagla's and philosophical analyses of abstract notions such as intuition and imagination can play an important clarifying role as research on innovative teachers develops.

Haley-Oliphant (1987) provided another example of research focusing on one 'imaginative' teacher. (Haley-Oliphant's study was actually part of a larger study involving three teachers in the United States and 21 teachers in Spain in an international cooperative research project aimed at broadening understanding of teachers' thought processes during teaching.) Haley-Oliphant's naturalistic study focused on one seventh grade science teacher in the United States and described that teacher's thoughts as she planned and delivered a series of inquiry activities called 'Mind Games.' Data collection methods included participant observation during planning and teaching, formal and informal interviews, and personal journals and documents collected from the teacher throughout one school year. The idea for 'Mind Games' came to the teacher after she said 'she saw the need' for inner city students to voice their opinions. The teacher designed the activities around questions of possibility, such as *what if*, *what would the world be like*, or *what might be*? Haley-Oliphant describes this teacher as seeking to:

> ... temporarily transform the adolescent student into a dreamer travelling through the wonderland of science, where impossibilities become possibilities, where ideas are the stuff of which progress is made and where imagination accompanied by reason transforms a current problem into a solution for tomorrow. (p. 10)

These Mind Games may be particularly effective activities in light of this teacher's goals. By documenting student-to-student interactions in the classroom as well, Haley-Oliphant demonstrated how the students developed the ability to argue and voice their opinions freely in class. In this naturalistic study, Haley-Oliphant described the teacher's activities in some detail but cautioned that a 'prescription for Mind Games could not be given ... without describing Mind Games within the context of Ms. Moran's (particular) goals, actions and knowledge, the effectiveness of the activity would be lost' (p. 29). The teacher was found to alter her instruction when she reflected on how a particular Mind Game was played and saw unfulfilled goals. The study underscores the value of careful descriptive methodology in continuing studies of innovative teaching because it demonstrated the importance of analyzing instructional activities in light of the teacher's goals, knowledge, and action.

Finally, there is a review by Woods (1990) of research on creative teaching conducted in primary and secondary schools in Great Britain over a twelve year period beginning in the late 1970s. Woods argued that 'opportunities to learn' are contingent upon 'opportunities to teach' and identified the skills and strategies used by teachers in these studies to balance opportunities and constraints for creative teaching. According to Woods, creativity involved innovation and ownership. Innovation here resulted from 'a new combination of known factors, or from the introduction of a new factor into a prevailing situation' (p. 32). Woods credited teachers with innovation (i.e., the innovation belonged to the teacher in that it was either the teacher's own idea or an adaptation of someone else's idea). Innovation, creativity, and change were again linked. As Woods wrote: 'Creative acts bring change. They change pupils, teachers, and situations' (p. 33).

To conclude, in some studies of education, invention and innovation have been linked with novelty. But the prevailing concept of innovation as externally directed change has overshadowed invention. Innovations bring change, but inventions bring change only when introduced into widespread use as innovations. In the teaching profession, externally generated inventions are insufficient for explaining how teachers work; an understanding of how teachers discover new solutions in context is needed as well (Rubin, 1985). Inventive teachers innovate; they change their instructional practices in response to the dynamic contexts of classrooms.

PREPARING TEACHERS TO INNOVATE

But how are teachers prepared to innovate? What teacher education experiences foster this predisposition? Thirty years of research on innovation diffusion has led to new understandings of what it takes to restructure schools. It has been well-documented that schools, classrooms, and students are as different as they are similar. Responding to the ever-changing contexts of schools and classrooms requires a growing understanding of the various paradigms and patterns accumulated by both research and practice. Responding to the individual and immediate needs of students in these ever-changing contexts demands teacher invention and improvisation.

The Current Paradigm for Change

Such new understandings of the change process and how teachers learn have underscored the need for teacher education to 'engage teachers in learning and development in the context of their particular classroom settings' (McLaughlin, 1991, p. 79). Teachers recognize that schools, classrooms, and students are constantly changing. Their goals are responsive to the diverse and dynamic contexts in which they teach. They view the needs of students, classrooms, and schools as demanding immediate attention, and waiting for research and policy to invent solutions is both inefficient and foolish (McLaughlin, 1993). Moreover, the school 'reform' policies now being pushed by politicians (e.g., national standards and examinations) are often antithetical to the innovative stance teachers wish to adopt (Darling-Hammond, 1993). The complex, dynamic, and unpredictable nature of schools and classrooms requires practitioners to be innovators.

In more responsible, contemporary models for reform, schools are viewed as professional communities where teachers are continual learners (Lieberman, 1992). A high level of innovativeness characterizes these professional communities where 'teachers are enthusiastic about their work and the focus is on devising strategies that enable all students to prosper' (McLaughlin, 1993). Recent fresh approaches to teaching and learning – alternatives to whole-group, teacher-centered instruction supported by the staff development practices of the seventies and eighties (Wasley, 1994) – demand invention, not the implementation of others' ideas.

Ushering in current thinking about school reform, researchers have called for teachers to adapt research findings to their particular classrooms (Joyce, Bennett, & Rolheiser-Bennett, 1990; McLaughlin, 1991; Sparks-Langer et al., 1990). Today's teachers are being encouraged to reflect critically on their practices and to provide opportunities for all students to learn. 'Critical review and construction of practice (is viewed as) a necessity' (McLaughlin, 1993, p. 96), and teachers are actively encouraged to replace externally developed innovations with their own inventions.

This new focus of school reform has also shifted from changing schools and teachers to understanding the changed nature of school contexts. Teaching in contemporary classrooms presents a particular challenge for today's teachers. Contemporary students bring with them to the classroom different cultures, different languages, and different attitudes toward learning than students of the past (McLaughlin, 1993).

One longitudinal study of secondary schools involving nearly 900 teachers in two states was conducted by the Stanford University Center for Research on the Context of Secondary School Teaching (McLaughlin, 1993; McLaughlin & Talbert, 1993). Through quantitative and qualitative analyses of survey and interview data, these researchers identified factors that facilitated or constrained teachers from teaching in ways that enabled all students to succeed. Teachers were found to respond to the challenges of contemporary teaching in different ways, but students were identified as the context variable that mattered most to teachers.

McLaughlin and Talbert (1993) extrapolated three broad patterns of teachers' responses:

1) One group of teachers responded by continuing to enforce traditional standards. These teachers often experienced burnout and cynicism.
2) Another group of teachers responded by lowering expectations for students. Teaching a less demanding curriculum resulted in boredom and disengagement for both teachers and students.
3) Teachers in a third group responded by changing their practices to include learner-centered instruction and a more active role for students.

Many teachers in this third group were unable to sustain these practices and experienced frustration. Some such teachers, however, were able to sustain changes in practice; these teachers were all members of a professional community that supported their efforts to transform their teaching (see also Lieberman, 1992).

A growing body of research provides evidence that membership in a professional community may support teachers in learning new teaching practices (see Lieberman, 1995). Peterson, McCarthey, and Elmore (1996) analyzed cases of restructuring experiments in three urban elementary schools. During this two-year naturalistic study, researchers collected views of classroom writing practices of two teachers in each school through interviews and observations. Exploring the connection between school organizational structures and classroom practices, these researchers concluded that organizational structures intended to promote change did not necessarily cause learning to occur.

Three schools were engaged in restructuring practices such as regrouping students, structuring time for team meetings, and providing professional development opportunities. Restructuring, however, occurred in accordance with each school's own vision of restructuring. For example, in one school teachers believed that each of them would have different beliefs and practices because teachers had different 'styles' of teaching and learning. Although the teachers believed they had changed their instructional strategies for teaching writing, teachers did little to facilitate the expression of students' own ideas. In this school, the researchers observed, teachers depended on each other for assistance in learning new practices. Without access to a larger professional community in which to expand their knowledge, teachers' knowledge of the writing process was superficial and limited.

In a series of descriptive case studies, Wasley (1994) described teachers who were 'stirring the chalkdust' in an effort to transform their teaching. Wasley's descriptions provide insights into what is involved in the current paradigm for school change. After watching five different teachers engaged in transforming their practice in different schools, Wasley concluded:

1) These teachers were collaborators; they collaborated with students and colleagues in forming new visions of teaching and learning. They engaged students in meaningful, intellectual tasks that included problem-solving and projects growing from student and community interests. These teachers were expert diagnosticians of individual students' intellectual growth; assessment was ongoing and an integral component of learning.

2) Teachers, principals, district officials, and policy makers need to share in the commitment to changing practices, not in a commitment to a

particular type of practice that disappears with each change of administration. Change, originating in the classroom, needs to be protected.

3) Traditional structures and procedures restrict teachers in their efforts to teach in ways that enable all students to succeed. Shared decision making, power, and responsibility among teachers, students, and school officials characterize restructuring schools.

4) Meaningful change takes time. Teachers need time to work with new ideas and practices. Teachers need to be exposed to new ideas through networks, seminars, reading, and discussion groups. Learning is a continuous process. (pp. 205-209)

In summary, restructuring schools and teaching requires continual growth for everyone. Engaging all learners in appropriate and intellectually challenging learning experiences demands an immediate and contextually based response to individual growth. Changing schools is a continuous process that requires teachers to be innovators.

Bringing Research to Practice: New Methodological Orientations

As we have seen through this review, traditional forms of staff development encouraged replication of research-based practices. To encourage invention over replication requires new understandings of what is involved in transforming teaching and learning. Invention demands new forms of staff development research and practice.

One exemplary staff development research project by Duffy (1993) was designed to help elementary teachers incorporate comprehension-strategy instruction into their literacy curriculum. Instead of providing teachers with materials or instructional kits to follow, Duffy communicated to teachers that they were expected to construct their own instruction. In monthly staff development sessions, teachers were provided with professional knowledge about research on reading and comprehension strategies. Additionally, the researcher and his colleagues worked in teachers' classrooms twice monthly to assist teachers. Through classroom observations and interviews with both teachers and targeted at-risk students, Duffy followed the progress of 11 teachers in four different school districts. Duffy asked what characterized instruction at various points in the teachers' progress toward becoming expert strategy instructors.

Results showed that teachers initially asked for prescriptions, much as students initially ask teachers for answers when they first encounter student-centered instruction. But, over time, these requests slowed, and teachers' practices suggested a continuum of nine points of progress. Teachers' progress was not linear, however. It was recursive. Teachers visited and revisited various points on the continuum throughout the project. Teachers, at times, modelled the strategies faithfully, expressed doubt and confusion, tried out the strategies tentatively, and implemented the strategies smoothly. At the 'creative-inventive' point on the continuum, teachers did not follow a prescribed list of strategies. At this point, the teachers decided what strategies to use, revised strategies, or invented new strategies by listening to their students. Not surprisingly, these teachers also expressed comfort with the ambiguities and uncertainties that new teaching situations presented.

Another example of innovative staff development research was conducted at the University of Michigan where researchers have collaborated with teachers to encourage and support project-based science instruction. Drawing from the literature on teacher change and learning to teach, Krajcik, Blumenfeld, Marx, and Soloway (1994) developed an alternative model for disseminating research to practitioners. The model, based on collaboration, classroom enactment, and reflection, was used to assist teachers in planning and implementing project-based science instruction supported by the National Science Foundation. From the 'curriculum enactment' perspective (Snyder et al., 1992), the researchers provided ten middle school teachers and one elementary school science teacher with materials, including a telecommunications network, that teachers could modify for their own classroom. In collaborative work sessions, the researchers provided teachers with information about the theoretical background of the project, model activities, and technology. They then documented teachers' classroom practices with video-taped classroom observations conducted from one to four times a week. Teachers also kept reflective journals recording their reactions and ideas. In addition to classroom observations and teachers' journals, interviews, and informal conversations with the teachers also provided data for written case studies.

Drawing on those case studies, Blumenfeld, Krajcik, Marx, and Soloway (1994) described what they learned about the collaborative model of staff development and how teachers' learning occurred. Like Duffy, these researchers found teachers initially reluctant to modify their activities:

> Rather, they continued to assume that they had to reproduce activities faithfully and follow specific topics in the curriculum. Their visions were still based on a transmission model founded on developing congruent practices. (p. 546)

Encouraged by the researchers, teachers gradually began to develop new activities. In the enactment of project activities, teachers learned more about the nature of project-based instruction, and the researchers learned more about the constraints of practice. Although 'change in practice was slow, idiosyncratic, and fragmented' (p. 548), gradually teachers' justifications for practices changed from rules to theoretical understandings of project-based instruction.

These studies suggest that researchers themselves can personally play a critical role in disseminating research to practitioners. Our own research follows a similar model. Each of these examples of the new staff development research may be referred to as *collaborative innovation*. Findings suggest that collaborations between researchers and practitioners can result in the development of new instructional practices and assessments when research-based concepts are embedded in particular content. In one study we carried out, one of us (Randi) taught secondary humanities as content. Randi designed, implemented, and assessed instruction based on theories she discussed with Corno about how students implicitly learn to become self-regulated learners. Collecting data on anything that might relate to self-regulated learning and its development in her classroom, Randi conducted what we termed a 'color field' case study (in the sense of a color field painting). Together, we analyzed and interpreted the data. Using one writer's description of a color field novel provides insight into how research conducted from teachers' perspectives can lead into their world:

> ... Randi's case (is) 'framed' by the limits of the research and ... (the teacher's) own observations and bounded by the immediate context of this classroom and curriculum. Like a color field painting, 'There is no structural focus, no vanishing point to tease the inner eye with the illusion of dimension.' ... It is this limitation of perspective, however, that allows entry to the two-dimensional world of the classroom as (the teacher) saw it. Like her, we researchers have 'no privileged information, no interpretive asides to clue us in. With only this teacher for guidance, we too become participants. We have no choice ...'
> (Corno, 1994, paraphrasing Flanagan, 1994, p. 29)

Building on this preliminary work, Randi (1996) interpreted the instructional practices of eight secondary teachers from their perspectives as they attempted to implement new instructional strategies learned in traditional staff development sessions. Unlike in traditional staff development programs, however, these teachers experienced interviews and classroom observations as Randi followed their progress through sequences of planning, delivering, and reflecting on lessons they themselves designed. Together, the researcher and the teachers also constructed narratives that traced the development of their lessons from the sources of the teachers' ideas to enactment in the classroom. Often, new instructional practices were found to be invented by these teachers based on ideas they had abstracted from the instructional models provided to them.

These teachers also interpreted through the researcher the changes they made in instructional strategies modelled in the original staff development sessions.

Their interpretations reflected the contexts in which they worked. Teachers' reasons for changed practices included: considerations of students' current and future needs, abilities, interests, and reactions to new practices; the nature of the subject area; and, factors beyond the immediate classroom and school context, such as state-mandated testing programs. As with our preliminary experiences with 'color-field' research, these teachers' interpretations were bounded by the contexts in which they worked, including the research study in which they participated. Their information was linked to sources that were both personal and collective. And some of the information these classroom teachers had access to was not generally available to researchers or external change agents (i.e., knowledge of their particular students and the unique cultures of their particular classrooms, subject area departments, and schools).

Our color-field studies, along with the other new staff development research we have discussed, have attempted to examine teaching from the perspective of practice. As Richardson (1994) has proposed, research conducted on practice helps 'to describe what it means to think like a teacher and what is entailed in teacher change' (p. 8). Drawing on the growing body of literature on teacher research, Richardson described teachers' inquiry into their own practice as 'practical inquiry.' She distinguished practical inquiry from formal research that contributes to the general knowledge base. Teachers undertake 'practical inquiry' to improve their own practice. What we have termed 'collaborative innovation' is a new form of staff development research somewhere between these two extremes.

Richardson also argued that formal research is insufficient to inform the unique contexts of practice and the immediate needs of teachers. We agree. However, practical researchers also need to recognize the limitations imposed on their own work by small and unrepresentative samples and non-experimental designs. They need to avoid interpretations that require substantial evidence. Far too often the research we found in our work for this chapter never acknowledged such limitations and moved instead into unwarranted, causal interpretations of data based on limited evidence and overgeneralization. Much of the research we reviewed was qualitative and descriptive and not conducted by teachers and researchers working as collaborators. The new staff development research we call 'collaborative innovation' overcomes some of these weaknesses with inherent checks and balances. At the same time, the process-oriented nature of collaborative innovation insures that there is an 'evidence trail' leading up to results.

CONCLUSION

Most studies we reviewed, like most studies we found as we organized this chapter, viewed teachers' new practices through the lenses of fidelity and implementation. Yet, the practice of adapting instructional innovations by teachers, even during the time when fidelity was targeted (Fullan & Pomfret, 1977), suggests that some teachers found a way 'to break through the mesh and coil of circumstance' (Dewey, 1904, p. 16) long before teachers were recognized as innovators. Some adaptations made by teachers did constitute innovations – as changes gradually and continually devised in response to the needs of particular students.

Similar practitioner-generated innovations have been observed in other professions related to teaching. In clinical psychotherapy, for example, practitioners in this field have been altering procedures learned in professional school based on their own experiences in practice.

> Few procedures are practiced with theoretical purity, to the great advantage of millions seeking help from psychotherapy. Fortunately, given our inadequate data base, therapists continue to innovate and often do hit upon successful procedures.... Similar statements could be made about educational or rehabilitation practices, and the like.... The successful experiences of practitioners must be observed, verified, and accumulated through empirical practice and accountability. (Barlow, Hayes, & Nelson, 1984, pp. 34–36)

We have found a small but growing body of literature documenting teachers' innovative practices as well (e.g., Paris, 1993; Wasley, 1994; Woods, 1990). But, for the most part, experienced teachers have seldom been invited to ask questions and act as critics of research products disseminated in staff development programs. Nor have they been sufficiently often invited to explain their reasons for adapting instructional innovations to particular classroom contexts (Little, 1993). Consequently, researchers have had few opportunities to approach implementation from teachers' perspectives – to conduct color-field studies and to participate in collaborative innovation research.

Researchers, writing about school change from the perspective of practitioners, have made it clear that there is a great deal to be learned from teachers (Miles, Saxl, & Lieberman, 1988). Lieberman (1992) envisioned a synthesis of research and practice in which 'we can learn from as well as about practice' (p. 27). We believe that closing the gap between research and practice requires, not just an understanding of how new ideas from research are imitated and refined in practice, but also an understanding of how new ideas are invented by teachers in their classrooms. In articulating a new paradigm of school restructuring, Darling-Hammond (1993) summarized the tension between the implementation of specific innovations developed outside the classroom in which they must be implemented and the generation of new practices in response to the ever-changing contexts in which teachers must work:

> They (teachers) must adapt and respond on the basis of individual needs and interactions to a complex, ever-changing set of circumstances – taking into account the real knowledge and experiences of learners, including their cultures, their communities, and the conditions in which they live. Yet this is what many current school reform policies seek to prevent teachers from doing (p. 758).

As we have seen here, there has been much research focused on change in education and how to accomplish it. During the time that external change agents attended to schools' problems and worked to devise carefully defined solutions, teachers have continued to face the ever-changing realities of classrooms. While reformers looked to transform schools, teachers looked to adapt to the daily and ever-changing exigencies of practice. Innovation has been no less a goal for some teachers than it has for school reformers. But teacher-generated innovations are immediate responses to the complex set of circumstances in which teachers work. The immediate demands of the classroom cannot wait for policy and research to develop and disseminate solutions. These complex and ever-changing conditions also make it difficult to argue for the long-term institutionalization of any innovation, whether it be internally or externally developed. Without a clearer understanding of how teachers generate new practices in response to the ever-changing contexts of their work, it is unlikely that research, policy, and staff development can support innovation at the classroom level.

And yet, long before reformers called for fresh practices, long before researchers discovered teachers' practical knowledge, and long before teachers were recognized as innovators, creative teachers were listening to their students, discovering how best to teach them, and inventing fresh practices. Through the lens of implementation, teachers' adaptations are variants from ideal, prescribed practices. Through the lens of *innovation*, teachers' adaptations are responses to the unique and varied contexts of teaching.

ENDNOTES

[1.] The authors wish to thank Bruce Biddle and Ivor Goodson for comments on an earlier draft.

REFERENCES

Aiken, W. (1942). *Adventure in American education, Vol. 1: Story of the eight year study*. New York: Harper and Brothers.

Amarel, M. & Chittenden, E. (1982, March). *A conceptual study of knowledge use in schools*. Paper presented at the annual meeting of the American Educational Research Association, New York. (ERIC Document Reproduction Service No. ED 240 203).

Anderson, L., Evertson, C., & Brophy, J. (1979). An experimental study of effective teaching in first-grade reading groups. *Elementary School Journal, 79*, 193-223.

Anderson, D. S. & Biddle, B. J. (Eds.). (1991). *Knowledge for policy: Improving education through research*. London: Falmer.

Bandura, A. (1977). *Social learning theory*. Englewood Cliffs, NJ: Prentice-Hall.

Bandura, A. (1986). *Social foundations of thought and action: A social cognitive theory*. Englewood Cliffs, NJ: Prentice-Hall.

Barlow, D. H., Hayes, S. C., & Nelson, R. O. (1984). *The scientist-practitioner: Research and accountability in clinical and educational settings*. New York: Pergamon Press.

Belfiore, E. (1984). A theory of imitation in Plato's Republic. *Transactions of the American Philological Association, 114*, 121-146.

Bennett, B. & Rolheiser-Bennett, C. (1992). A restructuring journey. In A. Costa, J. Bellanca, & R. Fogarty (Eds.), *If minds matter* (Vol. 1, pp. 103-123). Palatine, IL: Skylight Publishing.

Berlak, A. & Berlak, H. (1981). *The dilemmas of schooling: Teaching and social change*. London: Methuen.

Berliner, D. C. (1987). Ways of thinking about students and classrooms by more or less experienced teachers. In J. Calderhead (Ed.), *Exploring teachers' thinking* (pp. 60-83). London: Cassell.

Berliner, D. C. & Biddle, B. J. (1995). *The manufactured crisis: Myths, fraud, and the attack on America's public schools*. Reading, MA: Addison Wesley.

Berman, P. & McLaughlin, M. (1975). *Federal programs supporting educational change: The findings in review* (Vol. 4). Santa Monica, CA: Rand Corporation.

Berman, P. & McLaughlin, M. (1976). Implementation of educational innovation. *Educational Forum, 40*(3), 345-370.

Bird, T. (1986). Mutual adaptation and mutual accomplishment: Images of change in a field experiment. In A. Lieberman (Ed.), *Rethinking school improvement* (pp. 45-60). New York: Teachers College Press.

Blumenfeld, P. C., Krajcik, J. S., Marx, R. W., & Soloway, E. (1994). Lessons learned: How collaboration helped middle grade science teachers. *Elementary School Journal, 94*(5), 540-551.

Bolin, F. S. (1987). The teacher as curriculum decision maker. In F. S. Bolin & J. Falk (Eds.), *Teacher renewal: Professional issues, personal choices* (pp. 92-108). New York: Teachers College Press.

Borko, H., Cone, R., Russo, N. A., & Shavelson, R. J. (1979). Teachers' decision making. In P. Peterson & H. Walberg (Eds.), *Research on teaching* (pp. 136-160). Berkeley: McCutcheon.

Bussis, A., Chittenden, E., & Amarel, M. (1976). *Beyond surface curriculum*. Boulder, CO: Westview Press.

Calderhead, J. (Ed.). (1987). *Exploring teachers' thinking*. London: Cassell.

Carter, K. & Doyle, W. (1987). Teachers' knowledge structures and comprehension processes. In J. Calderhead (Ed.), *Exploring teachers' thinking* (pp. 147-160). London: Cassell.

Castle, D. (1988). Evaluating the effects and the process of staff development. *Journal of Staff Development, 9*(1), 20-27.

Clandinin, D. J. (1985). Personal practical knowledge: A study of teachers' classroom images. *Curriculum Inquiry, 15*(4), 361-385.

Clark, C. & Peterson, P. (1986). Teachers' thought processes. In M. Wittrock (Ed.), *Handbook of research on teaching* (3rd ed., pp. 255-296). New York: Macmillan.

Cochran-Smith, M. & Lytle, S. L. (Eds.). (1992). *Inside/outside: Teacher research and knowledge*. New York: Teachers College Press.

Cohen, D. K. (1988). *Teaching practice: Plus ca change* (Issue Paper No. 88-3). East Lansing, MI: Michigan State University, National Center for Research on Teacher Education.

Collins, A., Brown, J. S., & Newman, S. E. (1989). Cognitive apprenticeship: Teaching the craft of reading, writing and mathematics. In L. Resnick (Ed.), *Knowing, learning an instruction: Essays in honor of Robert Glaser* (pp. 453-493). Hillsdale, NJ: Erlbaum.

Connelly, F. M. & Ben-Peretz, M. (1980). Teachers' roles in the using and doing of research and curriculum development. *Journal of Curriculum Studies, 12*(2), 95-107.

Connelly, F. M. & Clandinin, J. (1988). *Teachers as curriculum planners*. New York: Teachers College Press.

Cornett, J. W. (1990). Teacher thinking about curriculum and instruction: A case study of a secondary social studies teacher. *Theory and Research in Social Education, 18*(3), 248-273.

Corno, L. (1977). Teacher autonomy and instructional systems. In L. Rubin (Ed.), *Curriculum handbook: Administration and theory* (pp. 234-248). Rockleigh, NJ: Allyn and Bacon.

Corno, L. (1994, April). *Implicit teachings and self-regulated learnings*. Invited address presented at the annual meeting of the American Educational Research Association, New Orleans, LA.

Crandall, D. P. (1983). The teacher's role in school improvement. *Educational Leadership, 41*(3), 6-9.

Crandall, D. P. & Loucks, S. F. (1983). *A roadmap for school improvement. Executive summary for people, policies and practices: Examining the chain of school improvement*. Andover, MA: The Network.

Crawford, J., Gage, N. L., Corno, L., Stayrook, N. G., Mitman, A., Schunk, D., Baskin, E., Stallings, J., & Harvey, P. (1978). The Stanford study of third-grade teaching and parent involvement: A nontechnical report. *Center for Educational Research at Stanford, Program on Teaching Effectiveness Report*. Stanford, CA: School of Education, Stanford University.

Cronbach, L. J. (1975). Beyond the two disciplines of scientific psychology. *American Psychologist, 30*(2), 116-127.

Cronbach, L. J. & Snow, R. E. (1977). *Aptitudes and instructional methods: A handbook for research on interactions*. New York: Irvington/Naiburg.

Cuban, L. (1990). Reforming again, again, and again. *Educational Researcher, 19*(1), 3-13.

Cuban, L. (1993). *How teachers taught: Constancy and change in American classrooms 1890-1990* (2nd ed.). New York: Teachers College Press.

Darling-Hammond, L. (1990). Instructional policy into practice: The power of the bottom over the top. *Educational Evaluation and Policy Analysis, 12*(3), 339-348.

Darling-Hammond, L. (1993). Reframing the school reform agenda. *Phi Delta Kappan, 74*(10), 753-761.

Dewey, J. (1904). The relation of theory to practice in the education of teachers. In C. McMurry (Ed.), *The third yearbook of the National Society for the Scientific Study of Education, Part I* (pp. 9-30). Chicago: University of Chicago Press.

Doyle, W. & Ponder, G. (1977). The practicality ethic in teacher decision-making. *Interchange, 8*(3), 1-12.

Drucker, P. (1985). *Innovation and entrepreneurship*. New York: Harper & Row.

Duckworth, E. (1986). Teaching as research. *Harvard Educational Review, 56*(4), 481-495.

Duckworth, E. (1987). *The having of wonderful ideas*. New York: Teachers College Press.

Duffy, G. G. (1993). Teachers' progress toward becoming expert strategy teachers. *Elementary School Journal, 94*(2), 109-120.

Eisner, E. (1985). *The educational imagination.* New York: Macmillan.

Eisner, E. (1994). *Cognition and the curriculum.* New York: Teachers College Press.

Elbaz, F. (1981). The teacher's 'practical knowledge': Report of a case study. *Curriculum Inquiry, 11*(1), 43-71.

Elbaz, F. (1983). *Teacher thinking: A study of practical knowledge.* London: Croom Helm.

Feiman-Nemser, S. & Buchman, M. (1985). Pitfalls of experience in teacher preparation. *Teachers College Record, 87*(1), 53-65.

Flanagan, M. (1994, January 2). Enter laughing. *The New York Times,* Section 7, p. 1.

Fullan, M. (1983). Evaluating program implementation: What can be learned from follow-through. *Curriculum Inquiry, 13*(2), 215-227.

Fullan, M. (1993). Innovation, reform, and restructuring strategies. In G. Cawelti (Ed.), *Challenges and achievements in American education* (pp. 116-133). Alexandria, VA: Association of Supervision and Curriculum Development.

Fullan, M., Bennett, B, & Rolheiser-Bennett, C. (1990). Linking classroom and school improvement. *Educational Leadership, 47*(8), 13-19.

Fullan, M. & Miles, M. (1992). Getting reform right: What works and what doesn't. *Phi Delta Kappan, 73*(10), 745-752.

Fullan, M. & Pomfret, A. (1977). Research on curriculum and instruction implementation. *Review of Educational Research, 47*(1), 335-397.

Gage, N. L. (1978). *The scientific basis of the art of teaching.* New York: Teachers College Press.

Gage, N. L. (1984). What do we know about teaching effectiveness? *Phi Delta Kappan, 66*(2), 87-93.

Glathorn, A. A. (1987). Cooperative professional development: Peer-centered options for teacher growth. *Educational Leadership, 45*(3), 31-35.

Goodlad, J. (1975). *The dynamics of educational change.* New York: McGraw-Hill.

Goodlad, J. (1984). *A place called school.* New York: McGraw-Hill.

Greene, M. (1988). What happened to imagination? In K. Egan & D. Nadaner (Eds.), *Imagination and education* (pp. 45-56). New York: Teachers College Press.

Gross, N., Giacquinta, J., & Bernstein, M. (1971). *Implementing organizational innovations: A sociological analysis of planned educational change.* New York: Basic Books.

Grossman, P. L. (1990). *The making of a teacher: Teacher knowledge and teacher education.* New York: Teachers College Press.

Grossman, P. (1992). *English as context: English in context* (S93-2). Stanford: Center for Research on the Context of Secondary Teaching.

Grossman, P. L. & Richert, A. E. (1986, April). *Unacknowledged knowledge growth: A re-examination of the effects of teacher education.* Paper presented at the annual meeting of the American Educational Research Association, San Francisco.

Gudmundsdottir, S. (1987, April). *Pedagogical content knowledge: Teachers' ways of knowing.* Paper presented at the annual meeting of the American Educational Research Association, Washington, DC.

Gudmundsdottir, S. (1990). Values in pedagogical content knowledge. *Journal of Teacher Education, 41*(3), 44-52.

Guskey, T. (1988). Teacher efficacy, self-concept, and attitudes toward the implementation of instructional innovation. *Teaching and Teacher Education, 4*(1), 63-69.

Guskey, T. (1990). Integrating innovations. *Educational Leadership, 47*(5), 11-15.

Haley-Oliphant, A. E. (1987). *Mind Games: A study of hypothetical questioning in a science classroom*. Paper presented at the annual meeting of the National Association for Research in Science Teaching, Washington, DC.

Hall, G. & Loucks, S. (1977). A developmental model for determining whether the treatment is actually implemented. *American Educational Research Journal, 14*(3), 263-276.

Hall, G., Loucks, S, Rutherford, W., & Newlove, B. (1975). Levels of use of the innovation: A framework for analyzing innovation adoption. *Journal of Teacher Education, 26*(1), 52-56.

Hargreaves, A. (1993). Individualism and individuality. In J. W. Little (Ed.), *Teachers' work* (pp. 51-76). New York: Teachers College Press.

Hargreaves, A. & Dawe, R. (1990). Paths of professional development: Contrived collegiality, collaborative culture, and the case of peer coaching. *Teaching and Teacher Education, 6*(3), 227-241.

Hashweh, M. (1987). Effects of subject matter knowledge in the teaching of biology and physics. *Teaching and Teacher Education, 3*, 109-120.

Hawthorne, R. K. (1992). *Curriculum in the making*. New York: Teachers College Press.

Highet, G. (1967). *The classical tradition*. London: Oxford University Press.

Hord, S. (1986). *A manual for using innovation configurations to assess teacher development programs*. Austin, TX: Research and Development Center.

Hord, S. & Hall, G. (1986). *Institutionalization of innovations: Knowing when you have it and when you don't*. Paper presented at the annual meeting of the American Educational Research Association, San Francisco.

Hord, S., Rutherford, W., Huling-Austin, L., & Hall, G. (1987). *Taking charge of change*. Alexandria, VA: Association for Supervision and Curriculum Development.

House, E. (1979). Technology versus craft: A ten year perspective on innovation. *Journal of Curriculum Studies, 11*(1), 1-15.

Huberman, A. M. & Miles, M. (1984). *Innovation up close: How school improvement works*. New York: Plenum Press.

Huberman, A. M. & Miles, M. (1986). Rethinking the quest for school improvement: Some findings from the DESSI Study. In A. Lieberman (Ed.), *Rethinking school improvement* (pp. 45-60). New York: Teachers College Press.

Jagla, V. M. (1989). *In pursuit of the elusive image: An inquiry into teachers' everyday use of imagination and intuition*. Unpublished doctoral dissertation, University of Illinois, Chicago.

Janesick, V. (1982). Of snakes and circles: Making sense of classroom group processes through a case study. *Curriculum Inquiry, 12*(2), 161-189.

Joyce, B., Bennett, B., & Rolheiser-Bennett, C. (1990). The self-educating teacher: Empowering teachers through research. In B. Joyce (Ed.), *Changing school culture through staff development* (pp. 26-40). Alexandria, VA: Association for Supervision and Curriculum Development.

Joyce, B. & Showers, B. (1980). Improving inservice training: The messages of research. *Educational Leadership, 37*, 379-385.

Joyce, B. & Showers, B. (1981). Transfer of training: The contribution of coaching. *Journal of Education, 163*, 163-172.

Joyce, B. & Showers, B. (1982). The coaching of teaching. *Educational Leadership, 40*, 4-10.

Joyce, B. & Showers, B. (1988). *Student achievement through staff development*. New York: Longman.

Joyce, B. & Weil, M. (1973). The teacher-innovator: Models of teaching as the core of teacher education. *Interchange, 4*(2-3), 47-60.

Joyce, B. & Weil, M. (1986). *Models of teaching*. Englewood Cliffs, NJ: Prentice-Hall.

Kagan, D. (1988). Teaching as clinical problem solving: A critical examination of the analogy and its implications. *Review of Educational Research, 58*(4), 482-505.

Krajcik, J. S., Blumenfeld, P. C., Marx, R. W., & Soloway, E. (1994). A collaborative model for helping middle grade science teachers learn project-based instruction. *Elementary School Journal, 94*(5), 483-498.

Lampert, M. (1985). How do teachers manage to teach? Perspectives on problems in practice. *Harvard Educational Review, 55*(2), 178-194.

Leinhardt, G. (1988). Situated knowledge and expertise in teaching. In J. Calderhead (Ed.), *Teachers' professional learning* (pp. 146-168). Philadelphia: Falmer Press.

Leinhardt, G. & Smith, D. A. (1985). Expertise in mathematics instruction: Subject matter knowledge. *Journal of Educational Psychology, 77*, 247-271.

Levitt, T. (1983). *The marketing imagination.* New York: Free Press.

Lieberman, A. (1992). The meaning of scholarly activity and the building of community. *Educational Researcher, 21*(6), 5-12.

Lieberman, A. (1995). Practices that support teacher development: Transforming conceptions of professional learning. *Phi Delta Kappan, 76*(8), 591-596.

Lieberman, A. & Miller, L. (1986). School improvement: Themes and variations. In A. Lieberman (Ed.), *Rethinking school improvement* (pp. 96-111). New York: Teachers College Press.

Lieberman, A. & Miller, L. (1992). The professional development of teachers. In M. C. Alkin (Ed.), *Encyclopedia of educational research.* (6th ed., Vol. 3, pp. 1045-1053). New York: Macmillan.

Little, J. W. (1989). District policy choices and teachers' professional development opportunities. *American Educational Research Journal, 11*(2), 165-179.

Little, J. W. (1993). Teachers' professional development in a climate of educational reform. *Educational Evaluation and Policy Analysis, 15*(2), 129-151.

Little, J. W. & McLaughlin, M. W. (Eds.). (1993). *Teachers' work: Individuals, colleagues, and contexts.* New York: Teachers College Press.

Loucks, S. F. (1983). *Defining fidelity: A cross study analysis.* Paper presented at the annual meeting of the American Educational Research Association, Montreal, Quebec, Canada. (ERIC Document Reproduction Service No. ED 249 659).

Loucks, S. & Crandall, D. (1982). *The practice profile: An all-purpose tool for program communication, staff development, evaluation, and improvement.* Andover, MA: The Network, Inc.

Loucks-Horsley, S. & Steigelbauer, S. (1991). Using knowledge of change to guide staff development. In A. Lieberman & L. Miller (Eds.), *Staff development for the education in the 90's* (pp. 15-36). New York: Teachers College Press.

McLaughlin, M. W. (1976). Implementation of ESEA Title I: A problem of compliance. *Teachers College Record, 80*(1), 69-94.

McLaughlin, M. W. (1987). Lessons from past implementation research. *Educational Evaluation and Policy Analysis, 9*(2), 171-178.

McLaughlin, M. W. (1990). The Rand Change Agent Study revisited: Macro perspectives and micro realities. *Educational Researcher, 19*(9), 11-16.

McLaughlin, M. W. (1991). Enabling professional development: What have we learned? In A. Lieberman & L. Miller (Eds.), *Staff development for education in the 90's* (pp. 61-82). New York: Teachers College Press.

McLaughlin, M. W. (1993). What matters most in teachers' workplace context? In J. W. Little & M. W. McLaughlin (Eds.), *Teachers' work: Individuals, colleagues, and contexts* (pp. 79-103). New York: Teachers College Press.

McLaughlin, M. W. & Marsh, D. (1978). Staff development and school change. *Teachers College Record, 80*(1), 69-94.

McLaughlin, M. W. & Talbert, J. E. (1993). *Contexts that matter for teaching and learning.* Stanford: Center for Research on the Context of Secondary Teaching.

McLaughlin, M. L., Talbert, J. E., & Bascia, N. (Eds.). (1990). *The contexts of teaching in secondary schools.* New York: Teachers College Press.

McTaggart, R. (1989). Bureaucratic rationality and the self-educating profession: The problem of teacher privatism. *Journal of Curriculum Studies, 21*(4), 345-361.

Marshall, J. (1988). A general statement on staff development evaluation. *Journal of Staff Development, 9*(1), 2-8.

Merryfield, M. M. (1993, April). *Shaping the curriculum in global education: The influence of student characteristics on teacher decision-making.* Paper presented at the annual meeting of the American Educational Research Association, Atlanta, GA.

Metz, M. H. (1993). Teachers' ultimate dependence on their students. In J. W. Little (Ed.), *Teachers' work* (pp. 104-136). New York: Teachers College Press.

Miles, M. B. (1983). Unraveling the mystery of institutionalization. *Educational Leadership, 41*(3), 14-19.

Miles, M. B., Saxl, E., & Lieberman, A. (1988). What skills do change agents need? An empirical view. *Curriculum Inquiry, 18*(2), 157-193.

Mitchell, D. E. & Kerchner, C. (1983). Labor relations and teacher policy. In L. Shulman & G. Sykes (Eds.), *Handbook of teaching and policy* (pp. 214-238). New York: Longman.

Mohlman, G., Coladarci, T., & Gage, N. (1982). Comprehension and attitude as predictors of implementation of teacher training. *Journal of Teacher Education, 33*(1), 31-36.

Munby, H. (1984). A qualitative approach to the study of a teacher's beliefs. *Journal of Research in Science Teaching, 21*(1), 27-38.

Noddings, N. & Shore, P. (1984). *Awakening the inner eye: Intuition in education.* New York: Teachers College Press.

Olson, J. (1980). Teacher constructs and curriculum change. *Journal of Curriculum Studies, 12*(1), 1-11.

Olson, J. (1981). Teacher influence in the classroom: A context for understanding curriculum translation. *Instructional Science, 10,* 259-275.

Paris, C. (1989, April). *Contexts of curriculum change: Conflict and consonance.* Paper presented at the annual meeting of the American Educational Research Association, San Francisco.

Paris, C. (1993). *Teacher agency and curriculum making in classrooms.* New York: Teachers College Press.

Pasch, M. & Harberts, J. (1992). Does coaching enhance instructional thought? *Journal of Staff Development, 13*(3), 40-44.

Patton, M. Q. (1982). Reflections on evaluating staff development: The view from an iron cow. *Journal of staff Development, 3,* 6-24.

Perkins, D. N. (1981). *The mind's best work.* Cambridge: Harvard University Press.

Perkins, D. N. (1986). *Knowledge as design.* Hillsdale, NJ: Lawrence Erlbaum.

Peterson, P., McCarthey, S., & Elmore, R. (1996). Learning from school restructuring. *American Educational Research Journal, 33*(1), 119-154.

Popkewitz, T., Tabachnick, R., & Wehlage, G. (1982). *The myth of educational reform.* Madison, WI: University of Wisconsin Press.

Randi, J. (1996) *From imitation to invention: The nature of innovation in teachers' classrooms.* Unpublished doctoral dissertation. New York: Columbia University, Teachers College.

Reynolds, A., Haymore, J., Ringstaff, C., & Grossman, P. (1988). Teachers and curriculum materials: Who is driving whom? *Curriculum Perspectives, 8*(1), 22-30.

Richardson, V. (1990). Significant and worthwhile change in education. *Educational Researcher,* *19*(7), 10-18.

Richardson, V. (1991). How and why teachers change. In S. Conley & B. Cooper (Eds.), *The school as a work environment: Implications for reform* (pp. 66-88). Boston: Allyn and Bacon.

Richardson, V. (1992). The agenda-setting dilemma in a constructivist staff development process. *Teaching and Teacher Education, 8*(3), 287-300.

Richardson, V. (1994). Conducting research on practice. *Educational Researcher, 23*(5), 5-10.

Richardson, V. & Anders, P. (1990). *Final report of the Reading Instruction Study.* Tuscon: University of Arizona.

Rogers, E. (1983). *The diffusion of innovations.* New York: Free Press.

Rubin, L. (1983). Artistry in teaching. *Educational Leadership, 40*(4), 44-49.

Rubin, L. (1985). *Artistry in teaching.* New York: Random House.

Sanders, D. P. & McCutcheon, G. (1988). The development of practical theories of teaching. *Journal of Curriculum Studies, 2*(1), 50-67.

Scheirer, M. A. & Rezmovic, E. L. (1983). Measuring the degree of program implementation. *Evaluation Review, 7*(5), 599-633.

Schon, D. (1983). *The reflective practitioner: How professionals think in action.* New York: Basic Books.

Schon, D. (1987). *Educating the reflective practitioner.* San Francisco: Jossey-Bass.

Shavelson, R. J. & Stern, P. (1981). Research on teachers' pedagogical thoughts, judgments, decisions, and behavior. *Review of Educational Research, 51*(4), 455-498.

Showers, B. (1984). *School improvement through staff development: The coaching of teaching.* Eugene: University of Oregon. (ERIC Document Reproduction No. ED 017 118).

Shulman, L. S. (1986). Those who understand: Knowledge growth in teaching. *Educational Researcher, 15*(2), 4-14.

Shulman, L. S. (1987). Knowledge and teaching: Foundations of the new reform. *Harvard Educational Review, 57*(1), 1-22.

Smith, L. M., Dwyer, D. C., Prunty, J. P., & Kleine, P. F. (1988). *Innovation and change in schooling: History, politics, and agency.* New York: Falmer Press.

Smith, L. M. & Keith, P. (1971). *Anatomy of educational innovation.* New York: Wiley.

Smith, L. M., Kleine, P. F., Prunty, J. P., & Dwyer, D. C. (1986). *Educational innovators: Then and now.* New York: Falmer Press.

Smith, L. M., Prunty, J. P., Dwyer, D. C., & Kleine, P. F. (1987). *The fate of an innovative school.* New York: Falmer Press.

Snyder, J., Bolin, F., & Zumwalt, K. (1992). Curriculum implementation. In P. Jackson (Ed.), *Handbook of research on curriculum* (pp. 4012-435). New York: Macmilllan.

Sockett, H. (1989). Research, practice, and professional aspiration within teaching. *Journal of Curriculum Studies, 21*(2), 97-112.

Sparks, G. M. (1986). The effectiveness of alternative training activities in changing teaching practices. *American Educational Research Journal, 23*(2), 217-225.

Sparks, G. M. & Simmons, J. (1989). Inquiry-oriented staff development: Using research as a source of tools, not rules. In S. Caldwell (Ed.), *Staff development: A handbook of effective practices* (pp. 126-139). Oxford, OH: National Staff Development Council.

Sparks-Langer, G., Simmons, J., Pasch, M., Colton, A., & Starko, A. (1990). Reflective pedagogical knowledge: How can we promote and measure it? *Journal of Teacher Education, 41*(4), 23-32.

Stallings, J. A. (1979). Follow-Through: A model for inservice training. *Curriculum Inquiry, 9*(2), 163-181.

Stenhouse, L. (1985). Defining the curriculum problem. In J. Rudduck & D. Hopkins (Eds.), *Research as a basis for teaching: Readings from the work of Lawrence Stenhouse* (pp. 61-64). London: Heinemann.

Stodolsky, S. (1988). *The subject matters: Classroom activity in math and social studies.* Chicago: University of Chicago Press.

Stodolsky, S. (1993). *A framework for subject matter comparisons in high schools. Teaching and Teacher Education, 9,* 333-346.

Sullivan, D. L. (1989). Attitudes toward imitation: Classical culture and the modern temper. *Rhetoric Review, 8*(1), 5-21.

Talbert, J. E., McLaughlin, M. W., & Rowan, B. (1993). Understanding context effects on secondary school teaching. *Teachers College Record, 95*(1), 45-68.

Wasley, P. (1994). *Stirring the chalkdust: Changing practice in essential schools.* New York: Teachers College Press.

Wilson, S. (1990). A conflict of interests: The case of Mark Black. *Educational Evaluation and Policy Analysis, 12*(3), 293-310.

Wilson, S. M., Shulman, L. S., & Richert, A. E. (1987). 150 different ways of knowing: Representations of knowledge in teaching. In J. Calderhead (Ed.), *Exploring teachers' thinking* (pp. 104-124). London: Cassell.

Woods, P. (1990). *Teacher skills and strategies.* London: Falmer.

Wu, P. C. (1988). Why is change so difficult? Lessons for staff development. *Journal of Staff Development, 9*(2), 10-14.

Yinger, R. J. (1987). *By the seat of your pants: An inquiry into improvisation and teaching.* Paper presented at the annual meeting of the American Educational Research Association, Washington, DC.

Zumwalt, K. K. (Ed.). (1986). *Improving teaching: 1986 ASCD yearbook.* Alexandria, VA: Association for Supervision and Curriculum Development.

Chapter 13: Teacher Learning: Implications of New Views of Cognition

RALPH T. PUTNAM, HILDA BORKO[1]

Michigan State University, University of Colorado

Current educational reform efforts in the United States are setting forth ambitious goals for schools, teachers, and students (e.g., National Council of Teachers of Mathematics, 1989; National Education Goals Panel, 1991; National Research Council, 1993). Schools and teachers are to help students develop rich understandings of important content, think critically, construct and solve problems, synthesize information, invent, create, express themselves proficiently, and leave school prepared to be responsible citizens and lifelong learners. Reformers hold forth visions of teaching and learning in which teachers and student engage in rich discourse about important ideas and participate in problem solving activities grounded in meaningful contexts (e.g., American Association for the Advancement of Science, 1989; National Council of Teachers of Mathematics, 1989, 1991). These visions of teaching and learning depart significantly from much of the educational practice that currently typifies American classrooms – practice that is based on views of teaching as presenting and explaining content and learning as the rehearsal and retention of presented information and skills.

Linda Anderson (1989a) provides a set of five dimensions that are useful for contrasting the ideas underlying the sorts of teaching and learning espoused by reformers with a more "traditional,' basic-skills, direct-instruction approach to schooling' (p. 313). Anderson argues that, although there is considerable variance among classrooms and teachers, in general the visions of teaching and learning being proposed differ from typical classrooms in several ways. In reform-oriented classrooms:

1) Academic goals focus on the 'development of 'expertise' that is demonstrated through strategic and flexible (i.e., decontextualized) use of knowledge' versus 'recall of facts and context-specific application of skills'.

2) The teacher's most important role is seen 'as mediating learning as it is constructed by students' rather than as 'conveying information to students.'

B.J. Biddle et al. (eds.), International Handbook of Teachers and Teaching, 1223-1296

3) Students play the role of 'active constructor of meaningful cognitive networks that are used during problem solving' rather than 'that of receptor[s] of information to be applied directly to practice activities.'

4) Academic tasks 'require students to define and represent problems and transform existing knowledge in one of many possible solutions' rather than serving as 'sites for application of algorithmic procedures to problems with single correct answers.'

5) 'Social environments may present conditions in which failure is accepted as a part of learning, self-regulation or cognition is valued more than other-regulation, and other students are viewed as resources for learning' rather than 'conditions in which failure has social consequences, the source of cognitive regulation is external to the student, and other students are viewed as hindrances to learning' (p. 312).

For teachers to move successfully toward these new visions of classrooms will require in many cases major changes in their knowledge, beliefs, and practice. The changes required are not a simple matter of learning new teaching procedures or techniques that someone else has developed. For the new, richer visions of teaching and learning are just that – visions. Reform documents stop short of offering concrete images and prescriptions for what this new reformed teaching should be like (Ball, 1994). Indeed, there is not a single reform vision; some have argued that we need different instantiations in different communities. In other words, the most appropriate paths toward the goals of educational reform may be different for students with different backgrounds and in different contexts (Delpit, 1988). To make the changes being asked of them, teachers must reflect deeply and critically on their own teaching practice, on the content they teach, and on the experiences and backgrounds of the learners in their classrooms. They must become more *adventurous* to engage in the kinds of ambitious teaching being called for (Cohen, 1989).

The need for teachers to make fundamental changes in how they teach and how they think about teaching raises questions about the adequacy of existing models of teacher education. How can pre-service and in-service teachers be supported in developing the knowledge, skills, and dispositions needed to teach in these rich new ways?

Recent scholarship about teacher learning and teacher education is leading to emerging images of successful teacher education experiences. Much of the spirit of these images is captured in an number of statements about the nature of teacher learning and effective teacher education programs:

– Teachers should be treated as active learners who construct their own understandings;

- Teachers should be empowered and treated as professionals;
- Teacher education must be situated in classroom practice;
- Teacher educators should treat teachers as they expect teachers to treat students.

These statements are rooted in important and valid ideas and have received virtually unanimous support in the teacher education community. Indeed, most of them have played a role in discussions of teacher education and in reforms advocated at various times over the past several decades (e.g., Feiman-Nemser, 1983). The statements have, however, become overused and oversimplified to the point of becoming almost like mantras. Closer examination of these truisms reveals hidden complexities and potential problems. For example:

- *Teachers should be treated as active learners who construct their own understandings.* Virtually all current psychological perspectives on learning consider it to be an active process in which learners construct new knowledge and understandings based on what they already know and believe. This prescription posits that, like their students, teachers can only learn new teaching practices and understandings to the extent that they can make sense of them through the lenses of their existing knowledge and beliefs. But if teachers can only interpret new instructional recommendations or ideas about teaching and learning through their existing conceptions, how can they ever come to learn new practices and ideas without distorting them to conform to their existing views?
- *Teachers should be empowered and treated as professionals.* This maxim often is enacted as the recommendation that teachers should determine the focus and nature of professional development activities. This choice can be especially important because teachers have so often been asked to implement the educational prescriptions of others, rather than being empowered to be reflective professionals responsible for and critical of their own practice. Teachers' ideas, however – about teaching, about learning, and about how their practice might change – are limited by their own experiences and thus may not transcend current practice. Empowering teachers to be self-directed may not, in and of itself, be enough to support them to make meaningful changes in their educational thinking and practice. This concern raises questions about appropriate roles for teacher educators, who must balance providing guidance with respecting teachers' professional knowledge.
- *Teacher education must be situated in classroom practice.* There have long been claims that field experiences provide the site for some of the most important learning that takes place in pre-service teacher

education. This position leads to arguments for early and substantial field experiences and sometimes for field experiences to be incorporated with or attached to *all* learning experiences (e.g., methods courses, foundations courses). In many cases, however, the settings available for pre-service fieldwork do not exemplify the kind of teaching that teacher education programs are trying to promote. Many teacher education programs try to help prospective teachers move beyond traditional instructional approaches that rely heavily on teacher presentation and student rehearsal to learn to teach in ways that enhance students' reasoning, problem solving, and understanding of important ideas. If the classrooms in which pre-service teachers are placed for fieldwork do not embody these new approaches, they may do little to support the learning of new instructional practices. This raises serious questions about the kinds of settings within which teachers learning should or can be set.

— *Teacher educators should treat teachers as they expect teachers to treat students.* This 'Golden Rule' of teacher education shows up as claims that teacher educators should model the kinds of teaching practices they want teachers to use with their students. Further, teacher educators should engage teachers in the activities and ways of interacting that are expected for students. Interpreted too simply, however, this approach overlooks important differences in the setting and goals for the learning of students and the learning of teachers. For example, many current reform efforts argue that students in schools should be engaged with meaningful problems of subject matter (e.g., science, mathematics, or literature). It is important for teachers, too, to engage with important subject-matter in new ways. The learning teacher, however, must ultimately go on to grapple with problems of pedagogy (i.e., the teaching of science, mathematics, or literature). Teachers must deal with issues of student learning and understanding, instructional techniques, and so forth, as well as the subject-matter content itself. To argue that teachers should participate in the same kinds of learning experiences as their students may overlook these important differences in what teachers and students need to learn.

Despite these and other complexities inherent in the mantras, they hold kernels of important ideas about teacher learning and teacher education. Indeed, in using terms such as *mantra* and *truism*, we want to both recognize the importance of the ideas underlying these statements and caution against their oversimplification and indiscriminate use.

Many of the ideas embedded in these mantras have long been a part of discussions of education and teacher education, for example the importance of grounding learning about teaching in field experiences. A number of them have resurfaced recently as people have viewed education through the lenses of current theories of cognition and learning (Greeno, Collins, & Resnick, 1996). In this chapter we use features of these theories to organize further consideration of the warrants for and problems with these mantras.

The first feature or theme is *the constructed nature of knowledge and beliefs*. Virtually all current cognitive theories of learning hold some form of a *constructivist* assumption – that knowledge is a form of interpretation based on a learners' existing conceptions, and that learning is the modification of those conceptions (Resnick, 1991). Because of the importance these constructivist assumptions place on a person's existing knowledge and beliefs, it is in the discussion of this theme that we consider the central role played by teachers' knowledge and beliefs in learning to teach, drawing on our previous reviews of research literature on teacher learning (Borko & Putnam, 1995, 1996). The subsequent three features, as framed by cognitive theory, are more recent arrivals on the research scene in North America, although they have roots in the thinking of educators and psychologists earlier in this century (e.g., Dewey, 1896; Vygotsky, 1978). The first of these (the second feature) is *the social nature of cognition*. Dissatisfied with overly individualistic accounts of learning and knowing, scholars are increasingly arguing for the importance of social and cultural factors in determining what and how we know and learn. The third feature is *the situated nature of cognition*. Knowledge and learning are increasingly viewed as being situated in particular physical and social contexts, challenging the view that knowledge exists in the mind of the individual, independent of its contexts of acquisition and use. Finally, the fourth feature is *the distributed nature of cognition*, the notion that cognition, rather than being a property solely of individuals, is distributed across persons and various artifacts such as physical tools and notation systems (Salomon, 1993).

Each of these four features of cognition has important implications for thinking about both the role of the teacher in the K-12 classroom and learning experiences for pre-service and in-service teachers. We consider both kinds of implications in the sections that follow, concluding the chapter by revisiting the mantras in light of our discussion of the four features.

CONSTRUCTED NATURE OF KNOWLEDGE AND BELIEFS

Virtually all current theories of learning view learners as active constructors of knowledge who make sense of the world and learn by interpreting events through their existing knowledge and beliefs. As Resnick (1991) writes,

The empiricist assumption that dominated many branches of psychology for decades, the assumption that what we know is a direct reflection of what we can perceive in the physical world, has largely disappeared. In its place is a view that most knowledge is an interpretation of experience, an interpretation based on schemas, often idiosyncratic at least in detail, that both enable and constrain individuals' processes of sense-making. (p. 1)

When thinking about students in classrooms, this general constructivist assumption suggests the need for increased attention to the existing knowledge and beliefs of students as they learn. Because the sense that people make of events is always somewhat idiosyncratic, one cannot assume that students in a classroom are learning the same thing or that they are learning by absorbing or recording in some literal sense what is taught. Indeed, there is considerable evidence that students often develop or cling to understandings that are markedly different from what curriculum developers and teachers intend. This has led to a good deal of research on the various misconceptions that students hold, particularly in science and mathematics (for a review see Confrey, 1990), and to proposals for how to help students confront and replace their erroneous conceptions (Posner, Strike, Hewson, & Gertzog, 1983; Smith, diSessa, & Roschelle, 1993).

As Smith et al. (1993) have argued, however, the idea of simply replacing erroneous conceptions is inconsistent with constructivist assumptions that all learning takes as its starting point the learner's current conceptions. All experience is filtered through the individual's existing cognitive structures; therefore, an individual's current understandings must provide the starting point for developing richer, more complex understandings. An important goal of curriculum and teaching, then, is to help students build on nascent understandings.

Role of Teachers' Knowledge and Beliefs

Teachers, like students, interpret experiences through the filters of their existing knowledge and beliefs. A teacher's knowledge and beliefs — about learning, teaching, and subject matter — thus are critically important determinants of how that teacher teaches. For example, teachers' conceptions of students' abilities and expectations for students from different backgrounds lead to differential treatment of students in classrooms (Good & Brophy, 1996; Ladson-Billings, 1995). At the same time, those knowledge and beliefs determine what and how the teacher learns from experiences in the classroom or from various professional development experiences. Like students, teachers can make sense of new instructional practices or ideas only through the lenses of what they already know and believe. This point is particularly relevant for thinking about the sorts of teaching that are being promoted in most current, scholarly reform movements – approaches that emphasize the importance of students' thinking and the development of powerful reasoning and understanding within subject-matter domains (e.g., National Council of Teachers of Mathematics, 1989; National Education Goals Panel, 1991; Resnick, 1987a). In many cases, reformers are calling for teachers to enhance, and sometimes supplant, the 'direct instruction' models of teaching that pervade today's public school classrooms by providing opportunities for students to explore ideas in rich contexts, rather than relying primarily on teacher presentation and student rehearsal. Because teaching for these goals entails thinking of subject-matter content in new ways and being attentive and responsive to the thinking of students, teaching cannot be prescribed in advance as a set of techniques to be carried out in a particular way. Rather, these approaches require teachers to think differently about students, subject matter, and the learning process and to become more 'adventurous' in their teaching (Cohen, 1989).

Thus, if teachers are to be successful in moving toward the sorts of ambitious instruction envisioned by reformers, their knowledge and beliefs must become the *targets* of change. At the same time, however, knowledge and beliefs are important *influences* on or *determinants* of change, serving as critical filters for what and how teachers learn (Cohen & Ball, 1990; Prawat, 1992; Putnam, Heaton, Prawat, & Remillard, 1992). Elsewhere we have used this notion of teachers' knowledge and beliefs playing a dual role as a perspective for reviewing research literature on the role of teachers' knowledge and beliefs in learning to teach (Borko & Putnam, 1995, 1996). Using a framework for categories of knowledge important for teaching developed by Shulman and his colleagues (Grossman, Wilson, & Shulman, 1989; Shulman, 1986b, 1987), we considered what sorts of changes are being called for in teachers' knowledge and beliefs in various domains (teachers' knowledge as targets for change), as well as what we know about teachers' learning in these various domains (teachers' knowledge as determinants of change). In the remainder of this section, we summarize some of the key points made in these previous chapters (Borko & Putnam, 1995, 1996). We organize our summary around three major categories of teacher knowledge: general pedagogical knowledge, subject-matter knowledge, and pedagogical content knowledge.

General pedagogical knowledge and beliefs.

General pedagogical knowledge includes a teacher's knowledge and beliefs about teaching, learning, and learners not specific to particular subject-matter domains. Our focus in this chapter is on conceptions of learning and instruction.

Linda Anderson (1989a) has argued that most current reform efforts are ground-ed in a *cognitive-mediational* conception, where learners are viewed as active problem solvers who construct their own knowledge and the teacher is respon-sible for stimulating students' cognitive activities needed for learning. This con-ception is quite different from a *receptive-accrual* view, often implicit in direct instruction models of teaching, in which learning is a matter of receiving and practicing information and skills presented by the teacher.

If teachers are to incorporate a cognitive-mediational conception of learning into their classroom teaching, they need knowledge of instructional strategies that can support focusing on students' thinking and facilitating their cognitive activities. Anderson (1989b) and# Brophy (1989) identified elements of general pedagogical knowledge shared by a number of instructional approaches that fo-cus on 'teaching for understanding and self-regulated learning.' These elements include understanding of the teacher's role as one of mediator of meaningful student learning, knowing how to create classroom environments that foster learning for understanding and self-regulation, and knowing methods of assess-ment that reveal students' thinking.

When teachers try to learn new instructional practices, their existing views of teaching and learning and their existing knowledge of instructional strategies can have a profound influence on the changes they actually make. For example, in a study of how California teachers interpreted new mathematics textbooks and calls for change in their teaching of mathematics, Putnam et al. (1992) found that teachers who viewed teaching as a process of presenting information sometimes 'announced' important ideas and assumed that children made sense of them. Teachers who believed that learning should be fun and engaging de-veloped instructional representations that portrayed the mathematics content in questionable ways. And teachers who believed that young students are not de-velopmentally ready to understand or that basic, factual information must be mastered before understanding can be acquired sometimes emphasized facts and procedures over thoughtfulness and understanding. In each of these instanc-es, teachers were trying to create more meaningful learning experiences for their students – by using more problem-solving oriented textbooks, more dis-cussion-oriented classroom activities, or more powerful instructional materials (i.e., manipulatives). But their use of these resources was shaped by what they already knew and believed about learning and teaching, resulting in changes that may have been quite superficial.

For experienced teachers trying to change, there is the additional issue that much of their knowledge has become routinized and automatic. Routines and automaticity are important aspects of the complex tasks of skilled teaching (Berliner, 1988; Leinhardt & Greeno, 1986). Skilled teachers develop rich knowledge of classroom situations, well-rehearsed routines for managing the classroom and conducting lessons, and the ability to quickly and automatically interpret classroom events and act accordingly. This automaticity or fluency is essential for coping with the managerial and cognitive complexity that is inherent in guiding the activities of a classroom full of students. At the same time, however, routinized knowledge can impede teachers' efforts to reflect on their own practices, to see things in new ways, or to learn new instructional approaches (Borko & Putnam, 1996).

There is also considerable evidence that pre-service teachers' beliefs about teaching and learning affect how they interpret their teacher education experiences (Borko & Putnam, 1996). Lortie (1975) has pointed out that prospective teachers experience more than 10,000 hours of classroom instruction as students prior to their formal teacher preparation programs. Through these 'apprenticeships of observation,' prospective teachers develop knowledge and beliefs that play powerful roles in shaping what they learn through various teacher education experiences. In our previous review of research literature on learning to teach (Borko & Putnam, 1996), several studies suggested that prospective teachers' beliefs that they already know enough to be good teachers may make them unrealistically optimistic about their future teaching performance and nonreceptive to learning from teacher education experiences (Brookhart & Freeman, 1992; Weinstein, 1990). Further, their specific beliefs about how students learn and about how teachers can facilitate that learning are often incompatible with the views of learning underlying instructional approaches advocated by teacher education programs. Some prospective teachers, for example, hold the view that *activities* which involve important content, and that are 'creative' and 'real-life,' will lead directly to learning of that content. They thus miss or downplay the role of learner mediation, prior knowledge, and substantive connections within the subject matter, as well as the teacher's role in mediating learning (Anderson & Holt-Reynolds, 1995). A number of researchers have found that prospective teachers' views of learning can shift toward more constructivist perspectives, but how much these views are taken on and how they are interpreted are influenced by the prospective teachers' incoming beliefs (Hollingsworth, 1989; Holt-Reynolds, 1992). Often, prospective teachers may take on new language that 'sounds' more 'constructivist,' but their underlying rationales for these ideas are not robust and are not tied to ideas about content.

Subject-matter knowledge and beliefs.

Although early studies found little or no relationship between teachers' subject-matter knowledge and the achievement of their students (e.g., Byrne, 1983), more recent research has documented some of the important ways that teachers' knowledge of the subjects they teach shapes their instructional practice. A number of studies have suggested that teachers with richer understanding of subject matter tend to emphasize conceptual, problem-solving, and inquiry aspects of their subjects, whereas less knowledgeable teachers tend to emphasize facts and procedures (Ball, 1988a; Carlsen, 1991; Fennema & Franke, 1992; Wilson, 1988). For example, Carlsen (1991) found that when teachers were teaching topics they knew well, they were more likely to use whole-class instruction, which provided students with opportunities to raise questions about science publicly, and to focus more on central ideas and links among them than when teaching topics they knew less well. Numerous teacher educators have argued that rich and flexible understanding of the subject is especially important in teaching that attempts to build on the thinking and problem-solving efforts of students, for teachers must be prepared to see connections between what students are thinking and important ideas in the discipline. Also, to help students come to understand important ideas in a discipline, teachers must understand the facts, procedures, and concepts they teach, as well as how these ideas relate to other ideas in the discipline (C. Anderson, 1989; McDiarmid, Ball, & Anderson, 1989). This sort of understanding concerns what Schwab (1964) has called the *substantive* structure of the discipline. It is also important for teachers to know about the *syntactic* structure of the discipline – the ways of establishing new knowledge and determining the validity of claims (e.g., Ball, 1991). These connections are important in deciding what aspects of students thinking to follow up on and how to guide students' thinking productively (Schifter & Fosnot, 1993).

Regarding substantive structure, novice and experienced teachers alike often lack the rich and flexible subject-matter knowledge that is needed in order to be responsive to students' thinking in ways that foster learning with understanding. Studies of prospective teachers' subject-matter knowledge reveal that 'many prospective teachers, both elementary and secondary, do not understand their subjects in depth' (McDiarmid et al., 1989, p. 199). For example, Ball (1990a, 1990b) found that entering teacher education students had weak understandings of elementary mathematics topics such as place value, division, fractions, and the relationship between area and perimeter. Their knowledge seemed to be based more on memorization than on conceptual understanding, and they showed virtually no evidence of understanding the connectedness of topics in mathematics. Similar weaknesses in conceptual understanding have been reported for physics (Clement, 1982) and history (Wilson, 1988). For experienced teachers, numerous writers have argued that teaching which emphasizes student understanding, reasoning, and problem solving requires richer and more flexible understandings of subject matter than many teachers have (Brown & Borko, 1992; Cohen, 1989; Roth, Anderson, & Smith, 1986). Limitations in subject-matter understanding can be exacerbated when teachers move away from textbook-based activities and toward more situated and meaningful problems and activities (Heaton, 1992; Putnam, 1992a).

With respect to syntactic structures, Ball (1988a, 1990a) found that in the subject area of mathematics, prospective teachers often hold naive conceptions of mathematics as an abstract, mechanical, and meaningless series of symbols and rules to be memorized. They look to experts (e.g., the teacher or the text) for establishing mathematical truth and know little about mathematical reasoning. Grossman et al. (1989) noted wide variation in beginning teachers' knowledge of syntactic structures of their disciplines. In history, for example, one novice teacher, a history major, saw history as both narrative and interpretation, with interpretation being central to historical inquiry. A political science major, in contrast, viewed history as limited to facts; he recognized the importance of interpretation but considered it to be the purview of political science, not history (Wilson & Wineburg, 1988). These differences in perspective dominated the organization and structure of the teachers' own knowledge and of the high-school history classes they taught.

Pedagogical content knowledge and beliefs.

Shulman (1986a, 1986b) coined the term *pedagogical content knowledge* to distinguish between the knowledge of a subject or discipline per se and the knowledge of a subject that is specifically related to teaching. For Shulman (1986b), pedagogical content knowledge includes 'the ways of representing and formulating the subject that make it comprehensible to others' and 'an understanding of what makes the learning of specific topics easy or difficult: the conceptions and preconceptions that students of different ages and backgrounds bring with them to the learning of those most frequently taught topics and lessons' (p. 9). Although pedagogical content knowledge integrates knowledge from several domains and cannot be sharply distinguished from subject-matter knowledge and general pedagogical knowledge, the domain is important, for it focuses on the knowledge and skills specific to teaching particular subject matter. In our previous reviews of the literature on teacher learning (Borko & Putnam, 1995, 1996) we organized our discussion of pedagogical content knowledge according to four categories described by Grossman (1990):

a) overarching conception of teaching a subject;
b) knowledge of instructional strategies and representations;
c) knowledge of students' understandings, thinking, and learning in a subject; and
d) knowledge of curriculum and curricular materials.

Here, we briefly review major findings in each area.

The teacher's *overarching conception of teaching a subject* is his or her knowledge and beliefs about the nature of the subject and what is important for students to learn (Grossman, 1990). Because this overarching conception serves as a 'conceptual map' for making judgments and decisions about learning goals, instructional strategies, assignments, curricular materials, and evaluation of student learning, it can have a profound influence in shaping instruction. For example, Grossman (1990) found that one new teacher who viewed textual analysis as central to the learning of secondary English taught a unit on *Hamlet* that entailed leading students through the play word by word to learn textual analysis skills. Another teacher, also teaching a unit on *Hamlet*, saw text as a springboard for discussion and broadening of students perspectives. His instructional goals were to interest students in the play and help them see connections to their own lives. Rather than reading *Hamlet*, his students read summaries and viewed videotapes in preparation for class discussions.

The influence of overarching conceptions of subject matter is particularly salient in the current climate of educational reform. Many reform efforts are calling for approaches to teaching subject matter that differ substantially from traditional teaching practice. In mathematics, for example, reformers are calling for decreased emphasis on isolated rules and procedures, arguing instead for an emphasis on problem solving, mathematical reasoning, and communicating mathematically (National Council of Teachers of Mathematics, 1989). Teachers' existing conceptions of mathematics, however, exert a powerful influence on the changes they make in their practice. In the case studies of California teachers by Putnam et al. (1992), teachers' overarching conceptions of mathematics and how it should be taught influenced their interpretations of various messages for change. In using new textbooks, for example, teachers who thought of mathematics as the learning of arithmetic facts and procedures skipped questions intended to promote open-ended discussion of mathematical ideas.

A second component of pedagogical content knowledge is *knowledge of instructional strategies and representations* for teaching particular topics, including the models, examples, metaphors, and so forth that a teacher uses to foster students' understanding. Effective teachers have extensive repertoires of powerful representations and ways to adapt these representations to meet the needs of specific learners. Novice teachers, however, often lack extensive repertoires of subject-specific instructional strategies and representations (Borko, Livingston, McCaleb, & Mauro, 1988; Eisenhart, Borko, Underhill, Brown, Jones, & Agard, 1993; Shulman & Grossman, 1987). Even experienced teachers have limited knowledge of subject-specific strategies and representations needed to teach for understanding. For example, in a study focused on science teaching, Smith and Neale (1991) found that elementary teachers used few conceptual change strategies before participating in an in-service program. Putnam and colleagues (1992) found some elementary school mathematics teachers' knowledge of instructional representations to be limited. In some cases, instructional representations that teachers devised to supplement or replace those in their textbooks were based more on the representations' motivational features than on their fit with the mathematics being taught, possibly leading to student misconceptions.

A third component of pedagogical content knowledge is *knowledge of students' understandings and potential misunderstandings* in a subject area. This domain differs from the more general knowledge and beliefs about learners and learning in that it is specific to particular content domains. In mathematics and science, for example, researchers have documented preconceptions, misconceptions, and alternative conceptions commonly held by learners for topics such as photosynthesis and negative numbers (for a review, see Confrey, 1990). To focus teaching on the development of subject-matter understanding by building on students' thinking, teachers need to have well-developed understandings of how students typically learn a particular subject and what topics they are likely to find difficult.

A final component of pedagogical content knowledge is *knowledge of curriculum and curriculum materials,* which includes familiarity with the range of textbooks and other instructional materials available for teaching various topics. It also includes knowledge of how topics and ideas are organized across the curriculum both within and across years. Research on pre-service and experienced teachers' knowledge and use of curricular materials is sparse, although there is evidence that pre-service teachers' knowledge in this area is limited (Borko & Livingston, 1989; Grossman, 1990). As teachers move toward reform visions of teaching, significant changes may take place in what curriculum is considered to be. If teaching is highly responsive to students' thinking and their current understandings, topics may no longer be sequenced in traditional ways. If teaching is organized around rich problems solved by groups of students, problems or projects may take on a more important role in the organization of curricular content. We discuss these ideas further later in the chapter.

Implications for Teacher Learning Experiences

The most obvious implication of the view that teachers, like students, are active constructors of knowledge is that their knowledge and beliefs are critically important in their learning and professional development. Teachers, whether novice or experienced, come to understand new practices through the lenses of their existing knowledge and beliefs. The new understandings they develop determine how new instructional strategies or activities are actually used in the classroom. Thus, teachers cannot simply be presented with prescriptions for new instructional practices and be expected to 'receive' them and use them as is. Rather teachers must be supported in enhancing their knowledge and changing their beliefs as they learn new instructional approaches. Like the students in their classrooms, teachers should be encouraged to impose meaning and organization on incoming information and recommendations by relating them to their existing knowledge and beliefs.

Learning of pre-service teachers.

For pre-service teacher education, this means attending seriously to the knowledge, beliefs, and expectations that prospective teachers bring to their teacher education programs, acquired through their own experiences in schools. Because these views about learners and learning often remain implicit and serve as the filters through which prospective teachers interpret and learn new instructional approaches, they are highly resistant to change (Ball, 1989; Borko, Eisenhart, Brown, Underhill, Jones, & Agard, 1992; Holt-Reynolds, 1992; McDiarmid et al., 1989). But teacher education courses and programs that challenge participants' preexisting beliefs can be successful in helping them develop knowledge and beliefs more consonant with those advocated by teacher educators. For example, McDiarmid (1990) and Ball (1988b) reported on the impact of a course they taught had on pre-service teachers' beliefs. The course, 'Exploring Teaching,' was designed to challenge prospective teachers to examine their 'web of beliefs' about the teacher's role, pedagogy, learning, diverse learners, subject matter, context, and learning to teach. In McDiarmid's section, students observed and interviewed an experienced teacher (Deborah Ball) who taught in ways likely to challenge their beliefs. Ball's students learned about permutations, watched Ball help a young child explore the concept, and tried to help someone else learn about permutations. Comeaux (1992) reported on a course designed to challenge students to examine their views of teaching and learning and support them to adopt a more constructivist world view. All three of these endeavors suggest that when courses explicitly challenge pre-service teachers' beliefs, changes in those beliefs can and do take place. It is not clear, however, how these changes vary across individuals, how lasting they are, or how much impact they have on the prospective teachers' classroom teaching.

Regarding subject-matter and pedagogical content knowledge, at least two research projects have found that few prospective teachers deepen their understandings of mathematics or their beliefs about the nature of mathematics during their teacher preparation programs (Eisenhart et al., 1993; National Center for Research on Teacher Education, 1991). It is easy to assume that the solution for limitations in teachers' subject-matter knowledge would be to require more courses in university arts and sciences departments, that it is in these courses outside of schools of education that teachers can gain the subject matter knowledge they need to teach successfully. Evidence for what prospective teachers (and other undergraduates) actually learn, however, in such disciplinary courses is sketchy (McDiarmid, 1994). There is a mismatch between the goals of professors in many academic courses – to socialize students into particular disciplines and to explain facts and concepts – and the need for prospective teachers to develop richer knowledge of the structure and functions of disciplinary knowledge and how it typically develops in individuals. It appears that prospective teachers typically have few opportunities to gain, either in education courses or in arts and science courses, the sorts of rich and flexible knowledge *of* and *about* subject matter they need to teach successfully for understanding.

There is also evidence, however, that pre-service teachers can be supported in enriching their subject-matter understanding, especially in courses that focus explicitly on the nature of the discipline and how it is learned (Civil, 1992; Schram, Wilcox, Lappan, & Lanier, 1989; Simon & Blume, 1994). In one project, for example, Schram and colleagues (1989) developed courses that emphasized helping prospective teachers rethink the nature of mathematics and how it is learned, as well as facilitating their learning of particular mathematical content. Students entered the program with a traditional view of mathematics as an abstract, mechanical, and meaningless series of symbols and rules. By the end of the first course, most students were beginning to value a learning environment organized around problem solving, group work, and opportunities to talk about mathematics, and to appreciate the importance of a conceptual understanding of mathematics. By the end of the second year, there were significant changes in participants' beliefs about themselves as learners of mathematics, what it means to know mathematics, and how mathematics is learned, with the prospective teachers showing a growing conceptual orientation to the study of mathematics (Wilcox, Schram, Lappan, & Lanier, 1990). Similarly, Simon (Simon, 1995; Simon & Blume, 1994) reported changes in mathematics understandings for prospective teachers participating in an experimental teacher preparation program designed to increase participants' mathematical knowledge and to foster their development of views of mathematics, learning, and teaching consistent with a reform vision of teaching.

Regarding their view of teaching and learning mathematics, however, the impact of experiences reported in these studies was mixed. In the program studied by Wilcox, Schram, and their colleagues (Schram et al., 1989; Wilcox et al., 1990), although pre-service teachers underwent significant changes in how they viewed mathematics for themselves, their views of mathematics for young children often remained unchanged. Even after the two-year program, many of novice teachers continued to associate elementary mathematics with basics — number facts and whole-number computations, hierarchically ordered content, and a need to master computational skills before problem solving – and they were inclined to teach in their elementary school classrooms in traditional ways. Civil (1992), Ball (1989), and Simon and colleagues (Simon & Brobeck, 1993; Simon & Mazza, 1993) also reported mixed results on the impact of pre-service courses on prospective teachers' pedagogical content knowledge and beliefs, leading Ball (1989) to suggest that teacher educators need to consider how to extend the form and duration of courses in ways to support teachers' learning from their own practice.

Learning of experienced teachers.

Experienced teachers, too, have existing knowledge and beliefs that influence how they learn new pedagogical ideas and practices. A number of staff development projects that have been successful in facilitating meaningful change in experienced teachers' instructional practices explicitly addressed teachers' pre-existing knowledge and beliefs and supported participants in examining and changing them (Carpenter, Fennema, Peterson, Chiang, & Loef, 1989; Richardson, Anders, Tidwell, & Lloyd, 1991; Schifter & Simon, 1992; Smith & Neale, 1991). All of these projects focused on helping teachers re-think their pedagogy within the context of teaching particular subject-matter domains (mathematics, science, or reading).

Three of the projects focused primarily on teachers' content knowledge and pedagogical content knowledge through intensive work in summer workshops followed by teachers' implementing new instructional practices in their own classrooms. The Cognitively Guided Instruction project (CGI – see Carpenter et al., 1989), a multi-year program of professional development, curriculum development, and research, was based on the premise that teaching is a problem-solving process best informed by in-depth knowledge of students and the subject matter being taught. In a summer institute, CGI developers provided first-grade teachers with opportunities to learn about the nature of addition and subtraction (the subject matter) and about how children typically solve addition and subtraction problems (pedagogical content knowledge). The teachers then drew on this new knowledge to reshape their mathematics teaching. In their Summer-Math for Teachers project, Simon and Schifter (1991; Schifter & Simon, 1992) focused on changing elementary and secondary teachers' beliefs about mathematics, teaching, and learning by providing opportunities for participants to learn mathematics themselves in a setting where the construction of meaning was encouraged and valued. The teachers reflected on those experiences to re-think their assumptions about subject matter, teaching, and learning, and to design new instructional sequences for their classrooms. Smith and Neale (1991), similarly, assumed that for elementary teachers to be successful with conceptual change teaching in science, they would need changes in their understandings of the scientific content they were teaching (light and shadows), their knowledge and beliefs about teaching science, and their knowledge about children's ideas. Teachers participated in a summer workshop in which they read research literature on children's misconceptions about light and shadow, interviewed students, participated in activities focused on their own understandings of light and shadow, and taught small groups of children. As in the other projects, these activities led to changes in the teachers' knowledge and beliefs as well as their teaching practice.

In a fourth approach to professional development, Richardson and her colleagues (Richardson & Anders, 1994; Richardson et al., 1991) worked with elementary teachers to change their beliefs and practices about reading instruction by examining their *practical arguments* (Fenstermacher & Richardson, 1993). A practical argument describes a person's reasoning about actions by specifying the rationales, empirical support, and situational contexts that serve as premises for the actions. Using practical argument as the basis for staff development entails having teachers make explicit their reasons for various instructional actions (i.e., their premises). Teachers then reconsider these premises through interaction with others and in light of new ideas, particularly those from the research literature. Richardson and Anders reported that working with reading teachers' practical arguments resulted in considerable shifts in the teachers' theories of reading, learning to read, and teaching reading and in their self-reported instructional practices. In general, shifts in beliefs were toward the literature end of a skills versus word – literature continuum and toward the construction end of a meaning-in-text – construction-of-meaning continuum. Changes in practices included less reliance on basal readers, use of more pre-reading activities designed to activate and build prior knowledge, and integration of literature into other subjects. The researchers concluded, based on these findings, that the practical argument staff development process has the potential to free teachers from external conditions for determining their beliefs and explaining their teaching (e.g., pressures from parents, administrators, and school board policies) to allow them to develop theoretical premises that justify their practices.

All of these successful professional development projects have in common a focus on supporting teachers in examining and changing their beliefs and knowledge as well as their instructional practices. They take teachers' existing knowledge and beliefs as important enough to subject to careful scrutiny and possible change. Additionally, all of the projects include an emphasis on the teaching of particular subject matter rather than focusing on generic teaching approaches. The general message they give is that, with systematic intensive work, it is possible for teachers to make substantial changes in their knowledge, beliefs, and practices – changes in directions compatible with a reform vision of teaching and learning.

Summary: Teachers' knowledge and beliefs.

In discussing the various domains of teachers' knowledge and beliefs – general pedagogical knowledge, subject-matter knowledge, and pedagogical content knowledge – we have focused on the importance of teachers' knowledge and beliefs for teaching in the ambitious ways called for by current reform movements and on the role played by prior knowledge and beliefs in teachers' learning. Many of these ideas are connected to the notion that the learning of all persons, including students and teachers, is highly influenced by their existing knowledge and beliefs because learning is an active process in which people interpret experiences through their existing conceptual structures to modify and expand their knowledge. In much of the rest of this chapter, we consider other salient ideas about cognition, including the social, situated, and distributed nature of knowledge, thinking, and learning. Each of these has implications for teachers' general pedagogical, subject-matter, and pedagogical content knowledge and beliefs. Thus, the preceding discussion of teachers' knowledge and beliefs will serve as a backdrop for considering various implications of the ideas about learning that follow.

THE SOCIAL NATURE OF COGNITION

The focus in the previous section on the role of individuals' existing knowledge and beliefs in learning might lead one to conclude that learning is primarily an individual activity. Indeed, the constructivist assumption that individuals actively construct knowledge is sometimes interpreted naively by teachers and other educators as a belief that by encouraging and supporting students' interactions with the physical world, powerful learning will take place through individuals' efforts to make sense (Cobb, 1994a; Driver, Asoko, Leach, Mortimer, & Scott, 1994; Prawat, 1992). This focus on the individual's constructive efforts, as important as it is for emphasizing the central role of personal engagement in the learning process, poses a dilemma for teachers – the dilemma of attending to, respecting, and encouraging individual students' thinking while simultaneously ensuring that students are learning the concepts, skills, and understandings of the curriculum (Ball, 1993; Cobb, Yackel, & Wood, 1988; Dewey, 1964; Lampert, 1988; Putnam, 1992b). The constructivist maxim that individuals actively construct their own understandings, when it is mistakenly translated into a romantic pedagogical view that the teachers' role is simply one of facilitating students' explorations (Cobb, 1994a), does not help teachers think through this tension between the individual and the curriculum. For it is not clear how facilitating a child's interactions with his or her environment will help the child develop the understandings expected by the curriculum. If the curriculum is understood as an aspect of the social environment – a product of society's expectations – then it becomes clear that dealing with this tension requires looking more carefully at the role of the social and cultural in learning and at how the social and cultural interact with individual efforts to construct meaning.

Increasingly, psychologists and educators are recognizing that the role of others in the learning process goes beyond providing stimulation and encouragement for individual construction of knowledge. They are coming to see the social and cultural as central to the learning process and indeed to what constitutes knowledge (Resnick, Levine, & Teasley, 1991). As Soltis (1981) writes,

> The earlier dominant philosophical view of mind, learning, and knowledge was 'egocentric,' focusing on the individual and how one acquired true knowledge of the world external to oneself. The newer view is 'sociocentric,' still considering the individual and the world but also taking into account the cultural nature of knowledge as a communal human construction that is both formed by and forms human beings. (p. 97)

This sociocentric view of knowledge and learning represents a confluence of ideas from numerous disciplines, including philosophy, anthropology, sociology, psychology, linguistics, and literary theory. In psychology, much of the current emphasis on the social aspects of learning and knowing has its basis in the work of Vygotsky (1978) and other Soviet activity theorists (Leont'ev, 1981). The role of the social and cultural has important implications both for how we think of the nature of knowledge – what it is that people learn – and how learning takes place.

Social nature of knowledge and knowing.

One important aspect of a sociocentric view is that what we take as knowledge and how we think are the products of the interactions of groups of people over time – the ways in which groups have come to order their experiences and make sense of their worlds. It is through sustained interaction that individuals come to share common ways of thinking and expressing ideas. Communities that share ways of thinking and communicating are sometimes referred to as *discourse communities* (Fish, 1980; Michaels & O'Connor, 1990; Resnick, 1991). A discourse community might be a scholarly discipline such as a science or history, or any group of people who share common interests and ways of talking, thinking, and writing (Resnick, 1991). Discourse communities also can be local and small – for example, a particular classroom or a group of teachers in a single school.

The various discourse communities within which we interact provide the ideas, theories, and concepts that we appropriate as our own through our personal efforts to make sense. Ideas or concepts, from this point of view, are essentially *cognitive tools* with which we think and reason (Brown, Collins, & Duguid, 1989b; Resnick, 1991). Understanding a concept, from this perspective, means being able to use that concept as a tool for both individual thinking and discourse with others (Greeno et al., 1996).

In addition to particular ideas or theories as culturally developed tools, the very way a person thinks and reasons is shaped largely through interactions with others. Central to Vygotsky's (1978) view of cognitive development is the notion that various kinds of complex thinking and reasoning first appear as interaction with others and then become internalized or appropriated as individual forms of thought. The quality of thinking, from this perspective, is determined, not by some absolute external criteria of what constitutes good thinking, but rather by the norms and expectations of a particular community. An important part of what it means to become competent in a particular discipline is to learn the forms of argument and discourse – the accepted ways of reasoning – within that disciplinary community. Learning a science, for example, entails

> … entering into a different way of thinking about and explaining the natural world; becoming socialized to a greater or lesser extent into the practices of the scientific community with its particular purposes, ways of seeing, and ways of supporting its knowledge claims. (Driver et al., 1994, p. 8)

A central goal of schooling, then, becomes enculturating students into various discourse communities and equipping them with competence in using the concepts and forms of reasoning and argument that characterize those communities (Lampert, 1990; Michaels & O'Connor, 1990; Resnick, 1988). To accomplish this goal, schools and teachers in classrooms must make decisions (consciously or unconsciously) about *which* discourse communities they will emulate and how to negotiate between the local school and classroom communities, on one hand, and the broader disciplinary communities on the other.

Learning as socially mediated.

The ideas thus far have been about how *what* we take as knowledge and how we think are determined by social and cultural influences. The *process* of learning is also a social one. Much of the work of sociocultural theorists has focused on how social interactions and participation in various culturally organized activities influence learning and development (Cobb, 1994b). One consequence of this work has been to conceptualize learning as coming to know how to participate in the discourse and practices of a particular community. From this view, learning is as much a matter of enculturation into particular ways of thinking and dispositions as it is a result of explicit instruction in particular concepts, skills, and procedures (Driver et al., 1994; Resnick, 1988; Schoenfeld, 1992).

The role of other people, especially more knowledgeable others such as parents or teachers, varies across views of learning. In the implicit theories of learning that underlie much of traditional school practice, more knowledgeable others are typically viewed as the source of knowledge which is presented or transmitted to learners. From an individual constructivist perspective, interactions with other people are a source of disequilibration (Piaget, 1985), the driving force for individual development. Thus the primary role of others in learning is to stimulate the individual's efforts at making sense (Tudge & Winterhoff, 1993). In contrast, in social constructivist views of learning, other persons play the role of model and supporter for learning. Individuals learn through observation of and interaction with more knowledgeable members of the culture, appropriating for themselves new ways of thinking.

A particularly influential construct for thinking about the role of knowledgeable others in learning is Vygotsky's notion of *zone of proximal development*, initially conceptualized as the region of activity between what a learner can accomplish unaided and what he or she can accomplish with the help of a knowledgeable other, typically an adult. Vygotsky used the idea of zone of proximal development to explain how learners can – through the support of others – engage in and learn (appropriate) increasingly complex activities. The more knowledgeable other models and guides the activity so that the learner gradually comes to share that view of the activity and becomes competent in carrying it out.

We close this overview of social views of cognition by revisiting the related issues of how individuals making idiosyncratic sense of the world come to common understandings and how teachers negotiate the tension between focusing on the thinking of individual students and bringing students to certain understandings expected by the curriculum. The view of knowledge as socially constructed is key to understanding these issues because the environment with which individuals interact is largely a social one; it is other people who provide learners with the conceptual or symbolic environment with which they interact.

In other words, it is people who provide learners with the cognitive tools that they re-construct or appropriate for themselves (Cobb, 1994b; Driver et al., 1994; Resnick, 1991). Cobb (1994b) argues that the individual and social constructivist views of learning should be seen as complementary perspectives, one focusing on the sense-making of individuals within a social context, and the other focusing on the social context and how it shapes individual thinking and learning. Thus, individuals can construct personal meanings only in the context of the ideas, conceptual tools, and modes of thought provided by the social environment, and discourse communities can 'transmit' these conceptual tools and modes of thought only to the extent that individuals can make personal sense of them.

Classroom Implications of a Social View of Cognition

The view that learning means learning how to participate in the discourse of particular communities implies that we should create classroom communities in which students can become enculturated into the ways of thinking and interacting that we value. Some have argued that classroom communities should be modelled after disciplinary communities of mathematicians, scientists, historians, and so on (Brown et al., 1989b). Lampert (1990), for example, has worked as a teacher and researcher to develop a teaching practice in a fifth-grade mathematics class which is 'congruent with ideas about what it means to do mathematics in the discipline' (p. 33). She has worked to create participation structures and discourse in the classroom within which students argue about mathematical ideas rather than accepting mathematical truths as given by the teacher or the textbook. Central to Lampert's effort is the assumption that students' conceptions of what it means to know and do mathematics will change by participating in a community of people engaging in mathematical discourse.

> I assumed that changing students' ideas about what it means to know and do mathematics was in part a matter of creating a social situation that worked according to rules different from those that ordinarily pertain in classrooms, and in part respectfully challenging their assumptions about what knowing mathematics entails. Like teaching someone to dance, it required some telling, some showing, and some doing it with them along with regular rehearsals. (Lampert, 1990, p. 58)

Similarly, other teachers and researchers have worked to develop classroom communities in which the discourse is modelled after discourse assumed to be important in various disciplinary communities (e.g., Ball, 1993, in mathematics; Roth, 1992, in science).

Not all scholars arguing for the importance of establishing discourse or learning communities see the discourse of disciplinary communities as central to classrooms. Ann Brown and colleagues (1993) argue that, rather than preparing students to participate in the professional cultures of mathematicians and historians, 'schools should be communities where students learn to learn' (p. 190). Their assumption is that by participating in activities designed to question and extend their own knowledge in various domains, students will become enculturated into ways of learning that will continue for the rest of their lives. Although direct teaching continues to play a role in these classrooms, the emphasis is on having students acquire the knowledge, skills, and dispositions to become lifelong learners by participating in active inquiry in various domains. In the 'guided learning classrooms' featured in Brown and colleagues' (1993) design experiments for grade school science, for example, students engage in research cycles during which they explore themes such as animal defense mechanisms, changing populations, and food chains. Teams of students generate questions, plan their research activities, and then gather information from a variety of sources such as books, videos, and experts available to them through an electronic mail system. Through these activities they learn the practices of scholarly research, as well as important science content. Thus, the students' learning of research skills and scientific knowledge occurs through interaction in a learning community.

In each of these cases, teachers and researchers are working to create discourse communities that are significantly different from those traditionally found in public school classrooms, on the assumption that through participation in those discourse communities, children will come to think and reason differently. Because students typically bring with them to such classrooms traditional values and assumptions, teachers must figure out ways to help students form discourse communities in which new ways of thinking, reasoning, and interacting are the norm. The establishment of participation structures that support the desired kinds of discourse is thus a key feature in successful attempts to create classroom communities with new norms for interaction. Lampert (1990), for example, emphasized the consistent use of a structure in which she presents a problem and students offer multiple potential solutions; they then proceed to discuss, compare, and challenge one another's solutions. Ann Brown and colleagues' (1993) guided learning classrooms made use of reciprocal teaching Palincsar & Brown, 1984) and the jigsaw method of cooperative learning (Aronson, 1978) as consistent structures within which students can interact. Structures such as these are important for establishing new shared norms and expectations for interaction in the classroom.

The idea of a more knowledgeable other guiding a learner in the zone of proximal development has led to a number of more particular instructional strategies such as modelling, coaching, fading, and scaffolding (Collins, Brown, &

Newman, 1989). When the teacher provides scaffolding, for example, learners are able to carry out various aspects of the task in the context of the entire task rather than practicing isolated skills. It is important that scaffolding enables students to take over increasing amounts of responsibility gradually and ultimately empowers them to carry out the cognitive skills they are to learn.

The ideas of modelling, coaching, and fading bear more than passing resemblance to the use of presentation, guided practice, and independent practice that are central in models of direct or active instruction (Rosenshine & Stevens, 1986). In both cases, the teacher gradually withdraws control over student actions as the student gains competence. A key difference, however, is in the nature of the task and the context in which it is situated. In traditional teaching, the tasks being presented and practiced might be isolated and decontextualized – for example, the steps in a computational algorithm. In contrast, theorists calling for scaffolding, modelling, and so forth, emphasize that tasks be situated in a meaningful context, so that individual skills are not learned and practiced in isolation.

The Teacher's Role

We are only beginning to understand the role of the teacher in classrooms designed to be discourse communities in which students can become enculturated into the mental habits, dispositions, and forms of argument that characterize various disciplines or other communities. Teachers will need new pedagogical skills and strategies, but we have much to learn about just what those skills are. Most educators working toward classrooms as communities of learning agree, for example, that direct, didactic teaching has a place in such classrooms but that it should play less of a role than it has in traditional classroom instruction. What is less clear is when and for what purposes direct teaching is appropriate, as well as what skilled teaching that relies more on scaffolding, coaching, and modelling should look like. As Ball (1994) pointed out about the reform visions of mathematics teaching and learning offered in documents such as that of the National Council of Teachers of Mathematics *Standards* (1989, 1991),

> ... despite their persuasive, inspiring vignettes, however, these documents are far from programs for practice. They sketch directions and commitments, principles and aspirations. They cannot provide guidance for the specifics of minute-to-minute practice or for the decisions met day to day. (Ball, 1994, pp. 3-4)

One aspect of the teacher's role that does seem clear is the importance of serving as a model for the kind of thinking and discourse students are expected to acquire. If the classroom is to be a community where sense-making and mathematical argument are the norm, for example, then the teacher must regularly model mathematical sense-making and argument. As Lampert (1990) explains, 'Given my goal of teaching students a new way of knowing mathematics, I needed to demonstrate what it would look like for someone more expert than they to know mathematics in the way I wanted them to know it' (p. 41). Similarly, if as in Ann Brown and colleagues' classrooms (Brown et al., 1993), the emphasis is on active learning and inquiry, then the teacher must serve as a model of how to engage in inquiry-oriented learning.

These changes – in pedagogical skills and strategies and in the teacher's role – will undoubtedly be accompanied by fairly deep changes in beliefs about knowledge, learning, and teaching. For example, teachers may come to view knowledge less as static bodies of facts, concepts, and procedures that exist apart from individuals and groups, and more as particular ways of making sense of the world and of participating in various communities of discourse.

Implications For Teacher Learning Experiences

This view of knowledge as socially constructed also has implications for learning experiences for teachers. One key implication is the importance of establishing new discourse communities in which teachers can participate as they work to change their teaching practice. In discussing such communities for experienced and pre-service teachers, we consider kinds of discourse that should be supported and the role of others, such as staff developers, teacher educators, and researchers, in supporting teachers' efforts to learn and change within these communities.

Discourse communities for practicing teachers.

Just as students need to learn new ways of reasoning, communicating, and thinking, and to acquire dispositions of inquiry and sense-making through their participation in classroom discourse communities, teachers need to construct their complex new roles and ways of thinking about their teaching practice within the context of supportive learning communities. Patterns of classroom teaching and learning have historically been resistant to fundamental change, in part because schools have served as powerful discourse communities that enculturate participants (students, teachers, administrators) into traditional school activities and ways of thinking (Cohen, 1989; Sarason, 1990). If teachers are to be successful in changing their thinking and practice, they will need opportunities to create new professional discourse communities that embody active learning, inquiry, and reasoning.

Many efforts to reform teaching over the years (e.g., Good & Brophy, 1973) have focused on restructuring schools in order to provide greater opportunities for professional collaboration among teachers. As helpful as restructuring efforts have been, however, they have not helped particularly in changing the nature of professional discourse communities. For example, efforts to restructure schools call for changes in the school day to allow the time to bring groups of teachers together but run the risk of simply reproducing the discourse of the dominant school culture. From a sociological perspective, McLaughlin and Talbert (1993) have argued that for teachers to rise successfully to the challenge of adapting their teaching practices to meet the expectations of the recent national reform agenda, they must have opportunities to participate 'in a professional community that discusses new teacher materials and strategies and that supports the risk taking and struggle entailed in transforming practice' (p. 15). In many cases, this means changing the nature of discourse among teachers in the schools.

Ball (1994) characterized typical discussions among teachers in many staff development sessions as 'style shows' in which teachers present classroom-based activities and ideas but fall short of critical and reflective examination of teaching practice. She described the consequences of this sort of discourse:

> The common view that 'each teacher has to find his or her own style' is a direct result of working within a discourse of practice that maintains the individualism and isolation of teaching. This individualism not only makes it difficult to develop any sense of common standards, it also makes it difficult to *disagree*. Masking disagreements hides the individual struggles to practice wisely, and so removes an opportunity for learning. Politely refraining from critique and challenge, teachers have no forum for debating and improving their understandings. To the extent that teaching remains a smorgasbord of alternatives with no real sense of community, there is no basis for comparing or choosing from among alternatives, no basis for real and helpful debate. This lack impedes the capacity to grow. (p. 16)

Teachers need opportunities to learn to be critical and reflective about their teaching. Further, if we take seriously the idea that complex thinking is derived from social interaction, then teachers will need discourse communities in which to learn and practice these skills and dispositions.

Some research projects focusing on the learning of experienced teachers have included an emphasis on establishing particular sorts of discourse communities. Richardson and Anders's (1994) practical argument approach to staff development, introduced earlier, is one example. Practical arguments provided a structure with which teachers could think about their own teaching practices and assumptions and hold them up for critical reflection in a group setting. Through group and one-on-one conversations, Richardson and Anders helped teachers to construct and reconstruct their practical arguments for reading comprehension instruction. By participating in these conversations, teachers were learning new ways of thinking and reflecting about their practice and simultaneously creating new forms of discourse for talking about teaching.

Goldenberg and colleagues (Goldenberg & Gallimore, 1991; Saunders, Goldenberg, & Hamann, 1992) also worked with teachers to establish a particular kind of discourse based on the concept of instructional conversations. Rather than 'training' the teachers in a previously articulated model of instruction, Goldenberg worked together with them over the course of a school year to develop such a model through 'joint productive activity.' The group came to describe instructional conversations as a mode of instruction that emphasizes active student involvement in goal- and meaning-oriented discussions. These discussions are interesting and engaging, concern an idea that appears to matter to the participants, and are characterized by features such as a coherent focus, high level of participation, and in-depth exploration of ideas. Working together, the researchers and teachers developed 10 principles of instructional conversations, several of which support ideas about social construction of knowledge and creation of discourse communities. For example, the teacher either 'hooks into' or provides students with pertinent background knowledge and stretches students' zones of performance by eliciting and promoting more extended language and expression. In leading instructional conversations, the teacher ensures that the atmosphere is challenging but nonthreatening, encourages all students to participate, and creates a discussion in which turns are interactive and connected and comments by teachers and students build upon and extend previous ones.

As the teachers developed these principles of instructional conversations, they were engaged in instructional conversations themselves, *as learners*, during weekly meetings that brought together other elements of the project, including video-taping of lessons, interviews, and observations. These instructional conversations, led by Goldenberg, entailed many of the same features the teachers identified as important for instructional conversations in classrooms. Goldenberg 'provided focus for the meetings, he was responsive to problems, issues, and questions raised by the teachers, he used elicitation techniques to promote analysis and to foster general participation, and he used direct teaching as necessary' (Saunders et al., 1992, p. 216). It was through these instructional conversations that the teachers conceptualized the instructional conversation as a method of teaching and developed increasingly analytic understandings of it. Thus Goldenberg helped these teachers establish a new kind of discourse within the staff development project, as they worked to define a parallel new kind of discourse for their own classrooms.

The roles of teachers and staff developers in fostering change.

An important feature of these examples was the establishment of new forms of reflective and critical discourse among teachers. This new discourse did not develop solely by providing teachers with opportunities to talk to one another in professional contexts. Rather, the staff developers and researchers played important roles in helping these teachers think about teaching in new ways. Just as students cannot learn science by interacting with the physical world without interaction with others who know science, teachers are unlikely to transcend their current views of teaching practice without an influx of ideas or ways of thinking about teaching, learning, and subject matter from another source. And just as we want to avoid the opposite extreme of having teachers simply 'tell' students important knowledge, we do not want professional development programs in which someone outside the classroom (e.g., the curriculum developer, or perhaps the district or state policy maker) develops a model of teaching and then trains teachers to carry out that model precisely. In thinking about what we do want, we are struck by two dilemmas.

The first is what Richardson (1992) refers to as the *agenda-setting dilemma*; the staff developer wants to see teachers' practice change in a particular direction while still empowering the teachers themselves to make the changes. This dilemma is analogous to that faced by the classroom teacher who wants to respect and build upon children's thinking, helping them make what they are learning personally meaningful, while simultaneously ensuring that students learn the subject-matter content that is expected of them. Staff developers, like teachers, must negotiate their way between the learners' current thinking and the subject matter or content to be learned. In the case of staff developers, the 'content' is often teaching practices and new ways of thinking about learners, subject matter, and teaching.

The second dilemma revolves around the role of the staff developer as more knowledgeable other; what is it that the staff developer knows and can do that can guide or contribute to the learning of teachers? As we discussed earlier, social constructivist views of learning emphasize the role of the more knowledgeable other – a person who provides modelling and scaffolding to foster meaningful learning within the learner's zone of proximal development. Such approaches assume that the teacher (as the more knowledgeable other) is proficient in the skills and thinking that are to be learned.

This assumption is problematic, however, for staff developers in their work with teachers. Most staff developers have not themselves engaged in these new forms of teaching at the K-12 level (Heaton & Lampert, 1993). Although people who conduct staff development (including ourselves) may have theoretical understandings of the knowledge and beliefs encompassed by reform visions of teaching and may have tried to enact these understandings in their own teaching of teachers, they are not expert practitioners who can provide modelling, coaching, or scaffolding to experienced teachers attempting to learning new instructional practices for K-12 classrooms.

What, then, do staff developers and university-based researchers have to offer in such a collaborative effort? First, they bring knowledge of research and scholarship on teaching and learning that can inform the thinking of teachers. This knowledge includes various teaching practices that have been tried and documented elsewhere, but perhaps more importantly, it also includes concepts and language that can serve as powerful tools for discourse about teaching and learning. Shulman (1986a) has argued that 'conceptual inventions, clarifications, and critiques' (p. 27) that can be used as tools for thinking differently about teaching and learning are a critically important contribution that research can make to the improvement of practice.

University-based staff developers can also bring to teacher discourse communities the critical and reflective stance and modes of discourse that are important norms for the academic community. The reflection, argument, and debate that are central to academic discourse are the kinds of communication patterns that, we are arguing, need to play a more prominent role in teacher discourse communities. Thus, it may be appropriate to think of the staff developer providing modelling, scaffolding, and coaching to help teachers become proficient with these forms of thought and discourse. Teachers, in turn, bring the equally important craft knowledge about pedagogical practices and their own students and classrooms. They bring their skill in working with students and their knowledge of the cultural and instructional contexts in which their students have been learning.

The bringing together of teachers and university-based staff developers or researchers essentially constitutes a new form of discourse community whose goal is to improve pedagogical practice. By working, thinking, and talking together, staff developers and teachers will come to new common understandings, essentially inventing new pedagogical practices as they go. Such an approach addresses the constructivist dilemma by avoiding the extremes of both top-down models in which teachers are viewed as mere implementors of someone else's pedagogical approach and models that assume that empowering teachers without the introduction of new pedagogical ideas is sufficient to produce meaningful change.

Richardson and colleagues' practical argument approach to staff development (Richardson, 1992; Richardson & Anders, 1994) illustrates these various roles. The staff development team brought research-based ideas about learning and instructional practices to the task of developing and examining practical arguments. Teachers provided knowledge about their students, the particular settings in which they taught, and their own teaching practice. Richardson (1992) argues that, to be effective, the staff developer in such a setting must have strong research-based knowledge at his or her fingertips, because presentation of this knowledge is most useful when it comes in response to issues that arise in the course of conversation. The staff developer must also be careful to be humble, even self-effacing, in presenting information and views in order to counteract the pervasive norm in schools to expect university-based staff developers to be the 'experts.'

Similarly, in the innovation program reported by Saunders et al. (1992), Goldenberg played a critical role in guiding instructional conversations with teachers, but the principles and understandings that emerged were very much 'joint productions.' The teachers brought intimate knowledge of their own classrooms and teaching practices to the conversations; through working together address the challenges that arose as teachers tried to implement this new (and emerging) mode of instruction, participants furthered the understanding of all involved.

Discourse communities for pre-service teachers.

Traditionally, pre-service teacher education programs have not emphasized the development of discourse communities among prospective teachers. Rather, they have focused more on the development of individual knowledge and competencies thought to be important for teaching through classes and fieldwork experiences. But the view of knowledge as socially constructed makes it clear that an important part of learning to teach is becoming enculturated into the teaching community – learning to think, talk, and act as a teacher. This claim is supported by research on the socialization of teachers into cultures of schools and teaching (for a review, see Zeichner & Gore, 1990).

In many professions, one could argue that this learning should take place by enculturating new practitioners into existing professionals' communities. For teachers, this argument holds as long as the existing teaching communities embody the sorts of thoughtful, reflective teaching practice we want to encourage. As we pointed out earlier, however, in many cases existing discourse communities of teachers carry with them some of the very norms and expectations that reformers would like to change. We address this concern further in a later section.

The establishment of strong cohorts of pre-service teachers – groups of students who move through a teacher education program's courses and experiences together – is a promising strategy for creating discourse communities for prospective teachers that can support them in acquiring professional knowledge and skills. Teacher educators and carefully chosen, practicing, mentor teachers can play a crucial role in guiding the establishment of norms of inquiry and reflection in these communities.

Another context that may provide reflective, critical discourse communities for pre-service teachers is professional development schools and related efforts. Most professional development schools have as a central component the establishment of new learning communities where inquiry, critique, and reflection are the norms. In these communities, in-service teachers, pre-service teachers, and university faculty and graduate students can study and learn together, working toward the overall improvement of teaching and learning.

Summary: The social nature of cognition.

We have argued that what people know and how they learn are being increasingly viewed as social phenomena. According to this perspective, knowledge and thinking are the products of interactions among groups of people over time. Learning is a highly social process in which individuals interact, often with more knowledgeable others, to acquire modes of thought and become enculturated into various communities. For the classroom, these views suggest that we should create communities in which students can become enculturated into the ways of thinking and interacting that we value – ways of thinking that will help them become lifelong learners. In such classrooms, the teacher takes on the role of coach, model, and facilitator. Regarding in-service and pre-service teacher education, we argued for the importance of establishing new kinds of discourse communities in which teachers engage in active learning, inquiry, reflection, and reasoning about teaching practice. Such communities might include both university-based researchers or staff developers – who bring knowledge of research and of scholarly discourse – and practicing teachers – who bring critical knowledge about teaching practices and the contexts in which they teach.

THE SITUATED NATURE OF COGNITION

Early cognitive theories typically treated knowledge and cognitive processes rather mechanistically, as the manipulation of symbols inside the mind of the individual. In contrast, many current cognitive theorists are concerned with the relationship between knowledge as it exists in the mind of the individual and the situations in which that knowledge is acquired and used (Brown et al., 1989b; Bruner, 1990). Theories of situated cognition, which focus explicitly on this relationship, assume that knowledge is inseparable from the contexts and activities in which it develops. These theories challenge the view of earlier cognitive approaches, such as information processing theories, which assume that there is a cognitive core independent of context and intention. They argue, instead, that the physical and social context in which an activity takes place is an integral part of that activity, and that the activity, in turn, is an integral part of the learning that takes place within the context. Thus, every cognitive act must be understood as a specific response to a specific set of circumstances (Resnick, 1991). How a person learns a particular set of knowledge and skills, as well as the situation in which a person learns, become fundamental parts of what is learned.

The view of cognition as situated has promoted renewed debate about the issue of *transfer* (e.g., Brown, Collins, & Duguid, 1989a; Greeno et al., 1996; Lave, 1988; Vera & Simon, 1993). From a traditional cognitive view, transfer of knowledge or skill to a new situation occurs when the individual has developed an abstract representation of the knowledge that can be applied to multiple situations. From the situated cognition perspective, transfer is made possible to the extent that knowledge is grounded in multiple contexts (Brown et al., 1989a). Explaining how transfer to new contexts does occur is an unresolved issue for proponents of a situated views of cognition. Because an extensive discussion of this issue is beyond the scope of this chapter, we turn directly to considering classroom implications of viewing cognition as situated.

Classroom Implications of a Situated View of Cognition

A number of scholars have examined implications of theories of situated cognition for classroom instruction (Brown et al., 1993; Brown et al., 1989b; Collins et al., 1989; Resnick, 1987b). Traditional instructional theories, grounded in behaviorist and early information-processing perspectives, assumed that learning is facilitated by breaking complex tasks into component parts to be taught and practiced in isolation (e.g., Gagné, 1985) and that concepts and skills can be learned independently of the situations in which they will be used. These theories supported instructional approaches such as teaching the meanings of words through dictionary-based activities and teaching mathematical algorithms without concern for the problems to which they can later be applied.

In contrast, the perspective of situated cognition implies that students should learn valued knowledge, skills, and dispositions as they occur in meaningful contexts, and that what is learned should be connected to situations of use. Brown, Collins, and Duguid (1989b) argue that this perspective suggests the importance of *authentic activities* in classrooms. They define authentic activities as the 'ordinary practices of a culture' (p. 34) – activities that are similar to what actual practitioners do. Such activities are contrasted to 'school activities' – tasks that typically do not provide the contextual features that would enable students to make connections between what they learn and related out-of-school performances. Ann Brown and colleagues (1993) offer another definition of authentic classroom activities – one that is derived from the role of formal education in children's lives. If we consider the goal of education to be preparing students to be lifelong intentional learners, then activities are authentic if they serve that goal. Activities are authentic, from this perspective, if they foster the kinds of thinking and problem-solving skills that are important in out-of-school settings, whether or not the activities themselves mirror what practitioners do. By engaging in the research cycle activities we described earlier, students in Brown and colleagues' classrooms, it is hoped, become enculturated into the community of scholars and lifelong learners.

Collins and colleagues (1989) have developed *cognitive apprenticeship* as an instructional model that relies heavily on the notion of authentic classroom activities. Key aspects of cognitive apprenticeship are that learning takes place in the context of complete, meaningful activities – that is, authentic activities – and that students learn by participating in these activities with the modelling and guidance of a 'master' (typically the teacher). Brown, Collins, and Duguid (1989) suggest that cognitive apprenticeship methods enculturate students into authentic practices through the selection of authentic activities and encouragement of social interaction around participation in the activities.

Collins and colleagues (1989) offer Schoenfeld's (1985) method for teaching mathematical problem solving as an example of cognitive apprenticeship that incorporates the elements of modelling, coaching, scaffolding, and fading. Central to Schoenfeld's approach was solving mathematical problems alongside his students. Schoenfeld formulated a set of heuristic strategies for how to approach mathematical problems that were similar to strategies used by expert mathematicians. He taught these strategies, along with 'control strategies' (e.g., generating and selecting among alternative courses of action, evaluating whether you are making progress toward a solution) and 'productive belief systems' (e.g., beliefs about oneself, about the work, and about mathematics) by first introducing a new heuristic and modelling its use in solving problems. He then gave the class problems to solve as a group. He provided scaffolding for their efforts by acting as a moderator – soliciting heuristics and solution strategies – while modelling various control strategies for making judgments about how best to proceed. He also challenged students to find difficult problems and, at the beginning of each class session, modelled solving one of the problems that they brought in. In addition, Schoenfeld had students participate in small group problem-solving sessions during which he acted as a 'consultant,' coaching students as needed, and gradually fading his prompts and questions so that those students took over more and more control of the problem-solving process. Finally, he alternated with students in conducting a 'postmortem analysis' of the problem solving process. This alternation between expert guidance and novice postmortem analysis provided additional modelling and scaffolding. Through the gradual introduction of new heuristics, careful sequencing of problems, and use of various teacher-led and student-centered activities, Schoenfeld thus taught mathematical problem solving as a meaningful activity rather than a set of discrete, isolated steps.

Teacher Knowledge and Beliefs: A Situated Cognition Perspective

A number of scholars have suggested that some, if not most, of teachers' knowledge is situated within the contexts of classrooms and teaching (Carter, 1990; Carter & Doyle, 1989; Leinhardt, 1988). This professional knowledge is not stored in teachers' minds as context-free abstract principles that are accessible and applicable in any teaching situation. Rather, it is developed in context, stored together with characteristic features of the classrooms and activities within which it is developed, and accessed for use in similar situations.

Carter and Doyle (1989), for example, suggest that much of expert teachers' knowledge is 'event-structured' or 'episodic.' This knowledge is organized around the tasks that teachers accomplish in classroom settings. According to Doyle (1986), teachers must accomplish two major types of classroom tasks: establishing and maintaining social order (problems of classroom management), and representing and enacting the curriculum (problems of learning). As teachers define problems specific to their classroom situations and create solutions for these problems, they store their newly developed knowledge of social order and academic work together with key features of the classroom situations in which that knowledge was developed. Rather than being organized as a set of abstract rules or principles about teaching, this knowledge is structured around classroom events and integrally connected to the classroom situations in which it is developed. It seems reasonable to assume that such situated knowledge coexists with context-free principles, theories, and research findings in teachers' systems of professional knowledge, and that teachers draw upon both types of knowledge when defining and solving problems of practice.

In contrast to theoretical and empirical work on classroom instruction and teacher knowledge, we know of no scholars who have examined teacher learning or teacher education programs explicitly from the perspective of situated cognition. Yet, this perspective has implications for both the content of teacher education (What knowledge, skills and understandings do teachers need in order to create classroom situations in which important student learning occurs?) and the process (In what types of contexts should learning activities for teachers be situated?). In the next section, we explore these questions. We focus first on experienced teachers and then on pre-service teachers, since potential learning opportunities for these two groups differ in ways that are important from a situated cognition perspective.

Implications for Teachers' Professional Development

At first glance, theories of situated cognition support the idea that professional development activities for experienced teachers should be situated in their ongoing practice. A closer examination, however, reveals several complexities and unanswered questions. Are the kinds of opportunities and support that staff development personnel can provide to teachers within their own classrooms ideal, or even sufficient, for helping the latter to explore new ways of teaching? Would other forms of assistance be more appropriate? Are there instances in which contexts other than classrooms are advantageous sites for staff development? We address these issues through an exploration of several different examples of professional development activities.

Classroom-based staff development.

To begin with an obvious implication, the notion of grounding professional development experiences in teachers' own practice suggests that staff development should occur at the school site, with a large component taking place in individual teachers' classrooms. For example, members of a staff development team might provide guidance and support for teachers based on observations of their instructional programs.

One example of this approach to staff development occurred in the University of Colorado Assessment Project (Borko, Mayfield, Marion, Flexer, & Cumbo, 1995). The project's purpose was to help teachers design and implement classroom-based performance assessments compatible with their instructional goals in mathematics and literacy. As one component of the project, a member of the research and staff development team spent one day a week, for approximately 6 weeks, in the classrooms of some participating teachers. During that time, she worked with children as they engaged in independent mathematics activities. She took notes to record her observations of the mathematical activities and children's performances, as well as her insights about the children's mathematical understandings. She then met with the teachers both to share her observations and insights and to discuss various ideas about record keeping. The teachers reported that these conversations gave them a better sense of what to look for when observing students, what questions to ask, and what information to record. The conversations also encouraged the teachers to modify their assessment practices to include classroom-based observations of student performances. Thus, by providing feedback and recommendations grounded in the teachers' ongoing classroom activities, the project staff member was able to help the teachers make changes compatible with the project goals and current reform recommendations.

Exploring examples of teachers' own practices.

A less obvious implication of this principle entails having teachers bring experiences (issues, problems, concerns, etc.) from their classrooms to staff development activities, rather than having the staff development personnel come to them. There is more evidence for the success of this approach than for classroom-based experiences, perhaps because it is typically a less labor-intensive and hence more feasible model for staff development. Three of the staff development projects we have already discussed included ongoing workshops in which teachers and the staff development and research team explored issues that arose in the teachers' instructional practices. In their Practical Argument Staff Development program (Richardson & Anders, 1994), group discussions were based in part on instructional issues and problems that teachers brought to the group. The practical argument sessions in which Richardson and Anders worked with teachers individually entailed viewing and discussing video-taped activities from the teacher's classroom.

In the CU Assessment Project Borko et al., 1995) one particularly effective approach to situating learning occurred when members of the staff development and research team introduced materials and activities in a workshop session, the teachers attempted to implement these ideas in their classrooms, and the group discussed their experiences in a subsequent workshop session. For example, on several occasions the mathematics educator on the project brought nonroutine mathematics problems to the workshops. One problem was the focus of a series of workshops on scoring rubrics at one of the schools. When the problem was first introduced, the teachers and researchers deliberated about features of student responses to consider when assigning scores, and they developed a scoring rubric for the problem. The teachers tried out the rubric in their classrooms during the next two weeks. At the subsequent workshop they reviewed both student responses and their scoring of these responses. On the basis of these discussions, the teachers made several changes in their scoring procedures. More generally, over the course of the year teachers made a number of significant changes in their assessment and instruction practices as a result of this sequence of a 'hands on' workshop, related classroom activities, and follow-up discussions in subsequent workshop sessions. For example, they made problem solving and explanation much more central components of their mathematics programs, and they developed scoring rubrics for assessing children's solutions and explanations for open-ended mathematics tasks.

Finally, as one component of Goldenberg and colleague's work with teachers on instructional conversations (Goldenberg & Gallimore, 1991; Saunders et al., 1992), teachers brought video-tapes of their instructional conversations to workshops to be analyzed by the group. Additionally, much of the focus of discussion throughout the workshops was the teachers' own classroom practice. Based on the success of their work with teachers, Goldenberg and Gallimore drew a number of conclusions about helping teachers learn skills as complex as instructional conversations. Two are related to situated learning: meetings should be productively organized around teachers' perceived needs in their own classrooms, and video-taping teachers' lessons and providing opportunities for them to review and analyze their efforts to do instructional conversation are indispensable.

Exploring ideas away from the classroom setting.

Must all activities designed to help teachers change their practices be drawn from the teachers' own classrooms? We believe that the answer to this question is no. In fact, on some occasions it may be advantageous for teachers to participate in activities that are not related to their own classrooms – either activities that are situated in other classrooms or ones that take place in non-classroom settings. We make this claim on conceptual as well as empirical grounds. Conceptually, theories of situated cognition stipulate that all knowledge is (by definition) situated. The question is not whether knowledge and learning are situated, but in what contexts they are situated. To design effective programs of teacher change, we must: first, consider what kinds of knowledge, skills, and understandings are likely to enable teachers to teach in ways that are compatible with the education reform agenda; next, ask what kinds of experiences constitute authentic activities with respect to these learnings; and then, determine appropriate contexts in which to situate these activities.

For some learning goals, situating teachers' experiences in summer workshops may have several advantages. For example, working with teachers in the summer affords them the luxury of exploring ideas without worrying about what they are going to do tomorrow. Further, it frees them from constraints of their own classroom and school situations. The summer institute that comprised the initial phase of their Cognitively Guided Instruction (CGI) project (Carpenter et al., 1989) is illustrative. The institute was designed to provide opportunities for teachers to learn specific subject matter and how children typically learn it, and to reflect on that knowledge and how it might shape their instructional strategies. Participating teachers were introduced to research-based ideas about children's learning of addition and subtraction through a variety of experiences that were situated primarily in children's mathematics activities. These experiences included, for example, watching and discussing video-tapes of children solving problems, and interviewing children about their mathematical understanding. Various assessments administered during the following school year indicated that the CGI teachers changed their beliefs, knowledge, and practices related to the teaching and learning of mathematics toward a more 'cognitively guided' perspective – one based on an understanding of children's mathematical thinking. For example, their responses reflected the beliefs that instruction should build on students' existing knowledge and that it should be organized to facilitate children's construction of knowledge (in contrast to teachers' presentation of knowledge). CGI teachers also knew more than control teachers about the strategies individual students used to solve problems, the kinds of problems that students find difficult, and different ways to pose those problems.

Combining situations for teacher change.

As the conceptual points and empirical research discussed in this section indicate, several types of professional development experiences, situated in a variety of contexts, are potentially valuable tools for helping teachers to change their instructional knowledge, beliefs, and practices. Determining the most appropriate type of situated experience depends on the specific goals of a professional development program. For example, summer workshops appear to be particularly powerful settings for teachers to develop new relationships to subject matter and new insights about individual students' learning. They may be less well suited to facilitating teachers' enactment of specific reform-based practices.

This analysis suggests that one strong model for staff development may be the combination of a summer workshop that introduces theoretical and research-based ideas and a program of ongoing support during the year as teachers attempt to adapt these ideas and introduce them into their classrooms. The CGI project provided such a combination for some of its participants (Fennema, Carpenter, Franke, Levi, Jacobs, & Empson, in press). In addition to the summer workshops, these participants received support in their classrooms by both a CGI staff member and a mentor teacher. Responsibilities of the support personnel included participating in ongoing workshop sessions with the teachers, visiting their classrooms, and generally providing support as the teachers attempted to base instruction on their children's thinking. At the end of the 4-year period during which 21 teachers were studied, the instruction of 90% of these teachers had become more cognitively guided. These teachers encouraged students to talk about their mathematical thinking, understood and appreciated the variety of solutions that their children constructed, and understood the value of using children's thinking to guide their instructional decisions. Further, most teachers came to believe more strongly that children can solve problems without being explicitly taught procedures for solving them, and that children can learn mathematics by solving many carefully selected problems. These beliefs were accompanied by changes in their perceptions of their own roles as teachers. Most teachers began the project with a view of teaching as demonstrating procedures and telling children how to think. By the end of the 4 years, they saw their role as one of helping children to develop their mathematical knowledge through creating learning environments, posing appropriate problems, and questioning children about their problem solutions. The combination of activities situated in both workshop and classroom contexts was successful in promoting changes in teachers' ideas and practices as well as changes in the students' mathematics achievement.

A similar model was adopted by the SummerMath for Teachers program (Schifter & Fosnot, 1993; Schifter & Simon, 1992; Simon & Schifter, 1991). During the program's two-week summer institute, teachers learned mathematics by participating in activities designed according to constructivist principles of knowledge and learning. They then designed instructional sequences that would provide their own students with mathematics learning opportunities similar to the ones in which they had participated. During the year following the summer institute, staff members visited the teachers' classrooms on a weekly basis and provided feedback, demonstration teaching, and opportunities for reflection. The teachers also attended workshops that provided opportunities for sharing their efforts to change their teaching; exploring issues related to mathematics, learning, and teaching more fully; and participating in small group planning sessions. As a result of these experiences, situated in two distinctly different contexts, many of the teachers began to develop different conceptions of mathematics and deeper understandings of mathematical learning and teaching. Moreover, as reported by the teachers, these changes in their beliefs affected their classroom teaching of mathematics. For example, many teachers expressed an increased commitment to teaching for student thinking and understanding, and they reported listening more to students. Almost all of the teachers who completed the summer institute and classroom follow-up reported implementing strategies such as group problem solving, the use of manipulatives, and new techniques for addressing nonroutine problems.

In sum, there are a number of different ways to situate experienced teachers' learning, ranging from having staff developers work alongside teachers in their own classrooms; to having teachers bring problems, issues, and examples of their teaching to group discussions; to creating activities focused on the teachers' own learning of subject matter. All of these experiences have their role in teacher learning, with a combination of approaches holding powerful potential for fostering meaningful change in teachers' thinking and practice.

Implications for Pre-service Teacher Education

Theories of situated cognition seem to suggest that teacher education experiences for prospective teachers, too, should be situated in classroom practice. Again, closer examination of this suggestion reveals complexities and concerns. For example, pre-service teachers do not have their own classrooms in which to situate learning activities or their own teaching experiences from which to draw in discussions about pedagogical issues. In this section we consider the kinds of learning environments that teacher educators can design to foster prospective teachers' exploration of pedagogical problems. Because goals and experiences for course work and student teaching components of pre-service teacher education differ, appropriate learning environments will differ as well. We therefore consider these two components of teacher education separately.

Learning environments for teacher education course work.

In thinking about the design of teacher preparation courses, we return to the definition of authentic activities provided by Brown and colleagues (1993) as activities that foster students' thinking, problem solving, and learning to learn. In some ways, the challenge to create authentic activities in teacher preparation courses is parallel to the challenge in K-12 classrooms. That is, teacher educators must create experiences in university courses that enable prospective teachers to wrestle with important substantive problems, using research and problem-solving skills. In this case, the particular focus should be on problems of pedagogy and the conceptual tools of teachers.

   One pedagogical approach that seems to hold promise is *case teaching* (Sykes & Bird, 1992). At present there is little research on case teaching in teacher education – either descriptive research on the use of cases or inferential research on the impact of case teaching on learning to teach. Our discussion draws upon essays about the advantages and limitations of cases and, in particular, on analytic pieces by scholars such as Carter (1990), Doyle (1990), Leinhardt (1990), and Sykes and Bird (1992).

   There is considerable variation in cases constructed for use in teacher education. However, they share a number of features, including a focus on particular situations rather than general principles and the provision of vicarious rather than direct encounters with those situations. Although not authentic in the sense of being actual classroom experiences, cases do allow pre-service teachers to explore real pedagogical problems. In fact, some proponents suggest that cases are preferable to field experiences because they afford the teacher educator more control over the situations that pre-service teachers encounter and the issues that they explore within those situations. They provide a shared experience for pre-service teachers to examine as a group, and they enable teacher educators to prepare for discussions and other activities in which the materials are used (Sykes & Bird, 1992).

Proponents of case teaching suggest a variety of uses for cases – in either written or video format – in teacher education. Perhaps the most common use, and one that certainly fits within the perspective of situated cognition, is as tools for developing skills in analyzing problematic teaching situations (Doyle, 1990; Merseth, 1990). In their analysis of cases of problematic teaching situations, prospective teachers can practice framing problems, generating various solutions to the problems, choosing among alternative solutions, and reflecting on implications of their choices. Some scholars (e.g., Leinhardt, 1988) advocate using cases of exemplary teaching to help pre-service teachers make connections between theories of instruction and their enactment under real conditions. This use is particularly appropriate in preparing teachers for reform-based teaching, as their opportunity to experience workable alternatives to conventional practice in actual classroom settings, much less exemplary models of such alternatives, is likely to be quite limited. The various uses are captured by Kleinfeld's (1992) suggestion that cases provide:

1) Vicarious experience with the kinds of problematic situations characteristic of teaching;
2) A model of how an expert teacher goes about framing and constructing educational problems;
3) A model of how a sophisticated teacher inquires about and reflects on such problems;
4) A stock of educational strategies for use in analogous problem situations;
5) A sense that teaching is an inherently ambiguous activity requiring continuous reflection. (pp. 34-35)

Cases, both written and video-taped, limit the information provided about any particular teaching situation and, as a result, simplify the problem-solving activity. If our aim in teacher education is to create experiences that more accurately reflect the complexity of teaching and the ill-structured (fuzzy) nature of pedagogical problems, then cases, as typically conceived, may be limited in their usefulness. What is needed, instead, is a much richer set of materials documenting classroom teaching and learning in a way that enables pre-service teachers to define and explore pedagogical problems of their choosing, using multiple sources of information in their explorations. Interactive multimedia cases and hypermedia environments have the potential to achieve these goals.

Materials being developed by Lampert and Ball as part of their Mathematics and Teaching Through Hypermedia (MATH) Project (Ball, Lampert, & Rosenberg, 1991; Lampert, Heaton, & Ball, 1994) and by Goldman and colleagues in the Cognition and Technology Group at Vanderbilt (1990) provide prototypes for such alternatives. For example, Ball and Lampert assembled a variety of materials documenting teaching and the learning of mathematics in the third- and fifth-grade classes where they taught on a regular basis. Materials include video-tapes of classroom mathematics lessons for the entire school year, instructional materials, journals containing Ball and Lampert's lesson plans and reflections, student journals, students' performances on quizzes and standardized tests, and interviews with students that explore their mathematical understandings. Lampert, Heaton, and Ball (1994) developed interactive media case materials and piloted them in Heaton's mathematics methods course. These cases include information about actual instances of teaching and learning in hard copy, video, and audio forms (e.g., video-tapes and transcripts of lessons, photocopies of students' work, and the teacher's journal), which Heaton and her students used to explore problems of pedagogical practice. Ball, Lampert, and colleagues are currently incorporating their multimedia information about the teaching and learning into hypermedia environments that will include tools for browsing, annotating, and constructing arguments.

The nonlinearity of hypermedia systems, the ability to visit and revisit various sources of information quickly and easily, and the ability to build and store flexible and multiple links among various pieces of information, make it possible for users to consider multiple perspectives on an event simultaneously. Further, the extensiveness of the data bases and ease of searching these data bases make it possible for users to define and explore problems of their own choosing (Merseth & Lacey, 1993). Like traditional cases, these multimedia and hypermedia materials have the advantage of being a shared context for the exploration of pedagogical problems. They enable pre-service teachers to be involved as active inquirers, participating in a learning community, and engaging in problem solving about teaching and learning parallel to the kinds of experiences we (as teacher educators) would like to see them create in their own classrooms (Lampert et al., 1994). However, they can be a 'simulated field experience' in a way that traditional cases cannot, coming much closer to mirroring the complexity of the problem space in which teachers work.

Cases and hypermedia systems are used to create authentic activities for preservice teacher education courses within the university setting. Grimmett and MacKinnon (1992), however, have suggested an alternative approach based on their commitment to incorporating craft knowledge into teacher education. They questioned the common practice of offering methods classes on campus, in the absence of children, and suggested that we redesign these classes to involve professors, experienced teachers, and pre-service teachers in the joint teaching of children in school settings. Using the school-based teacher education program documented by MacKinnon and Grunau (1991) as an example, they argued that 'all of the participants – beginning and experienced teachers, as well as professors – learned a great deal about teaching at one another's elbows' (p. 436), when pre-service teachers taught alongside their professors, and when video-tapes of that teaching were analyzed and critiqued. Although their recommendations do not come from a situated cognition perspective on teachers' knowledge, they clearly support this perspective.

Authentic activities and subject-matter knowledge.

The suggestions offered above focus on the development of prospective teachers' pedagogical knowledge and pedagogical content knowledge. In the section on The Constructed Nature of Knowledge and Beliefs, we presented evidence that prospective teachers often do not understand their subjects in sufficient depth to enact reform-based teaching, and we suggested that teacher education may need to focus on subject-matter knowledge as well as pedagogical knowledge and pedagogical content knowledge. We also reviewed some of the research on the learning of subject matter in pre-service teacher preparation programs.

An examination of the contexts in which pre-service teachers' learning of mathematics was situated reveals a pattern across studies. The research suggests that organizing courses about mathematics and mathematics teaching around solving nonroutine mathematical problems and opportunities to talk about mathematics can result in changes in participants' understandings of what it means to know mathematics and how mathematics is learned, as well as improving their substantive knowledge of mathematics content (Schram et al., 1989; Simon, 1995; Wilcox et al., 1990). Similarly, McDiarmid (1995) has worked with others to organize courses in the teaching of history around the examination of what and how historians think about critical topics. Prospective teachers in the latter program thus enhanced their own understandings of history as well as thinking about how they might develop such understandings in students. The perspective of situated cognition suggests that such findings would also generalize to other subject areas. In other words, activities that involve pre-service teachers in solving complex discipline-based problems and sharing their solutions with peers may be *generally* appropriate ways to situate teacher trainees' learning of subject matter for teaching.

Situating learning in the student teaching experience.

Undoubtedly the most common response to calls for situating pre-service teachers' learning is to focus on the student teaching experience. It is during student teaching that novices have the opportunity to practice enacting their pedagogical knowledge and beliefs in actual classroom settings. The student teaching experience has the potential to provide a supportive context in which novices can explore new instructional strategies and receive feedback on the lessons they teach. For this component of pre-service teacher education, the concept of an apprenticeship might be appropriate. That is, student teachers could be apprenticed to cooperating teachers and, through techniques like modelling, coaching, and feedback, could learn the skills and dispositions that make the cooperating teachers master teachers.

The picture, however, is not as clear-cut as it might appear at first glance. For example, despite the fact that it is the most widely studied aspect of teacher education, little is known about the student teaching experience. There continues to be much disagreement over the nature and degree of influence that student teaching has on prospective teachers' knowledge, beliefs, and practices (Glickman & Bey, 1990; Zeichner, 1985). Teachers consistently rate it as the single most beneficial component of their preparation programs (Guyton & McIntyre, 1990). In contrast, several scholars have cautioned that student teaching can have negative as well as positive consequences for prospective teachers (Feiman-Nemser, 1983; Zeichner, 1985). Others have suggested that student teaching may have little impact on teachers' development of pedagogical skills or reflective abilities (Hoover, O'Shea, & Carroll, 1988).

Even if research offered clear evidence that student teaching has a substantial influence on prospective teachers' ideas and practices, concerns about the ability of the experience to foster and support new ways of teaching would remain. Central among these concerns is the question of whether classrooms available for student teachers embody the kinds of teaching we want them to learn and can thus serve as a productive site for their learning – a concern we raised earlier in our discussion of social supports for teachers' learning. As Sykes and Bird (1992) caution:

> Finally, the situated cognition perspective draws on the image of apprenticeship in a guild or a professional community as a powerful form of learning. But this image requires a stable, satisfactory practice that the novice can join. If the aim of teacher education is a reformed practice that is not readily available, and if there is no reinforcing culture to support such practice, then the basic imagery of apprenticeship seems to break down. Teachers' knowledge is situated, but this truism creates a puzzle for reform. Through what activities and situations do teachers

learn new practices that may not be routinely reinforced in the work setting? (p. 501)

McNamara (1995) makes a similar point that for student teaching to do more than reproduce traditional teaching routines, teacher educators must ensure that the experience extends and transcends practices that student teachers encounter in particular schools.

If we take these cautions seriously, what are the implications for the design of the student teaching experience? Certainly this experience plays too central a role in pre-service education to consider eliminating it entirely. And the potential for student teaching to serve as a site for learning to enact reform-based practice seems too great to warrant such dramatic measures. One solution might be to place pre-service teachers in classrooms of teachers who, regardless of how they teach, are willing to let student teachers try out their new visions of learning and teaching. Then, university supervisors could serve roles similar to those of staff developers – not as masters to whom the student teachers would apprentice, but as experienced educators with a conceptual understanding of reform-based teaching who could provide coaching, feedback and support. Such an approach might even serve a dual purpose as a professional development experience for cooperating teachers interested in learning to teach in new ways.

Another possibility, not incompatible with the first, would be to offer seminars concurrently with the student teaching experience, conducted by university teacher educators, and designed to help student teachers critically analyze their learning-to-teach experiences. Within these seminars, student teachers would be able to examine the relationship between their ideas and practices, and to consider difficulties that arise when one tries to enact reform-based practice in settings that may not support such practice.

Summary: Situating Learning Experiences for Teachers

The perspective of situated cognition suggests that the contexts in which learning occurs are important determinants of what people learn. Thus, in designing experiences to promote reform-based visions of teaching, teacher educators must determine the kinds of knowledge, skills, and understandings that will enable teachers to teach in new ways; identify experiences likely to foster these learnings; and then determine appropriate contexts in which to situate these experiences. The analyses we presented in this section suggest that a combination of several types of experiences, situated in a variety of contexts, may best accomplish these goals. In the case of experienced teachers, for example, summer workshops appear to be particularly powerful settings for developing new understandings of subject matter and new insights about students' learning. Support and feedback over time, directly connected to actual classroom experiences, may be better suited to facilitating teachers' enactment of specific reform-based practices. A combination of multimedia cases for university-based coursework and student-teaching placements that encourage and support experimentation with new visions of teaching and learning may be a powerful design for pre-service teacher education.

THE DISTRIBUTED NATURE OF COGNITION

The essence of the concept of distributed cognition is that cognition is not solely a property of the minds of individuals. It is distributed or 'stretched over' (Lave, 1988) the individual, other persons, and symbolic and physical environments. In the world outside of school, intelligent activities typically are collaborative rather than solo performances, and they often depend upon resources beyond the individuals themselves such as physical tools and notational systems (Pea, 1993).[2] Pea stresses the idea that distribution of cognition should be seen as expansion rather than reallocation. In other words, by distributing cognition we expand a system's capacity for innovation and invention. Moll, Tapia, and Whitmore (1993) provide an example of a household in a predominantly Mexican, working-class community in Arizona, in which knowledge, labor, and material services are shared both within the household and across other households in the extended family and community. For example, households share knowledge about the government agencies and institutions with which they must deal, thus helping one another to apply for medical care, public housing, and food stamps. They also share labor services based on their expertise, working together on such tasks as repairing cars and building homes. Moll and colleagues make the case that such sharing, an example of the social distribution of cultural resources, is crucial to the families' survival.

Pea (1993) distinguishes between the distribution of cognition between persons and tools and the distribution among persons. With respect to the first aspect of distributed cognition, he notes that tools do not merely enhance cognition; in some cases they transform it. That is, the use of tools can result in qualitative as well as quantitative changes in thinking. The role of the compass in navigation provides an example (Resnick, 1987b). Before the invention of the compass, sailors navigated by the stars, locating constellations in the sky and performing complex geometric calculations to get their bearings. Simple magnetic compasses eliminated the need for some of these calculations. As compasses became more sophisticated (e.g., with built-in compensations for the variation between magnetic and true north), additional computational work was eliminated. Today, essentially all needed computations are performed by gyrocompasses; most cognitive tasks involved in navigating have been shifted from sailors to their tools.

The assertion that cognition is distributed among persons acknowledges that, for many cognitively complex tasks, no one participant in the task may have the knowledge and skills to complete it individually. Such solo performance is neither expected nor desired. Again, navigation provides an example. Hutchins (1990, 1993) described the navigational system on a technologically sophisticated U.S. Navy ship. Six people with three different job descriptions (and using several sophisticated cognitive tools) were involved in piloting the ship out of the harbor. Two people on the deck took visual sightings. Two others relayed the readings to a specialist on the bridge. That specialist recorded the readings in a book, while another plotted the ship's position on a navigational chart and projected where it would be at the next sighting. This information was used to decide what landmarks should be sighted next by the people on the deck. The knowledge needed to pilot the ship successfully was distributed throughout the entire navigational system. Important aspects of that knowledge were built into the tools. And the knowledge that resided in people was distributed across individuals such that no one person was able to pilot the ship alone. As this example indicates, cognitive properties of groups differ from those of individuals within the groups. The social organization of distributed cognition makes it possible for groups to accomplish cognitive tasks beyond the capabilities of any individual member (Hutchins, 1991).

Classroom Implications of a Distributed Model of Cognition

A number of scholars are urging formal education to incorporate the idea of distributed cognition into the design of classroom activities in order to prepare students for more adequate functioning in the world outside the classroom. Resnick (1987b) argues that,

> ... as long as school focuses mainly on individual forms of competence, on tool-free performance, and on decontextualized skills, educating people to be good learners in school settings alone may not be sufficient to help them become strong out-of-school learners. (p. 18)

Pea (1993) makes a similar point:

> Socially scaffolded and externally mediated, artifact-supported cognition is so predominant in out-of-school settings that its disavowal in the classroom is detrimental to the transfer of learning beyond the classroom. (p. 75)

He takes this position further, suggesting that

> we should reorient the educational emphasis from individual, tool-free cognition to facilitating individuals' responsiveness and novel uses of resources for creative and intelligent activity alone and in collaboration. (p. 81)

We may not want to go as far as Pea does in advocating a reorientation of formal education. If schooling, however, is to prepare students to engage in cognitively complex real-world activities, then we must thoughtfully design classrooms and classroom activities to incorporate the distribution of cognitive tasks across people and between persons and tools. Adopting such a position changes our notions of what students need to know and learn in substantial ways. With respect to distribution between persons and tools, the shift in emphasis that has accompanied the incorporation of calculators in K-4 mathematics classrooms — away from computational skills such as long division and to activities that focus on estimation, the meanings of operations, and selection of appropriate calculation methods — provides a compelling example. Micro-computer based laboratories (e.g., Linn, Songer, & Eylon, in press) provide another illustration; in these activities, students use the computer to investigate real-world phenomena in ways not possible with traditional laboratory equipment. They collect data using probes that plug into the computer and record information for variables such as temperature, pressure, light, and sound; and they interpret their data using computer-generated graphs of the relationships among these variables. In addition to collecting data and transforming them into data displays, the computer technology contributes to framing the students' investigations of the phenomena by enabling them to explore questions that could not be addressed using only traditional laboratory equipment.

Such shifts to learning activities that require tool-aided cognition are not without their concerns. As is the case with virtually all design decisions, there are inevitable trade-offs in the choice between tool-aided and tool-unaided cognition. For example, whereas tools may provide greater accessibility to higher-level, more complex cognitive activities, they may do so at the expense of students acquiring basic skills (e.g., mathematical computation) and certain lower-level understandings (Pea, 1993). Pea cautions us to be aware of these trade-offs and to make decisions that take into account both the trade-offs and our educational aims. Concerns and trade-offs notwithstanding, there seems to be a general acceptance of incorporating technology and cognitive tools into classroom learning activities. The mathematics education community's acceptance of this shift, for example, is evident in the *Curriculum and Evaluation Standards for*

School Mathematics (National Council of Teachers of Mathematics, 1989) which notes that 'calculators, computers, courseware, and manipulative materials are necessary for good mathematics instruction; the teacher can no longer rely solely on a chalkboard, chalk, paper, pencils, and a text' (p. 253).

Support for a shift in focus may not be as clear when it comes to the distribution of cognition across people. In fact, several features of the culture of schooling seem antithetical to the idea of distributing components of a cognitive task across participants. For example, independent thinking and individual accountability are highly valued in schools. As Resnick (1987b) notes,

> The dominant form of school learning and performance is individual. Although group activities of various kinds occur in school, students ultimately are judged on what they can do by themselves. Furthermore, a major part of the core activity of schooling is designed as individual work .... (p. 13)

Although we do not advocate eliminating a focus on individual competence in schools, we are persuaded by the arguments of Resnick (1987b), Brown and colleagues (1993), and others that, to prepare students for successful participation in society, schools need to place more emphasis on socially shared cognitive activities. To integrate such activities into classrooms successfully, we must strike a balance between a focus on individual competence and one on cooperation and collaboration.

Another characteristic of school culture that does not appear to fit well with the idea of distributed cognition is the practice of teaching all students (or, at least, all students of similar ability and achievement levels) the same body of knowledge and skills and then giving them the same test to determine what they have learned. One underlying rationale for this practice is the belief that there is a core body of knowledge and skills every child should learn in school. If cognitive tasks are distributed across individuals, then some students may not have the opportunity to acquire or develop these essentials. With respect to this issue, we again agree with Resnick (1987b) — in this case, that 'school should focus its efforts on preparing people to be good *adaptive_learners* (emphasis in original), so that they can perform effectively when situations are unpredictable and task demands change' (p. 18). From this learning-to-learn perspective, the essentials include skills such as problem solving and participating in joint cognitive activity, as well as the 'enabling' disciplines of reading, writing, and mathematics.' Rather than focusing on ensuring that all students learn a broad range of similar facts and concepts in various domains, the emphasis should be on a few powerful ideas that students are unlikely to discover on their own and that can help them make sense of a wide variety of more specific ideas (Brown et al., 1993; Prawat, 1991). The contrasting view, 'that all children of a certain age in a same grade should acquire the same body of knowledge at the same time ... is one of the reasons that contemporary school activities are to a large part inauthentic' (Brown et al., 1993, p. 224) and not conducive to producing adaptive learners.

If we accept the idea that components of cognitive tasks should be distributed among participants, then in order to ensure equity in opportunities to learn, we must be concerned with how components of different cognitive levels are distributed. Bereiter and Scardamalia (1989) hypothesized that 'the skills a student will acquire in an instructional interaction are those required by the student's role in the joint cognitive process' (p. 383). This hypothesis suggests the importance of considering individuals' roles in tasks that are shared by groups of students. For example, in a cooperative group working to solve a richly situated mathematics problem, one student might carry out the computations required, another student might record the group decisions, and another might do the higher level planning needed to solve the problem. In such situations, it is important that all students have the opportunity (across multiple tasks, if not within each task) to learn and practice higher-level as well as lower-level cognitive skills. This goal would not be met, for example, if higher level components of tasks were always assigned to high ability students. Such a division of efforts might be appropriate in nonschool settings, where the ultimate goal often is efficiency of task completion rather than learning. It is not appropriate, however, in classrooms where major goals are that all students learn how to learn and become lifelong learners.

Earlier, we described briefly the guided learning classrooms featured in the design experiments for grade school science conducted by Brown and colleagues (Brown, 1992; Brown et al., 1993). These classrooms provide an example of how cognition and expertise can be intentionally distributed across persons, and between persons and tools, in order to create a community of learners in which the major goal is that students are prepared as lifelong learners or 'learning experts.' Research cycles, a major activity in these classrooms, use a combination of the jigsaw method (Aronson, 1978) and reciprocal teaching (Palincsar & Brown, 1984) to distribute expertise across students. Students are assigned research themes (e.g., endangered species, changing populations), each divided into five subtopics. In research groups, each person becomes an expert on one of the subtopics. Then, in learning groups, the 'experts' use reciprocal teaching to lead discussions on their subtopics. Thus, each child in a learning group is an expert in one part of the material and is responsible for teaching it to others. Ultimately, all students in the group are tested on the entire unit. Features of the computer environment in the classroom also foster distributed cognition. For example, QuickMail (a version of electronic mail) gives students access to a wider community of learners and experts. It 'free[s] teachers from the burden of being sole guardians of knowledge and allow[s] the community to extend beyond the classroom walls' (Brown et al., p. 214).

As another example, the Kids as Global Scientists (KGS) Project, which involves students around the world in an Internet-based middle-school weather curriculum, features Global Exchanges based on a distributed expertise model of learning (Songer, in press-a, in press-b). Each Global Exchange begins with students collecting local weather data. Local understandings are then enhanced and expanded through use of the Internet and its resources. For example, students have access to real-time and archival satellite and weather imagery. Through electronic mail, they can correspond with peers and mentors worldwide who are participating in the Exchange. They are thus able to use the understandings about weather-related issues they develop based on familiar instances as a foundation for learning about these same issues on a much larger scale.

The Spring 1995 Exchange involved 1400 students at 30 middle schools, including students from nine international sites in countries such as Finland, Australia, and Hong Kong. Interviews with KGS teachers indicate that student motivation to learn was very high, at least in part because of the opportunity to share information with peers around the world. As a result of the extensive online conversations with mentors and peers, students' explanations were rich with personal stories of weather events intertwined with complex scientific explanations. Also, use of the computer seemed to facilitate working in cooperative groups. In general, participants valued the virtually unlimited access to information and new opportunities to learn that the telecommunication tools and world-wide participation provided (Songer, in press-a; Songer, in press-b).

Distributed Cognition The Teacher's Role

The teacher's role will be different in a classroom designed to foster and take advantage of distributed cognition than in a more traditional classroom that emphasizes independent, individual learning. To date, however, little has been written on the role of the teacher in classrooms that intentionally incorporate the design of distributed cognition. According to Brown and colleagues (1993), this role is still 'problematic' and 'largely uncharted' (p. 206). In this section, we explore ideas about the teacher's role, based on an analysis of the demands that teaching for distributed cognition will place on teachers.

Teacher as master inquirer.

One implication of the notion that cognition and expertise are distributed in the classroom is that the teacher can not be expected to claim expertise in all of the information domains explored in classroom tasks. Gone is the image of teacher as imparter of knowledge; it is replaced by one of teacher as guide to students' inquiry in multiple domains. In the role of guide, a teacher teaches as students become ready to learn rather than by following a set curriculum or rigid lesson plan. Brown (1992) cautions that such an approach does not imply absence of a curriculum. Rather, there are a few recurring themes that the teacher must help students come to understand. The teacher must be knowledgeable about these themes and skillful in supporting and guiding students as they explore them. Classroom learning activities must revisit the themes often throughout the year, each time at a deeper level of understanding. The teacher may also need a richer understanding of how these key ideas relate to the overall K-12 curriculum than is the case with a more teacher-directed instructional approach.

Brown and colleagues (1993) suggest that 'guiding learning is easier to talk about than to do. It takes clinical judgment to know when to intervene' (p. 207) and how to achieve a balance between fostering discovery and furnishing guidance. The transition to such a role is often not a comfortable one for teachers. As one teacher in the KGS project commented,

> I remember my first year. It's just uncomfortable when you don't know what's going to happen. And even now [3 years later], I think I have a lot of the bugs ironed out of this unit for myself, but even still, there are always things that you can't control .... I hate to use these trite words, but I think I'm more of a facilitator than a controller. (Hester & Songer, in press)

In addition to knowing how to guide inquiry, the teacher must be a role model for inquiry activities. In our earlier section, The Social Nature of Cognition, we pointed out that when teachers design classrooms to be discourse communities – places where students are enculturated into particular ways of acting and thinking – they must play a critical role in modelling the desired mental habits, dispositions, and modes of thought. Similarly, for a classroom focused on fostering the dispositions and skills for lifelong learning, the teacher must model inquiry him- or herself: 'If students are apprentice learners, the teacher is the master craftsperson of learning whom they must emulate' (Brown et al., 1993, p. 207). For example, the teacher must be able to recognize when she or he does not know an answer, be comfortable acknowledging when and what he or she does not know, and have the cognitive and physical resources to remedy this lack of knowledge. A KGS teacher described the shift in his role and its impact on his classroom:

> The learning environment of the class virtually took on a vibrant, inquisitive life of its own as my students and I became joint learners in discovering how to up- and download information to their new-found electronic pen pals. Mr. D, the teacher, became Mr. D, the facilitator, and my professional ego anxiety in not knowing exactly how everything worked gave place to a comfortable 'let's see if this will work' approach my students totally accepted and contributed to. (Songer, in press-b)

In making such shifts, teachers become models for inquiry.

Knowledge of technological tools.

Many classrooms designed to encourage the distribution of cognition across persons and cognitive tools incorporate fairly sophisticated technologies (e.g., e-mail, Internet, World Wide Web, CD-ROM) that 'explode' the sources of knowledge and expertise available to teachers and students. Brown and colleagues (1993) found that computer activities designed to extend cognition beyond the classroom were not readily incorporated into all classrooms where they were available. These activities were rapidly established only when teachers provided support and encouragement to students and, most importantly, modelled the use of the technologies. Similarly, a number of teachers in the KGS project reported that their personal inexperience with the Internet and programs such as *Blue Skies*, as well as insufficient access to computers, limited the extent to which they were able to integrate telecommunication into their weather units (Songer, in press-b). It sometimes took a number of years with the project before teachers were comfortable incorporating the technological tools into their science programs:

> To be honest, the first year I did KGS, I was just so nervous, … it was so uncomfortable that I really had to force myself to use the tool …. I just really think that I've personally come a long way in terms of not being afraid of the technology anymore. Actually wanting my kids to go to the computer lab and the fact that when I plan a unit, I actually think, 'I wonder how Internet could be a part of this.' You know, it's not just a chore anymore. It's something I'm completely comfortable with and now it's working into my actual unit planning and lesson planning as a tool. (Hester & Songer, in press)

Distributed Cognition: Learning Experiences for Teachers

In exploring implications of distributed cognition for pre-service and in-service teacher education, we are on speculative grounds – building on ideas about the teacher's role in a distributed cognition classroom but taking these ideas a step further to consider the kinds of learning experiences that will help teachers prepare for their new roles. We focus primarily on two areas of teacher responsibility: the creation of a classroom learning community; and the integration of technology and technological tools into classroom learning experiences.

Learning to create a classroom learning community.

Classrooms in which cognition is distributed across people are characterized by a culture of mutual respect, individual and joint responsibility, and a discourse community in which ideas are freely shared and explored. Brown and colleagues (1993) suggest that such a culture 'is difficult to describe and equally difficult to transmit to novice teachers except through demonstration, modelling, and guided feedback' (p. 199). Their caution leads naturally to the suggestion that novice teachers should be placed in classrooms like the ones created in their design experiments, so that they may participate in an apprenticeship form of learning. This suggestion is similar to our recommendation earlier in the chapter that student teachers' learning experiences should be situated in classrooms where they can observe and practice teaching according to a reform vision. But as our earlier analyses indicated, these recommendations will undoubtedly be difficult to follow because such classrooms are few and far between.

Another option, potentially easier to enact, is to create such cultures in our teacher education programs. Although the majority of teacher educators have not personally experienced learning or teaching in classrooms where distribution of cognitive tasks is common, teacher educators may be able to incorporate features of distributed cognition into our programs – learning along with the pre-service teachers. For example, we can assign group projects designed with the expectations that cognition is shared among group members and that tools such as computers are used to expand participants' communication beyond the classroom walls. We can play a role in these activities analogous to the role a K-12 teacher would play in his or her class – both guiding students' inquiry and modelling a stance of inquiry. Pre-service teachers can play the dual roles of students and students of teaching – first participating in the activities as they are assigned and then switching hats to examine their experiences and those of the teacher educator from the perspective of the teacher. They can then explore, as a group, whether and how they might organize and enact similar activities in their own classrooms.

One activity that holds promise as a tool for fostering important pedagogical conversations is the modelling of joint cognitive activities, as described by Bereiter and Scardamalia (1989). Careful analysis of the cognitive roles played by each participant in such an activity could serve as an excellent springboard for individual and shared reflection on roles and responsibilities in shared cognitive tasks, and on potential problems and dilemmas concerning the equitable distribution of cognition.

So far, we have focused on pre-service teacher education. It is likely to be at least as difficult for experienced teachers to modify their practices to develop a culture of shared cognition in their classrooms. Our recommendations for in-service teacher education are similar to those for pre-service. For example, we envision professional development experiences in which teachers participate in group activities that incorporate expectations for shared cognition. One implication of this recommendation is that professional development cannot occur in one-shot workshops. It will entail more long-term experiences that allow for the creation of learning communities and exploration of socially shared cognitive activities from the perspectives of both student and learning teacher.

Learning to distribute cognition across persons and technological tools.

Because classrooms designed to foster and take advantage of distributed cognition often use sophisticated technologies, teacher education programs should provide opportunities for teachers to learn about these new technologies and to explore how to incorporate them into classroom learning activities. As a first step toward accomplishing these goals, we can take advantage of most universities' telecommunication capabilities to introduce pre-service teachers to electronic mail and information resources available through the Internet. Informal conversations with our colleagues, as well as a perusal of programs for recent annual meetings of professional organizations such as the American Educational Research Association and National Council for Teachers of Mathematics, suggest that some teacher educators are beginning to incorporate computers and telecommunication tools into their course assignments. These assignments include, for example, ongoing e-mail conversations about course readings and evaluations of computer software relevant to the course subject matter.

Whereas teachers are introducing technology into K-12 classrooms by having students use technological tools to explore problems in mathematics, science, and other academic disciplines, teacher education students should use these tools to explore problems of pedagogy as well. The hypermedia environment being developed by Ball and Lampert within their MATH project (introduced in the section on situated cognition) provides one image of the possible (Shulman, 1983). Within this environment, students will be able to explore pedagogical problems that arise as they view and read about Ball's teaching of mathematics in a third-grade classroom and Lampert's in a fifth-grade classroom. Also, taking advantage of hypermedia, Blumenfeld, Krajcik, and colleagues have created instructional planning software that pre-service elementary teachers use to design science units and lessons (Krajcik, Blumenfeld, & Starr, 1993; Urdan, Blumenfeld, Soloway, & Brade, in press). Their two-year teacher preparation program emphasizes the teaching of science in the upper elementary grades and features an integrated set of foundations, science, and methods courses. As a program-wide assignment, pre-service teachers design a unit and series of lessons, drawing upon information from several of their courses. They use a computer-based system, Instruction by Design (IByD), that scaffolds the design of the unit and lessons. IByD is a computer-aided design (CAD) tool that enables students to build and store individual knowledge bases and to apply what they learn elsewhere in their program (e.g., courses, readings) to the design of instructional plans. A comparison of IByD users and other pre-service teachers suggested that novice teachers who used the tool internalized and benefited from the scaffolding provided by the program, producing plans that were more thorough than those of their colleagues not using IByD.

It is important for teachers to participate in technology-based activities in two roles – both as students learning to use the new tools and as teachers considering how to incorporate the tools into their own classroom activities and instructional programs. As we suggested with respect to the creation of classroom learning communities, it is not enough for teachers to learn to use new cognitive tools; they must step back and reflect on their experiences with technology and ask themselves how these experiences might profitably inform K-12 education.

A class for experienced and pre-service teachers at the University of Colorado included explicit attention to these two sets of priorities (P. Hester, personal communication). Goals for the 'Internet in the K-12 Classroom' course were that students understand methods of connecting to the Internet, become proficient using various Internet tools, become familiar with applications of Internet technology in the K-12 classroom, understand the issues surrounding use of the Internet in the K-12 classroom, and design at least one application of Internet technology in the K-12 curriculum. Students participated in on-line discussions focused on questions the instructor provided. They also kept journals where they recorded on-line activities they completed, reactions to those activities, questions or problems they encountered, and on-line resources they wished to share. Other on-line assignments had them join and participate in an educational listserve, become familiar with the World Wide Web, and explore a number of information sources on the Web. In-class and on-line discussions indicated that participants became familiar with the Internet and used it for course assignments. Several practicing teachers also began to incorporate Internet activities into their instructional programs. Participants indicated that the explicit instruction and technical support available through the course were important factors in their learning. The major limitation they reported was time – both to learn to use the Internet and to continue using it on an ongoing basis. Although courses such as this are labor-intensive and somewhat limited in reach, they afford an excellent opportunity for teachers to develop the technical skills and attitudes important for teaching in ways that facilitate distribution of cognitive activities across students and tools.

The support provided to teachers in the Kids as Global Scientists project provides additional ideas about the kinds of experiences that may assist teachers in their efforts to introduce technology into K-12 classrooms. Each year, participating teachers received the technology-based KGS Weather Curriculum, along with a packet of information intended to assist them in teaching the weather unit using computer telecommunications. The packet provided during the first year of the project included a bibliography and information on weather topics; a resource list of people, addresses, phone numbers and e-mail addresses; Internet Trek software and user's guide; and weather-measuring devices. KGS project personnel communicated with teachers at the 6 original sites via telephone and e-mail on a weekly basis and whenever problems arose. Thus, these teachers received individual assistance as they pilot tested the materials (Songer, in press-b).

During the summers before the second and third years of the project, some KGS teachers participated in workshops focused on modifying the curriculum and information packet. As a result of these workshops, the information packet has evolved into a bound curriculum guide that includes suggested experiments and demonstrations for each weather topic, information on Internet and non-Internet weather resources, technical support, advice on classroom management, suggested time lines, and examples of how teachers have enacted KGS instructional and assessment activities. As the number of sites has increased, telephone calls have become less common. Project personnel, however, maintain e-mail correspondence with all sites. In addition, teachers have begun to talk with each other via e-mail, exchanging experiences and suggestions as well as weather data. Preliminary analysis of surveys and interviews with the teachers indicates that they generally found materials in the teacher information packets very useful. Many respondents commented positively about the materials, and very few offered suggestions for additional support materials. Almost all concerns that the teachers expressed focused on technological issues (e.g., better connectivity, more access to computers) and time availability (Songer, in press-b).

Summary: The Distributed Nature of Cognition

Several prominent educators and cognitive scientists have recently advocated that formal education incorporate the idea of distributed cognition into the design of classroom activities (e.g., Brown et al., 1993; Pea, 1993; Resnick, 1987). They argue that such an approach will better prepare students for a world in which most complex tasks are accomplished by groups of people, often with the assistance of cognitive tools, rather than by individuals working in isolation. To enact such a shift in focus, the teacher must become a guide to students' inquiry – one who is very knowledgeable about important themes in the curriculum and is able to serve as a role model for inquiry activities.

In the absence of research that explicitly addresses the preparation of teachers for distributed cognition classrooms, we have speculated about the kinds of experiences that would help teachers take on these new roles and responsibilities. We suggested that both pre-service teacher education and professional development for experienced teachers address the creation of classroom learning communities and the integration of technology and technological tools into learning activities. We also recommended that teachers participate in such experiences as students and then step back to consider how they might organize and enact similar activities in their own classrooms. We hope to see these ideas subjected to empirical tests in the next few years, so that the next chapter written on learning to teach will have research findings, rather than merely the authors' speculations, to offer the teacher education community.

CONCLUSION: REVISITING THE MANTRAS

We began this chapter by describing a number of claims about teachers' learning that have become like mantras for the staff development community. We now return to those claims, exploring them in light of the various perspectives on cognition we have discussed. In revisiting the mantras, we try to clarify which aspects of them seem to hold important insights about teacher learning and which aspects seem problematic. In short, we try to make more complex the statements about teachers' learning that have been oversimplified. After discussing the mantras, we conclude by describing two additional issues that arise from our considerations of teacher learning.

Teachers Should Be Treated As Active Learners Who Construct Their Own Knowledge

Individuals learn by making sense of their worlds. This means that what they already know and believe is critically important in shaping what and how they learn. Early in the chapter, we reviewed considerable evidence concerning the important role played by teachers' knowledge and beliefs in how they teach, and in their learning to teach and to think about teaching in new ways. We saw that teaching in the rich and responsive ways held forth by current reform visions may require sometimes fundamental changes in what teachers know and believe about learning, teaching, and subject matter. We saw how influential teachers' existing views can be in their interpretation of new ideas and practices.

For teacher education or professional development experiences to be successful in supporting meaningful change, they must take into account and address teachers' knowledge and beliefs. This is one sense in which the mantra of treating teachers as active learners rings true. Just as subject-matter instruction planned around ideas in the curriculum without careful attention to how children make sense of those ideas is unlikely to succeed in promoting high levels of student understanding, teacher development efforts that suggest target-teaching practices to teachers with the expectation that they will be implemented without change are doomed to failure. What teachers know and believe will influence their interpretation and enactment of any new ideas for teaching.

We have also seen, however, that viewing learning as interpretation based on existing knowledge and beliefs does not imply that learning is an activity of individuals in isolation. Rather, the active process of individual sense-making takes place in a social and cultural environment. It is this social world that provides the language, concepts, and modes of thought with which we as individuals make sense of our worlds. By interacting within various discourse communities, in face-to-face interaction and through other means of communication such as books and electronic mail, individuals come to understand and think in ways that are common to those communities while simultaneously helping the thinking of the community develop and change. Thus, successful learning experiences for teachers must provide opportunities for teachers to interact with others — to become part of discourse communities within which they can reflect on their current and new teaching ideas and practices.

Teachers Should Be Empowered and Treated As Professionals

This mantra also gains support from the view that an individual's existing knowledge and beliefs play a central role in learning. If teaching depends fundamentally on teachers' knowledge and beliefs, then for meaningful changes in teaching to take place, teachers must be empowered to make those changes; they cannot simply be presented with new teaching strategies to implement. The complex, responsive forms of teaching envisioned by reformers require autonomy and flexibility on the part of teachers, and this means providing them with opportunities for expanding and changing their knowledge and beliefs about teaching, learning, and subject matter.

We have argued, however, that empowering teachers is not simply a matter of figuring out new structures and arrangements to give them more of a voice in educational decision making. Teachers also need to be supported in becoming more reflective and critical about their own teaching practice and encouraged to consider new ideas about teaching and learning. Social views of cognition suggest that this learning takes place through interaction with others, leading again to the importance of creating new kinds of discourse communities for teachers. For it is by interacting with others that teachers can learn to engage in the kinds of critical and reflective thinking that are essential to the reform visions of teaching.

Others have argued for the importance of bringing teachers and university-based educators together to bring about mutually enhanced changes in schools and teaching practice (Grimmett & MacKinnon, 1992; Richardson, 1992; Sarason, 1990). Our discussion of current views of cognition provides at least two kinds of support for this endeavor. First is the idea, discussed above, that individuals come to learn new ways of thinking through interaction in groups and with more knowledgeable others. Second is the idea that knowledge is distributed across people, thus different participants bring different but equally valuable expertise to conversations about teaching. Teachers bring knowledge about teaching practice, the students they teach, and the contexts in which they and their students think and learn – knowledge grounded in concrete experience. University-based staff developers and researchers bring more generalized research-based knowledge and skills of critique and reflection. It is only by bringing these kinds of expertise together through interaction that they can mutually shape changes in teaching practice.

Bringing different voices to the conversation about teaching highlights the dilemma of how to take into account potentially competing views about what constitutes good teaching. We argued earlier that neither an extreme top-down approach in which the ideas of people outside the classroom prevail, nor an extreme view that teachers already have all of the expertise they need for teaching, is tenable. A tension arises as we try to figure out how to ensure that the reform community's voice is heard while still empowering teachers; the reform community brings ideas that may be at odds with current teachers' thinking and practice, but it is the teachers who must ultimately make the changes. This tension is not a problem that can be solved once and for all but a dilemma that must be managed (Lampert, 1985). We suggest that a way to manage this tension between competing images of good teaching is by having individuals with different viewpoints work, think, and talk together as they strive to improve teaching practice. As Richardson (1992) pointed out, because of the long-standing norm in educational communities of viewing the staff-developer as the 'expert,' it is especially important for university educators in such settings to be humble and sensitive in promoting their views. It is important that all participants in such discourse communities view their thinking as both valued and open to change.

Teacher Education Should Be Situated in Classroom Practice

The view that knowledge is situated – integrally connected with the contexts in which it is acquired and used – clearly supports this maxim that teachers' learning experiences should be grounded in classroom practice. Our analysis, however, revealed a number of complexities in what seems at first blush like a straightforward recommendation.

Cognitive apprenticeship.

The first issue concerns the idea of cognitive apprenticeship, a pedagogical approach rooted primarily in the view of learning as situated in physical and social contexts. When applied to teachers' learning to teach in the ways envisioned in current reform movements, cognitive apprenticeship runs into problems. The cognitive apprenticeship model depends on the learner observing and participating in the activities of accomplished practice alongside more expert practitioners. There are few settings in which teachers, either novice or experienced, can work alongside 'master' teachers who can provide modelling, coaching, and scaffolding for learning the new teaching approaches being advocated by reformers. And, as we pointed out earlier, most university-based teacher educators and staff developers are not able to fill this role, for they too are unlikely to have enacted the reform visions of teaching in K-12 classrooms. Thus, models other than cognitive apprenticeship must serve as the basis for situating teacher learning in classroom practice.

Situating the learning of experienced teachers.

Our analysis also suggests that there is not just one way, or even one best way, to situate teacher learning in practice. Rather, there are different ways to situate learning, each suited particularly well to different components of teacher learning.

For experienced teachers, one model is to conduct staff development activities at the school site, with large components taking place in individual teachers' classrooms. Having a researcher or member of a staff development team in the classroom provides opportunities for the teacher and staff developer to work together to interpret classroom events in light of various ideas about teaching and learning.

A second approach is to have teachers bring experiences from their own classrooms – for example, video-tapes of classroom episodes or examples of students' work – to group staff development activities. This approach may provide opportunities for teachers to see different points of view and, through discussion, to develop a reflective stance toward their teaching practice and that of others.

Finally, the learning of experienced teachers can be situated in activities other than those that occur in their own classrooms – for example, activities from the classrooms of others or activities that do not directly involve teaching, such as engaging in the learning of subject matter themselves or watching video-tapes of students being interviewed about complex topics. Such activities may free teachers from the constraints of thinking about the immediate needs of their own classrooms, especially when they take place in summer workshops without the daily press of having to plan instruction.

The usefulness of these different ways of situating teachers' learning suggests that some combination of experiences situated in different settings may be most powerful for fostering meaningful change in teachers' thinking and practice. The power of such combined approaches is supported by the success of programs such as CGI and SummerMath, where professional development activities began with intensive summer workshops focused on teachers' learning of mathematics or students' thinking and learning, followed by extended interaction of staff developers and teachers over the school year as teachers worked to change their classroom teaching based on ideas considered in the workshops.

Situating the learning of pre-service teachers.

For pre-service teachers, too, our analysis suggests that there are multiple ways to situate learning experiences. The options differ to some extent from those for experienced teachers because prospective teachers do not yet have their own classrooms in which to situate their learning. They also have a lot of learning to do just to be able to carry out basic teaching tasks and function adequately in the classroom.

We suggested that case teaching holds promise for exploring problems of pedagogy (Sykes & Bird, 1992). Cases can provide sites for grounding the exploration of various theoretical ideas about teaching and learning in examples of practice. In addition, the instructor has more control of the particular situations that are explored by students with cases than with field-based experiences. Case-based approaches may be particularly effective when the case material is stored in hypermedia environments rather than in linear written or video-taped formats. Such environments allow for richer, more varied data sources related to single teaching episodes, thus enabling students to explore the represented situation in multiple ways.

We also presented evidence that novice teachers, like experienced teachers, can benefit from activities that situate their own learning of subject matter in new ways, if they are to model and coach students in the kinds of rich, complex thinking envisioned by current reforms. In mathematics, for example, prospective teachers may benefit from learning mathematics themselves in the context of group solving of non-routine problems.

Finally, student teaching continues to be a key site for the situating of novice teachers' learning in classroom practice. We raised key issues abut the usefulness of student teaching for fostering and supporting new ways of teaching rather than simply inducting new teachers into current modes of practice. The first issue is the difficulty of finding classrooms that exemplify the kinds of teaching the teacher education program is trying to foster. This leads to the second issue, the importance of providing novice teachers with opportunities for reflection on their student teaching experiences. These opportunities might be provided by seminars or other discourse communities which focus on the difficulties of enacting reform-based teaching in settings where that practice represents a departure from current practice.

In summary, although our analysis suggests that careful thought needs to be given to how pre-service and experienced teachers' learning is situated, the picture is considerably more complex than is suggested by the mantra that teachers' learning should be situated in classroom practice.

Teacher Educators Should Treat Teachers As They Expect Teachers to Treat Students

As we pointed out in the introduction, interpreting this recommendation as simply providing the same learning activities for teachers as we expect teachers to provide their students erroneously assumes that teachers and students have the same things to learn and are similar in what they bring to the learning setting. Typically, however, we want teachers to be thinking about issues of pedagogy and students' learning even as they learn about new ideas themselves, thus making their learning task more complex than what we expect for students. At the same time, it is important to plan teacher learning experiences based on assumptions about learning and how to foster it that are consistent with assumptions underlying the pedagogical approaches being used with students. For example, the assumption that prior knowledge and beliefs play a central role in what and how individuals learn means that existing conceptions need to be addressed in the learning experiences of teachers as well as students. Our discussion of teacher learning experiences throughout this chapter is based on this principle.

In the current climate of reforming K-12 education, there is another reason that it is important to make teachers' learning experiences consistent with those we expect for students. If our task were to educate teachers to teach in a system in which the content and methods of instruction remained stable over generations, teachers could draw on their own experiences as young learners for guidance. However, because teachers are being asked to make considerable changes in the nature and content of classroom instruction, it is essential that they themselves experience these new visions of education as learners and then reflect on them as learning teachers. In this chapter, we discussed three specific areas in which teachers should experience new visions: conceptions of subject matter, use of cognitive tools, and participation in learning communities.

New Issues in Learning to Teach

We close with two issues that arise from the views of teacher learning that we have been discussing. We hope that these issues will stimulate further thought, conversations, and research on pre-service and in-service teacher learning.

What ideas or content are essential in teacher education?

The idea that knowledge and thinking are distributed across persons and tools raises questions about what students and teachers need to know. In discussing how the idea of distributed cognition might play out in classrooms, we noted that different students will likely be developing different knowledge and skills – expertise in different areas. This phenomenon runs counter to the traditional view of schools as places for students to acquire a common core of knowledge and skills. We agreed with Resnick (1987) and Brown and colleagues (1987) that schools should focus on preparing students to be lifelong adaptive learners, with different individuals gaining specific expertise in different areas – a stance that is consistent with how knowledge is shared among individuals in most out-of-school settings. The same issue arises when thinking about teacher education experiences which take seriously the notion that learning and knowledge are distributed across persons and tools. Teachers cannot possibly be expected to 'master' all the content that students are likely to encounter as they make use of the vast information resources of the Internet. Furthermore, if we expect teachers to model for their students sharing information and thinking with others, we should see different teachers gaining expertise in different areas, drawing upon one another's knowledge and skills whenever possible. This raises for teachers and teacher educators, however, the issue of what are the essential skills, knowledge, and dispositions that all teachers must learn.

Interplay between teachers' knowledge and other available resources.

This issue, too, flows from the theme of distributed cognition, in particular the distribution of cognition across persons and tools. A common implicit assumption in much thinking about teacher education and staff development is that teachers 'carry' the knowledge and skill they need for teaching 'in their heads.' This assumption is clearly exemplified in research on the critical role of professional knowledge and beliefs in teaching and learning to teach. Like other teacher educators and researchers, we have emphasized the importance of teachers' knowledge, essentially assuming that, for the knowledge to be influential in teaching, it has to reside in the mind of the teacher. Thinking in terms of distributed cognition, however, shifts the focus from the knowledge of the individual teacher to the knowledge and resources of the teacher in conjunction with various available tools. These tools might include the vast information resources available with computers via the Internet and other people, such as university-based scientists, who might be connected to classrooms through electronic mail. But the tools also include the textbooks and other resources that have always been available in classrooms and libraries. As teacher educators and researchers, we need to think carefully about how to support teachers in augmenting their pedagogical thinking through the judicious use of such resources. We should assume that teachers will have a wide array of cognitive tools to support them in their instructional efforts, and we need to help them learn to use these resources as part of their teacher education experiences.

These are but two important issues that arise from some of the recent views of cognition we have discussed in this chapter. As researchers, teacher educators, and teachers continue to work together to enact richer visions of classroom teaching and learning, other issues and dilemmas will surely arise. For just as views of learning and teaching evolve, so too will the sorts of problems to be solved in enacting those views in classrooms and teacher education.

ENDNOTES

1. For their thoughtful comments on this chapter, we thank Tom Good, Ivor Goodson, Linda Anderson, Bill McDiarmid, Irene Rahm, and Nancy Songer. We take, of course, full responsibility for the ideas expressed.

2. In this chapter, we use distributed cognition and distributed intelligence synonymously. The distinction between them drawn by Pea (1993) is beyond the scope of this chapter. We also do not explore different conceptions of distributed cognition. Although we acknowledge that scholars present conceptions that differ – for example, in the extent to which they see cognition as primarily individual or distributed (Salomon, 1993b), we see these debates as beyond the scope of our discussion.

REFERENCES

American Association for the Advancement of Science. (1989). *Science for all Americans: A summary report of Phase I of Project 2061.* Washington, DC: Author.

Anderson, C. W. (1989). The role of education in the academic disciplines in teacher education. In A. Woolfolk (Ed.), *Research perspectives on the graduate preparation of teachers* (pp. 88-107). Englewood Cliffs, NJ: Prentice Hall.

Anderson, L. M. (1989a). Implementing instructional programs to promote meaningful, self-regulated learning. In J. Brophy (Ed.), *Advances in research on teaching: Vol. 1. Teaching for meaningful understanding and self-regulated learning* (pp. 311-343). Greenwich, CT: JAI Press.

Anderson, L. M. (1989b). Learners and learning. In M. C. Reynolds (Ed.), *Knowledge base for the beginning teacher* (pp. 85-99). Oxford: Pergamon.

Anderson, L. M. & Holt-Reynolds, D. (1995). *Prospective teachers' beliefs and teacher education pedagogy: Research based on a teacher educator's practical theory* (Research Report 95-6). East Lansing, MI: National Center for Research in Teacher Learning, Michigan State University.

Aronson, E. (1978). *The jigsaw classroom.* Beverly Hills, CA: Sage.

Ball, D. L. (1988a). *Knowledge and reasoning in mathematical pedagogy: Examining what prospective teachers bring to teacher education.* Unpublished doctoral dissertation, Michigan State University, East Lansing, MI.

Ball, D. L. (1988b). Unlearning to teach mathematics. *For the Learning of Mathematics, 8,* 40-48.

Ball, D. L. (1989, March). *Breaking with experience in learning to teach mathematics: The role of a preservice methods course.* Paper presented at the annual meeting of the American Educational Research Association, San Francisco.

Ball, D. L. (1990a). The mathematical understandings that prospective teachers bring to teacher education. *Elementary School Journal, 90,* 449-466.

Ball, D. L. (1990b). Prospective elementary and secondary teachers' understanding of division. *Journal for Research in Mathematics Education, 21,* 132-144.

Ball, D. L. (1991). Research on teaching mathematics: Making subject-matter knowledge part of the equation. In J. Brophy (Ed.), *Advances in research on teaching: Vol. 2. Teachers' knowledge of subject matter as it relates to their teaching practice* (pp. 1-48). Greenwich, CT: JAI Press.

Ball, D. L. (1993). With an eye on the mathematical horizon: Dilemmas of teaching elementary school mathematics. *Elementary School Journal, 93,* 373-397.

Ball, D. L. (1994, November). *Developing mathematics reform: What don't we know about teacher learning – but would make good working hypotheses?* Paper presented at Conference on Teacher Enhancement in Mathematics K-6, Arlington, VA.

Ball, D. L., Lampert, M., & Rosenberg, M. (1991, April). *Using hypermedia to investigate and construct knowledge about mathematics teaching and learning.* Paper presented at the annual meeting of the American Educational Research Association, Chicago.

Bereiter, C. & Scardamalia, M. (1989). Intentional learning as a goal of instruction. In L. B. Resnick (Ed.), *Knowing, learning, and instruction: Essays in honor of Robert Glaser* (pp. 361-392). Hillsdale, NJ: Erlbaum.

Berliner, D. C. (1988, February). *The development of expertise in pedagogy.* Paper presented at the annual meeting of the American Association of Colleges for Teacher Education, New Orleans.

Borko, H., Eisenhart, M., Brown, C. A., Underhill, R. G., Jones, D., & Agard, P. C. (1992). Learning to teach hard mathematics: Do novice teachers and their instructors give up too easily? *Journal for Research in Mathematics Education, 23*, 194-222.

Borko, H. & Livingston, C. (1989). Cognition and improvisation: Differences in mathematics instruction by expert and novice teachers. *American Educational Research Journal, 26*, 473-498.

Borko, H., Livingston, C., McCaleb, J., & Mauro, L. (1988). Student teachers' planning and post-lesson reflections: Patterns and implications for teacher preparation. In J. Calderhead (Ed.), *Teachers' professional learning* (pp. 65-83). New York: Falmer.

Borko, H., Mayfield, V., Marion, S., Flexer, R., & Cumbo, K. (1995, April). *Teachers' developing ideas and practices about mathematics performance assessment: Successes, stumbling blocks, and implications for professional development.* Paper presented at the annual meeting of the American Educational Research Association, San Francisco.

Borko, H. & Putnam, R. T. (1995). Expanding a teacher's knowledge base: A cognitive psychological perspective on professional development. In T. Guskey & M. Huberman (Eds.), *Professional development in education: New paradigms and practices* (pp. 35-65). New York: Teachers College Press.

Borko, H. & Putnam, R. T. (1996). Learning to teach. In D. C. Berliner & R. C. Calfee (Eds.), *Handbook of educational psychology* (pp. 673-708). New York: Macmillan.

Brookhart, S. M. & Freeman, D. J. (1992). Characteristics of entering teacher candidates. *Review of Educational Research, 62*, 37-60.

Brophy, J. (1989). Conclusion: Toward a theory of teaching. In J. Brophy (Ed.), *Advances in research on teaching: Vol. 1. Teaching for meaningful understanding and self-regulated learning* (pp. 345-355). Greenwich, CT: JAI.

Brown, A., Ash, D., Rutherford, M., Nakagawa, K., Gordon, A., & Campione, J. C. (1993). Distributed expertise in the classroom. In G. Salomon (Ed.), *Distributed cognitions: Psychological and educational considerations* (pp. 188-228). Cambridge: Cambridge University Press.

Brown, A. L. (1992). Design experiments: Theoretical and methodological challenges in creating complex interventions in classroom settings. *The Journal of the Learning Sciences, 2*, 141-178.

Brown, C. A. & Borko, H. (1992). Becoming a mathematics teacher. In D. A. Grouws (Ed.), *Handbook of research on mathematics teaching and learning* (pp. 209-239). New York: Macmillan.

Brown, J. S., Collins, A., & Duguid, P. (1989a). Debating the situation: A rejoinder to Palincsar and Wineburg. *Educational Researcher, 18*(4), 10-12.

Brown, J. S., Collins, A., & Duguid, P. (1989b). Situated cognition and the culture of learning. *Educational Researcher, 18*(1), 32-42.

Bruner, J. (1990). *Acts of meaning.* Cambridge, MA: Harvard University Press.

Byrne, C. J. (1983, April). *Teacher knowledge and teacher effectiveness: A literature review, theoretical analysis, and discussion of research strategy.* Paper presented at the 14th Annual Convention of the Northeastern Educational Research Association, Ellenville, NY.

Carlsen, W. (1991). Subject-matter knowledge and science teaching: A pragmatic perspective. In J. E. Brophy (Ed.), *Advances in research on teaching: Vol. 2. Teachers' subject matter knowledge and classroom instruction* (pp. 115-143). Greenwich, CT: JAI Press.

Carpenter, T. P., Fennema, E., Peterson, P. L., Chiang, C., & Loef, M. (1989). Using knowledge of children's mathematical thinking in classroom teaching: An experimental study. *American Educational Research Journal, 26,* 499-532.

Carter, K. (1990). Teachers' knowledge and learning to teach. In W. R. Houston, M. Haberman, & J. Silkula (Eds.), *The handbook of research on teacher education* (pp. 291-310). New York: Macmillan.

Carter, K. & Doyle, W. (1989). Classroom research as a resource for the graduate preparation of teachers. In A. Woolfolk (Ed.), *Research perspectives on the graduate preparation of teachers* (pp. 51-68). Englewood Cliffs, NJ: Prentice Hall.

Civil, M. (1992, April). *Prospective elementary teachers' thinking about mathematics.* Paper presented at the annual meeting of the American Educational Research Association, San Francisco.

Clement, J. (1982). Students' preconceptions in introductory mechanics. *American Journal of Physics, 50,* 66-71.

Cobb, P. (1994a). Constructivism in mathematics and science education. *Educational Researcher, 23*(7), 4.

Cobb, P. (1994b). Where is the mind? Constructivist and sociocultural perspectives on mathematical development. *Educational Researcher, 23*(7), 13-19.

Cobb, P., Yackel, E., & Wood, T. (1988). Curriculum and teacher development: Psychological and anthropological perspectives. In E. Fennema, T. P. Carpenter, & S. J. Lamon (Eds.), *Integrating research on teaching and learning mathematics: Papers from the First Wisconsin Symposium for Research on Teaching and Learning Mathematics* (pp. 92-130). Madison, WI: Wisconsin Center for Education Research, University of Wisconsin-Madison.

Cognition and Technology Group at Vanderbilt. (1990). Anchored instruction and its relationship to situated cognition. *Educational Researcher, 19*(5), 2-10.

Cohen, D. K. (1989). Teaching practice: Plus ça change ... In P. W. Jackson (Ed.), *Contributing to educational change: Perspectives on research and practice* (pp. 27-84). Berkeley: McCutchan.

Cohen, D. K. & Ball, D. L. (1990). Relations between policy and practice: A commentary. *Educational Evaluation and Policy Analysis, 12,* 331-338.

Collins, A., Brown, J. S., & Newman, S. E. (1989). Cognitive apprenticeship: Teaching the craft of reading, writing and mathematics. In L. B. Resnick (Ed.), *Knowing, learning, and instruction: Essays in honor of Robert Glaser* (pp. 453-494). Hillsdale, NJ: Erlbaum.

Comeaux, M. (1992, April). *Challenging students' views about teaching and learning: Constructivism in the social foundations classroom.* Paper presented at the annual meeting of the American Educational Research Association, San Francisco.

Confrey, J. (1990). A review of the research on student conceptions in mathematics, science, and programming. In C. B. Cazden (Ed.), *Review of Research in Education* (Vol. 16, pp. 3-56). Washington, DC: American Educational Research Association.

Delpit, L. (1988). The silenced dialogue: Power and pedagogy in educating other people's children. *Harvard Educational Review, 58,* 280-298.

Dewey, J. (1896). The reflex arc concept in psychology. *Psychological Review, 3,* 356-370.

Dewey, J. (1964). The child and the curriculum. In R. D. Archambault (Ed.), *John Dewey on education: Selected writings* (pp. 339-358). Chicago: University of Chicago Press.

Doyle, W. (1986). Classroom organization and management. In M. C. Wittrock (Ed.), *Handbook of research on teaching* (3rd ed., pp. 392-431). New York: Macmillan.

Doyle, W. (1990). Case methods in teacher education. *Teacher Education Quarterly, 17*(1) 7-15.

Driver, R., Asoko, H., Leach, J., Mortimer, E., & Scott, P. (1994). Constructing scientific knowledge in the classroom. *Educational Researcher, 23*(7), 5-12.

Eisenhart, M., Borko, H., Underhill, R., Brown, C., Jones, D., & Agard, P. (1993). Conceptual knowledge falls through the cracks: Complexities of learning to teach mathematics for understanding. *Journal for Research in Mathematics Education, 24*, 8-40.

Feiman-Nemser, S. (1983). Learning to teach. In L. Shulman & G. Sykes (Eds.), *Handbook of teaching and policy* (pp. 150-170). New York: Longman.

Fennema, E., Carpenter, T. P., Franke, M. L., Levi, L., Jacobs, V. R., & Empson, S. B. (in press). A longitudinal study of learning to use children's thinking in mathematics instruction. *Journal for Research in Mathematics Education.*

Fennema, E. & Franke, M. L. (1992). Teachers' knowledge and its impact. In D. A. Grouws (Ed.), *Handbook of research on mathematics teaching and learning* (pp. 147-164). New York: Macmillan.

Fenstermacher, G. D. & Richardson, V. (1993). The elicitation and reconstruction of practical arguments in teaching. *Journal of Curriculum Studies, 25*, 101-114.

Fish, S. (1980). *Is there a text in this class? The authority of interpretive communities.* Cambridge, MA: Harvard University Press.

Gagné, R. (1985). *The conditions of learning* (4th ed.). New York: Holt, Rinehart and Winston.

Glickman, C. D. & Bey, T. M. (1990). Supervision. In W. R. Houston (Ed.), *Handbook of research on teacher education* (pp. 549-566). New York: Macmillan.

Goldenberg, C. & Gallimore, R. (1991). Changing teaching takes more than a one-shot workshop. *Educational Leadership, 49*(3), 69-72.

Good, T. L. & Brophy, J. E. (1973). *Looking in classrooms* (1st ed.). New York: Harper & Row.

Good, T. L. & Brophy, J. E. (1996). *Looking in classrooms* (7th ed.). New York: Harper Collins.

Greeno, J. G., Collins, A., & Resnick, L. B. (1996). Cognition and learning. In D. Berliner, & R. Calfee (Eds.), *Handbook of educational psychology* (pp. 15-46). New York: Macmillan.

Grimmett, P. P. & MacKinnon, A. M. (1992). Craft knowledge and the education of teachers. *Review of Research in Education, 18*, 385-456.

Grossman, P. (1990). *The making of a teacher: Teacher knowledge and teacher education.* New York: Teachers College Press.

Grossman, P. L., Wilson, W. M., & Shulman, L. S. (1989). Teachers of substance: Subject matter knowledge for teaching. In M. Reynolds (Ed.), *Knowledge base for the beginning teacher* (pp. 23-36). New York: Pergamon.

Guyton, E. & McIntyre, D. J. (1990). Student teaching and school experiences. In W. R. Houston (Ed.), *Handbook of research on teacher education* (pp. 514-534). New York: Macmillan.

Heaton, R. M. (1992). Who is minding the mathematics content? A case study of a fifth-grade teacher. *Elementary School Journal, 93*, 151-192.

Heaton, R. M. & Lampert, M. (1993). Learning to hear voices: Inventing a new pedagogy of teacher education. In D. K. Cohen, M. McLaughlin, & J. Talbert (Eds.), *Teaching for understanding: Challenges for policy and practice* (pp. 43-83). San Francisco: Jossey-Bass.

Hester, P. & Songer, N. B. (in press). The techno-geeks are out to get us! The challenge of integrating internet-based resources and teaching practices. In Z. Berge & M. Collins (Eds.), *Wired together: The on-line classroom in K-12: Vol. 2. Case studies.* Creskill, NJ: Hampton Press.

Hollingsworth, S. (1989). Prior beliefs and cognitive change in learning to teach. *American Educational Research Journal, 26*, 160-189.

Holt-Reynolds, D. (1992). Personal history-based beliefs as relevant prior knowledge in coursework: Can we practice what we teach? *American Educational Research Journal, 29*, 325-349.

Hoover, N. L., O'Shea, L. J., & Carroll, R. G. (1988). The supervisor-intern relationship and effective interpersonal communication skills. *Journal of Teacher Education, 39*, 22-27.

Hutchins, E. (1990). The technology of team navigation. In J. Galegher, R. E. Kraut, & C. Egido (Eds.), *Intellectual teamwork: Social and technological foundations of cooperative work* (pp. 191-220). Hillsdale, NJ: Erlbaum.

Hutchins, E. (1991). The social organization of distributed cognition. In L. B. Resnick, J. M. Levine, & S. D. Teasley (Eds.), *Perspectives on socially shared cognition* (pp. 283-307). Washington, DC: American Psychological Association.

Hutchins, E. (1993). Learning to navigate. In S. Chaiklin & J. Lave (Eds.), *Understanding practice: Perspectives on activity and context* (pp. 35-63). New York: Cambridge University Press.

Kleinfeld, J. (1992). Learning to think like a teacher: The study of cases. In J. Shulman (Ed.), *Case methods in teacher education* (pp. 33-49). New York: Teachers College Press.

Krajcik, J. S., Blumenfeld, P. C., & Starr, M. L. (1993). Integrating knowledge bases: An upper elementary teacher preparation program emphasizing the teaching of science. In P. A. Rubba, L. M. Campbell, & T. M. Dana (Eds.), *Excellence in educating teachers of science* (pp. 37-54). Columbus, OH: ERIC Clearinghouse.

Ladson-Billings, G. (1995). Toward a theory of culturally relevant pedagogy. *American Educational Research Journal, 32*, 465-491.

Lampert, M. (1985). How do teachers manage to teach? *Harvard Educational Review, 55*, 178-194.

Lampert, M. (1988). Connecting mathematical teaching and learning. In E. Fennema, T. P. Carpenter, & S. J. Lamon (Eds.), Integrating research on teaching and learning mathematics: Papers from the First Wisconsin Symposium for Research on Teaching and Learning Mathematics (pp. 132-165). Madison, WI: University of Wisconsin-Madison, Wisconsin Center for Education Research.

Lampert, M. (1990). When the problem is not the question and the solution is not the answer: Mathematical knowing and teaching. *American Educational Research Journal, 27*, 29-63.

Lampert, M., Heaton, R., & Ball, D. (1994). Using technology to support a new pedagogy of mathematics teacher education. *Journal of Special Education Technology, 12*, 276-289.

Lave, J. (1988). *Cognition in practice: Mind, mathematics and culture in everyday life.* Cambridge: Cambridge University Press.

Leinhardt, G. (1988). Situated knowledge and expertise in teaching. In J. Calderhead (Ed.), *Teachers' professional learning* (pp. 146-168). London: Falmer.

Leinhardt, G. (1990). Capturing craft knowledge in teaching. *Educational Researcher, 19*(2), 18-25.

Leinhardt, G. & Greeno, J. G. (1986). The cognitive skill of teaching. *Journal of Educational Psychology, 78*, 75-95.

Leont'ev, A. N. (1981). The problem of activity in psychology. In J. V. Wertsch (Ed.) *The concept of activity in Soviet psychology* (pp. 37-71). Armonk, NY: M. E. Sharpe.

Linn, M. C., Songer, N. B., & Eylon, B. (in press). Shifts and convergences in science learning and instruction. In D. C. Berliner & R. Calfee (Eds.), *Handbook of educational psychology*. New York: Macmillan.

Lortie, D. (1975). *Schoolteacher.* Chicago: University of Chicago Press.

MacKinnon, A. & Grunau, H. (1991, April). *Teacher development through reflection, community, and discourse*. Paper presented at the annual meeting of the American Educational Research Association, Chicago.

McDiarmid, G. W. (1990). Challenging prospective teachers' beliefs during early field experience: A quixotic undertaking? *Journal of Teacher Education, 41*(3), 12-20.

McDiarmid, G. W. (1994). The arts and sciences as preparation for teaching. In K. Howey & N. Zympher (Eds.), *Informing faculty development for teacher educators* (pp. 99-137). Norwood, NJ: Ablex.

McDiarmid, G. W. (1995, April). *The role of a reinvented methods course in preservice history teachers' learning*. Paper presented at the annual meeting of the American Educational Research Association, San Francisco.

McDiarmid, G. W., Ball, D. L., & Anderson, C. (1989). Why staying ahead one chapter just won't work: Subject-specific pedagogy. In M. C. Reynolds (Ed.), *Knowledge base for the beginning teacher* (pp. 193-205). New York: Pergamon Press.

McLaughlin, M. & Talbert, J. E. (1993). *Contexts that matter for teaching and learning: Strategic opportunities for meeting the nation's educational goals*. Stanford, CA: Stanford University, Center for Research on the Context of Secondary School Teaching.

McNamara, D. (1995). The influence of student teachers' tutors and mentors upon their classroom practice: An exploratory study. *Teaching and Teacher Education, 11*, 51-61.

Merseth, K. (1990). Case studies and teacher education. *Teacher education quarterly, 17*(1), 53-62.

Merseth, K. K. & Lacey, C. A. (1993). Weaving stronger fabric: The pedagogical promise of hypermedia and case methods in teacher education. *Teaching and Teacher Education, 9*, 283-299.

Michaels, S. & O'Connor, M. C. (1990). *Literacy as reasoning within multiple discourses: Implications for policy and educational reform*. Paper presented at the Council of Chief State School Officers 1990 Summer Institute.

Moll, L. C., Tapia, J., & Whitmore, K. (1993). Living knowledge: The social distribution of cultural resources for thinking. In G. Salomon (Ed.), *Distributed cognitions: Psychological and educational consequences* (pp. 139-163). New York: Cambridge University Press.

National Center for Research on Teacher Education (1991). *Final report: The teacher education and learning to teach study*. East Lansing: Michigan State University, College of Education.

National Council of Teachers of Mathematics (1989). *Curriculum and evaluation standards for school mathematics*. Reston, VA: Author.

National Council of Teachers of Mathematics (1991). *Professional standards for teaching mathematics*. Reston, VA: Author.

National Education Goals Panel (1991). *The national education goals report: Building a nation of learners*. Washington, DC: Author.

National Research Council (1993). *National science education standards: An enhanced sampler. A working paper of the National Committee on Science Education Standards and Assessment*. Washington, DC: Author.

Palincsar, A. S. & Brown, A. L. (1984). Reciprocal teaching of comprehension-fostering and monitoring strategies. *Cognition and Instruction, 1*(2), 117-175.

Pea, R. (1993). Practices of distributed intelligence and designs for education. In G. Salomon (Ed.), *Distributed cognitions: Psychological and educational considerations* (pp. 47-87). New York: Cambridge University Press.

Piaget, J. (1985). *The equilibration of cognitive structures* (T. Brown & K. J. Thampy, Trans.). Chicago: University of Chicago Press.

Posner, G. J., Strike, K. A., Hewson, P. W., & Gertzog, W. A. (1983). Accommodation of a scientific conception: Toward a theory of conceptual change. *Science Education, 66*, 211-227.

Prawat, R. S. (1991). The value of ideas: The immersion approach to the development of thinking. *Educational Researcher, 20*(2), 3-10, 30.

Prawat, R. S. (1992). Teachers' beliefs about teaching and learning: A constructivist perspective. *American Journal of Education, 100*, 354-395.

Putnam, R. T. (1992a). Teaching the 'hows' of mathematics for everyday life: A case study of a fifth-grade teacher. *Elementary School Journal, 93*, 163-177.

Putnam, R. T. (1992b). Thinking and authority in elementary-school mathematics tasks. In J. Brophy (Ed.), *Advances in research on teaching: Vol. 3. Planning and managing learning tasks and activities* (pp. 161-189). Greenwich, CT: JAI Press.

Putnam, R. T., Heaton, R. M., Prawat, R. S., & Remillard, J. (1992). Teaching mathematics for understanding: Discussing case studies of four fifth-grade teachers. *Elementary School Journal, 93*, 213-228.

Resnick, L. B. (1987a). *Education and learning to think.* Washington, DC: National Academy Press.

Resnick, L. B. (1987b). Learning in school and out. *Educational Researcher, 16*(9), 13-20.

Resnick, L. B. (1988). Treating mathematics as an ill-structured discipline. In R. I. Charles & E. A. Silver (Eds.), *Research agenda for mathematics education: Vol. 3. The teaching and assessing of mathematical problem solving* (pp. 32-60). Hillsdale, NJ: Erlbaum.

Resnick, L. B. (1991). Shared cognition: Thinking as social practice. In L. B. Resnick, J. M. Levine, & S. D. Teasley (Eds.), *Perspectives on socially shared cognition* (pp. 1-20). Washington, DC: American Psychological Association.

Resnick, L. B., Levine, J. M., & Teasley, S. D. (Ed.). (1991). *Perspectives on socially shared cognition.* Washington, DC: American Psychological Association.

Richardson, V. (1992). The agenda-setting dilemma in a constructivist staff development process. *Teaching & Teacher Education, 8*, 287-300.

Richardson, V. & Anders, P. (1994). The study of teacher change. In V. Richardson (Ed.), *A theory of teacher change and the practice of staff development: A case in reading instruction* (pp. 159-180). New York: Teachers College Press.

Richardson, V., Anders, P., Tidwell, D., & Lloyd, C. (1991). The relationship between teachers' beliefs and practices in reading comprehension instruction. *American Educational Research Journal, 28*, 559-586.

Rosenshine, B. & Stevens, R. (1986). Teaching functions. In M. C. Wittrock (Ed.), *Handbook of research on teaching* (3rd ed., pp. 376-391). New York: Macmillan.

Roth, K. J. (1992). *The role of writing in creating a science learning community* (Elementary Subjects Center Series No. 56). East Lansing: Michigan State University, Institute for Research on Teaching.

Roth, K., Anderson, C., & Smith, E. (1986). *Curriculum materials, teacher talk and student learning: Case studies in fifth grade science teaching* (Research Series No. 171). East Lansing: Michigan State University, Institute for Research on Teaching.

Salomon, G. (Ed.). (1993). *Distributed cognitions: Psychological and educational considerations.* Cambridge: Cambridge University Press.

Sarason, S. (1990). *The predictable failure of educational reform: Can we change course before it's too late?* San Francisco: Jossey-Bass.

Saunders, W., Goldenberg, C., & Hamann, J. (1992). Instructional conversations beget instructional conversations. *Teaching & Teacher Education, 8*, 199-218.

Schifter, D. & Fosnot, C. T. (1993). *Reconstructing mathematics education: Stories of teachers meeting the challenges of reform.* New York: Teachers College Press.

Schifter, D. & Simon, M. A. (1992). Assessing teachers' development of a constructivist view of mathematics learning. *Teaching & Teacher Education, 8*, 187-197.

Schoenfeld, A. H. (1985). *Mathematical problem solving.* Orlando, FL: Academic Press.

Schoenfeld, A. H. (1992). Learning to think mathematically: Problem solving, metacognition, and sense making in mathematics. In D. Grouws (Ed.), *Handbook for research on mathematics teaching and learning* (pp. 334-370). New York: Macmillan.

Schram, P., Wilcox, S. K., Lappan, G., & Lanier, P. (1989). Changing mathematical conceptions of preservice teachers: A content and pedagogical intervention. In C. Maher, G. Goldin, & R. Davis (Eds.), *Proceedings of the eleventh annual meeting of the North American Chapter of the International Group for the Psychology of Mathematics Education* (pp. 296-302). New Brunswick, NJ: Rutgers University.

Schwab, J. J. (1964). Structure of the disciplines: Meanings and significances. In G. W. Ford & L. Pugno (Eds.), *The structure of knowledge and the curriculum* (pp. 6-30). Chicago: Rand McNally.

Shulman, L. S. (1983). Autonomy and obligation: The remote control of teaching. In L. S. Shulman & G. Sykes (Eds.), *Handbook of teaching and policy* (pp. 484-504). New York: Longman.

Shulman, L. S. (1986a). Paradigms and research programs in the study of teaching: A contemporary perspective. In M. C. Wittrock (Ed.), *Handbook of research on teaching* (pp. 3-36). New York: Macmillan.

Shulman, L. S. (1986b). Those who understand: Knowledge growth in teaching. *Educational Researcher, 15*(2), 4-14.

Shulman, L. S. (1987). Knowledge and teaching: Foundations of the new reform. *Harvard Educational Review, 57*(1), 1-22.

Shulman, L. S. & Grossman, P. L. (1987). *Final report to the Spencer Foundation* (Knowledge Growth in a Profession Technical Report). Stanford, CA: Stanford University, School of Education.

Simon, M. A. (1995). Reconstructing mathematics pedagogy from a constructivist perspective. *Journal of Research in Mathematics Education, 26*, 114-145.

Simon, M. A. & Blume, G. W. (1994). Mathematical modelling as a component of understanding ratio-as-measure: A study of prospective elementary teachers. *Journal of Mathematical Behavior, 13*, 183-197.

Simon, M. A. & Brobeck, S. (1993, October). *Changing views of mathematics learning: A case study of a prospective elementary teacher.* Paper presented at the annual meeting of the North American Chapter of the International Group for the Psychology of Mathematics Education, Monterey, CA.

Simon, M. A. & Mazza, W. (1993, October). *From learning mathematics to teaching mathematics: A case study of a prospective teacher in a reform-oriented program.* Paper presented at the annual meeting of the North American Chapter of the International Group for the Psychology of Mathematics Education, Monterey, CA.

Simon, M. A. & Schifter, D. (1991). Towards a constructivist perspective: An intervention study of mathematics teacher development. *Educational Studies in Mathematics, 22*, 309-331.

Smith, D. C. & Neale, D. C. (1991). The construction of subject-matter knowledge in primary science teaching. In J. Brophy (Ed.) *Advances in research on teaching: Vol. 2. Teachers' knowledge of subject matter as it relates to their teaching practice* (pp. 187-243). Greenwich, CT: JAI Press.

Smith, J. P., III, diSessa, A. A., & Roschelle, J. (1993). Misconceptions reconceived: A constructivist analysis of knowledge in transition. *Journal of the Learning Sciences, 3*, 115-163.

Soltis, J. F. (1981). Education and the concept of knowledge. In J. F. Soltis (Ed.), *Philosophy and education* (pp. 95-113). Chicago: National Society for the Study of Education.

Songer, N. (in press-a). Can technology bring students closer to science? In K. Tobin & B. Fraser (Eds.), *The international handbook of science education*. Dordecht, The Netherlands: Kluwer.

Songer, N. (in press-b). Exploring learning opportunities in coordinated network-enhanced classrooms: A case of kids as global scientists. *Journal of the Learning Sciences*.

Sykes, G. & Bird, T. (1992). Teacher education and the case idea. *Review of Research in Education, 9*, 457-521.

Tudge, J. & Winterhoff, P. (1993). Vygotsky, Piaget, Bandura: Perspectives on the relations between the social world and cognitive development. *Human Development, 36*, 61-81.

Urdan, T., Blumenfeld, P., Soloway, E., & Brade, K. (in press). IbyD – Computer support for developing unit plans: A first study. In S. Dijkstra (Ed.), *Instructional models in computer based learning environments*. Secaucus, NJ: Springer-Verlag.

Vera, A. H. & Simon, H. A. (1993). Situated action: A symbolic interpretation. *Cognitive Science, 17*, 7-48.

Vygotsky, L. (1978). *Mind in society: The development of higher psychological processes* (M. Cole, V. John-Steiner, S. Scribner, & E. Souberman, Eds. and Trans.). Cambridge, MA: Harvard University Press.

Weinstein, C. S. (1990). Prospective elementary teachers' beliefs about teaching: Implications for teacher education. *Teaching and Teacher Education, 6*, 279-290.

Wilcox, S., Schram, P., Lappan, G., & Lanier, P. (1990, April). *The role of a learning community in changing preservice teachers' knowledge and beliefs about mathematics education*. Paper presented at the annual meeting of the American Educational Research Association, Boston.

Wilson, S. M. (1988). *Understanding historical understanding: Subject matter knowledge and the teaching of history*. Unpublished doctoral dissertation, Stanford University, Stanford, CA.

Wilson, S. M. & Wineburg, S. S. (1988). Peering at history through different lenses: The role of disciplinary perspectives in teaching history. *Teachers College Record, 84*, 525-539.

Zeichner, K. (1985). The ecology of field experience: Toward an understanding of the role of field experiences on teacher development. *Journal of Research and Development in Teacher Education, 18*, 44-52.

Zeichner, K. M. & Gore, J. M. (1990). Teacher socialization. In W. R. Houston, M. Haberman, & J. Sikula (Eds.), *Handbook of research on teacher education* (pp. 329-348). New York: Macmillan.

Chapter 14: Cultures of Teaching and Educational Change

ANDY HARGREAVES

The Ontario Institute for Studies in Education

INTRODUCTION

Over the previous quarter century, research on educational change has come to attain stature and significance as an important and legitimate field of study in its own right. This evolving field of educational change is grounded in and has also influenced a complex collection of approaches to bringing about educational change in practice. Thus, studies of educational change have been variously concerned with the implementation of organizational innovations (Gross, Giacquinta, & Bernstein, 1971; Havelock, 1973; House; 1974; Huberman & Miles, 1984), with managed or planned educational change (Hall & Loucks, 1977; Leithwood, 1986), and with mandated educational reform (Berman & McLaughlin, 1978; McLaughlin, 1990; Sikes, 1992). Studies have also been conducted of how educational change is experienced or initiated by educators themselves in relation to the contingencies of their own practice (Richardson, 1991), their stage of career development (Huberman, 1993), the context of their school or subject department (Hargreaves, Davis, Fullan, Wignall, Stager, & Macmillan, 1992; Lieberman, Saxl, & Miles, 1988; Louis & Miles, 1990; McLaughlin & Talbert, 1993) and a host of other subjectively relevant phenomena as described in Fullan's (1991) definitive review of the field.

In the past few years, school restructuring has presented the most visible face of educational change at the highest levels of policy (Murphy, 1991) and in many individual efforts to bring about school-level change (Lieberman, 1995). Changing the structures of time and space in schooling along with the roles teachers play and the positions they occupy within those structures has been at the center of worldwide efforts to transform the most basic features of schooling in terms of classes, subjects, grades, and departments. Historians have demonstrated that these structures of schooling have proved especially resilient to change over the years and have repeatedly undermined successive efforts to bring about improvements in teaching and learning (Cuban, 1984; Tyack & Tobin, 1994). This is why structural reform now occupies much of the educational change agenda.

Yet, because of the way they have been implemented, many of the good intentions of school restructuring have placed literal and metaphorical imposi-

B.J. Biddle et al. (eds.), International Handbook of Teachers and Teaching, 1297-1319

tions upon the lives and work of teachers. Structural reforms have too often been built on teachers' backs, mandated without their involvement or consent. Many initiatives in school restructuring and reform have not even had good intentions to commend them. In some places, newly created national curricula have placed burdens of detailed content on teachers, content that has often been inappropriate for the diverse backgrounds and learning styles of the students who make up these teachers' classes (Hargreaves, 1989). Elsewhere, movements towards self-managing schools have not so much devolved real responsibility to teachers as loaded them up with the busy-work that used to be handled by central office (Smyth, 1993). Not surprisingly, principals and headteachers, whose managerial hand is often strengthened by self-management, seem to be much more enamoured of this educational change than classroom teachers whose time is eaten up by its consequences (Bishop & Mulford, 1996).

Given these limits of school restructuring as a sole strategy of educational change, other writers on, and advocates of change in, education have focused on developing the motivations and capacities of teachers and on building productive working relationships among them as an alternative approach to change. They have recommended *reculturing* schools as well as *restructuring* them (Fullan, 1993; Hargreaves, 1995).

It is this shift towards *cultural* alongside *structural* strategies of educational change that I want to address in this chapter. Elsewhere, I have emphasized the importance of culture in the life and renewal of organizations and as a vital area of investigation for understanding how the fundamental fabric of schooling persists or changes over time (Hargreaves, 1986, 1994). However, no educational changes are foolproof or flawless. All changes have drawbacks as well as advantages. Specific changes can benefit students and teachers but also do them great harm. It all depends on how they are interpreted and how they are used. All change efforts, even and especially those to which we are most passionately committed, therefore need to be subjected to periodic questioning, criticism, and review. We need to be vigilant about how changes can be misused and watchful of unintended negative consequences that our eagerness for improvement may initially prevent us from seeing.

It is time, I believe, for the concept of school *culture* and the strategy of *reculturing* schools to be opened to just this kind of questioning. In the very midst of growing interest in and advocacy for school *reculturing*, some stock-taking and soul-searching is now due – not so as to dismiss or demolish the concept of culture in educational change, but so as to review it and rebuild it in a more morally grounded and politically hard-headed way.

My task in this chapter, then, is to explore some rather more disquieting aspects of school cultures and their rise to prominence in the contemporary agenda of educational change. How are cultures of schooling and especially of teaching being promoted and represented? Which aspects of teacher cultures are being highlighted and which ones played down? What is it about the current context of educational change that seems to call forth cultural solutions? How can we explain this cultural turn in the theory and practice of educational change, and what stance should we take towards it? In order to address these questions, it is first necessary to examine the particular context of educational change in which the concept of culture is currently being used and understood.

CHAOS, COMPLEXITY AND CONTRADICTION IN TEACHING

Teaching in much of the Western world today is bedevilled by a number of fundamental paradoxes or contradictions. Among the more striking ones are that:

- Many vital areas of decision-making about curriculum content and responsibility for judging the performance of students are being taken out of teachers' hands and centralized. Conversely, moves towards decentralization are making teachers collectively responsible for the results they secure from their students and for making their schools places where such results are achievable.
- Individual school improvement (including collaborative teacher commitment to norms of continuous learning) is being promoted and celebrated with increasing urgency and enthusiasm. Meanwhile, many systems of state schooling, and the resources and supports they can offer teachers in their workplaces, are being actively dismantled and undergoing widespread deterioration.
- There is increasing support for teacher professionalism among governments who used to resist it, in terms of establishing professional standards, and in creating self-regulating bodies which will monitor and enforce these standards. At the same time, teacher redundancies, salary caps, and a multitude of reforms imposed on teachers without their involvement and consent, have significantly undermined the professional status and judgement that teachers value (Hargreaves & Goodson, 1996; Robertson, 1996).
- In many parts of the world, more and more women teachers are moving into positions of school leadership and are bringing more feminine and feminist orientations to the role with them. However, the 'leadership' of wider school systems and the policies that emanate from them are as non-negotiably masculine and managerial as ever, if not more so. (Blackmore, 1995)

Centralization is being accompanied by decentralization; professionalization by deprofessionalization. Commitments to individual school improvement are occurring alongside collapses of wider system support. More women are moving into school leadership while what they have to lead and manage seems less and less viable and defensible. What do these contradictions amount to? What do they mean? How should the teaching profession and the educational research community respond to them?

Some of the more avant-garde theorists of educational leadership and change do more than merely describe contradictions such as these. They virtually revel in them. Reinvented as paradoxes, chaos, and complexity, these deeply painful contradictions for practitioners have become symbolic tokens of hope and exhortation in what is often an academic ecstasy of change theory and change advocacy. In their book on *The Leadership Paradox*, #Deal and Peterson (1995) urge their readers to accept 'the seemingly contradictory approaches' to school leadership which emphasize its technical and expressive aspects respectively, 'as a paradox to be embraced and creatively addressed' (p. 9). Similarly, Handy (1994) argues that:

> Paradoxes are like the weather, something to be lived with, not solved, the worst aspects mitigated, the best enjoyed and used as clues to the way forward. Paradox has to be accepted, coped with and made sense of, in life, in work, in community and among the nations. (p. 18)

Senge (1990) points to dynamic complexity being a normal state of affairs in contemporary organizations. This complexity amounts to difficulties of tracing cause and effect when the consequences of our actions may not become evident until they are far removed in space and time. The existence of this dynamic complexity, argues Senge, is one of the fundamental reasons why we need to develop our organizations so that they have improved capacity to learn from and to solve ongoing problems. Taking up Senge's argument, one of Fullan's influential texts on educational change contends that 'as the scale of complexity accelerates in post-modern society, our ability to synthesize polar opposites where possible, and work with their co-existence where necessary, is absolutely critical to success' (Fullan, 1993, p. 41). While trying to take a more critical approach to educational paradoxes, some of my own writing has also overly emphasized their positive aspects and spoken more of paradoxes as exciting opportunities than crushing constraints (Hargreaves, 1995). It is not difficult to write books that celebrate the value of *Thriving on Chaos*, (Peters, 1988) when you are flying first-class to your next five-figure speech! Looking down at the chaos from the edge of the stratosphere can make it seem pretty interesting. Those who are surrounded by all the chaos aren't usually so convinced. The confusions and contradictions that infuriate teachers are the paradoxes and complexities admired by academics and their acolytes. As a source of authority on educational change, the scholarly pen, it seems, is considerably stronger than the teacher's word!

There are at least three reasons why it is not sufficient to explain the contradictions in teachers' work simply in terms of chaos theory, complex systems, or paradoxical demands.

First, the paradoxes, complexities, and uncertainties of present times are not just random, accidental, or mysterious. Take, for example, the growing social and moral uncertainty that we currently experience in education and elsewhere. This uncertainty propels educators into inventing missions and visions for their schools, leads parents to subscribe to charter schools and other schools of choice that accord with their own religious or social values, and pushes policy makers into imposing centralized curricula that bear the reassuring stamp of certainty upon them. This uncertainty is not just a product of systemic complexity, of organizational forces we cannot control that have no will or agency. It has very specific causes. Elsewhere, I have argued that the pervasive social and moral uncertainty which afflicts contemporary culture is part of a postmodern condition driven by changes in the circulation of information, ideas, and entertainment, by multicultural migration and international travel, and by international economic restructuring (Hargreaves, 1994; Kenway, 1995). These forces create increased moral uncertainty as ideas, information, and belief systems come into greater contact, they produce greater scientific uncertainty as information-flow is accelerated and knowledge is disconfirmed at an ever-increasing rate; and they help create contrary impulses to reinvent ideas of community and national identity (not least through education) in order to counter these trends toward globalization (Hargreaves, 1994; also Harvey, 1989).

Perhaps the most disturbing aspect of the advent of social and moral uncertainty is what Giddens (1995) calls *manufactured uncertainty*.[1] This is a condition where postmodern chaos and complexity to some extent result from wilful attempts by governmental, corporate, and financial powers to maximize their interests of profitability and control by keeping labor forces flexible, interest groups fragmented, and everyone off-balance (also Barlow & Robertson, 1994; Jameson, 1991).

When companies outsource their contracts, opt to use more temporary labor, and fire their employees only to rehire them again as consultants (but without pensions or other benefits), it is not coping with complexity or becoming a learning organization that is uppermost in their priorities, but making the labor force more exploitable and manipulable to protect company profits and achieve other management ends. The loss or reassignment of teachers' jobs similarly creates individual career uncertainties that are the product of states with shrinking budgets seeking higher control over their expensive professional labor costs. Lastly, the chaos of multiple innovation and of intensified reform efforts is often a sign of governments in panic — trying with increasing desperation to secure reforms through education when they know that in the context of world-wide economic restructuring, successful reform in employment and the economy may well continue to elude them. In a postmodern age of rapid information flow and associated economic and cultural change, much of our present uncertainty may be inevitable, and some of it may even be desirable (Slattery, 1995). But the origins of some of that uncertainty are also manufactured and malevolent. Many aspects of the contemporary paradoxes, chaos, and complexity in our social and educational condition should therefore not be causes for celebration but for fundamental critique. The literature of educational change has largely avoided this challenge.

The second problem of explaining the changes confronting teachers in terms of chaos and complexity is that some of these paradoxes and complexities are rooted in struggles for power and in conflicting visions of what educational change is for and who will benefit from it. For example, telling teachers that their classrooms should cultivate and recognize multiple intelligences marks an attempt to create more inclusive and equitable kinds of education where all students' chances for achievement are increased. Meanwhile, to judge schools and teachers by standardized test scores privileges one or two kinds of intelligence above all others and divides schools, teachers, and students in terms of their ability to succeed at them. Many teachers have to deal with this paradox of intelligence and expectation everyday – a paradox that is not a consequence of accident or muddle but of conflicting social and political values being played out in the classrooms of our nations. In much of the educational and organizational change literature, such paradoxes and complexities are presented as inevitable; the only challenge is how to work with them. Yet restructurings of labor, uncertainties of employment, erosions of equity, and intensified and expanded work expectations are parts of many contemporary paradoxes that are politically undesirable and morally indefensible. These are paradoxes that should be attacked, not accommodated.

Third, and most importantly for this chapter, some of the paradoxes and complexities that teachers experience amount to people taking or advocating interior psychic responses of an individual and interpersonal nature to external problems whose origins are more political and structural. This interior turn towards the self, personal relationships, and lifestyle choices as a focus for empowerment and change is a common characteristic of postmodern times. Many have been critical of this interior turn. Taylor (1991, p. 15) has argued that 'the culture of self-fulfilment has led many people to lose sight of concerns that transcend them. And it seems obvious that it has taken trivialized and self-indulgent forms.' Lasch (1979) has complained about the growth of a culture of narcissism where therapies and ideologies of personal growth and human potential are grounded in delusions of individual omnipotence, where people cannot see the boundaries between themselves and the world around them, where they confuse personal change with social change, or where they see the second as resulting from the first. And elsewhere I have explained the impact of what I call *the boundless self* on much of the theory and practice of teacher development, where teacher development has been described in terms of personal development or of 'storying' and 'restorying' one's life and career in ways that can easily become pious, narcissistic and self-indulgent (Hargreaves, 1994, 1996). It is odd and also ominous that when the work of teaching is being externally restructured like never before, vast areas of the literature and practice of teacher development are turning teachers inwards to individual reflection, personal wellness, and the telling of individual stories as the place where solutions can be found (Hargreaves & Goodson, 1996). It was the conservative Margaret Thatcher who said there is no such thing as society, there are only individuals — and there are few better moral warnings against the dangers of abandoning collective projects for individual ones than that!

Despite these problems, other writers have seen sources of strength in this interior turn towards lifestyle, the self, and personal relationships. Giddens (1991) persuasively argues that the collapse of scientific certainty and unquestioned expertise throws people back on their own reflexive resources for making their own choices and directing their own lives. Personal reflexiveness and self-help sought through others, he argues, can be sources of personal empowerment and positive social change compared to people's previous dependence on expert science or state control. This reflexiveness, Giddens claims, can bring about transformations in gender politics and the relationships of intimacy, as men become more able to turn inward to their emotional lives so that they have more insight into and awareness of their close relationships with others (Giddens, 1992). Elsewhere, Giddens (1995) extends his argument to claim that the interior turn towards self-development and personal reflexivity can even help dissolve the old distinctions between 'left' and 'right' as lifestyle politics brings together traditional conservatives and environmental radicals around 'green' issues that impact upon people's quality of life.

When self-reflexivity is connected to moral action and political consciousness, this can help us find a new moral ground and authority for our actions (Grimmett & Neufeld, 1994; Taylor, 1989). This kind of self-reflexivity is preferable to the narcissism and self-indulgence of personal self-development undertaken purely as a psychological quest. But it is hard not to wonder whether Giddens' celebrations of self-reflexivity and lifestyle politics reflect an abandonment of European class politics for Californian cults of personal growth as a source of theoretical inspiration. More than this, however, whether the interior turn towards the self is celebrated or critiqued, I want to argue that it is not just its *form* that may be problematic (as personally self-indulgent rather than morally and politically authentic), but the very *prominence* which this interior turn has come to occupy within the theory and practice of educational and social change.

We live in a world of widespread educational reform, where politically and structurally imposed problems are commonly seen as calling for personal and interpersonal solutions. School-level improvement is a popular response to the collapse of system-level support. More and more macho approaches to imposed educational reform are being implemented and accommodated through the relationship-centred and commitment-building qualities possessed by increasing numbers of women moving into school leadership. A fundamental irony of educational change in the postmodern world, therefore, is that externally imposed problems are being accompanied by discourses and practices of interior solutions, such as stress management, individual wellness, reflective practice, personal narrative, and school-level change.

The social-psychological, interior landscapes of schooling are places where much of the attention of policy and leadership is being focused to accommodate the pressures of global economic restructuring and sweeping educational reform. It is not wider systemic change which educators are increasingly asked to initiate, or indeed to resist, but the small local areas, the 15 per cent or so of their immediate work environment which, it is claimed, they will reasonably be able to control (Morgan, 1996). This is a dangerous seduction. It encourages teachers and principals to tend to their own gardens while leaving large-scale restructuring to others. It accepts that policy should be imposed on teachers and not be a process in which teachers should participate themselves (Darling-Hammond, 1995). It extols the virtues of gradualism but has no place for the courageous resistance of a Gandhi. The focus upon the interior landscapes of schooling along with attempts to redesign those interior landscapes are therefore important and troubling educational phenomena. Central to this inward shift of focus and energy is the concept of school culture. It is one aspect of this culture, the culture of teaching, that I want to address in the rest of this chapter.

THE SIGNIFICANCE OF TEACHER CULTURES

Culture is central to the life of schools, as it is to the life of any organization. For Williams (1961, p. 63), the study of culture involves 'the study of relationships between elements in a whole way of life' and 'the attempt to discover the nature of the organization which is the complex of these relationships.' For Page (1987, p. 82), the culture of a school comprises

> ... a set of beliefs, values and assumptions that participants share....
> while the beliefs are often tacit and regarded as self-evident by members

of the culture, they nevertheless provide a powerful foundation for members' understanding of the way they and the organization operate.

Among many writers, especially those whose concern is with analyzing corporate culture, it is what is shared subjectively among people that best defines the life of the organization. In a much repeated phrase of Deal & Kennedy's (1983, p. 5), culture can be defined as 'the way we do things around here.' For Schein (1985, p. 6), the essence of culture is 'the deeper level of basic assumptions and beliefs that are shared by members of an organization, that operate unconsciously, and that define in a basic, 'taken-for-granted' fashion, an organization's view of itself and its environment.'

Other writers are more inclined to suspend the notion of shared-ness being central to the definition of culture. Goodenough (1957), for example, has written that:

> ... culture is not a material phenomenon; it does not consist of things, people, behaviour or emotions. It is rather an organization of these things. It is the forms of things that people have in mind, their models for perceiving, relating and otherwise interpreting them. (p. 167)

Elsewhere, I have gone further than this and distinguished the *content* from the *form* of teacher cultures (Hargreaves, 1992, 1994). The *content* of culture refers to the substantive attitudes, beliefs, values, and ways of life that members of an organization, or a sub-group within it, hold in common. The content of a teacher culture may be found in allegiances to subject knowledge, commitments to child-centredness, acceptance of low standards, placing a strong focus on care and community, concentrating upon the academic elite, giving pride of place to sports and to its 'jocks,' and so forth.

The *form* of teacher cultures, by contrast, describes the patterns of relationship and forms of association among members of that culture. The form of teacher cultures may, for example, be *individualized* with teachers working independently and in isolation from each other (Flinders, 1988; Lortie, 1975; McTaggart, 1989), *collaborative* where teachers work together and share ideas and materials as a single professional community (Johnson, 1990; Nias, Southworth, & Yoemans, 1989); *balkanized* where teachers are separated into and work together in different sub-groups such as grade-levels or subject departments which are at best indifferent and at worst actively hostile to one another (Hargreaves & Macmillan, 1995); or characterized by *contrived collegiality* where collaboration is mandated, imposed, and regulated by managerial decree in terms of measures like compulsory team-teaching or required collaborative planning (Hargreaves, 1994). These four forms almost certainly do not exhaust all possible forms of teacher culture in schools. Sociometric and social network analyses may, in the future, establish complex maps of patterns of association among teachers, where other forms become apparent. One hypothetical possibility, for example, is *satellite cultures* where a core, dominant culture in the school is surrounded by several, peripheral, satellite subgroups.[2]

It is through cultures of teaching that teachers learn what it means to teach and what kind of teacher they want to be within their school, subject department, or other professional community. Cultures of teaching, in this respect, form frameworks for occupational learning. Concluding her study of two high schools, Page (1987, p. 96) remarked that 'understanding the cultures of schools is crucial to understanding the work of teachers.' As Waller (1932, p. 375) said, 'teaching makes the teacher.' It is a 'boomerang that never fails to come back to the hand that threw it.' And while there are characteristics of the occupation as a whole that shape the life, work, and culture of teaching (D. Hargreaves, 1980; Waller, 1932) *where* you are a teacher and *how* the work of teaching is organized in that place will significantly influence the kind of teacher you will become.

In his classic study of the *Culture of the School and the Problem of Change*, Sarason (1971, p. 59) argues that efforts to understand educational change must take account of three types of social relationship: 'those among the professionals within the school setting, those among the professionals and the pupils, and those among the professionals and the different parts of the larger society.' These relationships are what make up much of the culture of the school. In addition to teacher cultures being important for framing teachers' work and for filtering educational change, they also appear to have important consequences for student learning. In particular, cultures of collaboration among teachers seem to produce greater willingness to take risks, to learn from mistakes, and to share successful strategies with colleagues that lead to teachers having positive senses of their own efficacy, beliefs that their children can learn, and improved outcomes in that learning as a result (Ashton & Webb, 1986; Rosenholtz, 1989). How strong the professional cultures or communities of teaching are in particular departments, schools, or even whole systems seems to be really crucial for how satisfied teachers feel and how well students achieve in those places (McLaughlin, in press; McLaughlin & Talbert, 1993).

To sum up, cultures of teaching affect the actions of teachers in significant ways. They affect how teachers approach and define their work, how they respond to change, and how much agency they feel they have in making a difference in the lives and futures of their students. The importance for educational research and practice of understanding teacher cultures should therefore not be underestimated. Unfortunately, however, this understanding is often placed in the service of educational purposes that are distinctly suspect. These purposes even shape how the understanding of teacher cultures is pursued, how the research on cultures of teaching is constructed. Both the theory and the practical formation of teacher cultures are highly vulnerable to colonization by interests outside of teaching which seek to control it. One of the biggest problems facing the field of teacher cultures is its colonization by the purposes of educational management, by the kinds of change that educational managers and leaders want to bring about, and by the ways in which such change is typically implemented.

THE COLONIZATION OF TEACHER CULTURES

A criticism of early and classical anthropology and its study of different cultures has been its covert or unintended colonialism (Waite, forthcoming).[3] Classical anthropology, and ethnography, it is suggested, charted other cultures so they might be tamed and controlled more easily (Clifford & Marcus, 1986). It even arranged 'primitive' cultures along hierarchies which permitted them to be classified and evaluated accordingly (Vidich & Lyman, 1994). In this way, primitive cultures were colonized not only economically and religiously, but also intellectually through anthropological methods and forms of inquiry.

Contemporary studies of corporate cultures and school cultures often show the same tendencies to guide how we understand people's meanings in order to assist the interests of management. School cultures in general and teacher cultures in particular are frequently investigated and understood from the leader's point of view. Sergiovanni (1984), for instance, creates an understanding of school culture from the standpoint of the needs and priorities of the school leader. Much of the organizational culture literature takes a similar line, directing itself to the question of how leaders can build strong cultures to fulfil the organization's purposes. Bates (1987) has articulated a fundamental critique of this orientation. 'Company managers,' he says, 'have been attempting to construct and impose company cultures for a very long time' (p. 80). The literature on corporate management, he continues, emphasizes culture-building as a way for management to increase its control over members of the organization. Successful management depends on 'getting the culture right' (p. 81). Bates (1987) concludes that:

> ... advocates of corporate culture are conducting cultural analysis on behalf of managers. They are not, for example, incorporating a consideration of the interests of workers into their analysis, except for the assumption that what is good for the corporation, is good for workers too. (p. 82)

Conversely, Bates then wonders 'what an analysis of corporate culture might look like if it were conducted on behalf of the managed.' Just as cultural and economic imperialism colonized the cultures of primitive societies, so in many respects is corporate management colonizing and controlling the cultures of its workforces. This process of managerial colonization is happening in education too, with respect to teacher cultures, where much of the theoretical inspiration is drawn from the corporate domain. This colonization can be seen in four domains:

- in the literature of school leadership, which places high value on the culture-building behaviors of school principals or headteachers;
- in the creation and regulation of cultures of collaboration among teachers that are bureaucratic and managerialist in form;
- in value-laden representations of teacher cultures and of cultural change in teaching that highlight their positive, optimistic elements and neglect or suppress their more troubling or disturbing dimensions;
- in treating the cultural lives of teachers as a kind of 'bounded irrationality,' that should be open to management and manipulation by school leadership.

Leadership as Culture Building

Many contemporary models of educational leadership in the form of instructional, servant, or transformational leadership, identify culture-building (usually alongside problem-solving) as one of the main priorities of principalship (Deal & Peterson, 1995; Leithwood, 1992; Sergiovanni, 1984). Following the literature on corporate culture, where the chief executive's task is seen as establishing a vision, being the founder of the culture, rewarding those who commit to it, and 'letting go' those who don't (Deal & Kennedy, 1983), writing on educational leadership similarly sees culture-building among the staff as the prime responsibility of the principal (rather than anyone else). As Gronn (1995) noted, where they are seen to be effective at mobilizing team efforts, theoretically and conceptually, these leaders are accorded all the individual credit. Such leaders, he says, are poor models for democratic change. Although they may attempt to be inclusive and involving, and often place a sincere emphasis on caring, relationships and building collaborative cultures of trust and support, many of these principals, especially at the elementary school level, adopt paternalistic or maternalistic stances towards their staffs (e.g., Nias et al., 1989). In this respect, as I have argued elsewhere, it is more than a little ironic that many principals refer to their schools and their staffs as 'families' (Hargreaves, 1994). There is little ambiguity about who is the parent and who are the children here!

I do not wish to imply through this critique that principals should play no part in culture-building, that they should refrain from encouraging collaboration or shared professional learning, for example. But culture-building is other people's responsibility as well as the principal's. Teacher leadership and team leadership need to be given more practical and theoretical emphasis in the creation of school cultures in addition to the leadership offered by principals (e.g., Fullan, 1995). And it should be recognized that the cultures which *teachers* create and recreate are often divergent from and sometimes disruptive of those which their principals are trying to create. Nor do these cultures always amount to resistance which principals should overcome. They also offer possibilities for insight and learning that might help principals develop themselves. Interestingly, Macmillan (1996) has found that where it is the policy to rotate principals through different schools, enduring staff cultures often successfully resist the change efforts of leaders who are merely passing through. The robust cultures that teachers are often able to create frequently enable them to survive their principals and successfully 'wait them out.' These properties of teacher cultures receive less than their proper due in a leadership literature that is geared to managing and manipulating teacher cultures rather than learning from and strengthening them as independent sources of educational improvement and change.

Feminist scholarship has raised further questions about the cultural aspects of educational leadership. In an especially insightful paper, Blackmore (1995), has described how increasing numbers of women in the principalship are becoming 'the emotional middle-managers' of educational change – using women's ways of organizing, knowing, and caring (Belenky, Clinchy, Goldberger, & Tarule, 1986; Gilligan, 1982) to smooth the path of organizational development and change. Blackmore argues that these women principals are taking 'soft,' human-relations decisions as malleable middle-managers, while the top (largely male) executive and financial managers take the 'hard decisions' which circumscribe the scope of self-determination for individual schools in which the middle-managers work. This top-level culture is a predominantly masculine one that mandates system-wide changes, cuts jobs, shrinks budgets, imposes testing requirements, and demands detailed paperwork for administrative accountability. Under the aegis of empowerment, meanwhile, women principals use emotional management to build commitment and collaboration, offsetting resistance to the changes and stimulating the desire to make them work. The growth of such emotional middle-management in a broader policy context, where teachers have less representation and little voice, is one of the more disturbing features of the interior turn towards culture, emotions, and personal growth in school-level change; for all this is occurring at a time when schools are being privatized, public education is being dismantled, supports are being withdrawn, and the conditions of teachers' work are being restructured all around them. One of the more worrying effects of this pattern of change is on women principals themselves. Emotional labor takes its toll on their health and their personal lives as they try desperately to build caring cultures and positive change in policy contexts that are deeply inimical to them (see also Hochschild, 1983).

Contrived Collegiality

The attempted managerial colonization of teacher cultures by management is perhaps most evident in a phenomenon that I have called *contrived collegiality* (Hargreaves, 1992, 1994). Collaboration can be a burden as well as a blessing, especially once administrators take it over and convert it into models, mandates, and measurable profiles of growth and implementation. For the spontaneous, unpredictable, and dangerous processes of teacher-led collaboration, administrators sometimes prefer to substitute the safe simulation of contrived collegiality – more perfect, more harmonious (and more controlled) than the reality of collaboration itself.

Such *safe simulations* (Baudrillard, 1983; Eco, 1990) of collaboration among teachers occur when spontaneous, voluntary, and difficult-to-control forms of teacher collaboration are discouraged or usurped by administrators who capture it, contain it, and contrive it through compulsory cooperation, required collaborative planning, stage-managed mission statements, labyrinthine procedures of school development planning, and processes of collaboration to implement non-negotiable programs and curricula whose viability and practicality are not open to discussion.

The characteristic features of contrived collegiality are that it is:

- *administratively regulated.* It does not evolve from teachers' own initiative but is an administrative imposition that requires teachers to meet and work together.
- *compulsory.* It makes working together a matter of compulsion as in mandatory team teaching, peer coaching or collaborative planning. Contrived collegiality affords little discretion to eccentricity, individuality or solitude.
- *implementation-oriented.* It requires or 'persuades' teachers to work together so as to implement other people's mandates – be these the principal's, the district's, or those of the wider system. Collaboration here is secured in the service of goals defined by others.
- *fixed in time and space.* It occurs in particular places at particular times. Contrived collegiality requires teachers to work together in times and places that are administratively determined by others.
- *predictable.* It is designed to bring about relatively predictable outcomes. Control over its purposes and regulation of its time and placement are all designed to increase this predictability.

It is not so much that contrived collegiality is a manipulative, underhand way of tricking passive teachers into complying with administrative agendas. Teachers are very quick to see through such contrivances. Rather, the administratively simulated image of collaboration becomes a self-enclosed world of its own. In this sense, the major problem raised by safely simulated contrived collegiality is not one of control and manipulation but one of superficiality and wastefulness. Contrived collegiality does not so much deceive teachers, as delay, distract, and demean them.

The inflexibility of mandating collegiality makes it difficult for programs to be adjusted to the purposes and practicalities of particular school and classroom settings. It overrides the discretionary judgements of teacher professionalism, and it diverts teachers' efforts and energies into simulated compliance with administrative demands that are inflexible and inappropriate for the settings in which they work. Worst of all, by making collaboration into an administrative device, contrived collegiality can paradoxically suppress the desires that teachers have to collaborate and improve among themselves.

Value-laden Representations

A third way in which school and teacher cultures can and have become colonized by the purposes of management can be seen in how such cultures are commonly portrayed and represented in the relevant literature. While no representations or images of the world around us are free from value, some kinds of social scientific representation that portray patterns in human thinking and behavior are especially normative in nature. These kinds of conceptual patterning do not merely portray differences or variations in human conduct. The very way in which these variations are arranged strongly implies distinctions of good and bad, better and worse.

Bipolar, dichotomous representations draw such distinctions particularly sharply. Thus, Susan Moore Johnson (1990) eloquently represents cultures of teaching as follows:

> In the ideal world of schooling, teachers would be true colleagues working together, debating about goals and purposes, coordinating lessons, observing and critiquing each other's work, sharing successes and offering solace, with the triumphs of their collective efforts far exceeding the summed accomplishments of their solitary struggles. The real world of schools is usually depicted very differently with teachers sequestered in classrooms, encountering peers only on entering or leaving the building. Engaged in parallel piecework, they devise curricula on their own, ignoring the plans and practices of their

counterparts in other classrooms or grades.... Although such portrayals
are often exaggerated, they contain more truth than most of us would
like to believe. (p. 148)

Such portrayals present collaboration and collegiality as things to be aspired to,
while individualism and isolation are processes to be eradicated or avoided. Solitude, eccentricity, and creative individuality also have their place in teaching,
yet these bipolar portrayals of teacher culture present individualism and collaboration as mutually exclusive. They leave no room for individual and solitary
pursuits to be recognized and appreciated in the broader panoply of teachers'
work (Fullan & Hargreaves, 1996; Hargreaves, 1993).

Some analyses of teacher cultures present them not in dichotomous terms but
as an arrangement of points on a continuum. Little (1990), for example, has
identified four kinds of collegiality relations among teachers and has arranged
them along a continuum. She describes scanning and storytelling, help and assistance, and sharing as relatively weak forms of collegiality. She argues that if
collaboration is limited to anecdotes and help-giving only when asked, or to
pooling existing ideas without examining and extending them, it can confirm
the status quo. A fourth kind of collegial relation appears much further along
Little's continuum. This is joint work, and for Little it represents the strongest
form of collaboration. Joint work embraces activities like team teaching, shared
planning, mutual observation, action research, and mentoring. She argues that
it implies and creates stronger interdependence, shared responsibility, collective commitment, and greater readiness to participate in the difficult business of
review and critique.

The continuum is a popular device for representing variations in educational
practice. It allows finer discriminations to be made than straight polar opposites
allow. This is certainly true for cultures of teaching. There is much more to cultures of teaching than their being collaborative or individualized, good or bad.
A continuum of teacher collaboration holds out the promise of being able to
chart and push progress towards ever more sophisticated interpretations and im-
plementations of collaboration. But sometimes the urge to measure and manage
can obstruct the search for meaning. This can happen with educational continuums in two ways. First, quite complex and disparate behaviours may be clus-
tered amorphously together into a single stage, level, or point on the continuum
for the sake of simple and convenient measurement, when in practice the specific behaviors often do not belong together at all. One may, for instance, perform brilliantly in some areas of collaborative work but poorly in others. Great
team problem-solvers may be poor emotional supporters. Teachers who may be
excellent in nurturing junior colleagues may flinch when having to face conflicts with equals or superiors. It is impossible to capture these complexities and
distinctions on a single scale of collaborativeness.

A second point is that educational continuums often embody implicit values where movement along the continuum is construed as growth or progress towards a better state. However, progress along a continuum does not guarantee continuation towards progress. For example, Little's continuum tends to value forms of collaboration that are more intellectual, inquiry-based, and task-centred over ones which are organized more informally around principles and purposes of care, connection, and storytelling. In a critique of Little's work, Tafaaki (1992, p. 102) however, shows that in their exchange of narratives and stories, teachers are not merely 'gossiping' for amusement or moral support. Indirectly, through these stories, they are also learning about the moral principles which guide each other's work which, if sufficiently shared, might provide a basis for further associations among them. These 'communal caring' cultures are most likely to be found in the feminine, feminized, though not necessarily feminist world of elementary teaching (Acker, 1992). Such cultures may not operate like rational seminars of rigorous intellectual inquiry, but alongside and within the practices of care and connection, they do incorporate inquiry and reflection in more implicit, informal, and incidental ways. Representing teacher cultures along normative continuums of development and progress does not allow these sophisticated distinctions to be captured and portrayed.

Thus, we need to take care in how we portray teacher cultures – not just in crude polarities or normative continuums that guide us towards the researcher's or leader's visions of improvement and progress, but also in terms of more complex typologies or other kinds of representation which place the purposes of curiosity and understanding before the rush to betterment and action.

Bounded Irrationality

A fourth way in which teacher cultures have been managerially colonized really pervades the other three. The prior sections have revealed a growing normative tradition in writing on educational change, leadership, and schools as workplaces. In this tradition, teacher cultures are treated as embodying a kind of 'bounded irrationality' where the inefficient, irrational, dangerous, and resistant components of teachers' lives and work can be captured, contrived, and controlled for purposes of managerial manipulation. In a trenchant critique of the more general literature of organizational culture, Jeffcutt (1993, p. 32) observes that this literature 'is distinguished by heroic quests for closure.' It is a literature, he argues, that is dominated by two broad representational styles. *Epic* forms portray great cultural leaders who come into an organization and, in the face of failure and catastrophe, manage to turn its culture around. In education, case studies of great transformational leaders (Leithwood, 1992) or of principals who have worked with their staffs to turn failing schools around exemplify this *epic* mode. *Romantic* forms, meanwhile, stress placid or pulsating qualities of collaboration and teamwork that help to create cultures of organizational harmony. Case studies of exemplary principals building positive cultures of care and support (e.g., Nias et al., 1989) illustrate the presence of this *romantic* mode in educational writing.

Such representational strategies, Jeffcutt argues, 'expose an overriding search for unity and harmony that suppresses division and disharmony.' Much less common in the literature of leadership and change are representations of organizational culture that take *tragic* or *ironic* forms. Here, obstacles triumph, opponents gain their revenge, heroic quests are unsuccessful, and organizations collapse. In the educational research literature, such tragic and ironic accounts of marginalized, resistant, or subversive teacher cultures are less likely to be found in the expansive and improvement-oriented landscape of educational change than in the scholarly crevices of educational sociology and anthropology (e.g., Riseborough, 1980). In the general literature of school culture and educational change, however, what predominates are epic and romantic representational styles which embody '*bounded irrationality*, functioning to harmonize, integrate, and unify organization' (Jeffcutt, 1993, p. 32).

CONCLUSION

For me, this has been an unusual but important paper to write. I have devoted considerable time in recent years, both in my writing and in my practical work with teachers and administrators in the field, to building an understanding and appreciation of the *cultural* dimensions of teaching and of educational change. I have seen this as an especially important task, given a context of structural reforms that pay no heed to the humanity of teaching, to the motivations, dispositions, and capacities that teachers bring to their work, or to the collegial relationships and sheer emotional labor through which teaching is done. It remains a passionate mission of mine to have educational policy makers and administrators recognize how important the quality and character of human relationships among teachers are for the quality of their classroom work and to help them see the damage that can be done to these vital relationships when mandated reforms are oblivious to them. For these reasons, I believe that recognizing and embracing the cultural dimensions of teaching and educational change remain essential to understanding what teachers do, why they do it, and how they might do it better.

Yet it seems equally clear to me that the cultural turn in the literature and practice of educational change should not be celebrated prematurely or advocated naively. The interior turn that cultural strategies of educational change represent is not an innocent one. It occurs alongside and not instead of massive exterior strategies of school reform and restructuring in which many teachers appear to have little interest and even less involvement. While school-level cultural change may deserve praise and merit support in principle, in the context of parallel policy moves to dismantle public education and diminish the professional independence of teachers, its growing popularity should be seen as more suspect.

This chapter has been written to address this disturbing coalescence of seemingly contradictory forces. One of these forces turns leaders inwards to the cultural development of their staffs when the sources of their schools' problems should also be fought and contested 'out there.' It advocates cultural solutions to what are often structural and political problems. And it tries to harness the emotional energies of teachers and secure their commitment to imposed change while placing managerial boundaries around this 'irrationality' and around the unpredictable outcomes that unfettered collaborative cultures among teachers might otherwise unleash.

I am not recommending that we abandon teacher cultures as part of a proper focus for understanding or initiating educational change. But I *am* advising that we temper our enthusiasm about cultural approaches to change and take time to reflect on the ways in which teacher cultures are being widely colonized by the interests and purposes of management at this time of worldwide structural reform. In light of this analysis, while keeping teacher cultures within our investigative sights, I believe we would do well to pursue three courses of action in educational practice and research. First, we should recognize and support teachers as active agents in developing and maintaining their own cultures, not just as cultural construction materials which administrators can assemble in their own image. Second, we should cultivate and learn from studies of teacher cultures that are tragic and ironic as well as ones that are more epic or romantic. Third, our change theories and practices should address how teachers and principals can turn outwards in their change strategies to fight the assault on public education and the attrition of their professionalism, as well as turning inwards to develop the cultures and capacities of their own immediate staffs.

Cultures of teaching can be a vital key to positive educational change, or they can unlock a pandora's box of emotional adaptation to imposed reforms that hold out few benefits for students or their teachers. The keys of school culture have been cut. It is now up to teachers, administrators and educational researchers to open the right doors with them.

ENDNOTES

1. My use of the term here is somewhat different from Giddens. His usage is more general – manufactured uncertainty resulting from what humankind has created, rather than from plagues, famines, earthquakes or other natural events.

2. Jorges de Lima of the University of Azores in Portugal is currently undertaking such a social network analysis of teacher cultures in two secondary schools.

3. I am very grateful to Duncan Waite for the communication we have had around his work on school culture and anthropology for the way it has contributed to my understanding of colonization of culture.

REFERENCES

Acker, S. (1992). Creating careers: Women teachers at work. *Curriculum Inquiry, 22*(2), 141-163.

Ashton, P. & Webb, R. (1986). *Making a difference: Teachers' sense of efficacy and student achievement.* New York: Longman.

Barlow, M. & Robertson, H. J. (1994). *Class warfare: The assault on Canada's schools.* Toronto: Key Porter Books.

Bates, R. (1987). Corporate culture, schooling and educational administration. *Educational Administration Quarterly, 23*(4), 79-115.

Baudrillard, J. (1983). *Simulations.* New York: Columbia University, Semiotext.

Belenky, M. F., Clinchy, B. M., Goldberger, N. R., & Tarule, J. M. (1986). *Women's ways of knowing.* New York: Basic Books.

Berman, P. & McLaughlin, M. (1978). *Federal programs supporting educational change: V8 implementing and sustaining innovations.* Santa Monica, CA: Rand Corporation.

Bishop, P. W. & Mulford, R. (1996). Empowerment in four Australian primary schools: They don't really care. *International Journal of Educational Reform, 5*(2), 193-204.

Blackmore, J. (1995). *A taste for the feminine in educational leadership.* Unpublished manuscript, Deakin University, Faculty of Education, Geelong, Australia.

Clifford, J. & Marcus, G. E. (Eds.). (1986). *Writing culture: The politics and poetics of ethnography.* Berkeley: University of California Press.

Cuban, L. J. (1984). *How teachers taught: Constancy and change in American classrooms 1890-1980.* New York: Longman.

Darling-Hammond, L. (1995). Policy for restructuring. In A. Lieberman (Ed.), *The work of restructuring schools* (pp. 172-197). New York: Teachers College Press.

Deal, T. & Kennedy, A. (1983). Culture and school performance. *Educational Leadership, 40*(5), 14-15.

Deal, T. & Peterson, K. (1995). *The leadership paradox.* San Francisco: Jossey Bass.

Eco, U. (1990). *Travels in hyperreality.* San Diego, CA: Harcourt Brace Jovanovich.

Flinders, D. J. (1988). Teachers' isolation and the new reform. *Journal of Curriculum and Supervision, 4*(1), 17-29.

Fullan, M. (with S. Stiegelbauer) (1991). *The new meaning of educational change.* New York: Teachers College Press.

Fullan, M. (1993). *Change forces.* New York: Falmer Press.

Fullan, M. (1995). Broadening the concept of teacher leadership. *New directions.* Detroit: National Staff Development Council.

Fullan, M. & Hargreaves, A. (1996). *What's worth fighting for in your school?* (2nd ed.). New York: Teachers College Press.

Giddens, A. (1991). *Modernity and self-identity*. Cambridge: Polity Press.

Giddens, A. (1992). *The transformation of intimacy*. Stanford: Stanford University Press.

Giddens, A. (1995). *Beyond left and right*. Stanford: Stanford University Press.

Gilligan, C. (1982). *In a different voice*. Cambridge, MA: Harvard University Press.

Goodenough, W. H. (1957). Cultural anthropology and linguistics. In P. L. Garvin (Ed.), *Report of the Seventh Annual Round Table Meeting on Linguistics and Language Study* (pp. 167-173). Washington, DC: Georgetown University Press.

Grimmett, P. & Neufeld, J. (Eds.). (1994). *Teacher development and the struggle for authenticity*. New York: Teachers College Press.

Gronn, P. (1995). Greatness revisited: The current obsession with transformational leadership. *Leading and Managing, 1*(1), 14-27.

Gross, N., Giacquinta, J., & Bernstein, M. (1971). *Implementing organizational innovations: A sociological analysis of planned educational change*. New York: Basic Books.

Hall, G. E. & Loucks, S. (1977). A developmental model for determining whether the treatment is actually implemented. *American Educational Research Journal, 14*(3), 263-276.

Handy, C. (1994). *The age of paradox*. Cambridge, MA: Harvard Business Press.

Hargreaves, A. (1986). *Two cultures of schooling: The case of middle schools*. Lewes: Falmer Press.

Hargreaves, A. (1989). *Curriculum and assessment reform*. Toronto: OISE Press.

Hargreaves, A. (1992). Cultures of teaching: A focus for change. In A. Hargreaves & M. Fullan (Eds.), *Understanding teacher development* (pp. 216-240). London: Cassell and New York: Teachers College Press.

Hargreaves, A., Davis, J. Fullan, M., Wignall, R., Stager, M., & Macmillan, R. (1992). *Secondary school work cultures and educational change*. Toronto: The Ontario Institute for Studies in Education.

Hargreaves, A. (1993). Individualism and individuality: Reinterpreting the teacher culture. *International Journal of Educational Research, 19*(3), 227-245.

Hargreaves, A. (1994). *Changing teachers, changing times*. London and Cassell, NY: Teachers College Press and Toronto: OISE Press.

Hargreaves, A. (1995). Renewal in the age of paradox. *Educational Leadership, 52*(7), 14-19.

Hargreaves, A. (1996). Revisiting voice. *Educational Researcher*, (January/February), 1-8.

Hargreaves, A. & Goodson, I. F. (1996). Teachers' professional lives: Aspirations and actualities. In I. F. Goodson & A. Hargreaves (Eds.), *Teachers' professional lives* (p. 1). New York: Falmer Press.

Hargreaves, A. & Macmillan, R. (1995). The balkanization of teaching. In J. W. Little & L. S. Siskin (Eds.), *Subjects in question* (pp. 141-217). New York: Teachers College Press.

Hargreaves, D. (1980). The occupational culture of teaching. In P. Woods (Ed.), *Teacher strategies* (pp. 125-140). London: Croom Helm.

Harvey, D. (1989). *The condition of postmodernity*. Oxford: Basil Blackwell.

Havelock, R. (1973). *The change agent's guide to innovation in education*. Englewood Cliffs, NJ: Educational Technology Publications.

Hochschild, A. R. (1983). *The managed heart: Commercialization of human feeling*. Berkeley: University of California Press.

House, E. (1974). *The politics of educational innovation*. Berkeley, CA: McCutchan.

Huberman, M. (1993). *The lives of teachers*. London: Cassell and New York: Teachers College Press.

Huberman, M. & Miles, M. (1984). *Innovation up close*. New York: Plenum Press.

Jameson, F. (1991). *Postmodernism: Or the cultural logic of late capitalism*. London & New York: Verso.

Jeffcutt, R. (1993). From interpretation to representation. In J. Hassard & M. Pracker (Eds.), *Postmodernism and organizations* (pp. 25-48). London: Sage.

Johnson, S. M. (1990). *Teachers at work.* New York: Basic Books.

Kenway, J. (1995). *Reality bytes.* Unpublished manuscript, Deakin University, Faculty of Education, Geelong, Australia.

Lasch, C. (1979). *The culture of narcissism.* New York: W. W. Norton.

Leithwood, K. (Ed.). (1986). *Planned educational change through the processes of review, development and implementation.* Toronto: OISE Press.

Leithwood, K. (1992). The move toward transformational leadership. *Educational Leadership, 49*(5), 8-12.

Lieberman, A. (Ed.). (1995). *The work of restructuring schools.* New York: Teachers College Press.

Lieberman, A., Saxl, E. R., & Miles, M. B. (1988). Teachers' leadership: Ideology and practice. In A. Lieberman (Ed.), *Building a professional culture in schools* (pp. 148-166). New York: Teachers College Press.

Little, J. W. (1990). The persistence of privacy: Autonomy and initiative in teachers' professional relations. *Teachers' College Record, 91*(4), 509-36.

Lortie, D. (1975). *Schoolteacher.* Chicago: University of Chicago Press.

Louis, K. S. & Miles, M. (1990). *Improving the urban high school: The what and the how.* New York: Teachers College Press.

Macmillan, R. (1996). *The relationship between school culture and principals' practices at the time of succession.* Unpublished Ed.D. thesis, University of Toronto.

McLaughlin, M. (1990). The rand change agent study revisited: Macro perspectives and micro realities. *Educational Researcher* (December), 11-16.

McLaughlin, M. (in press). Rebuilding teacher professionalism in the United States. In A. Hargreaves & R. Evans (Eds.), *Beyond educational reform.* Buckingham: Open University Press.

McLaughlin, M. & Talbert, J. (1993). *Contexts that matter for teaching and learning.* Stanford: Stanford University, Centre for Research on the Context of Secondary School Teachers.

McTaggart, R. (1989). Bureaucratic rationality and the self-educating profession: The problem of teacher privatism. *Journal of Curriculum Studies, 21*(4), 345-361.

Morgan, G. (1996). *Finding your 15%: The art of mobilizing small changes to create large effects* (Working Paper). Toronto: Schuliah School of Business.

Murphy, J. (1991). *Restructuring schools: Capturing and assessing the phenomena.* New York: Teachers College Press.

Nias, J., Southworth, G., & Yeomans, R. (1989). *Staff relationships in the primary school.* London: Cassell.

Page, R. (1987). Teachers' perceptions of students: A link between classrooms, school cultures and the social order. *Anthropology and Education Quarterly, 18*, 77-97.

Peters, T. (1988). *Thriving on chaos. Handbook for management revolution.* London: Macmillan.

Richardson, V. (1991). How and why teachers change? In S. C. Conley & B. S. Cooper (Eds.), *The school as a work environment* (pp. 57-82). Needham, MA: Allyn and Bacon.

Riseborough, G. (1980). Teacher careers and comprehensive schooling. *Sociology, 15*(3), 355-381.

Robertson, S. (1996). Teachers' work, restructuring and postfordism: Constructing the new 'professionalism.' In I. F. Goodson & A. Hargreaves (Eds.), *Teachers' professional lives* (pp. 28-55). New York: Falmer Press.

Rosenholtz, S. (1989). *Teachers' workplace.* New York: Longman.

Sarason, S. (1971). *The culture of the school and the problem of change.* Boston: Allyn & Bacon.

Schein, E. (1985). *Organizational culture and leadership*. San Francisco: Jossey-Bass.

Senge, P. (1990). *The fifth discipline: The art and practice of the learning organization*. New York: Doubleday.

Sergiovanni, T. J. (1984). Leadership and excellence in schooling. *Educational Leadership, 41*(5), 4-13.

Sikes, P. (1992). Teacher development and imposed change. In M. Fullan & A. Hargreaves (Eds.), *Teacher development and educational change* (pp. 36-55). New York: Falmer Press.

Slattery, P. (1995). A postmodern vision of time and learning: A response to the National Education Commission Report, Prisoners of Time. *Harvard Educational Review, 65*(4), Winter, 612-633.

Smyth, J. (Ed.). (1993). *The socially critical self-managing school*. London and Philadelphia: Falmer Press.

Tafaaki, I. (1992). *Collegiality and women teachers in elementary and middle school settings: The caring relationship and nurturing interdependence*. Unpublished doctoral dissertation, University of Massachusetts, Boston.

Taylor, C. (1989). *Sources of the self*. Cambridge, MA: Harvard University Press.

Taylor, C. (1991). *The malaise of modernity*. Concord, Ontario: Anasi Press.

Tyack, D. & Tobin, W. (1994). The grammar of schooling: Why has it been so hard to change? *American Educational Research Journal, 31*(3), Fall, 453-480.

Vidich, A. J. & Lyman, S. M. (1994). Qualitative methods: Their history in sociology and anthropology. In N. K. Denzin. & Y. S. Lincoln (Eds.), *Handbook of qualitative research* (pp. 23-59). Thousand Oaks, CA: Sage.

Waite, D. (forthcoming). Anthropology, sociology and supervision. In G. R. Firth & E. F. Pajak (Eds.), *Handbook of research in school supervision*. New York: Macmillan.

Waller, W. (1932). *The sociology of teaching*. New York: John Wiley.

Williams, R. (1961). *The long revolution*. Harmondsworth: Penguin Books.

Chapter 15: A Bill of Goods: The Early Marketing of Computer-Based Education and Its Implications for the Present Moment[1]

DOUGLAS D. NOBLE

Cobblestone School and Rochester Institute of Technology

> The various companies are ... telling a school system, 'You take our package ... We'll give you the stuff, we'll rent you the machines, we'll train your teachers, and so on.' And who is big enough and honest enough and independent enough, and where can the countervailing power be mustered to call for order? (Cremin, 1968, p. 96)

INTRODUCTION

This chapter sketches the history of the marketing by Big Business of computer-based education (CBE), from the early 1960s to the present moment, as seen through the private papers of some of the major corporate players. Rather than being an exhaustive account or a synopsis of historical facts and figures, what follows is a sketch largely in the words of key participants about defining moments along the way. The point is to understand something of the driving impulses behind recurrent corporate computer-based forays into education – to examine the assumptions and visions, the motives, the marketing strategies, the business decisions, and the wider political contexts which have provided the opportunities through which the corporate elite have entered the schools with their high-tech wares.

Despite the many volumes that have been compiled about computer-based education over the last two decades, there is surprisingly little written on the history of this enterprise, and there is almost nothing written from the point of view of corporate strategists attempting to crack and technologize the education market. Instead, the vast bulk of the literature takes the perspective of the bewildered or the enthusiastic consumer and assumes the hyperbole of inevitability constructed by corporate marketeers as a given.

Yet what I hope to show above all is that from the start to the present Big Business has never really known what it was doing in this arena. Again and again, major firms have exploited political opportunities to break into the education market and have flailed wildly trying to make the killing they had con-

B.J. Biddle et al. (eds.), International Handbook of Teachers and Teaching, 1321-1385

vinced themselves was there for the taking. Far more often than not they have fallen on their faces, failing miserably and retreating to cut their losses ... only to lick their wounds and try again, equally oblivious, once the next opportunity arose or another technology product hit the market.

These repeated failures did not occur merely because Big Business has misunderstood the education market and the culture of the schools. These failures have resulted from the breathtakingly poor business sense of those corporate leaders most prominent in leading the charge to reform education through technological innovation. Repeatedly, these leaders of major Fortune 500 firms have insisted with blind determination on believing their own illusions and on following the predictions of information age fortune tellers, despite massive evidence to the contrary available to them, even from their own lieutenants. The hubris of these men in their self-appointed role to 'save' education, to pursue the holy grail of electronic teaching, to come up with the 'killer application' for their glorious computer gadgetry, has for three decades driven their firms to distraction if not destruction.

And this high-tech side show has created an appalling distraction for education and educators as well, as they have been taken for a ride on the roller coaster of computer development and marketing madness. The ride is by no means over, as telecommunications and entertainment giants jostle for favoured places on the education information superhighway into the nation's school and homes. Perhaps a little historical reflection will sober a few would-be enthusiasts among the present corps of teachers regarding not only the technologies themselves, but perhaps more importantly, the credibility and legitimacy of the self-appointed high-tech corporate saviours of education. Certainly, with state and federal politics once again greasing corporate entree into the education marketplace, and with the major teachers' unions now prostrate before visions of fibre optic utopia, there is little chance that reasonable reflection will stop the charade. Still, for what it's worth, this chapter offers a glimpse of the littered record of past performances.

What follows are case studies of three major corporate ventures into computer-based education. These studies are derived from proprietary documents – confidential memos, letters, strategic plans – now available in public archives. We look first at the initial attempts by Big Business to market computer-based education, in the mid-1960s, examining the joint ventures of IBM and SRA, and of GE and Time, through the private papers of key participants. We then examine Control Data Corporation's archival records documenting efforts to market its PLATO system in schools in the 1970s and early 1980s.

The final section of the chapter carries the insights from these case studies into the 1980s and 1990s, for which proprietary documentation from high-tech corporations is not yet readily available. Here we turn first to the 1980s, in which the combination of video games, microcomputer technology, the LOGO programming language for children, and a successful information age ideology of computer literacy led to the widespread introduction of computers into schools. We conclude with a dubious look at the recent hyperbole about multimedia, CD ROMs, and the information highway, and we note the new driving impulse of the entertainment, cable, and telecommunications industries in the latest marketing of a technology bill of goods to the schools.

BACKGROUND: MILITARY R&D AND CBE

The driving impulse behind early development of computer-based instruction was the Defense Department. (For a detailed account of the military origins of computer-based education, see Noble, 1991.) Most early research in the field took place under military sponsorship, and substantial military sponsorship of research in artificial intelligence, cognitive science, multimedia, and virtual reality applied to training and learning, continues to this day. 'Computers would probably have found their way into classrooms sooner or later,' wrote one knowledgeable observer in 1986, 'but without [ongoing military support] it is unlikely that the electronic revolution in education would have progressed as far and as fast as it has' (Fletcher & Rockaway, 1986, p. 18). In fact, military agencies have provided three-fourths of all funding for educational technology research over the last three decades, and each year the military spends as much on educational technology research as the Department (formerly Office) of Education has spent in a quarter century.

In the late 1950s, when it all began, military agencies and military contractors were pretty much the only players in the field of computer-based education. The field itself grew out of military research and development at the juncture of two fields: training science and what we now call computer science. Within training science, CBE grew out of research in programmed instruction, teaching machines, and other training devices and simulators developed in the decade after World War II. Within computer science, CBE grew out of research on 'human factors' problems in military computer-based information and command-and-control systems. These problems arose within attempts to link people with computers in large, real-time systems such as continental air defense systems; they involved man-machine communication, computer-based decision-making, and psychological studies of human information processing.

Research on 'automated instruction' – programmed instruction and teaching machines – had been proceeding in the military during the postwar decade, mostly within a host of military 'human engineering' laboratories such as the Air Force Personnel and Training Research Center and the Army's Human Resources Research Office. Many of the first experiments in CBE involved simulations of such teaching machines, with the computer generating and coordinating instructional frames.

Early CBE experiments in the late 1950s were taking place at a handful of sites scattered around the country. One was the SAGE air defense system site at Hanscom Field outside Boston. At SAGE, the goal was to arrange for the SAGE computers, off-line, to train the system's air controllers and radar operators (called 'human components') as the technology was continually updated or changed. The System Development Corporation in Santa Monica, California, the birthplace of the 'systems approach' and a spinoff of the Air Force's RAND Corporation, was also a key site for experiments in computer-based automated classrooms. One SDC researcher, Harry Silberman, compared CBE to computer programming: 'Instead of programming computer behaviour, the educator is programming human behaviour' (Silberman, 1967, p. 17). The vision of CBE at SDC was for educational institutions to become 'man-machine digital systems in their own right,' with 'attributes of real-time control systems' (Sackman, 1967, pp. 562, 568). At the University of Illinois, the first experiments with cost-effective automated instruction, via time-shared PLATO terminals, were lavishly funded by a wide range of military agencies.

At the military research firm Bolt, Beranek, and Newman in Cambridge, Massachusetts, still a major player in CBE development in the 1990s, research on human-machine communication and interaction led to early experiments in automated instruction. These experiments suggested to BBN researchers that CBE, with the 'deliberate exploitation of reinforcement and human engineering techniques, might be used to 'trap' the attention of students' (Licklider, 1967, p. 226). This view of CBE as a control system for students was also central in the research conducted at Stanford University's Institute for Mathematical Studies in the Social Sciences, the eventual birthplace of Computer Curriculum Corporation, still now a major CBE vendor. Here the focus was on early reading and mathematics instruction. Researchers were interested in studying children's mathematics learning under controlled laboratory conditions provided by precise computer-based sequencing. They were also interested in 'engineering' reading instruction through the design of an instructional control system in which the 'system to be controlled [was] the human learner' (Atkinson, 1968, p. 69). The ideal was to derive 'a differential equation for the motion of students through a course' and to map the 'student trajectory' through the system (Suppes, 1978, p. 279).

At IBM's Research Center at Yorktown Heights, New York, early CBE experiments focused on the simulation of Skinner's teaching machines which were then being manufactured by IBM. IBM was also interested in embedding training capabilities within their computers, as in the SAGE environment. IBM at the time was the prime contractor with the Air Force for the SAGE system.

IBM was also interested in exploring the possibility of new markets for their computer equipment.

These scattered experiments constituted the research base for CBE in the late 1950s and early 1960s. The experiments were rudimentary, using cumbersome equipment thrown together for the purpose, and utilizing local school children for experimentation either on site or in a local school. The primary focus in all sites was research, either on automated instructional delivery and control systems, or on man-machine communication and human learning.

A turning point came in the mid-1960s, when these isolated research efforts would suddenly become the darlings of Fortune 500 companies, and CBE researchers would be courted with lucrative offers for high-stakes commercial ventures. Most would be 'bought up' by large firms (Cremin, 1968, p. 95), and for some, this occasioned opportunities for 'gaining access to children of school age for ... experimental investigations' (Melton, 1959, p. 103). Computer-based education would suddenly leap from military-funded experimental tinkering to corporate panacea for the nation's schools.

CBE Becomes a Commercial Venture

By the late 1950s and early 1960s, military funding began to dry up. Defense contractors dependent on federal funding began to seek other sources of federal money and new subsidized markets. In the years 1958 through 1965, they found their answer in 'a powerful [new] base of operations [which] was established for the entrance of [these] American corporations into the profitable education industries' (Gandy, 1976, p. 61). With the passage of the National Defense Education Act in 1958, followed by the Vocational Education Act in 1963, the Equal Opportunity Act in 1964, and, finally, the Elementary and Secondary Education Act in 1965, major defense contractors found their new subsidized market. This new market was established overnight to lure defense contractors to apply their military-derived 'systems approach' to the newly discovered societal problems of poverty and educational failure. This new market answered the needs of a foundering defense industry as well as the desires of educational technology researchers seeking alternative sources of support and new 'living laboratories' for their experimentation.

Through massive new federal expenditures now filling the void of military cutbacks, computer-based educational technology was given its first chance for widespread commercialization. The education and poverty markets provided the perfect opportunity for warmed-over military hardware and systems to be refashioned as weapons in the war on poverty and educational failure. This latest subsidization of educational technology research, development, and commercialization was, in effect, 'the reselling of the Pentagon' (Gandy, 1976, p.

61). According to Oscar Gandy's dissertation by that title, the new social legislation enabled the capitalization of education with military technology and created an education market that did not exist before. Furthermore, the capitalization subsidy was producer-driven rather than consumer-driven, opening up a market for defense industry manufacturers rather than addressing any documented needs of schools, teachers or students.

Once established, industrial research and development in instructional technology became as much a marketing effort as a research effort, directed toward providing evidence or serving as models for the utilization of capital technologies. And 'once the subsidy [was] established, and a clientele lobby [of manufacturers] formed, political manoeuvring [became] focused more often on questions of 'how much,' instead of 'whether or not' (Gandy, 1976, p. 90). In short, once the door was opened that encouraged defense contractors to pursue the education technology market, it would never again be closed. The idea of the technological capitalization of education, and specifically that of computer-based teaching and learning systems, was an idea whose time had come (however prematurely), and the next three decades, up to the present moment, have witnessed the seemingly inevitable unfolding, with numerous episodic echoes, of this first euphoric moment in the early 1960s.

In the words of one spokesman for defense contractor, Westinghouse, whose Westinghouse Learning Corporation was one of the early beneficiaries of the new capitalization subsidy in education, the goal was 'to establish a beachhead' (Gandy, 1976, p. 185) in the emerging education market, which was in fact an 'unnatural market' (Gandy, 1976, p. 202), fattened repeatedly by government largesse far in advance of technological sophistication and far in advance of the capabilities of education consumers to use or even imagine.

The approaches of choice in the establishment of the beachhead were acquisition, diversification, and merger. Between 1964 and 1966, 120 combines and mergers were established to tap the education market. These hybrids typically coupled the 'hardware' of technology firms with the instructional materials, or 'software,' provided by publishing houses. In short order, these couplings brought together IBM and educational publisher SRA; General Electric and Time/Silver Burdett; Xerox and Ginn/American Education Publications; RCA and Random House; Raytheon and D. C. Heath; RCA and Prentice-Hall; Litton and American Book Company; CBS and Allyn and Bacon/Holt, Rinehart, and Winston; GTE/Sylvania and Reader's Digest; and 3M and Newsweek. These mergers and joint ventures continued the military model of engineering psychology in its attempt to wed the hard-nosed engineering disciplines to the 'softer' social and human sciences of instructional psychology and pedagogy. Their goal was to tap what was considered to be an enormous potential market in the new 'knowledge industry' of electronic publishing and 'electronic education.'

This was the grail motivating the sudden avalanche of unprecedented corporate interest in the public schools.

SRA AND IBM[2]

The first to leap into the fray was IBM which, as noted earlier, had been conducting basic experiments in computer-based instruction for half a dozen years at its Yorktown Heights, New York, Research Center. IBM was also the prime contractor for the nation's massive new SAGE air defense system, within which perhaps the very first military experiments in computer-based instruction were conducted.

In 1964 IBM bought Science Research Associates (SRA), a Chicago firm specializing in social science research (its earlier name had been Social Science Research Associates). SRA was then the largest commercial publisher of educational tests and modular reading materials in the country. The purchase of SRA was IBM's first acquisition in thirty years, and it was the crowning achievement of SRA's urbane and entrepreneurial founder and president, Lyle M. Spencer. Spencer's firm had been wooed by other corporate suitors, including Xerox, but Spencer chose to join IBM because of its 'incomparable depth and resources' ('IBM's Next Target,' 1966, p. 60) and because he had decided that 'computers had to be the wave of the future in education' ('IBM's Next Target,' 1966, p. 60). For its part, IBM's Chairman Thomas J. Watson, Jr., was attracted by SRA's highly successful modular reading kits and by its sophisticated familiarity with the education industry. Most of all he was persuaded by Spencer himself, whose negotiation with Watson was kept secret from all SRA personnel until the deal was a *fait accompli* (Larson, 1984).

SRA had been started in 1938, during the Depression, by Spencer and a college friend at the University of Chicago. They were prompted by a professor's suggestion that there was an urgent need for 'pharmaceutical houses' (Spencer, 1961b) in the sciences of human behaviour to concoct the same sorts of practical applications that had been done in the biological and physical sciences. This seemed like an exciting idea to the two young men, and it was the deciding factor in starting SRA. The first venture for the firm was the research and publication of occupational information for unemployed youths and was highly successful. During World War II Spencer was heavily involved in military selective service and aptitude testing as well as in studies of soldier morale, motivation, and attitudes. He developed the point score demobilization system under which millions of servicemen returned to civilian life. When he returned to the firm from this military exposure, he redirected its focus toward the development and marketing of aptitude testing and instructional materials. SRA soon began publishing selective service tests, the Kuder Preference Record, the Iowa Tests, and the Thurstone test batteries.

In the late 1950s, SRA became involved in the brief commercial effort by many companies to market teaching machines and programmed instruction to the schools. These ventures were generally hasty and ill-conceived; SRA's teaching machine division, according to Spencer, 'promptly fell on its clavicles' (Spencer, 1962a) soon after it was started. Nonetheless, Spencer had become smitten with the prospects of automated instruction and with the writings of Fritz Machlup on the knowledge explosion and its implications for publishing and for education. 'With vastly accelerating increases in the field of knowledge,' he insisted, 'improvements must be made in the rate of learning' (Spencer, 1961b). Spencer was frustrated by the inefficiency of children's learning, which he likened to 'that impressive hunk of machinery – the wood burning locomotive' (Spencer, 1966b). He figured that children were learning at 5 per cent efficiency and that SRA, with its 'major stake in the huge field of measuring man's capacity to learn,' must lead the effort to turn this around (Spencer, 1961a).

By 1962, Spencer was also already talking about 'learning systems' designed to 'take all students of a given group over a carefully planned route to a predetermined goal' (Spencer, 1962a). 'The material presented,' he insisted, 'must itself compel the student's attention, requiring a minimum of routine help from the teacher' (Spencer, 1962a). Spencer, a fervent champion of industrial automation, believed that such systems would improve the quality of education, speed it up, and reduce its cost. SRA had by then a successful learning system in its modular reading labs, which were SRA's big moneymaker ever since Donald Parker had sold SRA his method for cutting up books and putting them in boxes to individualize and 'teacher-proof' reading instruction. 'Leave the teacher out of this,' Parker later explained. 'That's the magic of this. *To hell with the teacher* ... She wouldn't know what to do. What I say to the teacher is, 'Teacher, I have raised you to a new level. You are now a learning consultant ... Mrs. Jones, you are really something now' (Parker, 1984). Whether or not the teacher was something, the reading lab certainly was. Its profits, based on the 'razor blade' principle, came from the sales of consumable workbooks rather than from the kits themselves, and despite recurring allegations that the kits' tests were rigged to ensure success (Larson, 1984), these modules 'put the company on the map' (Larson, 1984).

Despite the success of the reading labs, however, Spencer envisioned far more sophisticated electronic and even chemical enhancements of the learning process. Echoing the early SRA vision of a pharmaceutical house in the social sciences, Spencer saw great potential in exploring pharmaceutical education through LSD, RNA, and through what he called a 'love of learning lozenge' or LLL (Spencer, 1965e). But electronic engineering seemed the readiest route to learning efficiency. Spencer believed that 'greater sophistication in learning processes [would] require a wide variety of new technological contrivances' (Spencer, 1964). Relying on the new computer model of human intelligence, Spencer was most interested, specifically, in the 'process by which humans learn ... the input system to the brain, its analytic and logical process, and its data retrieval and output mechanism' (Spencer, 1965c). But computers were more than a model for intelligence for Spencer; they would be the principal vehicle for its improvement.

Spencer exulted in new possibilities of computer assisted instruction along with the use of slide projectors, closed circuit television, language laboratories, dictating equipment, microfiche, and video storage. 'Educational progress during the next decade,' he declared, 'can, for the first time, match the strides made by the hard science technologies' (Spencer, 1965e). 'We are banking on the fact that education and electronics do have more in common than their initial letter, e' (Spencer, 1968). Spencer estimated the educational technology market to be worth $500 million a year and he considered it 'the most exciting thing around these days' (Spencer, 1966d). He estimated that the largely untapped market for the application of computers to education was 'huge' – possibly a 'billion dollar business' (Spencer, 1965d), if it could successfully replace teachers. 'Today,' he even announced with confidence, 'we have for the first time in history an opportunity to wipe out poverty through education' (Spencer, 1966c). Despite his euphoria, however, Spencer was aware that 'no new technology – television, radio – developed specifically for educational purposes has made money. The hardware that has the greatest impact on education is the unexciting school bus' (Spencer, 1968).

In the fall of 1963 Spencer negotiated the purchase of SRA by IBM for the 'amazing price' of $66 million in IBM stock, over fifty times SRA's annual earnings. Spencer became a member of the IBM Board and suddenly owned more IBM stock, according to one account, than IBM Chairman Thomas J. Watson, Jr., himself, who was the man behind the deal for IBM (Keppel, 1983). IBM was in awe of the vast size of the education market, with $45 billion in overall expenditures in 1965 and with federal expenditures at $8.4 billion and rising. 'There was the great hope that [we] ... could open up an entirely new field' (Learson, 1982) and that the purchase of SRA would seed the movement by giving early users something to start with. One longtime SRA executive later explained the deal more succinctly: 'Tom [Watson] was looking for a way to introduce computers into schools, and Lyle sold him a bill of goods' (Van Ausdale, 1984).

Spencer was certainly a shrewd, competitive negotiator with 'an eye for money' (Bloom, 1985), someone who did not suffer fools gladly. 'If Spencer's business partners got in the way he had them for breakfast,' noted one longtime associate (Keppel, 1984). But Spencer was also awestruck by IBM and what it represented for him. 'Directly across from our hotel,' he told a group of executives, 'stands a brand new, starkly modern ... ten story IBM building, a fountain playing in the piazza, and computer reels whirring behind plate glass windows. It exudes modernity, high technology, the forward progressing look. It also says integrity, security through size, financial stability, good quality. IBM represents at least one order of magnitude of difference ... from any ... publishers' (Spencer, 1965d). He exulted that '1965 looks like the most important and dramatic of SRA's 26 years ... Now, for the first time, we have all the horses and backing anyone could ask for.' 'We are now,' he said, 'the guy to beat' (Spencer, 1965b).

Spencer apparently had achieved just the right combination for the task ahead: 'Just as IBM is famed for the application of engineering to the problems of business,' he wrote, 'so SRA is highly regarded for its ability to apply engineering to the problems of the classroom' (Spencer, 1965a). He also apparently was heading in the right direction: 'Our basic mission [is] the interface between IBM hardware and SRA learning systems,' he noted. 'Materials and hardware, built together. *Never been done*' (Spencer, 1965b). 'It is evident ... that nowhere yet has the problem of how modern technology can be applied most meaningfully to learning been tackled constructively, let alone grasped ... When first success occurs in this area – [it] will really change the industry' (Spencer, 1965b).

Spencer had 'a year of lead time' (Spencer, 1965a) before other corporate combines entered the field in 1965, as well as the perfect political context, for 'the huge injection of federal funds ... is lighting the fuse for a new era of educational progress without precedent in history' (Spencer, 1965e). Spencer also had some of the finest minds in education on his advisory board, including Ralph Tyler, Benjamin Bloom, and Francis Keppel; and he benefited from IBM's involvement with the CBE research of Patrick Suppes and Richard Atkinson at Stanford through their use of the new IBM 1500. Spencer fully believed Suppes's wildly exaggerated claims for computer-based education that it would soon provide an individual tutor for each child, an Aristotle for each Alexander. 'We call it CAI,' he stated with pride, insisting from the rudiments of Suppes's lab that it was 'possible to get remarkably sophisticated dialogue going between student and computer' (Spencer, 1965c). In July, 1966, he announced to the SRA staff, 'The first CAI program was recently delivered by the SRA-IBM team to Stanford University ... It marked the dawn of a new day in education' (Spencer, 1966a).

But Spencer's euphoria over the promise of CBE and about the invincibility of SRA/IBM proved remarkably short-sighted. Almost immediately after SRA and IBM joined forces, the competition began to mobilize. Within a year, over a hundred such combines entered the fray, uniting powerful technology firms with large publishing houses. And almost from the start, Spencer's frenzied motivation came more from glancing back over his shoulder at the competition than from any immediate product potential generated by his own operations.

'Our lead time is slipping away,' he warned in September, 1965 (Spencer, 1965d). By July, 1966, there was a real sense of urgency concerning the competition. Spencer was above all concerned about the new partnership between General Electric and Time, Inc. called the General Learning Corporation, which he felt had the greatest strength of all competitors (Spencer, 1965b). (As we shall see, GLC saw IBM/SRA as 'fearsome competition' as well.) Ironically, Spencer had earlier championed GE's advertising motto, insisting that 'SRA should be looking for an educational equivalent to GE's 'Progress Is Our Most Important Product'' (Spencer, 1962b), since the 'infinite improvability of man [sic]' – the idea of progress in education – was SRA's 'fundamental policy' (Spencer, 1962b). Now beating GLC had become its primary agenda. 'It seemed that we had a comfortable lead,' announced Spencer, but SRA experienced an 'unpleasant jolt in the last two weeks' when GE sold thirty of their terminals to education institutions (Spencer, 1966a). 'The implications for us are great, [and] we can expect many more [such jolts] in the next few years [despite] IBM's great capacity to counterpunch' (Spencer, 1966a).

Among the weapons in the IBM arsenal was the computer-based Yorktown Heights Research Center, which, Spencer believed, made available the facilities to experiment with many curriculum programs, 'and, within weeks, [to] prove or disprove them or help to improve their effectiveness (rather than [in] years, using current research methods)' (Spencer, 1964). SRA was also the first educational publisher selected by the new Office of Economic Opportunity to run a Job Corps Training Center with emphasis on tutorial and individual instruction. The SRA Job Corps Center, for which SRA received $8.7 million, was conceived by Spencer as 'a living laboratory' (Spencer, 1965a) in basic skills curriculum development which could eventually be incorporated into computer-based instructional software.

An early motto of SRA was: 'Go after the invalids; they represent someone else's mistakes. They represent the market for innovation in education, as well as the best guides to it' (Spencer, 1967a). In this spirit SRA/IBM focused its efforts on the newly discovered 'disadvantaged' student population, emphasizing the basic skills that had made its DISTAR reading program, originally purchased by SRA from the University of Illinois, such a successful product.

SRA had a sophisticated cadre of Ph.D.s in education, testing and measurement as well as a talented sales force. Its advisory board of distinguished educators were flown to exotic locations for high-powered brainstorming and strategy sessions. These strategies included the use of media and computers for more comprehensive learning systems as well as for more sophisticated methods of evaluating instructional results. There was also a focus on teacher training approaches, on student motivational techniques, and on tapping the education and training market in underdeveloped countries. Some strategies, according to the later reflections of one SRA veteran, were not always above board. One SRA vice president, for example, had staff associates sleuthing at the Educational Testing Service, a longtime rival of Spencer, to 'get something unsavoury' on ETS (Diamond, 1985). Another strategy was the creation of the Spencer Foundation itself. Spencer's notes from July, 1967, suggested that he '[e]xplore the idea of having a non-profit adjunct for corporations ... Could be enormously valuable to SRA and IBM in exploring learning ideas and accepting government contracts that are not appropriate for profit' (Spencer, 1967c).

Despite these varied strategies and directions, by 1967 Spencer observed that 'it may be three years before we bring a joint product to market. We are uneasy about the competitive aspects of this matter, because since our merger at least 11 other electronics firms have joined hands with education publishers. *They apparently assumed we knew what we were doing!*' (underline mine) (Spencer, 1967b). In reality, 'this combined approach turns out to be much more difficult an undertaking than either we or anyone else had anticipated' (Spencer, 1967b).

Among the unanticipated problems, in addition to competitive pressures and premature confidence in technological solutions, the overwhelming difficulty involved the wedding of an engineering staff with a group of educators and publishers. In 1968 Spencer's most vivid memory of the previous 'four tempestuous years' was of the 'amusing but impossible problems' of communication between the educators and the engineers (Spencer, 1968). Another unexpected set of obstacles involved popular resistance to corporate intrusion in the schoolhouse. Spencer quickly learned that '[w]e must not underestimate ... irrational fears about combining education and technology: dehumanization of teaching, replacing teachers, fear of control by the federal government or by big corporations forming an education-industrial complex' (Spencer, 1968). The U.S. population had not yet been prepared ideologically for this first technological assault on education.

The problems were also related to Spencer himself, who was 'very anxious about money,' 'couldn't keep to a course,' and made 'too many vacillations' (Harris, 1983). He loved new ideas but was extremely anxious about having them fail; [he] blew hot and cold' (Harris, 1983). He was an 'impatient man, a tough guy to work for, no good at having partners. He had to be in charge' (Keppel, 1984). Spencer was above all Spencerian, a social Darwinist who was only interested in 'tough, talented, bright people, people who could compete' (Keppel, 1984). This focus on elite talent was at the heart of his long-standing interest in the improvement and measurement of human achievement and learning, and it no doubt lay behind his hubristic faith in improving human intellectual capacities through technological prowess and ingenuity.

Spencer also had a legendary reputation for wine, women, and song. His drinking capacities were 'fantastic,' and, with the looks of Joseph Cotton, 'he was a Don Juan, stayed up drinking every night, [and] was never home, ... liv[ing instead] in Chicago nightclubs' (Keppel, 1984). Spencer died quite suddenly, in August, 1968, of pancreatic cancer at the age of 57. Despite two marriages and five sons, 'he wrecked his life. He killed himself' (Keppel, 1984). And when he died, his exaggerated visions for SRA/IBM died with him. Although SRA remained a division of IBM for another two decades before being eventually sold off to Macmillan/McGraw-Hill, 'the effect of SRA on IBM revenue ... never fulfilled what the original hopes were' (Learson, 1982). SRA never had a product to match the Reading Labs of the early 1960s, and its involvement in computer-based education remained marginal in the years that followed. Such was the fate of the very first Big Business venture hawking ill-conceived computer-based panaceas to the nation's schools. It would not be the last.

THE GENERAL LEARNING CORPORATION[3]

One of Lyle Spencer's close friends up to his death was Francis Keppel, an early SRA advisory board member who was so concerned about Spencer's lifestyle that he 'almost formed a club for the care and preservation of Lyle Spencer ... to control his supply of whisky and women' (Keppel, 1983).

It was Francis Keppel, who, first as U.S. Commissioner of Education and then as Assistant Secretary of Health, Education and Welfare, guided through Congress the ESEA legislation that opened the door to industry participation in the nation's schools. Keppel was a champion of technology in education, and in his book, *The Necessary Revolution in American Education* (Keppel, 1966), he outlined the path that such capitalization of education must take. He believed that private industry, in particular the powerful defense technology firms, could provide the ideas and hardware to fuel the 'revolution.' 'Seventy percent of the scientists that graduate don't go into universities,' Keppel explained. 'They go into industry. And if by legislation I'm kept from doing business with the private sector, I'm deprived of help from those brains ... We need ideas, the development of equipment and procedures. We need access to people like Western Electric' (Bowen, 1965g).

In March, 1965, during an interview with Time, Inc. executives (whom he would later join as head of the General Learning Corporation), Keppel shared his 'semi-private thoughts' on the upcoming ESEA legislation. He told about a 'loaded, missing clause' (Bowen, 1965g) in the bill's language which would, by omission, allow him to contract with the private sector and especially with large technology research firms. 'Look there,' he told the Time men, 'Read that. It's hidden language. What's left out: see if you can find it. There in Title IV.' The Time men read and could find only one passage permitting the Office of Education to make grants to private, non-profit organizations. 'It says 'No such grant may be made to a private agency ... other than non-profit,'' Keppel pointed out. 'But it doesn't say 'no contract'! So if this thing goes through that way, we can write contracts with private companies. It's the missing language that counts' (Bowen, 1965g). With this subterfuge Keppel opened the door through which many Fortune 500 corporations, including such major defense contractors as GE, ITT, RCA, Westinghouse, Raytheon, AT&T, Honeywell, Litton, and Xerox entered the field of public primary and secondary education for the first time.

One of the most formidable of these new ventures was the General Learning Corporation (GLC), established in January, 1966 as a joint venture by General Electric and Time, Inc. The origin of the partnership was a golf course conversation in the summer of 1964 between Time president James Linen and GE treasurer John Lockton (Prendergast, 1986, p. 210). Both companies were looking for ways to diversify, and both were intrigued by projections of the new education market, especially by the prospect of huge federal outlays for education. As Keppel was to explain later, after passage of ESEA promised ten-figure federal education aid annually, 'a billion dollars looking for a good, new way to be spent does not ordinarily turn the American businessman into a shrinking violet' (Keppel, 1967, p. 188).

Between the fall of 1964 and April, 1965, the deadline set for a decision on the joint venture proposal, the bright young men of Time, Inc., under orders from Chairman Henry Luce himself, scurried across the country investigating the state of the art of computer-based educational technology as well as the resources of giant GE, their proposed partner. Despite the profound skepticism of the investigating task force, the decision was made, the details were worked out, and the costly joint venture was launched with great public fanfare at the start of 1966. It took but a year, despite the frantic enlistment of prestigious officers and consultants from around the country, for the venture to collapse in March, 1967 and eventually to 'shrivel on the vine' before being sold (Solberg, 1984). The story of how this happened offers one dramatic account of how the barons of business and industry have impulsively and avariciously pursued their technological fantasies into the swollen yet uncharted and unproven market of education, taking educators and schools for a costly, worthless ride.

Time's initial interest in the joint venture grew from the runaway success of the Time-Life Book Division, with its mail-order educational feature books on The Sea, The Universe, The Cell, and so forth. Time executives immediately recognized that Time-Life had invented exemplary educational materials and that Time's publications were in fact educational tools, as Chairman Henry Luce had always contended. Time, Inc. proceeded to buy the elementary textbook publisher, Silver-Burdett, and was looking to plunge still further into the education market which Linen predicted would be worth $500 million to Time within ten years (Solberg, 1984).

In early 1964, Time-Life Books had launched an Educational Systems Project team to investigate Time's possible role in the post-Sputnik, university-based curriculum reform movement. Project team leader Ezra Bowen, the Director of Educational Research and Development for Time-Life Books, conveyed the team's optimism, even as it groped cautiously in the dark for new ideas and strategies. Bowen wrote, in a long-winded memo entitled 'Education Project X – Modus Operandi (seen from the beginning, darkly),' 'We are going to develop and produce the key materials for change in American classrooms: better, newer, brighter, more understandable, more exciting, more challenging materials to arouse the curiosity, the understanding, the sense of being important, of already being part of the world, of having the chance to shape the world, that kids have never had before. There is no limit to our market, because every kid needs these things' (Bowen, 1964a).

Bowen warned, however, that 'if we tell the world that now is the time for change in our schools, and Time-Life books is the agent for change, and here are our products, then we had better be brilliantly right the first time. Because if we are not, all the pedants and scholars and parents and teachers and mossbacks – not to mention our business rivals and the kids themselves, will boo us right off the stage' (Bowen, 1964a). Bowen was convinced that 'as we start out, … the bulk of the ideas and mechanical tools we need are already in existence' (Bowen, 1964a). All Time-Life had to do was tap the scholars, educators, and inventors doing this sort of work, 'leaving no stone unturned.' Its own contribution would be to bring together the scholars' knowledge, the educators' experience, and the inventors' scientific ingenuity, and to 'combine, interpret, and present them in the classroom better than ever before, and in ways that have never been done before' (Bowen, 1964a).

'The big hurdle' in all of this, Bowen reasoned, was marketing. 'The great hazard … is not in what we do, or in whether our primary audience (the kids) will accept it. The hazard is the great wall of parents, superintendents, teachers, legislators ad infinitum that we must win over in order to be permitted to bring our materials to the children. For this reason … we must … act with agonizing care, … in picking not only the right materials to present but also the moment and method and place of presentation, so that … the whole American community feels that the materials we produce are what the community wants, badly needs, and must have' (Bowen, 1964a).

Bowen and others visited Education Services Inc., the brainchild of MIT physicist Jerrold Zacharias, whose high school curriculum reform efforts had been generously sponsored by the National Science Foundation since just before the Sputnik scare in 1957. Bowen considered ESI to be 'the biggest, most comprehensive reform group of all, and alas, the most disorganized' (Bowen,

1964b). He referred to the presentations of Zacharias's film-based physics curriculum and of co-reformer Jerome Bruner's social studies curriculum as 'monkey shows' (Neil, 1965). He derided these university scholars as 'unbelievably naive' about publishing and collective work, and he accused ESI of 'intellectual snobbery' because anything 'popular' was deemed beneath them (Neil, 1965). Some of this hostility was no doubt because Time had done some earlier gratis work for ESI, receiving no feedback or credit. For all these reasons, Time and ESI never became partners, although Bruner would later become a consultant for GLC.

Bowen also investigated researchers in curriculum reform at Harvard, Cornell, and universities in Minnesota, Colorado, California. Bowen was especially keen on 'linking the names of Harvard and Time Inc. on a whole spread of materials' (Bowen, 1964b). Of one Harvard researcher, he noted: 'I admire his approach ... and I like the address' (Bowen, 1964b). None of these contacts led to any serious collaboration with Time, Inc., even though Bowen lobbied Keppel in Washington to recognize that 'the private sector can greatly assist the curriculum reform movement' (Bowen, 1964c) and later assured the Time-Life staff that 'Keppel at OE has been bearded and now realizes he may have to work out some way for his grantees to work with publishers in the early stages of their projects' (Bowen, 1964b).

In May, 1964, Charles Silberman, a *Time* writer later to become a prominent journalist of 1960s education reform, filed a report on the R&D project in education in which he outlined the shape of the coming 'education revolution.' He recommended that Time 're-examine our traditional policy of not dealing with hardware ... This could lead to the actual manufacture of hardware or working partnerships with hardware manufacturers' (Silberman, 1964, p. 5).

Enter GE, a giant electronics firm which had recently suffered a major loss when the Pentagon switched to ICBMs in the early 1960s leaving thousands of GE engineers unemployed. GE was looking for a way to diversify and to put those engineers to work in a profitable new market.

GE was IBM's single biggest private customer and in fact the most extensive private user of computers in the country (Solberg, 1964b). In the previous ten years they had 'jumped feet first' into two information-related businesses – computers and guidance-communication systems for space vehicles. In its largely military-sponsored research, the company was heavily invested in systems engineering, 'the planning and design of an aggregation of many factors to achieve a single best performance for all of them, together' (Solberg, 1964b). Some GE scientists were working at the cutting edge of man-machine interface design, enthusing about possibilities of developing 'cybernetic anthropomorphous machines,' or 'machines that are like men' (Solberg, 1964b).

Such research efforts were precisely those providing the military context for CBE research, and not surprisingly, GE was also involved in finding 'opportunities for automation in education' (Bowen, 1965a, p. 2). Several recent ventures with educational technology products had been aborted abruptly after failing to meet expectations. In 1961 GE's Educational Business Development program had developed a 'student response system' with control panel and response buttons and a rudimentary language lab 'in which, at one point, the student got the foreign language in one ear and the English language translation simultaneously in the other' (a concept quickly discontinued) (Bowen, 1965a, p. 9). A desktop test-scoring machine was also 'on the drawing boards, but nowhere else' (Bowen, 1965a, p. 4). After a year and a half, top management soured and killed the program, which had been started, inappropriately, in GE's Aerospace Division. But 'though the music stopped in 1962, the melody lingered on in [some] hearts' (Bowen, 1965a, p. 4), and in 1963 GE's radio department brought out poorly conceived 'electronic education kits' ('build your own analogue computer or PA system') which were soon dropped, although they enabled the company to rid itself of an oversupply of transistors (Bowen, 1965a, p. 5). In 1964, a five-month 'study of the opportunities in the education market' conducted by a team from marketing, engineering, and accounting (but not education), 'recommended that GE proceed into the education battle' (Bowen, 1965a, p. 5). Once again, top management killed the plan, although GE did come out with its successful though primitive 'Show and Tell' consumer educational toy.

By late 1964, GE was drawn to the promise of massive federal pump priming in education, and to dramatic increases in student enrolment, which meant to GE a larger potential education market and a greater need for technological teaching aids. The company projected that in ten years' time the market for such educational equipment would be almost $300 million (Solberg, 1964a, p. 3). The promotion of Fred Borch, GE's new young chairman, 'signalled the ascendancy of the marketing man' at GE (Solberg, 1964a, p. 3). Borch immediately directed the company to diversify into 'big, bold ventures' such as computers, nuclear power, and space, in order to counter the levelling off of capital and consumer spending for heavy electrical equipment and appliances. 'The overall theme [was] cosmic, ... reflecting the crystal balling of GE's high-powered, blue sky planning staff' (Solberg, 1964a, p. 3) which was intent on 'risking major resources in the development of new markets and technologies' (Solberg, 1964a, p. 3).

Such was the expansive context in which GE, parading the 'combat readiness' of its technological gear (Bowen, 1965a, p. 9), made an overture to Time, Inc. to enter the education market together. GE, with the second largest industrial research program in the country and with more patents than any other firm, was certain 'to be a big factor in [computers] in the years to come' (Solberg, 1964a, p. 3). It seemed quite a catch.

But Time, Inc. executives were far from convinced. Caution and skepticism toward a partnership with the electronics giant were the order of the day within the stately executive suites at Rockefeller Center.

Although GE's image in education was considered to be 'very good,' with its sponsorship of Mr. Wizard and College Bowl, still GE's contact with education and educators was considered 'tentative,' 'remote,' and 'frustrating' (Bowen, 1965a, p. 1). Bowen visited GE's Schenectady operations and reported, in January, 1965, 'GE's thoughts on education – though over-run with a kind of marketing mentality – are quite sound, but by no means sophisticated ... GE's educational equipment is rudimentary – surprisingly so. Basically they have built language labs, PA systems, computers, and TV sets. Little else. They have never tried to integrate a number of elements into a real system [and] at the moment, they are at a loss to know how to proceed. They smell a big market out there somewhere. But they are scared to death of the pitfalls ... after falling into two previous pits' (Bowen, 1965b, p. 2).

In an early position paper written in preparation for Time-GE talks in December, 1964, the Time task force warned that '... there is every need for caution. The information systems of the future are a bewitching rainbow. It is safe to predict that some solid companies will falter chasing after the pot of gold. Clearly, GE's proposal of collaboration must be viewed with utmost care' (Ellis & Mercer, 1964). The Time people were very wary of GE's control of the venture, asking, 'Do we want to be the bristles in somebody else's toothbrush?' (Ellis & Mercer, 1964). On the other hand, they wondered, 'Can Time, Inc. afford to remain aloof in the midst of a technological revolution?' (Ellis & Mercer, 1964).

From January 1 to April 1, 1965 a broad inquiry was conducted by a new Time task force to examine and evaluate current projects in CBE and to study the financial, marketing, and other problems and opportunities of collaboration with GE. In Ezra Bowen's 'rather negative preamble' (Bowen, 1965c) to the Task Force's charge, after a month of investigation he echoed Lyle Spencer's concern that 'we must face the fact that there is no precedent of financial success in the educational use of [technological] systems, or pieces thereof' (Bowen, 1965c). This new terrain was treacherous, but at the same time the spectre of the unknown engendered a collective giddiness; these were, after all, heady times when everything seemed possible. The skepticism persisted, however.

In mid-March, 1965, in a confidential memo, Bowen urged 'that we re-examine our intent very hard in the next few weeks. The decision we will be faced on April 16 will be of the first magnitude – perhaps the most important this company has made in ... years' (Bowen, 1965e, p. 5). He was wary of GE's intentions, especially their interest in controlling the joint venture. At this eleventh hour he was 'concerned at our lack of alternatives [besides GE], and the more or less passive position we now occupy because of that lack' (Bowen, 1965e, p.

5). Time staff were also wary of GE's interest in marketing educational toys. 'We have defined an educational system as an instructional learning loop' with education itself defined as 'the processes of teaching and learning.' [This] excludes entertainment as such. [None of us] wants anything to do with entertainment …, [so] if GE wants to go further into the entertainment business, it surely needs no help from Time, Inc.' (Bowen, 1965d).

There was skepticism, too, of the government's intentions. The task force wondered '… was the government luring industry into major commitments of time and people, commitments that would result in invaluable contributions of an R&D nature to education, but commitments which probably will never have the sort of mass payoff of which many industrialists dream?' (Bowen, 1965h, p. 2). Bowen reminded his colleagues, 'Let's not forget that part of our job is to decide whether Time, Inc. and GE should stay out of the educational system business' (Bowen, 1965d). He cited, as potential 'negative influences' in this business, teacher resistance as well as local resistance to costly innovation. He also feared '[n]ew breakthroughs in cognitive knowledge that may indicate that … personal motivation … and other factors involving human relationships are of transcendent importance in the learning process' (Solberg, 1966c, p. 24). He expressed concern, too, that '[n]ew breakthroughs in the field of pharmacology involving drugs that influence the nervous system and brain, may obviate the need for using computers for certain educational purposes' (Bowen, 1965d).

Despite such concerns, task force members visited CBE research sites around the country. They concluded that '[t]he technology in use in learning situations today amounts, in almost all cases, to no more than bits and pieces of systems' (Bowen, 1965c). IBM's Yorktown Heights educational computer programs were considered 'highly experimental and highly imperfect' (Bowen, 1965c), while SDC's machinery was viewed as 'somewhere between bland and downright insulting' (Bowen, 1965c). Bolt, Beranek, and Newman's human-to-computer dialogue project was 'no more than experimental' (Bowen, 1965c), as were Donald Bitzer's PLATO project at University of Illinois and Robert Glaser's project at Pittsburgh.

In February, Bowen concluded from these visits by him and others that '[t]he earliest I would speculate that we could have any piece of a system in any learning environment is one year from today [Feb., 1966]' (Bowen, 1965c). Bowen also visited Patrick Suppes' CBE project at Stanford in March, finding the operation 'highly imperfect' and 'so embryonic that every one pupil has one expert teacher hanging over him' (Bowen, 1965f). As incentive for Time to act quickly, Suppes told Bowen that he and Lyle Spencer were having a 'lively correspondence' and were almost 'at the point of no return' though the project was 'not yet in the embrace of IBM' (Bowen, 1965a, p. 13). Bowen, inquiring why Suppes focused on elementary schoolchildren, was 'stunned' that Suppes, then the father of young children, explained that such children 'don't ask difficult questions, [which would be] difficult to handle, technologically' (Bowen, 1965f). Bowen reiterated his warnings that 'April 1 brings us to a more decisive commitment than we now foresee for that date' (Bowen, 1965c, p. 15).

Despite the skepticism of the task force, the Time and GE leadership decided to go forward with the joint venture on April 16, 1965. After the decision, Time Publisher Rhett Austell wrote GE Vice President George Haller that '[n]otwithstanding our late entry in this field, we believe that our two companies are uniquely qualified to undertake this program on a scale and with a promise of success that no other companies can match' (Austell, 1965).

A timetable for the remainder of the year was then established to draw up a plan and a set of objectives for the new company which would be launched the following January. An augmented task force was established, now led by Norm Ross and Carl Solberg, director and assistant director of education, respectively, for Time-Life Books. These men accelerated the search for potential ideas and products linking technology with learning and teaching. They and their staff 'buzzed around romancing all the programmed-learning pioneers and other innovators from coast to coast' (Solberg, 1984), sizing up these researchers as possible consultants just as the researchers themselves paraded their wares before this formidable new potential sponsor.

In July several task force members attended the American Management Association (AMA) educational technology conference, the first major trade show by the recent entrants in the new educational technology market. Described by Bowen as 'something like the first, anxious encounter of the in-laws' (Ellis, 1965). Ellis added that '[i]t is very common to hear the new movers in education talk about the marriage of the public and the private sector ... In fact, the talk of matrimony is premature. It is more like a budding romance, with education playing the reluctant virgin to industry's ardent swain' (Ellis, 1965). But '[t]he educators are willing to compromise their virtue,' Ellis noted, reporting that the exhibition 'sounded like a convention of the Electronics Industries Association ...' (Ellis, 1965). He complained, 'Educators have been talking the [systems engineering] technicians' jargon with abandon in recent months, often with little understanding of its limitations. And many of the new products being exhibited, reported Ellis, 'appear to have been slapped together to cash in on the budding market ... full of bugs, ... gremlins ... [and] glitter, [mere] chrome-plated teaching machines' (Ellis, 1965).

At the AMA conference, it was extremely difficult for the technology-based giants to determine the size and shape of the market, which, all agreed, offered a 'breathtaking growth picture' (Ellis, 1965). The prediction considered most reliable by attendees saw public school outlays for teaching aids growing from $300 million a year in 1960 to $1.8 billion a year by 1975. The sales of text materials was projected to grow from $235 million to $1 billion in the same period. 'In the aggregate,' Ellis concluded, despite his apparent disappointment with the technology products on display, 'education looks like a sure bet for the future' (Ellis, 1965). Francis Keppel and Fritz Ianni, the two leaders of federal education policy, were on hand at the AMA convention to champion the new educational technology. Ianni, the Office of Education's director of research, exulted, 'I know of no other area which is so important as this one at present' (Ellis, 1965). Both men would soon be recruited by the new joint venture.

By mid-November, James A. Linen, Time, Inc. president and Time's 'mainspring' behind the joint venture, explained to his staff the finalized deal, which would amount to $37.5 million, with Time's half of the bargain in the form of its Silver-Burdett division. 'This will add a major new dimension to Time, Inc.'s involvement in the knowledge business' (Linen, 1965), he told them. On January 4, 1966, the new company was formally launched, with Richard Shetler from GE as president and Roy E. Larsen of Time, Inc. as chairman. Shetler was a former manager of GE's Missile Guidance Section and then became general manager of its entire Defense Programs Division. Larsen, a venerable member of Time's board, wasted little time in recruiting Francis Keppel to replace him as chairman. Other people who had been considered for the chairman slot included John W. Gardner, president of the Carnegie Foundation and a key education policy maker under President Kennedy, and Clark Kerr, Chancellor of the University of California. Keppel was considered to be a prime catch, lending immediate legitimacy to the joint venture.

The name for the new partnership, General Learning Corporation, was also chosen for reasons of immediate legitimacy. Norm Ross had urged for the use of the word 'Institute' in the name, thinking '[i]t transcends the commercial and, therefore, limiting ring of 'company' or 'corporation' ... It aspires to a place among the institutions of the academic community (e.g., MIT)' (Ross, 1965). Names originally considered and rejected along the way included 'Jefferson Institute,' 'Lincoln Institute,' 'Lifelong Learning Institute,' 'Learning, Inc.,' and 'Knowledge, Inc.'

The GLC business plan drawn up over the previous months called for marketing aimed, in order of priority, at schools, at OEO programs such as the Job Corps, at military and industrial training, and at the home. The plan noted that 'federal pump priming is, very likely, the factor that will put us in business' (Bowen, 1965c, p. 6). However, 'to be continually welcomed in the learning community,' Ezra Bowen added, 'systems must demonstrate a greater effectiveness over existing methods ... Thus we [must] give priority attention to demonstrating this greater effectiveness in certain selected situations where the results are, once again, measurable both in teaching terms and in dollar terms' (Bowen, 1965c, p. 6).

This research, development, and evaluation would lie at the heart of the marketing of new education products; it would itself, in fact, be marketing, and so the circumstances of implementation would have to appear scientifically precise while also affording optimal chances for success. Students, as always, would be the guinea pigs for such staged experimentation. 'The most promising circumstance in which to begin developing a system is a bonafide learning situation [such as] a school, where the problem can be pinpointed, the audience controlled, the results measured,' Bowen pointed out (Bowen, 1965c, p. 5). Furthermore, the site could not simply be any school system 'that thinks it might try to benefit in some vague, gratis way from working with GE and Time, Inc.' (Bowen, 1965c, p. 10). Bowen noted that a target school district would have to have a 'commitment to innovation, excellent administrative capacity, strong community support of ... innovation, a record of cooperation from a university, and the ability to acquire financing' (Bowen, 1965c, p. 10). These criteria, concluded Bowen, 'narrowed the choice to, at most, a half dozen school systems,' namely wealthy suburban school systems, such as those in Newton, Massachusetts, and Melbourne, Florida, already heavily penetrated by university and space research.

The new venture would also continue to target the OEO's Job Corps Program by running a center designed to provide basic skills to disadvantaged young men and women. The Job Corps charter was 'to engineer and design an educational system whereby these young men could develop into useful, socially adjusted, wage-earning members of the society' (Ellis, 1965, p. 7). GE had been running the Women's Job Corps Center in Clinton, Iowa, since June, 1965, and GLC would take over its operation. The Job Corps offered GLC considerable opportunities. The government was enthusiastic about adopting military training methods and technologies for use in its Job Corps operations. This was an invitation for further CBE experimentation, which Bob Ellis, GLC's new Planning Coordinator, called the 'brave new world of automated education' (Ellis, 1965, p. 8).

Ellis had reported in July that '[t]he government's list of industry partners in the Job Corps camps reads like the roster of the Apollo contractors: ITT, GE, Westinghouse, Litton, IBM ... For industry, the Job Corps offers the chance of getting the government to foot the research and development bill for developing educational systems ... Here at last was an opportunity to develop an educational system in which we did not have to concern ourselves with a traditional grading system, lock-step instruction, fixed class periods, parental and community interferences and many other factors contributing to educational inertia ... It could be advantageous for us to have the government provide both the massive financing for systems (which we may have trouble getting from schools), a controlled audience, and a learning situation totally committed to innovation' (Ellis, 1965, p. 4).

The Job Corps center as a research site also provided opportunity for marketing. As Carl Solberg noted a year later: 'To us it seems of course an opportunity to demonstrate the capabilities of the private sector in coping with unusually exacting – and exciting – problems of education' (Solberg, 1966d). Unfortunately, however, even though the first year's operation of the Clinton Job Corps Center by GE and then GLC seemed 'very successful,' the Center Director confessed that 'we don't really know why the good things are happening [t]here' (Solberg, 1966d). GLC even recommended hiring a sociologist to study the center closely in order to explain why it was working.

During the spring and summer months of 1966, GLC conducted a 'prodigious amount of investigation in computer-assisted learning.' In May, Ira Singleton of GLC's research and development staff visited Patrick Suppes at Stanford and reported that 'Suppes' work is highly experimental. It does not seem to be developed yet to the point where accurate and reliable commercial applications are possible.' Singleton confided, 'I cannot honestly credit [Suppes] with major educational achievements. It is true that he has attained a certain national renown, yet this could be due to his aggressiveness and to his glib outpourings of jargon. It could also be due to the fact that educators in his audience are bedazzled by the glitter of electronic equipment ... I see no wisdom in engaging Dr. Suppes as a consultant' (Singleton, 1966a). Fritz Ianni, now GLC consultant, seconded Singleton's concern that while 'Suppes is further along than anyone else ... the important question may be, 'Is he further along with something which will not eventually go?'' (Ianni, 1966).

Carl Solberg, Norm Ross, and others continued their visits to the laboratories of CBE researchers. Robert Glaser of Pittsburgh was hired as a principal consultant, and he in turn recommended others, including Robert Gagne, Robert Mager, and Robert Branson, although he recommended against the hiring of his former colleague at the American Institute of Research, John Flanagan, whom Glaser labelled primarily an 'extraordinary promoter' (Ellis, 1966) like Suppes. In June, Solberg revisited Wallace Feurzeig at BBN and William Uttal at the University of Michigan, who was instrumental in the early IBM CBE experiments at Yorktown Heights. In July, he visited Donald Bitzer at the University of Illinois, suggesting that GLC might use Bitzer's PLATO system.

GLC was motivated in these visits not only by research and development possibilities but by public relations as well. The company sought to provide support to key researchers in part because 'it would go a long way to create good will in the community we depend on for creation of new materials and their utilization' (Johnson, 1966, p. 4). GLC was concerned at this stage especially with its reputation. 'Anything that gives substance to the joint venture's genuine interest in improving education will be useful at all levels of our relations with people outside' (Johnson, 1966, p. 5).

Solberg also met again with Launor Carter and John Coulson at SDC to explore possible subcontracting or consulting by SDC. He found SDC's CBE research 'really rudimentary,' in fact 'ready for the Smithsonian' as a pioneering relic (Solberg, 1966a). Norm Ross reported to Solberg that, according to former

CBE researcher at SDC Harry Silberman, 'Once SDC had naive enthusiasm for the computer in learning, as he thinks others [such as GLC] do now' (Solberg, 1966a). Silberman insisted, said Ross, that CBE was not economically feasible in the mid-1960s and that when it gets to the actual day-to-day operations, 'it cools you off in a hurry' (Solberg, 1966a). Solberg was beginning to agree. After excursions to all the state-of-the-art CBE laboratories, Solberg concluded, yet again, in July, 1966 that '[c]omputer-assisted instruction is in the laboratory stage' (Solberg, 1966b).

But meanwhile, GLC staff were also meeting with research directors at the Navy and Air Force in order to determine areas of linkage in state-of-the-art education and training technology research. In June, 1966, the second major conference on educational technology was held under the joint sponsorship of the Office of Education, the Department of Defense, and a military-related industry group known as the National Security Industrial Association. This conference was held 'to develop support between industry, DOD, and OE in seeking solutions for educational and training problems' as well as 'to give industry an idea of the ... future market potentials in the $4 billion a year DOD education and training program' (Bernier, 1966). At the conference the new Office of Education Commissioner, Harold Howe, who had replaced Keppel, announced 'the eve of a major breakthrough in the use of electronic media and their organization into teaching systems that may change the character of education' (Bernier, 1966, citing *Christian Science Monitor* article, June 21, 1966, p. 12). Calling this moment 'unprecedented,' Howe continued the championing of private research and development by the Office of Education, even as reality was beginning to dawn on those in the know at GLC.

One incentive to ignore the truth was the furious competition among so many giants. Like Lyle Spencer at SRA/IBM, the GLC staff was forever looking over its shoulder at the formidable competition. The difference was that GLC and the competing companies in the 'education systems market' all had 'one thing in common: the fearsome competition of IBM,' due to its 'running start on the rest of the field, ... the sheer volume of its activity and the reputation it has gained through its hardware saturation policy' (Mebane, 1966, p. 1). Other competitors causing concern at GLC were Xerox, RCA/Random House, Raytheon/D. C. Heath, and Westinghouse. Control Data Corporation, which was supplying computers to the PLATO Project at the University of Illinois, was considered a 'smart, opportunistic company ... which could become an important factor in the market' (Mebane, 1966, p. 14). Many of these companies were busy making deals with the same small group of CBE researchers at Stanford, Pittsburgh, SDC, BBN, and elsewhere whom GLC was courting. As Lawrence Cremin observed, 'practically every one of the major guys who have been working in the field has been bought up' (Cremin, 1968, p. 95).

But some on the Time research and development staff were clearly becoming distressed. In one memo, Ira Singleton cautioned, 'The assumption that 'computers and computer-based systems will form an important part of the contribution which the joint enterprise can make' might prove false ... I have always been troubled that we have given short shrift to the possibility that computers are not of supreme value as teaching/learning devices, or that their values have yet to be demonstrated ... It may be that because of the nature of GLC itself, or because of the name and mission given to our task force, our thinking has been conditioned to a positive and affirmative view of computer-assisted learning. If so, our thinking will have been a little less than objective' (Singleton, 1966b, p. 2).

Singleton's concerns went still further. He wrote to Solberg, 'I wonder whether we should say that we will 'improve the quality of education' or 'improve the effectiveness of learning.' These seem brash statements – presumptuous ... In effect, we are saying that we will succeed where Dewey and countless others have failed. Would we insult educators, and would we raise doubts about our knowledge of the field and our competence to deal with it, if we advertised our intention to give education a 'one fell swoop' treatment that would straighten out all the kinks that still baffle researchers?' (Singleton, 1966b, p. 2).

By the start of the following year, one year after GLC was launched, things began to fall apart, long before any product was ready for market. Keppel was realizing that the technology was not there, and he was growing impatient with the technical preoccupations of his GE colleagues. Conflicts over contacts with government officials had already been brewing between the GLC office in Washington, DC, run by Shetler with his largely GE staff, and the New York office run by Keppel and the Time task force staff. With this came mistrust. Solberg confided in February, 1967 that 'the spectre of GE control looms larger ... I have visions of all kinds of monsters between Time-Life and the engineers ... I can't imagine GE letting other people have a significant say' (Solberg, 1967).

In March, 1967, the inevitable happened. More than 60 top officials and professionals at GLC lost their jobs in a 'massive shake-up' engineered by Keppel and the GLC board (Grant, 1967, p. A1). Dick Shetler was fired, with Keppel replacing him as president while still remaining chairman. The bitter shake-up stemmed from the drastically different views of the engineers and the educators about the direction of the company. 'To put it bluntly,' wrote Keppel in a confidential memo to the GLC board, 'I do not think that Dick and I have enough common understanding of the corporation's purpose ... to work together ... We differ on the extent to which the Corporation should build upon Federal contracts and upon ''hardware' as against learning materials' (Keppel, no date).

Thus software triumphed over hardware as Keppel came to realize that 'you can't take computers designed to put people on the moon and put them in the classroom' (Grant, 1967, p. A1). Almost all of the GE executives who were fired had formerly worked in GE's Apollo Support Division in Florida and were considered by Keppel to be 'gadgeteers' for whom the computer was the all-purpose panacea (Strogoff, 1967, p. 23). Keppel redirected the $37 million company toward the development of decidedly low tech learning materials targeted at academic and vocational education of disadvantaged students, abandoning the high flung promises for which the joint venture was originally launched.

Keppel later explained that 'technology was apparently of more interest to the technologist than to the teacher' (Keppel, 1971a), even though the available market for the new company had been expected to grow to $3.8 billion by 1980. 'Euphoric is not a bad word for [this original expectation],' wrote Keppel, but by 1970 'it was no longer taken for granted that ... modern technology would rescue Pauline from her perils ... Euphoria had turned into caution, perhaps even doubt' (Keppel, 1971a). Keppel continued to chart new strategies for the truncated firm, targeting areas opportunistically as they arose.

In 1970, for example, he predicted that '[a]ccountability may prove to be one of the major public policy issues of new relationships between education and business in the years to come' and so he suggested an emphasis on productivity, testing and, 'school-by-school measurement of cost inputs and learning outputs' (Keppel, 1970c, p. 357). He urged that GLC acquire a capability in testing, 'essential in the years to come,' and he even contemplated GLC being the marketer for the Educational Testing Service in order to get a toehold in the testing business (Keppel, 1970a).

Keppel also foresaw a role for GLC in 'performance contracting' and voucher plans then under consideration which would put private firms in charge of managing schools (the precursors of such private ventures today). Keppel recommended that GLC produce materials for everything from day-care centres to religious schools to proprietary schools, while also keeping a foot in 'government programs for the unemployed,' which, though 'wobbly enterprises,' would be useful to GLC for public relations (Keppel, 1971b). He even suggested that GLC might provide consultant services for the education system of Iran, since Time president James Linen was a friend of the Queen of Iran (Keppel, 1970b). Grabbing at such straws for several years, Keppel and the company stumbled on until 1974, when it was sold to textbook publisher Scott-Foresman for $20 million, after having lost $11 million for Time, Inc.

GE eventually squandered its opportunities in the overall computer business, too, through fragmented operations, overly ambitious projects, and a lack of commitment from top management. From 1957 to 1970 GE's domestic computer business lost $163 million, and in 1970 GE jettisoned its computer business altogether, selling it to Honeywell Information Systems.

Why had GLC failed? In a 1970 article Keppel blamed GLC's early failures on its exaggerated estimates of the capacity for industry to develop new technologies and the capacity for the fragmented education market to purchase any complex technology. Keppel came to acknowledge that education R&D proved to be 'a slow and very expensive process' and that 'business [would no longer] be able to underwrite any major portion of the R&D effort' (Keppel, 1970c, p. 355). Keppel's reservations attested to his integrity, in that he would not simply flood the market with useless products. Such integrity was rare, however. In fact, according to one published report in 1966, 'Office of Education officials were startled to learn that in the first year of the new Federal school aid program, local school officials spent $200 million of Federal funds for education hardware – much of it junk … Some of the shoddy equipment result[ed] from too hasty adaptations of machines and programs originally designed for the military' (Grant, 1966, p. A5). Fritz Ianni, GLC consultant and former OE director of research and development, conceded at the time that 'the whole question of education as a profit-making venture is an area that has not been carefully thought out' (Grant, 1966, p. A5).

In 1974, when GLC was sold, most observers faulted GLC's premature timing and reasoned that schools were not yet ready for advanced technology. Few noted that the technology itself was far from ready to enter the classroom. Solberg recounted in 1984 that GLC 'shrivelled on the vine' because 'GE's powerful computer wasn't all it was cracked up to be' (Solberg, 1984). Yet he lamented above all that he had 'buzzed around romancing all the … pioneers … and innovators … from coast to coast, [only] to discover that … the schools of America were not ready for the new technology, and the teachers would have nothing to do with it' (Solberg, 1984). Blaming the victim, he insisted that the timing of this 'resoundingly premature venture,' and not the bill of goods GLC and others were intent on hawking, was the 'the prime cause of our fiasco' (Solberg, 1984).

In a 1983 interview, Keppel explained that, 'in the middle 1960s, … there was then as there is now again, an enthusiasm, a euphoria for what modern information technology, computers, etc., could do for education … This was going to be the great system of changing education. It flopped. All the companies flopped' (Keppel, 1983, p. 38). These education companies, recounted Keppel, 'were put together out of idealistic dreaming and very little hard business sense' (Reichek, 1970, p. 32). One GLC top executive explained the 'fabulous failure' of GLC as just 'one of those mad rushes into the future that big corporations do now and then' (Prendergast, 1986, p. 214) – taking schools, teachers, and students along for the ride.

PLATO AND THE CONTROL DATA CORPORATION[4]

Only two years after the inglorious sale of GLC, and after most of the combines set up in the mid-1960s to tap the educational technology market had also dissolved for similar reasons, yet another major corporation embarked upon a 'mad rush into the future' in an effort to push CBE into the schools of America. Control Data Corporation (CDC) had been started in Minneapolis by William Norris in 1957 after leaving the Office of Naval Research, and it quickly rose to become a giant in computer and computer peripheral manufacturing and in worldwide data and computer services. At its peak, CDC employed 57,000 people worldwide and took in $3.6 billion a year in revenues. Norris was an unusual entrepreneur and business leader, one with a social conscience whose enduring legacy, according to his biographer, is that he 'showed the way to give capitalism a human face' (Worthy, 1987, p. 227). He also was a man with an *idee fixe*, an obsession for a system of computer-based education that eventually ruined the company.

The story of the CDC fiasco begins with the PLATO CBE system which was originated in 1960 by engineer Donald Bitzer and others at the military-sponsored Coordinated Science Laboratory at the University of Illinois. The PLATO project, whose acronym stood for 'Programmed Logic for Automatic Teaching Operations,' reflecting the military focus on automated instruction, had hardly begun when Norris at CDC was first told about it by a CDC salesman in Illinois. Norris was intrigued by the potential educational applications that might be developed for CDC computers at government expense, and in 1963 he entered into an agreement with the University of Illinois to provide the PLATO project with a CDC 1604 mainframe computer and subsequent updated mainframes in the following years.

Through the 1960s and 1970s, Bitzer's laboratory, which changed its name to Computer Based Education Research Laboratory (CERL), experimented with successive versions of PLATO, introducing such technological innovations as the plasma display screen for the terminals linked to the large mainframe computer. In 1966 military funding stopped, but generous funds from the National Science Foundation and other government agencies continued the support of the laboratory. CDC provided computer equipment and servicing but not direct funding. In 1971 CDC set up its own education department, hired university professors who had been working on computer courseware, and began using PLATO for internal training. Although both CDC and Bitzer's laboratory were slowly developing courseware, there was a proprietary mistrust by CDC toward the PLATO laboratory, which it viewed as potential competition down the road (Bitzer, 1988). Bitzer later referred to CDC's relationship with his lab as one of 'benign neglect' (Bitzer, 1988): 'They did their own thing; they tried to develop their own courseware, which was expensive ..., even though they could have tapped the courseware people at UI … for much less money' (Bitzer, 1988).

A 'market exploitation plan' drawn up by CDC in 1972 focused on promoting and selling computer science curricula, developing exchange agreements with universities, and promoting and selling continuing education materials. But, according to the plan, in 1972 'the market itself [was] as yet ill-defined [and] the true competitive picture [was] also cloudy' (Control Data Corporation, 1972, p. 106). CDC's 1974 budget for computer courseware development and acquisition included 92 per cent for courseware germane to the needs of business and industry but only 5 per cent for courseware germane to public and undergraduate education. However, given his penchant for attempting to solve social problems through for-profit business enterprise, Norris was most interested in the primary and secondary school markets. At least since 1970, Norris had been predicting that education, through PLATO, would eventually become CDC's principal source of revenue.

The formal effort to establish a commercial line of CDC PLATO services began in January, 1974, according to J. W. Dannemeyer, who directed the first education efforts at CDC (Dannemeyer, no date). PLATO was made compatible with the then current CDC Cyber operating system, and an architecture was developed for long-range PLATO evolution 'leading to profitable operation at prices competitive with traditional public school instruction costs' (Dannemeyer, no date). The most significant early problems encountered between 1973 and mid-1975, according to Dannemeyer, were 'internal CDC acceptance and the rationalization of a commercially viable product and services line' (Dannemeyer, no date). There was very significant resistance inside CDC to PLATO during this time, in part because of 'the lack of clear perspective regarding curriculum alternatives and acquisition' (Dannemeyer, no date). There were also severe jurisdictional pressures, as PLATO was subsumed under various departments prematurely, tapping resources needed for other projects. PLATO also had short-term negative effects on profits which concerned lower executive management personnel. A 'turning point' in PLATO commercial development, according to Dannemeyer, was the adoption of engineering methods in curriculum construction and the 'bootlegging' of a Mathematics Basic Skills development contract (Dannemeyer, no date).

By April, 1976 PLATO had 'increasing momentum within CDC' (Dannemeyer, no date), and so Norris determined that the PLATO system was ready for the commercial market. Although its initial target would be higher education and training operations in industry and government, CDC's ultimate goal was to bring CBE to children in schools and homes. With a flourish, Norris and Robert Morris, CDC vice president in charge of CBE products and services, held a New York press conference to announce the commercial offering of PLATO, whose acronym now stood for 'Programmed Learning and Teaching Operation'

(Pantages, 1976, p. 183). A *Datamation* report of the event, referring to the corporate CBE debacles of the 1960s, declared that '[y]esteryear promises of computer assisted instruction as the solution to staggering educational costs, illiteracy and poverty were reawakened' at the conference (Pantages, 1976, p. 183). Morris acknowledged such views, exulting, 'This is the biggest thing since the beginning' (Pantages, 1976, p. 183).

CDC's PLATO hit the ground running, with lucrative licensing and courseware royalty agreements negotiated with the University of Illinois, and with installations, orders, and 'learning centres' already in place. The deal with UI offered the university a mere 1 per cent on future sales and gave CDC control over any future PLATO work done by university researchers, who also lost government funding as a result of the commercial deal. One CERL source bitterly complained, 'I'm just upset, when you think of all the effort, that the University … [is] getting shafted' (Taylor, 1976, p. 7). Bitzer saw the deal as potentially lucrative for the university, however, even if some 'freedoms' were taken away with the new contract.

CDC also had plans with developing countries to help solve their massive manpower, education, and literacy problems with PLATO. Foremost was Iran, which a decade earlier was under consideration by GLC's Keppel as a potentially lucrative market for CBE. Although CDC appeared ready to take the CBE market by storm, however, there were problems. One was that although there were over 60 courses and over 1000 lessons written for PLATO, the quality of courseware was generally unexceptional, ranging from 'superb' to 'terrible' (Pantages, 1976, p. 187). Another problem was the high cost of PLATO terminal leasing, line costs, and mainframe access, which could run as high as $500,000 a year for a 64-terminal system. Despite these problems, Norris declared that the CBE industry was on a much more solid footing than the ventures of the 1960s. He predicted that PLATO would 'make possible terminals in employees' homes within a few years,' and that CBE 'would be the biggest consumer market this country has ever seen' (Smith, 1976, p. 5B).

Unlike GLC and SRA/IBM, CDC had a product, not simply a fantasy. But Norris and company had a fantasy as well, the same one that the high-tech corporate leaders of the 1960s had – to break into the school market and to revolutionize education. The PLATO system eventually did become 'the most extensively used computer-based instructional system in the world' by the early 1980s (Office of Technology Assessment, 1982, p. 129), primarily used for industrial and military training. But the fantasy, to revolutionize education by bringing PLATO into schools and homes, led Norris and CDC into a frenzy of corporate missteps that ultimately brought down the firm. The problem was this: PLATO might in some eyes have been ready for the external market, 'but the [school] market was not ready for PLATO. It had to be developed, and that proved more difficult than anticipated' (Worthy, 1987, p. 91).

CDC's earliest strategies to break into the schools and create a market there for PLATO was to proceed slowly and to focus on special populations of students. An early 1977 strategy session led by Norris concluded, 'The focus should be on finding niches where an education void exists or there are identifiable inadequacies which are recognized by those who require and will pay for the service' (Lacey, 1977a).

J. W. Lacey, president of the education company within CDC, wrote in 1977, 'I advocate a strategy of minimal initial confrontation with the established and traditional education and training modes ... Find niches that have a wide range of ability paced individuals, [where the] need for flexible schedules outweighs costs, [where] uniformity of educational content is necessary and desired by the customer, [where the] size of the market is large, [where there is] wide geographic disbursement of learners, and where present courseware is inadequate (e.g., the remedial market, small business, large, widespread corporations)' (Lacey, 1977a).

An early strategic report emphasized that CDC should proceed cautiously into the school market: 'U.S. elementary and secondary education is a limited market until 1980. Then it will emerge as a large market from 1980 to 1985. Our present marketing efforts should remain small ... [We should] develop full-scale PLATO CBE programs in several school systems which will clearly show the alternative advantage of CBE' (Conner, 1977). A report on the CDC 'Secondary Schools Strategy' concluded that it was 'unrealistic due to cost, political and product availability considerations to expect comprehensive introduction of PLATO into secondary schools. Instead, CD will concentrate on selected markets in areas of greatest need: rural, special education, inner city, gifted' (Control Data Corporation, 1978).

Special education or remedial education was considered a prime first target. CDC strategists shared Lyle Spencer's tactic at SRA to 'go after the invalids' because that was where the needs and the federal funds were. D. H. Wentworth, CDC vice president for educational products and services, responded in 1977 to a request for PLATO marketing strategies from the division's president, J. R. Morris, 'I believe we should devote our major marketing effort to only basic skills in a remedial type environment. It appears to me that this is an area needing considerable attention. It is not as cost sensitive and would have less resistance from educators. It would also have the possibility of displaying PLATO in a more positive light by providing training to those who are failing in the present education system' (Wentworth, 1977). Although 'basic skills should be number one priority' (Sheehan, 1977), J. M. Sheehan, another CDC education division executive, conceded to Morris that it would be 'a difficult task until hard data is available that tells educators that CBE achieves their objectives far better than traditional education or tutorial learning' (Sheehan, 1977).

A study of market focus and penetration strategies in 1977 recommended that the focus should be on 'special education' markets broadly construed, including corrections, American Indian programs, drug awareness programs, gifted programs, adult remedial education, the education of handicapped students, and summer school remediation. The rationale for this focus was clear: 'Special education students are 'hard to teach' [and] ... government monies are more readily available for special ed areas than for standard areas of education' (Ridley, 1978). But it was also clear from the start that this targeting of special education was a means to a grander end – the penetration of mainstream schooling itself. 'CBE can be the preferred alternative now for special education applications, then in a few years for traditional instruction' (Bevers, 1977) wrote one CDC executive. 'When the special education programs prove successful, courseware will be developed for penetration of 'mainstream' education' (Ridley, 1978).

Rural schools were another target that might eventually lead to comprehensive penetration of the schools. In 1977 and 1978, CDC engaged in a major study of Minnesota's public elementary and secondary schools, leading to a major proposal to the Minnesota legislature to place several hundred terminals in rural secondary schools. The proposal fell through, according to J. W. Dannemeyer, the first head of CDC's education operations, because it was politically mishandled and lacked curricular cohesiveness (Dannemeyer, no date, p. 2). In 1978, for example, there were 'operational difficulties' at the Osseo, Minnesota, field test site for language arts curriculum for learning disabled junior high students. The director of that rural project lamented, 'My major concern right now is to avoid frustrating teachers and students ... The word would spread rapidly to other local districts in the state and would, in my judgment, have a significantly negative impact on the future marketability of PLATO' (Valetta, 1978). CDC eventually lost the Osseo contract.

In 1979 CDC launched its 'Academic Equity for Rural Schools' project, otherwise known as the 'Little Fork-Big Falls Project' for its rural site. CDC requested public funding for the project through the Minnesota Council on Quality Education. Its stated purpose, exploiting a crisis, was to 'enable a rural school system that has had to cut back to a 'bare bones' curriculum in order to forestall closing or consolidation, to develop alternative teaching methods which will encourage a variety of self-instructional methods' (Muller, 1979).

A grassroots movement among educators against the so-called 'PLATO Bill' before the Minnesota House Aids Committee led the opposition to CDC's plan to place 30 terminals in the northern Minnesota school district. 'It is our understanding,' stated a leader of the opposition, 'that CDC is requesting State funds to match their own investment in the development of courseware to be employed in these terminals. We view this proposal as a CDC marketing effort for courseware development' (Bartel, 1979).

CDC's Dannemeyer eventually gave up the Little Forks/Big Forks project, rationalizing that 'no matter how strongly we can justify PLATO, *there will be resistance* – by consolidation advocates, by short-sighted militant teachers, by fundamental reactionaries, by lobbyists of other CBE purveyors' (Dannemeyer, 1978b). A 'Rural Schools Strategy' plan in 1978 suggested instead that CDC manoeuvre its efforts through the Minnesota Educational Computing Consortium, the state's public-funded computer curriculum development agency. 'The key to successful implementation of the plan is the MECC,' it concluded; '… our efforts at the state level [must] be coordinated with the MECC' (States, 1978b). A document entitled 'PLATO Strategy for the State of Minnesota' charted the plan succinctly: 'Objective: to establish PLATO as the CBE standard in the State of Minnesota. Strategy: to establish a master contract with the MECC and to establish significant initial market presentation through a 'seed' pilot project in Minnesota, both at the University of Minnesota and in school districts. Also, to gain high visibility with key personnel in state government and educational institutions' (Control Data Corporation, no date).

Unfortunately for CDC, MECC did not share its PLATO agenda. Dale La-Frenz, MECC Director of Instructional Services told CDC staff that 'MECC is willing to support whatever demand their customers have regarding PLATO; however, they do not see their role as marketeer. CDC must generate that interest and need' (Gingerella, 1979). CDC representatives botched their relations with the MECC from the start. MECC's LaFrenz was reported as complaining that 'CDC has always given MECC the illusion of not caring about MECC's feedback as to the educational use of computers and MECC has continually had to invite themselves into CDC seminars' (Gingerella, 1979). CDC representatives reported back from one meeting with LaFrenz that he thought CDC was 'missing the boat with our PLATO system … He repeatedly indicated off-line CAI was totally adequate and cheaper via micro than the PLATO route … Mr. LaFrenz doesn't believe we are aware of what users, including MECC, are doing with microprocessors today, and the potential for this business' (States, 1978a). Indeed, during the previous year MECC had become a strong supporter of APPLE II microcomputers, purchasing over 1000 Apples and developing Apple software available to Minnesota users at no cost.

MECC had not supported PLATO (only 32 terminals had been leased) due to the cost of the lease price. Dannemeyer had his own view of these circumstances, however. 'Unfortunately for CDC, … and especially [for] Minnesota rural kids, Apple [Computer, Inc.] moved in swiftly behind the rejected CDC proposal and, together with school administrators, perpetrated on the kids hundreds of the little Apple toys' (Dannemeyer, no date). This was CDC's first introduction to the Apple microcomputer competition; it would not be the last. MECC, not surprisingly, ultimately concluded that '… the need for a PLATO shared system [with MECC] no longer exists' (Gingerella, 1979). And with that, CDC's rural school plan bit the dust. But CDC had many plans, many strategies. It was also committed to the establishment of learning centres. The Learning Centres would be storefront education retail outlets, not just for PLATO terminals but for other technological innovations in education as well, including toys. Although learning centres were established in cities across the country, they proved not to be cost-effective (Smith, 1980, p. 15). It became apparent that the Learning Centres would have to be exceedingly large, even school-size, to be commercially viable. Nevertheless, they served other strategic purposes for the company. One CDC executive later explained the strategic importance of the learning center. 'It was extremely important in a strategic sense to demonstrate CD's commitment to the concept of a learning center, so that we were not thought to be in the market tentatively. Had the market felt that we were tentative or experimental, then no one would have expended the effort nor the dollars to begin with PLATO. The concept of the learning center network was very liable from a strategic point of view' (Smith, 1980, p. 15). Learning Centres were also considered by Norris to serve eventually as distribution points for home delivered educational programs.

The principal objective for CDC strategists was to define, to condition, and to penetrate the school market. Robert Morris, vice president of the CDC education company, insisted in 1977 that 'early market penetration ... must be considered as our single highest priority objective ... We are dealing with a dormant market. It exists, has needs and has money' (Morris, 1977). He was most distressed that '[p]otential customers do not share our sense of urgency for the implementation and use of computer-based education' (Morris, 1977). He therefore recommended a strategy designed 'to promote PLATO aggressively (e.g., on 60 Minutes), [to] promote success stories, [to] 'seed' terminals at government agencies (e.g., HEW, DOT, Smithsonian),' and to 'enlist prestigious world known authors to create courseware' (Morris, 1977). W. J. Ridley, head of the education company's academic division seconded this overriding concern about the market. 'The primary purpose of the Academic Division is market development. The express purpose is to condition, penetrate, and eventually establish a prominent position in the world of established education and attendant areas in terms of CBE products and services' (Ridley, 1978).

One approach to the development of a market was to exploit the recurring financial crises of the schools. After all, the CDC mission statement asserted that 'Control Data is committed to a strategy of addressing society's major needs as profitable business opportunities' (Varley, 1981). However high-minded Norris's intentions, this often translated into the profit-seeking exploitation of difficult times; the schools' scarcity and misery would be CDC's opportunity. One Norris-led strategy session in 1977 concluded that '[t]he current and growing financial crisis will hit its peak in 1979-80. It will be so severe as to cause a restructuring of the total U.S. educational process. This provides an opportunity for CD to work with several viable school systems to produce CBE alternatives that legislators and politicians can turn to for solutions' (Conner, 1977).

In 1980, a key educational consultant recommended that CDC exploit a fiscal crisis resulting from diminished federal funding to organize the citizenry behind CBE, since the 'financial squeeze' created more opportunity for CDC to pressure local groups of citizens and parents (Schilling, 1981a). CDC was also interested in giving school leaders and policy makers a public relations boost in difficult times by parading CBE as a 'modern' solution to school woes. 'At present,' wrote one CDC executive in 1979, 'dramatic needs confront school districts: demand for educational accountability, shortage of funds, lower enrolment, labour intensiveness, instructional management ... CDC has the opportunity to make an impact on the contemporary education market with a delivery system that will meet the needs of educators on the policy level, the management level, and on the instructional level' (Ridley, 1978).

'The potential market for PLATO products and services in the established education world is enormous,' announced the authors of the long-range strategic plan for CDC's educational company in 1979 (Ridley, 1978). 'Due mainly to the nature of labour-intensive practices, educational costs are increasing at a rate of 10-12 per cent a year. [Something must be done to prevent] the collapse of thousands of school districts over the next decade ... In addition to the cost problem, documentation is emerging at an increasing rate that indicates a decline in educational effectiveness, ... particularly in [the] basic[s] ... Fresh, individualized educational approaches are needed' (Ridley, 1978). Within some minds at CDC, things seemed ripe for PLATO.

But just about that time, things began to unravel for CDC and PLATO. Its plans to tap into Minnesota's rural schools had collapsed in the face of grassroots opposition, and by 1979 financial analysts had begun to doubt the wisdom of Norris's persistence with PLATO. From 1973 to 1979 PLATO lost about $38 million for CDC (Information Processing Department, 1979, p. 118). Some former employees reported that Norris ordered other CDC units rather than the education unit to bear part of PLATO's launching costs. One indicated that 'PLATO so thoroughly permeates all CDC businesses that the company has a problem accounting accurately for its revenues' (Worthy, 1987, p. 105). They also accused Norris of 'rushing headlong into the education industry without a solid marketing plan' (Information Processing Department, 1979, p. 123). Norris' opposition to market research was 'proverbial,' according to Bitzer (Bitzer, 1988, p. 170). Norris believed that the technology would sell itself. 'You don't need any fancy market research,' he told one reporter acidly, 'You know the market is there' (Information Processing Department, 1979, p. 123). In 1979, in response to analysts' recommendations for CDC to jettison PLATO for the sake of profits, Norris replied, 'No! I've stayed around to nurse this along, and we won't back away from it. For Control Data, PLATO is a way of life' (Information Processing Department, 1979, p. 123).

But the problems and the competition kept building. An education consultant hired by CDC to assess the situation in 1980 wrote: 'We have been attempting to address the 'Elementary-Secondary' market for CDC PLATO CBE in a somewhat formal manner for over two years now, with relatively little success. Even the introduction of the Special Education package at a new low price of $38,000 for 8 terminals failed to produce increase in customers ... We have presented papers, given speeches, and demonstrated PLATO at scores of education-related conferences. We have talked with hundreds of teachers and administrators, and we have visited many schools – to little purpose. We have even done some specific advertising in education journals this year – all with relatively little luck ... We have, in fact, attempted almost every avenue open to us except, perhaps, the deployment of a fully trained and committed cadre of 'education-only' sales people' (Mullin-Traynor, 1980, p. 6).

Bitzer had criticized CDC for using their regular hardware people, not educators, as sales people for the PLATO system. There was also, he said, a great deal of infighting among salespeople for pieces of the school turf. At one point the Federal Trade Commission went after CDC for having its salesmen posing as counsellors trying to sell CDC's counselling product (Hogg, 1978). Educators themselves faulted CDC for lack of courseware other than basic skills and GED, with no further plans to develop associated curricula. Of course, even if a total K-12 curriculum were developed, CDC had little guarantee it would be accepted by educators, which is partly why its focus was on special education and other market niches. PLATO was also thought to be too fraught with emotional reaction for educators. 'CDC failed to build a rapport, plus a desire on the part of schools, [teachers,] and superintendents, for PLATO. Combine this with the fear that PLATO replaces teachers, rather than [being] a powerful tool, and the grassroots forces were formed against CDC' (Gingerella, 1979). The 600-hour curriculum repertoire was 'just a hodgepodge,' conceded Dannemeyer (Dannemeyer, 1978b), with no real curriculum available other than Basic Skills and Computer Managed Instruction (CMI).

There was also the continual problem of excessive PLATO downtime and the growing prospect that PLATO cost effectiveness might not improve. Another problem was the diminishment of public funding to underwrite schools' PLATO costs. In public schools, wrote one CDC analyst, 'once again, we have the funding problem and until lower costs are achieved, penetration of this market is going to be weak' (Sheehan, 1977). Finally, as one CDC executive acknowledged as late as 1983, CDC still had a lot to learn about mass advertising and marketing. 'The tricky part for us has been trying to take a single product into multiple-market environments, each with different needs for the product' (Lewis, 1983, p. 13).

The competition also posed a problem. Like SRA/IBM and GLC before it, CDC was always looking over its shoulder at the competition. Back in 1978, before Apple and other microcomputers hit the market, the competition was thought to be the University of Illinois. Bitzer later recounted that CDC 'saw everyone as a potential competitor, even universities' (Bitzer, 1988). A CDC report in 1978 stated, 'It is our goal to differentiate our product from the UI's offering' (Morris, 1978, p. 3). IBM had abandoned its 1500 system by then, and it was not considered a major threat. A 1979 report entitled 'The Competition and Marketplace for PLATO's Basic Skills Package' reported that 'IBM's strategy appears to be a defensive one aimed at protecting its installed base rather than an aggressive pursuit of the CBE market ... It appears that courseware development within IBM is aimed almost entirely at IBM's internal training needs. IBM has no CMI system' (Lacey, 1977b).

The report in 1979 cited Computer Curriculum Corporation, the firm started by Patrick Suppes from the Stanford CBE project, as a potential threat but claimed that, with annual sales only around $4 million, 'Information on this company is hard to find because of its small size' (Merrill, 1979). The SRA Basic Reading Series was also considered a potential competitor to PLATO. But the report's authors were confident that PLATO was unique in its focus on older students learning the basic skills of grades 3-8, rather than focusing on standard elementary and secondary curriculum like most other vendors' software. At this point CDC was not aware that the 'microcomputer revolution' was underway with dire consequences for its PLATO product.

CDC pursued additional strategies to penetrate the school and home markets. It established a 'Home PLATO Program,' which set up 100 terminals in Twin Cities homes 'to assess consumer attitudes to PLATO and to home computers [and] to determine the optimal direction in marketing to consumers' (Bruning, no date). It continued to try to tap the Minnesota schools, but the Minneapolis Star and Tribune ran a series of critical articles reporting independent research findings on PLATO's effectiveness. The Tribune conceded that CDC had evidence of PLATO effectiveness for high school students and adults for whom its courses were originally designed, but none to back up its featured advertising with young children (Pinney, 1982, p. 1A). The Tribune was particularly critical of CDC's apparently specious advertising. One ad in 1979 read, 'You can't guarantee your child will do better in school. But we can.' Another showed a girl named Jane with her hand raised and a caption saying, 'A few months ago Jane could hardly read. Look at her now!' The company declined the newspaper's repeated requests for it to document PLATO's effectiveness with young children. Finally, in 1983, the Tribune noted that CDC suddenly and mysteriously dropped such advertising. When called by the newspaper, the company refused to comment (Pinney, 1983, p. 1A).

It was busy with other strategies. In early 1983, CDC announced that it would donate 440 desktop PLATO systems, with values totalling more than $6 million, to 110 colleges and universities. One magazine account reported, though, that 'some suggested that the gifts were a shrewd marketing ploy ..., the equivalent of automatically creating an ongoing market for the still-unprofitable PLATO' (Lewis, 1983, p. 13). Another school marketing plan suggested that CDC emphasize 'how PLATO is used to maintain order and discipline' (Williams, 1979).

With the increased public outcry for school accountability and testing, one CDC report urged that PLATO be targeted to the task of test preparation, a last-ditch ploy also attempted by Keppel's GLC. 'There are several important variables that increase the chance that a school would purchase the PLATO package,' noted the report. 'These variables include: does the school district require a competency test in order for its students to receive a high school diploma; does the school district meet the necessary requirements to receive *Federal ESSA (sic) Title I funds*?' (Merrill, 1979). This one-two punch, some inside CDC still believed, would be the winning combination for PLATO.

Ever vigilant for new opportunities, CDC also decided to exploit the new federal guidelines for special education that required school districts to maintain 'individual education plans' (IEPs) for all special education students. Public Law 94-142 was passed by Congress in 1975, and in 1977 Congress adopted the essential ingredients of the IEP for complex tracking and monitoring of goals, objectives, performance, plans, and of funding administration. CDC planned to use its expertise in PLATO CMI to provide this mandated monitoring. CDC had to assume that PL94-142 would be enforced, and that federal and state allocations would continue, despite threats by some states, including Florida which had an installed PLATO base, to ignore the federal mandates, and despite threats on the federal level to overturn the law. This niche was therefore fraught with obstacles, including strong competition. A 1980 CDC report, entitled 'Marketing Perspectives for the IEP Product Line,' noted that 'computer companies who already have an installed data processing base in schools [and] ... who also develop the administrative capabilities required for compliance with PL94-142 will be a serious source of competition ...' ('Marketing Perspectives,' no date).

As with CDC's other school strategies, the long-term goal, according to the report, remained 'to increase CD PLATO sales within the traditional education market of the U.S.' ('Marketing Perspectives for IEP Product Line,' no date). Therefore, the 'mission and scope' of the IEP strategy was '... to utilize the IEP system as the means to penetration of the academic market' (Mullin-Traynor, 1980). In 1981, CDC's education consultant Susan Schilling recommended 'renaming the project to something like Individual Planning Program to dissociate it from the legislation for the handicapped ... This would distinguish IEP [specifically targeting] … PL94-142 from … the capability and product for individualizing educational plans for a total school population … The procedure of evaluation-prescription-treatment-evaluation [in IEP] remains unchanged when applied to a 'normal' population' (Schilling, 1981b). (Perhaps for similar reasons, the meaning of the acronym 'PLATO' was itself changed by CDC sometime in the early 1980s from 'Programmed Logic for Automatic Teaching Operations' to the more user-friendly and generic 'Personal Learning and Training Opportunity.')

Seeing the handwriting on the wall, Schilling doubted the potential of the IEP strategy. 'I am concerned,' she wrote, 'that the current effort has proven to be a successful experiment, but an 'undeliverable' product' (Schilling, 1981a).

CDC had two strategies left. In 1981 CDC brought out a microcomputer, CDC110, in order to compete with Apple and IBM in the school and the home markets. It also entered into an agreement with Texas Instruments (TI) to market PLATO in diskette form for TI's stand-alone microcomputer. The following year TI left the personal computer market, leaving CDC high and dry. Dannemeyer saw CDC's foray in microcomputers as the sacrifice to the educational toy market of the original, bold PLATO mission. He had been distressed when Apple succeeded, where CDC had failed, in tapping into the Minnesota school market. He later wrote, 'The growing impact of such toys appears to have thrown CDC's PLATO people into a panic to produce their own stand-alone version of a functionally cut-down 'little PLATO'' (Dannemeyer, no date, p. 2).

Norris, too, was indignant at the fad-like manner in which schools were acquiring personal computers and accomplishing little beyond exposing young people to a few elementary tasks. No other computer companies were providing a total system for managing the teaching process. 'This fell far short of the revolutionary impact on education Norris had envisioned,' wrote Norris's biographer James C. Worthy in 1987 (Worthy, 1987, p. 99). Feelings about such revolutionary visions ran high among some at CDC. J. W. Dannemeyer, who was an early pivotal figure alongside Norris pushing PLATO within CDC, insisted in 1978: '… to see PLATO in public school in a big way – that's all I've wanted out of this whole thing since spring of 1974 – and *I will see it*. I stayed alive to see it through' (Dannemeyer, 1978a). W. J. Ridley shared Dannemeyer's frustrations as early as 1977, insisting that 'present institutions of learning *must be taught* to manage their business so that CBE is integral to the educational process and a normal funding requirement, as opposed to its present perception as being an unfunded increment to established educational methods' (Lacey, 1977c). Norris's biographer Worthy echoed these refrains in 1987. 'If working with computers is ever going to be anything more than an optional, supplemental activity subject to the whims of teachers and the vagaries of funding, computers will have to be integrated into *central*[ized] instructional processes' (Worthy, 1987, p. 101).

Despite these grand visions, even Norris began to recognize that PLATO marketing strategies were in trouble, but he remained undaunted by these CDC's repeated strategy failures with PLATO. While he acknowledged to an interviewer in 1983 that it had taken far longer to develop and market PLATO than he had anticipated, he still insisted that '[i]t's going to be a segment of our business down the road somewhere' (Lewis, 1983, p. 13). Norris and CDC by that time had spent over a billion dollars on PLATO (Flint, 1993, p. 45).

In 1984, in one last-ditch effort to market PLATO, CDC joined forces with Wicat Systems, Inc. of Orem, Utah, a 17-year old company with around $30 million in revenues, which had put around $50 million into developing its own large computer-managed 'curriculum-delivery system.' The two firms formed a 50/50 joint venture called Plato/Wicat Systems, which spent 'tens of millions of dollars ... to court schools' (Kahn, 1986, p. 59). The marriage lasted two years, during which time it was successful in selling 325 of Wicat's System 300 integrated learning systems. But in the fall of 1986, 'philosophical differences about how the market should be approached' led to the break-up of the venture (Barbour, 1987, p. 9). CDC wanted to tap into the installed base of stand-alone microcomputers already in the schools, while Wicat wanted to stick with its minicomputer-based system with terminals. Wicat was eventually sold to Jostens Learning Corporation, which, as we shall see, became for a brief time the market leader in integrated learning systems in the 1990s, before succumbing, too, to the hubris of the chairman of its parent company in wild pursuit of the CBE pot of gold.

Also in 1984, CDC had established a wholly owned subsidiary, United School Services of America (USSA), to consolidate educational products and services targeted at the public school market. Again, just like GLC's Keppel's GLC over a decade earlier, USSA explored the possibility of operating local schools on a fee-for-service basis (Worthy, 1987, p. 101). CDC never implemented these plans. After CDC folded in 1991, John Golle, a slick entrepreneur in corporate training, bought the rights to USSA research and models as the basis of his new company, Educational Alternatives, Inc. (EAI). EAI has recently managed schools in Miami Beach, Baltimore, and Hartford on a fee-for-service basis, in conjunction with Computer Curriculum Corporation (CCC), CDC's former competitor and now, with Josten Learning's demise, the market leader in large computer-managed integrated learning systems.

After Wicat, the game was up for PLATO, and things were turning sour for CDC as well. CDC tried to market its 'Local PLATO Delivery System,' a local area network that would attempt to hook up PC compatibles and Apple microcomputers to a file-server. But all the courseware developed by Plato-Wicat went back to Wicat in the break-up, so CDC did not have the integrated courseware it needed for the network to be viable. Because so much of CDC had become wrapped up in PLATO, the company began to disintegrate. In a 'free-fall through the 1980s,' it lost more than 90 per cent of shareholder value (Parker, 1993, p. 1F). According to one account, 'It was a terrifying, painful ride down,' with 'a seemingly endless stream of sell offs, spinoffs, layoffs and restructurings while the company struggled to find equilibrium' (Parker, 1993, p. 1F). In 1986, Norris was forced to step down and retired. But it was too late to save the company, which was dismembered finally in 1992. CDC was divided into two companies, Control Data Systems, which markets mainframes and computer peripherals, and CERIDIAN, which provides payroll services nationwide and owns Arbitron, which sells market ratings and audience demographics to radio stations. The PLATO system itself was sold to the firm NOVANET.

Norris' biographer James Worthy writes, 'Norris will be remembered for his vision of the part business as business can play in building a more humane society' (Worthy, 1987, p. 227). But at his last press conference in January, 1986, announcing his retirement from CDC, Norris was asked what was his proudest accomplishment. He answered, unhesitatingly, 'PLATO' (Worthy, 1987, p. 106).

LESSONS FOR THE PRESENT MOMENT

It is now almost a decade since William Norris retired from Control Data Corporation and over three decades since SRA/IBM and General Learning Corporation set out to revolutionize education through computer-based education and other educational technologies. How far have we come? For one thing, there are now 5.8 million computers in the nation's schools, and over $2 billion is being spent yearly by schools to purchase hardware and software for the 'information age.' Yet there is consensus that, except for a few futuristic demonstration projects, all of this money and hardware has had an insignificant effect on educational practice in the nation's schools,

The latest Office of Technology Assessment report on educational technology, just released in April, 1995, concludes that because teacher training has been largely ignored, the billions of dollars schools spent each year on computers, software, and other technologies have brought few benefits to classroom instruction, despite the millions of computers now in the nation's schools (West, 1995d, p. 1). Apple Computer, Inc., in a 1992 issue of MacWorld magazine entitled 'America's Shame,' found '[a]ntiquated computers, unused computers, computers used for games and not for teaching, schools and teachers unprepared to use computers that they own, mismanaged or misdirected policies, and unknown hundreds of millions of dollars spent over the last decade for little return' (Borrell, 1992, p. 3). 'The truth is,' the article concludes, 'that we are groping toward [yet] another ill-defined approach to the implementation of technology in the hope that the next effort will be the one that brings order from chaos' (Borrell, 1992, p. 5).

Time magazine, in its spring 1995 special issue 'Welcome to Cyberspace,' concedes as well that 'the promised revolution has failed to materialize,' despite the millions of computers and the billions of dollars. However, says Time, now a subsidiary of cable and entertainment giant Time Warner, the 'bold predictions' of CBE pioneers of the 1960s, including those at Time, Inc., 'were not wrong, just premature' (Wallis, 1995, p. 49). 'It may take 10 years, or more likely 20,' Time's paean to Cyberspace concludes, '… but the prophets of the post-Gutenberg age in education will finally be proved right' (Wallis, 1995, p. 49). In a word, despite a dubious past and present, the euphoria continues, in fact now more rancorous than ever, to revolutionize education with computer-based technology, linked up to Time Warner's and others' promised 'information highway.'

What lessons emerge from our three case studies of the early corporate marketing of computers in education that might be instructive in assessing the latest corporate efforts to revolutionize education with technology? In this section I first try to summarize these lessons. I then look briefly at how each in turn helps us to understand recent corporate efforts to change education with technology. The lessons include the following:

1) Schools are typically sold a bill of goods, not the goods themselves. (Penetration of the education market with computer-based technology has depended more on effective conditioning of the market through advertisement and ideological barrage than on the effectiveness of the technologies themselves.)

2) 'Mad rushes into the future' rather than altruism or business sense often drive corporate decisions and unlikely joint ventures within the education market – taking schools, teachers, and students along for the ride. (The leaders of large corporations, whose business leadership lends them credibility and whose high-tech firms are paraded as models for education, often subscribe irrationally to futuristic fantasies of vast market size and revolutionary technology.)

3) Corporate strategies for the marketing of computer-based education are chameleon-like, changing their colours to meet the needs of every new educational fad or government invitation or technological innovation that comes along.

4) Large-scale corporate ventures in computer-based education (typically supported by federal funds) exploit the financial crises of schools and the 'invalids' among the student population, thereby turning education's desperation into corporate opportunities to experiment with unproven wares.

5) Research with educational technology conducted in schools is as much or more a form of marketing and product development, using schools as laboratories, as it is an effort to serve schools or students.
6) Computer-based education is more about using schools and the education market in the service of technological product development and profits than it is about using technology in the service of education, schools, and students.

These lessons reflect the most recent developments in the marketing of computer-based education as they did the earliest efforts. In what follows, I show how each lesson in turn can be applied to more recent ventures in the field.

Lesson 1: Schools are typically sold a bill of goods, not the goods themselves.

Participants in the early ventures in CBE typically blamed their failure on the fact that the education market was not yet 'ready' for their technology. This is partly true, but not because the technology itself was ahead of its time; rather, the ideological leavening of the education market had not yet set. Although the glamour of technology captivated some, the schools were still not fully conditioned by the rhetoric of the information age and computer age to welcome the gadgetry into classrooms. The first real inroads came with tax-deductible donations of microcomputers to schools in the late 1970s and with the ideological campaign for computer literacy and thinking skills ('mindstorms') in the early 1980s. By 1984, with Time magazine's celebration of the computer as its 'man of the year' and the 1983 federal report, *A Nation At Risk*, calling for computer literacy and programming, a 'new basic skill,' the information age had seemingly arrived with the schools opened up to a flood of computers.

In 1982, Steven Jobs, chairman of Apple Computer, Inc., tried to get an 'Apple Bill' passed through the U.S. House of Representatives that would give the company tax deductions for computer donations to schools. It passed through the House but never made it to the Senate. However, later that year a similar bill passed the California legislature, to take effect from January, 1983 to June, 1984. The bill offered Apple a 25 per cent tax credit from their California taxes for computer equipment donations based on the fair market value of the donated equipment. This program, called 'Kids Can't Wait,' placed one Apple IIe computer in each of California's 9,250 eligible elementary and secondary schools and afforded Apple great public relations visibility for its products. IBM and Hewlett Packard soon followed suit.

Meanwhile, not entirely satisfied with these arrangements, Apple, Tandy, IBM, and other companies represented by the American Electronics Association, attempted to get Senate bills introduced during 1983 which would provide for deductions beyond the cost of donated equipment, up to a maximum of 200 per cent of the equipment cost, thereby ensuring a profit for donations (Uston, 1993, pp. 179-183). Apple and IBM were interested in the education market not to revolutionize education, though they saturated the schools with such rhetoric. Rather, they were intent on establishing very early brand loyalty among students who would eventually become adult computer users.

At the same time, in California, State Superintendent of Instruction William Honig began a national trend by requiring computer literacy courses for all California high school graduates. 'Computer Literacy' was a term no one could define, but most states soon followed Honig's lead and invested heavily in technology to bring computer literacy to their students and to prepare them for the information age. The term itself had been coined with just that scenario in mind. Andrew Molnar, director of the Office of Computing Activities at the National Science Foundation, later recounted that educational technophiles at NSF were deeply concerned about the scattered and uncoordinated programs in computer-based instruction (including PLATO and BBN's LOGO) that a skeptical NSF was reluctantly funding. They wanted a coordinated effort to bring CBE into the schools. 'We spent ... something like a half a billion dollars on technology in education, but they were so uncoordinated that you either had to be a liar, a thief, or corrupt in order to pull all of these things together to do a program that would involve technology in any significant way' (Molnar, 1991, p. 17).

Molnar and his colleagues took just such a deceptive route. 'We started computer literacy in '72,' Molnar recollected. 'We coined that phrase. It's sort of ironic. Nobody knows what computer literacy is. Nobody can define it. And the reason we selected computer literacy was because nobody could define it, and nobody knew what it was, and that it was a broad enough term that you could get all of these programs together under one roof' (Molnar, 1991, p. 18). Molnar and others then set about holding prestigious national conferences on computer literacy, and eventually in the early 1980s the term took on a life of its own, resulting in millions of computers in schools.

Hundreds of thousands of computers also entered the schools amidst exaggerated claims by Seymour Papert and Bolt, Beranek, and Newman that their LOGO software would bring thinking skills and 'powerful ideas' into the classroom through child-centered computer programming. In fact, LOGO was first conceived as a means to teach students grammar and then elementary mathematics; the idea that LOGO would teach generalized thinking came later. As one LOGO developer later recounted, '[T]he psychological dimension of LOGO, as represented by Papert's claim that LOGO programming would lead children to more explicit, better articulated reflection on their own cognitive processes and that this in turn would affect the character of their cognitive development, was in fact a late conceptual formulation' (Lawler, 1987, pp. 11, 12). This was, then, an afterthought, one still never proven in years of research on LOGO use by children in schools, but an extremely marketable notion nonetheless.

The LOGO-inspired movement to enable children to think and have powerful ideas using computers flooded the schools with new hardware and software, which now remain in the classrooms, even as their exaggerated rationale has long since been abandoned. In a recent retrospective on LOGO ('Rethinking the LOGO Culture,' 1995), its apologists and proselytizers, now reduced to an insular cadre at MIT's Media Lab, conceded that they had been 'naive' and that, once 'realism … set in,' they realized that the 'LOGO culture' was drastically – and prematurely – oversold to the nation's schools. Only a handful of schools still use LOGO now, and with severely reduced expectations of its benefits for children. Meanwhile the cognitive tinkerers at MIT's Media Lab, now bankrolled by Lego Corporation along with the Department of Defense and NSF, continue to play with ever more sophisticated technological versions of LOGO as a vehicle for science and mathematics exploration. But there is no more talk of enhanced 'thinking' or 'powerful ideas.'

The recent term 'information superhighway' also serves the purpose of saturating schools with computer technology, this time bringing fibre optic cable and on-line services into the schools at an estimated eventual cost of $10 billion. Vice President Albert Gore, a key promoter, has labelled this enterprise the National Information Infrastructure, and advocacy for it, appeared in President Bill Clinton's 1997 State of the Union address. A recent comprehensive report on the information highway notes that no two educators, technologists, and other telecommunications experts define the term the same way or 'agree on exactly how [its] development will affect education' (West, 1995a, p. 6). This information 'hypeway' is but the latest, and perhaps the most costly – or lucrative, depending on where one stands – bill of goods sold to the schools in the name of a computer-based educational revolution.

Lesson 2: 'Mad rushes into the future' rather than altruism or business sense often drive corporate decisions and unlikely joint ventures within the education market – taking schools, teachers, and students along for the ride.

Three examples over the last decade illustrate once again these insights from the early marketing of computer-based education. Douglas Carlston, chairman of educational software leader Broderbund, recounts the big software bust in the mid-1980s. In 1982, 'venture capitalists were entering the software industry in a big way at the same time market researchers started predicting phenomenal growth in the area of educational software. This led to the idea of the software publisher as a marketing company' (Carlston, 1985, p. 206). According to Carlston, marketing image was more important than substance, as was company name more the focus than individual products. 'Most of the significant new companies in 1982 and 1983 weren't especially interested in games. Their mandate was educational software, especially for young children. The futurists had said that educational software would be the area of greatest growth for the next few years, and it seemed auspicious that there were so few companies taking advantage of this particular market. A billion dollar pie was ... waiting to be cut up. Today's startups in the educational software field were bound to be tomorrow's success stories ... The fortunes of the near future were going to be made in educational programs' (Carlston, 1985, p. 207).

'Furthermore' writes Carlston, 'educational software was respectable. Video games were magnetic, but based on nonsense. Educational software would be a rational market, one in which senior programmers could implement designs formulated by professional educators and could bring out products that could be sold by truly professional marketers.' Many major firms jumped into the educational software market. Simon and Schuster and Reader's Digest 'began to look hungrily at this new market that seemed to have appeared overnight. CBS Software Division moved away from video games for the sake of games – toward educational software. By 1983 most of CBS Software's products were presented as 'educational'' (Carlston, 1985, p. 224).

By April, 1984, however, a slowdown began. Sales were abysmal. Carlston asks, echoing the post-mortems after GLC and CDC, 'What was going wrong? How could savvy and well-funded outfits ... fail so spectacularly?' He answers, 'Part of the problem was their collective inexperience. They insisted that software was just a form of literature that happens to run on a machine. Also book publishers didn't know the real size of the market. 'The area of young children's educational entertainment products ('edutainment') was opened and then filled in 1983 and 1984. By the summer of 1984, it was a terrible market for most companies. Large corporations were, once again, 'caught with their assumptions down' (Carlston, 1985, pp. 229-230).

A more recent example of a corporate leader taking his company to the brink of disaster by 'a mad rush into the future' of educational technology is the sudden demise of Jostens Learning Corporation, in 1993 the largest educational software firm in the country. H. William Lurton, chairman of Jostens, Inc., vendor of school graduation products such as class rings, yearbooks, and school photographs, decided to diversify into multimedia education. Although Lurton knew nothing about interactive educational software, he rationalized that Jostens was already in the educational market, so it would not be too great a stretch. Besides, Lurton saw the potential K-12 market for Jostens Learning products as 'huge.'

Lurton rushed into a hot business he knew nothing about, 'a cropper chasing a fad,' according to an account in *Forbes* (Schifrin, 1994, pp. 80-81). In 1988 he purchased a 25 per cent stake in Broderbund Software. Then he bought Education Systems Corporation, an interactive software company, and hired its chairman, 'a slick entrepreneur' named John Kernan, to become chief executive of a new subsidiary, Jostens Learning. From 1986 to 1991, 'Jostens Learning grew merrily,' and in 1992 Kernan persuaded Lurton to buy Wicat Systems, Inc., former PLATO partner and its biggest educational software competitor, for $102 million. This gave Jostens Learning more than 60 per cent of the market in 'integrated learning systems' focused on sophisticated multimedia presentation with sound, animation, and video. The same year, Lurton was chosen to be the new chairman of the U.S. Chamber of Commerce, with his principal goal 'to advance the education-related initiatives of business' such as President Bush's America 2000 and the Chamber's Center for Workforce Preparation and Quality Education. Lurton, Kernan, and Jostens Learning seemed exceptionally well-placed within the education business (Holzinger, 1992, p. 83).

But Jostens was really heading for disaster. The problem was that Jostens software could only run on its own computer systems which were very expensive. Educators were starting to choose software that could run on different computers, preferably those already installed in their schools. Jostens did not know enough about such trends in computing, and its market share began to erode. By mid-1993, Kernan had left, and Lurton was unceremoniously ousted after 22 years as Josten's boss. Kernan, a former cable executive, landed on his feet and is now chairman of a new education venture. Jostens Learning, however, is pretty much out of the learning business, leaving behind myriad school districts littered with its computer-based detritus.

As a final example, John Akers, John Sculley, and Kay Whitmore, former chairmen of IBM, Apple, and Kodak, respectively, have been key corporate figures in federal education policy in the late 1980s and 1990s. Under President Bush, Whitmore was on the board of the New American Schools Development Corporation, Bush's corporate foundation to invent high technology, 'break the mold,' schools. Akers was a prominent player on Bush's pivotal Educational Policy Committee and chaired the Education Task Force for the blue-chip Business Roundtable. Sculley represented corporate America in President Clinton's own high technology vision for the schools. All three leaders paraded their companies as models to be emulated in school restructuring, and their corporate philanthropy to schools lent them legitimacy as educational leaders.

None of the three is on the education scene any longer, however. They have all been ousted unceremoniously from their firms because of woeful mismanagement that led their companies to the brink of disaster. Akers left with the worst record of any chief executive in the history of IBM. Hundreds of thousands of jobs have been cut from these companies, which have all pulled way back from their commitment to educational reform as well as from the marketing and servicing of their educational technology products which remain, of course, in the schools, underutilized by teachers and students.

Lesson 3: Corporate strategies for the marketing of computer-based education are chameleon-like, changing their colours to meet the needs of every new educational fad or government invitation or technological innovation that comes along.

As we have seen, companies marketing computer-based education have typically invested themselves in a rapid series of strategic overhauls trying to attain access into the schools. The identical technology is dressed up in one guise after another in order to appear the perfect solution to the latest educational fashion, whether it be remediation, accountability, individualized instruction, or special education. Most recently, this list of fashions has come to include school restructuring and authentic assessment, as firms stumble over themselves to demonstrate that computers are the perfect solution both to portfolio assessment strategies and to the overall reinventing of school organization.

When President Bush's New American Schools Development Corporation, for example, announced the winners in its multimillion dollar competition to design new schools for the twenty-first century, 'the big winner,' according to the editors of *Educational Technology*, 'was technology' (Blaschke, 1992, p. 4). Computers, one reads again and again, are the key to restructuring the school. Andrew Molnar, the central figure in the NSF's support of computer-based education for over three decades, announced in a recent address, 'The current crisis in education and the current desire to restructure education offers us a 'window of opportunity.' It is now time to begin building a new, national infrastructure to make computing available to all' (Molnar, no date, p. 10). Meanwhile, the nationwide movement toward authentic, portfolio-type assessments of children's progress has been targeted as another set of problems for which the computer is the perfect solution (see, for example, Jenkins, 1994, pp. 6-8). Restructuring and assessment are among the latest examples of how computer-based technology is being marketed to the fashions of the education community.

A recent report on educational technology, released in April, 1995, by the Office of Technology Assessment, recounts how 'the advice of experts in education technology has changed dramatically over the past decade' (West, 1995d, p. 11). In 1983, teachers were told to use computers to teach students to program in BASIC, because 'it's the language that comes with your computer.' In 1984, they were told to teach students to program in LOGO in order to 'teach students to think, not just to program.' In 1986, they were told to teach with integrated drill-and-practice systems in computer labs in order to 'individualize instruction and increase test scores.' In 1988, they were told to teach word processing because children should 'use computers as tools like adults do.'

In 1990, they were told to teach with curriculum-specific tools such as science simulations, history databases, and data probes, in order to 'integrate the computers into the existing curriculum.' In 1992, they were told to teach hypertext multimedia programming because 'students learn best by creating products for an audience.' And in 1994, they were told to teach with Internet telecommunications in order to 'let students be part of the real world.' These rapid-fire changes in the prevailing wisdom of educational technology experts indicate that still, after thirty years, the implementation of computer-based technology in schools is in a highly experimental stage, despite the billions spent annually. More importantly, they reflect a powerful, unrelenting pressure from corporate marketers and their education allies to get the computers into the schools, one way or another.

Intense corporate pressures and competition continue to fuel the lucrative educational software market in the 1990s, in which developers are scrambling to create 'killer apps' for the coming education superhighway. To cite just one example, take John Kernan, former head of Jostens Learning Corporation. Kernan, media marketer turned 'educator,' explains his interest in education in succinct competitive terms. 'What I've always wanted to do with this business is beat Nintendo' (West, 1995c, pp. 10-11). Kernan, now head of Lightspan Partnership, is questing after the 'killer app,' the computer application that, as defined by *Education Week*, is 'so immediately useful – and so potentially lucrative – that it will create consumer demand' (West, 1995c, p. 10). For Kernan, the 'killer app' is in education, and he is gambling the company on finding the right combination of education, entertainment, multimedia, and telecommunications to get to the pot of gold before anyone else. Lightspan's production of an 'interactive, industrial-strength K-6 curriculum,' packaged as entertainment, has attracted over $35 million in investment from such corporate giants as Microsoft, TCI and Comsat, which are themselves gambling on such visions of the future (West, 1995c, p. 10).

Microsoft's chairman, Bill Gates, was also the original promoter of CD ROM multimedia in the late 1980s, triggering another corporate competitive frenzy which has found its way to the schoolhouse door in the past few years. Competition among computer hardware makers and software publishers has driven firm after firm to leap into a consumer and school CD ROM market that is in fact 'mainly wishful thinking' rather than a real market based on consumer demand (Losee, 1994, p. 127). Corporate marketers have thrust CD ROM capabilities, built into personal computers, on school and home consumers, not because an abundance of quality CD ROM-based multimedia software exists, or because CD ROM technology is the wave of the future, but rather because companies see the CD ROM market as a competitive strategy. According to one executive, it is 'a low-risk way to practice making content for interactive television (ITV)' on the information highway (Losee, 1994, p. 140).

Corporate executives admit that CD ROM technology and software is merely a 'bridge technology,' a stopgap on the way to the information highway: 'CD ROMs are the Quonset hut of media – temporary structures that have a way of becoming permanent' (Losee, 1994, p. 143). Explains one executive, 'You're not going to get to participate in ITV unless you get in early … It's a warm-up' (Losee, 1994, p. 141). 'Companies view CD ROM as a competitive advantage,' says one industry observer, and this competition to position the firm for the information highway has resulted in untold quantities of CD ROM drives and 'a proliferation of ill conceived and sloppily executed CD ROM [software]' being discounted or given away to schools in the wake of 'seller-fed hysteria' (Losee, 1994, p. 143). Once again, crazed competition, not educational benefit, or consumer demand, or even careful business sense, is what is driving the technology into an already bewildered school market.

Lesson 4: Large-scale corporate ventures in computer-based education (typically supported by federal funds) exploit the financial crises of schools and the 'invalids' among the student population, thereby turning education's desperation into corporate opportunities to experiment with unproven wares.

Just as we saw in earlier efforts to penetrate the schools through federally funded programs for disadvantaged children and for special education students, corporate marketers of new computer-based 'integrated learning systems' have targeted schools and districts with large populations of poor students eligible for federal Chapter One funds. Recent for-profit ventures in school management, too, such as Christopher Whittle's Edison Project and John Golle's Education Alternatives, Inc. (EAI), which depend upon intensive use of computer-based instruction to squeeze out a profit from schools, have targeted federally funded Chapter One schools and districts, typically those most desperate due to diminishing availability of local and state school revenues (see, for example, Conlin, 1991, pp. 62-67).

Integrated learning systems (ILSs) are computer networks of approximately thirty computers, typically located in a 'computer lab,' to which classes of students are assigned several hours a week. The ILS delivers individualized, self-paced instruction in reading, math, and other subjects, monitoring and recording student progress, and prescribing appropriate lessons based on previous student performance. Despite systematically biased research by vendors and scant evidence for the effectiveness of such systems, districts around the country have been buying them in unprecedented numbers. According to a recent article, 'the market for integrated learning systems seems to be entering a new, and far more lucrative, era,' one of 'extraordinary growth' (West, 1992, p. 8). In part this is because ILS vendors offer financially strapped districts the appearance of efficient and effective instructional delivery without additional expenditures on staff salaries. ILS vendors promise, even guarantee, results in student performance, especially in the performance of those students with the direst educational needs.

The vendors of ILSs and the marketers of for-profit school management have recently teamed up in their efforts to tap into the desperation of school districts for resources and for evidence of student achievement. For example, since Jostens' demise the new market leader in integrated learning systems, Computer Curriculum Corporation (CCC) joined with EAI in 1992 as strategic partner in EAI's contract to manage Chapter One schools in Baltimore and, more recently, in Hartford, Connecticut. This partnership has remarkably direct linkages to the early exploitation of school failure by computer-based education marketers in the 1960s. Patrick Suppes, CCC's founder and still its primary shareholder, was supported by IBM and courted by GLC in the mid-1960s, while EAI chairman John Golle based his for-profit venture in individualized instruction on research compiled by and purchased from Control Data Corporation in 1986. CCC is now a subsidiary of Paramount Communications, which, in turn, was recently purchased by Viacom, the telecommunications and entertainment giant whose major rival, Time Warner, has been a principal investor in the other celebrated for-profit schooling scheme, Chris Whittle's Edison Project. These giant corporate forces are now, as earlier, knocking on the schoolhouse door with computer-based technologies, once again targeting the most desperate school systems and the most desperate students within them.

Lesson 5: Research with educational technology conducted in schools is as much or more a form of marketing and product development, using schools as laboratories, as it is an effort to serve schools or students.

The earliest computer-based education in the schools consisted of a scattering of military and corporate research and development projects housed in 'real life' laboratories (i.e., schools). These efforts, it was hoped, would provide evidence for the effectiveness of absurdly primitive technologies, would result in new marketable products, and would enhance corporate public relations. Much recent corporate research on computer-based education in schools continues this self-serving pattern, under the guise of philanthropy and educational reform. Most recent philanthropic programs in education promoted by high technology firms amount to the funding of research by educational practitioners that might result in new market strategies, new product uses, or new evidence of effectiveness. These programs, such as IBM's two successive $25 million grant programs encouraging educators to find new ways to adapt IBM technologies to schools and classrooms, are also widely advertised as community-minded philanthropy, thereby greatly enhancing the corporate public image (West, 1994, p. 5).

As before, these corporate research and development projects in the schools, paraded as rigorous, social-minded experiments in school reform, are, in effect, more marketing schemes than anything else. The latest example of such an effort is Apple Computer's research program called 'Apple Classrooms of Tomorrow' (ACOT). Begun in 1985, the ACOT project has established a 'community of partners' with school districts and researchers across the country, focused on incorporating technology as 'a necessary and catalytic part of the effort required to fundamental [sic] restructure America's education system' (David, 1994, p. 1). According to a published ACOT progress report, ACOT began as an experiment about the effects of computers in education. In trade for equipment and technical support sufficient to 'saturate' classrooms with computer-based technologies, each district agreed to make its schools, teachers, and students 'available for study by Apple and Apple's consultants' (David, 1994, p. 2). ACOT staff has gradually played an increasingly directive role aimed at transforming the teaching and learning at the schools.

Apple's publications emphasize that the benefits to the firm lie strictly in its disinterested contribution to the enhancement of education. As its 'considerable benefit,' according to one ACOT document, 'Apple gets real-world laboratories in which to develop, test, and generate new knowledge about teaching and learning in a context clearly separated from company profits.' A benefit to the school district, but apparently not to the firm, says Apple, is the considerable 'positive publicity' ACOT classrooms receive in the form of national television exposure, published articles, and 'visitors from all over the world' (David, 1994, p. 3).

All too frequently, says Apple, 'educators tend to look at ACOT and dismiss it as unrealistic because of the concentrated resources' (David, 1994, p. 8). Yet even with its unparalleled computer saturation, clear, replicable results have not been forthcoming from a decade of ACOT research, and any positive changes in instruction and learning at ACOT sites, Apple concedes, might just as well be the result of new project-oriented methods of instruction and the teaming of teachers as from any contribution from the technology itself (Dwyer, 1994, pp. 4-10). In defense, as did their predecessors of the last three decades, Apple stresses the 'long term nature of the experiment, and the complexity of the questions.' If nothing else, Apple insists, 'technology stands out in [ACOT] classrooms as a symbol ... that schooling can and will change, that classrooms may have some bearing on the twenty-first century after all' (Dwyer, 1994, p. 9).

Apple's ACOT program is the most visible, and is considered the most progressive, corporate research and development project in computer technology within the nation's schools. As such, ACOT staff have been keenly sensitive about Apple not being perceived as self-serving and 'caring more about its product than about the teachers and students' (David, 1994, p. 9). In Apple's own assessment, 'an important turning point [in the project came with] a shift from perceived exploitation of the classrooms for Apple marketing purposes, to a clear signal from Apple that ACOT's purpose was long-term research and development aimed at producing new knowledge about technology and education. Sites no longer relied on local Apple sales representatives as their main source of assistance, nor were they asked to participate in surveys or other studies designed to provide fodder for sales and marketing units in Apple' (David, 1994, p. 10).

Apparently, once these signs of obvious merchandising and immediate profit making were removed, teachers and staff in ACOT schools accepted and trusted their new business partners. But long-term research and development is the stock in trade of high technology firms such as Apple, and research on learning is a key factor in the development of new, more sophisticated forms of the computer, often called the 'learning machine.' This is why Xerox has invested millions in its Institute for Research on Learning in California, why IBM, Arthur Andersen, and other technology giants are principal investors in the Institute for the Learning Sciences at Northwestern University, and why Apple itself is integrally involved in the Alliance for Restructuring Education along with the Learning Research and Development Center at the University of Pittsburgh. Learning research is a key component in basic computer research and development as well as in the search for new computer applications for the education market. Apple's careful orchestration of public relations surrounding ACOT conceals the fact that long term research and development in schools is, now as in the past, really marketing and product development in the guise of philanthropy and high-minded education reform.

Lesson 6: Computer-based education is more about using schools and the education market in the service of technological product development and profits than it is about using technology in the service of education, schools, and students.

A great deal of the school experimentation with computer-based education in the 1950s and 1960s was only marginally about education. The computer industry and military agencies were aggressively pursuing research in human-computer interaction, interface design, and automated tutoring systems for technical training. So-called educational research in this area, therefore, was in fact serving purposes very far afield from education. This is true in the 1990s as well, with the expansion of the 'information highway' into the schools, which arguably serves the interests of the entertainment and telecommunications industry rather than the needs or interests of education.

The latest merger frenzy now dominating the mad dash to the information superhighway is surprisingly reminiscent of the flurry of mergers between 'hardware' and 'software' companies that took place in the mid-1960s. A recent article offers a scorecard: 'MCI and News Corp, U.S. West and Time Warner, Creative Artists Agency and Nynex, Bell Atlantic and Pacific Telesis, Walt Disney and three other Baby Bells. There seems to be no end in sight to the coupling of the entertainment and communications giants ... The reason for the scramble to do a deal? The cable and phone companies are the infrastructure guys; ... [and] the entertainment companies have the content needed to fill those pipelines' (Clarkin, 1995, p. 29). In other words, we're seeing the convergence of hardware and software all over again. Only this time education is a mere afterthought, or more accurately, a niche in the coming interactive media deluge that will someday, it is widely believed, flow through the pipelines of the information superhighway.

Educational materials and instruction are now viewed by corporate America as one small category of 'software' or 'content' on the information superhighway, alongside computer games, electronic mail and bulletin boards, news, books, magazines, movies, pornography, television shows, interactive TV, consumer advertising, gambling, and home shopping capabilities. The target for all of these products is vast – the apparently limitless market for entertainment and other services pumped to homes and institutions along the information superhighway. And the motivations behind these latest corporate mega-ventures are even less noble or honourable than those driving the mergers into education in the sixties. Here there is not even a hint of social responsibility or philanthropy; these firms do not even pretend to be saving the schools or the poor or the underprivileged. In fact, they have had to be goaded by the federal administration into linking their telecommunications to the schools, since the education market is but a mere speck in their grandiose, and unashamedly greed-inspired, visions.

As in the 1960s, government leaders champion and encourage the latest technological assault on schools, decrying the woeful lack of an electronic infrastructure that, according to the chairman of the Federal Communications Commission, keeps students 'locked up in education cells' (West, 1995b, p. 7). Just as in the 1960s, Vice President Al Gore's promotion of a National Information Infrastructure linking schools to the Information highway has attempted to 'alert ... the telecommunications industry to a huge new market' (West, 1995a, p. 8). And just as in the 1960s and again in the 1980s, the FCC chairman has argued that 'networks into the classroom [will] be the greatest technological advance since the printing press' (West, 1995b, p. 7). His fantasy is that 'from their individual classrooms, teachers must be able to send and receive faxes, upload and download information from communications satellites, have access to interactive television programming, communicate with parents at home over telephone lines, and join virtual communities of their colleagues on-line' (West, 1995b, p. 7).

Despite these high-sounding prognostications (however removed from the real concerns of teachers), such communication capabilities are not what the information highway is actually all about. From the perspective of the corporate giants investing the billions to make it a reality, it's about entertainment – period – and education will perforce become steadily subsumed within entertainment when and if the information becomes reality. 'What's clear,' notes one Bell Atlantic executive, 'is [that] this is not so much an info highway, but an entertainment highway' (Michael Lasky, Bell Atlantic, quoted in Schwartz, 1995, p. 114). The reason is obvious to Bell Atlantic's CEO Ray Smith, who explained, when asked why the telecommunications giant was betting the company on interactive television and other interactive entertainment media: 'Why ...? Because that's where the people are' (Kline, 1995, p. 164). And, indeed, Americans spent about $340 billion on entertainment in 1993, compared with $270 billion spent on elementary and secondary education, both public and private (Landler, 1994, p. 66).

Already there are many signs of the coming marriage between education and entertainment with computer and telecommunications technology serving as matchmaker. The two cultures that dominate children's lives – education and entertainment – are merging, as entertainment companies seek to legitimize their products in the eyes of parents and educators by making them 'educational,' while educational technologists strive to incorporate the magical motivational ingredient of video games into their lessons. In the words of one observer, 'video games increasingly strive to instruct and learning software [increasingly] attempts to amuse ...' (Brody, 1993, pp. 52, 53).

Media and education critic Neil Postman offers a sober if unheeded reply in his book, *Amusing Ourselves to Death*: '[The entertainment industry's] principal contribution to educational philosophy is the idea that teaching and entertainment are inseparable. This entirely original conception is to be found nowhere in educational discourses, from Confucius to Plato to Cicero to Locke to John Dewey ... [Among educational philosophers,] no one has ever said or implied that significant learning is effectively, durably, and truthfully achieved when education is entertainment' (Postman, 1986, p. 146). And yet, in our world increasingly dominated by Time Warner and Viacom, Nintendo and MTV, the equation is rarely even questioned.

Publishing itself has become a component of software production, alongside movies, computer games, and other entertainment products, as most major publishing companies have been bought up by media and cable giants. This is true for educational publishing in particular, as textbook publishers and educational software developers are swallowed up into the vision of media conglomerates. Two examples are Broderbund and Davidson, ranked first and second in educational software. Broderbund, the firm of Doug Carlston, recently was about to be acquired by video-game giant Electronic Arts, Inc. before the deal fell through at the last minute. And Davidson and Associates, Inc., a leader in 'edutainment' software with its 'Math Blaster' series, recently entered into a five-year agreement with CCC at Paramount (now a part of media giant Viacom) to produce consumer software.

A groundbreaking meeting of textbook and technology publishers convened in February, 1993 to 'redefine instructional materials' and determine the 'implications for education and publishing.' It concluded that 'there is no longer a 'textbook' market and a technology market in schools … [Instead] it's an instructional materials market that needs to draw upon multiple media to deliver new curriculum to education' (Hill, 1993, p. 12). Echoing identical pronouncements in the sixties, the conference called for new 'strategic alliances' between technology and textbook companies in order to 'meet the multiple media needs of the schools [and homes].' And the common denominator of these needs is entertainment. According to Patrick Donaghy, president of Optical Data Corporation, the leading marketer of educational videodiscs, 'For companies that don't recognize that education and entertainment are coming together, there's not going to be a future' (Hill, 1993, p. 12).

In point of fact, the entertainment industry, rapidly merging with the telecommunications industry in the production and delivery of interactive media products along the superhighway, is the real engine of technological development in the 1990s, just as the military was its prime mover during former decades. According to the chairman of Silicon Graphics, a supplier of technology and software to the entertainment field, 'The entertainment industry is now the driving force for new technology, as defense used to be' (Mandel, Landler, & Grover, 1994, p. 60). And just as development of defense technology in computer-based instruction and human-computer interaction shaped the very first computer-based forays into the schools, now the technological visions of the entertainment and telecommunications industry are shaping the latest computer-based 'classrooms of the future,' as technologies developed for movies, interactive games, and theme parks are 'repurposed' (West, 1995a, pp. 6, 23) for delivery to the classroom. And educators, according to *Education Week*, are, 'at best, peripheral players in the game' (West, 1995a, pp. 6, 23).

Once again, because the moguls behind the new, highly competitive industry have no way to predict real consumer demand and therefore the real size of the market, the result could be devastation for many of the major corporate players and for those consumers – including schools – unlucky enough to hitch their futures to these players. 'The question is,' Viacom's chief executive asserts, 'will the market grow quickly enough to accommodate all the new players at the table? I think probably not' (Mandel et al., 1994, p. 61). Admits communications mogul Rupert Murdoch, 'We don't have the slightest idea what people are going to buy' (Mandel et al., 1994, p. 63).

And yet none of these corporate conglomerates of entertainment and telecommunications seem willing to bypass the high-stakes risks involved. No wonder, according to a story in *Business Week*, that '[o]f all the segments of the entertainment economy, the Information Highway generates the most angst among executives. They know it will be powered by entertainment. But the capital investments are gigantic' (Mandel et al., 1994, p. 63). They are all in it up to their corporate chins and so, by default it appears, are the rest of us. Especially now, as powerful new legislation to deregulate these industries has issued forth from Congress in mid-1995 successfully undercutting any hope for governmental roadblocks to the industry's rapacious hegemony. As for education, 'somebody's 'big wire' is going to be in every school,' notes one executive, 'and that presents a [huge] opportunity' (West, 1995a, p. 25) – one apparently too big for the Big Boys to miss out on. And so, still again, education is being sold a bill of goods by the relentless, rapacious marketers of a dubious technological future.

And so, as perhaps never before, it is appropriate to echo the query of education historian Lawrence Cremin who asked, in response to the first corporate assault on education with technology in the mid-1960s: '... who is big enough and honest enough and independent enough, and where can the countervailing power be mustered to call for order?' (Cremin, 1968, p. 96).

ENDNOTES

[1.] This article was written with the support of a National Academy of Education Spencer Postdoctoral Fellowship.

[2.] Most of the material in this section comes from either the Lyle M. Spencer Papers at the University of Chicago Archives or the Spencer Foundation Oral History Project of the Oral History Research Office of Columbia University.

[3.] Most of the information for this section comes from the Papers of Carl Solberg, Assistant Director of Research and Development for the General Learning Corporation, housed in the Special Collections, Millbank Memorial Library, Teachers College, Columbia University.

[4.] Most of the material from this section comes from the Control Data Corporation archives at the Charles Babbage Institute, Center for the History of Information Processing, University of Minnesota.

REFERENCES

Atkinson, R. C. (1968). Ingredients for a theory of instruction. In M. C. Wittrock, *Changing education: Alternatives from educational research* (pp. 65-82). Englewood Cliffs, NJ: Prentice Hall.

Austell, R. (1965, April 23). *Memo from Rhett Austell to George Haller* (Carl Solberg Papers, Box 1, Special Collections, Millbank Memorial Library). New York: Columbia University, Teachers College.

Barbour, A. (1987, March). After split, Plato and Wicat pursue differing goals. *Electronic Learning*, 9-10.

Bartel, B. W. (1979, March 23). *Letter from Bernhard W. Bartel, School Superintendent, Independent School District #831, to House Committee* (located in 'Rural Schools Task Force – Secondary Schools Committee' folder, Box 123568, Control Data Corporation Archives).

Minneapolis: University of Minnesota, Center for the History of Information Processing, Charles Babbage Institute.

Bernier, J. C. (1966, June 17). *Memo from Bernier to computer systems task force* (Carl Solberg Papers, Box 3, Special Collections, Millbank Memorial Library). New York: Columbia University, Teachers College.

Bevers, R. J. (1977, May 9). *Memo from R. J. Bevers to J. R. Morris* (Box 149752, Control Data Corporation Archives). Minneapolis: University of Minnesota, Center for the History of Information Processing, Charles Babbage Institute.

Bitzer, D. (1988, February 19). *Interview by Sheldon Hochheiter* (OH 141, Control Data Corporation Archives). Minneapolis: University of Minnesota, Center for Information Processing, Charles Babbage Institute.

Blaschke, C. (1992, August). Review of the NASDC awards. *Educational Technology*, p. 4.

Bloom, B. (1985). *Interview* (Spencer Foundation Oral History Project). New York: Columbia University, Oral History Research Office.

Borrell, J. (1992, September). America's shame: How we've abandoned our children's futures. *MacWorld*, pp. 3-5.

Bowen, E. (1964a, January 9). *Memo from Ezra Bowen to Norm Ross and Jerry Hardy on Education R&D* (Carl Solberg Papers, Box 1, Special Collections, Millbank Memorial Library). New York: Columbia University, Teachers College.

Bowen, E. (1964b, June 24). *Memo from Ezra Bowen to Norm Ross, Education R&D* (Carl Solberg Papers, Box 1, Special Collections, Millbank Memorial Library). New York: Columbia University, Teachers College.

Bowen, E. (1964c, September 3). *Memo from Ezra Bowen to Francis Keppel regarding 'Time Magazine story'* (Carl Solberg Papers, Box 7, Special Collections, Millbank Memorial Library). New York: Columbia University, Teachers College.

Bowen, E. (1965a, January 25). *Memo from Ezra Bowen to Joan Mebane regarding 'GE visit'* (Carl Solberg Papers, Box 1, Special Collections, Millbank Memorial Library). New York: Columbia University, Teachers College.

Bowen, E. (1965b, January 25). *Memo from Ezra Bowen to Norm Ross, 'ESP May 1965"* (Carl Solberg Papers, Box 1, Special Collections, Millbank Memorial Library). New York: Columbia University, Teachers College.

Bowen, E. (1965c, February 1). *Proposal to task force* (Carl Solberg Papers, Box 1, Special Collections, Millbank Memorial Library). New York: Columbia University, Teachers College.

Bowen, E. (1965d, February 4). *Memo from Ezra Bowen to ESP task force entitled 'Review of charge and initial function* (Carl Solberg Papers, Box 1, Special Collections, Millbank Memorial Library). New York: Columbia University, Teachers College.

Bowen, E. (1965e, March 12). *'Confidential memo' from Ezra Bowen to Ed Baker et al.* (Carl Solberg Papers, Box 1, Special Collections, Millbank Memorial Library). New York: Columbia University, Teachers College.

Bowen, E. (1965f, March 30). *Memo from Ezra Bowen to ESP task force* (Carl Solberg Papers, Box 1, Special Collections, Millbank Memorial Library). New York: Columbia University, Teachers College.

Bowen, E. (1965g, March 30). *Memo from Ezra Bowen to Roy Larsen and Norm Ross* (Carl Solberg Papers, Box 7, Special Collections, Millbank Memorial Library). New York: Columbia University, Teachers College.

Bowen, E. (1965h, July 16). *Confidential memo from Ezra Bowen to Norm Ross* (Carl Solberg Papers, Box 8, Special Collections, Millbank Memorial Library). New York: Columbia University, Teachers College.

Brody, H. (1993, Nov./Dec.). Video games that teach? *Technology Review, 96*(8), 52, 53.

Bruning, W. H. (no date). *Consulting and educational services – Strategic plan 1980-1984* (Box 149752, Control Data Corporation Archives). Minneapolis: University of Minnesota, Center for the History of Information Processing, Charles Babbage Institute.

Carlston, D. G. (1985). *Software people: An insider look at the personal computer software industry.* New York: Simon & Schuster.

Clarkin, G. (1995, May 11). Giants' mad dash to find partners. *New York Post* (Business Section), p. 29.

Conlin, E. (1991, July). Educating the market. *Inc.*

Conner, R. D. (1977, May 10). *Analysis and recommendation on CD education strategy* (Box 149752, Control Data Corporation Archives). Minneapolis: University of Minnesota, Center for the History of Information Processing, Charles Babbage Institute.

Control Data Corporation (no date). *PLATO strategy for the State of Minnesota* (in 'MECC: Minnesota Educational Computing Consortium' folder, Box 123568, Control Data Corporation Archives). Minneapolis: University of Minnesota, Center for the History of Information Processing, Charles Babbage Institute.

Control Data Corporation (1972, February 16). *Education market exploitation plan, Section II* (Box 107443, Control Data Corporation Archives). Minneapolis: University of Minnesota, Center for the History of Information Processing, Charles Babbage Institute.

Control Data Corporation (1978, October 11). *Draft: Secondary schools committee charter and policy guidelines* (Box 149045, Control Data Corporation Archives). Minneapolis: University of Minnesota, Center for the History of Information Processing, Charles Babbage Institute.

Cremin L. (1968). *Interview* (Carnegie Corporation Oral History Project). New York: Columbia University, Oral History Research Office.

Dannemeyer, J. W. (no date). *Source notes on the history of CDC PLATO* (Box AR, Control Data Corporation Executive History Narratives, Control Data Corporation Archives). Minneapolis: University of Minnesota, Center for the History of Information Processing, Charles Babbage Institute.

Dannemeyer, J. W. (1978a, January 13). *Memo from J. W. Dannemeyer to R. C. Chin, 'Private and confidential'* (Box 156958, Control Data Corporation Archives). Minneapolis: University of Minnesota, Center for the History of Information Processing, Charles Babbage Institute.

Dannemeyer, J. W. (1978b, February 7). *Memo from J. W. Dannemeyer to R. C. Chin and W. J. Ridley* (Box 156958, Control Data Corporation Archives). Minneapolis: University of Minnesota, Center for the History of Information Processing, Charles Babbage Institute.

David, J. L. (1994). *ACOT Report #2: Partnerships for change.* Cupertino, CA: Apple Computer.

Diamond, E. (1985). *Interview* (Spencer Foundation Oral History Project). New York: Columbia University, Oral History Research Office.

Dwyer, D. (1994, April). Apple classrooms of tomorrow: What we've learned. *Educational Leadership, 51*(7), 4-10.

Ellis, R. (1965, July 23). *Memo from Ellis to Beshoar, 'Special report on educational technology'* (Carl Solberg Papers, Box 1, Special Collections, Millbank Memorial Library). New York: Columbia University, Teachers College.

Ellis, R. (1966, September 16). *Memo from Robert Ellis to Norm Ross regarding 'American Institutes of Research'* (Carl Solberg Papers, Box 5, Special Collections, Millbank Memorial Library). New York: Columbia University, Teachers College.

Ellis, R. & Mercer, J. (1964, December 9). *Position paper: Time, Inc.-General Electric talks* (Carl Solberg Papers, Box 8, Special Collections, Millbank Memorial Library). New York: Columbia University, Teachers College.

Fletcher, J. D. & Rockaway, M. (1986). Computer-based training in the military. In J. A. Ellis (Ed.), *Military contributions to instructional technology* (pp. 171-222). New York: Praeger.

Flint, J. (1993, August 16). Vision is next month. *Forbes*, pp. 45-46.

Gandy, O. H., Jr. (1976). *Instructional technology: The reselling of the Pentagon*. Unpublished doctoral dissertation, Stanford University.

Gingerella, L. F. (1979, June 19). *Memo from L. F. Gingerella to W. N. Rose regarding 'State Department of Education meeting June 13, 1979"* (Box 149045, Control Data Corporation Archives). Minneapolis: University of Minnesota, Center for the History of Information Processing, Charles Babbage Institute.

Grant, G. (1966, July 3). School teaching 'hardware' a booming new business. *Washington Post*, pp. 12, 13.

Grant, G. (1967, March 21). 'Software triumphs over software' as Keppel shakes up general learning. *Washington Post*, p. 1.

Harris, I. (1983). *Interview* (Spencer Foundation Oral History Project). New York: Columbia University, Oral History Research Office.

Hill, M. (1993, May/June). Textbook, technology publishers meet on common ground. *Electronic Learning*, p. 12.

Hogg, J. F. (1978, May 9). *Letter from J. F. Hogg to J. R. Morris* (Box 149752, Control Data Corporation Archives). Minneapolis: University of Minnesota, Center for the History of Information Processing, Charles Babbage Institute.

Holzinger, A. G. (1992, April). A commitment to helping people. *Nation's Business*, p. 83.

Ianni, F. (1966, May 1). *Letter from Fritz Ianni to Carl Solberg regarding 'CAI task force'* (Carl Solberg Papers, Box 11, Special Collections, Millbank Memorial Library). New York: Columbia University, Teachers College. IBM's next target: The classroom. (1966, September 15). *Forbes*, p. 60.

Information Processing Department (1979, June 25). A social strategy aimed at profits. *Business Week*, pp. 118-119.

Jenkins, Y. L. (1994, March). Touching the mind: Technology and assessment. *Computing Teacher*, pp. 6-8.

Johnson, M. (1966, March 8). *Memo from Malcolm Johnson to Norm Ross regarding 'Requests for support to the joint venture'* (Carl Solberg Papers, Box 5, Special Collections, Millbank Memorial Library). New York: Columbia University, Teachers College.

Kahn, S. (1986, September). Very good! *Venture*, pp. 50-59.

Keppel, F. (no date). *Memo from Francis Keppel to Roy Larsen* (Francis Keppel Papers). Cambridge, MA: Harvard University Archives.

Keppel, F. (1966). *The necessary revolution in American education*. New York: Harper and Row.

Keppel, F. (1967, January). The business interest in education. *Phi Delta Kappan*, pp. 187-190.

Keppel, F. (1970a, June 29). *Memo from Francis Keppel to James Backe regarding 'Long-range planning'* (Francis Keppel Papers). Cambridge, MA: Harvard University Archives.

Keppel, F. (1970b, July 16). *Memo from Francis Keppel to James Backe* (Francis Keppel Papers). Cambridge, MA: Harvard University Archives.

Keppel, F. (1970c, July/August). New relationships between education and industry. *Public Administration Review, 30*(4), 353-359.

Keppel, F. (1971a, March 23). *Educational challenges of the 70s* (News release, Francis Keppel Papers). Cambridge, MA: Harvard University Archives.

Keppel, F. (1971b, December 23). *Memo from Francis Keppel to James Backe* (Francis Keppel Papers). Cambridge, MA: Harvard University Archives.

Keppel, F. (1983). *Interview* (Spencer Foundation Oral History Project). New York: Columbia University, Oral History Research Office.

Keppel, F. (1984). *Interview* (Spencer Foundation Oral History Project). New York: Columbia University, Oral History Research Office.

Kline, D. (1995, February). Align and conquer: An interview with Bell Atlantic's CEO Ray Smith. *Wired*, pp. 110-117, 164.

Lacey, J. W. (1977a, May 11). *Memo from J. W. Lacey to J. R. Morris regarding 'CBE strategy, 2-3 year range'* (Box 149752, Control Data Corporation Archives). Minneapolis: University of Minnesota, Center for the History of Information Processing, Charles Babbage Institute.

Lacey, J. W. (1977b, May 16). *Memo from J. W. Lacey to R. E. Morris regarding 'CBE market strategy and priority meeting'* (Box 131584, Control Data Corporation Archives). Minneapolis: University of Minnesota, Center for the History of Information Processing, Charles Babbage Institute.

Lacey, J. W. (1977c, May 16). *Memo from J. W. Lacey to R. E. Morris et al. regarding 'Comments by W. J. Ridley at CBE marketing strategy and priority meeting'* (Box 131584, Control Data Corporation Archives). Minneapolis: University of Minnesota, Center for the History of Information Processing, Charles Babbage Institute.

Landler, M. (1994, March 14). Are we having fun yet? Maybe too much. *Business Week*, pp. 66-70.

Larson, V. F. (1984). *Interview* (Spencer Foundation Oral History Project). New York: Columbia University, Oral History Research Office.

Lawler, R. W. (1987). Learning environments: Now, then, and someday. In R. W. Lawler & M. Yazdani, *Artificial intelligence and education* (Vol. 1, pp. 1-25). Norwood, NJ: Ablex.

Learson, V. (1982). *Interview* (Spencer Foundation Oral History Project). New York: Columbia University, Oral History Research Office.

Lewis, M. (1983, September 28). Selling PLATO. *Minneapolis/St. Paul Citibusiness*, pp. 12-13.

Licklider, J.C.R. (1967). Preliminary experiments in computer-aided teaching. In J. E. Coulson (Ed.), *Programmed learning and computer-based instruction* (pp. 217-239). New York: John Wiley.

Linen, J. A. (1965, November 19). *Memo from James A. Linen to Time, Inc., staff* (Carl Solberg Papers, Box 5, Special Collections, Millbank Memorial Library). New York: Columbia University, Teachers College.

Losee, S. (1994, September 19). Watch out for the CD-ROM hype. *Fortune*, pp. 127-143.

Mandel, M. J., Landler, M., & Grover, R. (1994, March 14). The entertainment economy. *Business Week*, pp. 58-66.

Marketing Perspectives for IEP Product Line. (no date). (In 'IEP reports' folder, Box 149045, Control Data Corporation Archives). Minneapolis: University of Minnesota, Center for the History of Information Processing, Charles Babbage Institute.

Mebane, J. (1966, August 17). *The market: Competitive influences* (Carl Solberg Papers, Box 3, Special Collections, Millbank Memorial Library). New York: Columbia University, Teachers College.

Melton, A. W. (1959). The science of learning and the technology of educational methods. *Harvard Educational Review, 29*(2), 97-105.

Merrill, B. E. (1979, February 12). *The competition and marketplace for PLATO basic skills package* (Box 123568, Control Data Corporation Archives). Minneapolis: University of Minnesota, Center for the History of Information Processing, Charles Babbage Institute.

Molnar, A. (no date). *Computers in education: A historical perspective of the unfinished task.* Unpublished speech, National Science Foundation.

Molnar, A. (1991, September 25). *Interview by William Aspray* (OH 234, Control Data Corporation Archives). Minneapolis: University of Minnesota, Center for the History of Information Processing, Charles Babbage Institute.

Morris, J. R. (1978). *Memo from J. R. Morris to J. W. Lacey regarding 'Proposed strategic plan'* (Box 149752, Control Data Corporation Archives). Minneapolis: University of Minnesota, Center for the History of Information Processing, Charles Babbage Institute.

Morris, R. E. (1977, May 10). *Memo from R. E. Morris to J. R. Morris* (Box 149752, Control Data Corporation Archives). Minneapolis: University of Minnesota, Center for the History of Information Processing, Charles Babbage Institute.

Muller, V. A. (1979, April 24). *Memo from V. A. Muller to W. J. Ridley regarding 'Little Fork/ Big Falls academic courseware review'* (Box 156958, Control Data Corporation Archives). Minneapolis: University of Minnesota, Center for the History of Information Processing, Charles Babbage Institute.

Mullin-Traynor, V. A. (1980, January 18). *Marketing perspectives for the IEP program product line* (Box 149045, Control Data Corporation Archives). Minneapolis: University of Minnesota, Center for the History of Information Processing, Charles Babbage Institute.

Neil, K. (1965, August 8). *Letter from Kaye Neil to Ezra Bowen, 'Confidential' on ESI* (Carl Solberg Papers, Box 1, Special Collections, Millbank Memorial Library). New York: Columbia University, Teachers College.

Noble, D. D. (1991). *The classroom arsenal: Military research, information technology, and public education.* London: Falmer Press.

Office of Technology Assessment (1982). *Information technology: Its impact on American education.* Washington, DC: U.S. Government Printing Office.

Pantages, A. (1976, May). *Control data's education offering: 'Plato would have enjoyed PLATO'.* Datamation, pp. 183-187.

Parker, D. (1984). *Interview* (Spencer Foundation Oral History Project). New York: Columbia University, Oral History Research Office.

Parker, W. (1993, July 12). What ever happened to control data? *St. Paul Pioneer Press*, pp. 1F-10F.

Pinney, G. W. (1982, August 22). Studies don't confirm claims for PLATO's teaching success. *Minneapolis Star and Tribune*, pp. 6A-7A.

Pinney, G. W. (1983, October 8). Control Data drops ads for PLATO courses, but won't say why. *Minneapolis Star and Tribune*, pp. 9B-10B.

Postman, N. (1986). *Amusing ourselves to death.* London: Heinemann.

Prendergast, C. (1986). *The world of Time, Inc.* (Vol. 3). New York: Atheneum.

Reichek, M. A. (Ed.). (1970, May 2). High marks in the teaching business. *Business Week*, p. 32.

Rethinking the LOGO Culture: What Lessons Have Been Learned? (1995, April 18). Symposium conducted at the Annual Meeting of the American Educational Research Association, San Francisco.

Ridley, W. J. (1978, June). *CDC Education Company long range strategic plan 1979-1983* (Box 149752, Control Data Corporation Archives). Minneapolis: University of Minnesota, Center for the History of Information Processing, Charles Babbage Institute.

Ross, N. (1965, December 6). *Memo from Norm Ross to Rhett Austell et al. regarding 'GLCJV-Name'* (Carl Solberg Papers, Box 5, Special Collections, Millbank Memorial Library). New York: Columbia University, Teachers College.

Sackman, H. (1967). *Computers, system science, and evolving society: The challenge of man-machine digital systems.* New York: John Wiley.

Schifrin, M. (1994, July 18). Look before you leap. *Forbes*, pp. 80-81.

Schilling, S. L. (1981a, March 10). *Memo from S. L. Schilling to W. J. Ridley regarding 'IEP Plan'* (Box 149045, Control Data Corporation Archives). Minneapolis: University of Minnesota, Center for the History of Information Processing, Charles Babbage Institute.

Schilling, S. L. (1981b, May 1). *Memo from S. L. Schilling to W. J. Ridley et al.* (Box 149045, Control Data Corporation Archives). Minneapolis: University of Minnesota, Center for the History of Information Processing, Charles Babbage Institute.

Schwartz, E. (1995, February). Ray Smith: The I-way, my-way. *Wired*, p. 113.

Sheehan, J. M. (1977, May 4). *Memo from J. M. Sheehan to J. R. Morris* (Box 149752, Control Data Corporation Archives). Minneapolis: University of Minnesota, Center for the History of Information Processing, Charles Babbage Institute.

Silberman, H. F. (1964, May 22). *Education and the new role of knowledge* (Final report of the R&D Project on Education, Carl Solberg Papers, Box 9, Special Collections, Millbank Memorial Library). New York: Columbia University, Teachers College.

Silberman, H. F. (1967). Characteristics of some recent studies of instructional methods. In J. E. Coulson (Ed.), *Programmed learning and computer based instruction* (pp. 13-24). New York: Wiley.

Singleton, I. C. (1966a, May 13). *Memo from Ira C. Singleton to Carl Solberg* (Carl Solberg Papers, Box 11, Special Collections, Millbank Memorial Library). New York: Columbia University, Teachers College.

Singleton, I. C. (1966b, August 10). *Memo from Ira C. Singleton to Carl Solberg regarding 'Task force report, Chapter 2"* (Carl Solberg Papers, Box 3, Special Collections, Millbank Memorial Library). New York: Columbia University, Teachers College.

Smith, G. G. (1980, October 6). *CDC executive history narratives* (Box AR, Control Data Corporation Archives). Minneapolis: University of Minnesota, Center for the History of Information Processing, Charles Babbage Institute.

Smith, W. D. (1976, April 15). Control data computer to be used in education. *The New York Times*, p 3A.

Solberg, C. (1964a, December 9). *Notes on GE-Time, Inc. meeting, 'GE: A versatile giant in search of new markets* (Carl Solberg Papers, Box 8, Special Collections, Millbank Memorial Library). New York: Columbia University, Teachers College.

Solberg, C. (1964b, November 23). *Briefing paper on GE from Carl Solberg to Jim Mercer and Bob Ellis* (Carl Solberg Papers, Box 1, Special Collections, Millbank Memorial Library). New York: Columbia University, Teachers College.

Solberg, C. (1966a, June). *Memo from Carl Solberg to task force regarding 'Visit to System Development Center'* (Carl Solberg Papers, Box 2, Special Collections, Millbank Memorial Library). New York: Columbia University, Teachers College.

Solberg, C. (1966b, July 27). *Carl Solberg, 'Notes of discussion with Lindy Saline and Al Boyd* (Carl Solberg Papers, Box 5, Special Collections, Millbank Memorial Library). New York: Columbia University, Teachers College.

Solberg, C. (1966c, August 16). *Computer systems task force report – Chapter III* (Carl Solberg Papers, Box 11, Special Collections, Millbank Memorial Library). New York: Columbia University, Teachers College.

Solberg, C. (1966d, November 16). *Memo from Carl Solberg to Winston Ehrmann regarding 'Clinton Job Corps Center'* (Carl Solberg Papers, Box 5, Special Collections, Millbank Memorial Library). New York: Columbia University, Teachers College.

Solberg, C. (1967, February 10). *Memo from Carl Solberg to Dana M. Cotton* (Carl Solberg Papers, Box 7, Special Collections, Millbank Memorial Library). New York: Columbia University, Teachers College.

Solberg, C. (1984, May 30). *Cover letter from Carl Solberg to David Ment, archivist, Millbank Library* (Carl Solberg Papers, Special Collections, Millbank Memorial Library). New York: Columbia University, Teachers College.

Spencer, L. M. (1961a, September 9). *Speech entitled 'Due diligence'* (Lyle M. Spencer Papers, Box 1). Chicago: University of Chicago Archives.

Spencer, L. M. (1961b, October 11.) *Address to new employees orientation meeting* (Lyle M. Spencer Papers, Box 1). Chicago: University of Chicago Archives.

Spencer, L. M. (1962a, September 20). *Problems of family-owned business* (Speech to the Young Presidents' Organization, Lyle M. Spencer Papers, Box 1). Chicago: University of Chicago Archives.

Spencer, L. M. (1962b). *Notes on SRA* (Lyle M. Spencer Papers, Box 2). Chicago: University of Chicago Archives.

Spencer, L. M. (1964, January 21). *Speech to IBM board of directors* (Lyle M. Spencer Papers, Box 1). Chicago: University of Chicago Archives.

Spencer, L. M. (1965a, March 23). *Speech to IBM entitled 'SRA and the war on poverty'* (Lyle M. Spencer Papers, Box 1). Chicago: University of Chicago Archives.

Spencer, L. M. (1965b, April 14). *Speech to SRA directors* (Lyle M. Spencer Papers, Box 1). Chicago: University of Chicago Archives.

Spencer, L. M. (1965c, June 3). *Speech to IBM Executive Computer Concepts Reunion* (Lyle M. Spencer Papers, Box 1). Chicago: University of Chicago Archives.

Spencer, L. M. (1965d, September 29). *Speech to SRA managers meeting entitled 'Planned educational growth'* (Lyle M. Spencer Papers, Box 1). Chicago: University of Chicago Archives.

Spencer, L. M. (1965e, November 12). *Speech to Joint Conference of Great Cities and ATPI, Los Angeles* (Lyle M. Spencer Papers, Box 1). Chicago: University of Chicago Archives.

Spencer, L. M. (1966a, July 12). *Speech to SRA staff associates* (Lyle M. Spencer Papers, Box 1). Chicago: University of Chicago Archives.

Spencer, L. M. (1966b, September 6). *Speech to the IBM Golden Circle Ladies* (Lyle M. Spencer Papers, Box 1). Chicago: University of Chicago Archives.

Spencer, L. M. (1966c, September 12). *Speech to SRA staff associates* (Lyle M. Spencer Papers, Box 1). Chicago: University of Chicago Archives.

Spencer, L. M. (1966d, December 7). *Untitled speech* (Lyle M. Spencer Papers, Box 1). Chicago: University of Chicago Archives.

Spencer, L. M. (1967a, February 24). *Speech at the National Junior College Seminar entitled 'A publisher looks at innovation'* (Lyle M. Spencer Papers, Box 1). Chicago: University of Chicago Archives.

Spencer, L. M. (1967b, June 27). *Speech to the IBM board of directors* (Lyle M. Spencer Papers, Box 1). Chicago: University of Chicago Archives.

Spencer, L. M. (1967c, September 28). *Notes on the Spencer Foundation* (Lyle M. Spencer Papers, Box 2). Chicago: University of Chicago Archives.

Spencer, L. M. (1968, June 12). *Speech to the IEEE International Conference on Communication* (Lyle M. Spencer Papers, Box 1). Chicago: University of Chicago Archives.

States, D. C. (1978a, September 20). *Memo from D. C. States to J. R. Morris regarding 'Meeting with MECC'* (Box 123568, Control Data Corporation Archives). Minneapolis: University of Minnesota, Center for the History of Information Processing,

States, D. C. (1978b, November 12). *Memo from D. C. States to Secondary Schools Task Force* (Box 123568, Control Data Corporation Archives). Minneapolis: University of Minnesota, Center for the History of Information Processing, Charles Babbage Institute.

Strogoff, A. (1967, January). Business takes a new look at education. *Education Forum, 31*(2), 23.

Suppes, P. (1978). Autobiography. In T. S. Krawiec, *The psychologists* (Vol. 3, pp. 261-287). Brandon, VT: Clinical Psychology Publishing.

Taylor, R. (1976, March 13). UI expects millions from PLATO sales. *Champagne-Urbana Courier*, pp. 1-2A.

Uston, K. (1993, October). 9,250 apples for the teacher. *Creative Computing*, 179-183.

Valetta, V. (1978, September 20). *Letter from Von Valetta, Deputy Commissioner of the Minnesota State Department of Education, to W. J. Ridley regarding 'Minnesota Project'* (Box 149045,

Control Data Corporation Archives). Minneapolis: University of Minnesota, Center for the History of Information Processing, Charles Babbage Institute.

Van Ausdale, L. (1984). *Interview* (Spencer Foundation oral history project). New York: Columbia University, Oral History Research Office.

Varley, T. D. (1981, May 28). *Academic mission statement* (Box 156958, Control Data Corporation Archives). Minneapolis: University of Minnesota, Center for the History of Information Processing, Charles Babbage Institute.

Wallis, C. (1995, Spring). The learning revolution [Special issue]. *Time, 145*(12), 49-51.

Wentworth, D. H. (1977, May 10). *Memo from D. H. Wentworth to J. R. Morris* (Box 149752, Control Data Corporation Archives). Minneapolis: University of Minnesota, Center for the History of Information Processing, Charles Babbage Institute.

West, P. (1992, December 16). Software maker's 'guarantee' of student performance questioned. *Education Week*, pp. 8, 9.

West, P. (1994, September 21). IBM launches $25 million 'entrepreneurship' project. *Education Week*, p. 5.

West, P. (1995a, January 11). Logged on for learning. *Education Week*, pp. 6, 8, 11, 23.

West, P. (1995b, January 11). Paving the way for the information highway. *Education Week*, p. 7.

West, P. (1995c, January 11). A soft sell. *Education Week*, pp. 10-11.

West, P. (1995d, April 12). OTA decries lack of focus on teachers. *Education Week, 14*(29), 1, 11.

Williams, T. T. (1979, September 7). *Memo from T. T. Williams to Secondary Schools Marketing Committee regarding 'Secondary schools strategy'* (Box 149045, Control Data Corporation Archives). Minneapolis: University of Minnesota, Center for the History of Information Processing, Charles Babbage Institute.

Worthy, J. C. (1987). *William C. Norris: Portrait of a maverick*. Cambridge, MA: Ballinger.

Chapter 16: Reform Efforts in American Schools: Will Faddism Continue to Impede Meaningful Change?

THOMAS L. GOOD, SALLY N. CLARK, DONALD C. CLARK[1]
University of Arizona

INTRODUCTION

Policy direction in American education is like the weather in the Midwest: constantly changing. However, unlike the weather which is driven by nature, people are responsible for fads in education. Education moves from problem to problem and typically defines problems too simply. Thus, the exaggerated answer to today's problem usually becomes tomorrow's problem. This 'disease orientation' in American education (identify *a* problem and devise a simple, quick solution) has drawn criticism from numerous educators, scholars and researchers (e.g., Cuban, 1993; Good, 1983; Good & Biddle, 1988; Slavin, 1989). The likelihood that any reform will be implemented is remote. Still, despite the fact that policy has resulted in few long-term solutions, the winds of change in the educational literature blow constantly.

In this chapter we document faddism in education and note that shifts in schooling are often extreme. (Seldom is fine tuning recommended!) To illustrate faddism, we examine how a single *instructional model* has often been seen as an answer to an educational problem only to be discarded for a new model. Thus, simple solutions that are perceived *not* to work are cast aside for new solutions in a continuing cycle. *Curriculum models* have also been proposed as solutions and, like instructional models, the popularity of individual models has risen and fallen over time. Although a fad may have useful effects (e.g., raising new questions), most fads are costly because they divert educators' attention from the careful understanding of educational problems in school and classroom contexts – thus preventing the search for more comprehensive solutions. However, some fads are more rhetoric (journal articles and policy advocacy) than fact, so that fads do not always affect classroom teaching. We discuss this phenomenon as well. Then we present an extended case example of how faddism has influenced a major reform effort – the middle school – to explore the problematical relation between policy advocacy and classroom practice. This example is especially instructive because this structure has been implemented long enough to permit evaluation of its effects.

B.J. Biddle et al. (eds.), International Handbook of Teachers and Teaching, 1387-1427

Next, we discuss reasons for faddism in American education and argue that a major cause of faddism is the multidimensional nature of successful schooling. Unfortunately, when educators advocate a single outcome measure or a dichotomous view of schooling, they define educational success as unidimensional. Any reform based on such a view is likely to have 'unanticipated consequences' that lead to yet another fad. Many reforms based on a more careful definition of problems and alternatives, however, are not backed with sufficient resources or time (i.e., for results to occur), especially when new programs are poorly defined (in terms of how classroom instruction should be modified) and when theory is far in advance of research. Finally, we provide five hypotheses about how educational reform can become more thoughtful.

CHANGING THE FORM OF INSTRUCTION AS A PANACEA

Documenting faddism in American schools is a straightforward task. For example, early in this century, educators supported large group instruction at a time when most classrooms were composed of students in several grades. In the 1920s educators became concerned about individualizing education; however, educators disagreed about the goals of individualization (for elite academic reasons, for life adjustment, citizenship skills) (Kliebard, 1986). A majority of educators could agree that the curriculum should be more 'individualized,' but obtaining a consensus about why has been difficult.

In the 1950s, social scientists discovered small-group instruction. Although serious conceptualization and research occurred on the method (e.g., Homans, 1950), most advocacy was relatively simplistic (e.g., provide new furniture) and focused on 'solutions.' In the 1960s the movement to individualized instruction reappeared. In the 1970s, there was great interest in humanistic education, and the call for 'open' classrooms and schools resounded across the educational landscape (Barth, 1969, 1970). Enthusiasm for humanistic instruction and open education quickly dissipated for a variety of reasons (e.g., teacher stress associated with team-teaching 90 students in an open space and lack of supporting empirical data). Indeed, open classrooms eventually were found to include not only

a) some of the worst manifestations of traditional teaching, but also
b) exciting, innovative teaching, and
c) innovative teaching that was ineffective and directionless.

Hence, open education took many forms and consequently had vastly different effects on students' affective, cognitive, and social development (Good, Biddle, & Brophy, 1975).

Enthusiasm for whole class teaching resurfaced in the late 1970s in the form of direct instruction. Policy makers urged teachers to become more structured and focused in their attempts to enhance student achievement and understanding. Although research showed the value of active teaching for some student outcomes (e.g., Good & Grouws, 1979), many policy makers over-applied it. Notably, this call for more structured teaching followed an era when many teachers had functioned as laissez faire leaders (i.e., in open classrooms). In the mid 1980s and into the 1990s policy makers and researchers focused on teachers' need to teach for understanding and to engage students in constructive whole class dialogue (Ball, 1991; Cohen, 1995). Now, in the mid 1990s, there is renewed interest in making schools more responsive to students as social beings *and* in addressing their needs as learners (Clark & Clark, 1994b; McCaslin & Good, 1996b).

CHANGING THE FORM OF INSTRUCTION IN THE 1990S

Two current arguments for the reform of teaching focus on small-group instruction and teaching for understanding.

Small-Group Instruction

Many of today's educators vigorously support small-group instruction and cooperative learning. Interest in small-group instruction has grown steadily for over a decade; however, advocacy for small-group instruction occurred after but little research on group processes (How do students learn in these settings? What is the nature of their intellectual and social exchange?). As is the case with most changes in education, research on small-group instruction followed advocacy rather than preceding it.

Subsequent research on small-group instruction has identified problems. For example, Bossert (1988-1989) reviewed research and found that students in control groups sometimes cooperated more than did students in treatment groups! Such data make it difficult to determine the veracity of arguments for the positive effects of small-group learning on students' motivation and achievement (such as the learning of facts or concepts). Moreover, McCaslin, Tuck, Wiard, Brown, LaPage, and Pyle (1994) noted that students' long-term memories of small-group experiences are much more favorable than their immediate reports. McCaslin et al. observed that students reconceptualize events in ways that are self-enhancing (exaggerating their roles, minimizing personal discomfort, etc.). Advocacy for small-group instruction is often based on questionnaires administered to students several days after instruction; however, data from such measures may mask important problems that occur during small-group instruction.

Observation of small-group instruction indicates that students use power in many ways (including humiliating other students) and that both the structure and quality of discussion vary notably between groups within a single class-room (McCaslin, Sisk, & Thompson, 1994-1995). Further, such variation exists in classrooms of teachers who have been trained to use small-group instructional models. Other recent research has indicated that small-group instruction often recreates the caste system that exists in the broader classroom (King, 1993; Mulryan, 1995).

Despite the limitations of the model, educators have enthusiastically advocated that teachers use such instructional models. Indeed, a former state Superintendent of Public Instruction in California, Bill Honig, went so far as to say, 'it's like we have a cure for polio, but we're not giving the inoculation' (Kantrowitz & Wingert, 1991, pp. 64-65). In our opinion, given the limited data base, equating small-group instruction with a vaccine for polio seems, at best, careless and thoughtless.

Teaching for Understanding

As we write this chapter, whole-class instruction in the form of whole-class dialogue is receiving considerable attention (Cohen, 1995). Despite such advocacy, there is already evidence that teachers have had difficulties implementing this reform to a level that would satisfy those who support the reform (e.g., Prawat, 1992).

Hiebert and Carpenter (1992) defined mathematical understanding as:

> A mathematical idea or procedure or fact is understood if it is part of an internal network. More specifically, the mathematics is understood if its mental representation is part of a network of representations. The degree of understanding is determined by the number and strength of the connections. The mathematical idea, procedure, or fact is understood thoroughly if it is linked to existing networks with stronger or more numerous connections. (p. 67)

These researchers and others who advocate teaching-for-understanding argue that students should construct knowledge. Some advocates of teaching-for-understanding believe active teaching should be eliminated. However, it is likely that some students need considerable structure (i.e., active teaching) and others little (cf. Vygotsky, 1978). Delpit (1995) criticized constructivist programs as vastly underestimating some students' need for active teaching.

Although there is much to admire in Hiebert and Carpenter's analysis, their writing contributes to a dichotomous orientation. In particular they posit studies of teachers' and students' thinking as the most valuable type of research. However, we wonder why students' and teachers' thinking in the classroom should be separated from students' scores on performance tests and their ability to apply mathematics outside the classroom. Advocating that research focus exclusively on students' thinking is especially problematic. Research has shown that some teaching-for-understanding curricula have not affected students' and teachers' classroom behavior or thinking in a generally positive fashion (e.g., Peterson, 1990). Students must understand mathematics (at some level), but they should also value it, enjoy it, and even be able to perform simple arithmetic tasks. Moreover, teachers' modelling, demonstrations, and explanations can help students construct knowledge.

Quality Versus Form of Instruction

If research on the form of teaching has shown anything, it is that schools and classrooms reflect extraordinary variation in teacher (and student) behavior. Observational studies in the 1970s indicated that there is considerable variation in curricula, teaching, and learning among classrooms in public schools. In some classrooms, virtually all allocated time is used for instruction; however, in other classrooms, as much as 40-50 per cent of allocated time is either used for other goals (some of which are important) or for managerial and clerical tasks (Berliner, 1979). Thus, teachers using whole-class models allocate time in different ways. However, changing the form of teaching may or may not change how students use time. For example, McCaslin et al. (1994-1995) report that there was more variation among small groups in students' use of time (e.g., academic vs. social) than among teachers in their allocation of time in whole-class settings.

Teachers vary in other ways as well. For example, early studies showed that in some classrooms, both low and high achievers participate in discussions; however, in other classrooms teachers allow high achieving students to dominate (e.g., Brophy & Good, 1974; Good, 1969). Moreover, female and minority students tend to receive less opportunity, less challenge, and less feedback which is likely to diminish their academic aspirations (Brophy & Good, 1974). Unfortunately, unequal response opportunities continue to characterize many classrooms (Jones & Gerig, 1994). Elementary school mathematics teachers have been found to vary notably in how much they focus on helping students to understand mathematics versus simply 'doing' mathematics mechanically (Good, Grouws, & Ebmeier, 1983). Blumenfeld (1992) notes, however, that small-group instruction does not necessarily increase the time students spend on understanding (vs. repetitive drill and practice). There is also considerable evidence that gender and achievement differences are not always reduced by small-group instruction (e.g., Mulryan, 1995).

We are not suggesting that approaches such as small-group instruction and peer tutoring (e.g., reciprocal teaching) have no positive effects; indeed, they have been successful in some contexts. Our point is that changing instructional format alone is not a panacea because the relationship between form of instruction and student opportunity is problematic. The real issue is the need to understand the quality of an instructional format, not its form (Good, 1983).

INNOVATIVE CURRICULA AS PANACEA

The movement from fad to fad in instructional format has been matched by abrupt changes in curriculum. Curriculum problems are also defined too simply (e.g., variation in quality of curriculum implementation is ignored), hence education moves from one curriculum to another.

Phonics Versus Whole Language

One long-standing historical and continuing controversy in education concerns the importance of phonics and word-attack skills versus sight reading versus whole-language approaches to teaching students to read. This pendulum has swung wildly.

On the basis of her research, Chall (1967) concluded that children generally benefit more from an initial reading curriculum that includes a strong phonics or word-attack component. Many educators and school districts, however, overreacted to Chall's argument and focused almost exclusively on phonics skills (far more than Chall had advocated). This occurred despite research indicating that although some teachers needed to emphasize phonics more, other teachers were already teaching enough phonics. For the latter group, an increase in time spent on phonics was unproductive and possibly harmful for students (because other goals such as reading for pleasure were neglected).

Reaction to the phonics curriculum and to basal readers came in the form of the whole language curriculum which was implemented to such extremes in some classrooms that it became the 'new' problem. To cite a recent example, the California Department of Education just lifted its mandate for a whole language curriculum that had been imposed a few years earlier.

New Math

Kilpatrick (1992) noted that in the 1950s the mathematics curriculum was under pressure from many sides. On the one hand, American schools were criticized by business and military leaders because young adults lacked basic computational skills. On the other, colleges criticized school mathematics programs because they failed to prepare students adequately for college work. Other groups were angry because mathematics was often taught more as a practical life skill than as a rigorous academic subject.

The Russians' launching of Sputnik created a wave of political uncertainty and a sense of crisis that resulted in a plethora of mathematics curriculum reform efforts. A concern that too few students were enrolling in university mathematics courses and that America was losing ground scientifically and militarily provided considerable justification for changing the curriculum. According to Kilpatrick (1992, citing Shulman, 1970),

> ... mathematicians and psychologists were brought together in curriculum development projects, and studies were undertaken that drew upon both new perspectives. A revival of interest in issues such as learning by discovery, readiness for learning, processes of learning and aptitude for learning, helped people from different disciplines see some common ground. (p. 23)

The efficacy of the 'new math' was never demonstrated empirically, and many teachers refused to (or could not) implement the model. The new math is an example of a theory well in advance of research. By the late 1970s, many policy makers were concerned about the mathematics curriculum, and researchers had demonstrated that in certain contexts more active teaching was associated with improvement in students' learning of basic mathematical facts and concepts (e.g., Good & Grouws, 1979). This research was, in turn, overgeneralized, which resulted in excessive enthusiasm for active teaching. Eventually, the overuse of structured teaching led to new calls for teachers to help students learn the meaning of mathematics (e.g., *Curriculum and Evaluation Standards for School Mathematics*, Commission on Standards for School Mathematics, 1989; *Everybody Counts*, National Research Council, 1989).

Lessons from the Past

That students learn what they have been taught is certainly not a new idea. Walker and Schaffarzick (1974) reviewed 32 studies of innovative curricula covering elementary school through college. They found that innovative curricula worked when the associated criterion tests matched the innovative curricula and that the traditional curriculum resulted in higher achievement when the associated test focused on content criteria emphasizing the traditional curriculum. Hence, to the extent that these data generalize, a given curriculum is likely to be more successful in terms of certain outcomes than others. Thus, it is important to *anticipate trade-offs* when curriculum decisions are made, recognizing that different types of students may be differentially affected by curricula and instruction (Good & Power, 1976; Good & Stipek, 1983) and that certain curriculum packages may be more useful for achieving some goals than for others.

Chall (1967) noted that *the teacher is as important as the curriculum* and that teachers can present the same curriculum in many different ways. Numerous researchers have found that the variation among teachers who are implementing the same curriculum is as great as the variation among teachers who are implementing different curricula. Hence, instructional *form* does not predict *quality* of implementation. For example, although a curriculum may focus more on understanding (and less on drill and practice), some teachers will incorporate more drill and practice in the new curriculum than others.

In summary, we have provided an overview illustrating faddism in American educational reform. In the next section we examine one reform movement in detail to illustrate how good ideas are mediated by a variety of factors when they are implemented. Such an examination is instructive in itself, but it also helps in the generation of hypotheses about reducing faddism and improving reform efforts in American education. We decided to discuss the middle school movement for two reasons. First, two of the authors are experts in this area (Clark & Clark, 1986, 1993). Second, schools have experimented with middle school education for the past 70 years.

MIDDLE LEVEL EDUCATION

Concern over appropriate educational programs for young adolescents began before the turn of the century and predates the establishment of the junior high school in 1909. Since those times educators have continued their calls for reform, emphasizing implementation of programs, instruction, and curricula that are developmentally appropriate to the needs of young adolescents.

This continuous pressure for reform is so much a part of the whole structure of middle level education that John Lounsbury (1991, p. 68) characterizes the development of middle level education as the '... longest-running, most extensive educational reform movement in the United States.' According to George and Oldaker (1985), the middle school movement is one of the largest and most comprehensive efforts at educational reorganization in the history of American public schools. Because of this long-standing emphasis on reform, middle level education (junior high and middle schools) serves as an appropriate example from which to examine the attempt to create successful educational practice. In this section we describe middle level education with an emphasis on the forces that influenced its development and the effects of those forces as identified by research in the 1980s and early 1990s. Then we examine trends in middle level education during almost a century of reform.

Forces Leading to the Establishment of Junior High and Middle Schools

Most middle level scholars agree that the first junior high schools were opened during the 1909-1910 school year in Columbus, Ohio, and Berkeley, California. The origins of the concept, however, can be traced to the late nineteenth century and early twentieth century. The idea of a separate school for young adolescents evolved slowly and was based primarily on concerns about the perceived failures of the organization of elementary and secondary schools into eight and four grades, respectively. Of particular concern was the belief that elementary schools were not dealing effectively with the needs of students in grades 7 and 8. As one examines the development of middle level education, it becomes increasingly apparent that the initial impetus was to solve major problems that existed in the then current school structure rather than to create a new organization. Hansen and Hern (1971, p. 4) suggest that: 'The history of the first middle school, the junior high school, indicates that it was conceived not as a movement to introduce something new into American education but as an expedient endeavour to ease several supposed deficiencies.' As we noted earlier, reform generally is a movement to solve a problem.

Leonard Koos (1927), another leading early junior high school educator, examined what he called the forces responsible for the establishment of junior high schools. 'Many forces ...,' he stated, 'are responsible for the movement for educational reorganization finding expression in the present widespread establishment of 'junior high schools' or 'intermediate schools" (p. 1). These forces identified by Koos (1927) included:

a) economy of time,
b) concern for high student mortality-dropout rates,
c) wide variations in learners, and
d) needs of young adolescents.

Economy of time.

The economy of time issue, originally conceived by Charles Eliot and others as a way to allow students to enter college at a younger age, soon took on a much broader focus. That focus was school reorganization. School reorganization issues in the early 1900s were focused, much as they are now, on grade-level organization, compression of time spent in school, pressures to push 'high school' course work into the lower grades, and departmentalization and specialization.

Pupil Mortality – Grade Retentions and Dropouts

The low number of students who completed high school during the early twentieth century was of great concern to educators of that time. They thought that reorganizing schools would increase the number of young people who would stay in school. In some instances they were right, for the percentages of students remaining in school districts with junior high schools did appear to be higher than those who maintained the 8-4 pattern of organization (Briggs, 1920). Closely aligned with high dropout rates was a concern about the high number of students (left-backs) who were 'repeating' a grade for a second or third time (Van Til, Vars, & Lounsbury, 1961). Several important issues evolved from these early concerns over pupil mortality and grade repetition, including provision of educational opportunity for all students, repeating courses – rather than an entire grade, a more relevant curriculum, and better instructional strategies.

Student learning differences.

The work of Thorndike (1907) and other researchers gave solid evidence of differences among learners in the typical classroom. As educational opportunity has broadened, student diversity has expanded. Not only must schools deal with variations in learning ability and achievement, they must provide for the needs of youth from a variety of socio-economic levels, family settings, and primary language backgrounds. Although Thorndike and others did increase the awareness of educators about individual differences and sparked efforts to provide for these differences in classrooms, the impact of their work was not altogether positive. Two major issues that became popular early in the twentieth century and that are of great concern to middle level educators of today are the legitimacy and importance of standardized testing and homogeneous grouping (ability grouping, tracking). As is so often the case, findings from basic research on these topics are often misrepresented and exaggerated when planning or implementing middle level programs.

The unique needs of young adolescents.

Since G. Stanley Hall (1905) first called attention to the unique needs of adolescents, the junior high school and the middle school have attempted to serve those special needs. Examination of the development of middle level education demonstrates that although designing programs to assist young adolescents as they undergo biological, psychological, and social change has always been a major goal, middle schools have not met this objective. Although many programs and activities adopted in the early junior high schools focused on the needs of young adolescents, the issues that have remained the most important over the years are content relevancy, student involvement in learning, and guidance.

Other Factors Influencing the Development of Middle Level Schools

From the earliest days of the junior high school to the current decade, three additional factors have influenced the development of middle level schools (Koos, 1927): overcrowding, momentum, and 'jumping on the bandwagon.'

Overcrowding.

The first factor described by Koos deals with creation of middle level schools to solve the problem of overcrowding at high schools. 'By removing pupils of the ninth grade from the high school building' he states, 'and housing them with those in the seventh and eighth grades in some older buildings, the problem is solved' (1927, p. 3). Koos continues:

> This easy emancipation from a housing difficulty has sometimes been the primary cause of a superficial reorganization; it has also sometimes been used to effect genuine reorganization where otherwise there might be too great opposition to a change for which the populace was not yet prepared. (1927, p. 3)

Throughout the evolution of middle level education, school districts have continued to view their middle level schools as the 'wild card' for solving enrolment problems (Alexander 1968; Valentine, Clark, Nickerson, & Keefe, 1981). In many cases when elementary schools are overcrowded, the sixth grade is moved to the middle level school; when high schools are overcrowded, the ninth grade is moved to the middle level school.

Momentum.

A second factor Koos (1927) identified was momentum. He believed that to the forces of economy of time, the problem with dropouts, the need to recognize individual differences, and the unique needs of young adolescents should be added the influence of momentum on the change process.

The first two decades of the junior high school (1910-1930) were marked by high visibility that included books, articles, reports, and conference presentations. This visibility, fuelled by rhetoric and research, initiated and sustained the momentum that led many educators to consider and establish junior high schools in their districts. This same type of momentum has re-emerged in American middle level schools during the past two decades. As a result of the leadership of the National Association of Secondary School Principals (NASSP) and the National Middle School Association (NMSA), and funding from the U.S. Department of Education and private foundations, middle level education has begun to gain recognition as a separate entity in the educational hierarchy. Of particular importance to this recognition is the work of the Carnegie Task Force on Education of Young Adolescents. Their 1989 report, *Turning Points: Preparing American Youth for the 21st Century*, has refuelled the momentum for change in middle level education.

Jumping on the bandwagon.

A third factor identified by Koos (1927) as important to the development of junior high schools was jumping on the bandwagon. He suggested that in examining the 'broad sweep of the movement for reorganization,' one of the most influential factors was the 'desire of some school authorities to be progressive' (p. 4).

> This factor is not unlike the force of a fad. It often operates without any clear understanding of the purposes of reorganization and it not uncommonly results in change which, rather than being fundamental, restricts itself to such a superficiality as the mere regrouping of grades. (p. 4)

As in the early years of the junior high school, many of today's educators want to be on the 'cutting edge' of innovations. These include reorganization of grade levels, implementing programs such as interdisciplinary teaming and teacher advisories, establishing collaborative decision-making structures, and implementing instructional strategies such as cooperative learning and computer-assisted learning.

Current Middle Level School Organization and Practice

From the early discussions about school reform that began in the 1870s and led to the establishment of the first junior high schools in 1910, middle level education has grown to include more than 12,000 middle level schools. Almost universally middle level school educators recognize the importance of schools that are responsive to the biological, psychological, and social needs of young adolescents. Although there is agreement on the *general* purpose of middle level schools, middle level educators – drawing from tradition, practice, rhetoric, and research – organize their schools and programs in a variety of ways (e.g., schools vary widely in how they attempt to address 'social needs'). What do these middle level schools of the 1980s and 1990s look like? How are they organized? What programs do they offer?

Descriptions of middle level schools of the 1980s and early 1990s are drawn from the following studies: the Dodge Foundation/NASSP National Study of Schools in the Middle (Valentine et al., 1981), the Association for Supervision and Curriculum Development (ASCD) Study of Middle Schools (Cawelti, 1988), Schools in the Middle: Progress 1968-1988 (Alexander & McEwin, 1992), Middle Grades: A National Survey of Practices and Trends – Center for Research in Elementary and Middle Schools – Johns Hopkins University (Epstein & Mac Iver, 1990), A Survey of Arizona Middle Level Schools (Clark & Clark, 1990), the NASSP National Eighth-Grade Shadow Study (Lounsbury & Clark, 1990), and the NASSP National Study of Leadership in Middle Level Education (Valentine, Clark, Irvin, Keefe, & Melton, 1993).

Data from these studies show that most middle level schools of today can be described as follows:

1) The grade-level configuration is 6-7-8 or 7-8 with an enrolment between 400 and 800 students.
2) Most teachers and students follow a traditional single subject schedule.
3) The guidance program is primarily the responsibility of a counsellor or counsellors.
4) The core curriculum consists of English-language arts, social studies, science, and mathematics and a limited exploratory program.
5) Instruction is largely teacher dominated, and student passiveness is a predominate element.
6) Most students are ability grouped for some subjects, and some students are 'tracked' for the entire day.

In these middle level schools there is about a 60 per cent chance that some form of interdisciplinary teaming will exist and about a 30 per cent chance of the existence of a teacher advisory program that features academic and social and academic support activities.

Trends and Issues in Middle Level School Reform

Success can be measured in many ways, and the middle level school reform movement can be judged successful if one considers that, from the two junior high schools established in the early 1990s to more than 12,000 schools in the 1990s, the middle level school has become the accepted place to educate young adolescents. Cuban (1993) examined the development of middle level schools and found that 'They [junior high schools] have met reform's tough standard of success: longevity' (p. 320). He goes on to say, 'But in surviving, junior high schools, like other social institutionalized social reforms, scaled down their goals, shifted their focus as they became absorbed into the school system, and ended up parroting senior high schools' (p. 320). Many middle level education scholars take exception to Cuban's characterization. However, although numerous organizational changes have taken place as part of middle level school reform, the curriculum and instruction that young adolescents experience in these schools are very similar to what they will receive in high school.

Although many trends have contributed and continue to contribute to middle level school reform during the twentieth century, we focus on three interrelated issues. These are:

a) organizational changes make little impact on the classroom,
b) implementation precedes knowledge and research, and
c) panaceas are simple solutions to complex problems.

Organizational changes make little impact on the classroom.

Over the last 90 years junior high and middle school educators have been successful in making structural changes in middle level schools. Researchers (Alexander & McEwin, 1992; Cawelti, 1988; Mac Iver, 1990; Valentine et al., 1993) document the following structural changes: changing the predominate junior high with grades 7-8-9 to a middle school with grades 6-7-8; and implementing guidance programs (counsellors, teacher advisories), nontraditional staff-utilization models (interdisciplinary teaming), and exploratory classes and experiences. These changes in organization were made with one primary objective in mind – to make middle level schools more developmentally responsive to the intellectual, social, emotional, and physical needs of young adolescents.

Research in the 1970s by developmental psychologists on young adolescent maturation indicated that young adolescents were experiencing biological changes 18 to 24 months earlier than they had 30 years earlier (Thornburg, 1980). This meant that many females were entering puberty while still enrolled in elementary school. This phenomenon prompted many middle level educators to reconsider the grade levels appropriate for middle level schools. They argued that if the junior high school in the 1940s and 1950s with grades 7-8-9 had been the appropriate grouping for young adolescents, the majority of whom were in the various stages of puberty, then it certainly seemed appropriate that the earlier initiation of puberty recognized in 1970s and 1980s required a response. That response was to reconfigure middle level schools to include the sixth and sometimes the fifth grade. Support of the inclusion of fifth and sixth grade was evident in the early 1980s when 54 per cent of the principals in the 1981 NASSP National Study of Middle Principals and Programs (Valentine et al., 1981) identified the 6-8 grade level configuration as the 'ideal.' By 1990 the 6-8 configuration was the most frequently used grade level configuration for schools for young adolescents (Valentine et al., 1993). When asked why their schools had changed to either 5-8 or 6-8 schools, principals reported that their major reason for change was to: 'provide a program best suited to the needs of the middle age student' (Valentine et al., 1993). These same educators also listed the following reasons for their change to a 'middle school' grade level organization: 'provide a better transition to high school,' 'employ new curriculum or instructional innovations,' 'employ ideas or programs successfully implemented in other schools,' 'solve concerns about a junior high program,' and 'adjust to enrolment needs.' When schools do indeed change their grade configuration to 'provide a program best suited to the needs of the middle age student,' then there is an initial recognition that adolescent needs are important and need to be addressed. That fact alone, however, does not appear to change the way most teachers teach (Lounsbury & Clark, 1990).

Although research to support one grade-level configuration over another is almost non-existent, one positive aspect of school grade-level reconfiguration involves data suggesting that developmentally appropriate programs are more likely to occur in schools organized around the 6-8 configuration (Lounsbury & Clark, 1990; Valentine et al., 1993). Whether or not grade level change affects the classroom is still a question in search of answers.

Guidance, long recognized as an important part of middle level schools, has undergone a major organizational change, one that has moved the primary function of guidance from counsellors to a responsibility shared by counsellors and teachers. The most widely used approach to broadening this concept of guidance in the middle level school is called teacher advisories (home base). In these programs a teacher is assigned to a group of 15 to 25 students and meets with these students regularly. The basic premise is that every student should be well known by or have at least one adult to serve as an advocate during his or her stay in the school (Carnegie Task Force on Education of Young Adolescents, 1989; George, 1987). According to the Carnegie Task Force on Education of Young Adolescents (1989, p. 40), teacher advisories 'enable teachers and other staff to provide guidance and actively monitor the academic and social development of students.' Although implementation of teacher advisories has not been as widespread as interdisciplinary teaming, exploratory programs, and other middle level programs, advisories are found in approximately 40 per cent of middle level schools in the United States (Alexander & McEwin, 1992; Valentine et al., 1993). The general concept of advisories is consistent with McCaslin and Good's (1996b) argument that teachers must spend more time listening to students if they are to respond to students both as learners *and* social beings.

Some research supports the importance of advisories in middle level schools. Mac Iver (1990) found that when teacher advisory groups focused on social and academic support activities, this helped to reduce dropouts. Connors (1986) found evidence that teacher advisory programs helped students to grow socially; contributed to a positive school climate; helped students learn about school, make friends, and get along with their classmates; and enhanced student and teacher relationships. George and Oldaker (1985) suggest that when teacher advisories are combined with other middle level programs such as interdisciplinary teaming and flexible scheduling, student self-concept improves, dropout rates decrease, and school climate becomes more positive. Needed now is more focused research which identifies the aspects of teacher advisories and other programs that contribute most to positive outcomes (i.e., address the issue of quality).

Interdisciplinary teaming is also considered by many middle level educators as one of the cornerstones of responsive middle level schools (Hafner, Ingels, Schneider, Stevenson, & Owings, 1990; Tye, 1985). When properly implemented, teaming facilitates teachers working together in smaller focus groups as recommended by Lipsitz (1984) and the Carnegie Task Force on Education of Young Adolescents (1989).

The potential advantages of interdisciplinary teaming are numerous. The structuring of smaller focus groups through the teaming of teachers facilitates strong support systems for both middle level students and their teachers, increases the flexibility of learning time, provides a better vehicle for instruction, and creates opportunities to make connections across the various subject areas (Alexander & George, 1981; Clark & Clark, 1987, 1992; George & Oldaker, 1985; Mac Iver, 1990).

Interdisciplinary teaming environments have been shown to benefit middle level learners in a variety of positive ways. Positive climates and smaller student focus groups, facilitated by interdisciplinary teams, directly influence psychosocial development and indirectly influence achievement (Epstein, 1981).

Research also confirms the strong linkage of interdisciplinary teaming organizations to developmentally appropriate practices for young adolescents (Arhar, 1992; Clark & Clark, 1992; Epstein, 1981; Fenwick, 1992; George & Oldaker, 1985; Mac Iver, 1990; Mitman & Lambert, 1992; Rutter, Maughan, Mortimore, Ouston, & Smith, 1979).

Numerous benefits for teachers also are found in interdisciplinary teaming organizations. Collaboration with other teachers facilitates communication, enhances satisfaction, and increases opportunities for professional development (Arhar, Johnston, & Markle, 1989). Other benefits include a support system among teachers that encourages innovation and the provision for professional autonomy and decision making about instructional and organizational issues (Clark & Clark, 1987).

Another essential part of the middle level curriculum, *the exploratory curriculum*, provides for less structured learning experiences (exploratory courses), student-selected enrichment courses, and participatory experiences (elective courses and activities). The exploratory curriculum needs to be more than just a sequence of courses. It should be a process that provides opportunities for students to 'explore their aptitudes, interests, and special talents and to develop an accurate and positive self-concept' across the entire range of the middle level school curriculum (NASSP Council on Middle Level Education, 1985, p. 4). The exploratory curriculum is a concept that should permeate the entire school curriculum. Lounsbury (1992, p. 3) also suggests that the middle level school should be an exploratory school 'and everything done therein should be approached in an exploratory mode.'

The major purpose of the exploratory curriculum in middle level schools is to allow young adolescents to achieve and demonstrate competence in a number of areas such as the arts, academics, athletics, and technology. In addition, the focus of the exploratory, as well as the core curriculum, is to provide opportunities for every student in the school to excel and be successful.

The exploratory curriculum continues to be an important part of the middle level school program. Although 77 per cent of middle level principals in the NASSP study consider the exploratory curriculum to be very important (Valentine et al., 1993), exploratory experiences have become much more restricted than was originally defined by Gruhn and Douglass (1947) and other junior high school reformers. More narrowly defined as 'exploratory courses, fine arts, and minicourses,' exploratory experiences have been reduced due to pressures by policy makers for higher academic achievement and the resultant increase in the number of required academic courses (Cawelti, 1988). State mandates calling for minimum competency testing in basic skills may also be playing an important role in restricting the opportunities of students to be exposed to skills and experiences that might prove useful (Becker, 1990).

There is ample evidence that over the last 90 years junior high and middle school reformers have been successful in bringing about *organizational changes* in their schools. Change in grade-level configurations and the wide acceptance and implementation of guidance, interdisciplinary teaming, and exploratory programs give testimony to their efforts. Researchers, however, are questioning the success of these organizational changes as they relate to teachers, their classrooms, and their students. In-depth studies of middle level schools such as the shadow studies conducted by John Lounsbury and others (Lounsbury & Clark, 1990; Lounsbury & Johnston, 1985, 1988) show that grade-level organization, interdisciplinary teaming, teacher advisories, and exploratory programs have had little impact on young adolescents and the instruction they receive. Most teachers in 6-8 schools teach no differently from teachers in 7-9 schools (Lounsbury & Clark, 1990; Lounsbury & Johnston, 1985); teacher advisories often become study halls and seldom address social issues and problems (Mac Iver, 1990); and most teachers in interdisciplinary teams still teach their subjects in rigid class periods with little or no content integration (Lounsbury & Clark, 1990).

In their calls for more developmentally appropriate programs that increase student achievement, improve social skills, and enhance emotional and physical health, middle level reformers 'sometimes forget that changing students depends to a large extent on changing teachers. If teachers continue to do the same old things, it is unlikely that student performance will improve' (Maeroff, 1988, p. 476). Schools must change more than their organization if they are going to affect the lives of students.

Implementation precedes knowledge and research.

The resurgence of interest in creating developmentally responsive middle level schools during the 1980s was evident in middle level educators' efforts to implement programs they believed to be appropriate to the needs of young adolescents. During the decade, the percentage of middle level schools with the grade level configuration of 6-8 expanded from 15 per cent to 50 per cent, and interdisciplinary teaming reported in 57 per cent of the schools became the norm rather than the exception (Valentine et al., 1993). Increases were also seen in the implementation of teacher advisory programs. Most of this implementation occurred with little reliance on research. Educators implemented these programs because they had read about them, heard about them at conferences and conventions, and visited schools that were using them. This oftentimes resulted in limited implementation and the installation of new program structures that had few effects on the way teachers engaged young adolescents in learning. Students in interdisciplinary teams were instructed in the same rigid time frames and single-subject classrooms as students assigned to teachers in traditional classrooms and schedules. In discussing this concern for lack of research, we address the following issues:

a) nature of research in middle level education;
b) lack of regard for research by educators;
c) lack of knowledge leads to uninformed and uneven implementation; and
d) wide variation in contexts leads to great variation in opportunity.

Much research conducted during the 1980s focused on reporting the frequency of implementation of structures in middle level schools. These studies included the NASSP Survey of Middle Level Principals and Programs (Valentine et al., 1981), the Association for Supervision and Curriculum Development study (Cawelti, 1988), and Alexander and McEwin's study (1992). Although these studies described the changing nature of middle level schools, they did not examine the impact of programs on teachers and students. Studies conducted by Epstein and Mac Iver (1990), Lipsitz (1984), Lounsbury and Clark (1990), and Lounsbury and Johnston (1985, 1988) were more helpful in that they described the impact of programs on young adolescents. Lipsitz's (1984) qualitative study of four successful middle level schools, for example, documented the successes school were having in educating young adolescents in four very different contexts. The shadow studies of ninth, sixth, and eighth grades (Lounsbury & Clark, 1990; Lounsbury & Johnston, 1985, 1988) indicated that programs such as interdisciplinary teaming and teacher advisories had few effects on instruction. Epstein and Mac Iver (1990) reported the incidence of implementation of various middle level programs and also studied factors that made these programs successful. This study was particularly helpful in the areas of interdisciplinary teaming and teacher advisories. Thus, although middle level reformers were introducing new structures into schools without the benefit of adequate research, until the latter part of the 1980s little research was available that would have been useful to them.

Would middle level educators use research and knowledge if they were available to assist them in developing appropriate educational experiences for young adolescents? The answer is perhaps not. Glickman (1991) suggests that *educators reject research* when it conflicts with their own knowledge. Drawing from major research in education, Glickman (1991) identifies 'what we know' and suggests that educators confront this knowledge. He believes that for years schools have been operated in ways that are not in the best interests of students. Educators have chosen, perhaps driven by their own beliefs or by community standards and values, to ignore or at least 'pretend ignorance' of the professional knowledge base. Educators must begin school restructuring by learning this knowledge base and confronting it, Glickman suggests. He identifies 11 issues supported by research and practice that educators need to examine and consider in their efforts to improve their schools. Five of those issues are particularly important to middle level educators:

a) tracking,
b) retention in grade,
c) corporal punishment,
d) learning from real activities and experiences, and
e) measuring school worth based on the learning students can display in authentic or real settings.

Educators' inability or unwillingness to consider the current knowledge base regarding issues such as these may be a major reason why many promising programs are not working as well as they should and why many middle level educators allow inappropriate practices to continue.

Lack of knowledge of research in many instances leads to uninformed and *uneven implementation* of programs that could be successful. Teachers and administrators must be informed about research and practice if they are going to make good decisions about programs for inclusion in their schools. Further, they need the ability to consider research and theory in relation to local values and contexts. Without this knowledge base, they are destined to make decisions that are not in the best interests of the young adolescents they serve, or, at best, the programs they implement will not function in the ways in which they were designed. Interdisciplinary teaming, for example, when combined with block scheduling, provides teachers in teams with the opportunity to use time flexibly, to instruct students in groups of various sizes, and to integrate curricula. Yet, the shadow studies of the 1980s (Lounsbury & Clark, 1990; Lounsbury & Johnston, 1985, 1988) showed that teachers in teams were not taking advantage of all of the possibilities available to them. This finding was confirmed by Alexander and McEwin (1992) who also were concerned that some schools in their study did not take full advantage of the opportunities offered by interdisciplinary teaming. In examining teacher advisory programs, Mac Iver (1990) found that, although 66 per cent of the schools in the Center for Research in Elementary and Middle Schools study reported using teacher advisory programs, only 28 per cent of those schools indicated the use of student support-type activities at least once a month.

The wide *variation in contexts* in middle level schools throughout the United States leads to great variation in educational opportunity. The wide variation of success or failure of programs – in the teachers who use them, in the students who participate in them, in the resources that are available to support them, and in the measurement and conceptualization of success – may also explain uninformed and uneven implementation. Much of the restructuring literature stresses that practitioners should be knowledgeable about and develop appropriate strategies for dealing within the contextual differences of each school (Clark & Clark, 1994a; David, 1991; Joyce, 1991; Levine, 1991). Successful reform is built on a strong knowledge base – a knowledge base that allows teachers and administrators to modify programs to fit the variety of teacher and student needs in relation to available resources, measurement and evaluation constraints, and school and district expectations of success. Resources to support professional development, information gathering, and technical assistance, for example, are critical in bringing about desired change (Levine, 1991). If, as in many cases, resources are unavailable to assist teachers and administrators in building the needed expertise to implement innovative programs fully, those programs are unlikely to achieve their potential effects.

Varying definitions of school success also affect middle level reform efforts. With the long-standing belief that middle level schools should provide a balanced curriculum that assists young adolescents in developing intellectually, socially, emotionally, and physically (Carnegie Task Force on Education of Young Adolescents, 1989; Clark & Clark, 1986; National Middle School Association, 1992; National Association of Secondary School Principals Council on Middle Level Education, 1985) middle level educators' definition of success is broadly based. This balanced approach to meeting young adolescents developmental needs often conflicts with district, state, and national initiatives that focus almost exclusively on academic achievement as measured by standardized tests. Many middle level schools that show good progress in promoting student achievement as measured by alternative assessment procedures may be judged unsuccessful if increasing students' achievement test scores is the only criterion for success.

The continuing pressure to use standardized test scores as the sole measure of school success disregards the successes that some middle level schools are achieving in developing good student social skills, healthy lifestyles, and strong self-concepts (Arhar, 1992; Clark & Clark, 1994a, 1994b; Mac Iver, 1990; Mitman & Lambert, 1992). An overemphasis on cognitive performance, particularly as measured by achievement tests, often pressures many middle level educators to place greater emphasis on academics. As a result, more time (increased academic course requirements) is given to the so-called 'basics,' and, as a result, students have fewer opportunities to participate in exploratory classes (music, art, technology, physical education, etc.), elective classes (band, orchestra, choral groups, etc.), and activities programs (intramural sports, clubs, community service). We believe that placing more emphasis on academic subjects takes the curriculum out of balance by denigrating the importance of social skills, physical development, and emotional health. Educators need to be concerned about both the social and academic needs of students (McCaslin & Good, 1996a, 1996b).

The conventional reaction by educators to pressures by legislators and policy makers for increased emphasis on academics is to return to a subject-centered approach with teacher lecture predominating (Lounsbury & Clark, 1990; Valentine et al., 1993). This regression to subject- and teacher-dominated education could be averted, however, by knowledgeable teachers and administrators. Vars (1991), for example, reported that in over 80 studies researchers found that students in student-centered interdisciplinary programs (e.g., curriculum integration around common themes) do as well as, and often better, on standardized tests than students taught in subject-centered single subject classes (focused on mathematics, science, social studies, or the language arts, for example) each taught in its own separate period. When properly informed, middle level educators are much less likely to compromise the integrity of promising innovations such as interdisciplinary teaming and curriculum by not implementing them in the ways they were intended.

Panaceas – Simple solutions to complex problems.

The history of middle level education shows that its initial purpose was to solve major problems that existed in early twentieth century schools and society. The organization of the junior high school was seen by many as a way to address the problems of a more rigorous curriculum at an earlier age, student failure, student learning differences, and the special needs of young adolescents. As with other reform efforts, there were early concerns that educators would fail to focus on these important issues and move to junior high schools for the wrong reasons. Koos (1927) discussed issues such as using the junior high and middle school as a way to solve overcrowding, an approach he thought led to superficial reorganization. For the duration of the middle level school movement, reformers have been implementing new organizational structures (e.g., advisories, interdisciplinary teams) perhaps for the wrong reasons (faddism; jumping on the bandwagon). Nevertheless, reformers thought they were making changes that would address the needs of young adolescents. Many of those changes, some positive and some negative, became part of the fabric of middle level education. In addressing student failure and student learning differences, early reformers attempted to solve two very difficult problems. Although their efforts to deal with these complex issues were commendable, hindsight shows that they were willing to settle for simplistic, insufficient solutions.

In the early 1900s only one-third of students reached the ninth grade, and slightly more than one in ten completed high school (Clark & Clark, 1994a). In addition,

> ... about one third of the school children in the early twentieth century were left back some time during their few years they spent in schools. About one out of every six children in any grade was a repeater in that grade. (Van Til et al., 1961, p. 15)

At that time educators became increasingly critical of conditions that led to so many 'left-backs' and dropouts. They argued that education could be better in democratic America. Consequently, when the new proposal for a junior high school was advanced, many educators hoped that the new seventh- through ninth-grade organization with improved methods and content more related to the learner's life might reduce the number of dropouts.

Junior high and middle school educators attempted to reduce the dropout rate in a number of ways. However, the most simplistic solution – repeating courses instead of the entire year – became widely accepted and implemented. As the end of the twentieth century nears, most middle level schools still approach the problem of student academic failure by having young adolescents repeat the course they failed, often with teachers using the same instructional approaches and materials. This simplistic answer has precluded a more proactive approach of identifying the reasons for failure and then taking steps to alleviate those reasons.

Another simple solution to a complex problem can be found in the way junior high schools in the past and middle schools of the present deal with individual learning differences. Homogeneous grouping (ability grouping or tracking) seemed 'logical' to early reformers. They thought that a good way to accommodate individual differences was to place all students of similar ability in the same group, classroom, or course. As a result, along with a departmentalized curriculum, most junior and senior high schools began the practice of tracking which grew in popularity and was almost universally supported by educators and the public. In his report on junior high schools, Conant (1960) strongly endorsed ability grouping and recommended that differentiation of programs begin in the junior high school (e.g., college preparatory, vocational).

About three decades ago, some educators and sociologists began to question the practice of ability grouping. In recent years, evidence of the deleterious effects of grouping on students, particularly on those from minority and low-income homes, has mounted (Braddock, 1990; Good & Brophy, 1994; Oakes, 1985). Middle level educators have been particularly outspoken about the negative effects of tracking on young adolescents, yet the practice continues in the vast majority of America's middle level schools (Braddock, 1990; George, 1988; Lounsbury & Clark, 1990; Valentine et al., 1993). It is ironic that an approach originally intended to accommodate individual student differences would 70 years later be found by many researchers to be harmful to students' achievement and self-concepts.

WHY FADDISM CONTINUES

Given the failure of radical reform (faddism) to improve education, why does it continue? This is a complex question with no simple answer. We certainly cannot answer this question in this chapter. However, we offer a few hypotheses to stimulate deliberation about why educators continue to offer simple solutions to complex educational problems and to challenge education to develop more comprehensive strategies for improving schooling.

Superficial Versus Real Change

Before offering reasons for faddism, however, we must differentiate between superficial and real change. Following Cuban (1993), we suspect that reforms often exist more in teacher educators' rhetoric and in journal articles than in classrooms. Seymour Sarason (e.g., 1971, 1995) has reminded educators that change is difficult and that individuals within institutions resist it. Although enthusiasm for reforms conveyed in educational journals may be sufficient to encourage school boards to try new programs, many teachers successfully resist change — whether for good or bad — by closing the door and doing as they please. We have heard teachers comment on a principal, or principals state about a central office administrator, … 'this person will be gone in 2 years … it's not even worth an argument … this too will pass.' Smylie and Crowson (1996) have distinguished between teacher persistence and teacher resistance. Whereas resistance suggests a conscious rejection, persistence suggests that the shared history of participants (culture, past practices) serve as conservative forces and constraints on participants' willingness to consider new behaviors.

Even though some fads do not affect classroom practice widely, they are still disruptive and costly. At a minimum, they stop the search for more sophisticated reform plans. Some fads lead to enormous dissipation of financial resources and personal energy. For example, buildings have been gutted to make way for open classrooms; subsequently, additional funds have been spent to rebuild walls. Language laboratories have been built, and expensive computers have been purchased, with little evidence that such expenditures have led to improvement in student learning. Indeed, considerable evidence shows that investments in technology cannot be justified in terms of improved instruction and learning [see the chapter by Noble in this volume].

Political Symbolism and Reform

There are countless reasons why reform has and continues to be popular. Some groups that advocate a reform do not believe the reform will actually improve learning. For these persons, the reform is political and is good simply because it symbolizes interest in education. Such groups may believe that educational problems are intractable; however, the symbolic value of possible improvement is an important myth. Hence, from this viewpoint, faddism is seen as a Hawthorne effect that may keep citizens, teachers, and parents working to keep the system going (e.g., to provide a rationale for teacher education programs). This relatively cynical hypothesis can take many forms. For some, the cynicism may be in the form 'this is the best strategy for obtaining funding for education.' However, others who engage in political symbolism may do so for extreme and self-serving political reasons (i.e., 'this is the best way to prevent funding').

In their book, *The Manufactured Crisis* (1995), Berliner and Biddle argue that some conservative groups (including appointed and elected officials) have created the myth that American education is in crisis (see also Bracey, 1996; Rose, 1995) and thus undeserving of financial support. If one can successfully promote such an idea, then radical reform of American schooling (e.g., public investments in charter schools or vouchers for private schools, etc.) can be seen as necessary. In contrast, if the public thinks that American schools are doing well, they are likely to view radical reforms with suspicion. Thus, entrepreneurs who have a vested interest in promoting charter schools or vouchers may be motivated to search for and publicize negative information about student performance. Along these same lines, one could argue that those who provide in-service training or prepare educational publications for school districts benefit from a crisis mentality that leads schools to invest resources in developing new and immediate solutions to problems.

Five Hypotheses for the 'Bandwagon' Phenomena in Reform

We could continue to list possible reasons for the popularity of reform; however, in the remainder of the chapter we want to present five hypotheses for explaining the 'bandwagon' phenomenon in teacher education and educational reforms.

Vague platforms and fuzzy definitions.

In reform movements, central propositions and assumptions are rarely spelled out in detail. For example, in the middle school movement appealing terms like 'developmentally appropriate for adolescents' or 'better transition to high schools' (Who could be against such sensible ideas?), are subject to multiple interpretations but are not defined precisely.

Part of the reason for fuzzy definitions is political. Similar to government coalitions and political parties, if an educational reform movement is to have sufficient breadth so that many people can attest to its importance, advocate the new ideas, and see the reform's relevance to their own interest, the 'platform' needs to be attractive but vague. Vagueness allows various people and groups to project their own interest on the 'platform.' After a bureaucracy (whether a teacher education program or a school board) has defined 'acceptable' practice, it takes considerable effort (many people writing about and calling for change) to encourage people to seriously consider implementing new ideas. For example, a precise definition of 'developmentally appropriate' is likely to offend or fail to convince some potential backers. Thus, there is some political motivation for describing reforms in vague terms.

Herbert Kliebard (1986, p. xi) described his difficulty in defining one of the most important curriculum influences in the last 100 years of American education – the progressive education movement:

> The more I studied this the more it seemed to me that the term encompassed such a broad range, not just of different, but of contradictory ideas on education as to be meaningless. In the end, I came to believe that the term was not only vacuous but mischievous. It was not just the word 'progressive' that I thought was inappropriate, but the implication that something deserving a single name existed and that something could be identified and defined if only we tried. My initial puzzlement turned to skepticism, my skepticism to indignation and finally to bemusement.

One of us had a similar experience in the mid 1970s trying to define individualized and open education (see Good et al., 1975). Some schools without walls were considerably more structured (e.g., in degree of flexibility and scheduling or amount of team planning, etc.) than were many traditional schools. Clark and Clark (1993) have described this phenomenon in middle schools.

A superintendent, policy maker, or teacher can judge a reform movement to be vacuous only if she or he is willing to read a considerable amount of material carefully. When a plethora of articles advocate a reform, it is easy to get carried away by the enthusiasm for change. Indeed, nearly 70 years ago, Koos (1927) noted the tendency of many educators to jump on the reform bandwagon because they wanted to use the latest techniques (i.e., to be on the cutting edge). The problem of faddism is especially likely to occur when the theory behind a reform is not spelled out in propositional form or with clear documentation (e.g., videos of teaching, etc.).

The tendency to advocate radical reform without offering precise definitions or empirical support continues today. For example, David Cohen (1995), who advocates teaching-for-understanding, encourages teachers to engage in more 'ambitious teaching.' But what does ambitious teaching mean? Does it mean different things in math and science, and for students of diverse backgrounds and varied academic aptitudes? How is ambitious teaching operationally defined at various grade levels?

We argue that advocates of reform should provide at least some operational definitions and propositional statements concerning what classrooms in which reforms are implemented should look like (Clark & Clark, 1994b). For example, reformers could compile an extensive video library illustrating the type of teaching advocated (and what is *not* advocated) and the new roles students are to play. Reformers also need to detail the in-service training and other support teachers will need to understand and implement new approaches to teaching. We recognize that a reform like teaching-for-understanding can be implemented in many ways, but teachers need help in visualizing the range of possibilities. They should provide results from pilot studies to show that the change can be beneficial.

Often teachers are blamed when an innovation fails, for example, because (it is said) they did not have sufficient knowledge, motivation, or ability to implement the change (e.g., Cohen, 1995). However, we suspect that reforms are at least as likely to fail because

a) they are ill-advised or
b) administrators and innovators fail to provide teachers with information and resources needed to implement the reforms.

Theories of reform should provide not only clear measures or concepts that can be used to evaluate the success of reforms but also compelling rationales as to why proposed student (or teacher) processes or outcomes are preferable to current ones. Unfortunately, most reform efforts continue at a global level, advocating, for example, more student participation or more student questions, without recognition that all types of student questions are not equally desirable and that, at times, student reflection and listening are better than student talk. To reiterate, reform tends to focus on *form* rather than *quality* of schooling. In large measure, this occurs because the underlying theory is fuzzy and at times contradictory.

Multiple purposes of schooling.

Educators have always raised questions about how to define success in schooling, and conceptions of success often differ radically. Berliner and Biddle (1995) addressed this issue in comparing American schools with those in other countries:

> This issue becomes crucial when one ponders the innate values reflected in American education. To begin with, Americans think that children should have a wide variety of experiences. Our middle-class neighbors seem to argue that their children should participate in organized sports such as little league, basketball, and soccer; engage in after-school activities such as piano lessons and dance; watch a good deal of TV; spend weekends in leisure pursuits; have their own cars and begin to date in high school; and so forth. This means, of course, that many American parents do not favor an educational system that assigns vast amounts of homework or that encourages students to become high-achieving drudges. By comparison, then, American teenagers probably have more nonacademic interests and a wider knowledge base than do students from countries that stress narrow, academic concerns. (p. 52)

Good (1996), in responding to the document *Prisoners of Time* (National Education Commission on Time and Learning, 1994), made a similar argument. Unless one focuses on the possible trade-offs, it is easy to become overly concerned about data showing that high schools in other countries (e.g., Japan, 3170 hours) spend more time than U.S. schools (1460 hours) teaching academic subjects. According to Good (1996), if educators and citizens want American youth to 'survive' their middle school years (and hence be able to benefit from more academic teaching in high schools) then some of the curriculum must be devoted to topics such as safety, violence, AIDS, drugs, and so forth. The argument for a differentiated curriculum is especially clear at this time when many believe that achievement differences between students in the U.S. and other countries have been exaggerated. 'Crisis thinking' narrows reformers' vision and leads to the use of resources to respond to a single problem.

As we noted earlier, the question of what constitutes success in United States schools involves more than international comparisons. For example, the movement from open classrooms to structured teaching to teaching-for-understanding has been influenced by competing definitions of what students should know and be able to do (e.g., understand a few concepts indepth vs. understand more concepts but in somewhat less depth?). Although educators, researchers, and policy makers often act as though these debates are new, they are long-standing and common. For example, in the United States, doctoral programs in the social sciences have emphasized breadth over depth in comparison to programs in Europe and Australia.

Focusing on a single outcome factor or a small set of highly related factors (e.g., achievement test scores in math and science) can make less than outstanding achievement scores appear inadequate. For example, educators might become concerned about why American students do not solve mathematical problems involving proportions better unless they consider a broad range of student and nonacademic factors. Students must learn many math concepts including estimation, probability, and basic facts. However, as McCaslin and Good (1996b) contend, students are more than academic learners, and they have to deal with many social and extracurricular activities (learn to make friends or the basketball team, say no to drugs, find part-time jobs, etc.). We believe that in the 1990s one cannot consider students' academic growth without at the same time considering their social and affective growth (Clark & Clark, 1986; McCaslin & Good, 1996b; Noddings, 1992).

In their book, *Listening in Classrooms*, McCaslin and Good (1996b) argue that a balanced curriculum (much like a balanced portfolio) is essential for success in American schools. They note that educators must recognize that students are social beings as well as learners and that any reform plan must consider students' social and affective needs as well as their cognitive needs. As the twenty-first century nears, conceptions of students must broaden to recognize that individual effort is an incomplete and antiquated model for judging school success, just as the model of teacher as lone 'cowperson or isolated performer' is obsolete (McCaslin & Good, 1996a). Given the massive inequalities that some students face (both outside and inside of the schools), it seems that for students to be successful in school, they will need more structural support than they are currently receiving (e.g., Clark & Clark, 1994a; Kaufman & Rosenbaum, 1992; Kozol, 1991; Rose, 1995; McCaslin & Good, 1992, 1996b). Whatever goals are deemed appropriate for United States students and citizens in the future, educators must invest not only in the academic lives of students but also in their social-emotional lives so that ultimately all students can play productive, societal roles. It is time to stop blaming parents *or* teachers, *or* administrators, *or* students, *or* teacher educators and to look for ways in which all of these groups can work together to solve the problems that confront American youth.

We hypothesize that widening the range of measures used to define success in school can lead to reform that is sophisticated problem solving and research rather than mere advocacy. In contrast, simple definitions of reform (and problems) are likely to produce only educational fads.

Undifferentiated, decontextualized problem statements.

We believe that simplistic, decontextualized conceptualizations of educational problems undermine reform. One important reason why educators move from fad to fad is that policy statements are incomplete, misleading, or flatly wrong. As noted earlier, in the past two decades considerable media attention has focused on the supposedly inadequate academic achievements of American students. If one accepts the premise that the U.S. educational system is fatally flawed, then it appears reasonable to explore alternatives, even radical ones (e.g., voucher plans, charter schools, and so on). In contrast, if a more accurate problem statement is presented (some schools are effective and some are not), then it is easier to justify the need for more research, more resources, and adaptive practices in order to address the problems of American education selectively and in particular *contexts*. If the problems of schooling vary from district to district and from school to school, it is essential that reformers look at quality of schooling and ignore the many superficial factors that critics of schools like to talk about.

Variation in American schools is easy to illustrate. As we noted, considerable research has documented variation among teachers in instruction and in effects of individual schools. Some teachers in some schools affect student achievement more than others (Good & Brophy, 1986, 1994; Rutter, 1983; Teddlie & Stringfield, 1993). Moreover, some schools and districts have more resources than others (Government Accounting Office, 1995), and in some cases this differential funding is extremely unequal with tragic consequences (Kozol, 1991, 1995). Although citizens want high-quality education in all settings (rural poor, suburban affluent, inner-city, etc.), appropriate steps toward improvement and the achievement of high-quality standards will vary in different school contexts.

Theory too far in front of research.

In education, as in the broader social sciences, theory is often far in advance of research. For example, Smylie (1995) recently noted:

> An increasing literature has accompanied the proliferation of teacher leadership programs and policies. The Educational Research Information Clearing (ERIC) lists over 2,100 published and unpublished papers on teacher leadership. It records additional entries on specific opportunities for teacher leadership. For example, ERIC contains almost 2,500 papers on participative decision making, 1,600 on career ladders, and approximately 1,300 on lead, master and mentor

teachers. Up to 50 per cent of the literature on teacher leadership opportunities has been produced over the last 5 years. (p. 4)

According to Smylie, although there has been an incredible increase in interest in teacher leadership, the literature has not changed. That is, most of the literature consists of position essays, with but few empirical investigations. Especially lacking are studies of teacher leadership based on an articulated theoretical framework that would organize and focus the research. Although we have long advocated improving conditions of teaching and increasing professional opportunities and resources for teachers, (Clark & Clark, 1983; Good & Brophy, 1973), we are against representing any single educational movement as a panacea or answer.

One theory that has been proposed frequently (but with little support and empirical data) is that school governance should be shifted from the principal and the school board to teachers and the community. Elmore (1995, p. 23) states his frustration with simple-minded approaches to structural reform: 'Imagine a school that embodies many of the remedies currently advocated by educational reformers. The school is governed by a site-based council, composed of teachers, administrators, parents, and community members.' He goes on to list a number of dimensions that many school reformers would see as the paragon of professional development and educational reform. He expresses his frustration this way:

> What would we expect to be the consequences of this kind of school restructuring for teachers and students? We might expect teachers to feel more energized, motivated, and positive about their work. We might expect students to experience a more stimulating educational environment, adapted more explicitly to the individual strengths and weaknesses. We might expect parents and community members to regard the school more positively. But would we expect teachers to teach differently and, as a consequence, students to learn more, to think differently, or to approach the acquisition of knowledge differently? (p. 23)

Although we share Elmore's surprise that anyone should think that structural reform in and of itself might lead to radical changes in students' thought, we are equally puzzled by part of his argument. He apparently believes that structural reform (empowerment of teachers) would inevitably energize teachers and improve their ability to identify students' individual strengths and weaknesses and to plan instruction accordingly. Given the plethora of studies illustrating immense variation among teachers in school climates, we wonder why anyone would expect giving teacher's control of the curriculum to energize an entire faculty (Good & Brophy, 1986; Good & Weinstein, 1986; Goodlad, 1983; Rosenholtz, 1989; Spencer, 1986). Rosenholtz (1989) described variation in the social organization of schools, including schools that she characterized as 'stuck' (schools in which teachers did not share ideas nor admit weaknesses). If teachers in 'stuck' schools were asked to expend more time developing curriculum or to admit 'uncertainty,' they would probably show polarized reactions to the new opportunities and an acute loss of morale, at least initially. Spencer (1986) noted that the lives of women teachers are complicated and that many have little discretionary time for participating in school reform. Goodlad (1983) hypothesized on the basis of his observational research that the internal organization and capacity of some schools were so limited that they could not make improvements unless they received *outside help*.

Our amazement at arguments (such as that of Elmore) suggesting simple relations between structural reform and educational practice turns to anger when we consider books like Kozol's *Savage Inequalities* (1991) and *Amazing Grace* (1995). Considering inequalities among schools and access to resources such as appropriate laboratory materials, books, well-qualified teachers, and discretionary budgets, how could anyone argue that teacher control over discretionary resources to purchase new supplies and materials and so forth are important variables when discretionary funds are so meagre in some schools?

There are many reasons why theory may be too far in advance of research. One reason is that advocates of reform who propose new theories often fail to do their homework. Clearly, if one does not know that a reform has already been attempted and has failed, it is easy to propose the reform again without dealing with the reasons for its failure. Similarly, persons who have not read the literature on change or on teaching and schooling are more likely to propose simple theories that are attractive and compelling and to believe that pilot studies are not needed. We believe that pilot studies should be completed in demonstration sites (with track records) and should be established before effusive dissemination of a new theory. Further, if complex change is expected, teachers need ample and continuous planning time and other resources.

Low expectations for public education.

Yet another hypothesis about the reason for faddism in education is that too few individuals are committed to providing the funding necessary to implement significant reforms. Low expectations for public education and an unwillingness to fund it operates at several levels. For example, Koos (1927) noted that innovation sometimes occurred for economic reasons, as when the problem of overcrowding in high schools was solved by removing ninth graders and putting them in junior high schools with seventh and eighth graders. This and similar decisions that have occurred over the last 50 years indicate that when policy makers make educational decisions, economic concerns are often compelling. Simple structural reform is considerably cheaper than improving the quality of instruction or curriculum. Thus, policy makers and educators attempt reform simply to show interest or because they see experimentation itself as good – for implementing inexpensive fads may be cheaper than attempting more dynamic reforms.

We argue that a basic reason for rampant faddism in American education is that citizens and policy makers are unwilling to pay for the research and development that should precede meaningful reform, as well as other needed educational expenses (e.g., books and computers for low-income schools). Some reasons for this unwillingness to fund education are related to the low status of education, economic perspectives, and narrow self-interest.

Unfortunately, public schools have few active advocates; however, they have many detractors who would prefer to see investments in public education used elsewhere. Especially in inner-city and many rural settings, citizens are not sufficiently powerful to compete for the appropriate funding of their schools and hence for highly qualified teachers. More powerful citizens often do not lobby for more school funding because the schools in their privileged districts are adequate.

Funding and new opportunities can make a difference in students' educational experience and in their subsequent lives (Kaufman & Rosenbaum, 1992). Although we do not advocate spending resources indiscriminately, public schools should be equally and appropriately funded in a democratic society. As Good (1996) noted, one unfortunate consequence of attacks on public schools (e.g., National Commission on Excellence in Education, 1983; National Education Commission on Time and Learning; 1994) is that support for public schools has become passive. Increased intelligent spending on the public school is not wasteful nor luxurious. Indeed, in a society that is becoming increasingly polarized economically, adequate funding of education for all is a practical necessity.

The largest advocacy group for public education is parents; however, their support tends to be for their local school. Seldom are they a political force that supports research and development funding. Given such a weak and localized base of political advocacy, it is not surprising to see that Americans are generally unwilling to spend money on public education and particularly on schools in poor districts. Thus, districts that have the most acute educational needs (and where additional resources would surely improve achievement) are unlikely to receive such funds. Although courts are beginning to intervene in some states, powerful interests often generate considerable opposition to spending more money in poorer districts.

Low societal expectations for education and educators result in other problems that make faddism more likely to occur. Because of low public expectation, some educational reformers may believe that new programs must produce large effects in a short time if they are to receive large funding and continuing interest. Policy makers and teacher educators, however, will have to become more candid in recognizing and expressing the fact that problems created by years of neglect and inadequate funding cannot be solved quickly.

CONCLUSION

We have argued that faddism is costly – sometimes due to the waste of resources, and always because it is illusionary. Moreover, simple reform ideas shift the focus away from significant problems. For reform to be more than faddism, several things must happen. Theory must become more contextual and specific. Observational research (which is labor intensive and expensive) must become more prevalent. Policy makers must recognize that 'confirmatory' studies based on questionnaires and on student performance that are not accompanied by an examination of instructional process and student and teacher thinking have but limited value. Indeed, such research is often more misleading than helpful. Research and theory building should occur together, and plans for reform must recognize the complexity of schooling and include several measure of student success. Following McCaslin and Good (1996b), we call for a balance between social, affective, and cognitive outcomes. It seems incomplete to settle for students to understand history and contemporary society but not their own attitudes and interests. It seems equally self-defeating to argue for self-understanding and students' self-esteem at the expense of not understanding history or other subject areas. However, we should make clear that our call for a balanced portfolio should not be translated into another shibboleth or Zeitgeist. There is no such phenomenon as *the* balanced portfolio without an explicit understanding of the particular instructional outcomes that are important in a given context with known and stated values. The argument here is simply that educators must recognize that students are social beings as well as learners and that reform plans must consider students' social needs as well as their cognitive ones, and this need for integration of affective, cognitive, and social needs will vary with students' socioeconomic backgrounds, developmental stage, and previous learning.

We argue that with more articulate theory, the need for empirical testing becomes apparent to more people more quickly. More precise language also tends to demystify reform and to help do away with simple calls for change (even though simple calls for change may be successful in mobilizing behavior and resources in the short run). In contrast, more complete theoretical analysis of reforms prior to implementation leads to a more sophisticated understanding of change (why the problem is larger in some settings than others) and leads to the need for more proactive research and funding. However, we have noted that citizens and policy makers have become increasingly unwilling to fund educational research and development in the last decade. Whether or not more complete thinking and more articulated plans (with more modest expectations and more realistic time lines) can lead to better funding is of course problematic and is an empirical question.

Crucially, future research and theory building should occur in tandem, and plans for reform must recognize the need for including multiple measures of student success. Before reforms are advocated, relevant pilot projects illustrating the possible effects of reforms should be conducted. Finally, the cost of educational reform (e.g., teachers' stress, stipends, professional development) need to be estimated and explicated.

Detailed arguments about how to achieve these conditions are beyond the scope of this paper. However, the five hypotheses we have advanced should yield a modest framework for combating faddism in American education. Although other factors beg for analysis (e.g., failure of teacher education to help teachers distinguish between faddism and meaningful reform), our framework should stimulate debate about meaningful change. Reform participants might use this framework to question one another. For example, teachers might request detailed information from researchers or administrators about supporting research and ask administrators for resources to support the development of new lessons, and so on. Similarly, researchers might ask administrators for more time for treatments to work (e.g., 18 months instead of 2 weeks). Or administrators might press teachers and researchers to relate general theory to the context of a particular school or classroom.

As we were putting finishing touches on this paper, we were overcome by feelings of *deja vu* as we read about the 'progress' of a two-day national summit of corporate leaders, state governors, and politicians concerned with education. Peter Applebome writing in the *New York Times* on Thursday, March 28, 1996 quoted President Clinton as saying on this occasion:

> I believe this meeting will prove historic, ... in 1983, we said we've got a problem in our schools ... in 1989, we said we need to know where we're going; we need goals. Here in 1996, you're saying you can have all the goals in the world, but unless somebody really has meaningful standards and a system of measuring whether you meet those standards, you won't achieve your goals. That is the enduring gift you've given to America's school children and America's future.

In his speech, the president implicitly suggested that public education was in a state of crisis and that vigorous action was needed, but the problem was not defined (hence the need for vigorous action was never made clear) However, even though the problem was left unspecified, the president, governors, and leaders of industry who attended the meeting were able to provide 'the solution' (i.e., higher standards for teachers, more technology, higher standards for students, and more charter schools)! If researchers want to be heard, it seems important for them to become more active disseminators and to become more vocal in public policy forums and publications. Politicians who make specious claims must be held accountable by researchers who are willing to present arguments based on evidence. Given what research tells us about the negative effects of thoughtless reforms that ignore the realities of teacher and student motivations, the dynamics of classroom teaching, and the serious inequities of educational funding in our country, it seems that much of what was recommended at the summit is ill-advised.

ENDNOTES

[1.] The authors gratefully acknowledge the assistance of Sharon Nichols who typed the manuscript and who made editorial suggestions. The authors want to also acknowledge Gail Hinkel who edited the paper and Mark Smylie for his helpful review.

REFERENCES

Alexander, W. M. (1968). *The emergent middle school*. New York: Holt, Rinehart and Winston.

Alexander, W. M. & George, P. S. (1981). *The exemplary middle school*. New York: Holt, Rinehart and Winston.

Alexander, W. M. & McEwin, C. K. (1992). Schools in the middle: Progress 1968-1988. In S. Clark & D. Clark (Eds.), *Schools in the middle: A decade of growth and change* (pp. 38-45). Reston, VA: National Association of Secondary School Principals.

Arhar, J. M. (1992). Interdisciplinary teaming and the social bonding of middle level students. In J. L. Irvin (Ed.), *Transforming middle level education: Perspectives and possibilities* (pp. 139-161). Needham Heights, MA: Allyn and Bacon.

Arhar, J. M., Johnston, J. H., & Markle, G. C. (1989). The effects of teaming on students. *Middle School Journal, 20*(3), 24-27.

Ball, D. (1991). What's all this talk about discourse? *Arithmetic Teacher, 39*, 44-48.

Barth, R. (1969). *Open education: Assumptions and rationales*. Unpublished qualifying paper, Harvard University, Cambridge, MA.

Barth, R. (1970). When children enjoy school: Some lessons from Great Britain. *Childhood Education, 46*, 195-200.

Becker, H. J. (1990). Curriculum and instruction in middle grade schools. *Phi Delta Kappan, 71*(6), 450-457.

Berliner, D. (1979). Tempus educare. In P. Peterson & H. Walberg (Eds.), *Research on teaching: Concepts, findings and implications* (pp. 120-135). Berkeley, CA: McCutchan.

Berliner, D. & Biddle, B. (1995). *The manufactured crisis: Myth, fraud and the attack on America's public schools*. New York: Addison-Wesley.

Blumenfeld, P. (1992). The task and the teacher: Enhancing student thoughtfulness in science. In J. Brophy (Ed.), *Advances in research on teaching* (Vol. 3, pp. 81-114). Greenwich, CT: JAI Press.

Bossert, S. (1988-1989). Cooperative activities in the classroom. In E. Rothkopl (Ed.), *Review of research in education* (Vol. 15, pp. 225-250). Washington, DC: American Educational Research Association.

Bracey, G. (1996). International comparisons and the condition of American education. *Educational Researcher, 25*, 5-11.

Braddock, J. H., II. (1990). Tracking in the middle grades: National patterns of grouping for instruction. *Phi Delta Kappan, 71*(6), 445-449.

Briggs, T. H. (1920). *The junior high school*. Boston: Houghton Mifflin.

Brophy, J. & Good, T. (1974). *Teacher-student relationships: Causes and consequences*. New York: Holt, Rhinehart and Winston.

Carnegie Task Force on Education of Young Adolescents. (1989). *Turning points: Preparing American youth for the 21st century*. Washington, DC: Carnegie Council on Adolescent Development.

Cawelti, G. (1988, November). Middle schools a better match with early adolescent needs, ASCD survey finds. In *ASCD curriculum update* (pp. 1-12). Alexandria, VA: Association for Supervision and Curriculum Development.

Chall, J. (1967). *Learning to read: The great debate*. New York: McGraw-Hill.

Clark D. C. & Clark, S. N. (1983, October). Staff development programs for middle level schools. In *Schools in the middle: A report on trends and practices* (pp. 1-12). Reston, VA: National Association of Secondary School Principals.

Clark, S. N. & Clark, D. C. (1986, September). Middle level programs: More than academics. In *Schools in the middle: A report on trends and practices* (pp. 1-4). Reston, VA: National Association of Secondary School Principals.

Clark, S. N. & Clark, D. C. (1987, October). Interdisciplinary teaming programs: Organization, rationale, and implementation. In *Schools in the middle: A report on trends and practices* (pp. 1-6). Reston, VA: National Association of Secondary School Principals.

Clark, S. N. & Clark, D. C. (1990). *Arizona middle schools: A survey report*. Phoenix: Arizona Department of Education.

Clark, S. N. & Clark, D. C. (1992). The pontoon transitional design: A missing link in research on interdisciplinary teaming. *Research in Middle Level Education, 15*(2), 57-81.

Clark, S. N. & Clark, D. C. (1993). Middle level school reform: The rhetoric and the reality. *Elementary School Journal, 93*, 447-460.

Clark, S. N. & Clark, D. C. (1994a). Meeting the needs of young adolescents. *Schools in the Middle, 4*(1), 4-7.

Clark, S. N. & Clark, D. C. (1994b). *Restructuring the middle level school: Implications for school leaders*. Albany: State University of New York Press.

Cohen, D. (1995). What is the system in systemic reform? *Educational Researcher, 24*, 11-17.

Commission on Standards for School Mathematics (1989). *Curriculum and evaluation standards for school mathematics*. Reston, VA: National Council of Teachers of Mathematics.

Conant, J. B. (1960). *A memorandum to school boards: Recommendations for education in the junior high school years*. Princeton, NJ: Educational Testing Service.

Connors, N. (1986). *A case study to determine the essential components and effects of an advisor/advisee program in an exemplary middle school*. Unpublished doctoral dissertation, Florida State University, Tallahassee, FL.

Cuban, L. (1993). *How teachers taught: Constancy and change in American classrooms 1890 through 1980*. New York: Longman.

David, J. L. (1991). What it takes to restructure education. *Educational Leadership, 48*(8), 11-15.

Delpit, L. (1995). *Other people's children: Cultural conflict in the classroom.* New York: New Press.

Elmore, R. (1995). Structural reform and educational practice. *Educational Researcher, 24(9),* 23-26.

Epstein, J. L. (1981). *Secondary school environments and student outcomes: A review and annotated bibliography* (Report No. 315). Baltimore, MD: Johns Hopkins University Center for Social Organization of Schools.

Epstein, J. & Mac Iver, D. (1990). *Education in the middle grades.* Columbus, OH: National Middle School Association.

Fenwick, J. (1992). *Managing middle grade reform – an 'American 2000' agenda.* San Diego, CA: Fenwick.

Government Accounting Office (1995, September). *School finance: Trends in U.S. education spending* (GAO/HEHS-95-235). Washington, DC: Author.

George, P. S. (1987). *Long-term teacher student relationships: A case study.* Columbus, OH: National Middle School Association.

George, P. S. (1988). Tracking and ability grouping. *Middle School Journal, 20*(1), 21-28.

George, P. S. & Oldaker, L. L. (1985). *Evidence for the middle school.* Columbus, OH: National Middle School Association.

Glickman, C. (1991). Pretending not to know what we know. *Educational Leadership, 48*(8), 4-11.

Good, T. (1969). *Student achievement level and differential opportunity for classroom response.* Unpublished doctoral dissertation, Indiana University, Bloomington, IN.

Good, T. (1983). Classroom research: A decade of progress. *Educational Psychologist, 18*, 127-144.

Good, T. (1996). Teaching effects and teacher evaluation. In J. Sikula, T. Buttery, & E. Guyton (Eds.), *Handbook of research on teacher education* (2nd ed., pp. 617-665). New York: Mellon.

Good, T. & Biddle, B. (1988). Research and the improvement of mathematics instruction: The need for observational resources. In D. Grouws & T. Cooney (Eds.), *Perspectives on research and effective mathematics teaching* (pp. 114-142). Hillsdale, NJ: Erlbaum.

Good, T., Biddle, B., & Brophy, J. (1975). *Teachers make a difference.* New York: Holt, Rinehart and Winston.

Good, T. & Brophy, J. (1973). *Looking in classrooms* (1st ed.). New York: Harper & Rowe.

Good, T. & Brophy, J. (1986). School effects. In M. C. Wittrock (Ed.), *Handbook of research on teaching* (3rd. ed., pp. 570-604). New York: Macmillan.

Good, T. & Brophy, J. (1994). *Looking in classrooms* (6th ed.). New York: Harper Collins.

Good, T. & Grouws, D. (1979). The Missouri Mathematics Effectiveness Project: An experimental study in fourth-grade classrooms. *Journal of Educational Psychology, 71*, 355-362.

Good, T., Grouws, D., & Ebmeier, H. (1983). *Active Mathematics Teaching.* New York: Longman.

Good, T. & Power, C. (1976). Designing successful environments for different types of students. *Journal of Curriculum Studies, 8*, 45-60.

Good, T. & Stipek, D. (1983). Individual differences in the classroom: A psychological perspective. In G. Fenstermacher & J. Goodlad (Eds.), *1983 NSSE yearbook* (pp. 9-43). Chicago: National Society for the Study of Education, University of Chicago Press.

Good, T. & Weinstein, R. (1986). Schools make a difference: Evidence, criticisms, new directions. *American Psychologist, 1*, 1090-1097.

Goodlad, J. (1983). *A place called school.* New York: McGraw-Hill.

Gruhn, W. T. & Douglass, H. R. (1947). *The modern junior high school.* New York: Ronald.

Hafner, A., Ingels, S., Schneider, B., Stevenson, D., & Owings, J. (1990). *National educational longitudinal study 1988: A profile of the American eighth grader.* Washington, DC: U.S. Department of Education, Office of Educational Research and Implementation.

Hall, G. S. (1905). *Adolescence.* New York: D. Appleton-Century.

Hansen, J. H. & Hern, A. C. (1971). *The middle school program.* Chicago: Rand McNally.

Hiebert, J. & Carpenter, T. (1992). Learning and teaching with understanding. In D. Grouws (Ed.), *Handbook of research on mathematics teaching and learning* (pp. 65-100). New York: Macmillan.

Homans, G. (1950). *The human group.* New York: Harcourt Brace Jovanovich.

Jones, G. & Gerig, T. (1994). Silent sixth-grade students: Characteristics, achievement, and teacher expectations. *Elementary School Journal, 95,* 169-182.

Joyce, B. R. (1991). The door to school improvement. *Educational Leadership, 48*(8), 59-62.

Kantrowitz, B. & Wingert, P. (1991, June 17). A dismal report card: Rich and poor, north and south, black, brown, and white, eighth graders flunked the national math test. What can be done about this scandal? *Newsweek,* pp. 64-65.

Kaufman, J. & Rosenbaum, J. (1992). The education and employment of low-income black youths in white suburbs. *Educational Policy and Evaluation, 14,* 229-240.

Kilpatrick, J. (1992). A history of research in mathematics education. In D. Grouws (Ed.), *Handbook of research on mathematics teaching and learning* (pp. 3-38). New York: Macmillan.

King, L. (1993). High and low achievers' perceptions and cooperative learning in two small groups. *Elementary School Journal, 93,* 399-416.

Kliebard, H. (1986). *The struggle for the American curriculum: 1893-1958.* New York: Routledge.

Koos, L. V. (1927). *The junior high school.* Boston: Ginn.

Kozol, J. (1991). *Savage inequalities: Children in America's schools.* New York: Crown.

Kozol, J. (1995). *Amazing grace: The lives of children and the conscience of a nation.* New York: Crown.

Levine, D. U. (1991). Creating effective schools: Findings and implications from research and practice. *Phi Delta Kappan, 72*(5), 389-393.

Lipsitz, J. (1984). *Successful schools for young adolescents.* New Brunswick, NJ: Transaction Books.

Lounsbury, J. H. (1992). Middle level schools—Once around the elephant. In S. Clark & D. Clark (Eds), *Schools in the middle: A decade of growth and change* (pp. 48-53). Reston, VA: National Association of Secondary School Principals.

Lounsbury, J. H. (1991). *As I see it.* Columbus, OH: National Middle School Association.

Lounsbury, J. H. & Clark, D. C. (1990). *Inside grade eight: From apathy to excitement.* Reston, VA: National Association of Secondary School Principals.

Lounsbury, J. H. & Johnston, J. H. (1985). *How fares the ninth grade?* Reston, VA: National Association of Secondary School Principals.

Lounsbury, J. H. & Johnston, J. H. (1988). *Life in the three sixth grades.* Reston, VA: National Association of Secondary School Principals.

Mac Iver, D. (1990). Meeting the needs of young adolescents: Advisory groups, interdisciplinary teaching teams, and school transition programs. *Phi Delta Kappan, 71*(6), 458-464.

Maeroff, G. I. (1988). Blueprint for the empowerment of teachers. *Phi Delta Kappan, 69*(7), 473-477.

McCaslin, M. & Good, T. (1992). Compliant cognition: The misalliance of management and instructional goals in current school reform. *Educational Researcher, 21,* 4-17.

McCaslin, M. & Good, T. (1996a). The informal curriculum. In D. Berliner & R. Calfee (Eds.), *Handbook of educational psychology* (pp. 622-670). New York: Macmillan.

McCaslin, M. & Good, T. (1996b). *Listening in classrooms*. New York: Harper Collins.

McCaslin, M., Sisk, L., & Thompson, E. (1994-1995). Motivation in the classroom. In *The dean's forum for the advancement of knowledge and practice in education: Proceedings 1994-1995* (pp. 15-16). Tucson: University of Arizona.

McCaslin, M., Tuck, D., Wiard, A., Brown, B., LaPage, J., & Pyle, J. (1994). Gender composition and small-group learning in fourth grade mathematics. *Elementary School Journal, 94*, 467-482.

Mitman, A. L. & Lambert, V. L. (1992). *Instructional challenge: A casebook for middle grade educators*. San Francisco: Far West Laboratory for Educational Research and Development.

Mulryan, C. (1995). Fifth and sixth graders' involvement and participation in cooperative small groups in mathematics. *Elementary School Journal, 95*, 297-310.

National Association of Secondary School Principals Council on Middle Level Education (1985). *An agenda for excellence at the middle level*. Reston, VA: Author.

National Commission on Excellence in Education (1983, November). A nation at risk: The imperative for educational reform. *Elementary School Journal, 84*(2), 113-130.

National Education Commission on Time and Learning (1994, April). *Prisoners of time*. Washington, DC: U.S. Government Printing Office.

National Middle School Association. (1992). *This we believe*. Columbus, OH: Author.

National Research Council (1989). *Everybody counts: A report to the nation on the future of mathematics education*. Washington, DC: National Academy of Sciences.

Noddings, N. (1992). *The challenge to care in schools*. New York: Teachers College Press.

Oakes, J. (1985). *Keeping track: How schools structure inequality*. New Haven, CT: Yale University Press.

Peterson, P. (1990). The California Study of Elementary Mathematics. *Educational Evaluation and Policy Analysis, 12*, 257-261.

Prawat, R. (1992). Are changes in views about mathematics teaching sufficient? The case of a fifth-grade teacher. *Elementary School Journal, 93*, 195-212.

Rose, M. (1995). *Possible lives: The promise of public education in America*. Boston: Houghton Mifflin.

Rosenholtz, S. (1989). *Teachers' workplace: The social organization of schools*. New York: Longman.

Rutter, M. (1983). School effects on pupil progress: Research findings and policy implications. In L. Schulman & G. Sykes (Eds.), *Handbook of teaching and policy* (pp. 3-41). New York: Longman.

Rutter, M., Maughan, B., Mortimore, P., Ouston, J., & Smith, A. (1979). *Fifteen thousand hours: Secondary schools and their effects on children* (pp. 114-142). Cambridge, MA: Harvard University Press.

Sarason, S. (1971). *The culture of school and the problem of change*. Boston: Allyn & Bacon.

Sarason, S. (1995). *School change: The personal development of a point of view*. New York: Teachers College Press.

Shulman, L. (1970). Psychology and mathematics education. In E. Begle (Ed.), *Mathematics education* (Sixty-ninth Yearbook of the National Society for the Study of Education, Part. 1, pp. 23-71). Chicago: University of Chicago Press.

Slavin, R. (1989). PET and the pendulum: Faddism in education and how to stop it. *Phi Delta Kappan, 70*, 752-758.

Smylie, M. (1995). New perspectives on teacher leadership. *Elementary School Journal, 96*, 3-7.

Smylie, M. & Crowson, R. (1996). Working within the scripts: Building institutional infrastructure for children's service coordination in schools. *Educational Policy, 10*(1), 3-21.

Spencer, D. (1986). *Contemporary women teachers: Balancing school and home.* White Plains, NY: Longman.

Teddlie, C. & Stringfield, S. (1993). *Schools make a difference: Lessons learned from a 10-year study of school effects.* New York: Teachers College Press.

Thornburg, H. (1980). Early adolescents: Their developmental characteristics. *High School Journal, 63*(6), 215-221.

Thorndike, E. L. (1907). *The elimination of pupils from schools* (Bulletin 1907, No. 4). Washington, DC: U.S. Department of Interior, Bureau of Education.

Tye, K. A. (1985). *The junior high: School in search of a mission.* Lanham, MD: University Press of America.

Valentine, J., Clark, D., Irvin, J., Keefe, J., & Melton, G. (1993). *Leadership in middle level education. Vol. 1: A national survey of middle level leaders and schools.* Reston, VA: National Association of Secondary School Principals.

Valentine, J. W., Clark, D. C., Nickerson, N. C., & Keefe, J. W. (1981). *The middle level principalship—Vol. 1: A survey of middle level principals and programs.* Reston, VA: National Association of Secondary School Principals.

Van Til, W., Vars, G. F., & Lounsbury, J. H. (1961). *Modern education for the junior high school years.* Indianapolis: Bobbs-Merrill.

Vars, G. F. (1991). Integrated curriculum in historical perspective. *Educational Leadership, 49*(2), 14-15.

Vygotsky, L. (1978). *Mind and society: The development of higher psychological processes.* Cambridge, MA: Harvard University Press.

Walker, D. & Schaffarzick, J. (1974). Comparing curricula. *Review of Educational Research, 44*, 83-111.

NAME INDEX

A

Acker, S. 31, 32, 138, 144, 156, 189–192, 200, 211–213, 216–218, 244, 448, 1313
Adair, A.V. 274
Adams, G.V. 512, 556, 557
Adams, R. 46
Addams, J. 202
Adelman, N.E. 558
Adkison, J.A. 181
Adler, P. 901, 902, 904, 922
Adler, P.A. 901, 902, 904, 922
Adler, S. 212, 224, 225
Adorno, T.W. 1147
Agar, M. 31, 32
Agard, P. 1234, 1236
Aggleton, P. 318, 319
Ahlbrand, W.P. 821
Ahlström, K-G. 332
Aiken, W. 1186
Ainscow, M. 527, 528, 546–548
Aitken, J.L. 81, 94
Akers, J. 1367
Akin, J.N. 1069
Alber, J.W. 751
Alec, E. 438
Alexander, D. 83, 96
Alexander, W.M. 1397, 1399, 1400, 1402, 1405, 1406
Alleman, J. 684, 687, 691, 826
Allen, J.R. 530, 542, 555, 560
Allen, L.R. 566, 947, 963
Allen, R.W. 941
Allen, V.L. 515
Allport, G.H. 538
Almack, J.C. 156, 170–172, 183, 187
Alonzo, R.C. 486
Alspaugh, D. 530, 555, 559
Altbach, P.G. 1018
Altenbaugh, R.J. 156
Altmaier, E. 471
Alton-Lee, A.G. 672, 683, 688, 731, 737, 744, 751, 754, 760, 761
Alutto, J.A. 486, 531, 533, 561, 564, 565
Alvermann, D.E. 717
Amarel, M. 1173, 1174, 1180
Ambrosie, F. 570
Amigues, R. 693
Ammon, P. 107
Amsler, M. 528, 542, 550, 553
Anastasi, A. 269
Ancess, J. 771, 1070

Anders, P. 862, 1184, 1238, 1239, 1248, 1249, 1251, 1258
Andersen, E.S. 718, 736
Anderson, A. 829
Anderson, B. 240
Anderson, B.D. 485
Anderson, B.T. 288, 290
Anderson, C.W. 672, 712, 720, 858, 1232
Anderson, D.S. 1165
Anderson, E.W. 169
Anderson, G. 555, 945, 947, 951, 952, 959, 1147
Anderson, J. 290, 771
Anderson, L. 4, 156, 671, 672, 1167, 1168, 1287
Anderson, L.M. 1223, 1230, 1231
Anderson, M.L. 160
Anderson, R.C. 729
Andersson, B.-E. 906
Andersson, C. 345
Anglin, L.W. 288, 289
Anthony, P. 183
Anweiler, O. 357, 387
Anyon, J. 271, 632
Appel, S. 1157
Apple, M.W. 67, 149, 155, 189, 193, 210, 217, 244, 594, 624, 630, 632, 634, 635, 638, 639, 939, 950, 960, 1000, 1045, 1063, 1146
Applebome, P. 1421
Applegate, J. 112
Archbald, D. 67
Archer, M. 431
Archer, M.S. 1022
Archibald, D.A. 835, 853, 855
Arendt, H. 996
Arfwedson, G. 342, 345
Argyris, C. 534
Arhar, J.M. 1403, 1407
Aristotle 1194
Armaline, W. 1131
Arnot, M. 202
Arnove, R. 1018
Arnstine, D. 506
Aronowitz, S. 5, 621, 624, 626, 627, 632, 640, 663, 664, 1146
Arons, S.C. 980
Aronson, E. 462, 845, 918, 919, 921, 1245, 1272
Arthur, J. 239
Ash, D. 708, 844
Ashenden, D.J. 163, 623, 631, 641, 648–650, 653, 661, 893, 917, 1135

H

S

SUBJECT INDEX

A

ability grouping 271, 1409
accountability of teachers 459–498
action research 114, 138
adaptive teaching 1072
adolescent culture 887 ff.
adult development 57
advisory programs for teachers 1404 ff.
African-American teachers 164, 186
age effects on peer culture 895–897
anti-racist schooling 262
anti-sexist schooling 221, 225
apolitical organizations 428
apprenticeship 95, 106 ff., 703
artefacts of teaching 807, 811
artifacts 834
assessment
    ambiguities 771 ff.
    authentic 1368
    of students' thinking 812, 834, 838
    outcomes 770
    performance 772, 855, 856
authentic tasks 834, 837, 1265
authenticity 29 ff.
authority 941
autobiographical research 13–34, 111, 146
automated instruction 1323
autonomy of teachers 218, 223, 447, 972, 976

B

background differences 93, 94, 146
bandwagon phenomena 1411–1420
basic skills 640, 1006, 1066, 1223
becoming a teacher 81 ff., 88 ff., 98 ff.
beginning teachers 83–87, 98 ff., 115, 120
behaviorism 820
beliefs of teachers 1227–1240
bilingualism 252
biographical research 224
bounded irrationality 1313, 1314
bureaucracy 1083
burn-out syndrome 149, 459–498, 1133
    alienational 465, 475, 484–489
    as a psychological concept 462, 463
    as a sociological concept 463, 464
    causes 461
    characteristics 470–473
    conceptualization 490
    consequences 461, 473, 474
    coping mechanisms 491
    development 466
    gender-related 472
    job-related 466
    longitudinal effects 492
    magnitude 468–470
    patterns 482–80
    rate 470

C

capacities of teachers 1298
careers 145–150
    concept 42 ff., 189
    entry 42
career ladders 14, 148, 528, 529, 550–555
    design features 551
    for women 189
    implementation 551 ff.
    participation 550, 551
    research 550 ff.
    teacher support 550, 551
case teaching 1263
casual mechanisms 35, 36
CD ROM technology 1369
centralization 1299
certification systems 293
changes
    in education 1177
    in paradigms 1205–1208
    in society 675
    in work 632, 1250–1252
    meaningful 1387–1428
    superficial 1410 ff.
chaos theory 1301 ff.
child-centered computer programming 1364
chosen peer cultures 888
class 245 ff., 256, 259
    effect on peer culture 890–892
classroom
    as writing environment 728, 729
    as context 217
    control 61
    creating a learning society 1276, 1277
    discourse 720 ff.
    evaluation of knowledge 744–750
    implications of a social view of cognition
        1244–1246
    instruction 387